Ber
B.A. Universida
M.A. University
Ph. D. Universi

HAMEL'S

COMPREHENSIVE BILINGUAL DICTIONARY
OF SPANISH FALSE COGNATES

GRAN DICCIONARIO BILINGÜE
DE TÉRMINOS EQUÍVOCOS
DEL INGLÉS

BILINGUAL BOOK PRESS

FIRST EDITION - 1998

HAMEL'S

COMPREHENSIVE
BILINGUAL DICTIONARY OF

SPANISH FALSE
COGNATES

FIRST EDITION
1998

GRAN DICCIONARIO
DE TÉRMINOS EQUÍVOCOS
DEL INGLÉS

√ **Close to 2,000 English & Spanish cognates**
√ **Over 10,000 definitions**
√ **Numerous examples to illustrate usage in context**
√ **Separate English & Spanish sections**

 THE FIRST COMPREHENSIVE AND TRULY
BILINGUAL DICTIONARY OF FALSE COGNATES

Bilingual Book Press

Quality Bilingual Publications

COMPREHENSIVE BILINGUAL DICTIONARY
OF SPANISH FALSE COGNATES

Series director: Bernard H. Hamel

Copyright © 1998

Published in the United States of America
by Bilingual Book Press, 10977 Santa Monica Blvd.
Los Angeles, Ca 90025

ISBN 1-886835-06-3

Library of Congress Catalog Card Number: 97-94773

A todos aquellos escritores, traductores y
profesionales de la lengua, para los que el cultivo
del idioma es motivo de orgullo y de constante superación,
y que consideran que el lenguaje no sólo es vehículo
de comunicación, sino manifestación o expresión artística.

A mi nietito Luke/Lucas de ascendencia hispano-norteamericana
con el voto de que algún día llegue a integrar este grupo selecto.

Table of Contents

Abbreviations/Abreviaturas

~	Example	Ejemplo
•	Expression, phrase, saying	Expresión, dicho, frase
adj.	Adjective	Adjetivo
adv.	Adverb	Adverbio
angl.	Anglicized word	Anglicismo
autom.	Automotive	Automóviles
biol.	Biology	Biología
bot.	Botany	Botánica
chem.	Chemistry	Química
cine	Cinema	Cinema
comm, com.	Commerce	Comercio
const.	Construction	Construcción
cost.	Sewing	Costura
culin.	Culinary	Culinario, cocina
dep.	Sport	Deportes
econ.	Economy	Economía
elect.	Electricity, electronics	Electricidad, electrónica
excl..	Exclamation	Exclamación
f.	Feminine	Femenino
ferro.	Railways	Ferrocarriles
fin.	Finance	Finanza
hum.	Humorous	Humorístico
interj.	Interjection	Interjección
jur.	Law, legal	Derecho, jurídico
m.	Masculine	Masculino
mech.	Mechanics, mechanical	Mecánica, mecánico
med.	Medicine	Medicina
mus.	Music	Música
naut.	Nautical	Náutica
min.	Mining	Minería
n.	Noun	Nombres, sustantivo
prep.	Preposition	Preposición
quim.	Chemistry	Química
rail.	Railways	Ferrocarriles
rel.	Religion	Religión
sew.	Sewing	Costura
v.	Verb	Verbo
zool.	Zoology	Zoología

INTRODUCTION

As everyone dealing with a foreign language has experienced, from the beginning student to the advanced language professional, be it a translator, a teacher, a writer, or even a lexicographer, false cognates constitute the major stumbling block in language translation and learning. As we know, false cognates are words which are similar in two languages, in this case English and Spanish, often deriving from a common origin (most commonly Greek and Roman) and having followed a different evolutionary path through the years, thus acquiring divergent meanings. The French fittingly call these deceitful pairs of words *faux-amis* (false friends).

These seemingly friendly words offer an easy but deceiving translation and contributes in no small way to the inducement of what aptly could be called spontaneous or instantaneous translation, a phenomenon which occurs when the translator, because of the close relationship between two words, *thinks* he knows the exact equivalent and translates it instinctively rather than reflexively. Most frequently this will happen: when dealing with false cognates such as *library* (*librería* instead of *biblioteca*); when assigning a literal meaning to a concept that may or may not be a false cognate, such as *hot-caliente* (un país *caliente* instead of *caluroso;* una bienvenida *caliente* instead of *cálida*); or when translating abstract words for which a number of options exists (and which the translator fails to explore thoroughly). These are the areas in which particular translation skill is required. Other categories of words, in contrast, offer no particular difficulties, such as the names of objects belonging to the physical world (which, we may add, make up the bulk of a dictionary): *table, chair, cup, garden, sun, moon, star,* to name only some of the most common ones; and as is the case with technical terms, since in most of these instances there exist only one possible translation. Translating technical papers may be tedious work because of the need to frequently consult a number of dictionaries but the translation itself involves little reflection lexically.

Unfortunately, even the most authoritative bilingual dictionaries are not immune to the misleading easiness that the similarity of the words offers (particularly those of recent years). The Oxford dictionary translates *controversy* solely as *controversia* and omits entirely *polémica,* the standard word for *controversy* until *controversia* made its debut in the Spanish Academy dictionary in 1984. The same dictionary translates the word *to contact,* as *poner en contacto con, contactar con,* but omits *comunicarse con, dirigirse a,* either expression a much more common and natural way of expressing this concept. Under *occupation* the Oxford dictionary list solely *ocupación* as a possible translation, and omits *profesión, oficio, pasatiempo.* In like manner the Larousse dictionary translates *cooperate* solely as *cooperar,* when *colaborar* is a much more common word. The word *preferential* is translated in the Larousse, Oxford and Collins dictionary as *preferencial,* a word which does not appear in the Spanish Academy dictionary[1]. Ironically, the Larousse does not include *preferencial* in the Spanish to English section. The word *inusual* is given as one of the possible translations of *unusual* in the Oxford and Collins dictionary, although this word does not appear in the Academy dictionary. The Oxford dictionary list *falacia* as the only translation of *fallacy,* although the meaning of *fallacy* as 'an error of judgment' does not translate as *falacia,* but rather by *error, sofisma, argumento falso*[2]. *Falacia* has the meaning of: "Engaño, fraude o mentira con que se intenta engañar a otro" (DRAE).

---

[1]"Hay muchos traductores que se dejan llevar por la comodidad y traducen *preferential* por *preferencial,* ya que casi todo su trabajo se reduce a cambiarle una letra a la palabra inglesa. (...) En español nunca hemos dicho "preferencial". La palabra no figura en el diccionario de la Academia ni le hace ninguna falta. Siempre hemos hablado de "acciones preferentes" y de "trato preferente". (A. Torrents dels Prats, *Diccionario de dificultades del inglés.* Ed. Juventud, Barcelona, 1989).

[2]Es impropiedad, debida a anglicismo, dar a este nombre el sentido de 'error, sofisma o argumento falso'. (Manuel Seco, *Diccionario de dudas y dificultades de la lengua española.* Espasa Calpe, Madrid, 1993).

Concerning our selection of false cognates for this work, we have omitted those cognates which we feel would not likely be misused, notwithstanding the close similarity between them and regardless of the level of proficiency of the speaker. Such translations as the following are not likely to occur in our opinion: "He has a very *accused* accent" (for "Tiene un acento muy *acusado*"); "He bought some new *rope*" (for: "Se compró *ropa* nueva"). Our assumption is that if the speaker is familiar with the word *rope*, he must also be familiar with its meaning. What may prompt the student or translator to substitute one word for a similar one in another language is the closeness of the concept rather than the outward appearance of the word. In the cases given above, the similarity is more visual than conceptual[1]. In our selection we have tried to stay as close as possible to those cognates we consider truly false, that is to say, cognates that share a common etymological root and which in many cases share common as well as divergent meanings. For example, **Aggravate** *v.* is a false cognate in the following instances: ‖ 1. Aumentar (pena, castigo, multa). *Augment, increase.* ‖ 2. Oprimir con gravámenes o tributos. *Increase taxation.* ‖ 3. Aumentar el peso de alguna cosa, hacer que sea más pesada. *To weigh down, make heavier.* However, in the following case, the meaning is the same in both English and Spanish: "Make, get worse (situation, problem, illness). *Agravar(se)*".

The zealousness of many authors to include in their work as many so-called false cognates as their imagination can conjure often results in the unfortunate pairing of a score of words of unrelated meaning and which, should they genuinely be a source of difficulty (which we don't believe they are), would produce some amusing statements indeed (we have taken the liberty of offering a few examples below[2]). What further contributes to the disparity of meanings between some of these cognates is the need that some authors of this type of work feel to pair all false cognates. We should point out that not all cognates are false in both languages. The English cognate *apply* is false in various of its meanings. However, its corresponding Spanish cognate *aplicar* has the same basic meanings as in English.

Whether false or not, we have indicated the corresponding cognate under each entry. When false, it appears with an arrow at the *end* of the entry section (⇨ ABUSAR) to

---

[1]Words of this type: **Exit** (way out)/*éxito* (success); **accost** (to approach)/*acostar* (put to bed); **affront** (insult)/*afrontar* (to face); **apuntar** (jot down)/*appoint* (nombrar); **avalar** (to guarantee)/*avail* (take advantage); **bale** (bundle)/*bala* (bullet); **barranda** (railing)/*veranda* (porch); **bark** (on tree)/*barco* (boat); **basement** (cellar)/*basamento* (plinth); **bigote** (mustache)/*bigot* (hater) !!!; **billete** (ticket)/*billet* (lodging); **blindar** (to reinforce)/*blind* (deprive of sight); **bufete** (office)/*buffet* (meal); **carpet** (rug)/*carpeta* (folder); **celoso** (jealous)/*zealous* (enthusiastic); **entender** (to understand)/*intend* (tener la intención); **entrenar** (to train)/*entrain* (to put on a train) !!!, **estofar** (to stew)/*stuff* (rellenar) !!!; **explanar** (to level, grade)/*explain* (make understandable); **fast** (quick)/*fasto* (annals), **flamante** (brand new)/*flaming* (burning); **inusitado** (unusual)/*unused* (not used); **lance** (Sp. adventure, episode)/*lance* (Engl. lance), **lid** (Engl. cover) **lid** (Span. battle); **sacar** (take out)/*sack* (to plunder); **suceso** (event)/*success* (good fortune); **vino** (wine)/**wino** (drunkard)!!!

[2]Ass-*as* [ace] (he's an *ass* at tennis!!!); bitch-*bicho* (!!!); champion-*champiñón* (Es el *champiñón* mundial de boxeo!!!); fuming-*fumando* (I was *fuming* a cigarrette!!!); gate-*gato* (por favor, ábreme el *gato*!!!); lentils-*lentes* (quisiera pedir una sopa de *lentes*!!!, I need a new pair of *lentils*!!!); limp-limpiar (she came to *limp* the house!!!); mallow-*malo* (he's a very mallow man!!!); mess-*mesa* (please set the *mess* so we can eat!!!), notch-*noche* (at what time did you come in last *notch*?!!!); pap-*papa* (He went to Rome to see the *Pap*!!!); piss-*piso* (!!!); play (theatre)-*playa* (fui al treatro a ver una *playa* de tres actos); poster-*postre* (This meal includes a *poster*!!!); rat-*rato* (I spent a very unpleasant *rat* at the party!!!, Esta casa está llena de *ratos*!!!); ratio-*ración* (I would like to order a *ratio* of beans); ray, *rey* (Los *reyes* del sol me dañan los ojos!!!); salt-*salto* (Esta ensalada tiene demasiado *salto*!!!); salute-*salud* (Here's in perfect *salute*!!!); tinted-*tinto* (I would like to order *tinted* wine!!!).

indicate that the corresponding cognate is also false and can be referenced in the opposite language section:

ABUSE[1]. *v.* To hurt or injure by prolonged mistreatment. *Maltratar, tratar cruelmente.* ~To ABUSE a child. *Maltratar a un niño.* ‖ 2. To speak insultingly, harshly, to or about; revile, malign. *Insultar, ofender.* ~The coach ABUSES his players. *El entrenador insulta a sus jugadores.* ‖ 3. To commit sexual assault upon. *Violar, ultrajar.* ⇨ABUSAR

When not false the corresponding cognate is indicated in closed brackets next to the entry word at the *beginning* of the section:

AMEND [ENMENDAR]. *v.* [Manuscript, text]. *Corregir.* ‖ **2.** To remove or correct faults in, rectify. *Sustituir, corregir.* Amend 'thin' to 'then'. *Sustituya 'thin' por 'then', ponga 'then' en lugar de 'thin'.* ‖ **3.** To change for the better, improve. *Mejorar.* ~To AMEND one's ways. *Mejorar su forma de vivir.* ‖ **4.** [Laws]. *Reformar, rectificar.* ‖ **5.** [Treaty, constitution]. *Modificar.*

The reason for including separate English and Spanish sections in this work is a practical one. The treatment of false cognates of both languages in the same section rather than in the strict bilingual dictionary form which we have followed in this work involves a series of explanations and commentaries which often proves confusing, frequently punctuated with expressions such as: "also means...", "without the meaning of...", "shares the same meaning but...", "without the connotation of...", etc., hindering the translator's ability to detach himself mentally from the 'false friend', escape its force of gravity, so to speak. Furthermore, it must be kept in mind that the corresponding cognate in the opposite language is irrelevant to the translation, serving merely to satisfy the translator's curiosity (how the meaning would have been affected had he used a false cognate). The knowledge of the particular meaning of the word in the opposite language is of no practical value.

For further clarity and ease of comprehension we have avoided the inclusion of related words under the same section. Words such as the following would be listed as separate entries: **Alternate** (noun), **alternate** (adj.), **alternate** (verb), **alternative**.

In closing I would like to express my sincere gratitude to my son Carlos for thoroughly reviewing the innumerable drafts of this work (as he has done in the past with my previous projects), making the needed corrections and providing valuable suggestions. Without his patience and diligence, the writing of this dictionary of false cognates would have been a much more laborious undertaking.

Bernard H. Hamel
Los Angeles, California, 1998

ENGLISH-SPANISH

A

ABILITY. *n.* Aptitud, adeptness, capacity. *Talento, capacidad, inteligencia, condiciones, competencia.* ~He has the ABILITY but he doesn't work. *Tiene condiciones pero no trabaja.* ~His ABILITY in French. *Su aptitud para el francés.* || **2.** Faculty. *Facultad.* ~Her ABILITY to walk is now severely impaired. *Su movilidad se ha visto seriamente afectada.* || **3.** *pl.* Talents, special skills or aptitudes. *Dotes.* ~You may be unaware of your child's ABILITIES. *Su hijo tiene dotes y usted no lo sabe.* || **4.** *PHRASES.* || •To have ABILITY (to do something). *Tener capacidad (para hacer algo).* || •She did it to the best of her ABILITY. *Lo hizo lo mejor que pudo.* || •People's ABILITY to pay. *Los recursos de que dispone la gente.* || •ABILITY to pay. *Solvencia.* || •My ABILITY to do it depends on. *El que lo haga depende de.* ⇨HABILIDAD

ABNEGATION [ABNEGACIÓN]. *n.* Self-denial, selfishness. *Renuncia, negativa.* ~ABNEGATION of his responsabilies. *Renuncia de sus obligaciones.*

ABORT. *v.* [Mission, flight]. *Cancelar, suspender, abandonar.* ~The flight was ABORTED because of heavy rains. *Se canceló (suspendió) el vuelo debido a lluvias torrenciales.* || **2.** [Computer]. *Interrumpir, detener prematuramente.* || **3.** [Negotiations, efforts, plan]. *Malograrse, fracasar.* ~The plans have been ABORTED. *Fracasaron los planes.* ⇨ABORTAR

ABORTION. *n.* Induced termination of pregnancy. *Aborto provocado, aborto médico, aborto accidental, pérdida del bebé, aborto criminal (in countries where abortions are illegal).* ▸There is no specific word in Spanish for *miscarriage.* ⇨ABORTO

ABRUPT. *adj.* [Manner of person]. *Brusco, áspero, cortante.* ~He was very ABRUPT. *Fue muy brusco, cortante.* || **2.** [Voice, tone]. *Áspero.* || **3.** Sudden (departure, conclusion, change, stop). *Repentino, súbito.* ~An ABRUPT halt. *Una parada repentina.* ~An ABRUPT change of plan. *Un repentino cambio de planes.* || **4.** [Style]. *Cortado, lacónico, entrecortado.* ~An ABRUPT literary style. *Un estilo literario entrecortado.* ⇨ABRUPTO

ABSENCE [AUSENCIA]. *n.* Lack. *Falta.* ~In the ABSENCE of any details. *~A falta de datos.* ~In the ABSENCE of suitable alternatives. *A falta de alternativas adecuadas.* || **2.** [Of mind]. *Distracción, despiste.*

ABSOLUTE [ABSOLUTO]. *adj.* Complete, full, total. *Completo, total.* ~You have ABSOLUTE freedom to go wherever you please. *Ud. tiene completa libertad de ir a donde le plazca.* ~We are in ABSOLUTE agreement. *Estamos totalmente de acuerdo.* ~The room was in ABSOLUTE silence. *En el cuarto reinaba el más completo silencio.* || **2.** Real, quite, truly. *Verdadero, auténtico.* ~This house is an ABSOLUTE palace. *Esta casa es un verdadero palacio.* ~He's an ABSOLUTE genius. *Es todo un genio.* He's an ABSOLUTE gentlemen. *Es todo un caballero.* He's considered an ABSOLUTE hero in this town. *~En el pueblo se le considera como un verdadero héroe.* || **3.** Unconditional, wholehearted (support, confidence, obedience]. *Incondicional, pleno, total.* ~You have my ABSOLUTE confidence and support. *Ud. tiene mi pleno (incondicional) apoyo y confianza.* || **4.** Complete, outright (fool, idiot, stupidity). *Perfecto.* ~An ABSOLUTE idiot. *Un perfecto idiota.* || **5.** Real (shame, disgrace, scandal). *Verdadero, auténtico.* ~It's an ABSOLUTE disgrace. ~*Es una verdadera (auténtica) desgracia.* ~It's an ABSOLUTE scandal. *Es simplemente escandaloso.* || **6.** Despotic, dictatorial, authoritarian. *Absolutista.* ~An ABSOLUTE government. *Un gobierno absolutista.* || **7.** Not mixed or adulterated, pure. *Puro.* ~ABSOLUTE alcohol. *Alcohol puro.* || **8.** Categorical, flat, downright, emphatic, firm. *Tajante, categórico, rotundo, terminante.* ~ABSOLUTE statements. *Afirmaciones tajantes.* ~An ABSOLUTE denial. *Una negativa rotunda.* || **9.** Irrefutable, indisputable, positive, unquestionable. *Indiscutible, incontrovertible.* ~An ABSOLUTE truth. *Una verdad incontrovertible.* ~An ABSOLUTE proof. *Una prueba indiscutible.* || **10.** *PHRASES.* || • An ABSOLUTE need. *Una necesidad ineludible, inaplazable.* || •An ABSOLUTE victory/success. *Un éxito/victoria rotundo.* || •An ABSOLUTE taste. *Un gusto perfecto.* || •It's ABSOLUTE nonsense! *Es pura tontería.*

ABSORB [ABSORBER]. *v.* [Heat, sound, blow, shock]. *Amortiguar.* The barrier ABSORBED the main impact of the crash. *El muro amortiguó en gran medida el impacto del accidente.* || **2.** [Energy, time]. *Ocupar.* ~Her family ABSORBS all her time and energy. *La familia ocupa todo su tiempo y energía.* ~The business ABSORBS a lot of my time. *El negocio me lleva mucho tiempo.* || **3.** Assimilate (information, experience). *Asimilar.* I didn't really have time to ABSORB everything he said. *La verdad es que no he tenido tiempo de asimilar todo lo que ha dicho.* || **4.** [Immigrants]. *Integrar, asimilar.* ~The country ABSORBED a thousand refugees. *El país dio entrada a mil refugiados, el país acogió a mil refugiados.* ~The power of Chinese civilization to ABSORB the new arrivals. *El poder de asimilación de la civilización china a los recien llegados.* || **5.** To pay for (costs, taxes). *Pagar, sufragar.* The company will ABSORB all the research costs. *La compañía sufragará todos los gastos.* ~The travelling costs will be ABSORBED by the employer. *Todos los gastos de viaje*

los pagará el patrón. || **6.** •To be ABSORBED in. *Engolfarse en, empaparse de, dedicarse de lleno al estudio de, enfrascarse en.* ~He was ABSORBED in his reading. *Estaba enfrascado en la lectura.* || **7.** To endure, stand. *Aguantar.* ~The champion ABSORBED a lot of punishment. *El campeón recibió mucho castigo.* ~He ABSORBED the blow without flinching. *Aguantó el golpe sin retroceder.* **8.** •She ABSORBED the atmosphere of the city. *Se impregnó del ambiente de la ciudad.* || **9.** •Industry will have to ABSORB the consequences. *La industría tendrá que asumir las consecuencias.* || **10.** •She ABSORBS chemistry readily. *La química le entra con facilidad.*

ABUSE[1]. *v.* To hurt or injure by prolonged mistreatment. *Maltratar, tratar cruelmente.* ~To ABUSE a child. *Maltratar a un niño.* || **2.** To speak insultingly, harshly, to or about; revile, malign. *Insultar, ofender.* ~The coach ABUSES his players. *El entrenador insulta a sus jugadores.* || **3.** To commit sexual assault upon. *Violar, ultrajar.* ⇨ABUSAR

ABUSE[2]. *n.* Evil. *Mal.* ~The police are doing all they can to stamp out such ABUSES. *La policia está haciendo todo lo posible para acabar con estos males.* || **2.** Insulting language. *Insultos, improperios.* ~A torrent of ABUSE. *Una lluvia de insultos.* || **3.** Physical abuse. *Malos tratos.* || **4.** •Child ABUSE. *Malos tratos a la infancia (de los hijos).* || **5.** •Alcohol ABUSE. *Alcoholismo.* || **6.** •Drug ABUSE. *Toxicomanía.* ⇨ABUSO

ABUSIVE. *adj.* Insulting. *Insultante, grosero, ofensivo, injurioso.* ~He began to use ABUSIVE language. *Empezó a lanzar improperios.* ~She received a number of ABUSIVE letters. ~*Recibió varias cartas insultantes.* || **2.** •To be (become) ABUSIVE. *Decir (empezar a soltar) groserías.* || **3.** •To use ABUSIVE language. *Insultar, injuriar.* ⇨ABUSIVO

ABYSMAL. *adj.* Extremely or hopelessly bad or severe. *Pésimo, desastroso, atroz, terrible, profundo, extremo.* ~To live in ABYSMAL poverty. *Vivir en la mayor miseria.* ~The most ABYSMAL ignorance. *La igno-*

rancia más profunda. ~An ABYSMAL result. *Un resultado malísimo.* ~An ABYSMAL performance. *Una pésima actuación.* ⇨ABISMAL

ACADEMIC [ACADÉMICO]. *adj.* Theoretical or hypothetical; not practical, realistic, or directly useful: an academic question; an academic discussion of a matter already decided. *Puramente teórico, que no tiene aplicación práctica, especulativo.* ~The question of where we go on vacation is purely ACADEMIC since we don't have any money. *Dónde vamos a pasar las vacaciones es una cuestión puramente teórica, ya que no tenemos dinero.* ‖ **2.** •ACADEMIC year. *Año escolar o lectivo.* ‖ **3.** •ACADEMIC gown. *Traje universitario.* ‖ **4.** •ACADEMIC freedom. *Libertad de enseñanza.* ‖ **5.** •ACADEMIC career. *Una carrera universitaria.* ▸*Académico* is increasingly being used in many of the instances listed above.

ACCEDE. *v.* To attain or assume an office, title, or dignity; succeed. *Tomar posesión de (puesto), subir a (trono).* ~Queen Victoria ACCEDED the throne in 1837. *La reina Victoria subió al trono en 1837.* ⇨ACCEDER

ACCENTUATE [ACENTUAR]. *v.* [Difference]. *Subrayar, hacer resaltar.* ‖ **2.** [Fact, necessity]. *Subrayar, recalcar.* ‖ **3.** [Eyes, features]. *Realzar, hacer resaltar.* ~A background of mountains ACCENTUATES the quiet beauty of the landscape. *En el fondo unas montañas ponen de relieve la apacible belleza de la naturaleza.* ‖ **4.** [Problem]. *Agudizar.* ~This only ACCENTUATES the problem. *Esto sólo agudiza el problema.*

ACCESSORY [ACCESORIO]. *n.* [Law]. Person who knowingly helps another in a crime or wrongdoing, often as a subordinate. *Cómplice, instigador (before the fact). Encubridor (after the fact).* ‖ **2.** •Toilet ACCESSORIES. *Artículos de tocador.*

ACCIDENT. Coincidence. *Casualidad.* ~It was quite by ACCIDENT. *Fue pura casualidad.* ~It is no ACCIDENT that. *No es una (mera) casualidad que.* ~It was pure ACCIDENT that their visits coincided. *Fue pura casualidad de que coincidieran sus*

visitas. ‖ **2.** Mishap. *Percance, contratiempo.* ~We arrived home without ACCIDENT. *Llegamos a casa sin percances (contratiempos).* ~He had a little ACCIDENT at school today. *Tuvo un pequeño percance en la escuela hoy.* ‖ **3.** *PHRASES.* ‖ •Their third child was an ACCIDENT. *Su tercer hijo fue un descuido.* ‖ •ACCIDENTS will happen (set phrase). *A cualquiera le puede pasar.* ‖ •It was an ACCIDENT on my part. *Lo hice sin querer.* ~I'm sorry, it was an ACCIDENT. *Lo siento, lo hice sin querer.* ‖ •That was an ACCIDENT waiting to happen (set phrase). *Tenía que suceder, es algo que tenía que suceder.* ⇨ACCIDENTE

ACCOMMODATION [ACOMODO]. *n.* Lodgings. *Alojamiento.* ~I can provide ACCOMODATIONS for five. *Puedo alojar a cinco personas.* ‖ **2.** Room. *Habitación.* ~Do you have ACCOMODATIONS for tonight? *¿Quedan habitaciones libres para esta noche?* ~To book ACCOMODATIONS in a hotel. *Reservar una habitación en un hotel.* ‖ **3.** Space. *Sitio.* ~We don't have the ACCOMODATIONS for so many people. *No tenemos sitio para tanta gente.* ‖ **4.** Agreement. *Acuerdo.* ~To reach an ACCOMODATION over something. *Llegar a un acuerdo sobre algo.* ‖ **5.** Loan (of money). *Préstamo.* ~He was able to obtain an ACCOMMODATION from his brother-in-law. *Consiguió un préstamo de su cuñado.* ‖ **6.** Commodity. *Comodidad.* ~Huts with no sanitary ACCOMODATIONS. *Cabañas sin servicios sanitarios.* ‖ **7.** Convenience, favor, help. *Favor, ayuda.* Would you take these letters to the post office as an ACCOMODATION to me? *Me podrías hacer el favor de llevar estas cartas al correo?* ~Tables and benches are installed for the ACCOMODATION of tourists. *Las mesas y los bancos son para la comodidad de los turistas.* ‖ **8.** Agreement. *Acuerdo.* ~The question is to reach an ACCOMODATION with Japan. *Lo importante es de llegar a un acuerdo con el Japón.* ‖ **9.** •Seating ACCOMODATIONS. *Asientos, plazas.* ~The plane has limited ACCOMODATIONS. *El avión tiene un número fijo de plazas.*

ACCOMODATE. *v.* To do a kindness or a favor to; oblige, cater to (someone's wish). *Complacer, contentar.* We will do our best to ACCOMODATE you. *Haremos lo posible para complacerle.* You just can't ACCOMODATE everyone. *No se puede contentar a todo el mundo.* ‖ **2.** Provide lodging for. *Alojar, hospedar.* The hotel can ACCOMODATE 100 guests. *El hotel tiene capacidad para cien personas.* ‖ **3.** Have or make room for. *Tener cabida para.* The restaurant can ACCOMODATE 20 people. *El restaurante tiene cabida para 20 personas.* ‖ **4.** To contain, house. *Contener, tener.* The library ACCOMODATES a fine collection of books. *La biblioteca alberga (contiene) una excelente colección de libros.* ‖ **5.** To take into account. *Tener en cuenta, contemplar, cubrir.* Our plans ACCOMODATES every eventuality. *Nuestro plan cubre cualquier eventualidad.* ‖ **6.** To resolve, settle. *Arreglar, resolver, allanar.* ~An attempt to ACCOMODATE the differences between them. *Un intento de allanar las diferencias entre ellos.* ‖ **7.** To adapt oneself to. *Amoldarse a, adaptarse a.* ~To ACCOMODATE oneself to a new situation. *Adaptarse, amoldarse a una nueva situación.* ‖ **8.** •To ACCOMODATE with a loan. *Falicitar un préstamo.* ⇨ACOMODAR

ACT. *v.*

❶ THEATER, CINEMA. [Theater]. *Hacer teatro, ser actor, actriz.* ‖ **2.** [Cinema]. *Hacer cine, ser estrella de cine.* ‖ **3.** •To act a part (role). *Desempeñar un papel, representar.* ~He ACTED as Macbeth in the Shakespeare festival. *Desempeñó el papel de Macbeth en el festival de Shakespeare.*

❷ TO ACT AS. To perform specific duties or functions. *Hacer de.* ~What does your husband do? -He's ACTING as court interpreter. *¿Qué hace tu marido? Hace de intérprete en la corte.* ‖ **2.** Work, function. *Funcionar, obrar como.* ~Aspirin ACTS as a stimulant. *La aspirina obra como estimulante.* ‖ **3.** [Brake, incentive, deterrent]. *Servir (de freno, aliciente, disuasivo).* Some people say that capital punishment ACTS as a deterrent. *Algunas personas dicen que la pena de muerte sirve de disuasivo.*

❸ VARIOUS. To pretend to have particular feelings, qualities, etc. *Fingir.* ~He's only ACTING. *Lo está fingiendo nada más.* ~He's ACTING ill. *Se está haciendo el enfermo.* ~To ACT the fool, to act dumb. *Hacerse el tonto.* ‖ **2.** To take action, take steps. *Obrar, actuar, tomar medidas.* ~The President must ACT to stop the war in Bosnia. *El Presidente debe tomar medidas para terminar la guerra de Bosnia.* ‖ **3.** To start to have an effect. *Surtir efecto, dar resultados.* ~The medicine is slow to ACT. *La medicina tarda en surtir efecto.* ‖ **4.** To reach, make, or issue a decision on some matter. *Tomar una decisión.* ~I am required to ACT before noon tomorrow. *Debo tomar una decisión (determinación) antes del mediodía mañana.* ‖ **5.** Behave, react. *Comportarse.* ~Why did she ACT that way? *Por qué motivo se comportó así?*

❹ EXPRESSIONS. •To ACT on somebody's advice. *Seguir los consejos de alguien.* ‖ •To ACT with the best intentions. *Obrar con las mejores intenciones.* ‖ •To ACT out (feelings). *Exteriorizar.* ‖ •To ACT up. *Funcionar mal (machine), dar guerra (child), doler (wound, injury).* ‖ •To ACT on behalf of somebody. *Representar a alguien, obrar en nombre de alguien.* ⇨ACTUAR

ACTION. *n.*

❶ LAW. A proceeding instituted by one party against another. *Demanda, proceso.* ‖ **2.** •To bring an ACTION (against). *Entablar (presentar) una demanda (contra).* ~She brought an ACTION against the hospital for negligence. *Entabló una demanda contra el hospital por negligencia.* ‖ **3.** •Take ACTION. *Proceder judicialmente.*

❷ MILITARY. •To go into ACTION. *Entrar en batalla.* The Navy went into ACTION. *La marina entró en batalla.* ‖ **2.** •Military ACTION. *Intervención del ejército.* ‖ **3.** •To see ACTION. *Combatir, luchar.* ‖ **4.** •Killed/wounded in ACTION. *Muerto/herido en combate.* ‖ **5.** •To see ACTION. *Combatir, luchar.* ~He saw ACTION in the Korean war. *Luchó en (estuvo en la guerra de) Corea.*

❸ EXCITING EVENTS. *Bullicio, diversión, animación, vida.* ~Where is the ACTION in this town? *¿Dónde hay vida en este lugar?* ~There's hardly any ACTION before dark. *Antes de la noche apenas hay animación.* ~He likes to be where the ACTION is. *Le gusta estar en medio del bullicio.* ❹ STEPS, MEASURES. *Medidas, actuación.* ~Prompt ACTION by the police saved several lives. *La rápida actuación de la policía salvó varias vidas.* We need to take immediate ACTION to prevent further ocurrences of such a tragedy. *Necesitamos tomar las medidas necesarias para que no vuelva a ocurrir tal tragedia.* Which course of ACTION do you recommend? *¿Qué medidas recomienda?* ❺ VARIOUS. Deed. *Acto.* Their ACTIONS show them to be untrustworthy. *Sus actos demuestran que no son dignos de confianza.* ‖ 2. Movement of the body, especially a particular type of movement. ~The horse's trotting ACTION. *La marcha de un caballo.* ❻ EXPRESSIONS. •To put something into ACTION. *Poner en práctica.* ‖ 2. •I want to see some ACTION here. *Quiero que todos pongan manos a la obra.* ‖ 3. •To be out of ACTION (machine). *Estar estropeado, averiado (machine), estar fuera de acción (persona).* ‖ 4. ACTIONS speak louder than words. *Hechos son amores y no buenas razones.* ‖ 5. •To take ACTION. *Tomar medidas.* ‖ 6. •ACTION replay. *Repetición (de la jugada).* ⇨ACCIÓN

ACTIVATE. *v.* MIL [Troops, unit]. *Movilizar.* When the Corean war broke out the 23rd batallion was ACTIVATED. *Cuando estalló la guerra de Corea se movilizó al 23º batallón.* ⇨ACTIVAR

ACTIVE [ACTIVO]. *adj.* Energetic. *Enérgico, vigoroso.* ~She may be 80 years old, but she's still very ACTIVE. *Tendrá unos 80 años pero sigue siendo una persona muy enérgica.* ‖ 2. [Interest]. *Vivo.* ~He developed an ACTIVE interest in sports. *Se interesó vivamente en los deportes.* ‖ 3. [Volcano]. *En erupción.* ‖ 4. [Law]. *Vigente.* ‖ 5. [Life]. *Ajetreado.* ~An ACTIVE life. *Una vida ajetreada.* ‖ 6. [Day, weekend]. *Movido, de gran actividad, ajetreado.* ‖ 7. ▶In the following examples note the substitution of *active*

by words denoting the activity in which the participants are involved (luchar, militar, trabajar, etc.). ~There are rebels ACTIVE in the region. *Hay rebeldes luchando en la zona.* ~To be politically ACTIVE. *Militar políticamente.* ~The friars were ACTIVE among the poor. *Los frailes trabajaban con los pobres.* ~She's very ACTIVE in charitable works. *Ella se dedica a muchas obras caritativas.*

ACTUAL. *adj.* Real, existing, not imaginary. *Real, verdadero.* ~He cited ACTUAL cases. *Citó casos reales (de la vida real).* ~It was not a dream but an ACTUAL occurrence. *No fue un sueño sino un hecho verdadero.* ‖ 2. Per se, in itself, as such. *Propiamente dicho.* ~There was no ACTUAL written agreement. *No hubo un acuerdo escrito propiamente dicho.* ~The ACTUAL show starts later. *El programa propiamente dicho empieza más tarde.* ‖ 3. Genuine, authentic. *Verdadero.* ~An ACTUAL case of heroism. *Un verdadero caso de heroismo.* ‖ 4. Very, precise. *Mismo.* ~The ACTUAL (very) day of the election. *El mismo día de las elecciones.* ‖ 5. Precise, exact. ~Those were her ACTUAL (precise) words. *Esas fueron sus palabras textuales.* ‖ 6. Concrete, specific. *Concreto, específico.* ~Let's take an ACTUAL case. *Tomemos un caso concreto.* ‖ 7. •ACTUAL application. *Aplicación práctica.* ‖ 8. •ACTUAL cash value. *Valor realizable en efectivo.* ‖ 9. ACTUAL disbursements. *Sumas efectivamente desembolsadas.* ⇨ACTUAL

ACTUALLY. *adv.* Really, in reality. *En realidad, de hecho.* ~He works as a teacher, but he's ACTUALLY a spy. *Trabaja de maestro, pero de hecho (en realidad) es un espía.* ‖ 2. Categorically, positively. *Positivamente, sin lugar a dudas.* ~Can you ACTUALLY say that you saw him that day? *¿Puede Ud. afirmar categóricamente que lo vio ese día?* ‖ 3. Honestly, truthfully. *A decir la verdad.* ~Actually (to be honest) I didn't go that day, like I told you. *A decir la verdad no fui este día como le dije.* ‖ 4. To be exact. *En concreto.* ~I stayed in France for 3 weeks, ACTUALLY 24 days. *Estuve en*

Francia 3 semanas, en concreto 24 días. ‖
5. Even. *Incluso, hasta, llegar a.* ~He ACTU-
ALLY hit her. *Incluso llego a pegarla.* ~We
ACTUALLY caught a fish. *Hasta cogimos un
pez.* ~He ACTUALLY paid for our meals! *¡Y
hasta nos pagó la comida!* ~He ACTUALLY
shook my hand. *Hasta me estrechó la
mano y todo.* ‖ **6.** •I never believed I'd
ACTUALLY win. *Nunca creí que llegaría a
ganar.* ‖ **7.** •Prices have stopped rising and
may soon ACTUALLY fall. *Los precios han
dejado de subir y puede que incluso bajen.*
‖ **8.** •It ACTUALLY stopped raining! *Aunque
parezca mentira, ha dejado de llover.*
⇨ ACTUALMENTE

ADDICT. *n.* Someone who is unable to
stop taking drugs. *Toxicómano, droga-
dicto (Acad.).* ‖ **2.** Someone who spends
too much time doing what he likes.
Fanático, entusiasta. He's a real television
ADDICT. *Es un verdadero fanático de la
televisión.* ‖ **3.** •I'm a guitar ADDICT. *Me
apasiona la guitarra.* ~I'm a detective
story ADDICT. *Soy un apasionado de la
novela policíaca.* ~He's a soccer ADDICT.
Es un hincha del fútbol. ⇨ ADICTO

ADDITION [ADICIÓN]. *n.* [Maths]. *Suma,
cálculo.* ~If my ADDITION is correct. *Si he
hecho bien el cálculo.* ~To learn ADDITION
and substraction. *Aprender a sumar y
restar.* •ADDITION sign. *Signo de cálculo.*
•To do ADDITION. *Hacer sumas.* ‖ **2.** Increase
(thing). *Aumento.* ~We made ADDITIONS to
our stock. *Aumentamos nuestras existencias.* ~These rooms are later ADDITIONS.
*Estas habitaciones se construyeron
después.* ‖ **3.** Increase (person). *Aumento.*
~ADDITIONS to the staff. *Aumento del
personal.* ~She's a valuable ADDITION to
our team. *Su incorporación a nuestro
equipo es muy valiosa.* ~We're expecting
an ADDITION to the family. *Dentro de poco
aumentara nuestra familia, tendremos un
nuevo miembro en la familia, tendremos
uno más en la familia.* ‖ **4.** Accompa-
niment, supplement. *Complemento.* ~A
bottle of wine would make a pleasant
ADDTION to the meal. *Una botella de vino
sería un agradable complemento para la*

comida. ~A useful ADDITION to your toolkit.
*Un práctico complemento para su caja
de herramientas.* ‖ **5.** Acquisition. *Adquisición.* These are our new ADDITIONS. *Estas
son nuestras nuevas adquisiciones.* ~This
is a welcome ADDITION to our books on
Europe. *Este aumenta valiosamente nuestros
libros sobre Europa.* ‖ **6.** •In ADDITION.
Además. ~In ADDITION, they're strangers.
Además son forasteros. •In ADDITION to.
Además de. ~In ADDITION to our previous
order. *Además de nuestro pedido anterior.*

ADDITIONAL [ADICIONAL]. *adj.* •This is
an ADDITIONAL reason for not telling her.
Es razón de más para no decírselo. ‖ **2.**
•Service is ADDITIONAL. *El servicio no está
incluido.* ‖ **3.** •Five ADDITONAL bodies were
recovered from the plane. *Se descubrieron
cinco cadáveres más en el avión.* ‖ **4.** •If
you wish ADDITIONAL information, please
contact your representative. *Si desea
alguna información suplementaria, le
rogamos comunicarse con su representante.* ‖ **5.** •ADDITIONAL flights will be
available during rush hours. *Están previs-
tos servicios extraordinarios durante las
horas de mayor demanda.* ‖ **6.** •This will
cost you an ADDITIONAL five dollars. *Eso le
va a costar cinco dólares más.* ‖ **7.** •ADDI-
TIONAL benefits. *Beneficios complementarios.* ▶Most uses of the literal translation
adicional is directly influenced by English
usage.

ADEPT. *n.* A skilled or proficient person;
expert. *Experto, perito.* ‖ **2.** *adj.* Very skilled;
proficient; expert. *Ducho, experto, hábil,
diestro.* ⇨ ADEPTO

ADEQUATE. *adj.* Sufficient. *Suficiente.*
~They took ADEQUATE food for the weekend.
*Llevaron suficiente comida para el fin de
semana.* ‖ **2.** Fair (performance), good but
not excellent, satisfactory. *Pasable, mediano,
acceptable.* ~Her performance was ADEQUATE
but lacked originality. *Su representación no
estuvo mal del todo, pero le faltaba algo
de originalidad.* ‖ **3.** •ADEQUATE consideration. *Consideración debida.* ‖ **4.** •ADE-
QUATE compensation. *Renumeración justa
o equitativa.* ‖ **5.** •To feel (prove) ADEQUATE

to a task. *Sentirse (mostrarse) competente para desempeñar un trabajo (una tarea).* ⇨ADECUADO

ADHERENCE. *n.* [To causes, etc.]. *Adhesión.* His wholehearted ADHERENCE to democratic principles. *Su incondicional adhesión a las ideas democráticas.* ‖ **2.** [To beliefs]. *Fidelidad.* ~Their ADHERENCE to the democratic system. *Su fidelidad al sistema democrático.* ‖ **3.** [To a rule]. *Observancia.* ~He was noted for his strict ADHERENCE to the rules. *Se le conocía como una persona que observaba religiosamente las reglas.* ⇨ADHERENCIA

ADJACENT [ADYACENTE]. *adj.* [Building, rooms]. *Contiguo.* ~The room ADJACENT to ours. *El cuarto contiguo al nuestro.* ‖ **2.** [Land]. *Colindante.* ~He would go horse-riding along the land ADJACENT to the road. *Paseaba a caballo por el territorio colindante al camino.* ‖ **3.** [Country]. *Limítrofe.* ~Spain and Portugal are ADJACENT countries. *España y Portugal son países limítrofes.*

ADJUDICATE. *v.* Give judgment, mediate. *Arbitrar, decidir.* ~He was asked to ADJUDICATE on the labor dispute. *Le pidieron que arbitrara en el conflicto laboral.* ‖ **2.** To act as a judge, to sentence. *Ser juez, sentenciar, dictaminar.* ‖ **3.** To be the judge in a competition. *Juzgar, actuar de juez (árbitro).* ‖ **4.** •To ADJUDICATE a claim. *Decidir sobre.* ‖ **5.** •To ADJUDICATE someone bankrupt. *Declarar a alguien en quiebra.* ⇨ADJUDICAR

ADJUDICATION. *n.* A judicial decision or sentence. *Decisión, juicio, sentencia.* ⇨ADJUDICACIÓN

ADJUST. *v.* Adapt. Adaptar. Her eyes slowly ADJUSTED to the gloom. *Sus ojos se fueron adaptando a la penumbra.* ~Writers must ADJUST their writing to reflect the new taste. *Los escritores necesitan adaptar sus escritos a los nuevos gustos.* ‖ **2.** [Person]. *Adaptarse a, amoldarse a.* It's not easy to ADAPT yourself to the local time when you travel. *Cuando se viaje tanto no es fácil adaptarse a la hora local.* ‖ **3.** Change,

rectify. *Modificar, cambiar, corregir.* ~Don't forget to ADJUST your watches. *No se olviden de cambiar la hora de su reloj.* We should ADJUST our approach. *Debemos modificar nuestro enfoque.* ~There's still time to adjust the error. *Todavía hay tiempo de corregir este error.* ‖ **4.** Straighten, correct, fix. *Arreglar.* ~He ADJUSTED his tie. *Se arregló la corbata.* ‖ **5.** To get used to. *Acostumbrarse.* ~I can't ADJUST to living alone. *No puedo acostumbrarme a vivir solo.* ‖ **6.** Regulate. *Regular, organizar.* ~To ADJUST one's daily schedule to leave time for everything. *Regular su horario para dejar tiempo para todo.* ‖ **7.** Settle, resolve (differences, conflicts). *Resolver.* ~Orderly ways of ADJUSTING conflicts. *Formas metódicas de resolver conflictos.* ‖ **8.** [Insurance claim]. *Liquidar.* ‖ **9.** [Volume, temperature, speed]. *Regular.* ~This wheel ADJUSTS the intensity of the light. *Esta rueda permite regular la intensidad de la luz.* ‖ **10.** [Engine]. *Arreglar.* ~To ADJUST the carburetor. *Arreglar el carburador.* ‖ **11.** [Methods]. *Variar.* ⇨AJUSTAR

ADJUSTMENT. *n.* [Persona]. *Adaptación.* ~Period of ADJUSTMENT. *Período de adaptación.* ‖ **2.** Change (to plan system). *Cambio, modificación.* ~We can always make an ADJUSTMENT. *Siempre podemos cambiarlo.* ~To make a small ADJUSTMENT in one's plans. *Modificar ligeramente sus proyectos.* ~The plan needs some minor ADJUSTMENTS. *El plan necesita algunos pequeños cambios (modificaciones).* ~We had to make some ADJUSTMENTS to our lifestyle. *Tuvimos que cambiar nuestro estilo de vida.* ‖ **3.** [Of differences]. *Composición, resolución.* The orderly ADJUSTMENT of disputes. *La resolución pacífica de discrepancias.* ‖ **4.** [To clothes]. *Arreglo.* ~This dress just needs minor ADJUSTMENTS. *Este vestido sólo necesita algunos pequeños arreglos.* ‖ **5.** Settlement (of insurance claim). *Liquidación.* ‖ **6.** [Commerce]. *Reajuste.* ~ADJUSTMENT of wages. *Reajuste salarial.* ‖ **7.** [Instrumento]. *Regulación, corrección.* ‖ **8.** •After ADJUSTMENT for inflation. *Después de tomar en cuenta la* *inflación.* ⇨ AJUSTE

ADMINISTER. v. [Country]. *Gobernar.* ||
2. [Justice, laws]. *Aplicar.* ~To ADMINISTER
a punishment. *Aplicar un castigo.* || **3.** Give,
deal (beating, blow). *Dar, proporcionar.*
The economic crisis ADMINISTERED a severe
blow to their hopes. *La crisis económica
asestó un duro golpe a sus esperanzas.* ||
4. [Questions]. *Formular, hacer.* ~The test
was ADMINISTERED fairly. *La prueba fue
imparcial.* || **5.** •To ADMINISTER an oath to
somebody. *Tomar juramento a alguien.*
⇨ ADMINISTRAR

ADMINISTRATION. n. The government
of the United States at a given time.
Gobierno. The Reagan ADMINISTRATION
followed President Carter's. *El gobierno del
presidente Carter dio paso al del presidente
Reagan.* || **2.** Term of office of the President
of the United States. *Mandato.* || **3.** •ADMINIS-
TRATION of the oath. *La toma del juramento.*
|| **4.** The management of any office, business,
or organization; direction. *Gerencia.* ~All
complaints must be directed to the ADMINIS-
TRATION. *Toda queja debe dirigirse a la
gerencia.* ⇨ ADMINISTRACIÓN

ADMIRE. v. •She was ADMIRING herself in
the mirror. *Se estaba mirando (contem-
plando) satisfecha en el espejo.* || **2.** •I was
just ADMIRING your tablecloth. *Me estaba
fijando en lo bonito que es el mantel.* || **3.**
•His performance was much ADMIRED. *Su
actuación tuvo mucho éxito.* ⇨ ADMIRAR

ADMISSION. n. Cost of entrance to an
event. *Entrada.* ~ADMISSION free. *Entrada
gratis.* ~ADMISSION is free on Sunday. *La
entrada es gratis los domingos.* || **2.**
Entrance (school, hospital). *Ingreso.* ~He's
seeking ADMISSION to a prestigious university.
*Está haciendo (efectuando) gestiones para
ingresar en una prestigiosa universidad.* ||
3. Acknowledgement, confession. *Reconocimiento, confesión.* ~That's an ADMISSION of
failure. *Eso es reconocer el fracaso.* ~He
made an ADMISSION of guilt. *Se confesó
culpable.* ~It would be an ADMISSION of
defeat. *Sería reconocer nuestra derrota.*
~By (on) his own ADMISSION. *Por confe-

sión propia.* || **4.** PHRASES. || •No ADMISSION.
Se prohibe la entrada. || •We gained
ADMISSION by a window. *Logramos entrar
por una ventana.* || •ADMISSION fee. *Cuota
de entrada.* || •ADMISSION forms (Univ.).
Impreso de matrícula. || •ADMISSIONS office.
Secretaría. ⇨ ADMISIÓN

ADMIT. v. To acknowledge, confess, recognize. *Confesar, reconocer (errores).* ~I
ADMIT I was wrong. *Reconozco que estaba
equivocado.* || **2.** PHRASES. •To be ADMITTED to
(hospital). *Ingresar, internar.* ~She was
ADMITTED this morning. *La internaron esta
mañana.* || •The small windows ADMIT very
little light in the room. *Las pequeñas
ventanas permiten (dejan entrar) poca luz.*
|| •To be ADMITTED to (an academy). *Ingresar.*
|| •Tickets that ADMIT two persons. *Entrada
para dos personas.* || •ADMITS one. *Entrada
individual.* || •To ADMIT to a crime. *Confe-
sarse culpable.* ⇨ ADMITIR

ADOPT. v. To select (candidate). *Nombrar,
designar.* || **2.** To accept (idea, suggestion).
Aceptar, seguir. ~After the Revolution they
ADOPTED a more open policy towards the
West. *Terminada la Revolución siguieron
una política más abierta hacia el Oeste.* ||
3. To formally accept, approve (agenda,
resolution, required textbook). *Aprobar.*
⇨ ADOPTAR

ADULT [ADULTO]. n. A person who is fully
grown up, mature person. *Persona mayor,
(law) mayor de edad.* || **2.** •ADULTS only.
*Sólo para mayores, autorizada para los
mayores de 18 años (película).*

ADVANCE [AVANZAR]. v. [Time, date].
Adelantar. ~They ADVANCED the wedding
date. *Adelantaron la fecha de la boda.* || **2.**
Promote (arts, sciences). *Fomentar, promo-
ver.* ~For the ADVANCEMENT of the arts. *Para
el fomento de las artes.* || **3.** [Interest].
Promover. || **4.** [Cause]. *Favorecer.* ~To
ADVANCE the cause of freedom. *Favorecer la
lucha en pro de la libertad.* || **5.** Propose.
*Proponer (an idea, theory), hacer (a
suggestion), dar (an opinion).* || **6.** [Salary].
Anticipar, adelantar. ~His employer
ADVANCED him a month's salary. *El empre-

sario le adelantó el salario de un mes. ‖ **7.** [Loan]. *Prestar.* ~Can you ADVANCE me a few dollars till tomorrow. *Me puede prestar algunos dólares hasta mañana.* ‖ **8.** Make progress. *Hacer progreso (person), progresar, adelantarse (technology), ascender (gain promotion).* ~We have greatly ADVANCED in our understanding of the human body. *Hemos adelantado mucho en nuestro conocimiento de cuerpo humano.* ‖ **9.** [An opinion]. *Exponer, emitir, sugerir.* ~A similar plan was ADVANCED by the British delegation. *Una propuesta parecida fue expuesta por la delegación inglesa.* ‖ **10.** [Claim]. *Presentar, formular.* ‖ **11.** Help. *Ayudar.* ~His election will ADVANCE our cause. *Su elección ayudará nuestra causa.* ‖ **12.** To promote (in rank). *Ascender.* ~They ADVANCED him to general. *Lo ascendieron a general.*

ADVANCED [AVANZADO]. *adj.* Having reached a late point in time or development. *Adelantado.* The project is very far ADVANCED. *El proyecto está muy adelantado.* ~He's very ADVANCED for his age. *Está muy adelantado para su edad.* ‖ **2.** Ahead or far or further along in progress, complexity, knowledge, skill, etc. *Superior.* ~An ADVANCED class in Spanish. *Un curso de español superior, curso de perfeccionamiento en español.* ‖ **3.** •ADVANCED degree. *Certificado de estudios superiores.* ‖ **4.** •ADVANCED education. *Educación superior.* ‖ **5.** •ADVANCED studies. *Estudios superiores o de perfeccionamiento.* ‖ **6.** •ADVANCED standing. *Reconocimiento de estudios universitarios realizados en otra institución.* ‖ **7.** •ADVANCED training. *Formación superior, especializada.* ‖ **8.** Using the most modern ideas, methods and equipment. *Muy moderno, ultramoderno, último modelo, de alto nivel.* ~ADVANCED technology. *La tecnología ultramoderna.* ‖ **9.** •To be ADVANCED in years. *Ser entrado en años.*

ADVERSE. *adj.* Unfavorable (effect, result). *Desfavorable.* ~Adverse PUBLICITY. *Publicidad desfavorable.* ‖ **2.** [Winds]. *Contrario.* ‖ **3.** [Balance]. *Negativo, deudor.*

‖ **4.** [To someone's interests]. *Contrario.* ~The agreement is ADVERSE to our interests. *El acuerdo es contrario a nuestros intereses.* ⇨ADVERSO

ADVICE. *n.* Suggestion, recommendation. *Consejo.* ~I'd like your ADVICE. *Quisiera que me aconsejara.* ‖ **2.** Technical or professional advice. *Asesoramiento.* ‖ **3.** *PHRASES.* ‖ •A piece of ADVICE. *Consejo.* ‖ •To seek someone's ADVICE. *Pedir consejo a alguien, consultar con alguien.* ~You should seek medical ADVICE. *Debería consultar con un médico.* ‖ •To take legal ADVICE on a matter. *Consultar el caso con un abogado, hacerse asesorar por un abogado.* ‖ •To take someone's ADVICE. *Seguir los consejos de alguien, hacerle caso a alguien, consultar a alguien.* ~Take my advice. *Hazme caso.* ‖ •Technical ADVICE. *Asesoramiento (técnico).* ⇨AVISO

ADVISE. *v.* Offer an opinion or suggestion as worth following, recommend. *Aconsejar, recomendar.* ~What do you ADVISE me to do? *¿Qué aconseja (recomienda) Ud. (que haga)?* ~The doctor ADVISES complete rest. *El médico recomienda descanso total.* ‖ **2.** To give professional advice *Asesorar.* ~He ADVISES on technical matters. *El nos asesora en los aspectos técnicos.* ‖ **3.** Inform, notify (in writing). *Notificar.* ~We will ADVISE you as soon as the merchandise is ready. *Le notificaremos tan pronto esté lista la mercancía.* ‖ **4.** To keep someone informed. *Tener a uno al corriente.* ~Keep me ADVISED. *Manténganme al corriente.* ‖ **5.** Inform. *Informar.* ~Have you been ADVISED of your rights? *¿Le han informado de sus derechos?* ‖ **6.** *PHRASES.* ‖ •To ADVISE against (doing something). *Aconsejar a alguien (que no haga algo).* ~They ADVISED him against marrying so young. *Le aconsejaron que no se casara tan joven.* ‖ •To ADVISE against (something). *Aconsejar en contra de.* He ADVISES against the plan. *Aconseja en contra del plan.* ‖ •To be well ADVISED to. *Sería aconsejable (+ infinitive), haría bien en.* ~You would be well ADVISED to consult a lawyer. *Sería* *aconsejable (haría bien en) consultar con un abogado.* || •To ADVISE with. *Consultar.* || •To ADVISE on. *Ser asesor en.* ⇨AVISAR

AFFECT. *v.* Influence. (price, decision, future). *Influir en.* ~Will the delay AFFECT the price? *¿Influirá el retraso en el precio?* ~It did not AFFECT my decision. *No influyó en mi decisión.* || **2.** [Medical]. *Atacar.* Countries AFFECTED by cholera. *Países atacados por el cólera.* || **3.** Touch emotionally. *Conmover, emocionar.* ~He seemed much AFFECTED. *Parecía muy emocionado, se conmovió mucho.* || **4.** Concern. *Tener que ver con.* ~It doesn't AFFECT me. *No tiene que ver conmigo.* || **5.** Harm. *Perjudicar.* ~The closing of the factory will AFFECT all the workers. *El cierre de la fábrica perjudicará a todos los trabajadores.* || **6.** Pretend, feign. He AFFECTED indifference. *Fingió ser indiferente.* ~She AFFECTED to cry. *Fingió llorar.* ⇨AFECTAR

AFFECTION. *n.* Fond attachment, devotion, or love; fondness (for someone). *Afecto, cariño.* His parents showed him very little AFFECTION. *Sus padres le demostraron muy poco cariño.* ~You could show him a little more AFFECTION. *Podrías ser un poco más cariñoso con él.* ⇨AFECCIÓN

AFFIRM. *v.* Assert (commitment, innocence). *Declarar.* ~Yes, they will, he AFFIRMED. *Sí, lo harán –aseveró (declaró).* ~A pilgrimage to AFFIRM their faith. *Una peregrinación para manifestar públicamente su fe.* ⇨AFIRMAR

AFFLUENCE. *n.* Wealth, prosperity. *Opulencia, prosperidad, riqueza, bienestar económico.* ~To live in AFFLUENCE. *Vivir en la abundancia, vivir con lujo.* ⇨AFLUENCIA

AFFLUENT. *adj.* Rich, prosperous, wealthy. *Rico, próspero, opulento.* ~The AFFLUENT society. *La sociedad opulenta, la sociedad de consumo, la sociedad de la abundancia, la sociedad próspera.* ⇨AFLUENTE

AGENCY. *n.* An administrative division of a government. *Ministerio, dirección general, servicio, dependencia, organismo, órgano.*|| **2.** Branch, office. *Filial, sucursal.* || **3.** Means, intercession, good offices. *Intermedio, mediación.* ~Through his doctor's AGENCY he received compensation. *Por mediación del médico recibió una indemnización.* || **4.** PHRASES. || •Independent AGENCIES (government). *Organismos autónomos (paraestatales).* || •International Atomic Energy AGENCY. *Organismo Internacional de Energía Atómica.* || •Employment AGENCY. *Oficina de empleo.* || •Free AGENCY. *Libre albedrío.* ⇨AGENCIA

AGENDA. *n.* A list, plan, outline, or the like, of things to be done, business to be discussed, matters to be acted or voted upon at a meeting; program. *Programa, orden del día.* ~The next item on the AGENDA. *El próximo asunto por tratar.* || **2.** PHRASES. || •The matter is at the top of the AGENDA. *Es un asunto prioritario.* || •That defeat was not on his AGENDA. *No tenía prevista esta derrota.* || •What's on the AGENDA for today. *¿Qué tiene programado para hoy?* || •I'm afraid my AGENDA for today is very heavy. *Lamento decirle que estoy muy atareado hoy.* ⇨AGENDA

AGITATED. *adj.* [Person]. *Inquieto, perturbado, nervioso.* ~In an AGITATED tone. *En un tono inquieto.* ~To be very AGITATED. *Estar muy inquieto (about something), estar en ascuas.* ~She was becoming increasingly AGITATED. *Se estaba poniendo cada vez más nerviosa.* ⇨AGITADO

AGGRAVATE. *v.* To annoy, irritate, exasperate. *Exasperar, sacar de quicio.* His questions AGGRAVATE me. *Sus preguntas me exasperan.* || **2.** •AGGRAVATED assault. *Amenaza de acometimiento grave.* || **3.** •To get AGGRAVATED. *Exasperarse.* **4.** •AGGRAVATED homicide. *Homicidio calificado.* || **5.** •AGGRAVATED burglary. *Robo calificado (con agravantes).* ⇨AGRAVAR

AGGRESSIVE. *adj.* [Person]. Bold, enterprising, energetic, particularly in the use of initiative and forcefulness in pursuing one's goals; assertive, forceful. *Audaz, emprendedor, dinámico.* ~An AGGRESSIVE salesman. *Un vendedor audaz, dinámico.* ~To AGGRESSIVELY promote a product.

Promover energicamente un producto.
►*Aggressive* is synonymous with zealous, *agresivo* is associated with hostility. ⇨AGRESIVO

AGITATE. *v.* Upset, alarm, disturb, worry. *Inquietar.* ~Do not AGITATE your mother, she doesn't feel well. *No inquietes a tu madre, no se siente bien.* ⇨AGITAR

AGONIZE [AGONIZANTE]. *v.* To suffer extreme pain or anguish; be in agony. *Sufrir angustiosamente, experimentar grandes angustias, pasar por momentos (trances) amargos, penosos, dolorosos.* ‖ **2.** To think about a difficult situation and with a lot of effort. *Atormentarse, torturarse, romperse la cabeza, darle vueltas (a un asunto), preocuparse mucho.* ~Stop AGONIZING, just do it. *No le des más vueltas al asunto y hazlo.* ‖ **3.** •To AGONIZE over something. *Estar indeciso, no saber que decisión tomar.* ~He AGONIZED over the decisión. *Le costó mucho decidirse.* ⇨AGONIZAR

AGONIZING [QUE AGONIZA]. *adj.* [Pain]. *Atroz, horroroso.* ‖ **2.** Decisión, experience. *Angustioso, penoso.* ~It was an AGONIZING experience. *Fue una experiencia penosa.* ‖ **3.** [Reappraisal]. *Doloroso.* ~After the war many countries had to go through an AGONIZING reappraisal in their participation in world affairs. *Después de la guerra, muchos países tuvieron que proceder a un doloroso replanteamiento de su participación en los asuntos mundiales (Prats).*

AGONY. *n.* Intense pain or suffering. *Dolor agudo, dolor punzante.* ~He was in AGONY. *Sufría unos dolores horrorosos.* ‖ **2.** Mental anguish, anxiety. *Angustia, afflicción, congoja.* ~The AGONY of defeat. *Una angustiosa derrota.* ‖ **3.** •To be in AGONY. *Estar desesperado de dolor, estar en un grito.* ~These shoes are absolute AGONY. *Estos zapatos me están matando.* ‖ **4.** •To suffer AGONIES of doubt. *Ser atormentado por las dudas.* She's going through AGONIES of doubt. *Las dudas le están atormentando (martirizando).* ⇨AGONÍA

ALIENATION [ALIENACIÓN]. *n.* Estrangement, isolation. *Distanciamiento, aleja-*

miento, apartamiento, aislamiento. ~The sense of ALIENATION felt by many black people in our culture. *El sentido de aislamiento que siente mucha de la población negra dentro de nuestra cultura.* ~His ALIENATION from the mainstream of American life. *Su distanciamiento de la corriente dominante de la vida norteamericana.* ~She feels a terrible sense of ALIENATION from everyone around her. *Se siente muy distanciado de la genta que la rodea.* ‖ **2.** •ALIENATION from society. *Marginación social.*

ALTER. *v.* To make a piece of clothing wider, longer, etc. *Arreglar, enmendar.* These suits are too large, they must be ALTERED. *Estos trajes son demasiado grandes, deben arreglarse (enmendarse).* ‖ **2.** To change or make something change. *Cambiar, modificar, retocar (painting), reformar (archit.), falsificar (evidence), corregir (text).* ~Her face hasn't ALTERED much over the years. *Su rostro no ha cambiado mucho en esos años.* ~We will have to ALTER our plans. *Tendremos que modificar nuestros planes.* ‖ **3.** MAR •ALTER one's course. *Cambiar de rumbo.* ⇨ALTERAR

ALTERATION. *n.* Change, modification or adjustment. *Cambio, modificacion.* She made major ALTERATIONS to the plan. *Cambió radicalmente los planes.* ~He's only made minor ALTERATIONS to the schedule. *Sólo ha introducido pequeños cambios (pequeñas modificaciones) en el programa.* ‖ **2.** Improvement, modification (building, store). *Obras, reformas.* ~The house needed extensive ALTERATIONS when we moved in. *Cuando fuimos a vivir en la casa necesitaba muchas reformas.* ‖ **3.** *pl.* Modification, repairs (to a garment). *Arreglos.* ~To make ALTERATIONS (garment). *Arreglar (traje, vestido).* ‖ **4.** •Closed for ALTERATIONS. *Cerrado por reformas.* ⇨ALTERACIÓN

ALTERNATE[1] [del verbo ALTERNAR]. *n.* Substitute (teacher, worker). *Sustituto, suplente.* ‖ **2.** •ALTERNATE member. *Miembro suplente.*

ALTERNATE[2] [del verbo ALTERNAR]. *adj.*

In place of another, substitute. *En lugar de, otro.* ~In this case, copper can be used as an ALTERNATE to iron. *En este caso, puede utilizarse cobre en lugar de hierro.* ~An ALTERNATE metal can be used. *También se puede construirse de cobre.* || 2. Every second one of a series. ~She works only on ALTERNATE Tuesdays. *Trabaja un martes sí y otro no.* ~Every ALTERNATE day. *Un día sí y otro no.*

ALTERNATE[3]. *v.* To take turns. *Turnarse.* Let's ALTERNATE in washing the dishes. *Vamos a turnarnos para lavar los platos.* ⇨ ALTERNAR

ALTERNATIVE. *n.* Choice between two mutually exclusive possibilities. *Alternativa.* You have the ALTERNATIVE of working hard and succeeding, or not working at all and failing. *Tiene la alternativa de trabajar con ahinco y tener éxito o no trabajar y fracasar.* || 2. A choice or the opportunity to choose among several possibilities. *Posibilidades.* ~You have various ALTERNATIVES to choose from. *Usted puede escoger entre varias posibilidades.* || 3. *PHRASES.* || •To have no other ALTERNATIVE than. *No tener (quedar) más remedio que.* ~If things go on like this I'll have no other ALTERNATIVE but to close the factory. *Si las cosas siguen así, no tendré más remedio que cerrar la fábrica.* || •You had better sign it because the ALTERNATIVE (if you don't it) can be very bad for you. *Harás bien en firmarlo, porque de lo contrario la cosa puede irle bastante mal.* || •There are ALTERNATIVES to flying. *Volar no es la única forma de viajar.* || •An ALTERNATIVE to this dilemma is. *Una posible solución a este problema es.* || •What other ALTERNATIVES are there? *¿Qué opciones hay?* || •An ALTERNATIVE proposal. *Una contrapropuesta.* ⇨ ALTERNA-TIVA

AMBITION [AMBICIÓN]. *n.* Legitimate and noble desire to succeed. *Empeño, dinamismo, iniciativa.* || 2. Drive, force, energy, will. *Voluntad, vigor, energía, ímpetu.* ~I awoke feeling tired and utterly lacking in AMBITION. *Al despertar me sentí cansado y sin fuerzas para hacer nada.* || 3. Aspiration,

yearning, longing. *Aspiración.* My AMBITION is to become a doctor. *Mi aspiración es ser médico.*

AMBITIOUS. *adj.* Energetic, enterprising. *Emprendedor, luchador, dinámico.* ▶The English *ambitious,* unless made clear by the content generally has a positive connotation, while the Spanish *ambicioso* more often than not has a negative overtone. An *ambitious* young man, is one to be admired and respected, while in Spanish un hombre *ambicioso* is one that will go to any lengths to achieve his goals, regardless of the consequences to others. Care must be taken to reflect that positive connotation whenever translating it literally to Spanish (ambicioso de gloria, de servir a su patria, de hacer el bien, etc.). The following translation of: "I wish to commend you, you're an AMBITIOUS young man" to: *Te felicito, eres un hombre ambicioso,* would achieve the reverse effect of what is intended, resulting more in an insult than a compliment. ⇨ AMBICIOSO

AMEND [ENMENDAR]. *v.* [Manuscript, text]. *Corregir.* || 2. To remove or correct faults in, rectify. *Sustituir, corregir.* Amend 'thin' to 'then'. *Sustituya 'thin' por 'then', ponga 'then' en lugar de 'thin'.* || 3. To change for the better, improve. *Mejorar.* ~To AMEND one's ways. *Mejorar su forma de vivir.* || 4. [Laws]. *Reformar, rectificar.* || 5. [Treaty, constitution]. *Modificar.*

AMENITIES. *n.* Pleasure, luxury, gratification. *Placeres, disfrute, lujos, esparcimiento.* ~The AMENITIES of life. *Las cosas agradables (placenteras) de la vida.* || 2. Fun, entertainment, amusement. *Actividades recreativas, distracciones, pasatiempos, entretenimiento, diversiones.* || 3. Conveniences, comfort, facilities. *Comodidad.* ~A house with a swimming pool, two fireplaces, and other AMENITIES. *Una casa con piscina, dos chimeneas y otras comodidades.* || 4. Appliances, appurtenances. *Accesorios.* ~Shower, telephone and other AMENITIES. *Ducha, teléfono y otros accesorios.* || 5. Rules of conduct. *Normas.* One of the AMENITIES which lawyers recognize is to refrain from stealing each others clients. *Una de las normas a la que se atienen los abogados es abstenerse de quitarse clientes los unos a los otros.* || **6.** Formalities. *Formalidades.* ~The visitor got the AMENITIES over quickly and got down to business. *Tras acabar apresuradamente con las formalidades, el visitante fue al grano inmediatamente.* || **7.** •Close to all AMENITIES. *Cercano a todo tipo de servicios públicos.* ⇨AMENIDAD

AMERICAN [AMERICANO]. *n/adj.* A citizen of the United States of America. *Norteamericano.*

AMOROUS. *adj.* Affectionate. *Cariñoso, tierno.* || **2.** [Look, mood]. *Apasionado.* ~An AMOROUS outburst of lyricism. *Un apasionado arrebato de liricismo.* || **3.** [Man]. *Mujeriego.* ~He made AMOROUS advances to his secretary. *Requebró de amores a su secretaria.* || **4.** In love, enamored. *Enamorado.* ~He's AMOROUS of the girl. *Está enamorada de la chica.* || **5.** Who falls in love easily. *Enamoradizo.* ⇨AMOROSO

AMPLE. *adj.* Plentiful, more than sufficient. *Abundante, de sobra.* ~They have AMPLE funds. *Tienen fondos abundantes.* ~He had AMPLE warning. *Se le avisó con sobrada anticipación.* ~There will be AMPLE opportunities to ask questions. *Habrá sobradas oportunidades para hacer preguntas.* || **2.** *PHRASES.* || •An AMPLE helping. *Una ración (porción) generosa.* || •To be in AMPLE supply. *Haber en abundancia.* || •We have AMPLE reasons to believe that ... *Tenemos razones sobradas para ...* || •To have AMPLE time. *Tener tiempo de sobra.* ⇨AMPLIO

ANGINA. *n.* Severe pain in a person's chest and left arm, caused by heart disease. *Angina de pecho.* ⇨ANGINA

ANGLE. *n.* Point of view. *Punto de vista, aspecto.* ~That is another ANGLE to the problem. *Ese es otro aspecto del problema.* ~To try to look at a problem from another ANGLE. *Intentar enfocar el problema desde otro punto de vista.* ⇨ÁNGULO

ANIMOSITY. *n.* Feeling of strong dislike. *Ojeriza, encono, antipatía, hostilidad, aversión, animadversión, cierta enemistad, mala voluntad.* ▸Although the Spanish Academy now accepts the word *animosidad,* of French and English derivation, in its dictionary, the use of the word, unless clear in context, may be confused with the classic meaning of *ánimo, valor, esfuerzo.* ⇨ANIMOSITY

ANNOUNCE. *v.* To say something in a loud and angry way. *Declarar.* ~Winston suddenly ANNOUNCED that he was leaving. *Winston declaró inesperadamente que se iba.* || **2.** To report, inform. *Comunicar, declarar.* ~It is ANNOUNCED from London that the Prime Minister is ill. *Se comunica desde Londres que el primer ministro está enfermo.* She ANNOUNCED that she was going home. *Declaró que se iba a casa.* || **3.** Publish, print. *Publicar, imprimir.* The book is ANNOUNCED for September. *El libro se publicará en septiembre.* || **4.** To serve as an announcer. *Ser locutor.* || **5.** •We regret to ANNOUNCE the death of. *Lamentamos participarle la muerte de.* ⇨ANUNCIAR

ANNOUNCEMENT. *n.* Tarjeta con que se invita a asistir a un acto social. *Invitación.* ~We have received your wedding announcement. *Ya hemos recibido su invitación de boda.* || **2.** Statement, declaration. *Declaración.* ~We were shocked by the ANNOUNCEMENT that the mayor was resigning. *Nos sorprendió enormemente la declaración de que el alcalde había dimitido.* || **3.** •An official ANNOUNCEMENT. *Un comunicado oficial.* ⇨ANUNCIO

ANTAGONIZE. *v.* Incur or provoke the hostility of someone. *Enemistarse con, suscitar el antagonismo de alguien.* ▸Although widely used, the word ANTAGONIZAR has not yet been acepted by the Real Academia.

ANTICIPATE. *v.* To expect. *Prever.* It was more difficult than ANTICIPATED. *Resultó más difícil de lo que se había previsto.*~The consequences of an earthquake in this area are difficult to anticipate. *No se pueden prever las consecuencias de un terremoto en esta zona.* || **2.** To expect (to await).

Esperar. Production was not as high as ANTICIPATED. *La producción no resultó tan alta como se esperaba.* ~We didn't ANTICIPATE such a large turnout. *No esperábamos tan nutrida concurrencia.* ~Are you ANTICIPATING any calls? *¿Está esperando algunas llamadas?* ~An eagerly ANTICIPATED event. *Un acontecimiento esperado con impaciencia.* || 3. To expect (foresee, contemplate). *Imaginarse, suponer.* ~I don't ANTICIPATE any problems. *Supongo (me imagino) que no habrá problemas.* || 4 Guess, surmise. *Suponer, calcular, figurarse, imaginarse.* I ANTICIPATE the interest rate will go up next month. *Calculo, me figuro, me imagino que subirán los intereses el mes que viene.* || 5. Calculate, take into consideration. ~All costs of the project have been ANTICIPATED. *Se han previsto todos los gastos del proyecto.* || 6. To expect, be confident, be hopeful, trust. *Esperar con firmeza y seguridad, confiar.* We ANTICIPATE a favorable response. *Confiamos en una pronta respuesta.* ~We ANTICIPATE your presence at dinner tomorrow. *Confiamos en que vendrá mañana.* || 7. Think, believe. *Creer, opinar.* Do you ANTICIPATE this will be easy. *¿Crees que esto va a resultar fácil?* || 8. Forestall, waylay. *Salir al paso de.* ~To ANTICIPATE criticism. *Salir al paso de las críticas.* || 9. To take actions in advance. *Adelantar.* ~To anticipate events. ADELANTAR los acontecimientos. || 10. •ANTICIPATED profits. *Ganancias previstas, beneficio esperado.* || 11. •ANTICIPATED cost. *Costo previsto.* || 12. •As ANTICIPATED. *De acuerdo con (según) lo previsto.* ⇨ANTICIPAR

ANTICIPATION. *v.* Expectation. *Ilusión.* ~We waited with growing ANTICIPATION. *Esperábamos con creciente ilusión.* || 2. Expectation. *Esperanza(s).* ~It did not come up to our EXPECTATIONS. *No correspondió a nuestras esperanzas.* || 3. Expectation. *Previsión.* ~I bought it in ANTICIPATION of her visit. *Lo compré en previsión de su visita.* || 4. Expectation. *Expectativa.* After months of ANTICIPATION. *Tras*

meses de expectativa. || 5. •In ANTICIPATION of. *A la espera de.* ~In ANTICIPATION of good weather. *A la espera de que hiciera buen tiempo.* ⇨ANTICIPACIÓN

ANXIETY [ANSIEDAD]. *n.* Concern. *Inquietud, desasosiego.* || 2. Worry. *Preocupación.* ~It's a great ANXIETY to us. *Nos preocupa mucho.* ~That child is a perpetual ANXIETY. *Este niño nos trae loco.* || 3. Eagerness. *Ansia(s), afán.* ~In his ANXIETY to leave he forgot his briefcase. *Tanto ansía salir que olvidó su maleta.* ~Their ANXIETY to please. *Su afán de agradar.*

ANXIOUS. *adj.* Eager (to do something). *Que tiene mucho interés (en hacer algo).* ~He's very ANXIOUS to please. *Tiene mucho afán de agradar.* ~ANXIOUS to please, he offered to cook dinner. *Deseoso de agradar, se ofreció a hacer la cena.* ~My parents are ANXIOUS to meet you. *Mis padres tienen ganas (mucho interés) en conocerle.* ~She's ANXIOUS to see you before you leave. *Se empeña (tiene interés) en verte antes de que te vayas.* || 2. Eager (for). To be ANXIOUS for. *Estar deseando, estar deseoso, estar ansioso.* || 3. Eager (that). *Querer vivamente que.* ~I'm very ANXIOUS that he should go. *Quiero a toda costa que vaya.* ~I'm not very ANXIOUS to go. *Tengo pocas ganas de ir.* || 4. Showing anxiety, apprehensive, worried, uneasy. *Inquieto, preocupado, angustiado.* ~I'm rather ANXIOUS about her health. *Su salud me tiene algo preocupado.* ~It's time to be going home, your mother will be ANXIOUS. *Mejor que te vayas a casa en seguida, tu madre se va a preocupar.* ~In an ANXIOUS voice. *En un tono angustiado.* ~With an ANXIOUS glance. *Con una mirada inquieta (llena de inquietud).* ANXIOUS about the future. *Preocupado por el futuro.* || 5. Causing or full of anxiety. *De gran preocupación, inquietud, desasosiego.* This was an ANXIOUS moment for all of us. *Fue un momento de gran preocupación para todos.* ⇨ANSIOSO

APERITIF. *n.* A drink of alchoholic liquor or wine taken to stimulate the appetite before a meal. *Trago, bebida (antes de la comida).* ⇨ APERITIVO

APPARENT. *adj.* Readily seen, evident,obvious. *Evidente, notorio, manifiesto, obvio.* His sadness was very APPARENT. *Su tristeza era muy evidente.* || **2.** •To be APPARENT. *Ser evidente, saltar a la vista, echarse de ver, ser notorio, ser manifiesto, verse claro.* || **3.** •To become APPARENT. *Hacerse patente, empezar a verse.* ~His weakness became APPARENT. *Se hizo patente su debilidad.* || **4.** • Heir APPARENT. *Presunto heredero.* || **5.** •There is no APPARENT difference. *No se advierte (nota) ninguna diferencia.* ⇨ APARENTE

APPEAL [APELAR]. *v.* Plead. *Rogar, suplicar.* To APPEAL for help. *Pedir (solicitar) ayuda.* ~The Minister went on television to APPEAL for calm. *El ministro apareció en la televisión para hacer un llamamiento a la calma.* || **2.** Attract, interest. *Atraer.* ~Teaching never APPEALED to me. *Nunca me atrajo la enseñanza.* ~It APPEALS to the imagination. *Estimula la imaginación.* ~I don't think it will APPEAL much to the public. *No creo que tenga atractivo para el público.* || **3.** •To APPEAL to arms. *Recurrir a las armas.*

APPEAR. *v.* [Publicly]. *Presentarse.* ~He APPEARED without a tie. *Se presentó sin corbata.* || **2.** [On stage]. *Actuar.* ~She's currently APPEARING on Broadway. *Actualmente está actuando en Broadway.* || **3.** [Before a court, committee]. *Comparecer.* ~To APPEAR before a magistrate. *Aparecer ante un juez.* ~She's APPEARING on a charge of murder. *Comparece acusada de asesinato.* || **4.** [In shop]. *Salir a la venta.* || **5.** [On television]. *Salir (en la televisión).* ~He has APPEARED on television many times. *Ha salido muchas veces por (en la) televisión.* || **6.** To play the role of. *Hacer el papel.* ~She APPEARED as Cinderella. *Hizo el papel de Cenicienta.* || **7.** To APPEAR on behalf of someone. *Representar a uno.* ⇨ APARECER

APPEARANCE [APARIENCIA]. *n.* [Becoming visible, coming into view]. *Aparición.* ~The APPEARANCE of smoke on the horizon raised the sailors' hope. *La aparición del humo en* el horizonte dio esperanza a los marineros. ~It was his first APPEARANCE on the stage. *Fue su primera aparición en las tablas.* ~Cast in order of APPEARANCE. *Reparto por orden de aparición.* || **2.** [Publicly]. *Presentación.* || **3.** [On stage]. *Actuación.* ~His APPEARANCE in 'Don Mendo'. *Su actuación en el papel de 'Don Mendo'.* || **4.** [Before court, committee]. *Comparecencia.* ~To make an APPEARANCE in court. *Comparecer ante el tribunal.* || **5.** [Of book]. *Publicación.* || **6.** [In shops]. *Salida a la venta.* || **7.** [Look, impression]. *Aspecto, presencia, impresión.* ~She was sickly in APPEARANCE. *Tenía (un) aspecto enfermizo.* ~Candidates must be of good APPEARANCE. *Los candidatos deben tener buena presencia.* ~She gives the APPEARANCE of being quite contented. *Dio la impresión de estar contenta con la vida.* His dishevelled APPEARANCE. *Su aspecto desaliñado.* || **8.** •To make one's first APPEARANCE. *Debutar.* || **9.** •To put in an APPEARANCE. *Hacer acto de presencia.*

APPLICATION [APLICACIÓN]. *n.* Formal request (for a job, school, loan, etc.). *Solicitud, petición, instancia.* ~His APPLICATION was turned down. *Su solicitud fue rechazada.* ~We received more than a hundred APPLICATIONS. *Recibimos más de cien solicitudes.* || **2.** Request for entrance at a school, university, etc.). *Solicitud de ingreso.* || **3.** Use. *Uso.* ~The machine has many APPLICATIONS. *La máquina tiene muchos usos.* ~APPLICATION of force. *Uso de la fuerza.* For external APPLICATION only (ointment, cream). *Para uso externo.* || **4.** *PHRASES.* || •To fill an APPLICATION. *Rellenar una solicitud.* || •To submit an APPLICATION. *Presentar una solicitud.* || •APPLICATION form (blank). *Formulario (impreso) de solicitud.* || •APPLICATION for employment. *Solicitud de empleo.* || •APPLICATION for membership. *Solicitud de ingreso.* || •APPLICATION for bail, injunction. *Petición.* •Sample (prices) on APPLICATION. *Pídanos (solicítenos) muestras (precios).* || •To submit an APPLICATION for membership (in an organization). *Pedir su ingreso en una organización.*

APPLY. *v.*

❶ TO REQUEST PERMISSION, A JOB. To request something formally. *Solicitar, presentarse.* ~He APPLIED to the government for financial help. *Solicitó ayuda financiera al gobierno.* ~It's a good job, why don't you APPLY? *Es un buen trabajo, ¿por qué no te presentas?* || **2.** •To APPLY for a job. *Solicitar un trabajo, postular para un trabajo.* || **3.** ~To apply (to a certain address). *Dirigirse, comunicarse con.* ~You can APPLY to the following address. *Puede dirigirse (comunicarse) a la siguiente dirección.* || **4.** •APPLY within. *Infórmase aquí, razón aquí.*

❷ AFFECT, RELATE TO, CONCERN. *Concernir, tener que ver con, ser aplicable a, referirse a. ser pertinente, interesar.* The law APPLIES to all. *La ley es aplicable a todos.* This doesn't APPLY to you. *Esto no te concierne.* ~Cross out what does not APPLY. *Táchese lo que no interese (no sea pertinente).* ~These were old regulations, they don't apply to you. *Esas son normas antiguas, ya no están en vigor.*

❸ TO USE. [Force, measures, rule]. *Usar, ejercer, recurrir a, utilizar.* ~Just APPLY common sense. *Use (utiliza) un poco de sentido común.* || **2.** Put to use. *Utilizar, emplear.* ~How can we best APPLY this money? *Como podemos utilizar mejor este dinero?* || **3.** To impose. *Imponer.* We intend to APPLY economic sanctions. *Nos proponemos imponer sanciones económicas.* ~Countries which have been the first to APPLY the death penalty. *Países que han sido los primeros en imponer la pena de muerte.* || **4.** [Word, label]. *Llamar, calificar.* ~The term 'mat' can be APPLIED to any small rug. *Se puede llamar 'alfombrilla' a cualquier alfombra pequeña.* || **5.** •To APPLY one's mind to something. *Concentrarse en algo.* || **6.** •To APPLY the brakes. *Apretar los frenos*

❹ VARIOUS. To be valid. *Ser válido.* This discount APPLIES only on purchases of a hundred dollars or more. *Este descuento sólo es válido para compras de más de cien dólares.* || **2.** Apply force, pressure. *Apretar.* ~APPLY your right foot to the acce-

lerator. *Apriete el acelerador con el pie derecho.*

❺ EXPRESSIONS. •This does not APPLY. *Eso no viene al caso, no interesa, no es pertinente.* || •To APPLY pressure (on someone). *Presionar, ejercer presión.* They're applying pressure on the workers to accept the offer. *Están presionando a los obreros para que accepten la oferta.* || •To APPLY pressure (on something). *Usar fuerza.* || •To APPLY the brakes. *Poner el freno, echar los frenos, frenar.* || •To APPLY oneself to a task. *Dedicarse a una tarea.* ~He APPLIED his mind to the problem. *Se dedicó a resolver el problema.* || •To APPLY for a pension. *Acogerse a jubilación.* || •To APPLY a match to. *Poner fuego (con un fósforo).* ⇨APLICAR

APPRECIABLE. *adj.* Considerable, sizeable, substantial, important. *Considerable, notable, importante.* There is an APPRECIABLE difference between socialism and communism. *Hay una notable diferencia entre el socialismo y el comunismo.* || **2.** Noticeable, perceptible. *Sensible, perceptible.* There is no APPRECIABLE change in the patient's condition. *No hay cambio sensible en el estado de salud del paciente.* ⇨APRECIABLE

APPRECIATE. *adj.* To be grateful or thankful for. *Agradecer.* ~I would greatly APPRECIATE that you would answer as soon as possible. *Mucho le agradecería que me contestara lo antes posible.* ~Your cooperation is much APPRECIATED. *Le agradecemos mucho su colaboración.* || **2.** To be fully conscious of, be aware of, recognize, understand. *Hacerse cargo, comprender, entender, darse cuenta.* ~I APPRECIATE your concern, but I can assure you that you have nothing to fear. *Me hago cargo de su preocupación, pero le aseguro que no tiene nada que temer.* ~I do APPRECIATE your reasons for being wary. *Entiendo (comprendo) muy bien los motivos de su recelo.* || **3.** To rise in value. *Aumentar de valor, subir.* ~Property in this area has been APPRECIATING at a rate of 10%. *La propriedad en esta zona ha ido aumentando el 10%.* || **4.** Value (art, music). *Saber apreciar, entender* *de.* ~Sabe APRECIAR el buen vino. *She appreciates good wine.* ⇨ APRECIAR

APPRECIATION. *adj.* Gratitude. *Reconocimiento, agradecimiento.* ~As a token of our APPRECIATION. *En señal de nuestro reconocimiento.* ‖ **2.** Awareness. *Conciencia, noción, entendimiento, dicernimiento.* ~An APPRECIATION of fine shades of meaning. *Una aptitud para captar los distintos matices de significado.* ‖ **3.** Rise in value. *Aumento, subida.* An APPRECIATION of 50% in property values. *Un aumento del 50% en los precios de las propriedades.* ‖ **4.** Appraisal. *Valoración (cosa), evaluación, estudio crítico (obra literaria).* ~An APPRECIATION of the life and work of Ernest Hemingway. *Un estudio crítico de la vida y obra de Ernest Hemingway.* ‖ **5.** •Art APPRECIATION classes. *Clases de iniciación al arte.* ‖ **6.** Understanding. *Comprensión.* ~Your APPRECIATION of the problems involved in this project is important. *Su comprensión de los problemas relacionados con este proyecto es de gran importancia.* ‖ **7.** •As a token of our APPRECIATION. *En señal de nuestro reconocimiento.* ‖ **8.** •To show one's APPRECIATION. *Mostrar su aprecio.* ⇨ APRECIACIÓN

APPRECIATIVE [APRECIATIVO]. *v.* Thankful, grateful. *Agradecido, de agradecimiento.* ~An APPRECIATIVE look. *Una mirada llena de agradecimiento.* ~He wasn't very APPRECIATIVE. *No se mostró muy agradecido.* ‖ **2.** [Audience]. *Atento.* ~New York audiences are very APPRECIATIVE. *El público neoyorquino suele ser muy atento.* ‖ **3.** Flattering (comments). *Elogioso, de aprobación.* ‖ **4.** •To be APPRECIATIVE of somebody's efforts. *Agradecerle los esfuerzos a alguien.*

APPREHEND. *v.* Arrest. *Detener, apresar.* ‖ **2.** Understand. *Comprender.* ‖ **3.** Become aware of. *Percibir, darse cuenta de.* ‖ **4.** Anticipate anxiously. *Temer.* ⇨ APREHENDER

APPREHENSION [APREHENSIÓN]. *adj.* Worry, anxiety about the future, dread. *Temor, miedo, recelo.* ~Although he is healthy he has the APPREHENSION that he is going to

die. *Aunque está sano, tiene miedo de morir.* ~He did it with a certain amount of APPREHENSION. *Lo hizo con cierto recelo.* ‖ **2.** Arrest, detention. *Detención, prendimiento.* ‖ **3.** Perception, awareness. *Percepción.* ‖ **4.** Understanding. *Comprensión.*

APPREHENSIVE [APREHENSIVO]. *adj.* Anxious or fearful about the future, uneasy. *Temeroso. miedoso, inquieto, preocupado.* ~I'm rather APPREHENSIVE about the consequences. *Estoy algo inquieto (preocupado) por lo que pueda pasar.*

APPROPRIATE[1]. *v.* To set aside for a specific use, allocate, earmark. *Consignar créditos, asignar, destinar fondos.* ~To APPROPRIATE funds for schools. *Destinar fondos para las escuelas.* ⇨ APROPIAR.

APPROPRIATE[2] [APROPIADO]. *adj.* Convenient (moment, comment). *Oportuno.* We should wait for an APPROPRIATE moment to announce the news to him. *Debemos esperar el momento oportuno para anunciarle la mala noticia.* ‖ **2.** Proper (authority). *Correspondiente, competente.* ~You must contact the APPROPRIATE authority. *Debe dirigirse a la autoridad competente.* ‖ **3.** Relevant. *Correspondiente.* ~Complete as APPROPRIATE. *Rellenar lo que corresponda.* ~Delete as APPROPRIATE. *Tachar lo que no corresponda.* ‖ **4.** *PHRASES.* ‖ •To take the APPROPRIATE measures. *Tomar las medidas pertinentes, correspondientes, del caso.* ‖ •APPROPRIATE committee. *Comité competente.* ‖ •This is the most APPROPRIATE thing to do. *Es lo más indicado.* ~He's the APPROPRIATE person for the job. *Es la persona más indicada para el puesto.* ‖ •Would it be APPROPRIATE for me to wear it. *¿Convendría que me lo pusiera?*

APPROVE. *adj.* [Person]. Admire, have a high regard for. *Gustar, agradar, caer bien.* ~Mother seems to APPROVE of him. *A mamá parece gustarle.* ~They don't APPROVE of my fiancé. *No les cae bien mi novio.* ~I don't APPROVE of his friends. *No me agradan sus amigos.* ‖ **2.** To be pleased with (something). *Gustarle a uno (algo).* ~I don't APPROVE of his conduct. *No estoy de acuerdo con (me parece mal) su conducta.* ‖ **3.** Accept, allow, permit. *Consentir.* ~Her father will never APPROVE of her marrying him. *Su padre no consentirá nunca que ella se case con él.* || **4.** To agree formally. *Dar su aprobación o visto bueno.* ~If the boss APPROVES, we can start right away. *Si el jefe da su aprobación, podemos empezar inmediatamente.* || **5.** To recognize officially. *Autorizar, acreditar (institución).* ~An APPROVED campsite. *Un camping autorizado.* ~An APPPROVED leave. *Una licencia autorizada.* || **6.** •APPROVE of + -ing. (I) To be favorable toward, have a favorable opinion of. *Estar de acuerdo, mirar con buenos ojos, gustar que.* ~She doesn't APPROVE of women smoking. *No mira con buenos ojos (no le gusta) que fumen las mujeres.* ~He doesn't APPROVE of smoking and drinking. *Está en contra del tabaco y del alcohol.* (II) Accept, favor, be partial to, believe, encourage. *Ser partidario de.* ~I don't APPROVE of her learning Latin. *No soy partidario de que aprenda latín.* || **7.** •In the APPROVED fashion. *Del modo acostumbrado.* || **8.** Do you APPROVE? *¿Está de acuerdo?* ⇨APROBAR

APPROXIMATION. *n.* Acercamiento. *Rough equivalent.* ~A good APPROXIMATION of a Tennessee accent. *Una buena imitación del acento de Tennessee.* ~At best it's an APPROXIMATION to the truth. *Como mucho podría decirse que se acerca a la verdad.* ⇨APROXIMACIÓN

APT. *adj.* Apt (to do something). Tending to, prone to. *Con tendencia a, susceptible de, propenso a.* ~He's APT to forget. *Tiende a (suele) olvidar.* ~She's APT to be car sick. *Tiende a marearse cuando viaja en coche.* || **2.** Likely. *Probable.* He's APT not to find me at home. *Es probable que no me encuentre en casa.* ~They're not APT to agree. *No es muy probable que acepten.* ~It is APT to be closed. *Lo más probable es que esté cerrado.* || **3.** Appropriate, fitting. (remark, reply, metaphor, quotation). *Apropiado, adecuado, acertado, pertinente, oportuno, justa (palabra).* || **4.** Clever, quick, intelligent. *Inteligente, talentoso, listo, capaz, despierto.* He's APT at languages. *Es muy bueno para*

los idiomas. || **5.** Gifted. *Dotado, aprovechado.* ~He's an APT pupil. *Es un alumno aprovechado.* || **6.** •I'm APT to be out on Mondays. *Por regla general no estoy los lunes.* || **7.** •We are APT to forget that ... *A menudo nos olvidamos que ...* ⇨APTO

ARCADE. *n.* [Of shops]. *Galería comercial, galerías (comerciales).* || **2.** Passageway. *Pasaje.* || **3.** [Round public square]. *Soportales.* || **4.** •Video ARCADE. *Sala de juego.* || **5.** •ARCADE game. *Videojuego.* || **6.** •Amusement arcade. *Salón de juegos.* ⇨ARCADA

ARDOR. *n.* Intense enthusiasm or eagerness: fervor, zeal. *Fervor.* His ARDOR cooled off in the course of the war. *Se apaciguó su fervor a lo largo de la guerra.* || **2.** Love. *Pasión.* ~Enough ARDOR in his tone to melt a heart of stone. *Suficiente pasión en la voz para derretir un corazón de piedra (para conmover a cualquiera).* ⇨ARDOR

AREA [AREA]. *adj.*

❶ PHYSICAL AREA. Size, square-footage area. *Extensión, superficie.* An AREA of 10 square meters. *Una superficie de 10 metros cuadrados.* || **2.** Space, room. *Lugar.* ~Is there enough AREA for the carpet? *¿Hay suficiente lugar para la alfombra?* || **3.** District, quarter, neighborhood. *Zona, barrio, vecindad, alrededores.* ~There have been many burglaries in the AREA. *Ha habido varios robos en la vecindad.* ~Residential area. *Zona residencial.* ~Shopping district. *Barrio comercial.* ~In the AREA we live in. *En el barrio en que vivimos.* ~The houses in the immediate AREA of the factory. *Las casas situadas en las inmediaciones (los alrededores) de la fábrica.* || **4.** Region (geographical). *Zona, región.* ~In the New York AREA. *En la zona de Nueva York.* ~AREA sales manager. *Gerente regional.* ~AREA office. *Oficina regional.* ~The AREA around the docks. *La zona del puerto.* ~The Caribbean AREA. *La región del Caribe.* || **5.** Part of a room, building, plot. ~Play AREA. *Zona de recreo.* ~Reception AREA. *Recepción.* || **6.** Region (patch, expanse, part). *Espacio, zona,*

parte. There are few open AREAS in the city. *Quedan pocos espacios abiertos en la ciudad*. ~Apply the ointment to the affected AREAS. *Aplicar el ungüento a las partes afectadas*. ~The wreckage of the plane was scattered over a wide AREA. *Los restos del avión siniestrados quedaron esparcidos sobre una extensa zona*. ‖ **7.** •Service AREA (on the highway). *Estación de servicio*.
❷ USED FIGURATIVELY. Field of knowledge, sphere. *Terreno, campo, materia, asunto*. ~I'm not a specialist in this AREA. ~*No soy especialista en este campo*. ~AREA of competence. *Terreno de competencia*. ~It's an AREA of difficulty (controversy). *Es un terreno difícil (polémico)*. ‖ **2.** Motivo, aspecto. Another AREA of concern... *Otro aspecto que preocupa es...* ‖ **3.** Sector. Sector. We want the participation of all AREAS of society. *Deseamos la participación de todos los sectores de la sociedad*. ‖ **4.** Discipline, subject, course. *Tema, materia, disciplina, rama*. ~This is an AREA I don't really know much about. *Esto es un tema que no conozco mucho*. ‖ **5.** Scope, range, extent. *Extensión*~We will assess the AREA of damage. *Examinaremos la extensión de los daños*. ‖ **6.** Section. *Parte*. His studies covers only one AREA of English history. *Sus estudios abarcan una sola parte de la historia de Inglaterra*. ‖ **7.** •It's a gray AREA. *Es un campo poco trabajado*.
❸ EXPRESSIONS. ‖ •AREA code (US). *Prefijo (local)*. ‖ •Postal AREA. *Distrito postal*. ‖ •Subject AREA. *Especialidad*. ‖ •AREA of agreement. *Margen de acuerdo*. ‖ •Distress AREA. *Zona damnificada*. ‖ •AREA of interest. *Sector de interés*. ‖ •AREA of responsibility. *Esfera de responsabilidad*. ‖ •Dining AREA. *Comedor*. ‖ •AREA of concern. *Motivo de preocupación*. ‖ •AREA of disagreement. *Zona de discrepancia*. ‖ •The library is a non-smoking AREA. *En la biblioteca no se puede fumar*. ‖ •AREAS of clouds across the South-West. *Nubosidad sobre el sudoeste*. ‖ •Disaster AREA. *Zona del desastre*, FIG *Situación desastrosa*.

~His life is a disaster AREA. *Tiene una vida personal desastrosa*. ⇨ AREA

ARGUMENT. *n.* Dispute, disagreement, quarrel. *Altercado, disputa, discusión, discordia*. ~There was a heated ARGUMENT. *Hubo una discusión acalorada*. ‖ **2.** (law) Plea, argument. *Alegato*. The judge rejected the defense ARGUMENT. *El juez desestimó el alegato de la defensa*. ‖ **3.** Synopsis, summary. *Resumen, síntesis, sumario, esquema*. ~I have read an ARGUMENT of his first work. *Leí un resumen de su primer libro*. ‖ **4.** Reason. *Motivo, razón*. There is a good ARGUMENT for postponing a decision. *Hay sobradas razones (motivos) para postergar la decisión*. ‖ **5.** Line of reasoning, contention. *Razonamiento*. Her ARGUMENT was that she needed a bigger house. *Razonaba que necesitaba una casa más grande*. ‖ **6.** Controversy. *Polémica*. ‖ **7.** *PHRASES*. ‖ •It's beyond ARGUMENT. *Es indiscutible, queda fuera de toda duda*. ‖ •His ARGUMENT is that ... *El sostiene que ...* ‖ •For the sake of ARGUMENT. *Pongamos por caso*. ‖ •The conclusion is open to ARGUMENT. *La conclusión es discutible*. ‖ •To have the better of an ARGUMENT. *Salir airoso de un debate*. ‖ •To follow someone's line of ARGUMENT. *Seguir el razonamiento de alguien*. ⇨ ARGUMENTO

ARM. *v.* [With tools, information]. *Proveer (a alguien de algo)*. ~I've ARMED myself with all the facts I need to prove my point. *Me he provisto de todos los datos para demostrar que estoy en lo cierto*. ARMED with pen and paper I set out to write. *Provisto de pluma y papel me puse a escribir*. ~An animal ARMED with a protective shell. *Una animal provisto de un caparazón protector*. ‖ **2.** To protect. *Proteger*. ~ARMED against the cold. *Protegido contra el frío*. ‖ **3.** To fit with some device. *To equip*. ~The divers were ARMED with cameras. *Los submarinistas iban equipados de máquinas fotográficas*. ⇨ ARMAR

ARREST. *v.* To detain, take into custody. *Detener*. The police ARRESTED more than 25 demonstrators. *La policía detuvo a más de 25 manifestantes*. ⇨ ARRESTAR

ARSENAL. *n.* Factory. *Fábrica de armamento.* ⇨ ARSENAL

ARTICULATE [ARTICULADO]. *adj.* Expressing oneself easily, clearly and effectively. *Que se expresa bien y con facilidad, expresivo.* ~He's very ARTICULATE. *Se expresa muy bien, sabe expresar sus ideas.* || **2.** Able to speak. *Capaz de hablar.* ~At two years of age a child is hardly ARTICULATE. *A los dos años de edad el niño es apenas capaz de hablar claramente.*

ARTIFICE. *n.* A clever trick (especially to deceive someone). *Estratagema, ardid.* ~They saw through the ARTIFICE. *Se dio cuenta del estratagema.* ⇨ ARTÍFICE

ASCEND. *v.* [Mountain]. *Subir a, escalar.* ~Few persons have ASCENDED Mount Everest. *Pocos han logrado escalar el monte Everest.* || **2.** [Throne]. *Subir, acceder.* ~Queen Victoria ASCENDED to the throne in 1837. *La reina Victoria subió al trono en 1837.* || **3.** To climb. *Subir.* To ascend the stairs. *Subir la escalera.* || **4.** [Smoke, balloon]. *Elevarse.* ⇨ ASCENDER

ASPIRATION. *n.* Wish, hope, dream. *Deseo, anhelo, ambición, ilusión.* ~As a boy his greatest ASPIRATION was to become a sailor. *De niño su mayor ilusión era de ser marinero.* ⇨ ASPIRACIÓN

ASSAULT. *n.* [Law]. *Agresión, violencia.* || **2.** Rape. *Violación.* || **3.** Onslaught. *Arremetida.* ~An ASSAULT on Everest. *Un intento de escalar el Everest.* ~The firm is preparing an ASSAULT on the market. *La empresa se dispone a conquistar el mercado.* || **4.** Violent attack. *Ataque.* ~Bayonet ASSAULT. *Ataque a la bayoneta.* || **5.** Violent criticism. *Ultraje.* || **6.** •ASSAULT and battery. *Lesiones.* || **7.** •Indecent ASSAULT. *Ofensa al pudor, atentado contra el pudor.* ⇨ ASALTO

ASSIGN. *v.* To appoint. *Destinar, designar, nombrar (personal).* They ASSIGNED him to the Paris embassy. *Le nombraron para la embajada de París.* ~A detective has been ASSIGNED to the case. *Se ha nombrado a un detective para que se ocupara del caso.* || **2.** Transfer (right, property). *Ceder, traspasar.* ~She ASSIGNED her property to her children. *Traspasó sus bienes a sus hijos.* || **3.** To designate (date) *Fijar, señalar.* On the day ASSIGNED for the trial. *En el día fijado (señalado) para el juicio.* || **4.** Ascribe (importance). *Dar, conceder.* We ASSIGN tremendous importance to training in our company. *En nuestra compañía concedemos mucha importancia a la preparación de nuestros empleados.* || **5.** Allocate, allot (room) *Destinar.* ~Which is the room which is ASSIGNED to me?. *¿Qué habitación es la que me destinan a mí?* || **6.** Attribute. *Atribuir.* Jealousy was ASSIGNED as the motive of the crime. *Se atribuyó el crimen a los celos.* ⇨ ASIGNAR

ASSIGNATION. *n.* Secret meeting. *Cita a escondidas.* ⇨ ASIGNACIÓN

ASSIGNMENT. *n.* Task. *Tarea.* || **2.** Lesson, homework. *Deber, tarea.* || **3.** Mission. *Misión.* ~To go on an ASSIGNMENT. *Salir a cumplir una misión.* ~Secret ASSIGNMENT. *Misión secreta.* || **4.** Job. *Trabajo.* His ASSIGNMENT was to collect evidence for the prosecution. *Su trabajo consistía en reunir pruebas para la acusación.* || **5.** Apppointment. *Nombramiento.* His ASSIGNMENT as vice-consul in London. *Su nombramiento como vice cónsul en Londres.* || **6.** LAW [To a case]. Designación. ~His ASSIGNMENT to the case was a surprise. *El haber sido designado para investigar el caso, causó mucha sorpresa.* || **7.** Transfer. *Cesión.* ⇨ ASIGNATURA

ASSIST. *v.* Give a hand, help, aid. *Ayudar.* ~He ASSISTED them in organizing the conference. *Los ayudó a organizar la conferencia.* || **2.** Further, promote, facilitate. *Favorecer, beneficiar.* ~The rumors will not ASSIST his election. *Los rumores no favorecerán su candidatura.* || **3.** To answer questions. *Interrogar.* ~A man is ASSISTING the police in their inquiries. *La policía está interrogando a un sospechoso.* ⇨ ASISTIR

ASSISTANCE. *n.* Help, aid. *Ayuda.* I couln't have done it without his assistance. *No lo podría haber hecho sin su ayuda.* || **2.** Cooperation. *Colaboración.* ~Your

ASSISTANCE in the search is greatly appreciated. *Se le agradece enormemente su colaboración en la búsqueda.* || **3.** •Can I be of any ASSISTANCE? *¿Puedo servirle en algo?* || **4.** •Public ASSISTANCE. *Subsidio (al necesitado).* || **5.** •To be of ASSISTANCE. *Prestarle ayuda a alguien.* ⇨ ASISTENCIA

ASSISTANT. *n.* Subordinate, helper. *Ayudante.* ~My ASSISTANT will help you. *Mi ayudante le atenderá.* || **2.** Clerk. *Dependiente, empleado.* The sales ASSISTANT will direct you to the glove department. *El encargado de ventas le indicará donde está la sección de guantes.* || **3.** PHRASES. || •ASSISTANT Secretary. *Subsecretario.* || •ASSISTANT Director. *Subdirector.* || •ASSISTANT Treasurer. *Subtesorero.* || •ASSISTANT Manager. *Subgerente, subdirector, director adjunto.* || •ASSISTANT Rector. *Coajutor.* || •ASSISTANT Professor. *Catedrático auxiliar (agregado).* || •ASSISTANT Dean. *Vicedecano.* || •ASSISTANT Teacher. *Profesor adjunto (escuela primaria), profesor ayudante (escuela secundaria).* || CIN •ASSISTANT cameraman. *Ayudante de operador.* || CIN ASSISTANT director. *Regidor de escena.* || •Clerical ASSISTANT. *Auxiliar administrativo.* || •Managerial ASSISTANT. *Ayudante de dirección.* || •ASSISTANT Chief. *Subjefe.* ⇨ ASISTENTE

ASSOCIATE [ASOCIADO]. *adj.* Accomplice. *Acómplice.* ~He and his ASSOCIATES have been sent to jail for conspiracy. *Él y sus cómplices fueron encarcelados por conspiración.* || **2.** Companion, friend. *Compañero, amigo.* ~He's a close ASSOCIATE of the author. *Es amigo íntimo del autor.* || **3.** [Business, profession]. Colleague. *Colega.* ~Let me introduce one of my associates. *Le quiero presentar a uno de mis colegas.* || **4.** Partner. *Socio.* ~One of his business ASSOCIATES. *Uno de sus socios.* || **5.** *adj.* •ASSOCIATE member. *Socio adjunto, socio adherido, socio correspondiente.* || **6.** •ASSOCIATE director. *Subdirector.* || **7.** •ASSOCIATE professor. *Profesor adjunto.*

ASSOCIATE. *v.* To be involved, connected with. *Estar vinculado.* She was ASSO-

CIATED with the movement. *Estaba vinculada con el movimiento.* || **2.** Mix with. *Juntarse, relacionarse con.* ~I don't like the people you ASSOCIATE with. *No me gustan las personas con quienes te juntas.* || **3.** •To be ASSOCIATED with. *Tener que ver con.* He refused to be ASSOCIATED with the scheme. *No quiso tener nada que ver con el asunto.* ~He was ASSOCIATED with a scandal many years ago. *Hace muchos años estuvo mezclado con un escándalo.* || **4.** •To ASSOCIATE with. *Tratar con, frecuentar (la companía de).* ~I don't ASSOCIATE with crooks. *No trato con ladrones.* || **5.** •To be ASSOCIATED with somebody (in a venture). *Participar juntamente.* ⇨ ASOCIAR

ASSUME. *v.* Suppose, presume, surmise. *Presumir, suponer, deducir.* ~ASSUMING that they arrive on time. *Suponiendo (en el supuesto de) que lleguen a la hora.* ~Let's SUPPOSE they're right. *Supongamos que tienen razón.* ~I SUPPOSE you've heard the news. *Supongo que se habrá enterado de la noticia.* ASSUMING that everything goes according to plan. *En el supuesto caso de que todo salga de acuerdo con lo previsto.* || **2.** To pretend, feign. *Afectar, adoptar, fingir (virtue).* ~He assumed to be surprised. *Fingió sorpresa.* He ASSUMED an air of cheerfulness. *Adoptó un aire de falsa alegría.* || **3.** To begin to use (name, attitude). *Adoptar.* He ASSUMED a foreign accent. *Adoptó un acento extranjero.* ~He ASSUMED a posture of arrogance. *Adoptó una postura arrogante.* || **4.** To become apparent. *Manifestarse.* The disease ASSUMES many forms. *La enfermedad se manifiesta de distintas maneras.* || **5.** Take for granted, suppose something to be a fact. *Dar por sentado.* ~We can ASSUME nothing. *No podemos dar nada por sentado.* ~We can safely ASSUME that ... *Damos por sentado que ...* || **6.** To acquire, take on, reach. *Adquirir, tomar, alcanzar, cobrar* ~The fire ASSUMED great intensity. *El incendio adquirió grandes proporciones.* ~The affair has ASSUMED a sinister character. *El asunto ha tomado (adquirido) un cariz siniestro.* || **7.** To consider.

Dar por. ~We ASSUMED him dead. *Le dimos por muerto.* || **8.** To take upon oneself, take charge of (debt, obligation, expenses). *Hacerse cargo.* He ASSUMED the mortgage on the house. *Se hizo cargo de la hipoteca de la casa.* || **9.** To appropriate, arrogate, seize, usurp. *Usurpar, apropriarse. arrogarse.* ~He ASSUMED to himself the right to make an amendment to the constitution. *Se arrogó por cuenta propia el derecho de enmendar la constitución.* || **10.** PHRASES. •An ASSUMED name. *Alias, nombre ficticio, nombre falso.* ~He's travelling under an ASSUMED name. *Viaja con un nombre ficticio.* || •Let's ASSUME that. *Pongamos por caso que.* || •You resigned, I ASSUME. *Me imagino que usted dimitió.* || •The ASSUMED culprit. *El presunto culpable.* ⇨ASSUMIR

ASYLUM. [Mental]. *Manicomio.* ⇨ASILO

ATMOSPHERE [ATMÓSFERA]. *n.* Surroundings. *Ambiente.* This café has a very nice ATMOSPHERE. ~*Este café tiene un ambiente muy agradable* ~The ATMOSPHERE is not very conducive to study. *El ambiente no es muy apropriado para el estudio.* ~A friendly ATMOSPHERE. *Un ambiente de cordialidad.*

ATTACK. *v.* To attack (a woman), rape. *Violar.* ~She was ATTACKED in broad daylight. *Fue violada en pleno día.* || **2.** Threaten. *Amenazar.* ~Traditional values are under ATTACK. *Los valores tradicionales se ven amenazados.* || **3.** Tackle, deal with (problem). *Abordar.* He ATTACKED the problem with determination. ~*Abordó el problema con mucha decisión.* || **4.** PHRASES || •To return to the attack. *Volver a la carga.* || •To be under ATTACK. *Ser el blanco de las críticas.* || •An ATTACK on someone's life. *Un atentado contra la vida de alguien.* || •Terrorist ATTACKS. *Antentados terroristas.* ||•To come under ATTACK. *Ser agredido.* || •An ATTACK of fever. *Un acceso de fiebre.* || •An ATTACK of nerves. *Una crisis de nervios.*|| •A heart ATTACK. *Un infarto.* ⇨ATACAR

ATTEND. *v.* To be present at, go to. *Asistir, concurrir, estar presente, presenciar, participar, tomar parte.* ~All children must ATTEND school. *Todos los niños deben asistir*

a la escuela. ~The meeting was well attended. *Asistió mucha gente a la reunión.* || **2.** To accompany, escort. *Acompañar.* ~She ATTENDED the princess during her tour of the country *Acompañó a la princesa durante su viaje por el país.* || **3.** [School, university, church]. *Ir a (un colegio, la universidad, la iglesia).* ~Which school did you children ATTEND? *¿A qué escuela fueron sus hijos?* || **4.** Look after, care for. *Cuidar.* ~Doctors were few and only ATTENDED the very sick. *Había pocos médicos y cuidaban únicamente a los enfermos de más gravedad.* || **5.** •I'll ATTEND to you later (threatening). *Luego me las arreglo con Ud.* || **6.** •To attend (on someone). Wait on, minister to. *Servir a alguien.* We have been waiting over half an hour to be ATTENDED on. *Llevamos más de media hora esperando que nos sirvan.* || **7.** •To ATTEND to. Take care of, deal with. *Ocuparse de, hacer caso de.* ~She will ATTEND to the arrangements for the meeting. *Ella se ocupará de hacer los arreglos para la reunión.* ~I may be late, I have got one or two things to ATTEND to. *A lo mejor llegue tarde, tengo que ocuparme de un par de cosas.* || **8.** •A well ATTENDED meeting. *Una reunión muy concurrida.* ⇨ATENDER

ATTRACTION [ATRACCIÓN]. *n.* Attractive feature. *Atractivo.* ~One of the ATTRACTIONS of owning a business is being your own boss. *Uno de los atractivos de tener negocio es el de ser su propio jefe.* || **2.** Charm. *Encanto.* ~One of the ATTRACTIONS of quiet life. *Uno de los encantos de la vida retirada.* || **3.** Incentive, inducement. *Aliciente.* ~The job has many ATTRACTIONS. *El trabajo tiene muchos alicientes.*

ATTRACTIVE [ATRACTIVO]. *adj.* Advantageous, interesting (offer, price, idea). *Interesante, atrayente, tentador.* ~An INTERESTING offer. *Una oferta interesante.* ~The idea isn't exactly ATTRACTIVE to me. *La idea no me atrae demasiado.* || **2.** [Prospect]. *Halagüeño.* ~It isn't a very ATTRACTIVE prospect. *No es una perspectiva muy halagüeña.* || **3.** [Child, girl].

Mona, guapa, linda. || **4.** [Man]. *Bien parecido, guapo, buen mozo.* || **5.** Pleasing. *Agradable.* ~He has an ATTRACTIVE personality. *Es una persona encantadora.*

AUDIENCE. *n.* Group of people listening to or watching a concert, show, film, etc. *Público, concurrencia, espectadores, auditorio (listeners), radioyentes(radio), telespectadores (television), lectores (of writer), audiencia (Acad.).* ~There was a big AUDIENCE. *Asistió un público numeroso.* ~The fight attracted a sizeable AUDIENCE. *La pelea atrajo a un buen número de espectadores.* ⇨AUDIENCIA

AUDITORIUM. [Room]. *Sala, salón de actos, anfiteatro.* ⇨AUDITORIO

AUTHORIZE. [Payment]. *Aprobar.* ~Payment of this invoice has not yet been AUTHORIZED. *Todavía no se ha aprobado el pago de esta factura.* ⇨AUTORIZAR

AUTOMATIC [AUTOMÁTICO]. Inevitable, unavoidable, certain. *Inevitable, inmediato.* ~Since the crime took place in the house, he is an AUTOMATIC suspect. *Como el delito tuvo lugar en su casa, inevitablemente es el sospechoso.* ~Citizenship is AUTOMATIC for children born in this country. *Los niños que nacen en este país se convierten de inmediato en ciudadanos.* || **2.** Mechanical. *Obligado.* ~The AUTOMATIC smile of a tired store clerk. *La obligada sonrisa de un dependiente cansado.* || **3.** Spontaneous. *Espontáneo.* The AUTOMATIC enthusiasm of the crowd. *El espontáneo entusiasmo de la multitud.*

B

BACHELOR. *n.* Unmarried man. *Soltero.* ~In my BACHELOR days. *En mi época de soltero.* || **2.** •Bachelor's degree. *Licenciatura.* || **3.** •BACHELOR of Arts. *Licenciatura en Filosofía y Letras.* || **4.** •BACHELOR in Sciences. *Licenciado en Ciencias.* ▸Licenciatura involves 5 years of studies equivalent to a Master's degree. ⇨BACHILLER

BAGGAGE. *n.* Trunks, bags, suitcases, etc., used in traveling. *Equipaje.* ~How many pieces of BAGGAGE do you have? *¿Cuántas maletas tiene?* || **2.** PHRASES. Baggage allowance. *Límite de peso, franquicia de (para) el equipaje.* || •BAGGAGE car. *Furgón de equipajes.* || •BAGGAGE check. *Talón de equipaje.* || •BAGGAGE room. *Consigna.* || •BAGGAGE locker. *Consigna automática.* || •BAGGAGE train. *Tren de equipajes.* || •BAGGAGE rack. *Redecilla de equipajes.* ⇨BAGAJE.

BALANCE. *n.* Equality of debits and credits in an account. *Saldo.* || **2.** Equilibrium. *Equilibrio.* ~To loose one's BALANCE. *Perder el equilibrio,* FIG *trastornarse.* ~To keep one's BALANCE. *Mantener (guardar) el equilibrio.* ~The wheel is out of BALANCE. *La rueda está desequilibrada.* ~Mental BALANCE. *Equilibrio mental.* || **3.** The amount still owed after a partial settlement. *Saldo.* ~There's a BALANCE of sixteeen hundred dollars in your account. *Su cuenta presenta un saldo de mil seiscientos dólares.* || **4.** Remainder. *Resto.* ~I would like to take the BALANCE of my vacation in September. *Quisiera tomar el resto de mis vacaciones en septiembre.* || **5.** Balance (of clock). *Volante.* || **6.** Good sense. *Buen sentido.* || **7.** Counterweight (to something). *Contrapeso (a algo).* || **8.** Scale. *Balanza.* ||

9. PHRASES. || •To throw somebody off BALANCE. *Hacer perder el equilibrio,* FIG *desconcertar a alguien.* || •To hang in the BALANCE. *Estar en juego, Estar pendiente de un hilo.* ~His reputation is in the BALANCE. *Su reputación está en juego.*|| •To strike a (proper) BALANCE. *Encontrar el punto medio, dar con el justo medio.* || •To catch off BALANCE. *Agarrar (coger) desprevenido.* || •To BALANCE an account. *Cuadrar una cuenta.* || •BALANCE due. *Saldo vencido.* || •BALANCE of power. *Equilibrio de potencias, de poder, de fuerzas.* || •Outstanding BALANCE. *Saldo pendiente.* || •BALANCE sheet. *Estado de cuenta.* || •Pay the BALANCE. *Saldar.* || •BALANCE in hand. *Saldo disponible.* || •Credit BALANCE. *Saldo acreedor.* || •On BALANCE. *A fin de cuentas, mirándolo bien.* ~On BALANCE, the changes have been beneficial. *En fin de cuentas, los cambios han resultado beneficiosos.* || •The BALANCE of the evidence. *Las pruebas consideradas en su conjunto.* || •The BALANCE of opinion. *La opinión general.* || •BALANCE of trade. *Balanza comercial.* || •BALANCE pole. *Balancín.* || •To hold the BALANCE. *Ser la voz cantante.* ⇨BALANCE

BALANCE². *v.* FIN [Budget]. *Equilibrar.* ~This year the government managed to BALANCE the budget. *Este año el gobierno logró equilibrar el presupuesto.* || **2.** To weigh (up). *Sopesar, comparar.* ~You have to BALANCE the risks against the likely profit. *Tiene que sopesar los riesgos y los posibles beneficios.* ~To BALANCE the advantages against the disadvantages. *Comparar las ventajas con los inconvenientes.* || **3.** [Load]. *Equilibrar.* ~To BALANCE the scales. *Para equilibrar la balanza.* || **4.**

[Object]. *Mantener, sostener (poner) en equilibrio.* ~He put out his arms to BALANCE himself. *Extendió los brazos para no perder el equilibrio.* ~To BALANCE a plate on the end of a stick. *Poner un plato en equilibrio en la punta de un palo.* || **5.** [Wheel of a car]. *Equilibrar, balancear (Lat. Am.).* || **6.** To counteract. *Servir de contrapeso.* || **7.** vi. To hold position. *Mantener el equilibrio.* || **8.** [Someone's power]. *Contrarrestar.* || **9.** PHRASES. •To BALANCE the budget. *Ajustar el presupuesto.* •To BALANCE out. *Compensarse.* ~It all BALANCES out in the end. *Al final una cosa compensa la otra.* ~The losses and the gains BALANCE out one another. *Las pérdidas y las ganancias se compensan.* •To BALANCE the books. *Hacer el balance.* ⇨ BALANCEAR

BALLOON. *n.* Small inflated rubber bag. *Globo.* ~She bought BALLOONS of all colors for the party. *Compró globos de diversos colores para la fiesta.* || **2.** Airtight bag that rises and floats above the earth, hot air balloon. *Balón de oxígeno, aerostático.* || **3.** Outline enclosing the words said by a character in a cartoon. *Bocadillo, globo.* || **4.** PHRASES. •To go up in a BALLOON. *Montar en globo.* || •Like a lead BALLOON. *Como un jarro de agua fría.* || •BALLOON glass. *Copa de coñac.* || •BALLOON loan. *Préstamo reembolsable al vencimiento.* ⇨ BALÓN

BAR. *n.* [Of chocolate]. *Tableta.* ~A candy BAR. *Una tableta de chocolate.* || **2.** [Of soap]. *Pastilla.* || **3.** [Of cage, prison]. *Barrote.* || **4.** Obstacle. *Obstáculo.* ~It is a BAR to progress. *Es un obstáculo para el progreso.* || **5.** Barrier. *Barrera.* || **6.** JUR Dock. *Banquillo.* || **7.** Court. *Tribunal.* || **8.** [Music]. *Compás.* || **9.** [On door]. *Tranca.* || **10.** Lever. *Palanca.* || **11.** Band of light, color. *Franja.* **12.** •Color BAR. *Segregación racial.* || **13.** •The BAR. *Abogacía (profession), Colegio de abogados (body of lawyers).* ⇨ BARRA

BARRACKS. *n.* *Cuartel.* ~To be confined to BARRACKS. *Ser acuartelado.* ⇨ BARRACA

BASE. *n.* Foot (of tree, mountain). *Pie.* ~He lived in a house at the BASE of a mountain.

Vivía al pie de una montaña. || **2.** [Of a column]. *Basa.* || **3.** [Of lamp]. *Pie.* || **4.** [Of statue]. *Pedestal.* || **5.** Camp (for expedition). *Campamento.* || **6.** [Of organization]. *Sede.* || **7.** [Of pie]. *Fondo.* || **8.** [Of word]. *Raíz.* || **9.** PHRASES. || •BASE line (tennis). *Línea de saque.* || FIG •To be off BASE. *Estar equivocado.* ~He's way off BASE. *Está totalmente equivocado.* || •Paint with a water BASE. *Pintura al agua.* || •Dishes with a rice BASE. *Platos a base de arroz.* || •BASE coat (of paint). *Primera capa, capa selladora.* || •BASE camp. *Campamento permanente.* || •To get to first BASE. *Alcanzar la primera meta, dar el primer paso, vencer la primera dificultad.* || •To catch someone off BASE. *Pillar a alguien desprevenido.* || •To touch BASES with. (I) To keep in touch with. *Mantenerse en contacto (con).* ~I called them just to touch bases. *Los llamé, para preguntarles como estaban.* (II) To cover thouroughly (subject). *Tratar detalladamente.* ~Her speech touched every BASE. *Su discurso tocó todos los puntos de interés.* ⇨ BASE

BASIC [BÁSICO]. *adj.* [Pay, interest, price]. *Base.* ~BASIC pay. *Sueldo base.* || **2.** Simple, rudimentary. *Elemental.* ~This textbook is very BASIC. *Este texto es muy elemental.* ~BASIC Spanish. *Español elemental.* || **3.** Fundamental, essential. *Fundamental.* ~Tourism is BASIC to the economy of the country. *El turismo es fundamental para la economía del país.* || **4.** [Industrías]. *De base.* ~BASIC industries. *Industrias de base.* || **5.** •BASICS. *Lo esencial, lo fundamental, la base.*

BATTERY. *n.* An unlawful attack upon another person. *Agresión, violencia.* || **2.** Large number of things, people or events. *Montón, multitud.* ~He is advised by a BATTERY of lawyers. *Lo asesora un verdadero ejército de abogados.* ~A BATTERY of questions. *Una descarga (sarta) de preguntas.* ~A BATTERY of cameras. *Una multitud de cámaras.* ~A BATTERY of tests. *Una serie de pruebas.* || **3.** A device that supplies electricity. *Pila (radio, flashlight), acumulador, batería (car).* || **4.** PHRASES. •Assault

and BATTERY. *Lesiones, agresión.* ‖ •BAT-
TERY acid. *Electolito.* ‖ •BATTERY farming.
Cría intensiva. ‖ •To recharge one's BATTE-
RIES. *Recuperar la energía.* ⇨BATERÍA

BEAST. *n.* [Wild]. *Fiera.* Lions and tigers
are WILD beasts. *Los leones y los tigres
son fieras.* ‖ **2.** Beast-like person. *Bruto,
animal, salvaje.* ~That BEAST of a policeman. *Aquel bruto de policía.* ‖ **3.** Livestock.
Reses, ganado. ‖ **4.** Sexually agressive man.
Fiera. ‖ **5.** Something unpleasant. *Cosa
difícil, desagradable.* ~Filing is a BEAST of
a job. *Archivar es un trabajo odioso.* ‖ **6.**
Animalistic nature. *Instinto animal.* ~Hun-
ger brought out the BEAST in him. *El
hambre puso de manifiesto su instinto
animal.* ‖ **7.** •BEAST of prey. *Depredador.* ‖
8. •The king of BEASTS. *El rey de los ani-
males.* ⇨BESTIA

BEAT. *v.* To hit (a person). *Pegar, golpear.*
~He BEATS his children. *Les pega a sus hijos.*
~He was BEATEN to death. *Lo mataron a
golpes.* ‖ **2.** [As punishment]. *Dar una
paliza.* ‖ **3.** [A drum]. *Tocar.* ‖ **4.** To defeat
(opponent). *Vencer, ganar, derrotar.* ~We
BEAT them. *Los ganamos.* ‖ **5.** Be better than
someone else. *Superar.* ~His cooking BEATS
mine. *Cocina mejor que yo.* ~You can't BEAT
home-made apple pie. *No hay como el pastel de manzana casero.* ‖ **6.** MUS To indicate (time). *Marcar, llevar.* ~She BEAT time
with her foot. *Llevaba el compás con el
pie.* ‖ **7.** Anticipate. *Llegar antes que.* ~He
left early to BEAT the heavy traffic. *Se
marchó temprano para evitar los embo-
tellamientos de tráfico.* ‖ **8.** [Heart]. *Latir.*
‖ **9.** Strike, pound. *Dar golpes.* ~Someone's
BEATING at the door. *Alguien está dando
golpes en la puerta.* ‖ **10.** [Carpet].
Sacudir. ‖ **11** To tread. ~They had BEATEN a
path across the field. *Habían dejado
marcado un sendero en el campo.* ‖ **12.** To
strike. *Azotar.* ~The waves BEAT on the
shore. *Las olas azotaban la playa.* ~The
sun BEAT down on them. *El sol caía de
lleno sobre ellos.* ‖ **13.** [Path]. *Abrir.* ~To
BEAT a path through the jungle. *Abrirse
paso en la selva.* ‖ **14.** Mystify, baffle.
Confundir, dejar perplejo. ~The police

confessed themselves BEATEN. *La policía
confiesa no tener pista alguna.* ~The problem has me BEATEN. *El problema me deja
totalmente perplejo.* ‖ **15.** Meter en la
cabeza. *To make someone see reason.* ~He
tried to BEAT some sense into him. *Intentó
meterle un poco de sentido común en la
cabeza, intentó hacerle entrar en razón.*
‖ **16.** •To BEAT around the bush. *Andarse
por las ramas.* ‖ **17.** •To BEAT the system.
Explotar el sistema. ⇨BATIR

BENEFIT. *n.* Advantage. *Ventaja, provecho.* ~The lecturer explained the BENEFITS of
public membership. *El conferencista explicó
las ventajas de la nacionalización.* ~She's
exploiting the situation for her own BENEFIT.
Ella explota la situación para su provecho.
~The BENEFITS of a good education. *Las
ventajas de una buena educación.* ~I didn't
derive much BENEFIT from the course. *No
saqué mucho provecho del curso.* ‖ **2.** *Help.
Ayuda. socorro.* ~The attack proceeded
without the BENEFIT of artillery. *El ataque
se realizó sin el apoyo artillero.* ‖ **3.** Good.
Bien. ~For the BENEFIT of your children. *Por
el bien de tus hijos.* ‖ **4.** Allowance. *Subsidio,
prestación.* ~Unemployment BENEFITS.
Subsidio (seguro) de desempleo. ~He's re-
ceiving unemployment BENEFITS. *Recibe
subsidios de desempleo.* ~The Minister said
that social security BENEFITS should be increased. *El ministro dijo que debían
aumentarse las prestaciones de la Seguridad Social.* ~They are not entitled to any
BENEFITS. *No tienen derecho a recibir
prestaciones de ningún tipo.* ‖ **5.** PHRASES.
‖ •For one's BENEFITS. (I) To (in order to) im-
press someone. *Para impresionar a alguien.*
~He wasn't really angry, that was just an act
for his girl friend's BENEFIT. *No fue más que
una comedia para impresionar a su amiga.*
(II) Intended for. *Destinado a.* ~Information
for the BENEFIT of new comers. *Información
destinada (de interés) para los recién
llegados.* ‖ •Fringe BENEFITS. *Ventajas laborales, ventajas extrasalariales, beneficios
complementarios.* ‖ •To be to the BENEFIT
of. *Ser provechoso.* ‖ •For one's BENEFIT.
(I) *En su honor.* She put on a new hat for

his BENEFIT. *Se puso un nuevo sombrero en su honor.* (II) *Para su gobierno.* ~Let me add for your BENEFIT that... *Añadiré para su gobierno que...* || •For the BENEFIT of. *En pro de, a favor de, en consideración a.* || •Without the BENEFIT of the clergy. *Sin sanción de la iglesia.* ⇨BENEFICIO

BLOCK [BLOQUE]. *n.* Any number of persons or things of the same type regarded as a unit. *Grupo, serie.* ~A BLOCK of seats. *Un grupo de asientos.* || **2.** Obstruction, hindrance. *Bloqueo, obstrucción.* || **3.** Deterrent, impediment, barrier. *Obstáculo, estorbo.* ~Her arrival should be no BLOCK to your leaving. *Su llegada no debe impedirle que se vaya.* || **4.** Auctioneer's platform. *Plataforma (para subastas).* || **5.** Traffic jam. *Atasco, embotellamiento.* || **6.** Section. *Sección.* ~A BLOCK of text. *Una sección de texto.* || **7.** Distance between two streets. *Manzana, cuadra (Lat.Am.).* ~It's five BLOCKS away. *Queda a cinco calles de aquí.* || **8.** Head (coll.). *Coco (fam.).* || **9.** Piece, chunk of wood. *Zoquete, tarugo.* || **10.** Blocklike stand for chopping, cutting, etc., such as a butcher's BLOCK. *Tajo.* || **11.** Piece of wood, linoleum, etc. engraved with a design or picture. *Clisé, cliché, grabado, plancha (metal).* || **12.** A length of track governed by signals. *Tramo.* || **13.** Thwarting of an opponent's play or movement (sport). *Parada.* || **14.** Form, mold. *Horma.* ~Hat block. *Horma de sombrero.* || **15.** Wooden head used for combing wigs or headdresses. *Fraustina.* || **16.** Anvil. *Cepo.* || **17.** Brake shoe, brake lining. *Zapata, almohadilla.* || **18.** Paving BLOCK. *Adoquín.* || **19.** *PHRASES.* || •Stumbling BLOCK. *Obstáculo.* || •To put on the BLOCK. *Vender en subasta.* ~They're putting their boat on

the BLOCK next week. *La semana que viene subastan su barco.* || •To run around the BLOCK. *Dar la vuelta a la manzana.* || •A mental BLOCK. *Un bloqueo mental.* ~He has a mental BLOCK about physics. *Tiene un bloqueo mental con la física.* || •A BLOCK of share. *Un paquete, una serie de acciones.* || •BLOCK vote. *Voto por delegación (representación).* || •BLOCK and tackle. *Aparejo de polea(s).* || •To KNOCK somebody's block off. *Romperle la crisma a alguien.* || •On the BLOCK. *A tocateja.* || •The executioner's BLOCK. *El tajo del verdugo.* || •Starting BLOCK (sport). *Taco de salida.* || •BLOCK letter. *Caracteres de imprenta (molde).* || •A chip off the old BLOCK. *De tal palo, tal astilla.* || •BLOCK of butter. *Pella de manteca.* || •Note BLOCK. *Bloc.*

BONANZA. *n.* Source of wealth. *Mina de oro, fuente de riqueza.* ~The movie was a BONANZA. *La película resultó una mina de oro.* || **2.** Plentiful supply. *Superabundancia.* ⇨BONANZA

BRIEF [BREVE]. Short. *Corto.* ~After a BRIEF stay in Italy. *Después de una estancia corta en Italia.* || **2.** Concise. *Conciso.* ~His letters are BRIEF but interesting. *Sus cartas son concisas pero interesantes.* || **3.** [Style]. *Lacónico.* || **4.** •Well, to be BRIEF. *Bueno, en resumen.* || **5.** Scanty (clothes). *Muy corto.* A BRIEF bathing suit. *Un traje de baño muy corto.*

BULLETIN [BOLETÍN]. *n.* A brief statement of the latest news. *Anuncio, comunicado, parte (med.).* ~The latest BULLETIN on his condition. *El último parte médico.* || **3.** •BULLETIN board. *Tablero, tablón de anuncios.*

C

CABIN. *n.* Cabin on a ship. *Camarote.* || **2.** Cabin (in the country). *Cabaña.* ~He has a CABIN in the country. *Tiene una cabaña en el campo.* || **3.** Hut. *Choza.* ~We had to spend the night in a farmworker's HUT. *Tuvimos que pasar la noche en la choza de un labrador.* || **4.** *PHRASES* || •CABIN cruiser. *Yate de recreo, motonave.* || •CABIN crew. *Tripulación de pilotaje.* || •CABIN class. *Clase de cámara, segunda clase.* || •CABIN boy. *Grumete.* || •CABIN baggage. *Equipaje de mano.* ⇨CABINA

CABINET. *n.* Wall cupboard used for storing or displaying things. *Armario de cocina (kitchen), botiquín (medicine), vitrina, escaparate (curio, china), mueble-bar (cocktail).* || **2.** Piece of furniture containing a radio or television set. *Caja, mueble.* || **3.** •Filing CABINET. *Archivador.* || **4.** •CABINET maker. *Ebanista.* || **5.** •CABINET meeting. *Sesión ministerial.* ⇨GABINETE

CALCULATE. *v.* To plan deliberately. *Planear deliberadamente.* ~It was CALCULATED to upset the plans. *Se planeó con la intención de estropear los planes.* || **2.** To intend, plan. *Creer, considerar, suponer.* ~I CALCULATED on arriving at about five. *Había pensado en llegar a eso de las cinco.* || **3.** •To be CALCULATED (to do something). *Proyectado para, hacer con el fin de.* ~This is CALCULATED to give him a jolt. *Esto tiene el propósito de darle una sacudida.* ~It's hardly CALCULATED to help us. *Esto apenas será ventajoso para nosotros.* ~His remarks were CALCULATED to offend. *Lo dijo con la intención de ofender.* ~Policies CALCULATED to attract younger voters. *Medidas destinadas a atraer el voto de los jóvenes.* || **4.** To CALCULATE on. *Contar con.* ~We are CALCULATING on having good weather. *Contamos con tener buen tiempo.* ⇨CALCULAR

CALCULATED [CALCULADO]. *adj.* [Insults]. Intentional, willful. *Intencionado, dicho con toda intención.* || **2.** [Act]. Deliberate. *Premeditado, deliberado, estudiado.* ~In a CALCULATED effort to destroy our power. *En un intento premeditado de destruir nuestro poder.* || **3.** With awareness. *Previsto, conocido, que se cuenta con ello.* Our country has taken a CALCULATED risk in lowering its import tariffs. *Nuestro país sabe a lo que se expone al reducir los derechos de importación (Prats).*

CANCEL. *v.* [In most cases]. *Anular (check, order, telephone call, invitation).* || **2.** Revoke, repeal. *Retirar, revocar, rescindir (decree).* || **3.** To stamp marks on a postage stamp. *Matasellar.* || **4.** [Flight, holiday, party]. *Suprimir, suspender.* || **5.** Delete, cross out. *Tachar, borrar, suprimir.* ~To CANCEL a name from a list. *Borrar un nombre de una lista.* || **6.** To balance, offset. *Contrarrestar.* ~The profits CANCEL the loss. *Los beneficios contrarrestan las pérdidas.* || **7.** •CANCEL out. *Anular, contrarrestar.* ~Those advantages are CANCELED out by the practical difficulties. *Las dificultades de orden práctico anulan estas ventajas.* || **8.** •They CANCEL each other out. *Se anulan mutuamente.* ⇨CANCELAR

CANDID. *adj.* Frank, open, sincere. *Sincero, franco, abierto.* ~To be quite CANDID with you. *Para serle completamente franco.* || **2.** Unposed, informal (shot, photograph). *Natural.* ~This is a very CANDID shot of you. *Pareces muy natural en esta foto.* || **3.** Just, impartial, objective. *Imparcial.* The speaker expressed a CANDID view of the proposals. *El* *conferenciante expuso un punto de vista imparcial de las propuestas.* || **4.** •He's less than CANDID. *Oculta algo.* || **5.** •To be quite candid. *Hablando con franqueza.* || **6.** •CANDID camara. *Cámara indiscreta.* ⇨CÁNDIDO

CAPITAL [CAPITAL]. *adj.* Very serious, grave. *Primordial.* ~Of CAPITAL importance. *De importancia primordial.* ~A CAPITAL consideration. *Una consideración primordial.* || **2.** PHRASES. || •CAPITAL punishment. *Pena de muerte.* || •CAPITAL letter. *Letra mayúscula.* ~Write your name in CAPITALS. *Escriba su nombre en mayúsculas.* || •CAPITAL sentence. *Condena de la pena de muerte.* || PRINT •Small CAPITALS. *Versalitas.* || •To make CAPITAL out of something. *Sacar provecho (partido) de algo.* They are seeking to gain political CAPITAL from this affair. *Intentan sacar provecho político del asunto.* || •CAPITAL assets. *Activo fijo.* || •CAPITAL gain. *Plusvalía.* || •Working CAPITAL. *Fondo de operaciones.*

CAPTURE. *v.* [Town, city]. *Tomar.* The king's forces CAPTURED the city. *Las fuerzas reales tomaron la ciudad.* || **2.** [Market]. *Acaparar, conquistar.* ~They CAPTURED 20% of the market. *Conquistaron el 20% del mercado.* || **3.** [Mood, atmosphere]. *Captar.* ~The painting CAPTURES the joyous mood of the time. *El cuadro capta el ambiente festivo de la época.* || **4.** [Person]. *Apresar, prender.* ~The police was able to CAPTURE the thief. *La policía ha logrado prender al ladrón.* || **5.** [Animal]. *Coger, apresar.* They CAPTURED the tiger with nets. *Cogieron al tigre con unas redes.* || **6.** Attract, hold (attention, interest). *Llamar, atraer, captar.* ~The idea has CAPTURED the public's imagination. *La idea cautivó la imaginación del público.* || **7.** ART *Captar, reproducir, representar fielmente.* ~The painter CAPTURED her expression very well. *El Pintor captó muy bien su expresión.* || **8.** [Ship]. *Apresar.* ~A Marroccan patrol boat CAPTURED a Spanish fishing boat for fishing in its waters. *Una patrullera marroquí apresó un pesquero español por faenar en sus aguas.* || **9.** Gain by effort (votes, title). *Conseguir.* ~He

CAPTURED the majority of the votes. *Consiguió la mayoría de los votos.* || **10.** [Championship]. *Ganar.* || **11.** [Amistad]. *Captarse, ganarse.* || **12.** [In chess]. *Comer.* ⇨CAPTURAR

CAR. *n.* Automovil. *Coche, auto.* || **2.** (I) [Of elevator] *cabina,* (II) [Of lift]. *Jaula, caja, cabina,* (III) [of balloon). *Barquilla.* || **3.** •Railway CAR. *Vagón.* || **4.** •CAR accident. *Accidente de circulación.* ⇨CARRO

CARBON. *n.* Chemical element. *Carbono.* ~CARBON dioxide. *Dióxido de carbono.* || **2.** •CARBON paper. *Papel calco.* || **3.** •CARBON black. *Negro de humo.* || **4.** •CARBON copy. *Copia exacta.* ~He's a CARBON copy of my uncle. *Es un calco (el vivo retrato) de su tío.* ⇨CARBÓN

CASE. *n.* Affair. *Asunto.* ~The Barcelona Tract CASE. *El asunto de Barcelona Tract.* || **2.** [Law]. *Causa, pleito, proceso, expediente.* ~To loose/win a CASE. *Perder/ganar un pleito (juicio).* || **3.** Argument, reasoning. *Motivo, razón, justificación.* ~There seems to be a CASE for reform. *Parece que hay razones para reformarlo.* ~There's a CASE for saying that... *Puede decirse razonablemente que...* ~I think you have a CASE here. *Su petición me parece legítima.* ~The CASE for Medicare. *La justificación de la medicina social.* ~There's a CASE for that attitude. *Hay argumentos en favor de esta actitud.* ~She has a strong CASE. *Sus argumentos son poderosos.* || **4.** Matter. *Cuestión.* ~It was a CASE of doing what we were told. *Era una cuestión de hacer lo que nos mandaran.* || **5.** PHRASES. || •All right, you have made your CASE. *Bien, usted ha justificado su posición.* || •An open and shut CASE. *Un caso claro, un caso que no tiene vuelta de hoja.* || •As in the CASE of. *Como pasó con.* || •Criminal CASE. *Asunto penal.* || •He's working on the train-robbery CASE. *Está haciendo investigaciones sobre el robo del tren.* || •If that's the CASE. *Si las cosas son así.* || •In a vast majority of CASES. *En la gran mayoría de las veces.* || •In no CASE. *Bajo ninguna circunstancia.* || •In the CASE of. *Tratándose de.* || •It's a CASE of. *Se trata de.* || •Solid

CASE. *Acusación fundada.* || •That alters the CASE. *Eso cambia la cosa.* || •That being the CASE. *De ser así.* || •The CASE for the defense. *La defensa, el conjunto de razones alegado por el acusado.* || •The CASE for the prosecution. *La acusación, el conjunto de acusaciones alegado por el fiscal.* || •To be a helpless CASE. *No tener cura.* || •To make a federal CASE out of something. *Hacer un drama de algo.* || •To make out a good CASE. *Presentar argumentos convincentes.* || •To rest one's CASE. *Terminar la presentación de su alegato.* || •To state one's CASE. *Presentar sus argumentos.* ⇨CASO

CASTIGATE. *v.* Criticize, censure. *Reprender, regañar, criticar severamente.* ~House Speaker CASTIGATES Reagan. *El Presidente de la Cámara de Representantes critica duramente a Reagan (Prats).* ⇨CASTIGAR

CASUAL. *adj.* Negligent, unconcerned, carefree. *Informal, vago, despreocupado, descuidado, desenfadado.* ~He has a CASUAL attitude towards life. *Lo trae todo sin cuidado.* ~He's rather CASUAL about keeping appointments. *Es bastante informal para cumplir sus compromisos.* || **2.** Not regular, at irregular intervals, occasional. *Temporero, eventual.* ~A CASUAL worker. *Un trabajador eventual.* || **3.** Haphazard, random, unsystematic. *Ligero, improvisado, a la ligera.* ~This cannot be done in a hasty or CASUAL manner. *Eso no puede hacerse precipitadamente ni a la ligera.* ~The report, citing merely one example of the CASUAL approach of governments ... *El informe que cita tan sólo un ejemplo de la despreocupada actitud de los gobiernos ... (Cit. Prats).* || **4.** Nonchalant, dispassionate. *Indiferente, displicente.* ~He tried to look CASUAL, but it was the handsomest house he had ever entered. *Trató de afectar indiferencia, pero era la casa más bonita que había visto en su vida (Cit. Prats).* ~In a casual way. *Con aire de afectada indiferencia.* ~He tried to sound CASUAL. *Se esforzó por parecer tranquilo.* ~He was very CASUAL about it. *No le daba importancia a la cosa.* ~Act CASUAL, there's a policeman coming. *Disimula, que ahí viene un policía.* || **5.** Informal, relaxed. *Natural, sencillo, familiar, campechano.* ~To some visitors the service in these hotels may seem too CASUAL. *A algunos turistas el servicio de estos hoteles pude parecerles demasiado familiar (Prats).* || **6.** Slight or superficial. *Intrascendente.* ~A CASUAL friend. *Un conocido (not a close friend).* ~In a CASUAL conversation I had with him. *En una conversación sin trascendencia que tuve con él.* || **7.** PHRASES. || •A CASUAL glance. *Una mirada al azar, una ojeada rápida.* || •A CASUAL meeting. *Un encuentro fortuito.* ||•A CASUAL remark. *Observación parentética, sin tracendencia, comentario sin importancia.* || •A CASUAL stroll. *Un paseo sin rumbo fijo.* || •A CASUAL suggestion. *Una sugerencia hecha de paso.* || •Casual dress. *Ropa para ocasiones no formales, ropa corriente, (de) sport.* || •Casual sex. *Relaciones sexuales promíscuas.* || •Casual work. *Trabajo ocasional.* ⇨ CASUAL

CASUALLY. *adv.* In a nonchalant, dispassionate manner. *Con aire de naturalidad, sin darle importancia.* ~As the four gunmen walked CASUALLY into the restaurant ... *Mientras los cuatro pistoleros entraban en el restaurante con aire de naturalidad ... (Cit. Prats).* || **2.** In an uninterested, relaxed, absent-minded manner. *Distraídamente.* ~She was looking CASUALLY through a magazine. *Ella ojeaba distraídamente una revista.* ⇨CASUALMENTE

CAUSE. *n.* [Reason, grounds]. *Motivo, razón.* ~She has no CAUSE for complain. *No tiene motivos para quejarse.* ~I have every CAUSE to regret it. *Tengo motivos sobrados para lamentarlo.* ~She was furious and with good CAUSE. *Estaba furiosa y con razón.* ⇨CAUSA

CAVITIES [CAVIDAD]. *n.* Tooth decay. *Caries.*

CELEBRATE. *v.* To have a good time. *Divertirse, pasarlo bien.* Let's CELEBRATE. *Vamos a divertirnos.* To conmemorate (anniversary, holiday) *Conmemorar.* ⇨ CELEBRAR

CELEBRATION. *n.* [Event]. *Fiesta.* ‖ **2.** Festivities. *Festividades, festejos.* ~He attended the CELEBRATION. *Asistió a las festividades.* ‖ **3.** Praise. *Canto.* ~The play is a CELEBRATION of life. *La obra es un canto a la vida.* ⇨ CELEBRACIÓN

CELESTIAL. *adj.* Pertaining to the sky or universe, as planets or stars. *Celeste.* ~The astronauts will use six telescopes to observe the sun and other CELESTIAL phenomena. *Los astronautas utilizarán 6 telescopios para observar el sol y otros fenómenos celestes.* ▶The spanish word *celestial* refers to the heavens or to divine beings. ⇨ CELESTIAL

CERTIFICATE [CERTIFICADO]. *n.* [Academic]. *Diploma, título.* ~She received her CERTIFICATE in Education. *Tiene diploma en pedagogía.* ‖ **2.** [Birth, marriage]. *Partida.* ‖ **3.** [Savings]. *Bono de ahorro.*

CERTIFIED. *adj.* [Copy]. Legalizado. ~A CERTIFIED copy of the document. *Una copia legalizada del documento.* ‖ **2.** [Profession]. *Diplomado, titulado.* ~His mother is a CERTIFIED nurse. *Su madre es enfermera diplomada.* ‖ **3.** Qualified. *Habilitado.* ~He's not CERTIFIED to teach in this state. *No está habilitado para ejercer la docencia en este estado.* ‖ **4.** •CERTIFIED public accountant. Contador público. ⇨ CERTIFICADO.

CHARACTER. *n.* A person in a play, story, novel, etc. *Personaje.* The play has six CHARACTERS. *La obra tiene seis personajes.* ‖ **2.** Odd, excentric person. *Tipo, sujeto.* ~He's quite a CHARACTER. *Es un tipo pintoresco. Es un original.* ~He's a very odd CHARACTER. *Es un tipo muy raro.* ‖ **3.** Moral strength, self-discipline, fortitude. *Buena reputación, excelencia moral, superioridad, virtud.* ~A person of good CHARACTER. *Una persona de buena reputación.* ‖ **4.** Personality. *Personalidad.* ~He has a lot of CHARACTER. *Tiene mucha personalidad.* ‖ **5.** *PHRASES.* ‖ •A suspicious CHARACTER. *Un tipo de mucho cuidado.* ‖ •CHARACTER assassination. *Defamación.* ‖ •To be in CHARACTER. *Ser característico, ser conforme al tipo.*

~Rudeness is very much in CHARACTER with him. *La mala educación es un rasgo típico en él.* ‖ •She's a shrewd judge of CHARACTER. *Es buena psicóloga.* ‖ •To vouch for someone's (good) CHARACTER. *Responder por alguien.* ‖ •To be out of CHARACTER. *Disonar de, desentonar, no ser típico.* ‖ •Chief CHARACTER (in a play). *Protagonista.* ‖ •CHARACTER reference. *Referencias.* ⇨ CARÁCTER

CHARGE. *n.*

❶ FINANCE. [Cost]. *Precio.* ~There's no CHARGE for the service. *No se cobra el servicio.* ~Admission CHARGE. *Precio de entrada.* ~Is there a CHARGE for delivery? *¿Se paga el transporte?* ‖ **2.** Fee (professional). *Honorarios.* ~This lawyer's CHARGES are quite high. *Los honorarios de este abogado son muy elevados.* ‖ **3.** •At no extra CHARGE. *Sin gasto adicional.* ‖ **4.** •At my own CHARGE. *A expensas mías.* ‖ **5.** •Bank CHARGES. *Comisión (por servicio bancario).* ‖ **6.** •CHARGE account. *Cuenta corriente, cuenta abierta.* ‖ **7.** •Extra CHARGE. *Suplemento.* ‖ **8.** •Free of CHARGE. *Gratis, sin cargo.* ‖ **9.** •No CHARGE for admission. *Entrada gratis.* ‖ **10.** •Service CHARGE. *Servicio.* •There's no CHARGE. *Esto no se cobra, esto es gratuito.* ‖ **11.** •To reverse the CHARGE. *Llamar a cobro revertido.*

❷ RESPONSIBILITY, OBLIGATION. *Cargo (office); encargo, cometido (task).* ~He assumed full CHARGE of the business. *Se hizo cargo del negocio.* ‖ **2.** Person cared for. *Personas al cuidado de uno.* ~The teacher and her CHARGES. *La maestra y sus alumnos.* ~The nurse and her CHARGES. *La enfermera y sus enfermos.* The nanny with her young CHARGES. *Una niñera con los niños a su cargo.* ‖ **3.** Peso. Load. My brother is a CHARGE on me. *Mi hermano es una carga para mí.* ‖ **4.** •To be in CHARGE of. *Estar a cargo de, mandar.* ~Who's in CHARGE here? *¿Quién manda aquí? ¿Quién es el encargado aquí?* ~I was in CHARGE of 20 children. *Tenía 20 niños a mi cargo.* ~He's in CHARGE of production. *Está al frente de la producción.* ‖ **5.** •To take CHARGE of. *Hacerse cargo de, encargarse de; asumir el mando de (men,* *expedition).* ~She took charge of the situation. *Se hizo cargo de la situación.* ~Take CHARGE of the administration. *Hazte cargo de la administración.*

❸ LAW. Formal accusation. *Cargo, acusación.* ~What is the CHARGE? *¿Cuál es el cargo (que se me hace)?* ~He's being tried on a CHARGE of murder. *Se le juzga por homicidio.* || **2.** Instruction, order (given by the court to the jury). *Orden, instrucción.* || **3.** •To appear on a CHARGE of. *Comparecer acusado de.* || **4.** •To bring a CHARGE against. *Formular una acusación contra alguien.* || **5.** To drop CHARGES. *Retirar la acusación (los cargos).* || **6.** •To beat the CHARGES. *Ser absuelto.* || **7.** •To face a CHARGE of. *Responder a una acusación de.*

❹ ATTACK. Attack, assault. *Ataque, asalto, carga.* ~Cavalry CHARGE. *Una carga de la caballería.* || **2.** [Of bull]. *Enbestida.* || **3.** [Sport]. *Ofensiva (en que se gana mucho terreno).*

❺ SUPPLY, ENERGY (explosive, electricity, dynamite, gunpowder, battery, furnace, firearm]. *Carga.* ~A CHARGE of dynamite/gunpowder. *Una carga de dinamita/pólvora.* ~The enemy placed a CHARGE of dynamite under the bridge. *El enemigo colocó una carga de dinamita debajo del puente.* ⇨CARGO

CHOCOLATE [CHOCOLATE]. *n.* •A box of CHOCOLATES. *Una caja de bombones.*

CIRCUIT [CIRCUITO]. *n.* [Journey, passage]. *Recorrido.* ~The CIRCUIT of the island takes three hours. *El recorrido de la isla tarda tres horas.* ~The moon's CIRCUIT around the earth. *La órbita de la luna alrededor de la tierra.* || **2.** [Events]. *Liga.* || **3.** [Of cinemas and theaters]. *Cadena.* || **4.** [Tour]. *Gira.* || **5.** [Track]. *Pista.* || **6.** [Lap by runner]. *Vuelta.* The athlete ran six CIRCUITS of the track. *El atleta dio seis vueltas a la pista.* || **7.** [Law]. *Distrito, juridicción.*

CIRCULATION. *n.* Average number of copies (newspaper, book, magazine). *Tirada.* ~This newspaper has a CIRCULATION of a hundred thousand copies. *Este periódico tiene una tirada de cien mil ejemplares.* ||

2. [Of news]. *Difusión.* ⇨CIRCULACIÓN

CLARIFY. *v.* Explain, make clear. *Aclarar.* The situation has not yet been CLARIFIED. *La situación todavía no se ha aclarado.* ⇨CLARIFICAR

CLEAR. *adj.* [Road, view, day]. *Despejado.* ~It was a CLEAR day in May. *Era un día despejado de mayo.* || **2.** [Conscience]. *Limpio, tranquilo.* ~I have a CLEAR conscience. *Tengo la conciencia tranquila (limpia).* || **3.** Complete, definite. *Neto, absoluto, amplio.* ~A CLEAR majority. *Una mayoría absoluta, una amplia mayoría.* ~Clear profit. *Beneficio neto.* ~He earns a CLEAR $2,000 a week. *Gana dos mil dólares semanales limpios.* || **4.** [Aire]. *Transparente.* || **5.** [Mind]. *Despejado.* ~To keep a CLEAR head. *Mantener la mente despejada.* || **6.** [Sonido]. *Audible, distinct.* ~The radio reception isn't very CLEAR. *La recepción de esta radio no es muy audible.* || **7.** Obvious. *Evidente.* A CLEAR case of murder. *Un caso evidente de homicidio.* ~It became CLEAR he was lying. *Se hizo patente (evidente) que estaba mintiendo.* || **8.** [Liquid, glass, plastic]. *Transparente.* || **9.** [Outline, picture]. *Nítido.* || **10.** Free, unobstructed (road, view, desk). *Libre.* ~Keep CLEAR. *No obstruya el paso.* ~He's CLEAR of debts. *Está libre de deudas.* ⇨CLARO

CLERICAL [CLERICAL]. *adj.* Pertaining to an office clerk. *Secretarial, de oficina.* ~We're in need of CLERICAL help. *Necesitamos oficinistas (personal de oficina, personal administrativo).* || **2.** •CLERICAL error. *Error de copia.* || **3.** •CLERICAL work. *Trabajo de oficina.*

CODE [CÓDIGO]. *n.* •CODE word. *Palabra clave.* || **2.** •Morse CODE. *Alfabeto Morse.* || **3.** •To break a CODE. *Descifrar una clave.* || **4.** •Telephone CODE number. *Prefijo.* || **5.** •In CODE. *En cifra, cifrado, en clave.* || **6.** •CODE of ethics. *Ética profesional.* || **7.** •Secret CODE. *Clave secreta.*

COLLAR. *n.* (of a shirt, dress). *Cuello.* Súbete el CUELLO del abrigo. *Turn your coat collar up.* || **2.** •Detachable COLLAR. *Cuello falso.* || **3.** •Blue COLLAR. *Obrero industrial.*

|| **4.** •Stiff COLLAR. *Cuello duro.* || **5.** •To get hot under the COLLAR. *Acalorarse, indignarse, sulfurarse, ponerse hecho una furia.* || **6.** •COLLAR size. *Medida del cuello.* || **7.** •To grab someone by the COLLAR. *Agarrar a alguien por el cuello.* || **8.** •Horse COLLAR. *Collera.* ⇨COLLAR

COLLECT [COLECTAR]. *v.* Gather. *Recoger.* ~He COLLECTED some shells on his walk. *Durante el paseo recogió algunas conchas.* ~We COLLECTED our belongings. *Recogimos nuestras cosas.* || **2.** [Stamps, records]. *Coleccionar, juntar.* ~He's COLLECTING the work of young unknowns. *Colecciona obras de artistas jóvenes desconocidos.* || **3.** [Taxes]. *Recaudar.* They COLLECTED a million dollars in taxes. *Recaudaron un millón de dólares en impuestos.* || **4.** [Wages, fares]. *Cobrar.* || **5.** [Money for charity]. *Recaudar, colectar.* || **6.** Pick up, fetch. *Recoger.* ~I COLLECTED my suit from the cleaner's. *Recogí el traje de la tintorería.* ~They COLLECT the garbage every Monday. *Todos los lunes pasan a recoger la basura.* ~I must COLLECT my bags from the station. *Tengo que recoger mi equipaje en la estación.* ~I'm COLLECTING Jean on the way. *De camino voy a pasar a recoger a Jean.* || **7.** [Dust, water]. *Retener.* || **8.** [Information, evidence, data]. *Reunir, recopilar, recabar.* || **9.** Attract, accumulate. *Juntar.* ~My books are COLLECTING dust. *Mis libros están acumulando polvo.* || **10.** Earn. *Ganar.* I COLLECTED $5,000 this month. *Este mes (me) gané unos 5,000 dólares.* || **11.** •COLLECT on delivery. *Entrega contra reembolso.* || **12.** •To COLLECT one's thoughts. *Poner en orden sus ideas.* ~Give me some time to COLLECT my thoughts. *Déjame pensar un poco.* || **13.** •To COLLECT oneself. *Recobrar la calma, serenarse.*

COLLECTION [COLECCIÓN]. *n.* [Of evidence]. *Recopilación.* || **2.** [Of rent, debts]. *Cobro.* || **3.** [Of taxes]. *Recaudación.* ~A debt COLLECTION agency. *Una agencia de cobro a morosos.* || **4.** Act of fetching. *Acto de recoger.* ~The goods are ready for COLLECTION. *Puede recoger (pasar a buscar) las mercancías.* ~Children must wait for COLLECTION by parents. *Los niños deben esperar a que los padres los recogan.* || **5.** [Of mail, refuse]. *Recogida.* ~Garbage COLLECTIONS are made every Tuesday morning. *Se recoge la basura todos los martes por la mañana.* || **6.** [Of money]. *Colecta.* ~To make a COLLECTION for the poor. *Hacer una colecta para los pobres.* || **7.** Group (of people). *Grupo.* ~There was an interesting COLLECTION of people at the wedding. *Había un interesante grupo de gente en la boda.* || **8.** Heap. *Montón.* ~A COLLECTION of broken bottles stood in the corner of the room. *En el ángulo del cuarto había un montón de botellas rotas.*

COLLEGE. *n.* Institution of higher learning. *Universidad.* ~I never went to COLLEGE. *Nunca fui a la universidad.* || **2.** School offering specialized instruction in some profession or occupation. *Escuela.* ~Military COLLEGE. *Escuela militar.* ~Teacher's (training) COLLEGE. *Escuela normal.* ~Technical COLLEGE. *Escuela de formación profesional.* ~Art COLLEGE. *Escuela de Bellas Artes.* || **3.** •COLLEGE course. *Cursos universitarios.* || **4.** •To go to COLLEGE. *Seguir estudios superiores.* ⇨COLEGIO

COLLOQUIAL [COLOQUIAL]. *adj.* Everyday. *Familiar.* In COLLOQUIAL language. *En lenguaje familiar.*

COMEDIAN. *n.* Comic actor or entertainer. *Actor cómico, humorista, cómico.* || **2.** Joker, clown. *Farsante.* ~He's a real COMEDIAN. *Es un verdadero payaso.* ⇨COMEDIANTE

COMFORTABLE [CONFORTABLE]. *adj.* [Chair, clothes]. *Cómodo.* ~A COMFORTABLE bed/armchair. *Una cama cómoda, un sillón cómodo.* || **2.** [Atmosphere, temperature]. *Agradable.* || **3.** [Patient]. *Tranquilo, estable.* ~She spent a COMFORTABLE night. *Pasó buena noche.* || **4.** At ease. *A gusto.* ~He doesn't feel COMFORTABLE with us. *No se siente a gusto con nosotros.* ~Choose a subject you're COMFORTABLE with. *Elija un tema en el que se sienta seguro.* || **5.** Substantial, ample. *Amplio.* ~To win by a COMFORTABLE margin. *Ganar por amplia mayoría.* || **6.** [Living]. *Holgado, tranquilo.* ~They enjoy a

COMFORTABLE lifestyle. *Llevan una vida desahogada.* || **7.** [Income]. *Adecuado, bueno, decente.* ~They're COMFORTABLE. *Está bien de dinero, son gente acomodada.* ~Comfortable income. *Buenos ingresos.* || **8.** [Truth]. *Agradable.* The truth is not so COMFORTABLE. *La verdad no es muy agradable.* || **9.** PHRASES. || •I don't feel altogether COMFORTABLE about it. *La cosa me trae algo preocupado.* || •It's so COMFORTABLE here. *Aquí se está de maravilla.* || •Make yourself COMFORTABLE. *Póngase cómodo.* || •To be (feel) COMFORTABLE. *Encontrarse a gusto.* || •To make oneself COMFORTABLE. *Acomodarse.* ~He made himself COMFORTABLE in an armchair. *Se acomodó en un sillón.*

COMMERCIAL [COMERCIAL]. *n.* Paid advertisement (radio, TV). *Anuncio (comercial).* || **2.** *adj.* •COMMERCIAL artist. *Dibujante publicitario.*

COMMISSION [COMISIÓN]. *n.* Charge. *Encargo.* ~She received a COMMISSION to design a hotel. *Le encargaron el diseño de un hotel.*| || **2.** Perpetration (of an offense). *Ejecución, perpetración, (de un crimen).* || **3.** MIL Certificate conferring rank. *Graduación, despacho de oficial, grado.* || **4.** Nomination (to a post, a task). *Nombramiento.* || **5.** PHRASES. || •To take something out of COMMISSION. *Retirar algo del servicio.* || •To put out of COMMISSION. *Inutilizar.* || •Ouf of COMMISSION. *Fuera de servicio (person), inservible (thing).* || •To put in COMMISSION. *Poner en servicio activo.* || •Done on COMMISSION, *Hecho por encargo.*

COMMIT. *v.* Dedicate. *Dedicar.* ~A large amount of money has been COMMITTED to this project. *Se ha dedicado una suma considerable a este proyecto.* ~If you want to be an actor you have to really COMMIT yourself to it. *Si quiere ser actor necesita dedicarse por completo a ello.* || **2.** To send into a battle. *Enviar a la batalla.* The commander has COMMITTED all his troops to the front lines. *El comandante envió todas sus tropas al frente.* || **3.** Entrust. *Entregar.* ~The goods were COMMITTED to various distributors of the region. *La mercancía fue entregada a* varios distribuidores de la zona. || **4.** Assign. *Asignar, consignar.* ~Her remains were COMMITTED to the grave. *Sus restos recibieron sepultura.* || **5.** To send. *Internar.* ~The judge COMMITTED her to prison. *El juez la mandó encarcelar.* ~To COMMIT someone to a mental hospital. *Internar a uno en un manicomio.* || **6.** To refer to a committee for consideration (Parliament). *Someter a la consideración de una comisión.* || **7.** Bind. *Comprometer, obligar.* ~That would COMMIT us to the purchase. *Eso nos comprometería a efectuar la compra.* ~The pact COMMITS both nations to ... *Con la firma del pacto ambas naciones se comprometen a ...* || **8.** State views. *Comprometerse.* He wouldn't COMMIT himself. *No quiso comprometerse.* || **9.** [To the flames, waves). *Entregar.* ~To COMMIT a manuscript to the flames. *Entregar un manuscrito a las llamas (al fuego).* || **10.** To pledge, promise, vow, undertake. *Hacer una promesa, declararse, comprometerse. a favor de.* ~We are deeply COMMITTED to this policy. *Nos hemos declarado firmemente a favor de esta política.* ~Without COMMITTING myself. *Sin compromiso por mi parte.* ~I'm COMMITTED to help him. *Me he comprometido a ayudarle.* || **11.** PHRASES. || •COMMIT one's soul to God. *Encomendarse a Dios.* || •To COMMIT something to paper. *Consignar por escrito.* || •To COMMIT something to memory. *Aprenderse algo de memoria.* || •To COMMIT something to somebody's care. *Confiar algo a (al cuidado de) alguien.* || •To COMMIT for trial. *Citar ante los tribunales.* || •To COMMIT suicide. *Suicidarse.* ⇨COMETER

COMMODITY. *n.* Basic staple. *Artículo de consumo, artículo de comercio, artículo de primera necesidad; producto, mercancía.* || **2.** Any useful thing. *Ventaja, lujo.* || **3.** *pl.* Food items. *Productos alimenticios.* || **4.** Raw materials. *Materias primas.* ⇨COMODIDAD

COMMOTION. *n.* Civil disturbance. *Disturbio, perturbación del orden público, tumulto.* || **2.** Noise, bustle. *Alboroto, jaleo.* || **3.** •To cause a COMMOTION. *Armar un*

escándalo (lío). || **4.** •What a COMMOTION!. *¡Qué escándalo!* ⇨CONMOCIÓN.

COMMUNICATE. *v.* Understand (each other). *Dialogar, entenderse.* ~We just don't COMMUNICATE. *No nos entendemos.* ⇨COMUNICAR

COMMUNITY [COMUNIDAD]. *n.* Society, the public. *Sociedad, público.* Unlike the present government, we believe in serving the COMMUNITY. *A diferencia del actual gobierno, nosotros estamos al servicio del público.* || **2.** Group of people living together as a social unit within a larger one, and having common interests. *Colonia.* ~The Argentinian COMMUNITY in Los Angeles. *La colonia argentina de Los Angeles.* || **3.** Local inhabitants. *Vecindario, vecindad, barrio, urbanización, colonia.* ~He's well known in the local COMMUNITY. *Es muy conocido por donde vive.* || **4.** Profession. *Clase.* The medical COMMUNITY. *La clase médica.* || **5.** Population. *Población.* The Black COMMUNITY. *La población negra.* || **7.** World, circle. *Mundo, mundillo.* In the theater COMMUNITY. *~En el mundillo teatral.* || **6.** PHRASES. || •The religious COMMUNITY. *Congregación, parroquia, feligresía.* || •COMMUNITY center. *Centro social.* || •COMMUNITY of interest. *Interés común.* || •COMMUNITY spirit. *Espíritu comunitario.* || •COMMUNITY chest. *Fondo para beneficiencia social.* || •COMMUNITY health center. *Clínica comunitaria.*

COMPARATIVE [COMPARATIVO]. *adj.* Involving comparison as a method (branch of study). *Comparado.* Comparative anatomy/literature. *~Anatomía/literatura comparada.* || **2.** Relative. *Relativo.* ~They live in COMPARATIVE luxury. *Viven con un lujo relativo.* || **3.** •He's a COMPARATIVE stranger. *Es practicamente un desconocido.*

COMPARATIVELY [COMPARATIVAMENTE]. *adv.* Relatively. *Relativamente.* ~Damages were COMPARATIVELY small. *Los daños causados fueron relativamente pequeños.*

COMPARE [COMPARE]. *v.* Put side by side (text). *Cotejar.* ~He COMPARED the writing with that on the envelope. *Cotejó la letra con la en el sobre.* || **2.** •COMPARED with (as opposed to, as contrasted with). *Frente a, en comparación con.* ~Airline rates for the U.S. post office are 29 cents per ton mile of mail transported, COMPARED with Air Canada's charge to the post office for 48 cents per ton per mile. *Las compañías de aviación americanas cobran a la Administración de Correos vientinueve centavos por tonelada-milla de correo transportado, frente a los cuarenta y ocho centavos cobrados por Air Canada (Cit. Prats).* ~It's tiny COMPARED to your house. *Es pequeñísima en comparación con tu casa.* || **3.** PHRASES. || •To COMPARE notes. *Cambiar impresiones.* || •Beyond COMPARE. *Sin comparación.* || •To COMPARE favorably with. *Ser superior a, superar a.* ~Our oranges COMPARE favorably with those produced abroad. *Nuestras naranjas son superiores a las cultivadas en el extranjero (Prats).* || •To COMPARE poorly. *Ser inferior a, desmerecer.* ~It COMPARES badly with other models in the same price range. *Desmerece en comparación con otros modelos de precio similar.* || •How do they COMPARE? *¿Cuáles son sus cualidades respectivas?* || •How do they COMPARE for speed? *¿Cuál tiene mayor velocidad?*

COMPENSATION. *n.* Salary, pay, remuneration. *Sueldo, paga, salario, remuneración, estipendio.* ~The COMPENSATION of government employees. *El sueldo de los empleados del gobierno.* || **2.** Reward. *Recompensa.* ⇨COMPENSACIÓN

COMPETENCE. *n.* Ability, fitness, capability. *Aptitud, eficacia, habilidad, capacidad.* ~No one questioned his COMPETENCE as a doctor. *Nadie puso en duda que estuviera capacitado para ejercer la medicina.* || **2.** •A certain level of COMPETENCE in French. *Un cierto nivel de conocimientos del francés.* ⇨COMPETENCIA

COMPETITION [COMPETICIÓN]. *n.* Rivalry in business. *Competencia.* Prices are low because of the fierce COMPETITION between companies making the same product. *Los bajos precios se deben a la intensa competencia entre compañías que fabrican los*

mismos productos. || **2.** Contest. *Concurso, oposición, certamen (literario).* ~An international chess COMPETITION. *Un concurso internacional de ajedrez.* || **3.** Rival. *Rival.* Who is my COMPETITION? *¿Quién es mi rival?* || **4.** *PHRASES.* || •In COMPETITION with. *En competencia con.* || •Unfair COMPETITION. *Competencia desleal.* || •Free COMPETITION. *Competencia libre.* || •To be in COMPETITION with someone. *Competir con alguien.* || •To enter a COMPETITION. *Presentarse a un concurso.*

COMPLACENT. *adj.* [Attitude]. DISPLICENTE. ~You've won the first round, but don't get COMPLACENT. *Has ganado la primera vuelta pero no te confíes (no te duermas sobre los laureles).* || **2.** Self-satisfied, smug. *Satisfecho consigo mismo, autosuficiente.* ⇨COMPLACIENTE

COMPLETE[1] [COMPLETAR]. *v.* To finish. *Acabar, concluir, finalizar, dar fin.* When we have COMPLETED our investigations. *Cuando hayamos concluido nuestras investigaciones.* || **2.** To fill out (a form). *Rellenar un impreso (formulario).* || **3.** •To COMPLETE (a sentence). *Cumplir.* || **4.** •Let me COMPLETE the picture. *Deje que termine de describir la situación.* || **5.** •To COMPLETE my happiness. *Para colmo de dicha.*

COMPLETE[2]. *adj.* Absolute. *Verdadero, perfecto.* He's a COMPLETE idiot. *Es un perfecto idiota.* || **2.** Total. *Total.* ~It was a COMPLETE failure. *Fue un fracaso total.* ~It was a COMPLETE waste of time. *Fue una pérdida de tiempo total.* ~He's a COMPLETE stranger. *Es totalmente desconocido.* || **3.** Finished, ended, concluded. *Acabado, terminado, concluido.* My report is still not quite COMPLETE. *Mi informe todavía no está terminado del todo.* || **4.** Consummate. *Consumado.* ~He's a COMPLETE pianist. *Es un pianista consumado.* || **5.** •COMPLETE with. *Con... incluido, con sus... correspondiente, con ... y todo.* ~The kit comes COMPLETE with tools and instructions. *El conjunto (equipo) viene con las herramientas e instrucciones incluidas.* The dog consumed twelve eggs COMPLETE with shells. *El perro se comió una docena de huevos con cáscara y todo (Prats).* ~He arrived COMPLETE with equipment. *Llegó con su equipo y todo.* ~He came dressed as a woodman, COMPLETE with axe. *Vino vestido de leñador, con hacha y todo.* ⇨COMPLETO

COMPLEXION. *n.* Skin (especially of the face). *Tez (in terms of color), cutis (skin type).* ~A good COMPLEXION. *Un buen cutis.* ~A dark/light complexion. *Una tez oscura/ clara.* || **2.** Aspect. *Cariz.* ~To put a different/ new COMPLEXION on something. *Darle otro/ un nuevo cariz a algo.* ~Matters took on a new COMPLEXION. *Los asuntos tomaron un nuevo cariz.* ⇨COMPLEXIÓN

COMPLIMENT[1] [-MENTO]. *n.* Praise. *Cumplido, (flirtatious) piropo.* I like COMPLIMENTS if they are sincere. *Los cumplidos, cuando son sinceros, me agradan.* || **2.** Courtesy, gift. *Obsequio.* ~COMPLIMENTS of the house. *Obsequio de la casa.* || **3.** Congratulations. *Felicidad, enhorabuena.* ~My COMPLIMENTS for the wonderful concert you gave yesterday. *Felicidades por el maravilloso concierto que Ud. dio ayer.* || **4.** Words of praise. *Palabras de elogio, elogios, palabras amables.* ~I want to thank my colleagues for the undeserved COMPLIMENTS they have addressed to me. *Quiero dar las gracias a mis colegas por los inmerecidos elogios que me han dedicado (Prats).* || **5.** *pl.* Regards, greetings, best wishes. *Saludos.* ~My COMPLIMENTS to you wife. *Saludos a su esposa.* || **6.** *PHRASES.* || •To pay one's COMPLIMENTS. *Dar saludos a.* || •To pay someone a COMPLIMENT. *Hacerle un cumplido a alguien.* || •With my COMPLIMENT. *De mi parte.* || •That's was meant as a COMPLIMENT. *Lo dije con buena intención.* || •I take that as a COMPLIMENT. *Agradezco la cortesía.* || •I take it as a COMPLIMENT that ... *Para mí es un honor que ...* || •To return the COMPLIMENT. *Devolver el cumplido.*

COMPLIMENT[2] [CUMPLIMENTAR]. *v.* To praise, congratulate. *Felicitar, alabar.* ~Allow me to COMPLIMENT you on your singing. *Permítame que le felicite por lo*

bien que canta. ~She COMPLIMENTED him on his new suit. *Le alabó el traje nuevo.*

COMPOSITION. *n.* Theme, essay, article. *Redacción.* The teacher required each of us to write a thousand word COMPOSITION every week. *El maestro nos exigió una redacción semanal de mil palabras.* ‖ **2.** Mixture, combination. *Mezcla.* ~The medicine was a COMPOSITION of various ingredients. *La medicina era una mezcla de varios ingredientes.* ⇨COMPOSICIÓN

COMPREHENSIVE. *adj.* [General]. *Completo, exhaustivo, de gran (máximo) alcance.* ~A COMPREHENSIVE list of customers. *Una lista completa de clientes.* ‖ **2.** Broad (view, knowledge). *Amplio, extenso.* ~He has a COMPREHENSIVE knowledge of computing. *Tiene amplios conocimientos de informática.* ‖ **3.** [Study, description]. *Detallado, global.* ~A COMPREHENSIVE account of the events. *Una descripción detallada de los acontecimientos.* ‖ **4.** [Insurance]. *A (contra de) todo riesgo.* ‖ **5.** •COMPREHENSIVE examination. *Reválida.* ⇨COMPRENSIVO

COMPROMISE[1]. *n.* Spirit, art of compromise. *Transigencia, contemporización.* ‖ **2.** Agreement. *Acuerdo mutuo, arreglo.* ~Better a poor COMPROMISE than a strong case. *Vale más un mal arreglo que un buen pleito.* ~Delegates predict that some COMPROMISE will be reached. *Los delegados preveen que se llegara a un acuerdo.* ‖ **3.** Mutual concessions. *Concesión.* ~It was necessary for the members to make COMPROMISES in order to achieve unity in the party. *Fue necesario hacer concesiones para conseguir la unidad del partido.* ‖ **4.** Middleway, happy medium. *Término medio.* ~My car is a COMPROMISE between a Volkswagen and a Cadillac. *Mi coche es un término medio entre un Volkswagen y un Cadillac (Prats).* ‖ **5.** Trade-off. *Equilibrio.* ~A COMPROMISE between price and quality. *Un equilibrio entre precio y calidad.* The COMPROMISE between idealism and reality. *El equilibrio entre el idealismo y la realidad.* ‖ **6.** •The art of COMPROMISE. *El*

arte de la negociación. ‖ **7.** •To reach a COMPROMISE. Llegar a un acuerdo. ⇨COMPROMISO

COMPROMISE[2]. *v.* Make concessions. *Llegar a un acuerdo, transigir, contemporizar.* ~If you don't agree with me, we will have to COMPROMISE. *Si no está de acuerdo conmigo, tendremos que llegar a un acuerdo.* ~I'm willing to COMPROMISE over the price. *Estoy dispuesto a transigir sobre el precio.* ‖ **2.** Endanger. *Poner en peligro, comprometer, arriesgar, exponer.* ~If you act rashly you may COMPROMISE the success of the project. *Si te precipitas puedes comprometer el éxito de la empresa.* ‖ **3.** Give way. *Ceder.* ~We cannot COMPROMISE on this point. *En este punto no podemos ceder.* ‖ **4.** Discredit (person, reputation). *Comprometer.* ~You're putting me in a COMPROMISING situation. *Me está poniendo en una situación embarazosa.* ~He vowed not to associate himself with people that might COMPROMISE him. *Juró no asociarse con personas que pudieran comprometerle.* ‖ **5.** To settle for. *Conformarse con.* ~If I couldn't retire in Spain I would COMPROMISE on Greece. *De no poder jubilarme en España, me conformaría con Grecia (Prats).* ⇨COMPROMETER

COMPULSIVE. *adj.* Compelling. *Absorbente.* ~This book is COMPULSIVE reading. *Este libro es absorbente.* ‖ **2.** Hardened, inveterate. *Incorregible, empedernido.* A COMPULSIVE gambler. *Un jugador empedernido.* ‖ **3.** •A COMPULSIVE eater. *Una persona que siente ganas de comer continuamente.* ⇨COMPULSIVO

COMRADE. *n.* Companion. *Compañero.* They were COMRADES in school. *Eran compañeros de clase.* ⇨CAMARADA

CONCEDE. *v.* Reconocer. *Admit (inability, failure, superiority).* ~That's true, he CONCEDED. *Eso es cierto —reconoció.* ~To concede defeat. *Admitir la derrota, rendirse, darse por vencido.* ‖ **2.** [Sport]. *Abandonar.* The opposing team CONCEDED defeat. *El equipo contrario abandonó el partido.* ⇨CONCEDER

CONCERN [CONCERNIR]. *v.* Affect, have to do with. *Involucrar, afectar, tener que ver con.* ~That doesn't CONCERN me. *Eso no me afecta, eso no tiene que ver conmigo.* ~My question CONCERNS money. *Mi pregunta se refiere al dinero.* ~It CONCERNS me closely. *Me toca de cerca.* ~The book CONCERNS a family. *Este libro trata de una familia.* ‖ **2.** To worry. *Preocuparse.* ~To CONCERN oneself with. *Preocuparse por, tomarse interés por.* ~ I would be CONCERNED. *Yo que tú me preocuparía.* ~CONCERN yourself with the problem in hand. *Ocúpate del problema que tiene entre manos.* ~Don't CONCERN yourself with politics. *No te metas en la política.* ‖ **3.** To interest. *Interesar.* ~We are CONCERNED in facts. *A nosotros nos interesan los hechos.* ~Money is the only thing that CONCERNS him. *El dinero es lo único que le interesa.* ~I'm more CONCERNED with quality than quantity. *Me interesa más la calidad que la cantidad.* ‖ **4.** Relate to. *Respecto a, en cuanto a.* ~My fears CONCERNING her health. *Mis temores en cuanto a su salud.* ~Where your interests are CONCERNED. *En cuanto a tus intereses.* ‖ **5.** •As far as I'm CONCERNED. *Por lo que a mí se refiere.* ~As far as women are CONCERNED. *Por lo que se refiere a las mujeres.* ‖ **6.** •To whom it may CONCERN (in letters). *A quien corresponda.*

CONCLUDE. *v.* [Treaty, alliance]. *Celebrar, convenir, concertar, pactar, firmar, suscribir.* ~Alexander III was compelled to CONCLUDE an alliance with Republican France. *Alejandro III tuvo que concertar una alianza con la Francia republicana.* ‖ **2.** Deduce, infer. *Llegar a la conclusión, deducir, sacar la conclusión.* ~He studied the document and CONCLUDED that the author was an eyewitness. *Después de leer el documento llegó a la conclusión de que debió hacer sido testigo presencial del asunto.* ‖ **3.** Decide. *Decidir, determinar, resolver.* ~He CONCLUDED that he would wait. *Decidió esperar.* ‖ **4.** Settle, arrange, come to an agreement. *Llegar (a un acuerdo), cerrar (un trato), convenir (en alguna cosa).* ~Having CONCLUDED their bargain they went their separate ways. *Tras haber cerrado el trato, cada uno se fue por su lado.* ‖ **5.** To end, finish. *Acabar, terminar, rematar, dar fin (a alguna cosa).* ~He CONCLUDED with this remark. *Terminó haciendo esta observación.* ~To be CONCLUDED (serial). *Terminará con el próximo episodio.* ⇨CONCLUIR

CONCLUSIVE [CONCLUSIVO]. *adj.* Final, decisive. *Concluyente, convincente, definitivo, terminante.* ~CONCLUSIVE evidence. *Prueba definitiva, concluyente o decisiva.* ‖ **2.** •A CONCLUSIVE victory. *Una victoria decisiva, contundente.*

CONCRETE[1] [CONCRETO]. *n.* Mixture of cement and various aggregates. *Cemento, hormigón.* ‖ **2.** •CONCRETE mixer. *Hormigonera.* •Reinforced CONCRETE. *Cemento o hormigón armado.*

CONCUR. *v.* To agree with. *Coincidir, estar de acuerdo, asentir.* ~The judge CONCURRED with the ruling. *El juez coincidió con el fallo.* ⇨CONCURRIR

CONDEMN. *v.* To declare unsafe. (I) [Building]. *Declarar ruinoso,* (II) [Meat, food product]. *Declarar no apto para el consumo.* ‖ **2.** To convert for public use (building). *Expropiar (por causa de utilidad pública).* ⇨CONDENAR

CONDITION[1]. *n.* State of health. *Estado de salud.* ~Her CONDITION is stable. *Su estado es estacionario.* ‖ **2.** Ailment, illness. *Afección, dolencia, enfermedad.* ~A heart CONDITION. *Una afección cardíaca.* ‖ **3.** Circumstances. *Circunstancias.* ~I will not work under those CONDITIONS. *No voy a trabajar en aquellas circunstancias.* ‖ **4.** *PHRASES.* ‖ •Under no CONDITION. *De ninguna forma.* ‖ •To be out of CONDITION. *No estar en forma.* ‖ •To keep oneself in good CONDITION. *Mantenerse en forma.* ‖ •Of humble CONDITION. *De clase humilde.* ‖ •Weather CONDITIONS. *El estado del tiempo.* ‖ •Weather CONDITIONS permitting. *Si el tiempo no lo impide.* ⇨CONDICIÓN

CONDITION[2]. *v.* To keep healthy (using cream, etc.). *Acondicionar (hair), tonificar (muscles).* ~This shampoo *conditions* your hair. *Este champú acondiciona el pelo.* ‖ **2.** To air-condition. *Acondicionar.* ⇨CONDI-CIONAR

CONDUCT. *adj.* [An orquestra]. *Dirigir.* ~He CONDUCTED the orquestra at that concert. *Dirigió la orquesta en ese concierto.* ‖ **2.** [Business]. *Llevar, dirigir.* ~He CONDUCTED his business from his home. *Dirigía su negocio en su casa.* ‖ **3.** Carry out. *Llevar a cabo, realizar (inquiry, experiment); mantener (conversación).* ~We have been CONDUCTING a survey of the region. *Hemos llevado a cabo un reconocimiento de esta zona.* ‖ **4.** Lead, direct (visitor, tour, party). *Guiar.* ~The guide CONDUCTED us around the castle. *El guía nos guió por los alrededores del castillo.* ‖ **5.** To behave (oneself). *Comportarse, portarse.* He CONDUCTED himself well at the party. *Se portó muy bien en la fiesta.* ‖ **6.** Lead, escort. *Acompañar.* The waiter CONDUCTED them to their table. *El camarero los acompañó hasta su mesa.* ‖ **7.** •A CONDUCTED tour. *Una visita acompañada.* ‖ **8.** •To CONDUCT a correspondence with. *Cartearse con, estar en correspondencia con.* ‖ **9.** •We were CONDUCTED through a passage. *Nos hicieron pasar por un pasillo.* ⇨CONDUCIR

CONDUCTOR. *n.* [Train]. *Encargado, vigilante, revisor.* ‖ **2.** [Bus] *Cobrador.* ‖ **3.** [Music]. *Director.* ⇨CONDUCTOR

CONFECTION. *n.* [Sweet]. *Dulce, confite.* ‖ **2.** Creation (fashion). *Creación.* ⇨CONFEC-CIÓN

CONFER. *v.* Discuss. *Consultar.* She CONFERED with her lawyer before giving her decision. *Antes de dar su decisión consultó con su abogado.* ⇨CONFERIR

CONFERENCE. *n.* Assembly. *Congreso.* ~The annual party CONFERENCE. *El congreso anual del partido.* ‖ **2.** League. *Liga.* ‖ **3.** Formal meeting. *Entrevista, reunión.* ~A CONFERENCE between a student and his adviser. *Una entrevista (reunión) entre un alumno y su consejero.* ‖ **4.** •At the CONFE-RENCE table. *En la mesa de las negociaciones.* ⇨CONFERENCIA

CONFIDENCE. *n.* Self-assurance, self confidence. *Seguridad en sí mismo, confianza en sí mismo.* She is full of/lacks CONFIDENCE. *Tiene mucha/le falta confianza (seguridad) en sí misma.* ~To gain CONFIDENCE. *Adquirir confianza.* ~To give someone confidence. *Infundir confianza.* ‖ **2.** Secrecy, confidentiality. *Confidencialidad, reserva.* ~I'm telling you in strict CONFIDENCE. *Te lo digo en confianza.* ~Write in strict CONFIDENCE. *Escribir con absoluta reserva.* ~Please apply in strict CONFIDENCE to ... *Dirigirse bajo reserva absoluta a ...* ‖ **3.** Trust, faith. *Confianza.* ~He doesn't inspire CONFIDENCE. *No inspira confianza.* ~I have every CONFIDENCE in her. *Tengo entera confianza en ella.* ‖ **4.** PHRASES. ‖ •In CONFIDENCE. *En confianza.* ‖ •To betray someone's CONFIDENCE. *Defraudar la confianza de alguien.* ‖ •To have every CONFIDENCE in someone. *Confiar en alguien.* ‖ •To take someone into one's CONFIDENCE. *Depositar su confianza en alguien.* ‖ •Vote of CONFIDENCE/no CONFI-DENCE. *Voto de confianza/censura.* ⇨CON-FIANZA

CONFLICT. *n.* Fight, battle, struggle. *Combate, lucha.* ‖ **2.** [Of interest, duty]. *Incompatibilidad, choque de principios opuestos.* ~A CONFLICT betwen work and family. *Una incompatibilidad entre el trabajo y la familia.* ‖ **3.** Clash, disagreement. *Diferencia, desacuerdo.* A CONFLICT of opinion. *Una discrepancia de opiniones.* ‖ **4.** PHRASES. ‖ •To be in CONFLICT with. *Estar en desacuerdo (oposición) con, chocar con.* ‖ •CONFLICT of evidence. *Contradicción de testimonios.* ‖ •The theories are in CONFLICT. *Las teorías están reñidas.* ‖ •To be in CONFLICT with. *Estar en pugna con, estar reñido con.* ⇨CONFLICTO

CONFORM. *v.* [Customs]. *Ajustarse.* An immigrant must CONFORM to the customs of his adopted country. *El inmigrante debe ajustarse a las costumbres del nuevo país.* ‖ **2.** [Rules]. *Someterse a, ajustarse a, cumplir con.* ~You must CONFORM to discipline. *Tiene que someterse a la disciplina.* ~To CONFORM to regulations. *Ajustarse a las reglas.* ~These fire extinguishers do not CONFORM with safety regulations. *Estos extinguidores no cumplen con (se ajustan a) las normas de seguridad.* ‖ **3.** [Religion]. *Seguir las directrices de la iglesia.* ⇨ CONFORMAR

CONFOUND. *v.* Bewilder. *Desconcertar.* ~His actions CONFOUND me. *Sus acciones me me desconciertan.* ‖ **2.** [Attempt]. *Thwart.* ‖ **3.** [Plan]. *Echar por tierra, desbaratar.* ‖ **4.** To foil. *Frustar.* Attacks which CONFOUNDED their opponents. *Ataques que frustraban sus adversarios.* ‖ **5.** INTERJ Damn. *Maldito.* ~CONFOUND the weather! *¡Maldito tiempo!* ~You CONFOUNDED fool~ *¡Imbécil!* ⇨ CONFUNDIR

CONFRONT. *v.* Come face to face with (danger, problem). *Afrontar, enfrentar, hacer frente a.* ~We try to help people CONFRONT their problems. *Ayudamos a la gente a hacer frente a sus problemas.* ~These hazards CONFRONT the miners everyday. *Los mineros hacen frente diariamente a estos peligros.* ~The police was CONFRONTED by a group of demonstrators. *La policía se vio enfrentada por un grupo de manifestantes.* ~The sight which CONFRONTED us on arrival. *El espectáculo con el que nos enfrentamos al llegar.* ‖ **2.** Face up to (fear, enemy, crisis). *Enfrentarse a, hacer frente a.* ~I decided to CONFRONT him on the matter. *Decidi encararme con él y plantearle la cuestión cara a cara.* ~The reader is CONFRONTED with a mass of statistics. *El lector se ve enfrentado con una gran cantidad de estadísticas.* ~To CONFRONT the attacker with his victim. *Poner el atacante y a su víctima cara a cara (frente a frente).* ‖ **3.** To arise, come up. *Surgir, presentarse.* ~The problems that CONFRONT us today. *Los problemas que se nos presentan hoy en día.* ⇨ CONFRONTAR

CONGESTED [CONGESTIONADO]. *adj.* Crowded (town, road). *Repleto, lleno.* ~A very CONGESTED street. *Una calle muy transitada.* ‖ **2.** [City]. *Superpoblado.*

CONGESTION [CONGESTIÓN]. *s.* [Traffic]. *Atasco, embotellamiento.* ~All roads leading to the city are CONGESTED during

rush hour. *Todas las carreteras de acceso a la ciudad tiene atasco en las horas puntas.* ‖ **2.** [De gente]. *Aglomeración.*

CONGRATULATE [CONGRATULAR]. *v.* To express pleasure to (a person), as on a happy occasion. *Felicitar, dar la enhorabuena.* ~I hear you have to be CONGRATULATED. *Me han dicho que hay que felicitarte (darte la enhorabuena).* ~I CONGRATULATED them on their new baby. *Los felicité por el nacimiento del niño.*

CONGREGATION. *n.* Assembly, gathering. *Reunión.* ‖ **2.** [Attending services]. *Fieles.* The CONGREGATION knelt to pray. *Los fieles se arrodillaron para rezar.* ‖ **3.** Parishioners. *Feligreses.* ⇨ CONGREGACIÓN

CONJURE. v. [By sleight of hands]. *Hacer aparecer.* ~To CONJURE a rabbit from a hat. *Hacer aparecer un conejo de un sombrero.* ‖ **2.** Evoke (memories). *Evocar, traer a la memoria.* ~It CONJURES (up) images of ... *Hace pensar en ...* ‖ **3.** [Spirits]. *Invocar.* ‖ **4.** *To summon.* ~He CONJURED up a delicious lunch. *Preparó un lindo almuerzo en un santiamén (como por arte de magia).* ‖ **5.** Perform tricks. *Hacer magia.* ~A name to CONJURE with. *Un nombre que abre todas las puertas.* ⇨ CONJURAR

CONNECT. *v.* Relate. *Relacionar, asociar.* ~Are these matters CONNNECTED? *¿Tienen alguna relación entre sí estas cuestiones.* ‖ **2.** Link together. *Comunicar.* ~The kitchen CONNECTS with the dining room. *La cocina comunica con el comedor.* ‖ **3.** To be on the same wave length, to be in tune with. *Sintonizar, estar en la misma onda.* ~We just don't CONNECT. *No sintonizamos, no estamos en la misma onda.* ‖ **4.** Make contact. *Dar en el blanco.* He CONNECTED with a blow to the head. *Le asestó un golpe en plena cara.* ‖ **5.** Associate with. *Vincular.* ~The town has always been CONNECTED with the textile trade. *La ciudad siempre ha estado vinculada a la industria textil.* ‖ **6.** Join (cables). *Empalmar.* ~El electricista ha estado EMPALMANDO los cables de la luz. *The electrician has been joining the light cables.* ‖ **7.** [Train, flight]. *Empalmar,* *enlazar.* ~The train only goes as far as Burgos, but there it CONNECTS with another that goes to Bilbao. *El tren va sólo hasta Burgos, pero allí empalma con otro que va hasta Bilbao.* ‖ **8.** Unite, link. *Unir.* An old road CONNECTS the two towns. *Una antigua carretera une los dos pueblos.* ‖ **9.** •To CONNECT somebody with. *Poner en comunicación con, poner al habla, comunicar con.* ~I'll CONNECT you with her office. *Le comunico con su despacho.* ⇨CONECTAR

CONNECTED [CONECTADO]. *adv.* Related by blood. *Emparentado.* The Jones are CONNECTED with the Smiths. *Los Jones están emparentados con los Smith.*‖ **2.** Having connections. ~To be well-CONNECTED. *Estar bien relacionado.* ‖ **3.** •What firm are YOU CONNECTED with *¿Con qué empresa trabaja?* ‖ **4.** •I never CONNECTED you with that. *Nunca creí que tuvieras algo con ver con eso.*

CONNECTION [CONEXIÓN]. *n.* Association, relationship. *Relación.* ~There is no CONNECTION with his company and mine. *No hay ninguna relación entre su firma y la mía.* ‖ **2.** Joint. *Juntura, union.* ‖ **3.** [Trains, buses]. *Enlace, empalme.* To go to Marseille you have to make a CONNECTION in Paris. *Para ir a Marsella necesita hacer empalme en París.* ‖ **4.** Relative. *Pariente.* ~He's English but he has Irish CONNECTIONS. *Es inglés pero tiene parientes irlandeses.* ‖ **5.** *PHRASES.* ‖ •In CONNECTION with. *Con respecto a, a propósito de.* ‖ •To have CONNECTIONS. *Tener enchufe.* ‖ •We have a bad CONNECTION. *No se oye bien la línea.*

CONQUER. *v.* [Enemy]. *Vencer.* ~Julius Ceasar conquered the French. *Julio César VENCIÓ a los galos.* ‖ **2.** [Miedo]. *Vencer, superar.* ~She was unable to CONQUER her fear of flying. *Fue incapaz de vencer (superar) el miedo a viajar en avión.* ~Love CONQUERS all. *El amor lo vence todo.* ‖ **3.** *vi.* Triumph. *Triunfar.* ~He was resolved to CONQUER or die. *Estaba dispuesto a triunfar o a morir.* ⇨CONQUISTAR

CONSCIOUS. *adj.* [Decision, irony, disdain]. *Intencional, deliberado, a*

propósito. ~It wasn't a CONSCIOUS effort to loose weight. It just happened. No *adelgazó a propósito. Ocurrió sin que se lo propusiera.* Was it CONSCIOUS or did you sit down next to him by chance? *¿Te sentaste a su lado a propósito, o fue una simple casualidad?* ‖ **2.** Real. *Verdadero.* ~She made a CONSCIOUS effort to be nice to them. *Se esforzó en ser amable con ellos.* ‖ **3.** Worried about. *Preocupado.* ~Safety-CONSCIOUS. *Preocupado por la seguridad.* ~A fashion-CONSCIOUS girl. *Una chica muy pendiente de la moda.* ~For your calorie-CONSCIOUS guests. *Para sus invitados preocupados por guardar la línea.* ‖ **4.** Uncomfortable, embarassed, awckward. *Incómodo, cohibido.* She was very CONSCIOUS of beeing stared at as a foreigner. *Le incomodaba que por ser extranjera todo el mundo la miraran.* ‖ **5.** •To become CONSCIOUS that. *Darse cuenta que.* ~He gradually became CONSCIOUS that he was the only man at the party who wasn't wearing a suit. *Se fue dando cuenta que era el único en la fiesta que no llevaba traje.* ‖ **6.** •To become CONSCIOUS. *Volver en sí.* ⇨CONSCIENTE

CONSEQUENCE [CONSECUENCIA]. *n.* Importance. *Importancia.* ~The only French player of any CONSEQUENCE. *El único jugador francés de cierta talla (que merece ser tenido en cuenta).* ‖ **2.** •Of no CONSEQUENCE. *Sin importancia.* ~That's of no CONSEQUENCE. *Eso no tiene importancia.*

CONSERVATIVE. *adj.* Moderate, cautious. *Moderado.* ~At a CONSERVATIVE estimate. *Calculando por lo bajo.* ~A CONSERVATIVE figure. *Una cifra moderada.* ‖ **2.** Traditional. *Conservador.* ‖ **3.** Prudent. *Prudente.* ~A CONSERVATIVE investment. *Una inversión prudente.* ‖ **4.** Not very modern in style. *Sobrio.* ~He dressed in a CONSERVATIVE manner. *Viste de forma sobria.* ⇨CONSERVATIVO

CONSERVE. *v.* Save. *Ahorrar.* ~To CONSERVE energy. *Ahorrar energía.* ⇨CONSERVAR

CONSIDER. *v.* Study, examine. *Examinar,*

estudiar. ~Kindly CONSIDER our offer. *Le ruego estudiar nuestra oferta.* ~We are CONSIDERING the matter. *Estamos estudiando el asunto.* || **2.** To contemplate (doing something). *Pensar (en la posibilidad).* ~He's CONSIDERING retiring. *Está pensando en la posibilidad de jubilarse.* ~Have you ever CONSIDERED going by train? *¿Ha pensado alguna vez ir por tren?* ~We're CONSIDERING him for a job. *Estamos pensando en él para el puesto.* || **3.** Keep in mind, take into account. *Tener en cuenta, tomar en consideración, hacer caso.* ~Offers under ten thousand dollars won't even be CONSIDERED. *Las ofertas por debajo de los diez mil dólares no serán siquiera tenidas en cuenta.* ~You must CONSIDER other people's feelings. *Hay que tomar en cuenta los sentimientos de los demás.* || **4.** To be interested in. *Interesar.* ~Would you CONSIDER buying it? *¿Le interesa comprarlo?* || **5.** Realize. *Darse cuenta.* ~When one CONSIDERS that ... *Cuando uno se da cuenta de que ...* || **6.** *PHRASES.* || •All things CONSIDERED. *Pensándolo bien.* || •CONSIDER it done. *Dalo por hecho.* || •I CONSIDER it an honor. *Lo tengo a mucha honra.* || •My CONSIDERED opinion is that ... *Estoy convencido de que ...* || •CONSIDER yourself lucky. *Date por afortunado.* ⇨ CONSIDERAR

CONSIDERATE [CONSIDERADO]. *adj.* Kind, thoughtful, friendly. *Atento, amable.* ~How CONSIDERATE of her! *¡Qué atenta!*

CONSIDERATION. *n.* Study. *Estudio, examen.* ~Their case has been given careful CONSIDERATION. *Su caso ha sido estudiado detenidamente.* ~The report is under CONSIDERATION. *El informe se está estudiando.* ~After due CONSIDERATION. *Después de un detenido examen.* || **2.** Factor. *Factor.* ~A major CONSIDERATION is the cost. *Un factor de tener muy en cuenta es el costo.* ~Her only CONSIDERATION was her own success. *Lo único que le interesaba era su propio éxito.* || **3.** Importance. *Importancia.* ~Of little/no CONSIDERATION. *De poca/ninguna importancia.* ~That is a CONSIDERATION. *Eso hay que tenerlo en cuenta.* || **4.**

Payment. *Suma, cantidad.* ~For a small CONSIDERATION. *Por una módica suma (cantidad).* || **5.** Respect. *Respeto.* ~Out of CONSIDERATION for. *Por respeto a.* || **6.** *PHRASES.* || •To give CONSIDERATION to. *Considerar.* || •Without due CONSIDERATION. *Sin reflexión, sin reflexionar.* || •On no CONSIDERATION will I do it. *No lo haré bajo ningún concepto.* ⇨ CONSIDERACIÓN.

CONSIGN. *v.* To hand over, entrust. *Encomendar, entregar, confiar.* ~The boy was CONSIGNED to the care of his aunt. *El niño fue encomendado a, confiado al cuidado de su tía.* || **2.** Relegate. *Relegar.* ~A writer CONSIGNED to oblivion. *Un escritor relegado al olvido.* ⇨ CONSIGNAR

CONSISTENCY. *n.* Regularity. *Regularidad, uniformidad.* ~There is CONSISTENCY in his pattern of behavior. *Hay cierta uniformidad en su conducta.* || **2.** Logical conclusion or connection. *Consecuencia lógica, coherencia.* ~Arguments lacking CONSISTENCY. *Argumentos que no tienen coherencia.* || **3.** Agreement, conformity. *Conformidad.* CONSISTENCY between versions. *Conformidad entre dos versiones.* ⇨ CONSISTENCY

CONSISTENT. *adv.* In accordance with, in keeping with. *De acuerdo con, consecuente.* ~His conduct is not CONSISTENT with his promises. *Su conducta no está de acuerdo con sus promesas.* ~His conduct is not CONSISTENT with his teaching. *Su comportamiento no es consecuente con sus enseñanzas.* || **2.** Steadfast (advocate, supporter). *Firme.* ~A CONSISTENT advocate of peace. *Un firme defensor de la paz.* || **3.** Constant (excellence, failure). *Constante.* ~There has been a CONSISTENT improvement in her attitude. *Ha habido una constante mejora en su actitud.* ~Her work is sometimes good, the problem is she's not very CONSISTENT. *Trabaja bien a veces pero el problema es que no tiene constancia.* || **4.** [Denial]. *Sistemático, constante.* ⇨ CONSISTENTE

CONSPICUOUS. *adj.* Striking (hat, tie). *Llamativo.* ~A CONSPICUOUS tie. *Una*

corbata llamativa. ‖ **2.** Easily seen. *Visible.* ~A CONSPICUOUS landmark. *Un punto de referencia visible.* ‖ **3.** [Color]. *Chillón.* ‖ **4.** Obvious (mistake, difference, omission, lack). *Patente, manifiesto.* ~A CONSPICUOUS violation. *Una infracción manifiesta.* ‖ **5.** Remarkable (for bravery, loyalty). *Destacado, sobresaliente, notable.* ~CONSPICUOUS gallantry. *Notable galantería.* ~The campaign has been a CONSPICUOUS success. *La campaña ha sido un notable éxito.* ‖ **6.** PHRASES. ‖ •To play a CONSPICUOUS part. *Desempeñar un papel importante.* ‖ •CONSPICUOUS consumption. *Consumo ostentoso.* ‖ •In a CONSPICUOUS position. *A la vista de todos.* ‖ •To make oneself CONSPICUOUS. *Llamar la atención.* ‖ •To be CONSPICUOUS by one's presence. *Brillar por su ausencia.* ⇨ CONSPÍCUO

CONSTANCY. *n.* Loyalty. *Lealtad, fidelidad.* ~CONSTANCY betweeen husband and wife. *Lealtad entre marido y esposa.* ‖ **2.** Endurance. *Fortaleza.* ~Resolute CONSTANCY in the face of odds. *Una inquebrantable fortaleza frente a los obstáculos.* ‖ **3.** Stability. *Invariabilidad.* ⇨ CONSTANCIA

CONSTIPATION [CONSTIPACIÓN]. *n.* Difficulty in moving one's bowels. *Estreñimiento.*

CONSUME. *v.* To destroy. (I) [By fire]. *Reducir a cenizas, devorar, arrasar.* ~The building was CONSUMED by fire. *El edificio fue devorado por las llamas, reducido a cenizas,* (II) [Jealousy, passion, hate, envy]. *Devorar.* ~He was CONSUMED by passion. *Le devoraba la pasión.* ~He was CONSUMED by (with) envy. *Se moría de envidia.* ‖ **2.** [Time]. *Ocupar, hacer perder.* ~This task CONSUMES too much of my time. *Esta tarea me ocupa demasiado tiempo.* ⇨ CONSUMIR

CONTACT[1] [CONTACTO]. *n.* Influential acquaintance. *Relaciones.* ~He has many CONTACTS. *Tiene muchas relaciones.* ~Business CONTACTS. *Relaciones comerciales.* ~He called one of his business CONTACTS. *Llamó a uno de sus colegas comerciales.* ‖ **2.** Dealings. *Trato.* We have little CONTACT with them. *Tenemos poco trato con ellos.* ~My CONTACT with him was purely professional. *Mi trato con él fue exclusivamente profesional.* ‖ **3.** PHRASES. ‖ •To come into CONTACT with. (I) *Tocar, (violently) chocar con.* ~The plane's wheels made CONTACT with the ground. *Las ruedas del avión tocaron tierra.* (II) To have dealings with someone. *Tratar a alguien.* ‖ •To loose CONTACT with someone. *Perder de vista a alguien.* ‖ •To make CONTACT with someone. *Comunicarse con alguien.* ‖ •CONTACT sport. *Deporte de choque.*

CONTACT[2] [CONTACT]· *v.* Get in touch with. *Comunicarse con, dirigirse a.* ~If you need more information please CONTACT our main office. *Si necesita más información diríjase a nuestra oficina central.*

CONTEMPLATE. *v.* To think of, plan, consider. *Pensar, proyectar, planear, estudiar la posibilidad.* ~He's CONTEMPLATING going to Spain for the summer. *Piensa pasar el verano en España.* Aren't you a little young to be CONTEMPLATING marriage? *Es usted muy joven para ir pensando en casarse.* ‖ **2.** To ponder. *Examinar a fondo, estudiar.* ~CONTEMPLATING the meaning of life. *Meditando sobre el sentido de la vida.* ‖ **3.** To yearn for. *Soñar, anhelar.* ~He was CONTEMPLATING going to Paris some day. *Anhelaba ir a París un día.* ‖ **4.** Expect. *Prever.* ~Are you CONTEMPLATING any difficulties? *¿Prevé alguna dificultad?* ⇨ CONTEMPLAR

CONTEND. *v.* Assert, claim. *Sostener; afirmar.* ~She CONTENDS that he was innocent. *Sostiene que él era inocente.* ‖ **2.** To compete. *Competir, disputarse.* ~Several people are CONTENDING for the job. *Varias personas compiten por (se disputan) el puesto.* Three parties are CONTENDING for power. *Tres partidos se están disputando el poder.* ‖ **3.** •To CONTEND with. To face (problems, difficulties). *Enfrentarse.* ~It's just one of the things that we have to CONTEND with. *Es una de las tantas cosas a las que tenemos que enfrentarnos.*

⇨ CONTENDER

CONTENTION. *n.* Dispute, controversy, disagreement. *Polémica.* ~Who was responsible is still in CONTENTION. *Todavía se discute quien tuvo la culpa.* ~The matter in CONTENTION. *El asunto en discusión.* ~Her motives are not in CONTENTION. *Nadie pone en tela de juicio sus intenciones.* || **2.** Point, claim, charge. *Punto de vista, opinión.* ~My CONTENTION is that ... *Mi opinión es que ..., sostengo que ...* ~Supporting his CONTENTION with biblical and mythological evidence. *Demostrando su punto de vista con citas de la biblia y de la mitología.* || **3.** Strife, struggle. *Contienda, rivalidad.* || **4.** Competition, contest, rivalry. *Competencia.* ~He's still in CONTENTION for a medal. *Todavía tiene posibilidades de llevarse una medalla.* ~She's out of CONTENTION in this race. *En esta carrera no tiene ninguna posibilidad.* ~To be in CONTENTION for something. *Competir por algo.* ~Teams in CONTENTION. *Equipos rivales.* || **5.** •Bone of CONTENTION. *Manzana de la discordia.* ⇨ CONTENSIÓN

CONTRIBUTE [CONTRIBUIR]. *v.* [One's share]. *Pagar.* || **2.** [Ideas, información]. *Aportar.* ~His story CONTRIBUTES nothing new. *La historia que nos contó no aporta nada nuevo.* || **3.** [In discussion]. *Participar, intervenir.* ~She CONTRIBUTES to class discussions. *Participa en clase.* || **4.** [Press]. *Colaborar.* ~To CONTRIBUTE to a journal. *Colaborar en una revista.* || **5.** [Article, poem, paper]. *Escribir.* ~He CONTRIBUTED two essays to the volume. *Escribió dos artículos para el libro.* ~She CONTRIBUTES regularly to «The Clarion». *Escribe regularmente para «The Clarion».*

CONTRIBUTION. *n.* [Of ideas, information]. *Aporte.* || **2.** [Press]. *Colaboración.* || **3.** [Money]. *Donativo, cuota.* || **4.** [Salary deduction]. *Cotización.* || **5.** [To discussion]. *Intervención.* ~His CONTRIBUTION to the debate was most enlightening. *Su intervención en el debate fue muy instructivo.* || **6.** [To a fund]. *Aporte.* || **7.** Gift. *Regalo.* This was his CONTRIBUTION to mankind. *Esto*

fue su aporte a la humanidad. ⇨ CONTRIBUCIÓN

CONTROL[1] [CONTROL]. *n.* Rule. *Dominio.* ~The zone was under Arab CONTROL. *La zona estaba bajo el dominio árable.* || **2.** Management, jurisdiction. *Mando.* The firm remains under the family's CONTROL. *La compañía sigue en manos (bajo el mando) de la familia.* || **3.** Authority. *Autoridad.* ~Parental CONTROL. *Autoridad de los padres.* He has no CONTROL over the children. *No tiene autoridad sobre los niños.* ~A former Italian territory which will soon become international under the CONTROL of the United Nations. *Un antiguo territorio italiano que pronto se internacionalizará bajo la autoridad de las Naciones Unidas.* || **4.** Restraint, check, curb. *Dominio.* ~She was in complete CONTROL of herself throughout. *En ningún momento perdió el dominio de sí mismo.* || || **5.** Power. *Dominio, mando.* || **6.** Self-restraint. *Dominio de si mismo.* || **7.** Verification, comparison, check. *Verificación, comprobación.* || **8.** Mean of controlling, check. *Regulación.* ~Wages CONTROL. *Regulación salarial.* ~Price CONTROL. *Regulación de los precios.* ~Birth CONTROL. *Regulación de natalidad.* || **9.** Handling. *Manejo.* Only in this way can the CONTROL of assets can be assured. *Sólo así puede asegurarse el manejo de esos fondos.* || **10.** Management. *Dirección, mando.* ~As a general manager he will CONTROL business management. *En su carácter de gerente tomará la dirección (el mando) de los negocios.* || **11.** Watch, vigilance. *Vigilancia, inspección.* ~In this way a stricter CONTROL of those dangerous elements can be maintained. *De esa manera se podrá ejercer una vigilancia más efectiva sobre esos elementos peligrosos.* || **12.** Repression, supression. *Represión.* ~These measures are necessary to CONTROL prostitution. *Estas medidas son necesarias para la represión de la prostitución.* || **13.** Device used to adjust or control. *Botón.* ~Volume CONTROL. *Botón del volumen.* || **14.** Fight (against disease). *Lucha (contra la enfermedad).* || **15.**

PHRASES. || •Who is in CONTROL here.? *¿Quién manda aquí?* || •Circumstances beyond our CONTROL. *Circunstancias ajenas a nuestra voluntad.* ~To loose CONTROL. *Perder los estribos.* || •Remote CONTROL. *Mando a distancia.* || •To take over the CONTROLS. *Tomar el volante (car), Tomar los mandos (avión).* || •CONTROL panel. *Tablero de instrumentos.* || •To be under private CONTROL. *Estar en manos de particulares.*|| •To get out of CONTROL. *Desmandarse.* || •To get under CONTROL. *Conseguir dominar.* ~He got the situation under CONTROL. *Consiguió dominar la situación.*

CONTROL[2]. *v.* To check, verify (account). *Comprobar.* || **2.** To regulate. *Regular.* ~To CONTROL the temperature of a room. *Regular la temperatura de una habitación.* || **3.** To hold in restraint, to check. *Atajar, contener.* || **4.** [Disease]. *Luchar, combatir.* ~To CONTROL malaria. *Luchar (combatir contra) el paludismo.* || **5.** To check closely, keep an eye on (employees). *Vigilar.* || **5.** [Traffic, business]. *Dirigir.* || **6.** [Immigration]. *Regular.* || **7.** [Emotion]. *Contener.* || **8.** [Temper]. *Dominar, refrenar.* || **9.** To direct, supervise. *Mandar, tener bajo su mando.* ~He CONTROLS more than 2,000 men. *Tiene autoridad sobre más de dos mil hombres, tiene más de 2,000 hombres bajo su mando.* || **10.** [One's feelings]. *Gobernar.* || **11.** [Person, animal]. *Dominar.* He was never able to CONTROL his son. *Nunca pudo dominar a su hijo.* || **12.** •To CONTROL a situation. *Dominar una situación.* || **13.** •To CONTROL oneself. *Sobreponerse, dominarse.* ⇨CONTROLAR

CONTROVERSIAL. *adj.* Debatable. *Polémico, discutible, controvertido, debatido, discutido.* ▶The word CONTROVERSIAL has been accepted by the *Real Academia.*

CONTROVERSY. *n.* Discussion, argument, disagreement. *Polémica.* ~It was the subject of endless CONTROVERSY. *Fue objeto de interminable polémica.* ▶CONTROVERSIA has been accepted by the *Real Academia.*

CONVENIENCE. *n.* Well-being, comfort. *Comodidad, confort.* ~An apartment with all the modern CONVENIENCES. *Un piso con todas las comodidades.* || **2.** Practicality, advantage. *Comodidad, ventaja.* I enjoy the CONVENIENCE of living downtown. *Me gusta la comodidad de vivir en el centro.* ~It is a CONVENIENCE to be so close. *Resulta muy práctico vivir tan cerca.* ~Living near one's work is a great CONVENIENCE. *Es una gran ventaja vivir cerca de donde uno trabaja.* || **3.** *PHRASES.* •At your CONVENIENCE. *Cuando guste, cuando le convenga, cuando le venga bien.* || •At your earliest CONVENIENCE. *Tan pronto como le sea posible, con la mayor brevedad (posible).* || •CONVENIENCE food. *Comida precocida, platos preparados; comidas en el acto, comida de preparación rápida.* || •For your CONVENIENCE an envelope is enclosed. *Para facilitar su contestación adjuntamos un sobre.* || •'All modern CONVENIENCES'. *'Todo confort'.* ⇨CONVENIENCIA

CONVENIENT. *adj.* Practical, neat (coll.). *Cómodo, práctico, útil.* ~A very CONVENIENT way of storing cassettes. *Una manera muy práctica de guardar los casetes.* || **2.** Easily accessible, near (to). *Accesible, céntrico.* ~A CONVENIENT location. *Una ubicación céntrica.* ~A CONVENIENT base from which to explore the region. *Una base muy bien situada desde donde explorar la región.* || **3.** Timely. *Oportuno.* ~Her death was certainly CONVENIENT for him. *Es cierto que su muerte le resultó muy oportuna.* At a CONVENIENT moment. *En un momento oportuno.* ~When it is CONVENIENT for you. *Cuando le venga bien.* ~His resignation was most CONVENIENT for the company. *Su renuncia fue muy oportuna para la empresa.* || **4.** Appropriate, suitable. *Apropiado.* ~We looked for a CONVENIENT place to stop. *Buscamos un sitio apropiado para parar.* || **5.** Handy, close, easy to reach. *Práctico, cerca (lugar).* ~I always go to the corner pharmacy, it's very CONVENIENT. *Siempre voy a la farmacia de la esquina, me queda muy a mano.* ~It's very CONVENIENT to have the school so near.

Resulta muy práctico tener la escuela tan cerca. ~He put it on a CONVENIENT chair. *Lo puso en una silla que estaba a mano.* ⇨ CONVENIENTE

CONVENTION [CONVENCIÓN]. *n.* Meeting, conference. *Asamblea, congreso.* ~A teacher's CONVENTION. *Un congreso de maestros.* || **2.** Agreement. *Convenio.* ~A copy of the Vienna CONVENTION will be circulated among the delegates. *Se distribuirá a los delegados el texto del convenio de Viena (Prats).*

CONVENTIONAL [CONVENCIONAL]. *adj.* Ordinary, usual. *Corriente, normal, habitual, clásico.* || **2.** Traditional, customary. *Tradicional, acostumbrado, sancionado por el uso.*

CONVERT [CONVERT]. *v.* To change from one system of measurement to another. *Reducir.* ~To CONVERT kiolometers to meters. *Reducir kilómetros a metros.* || **2.** Alter, improve, redecorate. *Arreglar, reformar.* ~He bought a house in the country which cost him $3,000 for CONVERSION. *Se compró una casa en el campo que le costó tres mil dólares en reformas (Prats).* || **3.** To alter (room, building) so that it can be used for a different purpose. *Convertir, transformar, convertir, adaptar.* The church has been CONVERTED into a museum. *La iglesía ha sido transformada en un museo.* ~They CONVERTED the study into a nursery when the baby was born. *Cuando nació el niño, transformaron la sala de estudio en habitación para él (Prats).* || **4.** JUR Appropriate. *Apropriarse indebidamente (ilícitamente).*

CONVERTIBLE [CONVERTIBLE]. *adj.* [Car]. *Descapotable.*

CONVICTIÓN. *n.* Proof of guilt. *Condena, declaración de culpabilidad.* With that evidence they managed to secure a CONVICTION. *Con esas pruebas lograron que se le condenara.* ~There were twelve CONVICTIONS for thefts. *Hubo doce condenas por robo.* || **2.** •He has no previous CONVICTIONS. *No tiene antecedentes penales.* ⇨ CONVICCIÓN

CONVICT. *n.* Criminal serving a sentence.

Presidiario, recluso, preso. || **2.** •Ex-convict. *Ex presidiario.* ⇨ CONVICTO

CONVOCATION. *n.* Academic assembly, meeting. *Reunión, asamblea, congregación.* ⇨ CONVOCATORIA

COOPERATE [COOPERAR]. *v.* To work together. *Colaborar.* ~If we all COOPERATE we can finish the job today. *Si todos colaboramos podremos terminar el trabajo hoy.* || **2.** •If the weather COOPERATES. *Si el tiempo no nos falla.*

COPY. *n.* [Newspaper]. *Número.* ~Back COPY. *Número atrasado.* || **2.** [Book]. *Ejemplar.* Please send me a COPY of the latest best-seller. *Favor de mandarme un ejemplar del último libro de mayor venta.* || **3.** Text. *Texto* ~A COPY of the Vienna Convention will be circulated among the delegates. *Se distribuirá a los delegados el texto del convenio de Viena (Prats).* || **4.** I hereby enclose three COPIES of Resolution A. *Le envío con la presente el texto de la Resolución A, por triplicado (Prats).* || **5.** Unprinted matters. *Manuscrito, original.* || **6.** Subject matter (for a journalist, novelist). *Tema, asunto.* ~A murder is always good COPY. *Un asesinato siempre es un buen tema.* ~Good news doesn't make good COPY. *Las buenas noticias no se venden bien.* ~It makes good COPY. *Es un asunto de interés.* || **7.** Article, news item. *Reportaje, artículo.* ~I got my COPY in by midnight. *Entregué el artículo (reportaje) antes de la media noche.* || **8.** PHRASE. || •COPY editor. *Corrector de manuscritos.* || •COPY preparation. *Composición.* || •COPY reader. *Corrector de manuscritos.* || •COPY desk. *Redacción.* || •Rough COPY. *Borrador.* ⇨ COPIA

CORPORATION [CORPORACIÓN]. *n.* [Business]. *Sociedad anónima.* || **2.** Municipal council. *Ayuntamiento, municipio.* || **3.** Artifical person. *Persona jurídica.*

CORPULENT. *adj.* Portly, stout, fat. *Gordo, obeso.* ⇨ CORPULENTO

CORRESPOND. *v.* To exchange letters with someone. *Escribirse, tener correspondencia con, intercambiar cartas, carte-*

arse con. ⇨ CORRESPONDER

COST [COSTO]. *n.* Price. *Precio.* ~What's the COST of this dress? *¿Cuál es el precio de este vestido?* ‖ **2.** Expense. *Gasto.* ~The COST of running a car. *Los gastos del mantenimiento de un coche.* ~To cover one's COSTS. *Reducir los gastos.* ~To meet the COST of something. *Correr con los gastos de algo.* ‖ **3.** Loss, sacrifice. *Sacrificio, esfuerzo.* She helped me out but at great COST to herself. *Sacrificó mucho al ayudarme.* ~At little COST to yourself, you could help one of these orphans. *Haciendo un pequeño sacrificio podrías ayudar a uno de estos huérfanos.* ~At great COST. *Tras grandes esfuerzos, tras grandes pérdidas.* ‖ **4.** Risk. *Riesgos.* ~Without counting the COST. *Sin pensar en los riesgos.* ~At little COST to himself. *Con poco riesgo para sí mismo.* ‖ **5.** Charge. *Cargo.* ~At no additional COST. *Sin cargo adicional.* ‖ **6.** PHRASES. ‖ •To pay the COST (jur.). *Pagar las costas.* ‖ •Whatever the COST. *Cueste lo que cueste.* ‖ •To count (consider) the COST. *Considerar las desventajas.* ‖ •At the COST of his life. *Pagó con su vida.* ‖ •At my COST. *A mis expensas.*

COURAGE. *n.* Bravery, valor. *Valor, valentía.* ~He has/lacks the COURAGE to do it. *Tiene/le falta valor para hacerlo.* ~To have/lack the COURAGE of one's convictions. *Ser/no ser fiel a sus convicciones, ser/no ser consecuente con sus principios.* ~To lose one's COURAGE. *Acobardarse, desanimarse.* ~He took COURAGE from her smile. *Su sonrisa le dió ánimo.* ‖ **2.** PHRASES. ‖ •To pluck up one's COURAGE. *Hacer de tripas corazón.* ‖ •You may take COURAGE from the fact that ... *Es alentador el hecho de que ...*‖ •Take COURAGE! *¡Ánimo!* ‖ •To take one's COURAGE with both hands. *Armarse de valor.* ⇨CORAJE

COURSE. *n.*
❶ CHOICE, OPTION, COURSE OF ACTION. *Camino, opción, remedio (used negatively).* ~Several COURSES are open to us. *Varios caminos se abren ante nosotros.* ~The only COURSE open to us. *El único camino que tenemos, nuestra única opción, no*

tenemos otro remedio que. The company has the CHOICE of three courses of action. *La empresa tiene tres opciones.* ‖ **2.** •His COURSE of action was to ... *Su opción fue.* ‖ **3.** •Your best COURSE is to say nothing. *Lo mejor es no decir nada.* ‖ **4.** •What COURSE do you suggest? *¿Qué es lo que me aconsejas?*

❷ DIRECTION. *Rumbo, camino.* ~Change COURSE and head for London. *Cambia de dirección y dirígete a Londres.* ~We continued on our COURSE. *Seguimos nuestro camino.* ‖ **2.** •To be on/off COURSE. *Seguir/perder el rumbo.* ~The plane had gone off COURSE. *El avión se había desviado de su rumbo.* ~The project is on COURSE for completion. *El proyecto va bien encaminado y se terminará en la fecha prevista.* ‖ **3.** •To change COURSE. *Cambiar de rumbo.* ~The party has changed COURSE. *El partido ha dado un nuevo rumbo.* ‖ **4.** •To set COURSE. *Poner rumbo.* ‖ **5.** •To set COURSE for. *Hacer rumbo a.* •To steer a COURSE for. *Ir rumbo a.* ‖ **6.** •The COURSE of true love. *El camino del verdadero amor.* ‖ **7.** •To be on COURSE. *Ir por buen camino.* ‖ **8.** •We are on COURSE for victory. *Nos encaminamos al triunfo.* ‖ **9.** •To take a middle COURSE. *Evitar los extremos.*

❸ PROGRESS, DURATION OF TIME. *Transcurso, paso.* ~During the COURSE of the interview. *Durante el transcurso de la entrevista.* ~In the COURSE of her duties, she handles a great deal of money. *En el desempeño (ejercicio) de sus funciones maneja una gran suma de dinero.* ~I hope that in the COURSE of the next few weeks they will have made up their minds. *Espero que dentro (en el transcurso) de estas próximas semanas se habrán decidido ya.* ‖ **2.** •COURSE of events. *Marcha de los acontecimientos.* ‖ **3.** •In due COURSE. *A su debido tiempo.* ~You will be informed in due COURSE. *Se le informará en su momento (a su debido tiempo).* ‖ **4.** •In the COURSE of construction. *En vías de construcción.* ‖ **5.** •In the normal COURSE of events. *Normalmente.* ‖ **6.** •In the COURSE of our conversation. *Mientras hablá-*

bamos. || **7.** •In the COURSE of time. *Con el tiempo, eventualmente.* || **8.** •To run its COURSE. *Finalizar, llegar a su fin, terminarse.* ~The affair has run its COURSE. *El asunto ha terminado.* || **9.** •We will let things take their COURSE. *Dejaremos correr los acontecimientos.* || **10.** •To hold one's COURSE. *Seguir el camino trazado.*

❹ VARIOUS. *Tratamiento.* ~The doctor put me on a COURSE of antibiotics. *El doctor me recetó antibióticos.* || **2.** Path, channel (river). *Recorrido, camino, corriente.* ~The COURSE of the Mississippi river. *El recorrido del río Mississippi.* || **3.** [Illness]. *Desarrollo.* || **4.** Trajectory. *Trayectoria.* ~The course of a bullet. *La trayectoria de una bala.* ~The COURSE of the Sun. *La trayectoria del sol.* || **5.** [Education]. *Cursillo (short), asignatura (univ.).* ~I have a COURSE in English grammar. *Tengo una asignatura de gramática inglesa.* || **6.** [Golf]. *Campo.* ~We rented a house overlooking a golf COURSE. *Alquilamos una casa con vista a un campo de golf.* || **7.** [Racing]. *Pista.* || **8.** [Horse-racing]. *Hipódromo.* || **9.** [Culinary]. *Plato.* ~A three-COURSE meal. *Una comida de tres platos.* •First COURSE.. *Entrada.* •Main dish. *Plato principal (fuerte).* •Last COURSE. *Postre.*

❺ PHRASES. || •This will happen as a matter of COURSE. *Eso ya vendrá por sí solo.* || •To last (stay) the COURSE. *Aguantar hasta el final.* || •To interfere with the COURSE of justice. *Entorpecer la acción de la justicia.* || •That is a matter of COURSE. *Eso cae de su peso.* || •A COURSE of lectures. *Un ciclo de conferencias.* ⇨CURSO

COURT [CORTE]. *n.*

❶ LAW. Place where legal matters are decided. *Tribunal.* || **2.** Audience. *Audiencia.* || **3.** Building. *Juzgado.*

•COURT case. *Causa, juicio.*
•COURT official. *Funcionario del juzgado.*
•COURT of last resort. *Tribunal de última instancia.*
•COURT order. *Orden judicial.*
•COURT proceedings. *Proceso.*
•COURT records. *Actas de juicios.*

•COURT hearing. *Vista.*
•COURT action. *Acción judicial.*
•COURT martial. *Consejo de guerra.*
•High COURT. *Tribunal supremo.*
•In open COURT. *En audiencia pública.*
•Juvenile COURT. *Tribunal de menores.*
•Las CORTES *The Spanish Parliament.*
•Out of COURT settlement. *Acuerdo extrajudicial.*
•The COURT is adjourned. *Se levanta la sesión.*
•The COURT will rise. *Póngase de pie.*
•To hold COURT. *Dar (recibir en) audiencia.*
•To laugh something out of COURT. *Rechazar algo poniéndolo en ridículo.* ~I'd be laughed out of COURT. *Se reirían de mí.*
•To take someone to COURT. *Demandar, llevar a uno ante los tribunales.*
•To settle out of COURT. *Llegar a un acuerdo sin ir a juicio, negociar una solución al margen de los tribunales.*
•To go to COURT. *Acudir a los tribunales.*
•To appear in COURT. *Comparecer ante el tribunal (los tribunales).*

❷ SPORT/BUILDING. [Tennis]. *Cancha, (Lat. Am.) pista.* || **2.** [Palace]. *Palacio.* || **3.** [Courtyard]. *Patio.* || **4.** [Of a church]. *Plaza.* || **5.** [Big room]. *Sala.*

COVER [CUBRIR]. *v.* [Cushion]. *Poner una funda.* || **2.** [Hole, bowl]. *Tapar.* ~COVER the pan. *Tape la cacerola.* || **3.** To protect a book. *Forrar.* || **4.** [Sofa]. *Tapizar, recubrir.* || **5.** To travel over, go the length of. *Recorrer.* ~We COVERED five miles in two hours. *Recorrimos cinco millas en dos horas.* || **6.** [Topic]. *Tratar, exponer.* ~Today our lesson will COVER the history of France. *La lección de hoy tratara sobre la historia de Francia.* || **7.** [Eventuality]. *Contemplar.* ~This case is not COVEREDED by present legislation. *La legislación vigente no contempla este caso.* || **7.** Apply to. *Aplicarse, afectar.* ~This legislation only COVERS large companies. *Esta legislación sólo se aplica a las empresas grandes.* || **8.** Hide. ~*Tapar.* She COVERED her eyes. *Se tapó los ojos.* || **9.** [Liabilities]. *Hacer frente a.* || **10.** [insurance]. *Asegurar, proteger.* This policy

COVERS you against all risks. *Esta poliza le proteje (asegura) contra todo tipo de riesgos.* || **11.** Substitute. *Suplir (substituir) a alguien.* || **12.** Conceal (truth). *Encubrir (la verdad).* || **13.** To aim a gun. *Apuntar.* || **14.** To include. *Abarcar, incluir, comprender.* || **15.** [Story]. *Hacer (realizar) un reportaje sobre, informar sobre algo.* || **16.** To put a cover on (saucepan). *Tapar.* || **17.** To be responsible (for a particular area). *Estar encargado de, ocuparse de.* ~He COVERS the north of the country. *Está encargado del norte del país.* || **18.** Overlook. *Dominar.* The house situated on a hill COVERS the entire region. *La casa situada en la colina domina toda la región.* || **19.** [Furniture, floor]. *Revestir.* || **20.** To take into account. *Tener en cuenta.* We must COVER all eventualities. *Debemos tener en cuenta todas las eventualidades.* || **21.** PHRASES. || •To COVER one's tracks. *No dejar rastro.* || •To COVER oneself. *Protegerse, asegurarse.* || •To COVER a great deal of ground. *Recorrer mucho camino.* || •To COVER for somebody. *Encubrir a alguien.* || •Will 10 dollars COVER it? *Alcanzará con 10 dólares?*

CREATIVE. *adj.* [Work]. *Original.* ~He came up with a really CREATIVE solution to the problem. *Encontró una solución muy original al problema.* || **2.** [Person]. *Creador.* ▶The word CREATIVO has been accepted by the *Real Academia.*

CREATIVITY. *n.* Quality of being creative. *Capacidad creadora.* ~The lack of CREATIVITY of Spanish producers. *La falta de capacidad creadora de los directores españoles (Prats).*

CREATURE. *n.* Human being. *Ser.* ~Creatures from another planet. *Seres de otro planeta.* || **2.** Animal. *Animal.* ~Sea-CREATURE. *Animal marino.* ~To be a CREATURE of habit. *Ser un animal de costumbre.* || **3.** LIT Tool, puppet. *Títere, instrumento, juguete.* || **4.** FIG *Creación, obra, producto, fruto.* ~A CREATURE of the imagination. *Una obra de la imaginación.* || **5.** •Poor CREATURE! *¡Pobre animal (animal)!, ¡Pobrecito (person)!* ⇨CRIATURA

CREDIBILITY [CREDIBILIDAD]. *n.* Confidence, trust. *Crédito, confianza.* ~He has very little CREDIBILITY. *No se le tiene confianza.* || **2.** Sincerity. *Sinceridad.* ~They are questioning the CREDIBILITY of his promises. *Dudan de la sinceridad de sus promesas.* || **3.** Authenticity. *Autenticidad.* A few touches of humor will add CREDIBILITY to your story. *Una pincelada de humor le dará mayor autenticidad a tu relato (Pratt).* || **4.** Truthfulness. *Veracidad.* ~The crucial issue is the CREDIBILITY of the witness. *El asunto fundamental es la veracidad del testigo.*

CREDIT. *n.* Recognition, acknowledgement. *Mérito, reconocimiento.* ~She deserves some CREDIT for trying. *Merece que se le reconozca el mérito de haberlo intentado.* ~To take the CREDIT for something. *Atribuirse el mérito.* ~I gave you CREDIT for more sense. *Te creía más inteligente.* || **2.** . Honor. *Honor.* ~It does you CREDIT. *Puede estar orgulloso.* ~To be a CREDIT to. *Hacer honor a.* ~He's a great CREDIT to the family. *Le hace mucho honor a su familia.* || **3.** Reputation. *Buena fama. reputación.* || **4.** [On balance sheet]. *Saldo acreedor, saldo a favor.* || **5.** [In accounting]. *Haber.* ~On the CREDIT side. *En el haber.* ~Debit and CREDIT. *Deber y haber.* || **6.** •To give CREDIT to (film, book). *Reconocer.* || **7.** •You have $200.00 to your CREDIT. *Tiene un saldo de 200 dólares.* ⇨CRÉDITO

CRIME. *n.* Violation of the law. *Delito.* ~To commit a CRIME. *Cometer un delito.* ~The scene of the CRIME. *El lugar del delito.* || **2.** Criminality. *Criminalidad.* ~An increase in CRIME. *Un aumento de la criminalidad.* || **3.** Criminal activity. *Delincuencia.* ~To prevent/punish CRIME. *Prevenir/castigar la delincuencia.* ~A life of CRIME. *Una vida de delincuencia.* || **4.** Something regrettable, deplorable. *Lástima, pecado.* It's a CRIME to waste all that time. *Es una lástima (un pecado) malgastar todo ese tiempo.* || **5.** •CRIME wave. *Ola delictiva.* || **6.** •CRIME doesn't pay. *No hay crimen sin castigo.* || **7.** •CRIME fiction. *Novelas policíacas.* ⇨CRIMEN

CRIMINAL[1] [CRIMINAL]. *adj.* •CRIMINAL lawyer. *Penalista.* || **2.** •CRIMINAL law. *Derecho penal.* || **3.** •CRIMINAL record. *Antecedentes penales.* || **4.** •CRIMINAL offender. *Infractor.* || **5.** •CRIMINAL assault. *Intento de violación.* || **6.** •CRIMINAL case. *Causa o proceso criminal.* || **7.** •CRIMINAL offense. *Delito penal.* || **8.** •CRIMINAL procedure. *Procedimiento del tribunal penal.* || **9.** •CRIMINAL proceedings. *Acción penal.*

CRIMINAL[2] [CRIMINAL]. *n.* Person guilty of a crime. *Delincuente.*

CROSS. *v.* Go against. *Contrariar (person), frustrar (plans).* ~She doesn't like to be CROSSED. *No le gustan que la contrarien.* || **2.** River (as obstacle). *Salvar.* || **3.** To mark with a cross. *Marcar con una cruz.* || **4.** *PHRASES.* || •To CROSS someone's mind (something). *Ocurrírsele algo a alguien.* Suddenly an idea CROSSED my mind. *De pronto se me ocurrió una idea.* || •To CROSS one's eyes. *Ponerse bizco.* || •I think we got our wires CROSSED. *Me parece que no hablamos el mismo idioma.* || •To CROSS oneself. *Persignarse, santiguarse, hacerse la señal de la cruz.* || •To keep one's fingers CROSSED. *Tocar madera.* || •CROSS my heart! *¡Te lo juro!* || •To CROSS from Dover to Calais. *Hacer la travesía de Dover a Calais.* || •To CROSS into another country. *Pasar la frontera a otro país.* || •To CROSS off (out). *Tachar.* || •To CROSS someone's palm with silver. *Llenar las manos de alguien de monedas de plata.* ⇨CRUZAR

CRUCIAL. *adj.* Fundamental. *Fundamental.* ~The CRUCIAL issue is the credibility of the witness. *El asunto fundamental es la veracidad del testigo.* || **2.** Critical, decisive. *Decisivo, crítico.* ~The next game will be CRUCIAL for us. *El próximo partido va a ser decisivo para nosotros.* || **3.** Key word. *Palabra clave.* ~The CRUCIAL words are 'in less than two months'. *La expresión clave es 'dentro de dos meses'.* || **4.** Essential. *De mucha importancia, importantísimo.* ~The correct ingredients are CRUCIAL. *Es importantísimo usar los ingredientes indicados.* ▶CRUCIAL has been accepted by the *Real Academia.*

CRUDE [CRUDO]. *adj.* [Tool]. *Primitivo.* ~CRUDE tools made of stone. *Toscas herramientas de piedra.* || **2.** [Steel]. *Bruto.* || **3.** [Object, workmanship, style]. *Tosco.* ~Crude furniture. *Muebles toscos.* || **4.** Vulgar. *Ordinario.* || **5.** Offensive, rude (joke, word, gesture). *Grosero.* ~A CRUDE remark. *Un comentario grosero.* || **6.** Unsophisticated. *Rudimentario, burdo.* ~A CRUDE comparison of engines. *Una comparación rudimentaria de motores.* || **7.** Unrefined, natural (sugar). *Sin refinar.* || **8.** Not skillfully performed, coarse (imitation, letters). ~The words 'Keep out' was painted in CRUDE letters on the door. *En la puerta las palabras 'Entrada prohibida' habían sido pintadas en burdas letras.*

CURE. *v.* [Habit, idea]. *Quitar.* || **2.** [Hide]. *Curtir.* || **3.** To remedy (evil, problem). *Remediar, poner remedio a.* ~Measures to CURE inflation. *Medidas para remediar la inflación.* || **4.** [By salting]. *Salar.* || **5.** [Rubber]. *Vulcanizar.* ⇨CURAR

CURIOUS. *adj.* Odd, singular. *Raro, extraño, sorprendente.* ~It's a CURIOUS way of putting it. *Es una manera muy extraña de expresarlo.* || **2.** Anxious. *Ansioso.* ~I'm CURIOUS to see Granada. *Tengo ganas de ver a Granada.* || **3.** Interested in. *Interesarle a alguien algo.* I'm CURIOUS to know how you did. *Me interesa saber como te salió la cosa.* ⇨CURIOSO

CURRENT. *adj.* In general use, prevalent (opinions, beliefs, tendency). *General.* ~CURRENT opinion. *La opinión general.* || **2.** [Word, phrase]. *Actual.* || **3.** [Year, month]. *En curso.* || **4.** Latest, most recent (magazine). *Último.* ~The CURRENT issue (number). *El último número.* || **5.** Existing (situation, policy, prices). *Actual.* || **6.** Valid (license, membership). *Vigente.* || **7.** Prevailing (opinion, practice). *Común, habitual.* || **8.** Up to date (figures, information, report). *Actualizado, al día.* || **9.** Of the present time. *Actual.* ~The CURRENT crisis. *La crisis actual.* My CURRENT boyfriend. *Mi actual* *novio.* || **10.** •CURRENT rate of exchange. *Cambio del día.* || **11.** •CURRENT affairs. *Actualidad.* || **12.** •CURRENT assets. *Activo disponible.* ⇨CORRIENTE

CYNICAL. *adj.* Suspicious, mistrustful. *Desconfiado, escéptico.* ~You're so CYNICAL; you don't believe in anything. *¡Qué desconfiado eres!, no crees en nada.* ~I think she takes a rather CYNICAL view of men. *Creo que es muy desconfiada de los hombres.* || **2.** Sneering, sarcastic. *Despreciativo, sarcástico.* ~He's a very CYNICAL man. *Es muy despreciativo.* ⇨CÍNICO

D

DAME. *n.* Strange woman. *Tipa, tía.* ‖ **2.** [In pantomine]. *Papel de anciana representado por un hombre.* ‖ **3.** Girl, chick. *Chica.* ⇨ DAMA

DEBATE. *v.* Wonder about, consider (idea, possibility). *Considerar, dar vueltas a, tratar de decidir.* ~They're still DEBATING on who to send. *Todavía están trantando de decidir a quién van a enviar.* ⇨ DEBATIR

DECEIVE. *adj.* To trick, mislead, fool. *Engañar.* ~Merchants who try to DECEIVE unwary customers. *Vendedores que tratan de engañar a los clientes desprevenidos.* ⇨ DECEPCIONAR

DECENT. *adj.* Adequate, suitable, appropriate. *Apropiado.* ~I need DECENT clothes to go to the wedding. *Necesito ropa apropiada para ir a la boda.* ‖ **2.** Fair, passable, acceptable. *Satisfactorio (aunque no excelente).* ~The food was DECENT. *La comida fue pasable.* ~She gave a DECENT performance. *Su actuación fue aceptable.* ‖ **3.** [Person]. *Bueno, honrado.* ~They're DECENT people. *Son gente honrada.* ‖ **4.** [Meal, wages]. *Adecuado.* ~They pay their employees DECENT wages. *Los sueldos que dan a sus empleados son adecuados (no están mal).* ‖ **5.** [Price]. *Módico.* ~They charge decent PRICES. *Cobran precios módicos.* ‖ **6.** Kind, obliging, generous. *Bueno, simpático, amable.* ~It's very DECENT of you to help. *Es muy amable de su parte ayudar.* ‖ **7.** Proper. *Lo que corresponde, lo correcto.* ~He did the DECENT thing and married her. *Hizo lo que debía y se casó con ella.* ‖ **8.** Quite good. *Bastante bueno.* She has quite a DECENT job. *Tiene un trabajo bastante bueno.* ‖ **9.** Wearing enough clothing to appear in public. *Presentable.* ~Are you DECENT? *¿Estás presentable?* ‖ **10.** Proper and fitting. *Apropiado.* ~A DECENT burial. *Un entierro apropiado.* ⇨ DECENT

DECEPTION. *n.* Deceit, fraud, trickery. *Fraude, engaño, embuste.* ~His wife was the victim of a DECEPTION. *Engañaron a su mujer.* ⇨ DECEPCIÓN

DECLINE[1]. *v.* Refuse (to do something), turn down (an offer, invitation). *Rechazar (una invitación, oferta), negarse (a hacer algo).* ~He DECLINED to answer. SE NEGÓ A CONTESTAR. ‖ **2.** Decrease. *Disminuir.* ~Their shares have DECLINED in value. *Sus acciones han disminuido de valor.* ‖ **3.** [Amount]. *Bajar.* ~The number of Congress members DECLINED from 371 to 361. *El número de congresistas bajo de 371 a 361.* ‖ **4.** [Business]. *Ir de baja.* ~After his father's death, his business began to DECLINE. *Después de la muerte de su padre, se fue de baja el negocio.* ‖ **5.** To worsen (health). *Empeorarse.* ~After the accident, his health began to DECLINE. *Después del accidente empezó a deteriorar su salud.* ‖ **6.** •To DECLINE in importance. *Ir perdiendo importancia.* ‖ **7.** •In my DECLINING years. *En mis últimos años.* ⇨ DECLINAR

DECLINE[2] [DECLINATION]. *n.* Deterioration. *Deterioro, decadencia.* ‖ **2.** [Health]. *Empeoramiento, debilitación.* ‖ **3.** Downward trend. *Ocaso, declive, decadencia.* ~The DECLINE and Fall of the Roman Empire. *La decadencia y caída del Imperio Romano.* ‖ **4.** Decrease. *Disminución, descenso.* ~A DECLINE in demand. *Una disminución en la demanda.* ~There has been a DECLINE in the party's popularity. *La popularidad del partido ha dismi-*

nuido. || **5.** Downward slope. *Declive.* ~Constructed on a slight DECLINE to allow the water to drain away. *Construido en un leve declive para permitir que se escurra el agua.* || **6.** •To go (fall) into DECLINE. *Empezar a decaer.* || **7.** •To be on the DECLINE. *Ir disminuyendo, ser menos frecuente, ir perdiéndose (traditions), ir a menos (prestige).* ~Interest in radio has been on the DECLINE lately. *El interés por la radio ha ido disminuyendo últimamente.*

DECORATE/DECORATION [DECORAR/ DECORACIÓN]. [Military]. *Condecoración/ condecorar.*

DEDICATE. *v.* Declare open (official building). *Inaugurar (oficialmente).* ~The playground was DEDICATED today. *Hoy se inauguró el patio de recreo.* ⇨DEDICAR

DEDICATION [DEDICACIÓN]. *n.* Commitment. *Entrega, devoción.* || **2.** In book, on music. *Dedicatoria.* || **3.** Opening. *Inauguración.*

DEFICIENT. *adj.* [Mentally]. *Retrasado, anormal.* || **2.** To be deficient (in something). *Carecer de, estar falto de.* ~Foods DEFICIENT in vitamins. *Alimentos de bajo contenido vitamínico.* ~A plan DEFICIENT in imagination. *Un plan carente de imaginación.* || **3.** Unsatisfactory. *Que deja mucho que desear.* ~Some of the methods used were DEFICIENT. *Se emplearon métodos que dejan mucho que desear.* || **4.** Insufficient, inadequate. *Insuficiente.* ~DEFICIENT knowledge. *Conocimiento insuficiente.* ⇨DEFICIENTE

DEFRAUD. *v.* Embezzle. *Desfalcar.* ~A group of employees DEFRAUDED the firm of millions of dollars. *Un grupo de empleado desfalcaron un millón de dólares.* || **2.** Swindle. *Estafar.* They DEFRAUDED their customers by selling them low quality products. *Estafaron a sus clientes vendiéndoles productos de calidad inferior.* ⇨DEFRAUDAR

DEGRADE. *v.* Despreciar, humillir. *Rebajar.* Films that DEGRADE women. *Películas que rebajan a mujeres.* || **2.** GEOL Wear down

(rocks, etc.). *Desgastar.* ~The wind and the rain DEGRADE the rocks. *La lluvia y el viento desgastan las piedras.* || **3.** Degenerate (race). *Degenerar.* `|| **4.** •To DEGRADE oneself (by doing something). *Rebajarse a hacer algo.* ⇨DEGRADAR

DELIBERATE [DELIBERADO]. *adj.* Intentional, studied (act, attempt). *Intencionado, premeditado, a propósito.* ~I could tell it was DELIBERATE. *Se veía que lo había hecho a propósito.* || **2.** Cautious, careful. *Prudente.* ~A DELIBERATE decision. *Una decisión hecha con reflexión.* || **3.** Unhurried. *Pausado, lento.* ~He began working in his usual DELIBERATE and meticulous manner. *Se puso a trabajar pausada y meticulosamente como era su costumbre.*

DELICATE. *adj.* [Health]. *Enfermizo, fragil, débil.* ~His health has always been DELICATE. *Siempre ha sido un muchacho enfermizo.* || **2.** [Workmanship]. *Fino, exquisito, primoroso.* ~A DELICATE pattern of butterflies and leaves. *Un primoroso diseño de mariposas y hojas.* || **3.** [Situación]. *Difícil.* ~The negotiations are at a DELICATE stage. *Las negociaciones se encuentran en un punto difícil.* || **4.** [Color]. *Suave.* ~A DELICATE shade of blue. *Un suave matiz azul.* || **5.** Subtle. *Sútil.* ~A DELICATE hint. *Una indirecta sútil.* ~A DELICATE distinction. *Una distinción sútil.* || **6.** [Smell]. *Fino.* Bees have a very DELICATE sense of smell. *Las abejas tienen un olfato muy fino.* || **7.** Capable of noticing very small changes or differences; sensitive (touch, instrument]. *Sensible.* ~The alarm is very DELICATE and goes off a the slightess movement. *La alarma es muy sensible y sueña con el más mínimo movimiento.* || **8.** •DELICATE balance. *Equilibrio precario.* ⇨DELICADO

DELICIOUS. *adj.* [Food]. *Rico.* ~These oranges are delicious. *Estas naranjas son riquísimas.* ⇨DELICIOSO

DEMAND[1]. *v.* Insist, order, command. *Exigir.* ~Jean DEMANDED to be told everything. *Juana exigió que le dijeran todo.* || **2.** [Pay raise, rights]. *Reclamar.* ~I DEMAND my rights. *Reclamo mis derechos.* ~The unions are DEMANDING better conditions. *Los sindicatos reclaman mejores condiciones.* ‖ **3.** To insist. *Insistir.* ~I DEMANDED to know why. *Insistí en saber por qué.* ~He DEMANDED to see the manager. *Insistió en (pidió) ver al gerente.* ‖ **4.** To require, call for, need. *Requerir.* ~The matter DEMANDS careful consideration. *La cuestión requiere un examen detenido.* ~The job DEMANDS care. *El trabajo exige cuidado.* ‖ **5.** To ask. *Preguntar.* ~And where do you think you are going, DEMANDED the police officer? *¿Y adónde pretende ir Ud. le preguntó el policía?* ⇨ DEMANDAR

DEMAND². *n.* Claim. *Exigencia.* The work makes great DEMANDS on me. *Me absorbe completamente el trabajo.* ~She did not feel equal to the DEMANDS of the job. *No se sentía capaz de hacer frente a las exigencias del trabajo.* ‖ **2.** Need. *Necesidad.* ~There is a pressing DEMAND for. *Hay una urgente necesidad de.* ~The pressing DEMANDS for housing. *La urgente necesidad de viviendas.* ‖ **3.** *PHRASES.* ‖ •On DEMAND. *A petición.* ‖ •To be in DEMAND. *Ser solicitado, solicitarse.* ~He's in great DEMAND as a magician. *Es un mago muy solicitado (popular).* ‖ •To make DEMANDS on someone. *Pedir mucho de alguien.* ‖ •The trial made enormous DEMANDS on his health. *El juicio puso a prueba su salud.* ‖ •Payable on DEMAND. *Pagadero a la vista.* ‖ •By popular DEMAND. *Por petición del público.* ‖ •Final DEMAND. *Ultimo aviso.* ⇨ DEMANDA

DEMOLISH [DEMOLER]. *v.* [Theory, proposal]. *Echar abajo, destruir.* ~He DEMOLISHED my argument in minutes. *Echó abajo mi razonamiento al instante.* ‖ **2.** To defeat. *Vencer.* ~She DEMOLISHED her opponent in less than half an hour. *Venció a su adversario en menos de media hora.*

DEMONSTRATION. *n.* Public show of feeling or opinion. *Manifestación.* He was arrested for his part in the DEMONSTRATION. *Fue detenido por su participación en la manifestación.* ⇨ DEMOSTRACIÓN

DEMONSTRATE. *v.* To make a public expression of dissatisfaction. *Hacer una manifestación (manifestarse) a favor o en contra de algo.* ~In 1968 many students DEMONSTRATED in the streets of Paris. *En 1968 muchos estudiantes hicieron una manifestación en las calles de París.* ‖ **2.** To show (a product) in use in an effort to sell it. *Hacer una demostración de.* ~Let me DEMONSTRATE how this machine works. *Déjeme hacerle una demostración de cómo funciona esta máquina.* ⇨ DEMOSTRAR

DENOMINATION. *n.* [Currency]. *Valor.* ~Coins of all DENOMINATIONS. *Monedas de distintos valores.* ~Bills in $10 and $20 DENOMINATIONS. *Billetes de $10 y $20 dólares.* ‖ **2.** Religion. *Secta religiosa.* ‖ **3.** Class, kind. *Clase, categoría, tipo.* ~Protestantism and Catholicism are both DENOMINATIONS of the same Christian faith. *El protestantismo y el catolicismo ambos provienen de la fe cristiana.* ⇨ DENOMINACIÓN

DEPARTMENT. *n.* Section (store). *Sección.* ~You can find this in the dress DEPARTMENT. *Lo puede encontrar en la sección de vestidos.* ‖ **2.** [Government]. *Ministerio.* ~The DEPARTMENT of Education. *El Ministerio de Educación.* ‖ **3.** Responsibility. *Responsabilidad.* Paying the bills is not my DEPARTMENT. *No es mi responsabilidad pagar las cuentas, no soy quien se encarga de pagar las cuentas.* ‖ **4.** Area of competence. *Terreno, aspecto.* I'm not that good in that DEPARTMENT. *Yo no soy muy bueno en este terreno.* ‖ **5.** [At a university]. *Facultad.* He's a professor in the DEPARTMENT of Romance Philology. *Es catedrático en la facultad de Filología Románica.* ‖ **6.** •The police/fire DEPARTMENT. *El cuerpo de policía/bomberos.* ⇨ DEPARTAMENTO

DEPEND. *v.* Rely, count on. *Fiarse (de), contar con, confiar en.* ~Can we DEPEND on you to do it? *¿Podemos contar contigo para hacerlo?* ~To DEPEND on one's work for one's living. *Vivir de su trabajo.* ~He has to DEPEND on his pen. *Tiene que vivir*

de su pluma. || **2.** To be sure (hum.). *Estar seguro.* You can DEPEND on her to be late. *Puede estar seguro de que va a llegar tarde.* You can't DEPEND on him to tell the truth. *No puede estar seguro de que va a decir la verdad.* ~He'll forget, you can DEPEND on it! *Se olvidará, puede estar seguro.* || **3.** •You may DEPEND on it. *Es cosa segurísima, cuente con ello, téngalo por seguro.* || **4.** •DEPENDING on the weather. *Según el tiempo que haga.* ⇨DEPENDER

DEPOSIT[1]. *n.* [Dregs] *Sedimento.* || **2.** [Mine]. *Yacimiento.* ~Rich DEPOSITS of gold in the hills. *Gran yacimiento de oro en las colinas.* || **3.** [Wine]. *Poso.* || **4.** [On the purchase of a home]. *Entrada.* ~Si tienes dinero para la ENTRADA del piso, para el resto puedes pedir un crédito. *If you have enough money to make a deposit on the house, you can finance the rest.* || **5.** Down payment. *Señal.* ~To leave a hundred dollar DEPOSIT on a refrigerator. *Dejar una señal de cien dólares para un refrigerador.* || **6.** •Is there a DEPOSIT on this bottle? *¿Cobran el envase?* || **7.** •To put a DEPOSIT on something. *Dejar una señal para algo.* || **8.** •DEPOSIT account. *Cuenta de ahorro.* ⇨DEPÓSITO

DEPOSIT[2]. *v.* Leave. *Dejar.* The taxi DEPOSITED me at the door. *El taxi me dejó en la puerta.* || **2.** [Luggage]. *Dejar en consigna.* ~I DEPOSITED my luggage at the station. *Dejé mis maletas en consigna en la estación.* || **3.** Pay (into account). *Ingresar.* ~I DEPOSITED a thousand dollars in my savings account. *Ingresé mil dólares en mi cuenta de ahorro.* ⇨DEPOSITAR

DEPRESS [DEPRIMIR]. *v.* To reduce (profits). *Reducir.* ~It would create mass unemployment and DEPRESS profits. *Causaría desempleo generalizado y reduciría las ganancias.* || **2.** [Trade]. *Dificultar, paralizar.* || **3.** [Prices, wages]. *Disminuir, hacer bajar.* ~Competition between workers DEPRESSES wage levels. *La competencia entre trabajadores hace rebajar el nivel de los sueldos.* || **4.** To press down (switch, lever). *Apretar, bajar.* ~To operate

the machine, DEPRESS the button. *Para hacer funcionar la máquina, apriete el botón.* || **5.** [Clutch, piano pedal]. *Pisar.* ~DEPRESS the clutch fully. *Pisa el embrague hasta el fondo.* || **6.** To weaken. *Debilitar.* Several factors combined to DEPRESS the economy. *El que se debilitara la economía se debe a varios factores.*

DERIVATION. *n.* Origin. *Origen.* ~The DERIVATION of this word is uncertain. *El origen de esta palabra es desconocido.* || **2.** Obtaining. *Obtención.* The DERIVATION of diesel from crude oil. *La obtención del diesel a partir del crudo.* ⇨DERIVACIÓN

DESCEND. *v.* Be inherited (tradition, custom). *Provenir.* ~This ring has DESCENDED through generations. *Este anillo ha ido pasando de generación a generación.* ~Concepts which DESCEND to us from the Greeks. *Conceptos que nos vienen, que hemos heredado de los griegos.* || **2.** Attack. *Lanzarse, caer sobre.* ~A plague DESCENDED on the town. *Una plaga se abatió sobre la ciudad.* || **3.** Invade. *Invadir.* ~The whole family will be DESCENDING on us at Christmas. *Nos va a invadir, a caer toda la familia para Navidad.* || **4.** [Stairs]. *Bajar.* The elderly man slowly DESCENDED the stairs. *El anciano bajo lentamente las escaleras.* || **5.** [Rain]. *Caer.* ~The rain DESCENDED in torrents. *Caía una lluvia torrencial.* || **6.** [Sun]. *Ponerse.* ~As the sun DESCENDED in the horizon. *Al ponerse el sol en el horizonte.* || **7.** •Night DESCENDED. *Se hizo noche.* ⇨DESCENDER

DESERT. *v.* [Place]. *Abandonar, huir.* ~They DESERTED their homes and fled to the hills. *Abandonaron sus casas y se refugiaron en los montes.* || **2.** [Post, friend, family, luck]. *Abandonar.* ~You've DESERTED us! *¡Nos abandonó!* ~He DESERTED his family. *Abandonó a su familia.* ~His luck DESERTED him. *Su suerte le abandonó.* || **3.** To fail. *Abandonar.* ~His courage DESERTED him. *Su valor lo abandonó.* ⇨DESERTAR

DESIGN [DISEÑAR]. *n.* Drawing. *Diseño, dibujo, esbozo.* ~She bought curtains and wallpaper with the same DESIGN. *Compró*

DESIGNED   **70**

cortinas y papel de empapelar con el mismo dibujo. ‖ **2.** Purpose, intention, aim. *Intención, propósito.* ~Was it by accident or by DESIGN? *¿Ocurrió por casualidad o a propósito?* ~She made no secrets of her DESIGNS. *Ella no escondió su intención.* ‖ **3.** Project, plan. *Projecto.* ~Have you seen the DESIGN for the new shopping center? *¿Has visto el proyecto para el nuevo centro de compras?* ‖ **4.** [Of dress]. *Patrón.* I made this dress from DESIGNS in a magazine. *Hice este vestido siguiendo los patrones de una revista.* ‖ **5.** [Of painting] *Bosquejo.* ‖ **6.** [Sculpture]. *Boceto.* ‖ **7.** [Course, test, computer program]. *Modelo.* ‖ **8.** [Room, city center]. *Disposición.* ‖ **9.** [Car]. *Líneas, estilo.* ‖ **10.** [Building]. *Estilo.* ~The building was originally Victorian in DESIGN. *Inicialmente el edificio tenía un estilo victoriano.* ‖ **11.** Ground plan of a building. *Distribución.* ‖ **12.** Plot, intrigue, scheme. *Intriga, conspiración.* ~His political rivals formulated a DESIGN to unseat him. *Sus rivales políticos urdieron una intriga para hacerle perder su peldaño.* ‖ **13.** Construction, making, manufacturing. *Fabricación, construcción.* ~There's a DESIGN fault in this folding table. *Hay una falla en la producción de esta mesa plegadiza.* ~This can opener has a good/bad DESIGN. *Este abrelatas esta bien/mal construído.* ‖ **14.** PHRASES. ‖ •Fashion DESIGN. *Creación (diseño) de modas.* ‖ •The DESIGN of the car was wrong. *El coche estaba mal concebido.* ‖ •The overall DESIGN. *El concepto, la idea general.* ‖ •To have DESIGNS on something or someone. *Tener puestas las miras en algo o en alguien.* ‖ •By DESIGN. *Intencionalmente, a propósito, deliberadamente.* ‖ •DESIGN Department. *Sección de proyectos.*

DESIGNED[2] [DISEÑADO]. *adj.* Intended, meant. *Destinado, encaminado a, orientado.* ~A statement DESIGNED to reassure the public. *Una declaración destinada a tranquilizar al público.* ~This dictionary was DESIGNED for translators. *Este diccionario está destinado a traductores.* ~A policy DESIGNED to fight inflation. *Una

política orientada a combatir la inflación.* ~These exercices are DESIGNED to harden the muscles. *Estos ejercicios están encaminados a endurecer los músculos.* ‖ **2.** Meant, planned, conceived. *Planeado, ideado, concebido.* ~The scheme was DESIGNED for small businesses. *El plan ha sido concebido (pensado) para la pequeña empresa.* ~The dinner was DESIGNED to coincide with your visit. *La cena fue planeada para coincidir con su visita.* ‖ **3.** To draw. *Dibujar.* ~Exhibition of jewels DESIGNED by Dalí. *Exposición de joyas dibujadas por Dalí.* ‖ **4.** Create. *Crear.* ~Who DESIGNED the costumes? *¿Quién creó los trajes?* ‖ **5.** To make or draw plans for. *Proyectar.* ~The engineer who DESIGNED the harbor died before it was completed. *El ingeniero que proyectó el puerto murió antes de verlo terminado.* ‖ **6.** •A well DESIGNED house. *Una casa bien distribuida.* ‖ **7.** •A well DESIGNED program. *Un programa bien concebido.*

DESIST. *v.* Desist from. *Dejar de, abstenerse de.* ~To DESIST from smoking. *Dejar, abstenerse de fumar.* ⇨DESISTIR

DESOLATE [DESOLADO]. *adj.* Uninhabited. *Deshabitado, desierto, desocupado, despoblado, solitario.* The house looked DESOLATE. *La casa parecía abandonada.* ‖ **2.** Barren. *Yermo.* ~DESOLATE land. *Terrenos yermos.* ‖ **3.** Forlorn, disconsolate (person). *Desconsolado, afligido.* ~She felt DESOLATE when her best friend moved away. *Cuando se fue de la ciudad su mejor amigo ella quedó desconsolada.* ‖ **4.** Dreary. *Triste.* ‖ **5.** [Outlook, existence]. *Sombrío, lúgubre.*

DESPERATE. *adj.* [Struggle]. *Encarnizado.* ‖ **2.** [Need]. *Urgente, apremiante, extremo.* ~The house is in DESPERATE need of repair. *La casa necesita arreglos urgentes.* ~Next week will do, it's not that DESPERATE. *La semana que viene está bien, no corre tanta prisa (no hay tanto apuro).* ‖ **3.** Very serious, extreme (situación). *Grave, difícil.* ~There is a DESPERATE shortage of food in the area. *Hay una *grave escasez de alimento en esta región.* ~DESPERATE ills require DESPERATE measures. *A grandes males, grandes remedios.* ‖ **4.** [Conditions]. *Malísimas.* ‖ **5.** Ultimate, final. *Supremo.* The doctors made one last DESPERATE effort to save his life. *Los médicos hicieron un supremo esfuerzo para salvarle la vida.* ‖ **6.** [Resistance]. *Heroico, enérgico.* ‖ **7.** Reckless, dangerous. *Peligroso, capaz de cualquier cosa.* ~He's a DESPERATE man. *Es un hombre sumamente peligroso.* ‖ **8.** Eager, anxious, dying (for something, to do something). *Que tiene apremio, deseoso.* I was DESPERATE to see her. *Quería verla a toda costa, me moría por verla.* ~I'm DESPERATE for a cup of tea. *Me muero por una taza de té.* ~I'm DESPERATE to get home. *No veo la hora de llegar a casa.*| **8.** Despair *Desesperanza.* ~We are getting DESPERATE. *Estamos perdiendo la esperanza.* ‖ **10.** •To be DESPERATE for. *Necesitar con urgencia.* ~He was DESPERATE for money. *Necesitaba dinero con urgencia.* ‖ **11.** Foolish, risky. *Imprudente. insensato.* ~Don't do anything DESPERATE. *No hagas ninguna locura.* ‖ **12.** Great, extreme. *Muchísima.* ~He was in a DESPERATE hurry. *Tenía muchísima prisa.* ~He has a DESPERATE desire to succeed. *Tiene un ardiente deseo de tener éxito.* ⇨ DESESPERADO

DESTINATION [-IÓN]. *n.* Place to which a person is going, or to which a thing is being sent. *Destino.* ~The letter never reached its DESTINATION. *La carta nunca llegó a su* destino. ~Their DESTINATION is London. *Van con destino a Londres.* ‖ **2.** •To reach one's DESTINATION. *Llegar a destino.*

DETAIL. *n.* Information. *Información.* ~Please send full DETAILS of your activities. *Rogamos envíe información completa sobre sus actividades.* ~He asked for further DETAILS. *Pidió más información, pidió información más detallada.* ‖ **2.** MIL Small detachment of soldiers for special duty. *Destacamento.* ~The commanding officer sent a DETAIL to occupy part of the territory. *El comandante envió un desta-*

camento para ocupar una parte del territorio. ‖ **3.** MIL Duty. *Cuadrilla.* ~To be on clean up/latrine DETAIL. *Estar en la cuadrilla de aseo/letrinas.* ⇨ DETALLE

DETAIN. *v.* To delay. *Retrasarse, demorar, entretenerse.* ~He was DETAINED by snow. *Se retrasó a causa de la nieve.* ~Don't let me DETAIN you. *No quiero entretenerlo.* ~I was DETAINED by a customer. *Me demoré con un cliente.* ~I was DETAINED by fog. *El retraso se debe a la niebla.* ~I won't DETAIN you any longer. *No le entretengo más.* ‖ **2.** [In a hospital]. *Retener, hacer quedar.* The doctor had him DETAINED in the hospital for a few more days. *El médico le hizo quedar en el hospital por unos días más.* ‖ **3.** [In class]. *Dejar castigado, hacer quedar después de la clase.* He was DETAINED for bad behavior. *Le hicieron quedar después de la clase por mala conducta.* ⇨ DETENER

DETECT [DETECTAR]. *v.* [Sarcasm, difference]. *Notar.* ~I DETECTED a note of sarcasm in his voice. *Noté cierto tonillo sarcástico en su voz.* ‖ **2.** [Smell, sound]. *Percibir.* ~He DETECTED a burning smell in the kitchen. *Percibió un olor a quemado en la cocina.* ‖ **3.** Discover (fraud, criminal, disease). *Descubrir.* ~Many forms of cancer can be cured if DETECTED early. *Se pueden curar varias clases de cáncer si se descubren a tiempo.* ‖ **4.** [Position]. *Localizar.* ~The submarines had to be DETECTED and destroyed. *Se tuvo que localizar los submarinos y destruirlos.*

DETENTION. *n.* EDUC •To be in DETENTION. *Estar castigado.* ~The teacher gave him DETENTION. *El profesor lo dejó castigado después de la clase.* ‖ **2.** •DETENTION home. *Correccional, reformatorio.* ⇨ DETENCIÓN

DETERIORATE. *v.* [In an abstract sense]. *Empeorar, decaer.* ~The situation is DETERIORATING. *La situación está empeorando.* ‖ **2.** DETERIORATE into. *Degenerar en.* ~The meeting soon DETERIORATED into a fight. *La reunión degeneró pronto en una pelea.* ⇨ DETERIORAR

DETERMINE[1]. *v.* Mark (boundary, edge,

limit). *Definir, demarcar.* ‖ **2.** [Date]. *Señalar, fijar.* ~The date of the court case has not yet been DETERMINED. *La fecha del pleito no se ha fijado todavía.* ‖ **3.** To decide, resolve. *Decidir.* ~He DETERMINED to leave at once. *Decidió partir de inmediato.* ~The last goal DETERMINED the game. *El último gol decidió el partido.* **4.** •To DETERMINE on. *Decidirse por, optar por.* ⇨ DETERMINAR

DETERMINED[2]. *adj.* Resolute. *Resuelto, decidido.* ~A DETERMINED person. *Una persona decidida.* ‖ **2.** [Attempt, effort]. *Enérgico, persistente.* ‖ **3.** •To be DETERMINED to do something. *Estar decidido (resuelto) a hacer algo.* ~I was DETERMINED not to say a word. *Estaba resuelto a no decir nada. Estar decidido (empeñado) en.* ~He was DETERMINED to achieve it. *Estaba empeñado en lograrlo.* ‖ **4.** LAW •To DETERMINE the merits of the case. *Pronunciarse sobre el fondo del caso.* ‖ **5.** •To be DETERMINED by. *Depender de.* ~His answer will be DETERMINED by what happens today. *Su repuesta depende de lo que pase hoy.* ⇨ DETERMINADO

DEVELOP. *v.*
❶ To COME UP WITH. ‖ **1.** To produce, manufacture, create, devise, design (products, machinery, engine, aircraft, drugs). *Producir, crear, construir, fabricar.* ~The company is spending a lot of money to DEVELOP new products. *La companía está gastando mucho dinero para crear nuevos productos.* ~Since the last war some outstanding aircraft and engines have been DEVELOPED. *Con posteridad a la segunda guerra mundial se han construido nuevos modelos de aviones y motores muy notables (Cit. Prats).* ~We had to stop the German from DEVELOPING the atomic bomb. *Teníamos que impedir que los alemanes consiguieran fabricar la bomba atómica (Prats).* ‖ **2.** Devise, draw up, work out (plan, program, policy, project]. *Elaborar, idear, trazar, redactar, formular.* ~The government will have to DEVELOP a new policy to deal with the problem. *El gobierno tendrá que idear*

(elaborar) un nuevo programa para resolver este problema. ~Various new procedures have been DEVELOPED to repair faulty exhaust pipes. *Se han ideado varios sistemas para reparar los caños de escape defectuosos.* ~The prisoners DEVELOPED (devised) a plan to escape from jail. *Los presos elaboraron un plan para escapar de la cárcel.* ~The mechanism which he DEVELOPED has been used by the industry. *El mecanismo que ideó ha sido utilizado por la industría.* ‖ **3.** [Skill, system, process]. *Perfeccionar.* ~Scientists are DEVELOPING new drugs to treat arthritis. *Los hombres de ciencia están perfeccionando (descubriendo) nuevas drogas para curar la artritis.* ~It has been under continuous DEVELOPMENT since that time. *A partir de dicha fecha ha sido objeto de perfeccionamientos constantes (Cit. Prats).* ‖ **4.** [A new technique]. *Realizar.* ‖ **5.** To invent, discover. *Inventar, crear.* ~Edison DEVELOPED the incandescent light. *Edison inventó la lámpara de incandescencia (Prats).* [...] this year cooks will DEVELOP five special new dishes. *Este año los cocineros crearán cinco nuevos platos especiales (Prats).* ‖ **6.** To discover, find. *Descubrir, hallar, encontrar.* ~They have DEVELOPED a formula that kills rats. *Han encontrado una fórmula para matar ratas.* ‖ **7.** To work on. *Confeccionar, elaborar, trabajar en la construccion de alguna cosa.* The company is DEVELOPING a new television system. *La compañía está trabajando en la construcción de un nuevo sistema de televisión.*

❷ TO ACQUIRE. [Interest, enthusiasm, hobby]. *Adquirir, interesarse en, aficionarse a.* ~She DEVELOPED an appreciation for classical music. *Empezó a apreciar la música clásica.* ~She has DEVELOPED an interest in French cuisine. *Ha empezado a interesarse (mostrar interés) por la cocina francesa.* ‖ **2.** [Inteligencia, aptitud, talento]. *Cultivar.* ~It is important to be born with talent but it gets you nowhere if you do not DEVELOP it. *Es importante nacer con* *inteligencia, pero de nada sirve si no se cultiva (Prats).* || **3.** [Habits]. *Contraer, adquirir.* ~She's DEVELOPED some very strange habits since she started to live on her own. *Ha adquirido costumbres muy raras desde que se fue a vivir por su cuenta.* || **4.** [Tendency]. *Revelar, manifestar.* || **5.** [Accent]. *Contraer* || **6.** [Taste]. *Coger (tomar).* ~He DEVELOPED a taste for gin. *Le ha cogido (tomado) el gusto a la ginebra.* ❸ TO APPEAR, ARISE, OCCUR (problem, complication, pain, illness). *Surgir, aparecer, empezar a tener o mostrar, producirse, manifestarse.* The car soon DEVELOPED engine trouble. *El motor del coche pronto empezó a fallar.* ~The prototype DEVELOPED several faults. *~Surgieron varios problemas con el prototipo.* ~He DEVELOPED a pain in his neck this morning. *Empezó a dolerle el cuello esta mañana.* ~Some alcoholics DEVELOP liver disease. *Algunos alcohólicos enferman del hígado.* ~Trouble is DEVELOPING in the cities. *Los problemas urbanos están en alza.* ~He soon developed spots. *Pronto le empezaron a salir granos.* || **2.** [Illness]. *Contraer, coger, empezar a sufrir de, mostrar los síntomas de.* ~He DEVELOPED other symptoms. *Empezó a presentar otros síntomas.* ~The study showed that one out of twelve women will DEVELOP breast cancer. *El informe indica que una en doce mujeres contraerán cáncer de los senos.* || **3.** [Leaves, flowers]. *To sprout.* The plant has already DEVELOPED many flowers. *La planta ya está echando flores.* ❹ To perform an activity with a view to benefit from its result (exploit, expand, upgrade, modernize, improve). || **1.** [Natural resources]. *Aprovechar, explotar, utilizar.* ~The DEVELOPMENT of the Mekong river. *El aprovechamiento del río Mekong.* ~The company plans to invest about 50 million dollars into DEVELOPMENT of coal deposits. *La compañia se propone invertir unos cincuenta millones de dólares en las actividades preparatorias para la explotación de los yacimientos de carbono.* || **2.** [Site, area]. *Urbanizar.* ~The area will be DEVELOPED soon. *Próximamente se urbanizará esta zona.* || **3.** To expand (range, business, site). *Ampliar.* ~Prestwick, the intercontinental airport in Scotland, has been DEVELOPED to accomodate larger jet aircrafts. *Prestwick, el aeropuerto intercontinental situado en Escocia, ha sido ampliado para atender a los grandes aviones de reacción (Prats).* || **4.** ~Turn, develop into. *Transformarse, convertirse.* ~They're planning to DEVELOP that whole site into a shopping complex. *Tienen planes para convertir toda esta zona en un centro de compras.* ❺ VARIOUS. To examine. *Tratar, examinar, estudiar.* ~We will DEVELOP some of these points in our next meeting. *Examinaremos (estudiaremos) algunos de estos temas en nuestra próxima reunión.* || **2.** Foster, encourage (trade, arts, industry). *Fomentar, promover.* || **3.** Develop into, turn into (feeling, situation). *Transformarse, convertirse.* ~Their friendship DEVELOPED into love. *Su amistad se convirtió (transformó) en amor.* ~The brawl DEVELOPED into an all out battle. *La disputa degeneró en una batalla campal (Prats).* || **4.** To go. *Ir.* How's the work DEVELOPING? *¿Cómo va el trabajo.* || **5.** [Photo]. *Revelar.* || **6.** Evolve, progress. *Evolucionar.* ~"Red Painting" completed before Kline's death in 1962, shows the direction in which the painter might have DEVELOPED. *«Pintura roja», que Kline terminó un año antes de su muerte, ocurrida en 1962, pone de manifiesto en qué dirección el pintor habría podido evolucionar (Cit. Prats).* || **7.** Spread, increase, expand. *Extenderse.* ~Cable TV DEVELOPED much more steadily in Canada and it DEVELOPED in both urban and rural areas, unlike the U.S. where it was blocked in the major cities until recently. *La televisión por cable se ha extendido mucho más gradualmente en el Canadá, tanto en la zonas urbanas como en las rurales, a diferencia de los Estados Unidos, país en el que hasta poco se hallaba concentrada en las grandes ciudades (Cit. Prats).* ⇨ DESARROLLAR

DEVELOPMENT. *n.* [Of trade, arts]. *Fomento.* ‖ **2.** Perfecting (of skill, system). *Perfeccionamiento.* ~These books are designed to help children with the DEVELOPMENT of reading and writing. *Estos libros están orientados a ayudar a los niños en el perfeccionamiento de la lectura y la escritura.* ‖ **3.** [Of plot, theme, plan]. *Elaboración.* ‖ **4.** [Of character, writer]. *Formación.* ‖ **5.** Advance, discovery (in technology). *Avance, descubrimiento, adelanto, conquista, mejora.* ~The latest DEVELOPMENTS in science. *Los últimos descubrimientos de la ciencia.* ~Technological DEVELOPMENTS in the last fifty years have surpassed all science-fiction written by Verne. *Los adelantos técnicos de los últimos cincuenta años han superado todas las fantasías científicas imaginadas por Julio Verne (Cit. Prats).* ‖ **6.** Change. (I) [General]. *Cambio, novedad.* ~There have been no new DEVELOPMENTS. *No ha sucedido nada nuevo.* ~There are no new DEVELOPMENTS. *No hay ninguna novedad.* (II) [in situation, policy, attitude]. *Rumbo, dirección* ~There have been new DEVELOPMENTS. *Las cosas han tomado un nuevo rumbo.* (III) [In personal status]. *Nueva circunstancia, modificación de una situación.* ~So that we may continue to provide the best of service, any DEVELOPMENTS which may affect your insurance should be brought to our attention promptly. *Con el fin de seguir prestándole el mejor servicio posible, le agradeceremos que nos comunique rápidamente toda (nueva) circunstancia que suponga una modificación de las condiciones de su poliza (Prats).* ‖ **7.** Exploitation. *Explotación, aprovechamiento, utilización.* ~The DEVELOPMENT of the Mekong river. *El aprovechamiento del río Mekong.* ‖ **8.** [Construction]. *Urbanización.* ~The area is ripe for DEVELOPMENT. *Están dadas las condiciones para urbanizar la zona.* ‖ **9.** Happening, event. *Acontecimiento, hecho.* ~We are awaiting further DEVELOPMENTS. *Estamos a la espera de nuevos acontecimientos.* ~The atmosphere of the meeting has been marred by some political DEVELOPMENTS. *El clima de la conferencia se ha visto enrarecido por determinados acontecimientos políticos (Prats).* ~So far, Nixon has not chosen to view the renewed attacks as a DEVELOPMENT warranting retaliation against targets in North Viet Nam. *Por ahora Nixon no ha querido considerar la reanudación de los ataques como un hecho que justifique la adopción de represalias contra los objetivos de Vietnam del Norte (Prats).* ‖ **10.** [Photo]. *Revelado.* ‖ **11.** Tendency. *Tendencia.* ~His works represent a new DEVELOPMENT in literature. *Sus obras señalan una nueva tendencia en la literatura.* ‖ **12.** Evolution, growth. *Evolución.* ~DEVELOPMENT of automobile sales in the last five years. *La evolución de la venta de automóviles en los últimos cinco años (Prats).* ~A course in the DEVELOPMENT of Greek thought. *Un curso sobre la evolución del pensamiento griego.* ‖ **13.** Creation, invention, introduction. *Invención, descubrimiento.* ~DEVELOPMENT of the electronic computer was mainly motived by its military use. *La invención de la calculadora electrónica se debió principalmente a su utilidad militar (Prats).* ‖ **14.** Formation, establishing, creation, organization. *Organización, creación, formación.* ~Funds have been approved for the DEVELOPMENT of a translation service. *Se han aprobado los créditos necesarios para la creación de un servicio de traducción (Prats).* ‖ **15.** Project (under study). *Estudio (para la construcción de una cosa).* ~All such systems are complicated and expensive. Several under DEVELOPMENT are still in the experimental state. *Todos estos dispositivos resultan complicados y caros. Hay varios en estudio, que no han pasado de la etapa experimental (Cit. Prats).* ‖ **16.** Group of dwellings built by the same constructor. *Conjunto residencial, complejo urbanístico, edificio para viviendas (condominium), bloque de viviendas (detached, individual homes).* ~A new housing DEVELOPMENT. *Un nuevo edificio de* *viviendas (condominium), un nuevo bloque de viviendas (detached, individual homes).* || **17.** Construction, construction work, work under construction. *Obra.* ~Major DEVELOPMENTS completed in 1966-67 include ... *Entre las varias obras terminadas en el período 1966-67 figuran* ... || **18.** Existence, instance, appearance, occurrence. *Aparición, manifestación, fenómeno.* ~Early in the seventeenth century the crew of a British ship made a voyage of four month's duration without the DEVELOPMENT of a single case of scurvy. *A principios del siglo XVII, la tripulación de un buque inglés realizó un viaje de cuatro meses sin que se produjera un solo caso de escorbuto (Prats).* ⇨DESARROLLO

DEVOTION [DEVOCIÓN]. *n.* [To friend, master]. *Lealtad, fidelidad.* ~They showed great DEVOTION to their king. *Demostraron gran lealtad a su rey.* || **2.** [To family, wife]. *Amor, cariño, afecto.* ~She's alway shown intense DEVOTION to her children. *Siempre ha demostrado un gran cariño por sus hijos.* || **3.** [To research, cause]. *Dedicación, entrega.* ~It demands total DEVOTION to the cause. *Requiere una total entrega a la causa.* || **4.** *pl.* [Prayers]. *Oraciones.* ~He was at his DEVOTIONS. *Rezaba.* || **5.** [Hobby, sport]. *Afición.* || **6.** •DEVOTION to duty. *Cumplimiento fiel de su deber.*

DIARY. *n.* Book for appointments. *Agenda.* ~Let me consult my DIARY. *Déjame consultar mi agenda.* || **2.** Notebook. *Libreta.* || **3.** •Desk DIARY. *Agenda de sobremesa.* ⇨DIARIO

DICTATE. *v.* [Order]. *Dar.* || **2.** Order about. *Dar órdenes.* Who's he to DICTATE what I should do? *¿Quién es él para darme órdenes?* ~I won't be DICTATED to! *¡A mí no me manda nadie!* || **3.** [Terms]. *Imponer.* ~They are in no position to DICTATE terms. *No están en posición de imponer condiciones.* ⇨DICTAR

DIFFER. *v.* To disagree. *No estar de acuerdo, disentir.* ~They DIFFER on that point. *No están de acuerdo sobre este punto.* || **2.** To be different. *Ser distintos,*

diferenciarse. ~How does this DIFFER from that? *¿En qué se diferencia éste de aquél?* ~They DIFFER widely in their tastes. *Tienen gustos completamente distintos.* || **3.** •I beg to DIFFER. *Permítame decirle que no estoy de acuerdo, siento tener que disentir.* ⇨DIFERIR

DILIGENT. *adj.* Thorough (work, study). *Esmerado, concienzudo, hecho a conciencia.* || **2.** [Search, inquiries]. *Minucioso, cuidadoso.* ~I have no doubt that DILIGENT research will produce results. *No tengo la menor duda de que una cuidadosa investigación surtira efecto.* ⇨DILIGENTE

DIRECT. *v.* Give directions to. *Indicarle el camino a.* ~Can you DIRECT me to the station? *¿Me podría indicar el camino a la estación?, ¿me podría decir como se va a la estación?* || **2.** To order. *Mandar, ordenar.* ~He DIRECTED me to draw up detailed plans. *Me mandó elaborar planes detallados.* ~Take as DIRECTED. *Tómese según prescripción facultativa, según indicación médica (Lat. Am.).* || **3.** [One's attention]. *Fijar.* Please DIRECT your attention to the following paragraph in the book. *Le ruego fijarse en el siguiente párrafo del libro.* ⇨DIRIGIR

DIRECTION. *n.* Instruction or guidance for making, using, etc. *Instrucciones.* •DIRECTIONS for use. *Instrucciones, modo (de uso, empleo).* || **2.** [To a place]. *Señas.* ~I had to ask for DIRECTIONS. *Tuve que preguntar el camino, tuve que pedir que me indicaran el camino.* ~Can you give me DIRECTIONS on how to go to your house? *¿Me puede indicar como se llega a su casa?* || **3.** Purpose. *Norte.* She seems to lack DIRECTION in her life. *No tiene un norte en la vida.* || **4.** [Task, assembly, use], *Instrucciones.* || **5.** Trend, tendency. *Tendencia.* || **6.** PHRASES. || •He has no sense of DIRECTION. *No tiene sentido de orientación.* || •In the opposite DIRECTION. *En sentido opuesto.* ~We were trying to go to London but we ended up going in the opposite DIRECTION. *Queríamos ir a Londres pero acabamos por tomar el* *sentido opuesto.* || •Am I going in the right DIRECTION? *¿Voy bien por este camino?* || •In all DIRECTIONS. *Por todos lados.* ~*They ran off in different directions. Salieron corriendo cado uno por su lado.* || •It's a step in the right DIRECTION. *Es un paso positivo.* ⇨DIRECCIÓN

DIRECTORY. *n.* [Telephone]. *Guía telefónica.* || **2.** [Street]. *Guía de calles.* || **3.** •DIRECTORY assistance. *Servicio de información telefónica, información.* ⇨DIRECTORIO

DISCARD. *v.* Dispose of (old things, unwanted things). *Deshechar, deshacerse de, tirar.* ~To DISCARD an old suit. *Desechar un traje viejo.* || **2.** [Idea, belief]. *Desechar.* ~This popular belief should be DISCARDED once and for all. *Esta creencia popular debe desecharse de una vez por todas.* || **3.** To shed (skin, leaves). *Mudar.* || **4.** To take off (clothing). *Desnudarse.* || **5.** [Habit]. *Renunciar a.* ⇨DESCARTAR

DISCERN. *v.* [With the senses: shape, sound]. *Distinguir, percibir.* ~Certain animals PERCEIVE sounds which humans can't hear. *Algunos animales perciben sonidos que el hombre no oye.* ~Upon entering the room he DISCERNED a very unpleasant odor. *Al entrar en la habitación percibió un olor desagradable.* || **2.** [Truth]. *Darse cuenta.* ~I DISCERNED that he was lying. *Me di cuenta de que mentía.* ⇨DISCERNIR

DISCONNECT. *v.* [Gas or electricity supply]. *Cortar.* ~I didn't pay my bills, so I was DISCONNECTED. *Me cortaron el teléfono (gas) por no pagar.* || **2.** [One part from the other]. *Separar.* ~Make sure you have DISCONNECTED the hose from the tap. *Compruebe que ha separado la manguera del grifo.* ~To DISCONNECT the fuse from a bomb. *Separar la espoleta de la bomba.* || **3.** [Wagons]. *Desenganchar.* ⇨DESCONECTAR

DISCONTINUE [DISCONTINUE]. *v.* [Work, visit]. *Interrumpir, suspender.* He DISCONTINUED his visits. *Interrumpió sus visitas.* || **2.** [Payment, service, production]. *Sus-*

pender. ~They have decided to DISCONTINUE the production of television sets. *Han decidido suspender la producción de televisores.* || **3.** [Newspaper]. *Anular el abono.* || **4.** •DISCONTINUED line. *Restos de serie.* || **5.** •'DISCONTINUED'. *Fin de serie.* || **6.** •A DISCONTINUED model. *Un modelo que ya no se fabrica.* || **7.** •To DISCONTINUE doing something. *Dejar de hacer algo.*

DISCOUNT. *v.* Disregard. (I) [Possibility, suggestion, view] *Descartar*, (II) [Claim, criticism]. *Pasar por alto, no tener en cuenta, no hacer caso* ~You can DISCOUNT most of what she says. *No hay que tener en cuenta la mayor parte de lo que dice.* || **2.** [Goods]. *Rebajar.* || **3.** [Price, debt]. *Reducir.* || **4.** [Report]. *Considerar exagerado.* || **5.** To leave out. *Dejar de lado.* || **6.** To anticipate. *Contar con.* ~We already had DISCOUNTED this loss. *Ya habíamos contado con esa pérdida.* ⇨descontar

DISCOVER. *v.* [Missing person, object]. *Encontrar, hallar.* They DISCOVERED the boy the next day at a friend's house. *Encontraron al muchacho al día siguiente en casa de un amigo.* || **2.** To realize [mistake, loss]. *Darse cuenta de.* ~I DISCOVERED that I'd lost my passport. *Me di cuenta de que había perdido el pasaporte.* || **3.** [Secret, reason]. *Aprender, enterarse de.* ~They DISCOVERED that they had been overpaid. *Se enteraron de que se les había pagado de más.* ⇨DESCUBRIR

DISCREET. *adj.* Cautious. *Circunspecto, prudente.* ~I followed at a DISCREET distance. *Seguí a una distancia prudencial.* || **2.** [Hat, house]. *Modesto.* || **3.** Restrained (elegance, colors). *Sobrio.* A DISCREET touch of rouge. *Una sobría pincelada de colorete.* ⇨DISCRETO

DISCRETION. *n.* Judgement. *Prudencia, juicio, criterio.* ~At the committee's DISCRETION. *A criterio (juicio) de la comisión.* || **2.** •Use your own DISCRETION. *Haz lo que te parezca (bien).* || **3.** •DISCRETION is the better part of valor. ~*La prudencia es la madre de la ciencia, una retirada a tiempo equivale a una victoria.* || **4.** •The years (age) of DISCRETION. *La madurez.* ⇨ DISCRECIÓN

DISCRIMINATE [DISCRIMINAR]. *v.* Differentiate. *Discernir, diferenciar, distinguir.* ~He cannot DISCRIMINATE between right and wrong. *No puede diferenciar el bien del mal.*

DISCRIMINATION [DISCRIMINACIÓN]. *n.* Discernment. *Discernimiento, perspicacia, criterio.* || **2.** Good taste. *Buen gusto.* He showed DISCRIMINATION in choosing the furniture. *Demostró buen gusto en escoger los muebles.* || **3.** Distinction. *Distinción.* DISCRIMINATION between these different shades of blue is difficult. *No es fácil distinguir entre estos dos matices de azul.* || **4.** Partiality. *Parcialidad.*

DISCUSS. *v.* Review, examine, consider. *Deliberar, examinar, considerar, estudiar.* ~Tomorrow the committee will DISCUSS the proposed tax increase. *Mañana la comisión examinará la propuesta de un aumento impositivo.* ~They will meet tomorrow to DISCUSS the matter. *Se encontrarán mañana para estudiar el asunto.* ~To DISCUSS (something) in detail. *Examinar algo a fondo.*|| **2.** Talk over, talk about. *Hablar de una cosa, conversar.* ~Should we go to the movies tonight? - I'm not sure, let's DISCUSS it. *¿Vamos al cine esta noche? -No sé, ¿por qué no lo conversamos?* ~He won't ever DISCUSS money. *Nunca quiere hablar de dinero.* ~They were DISCUSSING what they would do after the show. *Hablaban de lo que iban a hacer después de la función.* || **3.** Analyze. *Analizar.* ~We DISCUSSED the problem but came to no conclusions. *Expusimos el problema, pero no llegamos a ninguna conclusión.* || **4.** Debate, argue, take up. *Tratar de (alguna cosa).* ~The Board will DISCUSS tomorrow the proposed salary raises. *Mañana, la Junta tratará de los aumentos de sueldo propuestos (Prats).* || **5.** To expound, discourse in detail (book, lecture). *Comentar, explicar, referirse a, analizar.* The book DISCUSSES the rise of the city-state on the European continent. *El libro analiza (expone) el surgimiento de la ciudad estado en el continente europeo.* ⇨ DISCUTIR

DISCUSSION. *n.* Debate. *Debate, examen, estudio.* || **2.** Conversation. *Conversación.* ~With my DISCUSSIONS with Governments of the area [...]. *En mis conversaciones con los gobiernos de la región [...]* (Prats). ⇨ DISCUSIÓN

DISEMBARKATION [-IÓN]. *n.* [Of people]. *Desembarco.* || **2.** [Of goods). *Desembarque.*

DISFIGURE. *v.* To spoil (landscape, building). *Afear, estropear.* Pylons which DISFIGURE the landscape. *Postes que afean el paisaje.* ⇨ DESFIGURAR

DISGRACE. *n.* Shame. *Vergüenza.* ~There's no DISGRACE in being poor. *Ser pobre no es ninguna vergüenza.* ~This room is a DISGRACE. *Esta habitación es una vergüenza.* ~What a DISGRACE! *¡Qué vergüenza!* ~It's a DISGRACE. *Es una vergüenza.* || **2.** Dishonor. *Deshonra.* ~His conduct brought DISGRACE upon his family. *Su conducta trajo la deshonra a la familia.* || **3.** Downfall. *Caída.* •To be in DISGRACE (official). *Estar desacreditado.* || **4.** •To fall into DISGRACE. *Caer en la desgracia.* ⇨ DESGRACIA

DISGUST[1]. *n.* Loathing. *Asco, desprecio, revulsión, repugnancia.* ~It fills me with DISGUST. *Me da asco.* || **2.** Strong disapproval. *Indignación.* My DISGUST at their behavior surprised them. *Les sorprendió mi indignación hacia su comportamiento.* ~She stormed out of the room in DISGUST. *Salió indignada (furiosa) del cuarto.* ⇨ DISGUSTO

DISGUST[2]. *v.* To sicken, revolt, repel. *Repugnar, dar asco.* ~The smell/taste DISGUSTS me. *El olor/sabor me da asco.* ~The thought DISGUSTS me. *El pensamiento me repugna.* || **2.** To outrage. *Indignar.* ~I'm DISGUSTED by his disregard for others. *Me indigna su falta de consideración hacia los demás.* ~I'm DISGUSTED with your rudeness. *Tu falta de educación me indigna.*

⇨DISGUSTAR

DISHONEST. *adj*. Fraudulent. *Fraudulento*. ~A DISHONEST way of making money. *Una manera fraudulenta de ganar dinero.* ‖ **2**. Deceitful. *Embustero, tramposo.* ~You were DISHONEST on the test. *Hiciste trampa en el examen.* ~He's been DISHONEST with us about his past. *Nos engañó al no revelarnos su pasado.* ⇨DESHONESTO

DISHONOR. *v*. Renege on. (I) [Cheque]. *Rechazar, negarse a pagar, no pagar, devolver*, (II) [Agreement, treaty]. *No respetar*, (III) [Debt]. *No pagar*, (IV) [Promise]. *Faltar a, no cumplir.* ~To DISHONOR one's word. *Faltar a su palabra.* ⇨DESHONRAR

DISOBEY [DESOBEDECER]. *v*. [Law, rules]. *Contravenir, violar.* ~He was fined for DISOBEYING the law. *Se le dio una multa por infringir la ley.*

DISORDER. *n. med*. Upset. *Trastorno.* ~I have a stomach DISORDER. *Siento unos trastornos en el estómago.* ‖ **2**. Illness, ailment, trouble. *Enfermedad, afección.* Skin DISORDER. *Una afección de la piel.* ‖ **3**. [Mental, nervous]. *Trastorno.* ~Mental/nervous DISORDER. *Trastornos mentales/nerviosos.* ⇨DESORDEN

DISPATCH. *v*. To send (mail, parcel). *Expedir, remitir, enviar.* ~The package was DISPATCHED by air. *El paquete fue remitido por correo aéreo.* ‖ **2**. To finish quickly (food). *Zampar.* ~After dinner she DISPATCHED a dozen pastries all by herself. *Ella sola se ha zampado una docena de pasteles después de comer.* ‖ **3**. [persona]. *Enviar, mandar.* ~A reporter was DISPATCHED to Naples to cover the riot. *Se mandó a un periodista a Nápoles para informar sobre los disturbios.* ⇨DESPACHAR

DISPENSE. *v*. Administer (justice, sacraments). *Administrar.* ~A court of law to DISPENSE justice. *Un tribunal donde se administra la justicia.* ‖ **2**. [Grants, alms]. *Dar.* To DISPENSE alms to the poor. *Dar limosna a los pobres.* ‖ **3**. [Advice]. *Ofrecer, dar.* ~My aunt has gained a reputation for DISPENSING advice. *Mi tía es conocida por los buenos consejos que ofrece.* ‖ **4**. [Criticism]. *Hacer.* ‖ **5**. [Favors]. *Conceder.* ‖ **6**. [From a machine: soap, coffee]. *Expender.* ‖ **7**. [Drugs, prescription]. *Despachar, preparar~.* A pharmacist DISPENSES prescriptions. *El farmacéutico despacha recetas.* ‖ **8**. [Supplies, funds]. *Repartir, distribuir.* ~They've been given a budget of twenty million dollars to DISPENSE to developing countries. *Se les ha dado un presupuesto de veinte millones de dólares para repartir entre los países en vías de desarrollo.* ‖ **9**. Do without. *Prescindir.* ~Let's DISPENSE with formalities. *Prescindamos de las formalidades.* ‖ **10**. Make unnecessary. *Eliminar* . To see how many jobs could be DISPENSED with. *Para determinar cuantos trabajos podrían eliminarse.* ‖ **11**. [Laws, rules]. *Aplicar.* ⇨DISPENSAR

DISPLACE. *v*. [Bone]. *Dislocar.* He has displaced a bone in his right knee. *Se ha dislocado un hueso en la rodilla direcha.* ‖ **2**. Supplant, replace, take the place of. *Sustituir, reemplazar.* ~FICTION displaces facts. *La ficcíon sustituye a los hechos.* ~Television has DISPLACED books. *La televisión ha sustituido a los libros.* ‖ **3**. Discharge (oficial). *Destituir.* ‖ **4**. [Machine part]. *Sacar de su lugar.* ‖ **5**. •DISPLACED person. *Refugiado.* ⇨DESPLAZAR

DISPOSE. *v*. Get rid of, throw away. *Tirar, arrojar, deshechar, eliminar.* Nuclear waste is often DISPOSED of under the sea. *Con frecuencia se elimina los residuos (deshechos) nucleares tirándolos al mar.* ‖ **3**. Get rid of. *Deshacerse, librarse.* ~He doesn't want to DISPOSE of his books. *No quiere deshacerse de sus libros.* ‖ **4**. Deal with. *Despachar (asuntos, negocios).* ~I hope we can DISPOSE of these matters quickly. *Espero que podamos despachar estos asuntos rápidamente.* ‖ **5**. Settle (a problem). *Resolver.* ~We'll DISPOSE of the problem in due time. *Resolveremos este problema en su debido tiempo.* ‖ **6**. [Property]. *Traspasar, deshacerse.* ~To DISPOSE of one's assets. *Traspasar sus bienes.* ‖ **7**. [Free time]. *Emplear, ocupar.*

~The way I DISPOSE of my time is my own business. *Como ocupo mi tiempo es cosa mía.* || **8.** Determine. *Decidir.* || **9.** [Rights]. *Enajenar, ceder.* || **10.** [Food]. *Comerse, despachar, consumir.* ~She could DISPOSE of four hamburgers at one sitting. *Podía despachar cuatro hamburguesas de un tirón.* ~He doesn't know how to DISPOSE of all that food. *No sabe que hacer con toda esa comida.* || **11.** Finish. *Terminar, concluir.* ~The article DISPOSED of the matter in two paragraphs. *El artículo concluyó con el asunto con dos párrafos.* || **12.** Kill. *Matar, liquidar, despachar.* || **13.** To defeat an oponent. *Vencer.* ~It took him five minutes to DISPOSE of his opponent. *Tardó únicamente 5 minutos en vencer a su oponente.* || **14.** To destroy, shoot down (airplane). *Destruir, derribar (avión).* ~The air force DISPOSED of three enemy planes in one afternoon. *En una sola tarde la fuerza aérea derribó a tres aviones enemigos.* || **15.** Get rid of, throw away (clothes, trash). *Deshacerse, tirar.* ~When you're ready to DISPOSE of your clothes, please let me know. *Cuando quieres deshacerte de tu ropa, avísame.* ⇨DISPONER

DISPOSITION. *n.* Temperament, character. *Carácter, temperamento, natural.* ~He has a cheerful DISPOSITION. *Tiene un carácter alegre.* || **2.** Desire, tendency. *Inclinación.* ~I felt no DISPOSITION to punish him. *No me sentí inclinado a castigarlo.* ⇨DISPOSICIÓN

DISPUTE[1]. *n.* Disagreement. *Discusión, altercado.* || **2.** [Industrial]. *Conflicto.* ~Industrial DISPUTES are still a problem. *Los conflictos laborales siguen siendo un problema.* ~The management is in DISPUTE with the union. *Existe una situación de conflicto entre el sindicato y la patronal.* || **3.** Controversy, clash. *Polémica.* ~A border DISPUTE. *Un conflicto fronterizo.* || **4.** [Derecho]. *Litigio.* ~Under DISPUTE. *En litigio.* ~Territory in DISPUTE. *Territorio en litigio.* || **5.** Debate. *Discusión.* It's open to DISPUTE whether he acted reasonably. *Si actuó en forma razonable es discutible.* ~Her superiority in the field is beyond DISPUTE. *Su superioridad en este campo es indiscutible.* ⇨DISPUTA

DISPUTE[2]. *v.* To contest. *Discutir.* ~I don't DISPUTE the fact that it was a mistake. *No discuto que fue un error.* ~I DISPUTE the idea that. *Rechazo la idea de que.* ~It cannot be DISPUTED that the idea is attractive. *No se puede negar de que la idea resulta atrayente.* || **2.** To contest, challenge (will, decision). *Impugnar.* ~They DISPUTED his will alleging that he was not sound of mind. *Impugnaron su testamento alegando locura.* || **3.** Argue (point, question, subject, matter). *Debatir, discutir.* ~The circumstances of death have been hotly DISPUTED. ~A hotly DISPUTED affair. *Un asunto muy controvertido (polémico).* || **4.** [Claim, right]. *Refutar.* ~Critics have DISPUTED the official unemployment figures. *Algunos detractores han refutado la cifra oficial de desocupados.* ⇨DISPUTAR

DISSIPATE. *v.* Scatter, disperse (crowd). *Dispersar.* ~They DISSIPATED the enemy forces by unremitting gunfire. *Dispersaron a las fuerzas enemigas con un cañoneo sin tregua.* || **2.** To waste. *Derrochar.* ~He managed to DISSIPATE his fortune by the time he was thirty. *Derrochó toda su fortuna antes de llegar a los treinta.* || **3.** [Energy, talent]. *Desperdiciar.* ~Let's not DISSIPATE our energies in trivial occupations. *No desperdiciemos nuestras energías en actividades insignificantes.* || **4.** PHYS [Energy, heat]. *Difundir.* || **5.** [Fear, doubt]. *Desvanecer.* ~I hope that my explanation has DISSIPATED your doubts. *Espero que mi declaración haya desvanecido tus dudas.* ⇨DISIPAR

DISSIPATION. *n.* Waste (of resources). *Derroche, desperdicio.* ~We must learn to prevent the DISSIPATION of valuable resources such as oil and gas. *No debemos permitir el desperdicio de valiosos recursos como el petróleo y el gas.* || **2.** Debauchery. *Libertinaje.* ~His years of DISSIPATION soon ruined his health. *Todos aquellos años de libertinaje no tardaron en echar a perder su salud.* ⇨DISIPACIÓN

DISSOLVE [DISOLVER]. *v.* [Illusions]. *Disipar.* || **2.** To clear [clouds]. *Dispersar, desvanecer.* || **3.** [Crowd]. *Dispersar.* || **4.** To melt away (tablet, lump of sugar). *Desleír.* ~An aspirine DISSOLVED in a little water. *Una aspirina desleída en un poco de agua.* || **5.** [Contract]. *Rescindir.* || **6.** LIT To vanish. *Desvanecerse.* ~To DISSOLVE into thin air. *Desvanecerse, esfumarse.* || **7.** •To DISSOLVE into tears. *Deshacerse en lágrimas.*

DISTANT [DISTANTE]. *adj.* [Time]. *Lejano.* ~In those DISTANT times. *En aquellos lejanos tiempos.* || **2.** [Look]. *Distraído, ido, ausente.* ~With a DISTANT look in his eyes. *Con una mirada distraída.* || **3.** [Pariente]. *Lejano.* ~He's a DISTANT relative of mine. *Es un lejano pariente mío.* || **4.** Far away (land, place). *Lejano.* ~We would like to escape to a DISTANT spot. *Quisiéramos huir a un lugar lejos de aquí.*

DISTILL. *v.* [Information, ideas]. *Extraer.* ~All of which he DISTILLED from his constant reading. *Lo cual extrajo de sus frecuentes lecturas.* ⇨DESTILAR

DISTINCT . *adj.* [Smell, likeness, change, accent]. *Marcado.* ~A DISTINCT French accent. *Un marcado acento francés.* || **2.** [Idea, sign, intention]. *Claro, evidente.* ~What he was saying was far from DISTINCT. *No era muy claro lo que decía.* || **3.** [Tendency]. *Bien determinado.* || **4.** [Shape, outline]. *Nítido, claro, definido.* The town looked DISTINCT and toy-like in the pure morning air. *El pueblo se destacaba nítido y como de juguete en el aire puro de la mañana.* || **5.** [Improvement]. *Decidido, marcado.* His condition shows a DISTINCT improvement. *Su estado de salud muestra una marcada mejoría.* ⇨DISTINTO

DISTINGUISHED [DISTINGUIDO]. *adj.* Noted, eminent, famous. *Destacado, renombrado, famoso, conocido.* ~DISTINGUISHED artists took part in the festival. *Tomaron parte en el festival destacados artistas (Prats).*

DISTRACTION. *n.* Bewilderment, mental confusion. *Confusión, perplejidad.* ~They were in a state of extreme DISTRACTION when their daughter went missing. *Cayeron en un estado de total desconcierto cuando desapareció su hija.* || **2.** Amusement, entertainment. *Diversión.* ~Fishing is his major DISTRACTION. *La pesca es su mayor diversión.* || **3.** Distress. *Desconsuelo.* ~With DISTRACTION showing in his troubled countenance. *Con un semblante que reflejaba desconsuelo y preocupación.* || **4.** •To drive someone to DISTRACTION. *Sacar a alguien de quicio, volver loco a uno.* ~ That child will drive me to DISTRACTION. *Este niño me va a volver loco.* ⇨DISTRACCIÓN

DIVERSE. *adj.* Varied. *Variado.* ~Plant life in the area is extremely DIVERSE. *La vegetación en la zona es muy variada.* || **2.** Unlike, different. *Diferente, distinto.* ~Groups of people of DIVERSE cultures. *Grupos de personas con distintas costumbres.* ⇨DIVERSOS

DIVISION. *n.* Sharing out. *Repartimiento.* ~There were bitter battles after his death over the DIVISION of his money. *Tras su muerte se pelearon con encono acerca del repartimiento del dinero.* ~DIVISION of labor. *Repartimiento del trabajo.* || **2.** [Within a company]. *Sección, departamento.* ~He works in the international DIVISION of the company. *Trabaja en el departamento internacional de la compañía.* || **3.** Disagreement. *Desacuerdo, discordia.* ~Approved without a DIVISION. *Aprobado por unanimidad.* ~There's a DIVISION of opinion about this. *No todos estamos de acuerdo sobre eso.* || **4.** Area. *Zona.* || **5.** [Of a thermometer]. *Graduación.* ⇨DIVISIÓN

DOMESTIC [DOMÉSTICO]. *v.* Relating to a person's own country. *Nacional.* ~DOMESTIC flights/products. *Vuelos/productos nacionales.* || **2.** Relating to one's home. *Hogareño, casero.* DOMESTIC life/scene. *Vida/escena hogareña.* ~Women still perform more DOMESTIC chores than men. *Todavía la mujer se dedica más a las tareas hogareñas que el hombre.* || **3.** Home-loving. *Casero, hogareño, que gusta de la familia o del hogar.* ~He seldom goes out, he's very DOMESTIC. *Sale muy poco de casa, es muy hogareño.* || **4.** [Trade, policy]. *Interior.* ~DOMESTIC policy. *La política interior.* || **5.** [Strife]. *Interno, intestino.* || **6.** •DOMESTIC bliss. *Felicidad conyugal.* || **7.** •DOMESTIC troubles. *Problemas familiares.* || **8.** •DOMESTIC science. *Ciencia del hogar.* || **9.** •DOMESTIC violence. *Violencia en el hogar.* || **10.** •DOMESTIC appliance. *Electrodoméstico.*

DOUBLE [DOBLAR]. *v.* [Efforts]. *Redoblar.* The police are DOUBLING their efforts to find the murderer. *La policía está redoblando sus esfuerzos para encontrar al asesino.* || **2.** Have a dual role. *Servir al mismo tiempo.* ~The table DOUBLES as a desk. *La mesa se usa también como escritorio.* || **3.** [Fist]. *Cerrar.* ~He DOUBLED his fist in anger. *Cerró el puño con ira.*

DRAMATIC [DRAMÁTICO]. *adj.* Striking, considerable, major. *Notable, espectacular, impresionante, sensacional, asombroso, considerable.* There's been a DRAMATIC increase in unemployent recently. *Últimamente el desempleo ha aumentado considerablemente.* || **2.** [Moment]. *Emocionante, emocionado.* ~A DRAMATIC speech. *Un discurso emocionante.* ~The most DRAMATIC point in the story. *El momento más conmovedor del relato.* || **3.** Exagerated, impressive. *De gran efecto, efectista, teatral.* ~The hall's glossy purple painted walls make a DRAMATIC entrance. *Las*

paredes del vestíbulo, pintadas de un morado brillante, son de gran efecto (Prats).* || **4.** Vivid (colors). *Intenso.* || **5.** •DRAMATIC proportions. *Proporciones alarmantes.*

DRASTIC. *adj.* Severe. *Enérgico, radical.* ~DRASTIC measures. *Medidas enérgicas.* ~DRASTIC changes. *Cambios radicales.* || **2.** Important. *Importante.* ~Many employees had to take DRASTIC cuts in pay. *Muchos empleados sufrieron una importante reducción de sueldo.* || **3.** [Deterioration]. *Grave.* ▶The word DRÁSTICO has been accepted by the *Real Academia.*

DRUG. *n.* Medicine, medication. *Medicamento, medicina.* ~She takes DRUGS for her heart. *Toma medicamento para el corazón.* || **2.** Narcotic. *Narcótico, estupefaciente.* •DRUG addict. *Toxicómano.* || **3.** •DRUG addiction. *Toxicomanía.* || **4.** •DRUG traffic. *Contrabando de narcóticos.* ⇨DROGA

DUPLICATE. *v.* Repeat. *Repetir.* ~We were anxious not to DUPLICATE work already done. *No queriamos volver a hacer (repetir) el mismo trabajo.* || **2.** Imitate. *Imitar.* ~True art can never be DUPLICATED. *El verdadero arte no se puede imitar.* || **3.** Make copies. *Hacer copias.* ~Will you DUPLICATE these documents for me? *¿Me podría hacer copias de estos documentos?* || **4.** Reproduce (film, tape). *Reproducir.* ⇨DUPLICAR

E

EDIT. *v.* [Text, book] *Preparar, corregir.* ||
~Hours and hours EDITING the text. *Horas*
y horas corrigiendo el texto. **2.** [Newspaper] *Dirigir* ~She used to EDIT the
Washington Post. *Solía dirigir el*
Washington Post. || **3.** [Articles]. *Redactar*
|| **4.** Adapt. *Adaptar.* || **5.** [Radio, TV).
Montar. || **6.** [Film]. *Cortar, reducir.* ~The
film's 130 minutes were EDITED down from
150 minutes of footage. *La película que*
tenía 150 minutos de metraje fue reducida
a 130 minutos. || **7.** •EDITED by. *Compilado*
por, bajo la dirección de, prólogo y notas
de, edición de, a cargo de. || **8.** •To EDIT
something out. *Suprimir, eliminar.* ~To
EDIT a phrase out. *Eliminar una frase.*
⇨EDITAR

EDITION. *n.* Printing. *Tirada.* ~An EDITION
of 50,000 copies. *Una tirada de 50 mil*
ejemplares. || **2.** Version. *Versión.* An edited
VERSION of the speech. *Una versión preparada del discurso.* || **3.** •Paperback EDITION.
Edición en rústica. || **4.** •Hardback EDITION.
Edición en tela. || **5.** •A revised EDITION.
Una edición corregida. ⇨EDICIÓN

EDITOR. *n.* Person responsible for the
content of newspaper or publication.
Redactor (jefe), la redacción. || **2.** Author
who prepares a book for printing. *Autor*
de edición, anotador, compilador, revisador, corrector, adaptador. || **3.** Person
who supervises the content of a given
section of a newspaper (music, book, etc.).
Director, encargado, redactor, critico (de
una sección determinada de una publicación). ~The music EDITOR. *Persona que*
tiene a su cargo la sección musical de
una revista. || **4.** •Staff-EDITOR. *Redactor*
jefe. || **5.** •EDITOR's note. *Nota de la*

redacción. ⇨EDITOR

EDITORIAL. *n.* Leading article, opinion
article. *Artículo de fondo.* || **2.** *Adj.* •EDITORIAL staff. *La redacción.* ⇨EDITORIAL

EDUCATE. *v.* Teach. *Enseñar, instruir,*
formar (at school). ~Where were you
EDUCATED? *¿Dónde cursó sus estudios?*
~He was EDUCATED in Italy. *Se formó en*
Italia, estudió en Italia. ~The prince is
being privately EDUCATED. *El príncipe tiene*
un preceptor particular. || **2.** To teach a
better way of doing something. *Aleccionar,*
informar. ~The government is trying to
EDUCATE the public on the consequences
of drugs. *El gobierno está intentando*
informar al público de los daños provocados por las drogas. ⇨EDUCAR

EDUCATED. *adj.* Having education. *Culto,*
cultivado. ~He seems very well EDUCATED.
Parece muy culto. || **2.** •In EDUCATED speech.
En el habla culta. || **3.** •EDUCATED guess.
Estimación razonada, bien fundada, conjetura hecha con cierta base. ⇨EDUCADO

EDUCATION. *n.* Teaching, schooling.
Enseñanza, instrucción, preparación.
~She received a good EDUCATION. *Recibió*
una buena preparación. ~The teacher
emphasized the importance of reading in
acquiring a good EDUCATION. *La profesora*
subrayó la importancia de la lectura para
adquirir una buena formación. || **2.**
Knowledge, culture. *Cultura.* ~A man of
considerable/little EDUCATION. *Un hombre*
muy/poco culto. || **3.** The art of teaching.
Pedagogía. ~I had to take many EDUCATION
classes. *Tuve que tomar varios cursos de*
pedagogía. || **4.** Studies. *Estudios.* ~They
paid for his education. *Le pagaron los*

estudios. ~Their EDUCATION was interrupted by the war. *La guerra interrumpió sus estudios.* ~He didn't have a university EDUCATION. *No cursó estudios universitarios.* || **5.** Training. *Formación.* A liberal/technical EDUCATION. *Una formación liberal/ técnica.* || **6.** *PHRASES.* || •Adult EDUCATION. *Enseñanza para adultos.*|| •Health EDUCATION. *Clases de higiene.* || •Higher EDUCATION. *Cursos superiores, cursos universitarios.* || •I never had much EDUCATION. *Pasé poco tiempo en la escuela.* || •Meeting so many different people was an EDUCATION. *El conocer a tanta gente distinta fue algo muy instructivo.*|| •Primary/secondary EDUCATION. *Enseñanza primaria/secundaria.* ⇨ EDUCACIÓN

EFFECT. *n.* Consequences, results. *Consecuencias, resultados.* ~It had a disastrous EFFECT on exports. *Ha tenido nefastas consecuencias para las exportaciones.* ~Shortage of food was one of the EFFECTS of the war. *La escasez de alimentos fue uno de las consecuencias de la guerra.* || **2.** Impression. *Impresión.* ~Clothes which create the EFFECT of youthfulness. *Ropa que da la impresión de juventud.* ~The overall EFFECT is of absolute chaos. *La impresión general es de un caos total.* ~Pleasing EFFECT. *Impresión agradable.* || **3.** *PHRASES.* || •A message to the EFFECT that. *Un mensaje en el sentido de que.* || •An increase with immediate EFFECT. *Un aumento a partir de hoy.* || •He only did it for EFFECT. *Lo hizo sólo para llamar la atención.* || •In EFFECT. *Efectivamente.* || •Of no EFFECT. *Inútil.* || •She wore red with great EFFECT. *Causó sensación vestida así de rojo.* || •Side EFFECTS. *Reacciones adversas.* || •To be in EFFECT. *Estar vigente.* || •To be of no EFFECT. *No hacer mella.* ~The warnings had no EFFECT on him at all. *Las advertencias no hicieron mella en él.* ~I spoke to her repeatedly but to no EFFECT. *Le hablé repetidamente del tema, pero sin resultado.* || •To come into EFFECT. *Entrar en vigor.* || •To feel the EFFECTS of. *Resentirse.* ~She still feels the EFFECT of her illness. *Todavía se resiente de su enfer-*

medad. || •To good EFFECT. *Con éxito, con buenos resultados.* || •To have an EFFECT on. *Afectar.* ~This will have an EFFECT on prices. *Esto afectará los precios.* || •To have the EFFECT of. *Tener como resultado.* ~It had the EFFECT of increasing output. *Tuvo como resultado un aumento de la producción.* || •To no EFFECT. *Sin resultado alguno, inútilmente.* || •To remain in EFFECT. *Permancer vigente (en vigor, en vigencia).* || •To put into EFFECT. *Poner en vigor, poner en práctica.* ||•To take EFFECT. *Entrar en vigor.* || •To take EFFECT (drug). *Surtir efecto.* || •To this EFFECT. *Con este propósito.* || •Words to that EFFECT. *Algo por el estilo, algo parecido.* || •Personal EFFECTS. *Enseres.* ⇨EFECTO

EFFECTIVE. *adj.* Producing the desired result. *Eficaz.* ~These pills are very EFFECTIVE. *Estas píldoras son muy eficaces.* || **2.** [Person] *Capaz.* ~She's a very EFFECTIVE worker. *Es una trabajadora muy capaz.* **3.** In force. *Vigente.* || **4.** MIL Prepared and available for service. *Disponible.* || **5.** Successful. *Logrado, de mucho éxito.* His campaign was very EFFECTIVE. *Su campaña ha sido muy lograda.* In order to be EFFECTIVE, we need your support. *Para tener éxito, necesitamos su apoyo.* || **6.** Productive, operative. *Útil.* ~The EFFECTIVE life of the battery is six months. *La vida útil de la pila son seis meses.* || **7.** Impressive, striking (design, contrast). *Impresionante, logrado, llamativo.* The stage setting was very EFFECTIVE. *El decorado de la escena fue muy logrado.* || **8.** In force. *Vigente, en vigencia.* ~The rules EFFECTIVE at the present time. *Las normas vigentes en la actualidad.* || **9.** *PHRASES.* || •To become EFFECTIVE. *Entrar en vigor.* || •To be EFFECTIVE (thing). *Surtir efecto, dar buenos resultados.* ~The ads were simple, but remarkably EFFECTIVE. *Los avisos eran sencillos, pero dieron buenos resultados.* || •To be EFFECTIVE (person) *Tener dotes de.* She's a very EFFECTIVE speaker. *Tiene grandes dotes de oradora.* || •EFFECTIVE date. *Fecha de vigencia.* || •EFFECTIVE until. *Vigente hasta.* || •EFFECTIVE from. *En vigor* *a partir de.* ~The law becomes EFFECTIVE as of December 15. *La nueva ley entra en vigor a partir del 15 de diciembre.* ‖ •An EFFECTIVE way of ... *Una excelente manera de ...* ⇨EFECTIVO

EFFECTIVELY. *adv.* Successfully. *Eficazmente, con provecho.* ~Children have to learn how to communicate EFFECTIVELY. *Los niños debe aprender a expresarse bien.* ‖ **2.** In fact. *En efecto, de hecho.* ~EFFECTIVELY, what he's saying is that ... *En efecto, lo que está diciendo es que ...* ‖ **3.** •To speak EFFECTIVELY. *Hablar convincentemente.* ⇨EFECTIVAMENTE

EFFICIENT [EFICIENTE]. *v.* [Remedy, product]. *Eficaz.* ~These pills are the most EFFICIENT cure that I know against headaches. *Estas pastillas son el remedio más eficaz que conozco contra el dolor de cabeza.* ‖ **2.** Practical and economical. *Que rinde, de elevado rendimiento, que produce.* The steam engine is not a highly EFFICIENT machine. *La máquina de vapor no tiene un rendimiento muy elevado (Prats).* ~The least EFFICIENT mines. *Las minas menos rentables.* ~A very EFFICIENT heating system. *Un sistema de calefacción de elevado rendimiento.* ‖ **3.** [Employee]. *Apto, capaz, competente.* ‖ **4.** Organized. *Que funciona muy bien, muy bien organizado.* ~The city's transport system is one of the most EFFICIENT in Europe. *El sistema de transportación de la ciudad es uno de los mejores organizados en toda Europa.*

EFFORT [ESFUERZO]. *n.*
❶ ATTEMPT, TRY, STRUGGLE. *Tentativa, intento.* ~The constant EFFORT of the dreamer to attain his ideal. *La constante lucha del soñador por alcanzar su ideal.* ~The company's EFFORT to improve working conditions. *El empeño de la compañía en mejorar las condiciones de trabajo.* ~It was a good EFFORT. *Fue un buen intento.* Good EFFORT. *¡Bien hecho!* ~It wasn't bad for a first EFFORT. *Siendo su primer intento no es nada malo.* His EFFORT to be pleasant to her was unsuccessful. *Trató de ser amable con ella pero no lo consiguió.*

~Little EFFORT has been made to investigate this claim. *Se ha hecho muy poco en investigar esta petición.* ‖ **2.** •To make an EFFORT (to do something). *Intentar, procurar, tratar de.* Please make an EFFORT to be there before ten. *Procuren estar allí antes de las diez.* ~Repeated EFFORTS were made to contact him. *Se intentó repetidamente localizarlo.* ‖ **3.** •She couldn't even make the EFFORT to telephone. *Ni siquiera se molestó en llamar.*

❷ ACHIEVEMENT, ACCOMPLISHMENT, CREATION. *Obra, creación, logro, triunfo.* ~Their magnificent churches being justly ranked among the most wonderful EFFORTS of the human hand. *Sus suntuosas iglesias figuran con razón entre las más maravillosas creaciones surgidas de las manos del hombre.* A literary/artistic EFFORT. *Una obra literaria/artística.* ~What do you think of my latest EFFORT? *¿Qué te parece mi última obra?* ‖ **2.** Performance. *Exhibición.* ~It was a pretty poor EFFORT. *Fue una exhibición pobre.*

❸ DIFFICULTY, SACRIFICE. *Dificultad, sacrificio.* ~He spoke with EFFORT. *Habló con dificultad.* ~He refuses to do anything that requires mental EFFORT. *No quiere hace nada que exija concentración.* ~I was so weak that even standing up was an EFFORT. *Estaba tan débil que hasta ponerme de pie era un sacrificio, me resultó difícil.* ~Would it be too much of an EFFORT for you to do it? *¿Sería mucho sacrificio que lo hicieras tú, sería mucho pedir que lo hicieras tú?* ‖ **2.** •It's an EFFORT for me to climb de stairs. *Me cuesta mucho subir la escalera.*

❹ EXPRESSIONS. ‖ •The war EFFORT. *Campaña solidaria de la población civil durante la guerra.* ‖ •It's a waste of EFFORT. *Es tiempo perdido.* ‖ •Not to be worth the EFFORT. *No valer la pena.* ‖ •It was through his EFFORTS that we were able to raise the money. *Fue gracias a él que pudimos recaudar el dinero.* ‖ •In an EFFORT to. *Para, a fin de.* ~They've been working all night in an EFFORT to finish the bridge. *Han estado trabajando día y noche para poder terminar el puente.* || •It doesn't take much EFFORT to say thank you. *No cuesta tanto dar las gracias.* || •It requires a tremendous EFFORT of will. *Requiere una gran fuerza de voluntad.* || •If it's not too much of an EFFORT. *Si no es mucho pedir.* ~I'd like you to help me, if it's not too much of an EFFORT. *Quisiera que me ayudara, si no es mucho pedir.* || •To make every EFFORT to (do something). *Intentar todo lo posible para (hacer algo).*

ELABORATE[1]. *adj.* Detailed, comprehensive, exhaustive. *Detallado, minucioso.* ~An ELABORATE plan. *Un plan muy estudiado, un plan minucioso.* || **2.** [Style, work of art]. *Trabajado, esmerado, primeroso, rebuscado.* ~An ELABORATE mosaic consisting of thousands of tiny pieces. *Un trabajado mosaico compuesto de miles de diminutas piezas.* || **3.** [Meal]. *De muchos platos.* || **4.** [Courtesy]. *Exquisito.* || **5.** [Design, hairstyle, decoration]. *Intricado, complicado.* ~You want a plain blouse to go with this skirt. Nothing too ELABORATE. *Necesitas una blusa sencilla para ir con esta falda. Nada demasiado complicado.* || **6.** [Joke, excuse]. *Rebuscado.* ~He came up with such an ELABORATE excuse that I didn't believe him. *Su disculpa fue tan rebuscada que no le creí.* || **7.** •In ELABORATE details. *Con todo detalle, minuciosamente.* ⇨ELABORADO

ELABORATE[2]. *verb.* Explain, expand on. *Dar detalles, dar (más) explicaciones, extenderse, explicar detalladamente, entrar en detalles.* ~The Minister said that the bill would be soon introduced but he did not ELABORATE. *El ministro dijo que el proyecto de ley se presentará dentro de poco, pero no dio más explicaciones (Prats).* ~He refused to ELABORATE. *Se negó a dar más detalles.* || **2.** •To ELABORATE on something. *Explicar con más detalles.* ~Later on I'll ELABORATE on the methods we use. *Más adelante, explicaré con más detalles los métodos que empleamos.* ⇨ELABORAR

ELECT. *v.* To choose. *Decidir.* ~They ELEC-

TED to stay in their own country. *Decidieron (optaron por) quedarse en su propio país.* ⇨ELEGIR

ELEVATE. *v.* To promote (in rank). *Ascender, promover.* ~He was ELEVATED to the position of manager. *Fue ascendido a director.* || **2.** [Person]. *Exaltar.* || **3.** [Price]. *Aumentar.* || **4.** [Eyes, voice]. *Levantar, alzar.* || **5.** To elate. *Regocijar.* || **6.** [Someone's hopes]. *Alimentar (las esperanzas de uno).*|| ⇨ELEVAR

EMBARK. *v.* To start, undertake (career, new life). *Emprender.* In 1950 China EMBARKED on a major program of industrialization. *En 1950 China emprendió un programa de industrialización de gran envergadura.* ⇨EMBARCAR

EMBARRASS. *v.* To humble, humiliate. *Turbar, azorar, avergonzar, desconcertar.* ~I was EMBARRASSED by the question. *La pregunta me desconcertó.* ~I feel EMBARRASSED about it. *Me siento avergonzado por eso.* || **2.** [Husband, wife, friend.] *Hacer pasar vergüenza.* ~He EMBARRASSED me in front of my own family. *Me hizo pasar vergüenza delante de mi propia familia.* || **3.** To be (get) EMBARRASS. *Pasar vergüenza, turbarse.* ⇨EMBARAZAR

EMBARRASSING. *adj.* Awkward, humiliating, distressing. *Embarazoso, violento.* ~It's an AMBARRASSING situation. *Es una situación violenta.* ⇨EMBARAZADA

EMBRACE [ABRAZAR]. *v.* [Occasion, opportunity]. *Aprovechar.* ~To EMBRACE an opportunity. *Aprovechar una oportunidad.* || **2.** To accept (offer, proposal). *Aceptar.* || **3.** To cover, include, encompass. *Abarcar.* 'Democracy' EMBRACES many concepts. *La palabra 'democracia' abarca muchos conceptos.* || **4.** [Course of action]. *Adoptar.* || **5.** [Doctrine, party]. *Adherirse.* || **6.** [Profession]. *Dedicarse a.* || **7.** [Religion]. *Convertirse a.* ~She EMBRACED the Catholic faith. *Se convirtió al catolicismo.*

EMERGENCY [EMERGENCIA]. *n.* Sudden and unexpected events which require immediate action. *Urgencia, caso de urgencia, situación crítica.* ~EMERGENCY room. *Sala de urgencia.* ~EMERGENCY procedures. *Procedimientos de urgencia.* || **2.** Crunch, crisis, pinch. *Caso de necesidad, caso de apuro, caso improvisto.* ~It is wise to have some money saved for an EMERGENCY. *Conviene tener algún dinero ahorrado para un caso de apuro (Prats).* || **3.** Unexpected event. *Situación imprevista.* ~I must talk to you, it's an EMERGENCY. *Tengo que hablarte, es una situación inesperada.* || **4.** Crisis. *Crisis.* There's a national EMERGENCY. *Existe una crisis nacional.* || **5.** *PHRASES.* || •EMERGENCY landing. *Aterrizaje forzoso.* || •EMERGENCY measures. *Medidas de urgencia.* || •EMERGENCY stop. *Frenazo en seco.* || •State of EMERGENCY. *Estado de exepción.* ~A state of EMERGENCY was declared. *Se declaró el estado de exepción.* || •EMERGENCY brake. *Freno de seguridad.* || •In an EMERGENCY, in case of EMERGENCY. *En caso de urgencia.* || •To provide for EMERGENCIES. *Prevenir contra toda eventualidad (contingencia).* || •EMERGENCY meeting. *Reunión extraordinaria.* || •EMERGENCY power. *Poderes extraordinarios.* || •EMERGENCY service. *Urgencias.* || •EMERGENCY stop (aut.). *Parada en seco.* || •EMERGENCY ward. *Sala para casos de urgencia.* || •EMERGENCY ration. *Ración de reserva..* || •EMERGENCY road. *Camino provisional.* || •EMERGENCY door. *Puerta de socorro, salida de urgencia.*

EMIT. *v.* [Gas, smell, vapor]. *Despedir.* ~The factory has been EMITTING toxic gases into the atmosphere. *La fábrica ha estado despidiendo gases tóxicos en la atmósfera.* ~A sharp odor EMITTING from a broken gas line. *Un fuerte olor que despedía un caño de gas roto.* || **2.** [Sound, groan]. *Producir.* ~Recording the whistles EMITTED by dolphins. *Grabando los silbidos producidos por los delfines.* || **3.** [Smoke]. *Arrojar.* ~The chimney EMITTED clouds of smoke. *La chimenea arrojaba nubes de humo.* || **4.** [Cry]. *Dar.* ~He EMITTED a scream which startled the whole audience. *Dio un chillido que sobresaltó a toda la asistencia.* || **5.** [Heat]. *Desprender.* ~The engine EMITTED intense heat. *Del motor se*

desprendía un calor intenso. || **6.** Express. *Expresar.* ~They EMITTED constant complaints over the poor service. *Expresaron continuas quejas sobre el mal servicio.* ~In her book she EMITS her innermost thoughts. *En su libro expresa sus pensamientos más íntimos.* ⇨EMITIR

EMOTIONAL [EMOCIONAL]. *adj.* Moving (moment, experience, speech, appeal). *Emotivo, conmovedor.* ~An EMOTIONAL farewell. *Una despedida emotiva.* || **2.** Warm-hearted (person). *Sentimental.* || **3.** Taking things too hard. *Demasiado sensible.* || **4.** Showing excessive emotions. *Exaltado, exagerado.* || **5.** [Involvement, link]. *Afectivo.* || **6.** Affectionate, demonstrative. *Cariñoso.* We are an EMOTIONAL family, given to demonstrations of affection. *Somos una familia muy cariñosa, propensa a manifestar nuestro afecto.* || **7.** Impulsive, *Impulsivo.* ~It was a purely EMOTIONAL decision. *Fue una decisión puramente impulsiva.* || **8.** Psychological. *Psicológico.* He has EMOTIONAL problems. *Tiene problemas psicológicos.*

EMPHASIS [ÉNFASIS]. *n.* Importance, insistence. *Insistencia, importancia, atención especial.* ~His father's EMPHASIS had always been on discipline. *Su padre siempre había insistido en la disciplina (Prats).* ~He disliked the school EMPHASIS on classics. *Le molestaba que la escuela diera tanta importancia a los clásicos (Prats).* ~In this school the EMPHASIS is on languages. *En este colegio concedemos particular importancia a los idiomas.* || **2.** •To put (place) EMPHASIS on something. *Recalcar, subrayar, hacer resaltar, poner de relieve, hacer hincapié.* || **3.** •The new policy reflects a change of EMPHASIS. *La nueva política refleja un cambio en el orden de prioridades.*

EMPHASIZE. *v.* [General]. Stress, underline, highlight, accentuate, accent, underscore, draw attention to, spotlight. *Recalcar, subrayar, hacer resaltar, poner de relieve, hacer hincapié, destacar, acentuar.* ~The teacher EMPHASIZED the importance of reading in acquiring a good education. *La profesora subrayó la importancia de la lectura para adquirir una buena formación.* || **2.** Call attention to (problem, question). *Destacar, poner de relieve.* ~In his speech he EMPHASIZED the need to give fresh impetus to the economy. *En su discurso puso de relieve la necesidad de dar un nuevo impulso a la economía.* || **3.** Give importance to. *Subrayar, hacer hincapie en.* || **4.** Highlight, bring out. *Poner de relieve (fault, value); resaltar, hacer resaltar (shape, feature).* The dress EMPHASIZES her figure. *El vestido realza su figura.* || **5.** [Fact, point, warning]. *Recalcar, hacer hincapie en.* ~He EMPHASIZED the fact that we had to be more punctual. *Hizo hincapie en que teníamos que ser mas puntuales.* || **6.** Specify. *Poner de relieve.* || **7.** Insist. *Insistir.* ~I must emphasize that. *Debo insistir en que.* || **8.** [Art, photo]. *Realzar, dar realce.* || **9.** GRAM To lay stress (on a word in speaking). *Acentuar, poner el acento en.* ▶"En la vigésima edición del diccionario, la Academia aprobó el verbo *enfatizar* [...]. Nos limitaremos a decir que para obligarnos a emplear el verbo *enfatizar* tendrían que amenazarnos con tirarnos con paracaídas desde un avión, un mes de vacación en Ulan Bator, una suscripción a la revista 'Hola' u otras torturas de refinado parecido" (Prats).

ENCOUNTER[1]. *v.* To be faced with (a problem). *Tropezar con, topar con, enfrentarse a.* ~One ENCOUNTERS problems of all kinds in business. *En todos los negocios uno se enfrenta con dificultades.* || **2.** To meet by chance. *Tropezar con, topar con.* ~I first ENCOUNTERED him at summer school. *Lo conocí en la escuela de verano.* ⇨ ENCONTRAR

ENCOUNTER[2]. *n.* || •Sexual ENCOUNTERS. *Relaciones sexuales (fuera de una pareja estable).* || •His first ENCOUNTER with the law. *Su primer tropiezo con la ley.* || •My first ENCOUNTER with the works of Tennyson. *Mi primer toma de contacto con las obras de Tennyson.* ⇨ ENCUENTRO

ENTERTAIN. *v.* Amuse. *Divertir.* He ENTERTAINED troops overseas with songs and jokes. *Divertió a las tropas en el extranjero con canciones y chistes.* || **2.** Cherish, harbor (idea, hope). *Abrigar, acariciar (una idea, una esperanza).* ~To CHERISH the hope of a peaceful settlement. *Abrigar la esperanza de un acuerdo pacífico.* || **3.** Take into consideration (a proposal). *Estudiar, considerar (una propuesta).* Would you ENTERTAIN our proposal if we lowered the price to $15.00? *¿Consideraría nuestra propuesta si bajáramos el precio a $15.00?* || **4.** Give hospitality, receive as a guest. *Tener invitados, recibir, recibir en casa, invitar.* ~We enjoy ENTERTAINING friends. *Nos gusta recibir (a los amigos) en casa, nos gusta invitar a los amigos.* ~They ENTERTAIN a lot. *Invitan con mucha frecuencia.* ~They ENTERTAINED him with a dinner. *Lo invitaron a cenar.* || **5.** Make a fuss. *Festejar, agasajar.* The minister ENTERTAINED the diplomats. *El ministro agasajó a los diplomáticos.* || **6.** Meet, play against (a team). *Enfrentarse.* England will ENTERTAIN Spain at Wembley. *Inglaterra se enfrentará a España en el estadio de Wembley.* || **7.** [Conversation, relations]. *Mantener.* || **8.** Consider (idea, possibility). *Considerar.* ~I wouldn't ENTERTAIN it for a minute. *Tal idea es totalmente inconcebible para mí.* The general refused to ENTERTAIN the possibility of defeat. *El general se negó a aceptar (considerar) la posibilidad de una derrota.* || **9.** Treat (a subject). *Tratar.* ~I am not going to ENTERTAIN so large a theme at this time. *No voy a tratar en este momento de un tema tan complejo.* ⇨ ENTRETENER

ENTRY. *n.* Separate piece of information in a book, computer, etc. *Artículo, voz, vocablo, palabra.* || **2.** [Accounting]. *Anotación, partida, asiento, inscripción.* || **3.** Participant. *Participante, concurrente.* ~Now we'll announce the winning ENTRIES. *Ahora vamos a presentar a los ganadores.* || **4.** •Forcible ENTRY. *Allanamiento de morada.* || **5.** •No ENTRY. *Dirección prohibida, se prohibe la entrada.* || **6.** •ENTRY form. *Boleto de inscripción.* ⇨ENTRADA

EQUAL. *adj.* Capable, adequate. *Capaz, adecuado.* ~I don't feel EQUAL to the situation. *No me siento a la altura de las circunstancias.* ~I don't thing he's EQUAL to the task. *No lo creo capaz de hacerlo.* ~They were provided funds EQUAL to their needs. *Les concedieron fondos adecuados a sus necesidades.* ~She doesn't feel EQUAL to going to the party. *No se siente con fuerzas para ir a la fiesta.* ‖ **2.** Same. *Mismo.* ~With EQUAL indifference. *Con la misma indiferencia.* ~With EQUAL ease. *Con la misma facilidad.* ‖ **3.** [Treatment]. *Equitativo.* ~We give EQUAL treatment to everyone. *Tratamos equitativamente a todos* ‖ **4.** •EQUAL pay/rights. *Igualdad de salarios/derechos.* ‖ **5.** •EQUAL time. *Derecho de respuesta.* ⇨IGUAL

EQUIP. *v.* Prepare, make capable. *Preparar.* ~I was ill EQUIPPED for such a task. *No estaba bien preparado para una tarea así.* ~My training had not EQUIPPED me to handle such a situation. *Mi entrenamiento no me había preparado para enfrentarme a una situación como esá.* ‖ **2.** •To EQUIP somebody with something. *Proveer de.* ~The ship was not EQUIPPED with radar. *El barco no estaba provisto con radar.* ⇨EQUIPAR

EQUIPMENT. *n.* [Mental]. *Aptitud, dotes.* He has the necessary EQUIPMENT for law. *Tiene aptitud para ser abogado.* ‖ **2.** Tools. *Herramientas, instrumentos.* ~Dentists must take great care in sterilizing their EQUIPMENT. *Los dentistas deben cuidarse de que estén bien esterilizados sus intrumentos.* ‖ **3.** [Piece of equipment]. *Aparato.* ~The telephone is a wonderful piece of EQUIPMENT which has revolutionized the history of mankind. *El teléfono es un aparato maravilloso que ha revolucionado la historia de la humanidad (Prats).* ‖ **4.** •Office EQUIPMENT. *Material de oficina.* ‖ **5.** •Sports EQUIPMENT. *Artículos deportivos.* ⇨EQUIPO

ERRATIC [ERRÁTICO]. *adj.* Uncertain (performance, behavior). *Irregular, poco*

constante. ~The bus service into town is very ERRATIC. *El servicio de autobuses a la ciudad es muy irregular.* ‖ **2.** [Weather]. *Muy variable.* ‖ **3.** Odd, excentric (person). *Caprichoso, imprevisible.* ~She can be very ERRATIC, one day she's very friendly and the next day she hardly speaks to you. *Es una persona imprevisible (muy caprichosa), un día es muy amistosa y al otro día apenas le habla.* ‖ **4.** [Records, results, attempts]. *Desigual, poco uniforme.* ~The country's ERRATIC attempts to move into the future. *El desigual (poco uniforme) empeño por parte del país en adentrarse en el futuro.* ‖ **5.** [Respiration, pulse]. *Irregular.* ‖ **6.** Fluctuating (stock market). *Que sufre altibajos.* ~The stock market has been ERRATIC. *La bolsa ha sufrido muchos altibajos.* ‖ **7.** Uneven (writings). *Desigual.* His writings are ERRATIC. *Sus escritos son desiguales.* ‖ **8.** [Driving]. *Peligroso.* ~He was arrested for driving ERRATICALLY. *Fue detenido por manejar de una forma peligrosa.* ‖ **9.** Marked by irregular changes of direction. *Irregular.* ~The ERRATIC course of the river. *El curso irregular del río.*

ESCAPE[1]. *v.* Avoid or elude (a commitment, danger, etc.). *Evitar, librarse.* ~To ESCAPE punishment he hid in the garage. *Para evitar que le castigara se escondió en el garaje.* ‖ **2.** To forget, elude. *Olvidar, no recordar.* His name ESCAPES me at the moment. *No me acuerdo de su nombre en este momento.* ‖ **3.** Get completely free of (a person, grasp, etc.), get rid of, avoid. *Librarse.* He was unable to ESCAPE from her. *No pudo librarse de ella.* ‖ **4.** Slip out. *Dejar escapar.* A cry ESCAPED him. *No pudo contener un grito, dejo escapar un grito.* ‖ **5.** *PHRASES.* ‖ •He just ESCAPED being run over. *Por poco murió atropellado.* ‖ •They are looking for an ESCAPED convict. *Están buscando a un preso que se ha fugado de la cárcel.* ‖ •He ESCAPED with a warning. *Sólo recibió una reprimenda.* ‖•He ESCAPED with minor injuries. *Sólo sufrió heridas leves.* ‖ •There's no ESCAPING the fact that. *No se puede negar que.*

ESCAPE[2] [ESCAPE]. *noun.* Flight, breakout.

Huída, fuga. ~An attempted ESCAPE. *Un intento de fuga.* || **2.** [From reality]. *Evasión.* || **3.** *PHRASES.* || •To have a narrow ESCAPE. *Salvarse por los pelos.* || •ESCAPE clause. *Cláusula de excepción.* || •ESCAPE hatch. *Estilla de salvamento.* || •Fire ESCAPE. *Escalera de incendios.* || •ESCAPE chute. *Rampa de emergencia.* || •There's no ESCAPE. *No hay escapatoria posible.* ⇨ESCAPE

ESSAY. *n.* [Education]. *Redacción, composición.* || **2.** Attemp. *Atento, incursión.* ⇨ENSAYO

ESTABLISH. *v.* [Business]. *Montar.* ~Where are you thinking of ESTABLISHING the clinic? *¿Dónde montarás la clínica?* || **2.** [Habit]. *Consolidar.* || **3.** [Theory]. *Sentar.* || **4.** To affirm. *Hacer valer.* To ESTABLISH one's rights. *Hacer valer sus derechos.* || **5.** To prove. *Probar.* ~To ESTABLISH one's innocence. *Probar su inocencia.* ~The lawyers are trying to ESTABLISH the validity of his claim. *Los abogados están intentando probar la validez de su demanda.* || **6.** [Truth]. *Demostrar.* || **7.** Determine, fix, set. *Determinar, fijar.* The date of the meeting has not been ESTABLISHED yet. *La fecha de la reunión no se ha fijado todavía.* || **8.** [Committee, assembly] *Constituir, formar, crear, nombrar, instituir.* || **9.** To found, institute, bring into being. *Fundar.* ~ESTABLISHED in 1776. *Casa fundada en 1776 (Prats).* || **10.** To make known. *Cimentar, consagrar.* ~The book ESTABLISHED him as a writer. *El libro le consagró como escritor.* || **11.** [Relations]. *Entablar.* || **12.** Prove. *Comprobar.* ~If it can be ESTABLISHED that ... *Si se puede comprobar que ...* || **13.** Install. *Instalar.* ~He ESTABLISHED her in a flat. *La instaló en un piso.* His father ESTABLISHED him in business. *Su padre compró el negocio para él.* || **14.** To bring about permanently. *Imponer.* ~The army was sent to ESTABLISH order. *Se enviaron efectivos del ejército para imponer el orden.* || **15.** Cause people to accept. *Dejar sentado.* ~She saw it as a way to ESTABLISH her authority. *Lo veía como una manera de dejar sentado que era ella quien mandaba.* || **16.** *PHRASES.* •To

ESTABLISH oneself. *Crearse una reputación, hacer un negocio sólido.* || •ESTABLISH a reputation as. *Ganarse la fama de.* He soon ESTABLISHED a reputation as a womanizer. *Pronto se ganó la fama de ser un donjuán.* || •To ESTABLISH a precedent. *Sentar un precedente.* || •To ESTABLISH one's identity. *Acreditar su personalidad.* ⇨ESTABLECER

ESTABLISHED [ESTABLECIDO]. *adj.* [Habit]. *Arraigado.* || **2.** [Fact]. *Conocido, demostrado, admitido.* ~His reputation for carelessness was ESTABLISHED long before the latest problems arose. *Su fama de descuidado era bien conocida mucho antes que surgieran los últimos problemas.* ~This is an ESTABLISHED phenomenon, but how it happens is a total mystery. *Se trata de un fenómeno admitido por la ciencia, pero hasta ahora totalmente inexplicable. (Cit. Prats).* || **3.** •ESTABLISHED church. *Iglesia oficial del Estado.*

ESTIMATE[1] [ESTIMACIÓN]. *n.* Approximate cost of work to be done. *Presupuesto.* ~We got two or three ESTIMATES so we could pick the cheapest. *Pedimos dos o tres presupuestos para poder elegir el más barato.* || **2.** Assesment. *Valoración.* ~An expert will have to make an ESTIMATE of the damages. *Un perito tendrá que hacer la valoración de los daños.* **3.** Calculation. *Cálculo.* ~The influence of their work on the health and well-being of millions of Canadians is beyond ESTIMATE. *La influencia de su obra en la salud y el bienestar de millones de canadienses, no se puede calcular.* || **4.** Assesment, judgement. *Juicio, opinión.* ~By general ESTIMATE this is the company's best product to date. *Según la opinión general este es mejor producto que ha fabricado la compañía hasta la fecha.* || **5.** •Rough CALCULATION. *Cálculo aproximado.* ~At a rough ESTIMATE. *Haciendo un cálculo aproximado.* ▸ESTIMADO cannot be used as a noun.

ESTIMATE[2]. *v.* Consider, believe, guess. *Formar una opinión, calcular.* I ESTIMATE that our chances of winning are very low. *Calculo que las posibilidades que gane-*

mos son pocas. || **2.** Calculate approximately. *Calcular.* The company CALCULATES its loses at 7 million. *La compañía calcula que ha sufrido pérdidas del orden de 7 millones de dólares.* ~His estate has been CALCULATED at 400 million. *Se le calcula un patrimonio de 400 millones de dólares.* || **3.** Expected. *Previsto.* ~ESTIMATED time of arrival. *Hora de llegada prevista.* || **4.** Form judgement of. *Juzgar, pensar, creer* ~What do you ESTIMATE his chances are? *¿Qué posibilidades crees que tiene?* ⇨ESTIMAR

ESTIMATION. Opinion, judgement. *Juicio, opinión.* ~What is your APPRECIATION of him? *¿Cuál es su concepto de él?* ~In my ESTIMATION. *A mi juicio.* || **2.** Esteem. *Estima, aprecio.* ~To go up/down in someone's ESTIMATION. *Ganarse/perder la estima de alguien.* ⇨ESTIMACIÓN

EVADE. *v.* [Question, issue]. *Eludir.* ~To EVADE the issue. *Eludir la cuestión.* || **2.** [Regulations, military service]. *Eludir.* ⇨EVADIR

EVALUATE. *v.* Determine. *Determinar, precisar, fijar.* ~How can they EVALUATE your importance to the project? *¿Cómo pueden determinar su importancia en cuanto al proyecto?* || **2.** Study, analyze. *Analizar, estudiar.* ~We must first EVALUATE the success of the training program. *Debemos primero analizar el éxito del programa de entrenamiento.* **3.** To grade (exams). *Juzgar, calificar.* ⇨EVALUAR

EVENT. *n.* Happening, occurrence. *Acontecimiento, hecho, suceso.* ~The EVENTS of that night. *Los sucesos (acontecimientos) de aquella noche.* || **2.** [Sport]. *Prueba.* ~The 100 meter EVENT. *La prueba de los 100 metros.* || **3.** [Boxing]. *Encuentro.* || **4.** [Program]. *Número.* || **5.** [Shows]. *Programa de atracciones.* || **6.** [Civic] *Programa de actos.* || **7.** [Track}. *Atletismo en pista.* || **8.** Outcome. *Consecuencia, resultado.* ~There is no use of preparing for a disaster after the EVENT. *No tiene sentido de estar preparándose cuando ya es tarde.* || **9.** PHRASES. || •Coming EVENTS. *Sucesos veni-*

deros, atracciones venideras. || •Current EVENTS. *Actualidades.* || •In any EVENT. *En todo caso, pase lo que pase.* || •In the EVENT of. *En caso de.* ~In the EVENT of fire. *En caso de incendio.* || •In the EVENT that. *En caso de que.* ~In the EVENT of his refusing. *En caso de que no acepte.* || •In the normal course of EVENTS. *Si todo sigue su curso normal, en circunstancias normales.* || •It was quite an EVENT. *Fue todo un acontecimiento.* || •The EVENT will show. *Ya veremos lo que pasa.* || •To be waiting a happy EVENT. *Estar esperando un acontecimiento feliz.* ⇨EVENTO

EVENTUALLY. *adv.* Ultimately, finally, in the long run. *Inevitablemente, con el tiempo, finalmente, posteriormente, a la larga, tarde o temprano.* The plan seemed initially attractive but it was EVENTUALLY dropped. *Al principio el plan parecía atractivo, pero posteriormente se abandonó (Prats).* ~We EVENTUALLY managed to find a telephone booth. *Finalmente encontramos una cabina telefónica.* ~EVENTUALLY people became used to the idea. *Con el tiempo, la gente se acostumbró a la idea.* || **2.** Sooner or later, in due course. *Acabar por, llegar a.* ~I think he'll EVENTUALLY come. *Creo que acabará por venir.* ~EVENTUALLY there won't be enough food to go around. *Llegará un día que no habrá suficiente comida para todo el mundo.* ⇨EVENTUALMENTE

EVIDENCE. *n.* Testimony, statement, deposition. *Testimonio, deposición, declaración.* ~On the EVIDENCE of those present. *Según el testimonio (las declaraciones) de los que estuvieron presentes.* ~The EVIDENCE of the senses. *El testimonio de los sentidos.* •To give EVIDENCE. *Prestar declaración, dar testimonio.* •To call somebody in EVIDENCE. *Llamar a alguien como testigo.* •To turn state EVIDENCE. *Delatar a un cómplice.* || **2.** Proof, fact. *Prueba, documentos, datos, hechos.* ~There is no EVIDENCE against her. *No hay ninguna prueba en contra suya.* ~Anything you say may be taken down and used as EVIDENCE against you. *Lo que diga* *podrá utilizarse como prueba en su contra.* ~The revolver was introduced as EVIDENCE. *El revólver fue presentado como prueba.* •Circumstantial EVIDENCE. *Pruebas indirectas.* ‖ **3.** Sign, indication. *Indicio, señal, muestra.* ~The house showed EVIDENCE of neglect. *La casa se veía descuidada.* ~Some of the EVIDENCE suggests conspiracy. *Hay indicios que apuntan a una conspiración.* ‖ **4.** Grounds, supporting data. *Prueba.* What is the EVIDENCE that God exists? *¿Qué prueba hay de que Dios exista?* ‖ **5.** •In EVIDENCE. *Visible, manifiesto.* ~Poverty is very much in EVIDENCE in rural areas. *La pobreza de las zonas rurales es manifiesta.* ‖ **6.** •To be in EVIDENCE. *Estar a la vista. hacerse notar.* ‖ **7.** •He isn't much in EVIDENCE these days. *Ultimamente no se le ve mucho.* ⇨EVIDENCIA

EXAMINATION. [Medical]. *Reconocimiento.* ‖ **2.** Search, investigation, scrutiny. *Reconocimiento, estudio.* ~A careful EXAMINATION of the terrain showed no signs of human habitation. *Un cuidadoso reconocimiento del terreno indicó que allí no vivía nadie.* ‖ **3.** [Law]. *Interrogatorio.* ‖ **4.** [Accounting]. *Revisión.* ‖ **5.** [Customs]. *Registro.* ‖ **6.** Inspection (building). *Inspección.* ‖ **7.** •The matter is under EXAMINATION. *El asunto está bajo estudio.* ‖ **8.** •On closer EXAMINATION we discovered this mark. *Al examinarlo más de cerca descubrimos esta marca.* ⇨EXAMEN

EXAMINE. *v.* [Baggage]. *Registrar, revisar.* Customs officials EXAMINED their bags for contraband. *En la aduana registraron las maletas a ver si llevaba contrabando.* ‖ **2.** [Witness]. *Interrogar.* ‖ **3.** Inspect (accounts). *Revisar.* ‖ **4.** To inquire. *Investigar.* ‖ **5.** [Patient]. *Reconocer, revisar, hacer un reconocimiento médico.* ~The doctor EXAMINED the young man and found him in perfect health. *El médico reconoció al joven y lo encontró en perfecta salud.* ⇨EXAMINAR

EXCITE[1.] *v.* Arouse. *Despertar, suscitar, provocar.* ~His speech EXCITED suspicion. *Su discurso provocó sospechas.* ~The court case has EXCITED a great deal of public interest. *El pleito ha suscitado el interés general.* ~The book has EXCITED little comment on the side of the Atlantic. *El libro ha provocado pocos comentarios en este lado de Atlántico.* ‖ **2.** To move (emotionally). *Emocionar, conmover.* ~His playing is superb technically, but he doesn't EXCITE me. *Toca maravillosamente desde un punto de vista técnico, pero no me conmueve.* ‖ **3.** Enthuse. *Entusiasmar.* ~Don't get too EXCITED about it. *No te entusiasmes, no te hagas demasiadas ilusiones.* ‖ **4.** [Revolt]. *Instigar.* ‖ **5.** To make impatient, boisterous. *Alborotar.* ‖ **6.** To become upset. *Agitarse, ponerse nervioso.* ~You mustn't EXCITE yourself. *No debes agitarte.* ‖ **7.** To urge. *Incitar.* ⇨EXITAR

EXCITED[2] [EXCITADO]. *adj.* Moved (with emotion). *Emocionado.* ~The news has EXCITED me. *Las noticias me han emocionado.* ‖ **2.** Enthused. *Entusiasmado.* ~I'm so EXCITED about the trip. *Estoy tan entusiasmado con el viaje.* ‖ **3.** [Voice]. *Lleno de emoción.* ‖ **4.** Nervous, worried, upset. *Agitado, nervioso.* ~Don't get EXCITED. *No te pongas nervioso.*

EXCLUSIVE [EXCLUSIVE]. Select. *Selecto, distinguido, elegante.* ~They are seen in the most EXCLUSIVE nightclubs. *Se los ven en los clubes nocturnos más elegantes.* ‖ **2.** [Club, group]. *Cerrado.* An EXCLUSIVE circle of intimate friends. *Un grupo cerrado de amigos íntimos.* ‖‖ **3.** Expensive, deluxe. *Caro, lujoso.* ~This is a very EXCLUSIVE hotel. *Este hotel es muy caro (lujoso).* ‖ **4.** Only. *Único.* The EXCLUSIVE way of going home was by boat. *La única forma de llegar a casa era por barco.* ~This room is for the EXCLUSIVE use of guests. *Solo para invitados.* ~Singing is not her EXCLUSIVE interest outside of work. *El cantar no es su único interés fuera del trabajo.* ‖ **5.** Aristocratic, snobbish. *Presuntuoso, estirado, de muchas ínfulas, que se da mucho tono.* It's a very EXCLUSIVE family. *Es una familia que se da mucho tono.*

EXCUSE[1]. *v.* To forgive. *Disculpar, perdonar.* ~Please EXCUSE the bad handwriting.

Disculpe (perdone) la mala letra. ~I'll EXCUSE you this time, but next time try to be prompt. *Te perdono esta vez, pero de ahora en adelante trata de llegar a tiempo.* || **2.** Release from obligation. *Disculpar.* ~They asked to be EXCUSED. *Pidieron que se los disculparan.* || **3.** Justify. *Justificar.* ~That doesn't EXCUSE your behavior. *Eso no justifica su comportamiento.* || **4.** *PHRASES* || •To EXCUSE somebody. *Dispensar, eximir a una persona.* ~She was EXCUSED from attending class today. *Le dispensaron la asistencia a clase hoy.* || •EXCUSE my saying so. *Perdone mi atrevimiento.* || •May I be EXCUSED for a moment? *¿Puedo salir un momento? (children asking permission to go to the toilet) ¿Puedo ir al baño (servicio)?* || •EXCUSE me! (attracting attention). *¡Oiga!, por favor!, con permiso, ¿me permite?* ~EXCUSE me, can I get past? *¿Me permite pasar?* EXCUSE me, but where is the theatre? *~¡Oiga, por favor!, me puede indicar dónde está el teatro?* ~EXCUSE me, but aren't you forgetting something? *Oiga, creo que se le está olvidando algo.* ~EXCUSE me I must go. *Con permiso de Ustedes tengo que marcharme.* || •After 10 minutes he EXCUSED himself. *Después de 10 minutos pidió permiso y se fue.* ⇨EXCUSAR

EXCUSE². *noun.* Pretext, justification. *Pretexto, jutificación, disculpa.* ~There's no EXCUSE for this. *Esto no admite disculpa.* ~He's always making EXCUSES for himself. *Siempre trata de justificarse.* ~It's only an EXCUSE. *Es un pretexto nada más.* || **2.** •He gives poverty as his EXCUSE. *Alega pobreza.* || **3.** •To offer an EXCUSE. *Disculparse, pedir perdón (disculpas).* || **4.** •He's a poor (rotten) EXCUSE for a lawyer. *Es un mal abogado.* ⇨EXCUSA

EXECUTE. *v.* [Order]. *Cumplir.* || **2.** [Task, scheme]. *Realizar, llevar a cabo.* ~The directors made the decisions, but the managers had to EXECUTE them. *Los directores tomaron las decisiones, pero las llevaron a cabo los gerentes.* || **3.** *JUR* [Will]. *Cumplir.* ~To EXECUTE a will. *Cumplir un*

testamento. || **4.** [Music]. *Interpretar.* || **5.** [Duties]. *Desempeñar, ejercer.* ~To EXECUTE the duties of director. *Desempeñar las funciones de director.* || **6.** [A banker's order]. *Hacer.* || **7.** [Treaty, contract]. *Firmar.* || **8.** JUR [A document]. *Legalizar.* || **9.** [Play]. *Representar.* ~The whole play was EXECUTED with great precision. *La obra entera se representó con toda perfección.* ⇨EJECUTAR

EXECUTION. *n.* [Of order]. *Cumplimiento.* || **2.** [Of duties]. *Desempeño.* ~In the EXECUTION of his duties. *En el desempeño de sus obligaciones.* || **3.** Signing (of a treaty, contract). *Firma.* || **4.** LAW Implementation. *Cumplimiento.* || **5.** LAW [Of a document]. *Legalización.* || **6.** [Of task]. *Realización.* || **7.** MUS Delivery, rendering. *Interpretación.* || **8.** [Of act, crime]. *Comisión.* ⇨EXECUTION

EXHIBIT¹ [algo EXHIBIDO]. *n.* [Art]. *Objeto expuesto, pieza de museo, obra expuesta (painting).* The museum houses several hundred EXHIBITS. *El museo alberga unos centenares de obras.* •On EXHIBIT. *Las pinturas expuestas.*|| **2.** [Law]. *Prueba experimental.*

EXHIBIT². *v.* [Art]. *Exponer, presentar al público.* ~Local artists will EXHIBIT their works starting on Sunday. *A partir del domingo, presentarán sus obras artistas de esta ciudad.* || **2.** Manifest (signs, symptoms). *Mostrar, manifestar.* ~To EXHIBIT symptoms of hysteria. *Mostrar símptomas de histeria.* || **3.** [Film]. *Presentar.* || **4.** [Document, passport]. *Presentar.* ⇨EXHIBIR

EXHIBITION. *n.* [Art]. *Exposición.* Her works are on EXHIBITION in this gallery. *Sus obras están expuestas en esta galería.* || **2.** Display. *Muestra, demostración.* ~An EXHIBITION of bad temper. *Una demostración de mal genio.* || **3.** Trade fair. *Feria.* || **4.** •To be on EXHIBITION. *Estar actualmente expuesto.* || **5.** •To make an EXHIBITION of oneself. *Ponerse en ridículo.* || **6.** •EXHIBITION hall. *Sala (salón) de exposición.* ⇨EXHIBICIÓN

EXPAND. *v.* To enlarge. *Ampliar.* ~He

reads daily in order to EXPAND his vocabulary. *Lee todos lo días para ampliar su vocabulario.* ~He EXPANDED his business. *Amplió su negocio.* || **2.** [Gas, metal]. *Dilatar.* ~Heat EXPANDS metals. *El calor dilata los metales.* || **3.** To grow. *Crecer, ampliar.* ~His business has EXPANDED considerably these last few years. *Su negocio creció mucho estos últimos años.* || **4.** Become more friendly. *Abrirse.* || **5.** [Wings]. *Abrir, desplegar.* || **6.** [Math]. *Desarrollar.* || **7.** [Lungs]. *Dilatar, ensanchar.* || **8.** [Awareness]. *Aumentar.* || **9.** [Horizons]. *Ampliar, ensanchar.* || **10.** [Influence, role]. *Extender.* ~The minister sought to EXPAND his influence. *El ministro buscó extender su influencia.* || **11.** [Rubber band]. *Estirarse.* || **12.** To give further details. *Extenderse (sobre), explayarse (en).* || **13.** To broaden. *Ensancharse.* ~The river EXPANDS and makes a lake. *El río se ensancha y forma un río.* || **14.** •To EXPAND on. *Ampliar.* Can you EXPAND on your theory a little? *¿Podría ampliar un poco su teoría?* ⇨ EXPANDIR

EXPECT. *v.*

❶ TO AWAIT. *Esperar (algo o alguien).* ~I have been EXPECTING you. *Te estaba esperando.* ~I am EXPECTING an important letter from France. *Estoy esperando una carta importante de Francia.* ~She's EXPECTING a baby. *Espera un bebé.* ~We're EXPECTING rain. *Estamos esperando lluvia.* ~Great events are expected. *Se esperan grandes acontecimientos.* ~Is he EXPECTING you? *¿Tiene Ud. cita con él?*

❷ HOPE (FOR), PLAN, LOOK FORWARD TO. *Aspirar, esperar, querer.* The journey was not as nice as she had EXPECTED. *El viaje no fue tan agradable como se lo había imaginado.* ~Are you going to do some work, or would that be too much to EXPECT? *¿Vas a trabajar un poco o eso sería mucho que pedir?* ~He EXPECTS to be president one day. *Espera llegar a ser presidente algún día.* ~A job and a place to live, is all we EXPECT. *Lo único que queremos es un empleo y un lugar donde vivir.* ~We had EXPECTED to be consulted at the very least. *Lo menos que podrían haber hecho es consultarnos.* ~You can't EXPECT any money from your father. *No puedes esperar ningún dinero de tu padre.*

❸ ASSUME, SUPPOSE, IMAGINE, BELIEVE. *Creer, prever, suponer, imaginar.* ~The delinquency rate is EXPECTED to increase next year. *Se prevé que el próximo año aumentará el índice de criminalidad (Prats).* ~ I half-EXPECTED that to happen. *Suponía que iba a ocurrir.* ~I EXPECT she's in the office. *Imagino que estará en la oficina.* ~I expect so. *Supongo que sí.* ~I EXPECT he's there by now. *Me imagino que ya habrá llegado.*

❹ REGARD AS LIKELY TO HAPPEN, ANTICIPATE. *Prever, considerar segura o probable una cosa.* The police does not EXPECT violence. *La policía no prevé actos de violencia.* ~He is EXPECTED to arrive at eight o'clock in the morning. *Tiene prevista su llegada a las ocho de la mañana.* ~It is widely EXPECTED that a statement will be issued in the morning. *Se considera muy probable que se dé a conocer el informe mañana por la mañana.*

❺ DEMAND, REQUIRE, COUNT ON. *Contar con, pedir, requerir, exigir, solicitar; considerar que una persona tiene determinada obligación.* ~I EXPECT your cooperation. *Cuento con su colaboración.* ~A speech will be EXPECTED of you. *Se le pedirá que dé un discurso.* ~You're EXPECTED to work late if need be. *Se le exije que se quede trabajando si es necesario.* ~I EXPECT you to be punctual. *Cuento con que sea puntual.* ~Borrowers are EXPECTED to return books on time. *Se requiere que los usuarios devuelvan los libros a su debido tiempo.* ~I don't EXPECT you to pay me at once. *No pretendo que me pagues en seguida.* Employees are EXPECTED to be at work on time. *Los empleados deberán llegar puntualmente.*

❻ TO KNOW, BELIEVE. *Saber o creer que va a llegar a occurir algo a alguien, esperar, creer, pensar.* ~Nobody EXPECTED the strike to succeed. *Nadie creía que iba a tener éxito la huelga.* ~I EXPECTED her to complain. *Creí (pensé) que iba a protestar.* ~ I EXPECTED as much. *Ya me lo esperaba.* ~ I knew what to EXPECT. *Sabía a que atenerme.* ~I wouldn't have EXPECTED such behavior from you. *No esperaba tal comportamiento de su parte, no creía que se iba a comportarse así.* ~As one might EXPECT. *Como es de esperar.*

❼ OTHER MEANINGS. To deem, consider. *Considerar, juzgar.* The talks are EXPECTED to last two or three weeks. *Se considera que las negociaciones durarán unas dos o tres semanas.* ‖ **2.** To be faced with. *Aguardar.* ~He can EXPECT a life of hardship. *Le espera una vida de muchas privaciones.*

❽ EXPRESSIONS. ‖ •To be EXPECTING. *Estar embarazada.* ‖ •I EXPECT to have a good time. *Me prometo (cuento con) divertirme.* ‖ •When least EXPECTED. *El día menos pensado.* ‖ •What do you EXPECT me to do about it? *¿Qué pretendes que haga yo?* ‖ •How do you EXPECT me to go out like this? *¿Cómo pretendes que salga así?* ‖ •She can't be EXPECTED to know that. *No está obligada a saber eso.* ‖ •Tracey didn't leave a forwarding address but then what can you EXPECT? *Tracey no nos dejo su dirección, pero él es así (que otra cosa se puede esperar de él).*

EXPECTATION. *n.* •Our EXPECTATION is that. *Esperamos que.* ‖ **2.** •In EXPECTATION of. *Con la esperanza de.* ~We work with the expectation to be paid. *Trabajamos con la esperanza de que nos paguen.* ‖ **3.** •The performance came up to/fell short of our EXPECTATIONS. *La actuación estuvo/no estuvo a la altura de lo que esperábamos.* ‖ **4.** •Contrary to EXPECTATION. *Contrariamente a (en contra de) lo que se esperaba.* ‖ **5.** •Not to come up to somebody's EXPECTATIONS. *No alcanzar las expectativas de alguien.* ‖ **6.** •Beyond EXPECTATION. *Por encima de lo esperado.* ‖ **7.** •To exceed one's EXPECTATIONS. *Sobrepasar lo que se esperaba.* ‖ **8.** •To fall below one's EXPECTATIONS. *No llegar a lo que se esperaba.* ‖ **9.** •To have high EXPECTATIONS.

Tener muchas esperanzas de algo. ⇨EXPECTACIÓN

EXPEDIENT [EXPEDIENTE]. *adj.* Convenient, useful, desirable, suitable, appropriate. *Conveniente, oportuno.* They adopt the measure they deem the most EXPEDIENT. *Adoptan las medidas que juzgan más convenientes.* ~Count on him to do what is EXPEDIENT and ignore what is honest. *Puede estar seguro de que hará lo que es más oportuno y olvidará lo que es más honrado.*

EXPEDITE. *v.* Speed-up, hasten, execute promply. *Accelerar.* ~A measure intended to EXPEDITE the ship-building program. *Una medida para accelerar el proyecto de construccion naval.* ‖ **2.** [Business]. *Despachar.* ‖ **3.** [Progress]. *Facilitar.* ‖ **4.** [Legal matters, petition]. *Dar curso.* ⇨EXPEDIR

EXPERIENCE. *v.* [Difficulty]. *Tener, encontrarse con.* ~We EXPERIENCED great difficulty in selling our house. *Tuvimos muchos problemas en vender nuestra casa.* ‖ **2.** Feel (pain, pleasure, relief). *Sentir.* ~Did you EXPERIENCE any pain in your back? *¿Sintió algun dolor en la parte inferior de la espalda?* ‖ **3.** Live through, undergo, face (loss, setback, delays, fate). *Sufrir.* ~The reason death was feared was because no man could EXPERIENCE its impact. *El motivo que se temía a la muerte es que a ningún hombre le es dado sufrir su impacto.* ‖ **4.** •To EXPERIENCE hardship. *Pasar penurias.* ⇨EXPERIMENTAR

EXPIRE [EXPIRAR]. *v.* To become void. *Vencer, caducar (ticket).* ~Your subscription EXPIRES on the first of July. *Su suscripción vence el primero de julio.* My passport EXPIRES next week. *Mi pasaporte vence la semana que viene.* ‖ **2.** To end (term of office, treaty). *Terminar, finalizar.*

EXPLORE. *v.* Investigate. *Investigar.* ~What's over there? Let's go and EXPLORE. *¿Qué hay allí? Vamos a investigar.* ⇨ EXPLORAR

EXPOSE. *v.* To make known, disclose, or reveal (intentions, secrets, etc.) *Divulgar, revelar, poner al descubierto, sacar a la*

luz. ~To EXPOSE a voting fraud. *Poner al descubierto un fraude electoral.* || **2.** To reveal or unmask (a crime, fraud, impostor, etc.). *Desenmascarar.* ~The newspaper story EXPOSED him as a liar. *El artículo en el periodico demostró que era un mentiroso.* || **3.** [Weakness]. *Descubrir.* || **4.** [Falsity]. *Demostrar.* || **5.** || **6.** [ignorance, inefficiency, weakness]. *Descubrir.* || **7.** •To EXPOSE oneself. *Exhibirse desnudo.* ⇨ EXPONER

EXTEND. *v.* Enlarge (space). *Ampliar.* ~She wants to EXTEND her country home. *Quiere ampliar su casa de campo.* || **2.** Lengthen (road). *Alargar.* || **3.** Give, offer. *Dar, rendir, entregar.* He EXTENDED the letter to the manager. *Hizo entrega de la carta al director.* || **4.** [Invitation]. *Invitar, cursar (of a written invitation).* || **5.** [Welcome]. *Dar.* ~To EXTEND a warm welcome. *Dar una calurosa bienvenida.* || **6.** Prolong (time). *Prolongar, alargar, aplazar.* ~I asked them to EXTEND my travel insurance. *Solicité que prorrogaran el seguro de viaje.* ~Regular maintenance EXTENDS a car's life. *El mantenimiento regular alarga la vida de un coche.* ~EXTENDED illness. *Enfermedad prolongada.* ~He has been granted EXTENDED leave. *Se le ha permitido prolongar su permiso.* ~The deadline has been EXTENDED. *Se ha prorrogado el plazo.* || **7.** [Credit]. *Otorgar, conceder.* ~To EXTEND somebody extended credit. *Conceder a uno un crédito ilimitado.* || **8.** [Aid]. *Ofrecer.* || **9.** To tax the strength of. *Exigir el máximo esfuerzo.* ~We need exercises that will EXTEND our pupils. *Necesitamos ejercicios que exijan el máximo rendimiento de nuestros alumnos.* || **10.** [Simpathy]. *Manifestar, ofrecer.* || **11.** [Building]. *Ensanchar, ampliar.* ⇨ EXTENDER

EXTENSION. *n.* [Of time]. *Prórroga.* He was given an EXTENSION to finish his thesis. *Se le dio una prórroga para que pudiera terminar su tésis.* || **2.** [Passport]. *Renovación.* || **3.** [Building]. *Ensanche, ampliación.* ~They are having an EXTENSION built. *Están haciendo ampliaciones.* || **4.** Annex, wing (hotel, hospital, museum). *Anexo.*

~The hotel EXTENSION. *El anexo del hotel.* ~They are having an EXTENSION built. ~*Están construyendo un anexo, nuevo pabellón (a un hospital o museo).* || **5.** [Of road, canal]. *Prolongación.* ~A canal extension. *La prolongación de un canal.* || **6.** [Cable, cord]. *Prolongación.* || **7.** Appendage. *Prolongación.* The brush seemed an EXTENSION of his hand. *El pincel parecía una prolongación de su mano.* || **8.** •En toda la EXTENSIÓN del territorio nacional. *Throughout the country.* || **9.** •EXTENSION classes. *Cursos nocturnos (organizados por una universidad).* || **10.** •EXTENSION ladder. *Escalera extensible.* ⇨ EXTENSIÓN

EXTENUATE. *v.* To represent (a fault, offense, etc.) as less serious. *Aminorar, mitigar, disminuir (la gravedad de algo).* ⇨ EXTENUAR

EXTINGUISH. *v.* [Candle, cigar, fire]. *Apagar.* ~Please EXTINGUISH all cigarettes. *Sírvase apagar sus cigarrillos.* ~It took the firefighters more than three hours to EXTINGUISH the fire. *Los bomberos tardaron más de tres horas en apagar el incendio.* || **2.** LIT [Hope, memory]. *Apagar.* || **3.** [Debt]. *Cancelar.* || **4.** [Obligation]. *Cumplir con.* || **5.** [Title]. *Suprimir.* ⇨ EXTINGUIR

EXTRA [EXTRA]. *adj.* Spare. *De sobra.* ~I have two EXTRA tickets. *Tengo dos entradas de sobra, me sobran dos entradas.* || **2.** More. *Más.* ~We need two EXTRA chairs. *Necesitamos dos sillas más.* ~We will have to work EXTRA. *Tendremos que trabajar más.* || **3.** Special. *Especial, excepcional.* ~To take EXTRA care. *Ir con especial cuidado.* ~You must make an EXTRA effort. *Tiene que hacer un esfuerzo excepcional.* ~That little EXTRA something. *Ese algo especial.* || **4.** Maximun. *Mayor.* ~For EXTRA security. *Para mayor seguridad.* || **5.** Subject to additional charge. *Más, aparte, no incluido.* ~A shower is two dollars EXTRA. *Con ducha cuesta dos dólares más* ~The wine is EXTRA. *El vino se cobra aparte, el vino no está incluido.* ~Service EXTRA. *El servicio no está incluido (en el precio).* ~Singing lessons are EXTRA. *La* *clases de canto son aparte.* || **6.** [Part]. *Recambio, repuesto.* || **7.** *PHRASES.* || •EXTRA charge. *Suplemento, recargo.* || •EXTRA luggage. *Exceso de equipaje.* || •EXTRA pay. *Sobresueldo.* || •EXTRA time (in soccer). *Prórroga, tiempo suplementario.* || •EXTRA weight. *Sobrecarga.* || •EXTRA work. *Horas extraordinarias.* || •I brought an EXTRA pair of socks. *He traido un par de calcetines de más (de repuesto).* || •To make some EXTRA copies. *Hacer unas copias de más.* || •We install it at no EXTRA charge. *La instalación viene incluida.*

EXTRAVAGANT. *adj.* Lavish, prodigal. *Pródigo.* || **2.** Wasteful. *Despilfarrador, derrochador.* || **3.** Luxurious. *Lujoso, suntuoso, de lujo, dispendioso.* ~It seems very EXTRAVAGANT to have three cars. *Parece un lujo excesivo tener tres coches.* ~Let's be EXTRAVAGANT. *Démonos este lujo.* ~He has EXTRAVAGANT tastes. *Tiene gustos dispendiosos.* || **4.** [Price]. *Exhorbitant.* ~She paid an EXTRAVAGANT price for it. *Le costó un disparate.* || **5.** [Praise, claim, compliment]. *Exagerado, excesivo, desmesurado.* ~EXTRAVAGANT claims about the effectiveness of the system. *Afirmaciones exageradas (excesivas) sobre la eficacia del sistema.* ⇨EXTRAVAGANTE

EXUBERANT [EXUBERANTE]. *adj.* [Person]. *Eufórico, efusivo, rebosante.*

F

FABRICATE. *v.* Forge. *Falsear, falsificar (documentos).* ~He admitted to having FABRICATED the data in his application. *Confesó que la información en el formulario era falsa.* ~The police was accused of FABRICATING evidence. *Se le acusó a la policia de falsificar las pruebas.* ‖ **2.** [Story, lie]. *Inventar.* ~Numerous lies FABRICATED by politicians were already in circulation. *Andaban en boca de todos un montón de mentiras ideadas (inventadas) por los políticos.* ‖ **3.** [Metal]. *Labrar.* ~To FABRICATE steel into plates. *Labrar, acerar en chapas.* ⇨FABRICAR

FABRICATION. *n.* Story, lie. *Falsedad, mentira, invención, cuento.* ~It is pure FABRICATION. *Es pura invención (ficción).* ⇨FABRICACIÓN

FACILITY. *n.* Works, installations. *Obras, instalaciones.* ~The port FACILITIES. *Las obras del puerto.* ~A sports FACILITY. *Unas instalaciones deportivas.* ‖ **2.** Feature. *Ventajas, prestaciones.* ~This computer offers a wide range of FACILITIES. *Esta computadora ofrece una amplia gama de prestaciones.* ‖ **3.** Services, conveniences, amenities, accomodations. *Servicios, comodidades, ventajas.* The village lacks certain basic FACILITIES. *Al pueblo le faltan algunos servicios básicos.* ~The hotel has conference FACILITIES. *El hotel dispone de una sala de conferencia.* ~Cooking FACILITIES in all rooms. *Se puede cocinar en todas las habitaciones.* ~Cooking FACILITIES. *Derecho a cocina.* ‖ **4.** Buildings, equipment and services provided for a particular purpose. *Complejo, centro, instalación, local.* ~Military, sports, recreational FACILITIES. *Instalaciones militares, deportivas, recreativas.* ~FACILITIES for the disabled. *Instalaciones para minusválidos.* ⇨FACILIDAD

FACTION. *n.* A group or clique within a larger group. *Grupo, sector.* ⇨FACCIÓN

FACTORY [FACTORÍA]. *n.* Works, mill, plant. *Fábrica.* ‖ **2.** •FACTORY worker. *Obrero.*

FACULTY. Teaching body. *Profesorado, cuerpo docente.* ⇨FACULTAD

FAIL. *v.* [Exam]. *Suspender.* ~She FAILED biology. *La suspendieron en biología.* ‖ **2.** [Show, film, attempt]. *Fracasar.* ~The attempt FAILED. *El intento fracasó.* ‖ **3.** [Crops, harvest]. *Perderse, malograrse.* ‖ **4.** Go bankrupt, go out of business. *Quebrar.* ‖ **5.** Forget, neglect. *Dejar de.* ~Don't FAIL to come. *No dejes de venir.* ~She never FAILS to attend. *Nunca falta.* ‖ **6.** [Health]. *Deteriorarse, decaerse, debilitarse.* ~He could no longer read because of his FAILING eyesight. *La vista se le había deteriorado tanto que ya no podía leer.* ‖ **7.** Not do (something). *No hacer (algo), no lograr, conseguir hacer (algo).* ~He FAILED to score. *No logró marcar.* ~He FAILED to live up to our expectations. *No dio todo lo que se esperaba de él.* ~The engine FAILED to start the first time. *El motor no arrancó de entrada.* ~You FAILED to mention the crucial point. *No has mencionado el punto esencial.* ~Doctors FAILED to save his life. *Los médicos no lograron salvarle la vida.* ►"To fail to do something may often be translated into Spanish by a simple negative: He FAILED to come. *No vino.* He FAILED to answer the invitation. *No contestó a la invitación"* (Gran Diccionario Larousse). ‖ **8.** [Hopes]. *Frustrarse.* ‖ **9.** To run out, fall short. *Acabarse.* ~When the supplies FAILED. *Cuando se acabaron* *los víveres.* || **10.** To stop functioning or operating. *Descomponerse, dejar de funcionar.* The electricity FAILED during the storm. *Se descompuso la electricidad durante la tempestad.* || **11.** Let down, forsake. *Abandonar.* His friends FAILED him. *Sus amigos le abandonaron.* || **12.** PHRASES. || •I FAIL to see why. *No veo por qué.* ~I FAIL to see why he did not admit it. *No veo por qué no se lo confesó.* || •If everything else FAILS. *Como último recurso.* ~If everything FAILS we'll request a loan. *Como último recurso solicitaremos un préstamo.* || •It never FAILS to amaze me. *Nunca deja de sorprenderme.* || •To FAIL in one's duty. *Faltar a (no cumplir) su deber.* || •Without FAIL. *Sin falta.* ~I'll be there at ten without FAIL. *Estaré allí a las diez sin falta.* || •Words FAIL me. *No encuentro palabras.* ~In describing Mozart's genius, words FAIL me. *No encuentro palabras para describir el genio de Mozart.* ⇨FALLAR

FALLACY. *n.* Mistaken idea, misconception. *Error, sofismo, idea falsa o errónea, argumento falso o equivocado.* ~It's a common FALLACY that women are worse drivers than men. *Es errónea la idea generalizada de que las mujeres manejan peor que los hombres.* ~Many people believe sincerely in the FALLACY of neutrality. *Mucha gente cree sinceramente en la mentira de la neutralidad.* ~The tenet that war is the natural condition of man is an abominable FALLACY. *El apotegma de que la guerra es el estado natural del hombre es un sofismo abominable.* ⇨FALACIA

FALSE. *adj.* Not genuine (eyelashes, fingernails, teeth]. *Postizo.* || **2.** Incorrect, wrong, erroneous, mistaken (belief, idea, impression). *Erróneo, equivocado.* ~We often make FALSE assumptions about people of other cultures. *Con frecuencia hacemos suposiciones erróneas sobre personas que pertenecen a otras culturas.* ~You'll get a FALSE impression of the town if you only visit the university. *Vas a tener una idea errónea (equivocada) de la ciudad si sólo visitas la universidad.* || **3.** Not faithful or loyal (friend, wife). *Infiel.* || **4.** Insincere.

Forzado. A FALSE laugh. *Una sonrisa forzada.* || **5.** EXPRESSIONS. || •FALSE ceiling. *Cielo raso.* || •FALSE claims. (I) *Reclamaciones fraudulentas,* (II) *Pretensión infundada.* || •FALSE move. *Paso en falso.* ~One FALSE move and you're dead! *¡Un paso en falso y te mato!* || •FALSE bottom. *Fondo doble.* || •FALSE imprisonment. *Detención ilegal.* || •FALSE start (sport). *Salida nula.* || •Under FALSE pretenses. *Por (con, mediante) fraude, con engaño(s).* ~He acquired the title under FALSE pretenses. *Obtuvo el título por medios fraudulentos.* || •True or FALSE? *¿Verdad o mentira?* ⇨FALSO

FALSIFY [FALSIFICAR]. *v.* Misrepresent (story, issue, truth, situation). *Falsear.* He FALSIFIED the history of his family to conceal his humble origins. *Falseó la historia de su familia para esconder su humilde origen.* || **2.** To distort, misrepresent (history). *Desvirtuar.* || **3.** [Liquor, wine]. *Adulterar.* ~Producing FALSIFIED champagne for sale in hotels. *Produciendo champán adulterado para vender en los hoteles.* || **4.** To prove to be false (theory, judgement). *Desmentir, refutar.* || **5.** [Hopes]. *Frustrar.*

FAMILIAR. *adj.*
❶ COMMON, WELL-KNOWN (Song, word, expression, face). *Común, conocido.* ~A FAMILIAR song. *Una canción muy conocida.* ~FAMILIAR faces. *Caras conocidas.* It's a FAMILAR expression. ~*Es una expresión muy conocida.* ~It's a FAMILIAR feeling. *Es un sentimiento común, es un sentimiento que conocemos todos.* ~He was a FAMILIAR sight around the bars of the district. *Se le veía con frecuencia en los bares de la zona.* ~These violent scenes are becoming all too FAMILIAR. *Estas escenas violentas se dan con demasiada frecuencia.* || **2.** Easily recognizable. FAMILIAR scents which carry you back to early childhood. *Aromas que hacen recordar nuestra infancia.* || **3.** •A FAMILIAR story. *Un cuento de todos los días.* ~The old lady was a FAMILIAR sight in the village. *La anciana era muy conocida en el pueblo.* || **4.** •His name is FAMILIAR. *El nombre me suena.* || **5.** •It's the old FAMILIAR story. *Es la historia de siempre.*

❷ KNOWING PERSONALLY (PERSON). Intimate, close, friendly. *De confianza, íntimo.* ~He's a FAMILIAR friend. *Es un amigo íntimo.* || **2.** Unduly intimate; too personal; taking liberties. *Que se toma demasiadas libertades con alguien, demasiado amigable.* ~The duchess dislikes FAMILIAR servants. *A la duquesa no le gusta que los criados se tomen demasiadas libertades.* ~He's too FAMILIAR with my wife. *Es demasiado amigable con mi esposa.* || **3.** •To be on FAMILIAR terms. *Conocer (person).* ~He's on FAMILIAR terms with all the teachers. *Conoce personalmente a (tiene confianza con) todos los maestros.*
❸ VARIOUS. [Excuse]. *Consabido.* || **2.** Usual, cutomary, habitual. *Acostumbrado.* ~We walked along the FAMILIAR path that leads to my grandmother's house. *Anduvimos por el acostumbrado camino que conduce a la casa de la abuela.* || **3.** Informal (speech, writing). *Sencillo, simple, llano.* To write in a FAMILAR style. *Escribe en un estilo llano.*
❹ EXPRESSIONS. || •To be FAMILIAR with. *Estar al corriente, conocer, estar enterado de.* ~I'm FAMILIAR with the details. *Estoy al corriente de los detalles.* ~Are you FAMILIAR with this type of machine? *¿Conoces esta clase de máquina?* ~Are you FAMILIAR with the works of Shakespeare? *¿Has leído las obras de Shakespeare?* ⇨FAMILIAR

FASTIDIOUS. *adj.* Demanding, hard to please. *Quisquilloso, melindroso.* ~The boss is very FASTIDIOUS when he checks the reports. *El jefe es muy quisquilloso cuando revisa los informes.* || **2.** [About cleanliness]. *Exigente.* ~I'm FASTIDIOUS about cleanliness. *Soy muy exigente en cuanto a la limpieza.* || **3.** [Taste]. *Fino.* || **4.** [Mind]. *Refinado.* || **5.** Too fussy. *Maniático, mañoso* (Lat. Am.). || **6.** Painstaking. *Sumo.* •Chosen with FASTIDIOUS care. *Elegido con sumo cuidado.* ~He dresses with FASTIDIOUS care. *Viste con suma elegancia.* || **7.** [Food]. *Delicado.* The child is very FASTIDIOUS with the food. *~El niño es muy delicado en la comida.* ⇨FASTIDIOSO

FATAL. *adj.* Deadly, lethal. *Mortal.* ~It is not known who fired the MORTAL shot. *No se sabe quién disparó el tiro que le causó la muerte.* ~A FATAL dose of poison. *Una cantidad mortal de veneno.* || **2.** Disastrous, damaging, harmful (decision, mistake). *Funesto, de funestas consecuencias.* ~To delay was FATAL to the project. *El retraso tuvo consecuencias funestas para el proyecto.* It would be FATAL to say that ... *Sería funesto (tendría funestas consecuencias) asumir que* ... || **3.** Decisively important, fateful. *Fatídico, decisivo.* ~The FATAL day arrived for David to take a decision. *Llegó para David el día fatídico de tomar una decisión.* || **4.** •That was FATAL. *Eso fue el colmo.* || **5.** •It's FATAL to say that. *Es peligroso decir eso.* ⇨FATAL

FATALITY. *n.* Death resulting from a disaster. *Victima, muerto.* ~There were no FATALITIES. *No hubo muertos.* || **2.** Disaster. *Calamidad, desgracia.* ~Floods, earthquakes and other FATALITIES. *Inundaciones, terremotos y otras calamidades.* ⇨FATALIDAD

FATUOUS. *adj.* Silly, foolish. *Necio, tonto.* ~He made some FATUOUS remarks. *Hizo comentarios tontos.* He's a FATUOUS man. *Es un necio.* ⇨FATUO

FAULT. *n.* Defect (in character). *Defecto.* ~He has many FAULTS. *Tiene muchos defectos.* || **2.** [In manufacturing}. *Desperfecto, imperfección.* || **3.** Blame. *Culpa.* ~It's their FAULT. *Es culpa suya.* || **4.** GEOL *Falla.* || **5.** Breakdown (of machinery]. *Avería.* ⇨FALTA

FELONY. *n.* Crime *Crimen, delito mayor (grave).* ⇨FELONÍA

FIGURATIVE [FIGURATIVO]. *adj.* Abstract. *Figurado, metafórico.* In a FIGURATIVE sense. *En sentido figurado.*

FIGURE[1]. *verb.* To reckon, imagine. *Imaginarse, suponer, calcular, pensar.* ~I never FIGURED that he would get angry. *Nunca me imaginé que se iba a enojar.* ~I never FIGURED her to be the guilty one. *Nunca me imaginé que ella era la culpable.* ~I FIGURED you'd want to rest after the journey. *Pensé que después del viaje quisieras descansar.*

FIGURE **100**

~They FIGURED on about 20 people being there. *Calcularon que iban a venir unas 20 personas.* || **2.** Conclude, decide. *Llegar a la conclusión.* ~He FIGURED it was no use to complain. *Llegó a la conclusión de que era inútil quejarse.* || **3.** Regard, consider (oneself). *Considerarse, juzgarse.* ~He FIGURES himself a good candidate to the presidency. *Se considera como un buen candidato a la presidencia.* || **4.** To be important or conspicuous. *Sobresalir, destacarse.* ~He FIGURED prominently in last year's elections. *Ocupó un lugar destacado en las últimas elecciones.* ~Kennedy's descendants were to FIGURE prominently in the history of the country. *Los descendientes de Kennedy habian de destacarse en la historia de la nación.* || **5.** [With *on*]. (I) To count or rely on. *Esperar, contar con.* ~They hadn't FIGURED ON our finding their hideout. *No contaba con que encontraríamos su escondite.* ~You mustn't FIGURE ON his help. *No puede contar con su ayuda,* (II) To take into consideration; plan on, consider (doing something). *Pensar, tener pensado, tener la intención.* ~He doesn't FIGURE ON going to Paris soon. *No tiene planes inmediatos de ir a París.* ~How soon are you FIGURING ON getting married. *Cuando piensa (tiene pensado) casarse.* ~We'd FIGURED ON helping you. *Teníamos pensado ayudarles, nuestra intención era ayudarles.* || **6.** [With *out*]. (I) Understand. *Comprender, entender, explicarse.* ~He couldn't FIGURE OUT where all the money had gone. *No se explicaba donde había ido a parar el dinero.* ~I can't FIGURE OUT why he did it. *No me explico por qué lo hizo.* ~I can't FIGURE him out. *No le entiendo,* (II) Descifrar. *Decipher, make out.* ~I can't FIGURE OUT his writing. *No puedo decifrar su letra,* (III) Calculate, work out, compute (sum, profit). *Calcular.* I didn't have time to FIGURE OUT last year's profits. *No he tenido tiempo de calcular las ganancias del año pasado, (IV)* Find, come up with, solve, decide. *Encontrar manera de, resolver, decidir.* ~I haven't FIGURED OUT how to do

it yet. *~Todavía no he encontrado la manera de hacerlo.* || **7.** [With *in*]. Add, include. *Añadir, incluir.* ~Don't forget to FIGURE IN the rent and the telephone on the bill. *No te olvides de incluir el alquiler y el teléfono en la cuenta.* || **8.** Picture mentally. *Representarse.* || **9.** Appear. *Aparecer.* This theme FIGURES largely in her work. *Este tema ocupa un lugar prominente en su obra.* || **10.** To make sense, be reasonable, be expected. *Ser lógico, ser de esperar.* ~They're getting divorced -that FIGURES! *Se van a divorciar. -¡No me extraña nada!* ~It rained the entire weekend. Oh, that FIGURES (that was to be expected). *Llovió todo el fin de semana. ¡Cuándo no!* || **11.** To compute, calculate. *Calcular.* ~He FIGURED his expenses for the month. *Calculó los gastos del mes.* ⇨ FIGURAR

FIGURE[2] [FIGURA]. *n.* Number. *Número.* ~Add together this column of FIGURES. *Suma esta columna de números.* ~In round FIGURES. *En números redondos.* || **2.** [With *double, three, four, etc*]. *Número o cantidad entre 10 y 99, 100 y 999, 1000 y 9999, etc.* ~Inflation is now into double FIGURES. *La inflación pasa del 10%.* ~Her salary is well into six FIGURES. *Gana bastante más de 100.000.00 dólares.* || **3.** [Officially published number; often used with the adjectives *low* or *high*]. *Cifra.* ~The PRODUCTION figures are low. *Las cifras de producción son bajas.* A high FIGURE of mortality. *Una cifra elevada de mortalidad.* || **4.** A particular amount of money. *Cantidad, suma.* ~An estimated FIGURE of a million dollars. *Una (cantidad) suma aproximada de un millón de dólares.* || **5.** Price. *Precio.* ~I know it's worth a lot of money but I couldn't put a FIGURE on it. *Sé que cuesta mucho, pero no sabría adivinar el precio.* || **6.** Shape of one's body (especially of a woman). *Tipo, línea.* ~She has a great FIGURE. *Tiene buen tipo, tiene un tipo estupendo.* ~To keep/loose/watch one's FIGURE. *Guardar/perder/cuidar la línea.* || **7.** Look, aspect. *Presencia, aspecto.* He has a good FIGURE. *Tiene* *mucha presencia.* ~A fine FIGURE of a man. *Un hombre bien plantado.*‖ **8.** Performance. *Actuación, papel.* To cut a brilliant FIGURE. *Hacer un buen papel.* ~To cut a sorry FIGURE. *Salir desairado, parecer ridículo.* ‖ **9.** Object noticeable only as a shape. *Silueta.* ~A FIGURE loomed out of the mist. *Apareció una silueta en la niebla.* ‖ **10.** Drawing, diagram (in a book). *Dibujo, grabado, ilustración.* ‖ **11.** •Figure SKATING. *Patinaje artístico.*

FINAL. *adj.* Conclusive, decisive. *Definitivo.* ~He reached a FINAL decision. *Su decisión fue definitiva.* ‖ **2.** Last. *Último.* ~He died on the FINAL days of combat. *Murió en los últimos días de la contienda.* ~And that's my FINAL offer. *Es mi última oferta.* ~The FINAL chapter of a book. *El último capítulo de un libro.* ‖ **3.** *PHRASES.* ‖ •FINAL demand (of payment). *Último aviso de pago.* ‖ •And that's FINAL. *Y no hay más que hablar.* ~You can't go and that's FINAL. *No puedes ir y no hay más que hablar.* ‖ •The judges' decision will be FINAL. *Las decisiones de los jueces serán inapelables.* ‖ •I would like to make one FINAL point. *Y por último quisiera señalar que ...* ‖ •That's my FINAL word on the subject. *Y no se hable más del asunto.* ‖ •In the FINAL analysis. *A fin the cuentas.* ⇨FINAL

FINALITY. *n.* Conclusiveness or decisiveness (of decision, statement, answer). *Resolución, irrevocabilidad, carácter definitivo. De modo tajante (terminante).* ~He said it with FINALITY. *Lo dijo de modo terminante.* ⇨FINALIDAD

FINALIZE. *v.* [Plans, arrangements]. *Ultimar, concretar.* Plans have not yet been FINALIZED. *No se se han concretado los planes todavía.* ~The couple FINALIZED plans to marry at once. *La pareja ha terminado los últimos preparativos para su pronto casamiento.* ‖ **2.** [Date]. *Fijar, concretar.* ‖ **3.** To give final approval. *Aprobar de modo difinitivo.* ~We FINALIZED the agreement yesterday by signing the contract. *Firmamos el contrato ayer aprobando así el acuerdo de modo definitivo.* ‖ **4.** Finish, complete.

Acabar, terminar, concluir. ~Soon my conclusions will be FINALIZED. *Pronto concluiré mis conclusiones.* ⇨FINALIZAR

FINALS *n.* [University]. *Exámenes de fin de curso.* ⇨FINALES

FINE. *adj.*
❶ EXCELLENT, SUPERIOR (in quality or appearance). *Excelente, magnífico, admirable.* ~A FINE piece of work. *Un excelente trabajo.* ~A FINE performance. *Una excelente representación.* ~It's a FINE thing what you're doing. *Es algo admirable lo que estás haciendo.* ~He's a FINE person. *Es una excelente persona.* ~A FINE future. *Un mágnifico porvenir.* ‖ **2.** Refined, discriminating (taste). *Refinado, delicado.* ~Only the FINEST of palates will appreciate this meal. *Sólo los paladares más refinados (delicados) apreciarán esta comida.* ‖ **3.** [Wine, ingredients]. *Selecto, de primera calidad.* ~Goods of the FINEST quality. *Artículos de la mejor calidad.* ‖ **4.** Brilliant. *Brillante.* ~The country's FINEST minds. *Los cerebros más brillantes del país.* ‖ **5.** Beautiful, elegant, smart (woman, clothes). *Elegante.* ~FINE clothes. *Ropa elegante.* ‖ **6.** Exquisite. *Primoroso.* ~FINE hand. *Letra primorosa.* ‖ **7.** Highly skilled or accomplished. *Excelente, magnífico.* ~A FINE pianist. *Un excelente pianista.* ‖ **8.** Best. *Mejor.* ~The FINEST collection of Impressionist paintings are in the Musée d'Orsay in París. *La mejor colección de cuadros impresionistas está en el Musée d'Orsay en Paris.* ‖ **9.** •A FINE young man. *Un hombre bien parecido.* ‖ **10.** •Down to a FINE art. *A la perfección.* ~You really got making pizzas down to a FINE art. *Ud. cocina las pizzas a la perfección.* ~He's got making omelettes down to a fine art. *Se ha convertido en experto en hacer tortillas.* ‖ **11.** [Feature]. *Delicado.* ~She inherited her mother's FINE features. *Ha heredado los rasgos delicados de su madre.*
❷ SMALL, THIN, SHARP. Small (particle, print]. *Menudo.* FINE drops of rain were falling. *Caían menudas gotas de lluvia.* ~Before you sign the contract you should

look at the FINE print. *Antes de firmar el contrato no dejes de leer la letra menuda (pequeña).* || **2.** [Line]. *Tenue.* || **3.** [Point of a pencil]. *Delgado.* || **4.** [Edge, point]. *Muy afilado, agudo.* ~Sharpen the pencil to a FINE point. *Afilar bien el lápiz.* || **5.** [Thread]. *Delgado.*

❸ OTHER MEANINGS. Subtle (distinction, points). *Sútil.* ~A fine distinction. *Una diferencia sútil.* ~The FINER points of the argument. *Los puntos más sútiles del argumento.* ~The FINER points of poetry are often lost in translation. *Los matices más sútiles de la poesía a menudo se pierden en la traducción.* ~There's a very FINE line between eccentricity and madness. *La línea divisoria entre la excentricidad y la locura es muy tenue.* || **2.** [Adjustment]. *Preciso.* || **3.** Detailed (embroidery, engraving, workmanship). *Delicado.* || **3.** [Judgement]. *Certero.* || **4.** [Balance]. *Delicado.* || **5.** Pure (gold, silver). *Puro.* ~This gold is 98% FINE. *Este oro tiene una pureza del 98%.* || **6.** •To have a FINE eye for detail. *Ser muy observador, ser muy detallista.* || **7.** Pleasant. *Agradable.* ~A FINE feeling. *Una sensación agradable.* ~Thank you for inviting us to such a FINE party. *Le agradecemos el invitarnos a una fiesta tan agradable.* || **8.** Sharp. *Agudo.* ~A FINE sense of justice. *Un agudo sentido de la justicia.* || **9.** Showy (feathers). *Vistoso.* A bird of FINE plumage. *Un ave de vistoso plumaje.* ⇨FINO

FOCUS. *v.* To concentrate. *Concentrar.* ~I can't FOCUS my mind on my work. *No puedo concentrarme en el trabajo.* ~All eyes were FOCUSED on her. *Todas las miradas estaban puestas (clavadas) en ella.* || **2.** [Light]. *Hacer converger.* || **3.** [Attention]. *Fijar, concentrar.* ~To FOCUS one's attention on a problem. *Fijar su atención en un problema.* ⇨ENFOCAR

FOOTBALL. *n.* [Played in the United States] *Fútbol (futbol) norteamericano.* ⇨FÚTBOL

FORCE. *v.* To bring about, obtain (action, change). *Provocar.* ~To FORCE a vote (on something). *Hacer que algo se someta a votación.* || **2.** Extort. *Arrancar.* ~They had to FORCE the secret out of him. *Tuvieron que arrancarle el secreto a la fuerza.* || **3.** Impose. *Obligar, imponer.* ~I didn't want to accept the money, but she FORCED it on me. *No quería el dinero pero me obligó a acceptarlo.* ~It's been FORCED on us by management. *La dirección nos lo ha impuesto.* || **4.** Speed up (plant). *Acelerar el crecimiento de.* || **5.** [Pace]. *Apresurar.* || **6.** Cause. *Hacer que.* ~To FORCE a car off the road. *Hacer que un coche salga de la calzada.* ~To FORCE somebody into bankruptcy.* || **7.** *WITH PREPOSITIONS.* || •FORCE back. *Contener.* She could FORCE back her tears no longer. *Ya no podía contener el llanto.* || •FORCE out. ~She was FORCED out of the race by engine trouble. *Se vio obligada a retirarse de la carrera por problemas de motor.* || •To FORCE off. ~He FORCED the lid off. *Le sacó la tapa a la fuerza.* || •To FORCE through. ~To FORCE a bill through Congress. *Hacer que se apruebe un proyecto de ley.* || •To FORCE in. *Entrar por fuerza.* ~They FORCED their way in. *Entraron por fuerza.* || •FORCE back (an enemy). *Hacer retroceder.* || •FORCE down. (I) [Plane] *Obligar a aterrizar,* (II) [Food]. *Tragar a duras penas.* ⇨FUERZA

FORM. *n.* Blank (document). *Formulario, impreso, planilla, modelo, hoja.* ~To fill in a FORM. *Rellenar un formulario (impreso).* ~Application FORM. *Formulario de solicitud.* || **2.** Type, kind. *Clase, especie, tipo.* ~Birds are a higher FORM of life than insects. *Las aves son una especie superior a los insectos.* ~The recipe requires fat in some FORM or other. *En la receta hay que usar algún tipo de grasa.* ~They require some FORM of explanation. *Necesitan algún tipo de explicación.* || **3.** Way. *Manera.* There are many FORMS of saying it. *Hay varias maneras de decirlo.* ~It's only a FORM of speech. *Es un decir.* || **4.** [Mood]. ~To be in good FORM. *Estar de buen humor.* || **5.** System. *Sistema.* ~A new FORM of government. *Un nuevo sistema de gobierno.* || **6.** Shape (of a person). *Figura.* ~The female FORM. *La figura* *humana.* || **7.** Etiquette. *Educación, etiqueta, gusto.* ~As a matter of FORM. *Por educación (cortesía).* ~Bad FORMS. *Malos modales.* It's bad FORM. ~*Es mala educación, es mal gusto.* || **8.** Mold. *Molde.* || **9.** Aspect, appearance. *Aparencia, aspecto, manifestación, característica.* ~What FORM does the disease take? *¿Cómo se manifiesta la enfermedad?* What FORM will the ceremony take? *¿En qué consistirá la ceremonia?* ~It took the FORM of a cash prize. *Consistio en un premio en metálico.* ~The invitation came in the FORM of a letter. *Nos invitó por carta.* What FORM should our protest take? *¿Cómo deberíamos manifestar nuestra protesta?* || **10.** PHRASES. || •True to FORM. *Como es de esperar.* || •For FORM sake. *Para salvar las aparencias, para cumplir, para que no se diga.* || •To be out of FORM. *Estar desentrenado.* || •In due form. *Como es debido.* ⇨FORMA

FORMAL. *adj.* Ceremonious. *Ceremonioso, serio, solemne.* ~He spoke to me in a FORMAL manner. *Me habló de una manera ceremoniosa.* ~A FORMAL speech. *Un discurso solemne.* || **2.** Conventional. *De etiqueta (party), de vestir (dress), de cumplido (visit), correcto (style, language).* ~We had to make a FORMAL visit. *Tuvimos que hacer una visita de cumplido.* ~They paid a FORMAL call on the new Ambassador. *Hicieron una visita oficial (de protocolo) al nuevo embajador.* || **3.** Valid, official, authorized. *Oficial, de protocolo, con las debidas formalidades, reglamentario.* ~A FORMAL receipt. *Un recibo en debido forma.* ~A FORMAL proposal. *Una propuesta oficial.* ~A FORMAL order. *Un pedido en firme.* || **4.** FORMAL education. *Formación académica.* || **5.** FORMAL suit. *Traje de vestir.* || **6.** FORMAL training. *Educación profesional.* ⇨FORMAL

FORMIDABLE. *adj.* Impressive, imposing. *Imponente.* ~With his *formidable* stature. *Con su figura imponente.* || **2.** Daunting, intimidating. *Temible.* ~A FORMIDABLE opponent. *Un rival temible.* || **3.** [Problem, obstacle, temper]. *Tremendo.* ~He has a FORMIDABLE temper. *Tiene un genio tremendo (impresionante).* ~The mountains were a FORMIDABLE barrier to our progress. *Las montañas constituían una enorme barrera a nuestro progreso.* ~The race is a FORMIDABLE test for both car and driver. *La carrera es una prueba tremenda tanto para el coche como para el conductor.* || **4.** Prodigious, outstanding (talent, mind). *Grande, fabuloso.* ~He has a FORMIDABLE mind. *Tiene gran intelecto, tiene un intelecto fabuloso.* || **5.** Terrible. *Terrible.* ~The director and his FORMIDABLE wife. *El director y la terrible mujer que tiene.* ⇨FORMIDABLE

FORMULA. *n.* [For baby]. *Preparado para biberón, para lactantes.* ⇨FORMULA

FORTUNE. *n.* A lot of money. *Platal, dineral.* ~It cost a FORTUNE. *Costó un dineral.* || **2.** Fate. *Trayectoria, peripecia.* ~I followed his FORTUNE(s) with interest. *Seguí su trayectoria con interés.* || **3.** Destiny. *Destino, sino.* ~I felt it was useless to struggle against FORTUNE. *Pensé que era inútil luchar contra el destino.* || **4.** Luck. *Suerte.* ~He had the good FORTUNE to escape. *Tuvo la suerte de poder escapar.* || **5.** •To tell/read somebody's FORTUNE. *Decirle/leerle la buenaventura a alguien.* || **6.** •The FORTUNES of war. *Las vicisitudes de la guerra.* ⇨FORTUNA

FOUNDATION [FUNDACIÓN]. *n.* Basis, grounds. *Fundamento, base.* ~Without FOUNDATION. *Sin fundamento.* ~Statement devoid of FOUNDATION. *Declaración que carece de fundamento.* ~The suspicion is without FOUNDATION. *La sospecha es infundada (carece de fundamento).* || **2.** [Cosmetic]. *Maquillaje de fondo, base.* ~FOUNDATION cream. *Crema base.* || **3.** [Figurative]. *Piedra angular.* ~The family is the FOUNDATION of our society. *La familia es la piedra angular de nuestra sociedad.* || **4.** -s. [Construction]. *Cimientos.* ~To lay the FOUNDATIONS (of a building). *Poner (echar) los cimientos (de un edificio).* || **5.** Groundwork. *Trabajo preliminar (de base).* ~He laid the FOUNDATIONS of the venture's success by careful planning. *Su cuidadosa planificación cimentó el éxito de la empresa.* || **6.** •FOUNDATION stone. *Primera piedra,*

piedra fundamental (fig.). ‖ **7.** •FOUNDATION course. *Curso común, preparatorio.*

FOUNTAIN. *n.* [Of a river]. *Manantial.* ‖ **2.** [Of water]. *Surtidor.* ~I had some water at a FOUNTAIN in the park. *Bebí agua en un surtidor del parque.* ‖ **3.** [For ink, oil]. *Depósito.* ‖ **4.** Spray, jet. *Chorro.* ~A FOUNTAIN of blood oozed out of his wound. *De la herida brotó un chorro de sangre.* ‖ **5.** •Fountain pen. *Pluma estilográfica.* ⇨FUENTE

FRATERNITY [FRATERNIDAD]. *n.* [Religious]. *Hermandad, cofradía.* ‖ **2.** Society. *Asociación.* ‖ **3.** [University club]. *Club, asociación estudiantil.* ‖ **4.** [Cummunity]. ~The legal, medical, teaching FRATERNITY. *Los abogados, los médicos, el profesorado.*

FRESH. *adj.*
❶ NEW, RECENT. *Nuevo.* It needs a FRESH coat of paint. *~Necesita una nueva mano de pintura.* ~FRESH clues. *Nuevos indicios.* ~Open a FRESH packet. *Abre otro paquete.* ~To start a FRESH life. *Empezar una vida nueva.* ‖ **2.** Newly arrived, produced. *Recien llegado, importado, salido, etc.* ~FRESH off the press. *Recien salido de la imprenta.* ~FRESH from Spain. *Recien llegado (importado) de España.* ~FRESH from the oven. *Acabadito de salir del horno.* ~FRESH from school. *Recién salido de la escuela.* ‖ **3.** Inexperienced. *Nuevo.* She comes FRESH to television. *Esta es su primera experiencia en la televisión.* ‖ **4.** •To make a FRESH start. *Empezar de nuevo.* ‖ **5.** •To put FRESH courage into somebody. *Reanimar a alguien, dar ánimos a alguien.*
❷ PURE, CLEAN, HEALTHY. [Aire]. *Puro.* ~In the FRESH air. *Al aire libre.* ‖ **2.** Without salt (water). *Dulce.* FRESH water. *Agua dulce.* ‖ **3.** [Bread]. *Del día, tierno.* ~This is FRESH bread. *Es pan tierno.* ‖ **4.** [Complexion, face]. *Sano, de buen color, lozano.* ‖ **5.** Not tired. *Descansado.* ~Do it when you're FRESH. *Hazlo cuando estés descansado.* ‖ **6.** [Clothes, linen]. *Limpio.* ~As I arrived at the hotel I went into my room and put on a FRESH shirt. *Al llegar al hotel fui a la habitación y me puse una camisa limpia (Prats).* ‖ **7.** Natural. *Natural.* ~A FRESH lemonade. *Una*

limonada natural. ‖ **8.** Not canned or frozen (food). *Natural.* ~FRESH vegetables. *Verdura natural.* ‖ **9.** •To feel perfectly FRESH. *Estar lleno de vigor.* ‖ **10.** •As FRESH as a daisy. *Tan fresco como una lechuga.*
❸ TAKING LIBERTIES. •To get FRESH with somebody. *Propasarse, insolentarse, ser insolente con alguien.* ~She was FRESH with her grandfather. *Se insolentó con el abuelo.* ‖ **2.** Cheeky. *Descarado, impertinente.* ~A FRESH remark. *Un comentario impertinente.* ‖ **3.** •Don't get FRESH with me! *¡Basta de familiaridades!* ⇨FRESCO

FRICTION. *n.* Antagonism. *Tirantez, roces.* ~Domestic FRICTION. *Roces familiares.* ~That is bound to lead to FRICTION. *Sin duda eso va a provocar tirantez.* ⇨FRICCIÓN

FRIGID [FRÍGIDO]. *adj.* [Clima]. *Glacial, frío.* ~The FRIGID climate of the North Pole. *El frío glacial del Polo Norte.* ‖ **2.** Unfriendly (welcome, greeting, smile). *Glacial.* ~The guard looked at us with a FRIGID stare. *El guarda nos dirigió una mirada glacial.*

FRONT [FRENTE]. *n.* Forward location. *Parte delantera.* ~You'll find him in the FRONT of the train. *Está en la parte delantera del tren.* ‖ **2.** [Of a shop]. *Escaparate.* ‖ **3.** [Of a building]. *Fachada.* ~The FRONT of the museum is very impressive. *La fachada del museo es imponente.* ‖ **4.** Beginning, head. *Principio.* ~He's at the FRONT of the line. *Está al principio de la cola.* ‖ **5.** [Of a shirt]. *Pechera.* ‖ **6.** An area of activity, conflict, or competition. *Nivel, terreno.* ~The news on the home FRONT is encouraging. *Las noticias al nivel nacional son alentadoras.* ~Has she made any progress on the work FRONT? *¿Ha progresado en el trabajo?* ‖ **7.** Outward show. *Fachada.* ~The florist's shop served as a FRONT for dope smugglers. *La florería servía de fachada a los traficantes de droga.* His friendliness is only a FRONT. *Su simpatía no es más que una fachada.* ‖ **8.** [For illegal activities]. *Pantalla.* ‖ **9.** [Overlooking the sea]. *Paseo marítimo, malecón, rambla (Lat.Amer.).*

FUNCTION[1] *v.* Serve as (person) *Actuar, desempeñar una función, realizar una tarea.* ~He will FUNCTION as host in my absence. *En mi ausencia actuará de presentador.* ‖ **2.** To serve as (thing). *Hacer las veces de, servir de.* ~This orange crate can FUNCTION as a chair. *Este cajón para naranjas puede hacer las veces de una silla.* For many years Athens FUNCTIONED as the intellectual center of the world. *Durante muchos años Atenas sirvió como centro cultural del mundo entero.* ‖ **3.** •I'm so tired, I can hardly FUNCTION. *Estoy tan cansado que casi no puedo hacer nada.* ⇨ FUNCIÓNAR

FUNCTION[2]. *n.* Reception, party. *Recepción, reunión social.* ‖ **2.** Ceremony. *Acto, ceremonia.* ‖ **3.** Duty, role, position. *Papel, oficio, cargo.* ~In my FUNCTION as treasurer. *Como (en mi calidad de) tesorero.* ~It's not part of my FUNCTION. *No corresponde a mi cargo.* ‖ **4.** Purpose. *Razón de ser.* ~This seems to be my FUNCTION in life. *Esa parece ser mi misión en la vida.* ~It's his only useful FUNCTION. *Es para lo único que sirve.* ⇨ FUNCIÓN

FUNCTIONAL [FUNCIONAL]. *adj.* Practical. *Práctico.* ~FUNCTIONAL clothes. *Ropa práctica.* ‖ **2.** Functioning (machine, weapon, part). *En buen estado, que funciona.* ~The flashlight was still FUNCTIONAL after being dropped. *La linterna seguía funcionando después de haberse caído.* ‖ **3.** [Law, rule, principle]. *Vigente.*

FUNDAMENTAL [FUNDAMENTAL]. *adj.* Elementary. *Elemental.* ~A grasp of FUNDAMENTAL mathematics. *Un conocimieno de matemática elemental.* ‖ **2.** Essential (skill, constituent). *Esencial, indispensable.* ~A qualification in computer study is a FUNDAMENTAL requirement. *Es requisito esencial tener estudios de informática.* ~Water is FUNDAMENTAL to survival. *Sin el agua no se puede sobrevivir.* ‖ **3.** Intrinsic (Absurdity, truth). *Intrínsico.* ‖ **4.** [Optimism]. *Innato.*

FUNERAL[1]. *n.* Ceremonies for a dead person prior to burial. *Entierro, sepelio.* ‖ **2.** FAM •That's her FUNERAL. *Allá ella, con su pan se lo coma.* ~That's not my FUNERAL. *Me trae sin cuidado.* ‖ **3.** •State FUNERAL. *Exequias nacionales.* ⇨ FUNERAL

FUNERAL[2] [FUNERAL]. *adj.* Of or pertaining to a funeral. *Fúnebre.* •FUNERAL home (parlor). *Funeraria, casa de pompas fúnebres.* ‖ **2.** •FUNERAL procession (march). *Cortejo (comitiva) fúnebre.* ‖ **3.** •FUNERAL service. *Misa de cuerpo presente.* ‖ **4.** •Webster and Sons. FUNERAL Directors. *Funeraria Webster e Hijos, Webster e Hijos. Pompas Fúnebres.* ‖ **5.** •FUNERAL chant. *Canto fúnebre.*

FURIOUS. *adj.* Violent, intense. (1) Struggle. *Feroz,* (II) [Speed, pace]. *Vertiginoso,* (III) [Storm]. *Violento,* (IV) [Activity, effort]. *Febril, frenético.* ⇨ FURIOSO

G

GAIN. *v.*

❶ ACQUIRE, ACHIEVE, GET, OBTAIN. ‖ **1.** [Independence, control]. *Conseguir, obtener.* Latin America GAINED its independence from Spain. *Hispanoamérica consiguió independizarse de España.* ‖ **2.** [Experience, confidence, reputation, popularity]. *Adquirir.* ~He gradually GAINED confidence in himself. *~Fue adquiriendo cada vez más confianza en sí mismo.* ‖ **3.** [Recognition]. *Obtener, ganarse.* ‖ **4.** [Friends]. *Hacerse.* ‖ **5.** [Qualification, degree]. *Obtener.* ‖ **6.** [Attention]. *Atraer, captar.* ~I succeeded in GAINING their attention. *Logré atraer (captar) su atención.* ‖ **7.** [Votos]. *Obtener.* ~The Democrats have GAINED 15 house seats from the Republicans. *Los Demócratas han obtenido 15 escaños que antes ocupaban los Republicanos.*

❷ INCREASE (In weight, speed, height, amount). ‖ **1.** [Weight]. *Aumentar (de peso), engordar.* ~After he stopped smoking he GAINED 8 pounds. *Después de que hubo dejado de fumar, aumentó ocho libras.* ‖ **2.** [Speed]. *Acelerar.* ~The car GAINED speed going down the hill. *El coche aceleró al bajar la pendiente.* ‖ **3.** [Shares]. *Aumentar de valor, subir.* ~The shares GAINED five points. *Las acciones subieron cinco enteros.* ~The shares have GAINED in value. *Las acciones subieron (aumentaron) de valor.* ‖ **4.** •The day was GAINING in warmth. *El día se ponía cada vez más caluroso.*

❸ OTHER MEANINGS. [Health]. *Mejorar.* ~He's GAINING in fitness. *Su estado físico ha mejorado mucho.* ‖ **2.** [Clock]. *Adelantar.* ~My watch is GAINING five minutes a day. *Mi reloj (se) adelanta cinco minutos por día.* ‖ **3.** [Ground, yards]. *Avanzar.* ~The offensive GAINED two miles. *La ofensiva avanzó dos millas.* The football team GAINED three yards. *El equipo de fútbol avanzó 3 yardas.* ‖ **4.** Profit, benefit. *Aprovechar, aprender, beneficiar.* ~We hope to GAIN from the company's success. *Esperamos sacar provecho del éxito de la compañía.* ~He hopes to GAIN considerably from his investment. *Espera sacar muchos beneficios de sus inversiones.* ‖ **5.** Reach. *Llegar.* ~I finally GAINED the shore. *Alcancé finalmente la orilla.*

❹ EXPRESSIONS. •To GAIN on someone. *Alcanzar.* ~You'll have to drive faster, they're GAINING on us. *Vas a tener que acelerar, nos están alcanzando.* ‖ **2.** •To GAIN entrance to a building. *Lograr entrar a un edificio.* ‖ **3.** •To GAIN port (a ship). *Llegar a puerto.* ~The ship GAINED port. *El barco llegó a puerto.* ‖ **4.** •To GAIN in popularity. *Resultar más popular, adquirir mayor popularidad.* ⇨ GANAR

GALLANT [GALANTE]. *adj.* Brave, intrepid. *Valiente, intrépido.* Three GALLANT soldiers held off the enemy attack. *Rechazaron el ataque enemigo tres valientes soldados.* ‖ **2.** Stately, splendid. *Imponente, elegante, espléndido.* ~The tall and GALLANT ship speeding over blue water. *La majestuosa y imponente nave navegando a toda velocidad por el agua azul.* ‖ **3.** Showy. *Lucido, gallardo.* ‖ **4.** Attentive towards women, chivalrous. *Atento.* ~What man is so GALLANT today as to give up his seat on a bus to a lady. *¿Cuál es el hombre suficiente atento hoy en día para ofrecer a una dama su asiento en el autobús?*

GALLERY. *n.* Museum. *Museo (de Bellas*

Artes). || **2.** [For press, spectators]. *Tribuna.* || **3.** [Golf spectators]. *Público.* || **4.** [Theatre]. *Gallinero, paraíso.* || **5.** [Ship]. *Galera.* •SHOOTING gallery. *Tiro al blanco.* ⇨GALERIA

GARAGE [GARAJE]. *n.* [For repairs]. *Taller mecánico.* ~My car's at the GARAGE. *Tengo el coche en el taller mecánico.* || **2.** Filling station. *Gasolinera, estación de servicio.* || **3.** •Garage sale. *Venta de trastos viejos (en una casa particular).*

GENEROUS [GENEROSO]. *adj.* Plentiful (helping, amount, supply, quantity). *Copioso, abundante.* ~A GENEROUS helping. *Una buena ración.* || **2.** [Soil]. *Fértil, rico.*

GENIAL. *adj.* Cordial, cheerful, warm, friendly (of persons). *Cordial, afable, sociable, simpático.* || **2.** [Welcome]. *Warm.* || **3.** [Smile]. *Amistoso, cordial* || **4.** Pleasant (climate). *Agradable.* ~In these genial regions one's wants are naturally diminished. *En estas zonas de clima agradable, como es de esperar, no se necesitan tantas cosas.* ⇨GENIAL

GENIUS. *n.* Gift. *Don, talento.* ~To have a GENIUS for business. *Tener un don especial para los negocios.* She has a GENIUS for music. *Tiene talento para la música.* || **2.** Powerful influence. ~An evil GENIOUS. *Una influencia maligna.* ⇨GENIO

GENTLE. *adj.* [Person]. *Dulce, tierno.* ~She a GENTLE person. *Ella es muy dulce.* || **2.** Noble. *Noble.* ~Of GENTLE birth. *De ascendencia noble.* || **3.** Soft or low (sound, voice]. *Dulce.* || **4.** [Push, touch]. *Ligero.* || **5.** Slow. *Lento, pausado, leve.* ~The gentle ROCKING of his mother's chair. *El pausado balanceo de la silla al mecerse su madre.* ~I shook her GENTLY and she opened her eyes. *La toqué levemente y abrió los ojos.* || **6.** [Hint, reminder]. *Discreto.* || **7.** Easily handled or managed (animal). *Manso, dócil, apacible.* || **8.** Moderate (slope), *Poco empinado.* || **9.** Moderate (exercise). *Moderado.* || **10.** [Shampoo]. *Suave.* || **11.** Mild [wind, movement]. *Suave.* A GENTLE wind. *Una suave brisa.* A GENTLE tap on the shoulder. *Un suave golpecillo en la* espalda. ~It is GENTLE on your stomach. *No hace daño al estómago.* || **12.** Good birth. *Alcurnia.* ~Of GENTLE birth. *De buena cuna, bien nacido.* || **13.** Dear, kind, distinguished (reader). *Estimado, amado, distinguido.* Consider, GENTLE reader, my terrible predicament at this juncture. *Tenga en cuenta, estimado (amado) lector, mi problema en este momento.* || **14.** Kind (words). *Amable.* || **15.** Affectionate. *Cariñoso.* ~He was very GENTLE with her during her illness. *Estuvo muy cariñoso con ella durante su enfermedad.* ~She sat GENTLY caressing the baby in her lap. *Estaba sentada acariciando cariñosamente al niño que tenía en las rodillas.* || **16.** •The GENTLE sex. *El sexo débil.* || **17.** •Be GENTLE with that vase. *Tenga cuidado con ese jarrón.* ⇨GENTIL

GENUINE [GENUINO]. *adj.* [Work of art]. *Original.* The painting was discovered to be GENUINE. *El cuadro resultó ser un original.* || **2.** Sincere. *Sincero.* ~His feelings for her were GENUINE. *Sus sentimientos hacia ella eran sinceros.* || **3.** Decent (people). *Buena.* ~They were GENUINE people. *Era gente buena.* || **4.** True. *Verdadero.* ~It was a GENUINE misunderstanding. *Fue realmente un malentendido.* ~My first encounter with a GENUINE Spanish bullfighter. *Mi primer encuentro con un verdadero torero español.* || **5.** [Leather]. *Legítimo, auténtico.* || **6.** [Signature, antique]. *Auténtico.* || **7.** •GENUINE callers only, please. *Curiosos abstenerse.*

GESTURE [GESTO]. *n.* Small token, symbolic act. *Muestra.* || **2.** Demonstration, indication. *Demostración.* ~As a GESTURE of friendship. *En señal de amistad.* ~As a GESTURE of support. *Para demostrar nuestro apoyo.* ~He did it as a GESTURE of good will. *Lo hizo para demostrar su buena voluntad.* || **3.** Act of kindness or courtesy. *Detalle.* What a nice GESTURE! *¡Qué detalle!* ~The letter arrived late, but it was a nice GESTURE. *La tarjeta llegó tarde, pero fue todo un detalle.* ~It was a kind GESTURE on your part to drive me home. *Ha sido* *muy amable en llevarme a casa con su coche.* ‖ **4.** Ploy. *Táctica, truco, estratagema.* ~A political GESTURE. *Una táctica política.* ‖ **5.** •Empty GESTURE. *Pura formalidad.*

GLOBAL. *adj.* Of the world, world-wide, universal. *Mundial.* ~The dream of GLOBAL peace. *La esperanza de una paz universal.* ‖ **2.** [Warfare, problem]. *A escala mundial.* ‖ **3.** Spherical. *Esférico.* ~The earth is a GLOBAL mass. *La tierra es una masa esférica.* ‖ **4.** Comprehensive. *Exhaustivo.* ~A catalogue noted for its GLOBAL coverage. *Un catálogo famoso por su contenido exhaustivo.* ‖ **5.** Overall. *Total.* ~The GLOBAL output of the factory. *La producción total de la fábrica.* ⇨GLOBAL

GLORIOUS [GLORIOSO]. *adj.* Splendid, superb. *Magnífico, espléndido, maravilloso.* ~The weather is GLORIOUS at the moment. *Hace un tiempo espléndido.* ~What A GLORIOUS day! *Qué día más hermoso!* ~A GLORIOUS spring morning. *Una espléndida mañana de primavera.* ~A glorious work of art. *Una magnífica obra de arte.* ‖ **2.** [Ironic]. *Mayúscula, colosal, garrafal, de antología.* ~It was a GLORIOUS muddle. *Resultó un lío colosal.* ~Some GLORIOUS errors. *Unos errores garrafales (mayúsculos).* ‖ **3.** Extremely pleasant, intensely delightful, highly enjoyable. *Sumamente agradable o ameno; maravilloso.* ~I had the GLORIOUS feeling that ... *Tenía la maravillosa sensación de que ...* ~I had a GLORIOUS time at the party. *Me he divertido de lo lindo en la fiesta.* ~I enjoyed a GLORIOUS weekend at the beach. *Disfruté de un espléndido fin de semana en la playa.* ‖ **4.** Illustrious, praiseworthy. *Ilustre.* He had a GLORIOUS career. *Tuvo una ilustre carrera.* ‖ **5.** Bright, brilliant (color). *Brillante, intenso, llamativo.* The walls were covered with frescoes in GLORIOUS colors. *La pared estaba cubierta de frescos de colores intensos.*

GLORY. *n.* Splendor. *Esplendor.* The glory of Spring. *La esplendorosa primavera.* ~And there in all its GLORY was our old Chevrolet. *Y ahí estaba, en todo su esplen-*dor, *nuestro viejo Chevrolet.* ~The GLORY of the system is that ... *Lo espléndido del sistema está en qué ...* ~Her photographs depict the Himalayas in all their GLORY. *Sus fotografías muestran el Himalaya en todo su esplendor.* ‖ **2.** Triumph. *Triunfo.* ~I'm entitled to bask in a little reflected GLORY. *Tengo derecho a disfrutar un poco del triunfo ajeno.* ‖ **3.** Merit, honor. *Mérito, honores.* I mustn't take all the GLORY. *El mérito no sólo es mío.* ~She deserves more of the GLORY that in fact she received. *Se merecía más honores de los que de hecho recibió.* ‖ **4.** •To GLORY in something. *Jactarse de algo.* ‖ **5.** •GLORY be! *¡Gracias a Dios!* ⇨GLORIA

GOAL [GOL]. *n.*
❶ USED FIGURATIVELY. Aim, objective, ambition. *Meta, objetivo, ambición.* ~To reach one's GOAL. *Lograr (alcanzar, llegar a) una meta, realizar una ambición.* ‖ **3.** •To set GOALS for oneself. *Proponerse metas (objetivos).* ~I set myself the GOAL of finishing the job by Friday. *Me propongo (como meta) terminar el trabajo para el viernes.* ‖ **4.** Destination. *Destino, meta.*
❷ SPORT. goal. *n. Tanto, gol (Acad.).* ‖ •GOAL post. *Poste.* ‖ •GOAL scorer. *Goleador.* ‖ •GOAL posts. *Portería, arco (L.Am.).* ‖ •GOAL area. *Área de meta.* ‖ •GOAL line. *Línea de meta.* ‖ •GOAL kick. *Saque de meta.* ‖ •GOAL average. *Promedio de tantos (goles).* ‖ •To keep (play in) GOAL. *Ser (jugar de) portero, arquero (L.Am.).* ‖ •To score a GOAL. *Marcar (meter) un tanto (gol).* ‖ •To shoot at GOAL. *Tirar a puerta.*

GRACE. *n.* Gracefulness. *Finura, elegancia.* ‖ **2.** Courtesy. *Cortesía, gentileza.* ~He had the GRACE to apologize. *Tuvo la cortesía de pedir perdón.* ‖ **3.** Delay. *Demora.* ~3 day's GRACE. *3 días de plazo.* ‖ **4.** Blessing. *Bendición.* ~To say GRACE. *Bendecir la mesa.* ‖ **5.** Good quality. *Cualidad.* ~Her saving GRACE is her sense of humor. *Lo que la salva es que tiene sentido del humor.* ‖ **6.** Forgiveness. *Perdón.* ‖ **7.** [Of shape, form]. *Armonía, elegancia.* ‖ **8.** [Of movement]. *Garbo,* *donaire.* ‖ **9.** [Of style]. *Elegancia, amenidad.* ‖ **10.** [Of expression]. *Elegancia.* ‖ **11.** EXPRESSIONS. ‖ •Social GRACES. *Modales.* ~She has no social GRACES. *No sabe como comportarse, no tiene modales (roce).* ‖ •To fall from GRACE. *Caer en desgracia.* ‖ •Yes, your GRACE. *Sí, su Excelencia.* ‖ •To get into somebody's good GRACES. *Congraciarse con uno, gozar del favor de alguien.* ‖ •With good GRACE. *Con buen talante, de buena gana.* With a bad GRACE. *Con mal talante, de mala gana.* ‖ •In good GRACE. *Con la conciencia tranquila.* ‖ •To be in somebody's good GRACES. *Estar en buenas relaciones con alguien.* ⇨GRACIA

GRACEFUL [GRÁCIL]. *adj.* [Dancer, movement]. *Lleno de gracia.* ~She's very GRACEFUL. *Se mueve con mucha gracia (mucho garbo).* ‖ **2.** [Style]. *Elegante.* ‖ **3.** [Apology, retirement]. *Digno.* ~When I'm no longer needed, I will retire GRACEFULLY. *Cuando ya no pueda trabajar, me jubilaré con dignidad.*

GRACIOUS. *adj.* Courteous. *Atento, cortés, educado.* ~They were GRACIOUS enough to apologize. *Tuvieron la gentileza de pedir disculpas.* ‖ **2.** Lenient, merciful. *Indulgente, misericordioso.* ‖ **3.** Elegant, urbane. *Elegante, refinado.* ~Gracious living. *Vida elegante o de lujo.* ‖ **4.** Kind. *Amable.* He was very GRACIOUS with me. *Fue muy amable conmigo.* ‖ **5.** •GRACIOUS me! *¡Dios mío!* ⇨GRACIOSO

GRADE. *n.* Mark. *Nota, calificación.* ~To get good GRADES. *Sacar buenas notas.* ‖ **2.** Rank (hierarchy, staff). *Categoría.* ~To be promoted to a higher GRADE. *Ser ascendido a un grado superior.* ‖ **3.** [Military]. *Rango.* ‖ **4.** Class. *Clase, categoría.* ~It divides hotels into four GRADES. *Divide a los hoteles en cuatro categorías.* ‖ **5.** Level. *Nivel.* ‖ **6.** Slope, gradient. *Pendiente, cuesta.* ‖ **7.** Quality. *Calidad.* ~GRADE A tomatoes. *Tomates de la primera calidad.* ~Leather of the highest GRADE. *Cuero de alta calidad.* ~Different GRADES of paper. *Papel de distinta calidad.* ‖ **8.** Size. *Tamaño.* ~GRADE 3 eggs. *Huevos del*

tamaño número 3. ‖ **9.** Antigüedad (en un puesto). *Seniority.* ‖ **10.** Course, school year. *Curso, año.* ~He finished the fourth GRADE. *Terminó el cuarto año (de clase).* ‖ **11.** Elementary school system. *Escuela primaria.* ~She teaches in GRADE school. *Enseña en la escuela primaria.* ‖ **12.** PHRASES. ‖ •To make the GRADE. *Llegar al nivel deseado, tener éxito, triunfar.* ~She's talented enough to make the GRADE. *Tiene suficiente talento para triunfar.* ~He wanted to be an actor but he didn't make the GRADE. *Quería ser actor pero no tuvo éxito.* ‖ •GRADE school. *Escuela primaria.* ‖ •GRADE crossing. *Paso a nivel.* ‖ •Administrative GRADES. *Escalafón administrativo.* ‖ •Salary GRADES. *Escala salarial.* ⇨GRADO

GRADUATE. *v.* [Education]. *Sacarse el título.* ‖ **2.** [With a diploma]. *Diplomarse (en).* ‖ **3.** [From a university]. *Licenciarse, graduarse, obtener el título (en).* ~She GRADUATED from Cambridge in 1974. *Se licenció en la Universidad de Cambridge en 1974.* ~He GRADUATED in history. *Se licenció en historia.* ‖ **4.** Progress. *Pasar a.* ~To start with a small one and then GRADUATE to a bigger one. *Empezar con uno pequeño y pasar a uno mayor.* ~They often GRADUATE from marijuana to heroin. *A menudo pasan de la marihuana a la heroína.* ‖ **5.** [From high school]. *Terminar el bachillerato, recibirse de bachiller.* ‖ **6.** [Payments, contributions]. *Escalonar.* ‖ **7.** •To GRADUATE as. *Recibirse de.* ⇨GRADUAR

GRAIN. *n.* Cereals. *Cereales.* ‖ **2.** [In wood]. *Fibra.* ‖ **3.** [In stone]. *Veta, vena.* ‖ **4.** [In leather]. *Flor.* ‖ **5.** [In cloth]. *Granilla.* ‖ **6.** [In direction of fiber]. *Hilo.* ‖ **7.** [Of fabric]. *Hilo.* ‖ **8.** •There's not a GRAIN of truth in what he says. *No hay ni una pizca de verdad en lo que dice.* ‖ **9.** •Against the GRAIN (in carpentry). *Contra el hilo.* ⇨GRANO

GRATIFICATION. *n.* Pleasure. *Placer, satisfacción.* ~I play the piano for my own GRATIFICATION. *Toco el piano por satisfac-*

ción personal. ⇨GRATIFICACIÓN

GRATIFY. *v.* To please, satisfy (one's wish). *Halagar, complacer, dar gusto.* ~Hoping to GRATIFY my curiosity, I opened the door. *Para satisfacer mi curiosidad, abrí la puerta.* ⇨GRATIFICAR

GUARANTEE [GARANTIZAR]. *v.* Assure, insure, promise. *Asegurar.* ~I can't GUARANTEE it. *No se lo puedo asegurar.* ~An extra $2 will GUARANTEE you a seat. *Por dos dólares más tiene el asiento asegurado.* ~Take this opportunity and I GUARANTEE you will not regret it. *Aprovecha esta oportunidad y te aseguro que no te vas a arrepentir.* || **2.** Take responsability for. *Responder por.* || **3.** [Debt, treaty]. *Avalar.*

GUARD[1]. *v.* Protect, shield. *Defender, proteger.* ~There's no one to GUARD these isolated farms against a possible attack. *No hay nadie que pueda defender estas remotas granjas de un posible ataque.* || **2.** Keep watch over (building, vehicle, prisoner). *Vigilar.* ~The door is heavily GUARDED. *Tienen la puerta muy vigilada.* ~I asked him to WATCH the suitcases. *Le pedí que vigilara las maletas.* ~To GUARD a prisoner. *Vigilar a un prisionero.* || **3.** To escort. *Escoltar.* || **4.** [Piece, position in chess or cards]. *Cubrir, defender.* || **5.** To prevent (against). *Impedir.* ~We must GUARD against that happening. *Tenemos que impedir que eso ocurra.* || **6.** To take precautions (against). *Precaverse.* ~You have to GUARD against danger. *Hay que precaverse del peligro.* || **7.** Watch, control. *Tener cuidado.* ~You must GUARD your temper. *Ten cuidado con tu genio.* || **8.** •To

guard one's tongue. *Cuidar lo que uno dice.* ⇨GUARDAR

GUARD[2]. *n.* Safeguard. *Resguardo.* || **2.** [On machine]. *Seguro, diapositivo de seguridad.* || **3.** [Of sword]. *Guarda, guarnición, guardamano.* || **4.** Sentry. *Sentinela.* || **5.** Escort. *Escolta.* || **6.** [Prison]. *Encarcelero, oficial de cárceles.* || **7.** [In US football]. *Defensa.* || **8.** [In basketball]. *Escolta.* || **9.** [Fire]. *Guardallamas.* || **10.** [Around trigger]. *Seguro.* || **11.** Precaution. *Protección, prevención.* ~A GUARD against errors/infection/theft. *Una protección contra los errores/la infección/los robos.* ~As a GUARD against mistakes. *Para prevenir errores.* || **12.** PHRASES. || •He's one of the old GUARD. *Es uno de los viejos.* || •To be on one's GUARD. *Estar alerta, estar sobre aviso.* || •To drop one's GUARD. *Descuidarse.* || •Fire GUARD. *Pantalla.* •To be on guard (at a post). *Estar de guardia.* ~Who was on GUARD when the fire broke out? *¿Quién estaba de guardia cuando empezó el incendio?* || •To catch (throw, take) someone off GUARD. *Coger, agarrar (Lat. Am.) desprevenido.* ⇨GUARDIA/GUARDA

GUIDE. *n.* Adviser. *Consejero.* ~Spiritual GUIDE. *Consejero espiritual.* ~Let conscience be your GUIDE. *Que la conciencia sea tu consejera.* || **2.** Example. *Ejemplo.* || **3.** •It's a rough GUIDE. *Es una aproximación.* ⇨GUÍA

GUSTO. *n.* Energy, eagerness, enthusiasm. *Entusiasmo.* ~With GUSTO. *Con entusiasmo.* ~He always sings with great GUSTO. *Siempre canta con mucho entusiasmo.* ⇨GUSTO

H

HABIT [HÁBITO]. *n.*
❶ HABITUAL BEHAVIOR. *Costumbre.*
~As was her HABIT. *Como tenía por costumbre.* ~Don't make a HABIT out of it! *¡Que no se repita!* ~I got into the HABIT of reading the newspaper at breakfast. *He tomado la costumbre de leer el periódico a la hora del desayuno.* ~I'm not in the HABIT of lying to my friends. *No acostumbro decir mentiras a los amigos.* ~The book-buying HABIT could spread to a much wider population. *La costumbre de comprar libros bien podría extenderse a un círculo mucho más amplio.*
❷ ANNOYING BEHAVIOR. *Vicio, mala costumbre.* Children get into bad HABITS. *(A veces) los niños adquieren (adoptan) malas costumbres.* ~I was taught to drive by my boyfriend, but I'm afraid I've picked up some of his bad HABITS. *Me enseñó a manejar mi novio y desgraciadamente adquirí algunas de sus malas costumbres.* ‖ **2.** • To kick the HABIT. *Dejar un vicio.* ‖ **3.** •To break, cure a bad HABIT. *Perder una mala costumbre.* ~I'm trying to make him break the HABIT of switching the television on every time he comes home. *Estoy tratando de hacerle perder la costumbre de encender la televisión cada vez que llega a casa.* ~He has been waking me up at five o'clock in the morning the last two weeks; let's hope he doesn't make a HABIT of it. *Me estuvo despertando a las cinco de la mañana estas últimas semanas. Espero que no siga haciéndolo.*
❸ EXPRESSIONS. ‖ •From force of HABIT, out of HABIT, from HABIT. *Por costumbre.* ~I always buy the same brand of toothpaste just out of HABIT. *Por costumbre, siempre compro la misma marca de dentrífico.* ‖ •To get out of the HABIT of. *Perder la costumbre de, dejar de.* ‖ •To get out of the HABIT (of doing something). *Dejar de (hacer algo).* ~I used to swim twice a week, but I seem to have gotten out of the HABIT recently. *Solía nadar dos veces por semana, pero últimamente dejé de hacerlo.* ‖ •To make a HABIT of. *Seguir haciendo algo.*

HISTORY. *n.* Record, background. *Historial.* ~Personal/family HISTORY. *Historial personal/familiar.* ~Medical HISTORY. *Historial médico (clínico).* ‖ **2.** MED •To have a HISTORY of. *Haber tenido o sufrido.* ~He has a HISTORY of heart trouble. *Ha tenido problemas cardíacos.* ⇨HISTORIA

HONEST. *adj.* Trustworthy, upright. *Honrado, recto.* She's poor but HONEST. *Es pobre pero honrada.* •He's as HONEST as the day is long. *Es una persona sumamente honrada.* ‖ **2.** Sincere, truthful. *Sincero, franco.* ~Give me your HONEST opinion. *Dime sinceramente lo que opinas, ¿qué piensas francamente de esto?.* ~To be HONEST I don't know what to say. *Sinceramente, no sé lo que decir.* ~To be HONEST with you, I don't think it will be possible. *Si quieres que te diga la verdad, no creo que sea posible.* •To be perfectly HONEST with you. *Para decirlo con toda franqueza.* •Be HONEST. *¡Di la verdad!* ‖ **3.** [Of work]. Done without cheating, using one's own efforts]. *Honradamente, bien adquirido.* ~I do not intend to become a millionaire, I just want to make an HONEST buck. *No aspiro a hacerme millonario. Lo único que quiero es ganarme unas pesetas honradamente (Prats).* •To make an HONEST living.

Ganarse la vida honradamente. ~It's time to stop being a student and make an HONEST living (get a job and earn money). *Es tiempo ya que dejes de ser estudiante y empieces a ganarte la vida honradamente.* || **4.** Simple, plain. *Simple, modesto, humilde.* I'm perfectly happy with an HONEST hamburger. *Todo lo que me apetece es una simple hamburguesa (Prats).* || **5.** Genuine, real. *Simple.* ~I made an HONEST mistake. *Me equivoqué simplemente, fue una simple equivocación.* || **6.** Truthful or creditable. ~Honest weight. *Peso de ley (medida legítima).* || **7.** *PHRASES.* || • HUM He made an HONEST woman out of her. *Cumplió y se casó con ella.* || •An HONEST face. *Una cara abierta.* || •By HONEST means. *Por medios legales.* || •HONEST! *¡Te lo juro! ¡En serio¡* ~I didn't do it, HONEST. *En serio, no lo hice; de veras que no fui yo.* || •The HONEST truth. *La pura verdad.* || •To do an HONEST day's work. *Hacer una buena jornada.* ~To tell the truth, I don't think he worked an HONEST day in his life. *A decir la verdad, no creo que haya trabajado un sólo día en su vida.* ⇨HONESTO

HONESTY. *n.* Rectitude, uprightness. *Honradez, rectitud.* || **2.** Freedom from deceit or fraud. *Honrado.* ~As he will deal with large amounts of money, his HONESTY cannot be in question. *Como tendrá a su cargo una gran cantidad de dinero, necesitamos estar seguro de que es un hombre honrado.* || **3.** Frankness, sincerity. *Franqueza, sinceridad.* ~You may not like what he says, but you have to admire his honesty. *Puede no gustarle lo que dice, pero debe admirar su sinceridad.* ~To be honest, you have to admit that ... *Para ser*

sincero, hay que reconocer que ... || **4.** *PHRASES.* •HONESTY is the best policy. *La honradez es la mejor política, lo mejor es ser franco.* •In all HONESTY. *Con toda franqueza.* ~I must tell you, in all HONESTY, that the task ahead of you will be very difficult. *Debo decirle, con toda franqueza, que la labor que le espera va a ser muy ardua.* ▸«La honradez es la conducta limpia de la cintura para arriba, y la honestidad lo es de la cintura para abajo.» (Salvador de Madariaga. Cit. por Dels Prats). ⇨HONESTIDAD

HONOR. *v.* Fulfill (obligation, treaty). *Cumplir.* ~I intend to HONOR the contract. *Tengo toda la intención de cumplir con el contrato.* || **2.** [Check]. *Aceptar y pagar.* ~To HONOR a check. *Aceptar y pagar un talón bancario.* || **3.** •To honor ONE'S words. *Cumplir con su palabra.* || **4.** [Bill, debt]. *Satisfacer, pagar.* || **5.** [Credit card, signature]. *Aceptar.* ~All credit cards are HONORED here. *Aquí se aceptan todas las tarjetas de crédito.* || **6.** To pay honor *Rendir homenaje.* ⇨HONRAR

HONORARY [HONORARIO]. *adj.* [Of duties]. *Honorífico.* || **2.** •To receive an HONORARY degree. *Ser nombrado doctor honoris causa.* ~He was given an HONORARY degree. *Le concedieron un doctorado honoris causa.*

HOUR. *n.* Particular moment. *Momento.* ~It was his finest HOUR. *Fue su mejor momento.* ~In my HOUR of need they all deserted me. *Todos me abandonaron cuando más los necesitaba.* ~The man/ question of the hour. *El hombre/tema del momento.* ⇨HORA

I

IDENTIFY [IDENTIFICAR]. *v*. Introduce. *Darse a conocer, presentarse*. ~The police officer IDENTIFIED himself. *El agente de policía se dio a conocer*. I IDENTIFIED myself to the usher as a lawyer and he let me in right away. *Me presenté al ujier y me dejó entrar en seguida (Prats)*. || **2.** Recognize, distinguish. *Reconocer, distinguir*. Even the smallest baby can IDENTIFY its mother by her voice. *Hasta el niño más pequeño puede reconocer, por su tono de voz, a la madre*. || **3.** Indicate. *Indicar*. ~Subjects of special interest are IDENTIFIED by an asterisk. *Los asuntos que presentan un interés especial vienen indicado con un asterisco (Prats)*. || **4.** [A problem]. Discover, recognize, determine, show, reveal. *Determinar (el origen, naturaleza o características de alguna cosa), descubrir, averiguar*. What the report does quite clearly is IDENTIFY that there is racial inequality. *El informe revela que no se puede negar que existe discriminación racial*. ~The committee shall IDENTIFY the problem which deserves first consideration. *El comité determinará los problemas que deben ser examinados en primer lugar (Prats)*. || **5.** [Followed by *with*]. Align with, involve with. *Relacionar, asociar*. ~He was IDENTIFIED with the Labor Party. *Se le relacionaba con el partido laborista*. ~During the 1950's he was IDENTIFIED with many radical groups. *Durante los años 50 estuvo relacionado (involucrado] con varios grupos de tendencia radical*. || **6.** Ascertain, determine, establish. *Establecer*. The plane was IDENTIFIED as American. *Se estableció que el avión era norteamericano*. || **7.** To name. *Nombrar*. There are some people who can IDENTIFY every car as it passes by. *Hay algunas personas que pueden nombrar cada coche que ven pasar por la calle*. ~One of the employees, who asked not to be IDENTIFIED *Uno de los empleados, que pidió que no se le nombrara*. ~The guard was IDENTIFIED as Victor Kowalski. *El guardia se llama Victor Kowalski*. || **8.** Sympathize with, relate to. *Tener en común*. ~People with whom English-speaking readers could IDENTIFY. *Personas de habla inglesa con los que los lectores tienen mucho en común*. ~I can IDENTIFY with him. *Los dos tenemos mucho en común*. ||. **9.** [Body]. *Reconocer*. ~To IDENTIFY the body of a relative. *Reconocer el cadáver de un familiar*.

IDENTITY. *v*. Personality, individuality, uniqueness. *Personalidad*. ~Many who join the army loose their IDENTITY. *Muchos de los que ingresan en el ejército pierden su personalidad propia*. Every country has its own cultural IDENTITY. *Cada país tiene su propia personalidad cultural*. || **2.** Name. *Nombre*. ~He said a third person was interested in the business but he refused to reveal its IDENTITY. *Dijo que había un tercero interesado en adquirir el negocio, pero se negó a dar su nombre (Prats)*. ~The IDENTITY of the killer is still unknown. *Todavía se desconoce el nombre del asesino*. || **3.** Who a person is. *Señas personales*. ~Police say that they know the name of the murderer but not his IDENTITY. *La policía dijo que sabía el nombre del asesino, pero no tenía conocimiento de sus señas personales (Prats)*. || **4.** •IDENTITY card. *Cédula personal*. ⇨IDENTIDAD

IDIOM. *n*. Expression, set phrase. *Modismo, locución, expresión idiomática, frase hecha*. "To bite off more than one can chew" is an IDIOM which means to try to do something that is too difficult. *"El que mucho abarca poco aprieta" es un modismo que significa intentar hacer algo demasiado difícil.* ⇨IDIOMA

IGNORE. *n.* [General]. Overlook, disregard. *Pasar por alto, prescindir (de una cosa), hacer caso omiso, no hacer caso, cerrar los ojos (ante un hecho).* ~How can the government IGNORE the wishes of the majority? *¿Cómo puede el gobierno hacer caso omiso de lo que quiere la mayoría?* || **2.** [Warning, remark, plea]. *No hacer caso de, hacer caso omiso de.* ~He chose to IGNORE the remark. *Prefirió pasar por alto el comentario.* ~He IGNORED their warnings. *No hizo caso de sus advertencias.* || **3.** [Behavior, fact]. *Pasar por alto, no tener en cuenta* ~I try to IGNORE the insults and answer the arguments. *Paso por alto los insultos y contesto los argumentos.* ~We can't IGNORE the fact that. *No podemos dejar de tener en cuenta el hecho de que.* || **4.** [Letter, message]. *Dejar sin contestar.* || **5.** [Person]. To snub. *Desairar, no hacer (el menor) caso, hacer como si no existiera.* ~He IGNORED me. *Afectó no verme, hizo como no me viera.* I smiled but she IGNORED me. *Le sonreí pero hizo como no me viera.* ~Just IGNORE him. *No le hagas caso, haz como si no existiera.* || **6.** Neglect. *Desatender, descuidar.* His needs were IGNORED. *Se desatendieron sus necesidades.* ⇨IGNORAR

ILLUMINATE. *v.* Clarify (subject). *Esclarecer, dilucidar, aclarar.* ~His lecture ILLUMINATED many scientific phenomena. *Su conferencia esclareció muchos fenómenos científicos.* || **2.** Decorate with lights. *Poner luminarias.* ⇨ILUMINAR

ILLUSION. *n.* False hope, wishful thinking. *Quimera, fantasía.* ~I was thinking of going to Spain when I retired, but now I know it was just an ILLUSION. *Pensaba viajar a España cuando me jubilara, pero ahora me doy cuenta que fue una quimera.* || **2.** False Appearance. *Impresión.* ~The mirrors gave the ILLUSION

that the room was larger. *Los espejos daban la impresión de que la habitación era más grande.* ~It gives an ILLUSION of space. *Crea una impresión de espacio.* || **3.** False idea, error, delusion. *Engaño.* ~I was under the ILLUSION that he lived there. *Tenía la impresión de que vivía allí.* ~He's under the ILLUSION that he's a great pianist. *Se está engañando pensando que es un gran pianista.* ~He cherished the ILLUSION that she loved him. *Se engañaba pensando que ella lo quería.* ~He was under no ILLUSIONS. *No se engañaba.* ⇨ILUSIÓN

ILLUSTRATE. *v.* Explain by examples (point, theory, subject). *Aclarar.* ~To prevent misunderstandings, let me ILLUSTRATE. *Para evitar malentendidos, déjeme aclararle el asunto.* || **2.** Show. *Demostrar.* ~This example ILLUSTRATES how serious the problem is. *Este ejemplo demuestra la gravedad del problema.* ⇨ILUSTRAR

ILLUSTRATION. *n.* Example. *Ejemplo.* ~By way of ILLUSTRATION. *Como (a modo de) ejemplo.* **2.** Clarification. *Aclaración, explicación.* ~He gave an ILLUSTRATION of what he meant. *Aclaró lo que quería decir.* || **3.** [In book]. *Grabado, lámina.* ⇨ILUSTRACIÓN

IMAGE. *n.* Fame, reputation. *Reputación, fama.* ~The company is trying to improve its IMAGE. *La compañía está tratando de mejorar su reputación.* || **2.** Idea, concept. *Idea, concepto.* She had a clear IMAGE of what she would look like in 20 years. *Tenía una idea clara de como se vería dentro de 20 años.* Miller dismisses the classic IMAGE of American democracy as a «fairy tale». *Miller rechaza el concepto clásico de la democracia americana calificándola de «cuentos de hadas» (Cit. Prats).* ~The IMAGE that most people have of the French. *El concepto que la mayoría de la gente tiene de los franceses.* || **3.** Embodiment. *Personificación.* She was the IMAGE of frustration. *Era la imaginación viva de la desesperación.* || **4.** •He's the spitting (living) IMAGE of his father. *Es el vivo retrato de su padre.* || **5.** •To have a bad IMAGE of someone. *Tener* *mal concepto de alguien.* ⇨IMAGEN

IMAGINATION [IMAGINACIÓN]. *n.* Inventiveness, resourcefulness. *Inventiva, ingenio.* A job that requires imagination. *Un puesto que requiere inventiva.* ‖ **2.** Creative ability. *Poder creador, ingenio.* What a fertile IMAGINATION he must have, to have written such spellbound stories. *Que gran ingenio hubo de tener para escribir historias tan cautivantes.* ‖ **3.** [Capture the IMAGINATION of]. To fascinate, interest. *Deleitar, deslumbrar, cautivar, apasionar, suscitar el interés de.* ~His music captured the IMAGINATION of a whole generation of young people. *Su música deslumbró a toda una generación de jóvenes.* ‖ **4.** *PHRASES.* ‖ •It's a figment of your IMAGINATION. *Son imaginaciones tuyas.* ‖ •The product failed to capture the public IMAGINATION. *El producto no despertó el interés del público.* ‖ •By no stretch of the IMAGINATION. *Ni remotamente.* ~He couldn't by any stretch of the IMAGINATION be called a handsome man. *Ni remotamente se le puede considerar hombre bien parecido.*

IMMACULATE. *adj.* Tidy. *Perfectamente ordenado.* ~The room was IMMACULATE. *El cuarto estaba perfectamente ordenado.* ‖ **2.** [Clothes, appearance]. *Impecable.* ~He was elegantly dressed, with a suit that was IMMACULATE. *Iba muy elegante y con un traje impecable.* ‖ **3.** [Work, style]. *Perfecto.* ~Your timing is IMMACULATE. *Llegaste justo a tiempo.* ~They're expensive, but their service is IMMACULATE. *No son baratos, pero su servicio es perfecto.* ‖ **4.** Flawless (performance, taste). *Impecable.* ~He gave an IMMACULATE performance. *Su actuación fue impecable.* ‖ **5.** [Conduct]. *Impecable.* ⇨INMACULADO

IMMATERIAL [INMATERIAL]. *adj.* Irrelevant. *Que no viene al caso, que no tiene que ver con (lo tratado).* ~It's IMMATERIAL to me whether we win or not. *Me trae sin cuidado si ganamos o no.* ~My views are IMMATERIAL. *Lo que opino no viene al caso.* ‖ **2.** •That's IMMATERIAL. *Eso no tiene importancia, eso no viene al caso.* ‖ **3.** [Law]. *No pertinente.*

IMMEDIATE [INMEDIATO]. *adj.* Urgent, pressing (aim, problem, need, concern). *Urgente, apremiante.* ~The IMMEDIATE problem is to find out how to get out of this place. *El problema de más urgencia es encontrar la manera de salir de este lugar.* ‖ **2.** Close, near (area, family). *Cercano, próximo.* ~Only his IMMEDIATE family was present. *Sólo asistieron sus familiares más cercanos.* ~IMMEDIATE future. *Futuro próximo.* ‖ **3.** [Danger]. *Inminente.* ~There's an IMMEDIATE danger of a flood. *Es inminente el peligro de inundación.* ‖ **4.** [Heir]. *En línea directa.* ‖ **5.** [Relief]. *Instantáneo.* ~These tablets provide IMMEDIATE relief. *Estas tabletas proporcionan un alivio instantáneo.* ‖ **6.** Instinctive (reaction). *Instintivo.* ~My IMMEDIATE reaction was to say no. *Instintivamente dije que no.* ‖ **7.** Direct, prime (cause). *Principal, directo.* The IMMEDIATE cause of death was poison. *Su muerte fue ocasionada directamente por el veneno.* ‖ **8.** No secondary or remote; direct. *Directo.* ~The IMMEDIATE parties to the quarrel. *Las personas directamente involucradas en el pleito.* ‖ **9.** *PHRASES.* ‖ •The IMMEDIATE area. *Las inmediaciones.* ‖ •IMMEDIATE need. *Primera necesidad.* ‖ •To have IMMEDIATE rapport (with someone). *Simpatizar en seguida (con alguien).* ‖ •We have no IMMEDIATE plans to go to Paris. *No tenemos proyectado ir a París de momento.*

IMMENSELY [-MENTE]. *adj.* [Rich, gifted). *Enormemente.* ~He's IMMENSELY rich. *Tiene una enorme fortuna.* ‖ **2.** [Interesting, difficult]. *Sumamente.* ~The meeting was IMMENSELY interesting. *La reunión resultó sumamente interesante.* ‖ **3.** Very much. *Muchísimo.* ~We enjoyed ourselves IMMENSELY. *Lo disfrutamos muchísimo, lo pasamos en grande.* ~It was IMMENSELY helpful. *Fue de muchísima ayuda.*

IMMERSION. *n.* [In work, study]. *Absorción, enfrascamiento.* ~Her IMMERSION in her books was total. *Estaba totalmente enfrascada en su lectura.* ⇨INMERSIÓN

IMPACT [IMPACTO]. *n.* Collision, shock. *Choque, golpe.* ~He felt the terrific IMPACT of the blow. *Sintió el tremendo efecto del choque.* || **2.** Influence, effect. *Influencia, huella, repercusión, consecuencias, efecto.* ~The IMPACT of wage increase on production costs. *La repercusión de los aumentos de salarios en los costes de producción.* ~This will have very little IMPACT on the budget deficit. *Eso hará muy poca mella en el déficit presupuestario.* The IMPACT of Einstein on modern physics. *La influencia de Einstein en la física moderna.* || **3.** Influence, effect (of a book, movie). *Sensación, impresión, conmoción, interés.* The poem had a great IMPACT on me. *~El poema me impresionó mucho.* ~The book had a great IMPACT on its readers. *El libro conmovió profundamente a sus lectores.* ~The speech made no IMPACT. *El discurso no hizo mella.* || **4.** •The force of the IMPACT. *La intensidad (fuerza) del choque.*

IMPART. *v.* To make known (news, information). *Comunicar, hacer saber, difundir.* ~The role of a university is to IMPART knowledge. *La universidad tiene como función difundir conocimientos.* || **2.** [Secret]. *Divulgar.* || **3.** [Feeling, quality]. *Conferir, dar.* ~Oregano IMPARTS a delicious flavor to the stew. *El orégano le da un rico sabor al guiso.* The leafy green stage IMPARTS a feeling of tranquility to the first act of the play. *El escenario asi adornado de verdes hojas le confiere una sensación de serenidad al primer acto de la obra.* || **4.** [Motion]. *Transmitir.* || **5.** Conceder. *To grant.* ~His manner of speaking IMPARTED authority to a mediocre plan. *Su forma de hablar concedió seriedad a un proyecto que se consideraba mediocre.* ⇨IMPARTIR

IMPEDE. *v.* Hinder (progress, communications). *Estorbar, dificultar.* ~Storms at sea IMPEDED our progress. *Un temporal dificultó nuestra travesía.* ~Although he's shy it hasn't IMPEDED his career. *Aunque es tímido, ello no ha sido un estorbo para su carrera.* || **2.** Obstruct. *Poner obstáculos, trabas a.* ~To IMPEDE the flow of traffic. *Obstruir el tráfico.* ⇨IMPEDIR

IMPERATIVE [IMPERATIVO]. *adj.* [Tone, voice]. *Imperioso.* ~He spoke to me in an IMPERATIVE tone of voice. *Me habló en un tono imperioso.* || **2.** Urgent, pressing (need). *Urgente, apremiante.* ~There was an IMPERATIVE need to solve this matter. *Había una necesidad apremiante de resolver este asunto.* || **3.** Authoritative. *Perentorio, autoritario.* ~An IMPERATIVE manner. *Una actitud autoritaria.* || **4.** Essential. *Imprescindible, fundamental.* ~It's IMPERATIVE that the work be completed by Friday. *Es imprescindible que el trabajo esté listo para el viernes.*

IMPLEMENT [IMPLEMENTAR]. *v.* [General]. *Llevar a cabo, realizar, poner en práctica.* ~We have decided to IMPLEMENT the committee's suggestions in full. *Hemos acordado llevar a cabo todas las sugerencias de la comisión.* || **2.** [Promise]. *Cumplir.* ~He continued to clamor for action to IMPLEMENT the promise. *Siguió insistiendo que se tomaran medidas para cumplir la promesa.* || **3.** [Law, policy]. *Aplicar.* ~The new national health system will be implemented next year. *El nuevo programa de salud pública se aplicará el año que viene.* || **4.** [Decisions, measure]. *Poner en práctica.*

IMPLICATE. *v.* To involve. *Comprometer, enredar, envolucrar.* ~They are IMPLICATED in the crime. *Están involucrados en el crimen.* ~He was IMPLICATED in the scandal. *Fue comprometido en el escándalo.* ~Are you IMPLICATED in this? *¿Estás metido en eso?* ⇨IMPLICAR

IMPLICATION. *n.* Consequence, effect. *Consecuencia, repercusión, proyección, efecto.* One cannot tell what the IMPLICATION of his action will be. *No se puede decir cuáles serán las consecuencias de su acción.* ~We will have to study all the IMPLICATIONS. *Tendremos que estudiar todas las consecuencias.* || **2.** Involvement (in a crime). *Complicidad, participación.* ~His *implication* in the crime has not yet been determined. *Todavía no se ha comprobado su participación en el delito.* || **3.** The act of implying, suggestion, hint. *Insinuación.*

~I resent the IMPLICATION that I would have lied to you. *Me ofende la sugerencia de que yo te mentiría.* ~By IMPLICATION, he is blaming us. *Indirectamente nos está acusando.* || **4.** Significance. *Transcendencia, importancia.* ~He did not realize the IMPLICATION of his words. *No se dio cuenta de la transcendencia de sus palabras.* || **5.** •By IMPLICATION then ... *De ahí se deduce, pues ...* ⇨ IMPLICACIÓN

IMPLICIT [IMPLÍCITO]. *adj.* [Belief, trust]. *Absoluto.* ~IMPLICIT ignorance. *Una ignorancia absoluta.* || **2.** Unquestioning, wholehearted (faith, obedience). *Incondicional, ciego.* ~They followed him with IMPLICIT obedience. *Le seguían con fe ciega.*

IMPOSE. *v.* Take advantage of. *Abusar, aprovecharse de.* ~To IMPOSE on someone's generosity/goodwill/hospitality. *Abusar de la generosidad/buena voluntad/hospitalidad de alguien.* || **2.** To bother, trouble. *Molestar, importunar.* ~I think I've IMPOSED on him enough already. *Me parece que ya lo he molestado bastante.* ⇨ IMPONER

IMPOSITION. *n.* Taking unfair advantage of. *Abuso.* ~It really was an IMPOSITION on her hospitality. *La verdad es que fue abusar de su hospitalidad.* || **2.** Bother. *Molestia.* ~Would it be an IMPOSITION if? *¿Le molestaría si?* ⇨ IMPOSICIÓN

IMPRESS. *v.* To create a favorable impression *Causar una buena impresión, gustar, encantar.* ~We were IMPRESSED by your work. *Su obra nos causó una muy buena impresión.* ~I was not IMPRESSED by the film. *No me gustó sobremanera la película.* ~He IMPRESSED us as a sincere young man. *Nos causó la impresión de ser un muchacho sincero.* What IMPRESSED me most about the book was its vivid language. *Lo que más me gustó del libro fue su lenguage expresivo.* ~We were IMPRESSED by his acting. *Quedamos admirado de su actuación.* ~As an actress she fails to IMPRESS. *Como actriz no llama la atención.* ~He only did it to impress her. *Lo hizo sólo para dejarla admirada.* || **2.** Mark. *Imprimir, marcar.* ~Patterns IMPRESSED in the clay. *Diseños*

impresos en la arcilla. || **3.** [Upon one's mind]. *Quedar grabado.* ~It IMPRESSED itself on my mind. *Quedó grabado en mi memoria.* ~Her advice remained IMPRESSED on my mind. *Sus consejos quedaron grabados en mi memoria.* || **4.** [Pattern]. *Estampar.* || **5.** To convince. *Convencer.* I tried to IMPRESS the importance of the job on him. *Traté de convencerle de la importancia del puesto.* My excuse did not IMPRESS them. *Mi excusa no les convenció.* || **6.** [Followed by *upon*]. To stress, emphasize. *Recalcar.* ~They IMPRESSED upon us that it could be dangerous. *Nos recalcaron el hecho de que podría ser peligroso.* He tried to IMPRESS upon him the gravity of the situation. *Le recalcó lo peligroso de la situación.* || **7.** Inculcate, stress the importance of. *Inculcar.* ~My father IMPRESSED upon me the importance of work. *Mi padre me inculcó la importancia del trabajo.* ⇨ IMPRESIONAR

IMPROPER. *adj.* [Conditions, method]. *Inadecuado.* I will not work in IMPROPER conditions. *No pienso trabajar en condiciones inadecuadas.* || **2.** Indecent. *Indecente, indecoroso.* ~An IMPROPER suggestion. *Una insinuación indecorosa (indecente).* || **3.** [Behavior, actions]. *Deshonesto.* ~IMPROPER conduct. *Comportamiento poco honrado.* || **4.** Wrong (use, diagnosis). *Incorrecto, equivocado.* ~It was an IMPROPER diagnosis. *Fue un diagnosis equivocado.* ⇨ IMPROPRIO

INADEQUATE. *adj.* [Service]. *Deficiente.* ~The food was good but unfortunately the service was INADEQUATE. *No era mala la comida, pero desafortunadamente el servicio resultó deficiente.* ⇨ INADECUADO

INAUGURATE. *v.* [President, official]. *Investir.* ~He was INAUGURATED president. *Fue investido como presidente.* || **2.** [Statue]. *Descubrir.* ⇨ INAUGURAR

INAUGURATION [INAUGURACIÓN]. *n.* [Presidential]. *Toma de posesión, investidura.*

INCENTIVE [INCENTIVO]. *n.* Stimulus. *Estímulo, aliciente.* ~Increasing needs are often an INCENTIVE to invention. *In muchos casos ocurre que las necesidades apremiantes sirven de estímulo para la creación.*

INCIDENCE. *n.* Occurrence. *Frecuencia, volumen, intensidad.* ~The high INCIDENCE of false calls. *El elevado incremento de las falsas alarmas.* ~The high INCIDENCE of death among ... *El alto índice de muerte en ...* ⇨INCIDENCIA

INCLINATION. *n.* Desire. *Deseo, ganas.* ~I have neither the time nor the INCLINATION to see you. *Yo no tengo ni tiempo ni deseos de verlo.* ~She shows no INCLINATION to relinquish her post. *No da muestras de querer dejar su puesto.* ~My INCLINATION is to stay. *Yo prefiero quedarme.* ⇨INCLINACIÓN

INCLUDING [INCLUYENDO]. *prep.* Among which. *Entre ellos, entre los que figuran.* He wrote many books, INCLUDING two on Mexico. *Escribió numerosos libros entre los que figuran dos sobre México.* || **2.** Like. *Como son, como por ejemplo.* There are many things he wouldn't recognize if he came back, INCLUDING the new school and the new City Hall. *De volver habría muchas cosas que no reconocería, como por ejemplo la escuela y el Ayuntamiento, que son nuevos (Cit. Prats).* || **3.** Even. *Hasta.* It's a play where everybody dies, INCLUDING the prompter. *Es una de esas comedias en las que muere hasta el apuntador (Prats).* ~I stayed up to and INCLUDING Friday. *Me quedé hasta el viernes inclusive.* ~They all liked it, INCLUDING Paul. *A todos les gustó, contando (incluso) a Paul.* || **4.** If you include. *Contando.* ~We have six children INCLUDING the baby. *Tenemos seis hijos contando el bebé.* INCLUDING the introduction, the book runs to 300 pages. *Contando la introducción, el libro tiene 300 páginas.* ~I have five INCLUDING this one. *Con éste tengo cinco.*

INCONSISTENCY. *n.* Incongruity, incompability, contradiction. *Incongruencia, contradicción, anomalía, falta de concordancia.* ~I see an INCONSISTENCY here. *Aquí veo una contradicción.* ⇨ INCONSISTENCIA

INCONSISTENT. *adj.* Contradictory. *Contradictorio, ilógico.* ~Your evidence is INCONSISTENT with the facts. *Su testimonio no concuerda con los hechos.* || **2.** Unpredictable, unreliable. *Inconsecuente, desigual (performance).* ~The team's performance this season has been highly INCONSISTENT. *La actuación del equipo esta temporada ha sido muy desigual.* ⇨ INCONSISTENTE

INCONVENIENCE. *n.* Bother, trouble. *Molestia, contrariedad, inconveniente.* ~Please excuse the INCONVENIENCE. *Disculpe la molestia.* ⇨INCONVENIENCIA

INCONVENIENT. *adj.* [Persona]. *Molesto.* || **2.** [Place]. *Mal situado, incómodo.* ~The phone is in an INCOVENIENT place. *El teléfono está mal situado.* ~It's a very INCONVENIENT place to hold the meeting. *Es un lugar muy incómodo para tener la reunión.* || **3.** [Time]. *Inoportuno, mal escogido.* ~An INCONVENIENT time for a visit. *Un momento inoportuno para tener visita.* || **4.** [Arrangement, design]. *Poco práctico.* ~The furniture layout is very INCONVENIENT. *La disposición de los muebles es poco práctica.* || **5.** Difficult. *Difícil, incómodo.* ~It's a bit INCONVENIENT for me to get to the center of town. *Es algo difícil para mi llegar al centro.* ~It's INCONVENIENT for me to not to have a car. *Me es incómodo no tener coche.* ⇨INCONVENIENTE

INCORPORATE. *v.* To include, contain. *Incluir, comprender.* Great Britain INCORPORATES England, Scotland and Wales. *Gran Bretaña comprende Inglaterra, Escocia y Gales.* || **2.** [Business, enterprise]. *Constituir.* A company INCORPORATED in the State of New Jersey. *Una compañía constituida en el estado de New Jersey.* || **3.** Contain. *Contener.* ~A product INCORPORATING vitamin Q. *Una producto que contiene vitamina Q.* ⇨INCORPORAR

INCUR. *v.* Come into, acquire. *Contraer.* ~To INCUR obligations. *Contraer obligaciones.* || **2.** To cause, make. *Realizar, hacer, causar, ocasionar.* ~Expenses INCURRED by the passengers. *Gastos realizados (hechos) por los pasajeros.* ⇨INCURRIR

INDICATION. *n.* [Sign, hint]. *Indicio.* ~We were given no INDICATION of what was going to happen. *No se nos dio ningún indicio (ninguna pauta) de lo que iba a ocurrir.* ~There's every INDICATION that. *Todo parece indicar que.* ~The footprints gives us an INDICATION of the animal's size. *Las huellas nos da una idea del tamaño del animal.* ⇨ INDICACIÓN

INDIVIDUAL. *adj.* Separate. *Suelto, por separado.* They won't sell you INDIVIDUAL volumes. You have to buy the whole series. *No te venderán tomos sueltos. Tienes que comprar toda la colección (Prats).* ‖ **2.** Separate. *Cada uno, particular de cada caso; varios, distintos.* ~The statistics for INDIVIDUAL airports are shown on page 4. *Las estadísticas correspondientes a cada aeropuerto se indican en la página 4 (Prats).* ~The system may be changed to meet the INDIVIDUAL requirements of aerodromes. *El sistema puede modificarse de acuerdo con las necesidades particulares de cada aeródromo.* ‖ **3.** Personal. *Personal.* ~INDIVIDUAL tastes. *Gustos personales.* ~She has her INDIVIDUAL style of dressing. *Tiene un estilo muy personal de vestirse.* ‖ **4.** Own, particular, separate. *Propio, particular.* ~Each one of you will be given an INDIVIDUAL copy. *Cada uno tendrá su propia copia.* ~Each case will be judged on its INDIVIDUAL merit. *Cada caso se juzgará según sus propios méritos.* ‖ **5.** Each. *Cada uno.* ~Individual parts of a tea set. *Cada pieza (cada una de las piezas) de un juego de té.* ▶At times this word is not translated in Spanish. ~A collection comprising 25 INDIVIDUAL volumes. *Una colección de 25 tomos.* ⇨ INDIVIDUAL

INFER. *v. Deduce.* ~We INFERED from comments they had made to friends that they were not willing to support us. *Por lo que comentaron a unos amigos, deducimos que no estaban dispuestos a apoyarnos.* ⇨ INFERIR

INFLAME. *v.* [Curiosity]. *Excitar, avivar.* ‖ **2.** [Crowd]. *Excitar.* ~His remarks INFLAMED the crowd. *Sus comentarios excitó a la muchedumbre.* ‖ **3.** [Situación]. *Exacerbar.*

‖ **4.** [Passion, anger]. *Encender.* Anger INFLAMED her cheeks. *La cólera encendía sus mejillas.* ‖ **5.** •To be INFLAMED with rage. *Rabiar.* ⇨ INFLAMAR

INFORMAL. *adj.* [Visit, gathering, discussion, occasion]. *De confianza, íntimo, entre amigos, sin ceremonias.* ~They speak to their superiors in an INFORMAL manner. *Hablan a sus superiores sin ceremonias.* ~An INFORMAL dinner. *Una cena entre amigos.* ‖ **2.** [Language, treatment, tone, manner]. *Familiar.* ~In INFORMAL English. *En inglés familiar.* ~The atmosphere at work is fairly INFORMAL. *En el trabajo hay un ambiente muy familiar.* ‖ **3.** Unofficial. *No oficial, extraoficial.* ~An INFORMAL gathering of friends. *Una reunión entre amigos.* ‖ **4.** [Persona]. *Desenvuelto, afable, poco ceremonioso.* ‖ **5.** [Dance]. *Sin etiqueta.* ⇨ INFORMAL

INGENIOUS. *adj.* Bright, gifted, able, resourceful. *Hábil, mañoso.* ‖ **2.** [Scheme]. *Genial.* ~That was certainly an INGENIOUS idea. *No cabe duda de que fue una idea genial.* ⇨ INGENUOSO

INGENUITY. *n.* The quality of being cleverly inventive or resourceful, inventiveness. *Inventiva, habilidad, ingeniosidad, ingenio.* ‖ **2.** [Gadget, tool, idea]. *Lo genioso.* ‖ **3.** •To test one's INGENUITY. *Aguzar el ingenio.* ⇨ INGENUIDAD

INHALE [INHALAR]. *v.* [Air]. *Aspirar, respirar.* ‖ **2.** Cigarette smoke. *Tragar.* ‖ **3.** *vi.* [Smoker]. *Tragarse el humo.*

INHERENT [INHERENTE]. *adj.* •With all the INHERENT difficulties. *Con todas las dificultades inevitables.* ‖ **2.** •The risks INHERENT in climbing. *Los riesgos propios del montañismo.* ‖ **3.** •With all its INHERENT difficulties. *Con todas las dificultades que conlleva.*

INHIBIT [INHIBIR]. *v.* [Freedom, activity]. *Limitar, restringir.* This law INHIBITS freedom of speech. *Con esta ley se restringe la libertad de expresión.* ‖ **2.** [Person]. *Cohibir.* ‖ **3.** [Sales, growth]. *Limitar.* ~Failure to set up a good transport network INHIBITED the expansion of trade. *El no haber sabido elaborar un buen sistema de transporte ha limitado la expansión del comercio.* || **4.** To prevent. *Impedir.* ~Don't let my presence INHIBIT the discussion. *No quiero que mi presencia impida la discusión.* ~Her shyness INHIBITED her from saying more. *Su timidez le impidió decir algo más.*

INITIATE. *v.* [Plan, reform]. *Promover, poner en marcha.* The government INITIATED a road-building program. *El gobierno puso en marcha un programa de construcción de carreteras.* || **2.** [Lawsuit, proceedings]. *Entablar.* ~He INITIATED court proceedings in order to recover his debts. *Entabló una demanda judicial para recobrar el dinero que se le debía.* || **3.** Admit (into a secret society). *Admitir.* ~The club will INITIATE new members Tuesday. *El martes el club admitirá nuevos miembros.* || **4.** [Fashion]. *Introducir.* ~To INITIATE a change in fashions. *Introducir una nueva moda.* ⇨ INICIAR

INJECT [INYECTAR]. *v.* [With a vaccine]. *Vacunar.* || **2.** [Capital]. *Invertir.* ~A large amount of money will have to be INJECTED into the company. *Se tendrá que invertir una gran suma de dinero en la compañía.* || **3.** [Life, hope]. *Infundir.* ~To INJECT new life into a club. *Infundir un espíritu nuevo a un club.*

INPENETRABLE. *adj.* [Mystery, thoughts]. *Insondable.* || **2.** [Character, smile]. *Inescrutable.* || **3.** Incorrigible. *Incorrigible.* ⇨ IMPENETRABLE

INQUIRE [INQUIRIR]. *v.* Ask. *Preguntar.* ~She INQUIRED what the matter was. *Preguntó que pasaba.* ~I INQUIRED how to get to the cathedral. *Pregunté como se llegaba a la catedral.* ~INQUIRE at the reception desk. *Pregunte (infórmese) en recepción.* || **2.** Find out. *Averiguar, informarse de.* I'm INQUIRING about the job advertised in the newspaper. *Llamo para informarme sobre el trabajo que anuncia en el periódico.* || **3.** *PHRASES.* || •INQUIRE about. *Pedir informes sobre.* ~Shall I INQUIRE about the price of the tickets? *¿Quiere Ud. que pida informes sobre el precio de los billetes?* || •INQUIRE after (a person's

health). *Preguntar por.* Someone was INQUIRING about you. *Alguien preguntó por Ud.* || •INQUIRE into (case, matter). *Investigar, indagar.* ~The police are INQUIRING into his sudden death. *La policía está haciendo investigaciones sobre su muerte repentina.* || •I was only INQUIRING. *Era una simple pregunta.* || •INQUIRE within. *Razón aquí.*

INSENSIBLE. *adj.* Unconscious. *Inconsciente, sin conocimiento.* || **2.** Unaware. *Inconsciente.* ~I'm not INSENSIBLE to the risks involved. *Soy consciente de los riesgos que acarrea.* ~The blow knocked him INSENSIBLE. *El golpe le hizo perder el conocimiento.* || **3.** Indifferent. *Indiferente.* ~She is quite INSENSIBLE to his distress. *Su angustia le es totalmente indiferente.* ⇨ INSENSIBLE

INSPECT [INSPECCIONAR]. *v.* [Luggage]. *Registrar, revisar.* || **2.** [Troops]. *Pasar revista.* ~The king INSPECTED the troops. *El Rey pasó revista a las tropas.* || **3.** Look closely at (car, camera). *Examinar, revisar.* ~INSPECT the documents for any discrepancies. *Revisen los documentos para comprobar si hay alguna discrepancia.*

INSPIRE [INSPIRAR]. *v.* [Respeto, hope, courage]. *Infundir.* ~The news INSPIRED us with new hopes. *La noticia nos infundió nuevas esperanzas.* || **2.** To influence, encourage. *Estimular, animar.* ~It INSPIRED me to try harder. *Me animó a esforzarme más.* ~What inspired you to do that? *¿Qué te movió (llevó) a hacer eso?*

INSTANCE. *n.* Example. *Ejemplo.* •To cite a few INSTANCES. *Para citar algunos ejemplos.* •For INSTANCE. *POR EJEMPLO.* || **2.** Case. *Caso.* •In this INSTANCE. *En este caso, en esta situación.* •In many INSTANCES. *En muchos casos.* •In the present INSTANCE. *En el caso presente.* •Let's take an actual INSTANCE. *Tomemos un caso concreto.* •In the first INSTANCE. *En primer lugar.* ⇨ INSTANCIA

INSTANT [En el INSTANTE]. *adj.* Immediate. *Inmediato.* ~Bourgeois cartoons hold the major quality required in the field; they have INSTANT impact. *Las caricaturas de Bour-*

geois poseen la cualidad más importante que se requiere en este género: producen un efecto inmediato (Cit. Prats). || **2.** [Need]. *Imperioso, urgente.*

INSTITUTION. *n.* [Cultural]. *Instituto.* || **2.** [Home for the aged]. *Asilo.* || **3.** Asylum. *Manicomio.* || **4.** [For abandoned children]. *Hospicio.* || **5.** Long-established person, fixture. *Persona conocidísima.* ⇨ INSTITUCIÓN

INSTRUCTION. *n.* Order. *Orden.* ~On the INSTRUCTIONS of the boss. *Por orden del jefe.* ~We have given INSTRUCTIONS for the transfer of ... *Hemos cursado órdenes para la transferencia de ...* ~I'm under DIRECTIONS to be back at eight. *Tengo órdenes de estar de vuelta a las ocho.* || **2.** •Driving INSTRUCTION. *Clases de conducir.* || **3.** •To give INSTRUCTION. *Enseñar.* ~To give somebody INSTRUCTION in fencing. *Enseñar esgrima (a uno).* || **4.** •INSTRUCTIONS for use. *Modo de empleo.* ⇨ INSTRUCCIÓN

INTEREST [INTERÉS]. *n.* Advantage. *Provecho, beneficio.* ~In the INTEREST of peace. *En pro de la paz.* ~In the INTEREST of safety. *Para mayor seguridad.* ~It's not in my best INTEREST. *No salgo ganando.* ~To act in one's own INTEREST. *Obrar en beneficio propio.* ~It is in your own INTEREST to confess. *Le conviene confesar.* ~ It is not in Ruritania's INTEREST to leave the base. *Le perjudicará a Ruritania abandonar la base.* ~In the INTEREST of easing international tension. *Con el fin de relajar la tensión internacional.* ~I have your INTERESTS at heart. *Lo hago por su bien.* || **2.** Hobby, pastime, leisure time activities. *Pasatiempos, aficion, curiosidad, interés por las cosas .* ~Her main INTERESTS are tennis and dancing. *Sus pasatiempos predilectos son el tenis y el baile.* ~He has a wide range of INTERESTS. *Tiene una gran curiosidad (cultural, científica, intelectual), tiene muchas aficiones, se interesa en muchas cosas.* || **3.** Share (part, stake). *Participación.* ~He has a controlling INTEREST in the firm. *Tiene participación mayoritaria en la empresa.* ~I have a small INTEREST in a diamond mine. *Tengo una pequeña participación en una mina de diamantes.* || **4.**

Share (of stock). *Acción.* ~These are shares that yield a high INTEREST. *Son acciones que rinden bien.* || **5.** Business. *Negocio.* ~He has a number of business INTERESTS abroad. *Tiene varios negocios en el extranjero.* ~She travels abroad to look after her INTERESTS. *Viaja al extranjero para atender sus negocios, los asuntos de su negocio.* [Business interests] *Los negocios, el mundo de los negocios, los empresarios,* [Powerful group] *Las altas empresas, la alta finanza.* || **6.** Industry. *Industria.* ~The coal INTEREST. *La industria hullera.* || **7.** [Personal]. Stake *Motivos personales.* ~I have a personal INTEREST to see that justice is done. *Tengo motivos personales para asegurarme que se haga justicia.* || **8.** •To repay with INTEREST. *Pagar con creces.* ~He repaid my affection with INTEREST. *Me devolvió con creces el cariño que le había dado.* They'll pay me back with INTEREST! *¡Me las van a pagar con creces!*

INTERFERE [INTERFERIR]. *v.* To meddle, get involved. *Entrometerse, meterse.* ~She started INTERFERING as usual. *Empezó a entrometerse como de costumbre.* ~Who told you to INTERFERE? *¿Quién te mete a tí en eso?* ~Don't INTERFERE in her affairs! *¡No te metas (entrometas) en sus asuntos!* ~I wouldn't want to INTERFERE with your personal matters, but I think you should find another school for your son. *No quisiera meterme en tus asuntos personales, pero creo que deberías cambiar a tu hijo de escuela (Prats).* || **2.** To tamper. *Forzar, descomponer.* ~The lock had clearly been INTERFERED with. *Era obvio que alguien había tratado de forzar la cerradura.* || **3.** To spoil, damage, ruin. *Estropear, echar a perder.* Our neighbor's arrival INTERFERED with our plan. *La llegada de nuestro vecino echó a perder nuestros planes.* || **4.** To touch. *Tocar.* Don't INTERFERE with my papers. *No toques mis papeles.* || **5.** To disrupt. *Entorpecer, obstaculizar, poner trabas, estorbar.* As long as it doesn't INTERFERE with my studies. *Mientras no estorbe mis estudios.* ~Anxiety can INTERFERE with a child's performance at school. *La angustia* *puede entorpecer (obstaculizar) el rendimiento de los niños.* || **6.** To hinder. *Dificultar.* ~She never had children because they would have INTERFERED with her dancing career. *Nunca tuvo hijos porque le hubieran dificultado su carrera de bailarina.* || **7.** To bother, annoy, inconvenience. *Distraer, molestar.* ~Don't INTERFERE when I'm working. *No me molestes cuando estoy trabajando.* ~I'll come to see you later. I don't want to INTERFERE with your work. *Pasaré a verte después. No quiero distraerte de tu trabajo (Prats).* ~Dance music will be played in the first class lounge and will not INTERFERE with economy class passengers. *La música de baile se tocará en el salón de primera clase y no molestará a los pasajeros que viajan en clase económica (Prats).*

INTERPRET. *v.* Translate (orally). *Traducir.* ⇨INTERPRETAR

INTERROGATION [INTERROGACIÓN]. *n.* Questioning. *Interrogatorio.* ~He died under INTERROGATION. *Murió durante el interrogatorio.*

INTERSECT [intersectarse]. *v.* [Road]. *Cortar, cruzar.* ~Where the expressway INTERSECTS the highway. *Donde el autopista cruza la carretera.* || **2.** *vi.* [Roads, paths]. *Cruzarse.* ~INTERSECTING roads. *Caminos que se cruzan.*

INTERSECTION [INTERSECCIÓN]. *n.* Crossroads. *Cruce.* || **2.** Junction. *Bocacalle.*

INTERVENE. *v.* To happen, occur. *Sobrevenir, ocurrir, surgir.* ~If nothing INTERVENES to prevent it. *Si no surge nada que lo impida.* He was about to continue, but the bell INTERVENED. *Iba a continuar, pero sonó la campana.* ~Rain INTERVENED and we postponed the match. *Empezo a llover y tuvimos que aplazar el partido.* || **2.** [Time]. *Transcurrir, mediar.* ~One year INTERVENED before we met again. *Transcurrió un año antes de que nos volviéramos a ver.* ~What happened in the INTERVENING period? *¿Qué pasó en el interín?* || **3.** To be or lie between. *Que ocupa un lugar intermedio.* ~In the INTERVENING chapters. *En los capítulos*

intermedios. ~In the INTERVENING days. *Durante los días intermedios.* ~The INTERVENING hills. *Las colinas intermedias.* || **4.** Interrupt. *Interrumpir.* ~Can I just INTERVENE for a moment? *¿Puedo interrumpir un momento?* ⇨INTERVENIR

INTOXICATED. *adj.* Drunk. *Borracho.* || The driver was clearly INTOXICATED. *Se veía a las claras de que el conductor estaba borracho.* **2.** Mentally or emotionally exhilarated. *Embriagado.* INTOXICATED with dreams of fortune. *Embriagado con la ilusión de que un día llegaría a ser rico.* ⇨INTOXICADO

INTRODUCE. *v.* To present someone to another person. *Presentar.* ~Allow me to INTRODUCE my friend Peter to you. *Permítame que le presente a mi amigo Pedro.* || **2.** To begin, lead into, preface. *Empezar una frase.* ~To INTRODUCE one's speech with an amusing anecdote. *Empezar una frase con una anécdota divertida.* || **3.** [Legislative bill]. *Presentar.* ~To INTRODUCE a bill to Congress. *Presentar un proyecto de ley en el Congreso.* || **4.** To initiate. *Iniciar a alguien en algo.* ~I was INTRODUCED to chess when I was eight years old. *Empecé a jugar al ajedrez cuando tenía ocho años.* ~I was INTRODUCED to Milton too young. *Me hicieron leer a Milton demasiado temprano.* ~He INTRODUCED me to the classics. *Me inició en la lectura de los clásicos.* || **5.** To create, bring into use (new product). *Lanzar, dar a conocer.* To INTRODUCE a new toothpaste. *Lanzar una nueva pasta dentífica.* || **6.** Present formally, announce (a speaker, performer). *Presentar.* INTRODUCING Juan Romero as Don Félix. *Presentamos por primera vez a Juan Romero en el papel de don Félix.* || **7.** Propose, mention, suggest (topic, question). *Proponer, sugerir, plantear.* ~It was she who INTRODUCED the issue of bacteria in canned goods. *Fue ella quien planteó el problema de la bacteria en los alimentos en lata.* || **8.** Bring up (subject). *Abordar.* ~Be careful how you INTRODUCE the subject. *Hay que abordar el tema con mucho cuidado.* || **9.** To preface (a book). *Prologar.* || **10.** •I was INTRODUCED into a dark room. *Me hicieron entrar en un cuarto oscuro.* || **11.** •I was INTRODUCED into his presence. *Me llevaron ante él.* ⇨ INTRODUCIR

INTRODUCTION [INTRODUCCIÓN]. *n.* [Of person]. *Presentación.* ~To make the INTRODUCTIONS. *Hacer las presentaciones.* || **2.** [En el arte]. *Iniciación.* ~An INTRODUCTION to European drama. *Un curso de iniciación al teatro europeo.* || **3.** [Of product]. *Lanzamiento.* ~Since their INTRODUCTION, compact discs have taken over from records. *Desde su lanzamiento, los discos compactos han reemplazado los discos.* || **4.** [Of topic]. *Planteamiento.* || **5.** Experience. *Experiencia.* ~My INTRODUCTION to life in Cadiz. *Mi primera experiencia de la vida en Cádiz.* ~That was my INTRODUCTION to France. *Esa fue mi primera toma de contacto con Francia.* || **6.** [Of legislative bill]. *Presentación.* || **7.** [Music]. *Preludio.* || **8.** •Letter of INTRODUCTION. *Carta de recomendación.*

INTRODUCTORY [INTRODUCTORIO]. *adj.* [Remarks, notes]. *Preliminar.* ~INTRODUCTORY remarks. *Palabras preliminares.* || **2.** [Price, offer]. *De lanzamiento.* || **3.** [Course, lesson]. *Elemental.* An INTRODUCTORY course in French. *Un curso elemental de francés.*

INTRUSION [INTRUSIÓN]. *n.* [[On privacy, mood]. *Invasión.* ~The recording of this conversation constitutes an INTRUSION of privacy. *La grabación de esta conversación supone una invasión de mi intimidad.*

INVENTORY [INVENTARIO]. *n.* Stock. *Existencias.* When the order came in, the INVENTORY was very low. *Cuando llegó el pedido apenas quedaban existencias.*

INVESTIGATION. *n.* Detailed examination. *Examen, estudio.* ~Upon closer INVESTIGATION. *Tras un examen más detenido.* ~Her claim is under INVESTIGATION. *Se está estudiando su petición.* || **2.** •She's under INVESTIGATION by the police. *La policía está haciendo averiguaciones sobre ella.* || **3.** •He was hospitalized for further INVESTIGATION. *Lo hospitalizaron para hacerles más pruebas.*

⇨ INVESTIGACIÓN

INVITE [INVITAR]. *v.* To request politely. *Rogar con cortesía.* ~I was INVITED for an interview. *Me pidieron que fuera a entrevistarse.* ~He was INVITED for an interview. *Lo citaron para una entrevista.* ~To INVITE donations. *Solicitar donaciones.* || **2.** Request (comment, questions, offers). *Solicitar, pedir, rogar.* ~He INVITES our opinion. *Solicita nuestra opinión.* || **3.** To cause (disaster, criticism). *Provocar.* ~His suggestion INVITED a lot of criticism. *Su sugerencia provocó muchas críticas.* || **4.** Encourage. *Incitar.* ~You are INVITING problems. *Te estás buscando problemas.* ~It INVITES people to draw the wrong conclusions. *Se presta a que la gente saque conclusiones erróneas.* His work INVITES comparison with the classics. *Su obra sugiere comparaciones con los clásicos.* ~It INVITES doubts about her suitability for the post. *Hace dudar sobre su idoneidad para el puesto.* || **5.** •To INVITE someone to have a drink. *Convidar a uno a tomar algo.* || **6.** •She seems to INVITE stares. *Parece que le gusta que la mire la gente.*

INVOLVE [INVOLUCRAR]. *v.* To imply, entail, require, demand. *Entrañar, implicar, significar, suponer.* This change will INVOLVE a lot of extra work. *Este cambio va a significar mucho trabajo extra.* || **2.** To be a matter of. *Tener que ver con, tratarse de.* ~What is INVOLVED is a matter of principle. *Se trata de una cuestión de principios.* ~Don't you realize it's my reputation that's INVOLVED here? *¿No te das cuenta que es mi reputación lo que está en juego?* ~Whenever there's money INVOLVED. *Siempre que hay dinero de por medio.* || **3.** Consist of, have to do with. *Consistir.* ~What exactly does your work INVOLVE? *¿En qué consiste exactamente su trabajo?* ~What's INVOLVED? *¿De qué se trata?* || **4.** To concern, affect. *Afectar, atañer, concernir.* ~This problem INVOLVES all of us. *Este problema nos concierne (afecta) a todos.* The changes don't INVOLVE me. *Los cambios no me afectan.* || **5.** Require, demand. *Requerir, exigir.* The post INVOLVES (requires) traveling. *El puesto exige viajar.* || **6.** To give rise to, lead to, result in.

Acarrear, ocasionar. ~It INVOLVED a lot of expenses. *Nos acarreó muchos gastos.* || **7.** [Time]. LLEVAR, TOMAR. ~This project will INVOLVE long hours of work. *Este proyecto nos llevará muchas horas de trabajo.* || **8.** To complicate. *Complicar, enredar, comprometer, confundir.* Let's not INVOLVE things. *No confundamos las cosas.* || **9.** To preoccupy, absorb. *Absorber, interesar, atraer.* ~Politics INVOLVES him too much. *La política le absorbe demasiado.* You are much too INVOLVED with the problem to see it clearly. *~Está demasiado absorto en el problema para verlo directamente.* || **10.** To be engrossed. *Enfrascarse.* He was INVOLVED in a book by Shakespeare. *Estaba enfrascado en la lectura de un libro de Shakespeare.* || **11.** To be busy with. *Estar ocupado con.* He said that since he was so INVOLVED with his projects that he would not be able to attend the meeting. *Dijo que estaba tan ocupado con sus proyectos que no iba a poder asistir a la reunión.* ~He's very INVOLVED with his new show at the moment. *En este momento está muy ocupado con su nuevo espectáculo.* || **12.** Afect. *Afectar, alcanzar, comprender.* ~The strike INVOLVES 1,000 workers. *La huelga afecta a mil trabajadores.* || **13.** To be implicated. *Estar implicado.* ~They tried to INVOLVE her in the scandal. *Trataron de implicarla en el escándalo.* ~Was he involved? *¿Estuvo él metido en ello?* ~How did you come to be INVOLVED? *¿Cómo llegaste a estar envuelto en eso?* || **14.** Allow to participate. *Dar participación.* We try to INVOLVE as many people as possible in decision making. *Tratamos de darle participación al mayor número de gente posible en la toma de decisiones.* || **15.** Take part in. *Tomar parte.* ~He doesn't INVOLVE himself in the day-to-day running of the business. *No toma parte en la gestión diaria del negocio.* ~Whenever there's an argument in the family, he has to get INVOLVED. *Siempre que hay una pelea en la familia, tiene que meterse.* || **16.** To get mixed up in something. *Mezclar, involucrar.* ~Don't try to INVOLVE me in

your problems. *No intentes mezclarme en tus problemas.* || **17.** [Emotionally]. To be/get INVOLVED. *Tener relación con alguien.* ~She's INVOLVED with a married man. *Tiene relación con un hombre casado.* ~She doesn't want to get to INVOLVED with him. *No quiere llegar a una relación seria con él.* ~He became involved with a girl. *Tuvo un lío con una joven.* || **18.** To take interest in something. *Interesarse por algo, tomar parte en.* || **19.** PHRASES. || •The issues INVOLVED. *Las cuestiones en juego.* || •The people INVOLVED. *Los interesados.* || •To be INVOLVED in an accident. *Sufrir un accidente.* || •To be deeply INVOLVED in something. *Estar muy metido en algo.* || •The people you're INVOLVED with. *La gente con la que andas metido.* ▸"El parecido morfológico entre *involve* y la palabra española *involucrar* induce a algunos traductores utilizarla frecuentemente como solución de traducción. Nos limitaremos a observar que la definición de *involucrar* (según el Dic. Acad.) es la siguiente: Abarcar, incluir, comprender. || **2.** Injerir en los discursos o escritos cuestiones o asuntos extraños al principal objeto de ellos" (Prats).

IRRELEVANT [IRRELEVANTE]. *adj.* Not relevant, not pertinent. *No pertinente, ajeno (al tema tratado).* ~Questions that are IRRELEVANT to the subject being discussed. *Cuestiones que no tienen nada que ver con el tema discutido, ajenas al tema discutido.* || **2.** PHRASES. •IRRELEVANT remark. *Un comentario fuera de lugar.* •That's IRRELEVANT. *Eso no viene al caso.* ~The size of the building is IRRELEVANT. *El tamaño del edificio no tiene importancia, no viene al caso.* •Whether I agree or not seems to be IRRELEVANT. *Mi opinión no parece contar para nada.* •To be IRRELEVANT to something. *No tener relación con.* •To be IRRELEVANT to somebody. *Serle indiferente a alguien.*

IRRIGATE [IRRIGAR]. *v.* To supply (land) with water by artificial means. *Regar.* Lands are IRRIGATED with water from the canal. *Riegan la tierra con el agua del canal.*

J

JOURNAL [JORNAL]. *n.* Periodical. *Boletín, revista, publicación.* ~A weekly news JOURNAL. *Revista semanal de noticias.* ‖ **2.** Diary. *Diario.* ‖ **3.** Newspaper. *Periódico.* ‖ **4.** [Bookkeeping}. *Libro de diario.* ‖ **5.** [Government, law]. *Actas.* ‖ **6.** [Nautical]. *Diario de a bordo.* ‖ **7.** [Club, learned society]. *Boletín.* The JOURNAL of the American Medical Association. *El boletín de la Asociación Norteamericana de Medicina.*

JOURNEY. *n.* Trip. *Viaje.* ~To go on a JOURNEY. *Salir de viaje.* ~It's a two days JOURNEY from here. *Son dos días de viaje desde aquí.* ~A long JOURNEY. *Un largo viaje.* ‖ **2.** Distance. *Trayecto.* ~a 20 mile JOURNEY. *Un trayecto de 20 millas.* ‖ **3.** Trajectory. *Trayecto.* The capsule's JOURNEY through space. *El trayecto de la capsula por el espacio.* ‖ **4.** Way. *Camino.* ~We'll eat on the JOURNEY. *Comeremos por el camino.* ~I pass it on my JOURNEY to work. *Paso por allí de camino al trabajo.* ‖ **5.** Destination. *Destino.* Our JOURNEY's end is San Francisco. *Nuestro destino es San Francisco.*

‖ **6.** FIG Progress, passing, way. *Paso, camino.* ~On your JOURNEY through life. *En su paso por la vida.* ~The JOURNEY to success. *El camino hacia el éxito.* ⇨ JORNADA

JUBILATION. *n.* Joy, exultation. *Regocijo, alborozo, júbilo.* ⇨ JUBILACIÓN

JUST. *adj.* Deserved. *Merecido.* ~To get one's JUST rewards. *Recibir su merecido.* ‖ **2.** Well-founded. *Justificado, fundado.* ~A JUST battle. *Una batalla justificada.* ~JUST grounds for complaints. *Motivo justificado de queja.* ‖ **3.** Accurate. *Correcto, exacto.* ~JUST proportions. *Proporciones exactas.* ‖ **4.** [Account, representation). *Que se ajusta a la realidad.* ⇨ JUSTO

JUVENILE. *adj.* Childish, immature. *Infantil.* ~Don't be so JUVENILE! *¡No seas tan infantil!* ‖ **2.** [Publishing, literature]. *Infantil y juvenil.* ‖ **3.** [Theater]. •JUVENILE lead. *Papel de galán joven (part), galán joven (actor).* ‖ **4.** •JUVENILE books. *Libros para niños.* ‖ **5.** •JUVENILE court. *Tribunal de menores.* ⇨ JUVENIL

L

LABOR[1]. *n.*

❶ PRODUCTIVE ACTIVITY. Work. *Trabajo.* There is much LABOR involved in redecorating a house. *El renovar una casa significa mucho trabajo.* •LABOR of love. *Trabajo placentero (agradable), tarea muy grata, trabajo realizado con amor, trabajo desinteresado, trabajo hecho por amor al arte.* || **2.** Task. *Tarea.* ~Translation is a LABOR that must be done afresh for each succeeding age. *El traducir es una clase de tarea (trabajo) que debe volver a hacerse cada nueva generación.* || **3.** Hard task, toil. *Esfuerzos, pena, fatiga.* ~The fruits of their LABOR. *Los frutos de sus esfuerzos.* ~With enormous LABORS he made himself into a popular writer. *Tras muchos esfuerzos llegó a ser un escritor muy conocido.*

❷ CHILDBIRTH. *Parto.* ~A difficult LABOR. *Un parto difícil.* || •LABOR pains. *Dolores del parto.* || •To be in LABOR. *Estar de parto.* || •LABOR ward. *Sala de partos.*

❸ WORKERS. *Mano de obra, trabajadores.* || •Cheap LABOR. *Mano de obra barata.* || •division of LABOR. *La división del trabajo.* || •Hard LABOR. *Trabajos forzados.* ~5 years of hard LABOR. *5 años de trabajos forzados.* || •LABOR camp. *Campo de trabajos forzados.* || •LABOR cost. *Costes de la mano de obra.* || •LABOR Day. *Día del Trabajo.* || •LABOR dispute. *Conflicto laboral.* || •LABOR leader. *Dirigente sindical.* || •LABOR movement. *Movimiento obrero.* || •LABOR Party. *El Partido Laborista, los laboristas.* || •LABOR shortage. *Escasez de mano de obra.* •LABOR union. *Sindicato.* || •Lost LABOR. *Trabajo en vano.*

•Manual LABOR. *Trabajo manual.* || •Ministry of LABOR. *Ministerio del trabajo.* || •Organized LABOR. *Sindicación.* || •Skilled LABOR. *Mano de obra especializada.* ⇨LABOR

LABOR[2] [LABORAR]. *v.* Work. *Trabajar (duro).* ~When a writer LABORS long over a single paragraph. *Cuando un escritor se detiene por mucho tiempo en un sólo párrafo.* || **2.** Move. *Avanzar penosamente.* ~To LABOR up a hill. *Subir penosamente una cuesta.* || **3.** [Engine]. *Funcionar con dificultad.* ~The engine is beginning to labor. *El motor funciona con dificultad.* || **4.** To stress, linger on, dwell on. *Machacar, insistir en.* ~I won't LABOR the point. *No hace falta insistir en eso.* ~He did rather LABOR the subject. *Se extendió demasiado sobre el tema.* || **5.** To strive, as toward a goal. *Afanarse por.* ~To LABOR for peace. *Afanarse por lograr la paz.* || **6.** *PHRASES.* || •To LABOR in vain. *Trabajar en vano.* || •To LABOR at something. *Trabajar incansablemente en algo.* || •To LABOR under a delusion. *Hacerse ilusiones, estar equivocado.* ~He was LABORING under the delusion that ... *Se engañaba pensando que ...*

LABORIOUS. *adj.* Requiring much work or perseverance. *Penoso, trabajoso, pesado, difícil.* ~Months of LABORIOUS research. *Meses de penosa investigación.* || **2.** [Style, prose]. *Poco fluído, farragoso.* || **3.** •LABORIOUS in detail. *Con excesivo detalle.* ⇨LABORIOSO

LAMENT. *v.* Mourn (death, loss). *Llorar.* She was LAMENTING the death of her beloved father. *Lloraba la muerte de su querido padre.* ⇨LAMENTAR

LAMP [LÁMPARA]. *n.* [In street]. *Farol.* || **2.**

[Auto, rail]. *Faro.* || **3.** Bulb. *Bombilla.* || **4.** [Figuratively]. *Antorcha.* || **5.** [Miner]. *Linterna.* || **6.** •Rear lamp. *Faro trasero.* || **7.** •LAMP shade. *Pantalla.*

LANGUAGE [LENGUAJE]. *n.* [Of a country]. *Idioma, lengua.* ~Dead LANGUAGE. *Lengua muerta.* ~The English LANGUAGE. *El idioma inglés.* ~We STUDY language and literature. *Estudiamos lengua y literatura.* ~LANGUAGE lab. *Laboratorio de idiomas.* ~LANGUAGE school. *Escuela (academia) de idiomas.* ~Living LANGUAGE. *Lengua viva.* ~Modern LANGUAGES. *Lenguas modernas.* || **2.** *PHRASES.* || •Native LANGUAGE. *Lengua materna.* || •LANGUAGE barrier. *Barrera lingüística.* || •Bad (strong) LANGUAGE. *Palabrotas.* || •To use bad LANGUAGE. *Ser mal hablado.* || FIG •We speak the same LANGUAGE. *Estamos de común acuerdo.*

LARGE. *adj.*
❶ IN SIZE. Big. *Grande.* ~A LARGE garden. *Un jardín grande.* ~A LARGE man. *Un hombre grandote.* ~She has a LARGE nose. *Tiene una nariz grande.* ~Try on a LARGER size. *Pruébate un talle más grande.* ~LARGE print. *Letra grande.* ~These trousers are too LARGE for me. *Estos pantalones me quedan grandes.* ~She had LARGE black eyes. *Tenía grandes ojos negros.* || **2.** [Parcel]. *Bultoso, voluminoso.* || **3.** •The LARGE size. *La talla grande.*
❷ AMOUNT, QUANTITY. Considerable, important. *Importante, considerable, grande.* ~A LARGE proportion of my income. *Una gran parte de mis ingre*sos. ~A LARGE sum of money. *Una gran cantidad (una suma considerable) de dinero.* || **2.** [Meal, harvest]. *Abundante, copioso.*
❸LARGE GROUP OF PEOPLE OR THINGS. [Family, crowd]. *Numeroso.* || **2.** Long, extensive (list). *Extensa.* ~A LARGE wine list. *Una extensa carta de vinos.*
❹IN SCOPE. Extensive, broad (power, issue, question, view). *Amplio, extenso.* ~To have LARGE views. *Tener miras amplias.* ~A useful book about the

conflict, which helps to explain the LARGER picture. *Un libro práctico sobre el conflicto que nos proporciona una perspectiva más amplia.* || **2.** Main, chief. *Principal.*
❺ EXPRESSIONS. || •There it was as LARGE as life. *Se nos apareció de modo inconfundible.* || •It looked LARGER than life. *Parecía más grande de lo que era en realidad.* || •There he was as LARGE as life. *Allí estaba en persona.* || •By and LARGE. *Por lo general.* || •To be at LARGE (prisoner). *Estar libre, estar en libertad, andar suelto.* || •The public at LARGE. *El público en general.* || •On a LARGE scale. *A gran escala.* || •To a LARGE extent. *En gran parte.* ⇨ LARGO

LATITUDE. *n.* Freedom to choose. *Libertad, flexibilidad.* Such LATITUDE leads to indiscipline. *Tanta libertad conduce a la indisciplina.* ⇨ LATITUDES

LAVATORY. *n.* [Room in house]. *Cuarto de baño.* || **2.** [Public]. *Aseos, baños, servicios.* ⇨ LAVATORIO

LAX [LAXO]. *adj.* Careless, negligent. *Descuidado, negligente.* ~He's been very LAX lately with his homework. *Ultimamente ha estado muy descuidado con sus deberes.* || **2.** Loose, not taut. *Flojo, suelto.* || **3.** [Discipline, supervision, laws]. *Poco estricto.* ~LAX laws. *Leyes poco estrictas.*

LECTURE. Speech delivered before an audience. *Conferencia, charla (informal).* ~A LECTURE on medieval art. *Una conferencia sobre el arte medieval.* || **2.** Reproof, reprimand. *Reprimenda, sermón.* ⇨ LECTURA

LIBRARIAN [LIBRERO]. *n.* Person engaged in library service. *Bibliotecario.*

LIBRARY. *n.* Building where books may be read or borrowed. *Biblioteca.* ⇨ LIBRERÍA

LICENSE. *n.* Freedom. *Libertad.* ~You can allow some LICENSE in translation. *Se puede permitir cierta libertad en la traducción.* || **2.** Excess. *Libertinaje.* ~A wave of reforms for the correction of what was regarded as LICENSE. *Una ola de reformas para enmendar lo que se consideraba una clase de libertinaje.* || **3.** Permission.

Permiso. ~To give a criminal a gun is to give him a LICENSE to kill. *Dar a un crimal una pistola es darle permiso de matar.* || **4.** •Driving LICENSE. *Carnet de conducir.* || **5.** •LICENSE number. *Número de matrícula.* || **6.** •LICENSE plate. *Placa de matrícula.* ⇨ LICENCIA

LIGHT. *adj.* [Not heavy]. *Ligero.* ~It's LIGHTER than the other one. *Es más ligero que el otro.* || **2.** [Beer]. *Clara.* || **3.** Bright. *Claro.* ~It gets LIGHT very early these days. *Ahora aclara (amanece) muy temprano.* ~It's already LIGHT. *Ya es de día, ya está claro.* || **4.** [Color]. *Claro.* ~LIGHT green curtains. *Cortinas de un verde claro.* || **5.** [Hair]. *Rubio.* || **6.** [Skin]. *Blanco.* ~Her skin is LIGHTER than the rest of the family. *Tiene la tez más blanca que los demás de la familia.* || **7.** [Fabric]. *Liviano.* ~A LIGHT summer dress. *Un vestido de verano liviano.* || **8.** [Breakfast, meal]. *Ligero.* || **9.** [Breeze, wind]. *Suave.* || **10.** Not strenous (work, duties). *Ligero, fácil.* || **11.** Not serious (music, comedy, ready). *Ligero.* A program of LIGHT entertainment. *Un programa de variedades.* || **12.** [Sound]. *Débil.* || **13.** Sparse (traffic). *Liviano.* ~Traffic is LIGHT at this time. *A esta hora hay poco tráfico.* || **14.** •The losses were fairly LIGHT. *Las pérdidas fueron de poca consideración (de poca monta).* || **15.** •LIGHT rain. *Llovizna.* || **16.** •A LIGHT covering of snow. *Una fina capa de nieve.* ⇨ LEVE/LIGERO

LINE [LÍNEA]. *n.*
▶ LONG THIN MARK. [Made with a pen, or used figuratively]. Pencilmark (penmark), stroke, marking. *Raya, trazo.* || **2.** Border, boundary. *Frontera.* ~We crossed the LINE into Italy. *Cruzamos la frontera de Italia.* || **3.** Wrinkle. *Arruga.* ~He has many LINES around his eyes. *Tiene muchas arrugas alrededor de los ojos.* || **4.** •To draw a LINE though something. *Tachar algo.* || **5.** •To draw a LINE under something. *Subrayar.* || **6.** •State LINE. *Límite de un Estado.* || **7.** •To be a fine LINE between. *Haber sólo un paso entre.* ~There's a FINE line between bluntness and rudeness. *De la franqueza*

a la mala educación hay sólo un paso. || **8.** •To draw the LINE (at something). *Decir basta (a algo), no pasar más allá de.* ~One has to draw the LINE somewhere. *En algún momento hay que decir basta.* || **9.** •To know where to draw the LINE. *Saber cuando hay que parar.* || **10.** •To thread (walk) a thin (fine) LINE. *Caminar en la cuerda floja.* **11.** • FIG To sign on the dotted LINE. *Aprobar a ciegas.*

▶ WAY OF THINKING. ~The government official LINE has always been ... *La filosofía (política) mantenida por el gobierno siempre ha sido ...* || **2.** •To follow the party LINE. *Seguir la política impuesta por el partido.* •LINE of argument. *Argumento.* ~Which LINE of argument is Clark likely to take? *Nos preguntamos que argumento presentará Clark.* || **3.** •LINE of thought. *Hilo del pensamiento.* || **4.** •To be in LINE with. *Estar conforme con.* || **5.** •In LINE with. *De acuerdo con.* || **6.** •Something along these LINES. *Algo por el estilo.* ~I was thinking of something along the LINES of ... *Pensaba en algo parecido a ..., por el estilo de ...* || **7.** ~We're thinking along similar LINES. *Pensamos de igual manera.*

▶ ATTITUDE. Stance, position. *Postura, actitud.* || **2.** •To take a strong/firm/hard/strict LINE. [On something]. *Tener una actitud, adoptar una postura firme sobre algo.* ~The court should take a tougher LINE with ... *El tribunal debería tomar medidas más rigorosas en cuanto a ...* [On someone]. *Emplear mano dura con (una persona).* ~If you don't take a hard LINE with him, he won't perform his work. *Si no empleas una mano dura con él, no va cumplir su trabajo.*

▶ TELEPHONE LINE. •Your father is on the LINE. *Su padre está en el teléfono.* || **2.** •It's a very bad LINE. *Se oye muy mal.* || **3.** •Hold the LINE! *¡No cuelgue!, ¡no se retire¡* || **4.** •Hot LINE. *Teléfono rojo.* || **5.** Wire or cable transmitting electricity of telephone signal. *Tendido.* ~The LINES were damaged by a storm. *El tendido quedó averiado por la tormenta.*

▸ STRING. Cable, rope. *Cuerda.* [Clothes, washing]. *Cuerda (de tender la ropa).* [Power]. *Cable eléctrico.* [For fishing]. *Hilo, sedal (de pescar).*

▸ WRITING/WORDS. [Poetry]. *Verso.* || **2.** [Actor's line]. •He forgot his LINES. *Se olvidó de lo que le tocaba decir.* ~The actor wasn't sure of his LINES. *El actor no se sabía bien su papel.* || **3.** •To learn one's LINE. *Aprenderse el papel.* || **4.** •New LINE. *Punto aparte.* || **5.** Short letter, note. *Cuatro líneas.* ~Drop me a LINE when you arrive. *Escríbenos unas (cuatro) líneas cuando llegues.* || **6.** [Of a story]. Theme, main ideas, outline. *Tema, fondo, idea, significado.* ~In spite of these gaps, the broad LINES of the story remain clear. *A pesar de esas lagunas, el sentido de la obra queda clara.*

▸ ROW OF PEOPLE/THINGS, SERIES. Queue. *Cola.* ~Please wait in LINE. *Póngase en la cola por favor.* || **2.** Row. *Fila.* ~They formed a LINE behind their teacher. *Se pusieron en fila detrás del profesor.* || **3.** [Of trees, cars]. *Hilera.* ~A LINE of cars. *Una hilera de coches.* || **4.** Series. *Serie.* ~He's the latest in a long LINE of radical leaders. *Es el último de una larga serie de dirigentes radicales.* ~A long LINE of disasters. *Una larga serie de desastres.* ~A prestigious LINE of authors from Kafka to Marcuse. *Una serie de renombrados escritores desde Kafka hasta Marcuse.* || **5.** •Somewhere along the LINE. [At a given time]. *En algún momento.* ~We must have made a mistake somewhere along the LINE. *Nos habremos equivocado en algún momento.*

▸ LIES/EXCUSES. Story, (sale) pitch, song and dance. *Rollo, cuento.* ~Don't give me that LINE. *No me vengas otra vez con este cuento.* || **2.** •To shoot a LINE. *Fanfarronearse.*

▸ RAILWAY LINE. Railroad track. *Vía.* ~The accident on the southern LINE is delaying all the trains. *El accidente ocurrido en la vía meridional retrasó a todos los trenes.*

▸ WORK/INTEREST. Occupation, area of activity. *Oficio.* ~What's his LINE? *¿Qué hace, en qué se ocupa, a qué se dedica?* ~In my LINE of business. *En mi trabajo, en mi oficio.* ~Opera isn't really my LINE. *La ópera no es lo mío.* ~I'm in the building LINE. *Estoy en el ramo de la construcción.* || **2.** Company. *Compañía, empresa.* ~Shipping LINE. *Compañía naviera.*

▸ OBEY. •To bring somebody into LINE. *Pararle los pies a alguien, meter en vereda a alguien.* ~He needs to be brought into LINE. *Hay que meterle en vereda.* || **2.** •To step out of LINE. *Salirse de las reglas.* || **3.** •To tow the LINE. *Acatar la disciplina, obedecer órdenes.* || **4.** •To step out of LINE. *Mostrar disconformidad, desobedecer, escapar al control.* || **5.** •To keep someone in LINE. *Mantener bajo control ((a miembros de un grupo o partido).* •MIL To keep (one's men) in LINE. *Mantener la disciplina (entre sus hombres).* || **6.** •To follow the party LINE. *Seguir la política impuesta por el partido.* || **7.** [Of conduct]. *Directiva.*

▸ WAR. Front line. *Frente.* These men have been on the LINE for weeks. *Hace varias semanas que estos hombres han estado en el frente.* ~Beyond enemy LINES. *Detrás del frente enemigo.* || **2.** •He died in the LINE of duty. *Murió cumpliendo su deber.*

▸ DO THE SAME. •In LINE with. *A la par de.* ~Wages haven't risen in LINE with inflation. *Los sueldos no han aumentado a la par de la inflación.* || **2.** •In LINE with other manufacturers, we have ... ~Al igual que otros fabricantes, hemos ...

▸ REMARK. ~His speech was full of memorable LINES. ~He kept giving me that LINE about ... ~Who was it who came up with that FAMOUS line ... || **2.** •The best LINE in the movie. *La mejor frase de la película.*

▸ PRODUCT/SELECTION. [Business]. Class. *Especialidad, ramo.* || **2.** Range of goods. *Surtido.* || **3.** [Goods]. *Género.* || **4.** [Jokes, stories]. Repertoire, collection. *Repertorio, surtido.* He has a nice LINE in mother-in-law jokes. *Tiene un buen repertorio (surtido) de chistes de suegras.*

▸ ROUTE/DIRECTION. Route. *Vía.* || **2.** Trajectory. *Trayectoria.* ~The LINE of a ball/

bullet. *La trayectoria de una pelota/bala.* || **3.** •LINE of vision. *Campo visual.* || **4.** •LINES of communication. *Vías de comunicación.* || **5.** •To be on the right LINE. *Ir por buen camino.*

▶ INFORMATION/INVESTIGATION. Clue. *Indicación, pista.* || **2.** •To give somebody a LINE on something. *Darle una pista de algo a alguien.* || **3.** •A LINE on. *Información de buena fuente.* || **4.** •To get a LINE on somebody. *Descubrir un secreto sobre alguien, informarse sobre.* Interpol is trying to get a LINE on where he might be found. *La Interpol está tratando de averiguar donde vive.* ~She got a LINE on their plan. *Consiguió información sobre su projecto.* ~Police are following several LINES of inquiry. *La policia está siguiendo varias pistas.*

▶ INCLUSIVE/EXHAUSTIVE. •All along the LINE. (I) [At every state]. *Desde el principio.* ~She's had bad luck all along the LINE. *Tuvo mala suerte desde el principio,* (II) [In detail]. *Con todo detalle.* || **2.** •Down the LINE. *Del Primero al último.* ~These changes will affect everyone down the LINE. *Estos cambios afectarán a todos, del primero al último.*

▶ OTHER MEANINGS. [Of descent]. *Linaje.* ~He comes from a long LINE of horsemen. *Proviene de un largo linaje de jinetes.* •Royal LINE. *Familia Real.* || **2.** [Of a dress]. *Corte.*

▶ PHRASES. || •Asembly LINE. *Cadena de montaje.* || •To be in LINE. *Corresponder, coincidir.* || •To be on the LINE. *Estar en peligro, peligrar.* ~My job is on the LINE. *Hay peligro de que pierda el trabajo.* || •To be out of LINE. *Estar fuera de lugar.* ~This remark was out of LINE. *Este comentario estuvo fuera de lugar.* || •To be out of LINE. *No coincidir, no corresponder.* ~His ideas are out of LINE with mine. *Sus ideas no coincidían con las mías.* || •To hold the LINE against. *Impedir.* ~He's trying to hold the LINE against further cuts. *Está tratando de impedir que sigan haciendo recortes.*|| •To lay on the LINE. *Pagar (dinero).* || •To lay it on the LINE. *No andarse con rodeos.*

~I'm going to lay it on the LINE with you. *Te lo voy a decir claramente.* || •To lay something on the LINE. *Jugarse.* I laid my life on the LINE for you. *Me jugué la vida por tí.* || •To reach or come to the end of the LINE. *Llegar al final.* || •To be in LINE for (under consideration, in the running for). *Ser candidato a, tener muchas posibilidades (de conseguir un empleo, una promoción).* ~He's in LINE for the post. *Es candidato al puesto.* ~He's in LINE for a promotion. *Va a ser ascendido.* ~He's in LINE for the presidency. *Es candidato a la presidencia.* || •LINE of least resistance. *Ley del mínimo esfuerzo.* || SPORT •Finishing LINE. *Banda.*

LIQUOR. *n.* Alcoholic beverage. *Aguardiente, bebida, bebida alcohólica.* ⇨LICOR

LITERALLY [LITERALMENTE]. *adv.* In a literal sense. *Así como suena, materialmente, al pie de la letra.* •To take LITERALLY. *Tomar al pie de la letra.* ~I took what he said LITERALLY. *Tomé lo que me dijo al pie de la letra.* || **2.** Actually, without exaggeration. *Materialmente.* ~It was LITERALLY impossible to work. *Era materialmente imposible trabajar.*

LITERATURE [LITERATURA]. *n.* Promotional material. *Impreso, folleto, circular, información, publicidad.* ~They asked for volunteers to distribute campaign LITERATURE. *Pidieron voluntarios para repartir propaganda electoral* (Cit. Prats). ~Do you have any LITERATURE on this product? *¿Tiene algún folleto sobre este producto?* || **2.** Books and articles written on a particular subject. *Publicaciones, tratados, obras, trabajos, material publicado, bibliografía.* ~The first task of any scientist is to look up the existing LITERATURE. *La tarea de todo científico consiste en consultar todo lo publicado sobre el tema* (Prats).

LIVID [LÍVIDO]. *adj.* Angry. *Furioso, furibundo.* || **2.** Lead-colored. *Plomizo.*

LOCAL. *adj.* Pertaining to a city, town, or small district rather than an entire state or country. *Del barrio, del pueblo, de la*

zona, de esta ciudad, del país, de aquí, del lugar, de la localidad. ~I don't buy from the LOCAL shops. *No compro en las tiendas del barrio, de la zona.* ~LOCAL wine. *Vino de la región, del país.* ~The LOCAL community. *Los vecinos o habitantes de la zona.* ~A LOCAL specialty. *Una especialidad de la region, etc.* ~Here's the LOCAL forecast. *Este es el pronóstico del tiempo para la región.* ~The LOCAL doctor. *El médico del pueblo.* ~He's a LOCAL man. *Es de aquí, es un hombre del lugar.* ~The LOCAL priest. *El cura de la parroquia, del pueblo.* ~LOCAL quarrels. *Luchas pueblerinas.* ‖ **2.** Regular. *Habitual.* Get it from your LOCAL dealer. *~Adquiéralo en su proveedor habitual.* ‖ **3.** Of the country. *Nacional, del propio país.* ~LOCAL currencies. *Las respectivas monedas nacionales.* ‖ **4.** [Election, council, government]. *Municipal.* ~LOCAL government. *Gobierno municipal.* ‖ **5.** PHRASES. ‖ • LOCAL call. *Llamada urbana.* ‖ •LOCAL color. *Ambien-*

tación. ‖ •LOCAL telephone service. *Servicio telefónico urbano.* ⇨ LOCAL

LOCATE [LOCALIZAR]. *v.* Situate. *Situar, ubicar(Lat. Am.).* ~Where is your house LOCATED. *¿Dónde está situada su casa?* ‖ **2.** To find. *Encontrar.* ~The switch is LOCATED under the seat. *El interruptor se encuentra debajo del asiento.* ~Can you LOCATE the town on this map? *¿Puede encontrar la ciudad en este plano?* ‖ **3.** Settle. *Establecerse, domiciliarse.* ~They have LOCATED in California. *Se han establecido en California.*

LUNATIC [LUNÁTICO]. *adj.* [Scheme, idea]. *Alocado, descabellado, disparatado.* ‖ **2.** [Noise, atmosphere]. *Demencial.* ‖ **3.** Radical, extremist. *Fanático, radical.* ~The LUNATIC fringe. *El sector más fanático (radical).* ‖ **4.** Whimsical, temperamental, moody. *Caprichoso.* ‖ **5.** •There's always a LUNATIC element who ... *Siempre tiene que haber algún loco que ...*

M

MAINTAIN. *v.* Preserve (order, balance, conversation]. *Sostener.* ~They MAINTAINED a long conversation. *Sostuvieron una larga conversación.* ‖ **2.** [Silence, appearances, advantage]. *Guardar.* ~You must MAINTAIN silence in church. *En la iglesia debes guardar silencio* ‖ **3.** [Custom]. *Conservar.* ~Members of the tribe MAINTAIN their native customs with ceremonial dances. *Los miembros de la tribu conservan sus costumbres autóctonas a través de bailes ceremoniales.* ‖ **4.** Keep in good condition (road, building, car, machine, house, garden). *Conservar en buen estado, ocuparse del mantenimiento de.* ‖ **5.** Claim, assert. *Sostener, afirmar.* ~He MAINTAINS that he's innocent. *Sostiene que es inocente.* ~He MAINTAINED that he had never seen the woman before. *Afirmó que nunca había visto a esa mujer.* ‖ **6.** [War, siege]. *Continuar, sostener.* ‖ **7.** [Opposition]. *Afirmar.* ‖ **8.** [Student]. *Pagar los estudios de.* ‖ **9.** [Project]. *Costear.* ‖ **10.** •To MAINTAIN one's ground. *Mantenerse en sus treces.* ⇨MANTENER

MALICE. *n.* Evil intent, ill will. *Maldad, mala intención.* ~He did it without MALICE. *Lo hizo sin mala intención.* ~She did it out of sheer MALICE. *Lo hizo de pura maldad.* ‖ **2.** Bitterness. *Rencor.* ~To bear someone MALICE. *Guardar rencor a uno.* ‖ **3.** [Law]. *Dolo, intención delictiva.* ‖ **4.** •With MALICE afterthought. *Con premeditación.* ⇨MALICIA

MALICIOUS. *adj.* Bitter. *Rencoroso.* ‖ **2.** Wicked. *Malo, malévolo.* ~With a MALICIOUS look in his eyes. *Con expresión malévola en los ojos.* ‖ **3.** [Law]. *Delictuoso, delictivo.* ‖ **4.** •MALICIOUS damages.

Daños intencionales. ‖ **5.** •MALICIOUS slander. *Calumnia intencionada.* ‖ **6.** •A MALICIOUS tongue. *Una lengua viperina.* ⇨MALICIOSO

MANAGE. *vt.* [Company]. *Llevar, dirigir, administrar.* ~Who MANAGES this branch? *¿Quién dirige esta sucursal?* ‖ **2.** [Land, finance, fund]. *Administrar.* ~She has never been very good at MANAGING her money. *Nunca supo administrar su dinero.* ‖ **3.** [Household]. *Llevar.* ‖ **4.** [Money, affairs]. *Manejar.* ‖ **5.** [Child, person]. *Llevar, manejar.* ~She can't MANAGE children. *No puede con los niños.* ~I can MANAGE him. *Yo sé llevarlo.* ‖ **6.** [Animal]. *Domar.* ~Will you be able to MANAGE such a frisky horse? *¿Vas a poder domar a un caballo tan fogoso?* ‖ **7.** [Tool]. *Manejar, manipular.* ‖ **8.** [Car]. *Conducir.* ‖ **9.** [Ship]. *Gobernar.* ‖‖ **10.** [Life, time]. *Organizar.* ~He seems unable to MANAGE his life. *Parece incapaz de organizar su vida.* ‖ **11.** [Undertaking]. *Dirigir, conducir.* ~To MANAGE the affairs of the nation. *Dirigir los asuntos de un país.* ~Has she had any experience in MANAGING large projects? *Tiene experiencia en dirigir proyectos importantes.* ‖ **12.** To dominate. *Dominar.* To MANAGE one's husband. *Dominar a su marido.* ‖ **13.** To be in charge. *Encargarse, ser el encargado de.* ~Mr. López MANAGES the glove department. *El Señor López es el encargado del departamento de guantes.* ‖ **14.** To get along. *Arreglárselas.* ~We'll MANAGE. *Nos las arreglaremos.* ⇨MANEJAR

MANIA. *n.* Craze. *Pasión, furor, fiebre, locura.* ~She has a MANIA for fashions. *Es una apasionada de las modas.* ⇨MANÍA

MANIFESTATION. *n.* [Of a ghost]. *Apari-*

ción. ⇨ MANIFESTACIÓN

MANNERS. *n.* Way of behaving. *Modales, educación.* ~Didn't they teach you MANNERS at school? *¿No te enseñaron modales en el colegio?* ~Have you forgotten your MANNERS. *¿Dónde están tus modales?* ~His table MANNERS leave much to be desired. *Sus modales en la mesa dejan mucho que desear.* •Good MANNERS. *Buenos modales. educación.* ~Good manners demand that ... *La educación exige que ...* •Bad MANNERS. *Falta de educación, malos modales.* ~It's bad MANNERS to speak with one's mouth full. *Es de mala educación hablar con la boca llena.* •To have bad/no MANNERS. *No tener educación, ser mal criado (educado).* ~She has no MANNERS. *Ella no tiene educación.* •To forget one's MANNERS. *Descomedirse.* •To teach someone MANNERS. *Enseñarle a uno a portarse bien.* || **2.** Way of behaving, aspect. *Manera de ser, comportamiento, aire.* ~I don't like his MANNER. *No me gusta su comportamiento.* ~He had the MANNER of an old man. *Tenía aire de viejo.* ~There's something odd about his MANNER. ~She has an abrupt MANNER. *Es brusca.* ~I thought I noticed a certain coldness in his MANNER. *Noté cierta frialdad en su manera de ser.* || **3.** Attitude. *Trato.* ~A good telephone MANNER is essential. *Es imprescindible tener buen trato por teléfono.* ~She has a very pleasant MANNER. *Tiene un trato muy agradable.* || **4.** Type, class. *Clase, suerte, índole.* ~All MANNER of gifts. *Toda clase de regalos.* ~What MANNER of man is he? *¿Qué tipo de hombre es?* || **5.** Customs. *Costumbres.* ~A novel of MANNERS. *Una novela de costumbres.* ~A comedy of MANNERS. *Una comedia costumbrista (de costumbres).* || **6.** Mode. *Manera, modo.* ~Adverb of MANNER. *Adverbio de modo.* •MANNER of payment. *Modo de pago.* || **7.** Style. *Estilo.* ~The house was decorated in the French MANNER. *La casa estaba decorada al estilo francés.* ~A painting in the MANNER of the Impressionists. *Un cuadro al estilo de los impresionistas.* ~A

painter in the grand MANNER. *Un pintor de cuadros grandiosos.* || **8.** *PHRASES.* || •By no MANNER of means. *De ningún modo.* ~I'm not the only one by no MANNER of means. *De ningún modo soy el único.* || •In a MANNER of speaking. I. [In a way; as it were; so to speak]. *Por así decirlo.* We were, in a manner of SPEAKING, babes in the woods. *Estamos, por así decirlo, totalmente perdidos.* II. [Up to a point]. *Hasta cierto punto.* ~Did you solve the problem? -in a MANNER of speaking. *¿Revolviste el problema? -hasta cierto punto.* || •It's just a MANNER of speaking. *Es un decir, como quien dice.* || •No MANNER of doubt. *Sin ninguno género de duda.* || •To have an easy MANNER. *Tener un aire desenvuelto.* ⇨ MANERA

MANSION [MANSIÓN]. *n.* Stately residence. *Palacio, hotel, casa grande.* ~My house is not a mansion. *Mi casa no es un palacio.* || **2.** [Of ancient family]. *Casa solariega.*

MANTLE. *n.* Cloak. *Capa, manto.* ~Beneath a MANTLE of snow. *Bajo una capa de nieve.* || **2.** [Of role]. *Responsabilidad, valía.* The MANTLE of responsibility passed on to Hugh. *Hugh asumió la responsabilidad.* ~The MANTLE of office weighed heavily upon his shoulders. *La responsabilidad del cargo le abrumaba.* ⇨ MANTEL

MANUAL [MANUAL]. *adj.* [Work]. *Físico.* ~Manual work. *Trabajo físico.* || **2.** [Freno]. *De mano.* || **3.** •MANUAL training. *Enseñanza de artes y oficios.* || **4.** •MANUAL worker. *Trabajador.* || **5.** •MANUAL alphabet. *Alfabeto para sordomudos.*

MAP [MAPA]. *n.* [Of the world]. *Mapamundi.* || **2.** [Of the subway]. *Plano.* || **3.** [Of street, town, transport system]. *Plano.*

MARCH. *v.* Demonstrate. *Manifestarse, hacer una manifestación.* ~The protesters MARCHED on the Capitol. *Los manifestantes se dirigieron al Capitolio.* || **2.** Take (a person somewhere). *Llevar.* They MARCHED him off to prison. *Lo llevaron a la cárcel, lo llevaron preso.* || **3.** Stride. *Irrumpir, entrar decidido, resuelto.* ~She MARCHED into the office and started shouting.

Irrumpió en la oficina y se puso a gritar. ~He MARCHED up to the referee. *Se dirigió resueltamente al árbitro.* || **4.** To bring in (a person). *Hacer entrar.* ~The prisoner was MARCHED in. *Hicieron entrar al prisionero.* || **5.** To go forward; advance; proceed. *Seguir.* Time MARCHES on. *El tiempo sigue su curso.* || **6.** To parade. *Desfilar.* ~The band MARCHED through the streets. *La banda desfiló por las calles.* || **7.** •To MARCH out. *Salir enfadado.* || **7.** •To MARCH past. *Desfilar.* ~They MARCHED past the visiting dignitaries. *Desfilaron ante los dignatarios visitantes.* ⇨MARCHAR

MARGINAL [MARGINAL]. *adj.* Minor. *Pequeño, escaso, insignificante.* ~Of MARGINAL importance. *De escasa importancia.* ~It was a MARGINAL improvement. *Fue una mejora de poca monta.* || **2.** [Case]. *Incierto, dudoso.* || **3.** [Interest, matter]. *Periférico.* || **4.** Not very productive (land). *Poco rentable, de muy bajo rendimiento.* ~MARGINAL land. *Tierra de muy bajo rendimiento.*

MARINA. *n.* A boat basin offering dockage and other services for small craft. *Embarcadero, puerto deportivo.* ⇨MARINA

MARK[1]. *n.*
❶ CHARACTERISTICS, DISTINCTIVE TRAITS. ~It's the MARK of a gentleman. *Es señal de caballerosidad.* ~Tolerance is the MARK of a civilized society. *Una sociedad civilizada se distingue por su tolerancia.* ~This work bears the MARK of a true genius. *Tiene todas la características de un veradero genio.*
❷ PROFICIENCY, ATTAINMENT. [In exam]. *Nota, calificación.* ~To get high MARKS in English. *Sacar una buena nota en inglés.* ~She always gets top MARKS. *Siempre saca las mejores notas (la máxima calificación).*
❸ TRACE, IMPRINT. *Huella.* ~The MARKS of age. *Las huellas de la edad.* ~Margaret Thatcher made an unforgettable MARK on British politics. *Margaret Thatcher dejo huellas inconfundibles en la política de Inglaterra.* ~~The tires left MARKS on the road. *Los neumáticos dejaron huellas en la carretera.*
❹ SIGN, TOKEN, INDICATION. *Señal.* ~As a MARK of respect. *En señal de respeto.* Sign, indication. *Señal.* ~As a MARK of my disapproval. *En señal de mi desaprobación.* ~As a MARK of our gratitude. *En señal de nuestro agradecimiento.* ~It's the MARK of good weather. *Es señal (indicio de buen tiempo).*
❺ VISIBLE IMPRESSION LEFT ON SKIN (spot, bruise, burn, scratch). [Smallpox]. *Picadura.* || **2.** [Burn]. *Quemadura.* || **3.** [Scratch]. *Rasguño.* || **4.** [Left by blow]. *Señal.* ~He left the ring without a MARK on his body. *Salió del cuadrilátero sin llevar señal alguna en el cuerpo.*
❻ TARGET. Target. *Blanco.* ~To hit the MARK. *Dar en el blanco,* FIG *acertar, dar en el clavo.* || **2.** Aim. *Objetivo.* || **3.** FIG •To be wide off the MARK. *Estar lejos de la verdad, estar muy equivocado.*
❼ VARIOUS. Stain. *Mancha.* ~I can't get these MARKS off my T shirt. *No puedo sacar estas manchas de mi camiseta.* ~Greasy MARKS. *Manchas de grasa.* || **2.** Symbol. *Signo, señal.* ~Punctuation MARK. *Signo de puntuación.* || **3.** [Instead of signature]. *Cruz.* || **4.** Proof. *Prueba, testimonio.* ~MARKS of friendship. *Pruebas de amistad.* || **5.** [Of score]. *Tanto.* || **6.** [Sport]. *Línea de salida.* || **7.** Label. *Etiqueta.* || **8.** TECH Model. *Serie.* ~A MARK 3 engine. *Un motor de tercera serie.* || **9.** Level. *Nivel.* ~The collection has reached the 3 million dollar MARK. *La colecta ha alcanzado el total de 3 millones de dólares.* ~Water MARK. *Nivel de agua.* || **10.** •On your MARKS!, get set!, go! *¡Preparados!, ¡listos!, ¡ya!*
❽ EXPRESSIONS. || •Distinguishing MARKS. *Señas de identidad.* || •To leave one's MARK. *Dejar sus huellas.* || •To make one's MARK. *Distinguirse, señalarse, destacarse.* ⇨MARCA

MARK[2]. *v.* To stain. *Manchar.* || **2.** Indicate. *Señalar, indicar.* ~It MARKS a change of direction. *Indica un cambio de dirección.* ~Stones MARK the path. *Unas piedras señalan el camino.* || **3.** To correct (exam, exercise). *Corregir.* || **4.** To give MARKS to. *Puntuar, calificar, dar notas a.* || **5.** [Price]. *Indicar, poner precio.* ~'10% off MARKED price'. *'Descuento del 10% sobre el precio indicado'.* || **6.** Pay atention to, heed. *Fijarse en, prestar atención a.* ~MARK my words. *Fíjate en lo que te digo, ¡ya verás!* ~But she has lied before, MARK you. *Pero ten en cuenta que nos ha mentido antes.* || **7.** [Anniversary, retirement]. *Celebrar.* || **8.** [Beginning, watershed]. *Señalar.* ~This event MARKED the beginning of the revolution. *Este acontecimiento señaló el comienzo de la revolución. 1997* MARKS the centenary. *En 1997 se cumple el centenario.* || **9.** Characterize. *Caracterizar.* ~A period MARKED by constant riots. *Un período caracterizado por constantes disturbios.* ~The friendship which has MARKED our relations. *La amistad que ha caracterizado nuestras relaciones.* || **10.** To note, observe. *Darse cuenta, observar.* ~MARK that there's a difference. *Dese cuenta de que hay una diferencia.* || **11.** Chart, delineate. *Trazar.* || **12.** WITH PREPOSITIONS. || •MARK down. (I) Note down. *Apuntar.* (II) [Price]. *Rebajar.* (III) [Goods]. *Rebajar el precio de.* || •MARK off. (I) Separate. *Separar, dividir, distinguir.* (II) [Area]. *Delimitar.* (III). Cross out. *Tachar.* || •MARK out. (I) [Area]. *Delimitar.* (II) [Boundary, course, direction]. *Trazar.* The course that Italy has MARKED out for itself. *El camino que Italia ha elegido,* (III) [Field]. *Jalonar,* (IV) Single out. *distinguir.* ~It is what MARKS Bach's music off from that of his predecessors. *Es lo que distingue la música de Bach de la de sus predecesores.* || **13.** PHRASES. || •MARK up (price). *Aumentar.* || •To MARK time. (1) [Kill time]. *Hacer tiempo.* (II) [Await one's chance]. *Esperar el momento oportuno.* ⇨MARCAR

MARMALADE. *n.* Jelly. *Mermelada de naranja.* ⇨MERMELADA

MASS. *n.*
❶ QUANTITY. *Gran cantidad.* ~She has MASSES of confidence. *Tiene muchísima confianza en sí misma.* || **2.** [Of things].

Montón. ~MASSES of clothes. *Montones de ropa.* ~We received MASSES of complaints. *Recibimos montones (cantidades) de quejas.* ~We have MASSES. *Tenemos montones.* || **3.** [Of people]. *Multitud, muchedumbre.* || **4.** Majority. *Mayoría, mayor parte.* The MASS of people. *La mayoría de la gente.* || **5.** [Nubes]. *Cúmulo.*
❷ VARIOUS. Vague shape. *Bulto.* || **2.** [Of nerves]. *Manojo, madeja.* He's a MASS of nerves. *Es una madeja de nervios.* || **3.** [De problemas, virtudes, contradicciones]. *Cúmulo.* ~A MASS of contradictions. *Un cúmulo de contradicciones.* || **4.** Conjunto. Body, bulk. ~Her hair was a MASS of curls. *Tenía la cabeza cubierta de rizos.* ~The cherry tree was a MASS of pink. *El cerezo era una nube de flores rosadas.* ~He is a MASS of bruises. *Está cubierto de cardenales.* The garden is a MASS of yellow. *El jardín está repleto de flores amarillas.* || **5.** [Of mountain]. *Macizo.* ⇨MASA

MASSACRE [MASACRE]. *n.* Slaughter. *Matanza.* ~Los ecologistas tratan de evitar la MATANZAS de focas y otros animales. *Ecologists attempt to prevent the slaughter of seals and other animals.* || **2.** Heavy defeat. *Paliza, derrota aplastante.* The team lost in a 9-0 MASSACRE. *El equipo perdió en una derrota aplastante de 9 a 0.*

MASSIVE [MASIVO]. *adj.* [Gold, wall]. Solid, weighty. *Macizo.* ~The castle's MASSIVE walls. *La paredes macizas del castillo.* || **2.** [Support, increase, task]. Huge. *Enorme, descomunal.* || **3.** Imposing. *Imponente.* || **4.** [Of head]. *Abultado, grande.* || **5.** •A MASSIVE majority. *Una mayoría aplastante.*

MASTER[1] [MAESTRO]. *adj.* Main. *Principal.* ~The MASTER bedroom. *El dormitorio principal.* ~MASTER joint. *Junta principal.* || **2.** Masterly. *Magistral.* ~A MASTER stroke. *Un toque magistral.* || **3.** Dominant. *Superior.* ~The MASTER race. *La raza superior.* || **4.** Imminently skilled. *Consumado.* ~A MASTER pianist. *Un pianista consumado.* || **5.** •MASTER copy. *Original.* •MASTER plan. *Plan general.*

MASTER[2]. *n.* [Dog, servant, slave]. *Amo.* ~The slave looked at his MASTER with hate in his eyes. *El esclavo miró a su amo con los ojos llenos de odio.* || **2.** [Of household]. *Señor, amo.* ~The MASTER of the house. *El señor de la casa.* || **3.** Owner. *Dueño.* ~To be one's own MASTER. *Ser dueño de sí mismo.* || **4.** [Of a ship]. *Capitán.* || **5.** [As title to a young boy]. *Señor.* ~MASTER James Brown. *El señor James Brown.* ~The young MASTER. *El señorito.* || **6.** Original. *Original.* ~I gave him the MASTER to copy. *Le di el original para que sacara una copia.* || **7.** [Of a military order]. *Maestre.* ~Lope de Vega was grand MASTER of Calavera. *Lope de Vega fue maestre de Calavera.* || **8.** Victor, conqueror. *Vencedor.* ~I finally met my MASTER. *Por fin encontré quien me venciera.* || **9.** PHRASES. || •I will be MASTER in my house. *En esta casa mando yo.* || •MASTER sergeant. *Sargento mayor.* || •MASTER spy. *Jefe de espías.* || •MASTER switch. *Interruptor central.* || •MASTER'S degree. *Licenciatura.* || •Old MASTER. *Pintor clásico (man), obra clásica (work).* || •To be a MASTER at politics. *Ser un político consumado.* || •To be one's own MASTER. *Ser independiente, no tener que dar cuentas a nadie, no depender de nadie; trabajar por su propia cuenta.* ~I started this business because I wanted to be my own MASTER. *Empecé este negocio porque quería ser independiente.* || •To be the MASTER of one's fate (destiny). *Decidir su propio destino.* ~Without these economic changes, Africa cannot be the MASTER of its destiny. *Sin estos cambio en el orden económico, Africa no puede decidir su propio destino.* || •To be the MASTER of the situation. *Dominar la situación.* || •To make oneself MASTER of. *Apoderarse de.* || •To meet one's MASTER. *Encontrar la horma de su zapato.* || •You can't serve two MASTERS. *No se puede servir a Dios y al Diablo.* ⇨MAESTRO

MATERIAL [MATERIAL]. *n.* Cloth. *Tejido, tela.* ~What kind of MATERIAL do you prefer for the curtains. *¿Qué clase de tela prefiere para las cortinas?* || **2.** •He's artist MATERIAL. *Tiene madera de artista.* || **3.** •This is BESTSELLER material. *Este es un bestseller en potencia.*

MATERIALIZE [MATERIALIZAR]. *v.* Happen, take place, occur. *Realizarse, convertirse en (hacerse) realidad (una cosa).* ~My hopes have not MATERIALIZED. *Mis esperanzas no se han realizado.* || **2.** [Plan, idea]. *Concretarse, tomar forma.* || **3.** Appear, show up. *Aparecer, presentarse.* ~I waited for an hour, but he never MATERIALIZED. *Esperé más de una hora, pero no apareció.*

MATRIMONY. *n.* Married life. *Vida conyugal.* ⇨MATRIMONIO

MATURE. *adj.* Developed (animal, plant, tree). *Adulto.* The mature EAGLE has a wingspan of over six feet. *El águila adulta tiene una envergadura de más de seis pies.* || **2.** Due, payable (policy, bond, debenture). *Vencido.* ~The bond MATURES in 20 years. *La obligación vence en 20 años.* || **3.** [Culinary]. *Añejo (whiskey), curado (cheese), añejo, de crianza (wine).* || **4.** [Deliberation, reflexion, consideration}. *Largo, detenido.* ~After MATURE deliberations. *Después de largas deliberaciones.* ~On mature REFLEXION we have decided to decline their offer. *Tras pensarlo detenidamente hemos decidido no acceptar la propuesta.* || **5.** [Estudiante]. *Mayor (de 25 años).* || **6.** [Physically]. *Desarrollado.* ~At that age most girls are physically MATURE. *A esa edad la mayoría de las niñas ya se han desarrollado.* || **7.** Older. *De edad madura.* ~A respectable gentleman of MATURE years. *Un distinguido señor de edad madura.* ⇨MADURO

MEMBER [MIEMBRO]. *n.* [Of society, club]. *Socio.* || **2.** [Of Parliament]. *Diputado.* || **3.** [Of church]. *Feligrés.* || **4.** [Of company]. *Empleado.* || **5.** [Group]. *Integrante.* ~Anyone can become a MEMBER of our group. *Cualquiera puede integrarse a nuestro groupo.* || **6.** Person, individual. *Persona, individuo.* ~A MEMBER of the opposite sex. *Una persona del sexo opuesto.* ~Babies on average have less colds than other MEMBERS of the family. *Los* *niños pequeños generalmente tienen menos resfríos que otros miembros de la familia.* || **7.** *PHRASES.* || •'MEMBERS only'. *'Sólo para socios'.* || •MEMBER of the crew. *Tripulante.* || •If any MEMBER of the audience ... *Si cualquiera de los asistentes ...* || •He's a MEMBER of the party/union. *Es afiliado al partido/sindicato.* || •The offer is open to any MEMBER of the public. *La oferta está abierta al público en general.* || •They treat me like I was a MEMBER of the family. *Me tratan como si fuera de la familia.* || •MEMBER of the bar. *Abogado.* || •Dogs and wolves are MEMBERS of the same species. *Los perros y los lobos pertenecen a la misma especie.*

MEMORY [MEMORIA]. *n.* Recollection. *Recuerdo.* ~She has fond MEMORIES of her childhood. *Tiene gratos recuerdos de su infancia.*

MERIT [MÉRITO]. *n.* Advantage, quality. *Ventaja, virtud, bondad, cualidad.* ~One of the MERITS of the system is its simplicity. *Una de las ventajas del sistema es su simplicidad (Prats).* ~The plan was accepted on its financial MERITS. *Se aceptó el plan por sus ventajas económicas.* ~Patience is one of his greatest MERITS. *La paciencia es una de sus mayores cualidades.* || **2.** Praiseworthy quality. *Justo valor, valor intrínsico.* ~Each case will be judged on it's own MERIT. *Se juzgará cada caso por separado (individualmente).* || **3.** *PHRASES.* || •To look into the MERIT of something. *Examinar los argumentos a favor y en contra.* || •There is no MERIT in prolonging the dispute. *No tiene ningún sentido prolongar el conflicto.* || •To pass with MERIT. *Aprobar con mención especial.* || To judge the MERIT of a case. *Juzgar el fondo de un caso.*

MESSAGE. *n.* [Non-official communication from person to person]. *Recado.* ~There's a MESSAGE for you. *Hay un recado para usted.* ~Could you give him a MESSAGE? *¿Podría darle un recado?.* || **2.** Note. *Nota, aviso, anuncio.* ~I left him a MESSAGE to call me up when he arrived. *Le*

dejé una nota de llamarme en cuanto llegara. || **3.** Wording. *Texto.* ~The MESSAGE of the telegram. *El texto del telegrama.* || **4.** Speech, address. *Discurso.* || **5.** •To get the MESSAGE. *Comprender, caer en la cuenta, darse por enterado.* ~Do you think he got the MESSAGE? *¿Crees que se dió por enterado?* || **6.** •MESSAGE board. *Tablero.*

MINIMIZE [MINIMIZAR]. *v.* Reduce (risks, costs). *Reducir al máximo.* ~Our stringent safety measures MINIMIZE our chances of an accident. *Nuestras estrictas medidas de seguridad reducen al máximo la posibilidad de un accidente.* || **2.** Play down. *Quitarle importancia a.* ~Being modest, she MINIMIZES her role in the organization. *Como es modesta, le quita importancia a su papel en la organización.* || **3.** To underestimate. *Menospreciar.*

MINISTER [MINISTRO]. *n.* [Religious]. *Pastor.*

MINUTE [MINUTO]. *n.* Moment. *Momento.* ~She could arrive any MINUTE now. *Llegará de un momento a otro.* ~Just a MINUTE. *Espere un momento.* ~We expect him any MINUTE. *Le esperamos de un momento a otro.* Never for a MINUTE have I regretted my decisión. *Ni por un momento he lamentado mi decisión.* ~I've enjoyed every MINUTE of the holiday. *Disfruté de las vacaciones al máximo.* ~The MINUTE I saw the house, I liked it. *En cuanto vi la casa, me gustó.* ~It was difficult, but worth every MINUTE. *Fue difícil pero mereció la pena.* ~I'm feeling better by the MINUTE. *Me siento cada vez mejor.* ~Tell me the MINUTE he comes. *Avíseme en cuanto llegue.* ~They'll be here any MINUTE now. *Llegarán de un momento a otro.* ~It was all over in a MINUTE. *Todo eso ocurrió en un instante.* ~The ambulance was there within MINUTES. *La ambulancia llegó en seguida.* •At this very MINUTE. *En este preciso instante.* •To leave things until the last MINUTE. *Dejar las cosas hasta última hora.* •This very MINUTE. *Ahora mismo.* •There's one born every MINUTE. *¡Hay cada idiota!* •At the last *minute. A última hora.* •Every MINUTE counts. *No hay tiempo que perder.* ‖ **2.** Note. *Nota, minuta.* ‖ **3.** •To the MINUTE. *Con suma precisión.* ‖ **4.** •Up to the MINUTE news. *Noticias de última hora.* ‖ **5.** •Up to the MINUTE style. *El último grito, la última moda.* **6.** •MINUTES. *Acta.* ~The MINUTES of the reunion. *El acta de la reunión.*

MISERABLE. *adj.* Unfortunate. *Desdichado, desgraciado.* ~I've never seen a man so MISERABLE. *Nunca vi a un hombre tan desdichado.* ~He feels MISERABLE since he lost his last tournament. *Se siente muy desgraciado desde que perdió el último campeonato.* ‖ **2.** In low spirits, sad, despondent. *Triste, deprimido.* ~It makes me MISERABLE. *Me deprime mucho.* ~I feel MISERABLE today. *Hoy me siento sin fuerzas para nada.* ~We were tired and MISERABLE. *Estábamos cansados y con el ánimo por el suelo.* ~He's been MISERABLE since his dog died. *Desde que se le murió el perro está desconsolado.* ‖ **3.** Indisposed, ill, under the weather. *Malo, incómodo, molesto, indispuesto.* ~I feel MISERABLE. *Me siento malísimo.* ‖ **4.** [Weather]. *Malo, de perro.* ~All weekend we had a MISERABLE weather. *Todo el fin de semana tuvimos mal tiempo (un tiempo de perro).* ‖ **5.** Illtempered, unpleasant (person). *Desagradable.* ‖ **6.** Complete. *Rotundo.* ~It was a MISERABLE failure. *Fue un fracaso rotundo.* ‖ **7.** Paltry. *Mísero.* He was left with only a few MISERABLE dollars in his pocket. *En el bolsillo sólo le quedaba dos míseros dólares.* ‖ **8.** •Don't make yourself MISERABLE. *No te amargues la vida.* ‖ **9.** •To make someone's life MISERABLE. *Amargarle la vida a uno.* ⇨MISERABLE

MISERY. *n.* Mental anguish. *Angustia, pena, tristeza.* ‖ **2.** Suffering. *Sufrimiento.* The MISERY of a tooth ache. *El suplicio de un dolor de muela.* •To put an animal out of its MISERY. *Acortarle la agonía a un animal, matar a un animal que sufre.* ~They put the dog out of his MISERY. *Sacrificaron al perro para que no sufriera más.* ~Go on, tell, put me out of my MISERY. *Anda, dímelo, no me hagas esperar.* ~To put them out of their MISERY he told them

the final score. *Para que no siguieran torturándose, les dijo el resultado final.* ⇨MISERIA

MISSION. *n.* Group of delegates. *Delegación.* ‖ **2.** Embassy. *Embajada.* ‖ **3.** •Trade MISSION. *Delegación comercial.* ‖ **4.** •MISSION control. *Centro de control.* ⇨MISIÓN

MODERATE [MODERADO]. *adj.* [Price]. *Módico.* ~Quality products at MODERATE prices. *Productos de primera a precios módicos.* ‖ **2.** Average. *Regular, mediano.* ~A MODERATE income. *Una entrada mediana.* ‖ **3.** [Talent, ability]. *Mediocre.* ~A student of MODERATE ability. *Un estudiante mediocre.* ‖ **4.** [Clima]. *Templado.*

MODEST [MODESTO]. *adj.* Chaste, decent, reserved (person, dress). *Púdico, recatado, pudoroso.* ~A MODEST woman. *Una mujer recatada.* ‖ **2.** [Price, wage]. *Módico.* ‖ **3.** [Success, ambition]. *Discreto.* ~A MODEST success. *Un éxito discreto.* ‖ **4.** Moderate (demand, improvement, increase, success]. *Moderado.* ~To be MODEST in one's demands. *Ser modesto en sus reclamaciones.* ~The workers' DEMANDS seem modest enough. *Parece que las reclamaciones de los obreros eran moderadas.* ‖ **5.** [Allowance]. *Pequeño, reducido.* ~He receives a MODEST monthly allowance. *Recibe una pequeña mensualidad.*

MOLEST. *v.* To make indecent sexual advances to. *Acosar (sexualmente).* ⇨MOLESTAR

MORAL. *n.* [Story]. *Moraleja.* ~I didn't understand the MORAL of this fable. *No he entendido bien la moraleja de la fábula.* ‖ **2.** *pl.* Principles. *Sentido ético.* ~Have you no MORALS? *¿No tiene ningún sentido ético?* ‖ **3.** Behavior, conduct. *Conducta, manera de proceder.* Who are you to criticize my MORALS. *¿Quién es usted para criticar mi conducta?* ⇨MORAL

MORBID. *adj.* [Mind]. *Morboso, enfermizo.* ‖ **2.** [Curiosity]. *Malsano.* ‖ **3.** Depressed. *Pesimista.* ⇨MORBIDO

MOTIVATE. *v.* Stimulate. *Animar, alentar, estimular.* ~A good teacher has to be able to MOTIVATE her students. *Un buen profesor necesita poder estimular a los estudiantes.* || **2.** Incite, impel, induce. *Impulsar, incitar, mover.* Would you say he was MOTIVATED by a desire for power? *¿Opina usted que fue impulsado por un afán de poder?* ~What MOTIVATES him is pure greed. *Lo que le incita a actuar de esta manera es pura codicia.* || **3.** Bring about, cause. *Ocasionar, deberse a.* ~The closure of the school was a financially MOTIVATED act. *El cierre de la escuela fue ocasionado por necesidad económica.* ~My decision to make this trip was MOTIVATED by a simple desire to leave the country. *La decisión de hacer este viaje se debe únicamente a mi deseo de abandonar el país.* || **4.** •To be highly MOTIVATED. *Entusiasmarse (por una cosa).* ⇨MOTIVAR

MOTIVATION [MOTIVACIÓN]. *n.* Encouragement, incentive. *Estímulo, móvil, aliciente.* ~The salary increase serves as a MOTIVATION for working harder. *Este aumento de sueldo es un estímulo para que trabajemos más.* || **2.** Reason. *Motivo.* ~The MOTIVATION for the decision is to improve our service to customers. *El motivo de nuestra decisión es de mejorar nuestro servicio a los clientes.*

MOTIVE. *n.* Purpose, aim, intention. *Propósito, razón.* ~Their MOTIVE for running away was to avoid problems. *Huyó para que no hubiera problemas.* || **2.** [Jury]. *Móvil.* ~The MOTIVE of a crime. *El móvil de un crimen.* || **3.** •With the best of MOTIVES. *Con la mejor intención.* ⇨MOTIVO

MOTORIST. *n.* Person who drives an automobile. *Conductor.* ⇨MOTORISTA

MOVE[1]. *v.*

❶ AFFECT EMOTIONALLY. To move. *Conmover, enternecer, impresionar.* ~She's easily MOVED. *Es muy sensible.* ~I was deeply MOVED by what I saw. *Lo que vi me conmovió profundamente.* || **2.** •When I feel so MOVED. *Cuando estoy con el ánimo para eso.* || **3.** To prompt, persuade, convince. *Inducir, impulsar a, incitar a.* ~This MOVED her to remonstrate.

Esto la indujo a protestar. ~He was MOVED to express his indignation. *Se sintió impulsado a expresar su indignación.* || **4.** •To MOVE somebody to anger. *Encolerizar.* || **5.** •To MOVE someone to tears. *Hacer llorar a alguien.* ~At the end of the film, when she left him, I was MOVED to tears. *La película me hizo llorar cuando al final ella lo dejo a él.*

❷ DESTINATION. Go to. *Ir, arrimarse, acercarse, desplazarse..* ~Let's MOVE into the garden. *Vamos al jardín.* ~Why don't you MOVE near the fire? *¿Por qué no te arrimas (acercas) al fuego?* ~The government troops have MOVED into the area. *Tropas del gobierno se han desplazado a la zona.* || **2.** Leave. *Irse, marcharse.* ~It's time we were MOVING. *Es hora de irnos.* || **3.** •To MOVE to and fro. *Ir y venir, ir de acá para allá.* || **4.** To start to leave. *Ponerse en marcha.* ~The procession began to MOVE. *La procesión se puso en marcha.*

❸ CHANGE. [House, office] *Mudarse, trasladarse.* ~The family MOVED to a new house. *La familia se mudó a una casa nueva.* || **2.** [Furniture]. *Cambiar de sitio, trasladar.* ~Why have you MOVED the television set? *¿Por qué has cambiado el televisor de sitio.* || **3.** [Opinion]. *Hacer cambiar.* ~He will not be easily MOVED. *No va a ser fácil hacerle cambiar de idea.* || **4.** Transfer. *Trasladar.* ~He was MOVED to Quito. *Lo trasladaron a Quito.* || **5.** •To MOVE TO another seat/job. *Cambiarse de asiento/trabajo.* ~We could MOVE to another table. *Podríamos cambiarnos de mesa.* || **6.** •The company that MOVED us. *La compañía que nos hizo la mudanza.*

❹ MOVEMENT. *Remover, sacudir, agitar.* ~The breeze MOVED the leaves gently. *La brisa agitaba dulcemente las hojas.* || **2.** Propel. *Propulsar, impeler.* ~The wind MOVES the windmills. *El viento propulsa los molinos de viento.* || **3.** Remove. *Quitar.* MOVE that motorbike off the lawn! *¡Quita esta moto del césped!* ~MOVE out of the way! *¡Quítate de en medio¡* || **4.** Carry oneself. *Andar con garbo.* ~She MOVES with grace. *Anda con garbo.* || **5.** *Travel,* go at. ~It MOVES at high speed. *Va a gran velocidad.* || **6.** MOVE to one side. *Correr.* ~MOVE your chair a little. *Corre un poco la silla.* || **7.** Activate. *Accionar.* ~Moved by electricity. *Accionado electricamente.* ❺ TAKE THE INITIATIVE. Propose. *Proponer.* ~I MOVE that the meeting be closed. *Propongo que se cierre la reunión.* || **2.** Persuade. *Persuadir.* || **3.** •To MOVE heaven and earth. *Remover cielo y tierra, hacer lo imposible.* ~I'll MOVE heaven and earth to get it. *Haré lo imposible para conseguirlo.* || **4.** Take action. *Tomar medidas, dar el primer paso, hacer gestiones, actuar.* She MOVED quickly to quell rumors. *Tomó medidas en seguida para acallar los rumores.* ~The government must MOVE first. *El gobierno necesita dar el primer paso.* ~The council MOVED to stop the abuse. *El consejo hizo gestiones para corregir el abuso.* ~We must MOVE now. *Tenemos que actuar ahora.* ❺ ADVANCE, PROGRESS, DEVELOP. Progress. *Hacer progresos, adelantar, marchar.* ~Things seem to be MOVING. *Parece que las cosas marchan, parece que se están haciendo progresos.* || **2.** Develop. *Desarrollar.* ~Events MOVED rapidly. *Se precipitaron los acontecimientos.* ~A fast-MOVING adventure story. *Una historia de ritmo muy ágil.* || **3.** Keep up. *Mantenerse al día.* ~You have to MOVE with the times, granny. *Hay que mantenerse al día, abuelita.* || **4.** To get ahead. *Tomar la delantera, pasar a ocupar.* ~To MOVE into the lead/into second place. *Pasar a ocupar el primer/segundo lugar.* ~The Socialists have MOVED ahead in the opinion of the polls. *Los socialistas han tomado la delantera según los sondeos.* ❻ OTHERS. Sell (merchandise). *Colocar, vender.* || **2.** [Game]. *Jugar, hacer una jugada.* ~Who MOVES next? *¿A quién le toca jugar?* White MOVES. *Blanco juega.* || **3.** Transport. *Transportar, trasladar.* I need to MOVE these boxes to the warehouse. *Tengo que transportar estas cajas al almacén.* ~He was too ill to be MOVED. *Estaba demasiado enfermo para que*

pudieran transportarlo.

MOVE ABOUT. *Cambiar de sitio.* ~When I arrived they were MOVING the furniture about. *Cuando llegué estaban cambiando los muebles de sitio.* •To MOVE about freely. *Circular libremente.*

MOVE ACROSS. Run through. *Pasar.* ~She MOVED her finger across the page. *Pasó el dedo por la página.*

MOVE ALONG. [Crowd]. *Hacer circular.* ~MOVE along, please, there's nothing to see! *¡Circulen, por favor, no hay nada que ver.* || **2.** [To a person on a bench] *Correrse.* ~MOVE along! *¡Corréte!, ¡haz sitio!* || **3.** [Passengers]. *Hacer pasar hacia adelante.* || **4.** I'll be MOVING along now. *Ya me voy.* || **5.** To make progress. *Adelantar, avanzar.* ~I'm MOVING along fine. *Estoy adelantando mucho.* || **6.** Keep on going. *Avanzar, ir (pasar) hacia adelante.*

MOVE APART. [Friends]. *Distanciarse.* ~We MOVED apart since she got married. *Nos hemos distanciado desde que se casó.*

MOVE AROUND. [Change residence]. *Mudarse, cambiarse a menudo.* || **2.** [Change jobs]. *Cambiar de trabajo a menudo.* || **3.** Revolve, turn. *Girar.* ~The earth MOVES around the sun. *La tierra gira alrededor del sol.*

MOVE ASIDE. *Apartarse, ponerse a un lado, quitarse de en medio.* ~Please move aside. *Apártese, quítese de en medio.* || **2.** *Apartar (object).* ~He moved the book aside. *Apartó el libro.*

MOVE AWAY. Depart. *Irse, marcharse.* ~Her children had MOVED away and she was left alone in the house. *Los hijos se habían marchado y se quedó sola en la casa.* || **2.** [Object, person]. *Alejar, apartar.* || **3.** Move from a house. *Mudar de casa.*

MOVE BACK. [Crowd]. *Hacer retroceder.* ~The police MOVED back the crowd. *La policía hizo retroceder a la multitud.* || **2.** Return an object to its original place. *Devolver a su lugar.* || **3.** To return a person to his original place. *Volver a.* ~He MOVED back with his parents. *Volvió (a vivir) con sus padres.* || **4.** [Withdraw, retreat]. *Retroceder, retirarse.* || **5.** [Person]. Retroceder.

~They MOVED back to let him pass. *Retrocedieron para dejarlo pasar.* || **6.** [An object]. *Colocar más atrás.* ~MOVE the microphone back a little. *Coloca el micrófono un poco más atrás.* || **7.** Postpone (date). *Aplazar, postergar.* ~She MOVED the date of the meeting back again. *Ha vuelto a aplazar (postergar) la fecha de la reunión.* || **8.** •Media attention has MOVED back to domestic issues. *Los medios de comunicación han vuelto a centrar su atención en los asuntos internos.*

MOVE DOWN. Fall, drop. *Bajar.* ~This song has MOVED down five places. *Esta canción ha bajado cinco puestos.* || **2.** Change. To MOVE down into second gear. *Cambiar a segunda.* || **3.** [Bus, train]. *Correrse.* ~MOVE to the back, please! *¡Córranse al fondo, por favor!*

MOVE FORWARD. *Ponerse más adelante.* ~I MOVED forward to get a better view. *Me puse más adelante para ver mejor.* || **2.** [Date]. *Adelantar.* ~The date has MOVED forward to July. *Han adelantado la fecha a julio.* || **3.** [Troops]. *Hacer avanzar.* || **4.** [Help, progress]. *Avanzar, adelantar.*

MOVE IN. To set up home, take possession. *Mudarse, cambiarse a, instalarse en.* ~We MOVED in last week. *Nos mudamos (cambiamos) la semana pasada.* || **2.** To draw closer. *Acercarse.* || **3.** Go into action. *Intervenir.* ~The referee MOVED in to separate the two boxers. *El árbitro intervino para separar los dos boxeadores.* ~They MOVED in at dawn. *Atacaron al amanecer.* || **4.** [Furnitute]. *Colocar, instalar.* || **5.** [Transport]. *Transportar.* ||

MOVE IN ON. Advance upon (enemy). *Avanzar sobre.* || **2.** Encroach upon (territory, business). *Invadir.*

MOVE IN WITH. To go and live with. *Irse a vivir con alguien.* ~She wants her boyfriend to MOVE in with her. *Quiere que su novio vaya a vivir con ella.*

MOVE INTO. Go into. *Introducirse, intervenir.* ~The company plans to MOVE into the hotel business. *La compañía tiene planes de introducirse en el ramo hostelero.*

MOVE OFF. To start to leave. *Ponerse en marcha.* ~The conductor blew his whistle and the train slowly MOVED off. *El revisor tocó un silbato y el tren se puso lentamente en marcha.*

MOVE ON. To walk further. *Seguir adelante.* || **2.** Continue journey. *Seguir (reanudar) su viaje.* ~Let's stay here tonight, and MOVE on tomorrow. *Nos quedaremos aquí está noche y mañana por la mañana seguiremos nuestro viaje.* || **3.** Proceed. *Pasar.* Time is MOVING on. *El tiempo pasa.* ~Shall we MOVE on? *¿Pasamos al punto siguiente?* ~The Committee MOVED on to discuss finance. *La comisión pasó a discutir la financiación.* •To MOVE on to higher things. *Pasar a hacer cosas más importantes.* || **4.** [Progress]. *Avanzar, progresar.* || **5.** Cause to disperse (spectators, loiterers). *Hacer circular.* ~The police made us MOVE on because we were making too much noise. *La policía nos hizo dispersar por causar mucho ruido.* || **6.** To change. *Cambiar.* ~Things have MOVED on since your last visit. *Las cosas han cambiado desde tu última visita.* || **7.** Go on to something else. *Cambiar de tema, seguir adelante, pasar a otro tema.* ~I think we covered this topic -should we MOVE on? *Opino que hemos agotado el tema -¿seguimos adelante?*

MOVE OUT. Leave accomodations. *Irse, mudarse, cambiarse de, abandonar (una casa, local).* ~We're waiting for the tenants to MOVE out. *Estamos esperando a que se vayan los inquilinos.* ~They want to MOVE out of their apartment and find a house. *Quieren mudarse de su apartamento y buscar casa.* || **2.** Withdraw (troops). *Retirar.* ~They MOVED their soldiers out of the beleaguered city. *Retiraron sus tropas de la ciudad asediada.* || **3.** Remove from accomodations. *Desalojar.* || **4.** To leave. *Irse.* Do you have everything packed? Then let's MOVE out. *¿Tienes todo preparado? Entonces, vámonos.*

MOVE OVER. Make room. *Correrse.* MOVE over, so that we can all sit down. *Córrete para que todos quepamos.*

MOVE OVER TO. To change to a different system. *Cambiar a.* ~We should MOVE over to a different system. *Nos conviene cambiar a otro sistema.*

MOVE TOGETHER. Join. *Juntar.* ~We could MOVE the tables together. *Podríamos juntar las mesas.*

MOVE TOWARD. To be more and more convinced. *Convencerse cada vez más.* ~I'm MOVING toward the view that. *Cada vez me convenzo más que.*

MOVE UP. *Progresar.* They have MOVED up in the world. *Han progresado mucho.* ~This song has MOVED up five places. *Está canción ha subido cinco puestos.* || 2. Make room. *Correrse.* There's room for one more person if everybody MOVES up a little. *Cabe otra persona más si cada uno se corre un poco.* || 3. Change (gear). *Cambiar.* ~I MOVED up into third gear. *Cambiar a tercera.* || 4. Bring closer. *Acercar.* || 5. Promote. *Ascender.* •To be MOVED up (pupil). *Pasar a la clase superior.* || 6. Go up. *Subir.* || 7. Walk further. *Avanzar.* ~Move up so you won't loose your place in line. *Avanza para que no te tomen el puesto en la cola.* || 8. Advance. *Avanzar, ascender.* ~She MOVED swiftly up the executive ladder. *Ha ascendido rápidamente en el escalón ejecutivo.* ⇨ MOVER

MUNDANE. *adj.* Comments. *Vulgar, banal.* ~A reviewer is not expected to mention anything so MUNDANE as the price of books. *No es de esperar que un crítico aluda a cosa tan vulgar como el precio de los libros.* ~Nothing but MUNDANE businessmen. *Simples negociantes vulgares.* || 2. [Job, life, activtiy). *Rutinario, prosaico* ~The occupations and distractions of MUNDANE life. *Las ocupaciones y preocupaciones de la vida diaria.* || 3. [Person]. *Ramplón.* || 4. Earthly. *Terrestre, terrenal.* ⇨ MUNDANO

MURMUR. *n.* [Of distant traffic]. *Rumor.* || 2. Complaint. *Queja.* ~We have not heard any MURMURS since everyone had an increase in salary. *No se ha oido una sola queja desde que se dio aumento de sueldo a todos.* || 3. The ripple (of leaves, wind, stream)]. *Susurro.* ~The wind MURMURED through the trees. *Se oía el susurro del viento a través de los árboles.* || 4. *PHRASES.* || •Without a MURMUR. *Sin chistar (rechistar).* ~He did it without a MURMUR. *Lo hizo sin rechistar.* || •To speak in a MURMUR. *Hablar en voz baja.* ~"But I came especially to see you", he MURMURED. *"Pero he venido específicamente para verlo", dijo en voz baja.* || •I don't want to hear a MURMUR out of you. *¡No quiero oir ni un suspiro!* || •Heart MURMUR. *Soplo cardíaco.* ⇨ MURMURAR

MYSTIFY. *v.* To baffle. *Dejar perplejo, desconcertar, desorientar, despistar.* ~He MYSTIFIED all of us by pouring his drink out of the window. *Nos desconcertó a todos cuando echó su trago por la ventana.* || 2. •I was completely MYSTIFIED. *Me quedé pasmado.* ⇨ MISTIFICAR

N

NAME [NOMBRE]. *n.* Reputation. *Reputación, fama, renombre.* ~The firm has a good NAME. *La empresa tiene una buena reputación.* ~He has a NAME for carelessness. *Tiene fama de descuidado.* •To give a bad NAME. *Dar mala reputación a.* ‖ **2.** Celebrity. *Figura, personaje.* ~She's a big NAME in the fashion world. *Es una de las grandes figuras de la moda.* ~He's one of the big NAMES in the business. *Es uno de los personajes importantes en ese campo.* This show has no big NAMES. *Este espectáculo no tiene grandes figuras.* •He's a big NAME. *Es todo un personaje.* ‖ **3.** Surname. *Apellido.* ‖ **4.** Nickname. *Apodo.* ~His middle NAME is 'lover'. *Le han apodado 'el amante'.* ‖ **5.** Pseudonym. *Seudónimo.* She writes under the NAME of. *Escribe bajo el seudónimo de.* ‖ **6.** PHRASES. ‖ •A lady by the NAME of Dulcinea. *Una señora llamada Dulcinea.* ‖ •By NAME only. *En aparencia.* ~He was king in NAME only. *Era rey sólo en aparencia.* ‖ •He hasn't a penny to his NAME. *No tiene donde caerse muerto.* ‖ •He started without a penny to his NAME. *Empezó sin un solo centavo.* ‖ •Maiden NAME. *Apellido de soltera.* ‖ •Married NAME. *Apellido de casada.* ‖ •To make a NAME for oneself. *Hacerse famoso.* ‖ •One of these bullets had my NAME on it. *Una de esas balas iba dirigida a mí.* ‖ •She goes by the NAME of Shirley Lane. *She hace llamar Shirley Lane.* ‖ •That's the NAME of the game. *Así es la cosa.* ‖ •To call someone NAMES. *Poner verde a uno.* ‖ •To drop NAMES. *Mencionar a gente importante (para darse tono).* ‖ •To make a NAME for oneself. *Darse a conocer.* ‖ •To make one's NAME. *Llegar a ser famoso.* ‖ •To put one's NAME down. *Apuntarse.* They've put the baby's NAME down for the local school. *Han apuntado al niño en el colegio de la zona.* ~He's put his NAME down for a transfer. *Ha solicitado un traslado.* ‖ •To take somebody's NAME (policeman). *Pedirle la documentación a alguien.* ‖ •To take somebody's NAME and address. *Apuntar las señas de uno.* ‖ •What NAME shall I say? (announcing arrival). *¿De parte de quién?* ‖ •Without mentioning any NAMES. *Sin mencionar a nadie.*

NATIONAL. *adj.* [Traje]. *Típico.* ~They were wearing their NATIONAL costumes. *Llevaban sus trajes típicos.* ‖ **2.** •NATIONAL debt. *Deuda pública.* ‖ **3.** •NATIONAL insurance. *seguridad social.* ⇨ NACIONAL

NATIVE[1] [NATIVO]. *adj.* [Place, ciudad]. *Natal.* ‖ **2.** [Land]. *Patria.* ~Her NATIVE land is England. *Inglaterra es su patria.* ‖ **3.** [Language]. *Materna.* ~She's not a NATIVE Dutch speaker. *El holandés no es su lengua materna.* ‖ **4.** [Plant, animal]. *Originario de.* ~The animal is NATIVE to Africa. *El animal es originario de Africa.* ‖ **5.** Innate. *Inato.* ‖ **6.** Artless. *Natural, sencillo.* ~NATIVE ability. *Habilidad natural.* ‖ **7.** Indigenous. *Indígena, autóctono.* ‖ **8.** [Product, resources]. *Nacional, del país.* ‖ **9.** •To go NATIVE. *Adoptar las costumbres de los naturales del país.*

NATIVE[2] [NATIVO]. *n.* Person born in a particular place. *Natural.* ~She's a NATIVE of Edinburgh. *Es natural de Edinburgo.* ‖ **2.** Original inhabitant. *Indígena.* ‖ **3.** •NATIVE wit. *Sentido común.*

NATURAL. *adj.* Normal. *Normal.* ~It's not NATURAL for a child of his age to be so quiet. *No es normal que un niño de su edad sea*

tan callado. || **2.** [Born]. *Nato.* A NATURAL actor. *Un actor nato.* ~These animals are NATURAL enemies. *Estos animales son enemigos por naturaleza.* || **3.** Logical. *Lógico.* ~I'm sure there's a perfectly NATURAL explanation. *Estoy seguro de que hay una explicación muy lógica para ello.* || **4.** •For the rest of your NATURAL life. *Por el resto de tu vida, de por vida.* || **5.** [Child, parent]. *Biológico.* || **6.** •NATURAL childbirth. *Parto sin dolor.* ⇨NATURAL

NAVIGATE. *v.* [Aircraft]. *Pilotear.* || **2.** [Figuratively]. *Guiar, conducir.* ~To NAVIGATE by the stars. *Guiarse (orientarse) por las estrellas.* || **3.** [In car]. *Hacer de copiloto.* I'll drive, you NAVIGATE. *Yo manejo (conduzco) y tú miras el mapa (haces de copiloto).* || **4.** Steer (ship, plane). *Conducir, llevar, gobernar.* || **5.** •Having sucessfully NAVIGATED the lobby. *Una vez salvada la entrada.* || **6.** •To NAVIGATE a bill through Parliament. *Llevar un proyecto de ley a buen término.* ⇨NAVEGAR

NEBULOUS. *adj.* [Argument, concept]. *Vago, impreciso.* ⇨NEBULOSO

NEGOTIATE. *v.* [Sale, loan]. *Gestionar, tramitar.* ~To NEGOTIATE the sale of an estate. *Gestionar la venta de una finca.* || **2.** [Obstacle]. *Salvar, franquear.* || **3.** [River]. *Pasar, cruzar.* || **4.** [Bend]. *Tomar.* ~To NEGOTIATE a bend. *Tomar una curva.* || **5.** [Difficulty]. *Superar.* ~She had difficulty NEGOTIATING the stairs. *Le costó subir la escalera.* || **6.** [Hill]. *Subir.* ⇨NEGOCIAR

NERVE. *n.* Courage. *Valor.* ~I didn't have the NERVE to do it. *No tuve el valor de hacerlo.* || **2.** Audacity, impudence, impertinence. *Caradura, descaro.* ~He had the NERVE to call me. *Tuvo el descaro de llamarme por teléfono.* || **3.** PHRASES. || •He gets on my NERVES. *Me fastidia terriblemente.* || •It takes some NERVE to do that. *Hace falta mucha sangre fría para hacer eso.* || •To strain every NERVE to. *Hacer un esfuerzo supremo (sobrehumano) por.* || •To touch a NERVE. *Poner el dedo en la llaga.* || •To loose one's NERVE. *Rajarse.* || •What a NERVE! *¡Qué cara!* ⇨NERVIO

NERVOUS. *adj.* Afraid. *Miedoso.* ~I've always been NERVOUS of dogs. *Siempre les he tenido miedo a los perros.* ~I was NERVOUS about making a mistake. *Tenía miedo de equivocarme.* ~She's NERVOUS in traffic since the accident. *Desde el accidente le tiene miedo al tráfico.* || **2.** Timid. *Tímido.* || **3.** Worried. *Inquieto, preocupado.* ~I was so NERVOUS about my exams that I couldn't sleep all night. *Estaba tan preocupado de los exámenes que no pude dormir toda la noche.* || **4.** •NERVOUS breakdown. *Depresión nerviosa.* ⇨NERVIOSO

NICHE [NICHO]. *n.* Specialization. *Especialidad.* || **2.** Place, position. *Colocación conveniente, buena posición, hueco.* ~She's found a little NICHE for herself in the business. *Se ha hecho su huequito en la empresa.*

NOMINATE [NOMINAR]. v. Propose. *Proponer, designar.* ~This movie has been NOMINATED for the best sound track. *Esta película ha sido propuesta para la mejor banda musical.* || **2.** Appoint. *Nombrar.* ~He was 70 years old when he was NOMINATED for president. *Cuando fue nombrado presidente tenía 70 años.*

NOMINATION [NOMINACIÓN]. *n.* Proposal. *Propuesta.* || **2.** Candidacy. *Candidatura.* || **3.** Appointment. *Nombramiento.* ~The Senate approved all the president's NOMINATIONS. *El Senado aprobó todos los nombramientos del presidente.*

NOTABLE [NOTABLE]. *adj.* Appreciable, noticeable, considerable (improvement, difference). *Considerable, marcado.* ~A NOTABLE lack of interest. *Un gran desinterés.* || **2.** Outstanding, remarkable. *Digno de notar.* ~Una actuación NOTABLE. *An outstanding performance.* ~Posee una NOTABLE inteligencia. *She's remarkably intelligent.* || **3.** [Author, actor]. Distinguido. ~A nation which produced some of the most NOTABLE thinkers in Europe. *Un país que originó algunos de los más distinguidos (grandes) pensadores de Europa.*

NOTE. *n.* Key. *Tecla.* ~The black/white

NOTES. *Las teclas negras/blancas.* || **2.** [Finance]. *Billete de banco.* ~A ten pound NOTE. *Un billete de diez libras.* || **3.** Annotation. *Apuntes.* ~I have to look it up in my NOTES. *Tendré que mirarlo en mis apuntes.* ~To speak from NOTES. *Pronunciar un discurso a base de apuntes.* || **4.** Sign, stigma. *Marca, señal.* || **5.** Comment. *Comentario.* ~She wrote the catalogue NOTES. *Escribió el comentario del catálogo.* || **6.** Sound. *Sonido.* || **7.** [Of a bird]. *Canto.* || **8.** *PHRASES.* •It strikes a familiar NOTE. *Suena conocido.* || •Nothing worthy of NOTE. *Nada digno de mención.* || •Nothing of NOTE. *Nada importante.* ~Nothing of NOTE came of their research. *Su investigación no produjo ningunos resultados importantes.* || •Of NOTE. *Iminente, renombrado, notable.* ~A surgeon of NOTE. *Un cirujano de renombre, un iminente cirujano.* || •Promissary NOTE. *Pagaré.* || •To end something on a high NOTE. *Cerrar con broche de oro.* || •To hit the wrong NOTE. *Desentonar.* || •To compare NOTES. *Cambiar impresiones, discutir los resultados.* || •To strike the right NOTE. *Acertar, hacer o decir lo apropiado.* || •To take NOTE of. *Fijarse en, prestar atención a, ocuparse de.* ~Only the critics took NOTE of this book. *Sólo lo críticos se ocuparon del libro.* ~I shall take full NOTE of your objections. *Tendré muy en cuenta sus objeciones.* || •To take NOTE of. *Prestar atención a.* ⇨NOTA

NOTE². *v.* Observe, notice. *Observar, fijarse en.* ~NOTE the red markings on its head. *Fijense en (observen) las manchas rojas de la cabeza.* || **2.** Write down. (information, details). *Anotar, apuntar.* ~We ask for the decision to be NOTED in the minutes. *Pedimos que la decisión constara en acta.* || **3.** Take into account. *Tomar en cuenta.* ~Your remarks have been NOTED. *Hemos leído con atención sus observaciones.* || **4.** •Will customers kindly NOTE that smoking is not permitted. *Se les recuerda a los señores clientes que está prohibido fumar.* ⇨NOTAR

NOTICE. *n.*

❶ ATTENTION/IMPORTANCE/INTEREST. Attention. *Atención.* ~It has been brought to my NOTICE that. *Ha llegado a mi conocimiento que.* || **2.** •To attract NOTICE. *Llamar la atención.* ~It was an event which attracted a lot of NOTICE. *Fue un acontecimiento que llamó mucho la atención.* || **3.** •To avoid NOTICE. *Procurar pasar inadvertido.* || **4.** •To escape NOTICE. *Pasar inadvertido.* || **5.** •To take (special) NOTICE of something. *Hacer caso de algo, prestar (especial) atención a (algo).* ~Take special NOTICE of these instructions. *Preste especial atención a estas instrucciones.* || **6.** •To take no NOTICE of something. *No hacer caso.* ~I asked him to drive more slowly but he took no NOTICE. *Le rogué que manejara más despacio pero no se dió por aludido (no me hizo caso).* || **7.** •To sit up and take NOTICE. *Aguzar las orejas.*

❷ NOTIFICATION. Warning. *Advertencia.* || **2.** Sign, poster. *Cartel, letrero.* ~The NOTICE said «keep of the grass». *El letrero decía «no pisar el cesped».* || **3.** •Until further NOTICE. *Hasta nuevo aviso.* ~The beaches are closed until further NOTICE. *Cerradas las playas hasta nuevo aviso.* || **4.** •Without prior NOTICE. *Sin previo aviso.* || **5.** •At a moment's NOTICE. *En el acto, inmediatemente.* ~I can't drop everything at a moment's NOTICE. *No puedo abandonarlo todo asi, de un momento a otro.* ~You must be ready to leave at a moment's NOTICE. *Tiene que estar listo para salir inmediatemente.* || **6.** •At short NOTICE. *A corto plazo, en seguida.* ~It's impossible to do it at such short NOTICE. *Es imposible hacerlo a tan corto plazo.* || **7.** •To give two months' NOTICE. *Avisar con dos meses de antelación (anticipación).* || **8.** •At 7 day's NOTICE. *Con 7 días de antelación.* || **9.** •To give (serve) NOTICE that. *Avisar a uno que.* || **10.** •NOTICE is hereby given that. *Se pone en conocimiento del público que.*

❸ TERMINATION OF EMPLOYMENT. Formal announcement of intention to terminate employment. *Preaviso.* ~I have to give the company a month's NOTICE.

Tengo que dar un mes de preaviso. ‖ **2.** Order to leave job (by employer). *Despido.* ~The firm gave him his NOTICE. *La compañía le comunicó su despido.* ~She was given her NOTICE. *La despidieron.* •To give somebody a week's NOTICE. *Despedir a uno con una semana de plazo.* •To get one's NOTICE. *Ser despedido.* ‖ **3.** Intention to leave job (by employee). *Renuncia, dimisión.* ~He handed in his NOTICE. ~*Presentó su dimisión.*

❹ OTHERS. Recognition. *Reconocimiento.* ~They deserve NOTICE and respect. *Merecen el reconocimiento y respeto de todos.* ~He achieved public NOTICE in later life. *Alcanzó reconocimiento general en la edad madura.* ‖ **2.** Announcement. *Aviso, anuncio.* ‖ **3.** Write-up. *Crítica, reseña.* ~To get good NOTICES (play, performance). *Recibir críticas favorables.* ⇨ NOTICIA

NOTORIOUS. *adj.* Widely and unfavorably known. *De mala reputación, de mala fama, infame.* ~She's a NOTORIOUS liar. *Tiene fama de mentirosa.* ⇨ NOTORIO

O

OBEY. *v.* [Instincts]. *Seguir.* || **2.** [Law]. *Cumplir, observar, obrar de acuerdo con, acatar.* ~|| **3.** [Needs]. *Responder a.* ~She dropped out of the race because her legs wouldn't OBEY her anymore. *Tuvo que abandonar la carrera porque ya no le respondían las piernas.* || **4.** Pay heed to. *Hacer caso de.* || **5.** [Summons]. *Acudir a.* || **6.** [Instruction, order]. *Cumplir.*~The soldiers refused to OBEY orders. *Los soldados se negaron a cumplir las órdenes.* || **7.** [Rules]. *Observar.* ~You have to OBEY the rules if you wish to live here. *Si quiere vivir aquí, tiene que observar las reglas.* || **8.** [Instructions]. *Seguir.* To assemble the bookshelf, follow the INSTRUCTIONS. *Para montar la estantería, siga las instrucciones.* || **9.** •Just OBEY your conscience. *Haz lo que te dicte la conciencia.* ⇨ OBEDECER

OBJECTION [OBJECIÓN]. *n.* Difficulty. *Inconveniente, obstáculo, dificultad.* ~What are the OBJECTIONS? *¿Cuáles son las dificultades?, ¿qué obstáculos hay?* ~There is no OBJECTION to your going. *No hay inconveniente en que vayas.* || **2.** Disapproval, dislike. *Oposición.* The plan met with the OBJECTION of the clergy. *El plan se encontró con la oposición del clero.* ~I have no OBJECTION to her. *No tengo nada en contra de ella.* || **3.** •OBJECTION! *¡Protesto!* || **4.** •OBJECTION overruled. *No ha lugar a la protesta.* || **5.** •OBJECTION sustained (upheld). *Ha lugar a la protesta.*

OBLIGATION [OBLIGACIÓN]. *n.* Commitment. *Compromiso.* ~Professional OBLIGATIONS prevented me from attending. *Compromisos profesionales me impidieron asistir.* ~The firm was unable to meet its OBLIGATIONS. *La empresa no pudo hacer frente a sus compromisos.* || **2.** PHRASES. || •To fail to meet one's OBLIGATIONS. *No poder cumplir sus compromisos.* || •To assume an OBLIGATION. *Contraer un compromiso.* || •To meet one's OBLIGATIONS. *Cumplir (hacer honor a) sus compromisos.* ~She always meets her OBLIGATIONS. *Siempre cumple sus compromisos.* || •To be under an OBLIGATION to. *Haberse comprometido a, poner en el compromiso de.* ~It has placed me under an OBLIGATION to help her. *Me ha puesto en el compromiso de ayudarla.* || •To be under an OBLIGATION to someone. *Deberle favores a uno.* || •Without OBLIGATION (in advertising). *Sin compromiso.* ~Send for our brochure without OBLIGATION. *Solicite sin compromiso alguno nuestro folleto informativo.*

OBLIGE. *v.* To gratify. *Complacer.* ~She OBLIGED the guests with a song. *Complació a los invitados cantando una canción.* || **2.** Help, do a favor. *Ayudar, hacer un favor.* ~He was always ready to OBLIGE a friend. *Estaba siempre dispuesto a hacerle un favor a un amigo.* || **3.** Be grateful. *Estar agradecido.* ~We are greatly OBLIGED to you for your help. *Le estamos muy agradecido por su ayuda.* ⇨ OBLIGAR

OBLITERATE [OBLITERAR]. *v.* To destroy (city, population). *Arrasar, destruir totalmente.* || **2.** [Words, memories]. Borrar. ~Centuries of winds and rain had OBLITERATED the words carved on the gravestones. *Siglos de viento y lluvia habían borrado las palabras grabadas en las lápidas.* ~Nothing could OBLITERATE the memories of those tragic events. *Nada podría borrar de la memoria aquellos* *acontecimientos trágicos.* To remove. *Quitar.* || **3.** To cross out. *Tachar.* || **4.** To wipe out. *Eliminar.* || **5.** [A stamp]. *Matar, poner el matasellos sobre.*

OBSCURE. *adj.* Not clear or plain, vague (impression, feeling, memory, meaning). *Poco claro, confuso, vago.* ~ An OBSCURE sentence in the contract. *Una frase poco clara en el contrato.* OBSCURE legal phrases. *Frases legales poco claras.* || **2.** Hidden, remote (island, town). *Recóndito, perdido.* ~An OBSCURE provincial town in an OBSCURE island in the Pacific. *Un recóndito pueblo provinciano en una isla perdida del Pacífico.* ~He lives in an OBSCURE place in the country. *Vive en un lugar recóndito del campo.* || **3.** Little known (writer, book, origin). Desconocido, poco conocido. ~The origin of this design is OBSCURE. *El origen de este estilo es desconocido, se desconoce el origen de este estilo.* ~An OBSCURE 12th century mystic. *Un desconocido místico del siglo doce.* ~OBSCURE operas. *Óperas poco conocidas.* || **4.** [Subject]. *Críptico, hermético.* ~He's an authority of some OSBSCURE subject like Coptic calligraphy. *Es una autoridad sobre un tema medio críptico algo como la caligrafía copta.* || **5.** Hard to understand, inexplicable. *Inexplicable, extraño.* Official policy has changed, for reasons that remain OBSCURE. *Por motivos todavía inexplicables, ha cambiado la política oficial.* ~For some OBSCURE reason he refused my help. *Por alguna extraña razón se negó a que le ayudara.* || **6.** Indistinct. *Indefinido, impreciso, borroso.* ~He saw the hideous, OBSCURE shape rise slowly to the surface. *Vio esta horrosa y borrosa figura aparecer lentamente en la superficie.* ⇨OSCURO

OBCURE[2]. *v.* To conceal (object, beauty, sun). *Ocultar.* ~Her view of the stage was OBSCURED by the man in front of her. *El hombre que tenía delante le impedía ver todo el escenario.* ~He was suddenly OBSCURED from sight. *De repente quedó oculto a la vista.* || **2.** Make unclear, cover ᴜᴘ. ~He's just trying to OBSCURE the issue.

Lo que quiere es confundir, complicar las cosas. ~These irrelevant details OBSCURE the central problem. *Estos detalles supérfluos impiden ver claramente el problema central.* || **3.** [Truth]. *Disimular.* ~Words that OBSCURE the truth must be discarded. *Se tienen que eliminar las palabras que disimulan la verdad.* || **4.** Eclipsar. Overshadow. ⇨OSCURECER

OBSEQUIOUS. *adj.* Servile. *Servil.* ~The salesman's OBSEQUIOUS manner was beginning to irritate me. *La manera de ser (comportamiento) del vendedor me empezaba a molestar.* ⇨OBSEQUIOSO

OBSERVE [OBSERVAR]. *v.* [Suspect]. *Vigilar.* ~The police OBSERVED the suspect closely. *La policía vigilaba el sospechoso de cerca.* || **2.** [Remark]. *Advertir, señalar.* ~As Mr. Brown has OBSERVED. *Como ha señalado el Sr. Brown.* || **3.** [Silence]. *Guardar.* || **4.** Religious festival. *Guardar, celebrar.* ~To OBSERVE the fast of Ramadan. *Guardar ayuno durante el Ramadán.* || **5.** [Anniversary]. *Celebrar.* ~We always CELEBRATE birthdays at home. *Siempre celebramos los cumpleaños en casa.* || **6.** [Ley]. *Cumplir con.* || **7.** See, notice. *Ver, notar.* ~I OBSERVED him steal the duck. *Lo vi robar el pato.* ~He was OBSERVED entering the building. *Se le vio entrar en el edificio.* || **8.** To regard with attention. *Fijarse en.* ~I want you to OBSERVE how she reacts. *Fíjate bien como reacciona.* ~She OBSERVES things keenly. *Se fija mucho en las cosas.* ~OBSERVE closely. *Fíjate bien en esto.*

OBSOLETE [OBSOLETO]. *adj.* [Language]. *Caído en desuso.* ~OBSOLETE word. *Palabra caída en desuso.* || **2.** Out of fashion. *Pasado de moda.* Gas lamps are now OBSOLETE. *Las lámparas a gas ya no se usan.* || **3.** Expired. *Que ha caducado.* || **4.** No longer in general use. *Viejo, gastado, inservible, desgastado.* ~OBSOLETE equipment. *Maquinaria en desuso.*

OBSTINATE [OBSTINADO]. *adj.* [Pain]. *Persistente, tenaz.* He complained of his OBSTINATE headaches. *Se quejaba de sus*

tenaces dolores de cabeza. || **2.** [Of illness]. *Rebelde, pertinaz.* ~An obstinate disease. *Una enfermedad rebelde.* || **3.** [Efforts, resistance, pursuit, stains]. *Tenaz.* ~Strong enough to remove the most OBSTINATE stains. *Suficientemente fuerte para eliminar hasta las manchas más tenaces.*

OBSTRUCT. *v.* [View]. *Tapar.* They erected a building in front of his house which OBSTRUCTS his view of the city. *Ante su casa han levantado un edificio que tapa su vista de la ciudad.* || **2.** Hinder. *Estorbar.* ~To OBSTRUCT the traffic. *Estorbar el tránsito.* ~This chair is OBSTRUCTING passage. *Esta silla estorba el paso.* || **3.** [Progress]. *Dificultar.* || **4.** [Bill]. *Obstaculizar la aprobación.* || **5.** [Sport]. *Bloquear.* ⇨OBSTRUIR

OBVIOUS [OBVIO]. *adj.* Lacking in subtlety. *Poco sútil.* ~It was such an OBVIOUS ploy. *~Se veía a la claras que se trataba de una ardid.* •Not to be too OBVIOUS in doing something. *Hacer algo con disimulo, ser astuto (al hacer algo).* ~Try to hear what they're saying, but don't be too OBVIOUS about it. *Trata de oir lo que dicen pero con disimulo.* ~We must not be too OBVIOUS about it. *En esto conviene ser algo astuto.* || **2.** Clear. *Claro.* ~It's not OBVIOUS to me. *No es tan claro para mí.* ~If there is a connection, it's not at all OBVIOUS to me. *Si es que hay alguna relación, yo no la veo nada clara.* ~It was perfectly OBVIOUS that she was lying. *Estaba clarísimo que mentía.* || **3.** Unmistakable. *Indiscutible.* ~It's an OBVIOUS lie. *Es claramente mentira.* ~She's the OBVIOUS candidate for the job. *Es la candidata indiscutible para el puesto.* || **4.** Showy. *Vistoso, llamativo.* || **5.** PHRASES. || •An OBVIOUS remark. *Una perogrullada.* || •An OBVIOUS fact. *Un hecho patente.* || •It was the OBVIOUS thing to do. *Era lo que había que hacer.* || •It's the most OBVIOUS thing to do. *El lo más indicado.* || •To make (something) OBVIOUS. *Hacer patente.* They made it very OBVIOUS that they did not enjoy the party. *Hicieron muy patente el hecho de que no les había gustado la fiesta.* || •To be glaringly OBVIOUS. *Saltar a la vista.*

OCCASION. *n.* Opportunity, chance, suitable time. *Coyuntura, oportunidad, momento propicio.* ~I have not had the OCCASION to thank you properly. *No he tenido la oportunidad de agradecérselo debidamente.* ~The banquet was a good OCCASION for talking. *El banquete fue una buena oportunidad para hablar.* ~He was awaiting a suitable OCCASION. *Aguardaba un momento propicio.* •To take OCCASION to do something. *Aprovechar la oportunidad para hacer algo.* •To leave something for another OCCASION. *Dejar algo para otra oportunidad.* || **2.** Cause. *Motivo, razon.* ~I have no OCCASION for complaint. *No tengo motivo de queja, no tengo porque quejarme.* ~There's no OCCASION for alarm. *No hay motivo para inquietarse.* ~If you have OCCASION to use it. *Si te ves en el caso de usarlo.* •On the OCCASION of. *Con motivo de.* •To give OCCASION for scandal. *Provocar el escándalo.* || **3.** Occurrence, instance, times. *Veces, ocasión.* ~On the OCCASION of the world cup final. *Cuando la final de la copa mundial.* •On OCCASION. *De vez en cuando, algunas veces.* ~I have on occasion visited her home. *Algunas veces estuve en su casa.* •On one OCCASION. *Una vez.* •On other OCCASIONS. *Otras veces.* •On that OCCASION. *Esa vez.* || **4.** Situation, circumstances. *Caso, circunstancia.* ~Should the OCCASION arise, please mention my name. *Si viene al caso le ruego mencionarle mi nombre.* ~A speech prepared for the OCCASION. *Un discurso preparado para las circunstancias.* ~I'm ready to defend my policies should the OCCASION arise. *Si lo exige las circunstancias, estoy dispuesto a defender mi programa.* •As the OCCASION requires. *Según el caso.* •To be equal (rise) to the OCCASION. *Estar (ponerse) a la altura de las circunstancias.* || **5.** Special event. *Acontecimiento.* ~We cracked a bottle of champagne to mark the OCCASION. *Descorchamos una botella de champán para celebrarlo.* •To be quite an OCCASION. *Ser todo un acontecimiento.* ~His birthday was quite an OCCASION. *Su cumpleaños fue todo un acontecimiento.* •What is the OCCASION? *¿Qué se celebra?* •Let's make it an OCCACION! *¡Vamos a celebrarlo!* ⇨OCA-SIÓN

OCCASIONAL. *adj.* Intermittent, sporadic, irregular. *Aislado, esporádico.* OCCASIONAL showers in Galicia. *Chubascos aislados en Galicia.* || **2.** Occurring from time to time. *Que ocurre de vez en cuando.* ~I like an OCCASIONAL glass of wine. *De vez en cuando me gusta tomarme un vaso de vino.* ~The magazine runs an OCCASIONAL feature on cookery. *De vez en cuando aparece en la revista un artículo de cocina.* || **3.** For special occasions (verse, music). *Compuesto especialmente para la ocasión.* ~An OCCASIONAL poem. *Un poema para el caso.* || **4.** [Table, chair]. *Para casos de necesidad, auxiliar.* ~An OCCASIONAL chair. *Una silla para casos de necesidad.* ⇨OCASIONAL

OCCASIONALLY. *adv.* Sometimes, now and then, from time to time. *De vez en cuando, a veces. alguna que otra vez.* ~Do you smoke? -only very OCCASIONALLY. *¿Fumas? -(sólo) muy de vez en cuando.* •Very OCCASIONALLY. *Muy de tarde en tarde.* ⇨OCASIONALMENTE

OCCUPATION [OCUPACIÓN]. *n.* Craft, trade, profession. [General]. *Profesión.* ~What is your OCCUPATION? *¿Cuál es su profesión?* [Specific]. *Oficio.* ~A tailor by OCCUPATION. *De oficio sastre.* || **2.** Job, work, employment. *Trabajo, empleo, puesto.* ~It provides OCCUPATION for 50 men. *Emplea (da trabajo) a 50 hombres.* ~A poorly paid OCCUPATION. *Un trabajo mal renumerado.* || **3.** Pastime. *Pasatiempo, entretenimiento.* ~A harmless enough OCCUPATION. *Un pasatiempo inocente.* ~Reading was his favorite OCCUPATION. *Su mayor pasatiempo era la lectura.* ~This will give OCCUPATION to your mind. *Esto le servirá para entretener la inteligencia.*

OCCUR [OCURRIR]. *v.* [Of change]. *Producirse.* A complete change has OCCURRED. *Se ha producido un cambio completo.* || **2.**

[Opportunity]. *Presentarse.* ~If another opportunity OCCURS. *Si se presenta otra ocasión.* || **3.** Be found, appear. *Encontrarse, exisitir, darse, aparecer.* ~That phrase OCCURS repeatedly in her writings. *Esa frase aparece repetidamente en sus escritos.* ~A sound that doesn't OCCUR in our language. *Un sonido que no existe (no se da) en nuestra lengua.* || **4.** Tener lugar. To take place. ~A festival that OCCURS every five years. *Un festival que tiene lugar cada cinco años.*

OCCURRENCE. *n.* Event, happening. *Acontecimiento, suceso, hecho.* ~An everyday OCCURRENCE. *Un hecho cotidiano, un hecho que ocurre con frecuencia.* ~Murders are an everyday OCCURRENCE here. *Aquí los asesinatos son cosas de todos los días.* ~The unusual OCCURRENCE of last evening. *Los extraños acontecimientos de la noche anterior.* •It's a common OCCURRENCE. *Ocurre con frecuencia, ese caso se da con frecuencia.* ~A common OCCURRENCE. *Un caso frecuente.* || **2.** Instance. *Caso.* ~There were two separates OCCURRENCES. *Hubo dos casos independientes.* || **3.** Existence. *Existencia, aparición.* It's OCCURRENCE in the south is well known. *Es conocida su existencia en el sur.* It's OCCURRENCE here is unexpected. *Su aparición aquí es inesperada.* || **4.** Incidence, frequency, rate. *Incidencia, frecuencia.* ~The OCCURRENCE of cancer among children. *La incidencia del cancer en los niños.* || **5.** Presence (of minerals, plants). *Presencia.* ~Evidence of oil OCCURRENCE in the region. *Indicios de la presencia de petróleo en la zona.* ⇨OCURRENCIA

OFFEND [OFENDER]. *v.* Disgust. *Disgustar, repeler.* ~The sight of a few dirty dishes OFFENDS her. *La vista de unos pocos platos sucios le resulta repelente.* || **2.** To violate (decency, justice, reason). *Ir en contra, atentar contra.* ~Their behavior OFFENDS one's sense of justice. *Su conducta atenta conra el sentido que cualquiera tiene de la justicia.* ~His argument OFFENDS reason. *Su argumento va en contra de toda razón.* || **3.** [The eyes, the ears]. *Herir, lastimar.* ||

4. To shock. *Escandalizar.*

OFFENSE. *n.* Breach of law, regulations. *Delito, falta (sport), crimen, infracción de la ley.* ~A traffic offense. *Una infracción de tráfico.* •Second OFFENSE. *Reincidencia.* •It is an OFFENSE to. *La ley castiga a los que.* || **2.** [Moral]. *Transgresión.* || **3.** Something that outrages the moral or physical senses. *Atentado.* ~An OFFENSE against decency. *Un atentado contra la moral.* To be an OFFENSE to the ear. *Herir (lastimar) el oído.* || **4.** Scandal. *Escándalo.* || **5.** Assault. *Ofensiva.* || **6.** The act of attacking. *Ataque.* ⇨OFENSA

OFFENSIVE [OFENSIVO]. *adj.* Repulsive, disgusting, revolting, degrading. *Repugnante, degradante.* ~Loud, OFFENSIVE behavior. *Conducta ruidosa y degradante.* || **2.** Objectionable. ~An OFFENSIVE joke. *Un chiste de mal gusto.* ~An OFFENSIVE remark. *Un comentario insultante.* || **3.** Unpleasant (smell, sight). *Desagradable.* || **4.** Shocking. *Chocante.* || **5.** Irritating, annoying. *Pesado, molesto, fastidioso.* OFFENSIVE commercials. *Anuncios pesados, molestos.* || **6.** •Morally OFFENSIVE (book, movie). *Que ofende la moral.* || **7.** •Words OFFENSIVE to the ear *Palabras groseras (malsonantes).* || **8.** •To be OFFENSIVE. *Ofender, insultar a alguien.*

OFFER. *v.* Propose (idea, solution, plan). *Proponer, sugerir.* ~He never even OFFERED any suggestions. *Ni siquiera hizo ninguna sugerencia.* || **2.** Provide (opportunity, prospect). *Proporcionar, brindar, facilitar, deparar.* || **3.** Arise. *Presentarse.* ~I'll talk to him whenever a suitable occasion OFFERS itself. *Le hablaré en cuanto se presente la oportunidad.* || **4.** Propose marriage. *Proponer el matrimonio.* || **5.** [Comment, remark]. *Hacer.* ~He OFFERED no comment. *No hizo ningún comentario.* ~I wish to OFFER two comments. *Quiero hacer dos observaciones.* || **6.** [Excuse, alibi]. *Presentar.* || **7.** [Opinion]. *Expresar, manifestar.* || **8.** PHRASES. •I OFFERED him my hand, but he refused. *Le tendí la mano, pero la rechazó.* || •May I OFFER you a drink? *¿Quisiera*

tomar algo? || •The garden OFFERS a fine spectacle. *El jardín se muestra espléndido.* || •To OFFER oneself for a post. *Presentarse para un puesto.* || •To OFFER goods for sale. *Vender mercancías.* || •To OFFER one's soul to God. *Ofrendar su alma a Dios.* || •To OFFER an apology. *Pedir disculpas.* || •To OFFER one's flank to the enemy. *Exponer su flanco al enemigo.* || •To OFFER battle. *Presentar batalla.* ⇨OFRECER

OFFICE [OFICINA]. *n.*
❶ PLACE. Federal agency. *Agencia gubernamental.* || **2.** [Room]. *Despacho.* ~The manager made an appointment to see him at five o'clock in his OFFICE. *El gerente lo citó en su despacho a las cinco.* || **3.** [Lawyer's]. *Bufete.* || **4.** [As part of organization]. *Sección.* || **5.** Ministry. *Ministerio.* || **6.** Branch. *Sucursal.* ~They have OFFICES in Paris, London and Madrid. *Tienen sucursales en París, Londres y Madrid.* || **7.** [Doctor's]. *Consultorio.* ~There's a stretcher in the doctor's OFFICE. *En el consultorio del médico hay una camilla.* || **8.** [Architect's]. *Estudio.*
❷ FUNCTION. Duty. *Función, cometido.* || **2.** Position, post. *Cargo.* ~She has held this OFFICE twice. *Había ocupado dos veces este cargo.* ~To hold OFFICE. *Ocupar un cargo.* ~To leave OFFICE. *Dimitir.*
❸ VARIOUS. Assistance, service. *Mediación, buenos oficios.* ~Through someone's good OFFICES. *Gracias a los buenos oficios de uno.* || **2.** Power. *Poder.* ~The government in OFFICE. *El gobierno que está en el poder.* || **3.** [Religion]. *Oficio.* ~OFFICE for the Dead. *Oficio de difuntos.* ~Holy OFFICE. *Santo Oficio.*

OFFICER. *n.* [Police]. *Policía, agente.* || **2.** [In government service]. *Funcionario.* || **3.** [Of union, party]. *Dirigente.* || **4.** [Of club]. *Directivo.* || **5.** [Of society]. *Dignatario.* || **6.** [Of local government]. *Magistrado.* || **7.** [Of a company]. *Director.* ⇨OFICIAL

OFFICIAL. *n.* [Who holds a public appointment]. *Funcionario, dignatario.* ~An OFFICIAL of the Ministry. *Un funcio-*

nario del Ministerio. •High OFFICIALS. Altos funcionarios. || **2.** Referee, umpire. *Árbitro.* ~The OFFICIALS for tonight's game. *Los árbitros para el partido de hoy.* || **3.** [Party, union]. *Dirigente.* ~The OFFICIALS of the Republican Party. *Los dirigentes del partido republicano.* ⇨ OFICIAL

OMINOUS. *adj.* Foreboding, threatening. *De mal agüero, siniestro, amenazador.* ~The silence was OMINOUS. *El silencio no auguraba nada bueno.* ~In an OMINOUS tone. *En tono amenazador.* ~That's OMINOUS. *Eso es mala señal.* || **2.** [Prophetic]. *Agorero, inquietante.* ⇨ OMINOSO

OMIT [OMITIR]. *v.* Overlook. *Pasar por alto.* They OMITTED his name on the list. *Pasaron su nombre por alto en la lista.* || **2.** Forget. *Olvidarse.* ~Don't omit any names on the list. *No te olvides de ningún nombre en la lista.* ~I omitted to mention it. *Se me olvidó mencionártelo.* || **3.** Delete, supress. *Suprimir.* ~This chapter can be omitted. *Este capítulo se puede omitir.*

OPERATE[1] [OPERAR]. *v.* [Intransitive use]. To function. *Funcionar.* ~A machine OPERATED by electricity. *Una máquina que funciona con electricidad.* ~It OPERATES on two levels. *Funciona a dos niveles.* ~The elevator is not OPERATING. *El ascensor no funciona.* || **2.** To be in existence. *Actuar.* ~In the 20 years the committee has been OPERATING. *Durante los 20 años de actuación del comité.* || **3.** To act, work. *Actuar, obrar, proceder.* ~Various trends are OPERATING in favor of integration. *Varias tendencias obran en favor de la integración.* ~The law OPERATES to our advantage. *La ley nos favorece.* ~We have to OPERATE within the laws of the country. *Tenemos que actuar (proceder) de acuerdo a las leyes del país.* ~Soldiers cannot OPERATE effectively without good food. *El ejército no puede actuar si no tiene buena comida.* ~That's the way she OPERATES. *Así actúa ella.* || **4.** [Of a drug]. To produce the effect intended. *Surtir efecto.* Is the aspirin OPERATING yet? *¿Ha surtido efecto ya la aspirina?* || **5.** [Rules, laws]. Be applicable.

Regir. || **6.** Work. *Trabajar.* ~How can I OPERATE under these conditions? *¿Cómo puedo trabajar en estas condiciones?* The company OPERATES on an international scale. *La compañía trabaja a escala internacional.* ~We have representatives OPERATING in most countries. *Tenemos representantes trabajando en la mayoría de los países.* || **7.** [Criminal]. *Cometer un delito.* ~The thief OPERATED at night. *El ladrón cometía sus robos por la noche.* || **8.** Influence. *Influir.* Their propaganda is beginning to OPERATE on the minds of the people. *Su publicidad esta empezando a influir a la gente.*

OPERATE[2] [OPERAR]. *v.* [Transitive use]. [Machine]. *Hacer funcionar, manejar.* ~He OPERATES the company's complicated machinery. *Maneja con gran habilidad la complicada maquinaria de la empresa.* ~Do you know how to OPERATE it? *¿Sabes cómo funciona?* Can you OPERATE this tool? *¿Sabes manejar esta herramienta?* ~How do you OPERATE the remote control unit? *Como haces funcionar este mando a distancia?* || **2.** To run, manage. (I) [A business]. *Dirigir, gobernar, llevar,* (II) [Store]. *Tener, ocuparse en, dedicarse a, ser proprietario de.* ~He's been OPERATING his business for 3 years. *Hace 3 años que se ocupa del negocio.* ~He OPERATED a small store with which he supported his family. *Tenía una pequeña tienda con la que mantenía a su familia.* ~She OPERATES a small business from home. *Lleva un pequeño negocio desde su casa.* ~We OPERATE a bus service. *Tenemos un servicio de autobuses.* || **3.** [Country]. *Administrar.* ~The Virgin Islands have been OPERATED ... *Las Islas Vírgenes se han venido administrando hasta ahora ... (cit. Prats).* || **4.** [Mine]. *Labrar, trabajar, explotar.* || **5.** To be in charge of. *Atender a, encargarse de.* ~To OPERATE a switchboard. *Atender a una centralilla telefónica.* || **6.** [Car]. *Conducir, manejar, dirigir.* || **7.** To work or use a machine, *Utilizar.* ~These machines can be OPERATED without difficulty by anyone. *Estas máquinas se pueden utilizar sin* *dificuldad por cualquiera.* ‖ **8.** Put into Service. *Realizar, poner.* The company announced that starting next month they will OPERATE 3 extra flights to New York. *Ha anunciado la compañía que a partir del mes próximo realizaran 3 vuelos más.* ‖ **9.** To have. *Tener.* ~Does the company OPERATE a retirement system? *¿Tiene la compañía programa de jubilación?*

OPERATION [OPERACIÓN]. *n.* [Machine]. *Funcionamiento.* ~The OPERATION of the valves is bad. *El funcionamiento de las válvulas es malo.* ‖ **2.** [Using, running]. *Manejo.* Designed for one-person OPERATION. *Concebido para ser manejado por una sola persona.* ~The OPERATION of a crane. *El manejo de una grúa.*‖ **3.** [Military]. *Maniobra.* ‖ **4.** [Company]. *Actividad.* ~The company's OPERATIONS during the year. *Las actividades de la compañía durante el año.* ‖ **5.** [Gang]. *Activity.* ~The gang's OPERATIONS. *Las actividades de la pandilla.* ‖ **6.** Work. *Obras.* OPERATIONS begin tomorrow. *Las obras empiezan mañana.* ‖ **7.** •To be in OPERATION. [Machine]. *Estar funcionando, estar en funcionamiento, funcionar, estar funcionando,* [Of law]. *Vigente, en vigor,* [System]. *Regir.* ~To be in full OPERATION. *Estar en pleno funcionamiento.* ~The new computer is not yet in OPERATION. *La nueva computadora todavía no ha entrado en funcionamiento.* ~A bus service will be in OPERATION in May. *Habrá un servicio de autobuses a partir de mayo.* ‖ **8.** •To put into OPERATION (a plan). *Poner en marcha.* ‖ **9.** •Shady OPERATIONS. *Maniobras turbias.*

OPERATOR [OPERADOR]. *n.* [Telephone]. *Telefonista.* ‖ **2.** {Machine]. *Maquinista.* ‖ **3.** [Radio]. *Radiotelegrafista.* ‖ **4.** [Mine]. *Explotador.* ‖ **5.** Dealer. *Negociante.* ‖ **6.** [Elevator]. *Ascensorista.* ‖ **7.** Person who trades in securities. *Corredor (de bolsa), bolsista.* ‖ **8.** •Tour operator. *Agente de viajes.* ‖ **9.** •Smart, smooth, slick operator. *Tío vivo.*

OPPRESSIVE [OPRESIVO]. *adj.* [Of atmosphere]. *Agobiante.* ‖ **2.** [Of heat].

Sofocante. ~We were unable to sleep because of the OPPRESSIVE heat. *No pudimos dormir debido al calor sofocante.* ‖ **3.** [Burden]. *Agobiante, oneroso.* ‖ **4.** [Tax]. *Gravoso.*

OPTIMISTIC [OPTIMISTA]. *adj.* Encouraging, promising. *Alentador, esperanzador.* ~OPTIMISTIC signs. *Indicaciones alentadoras.*

OPTIONAL [OPCIONAL]. *adj.* Not compulsory, voluntary. *Optativo, facultativo, discrecional.* ‖ **2.** [Course, subject]. *Optativo.* ‖ **3.** [Attendance]. *No obligatorio.* ~Attendance is OPTIONAL. *La asistencia no es obligatoria.* ‖ **4.** [Dress]. ~Evening dress is OPTIONAL. *El traje de etiqueta no es de rigor, traje de etiqueta o de calle.* ‖ **5.** •It's OPTIONAL whether you go or stay. *Puede irse o quedarse.*

ORDER. *v.* Request. *Pedir (dish, drink), encargar (place an order for), mandar hacer (a suit), llamar (a taxi).* ~Can you ORDER me a copy? *¿Me puede encargar un ejemplar.* ~Are you ready to ORDER? *¿Ya han decidido lo que van a tomar (pedir)?* ‖ **2.** Organize. *Organizar.* ~To ORDER one's life properly. *Organizar bien su vida.* ~To ORDER one's affair. *Poner en orden sus asuntos.* ‖ **3.** To have someone do something. *Mandar.* The doctor ORDERED him to stay in bed. *El médico le mandó quedarse en la cama.* ‖ **4.** To prescribe. *Recetar.* The doctor ORDERED a course of antibiotics. *El médico le recetó unos antibióticos.* ‖ **5.** To expel. *Expulsar.* The referee ORDERED the player off (the field). *El árbitro expulsó al jugador.* ⇨ORDENAR

ORDER¹. *n.*

❶ REQUEST FOR GOODS. *Pedido, encargo.* ~The shop called to say that your order had come in. *Llamó la tienda para decir que había llegado su pedido.* ‖ **2.** •To be on ORDER. *Estar pedido (encargado).* ~The books are on ORDER. *Se han pedido los libros, los libros están pedidos.* ‖ **3.** •To place an ORDER. *Hacer un pedido, encargar, pedir.* ~I placed an ORDER with her for two pastries. *Le encargué dos* *pasteles.* ~We're taking ORDERS for the new model. *Estamos recibiendo pedidos para el nuevo modelo.* || **4.** •ORDER form. *Hoja de pedido.* || **5.** •ORDER department. *Sección de pedidos.* || **6.** •ORDER number. *Número de pedido.* || **7.** •Unfilled ORDERS. *Pedidos pendientes.* || **8.** •Side ORDER (of food). *Ración.* ~An ORDER of French fries. *Una ración de patatas (papas) fritas.* || **9.** •Made to ORDER (suit). *Hecho a la medida.* ~A suit made to ORDER. *Un traje hecho a la medida.* || **10.** || •To ORDER. *Por encargo.* ~We only make wedding cakes to ORDER. *Hacemos tortas (pasteles) de boda únicamente por encargo.* || **11.** To be on ORDER. *Estar pendiente (un pedido).* ~Do you have an ORDER with our store? *¿Tiene un pedido pendiente con nosotros?* || **12.** •Mail ORDER. *Pedido por correspondencia.* ❷ CONDITION. *Estado.* ~In good ORDER. *En buen estado, en condiciones.* What sort of ORDER is it in? *¿En qué estado está?* ~His financial affairs were in good ORDER. *Estaba bien economicamente.* || **2.** •In working ORDER. *Que funciona, en funcionamiento.* ~The car was in perfect working ORDER. *El coche funcionaba perfectamente bien.* || **3.** •To be out of ORDER. *Estar descompuesto (averiado, estropeado), no funcionar.* || **4.** •To get out of ORDER. *Descomponerse, estropearse.* ❸ CORRECT BEHAVIOR. •Out of ORDER. Inappropriate, unsuitable, uncalled for. *Fuera de lugar.* His remark was certainly out of ORDER. *Su comentario estuvo fuera de lugar.* ~We were out of ORDER asking her where she was going. *Estuvimos mal en preguntarle dónde iba.* ❹ FITTING/APPROPRIATE/SUITABLE. •In ORDER. Would it be in ORDER for me to attend? *¿Habría algún inconveniente en que yo asistiera?* An apology is in ORDER. *Lo indicado sería disculparse.* ~Celebrations are in ORDER. *Esto hay que celebrarlo.* ~A piece of toast would be in ORDER right now. *Una tostada me vendría muy bien en este momento.*

❺ IN A STATE OF PROPER ARRANGEMENT, PREPARATION, OR READINESS. •In ORDER. || **1.** *Listo, dispuesto.* Everything is in ORDER for the departure. *Todo está dispuesto para la salida.* ~Is everything in ORDER for tomorrow's performance? *¿Está todo dispuesto para la función de mañana?* || **2.** [Legal document, passport]. *En regla.* ~Is your passport in ORDER? *¿Tiene el pasaporte en regla?* ❻ TYPE/KIND. *Tipo, índole.* ~Problems of a different ORDER. *Problemas de distinto tipo.* || **2.** •On the ORDER of. Of the caliber of. *Del calibre de.* ~No es una cantante del calibre de Ella Duncan. ~I would like a dress on the ORDER of the one in the window. *Quiero un vestido parecido al que está en el escaparato.* || **3.** •Of the highest ORDER. *De primera calidad.* ❼ *PHRASES.* || •ORDER in the court! *¡Silencio en la sala!* || •In the ORDER of. Approximately. *Alrededor de, aproximadamente.* || •In short ORDER. *Inmediatamente.* ~The merchandise arrived in SHORT order. *La mercancía llegó en seguida.* || •It's in the ORDER of things that difficulties should arise. *Es normal que surjan dificultades.* || •Postal ORDER. *Giro postal.* || •Sailing ORDERS. *Ultimas instrucciones (dadas al capitán de un barco).* || •That's a tall ORDER. *Es mucho pedir.* ~It's a tall ORDER, but I'll see what I can do. *Es algo difícil, pero veré que puedo hacer.* || •To call the meeting to ORDER. *Abrir la sesión.* || •To get one's marching ORDERS. *Ser despedido.* || •To be the ORDER of the day. *Estar de moda.* || •To be under the ORDER of. *Estar bajo el mando de.* || •To give ORDERS. *Mandar (que se haga algo).* ⇨ ORDEN

ORDINARY. *adj.* [Things]. Usual, habitual, everyday, normal. *Normal, habitual, de todos los días.* Ordinarily I would help you. *Normalmente (en circunstancias normales) le ayudaría.* ~I'll just wear my ORDINARY clothes. *Me pondré la ropa de todos los días.* ~In ORDINARY use. *Empleado normalmente (habitualmente).* ~It's not what you'd call an ORDINARY present. *No es lo que se diría un regalo de todos los días.* ~In the ORDINARY way. *En la forma habitual.* || **2.** [Person]. Average, regular. *Simple, medio.* He was just an ORDINARY tourist. *No era más que un simple turista.* An ORDINARY citizen. *Un simple ciudadano.* ~The ORDINARY Spaniard. *El español medio.* For the ORDINARY reader. *Para el lector medio.* ~The ORDINARY citizen. *El ciudadano de a pie, el hombre de la calle.* || **3.** Mediocre, poor, inferior. *Mediocre.* ~A very ORDINARY team. *Un equipo muy mediocre.* ~The present they gave her was very ORDINARY. *El regalo que le hicieron no fue nada del otro mundo.* || **4.** Unpretentious, simple, modest. *Modesto, sencillo.* ~ORDINARY people. *Gente modesta, gente sencilla.* ~An ORDINARY little house in the suburbs. *Una casita normal y corriente en las afueras.* || **5.** [En forma negativa]. Just any. *Cualquiera.* It cannot be done with an ORDINARY pencil. *No se puede hacer con un lápiz cualquiera.* ~This is no ordinary day. *Hoy no es un día cualquiera.* || **6.** •Out of the ORDINARY. *Fuera de lo común, excepcional, extraordinario.* ~A man above the ORDINARY. *Un hombre fuera de serie, un hombre que no es uno del montón.* ⇨ORDINARIO

ORIGINAL [ORIGINAL]. *adj.* First. *Primeros, originarios.* ~The ORIGINAL inhabitants. *Los primeros habitantes, los habitantes originarios.* ~One of the ORIGINAL members. *Uno de los primeros miembros.*

P

PACKAGE [PAQUETE]. *n*. Bundle. *Bulto*. ‖ **2**. Agreement. *Convenio, acuerdo*. ‖ **3**. Embalaje. *Packing*. ‖ **4**. [Sale]. *Venta global de varios artículos, lote, conjunto*. •PACKAGE deal. *Convenio general, acuerdo global*. ‖ **5**. •PACKAGE holiyday (tour). *Viaje organizado todo incluído, viaje todo comprendido*. ~PACKAGE vacations. *Vacaciones todo pagado*. ‖ **6**. •All in one PACKAGE. *Todo junto*. ~Humor, reflexion and wit all in one PACKAGE. *Humor, reflexión e ingenio todo junto*.

PAIR. *n*. [People, cards, animals, stamps]. *Pareja*. ~The happy PAIR. *La feliz pareja*. ‖ **2**. [Of oxen]. *Yunta*. ‖ **3**. [Of rabbits]. *Casal*. ‖ **4**. [Tennis]. *Dobles*. ‖ **5**. [Of horses]. *Tronco*. ‖ **6**. PHRASES. ‖ •Arranged in PAIRS. *Colocados de dos en dos*. ~The seats were arranged in PAIRS. *Los asientos estaban colocados de dos en dos*. ‖ •I only have one PAIR of hands. *Sólo tengo dos manos*. ‖ •You need to have a sharp PAIR of eyes. *Tienes que tener vista de lince*. ‖ •A PAIR of scissors. *Unas tijeras*. ‖ •A PAIR of pajamas. *Un pijama*. ‖ •A PAIR of trousers. *Un pantalón, unos pantalones*. ‖ •To make a PAIR. *Hacer pareja, hacer juego*. ~These two candlesticks make a PAIR. *Esos dos candeleros hacen juego*. ⇨PAR

PALE [PÁLIDO]. *adj*. [Color]. *Claro*. ~A PALE blue dress. *Un vestido azul claro*. ‖ **2**. [Light]. *Débil, tenue*. ~In the PALE light of early morning. *En la luz tenue de las primeras horas de la mañana*. ‖ **3**. [Beer]. *Rubia*. ‖ **4**. [Person]. *Blanco (naturally pale), pálido (from fright, etc.)*.

PAMPHLET. *n*. Publication of generally 'ess than 80 pages stitched or stapled gether and usually having a paper cover; booklet. *Folleto*. I picked up a PAMPHLET on places to visit in the region. *Saqué un folleto sobre los lugares que se pueden visitar en la zona*. ⇨PANFLETO

PANEL [PANEL]. *n*. Team, group. *Grupo, equipo*. ~A PANEL of experts. *Un grupo de expertos*. ‖ **2**. [Flat surface]. *Tablero, tabla*. ‖ **3**. [Of control, instrument]. *Tablero*. ‖ **4**. [Of celing]. *Artesón*. ‖ **5**. Jury. *Jurado*. ‖ **6**. [Contestant on TV, radio]. *Concursantes*. ‖ **7**. [Of door]. *Entrepaño*. ~A beautiful old door with oak PANELS. *Una hermosa puerta antigua con entrepaños de roble*. ‖ **8**. [Of garment]. *Pieza*. ‖ **9**. [Architecture]. *Lienzo*. ‖ **10**. [Dress]. *Paño*. ‖ **11**. [Plywood]. *Tablero*. ‖ **12**. •PANEL discussion. *Mesa redonda, debate*. ‖ **13**. •PANEL game. *Concurso por equipo*.

PAPER. *n*. Newspaper. *Diario, periódico*. ~I read it in the PAPER. *Lo leí en el diario (periódico)*. •PAPER boy. *Repartidor de periódicos*. ‖ **2**. Documents. *Documentos*. ‖ **3**. [Identity]. *Documentación*. ~Your PAPERS, please. *La documentación, por favor*. ‖ **4**. Examination. *Examen*. ~By tomorrow I'll have your PAPERS corrected. *Tendré sus exámenes listos para mañana*. ‖ **5**. Essay. *Trabajo (escrito)*. ~To write a PAPER (on a subject). *Hacer un trabajo (sobre un tema)*. ~A research PAPER. *Un trabajo de investigación*. ‖ **6**. PHRASES. ‖ •To give someone his walking PAPERS. *Poner alguien de patitas en la calle*. ‖ •To write for a PAPER. *Ser periodista*. ‖ •Weekly PAPER. *Semanario*. ‖ •On PAPER. *En teoría*. ~The scheme looks excellent on PAPER. *En teoría el plan es excelente*. ‖ •PAPER cutter. *Guillotina*. ‖ •PAPER knife. *Abrecartas, abrepapeles*. ‖ •PAPER profits. *Beneficio* *ficticio (no realizado).*|| •To put something down on PAPER. *Poner algo por escrito.* || •It isn't worth the PAPER it's written on. *Es papel mojado, no vale para nada.* || •PAPER cup. *Taza de cartón.* ⇨PAPEL

PARDON. *v.* LAW [Offender]. *Indultar.* ~The prisoner was PARDONED for good conduct. *Han indultado al prisionero por haberse portado bien en la cárcel.* ⇨PERDONAR

PARENT. *n.* *Padre* (father), *madre* (mother), *padres* (father and mother). ~It has to be signed by a PARENT. *Tiene que firmarlo uno de los padres.* His PARENTS live in Ohio. *Sus padres viven en Ohio.* || 2. FIG Source. *Origen, madre, causa.* ~Wealth is the PARENT of idleness. *La riqueza es madre de la ociosidad.* || 3. •The PARENT company. *La casa madre, la casa matriz.* ⇨PARIENTE

PARK [APARCAR]. *v.* To place or leave (a vehicle) in a certain place for a period of time. *Aparcar (Spain), estacionar(se), (Latin America).*

PAROCHIAL [PARROQUIAL]. *adj.* Provincial, narrow-minded (person). *Estrecho, limitado, restringido, de miras estrechas.* || 2. [Outlook, attitude]. *Provinciano, pueblerino.* ~To have a PAROCHIAL outlook. *Tener una mentalidad pueblerina.* || 3. •PAROCHIAL school. *Colegio privado religioso.* || 4. [Of a civil parish]. *Municipal.*

PARSIMONIOUS. *adj.* Stingy. *Tacaño, mezquino.* ~There's no need to be so PARSIMONIOUS with the butter. *No hay necesidad de ser tan mezquino con la mantequilla.* || 2. Frugal. *Frugal, escaso, parco.* ~A PARSIMONIOUS meal. *Una comida frugal.* ⇨PARSIMONIOSO

PART[1]. *n.*

❶ PARTICIPATION, INVOLVEMENT, INFLUENCE. *Participación, influencia, contribución.* He was arrested for his PART in the demonstration. *Fue detenido por su participación en la manifestación.* || 2. •To take PART in. *Intervenir en, participar en, tomar parte en.* || 3. •To have no PART in

something. (I) [Not to be active]. *No participar en algo,* (II) [Have nothing to do with]. *No tener nada que ver con algo, ser ajeno a algo, desentenderse de algo.* ~He had no PART in stealing. *No tuvo que ver con el robo.*~I want no PART in it. *No quiero saber nada de ello.* || 4. •To play a PART (in something). *Contribuir, influir.* The climate has played a PART in ... *El clima ha contribuido a ...* ~That played no PART in my decision. *Eso no influyó mi decisión.* ~Accounting now plays a much more active PART in international business. *La contabilidad está contribuyendo cada vez más al comercio inernacional.*

❷ PLACE, REGION, AREA. *Lugar, region.* ~He's not from these PARTS. *No es de aquí.* ~In these PARTS. *Por estos lugares, por aquí, en estos pagos, en estos contornos.* ~What PART are you from? *¿De dónde es usted?* ~A lovely PART of the world. *Una region preciosa.* ~In tropical PARTS. *En regiones tropicales.* ~A journey to foreign PARTS. *Un viaje al extranjero.*

❸ A PERIOD OF TIME (within a larger period of time). ~In the early PART of the week. *Al principio de la semana.* ~In the latter PART of the year. *En los últimos meses del año.* •The best PART of. Almost. *Casi.* ~It went on for the best PART of an hour. *Continuó casi una hora.* ~We lost the best PART of a month. *Perdimos casi un mes.*

❹ PARTICULAR ASPECT (of a situation or an activity). ~The funny (funniest) PART is that. *Lo más gracioso es que, lo gracioso del asunto (caso) es que.* ~The worse PART of it was that. *Lo peor de todo fue que.* ~You haven't heard the best PART yet. *Todavía no te he dicho lo mejor.* ~The hardest PART will be to find the money. *Lo difícil va a ser juntar el dinero.*

❺ TO A CERTAIN EXTENT, LARGELY, BY AND LARGE. •For the most PART, in (good, great) PART. *Ante todo, más que nada.* ~His success is in good PART ascribable to dogged determination. *Más que nada, debe su éxito a su obstinada determinación.* This is in great PART due to ... *Esto se debe ante todo a, más que nada esto se*

debe a ... ~They are good students, for the most PART. *La mayoría son buenos estudiantes.* ~He was, for the most PART, friendly. *En general era simpático.* ~The shops are for the most PART closed on Sundays. *Las tiendas generalmente cierran los domingos.*
❻ ACTING. *Papel.* ~He played the part of Hamlet. *Representó (hizo) el papel de Hamlet.* ~He's not sincere, he's just acting the PART. *No es sincero, está haciendo el papel.* ‖ 2. •Bit PART. *Papel secundario.* ‖ 3. •To look the PART. *Encajar bien en un papel.* ~He just doesn't look the PART. *No tiene el aspecto adecuado para el papel.*
❼ OTHER MEANINGS. Episode. *Capítulo.* An eight-PART series. *Una serie en ocho episodios.* ‖ 2. Serial. *Fascículo.* ~Buy PART one and get part two free. *Compre el primer fascículo y recibirá el segundo gratis.* ‖ 3. Ability. *Habilidad, talento.* ~A man of many PARTS. *Un hombre de mucho talento.* ‖ 4. Duty, contribution. *Deber, contribución, colaboración.* To do one's PART. *Cumplir con su deber, sus obligaciones.* Everyone must do their PART. *Todos necesitan contribuir.* ‖ 5. Characteristic, feature. *Aspectos.* ~Some PARTS of housekeeping are pleasant. *Algunos aspectos de las faenas domésticas son agradables.* ‖ 6. [In hair]. *Raya.* ‖ 7. PHRASES. •To take somebody's PART. *Tomar partido por alguien, apoyar a alguien.* ‖ •PART owner. *Copropietario.* ‖ •PART of me wants to forgive you. *Por un lado quisiera perdonarte.* ‖ •The best PART of. *Casi.* ‖ •For my PART. *Para mí, en lo que a mí respecta.* ‖ •Spare PARTS. *Piezas de recambio, repuesto.* ⇨PARTE

PART[2]. *v.* Separate. *Separar.* ~Till death us do PART. *Hasta que la muerte nos separe.* ~They were PARTED during the war. *La guerra los separó.* ~They PARTED five years ago. *Se separaron hace cinco años.* ~The best of friends must PART. *Los mejores amigos han de separarse alguna vez.* ‖ 2. To say goodby. *Despedirse.* ~When we ᴿᵀᴱᴰ from Sevilla. *Cuando nos despeᵗᵒˢ de Sevilla.* ‖ 3. [Crowd]. *Apartarse.*

~The branches PARTED. *Se apartaron las ramas.* ~The people PARTED to let her through. *La gente se hizo a un lado para dejarla pasar.* ‖ 4. [Road]. *Bifurcarse.* ‖ 5. Snap, break (rope, cable). *Romperse, partirse.* ~The rope PARTED in the middle. *La cuerda se rompió por la mitad.* ‖ 6. Open up (curtains, lips). *Abrirse.* ‖ 7. PHRASES. •To PART as friends. *Separarse amistosamente.* ~They PARTED as friends. *Quedaron como amigos.* ‖ •To PART company with. (I) To leave. *Despedirse de alguien.* (II) Quarrel with. *Reñir con alguien.* ‖ •To PART one's hair. *Hacerse la raya (en el pelo).* ~She PARTS her hair down the middle. *Se peina con la raya en el medio.* ‖ •To PART with. (I) Get rid of. *Deshacerse, desprenderse de.* ~I'm sorry to have to PART with it. *Siento perderlo.* (II) [Money]. *Pagar, dar, soltar.* ~It's difficult to get them to PART with their money. *Es difícil hacerle soltar dinero.* ⇨PARTIR

PARTIAL. *adj.* •To be PARTIAL to. *Ser aficionado a.* ~David is very PARTIAL to claret. *David es muy aficionado al clarete.* ⇨PARCIAL

PARTICULAR[1]. *adj.* Specific. *Determinado, concreto.* ~There is no PARTICULAR subject. *No hay ningún tema determinado.* ~If a PARTICULAR dose is exceeded. *Si se excede una determinada dosis.* ~At one PARTICULAR time in his life. *En determinado momento de su vida.* ~In your PARTICULAR case. *En tu caso concreto.* ~He didn't tell me any PARTICULAR time. *No me dijo ninguna hora concreta.* ‖ 2. Special. *Especial.* ~For no PARTICULAR reason. *Sin ninguna razón especial.* ~Nothing in PARTICULAR. *Nada en especial.* ~For no reason in PARTICULAR. *Por ningún motivo especial.* ~Are you looking for anything in PARTICULAR? *¿Busca algo en especial?* ~To take PARTICULAR care. *Tomar especial cuidado.* ~It is of PARTICULAR interest. *Es de especial interés.* ‖ 3. Fussy, fastidious. *Exigente, quisquilloso, delicado (food).* ~I'm not PARTICULAR. *Me da igual, me da lo mismo.* ~He's very PARTICULAR about his food. *Es muy delicado con la comida.* He's very PARTICULAR about cleanliness. *Es muy exigente para la limpieza.* He's PARTICULAR about his car. *Cuida mucho el coche.* ~I'm PARTICULAR about my friends. *Escojo mis amigos con mucho cuidado.* || **4.** Individual, distinct, personal. *Individual, personal, propio.* It varies according to the PARTICULAR case. *Varía según el caso individual.* ~My own PARTICULAR sentiments. *Mis propios sentimientos personales.* Each person has his own PARTICULAR point of view. *Cada persona tiene su propio punto de vista.* ⇨ PARTICULAR¹

PARTICULARS². *n.* Details. *Detalles, pormenores.* ~I'm not familiar with the PARTICULARS of this case. *No estoy enterado de los pormenores de este asunto.* || **2.** •To receive full PARTICULARS (about something). *Recibir información detallada (sobre algo).* || **3.** •To take down somebody's PARTICULARS. *Tomar nota de los datos personales de alguien.* || **4.** •Correct in all PARTICULARS. *Correcto en todos los detalles.* || **5.** •For further PARTICULARS apply to. *Para más informes escriban a.* || **6.** •To give PARTICULARS. *Citar los detalles.* ~Please give full PARTICULARS. *Se ruega dar un informe detallado.* || **7.** •To go into PARTICULARS. *Entrar en pormenores.* ⇨ PARTICULAR²

PARTITION [PARTICIÓN]. *n.* Thin wall. *Tabique.* ~A glass PARTITION. *Un tabique de cristal.*

PASS. *v.*
❶ MOVEMENT. To go past (someone). *Cruzarse con.* ~We PASSED him on the street. *Nos cruzamos con él por la calle.* ~We PASSED on the stairs. *Nos cruzamos en la escalera.* || **2.** To go PASS (something). *Pasar delante de.* ~We are now PASSING the Tower of London. *Pasamos ahora delante de la Torre de Londres.* || **3.** To cross (mountain, border). *Cruzar, atravesar.* || **4.** Overtake (car). *Adelantar.* ~He'll try to PASS us on this bend. *Nos va a querer adelantar en esta curva.* ~No PASSING. *Prohibido adelantar.* || **5.** [Procession]. *Desfilar.* || **6.** To go down. *Bajar.* ~The liquid

PASSES through the tube. *El líquido baja por el tubo.* || **7.** •To PASS over (plane). *Sobrevolar.* ~We are now PASSING over Washington. *Estamos sobrevolando Washington.*

❷ APPROVAL. To succeed in (exam, test). *Aprobar, ser aprobado (en).* ~Did you PASS in chemistry? *¿Aprobaste en química?* || **2.** [Motion, plan, law]. *Aprobar.* ~The motion was PASSED unanimously. *La aprobación de la propuesta fue unánime.* || **3.** Be acceptable. *Ser aceptable, admitirse.* What PASSES in New York may not be good enough here. *Lo que se admite en Nueva York puede resultar inaceptable aquí.* || **4.** Meet approval. *Someterse, cumplir.* All our products must PASS a rigorous inspection. *Todos nuestros productos son sometidos a una rigurosa inspección.* ~The design PASSES all the safety requirements. *El diseño cumple con todos los requisitos de seguridad.* || **5.** Qualify. ~He was PASSED fit for military service. *Fue declarado apto para el servicio militar.* [After illness]. *Dar de alta.* || **6.** To censure. *Dar el visto bueno.* ~The censor has PASSED the play. *La censura ha dado el visto bueno a la obra.*

❸ CONVEY, EXPRESS. [Opinion]. *Expresar, dar (su opinión).* ||| **2.** [Remark]. *Hacer una observación (comentario).* || **3.** Exchange (words). *Cambiarse.* ~Words PASSED between them. *Se cambiaron algunas palabras.* || **4.** Pass on. Convey (message). *Transmitir, comunicar.* ~She said she would PASS the information on to the other students. *Dijo que comunicaría la información a los demás estudiantes.* || **5.** Notify. *Avisar.* Could you PASS the word on to the others? *¿Podrías avisar a los demás?*

❹ TRANSMIT (With *on*). Infect with. *Contagiar.* ~She has PASSED her flu on to me. *Me ha contagiado la gripe que tenía.* || **2.** [Cost, increase, price].To be detrimental to *Repercutir, perjudicar.* ~The costs are PASSED on to the customer. *Los costos, los paga el cliente.* Unfortunately any increase in price will have to be PASSED on to the dealers. *Desgraciadamente, todo* aumento de precio afectará desfavorable-mente a los distribuidores. ‖ **3.** [Savings, benefits]. To benefit. *Beneficiar.* ~We PASS on these savings to you! *¡Ud. se beneficia de estos ahorros!*

❺ REPRESENT FALSELY (with *off*). *Hacer pasar.* ~He tried to PASS it off as a genuine Dali. *Trató de hacerlo pasar por un Dalí auténtico.* ‖ **2.** Impersonate, pass oneself as. *Hacerse pasar.* ~He PASSED himself off as a journalist. *Se hizo pasar por perio-dista.* ‖ **3.** Brush aside. *Quitarle impor-tancia a una cosa, dar la impresión de que.* ~He PASSED it off as a bout of indi-gestion. *Le quitó importancia diciendo que no era más que una indigestión.* ~She tried to PASS off the entire episode as a coincidence. *Quiso dar la impresión que todo había sido una simple casualidad.*

❻ VARIOUS. Exceed, surpass. *Sobrepasar, superar.* She PASSED her own expectations in winning the scholarship. *Superó sus expectivas al recibir la beca.* ‖ **2.** To happen. *Ocurrir, acontecer.* ~It came to PASS that ... *Aconteció que ..., sucedió que ...* ‖ **3.** To loose (an opportunity). *Perderse.* ~I had a chance of going to college, but I let it PASS. *Me perdí la oportunidad de asistir a la universidad.* ‖ **4.** Be considered. *Considerarse.* ~What PASSES for good manners. *Lo que se considera buena edu-cación.* ~In her day she PASSED for a great beauty. *En sus tiempos se le consideraba una gran belleza.* ~What PASSES nowdays for a hat. *Lo que se llama sombrero hoy día.* ‖ **5.** [Kidney stone]. *Expulsar.*

❼ WITH PREPOSITIONS. PASS away. *Morir.* ‖ **2.** PASS by. (I) *Pasar de largo.* ~Life has PASSED him by. *Ha disfrutado poco de la vida, no ha vivido.* (II) [Not affect]. *Permanecer al margen.* The eco-nomic recovery is PASSING this region by. *Esta región permanece al margen de la reactivación de la economía.* ~Don't let love PASS you by. *No dejes que el amor te deje de lado.* ‖ **3.** PASS down. *Transmitir.* ~They PASSED their knowledge down from ne generation to the next. *Transmitieron conocimientos de generación en gene-*

ración. ‖ **4.** PASS for. Be mistaken for. *Parecer.* ~She wrote a book about a grand-mother who PASSED for twenty. *Escribió un libro acerca de una abuela que pare-cía tener veinte años.* ‖ **5.** PASS into. Disappears. To PASS into darkness. *Desa-parecer en la oscuridad.* ‖ **6.** PASS out. (I) To faint. *Desmayarse, perder el cono-cimiento.* ~I must have PASSED out. *Debo haberme desmayado.* ~I nearly PASSED out with fright. *Casi me desmayé del susto.* (II) Distribute (leaflets). *Repartir, distribuir.* ~Their teacher PASSED out the dictionaries. *El profesor repartió los diccionarios.* ‖ **7.** PASS over. (I) Overlook. *Omitir, pasar por alto.* ~You PASSED over a very importan fact. *Ha pasado por alto algo muy importante.* (II) Overlook, ignore, disregard. *Pasar por alto, omitir.* ~I shall PASS over his latest misdeeds without comment. *No aludiré a sus últimas diabladuras.* (III) Disregard for promotion. *Pasar por encima.* ~He has been PASSED over three times now. *Lo han pasado por encima tres veces.* ‖ **8.** PASS through. (I) *Estar de paso.* ~I'm just PASSING through. *Sólo estoy de paso.* (II) Cross. We PASSED through Germany in two days. *Cruzamos Alemania en dos días.* ‖ **9.** PASS up. (I) (opportunity). *Dejar pasar, desper-diciar.* (II) [Offer]. *Rechazar.* (III) [Hopes]. *Renunciar.* ‖ **10.** To PASS across. *Cruzar.* ~To PASS across the street. *Cruzar la calle.*

❽ EXPRESSIONS. ‖ •He PASSED into a coma. *Entró (cayó) en coma.* ‖ •Spring PASSED into summer. *La primavera dejó paso al verano.* ‖ •In PASSING. *De paso.* ~Be it said in PASSING. *Sea dicho de paso.* ‖ •Let it PASS. *Conviene dejarlo.* ‖ •Not a drop has PASSED my lips. *No he bebido ni una gota.* ‖ •Not to let something PASS. *No consentir.* ~We can't let that PASS! *¡Eso no lo podemos consentir¡* ‖ •PASS a cloth over something. *Limpiar algo con un paño (trapo).* ‖ •PASS one's hand between two bars. *Introducir la mano entre dos rejas.* ‖ •PASS out of sight. *Perderse de vista.* ~We watched until he PASSED out of sight. *Nos quedamos mirando hasta que se perdió de vista.* ‖ •PASS sentence. *Fallar, dictar sentencia.* ‖

•To let something PASS. Ignore. *Pasar por alto, tolerar.* He made some comments about my work, but I let it PASS. *Hizo algunos comentarios acerca de mi trabajo, pero no le hice caso.* || •To PASS into oblivion. *Ser olvidado.* ⇨PASAR

PASSAGE. *n.* Hallway. *Corredor, galería, pasillo, pasadizo (narrow).* ~A secret PASSAGE. *Un pasadizo secreto.* || **2.** Cost of a journey on a ship or plane). *Viaje.* ~My parents couldn't afford the PASSAGE to America. *Mis padres no podían pagarme el viaje a Los Estados Unidos.* || **3.** [Of time]. *Paso.* ~With the PASSAGE of time he became more mellow. *Con el paso del tiempo se volvió más sosegado.* || **4.** Crossing. *Travesía.* ~The PASSAGE lasted two hours. *La travesía en barco duró dos horas.* || **5.** [Law]. *Aprobación.* ~The PASSAGE of a bill through Parliament. *La aprobación de un proyecto de ley por el Parlamento.* || **6.** Extract (Literature, music). *Trozo, selección.* ~Selected PASSAGES from 'Ceasar'. *Selecciones de 'César'.* || **7.** Transition. *Paso.* The PASSAGE of boyhood to manhood. *El paso de la juventud a la madurez.* •Birds of PASSAGE. *Aves de paso.* ~The PASSAGE of barbarism to civilization. *El paso de la barbarie a la civilización.* || **8.** Way, road. *Camino.* We forced a PASSAGE through the crowd. *Nos abrimos camino a través de la multitud.* || **9.** Movement. *Tránsito.* The bridge isn't strong enough to allow the PASSAGE of heavy vehicles. *El puente no es lo suficiente fuerte para permitir el tránsito de vehículos pesados.* || **10.** Transit, passing. *Paso.* ~The PASSAGE of air through the lungs. *El paso del aire por los pulmones.* ~The PASSAGE of an electric current through the wire. *El paso de la corriente eléctrica por el cable (cordón, hilo).* || **11.** •Free PASSAGE. *Paso franco (libre).* || **12.** •To grant someone a safe PASSAGE. *Darle a alguien un salvaconducto.* ⇨PASAJE

PASSION [PASIÓN]. *n.* Rage. *Rabia, furia, vehemencia.* ~She spoke with PASSION. *Habló con vehemencia (ardor).* || **2.** PHRASES. || •To be in a PASSION. *Estar fuera de sí.* || •To fly into a PASSION. *Encolerizarse, ponerse furioso.* || •In a fit of PASSION. *En un arrebato de ira.* || •To have a PASSION for. *Encantarle a uno (algo).* ~He has a PASSION for strawberries. *Le encantan las fresas.* || •Crime of PASSION. *Crimen pasional.* || •He has a PASSION for opera. *Le apasiona la ópera.* || •PASSIONS were aroused by the controversy. *La polémica exaltó los ánimos.*

PASSIONATE [APASIONADO]. *adj.* Angry. *Colérico, furioso.* || **2.** [Desire, admirer, follower]. *Ardiente, ferviente.* ~She's a PASSIONATE supporter of women's rights. *Es un ardiente partidario de los derechos de la mujer.* || **3.** [Speech]. *Vehemente, ardoroso.* ~She was PASSIONATE in her defense of the party. *Fue vehemente en su defensa del partido.* || **4.** [Hatred]. *Mortal.*

PATERNAL [PATERNAL]. *adj.* [Pride]. *De padre.* ~With PATERNAL pride. *Con orgullo de padre.* || **2.** [Trait, inheritance]. *Paterno.* ~He passed his childhood on the PATERNAL farm. *Vivió toda su juventud en la finca paterna.* || **3.** [Through father's line]. *Paterno.* ~PATERNAL grandmother. *Abuela paterna.*

PATHETIC. *adj.* Hopeless, arousing pity. *Digno de lástima, conmovedor.* ~She was a PATHETIC sight. *Daba lástima (pena) verla así.* || **2.** Terrible. *Malísimo, pésimo.* ~The music was PATHETIC. *La música era malísima.* ~It was a PATHETIC performance. *Fue una exhibición pésima.* ~His jokes are PATHETIC. *Sus chistes son pésimos.* || **3.** Feeble, inadequate. *Pobre.* ~What a PATHETIC excuse! *¡Qué excusa más pobre!* ~In return for our investment we get a PATHETIC three percent interest. *Sobre lo que hemos invertido recibimos un mísero tres por ciento de interés.* ⇨PATÉTICO

PATRON. *n.* Sponsor (of charity, cause). *Patrocinador.* ~|| **2.** [Of arts]. *Mecenas.* || **3.** Customer. *Cliente habitual.* ⇨PATRÓN

PAVEMENT. *n.* [Along street]. *Acera.* ~He was fined for parking on the *pavement. Le pusieron una multa por aparcar en la acera.* ⇨PAVIMENTO

PECULIAR. *adj.* [Person]. Excentric, strange, odd. *Raro, excéntrico, extraño.* ~Her PECULIAR behavior. *Su extraño comportamiento.* ~All great writers have been PECULIAR. *Todos los grandes escritores han sido excéntricos (raros).* || **2.** [Thing]. *Raro, extraño.* ~This meat has a PECULIAR taste. *Esta carne tiene un gusto raro.* ~He has a very PECULIAR way of showing his gratitude. *Tiene una manera muy extraña de demostrar su agradecimiento.* || **3.** Special. *Especial.* ~The region has its own PECULIAR dialect. *La región tiene su dialecto especial.* || **4.** •To feel PECULIAR. *Tener una sensación extraña.* ⇨ PECULIAR

PEEL. *v.* [Paint]. *Desconcharse.* || **2.** [Wallpaper]. *Despegarse.* || **3.** [Bark]. *Descortezar.* ~The bark had been PEELED from the trees. *Habían descortezado los árboles.* || **4.** [Nuts]. *Descascarillar.* || **5.** [Nails]. *Descascarillarse.* || **6.** Remove. *Quitar.* ~As he lifted the dressing, he PEELED away a layer of skin. *Al quitar la venda arrancó (levantó) una capa de piel.* || **7.** •PEEL back. *Quitar, despegar.* ~He PEELED back the plastic film. *Quitó (despegó) la película de plástico.* || **8.** •To PEEL off one's clothes. *Quitarse la ropa, desnudarse.* ⇨ PELAR

PENALIZE [PENALIZAR]. *v.* Punish. *Castigar, imponer sanciones, sancionar.* ~Leningrad and other cities have instituted programs to PENALIZE workers who quit their jobs more than twice a year. *En Leningrado y otras ciudades se han dictado normas para imponer sanciones a los trabajadores que cambian de empleo más de dos veces al año (Cit. Prats).* || **2.** To handicap, put at a serious disadvantage. *Perjudicar.* ~This policy PENALIZES the poor. *Esta política perjudica a los pobres.* ~The tobacco tax PENALIZES the smoker. *Los impuestos sobre el tabaco perjudican al fumador.* || **3.** [Sport]. *Castigar, sancionar, penalizar (Acad.).* ~To be PUNISHED for a foul. *Ser castigado por una falta.* || **4.** [Education]. *Quitar puntos, bajar la nota.* ~Candidates will be PENALIZED for bad spelling. *Se sacarán*

puntos a los solicitantes por mala ortografía.* || **5.** Make punishable. *Penar.* ~PENALIZED by law. *Penado por la ley.* || **6.** To fine. *Multar.* ~To PENALIZE unlicensed drivers. *Multar a los conductores que no tienen matrícula.*

PENALTY. *n.* Punishment. *Pena, castigo.* || **2.** [Sport]. *Castigo.* || **3.** Handicap]. *Desventaja, inconveniente.* ~One of the PENALTIES of fame. *Parte del precio que hay que pagar por ser famoso.* | **4.** Fine. *Multa.* || **5.** [Golf]. *Penalización.* || **6.** [Bridge]. *Multa, castigo.* || **7.** •On PENALTY of death. *So pena de muerte.* || **8.** •To pay the PENALTY for something. *Cargar con (pagar) las consecuencias de algo.* ~The doctor paid the full PENALTY for his negligence. *El médico pagó cara su negligencia.* || **9.** •Death PENALTY. *Pena de muerte.* || **10.** •PENALTY clause. *Cláusula de penalización, cláusula penal, punitiva.* || ⇨ PENALIDAD

PENETRATE. *v.* [Clothing, armor]. *Atravesar, traspasar.* ~The shell PENETRATED the hull. *El proyectil atravesó el casco.* || **2.** [Enemy lines]. *Adentrarse en.* ~To PENETRATE deep behind enemy lines. *Adentrarse considerablemente en territorio enemigo.* || **3.** To enter (an organization). *Infiltrarse en.* ~The organization had been PENETRATED by a spy. *Un espía se había infiltrado en la organización.* || **4.** [Market]. *Introducirse en, entrar en.* ~The company has been successful in PENETRATING overseas markets this year. *Este año la compañía logró introducirse en el mercado exterior.* || **5.** To see through, understand (secret, mystery, meaning). *Entender.* ~She explained it again, but it took a long time to PENETRATE. *Me lo volvió a explicar pero tardé mucho en entenderlo.* || **6.** To permeate. *Transcender, extenderse por.* ~The smell PENETRATED the whole house. *El olor se extendió por toda la casa.* ⇨ PENETRAR

PENETRATING. *adj.* [Mind]. *Perspicaz.* ~He has a very PENETRATING mind and grasps everything immediately. *Es muy*

perspicaz y todo lo entiende en seguida. ‖ **2.** [Cry]. *Agudo.* ~A PENETRATING whistle. *Un silbido agudo.* ⇨ PENETRANTE

PERCEIVE. *v.* Realize. *Darse cuenta de.* ~He PERCEIVED that he was being watched. *Se dio cuenta de que lo observaban.* ‖ **2.** Notice. *Notar.* ~Do you PERCEIVE anything strange? *¿Notas algo raro?* ‖ **3.** To regard. *Ver, considerar.* ~He's PERCEIVED as a latter-day Robin Hood. *Se lo ve (considera) como un Robin Hood moderno.* ‖ **4.** Hear. *Oir.* ~He PERCEIVED a faint sound. *Oyó un leve ruido.* ‖ **5.** Divisar. *To see.* ~I PERCEIVED a boat in the distance. *Divisé un barco a lo lejos.* ‖ **6.** Comprender. *To understand.* ~I cannot PERCEIVE how it can be done. *No comprendo cómo se puede hacer.* ⇨ PERCIBIR

PERCEPTIBLE [PERCEPTIBLE]. *adj.* Audible. *Audible.* ~A barely PERCEPTIBLE sound. *Un sonido que apenas se oye.* ‖ **2.** Noticeable. *Sensible.* ~A perceptible difference. *Una diferencia sensible.* ‖ **3.** Visible. *Visible.* ~Barely PERCEPTIBLE through the fog. *Que apenas se podía ver a través de la niebla.*

PERCEPTION. *n.* Idea, image. *Idea, imagen.* ~People's PERCEPTION of class differences. *La idea que la gente tiene de las diferencias sociales.* ~The PERCEPTION of the president as. *La imagen del presidente como.* ~The PERCEPTION of oneself. *La idea que tiene uno de sí mismo.* ‖ **2.** Impression. *Impresión.* ~The PERCEPTION is that there's been undue pressure from the American Jewish community. *Existe la impresión de que la comunidad judía norteamericana ha ejercido una presión excesiva (Cit. Prats).* ~It's my PERCEPTION that. *Tengo la impresión de que.* ‖ **3.** Insight. *Perspicacia, agudeza.* An artist of rare PERCEPTION. *Un artista de gran perspicacia.* ‖ **4.** Understanding. *Comprensión.* ‖ **5.** Interpretation. *Interpretación.* An endeavor to correct their PERCEPTION of what is beautiful. *Un intento de modificar su interpretación de lo bello.* ⇨ PERCEPCIÓN

PERFECT[PERFECTO]. *adj.* [Behavior,

reputation]. *Intachable.* ‖ **2.** Ideal. *Idóneo, ideal.* ~This is the perfect tool for the job. *Esta es la herramienta ideal para el trabajo.* ‖ **3.** Absolute, utter. *Perdido (fool), consumado, verdadero (gentleman), auténtico (waste of time), absoluto (silence).* ‖ **4.** Complete. ~She has a PERFECT right to be here. *Tiene todo el derecho del mundo a estar aquí.* ~He's a PERFECT stranger to us. *Nos es totalmente desconocido.* ~With PERFECT assurance. *Con la más completa confianza.*

PERIOD [PERÍODO]. *n.* [Time limit]. *Plazo.* ~Within a three month PERIOD. *Dentro de un plazo de tres meses.* ‖ **2.** [Sport]. *Tiempo.* ‖ **3.** [School]. *Hora, clase.* ~The school day is divided into seven PERIODS. *El día escolar está dividido en siete clases.* ‖ **4.** Full stop. *Punto.* I said no, PERIOD. *He dicho que no, y se acabó (punto).* ‖ **5.** [Historical, artistic]. *Época.* ~The Elizabethan PERIOD. *La época isabelina.* ~The author accurately conveys the atmosphere of the PERIOD. *El autor refleja fielmente el ambiente de la época.* ~The romantic PERIOD. *La época romántica.* ~A painting of his early PERIOD. *Un cuadro de su primer época, un cuadro de su juventud.* ‖ **6.** [Grammar]. *Punto.* ‖ **7.** Natural pause in speaking. *Pausa.* ‖ **8.** *adj.* [Dress]. ~In PERIOD dress. *En traje de la época.* ‖ **9.** [Furniture]. *De época, clásico.* ~PERIOD piece. *Mueble clásico.* ‖ **10.** PHRASES. ‖ •The holiday PERIOD. *La temporada de vacaciones.* ‖ •The post-war PERIOD. *La posguerra.* ‖ •Free PERIOD. *Hora libre.* ‖ •This is a bad PERIOD for. *Esta es una mala época para.*

PERIODICAL. *n.* Magazine. *Revista, publicación periódica.* ⇨ PEDIÓDICO

PERMANENT [PERMANENTE]. *adj.* [Address, job]. *Fijo.* ~I'm not PERMANENT here. *Yo no estoy fijo aquí.* ~I need a PERMANENT job. *Necesito un trabajo fijo.* ‖ **2.** [Damage]. *Irreparable.* ~Water may cause PERMANENT damage to the mechanism. *El agua puede causar un daño irreparable al mecanismo.* ‖ **3.** [Relationship]. *Estable.* ‖ **4.** [Dye, ink]. *Indeleble.* ‖ **5.** Lasting, *Dura-*

dero. ‖ **6.** [President]. *Vitalicio*.

PERSIST [PERSISTIR]. *v.* Insistir. *Empeñarse en*. ~He PERSISTS in calling me 'darling'. *Se empeña en llamarme 'cariño'*. ‖ **2.** [Rain]. *Continuar*. ~If the rain PERSISTS. *Si continúa (sigue) lloviendo*. ‖ **3.** To PERSIST in one's opinion. *Aferrarse a su opinión*.

PERSISTENT [PERSISTENTE]. *adj.* [Pain, disease]. *Pertinaz*. A PERSISTENT flu. *Una gripe pertinaz*. ‖ **2.** [Offender, smoker]. *Habitual*. ~The neighborhood police has arrested a PERSISTENT offender. *La policía del barrio ha detenido a un delincuente habitual*. ‖ **3.** Unceasing. *Continuo, constante, repetido*. ~Despite our PERSISTENT warnings. *A pesar de nuestras continuas advertencias*. ‖ **4.** Persevering. *Perseverante, firme*. PERSISTENT in his intention to. *Firme en su intención de*.

PERSONAL [PERSONAL]. *adj.* Private. (secretary, helicopter, boat). *Particular*. ~He took me for a ride in his PRIVATE helicopter. *Me llevo a dar una vuelta en su helicóptero particular*. ‖ **2.** Indiscreet. *Indiscreto*. ~Don't ask PERSONAL questions. *No hagas preguntas indiscretas*. ‖ **3.** [Friend, life, hygiene]. *Íntimo*. ~He's a PERSONAL friend of mine. *Es un amigo íntimo mío*. ~Don't meddle in my PERSONAL life. *No se entremeta en mi vida íntima*. ‖ **4.** [Liberty]. *Individual*. ‖ **5.** In person. *En persona*. ~To make a PERSONAL appearance. *Aparecer en persona*.

PERVERSE. *adj.* Stubborn. *Terco, obstinado*. ‖ **2.** Wayward (youth). *Caprichoso*. ‖ **3.** Contrary. *Adverso, contrario*. ~PERVERSE circumstances. *Circunstancias adversas*. ⇨ PERVERSO

PEST. *n.* Small animal or insect that destroys crops. *Insecto (animal) nocivo (dañino), bicho, parásito*. ‖ **2.** [Botany]. *Planta nociva*. ~This will kill the PEST in your roses. *Esto matará los insectos nocivos de sus rosas*. ‖ **3.** [Person]. *Pelma*. What a PEST that child is! *¡Cómo me fastidia este niño!* ‖ **4.** [Thing]. *Lata, molestia*. ~It's a PEST having to go. *Es una lata tener que ir*. ‖ **5.** Plague. *Plaga*. ~The moth is a PEST of pinewoods. *La mariposa es una plaga de los pinares*. ⇨ PESTE

PETULANT. *adj.* Irritable, peevish, fretful, pettish, touchy. *Malhumorado, irritable, de mal genio, irrascible, susceptible, enojadizo*. ‖ **2.** [Frown]. *De niño caprichoso*. ~He became PETULANT because he could not get his way. *Se enfurruñó porque no se pudo salir con la suya*. ⇨ PETULANTE

PHASE [FASE]. *n.* FIG State. *Etapa, época*. ~A transitional PHASE. *Una época de transición*.

PHYSICAL [FÍSICO]. *adj.* Material. *Material*. ~The PHYSICAL universe. *El mundo material*. FIG ~A PHYSICAL impossibility. *Una imposibilidad material, materialmente imposible*. ‖ **2.** [Sport]. *Duro*. ~It was a very PHYSICAL game. *Jugaron muy duro*. ‖ **3.** [Medical]. •PHYSICAL examination. *Reconocimiento médico*. ‖ **4.** •The PHYSICAL effects of alcohol consumption. *Los efectos del alcohol en el organismo*. ‖ **5.** •Latin people tend to be more PHYSICAL. *Los latinos recurren más al contacto físico*. ‖ **6.** •It's very PHYSICAL work. *Es un trabajo que requiere mucho esfuerzo físico*.

PHYSICIAN. *n.* Doctor. *Médico*. ⇨ FÍSICO

PIECE. *n.* Part of something broken, torn, cut or divided. *Pedazo, trozo*. ~A PIECE of bread. *Un pedazo (trozo) de pan*. ~She ripped the letter into PIECES. *Rompió la carta en pedacitos*. •To fall to PIECES. *Hacerse pedazos*. ‖ **2.** [Of land]. *Terreno (for building), parcela (for farming)*. ‖ **3.** Coin. *Moneda*. ‖ **4.** [Of cake]. *Porción*. ‖ **5.** ▶Note that in the following example, the word 'piece' is not translated. ~A PIECE of advice. *Un consejo*. ~A PIECE of chewing gum. *Un chicle*. ~A PIECE of clothing. *Una prenda (de vestir)*. ~A PIECE of furniture. *Un mueble*. ~An excellent PIECE of work. *Un trabajo excelente*. ‖ **6.** *LOCUCIONES*. ‖ •They got back in one PIECE. *Volvieron sanos y salvos*. ‖ •I dropped it, but it's still in one PIECE. *Se me cayó, pero está intacto*. ‖ •She smashed the vase to PIECES. *Hizo añicos el jarrón*. ‖ •The toy lay in *pieces* on the floor. *El juguete estaba en el suelo, hecho pedazos.* ⇨PIEZA

PILE. *n.* Stack, heap (of books, things). *Montón.* ~There was nothing left of the house but a PILE of rubble. *De la casa no quedaba más que un montón de escombros.* ~PILES of work. *Montones de trabajo.* ~To put things into a PILE. *Amontonar cosas.* || **2.** Estaca. *Stake.* ~To drive PILES in the ground. *Clavar estacas en la tierra.* || **3.** [Of carpet]. *Pelo.* || **4.** •To make one's PILE. *Hacer fortuna, hacer su agosto, forrarse.* ~He made his PILE in oil. *Se hizo una fortuna en el petróleo.* ⇨PILA

PINCH. *v.* Steal. *Robar, birlar.* || **2.** Arrest. *Pescar, agarrar, atrapar.* ~She got PINCHED for a parking offense. *Le pescaron en una infracción de aparcamiento.* || **3.** [Shoes]. *Apretar.* ~These shoes PINCH my feet. *Estos zapatos me aprietan (los pies).* ~To know where the shoe PINCHES. *Saber donde aprieta el zapato.* || **4.** [With finger]. *Pellizcar, dar un pellizcón.* || **5.** Squeeze, crush. *Apretar, estrujar, aplastar.* || **6.** •To PINCH and scrape. *Escatimar gastos.* ~We had to PINCH and scrape. *Tuvimos que hacer muchas economías.* ~We had to PINCH and scrape to send her to college. *Nos privamos de muchas cosas a fin de enviarla a la universidad.* || **7.** •PINCH the pastry to make little folds. *Hacer un repulgo en la masa.* ⇨PINCHAR

PIONEER [PIONERO]. *n.* Forerunner. *Precursor.* || **2.** Explorer. *Explorador.* || **3.** Early settlers. *Colonizador.* ~In PIONEER days. *En tiempo de lo colonizadores.* || **4.** [Of scheme, in study]. *Iniciador, promotor.* ~He was a PIONEER in the study of bats. *Fue uno de los primeros en estudiar a los murciélagos.*

PIPE. *n.* [For water, gas]. *Conducto, tubería, tubo, caño, cañería.* ~A PIPE burst in the kitchen and innundated the floor. *La cañería de la cocina reventó y inundó todo el suelo.* || **2.** Flute. *Flauta.* || **3.** [Of organ]. *Tubo, cañón.* || **4.** [Of hose]. *Manga.* || **5.** [Of wind instrument]. *Caramillo.* || **6.** Whistle. *Pito.* || **7.** PIPE dream. *Sueño*

imposible. || **8.** •The PIPES. La gaita. ⇨PIPA

PLAGUE [PLAGA]. *n.* [Disease]. *Peste.* || **2.** [Insects, social scourge]. *Plaga.* || **3.** Annoyance. *Molestia, fastidio.*

PLAN[1] [PLANEAR]. *v.* |[House]. *Hacer los planos de.* || **2.** Intend. *Pensar, tener la intención de, proponerse.* ~We PLAN to go out tonight. *Pensamos salir esta tarde.* ~We weren't PLANNING to. *No teníamos tal intención, no se nos había ocurrido.* ~How long do you PLAN to stay? *¿Cuánto tiempo piensas quedarte?* || **3.** To prepare. *Preparar.* ~They're PLANNING a surprise for her birthday. *Le están preparando una sorpresa para el cumpleaños.* ~The trip was PLANNED by him. *Este viaje lo preparó él.* || **4.** Organize. *Organizar.* ~A number of social activities have been PLANNED to entertain the participants at the meeting. *Se han organizado diversos actos sociales para agasajar a los congresistas* (Prats). || **5.** •To PLAN on. (I) *Pensar, tener pensado.* ~I PLANNED on going out. *Había pensado salir.* (II) Expect, count on. *Contar con.* ~I hadn't PLANNED on having to look after her. *No contaba con tener que cuidarla.* ~We are PLANNING for about 50 guests. *Contamos que vendrán unos 50 invitados.*

PLAN[2] [PLAN]. *n.* [Map, diagram]. *Plano.* ~Work out a PLAN before you begin. *Hazte un esquema antes de empezar.* ~To make a PLAN of. *Trazar el plano de.* || **2.** Personal project. *Proyecto.* ~The PLAN is to come back later. *Pensamos volver más tarde, tenemos la idea de volver más tarde.* || **3.** [Book, essay]. *Esquema.* || **4.** PHRASES. || •We bough it on an installment PLAN. *Lo compramos a plazos.* || •Everything went according to PLAN. *Todo salió como estaba previsto.* || •What's our PLAN of action? *¿Qué nos proponemos hacer?* || •The Divine PLAN. *El diseño divino.* ⇨PLAN

PLANT. *v.* [Seeds, vegetables, suspicion]. *Sembrar.* ~To PLANT a field with turnips. *Sembrar un campo de nabos.* ~The field is PLANTED with wheat. *El campo está sembrado de trigo.* ~He PLANTED the seed of suspicion in her mind. *Sembró la*

PLATE **166**

sospecha en ella. || **2.** [Bomb]. *Poner, colocar.* || **3.** [Idea]. *Introducir, inculcar.* ~To PLANT an idea in somebody's mind. *Introducir una idea en la mente de alguien.* ~To PLANT a love of learning in young people. *Inculcar el afán de conocimiento en los jóvenes.* || **4.** [People, building]. *Establecer, instalar.* ~Engaged in PLANTING a colony of Germans in the valley. *Ocupados en establecer una colonia alemana en el valle.* ~They PLANTED the first church in that part of the colony. *Establecieron la primera iglesia en esta parte de la colonia.* || **5.** [Spy, informer]. *Infiltrar, colocar, introducir.* || **6.** [Blow]. *Asestar.* ~He PLANTED him a blow on the nose. *Le asestó un puñetazo en la nariz.* || **7.** •To PLANT something on somebody. *Comprometer a uno escondiendo un objeto robado en su ropa o habitación.* ~They PLANTED marked notes in the drawer. *Colocaron a escondidas billetes marcados en el cajón.* ⇨PLANTA

PLATE. *n.* [For church offerings]. *Platillo, bandeja.* || **2.** Sheet (of metal). *Placa, chapa.* || **3.** Tableware. *Vajilla.* || **4.** Illustration. *Grabado, lámina.* || **5.** [Of glass]. *Placa.* || **6.** [Fotografía]. *Placa.* || **7.** [Art, print]. *Plancha.* || **8.** Homeplate (in baseball). *Base del bateador.* || **9.** Grill. *Plancha.* ~Gambas a la PLANCHA. *Grilled shrimps.* || **10.** Coating. *Revestimiento, enchapado.* || **11.** Food and service for one person, as at a banquet, fund-raising dinner, or the like. *Cubierto.* ~The wedding breakfast cost $20 a PLATE. *El banquete nupcial cuesta $20 por cubierto.* || **12.** [Printing]. *Clisé, estereotipo, plancha.* || **13.** [Armor]. *Blindaje.* || **14.** Prize (in horse racing). *Premio, copa de oro o plata.* || **15.** Sign (generally made of metal). *Placa.* ~The PLATE on the door said 'Dr. Rothman'. *La placa en la puerta decía 'Dr. Rothman'.* || **16.** [Earth's surface]. *Placa.* || **17.** License or number plate (of a car). *Placa, matrícula, patente.* ~The car had German (number, license) PLATES. *El coche tenía matrícula alemana.* || **18.** PHRASES. || •To have a lot on one's PLATE. *Tener tela de*

que cortar. || •Dental PLATE. *Dentadura postiza.* || •To hand something to someone on a PLATE. *Servir algo a uno en bandeja de plata.* ~The American company was handed the contract on a PLATE. *A la compañía norteamericana se le entregó el contrato en bandeja de plata.* || •Hot PLATE. *Placa eléctrica.* || •Gold/silver PLATE. *Chapa de oro/plata.* ⇨PLATO

PLATFORM. *n.* [Of railway station]. *Andén, vía.* ~People waiting on the PLATFORM. *Gente esperando en el andén.* ~The 5:15 is on PLATFORM 8. *El tren de las 5:15 está en la vía número ocho.* ~The train standing at PLATFORM 3. *El tren que está en la vía número 3.* || **2.** [Opportunity to air views]. *Tribuna.* ~Last year they shared the PLATFORM. *El año pasado ocuparon la misma tribuna.* || **3.** [Stage]. *Estrado.* || **4.** [Politics]. *Programa.* ~Political PLATFORM. *Programa electoral.* || **5.** [Roughly built]. *Tarima, tablado (for dancing).* || **6.** Freight platform (railways). *Muelle.* || **7.** [For orator]. *Estrado, tribuna.* || **8.** [Band]. *Estrado.* || **9.** [Of builders]. *Andamio.* || **10.** Place for public discussion, forum. *Foro.* ⇨PLATAFORMA

PLAUSIBLE. *adj.* Reasonable (argument, excuse, explanation, answer). *Admisible, verosímil, creíble.* His explanation sounds fairly PLAUSIBLE to me. *Su explicación me parece bastante verosímil.* ~It's perfectly PLAUSIBLE that. *Es perfectamente posible que.* || **2.** [Liar, salesman, politician]. *Convincente pero poco de fiar.* ⇨PLAUSIBLE

POINT. *n.*
❶ SIGNIFICANCE, RELEVANCY, APPROPRIATENESS. *Significado, importancia, lo esencial.* ~We found it difficult to see the POINT of the argument. *No acertamos a entender el argumento.* ~The POINT of the story. *El significado del relato.* ~The POINT is they are doing as well as they can. *Lo esencial es que están haciendo cuanto es posible.* || **2.** •To come to the POINT. *Ir al grano, llegar al meollo de la cuestión.* The judge became impatient with the witness and asked him to come to the POINT.

El juez se impacientó con el testigo y le dijo que se ciñara a lo esencial. || **3.** •To get (wander) off the POINT. *Salirse, apartarse del tema.* || **4** •It's beside (not) the POINT. *Eso no viene al caso, no se trata de eso.* ~There's no POINT in going. *No merece la pena ir.* || **5.** •To miss the POINT. *No seguir la corriente, no entender.* ~He seems to have entirely missed the POINT. *Parece no haber entendio nada de que se trataba.* || **6.** •To speak to the POINT. *Hablar acertadamente, hablar con tino.* || **7.** •To get back to the POINT. *Volver al tema.* ~Now, to get back to the POINT. *Bueno, para volver (volviendo) al tema.* || **8.** •The main POINT. *Lo esencial.* I see your POINT. *Entiendo lo que quieres decir.* || **9.** To keep (stick) to the POINT. *No salirse del tema, no irse por las ramas, ceñirse al tema.* ~Ask them not to digress and keep to the POINT. *Díganles que no se vayan por las ramas.* || **10.** •That just the POINT! *¡Justamente!, ¡precisamente!* || **11.** •The (whole) POINT is that ... *Lo importante es ..., lo único que importa es, el hecho es que.* || **12.** •That's just the POINT! *¡Eso es!, ¡si eso es lo más importante!* || **13.** •That's not the POINT. *No es eso.* || **14.** •The POINT of the joke is that ... *La gracia del chiste es que ...* || **15.** •To the POINT. *Directo.* ~He was brief and to the POINT. *Fue breve y conciso.* ~I don't need a car, and more to the POINT ... *No necesito coche, y lo que es más ...* || **16.** •To give POINT to an objection. *Dar valor (importancia) a una objeción.*

❷ ARGUMENT. *Argumento, caso, razón.* ~I think he has a POINT. *Creo que tiene razón.* ~It was a POINT which never occurred to me. *Era algo que nunca se me había ocurrido.* ~I see your POINT about being boring. *Ya veo que querías decir con lo que era aburrido.* I'd like to make one more POINT. *Quisiera hacer otra observación.* ~On that POINT we agree. *Sobre eso estamos de acuerdo.* ~He has unquestionably won his POINT. *No cabe duda de que tiene razón.* || **2.** •To prove a POINT. *Demostrar que uno tiene razon.* ~That proves my POINT that we need more staff.

Eso me da la razón de que necesitamos más personal. ~She's doing it simply to prove a POINT. *No lo hace más que para demostrar que tiene razón.*|| **3.** •To make a POINT. *Expresar, decir, manifestar, observar, señalar, plantear, etc.* ~What POINT are you trying to make? *¿Qué estás tratando de decir?* ~It was a very interesting POINT you made. *Lo que señalaste (dijiste, planteaste) es muy interesante.* ~All right, you made your POINT. *Bueno, ya has dicho lo que querías decir.* || **4.** •To make it a POINT (to do something). To make an effort to, emphasize, stress. *Poner empeño en hacer algo, no dejar de, insistir en, encargarse de, preocuparse por, proponerse (hacer algo).* || **5.** •To press the POINT that. *Insistir en que, hacer hincapie en que.* || **6.** •To make the POINT that ... *Observar que ...* || **7.** To make one's POINT (See || **2.** To prove a point). || **8.** •It's a case in POINT. *Es un ejemplo de ello.* || **9.** •In POINT of fact. *De hecho, en realidad.* || **10.** •I think she has a POINT. *Creo que tiene un poco de razón.* || **11.** •It gave POINT to the argument. *Hizo ver la importancia del argumento.* || **12.** •You made your POINT. *Nos has convencido.* || **13.** •He made the following POINT. *Dijo lo siguiente.* || **14.** •To make the POINT that ... *Hacer ver (comprender) que.* || **15.** •To make a POINT of. *No dejar de, insistir en.* ~She always made it a POINT of talking to everyone. *Siempre se preocupaba por (se proponía) conversar con todo el mundo.* ~I'll make it a POINT of watching them closely. *Me encargaré de vigilarlos de cerca.* || **16.** •To press the POINT. *Insistir en.* || **17.** POINT taken! *¡De acuerdo!, ¡Tienes razón!*

❸ PURPOSE, USEFULNESS. *Finalidad, objeto, utilidad.* ~The whole POINT of my trip was to see you. *El único propósito del viaje era verte a tí.* ~There is some POINT to it. *Tiene su sentido (razón de ser).* ~He wondered if there was any POINT in seeing her. *Se preguntó si valía la pena (convenía) verla.* || **2.** •To not see the POINT of (doing something). *No ver el sentido (la necesidad) de.* ~He did not see the

POINT of continuing the discussion. *No vio la necesidad de seguir con el debate.* ~I don't see the POINT. *¿Para qué?, ¿qué sentido tiene?, ¿De qué sirve?, de nada sirve.* ~I don't see the POINT of doing it. *No entiendo porque sea necesario hacerlo, no veo el motivo por hacerlo.* ~I can't see much POINT in a resumption of talks. *No veo de qué va a servir que se reanuden las conversaciones.* ~There's no POINT in feeling sorry for yourself. *No sirve nada compadecerse.* || **3.** •What's the POINT? *¿Para qué?, no sirve, no veo el sentido de.* ~What's the POINT of trying? *¿De qué sirve esforzarse?* What's the POINT of railways? *¿Qué utilidad tienen (a qué sirven) los ferrocarriles?* What's the POINT of arguing? *¿De qué sirve discutir?*

❹ TIME. Momento. *Juncture, precise moment.* •At that POINT, at one POINT. *Entonces, en este (aquel) momento.* ~At that POINT, a soldier opened fire on the car. *En aquel momento un soldado disparó sobre el coche.* ~I was completely lost at one POINT. *En ese momento estaba completamente perdido.* ~At this POINT in the game. *En este momento del juego.* ~At what POINT did you begin to suspect? *¿En qué momento empezó Ud. a sospechar?* ~At no POINT did they mention money. *En ningún momento hablaron de dinero.* ~From this POINT on. *A partir de este momento.* || **2.** •From that POINT onward. *Desde entonces.* || **3.** •At the POINT of death. *Al borde de la muerte.* || **4.** •We've reached the POINT of no return. *Ahora ya no nos podemos echar atrás, ahora tenemos que seguir adelante.* || **5.** To be on the POINT of. *Estar por.* ~He was on the POINT of telling him to stay when ... *Estaba por decirle que se quedara cuando ...*

❺ PLACE. Lugar, sitio. ~At the POINT where the road forks. *Donde se bifurca el camino.* ~The bomb struck the target at a POINT just left of the center. *La bomba estalló inmediatamente a la izquierda del centro.* ~They stopped at a number of POINTS along the road. *Se detuvieron en varios lugares en el camino.*

❻ DEGREE. Grado. •To the POINT of. *Que raya en, hasta.* ~He's outspoken to the POINT of being rude. *Es franco para no decir grosero.* ~To be severe to the POINT of cruelty. *Su severidad raya en la crueldad.* ~She is reserved to the POINT of coldness. *Es tan reservada, que llega a ser fría.* ~His writing is untidy to the POINT of being illegible. *Tiene tan mala letra que lo que escribe resulta ilegible.* ~We worked to the POINT of exhaustion. *Trabajamos hasta quedar agotados.* || **2.** [Preceded by an adjective]. To reach, be at. *Alcanzar, estar, estar a punto de.* ~The trains were at a bursting POINT. *Los trenes iban repletos.* ~His nerves were at a breaking POINT. *Estaba a punto de estallar.* The children have reached a saturation POINT. *Los niños están saturados.* || **3.** [Thermometer]. Grado. ~To rise two POINTS. *Subir dos grados.* || **4.** [Share]. Entero. ~The shares dropped three POINTS. *Las acciones bajaron de tres enteros.* || **5.** •Up to a POINT. *Hasta cierto punto, en cierto modo.*

❼ CHARACTERISTIC, FEATURE, QUALITY. Rasgo, característica, cualidad. ~To have one's good POINTS. *Tener sus cualidades.* ~Generosity is not one of his main POINTS. *La generosidad no es una de sus mejores cualidades.* || **2.** •Good (strong) POINT(s). (I) Cualidad. He's boring, but I guess he has his good POINTS. *Es aburrido, pero me imagino que algunas cualidades debe de tener.* ~Her kindness is one of her strong POINTS. *Se destaca por su amabilidad.* (II) Ability. Habilidad, fuerte. ~Math is not a strong POINT of mine. *Nunca he sido muy fuerte en matemáticas.* || **3.** •Bad POINT. Defecto. ~She doesn't see his bad POINTS. *No ve sus defectos.* || **4.** •The good and bad POINTS of. *Los pros y contras de, las cualidades y defectos de.* ~The good and bad POINTS of the system. *Los pros y contras del sistema.* ~He said he was aware of the good and bad POINTS of the teacher. *Dijo que estaba al tanto de las cualidades y defectos del profesor.*

❽ SHARP END. Punta. •With a sharp

POINT. *Puntiagudo.* || **2.** •POINT of entry (bullet). *Orificio de entrada.* || **3.** [Geography]. *Punta, promontorio, cabo.* || **4.** •At the POINT of a gun. *A mano armada.* || **5.** •To sharpen THE point of a pen. *Sacar punta a un lápiz.* || **6.** •The POINT of the arrow. *La punta de la flecha.* || **7.** •To taper to a POINT. *Terminarse en punta.*
❾ VARIOUS. [Score]. *Tanto.* •To score POINTS. *Marcar puntos.* || **2.** Pointer, hint, suggestion, piece of advice. *Sugerencia, consejo.* The golf pro at the club gave me some good POINTS for improving my game. *El golfista profesional en el club me dio varios consejos para jugar mejor.* || **3.** Item, particular, issue, subject. *Detalle, cosa, asunto, materia.* ~These are the POINTS to look for. *Estos son los detalles en que hay que fijarse.* ~He said there were two POINTS in the proposal that were important. *Dijo que había dos cosas (asuntos) en la propuesta que eran importantes.* || **4.** Matter, question, case. *Cuestión, caso.* ~A POINT of honor. *Una cuestión de honor.* ~A POINT of law. *Una cuestión de derecho.* •A POINT of conscience. *Un caso de conciencia.* ~It's a POINT of controversy. *Es motivo de polémica.* || **5.** Thought, idea, notion, consideration, something. *Posibilidad, idea, algo.* It's a POINT to keep in mind if you buy another boat. *Es algo que no hay que olvidar cuando compres otro barco.* || **6.** [Of a joke]. *El chiste.* ~I fail to see the POINT of the joke. *No veo la gracia (el chiste) de la broma.* || **7.** [Type]. *Cuerpo.* 9 POINT black. *Negritas del cuerpo 9.* || **8.** •To make POINTS with someone. *Hacer méritos con alguien.* ⇨ PUNTO

POLICY. *n.* Course of action. *Norma (de actuación), línea de conducta.* ~The firm has consistently followed the POLICY of only selling prime quality goods. *Esta casa ha tenido siempre por norma vender únicamente artículos de primera calidad (Prats).* Our POLICY is to do this. *Tenemos por norma hacer esto.* || **2.** Government. *Política.* ~They adopted a POLICY of neutrality. *Adoptaron una política de neutralidad.* ~This government has no

POLICY on wages. *Este gobierno no tiene una política salarial.* •Foreign POLICY. *Política exterior.* || **3.** [Business]. Standard practice. *Norma.* ~Our POLICY is to satisfy our customers. *Tenemos por norma satisfacer a nuestros clientes.* ~This firm has consistently followed a POLICY of only selling prime quality goods. *Esta casa ha tenido siempre por norma vender únicamente artículos de primera calidad (Prats).* || **4.** [Insurance]. *Poliza (de seguros).* ~To take out an insurance POLICY. *Hacerse un seguro, sacar una poliza.* ~He took out a new POLICY. *Sacó un nuevo seguro.* || **5.** [Of party, at election]. *Programa.* || **6.** Wisdom. *Prudencia.* || **7.** Philosophy. *Principio.* It's always my POLICY to ask people's opinion. *Tengo por principio pedir a la gente su opinión.* || **8.** Plan. *Táctica.* ~Her POLICY is to ignore him. *Su táctica es de no hacerle caso.* ~It's a good/ bad policy. *Es buena/mala táctica.* ~To change one's POLICY. *Cambiar de táctica.*|| **9.** *PHRASES.* || •It's good/bad POLICY. *Es/no es recomendable.* || •It would be contrary to public POLICY to ... *No sería conforme con el interés nacional ...* || •As a matter of POLICY. As a rule. *Tener por norma.* I always ask her first as a matter of POLICY. *Tengo por norma preguntarle primero a ella.* || •Good-neighbor POLICY. *Política de buena vecindad.* ⇨ POLÍTICA

POLISH. *v.* [Furniture, floor]. *Encerar, sacar brillo, lustrar (L.Am.).* || **2.** [Nails]. *Pintar con esmalte.* || **3.** [Shoes]. *Limpiar.* || **4.** [Mechanically, industrially]. *Pulimentar.* || **5.** •To POLISH up. (I) [One's French]. *Repasar, refrescar, perfeccionar,* (II) [Person], *Civilizar,* (III) [Manners]. *Refinar.* || **6.** •To POLISH one's nails. *Pintarse las uñas.* ⇨ PULIR

POLUTION. *n.* The introduction of harmful substances or products into the environment. *Contaminación.* || **2.** •ENVIRONMENTAL pollution. *Contaminación ambiental (del medio ambiente).* ⇨ POLUCIÓN

PONDER. *v.* Meditate. *Reflexionar, pensar,*

meditar, cavilar. ~PONDERING her fate. *Cavilando sobre su destino.* He was left to PONDER whether he had made the right decision. *Quedó preguntándose si su decisión habría sido acertada.* ~While I PONDERED over the whole business an idea struck me. *Mientras reflexionaba sobre el asunto, de repente se me ocurrió una idea.* || **2.** To weigh carefully, consider. *Considerar, examinar, sopesar.* ~We were PONDERING over the various alternatives. *Estábamos sopesando las diferentes posibilidades.* ⇨ PONDERAR

POPULAR. *adj.* Well-liked. *Estimado.* ~He's POPULAR with his colleagues. *Sus colegas le estiman mucho.* ~You won't be POPULAR with your neighbors if you don't do it. *No ganarás la simpatía de los vecinos si no lo haces.* ~He's very POPULAR with the girls. *Tiene éxito con las muchachas.* ~I'm not very POPULAR in the office right now. *Por ahora no me quieren mucho en la oficina.* || **2.** Fashionable. *De moda.* ~Until recently, opera was not very POPULAR in England. *Hasta hace poco no era muy de moda la ópera en Inglaterra.* || **3.** Common. *Común, corriente.* ~A POPULAR color. *Un color muy visto.* ~A very popular song. *Una canción muy conocida.* || **4.** Frequently used. *Muy concurrido, frecuentado* (resort, restaurant). ~The most POPULAR reason cited by respondents. *La respuesta más frecuente entre los encuestados.* || **5.** [Price]. *Económico.* ~At POPULAR prices. *A precios económicos.* || **6.** Widespread (belief, notion, misunderstanding). *Generalizado.* || **7.** •By POPULAR request. *A petición del público.* || **8.** •POPULAR opinion. *Opinión general.* ~There is POPULAR belief that. *Existe una idea muy generalizada de que.* ⇨ POPULAR

PORTENT. *n.* Augury, warning. *Augurio, presagio.* ~A PORTENT of doom. *Un presagio de la catástrofe.* ⇨ PORTENTO

PORTENTOUS. *adj.* [Remark, tone]. *Solemne.* || **2.** Significant (dream). *Profético.* ⇨ PORTENTOSO

PORTER. *n.* Baggage carrier (at station, airport). *Maletero, mozo.* || **2.** [Sleeping-car attendant]. *Mozo, camarero.* || **3.** [On expedition]. *Porteador.* || **4.** [Hospital]. *Camillero.* || **5.** [In college]. *Bedel.* || **6.** Beer. *Tipo de cerveza negra.* || **7.** Doorkeeper (in government buildings). *Conserje.* ⇨ PORTERO

POSITION [POSICIÓN]. *n.*

❶ PLACE. *Lugar, sitio.* ~From this POSITION you can see the whole field. *Desde este sitio se puede ver todo el campo.* ~They took up their POSITIONS in the parade. *Tomaron sus puestos en el desfile.* || **2.** •To place in POSITION. *Colocar.* || **3.** •To be in/out of POSITION. *Estar en su sitio/fuera de lugar.* || **4.** •From this POSITION. *Desde aquí.* || **5.** •To hold something in POSITION. *Sujetar algo.*

❷ SITUATION, STATE. *Situación.* ~The country's economic POSITION. *La situación económica del país.* ~Our POSITION is improving. *Estamos mejorando de situación.* ~I'm in the fortunate SITUATION of having a private income. *Tengo la suerte de disponer de rentas.* || **2.** •If I were in your POSITION. *Si estuviera en su lugar.* || **3.** •To be in an awkward POSITION. *Estar en una situación delicada.* || **4.** •To be in no POSITION to. *No estar en condiciones para.* ~You're in no SITUATION to criticize. *No eres la persona más indicada para criticar.* ~I'm not in a POSITION to help them right now. *En este momento no estoy en condiciones de ayudarlos.* || **5.** •Put yourself in my POSITION. *Ponte en mi lugar.*

❸ OPINION. *Opinión, actitud, postura, punto de vista.* What is our POSITION on Greece? *¿Cuál es nuestra actitud hacia Grecia?* ~You know my POSITION on this matter. *Ya sabes lo que opino sobre este asunto.* || **2.** •To take up a POSITION on a matter. *Adoptar una postura en un asunto.* || **3.** •To state one's POSITION. *Manifestar su opinión.*

❹ OF BODY. *Postura.* ~In a comfortable POSITION. *En una postura cómoda.*

❺ JOB. *Puesto, empleo, cargo.* ~A POSITION of responsibility. *Un puesto de responsabilidad.* ~To apply for the POSITION of

cook. *Solicitar el puesto de cocinero.*
❻ IN A LEAGUE. *Puesto, lugar.* •In first/
last POSITION. *En primer/último lugar.* ‖ **2.**
•To loose one's POSITION at the top of the
league. *Perder su puesto en la cabeza de
la liga.* ‖ **3.** •What POSITION does he play.
¿De qué juega?
❼ VARIOUS. Rank. *Rango.* ‖ **2.** High
standing. *Categoría social.* ~A woman of
her POSITION. *Una mujer de su categoria
social.*

POSITIVE [POSITIVO]. *adj.* [Criticism].
Constructivo. ‖ **2.** [Sign], *Favorable.* ‖ **3.**
[Proof]. *Incontrovertible.* ‖ **4.** [Refusal].
Categórico, tajante. ‖ **5.** Sure, certain.
Seguro. ~To be POSITIVE about something.
Estar seguro de algo. ~You don't seem to
be very POSITIVE. *No pareces muy seguro.* ‖
6. Absolute, sheer, utter. *Auténtico, verdadero.* ~It was a POSITIVE disaster. *Fue un
auténtico desastre.* It's a POSITIVE disgrace.
Es una verdadera desgracia. ‖ **7.** [Proof].
Definitivo, concluyente. ~There's no POSI-
TIVE evidence. *No hay pruebas conclu-
yentes (definitivas).* ‖ **8.** Decisive. *Categórico.* ~She's very POSITIVE in her likes
and dislikes. *Es muy categórica en sus
preferencias.* ~What we need is POSITIVE
leadership. *Lo que necesitamos es un
liderazgo firme.* ‖ **9.** Confident, convinced.
Seguro, convencido. He is POSITIVE that he
will win the contest. *Está convencido de
que va a ganar el concurso.* ‖ **10.** Optimistic. *Optimista.* ~She's taking a more
POSITVE attitude. *Está adquiriendo una
actitud más optimista* ‖ **11.** Self-assured.
Seguro de sí mismo. ~He has a very POSI-
TIVE attitude. *Está muy seguro de sí mismo.*
‖ **12.** Favorable. *Favorable.* ~There was a
POSITIVE reaction to the speech. *El discurso
tuvo buena acogida.* ‖ **13.** Likely to
succeed or improve. *Esperanzador, alentador.* ~All the signs are POSITIVE, he will
get well soon. *Los indicios son muy alen-
tadores, pronto se va a recuperar.* ‖ **14.**
Good, useful. *Ventajoso, provechoso.* ~At
least something POSITIVE has come out of
the situation. *Por lo menos algo ventajoso resultó de la situación.* ‖ **15.** Morally

good. *Bueno (moralmente).* ‖ **16.** Forceful.
Enérgico. ~That was a very POSITIVE
decision. *Fue una decisión muy enérgica.*
‖ **17.** Explicit. *Claro, concreto.* ~But I gave
you POSITIVE instructions. *Pero yo le di
instrucciones bien claras.* ‖ **18.** Active.
Activo. People should have a more POSITIVE
voice in government. *El pueblo debería
tener participación más activa en el
gobierno.*

POSITIVELY [POSITIVAMENTE]. *adv.* Definitely. *Decididamente, resueltamente,
francamente, realmente, verdaderamente.*
~The food was POSITIVELY revolting. *La
comida daba auténtico asco.* ~He was
POSITIVELY rude. *Estuvo francamente
grosero.* ~It's POSITIVELY marvelous! *¡Es
verdaderamente maravilloso!* ~He's
POSITIVELY stupid. *Es realmente (totalmente) estúpido.* ‖ **2.** Absolutely. *Terminantemente, categoricamente.* ~POSITIVELY
no parking. *Terminantemente prohibido
estacionar.* ~This is POSITIVELY your last
chance. *Decididamente, ésta es tu última
oportunidad.* ~I POSITIVELY refuse to go to
the wedding. *Me niego categoricamente
a ir a la boda.* ‖ **3.** Energetically. *Energicamente.* •To speak POSITIVELY. *Hablar con
convicción.* ‖ **4.** Definitely. *De forma
concluyente.* The body has not yet been
POSITIVELY identified. *No se ha hecho una
identificación definitiva del cadáver.* ‖ **5.**
For sure. *Con certeza.* I can't speak POSI-
TIVELY. *No puedo asegurar nada.* ‖ **6.**
Emphatically. He said quite POSITIVELY that
he was coming. *Aseguró que iba a venir.* ‖
7. In a good way. ~I don't respond POSI-
TIVELY to being bossed around. *No me
gusta que me manden.* ‖ **8.** INTERJ. Used to
express strong affirmation. Do you plan to
go to the party? POSITIVELY! *¿Vas a la
fiesta? Con toda seguridad.*

POSTULATE. v. Assume. *Suponer, dar
por sentado.* ⇨ POSTULAR

POWER. *n.*
❶ ENGINEERING, PHYSICS. Force,
strength. *Potencia.* ~The engine lacks
POWER. *Al motor le falta potencia.* ‖ **2.**

Energy. *Energía.* ~NUCLEAR power. *Energía nuclear.* ‖ **3.** [Electricity]. *Corriente.* ~To cut off the POWER. *Cortar la corriente.* ‖ **4.** [Drill, saw]. *Mecánico, eléctrico.* ~POWER drill. *Taladro mecánico.* ‖ **5.** Performance, output. *Rendimiento.* ‖ **6.** [Math]. *Potencia.* ~Two to the POWER of four. *Dos elevado a la potencia de cuatro.* ‖ **7.** [Of lens, loudspeaker]. *Potencia.* ‖ **8.** *PHRASES.* ‖ •POWER lines. *Cables de alta tensión.* ‖ •POWER steering. *Dirección asistida.* ‖ •POWER failure. *Corte del suministro eléctrico.*
❷ ABILITY, CAPACITY. ~I did everything in my POWER. *Hice todo lo que estaba en mis manos, hice todo lo que me era posible.* ~It doesn't lie within my POWER. *No está en mis manos.* ~She has the POWER to see into the future. *Es capaz de predecir el futuro.* ‖ **2.** Faculty. *Facultad, capacidad.* ~Test your MENTAL powers. *Pon a prueba tu inteligencia (tus facultades mentales).* ~Her creative/imaginative POWERS. *Su capacidad creativa/imaginativa.* ~He was at the height of his POWER. *Estaba en la plenitud de sus facultades mentales.* ~The POWER of speech. *La facultad del habla.*
❸ VARIOUS. Nation. *Potencia.* ~The great POWERS. *Las grandes potencias.* ‖ **2.** Influence. *Influencia.* ~To have POWER over somebody. *Tener influencia sobre alguien.* ~The immense POWER of television. *La enorme influencia de la televisión.* ‖ **3.** Right. *Derecho.* ~The POWER of veto. *El derecho de veto.* ‖ **4.** Dominance, supremacy. *Dominio, poderío.* ~Sea POWER made us great. *El dominio del mar, nuestro poderío marítimo nos hizo grande.* ‖ **5.** •The ship returned to port under her own POWERS. *El buque volvió al puerto impulsado por sus propios motores.* ‖ **6.** •The POWER of darkness. *Las fuerzas del mal.*
⇨ PODER

POWERFUL [PODEROSO]. *adj.* Strong (person). *Fuerte, fornido.* ‖ **2.** [Remedy]. *Eficaz.* ‖ **3.** [Engine, machine]. *Potente.* ‖ **4.** [Emotion]. *Fuerte.* ‖ **5.** [Speech, film]. *Conmovedor, emocionante.* ~It's a POWERFUL film. *Es una película muy emocio-*

nante. ‖ **6.** [Argument]. *Convincente.* ‖ **7.** [Performance]. *Magistral.* ~It was a POWERFUL performance. *Su actuación fue magistral.* ‖ **8.** [Arms, shoulders]. *Fuerte.* ‖ **9.** [Engine, loudspeaker, weapon]. *Potente.* ‖ **10.** [Drug, detergent]. *Potente, fuerte.* ‖ **11.** [Smell, current]. *Fuerte.*

PRACTICAL [PRÁCTICO]. *adj.* Sensible, reasonable. *Sensato, razonable.* ~Be PRACTICAL. We can't afford both the car and the vacation. *Sé realista. No nos alcanza el dinero para comprar coche e ir de vacaciones.* ‖ **2.** Feasible, possible. *Factible, viable, posible.* ~The only PRACTICAL solution is to sell the company. *La única solución viable es de vender la companía.* ~A PRACTICAL alternative would be. *Otra posibilidad sería.* ‖ **3.** Virtual. *Casi.* ~The first night was a PRACTICAL disaster. *El estreno fue casi un fracaso.* ‖ **4.** Suitable. *Apropiado.* ~Jeans would be the most PRACTICAL thing to wear. *Lo más apropiado sería llevar (pantalones) vaqueros.* ‖ **5.** Real. *Verdadero.* ~Much of the information was of no PRACTICAL use. *En verdad, gran parte de la información no servía para nada.* ‖ **6.** Handy. *Habilidoso.* He's very PRACTICAL with cars. *Es muy habilidoso con los coches, tiene mano con los coches.* ‖ **7.** *PHRASES.* ‖ •PRACTICAL joker. *Bromista.* ‖ •PRACTICAL joke. *Broma pesada.* ‖ •PRACTICAL nurse. *Enfermera auxiliar (sin título).* ‖ •For all PRACTICAL purposes. *En la práctica.*

PRACTICE[1] [PRÁCTICA]. *n.*
❶ CUSTOM, HABIT. *Costumbre.* ~It is their PRACTICE to ask for references. *Acostumbran pedir informes.* ~It's the usual PRACTICE. *Es la costumbre.* ~It's not our PRACTICE to. *No acostumbramos.* ~This is common PRACTICE in Spain. *Esto es lo que se suele (acostumbra) hacer en España.* ‖ **2.** •To make a PRACTICE of doing something. *Tener la costumbre de hacer algo.* ~He made a PRACTICE of dining early. *Tenía la costumbre de cenar temprano.*
❷ SPORT, PHYSICAL EXERCISE. Training. *Entrenamiento, adiestramiento.*

~It takes years of PRACTICE. *Requiere años de entrenamiento.* || **2.** Exercise. *Ejercicios.* || **3.** •PRACTICE match. *Partido de entrenamiento.* || **4.** •To be out of PRACTICE. [Physically] *No estar en forma, estar desentrenado.* [Mentally]. *Tener olvidado.* ~I once played a good game of chess, but I'm out of PRACTICE now. *Solía jugar muy bien al ajedrez, pero se me ha olvidado.* || **5.** •To keep in PRACTICE. *Mantenerse en forma.*
❸ DOCTOR/LAWYER. Exercise (of profession). *Ejercicio.* ~The practice of MEDICINE. *El ejercicio de la medicina.* || **2.** Place. [Of doctor]. *Consultorio, consulta.* || **3.** [Of lawyer]. *Bufete, gabinete, estudio jurídico.* || **4.** Patients (doctor). *Pacientes, clientela.* ~A dentist with a large PRACTICE. *Un odontólogo con una numerosa clientela.* || **5.** Clients (lawyer). *Clientela.* || **6.** PHRASES. || •Private PRACTICE. *Consulta privada.* || •To be in PRACTICE. *Ejercer la medicina (doctor), ejercer la abogacía (lawyer).* ~He was in PRACTICE in Bilbao. *Ejercía en Bilbao.* ~He's no longer in PRACTICE. *Ya no ejerce.* || •She's no longer in PRACTICE. *Ya no ejerce.* || •To set up PRACTICE as a doctor. *Establecerse como médico.* || •General PRACTICE. *Medicina general.*
❹ MUSICAL INSTRUMENTS. *Ensayo.* ~Musicians must keep in PRACTICE. *Los músicos tienen que ensayar continuamente.* || **2.** •Choir PRACTICE. *Ensayo coral.* || **3.** •Piano PRACTICE. *Ejercicios en el piano.* || **4.** •PRACTICE session (music). *Ensayo.*
❺ VARIOUS. Experience. *Experiencia.* ~It needs a lot of PRACTICE. *Hace falta bastante experiencia.* || **2.** Rule. *Norma.* ~He made a PRACTICE of always consulting his subordinates. *Tenía como norma consultar a sus subordinados.* ~Restrictive PRACTICES. *Normas restrictivas.* || **3.** Technique, procedure. *Técnica, modo, método, manera de proceder.* ~This is standard PRACTICE with our company. *Nuestra compañia siempre ha actuado de esta forma.* ~The authorities agreed to review his residence permit, against normal PRACTICE. *Las autoridades*

consentieron en revisar su permiso de residencia, lo cual era en contra del procedimiento normal.* || **4.** Scheme, plot. *Mañas.* ~Sharp PRACTICES. *Mañas.* || **5.** Professional business. *Empresa (compuesta de profesionales).* ~A lucrative PRACTICE. *Una empresa próspera.* || **6.** •Put something in PRACTICE. *Llevar a cabo, realizar.* He never had a chance of putting his projects into PRACTICE. *Nunca tuvo la oportunidad de realizar (llevar a cabo) sus proyectos.* || **7.** •PRACTICE makes perfect. *El uso hace el maestro.* || **8.** •In PRACTICE. *De moda, en boga.*

PRACTICE². *v.* [Method]. *Seguir.* ~We PRACTICE this method. *Nosotros empleamos (seguimos) este método.* || **2.** [Principle]. *Poner en práctica.* ~We PRACTICE what we preach. *Ponemos en práctica lo que enseñamos.* || **3.** [Song, act]. *Ensayar.* || **4.** [Piano]. *Estudiar.* || **5.** [Profession]. *Ejercer.* ~To PRACTICE medicine/law. *Ejercer la medicina/abogacía.* || **6.** [Sport]. *Entrenar.* || **7.** To have. *Tener.* ~To PRACTICE patience, good manners. *Tener paciencia, buenos modales.* ⇨ PRACTICAR

PRECINCT. *n.* Enclosure, grounds. *Recinto.* ~The cathedral PRECINCTS. *El recinto de la catedral.* || **2.** Voting district. *Distrito electoral.* || **3.** Police station. *Comisaría.* || **4.** Boundary. *Límite, frontera.* || **5.** Neighborhood. *Barrio.* || **6.** *pl.* [Of a city, town]. *Contornos, alrededores.* || **7.** •Within the PRECINCTS of. *Dentro de los límites de.* •Pedestrian PRECINCT. *Zona reservada para peatones.* || **8.** •Shopping PRECINCT. *Zona comercial (reservada para peatones).* ⇨ PRECINTO

PRECIOUS. *adj.* Priceless. *Inapreciable.* A PRECIOUS friendship. *Una amistad inapreciable.* || **2.** Exhibiting preciosity. *Preciosista.* A PRECIOUS writer. *Un escritor preciosista.* || **3.** [Style]. *Rebuscado.* ~A PRECIOUS turn of phrase. *Una locución rebuscada.* || **4.** [Manners]. *Afectado.* || **5.** [Beloved]. *Querido.* He'll be furious if you damage his PRECIOUS car. *Se pondrá furioso si estropeas su querido coche.* || **6.** [Moment]. *Grato, preciado.* Capture those

PRECIOUS moments with your camera. *Capte esos momentos tran preciados con su cámara fotográfica.* || **7.** To be PRECIOUS (something to someone). *Querer, tenerle cariño a una cosa (memories, bracelet).* ~That bracelet was very PRECIOUS to her. *Le tenía mucho cariño a esta pulsera, quería mucho esta pulsera.* ⇨PRECIOSO

PREDICAMENT. *n.* Unpleasantly difficult situation. *Apuro, aprieto.* ~With no money, no job and nowhere to live, he found himself in a real PREDICAMENT. *Al no tener ni dinero, ni trabajo, ni dónde vivir, se encontraba en un verdadero aprieto.* || **2.** •To be in a PREDICAMENT. (I) Difficult situation. *Estar en un apuro.* (II). Dilemma. *Estar en un dilema.* || **3.** •What PREDICAMENT to be in!. *¡Qué lío!* ⇨PREDICAMENTO

PREDICTION [PREDICCIÓN]. *n.* Forecast. *Pronóstico.* || **2.** Prophesy. *Profesía.* || **3.** •To make a PREDICTION. *Predecir, pronosticar.* ~We can't make a PREDICTION about when the next earthquake will happen. *No se puede pronosticar cuando ocurrirá otro terremoto.*

PREFERENTIAL [PREFERENCIAL]. *adj.* Showing preference. *Preferente.* ~To give PREFERENTIAL treatment to somebody. *Dar trato preferente a alguien.* || **2.** [Creditor, debt]. *Privilegiado.* || **3.** Favored (country, trade relations). *Privilegiado.*

PREMISES [PREMISA]. *n.* Building, site. *Edificio, local.* ~They've moved to new PREMISES. *Se han mudado a un nuevo local (nuevas oficinas).* || **2.** *PHRASES.* || •Business PREMISES. *Local comercial.* || •Licensed PREMISES. *Local autorizado para la venta de bebidas alcohólicas.* || •On/off the PREMISES. *En el/fuera del local.* || •Meals are cooked on the PREMISES. *Las comidas se preparan en el establecimiento.* || •Animals may not be kept on these PREMISES. *Prohibido tener animales en este edificio.* || •They were escorted off the PREMISES. *Se les hizo salir del local.*

PREMONITION [PREMONICIÓN]. *n.* Foreboding, portent, omen, sign. *Presentimiento.* ~A PREMONITION of death. *Un*

presentimiento de la muerte. || **2.** •To have a PREMONITION that. *Presentir que.* ~When Anne didn't arrive, John had a PREMONITION that she was in danger. *Cuando no llegó Ana, Juan presintió que algo le había pasado.*

PREOCCUPIED [PREOCUPADO]. *adj.* •To be PREOCCUPIED. *Estar absorto en.* He was too PREOCCUPIED to notice. *Estaba demasiado absorto para darse cuenta.* ~I was so PREOCCUPIED with my own thought that. *Estaba tan absorto en mis pensamientos que.*

PREPARATION. *n.* Arrangements. *Preparativos.* ~Have you made all the PREPARATIONS for the trip? *¿Ha hecho todos los preparativos para el viaje?* || **2.** [Chemistry]. *Preparado.* || **3.** Homework. *Deberes.* || **4.** •Titles in PREPARATION. *Próximos títulos.* || **5.** •In PREPARATION for. *Para.* I baked all afternoon in PREPARATION for the party. *Me pasé toda la tarde haciendo pasteles para la fiesta.* ⇨PREPARACIÓN

PREPARED. *adj.* Ready. *Listo.* ~We were not PREPARED for this. *Esto no lo esperábamos, no contamos con esto.* || **2.** Willing. *Dispuesto.* ~He was not PREPARED to listen to us. *No estaba dispuesto a escucharnos.* ~You have to be PREPARED to take risks in this kind of work. *Tiene que estar dispuesto a tomar riesgos en este tipo de trabajo.* ~How much are you PREPARED to pay. *¿Cuánto esta dispuesto a pagar?* || **3.** To expect. *Prever.* ~We were PREPARED for it. *Lo habíamos previsto.* ~I wasn't PREPARED for all these questions. *No había previsto tantas preguntas.* || **4.** •Be PREPARED (scout motto). *Siempre listos.* ⇨PREPARADO

PRESCRIBE [PRESCRIBIR]. *v.* [Medicine]. *Recetar.* ~The doctor PRESCRIBED antibiotics for her ear infection. *El médico le recetó antibióticos para la infección en el oído.* •The PRESCRIBED dose. *La dosis recomendada.* || **2.** [Figurative]. Recommend. ~He PRESCRIBED complete rest. *Recomendó el reposo completo.* ~What do you PRESCRIBE? *¿Qué recomienda?* || **3.** Required. *Obligatorio.* ~PRESCRIBED reading.

Libros de lectura obligatoria. ‖ **4.** [Law]. To lay down a rule. *Establecer (fijar) una norma.* •In the PRESCRIBED way. *De conformidad con la ley, en el modo que ordena la ley.* ‖ **5.** •In the PRESCRIBED time. *Dentro del plazo que fija la ley.*

PRESCRIPTION. *n.* Prescribed medicine. *Receta (médica).* It's available only on PRESCRIPTION. *Se vende sólo con receta médica, en venta solemente bajo receta.* ~To fill a PRESCRIPTION. *Preparar una receta.* ‖ **2.** Instructions, rule. *Norma, regla, precepto.* ~There are no PRESCRIPTION about what the members can do. *No hay reglas en cuanto a la conducta de los socios.* ~Do you think that it's possible to give any PRESCRIPTIONS about how to achieve success? *¿Usted cree que se puede establecer normas para alcanzar el éxito?* ⇨ PRESCRIPCIÓN

PRESENT. *v.* [As a gift]. *Regalar, obsequiar.* ~She was PRESENTED with a silver tray. *Le regalaron una bandeja de plata.* ‖ **2.** [Problema]. *Plantear.* ~That PRESENTS some problems. *Eso plantea algunos problemas.* ~The boy PRESENTS a problem. *El chico nos plantea un problema.* ‖ **3.** Provide (opportunity, sight, view, perspective). *Ofrecer.* ~It PRESENTS a magnificent sight. *Ofrece un espectáculo maravilloso.* ~To PRESENT a dismal aspect. *Ofrecer un aspecto lúgubre.* ‖ **4.** [Play]. *Representar.* ‖ **5.** Expound (case, plan). *Exponer.* ‖ **6.** Give, hand over. *Entregar.* ~The daughter will PRESENT the bouquet to her. *La hija le entregará el (le hará entrega del) ramo de flores.* ‖ **7.** To confront. ~I was PRESENTED with a bill for $50.00. *Me pasaron una cuenta por $50.00.* ~We were PRESENTED with a very difficult situation. *Nos vimos frente a una situación muy difícil.* ‖ **8.** To constitute. *Constituir.* ~They PRESENTED an easy target. *Eran un blanco fácil.* ~It PRESENTS an obstacle for future development. *Puede significar (constituir) un obstáculo para el desarrollo futuro.* ⇨ PRESENTAR

PRESENTATION. *n.* Exposition. *Exposición.* ~A more detailed PRESENTATION of these concepts can be found on page 9. *En la página 9 figura una exposición más detallada de estas ideas (Prats).* ‖ **2.** Lecture, talk. *Disertación, conferencia, charla.* ~I have been asked to give a brief PRESENTATION on the aims of the project. *Me pidieron que diera una breve charla sobre el propósito del proyecto.* ‖ **3.** Exhibition, performance. *Exhibición, representación.* ~There are two PRESENTATIONS of the show every day. *Hay dos representaciones diarias del espectáculo.* ‖ **4.** Bestowal (of a gift, medal, prize). *Acto de entrega (premio, regalo).* ‖ **5.** [Case]. *Exposición.* ‖ **6.** Gift, prize. *Regalo, premio.* ‖ **7.** [Ceremony]. *Entrega (ceremoniosa de de un regalo).* ~The PRESENTATION of the prize will be at the annual dinner. *La entrega de los premios se realizará en la próxima cena anual.* ~Everyone is invited to the PRESENTATION. *Todos están invitados a la ceremonia de entrega de premios.* ‖ **8.** [School, university]. *Exposición oral de un ejercicio escrito.* ‖ **9.** Demonstration (business). *Demostración.* ‖ **10.** [Show, production]. *Producción.* ‖ **11.** •PRESENTATION copy. *Ejemplar de cortesía, un ejemplar con la dedicatoria del autor (of a book).* ⇨ PRESENTACIÓN

PRESERVE. *v.* Maintain, keep. *Mantener, conservar.* ~To PRESERVE one's dignity/sense of humor. *Mantener la dignidad/el sentido de humor.* ‖ **2.** [Culinary]. *Conservar, guardar, poner en conserva.* ‖ **3.** Save, protect. *Proteger, guardar.* ~May God PRESERVE you. *Que Dios te guarde.* ⇨ PRESERVAR

PRESIDENT. *n.* [Bank]. *Director.* ‖ **2.** [University]. *Rector.* ⇨ PRESIDENTE

PRESS [PRESIONAR]. *v.*
❶ SQUEEZE, DEPRESS, PUSH (button, level, trigger, switch, doorbell). To push. *Apretar.* ~Position the tile and PRESS firmly. *Coloque el azulejo y apriete con fuerza.* ‖ **2.** [Keys on typewriter]. *Pulsar.* ‖ **3.** To squeeze (hand, trigger). *Apretar.* She PRESSED his arm to get his attention. *Le*

apreto el brazo para que le prestara atención. ~To press the trigger. *Apretar el gatillo.* || **4.** [Hand] (painfully). *Apretujar.* || **4.** [Pedal, footbrake]. *Pisar.*

❷ SQUEEZE, CRUSH, COMPRESS (fruit, grapes). *Estrujar.* || **2.** [Fruit]. *Exprimir, estrujar.* ~To press the juice out of an orange. *Exprimir el zumo de una naranja.* || **5.** [Grapes]. *Pisar, prensar.*

❸ TO MAKE FLAT. [Flowers]. *Prensar.* || **7.** To iron (suit, dress). *Planchar.* ~This suit presses easily. *Este traje es fácil de planchar.* || **2.** [Metal]. *Prensar.*

❹ TO PRESS AGAINST. •He pressed his lips to hers. *Le besó en la boca.* || **2.** •He pressed his face to the window. *Pegó la cara al cristal.* || **3.** •To press somebody to one's heart. *Abrazar a uno estrechamente.* || **4.** •To press books into a case. *Meter libros apretadamente en una maleta.* || **5.** •She pressed the child to her. *Estrechó el niño contra su pecho.*

❺ TO PUT PRESSURE ON SOMEONE. *Apremiar.* ~They're pressing me to get the job finished. *Me están apremiando para que termine el trabajo.* ~Estamos apremiados de tiempo. *We are pressed for time.* || **2.** [Enemy, creditors]. *Hostigar, acosar.* ~He was being pressed by his creditors. *Le acosaban los acreedores.* | **3.** [In game]. *Apretar.* || **4.** [In pursuit]. *Seguir de cerca, pisar los talones.* || **5.** To insist, urge. *Insistir, exigir, instar.* ~I pressed him for an answer. *Insistí en (exigí) que me diera una respuesta* ~He pressed us to stay for dinner. *Insistió en que nos quedáramos a cenar.* ~I didn't press the point. *No insistí más.* ~To press for an answer. *Exigir una respuesta.* || **6.** To be urgent. *Apremiar.* ~To be pressed for money. *Andar muy escaso de dinero.* ~To be pressed for time. *Not tener mucho tiempo, tener mucha prisa.* || **7.** JUR [Charges]. *Presentar, formular.* || **8.** To impose. *Imponer.* ~To press one's opinions on others. *Imponer sus opiniones a otros.*

❻ VARIOUS. |To hurry. *Apresurarse.* ~The crowd pressed towards the stage. *El público se apresuró hacia el escenario.* ||

2. [Crowd]. *Apiñarse.* ~The people pressed around him. *La gente se apiñó en torno a él.* || **3.** [Disk, album]. *Imprimir, prensar.* || **4.** Emphasize. *Hacer hincapié, recalcar.* ~To press a point. *Recalcar un punto.*

PRESUME. *v.* Assume, take for granted. *Suponer.* ~I presume you know why I'm asking. *Supongo (me imagino) que sabe porque lo pregunto.* ~I presume so. *Supongo que sí.* ~A defendant is presumed innocent until proven guilty. *Un acusado es inocente hasta que se demuestre lo contrario.* || **2.** Venture, dare. *Aventurarse, atreverse, permitirse.* ~If I may presume to advise you. *Si me permite ofrecerle un consejo.* ~I would never presume to question your authority. *No me atrevería nunca a poner en duda su autoridad.* || **3.** Impose upon. *Abusar.* I've already presumed enough on you generosity. *Ya he abusado bastante de su generosidad.* || **4.** •Missing, presumed dead. *Desaparecido, dado por muerto.* || **5.** •Doctor Livingston, I presume. *Usted debe de ser el doctor Livingston, ¿o me equivoco?* ⇨ PRESUMIR

PRETEND. *v.* To feign. *Fingir, aparentar, hacer pasar por, hacer como si ...* ~He pretended to be alone. *Fingió estar solo.* ~She pretended to be asleep. *Fingió estar dormida.* ~He pretends he doesn't care. *Hace como si no le importara.* ~They pretended to be students. *Se hicieron pasar por estudiantes.* ~She's not as stupid as she pretends (to be). *No es tan tonta como quiere aparentar.* || **2.** Make believe. *Simular, suponer, hacer cuenta de que.* ~Let's pretend we're on a desert island. *Vamos a suponer que estamos en una isla desierta.* The boy is pretending to be an elephant. *El niño simula ser un elefante.* || **3.** •Stop pretending! *¡Déjate de mentiras¡* ⇨ PRETENDER

PRETENSE. *n.* Excuse. *Pretexto, excusa.* ~Under the pretense of friendship. *So pretexto de amistad.* ~Under the pretense of wanting to help. *Con el pretexto de querer ayudar.* || **2.** Deception. *Fingimiento, simulacro.* ~It's all a pretense. *Es*

todo fingido. •To make a PRETENSE of doing something. *Fingir hacer algo.* ‖ **3.** [Law]. •Under false PRETENSES. *De manera fraudulenta.* ‖ **4.** [Display]. *Ostentación, afectación.* ~Her air of confidence is a PRETENSE. *Este aire de seguridad suyo no es más que una fachada.* •Without (devoid of all) PRETENSE. *Sin ostentación, sin afección.* ⇨ PRETENCIÓN

PREVAIL [PREVALECER]. *v.* Continue to exist, be current. *Regir, predominar, reinar, imperar.* ~The customs which prevailed. *Las costumbres que regían.* ~The conditions that now PREVAIL. *Las condiciones que ahora imperan.* ‖ **2.** Persuade, convince. *Persuadir, convencer.* ~To prevail upon (on) someone to do something. *Convencer (persuadir) a alguien que haga algo.* ‖ **3.** Gain mastery. *Imponerse.* ~To prevail against (over) one's enemies. *Triunfar sobre los enemigos.* ~Finally good sense prevailed. *Por fin se impuso el buen sentido.* ~Eventually peace prevailed. *Por fin se restableció la paz.* ‖ **4.** [Sunshine, winds]. *Predominar.* ~A region where strong winds prevail. *Una región donde predominan vientos fuertes.*

PREVENT. *v. Hinder. Impedir.* ~The rain PREVENTED us from going for a walk. *La lluvia nos impidió ir a dar un paseo.* ~What PREVENTED you from coming yesterday? *¿Qué te impidió venir ayer?* ‖ **2.** Avoid. *Evitar.* ~To PREVENT something from happening. *Evitar que pase algo.* ⇨ PREVENIR

PREVIOUS. *adj.* Earlier (occasion, attempt, page). *Anterior.* ~Because of a PREVIOUS engagement. *Por tener compromiso anterior.* ~In previous years. *En años anteriores.* ~The PREVIOUS afternoon. *La tarde anterior.* ‖ **2.** Hasty. *Prematuro.* ~This seems somewhat PREVIOUS. *Esto parece algo prematuro.* ‖ **3.** PHRASES. ‖ •On a PREVIOUS occasion. *En otra ocasión.* ‖ •PREVIOUS conviction. *Antecedente penal.* ‖ •To be PREVIOUS. *Precipitarse.* ‖ •PREVIOUS to. *Anterior a.* ~The period just PREVIOUS to the coup. *El periodo inmediatamente*

anterior al golpe. ‖ •PREVIOUS to this. *Anteriormente.* ⇨ PREVIO

PRIMITIVE. *adj.* [Method, tool]. *Rudimentario, básico.* ~PRIMITIVE weapons. *Armas rudimentarias.* ‖ **2.** Old-fashioned. *Anticuado.* ~PRIMITIVE ideas. *Ideas anticuadas.* ‖ **3.** [Urge, instincts]. *Primario.* ~PRIMITIVE passions. *Pasiones primarias.* ‖ **4.** Uncivilized. *Inculto.* ‖ **5.** Sordid. *Sucio.* ⇨ PRIMITIVO

PRINCIPAL [PRINCIPAL]. *n.* [Of school]. *Director.* ‖ **2.** [Of university]. *Rector.* ‖ **3.** [Theatre]. *Protagonista.* ‖ **4.** [Violinist]. *Primer violín, concertino.* ‖ **5.** [Tenor]. *Primer tenor.* ‖ **6.** [Of a crime]. *Author.*

PRIORITY [PRIORIDAD]. *n.* Importance, important thing, most important thing. *(Grado de) importancia, urgencia.* ~My top PRIORITY at the moment is to find a place to live. *El asunto de mayor importancia para mi en este momento es encontrar casa.* ~The problems were dealt with in order of PRIORITY. *Los problemas se trataran en orden de importancia.* ~They have given PRIORITY to reducing inflation. *El problema de mayor urgencia para ellos es la reducción de la inflación.* ~Women's issues are often seen as low PRIORITY. *Con mucha frecuencia las cuestiones femenistas se consideran de menor importancia (urgencia).* ~My first (number one) PRIORITY is. *Para mí lo primero (lo más importante) es.* ~First let's decide what our PRIORITIES are. *Primero tenemos que decidir que es lo más importante.* ‖ **2.** Preference. *Preferencia.* Banks normally give PRIORITY to large businesses when deciding on loans. *Los bancos suelen dar preferencia a las grandes empresas a la hora de otorgar préstamos.* ~If medical supplies are short, children will be given PRIORITY. *De llegar a escasear los medicamentos se dará preferencia a los niños.* ‖ **3.** [In time]. *Anterioridad.*

PRIVACY [PRIVACIDAD]. *n.* Free from public scrutiny. *Intimidad, vida privada.* ~In the PRIVACY of one's home. *En la intimidad del hogar.* ~One's right to PRIVACY. *Su*

derecho a la intimidad. ~There is no PRIVACY in these apartments. *En estos pisos no hay vida privada.* || **2.** Secrecy. *Secreto, reserva.* ~The affair is shrouded in the utmost PRIVACY. *El asunto está envuelto en el mayor secreto (Prats).* || **3.** Isolation, solitude. *Soledad, recogimiento, aislamiento.* ~In the PRIVACY of my study I have the most brilliant ideas. *En la soledad de mi cuarto se me ocurren las ideas más brillantes (Prats).* ~Desire for PRIVACY. *Deseo de soledad, deseo de estar a solas.*

PRIVATE [PRIVADO]. *adj.* Personal. *Personal.* The President sent a PRIVATE message of sympathy. *El Presidente mandó una nota personal de condolencia.* ~The Bishop acted in a PRIVATE capacity. *El obispo actuó a título personal.* || **2.** Reserved, withdrawn. *Reservado.* He's a very PRIVATE person. *Es una persona reservada.* || **3.** Alone. *Solo, a solas.* ~They want to be PRIVATE. *Quieren estar a solas.* || **4.** Secret. *Secreto.* Please keep what I will tell you PRIVATE. *Le ruego no divulgar a nadie lo que le voy a decir.* || **5.** Secluded. *Apartado, retirado, aislado.* ~This place is quiet and PRIVATE. *Este lugar es apacible y apartado (retirado).* A PRIVATE place of meditation. *Un lugar apartado donde meditar.* || **6.** [Classes, secretary, car, house, room, teacher]. *Particular.* || **7.** [School]. *De pago.* || **8.** [Bank account]. *Personal.* || **9.** [Motives, opinion, income, use]. *Personal.* ~It's my PRIVATE opinion that ... *Por mi parte pienso que ..., personalmente opino que ...,* ~For his PRIVATE use. *Para su uso personal.* || **10.** [Letter, conversation]. *Confidencial.* || **11.** [Celebration, wedding]. *Intimidad.* It will be a PRIVATE celebration. *Se celebrará en la intimidad.* || **12.** [Hearing, meeting]. *Secreto, a puertas cerradas.* ~The committee sat in PRIVATE. *La comisión se reunión a puertas cerradas.* || **13.** PHRASES. || •In PRIVATE. (I) *Confidencialmente.* ~I have been told in PRIVATE that ... *Me han dicho confidencialmente que ...* (II) *En la intimidad.* ~What you do in PRIVATE is your own affair. *Lo que hagas en la intimidad es cosa tuya.* || •Private PARTS.

Partes pudendas. || •A gentleman of PRIVATE means. *Un señor que vive de sus rentas.* || •In PRIVATE life. *En la intimidad.* || •It's a PRIVATE joke. *Es un chiste que los dos entendemos.* ▸*Privado* most often refers to entities or activities which are official or public (company, sector, property, education, bank), while *particular* denotes an object considered as your very own such as personal belongings (car, room, boat) or to some activities which are normally carried on as group (lesson, teacher, secretary).

PROBATION [-CIÓN]. *n.* Trial period (in employment). *Período de prueba.* ~To be on two months' PROBATION. *Trabajar dos meses de prueba.* ~She's on PROBATION. *Está cumpliendo su período de prueba.* || **2.** [Law]. *Libertad condicional.* ~To be on PROBATION. *Estar en libertad condicional.* || **3.** •PROBATION officer. *Encargado oficial de vigilar a los que están en libertad condicional.* || **4.** •Release on PROBATION. *Libertad a prueba.*

PROBLEM [PROBLEMA]. *n.* Difficulty. *Dificultad.* ~This should represent no PROBLEM for an experienced musician. *Esto no debería ofrecer ninguna dificultad a un músico con experiencia.* || **2.** PHRASES. || •What's your PROBLEM? *¿Qué te ocurre?, ¿qué te preocupa?, dime qué te ocurre, ¿qué pasa?.* || •That's your PROBLEM. *Eso es asunto tuyo, allá tú.* || •They have lots of PROBLEMS. *Pasan muchos apuros, tiene muchas preocupaciones.* || •PROBLEM child. *Niño difícil.* || •Problem drinker. *Alcohólico.* || •The PROBLEMS of history. *Los interrogantes de la historia.* || •He has a drinking PROBLEM. *Tiene tendencia al alcoholismo, bebe demasiado.* || •The housing PROBLEM. *La crisis de la vivienda.* || •It's not my PROBLEM. *No tiene que ver conmigo.* || •I'm having a PROBLEM deciding. *No acabo de decidirme, me está costando decidirme.* || •Your PROBLEM is that you just don't want to work. *Lo que pasa es que no quieres trabajar.*

PROCEDURE [PROCEDIMIENTO]. *n.* Course

of action, steps, measure. *Medida, medio.* ~What PROCEDURE will you follow to regain the stolen property. *~Qué medida tomará para recuperar los bienes robados.* ~One of the first PROCEDURES was to examine the reports. *Lo primero que se hizo fue examinar los informes.* || **2.** Process. *Sistema.* ~We must follow the democratic PROCEDURE. *Debemos seguir el sistema democrático.* || **3.** Particular way of doing something, conduct, behavior. *Conducta, manera de actuar.* ~He told me he didn't especially like my PROCEDURE. *Me dijo que no le gustaba nada mi manera de actuar.*|| **4.** Método, técnica. *Method, technique.* Scientific/surgical/therapeutic PROCEDURE. *Método científico/quirúrgico/terapéutico.* || **5.** Usual, normal or standard way of doing something. *Forma, manera.* ~He told him it was not the PROCEDURE of a citizen of that country to act in that way. *Me dijo que por lo general no actuaban así los ciudadanos de este país.* || **6.** Protocol, convention, rules, policy. *Protocolo, norma, reglamento.* ~These people are sticklers for PROCEDURES. *Esta gente se rige estrictamente por las reglas (normas).* ~The ship's captain has not followed evacuation PROCEDURES. *El capitán del barco no ha observado las normas (reglamentos) de la evacuación (Prats).* || **7.** [Legal, business]. *Gestión, trámite.* ~Joining the library is a normal PROCEDURE. *El trámite para hacerse socio de la biblioteca es sencillo.*

PROCEED. *v.* Move forward (person, vehicle). *Avanzar, dirigirse, andar, ir, pasar.* ~I was PROCEEDING along the street when I met Mary. *Andaba por la calle cuando vi a María.* Please PROCEED to gate five. *Le rogamos se dirijan a la puerta número cinco.* ~In crossing a mine field you must PROCEED with caution. *Al cruzar un campo de minas se debe avanzar con cuidado.* ~The car PROCEEDED at 30 kilometers per hour. *El coche iba a 30 kilómetros por hora.* ~Let's PROCEED to the dining room. *Pasemos al comedor.* ~PROCEED to the next corner and then turn right. *Vaya hasta la próxima esquina y tuerza a la derecha.* || **2.** To continue. *Seguir, continuar, proseguir.* ~Before we PROCEED any further. *Antes de seguir.* ~PROCEED, Mr. Thomas. *Siga, Sr. Thomas.* ~Do you intend to PROCEED with the case? *¿Piensa seguir adelante con el caso?.* || **3.** To go on to. *Pasar a.* ~Let us PROCEED to the next item. *Pasemos al siguiente punto.* ~She PROCEEDED to tell us why. *Pasó a explicarnos por qué.* ~Well, he PROCEEDED, it was like this. *Bueno, prosiguió, fue así.* || **4.** [Progress]. *Marchar.* ~Everything is PROCEEDING according to plans. *Todo marcha conforme a lo programado.* || **5.** Emerge. *Salir, provenir.* ~Sounds PROCEEDED from the box. *Unos ruidos salían de la caja.* || **6.** To stem, result, arise from, originate. *Provenir.* ~This PROCEEDS from ignorance. *Esto proviene de la ignorancia.* ~The confusion PROCEEDED from a misunderstanding. *La confusión lo ocasionó un malentendido.* || **7.** To take place. *Desarrollar, tener lugar.* ~The negotiations now PROCEEDING in our country. *Las negociaciones en curso en nuestro país.* || **8.** To begin to (say or do something). *Empezar.* ~She accepted a ride in my car and then PROCEEDED to lecture me on the evils of traffic. *Consintió en subir a mi coche e inmediatemente empezó a despotricar contra el tráfico.* || **9.** •To PROCEED to blows. *Llegar a las manos.* || **10.** •To PROCEED against somebody (in court). *Demandar.* ⇨ PROCEDER

PROCEEDING[1] [PROCEDIMIENTO]. *n.* [Way of acting]. *Proceder.* ~A somewhat dubious proceeding. *Un proceder sospechoso.*

PROCEEDINGS[2] [PROCEDIMIENTO]. *n.* [Of meeting, learned society]. *Actas.* ~PROCEEDINGS of the Royal Society. *Actas de la Real Sociedad.* || **2.** [Of ceremonies]. *Acto, actos, función.* ~The PROCEEDINGS began at 7 o'clock. *El acto empezó a las 7:00.* || **3.** Measures. *Medidas.* ~There will be no disciplinary PROCEEDINGS. *No se tomaran medidas disciplinarias.* || **4.** [Law]. *Proceso.* || **5.** •To take (start, institute) legal PROCEEDING against someone. *Proceder* *(presentar una demanda) contra alguien.*

PROCESS[1]. *v.* To handle. *Tramitar.* ~Your application will be PROCESSED immediately. *Su solicitud será tramitada inmediatemente.* || **2.** [Food]. *Tratar.* ~PROCESSED cheese. *Queso tratado.* || **3.** [Film]. *Revelar.* || **4.** [Data]. *Tratar, manejar.* || **5.** Attend to, deal with. *Despachar.* ~He PROCESSED the early morning mail-first, then went on to the rest of his chores. *Primeramente despachaba el correo de la mañana y después procedía a realizar los demás trabajos (Cit. Prats).* ⇨ PROCESAR

PROCESS[2] [PROCESO]. *n.* Method. *Método, sistema.* || **2.** [Law]. (I) Proceedings. *Acción judicial.* (II) [Writ]. *Demanda.* || **3.** [Course]. ~In PROCESS of construction. *Bajo construcción, en construcción.* ~In the PROCESS of cleaning the picture, they discovered that ... *Mientras limpiaban el cuadro, descubrieron que ...* ~We're in the PROCESS of moving. *Estamos en vías de trasladarnos.* || **4.** Procedure. *Trámite.* The PROCESS of obtaining a permit. *El trámite para obtener un permiso.* || **5.** *PHRASES.* || • In the PROCESS of time. *Andando el tiempo, con el tiempo.* || •The aging PROCESS. *El envejecimiento.* || •I'm in the PROCESS of writing to him right now. *En este preciso momento le estoy escribiendo.* || •We're in the PROCESS of buying the house. *Estamos con los trámites de la compra de la casa.* || •He made money, but lost many friends in the PROCESS. *Hizo dinero pero al mismo tiempo perdió muchos amigos.*

PROCESSION [PROCESIÓN]. *n.* [Of people, floats]. *Desfile.* || **2.** Serie, sucesión. *Series, succession.* ~An endless PROCESSION of gray days. *Una interminable sucesión de días grises.* || **3.** [Of funeral]. *Cortejo, comitiva.* || **4.** [Royal, wedding]. *Cortejo.*

PROCURE [PROCURAR]. *v.* To obtain. *Conseguir, obtener, lograr, gestionar.* ~To procure the release of the hostages. *Lograr (conseguir) la libertad de los rehenes.* || **2.** [For prostitution]. *Llevar a la prostitución.* ⇨ PROCURAR

PRODUCE. *v.* [Industry]. *Fabricar.* ~The factury PRODUCES more than 100 cars per hour. *La empresa fabrica más de 100 coches por hora.* || **2.** [Teatro]. *Dirigir.* ~Who PRODUCED that play? *¿Quién dirigió esa obra?* || **3.** [Radio, TV]. *Realizar.* || **4.** Give birth to. *Dar a luz.* || **5.** Show. *Enseñar, presentar.* ~Please PRODUCE your tickets. *Se ruega mostrar (presentar) los boletos.* ~I had to PRODUCE my passport. *Tuve que enseñar el pasaporte.* || **6.** Bring out. *Sacar.* ~She PRODUCED a sweet from her pocket. *Sacó un caramelo del bolsillo.* || **7.** Cause. *Causar, ocasionar.* ~It PRODUCED great alarm. *Causó mucha alarma.* ~What impression does it PRODUCE on you? *¿Qué impresión te causa?* || **8.** [Proof, evidence, witness]. *Aducir, presentar, aportar.* ~He could PRODUCE no witnesses. *No pudo nombrar a ningún testigo.* ~She PRODUCED no evidence to support her argument. *No aportó ninguna prueba para apoyar su argumento.* || **9.** Create. *Crear, dar.* ~A university which has PRODUCED many scientists. *Una universidad que ha dado muchos grandes científicos.* ~He PRODUCES a novel a year. *Escribe una novela por año.* ~It PRODUCED very little interest. *Suscitó muy poco interés.* ~To PRODUCE a great painting. *Pintar (crear) un magnífico cuadro.* ~She PRODUCED a fantastic meal. *Cocinó una comida sabrosísima.* ⇨ PRODUCIR

PRODUCTION. *n.* [Manufacture]. *Fabricación.* ~The car goes into PRODUCTION next year. *El coche empezará a fabricarse el año que viene.* ~To take something out of PRODUCTION. *Dejar de fabricar algo.* ~Mass PRODUCTION. *Fabricación en serie.* || **2.** [Performance]. *Presentación, representación.* || **3.** [Artistic work]. *Obra.* || **4.** [By producer, of actor]. *Dirección.* || **5.** [Cinema, TV]. *Realización.* || **6.** Output. *Rendimiento.* ⇨ PRODUCCIÓN

PROFESS]. *v.* [Opinión]. *Declarar, proclamar.* || **2. [Regret]. *Manifestar.* || **3.** To claim. *Pretender.* ~I don't PROFESS to be an authority on the matter. *No pretendo ser experto en el tema.* ~He PROFESSES not to know anything about the matter. *Dice que no sabe nada del caso.* ‖ **4.** [Ignorance]. *Confesar.* ‖ **5.** To declare, state. *Decir, afirmar, declarar.* ~She PROFESSES to be 25. *Dice (afirma) tener 25 años.* ⇨ PROFESAR.

PROFESSOR. *n.* University teacher. *Catedrático.* ⇨ PROFESOR

PROFICIENT [-IENTE]. *adj.* [In languages]. *Experto.* ‖ **2.** [In skill]. *Hábil, perito, muy competente.* ‖ **3.** •She's fully COMPETENT in English. *Domina el inglés (a la perfección).*

PROGRESSIVE [PROGRESIVO]. *adj.* [Attitude, measure, political party]. *Progresista.*

PROJECT[1] [PROYECTO]. *n.* [Education]. *Estudio, trabajo.* ‖ **2.** [Housing]. *Complejo de viviendas subvencionado.* ~If you're in need of low-cost housing, there's a possibility that you can rent an appartment built by the city in one of its public housing PROJECTS. *Si necesita una vivienda de alquiler bajo tiene la posibilidad de arrendar un apartamento en los bloques de viviendas de renta limitada construídos por el Ayuntamiento (Prats).* ‖ **3.** [Activity]. *Actividad.* ~Our company is involved in many technical assistance PROJECTS abroad. *Nuestra compañía participa en muchas actividades de asistencia técnica en el extranjero (Prats).* ‖ **4.** Operation. *Operación.* ~PROJECT Apolo. *Operación Apolo.* ‖ **5.** Undertaking. *Empresa.* Paddling along an African river in a canoe appealed to my sense of adventure but I was not unaware of the risks involved in the PROJECT. *Navegar por un río africano en una canoa excitaba mis ansias de aventura, pero no se me ocultaba los peligros de la empresa (Prats).* ‖ **6.** (Piece of engineering work: bridge, building, etc., under construction). *Obra.* Hydraulic PROJECTS. *Obras hidráulicas.*

PROJECT[2]. *v.* Impel (missile). *Lanzar.* ~Upon impact they were PROJECTED forward. *Salieron despedidos hacia adelante con el impacto.* ‖ **2.** [Forecast].

Pronosticar. PRONOSTICAN un aumento de 3% en el precio del azucar. *An increase of 3% is projected on the price of sugar.* ‖ **3.** Protrude, jut out. *Sobresalir.* ~The land PROJECTS out into the sea. *La tierra se adentra en el mar.* ⇨ PROYECTAR

PROMINENT [PROMINENTE]. *adj.* [cheekbone, tooth]. *Saliente.* ‖ **2.** [Eye]. *Saltón.* ‖ **3.** Important. *Importante, destacado.* ~To play a PROMINENT part in something. *Desempeñar un papel importante en algo.* ~He was PROMINENT in literary circles. *Era una figura destacada en el ambiente literario.* ‖ **4.** Conspicuous. *A la vista.* ~The most PROMINENT article in the window. *El artículo que más salta a la vista en el escaparate.* ~Put it in a PROMINENT position. *Ponlo muy a la vista.* ‖ **5.** Outstanding. *Notable.* ~The most PROMINENT feature of this theory. *El aspecto más notable de esta teoría.*

PROMOTE [PROMOCIONAR]. *v.* Advocate. *Promover, fomentar, impulsar.* ~A meeting to PROMOTE trade between the two countries. *Una reunión para fomentar el comercio entre ambos países.* ‖ **2.** Raise in rank. *Ascender.* ~He was PROMOTED to colonel. *Lo ascendieron a coronel.* ‖ **3.** Advertise. *Organizar una campaña de ventas, fomentar (la venta de algún producto), hacer propaganda, lanzar, dar publicidad.* ~A tour to PROMOTE their latest album. *Una gira para dar(le) publicidad a su último álbum.* ‖ **4.** [In league]. *Hacer subir.* ~Our team has been PROMOTED to the first division. *Nuestro equipo ha sido subido a primera división.* ‖ **5.** Encourage (good relations, friendship]. *Fomentar.* ~The Institute is intended to PROMOTE Arab culture. *El Instituto busca fomentar la cultura árable.* ‖ **6.** [Campaign]. *Apoyar.* ‖ **7.** [Discussion]. *Estimular, favorecer, facilitar.* ‖ **8.** [Bill]. *Presentar.* ‖ **9.** [Company]. *Fundar, crear, financiar.* ‖ **10.** [Growth]. *Estimular.* To PROMOTE the economy. *Estimular la economía.* ‖ **11.** [Hatred]. *Suscitar, provocar.* ‖ **12.** [Concert, boxing match]. *Organizar.*

PROMOTION. *n* [In rank]. *Ascenso.* ~To

get a PROMOTION. *Ser ascendido.* || **2.** [Of product]. *Propaganda, publicidad, campaña de ventas.* || **3.** [Of arts, ideas]. *Fomento.* || **4.** [Bill]. *Presentación.* ⇨PROMOCIÓN

PROPAGANDA. *n.* (Information, ideas, or rumors deliberately spread widely to help or harm a person, group, movement, institution, nation, etc.). *(Diseminación de doctrinas, opiniones e información falsas con el fin de promover o desprestigiar una causa).* ⇨ PROPAGANDA

PROPERTY [PROPIEDAD]. *n.* [Personal possessions]. *Bienes.* ~He left all of his PROPERTY to the poor. *Dejó todos sus bienes a los pobres.* || **2.** [Building]. *Inmueble, edificio.* ~There are many PROPERTIES for sale on this block. *En esta cuadra hay muchas casas (edificios) a la venta.* || **3.** [House]. *Casa.* || **4.** [Piece of land]. *Terreno, solar, parcela.* || **5.** [Person, book, movie]. *Éxito.* ~She's the hottest PROPERTY in pop music. *Es el gran éxito del mundo de la música pop.* || **6.** [Theater]. *Accesorio.* || **7.** *PHRASES.* || •That's my PROPERTY. *Eso es mío.* Whose PROPERTY is this? *¿De quién es esto?, ¿a quién pertenece esto?* || •It doesn't seem to be anyone's PROPERTY. *No parece que tenga dueño. No parece pertenecer a nadie.* || •That news is common PROPERTY. *Eso lo saben todos ya, esa noticia es ya del dominio público.* || •Don't damage other people's PROPERTY. *No dañes las cosas ajenas.* || •Public PROPERTY. *Dominio público.*

PROPOSE [PROPONER]. *v.* Suggest. *Sugerir.* He PROPOSED dealing directly with the suppliers. *Sugerió que se tratara directamente con los distribuidores.* || **2.** [Marriage]. *Hacer una propuesta de matrimonio.* || **3.** To plan, intend. *Pensar, pretender.* ~What do you PROPOSE to do? *¿Qué piensa hacer?* || **4.** To recommend. *Recomendar.* ~What course do you PROPOSE? *¿Qué línea de acción nos recomienda?* || **5.** [To a girl]. *Declararse.* || **6.** To toast. *Brindar por.*

PROPOSITION [PROPOSICIÓN]. *n.* Offer,

proposal, suggestion. *Propuesta, oferta, sugerencia.* ~Her PROPOSITION that we should work together. *Su propuesta de trabajar juntos.* ~They made me an attractive PROPOSITION concerning the house. *Me hicieron una oferta interesante por la casa.* || **2.** [Prospect]. *Perspectiva.* Living alone was an inviting PROPOSITION. *La atraía la idea de vivir sola.* ~That's a different PROPOSITION (altogether). *Eso ya es otro cantar, eso es harina de otro costal.* ~That's a tough PROPOSITION. *Es un asunto difícil de resolver.* || **3.** [Business]. *Trato, negocio.* ~A paying PROPOSITION. *Un negocio rentable.* || **4.** [Plan]. *Proyecto.* || **5.** [Job]. *Tarea.* || **6.** Undertaking. *Empresa.* || **7.** [Problem]. *Problema.* || **8.** [Objective]. *Propósito.* || **9.** [Sexual]. *Invitación a la cama.*

PROSPECT. *n.* Outlook. *Perspectiva.* ~Future PROSPECTS. ~*Perspectivas para el futuro.* ~PROSPECTS are very good. *Las perspectivas son francamente buenas.* ~It's a grim PROSPECT. *Es una perspeciva nada atractiva.* ~PROSPECTS for a good harvest are poor. *La cosecha se anuncia más bien mediocre.* || **2.** Chance. *Posibilidad.* ~There's little PROSPECT of that happening. *Hay pocas probabilidades que eso ocurra.* ~The PROSPECT of an early peace. *La posibilidad de una pronta paz.* ~There is little PROSPECT of his coming. *Hay pocas posibilidades de que venga.* ~I see no PROSPECT of that. *Eso no lo creo probable.* || **3.** Hope. *Esperanza, expectativa.* There is no PROSPECT of their leaving. *Hay pocas esperanzas de que se vayan.* || **4.** View, panorama. VISTA. ~A PROSPECT of Toledo. *Una vista de Toledo.* || **5.** Future. *Porvenir.* ~His PROSPECTS are extremely good. *Le espera un gran porvenir.* ~The job has PROSPECTS. *Es un trabajo con porvenir.* || **6.** •'Good PROSPECTS' (advertisement for a job). *Buen porvenir, posibilidades de superación.* || **7.** [Person]. (I) *Persona en perspectiva.* ~He's not much of a PROSPECT for her. *No vale gran cosa como partido para ella.* (II) Possible client. *Cliente o comprador* *eventual.* ⇨ PROSPECTO

PROVE. *v.* Turn out. *Resultar.* It PROVED to be disastrous. *Resultó desastroso.* ‖ **2.** Show. *Demostrar.* ~This PROVES that ... *Esto demuestra que ...* ~To PROVE one's point. *Demostrar que uno tiene razón, que uno está en lo cierto.* ~History PROVED him right. *La historia le dió la razón.* To PROVE oneself. *Dar pruebas de valor.* ~To PROVE somebody's innocence. *Demostrar la inocencia de alguien.* ~Can you PROVE it? *¿Tiene usted prueba (de ello)?* ‖ **3.** Confirm. *Confirmar.* The exception PROVES the rule. *La excepción confirma la regla.* ‖ **4.** [Will]. *Verificar, comprobar.* ⇨PROBAR

PROVIDE [PROVEER]. *v.* Furnish, supply, give. *Facilitar, proporcionar, sumistrar, dar, surtir.* ~The foreman will PROVIDE all the necessary tools. *El encargado le facilitará todas las herramientas que necesite.* ~The firm will PROVIDE you with a car. *La empresa le facilitará un coche.* ~We PROVIDED them with food and blankets. *Les proporcionamos comida y mantas.* ~Can you PROVIDE a substitute? *¿Puede encontrar un suplente?* ~The government PROVIDED half the money. *El gobierno proporcionó la mitad del dinero.* ~It PROVIDES shade for the cows. *Da sombra a las vacas.* ~They are alleged to have PROVIDED arms to the rebels. *Se dice que les suministraron armas a los rebeldes.* ‖ **2.** Install, equip. *Equipar, dotar, instalar.* ~I have PROVIDED my car with a radio. *He instalado una radio en mi coche.* ‖ **3.** Look after, care for. *Atender a las necesidades de uno, mantener.* A man must be able to PROVIDE for his familty. *Un hombre ha de poder mantener a su familia.* ~I have to PROVIDE for old age. *Tengo que asegurarme el bienestar en la vejez.* ‖ **4.** Stipulate. *Estipular, prescribir, disponer.* ~As PROVIDED for in the 1990 contract. *De acuerdo con lo estipulado en el contrato de 1990.* ~The law PROVIDES that ... *La ley estipula que ...* ‖ **5.** Make arrangements. *Disponer, organizar, adoptar las medidas necesarias.* ~Airlines should be able to PROVIDE their own ground handling

services. *Las compañías de aviación deberían poder organizar sus propios servicios de escala (Prats).* ‖ **6.** Offer. *Ofrecer, constituir.* The meeting PROVIDED an opportunity to put forward new proposals. *La reunión ofreció (brindó) la oportunidad de presentar nuevas propuestas.* ‖ **7.** Anticipate, plan, make allowance for. *Prever.* ~Everything has been PROVIDED for. *Todo está previsto.* ~To provide for every contingency. *Prevenir cualquier posibilidad.* ‖ **8.** [Building, construction]. *Construir, instalar, montar.* ~The Government is responsible for the PROVISION of highways. *El Estado es el encargado de construir carreteras (Prats).* ‖ **9.** To yield, produce. *Producir, abastecer.* ~The garden PROVIDES enough vegetables for the family. *El huerto abastece a la familia de verduras.* ‖ **10.** To have, own, have available. *Tener, disponer.* ~The company PROVIDES sport facilities for its staff. *La compañía cuenta con instalaciones deportivas para uso del personal.* ‖ **11.** Render, lend. *Prestar.* ~To PROVIDE a service. *Prestar un servicio.* ~To PROVIDE military aid. *Prestar ayuda militar.* ~To PROVIDE support. *Prestar apoyo.* ‖ **12.** PHRASES. •To PROVIDE against. *Tomar medidas contra.* ~To PROVIDE against misfortune. *Tomar medidas contra cualquier desgracia.* ‖ •To PROVIDE for the future. *Ahorrar para el futuro.* ‖ •They are well PROVIDED for. *Tienen recursos adecuados.* ‖ •To PROVIDE for one's dependents. *Asegurar el porvenir de su familia.* ‖ •Not to PROVIDE a decent living. *No dar lo suficiente para vivir.*

PROVINCE [PROVINCIA]. *n.* Field of knowledge. *Campo, esfera, especialidad, terreno, incumbencia.* ‖ **2.** [Area of responsibility]. *competencia.* ~That's not my PROVINCE. *No es de mi competencia.*

PROVISION [PROVISIÓN]. *n.* Supply (of food, supplies). *Suministro, abastecimiento.* ‖ **2.** Condition, stipulation (treaty, law). *Disposición.* ~According to the PROVISIONS of the treaty. *De acuerdo con lo estipulado en el tratado.* ~There is no

PROVISION to the contrary. *No hay estipulación que lo prohiba.* ~There is no PROVISIÓN for this in the agreement. *Esto no está previsto en el acuerdo.* || **3.** Preparatory arrangements. *Previsiones.* ~To make PROVISION for the future. *Hacer previsiones para el futuro.* Inadequate PROVISION has been made for these cases. *No se han hecho previsiones adecuadas para estos casos.* ~She made no PROVISION in her will. *No le dejo nada en el testamento.* ~We've made PROVISION for all eventualities. *Hemos previsto cualquier eventualidad.* ~To make PROVISION for one's family. *Asegurar el porvenir de su familia.* ~To make PROVISION for the future. *Ahorrar para el futuro.* ~To make PROVISION for somebody. *Atender las necesidades de alguien.* || **4.** Condition. *Condi-* *ción.* ~I'll do it subject to one PROVISION. *Lo haré con una condición.* ~I'll do it with the PROVISION that they sell it. *Lo haré con la condición de que lo vendan.*

PURSUE. *v.* [Person, animal]. *Seguir.* ~He PURSUED the girl home. *Siguió a la chica hasta casa.* ~They PURSUED the fox into the woods. *Siguieron la zorra dentro del bosque.* || **2.** Seek, strive for (pleasure, happiness). *Buscar.* || **3.** To carry out. *Llevar a cabo.* || **4.** [Studies]. *Dedicarse a, seguir.* || **5.** [Profession, career]. *Ejercer.* || **6.** [Hopes, rights]. *Luchar por, reivindicar.* || **7.** [Policy, course of action, research, study]. *Continuar con.* ~We can PURSUE the matter further in our next meeting. *Podemos continuar con el tema en nuestra próxima reunión.* ⇨ PERSEGUIR

Q

QUALIFICATION. *n.* Ability. *Aptitud, capacidad, competencia.* To have/not have the QUALIFICATIONS to ... *Estar/no estar capacitado para ...* ‖ **2.** Requirement. *Requisito.* ~The essential QUALIFICATION is enthusiam. *El requisito esencial es tener entusiasmo.* ~She has the right QUALIFI-CATIONS for the job. *Es la persona idónea para el puesto.* ~The QUALIFICATIONS for membership. *Lo que se requiere para ser socio.* ‖ **3.** Diploma. *Título.* ~What are his QUALIFICATIONS? *¿Qué título tiene?* ~She has a teaching QUALIFICATION. *Tiene título de maestra.* ‖ **4.** Reservation. *Reserva.* ~To accept without QUALIFICATIONS. *Aceptar sin reserva.* ‖ **5.** Restriction. *Limitación.* ‖ **6.** Background. *Preparación.* With all his QUALIFICATIONS, he still couldn't get a job. *A pesar de su excelente preparación, no pudo conseguir trabajo.* ‖ **7.** Eligibility. *Derecho.* Their QUALIFICATION for financial assistance. *Su derecho a percibibir ayuda económica.* ‖ **8.** Being accepted. *Clasificación.* QUALI-FICATION for the finals was all they hoped for. *No esperaban más que clasificarse para la final.* ‖ **9.** Points, failing. *Salve-dad.* ~I should like to add a few QUALIFI-CATIONS. *Quisiera hacer algunas salve-dades.* ⇨CALIFICACIÓN

QUALIFY. *v.* Make eligible, entitle. *Capacitar, habilitar.* ~The letter QUALIFIED him for membership. *La carta le dio derecho a hacerse socio.* Her skills QUALI-FIES her for the job. *Reune las condiciones necesarias para el puesto.* ~That's doesn't QUALIFY him to speak on this. *Eso no le da derecho para hablar sobre este asunto.* ‖ **2.** Modify (report). *Modificar.* ‖ **3.** [Decla-ration]. *Matizar.* ~I would like to QUALIFY

what I said earlier. *Quisiera matizar lo que expresé anteriormente haciendo algunas salvedades.* ‖ **4.** Obtain diploma. *Sacar el título de.* ~She QUALIFIED as a doctor. *Obtuvo el título de médico.* ~He hopes to QUALIFY as an architect next year. *Espera sacar el título de arquitecto el año que viene.* ‖ **5.** [In competition]. *Quedar clasi-ficado, clasificarse.* ‖ **6.** Diminish, mitigate, moderate. *Atenuar, moderar, disminuir.* ‖ **7.** To be entitled to. *Tener derecho.* ~Their low income QUALIFIES them for some benefits. *Sus bajos ingresos les dan derecho a recibir ciertas prestaciones.* ‖ **8.** [For a loan]. *Aprobar, otorgar.* ~He didn't qualify for the loan. *No le aprobaron (otorgaron) el préstamo.* ‖ **9.** ⇨CALIFICAR

QUALITY. *n.* Degree of excellence. *Calidad.* ~Of poor QUALITY. *De calidad inferior.* ~Of excelent QUALITY. *De primera calidad.* ~Good QUALITY products. *Produc-tos de buena calidad.* ⇨CALIDAD

QUESTION. *v.* To doubt. *Discutir, poner en duda, poner en tela de juicio.* ~I don't QUESTION your honesty. *No pongo en tela de juicio su honradez.* ‖ **2.** Interrogate. *Hacer preguntas a, interrogar (police).* ‖ **3.** [By examiner]. *Examinar.* ‖ **4.** [At meeting]. *Interpelar.* ►«Aunque CUESTIONAR figura en el diccionario de la Academia [...], lo cierto es que no se utilizaba ya en la práctica hasta que lo resucitaron los que practican la traducción literal, para verter al castellano el verbo inglés *to question*, que significa discutir, poner en duda, poner en tela de juicio. Nosotros lo evitamos» (Prats). ⇨CUESTIÓN

QUIET. *adj.* Silent. *Silencioso.* ~Keep quiet! *¡Silencio!, ¡cállate!* ~A QUIET

QUOTA **186**

engine. *Un motor silencioso.* ~QUIET footsteps. *Pasos silenciosos.*|| **2.** Peaceful, calm. *Tranquilo.* ~She leads a very QUIET life. *Lleva una vida muy tranquila.* || **3.** [Business]. *Apagado, flojo.* ~Business is QUIET today. *Hoy hay poco negocio.* ~The market was QUIET. *El mercado estaba apagado.* ~Business is very QUIET. *El negocio está muy flojo.* || **4.** Unobstrusive. *Callado, reservado, sosegado.* ~A QUIET man. *Un hombre reservado.* A QUIET disposition. *De carácter reservado.* ~You're very QUIET today. *Hoy estás muy callado.* ~He's a QUIET boy. *Es un muchacho callado.* || **5.** Secret. *Confidencial.* I'd like a QUIET word with him. *Quiero hablarle en secreto.* ~Keep it QUIET. *No se lo digas a nadie.* || **6.** Without fuss. ~A QUIET supper. *Una cena sencilla.* ~It was a QUIET wedding. *La boda se celebró en la intimidad.* ~We spent a QUIET evening at home. *Pasamos una tarde tranquila en casa.* || **7.** Not showy *Sobrio, poco llamativo (of clothes], suave, apagado (of colors).* || **8.** [Not excited]. *Tranquilo, reposado.* || **9.** •A QUIET voice. *Una voz suave.* ~She has a very QUIET voice. *Tiene una voz muy suave, habla muy bajo.* || **10.** ~All QUIET on the Western Front. *Sin novedad en el frente del oeste.* ⇨QUIETO

QUOTA. *n.* Prescribed amount. *Cupo.* ~Import QUOTA. *Cupo de importación.* || **2.** Part. *Parte.* ~I've done my QUOTA. *He hecho mi parte.* ⇨CUOTA

R

RARE. *adj.* Unfrequent, uncommon. *Poco frecuente, poco común.* ~In a moment of RARE generosity. *En un momento de generosidad poco frecuente en él.* ~The plant is RARE in Wales. *La planta es poco común en Gales.* ‖ **2.** Unusually good. *Excepcional, singular.* ~She was a RARE beauty. *Era de una singular belleza.* ~Her RARE gift for comedy. *Su excepcional talento para la comedia.* ‖ **3.** Rarified (air). *Enrarecido.* ‖ **4.** [Culinary]. *Vuelta y vuelta (meat).* ‖ **5.** •At RARE intervals. *Muy de tarde en tarde.* ⇨RARO

RATIO [RATIO]. *n.* Proportion, relationship. *Razón, relación, proportion.* ~In the RATIO of 5 to 2. *A razón de 5 a 2.* ~The RATIO of wages to raw materials. *La relación entre lo sueldos y las materias primas.* The RATIO of men to women is two to three. *La proporción entre los hombres y las mujeres es de dos a tres.* ~The RATIO of girls to boys. *La proporción de niñas con respecto a niños.*

REALIZE. *v.* Become aware of. *Darse cuenta de, comprender, caer en la cuenta.* ‖ **2.** To be aware of, know. *Darse cuenta de, saber.* ~I didn't REALIZE he was his brother. *No me había dado cuenta de que era su hermano.* I REALIZE it's expensive, but it's worth it. *Reconozco (sé, entiendo) que es caro, pero vale la pena.* ~I REALIZE your position. *Comprendo su posición.* ‖ **3.** Achieve. *Hacer realidad (ambition, wish), producir (profit).* ~Her wish was REALIZED at last. *Su deseo al fin se hizo realidad.* ‖ **4.** [Potential]. *Desarrollar.* ~She isn't really REALIZING her potential. *Lo que pasa es que ella no está desarrollando sus capacidades.* ‖ **5.** [Plan]. *Llevar a cabo.* ~He REALIZED his project at last. *Finalmente llevó a cabo su proyecto.* ‖ **6.** Think, believe. *Creer, imaginar.* ~He's much more intelligent that you REALIZE. *Es mucho más inteligente de lo que usted se imagina.* ⇨REALIZAR

REASONABLE [RAZONABLE]. *adj.* Average. *Regular, pasable.* ~What was the food like? –REASONABLE. *¿Cómo era la comida? – Pasable.* ‖ **2.** Fairly good. *Bueno, bastante.* ~You stand a REASONABLE chance of winning. *Tiene bastantes posibilidades de ganar.* ~The book had a REASONABLE success. *El libro tuvo bastante éxito.* ~There is REASONABLE hope of a final favorable reply. *Hay buenas esperanzas de que nos den una respuesta favorable (Prats).* ‖ **3.** [Price]. *Moderado, módico.* We have very REASONABLE prices. *Nuestros precios son módicos.* ~Their shoes are very REASONABLE. *Sus zapatos están muy bien de precios, no son nada caros.* ‖ **4.** [Person]. *Sensato, juicioso, tolerante, comprensivo* ~Talk to him. He's a REASONABLE man, he'll listen to you. ~Háblale. *Es muy comprensivo, te escuchará.* ‖ **5.** Logical, legitimate, justified. *Legítimo, lógico, fundado.* ~Any writer who uses this formula lay himself open to enterely REASONABLE suspicion on the part of the readers. *Todo escritor que utilice esta fórmula se expone a infundir sospechas perfectamente justificadas en el ánimo de sus lectores (Prats).* ‖ **6.** Sensible. *Prudential.* ~A REASONABLE length of time. *Un tiempo prudencial.* ‖ **7.** •It must be proved beyon REASONABLE doubts. *Tiene que ser demostrado sin que quede lugar a duda.* ‖ **8.** •REASONABLE evidence. *Indicios racio-*

nales de criminalidad.

RECENT [RECIENTE]. *adj.* Last. *Último.* ~In RECENT years. *En los últimos años.* ‖ **2.** Recently. *Recientemente.* ~In a RECENT speech in Chicago. *En un discurso pronunciado recientemente en Chicago.*

RECEPTION. *n.* Response, reaction. *Recibimiento, acogida.* ~The project had a favorable RECEPTION. *El proyecto tuvo una acogida favorable, el proyecto fue bien recibido.* ⇨ RECEPCIÓN

RECESS [RECESO]. *n.* [In school]. *Recreo.* ‖ **2.** Rest period. *Descanso.* ‖ **3.** [Tribunal, parliament]. *Suspensión, período de vacaciones.* ~Parliament is in RECESS. *La sesión del parlamento está suspendida.* ‖ **4.** [Between sittings: of committee, etc.]. *Intermedio, interrupción.* ‖ **5.** [Technical]. *Rebajo.* ‖ **6.** [Architecture]. *Hueco (in a wall), nicho (for a statue), alcoba (for a bed).* ‖ **7.** Secluded place. *Escondrijo, recoveco, lugar escondido (oculto).* ~The RECESSES of the mind. *Los recovecos de la mente.* ~In the inmost RECESSES of the soul. *En los lugares más recónditos del alma.* ‖ **8.** Remote place. *Lugar apartado.* ~In the farthest RECESSES of Argentina. *En los lugares más apartados de Argentina.* ‖ **9.** [Of water]. *Retroceso.*

RECIPIENT. *n.* A person or thing that receives, receiver: *El que recibe.* ~She was the RECIPIENT of an honorary doctorate. *Le confirieron un doctorado honoris causa.* ‖ **2.** [Of letter]. *Destinatario.* The letters kept by the RECIPIENTS. *Las cartas que guardan los destinatarios.* ‖ **3.** [Of a gift]. *Beneficiario.* ‖ **4.** Winner. *Ganador.* He's the RECIPIENT of this year's Nobel prize. *Es el ganador del premio Nobel de este año.* ‖ **5.** Object. *Objeto.* ~He was the RECIPIENT of much criticism. *Fue objeto de muchas críticas.* ‖ **6.** MED [Of an organ]. *Receptor.* ⇨ RECIPIENTE

RECIPROCATE [RECIPROCAR]. *v.* To share the same feeling with someone. *Corresponder.* ~His love was not RECIPROCATED. *Su amor no era correspondido.* ‖ **2.** Return (a favor), repay (compliment). *Devolver.*

~RECIPROCATE the compliment just paid them. *Devolver los elogios que se les acababan de hacer.*

RECOLLECTION. *n.* Memories. *Recuerdos.* ~I have fond RECOLLECTIONS of my childhood. *Tengo gratos recuerdos de mi infancia.* ‖ **2.** Recall. *Recuerdo.* ~My RECOLLECTION of the incident is quite different. *Según lo que yo recuerdo las cosas fueron muy distintas.* ⇨ RECOLECCIÓN

REDUCE. *v.* To diminish. *Disminuir.* ~To reduce output. *Disminuir la producción.* ~REDUCE the risk of war. *Disminuir las posibilidad de una guerra.* ‖ **2.** To demote (in the army). *Degradar.* ‖ **3.** [Culinary]. *Espesar, trabar.* ~To REDUCE a sauce. *Trabar una salsa.* ‖ **4.** [Medical]. *Recomponer.* ~To REDUCE a fracture. *Recomponer una fractura.* ‖ **5.** Force. *Forzar.* ~To REDUCE somebody to tears. *Hacer llorar a una persona.* ~He was REDUCED to borrowing money. *Se vio en la necesidad de pedir dinero prestado.* ~Their policies have REDUCED the country to poverty. *Sus políticas han sumido el país en la pobreza.* ‖ **6.** [Weight]. *Adelgazar.* ~I REDUCED weight by going on a diet. *Adelgacé a base de un dieta.* ‖ **7.** [Price]. *Rebajar.* ~We were hoping they would REDUCE the rent a little. *Esperábamos que rebajarían un poco el alquiler.* ~We bought a television set that was REDUCED from $300. to $200. *Compramos un televisor que había sido rebajado de $300. a $200.* ‖ **8.** [Speed]. *Aminorar, disminuir.* The plane REDUCED speed as it approached the airport. *El avión disminuyó la velocidad al acercarse al aeropuerto.* ‖ **9.** To destroy. *Destruir.* ~The building was REDUCED to rubble. *El edificio fue completamente destruido.* **10.** Capture (a town, city). *Conquistar, tomar.* ‖ **11.** [Pain]. *Aliviar.* ‖ **12.** To shorten (in length). *Acortar.* ‖ **13.** [In width]. *Estrechar.* ⇨ REDUCIR

REDUCTION. *n.* [In prices, charges]. *Rebaja, descuento.* ~A REDUCTION of 5%. *Una rebaja (descuento) del 5%.* ~«Great REDUCTIONS». *«Grandes rebajas».* ‖ **2.** [Foto]. *Copia en tamaño reducido.* ‖ **3.**

Decrease. *Disminución.* ~There has been no REDUCTION in demand. *No ha disminuido la demanda.* || **4.** [In length]. *Acortamiento.* || **5.** [In width]. *Estrechamiento.* || **6.** [In weight]. *Adelgazamiento.* || **7.** MIL [To a lower rank]. *Degradación.* || **8.** [In temperature]. *Baja.* || **9.** [Of voltage]. *Disminución.* ⇨ REDUCCIÓN

REFER. *v.* To send. *Mandar, enviar.* ~I was REFERRED to a specialist. *Me enviaron a un especialista.* ~They REFERED me to the manager. *Me mandaron hablar con el gerente.* || **2.** [To a tribunal]. *Remitir.* ~To REFER a matter to a tribunal. *Remitir un asunto a un tribunal.* || **3.** Consult. *Consultar, remitirse.* ~To REFER to one's note. *Consultar los apuntes.* ~For more imformation REFER to the manual. *Para mayor información consulte el (remítase al) manual.* || **4.** Direct (to source of information). *Remitir.* ~The reader is REFERED to page 15. *Se remite al lector a la página 15.* || **5.** Submit (problem, proposal). *Remitir.* ~I shall REFER the proposal to the board. *Remitiré su propuesta a la junta.* || **6.** Mention, make reference to. *Aludir, hacer referencia, mencionar.* ~She didn't REFER to the subject. *No aludió (hizo referencia) al tema.* ~We will not REFER to it again. *No lo volveremos a mencionar.* || **7.** Apply to, concern. *Atañer.* ~This criticism doesn't REFER to you. *Esta crítica no va por tí.* || **8.** [An event to a date]. *Situar.* ~Historians REFER this event to the sixteenth century. *Los historiadores sitúan este acontecimiento en el siglo dieciséis.* || **9.** To attribute. *Atribuir.* ~The discovery of gunpower is usually REFERRED to China. *Se suele atribuir el descubrimiento de la pólvara a China.* || **10.** [An effect to its cause]. *Atribuir, achacar.* ~He REFERS his emotional problems to his childhood. *Atribuye sus problemas emocionales a su infancia.* || **11.** Classify. *Clasificar.* ~This insect is to be REFERED to the genus Pieris. *Este insecto ha de clasificarse en el género Pieris.* || **12.** •REFER to drawer (on back of check). *Devolver al librador (por falta de fondos).* ⇨ REFERIR

REFERENCE [REFERENCIA]. *n.* [Manual]. *De consulta.* Reference works. *Obras de consulta.*

REFLECT [REFLEXIONAR]. *v.* To think. *Reflexionar, meditar.* ~REFLECT before you act. *Reflexione antes de obrar.* ~If we but REFLECT a moment. *Si sólo reflexionamos un instante.* || **2.** Discredit. *Perjudicar, decir mal de, desacreditar.* Your conduct REFLECTS on the company. *Su conducta desacredita a la companía.* || **3.** Be a credit to. *Decir mucho de.* || **4.** To result in. *Traducirse en, redundar en, dar lugar a.* ~Improved methods of agriculture were soon REFLECTED in larger crops. *La mejora de los métodos agrícolas se tradujo pronto en unas mayores cosechas (Cit. Prats).*

REFLECTION [REFLEXIÓN]. *n.* Image. *Reflejo.* ~It's not an accurate REFLECTION of the situation. *No es un fiel reflejo de la situación.* ~A pale REFLECTION of past glories. *Un pálido reflejo de glorias pasadas.* || **2.** Disparagement. *Crítica, reproche.* ~This is no REFLECTION on your honesty. *Esto no es ningún reproche a su honradez.* ~It's a sad REFLECTION on human nature. *No dice mucho en favor de la humanidad.* || **3.** Comment. *Observation.* || **4.** Reconsideration. ~On REFLECTION. *Pensándolo bien.*

REFRESHMENTS [REFRESCO]. *n.* Food or drink, especially for a light meal. *Refrigerio.* ~Light REFRESHMENTS will be served. *Se servirá un pequeño refrigerio.*

REFUSE [REHUSAR] . *v.* To decline to accept (something offered), reject. *Rechazar.* ~He REFUSED the award. *Rechazo el premio.* ~He has been REFUSING food for several days. *Lleva varios días rechazando la comida.* ~I regret to have to REFUSE your invitation. *Siento no poder acceptar su invitación.* || **2.** To be unwilling (to do something). *Negarse (a hacer algo), decir que no (a una cosa).* ~He REFUSED to answer the question. *Se negó a contestar a la pregunta.* ~They asked me but I REFUSED. *Me lo pidieron pero dije que no.* ~He REFUSED to go to the meeting. *No quiso ir a la* reunión. || **3.** To deny someone something. *Negar.* ~They REFUSED her a visa. *Le negaron el pasaporte.* || **4.** To REFUSE oneself something. *Privarse.* They REFUSED themselves the simple luxuries of life. *Se privaban de las pequeñas comodidades de la vida.* || **5.** •They can REFUSE her nothing. *Son incapaces de privarla de nada.* || **6.** •I have never been REFUSED here. *Aquí no se han negado nunca a servirme.*

REGISTER. *v.* [For a course]. *Matricularse.* I've REGISTERED for three English classes. *Me matriculé para tres clases de inglés.* || **2.** [Letter]. *Certificar, mandar certificado.* ~A REGISTERED letter. *Una carta certificada.* || **3.** To list, enter (on an official list). *Inscribir.* ~To REGISTER the birth of a child. *Inscribir el nacimiento de un niño.* || **4.** To show (a feeling). *Marcar, reflejarse, acusar.* ~His face REGISTERED fear. *En su rostro se reflejaba el miedo.* ~He REGISTERED no surprise. *No acusó sorpresa alguna.* || **5.** [Thermometer]. *Marcar.* The thermometer REGISTERED forty degree centigrade. *El termómetro marcaba los cuarenta grados.* || **6.** Understand, remember, realize, sink in. *Fijarse, sonarse, caer en la cuenta, acordarse.* ~Finally it REGISTERED who he was. *Por fin me acordé, caí en la cuenta de quien era.* ~His name didn't REGISTER with me. *No me sonaba su nombre.* ~We're loosing our jobs, hasn't that REGISTERED with you. *No vamos a quedar sin trabajo, a ver si te entra eso en la cabeza.* || **7.** Experience. *Experimentar.* ~Production has REGISTERED a big fall. *La producción ha experimentado un descenso considerable.* || **8.** To have some effects, make some impression. *Producir impresión, caer en la cuenta, pasar inadvertido.* ~It doesn't seem to have REGISTERED with her. *Parece no haber producido impresión en ella.* ~Things like that just don't REGISTER. *Las cosas así pasan inadvertidas.* || **9.** To be on a list. *Estar inscrito.* ~Are you REGISTERED with Dr. Adams? *¿Está inscrito como paciente del Dr. Adams?* || **10.** To lodge (a complaint). *Presentar (una queja).* || **11.** [Luggage]. *Facturar.* || **12.** Show up,

record. *Ser detectado.* ~It weighed so little that it didn't REGISTER on the scale. *Pesaba tan poco que el peso no se detectaba en la balanza.* ~The geiger counter REGISTERED a dangerous level of radioactivity. *El contador Geiser detectó un peligroso nivel de radioactividad.* ~The earthquake was too small to be REGISTERED on the Richter scale. *Por ser muy leve el terremoto no pudo ser detectado en la escala de Richter.* || **13.** [Protest]. *Hacer constar.* The delegation REGISTERED their protests at the White House meeting. *La delegación hicieron constar su descontento en la reunión de la Casa Blanca.* || **14.** [Opposition]. *Manifestar.* Thousand of miners demonstrated in the streets to REGISTER their opposition. *Miles de mineros hicieron una manifestación para expresar su oposición.* || **15.** [Victory]. To score a win. *Ganar, apuntarse una victoria.* ⇨REGISTRAR

REGULAR. *adj.* Norma, usual, customary. *Normal, corriente.* Do you want the large or the REGULAR size. *¿Lo quiere tamaño familiar o normal?* ~Our REGULAR waiter. *El camarero que suele servirnos.* ~The REGULAR travellers on a train. *Los que siempre viajan en un tren.* ~The REGULAR word is 'looking glass'. *La palabra corriente es 'espejo'.* || **2.** [Customer]. *Cliente habitual (in shop), asiduo (of bar).* || **3.** Permanent. *Permanente.* ~A REGULAR job. *Un trabajo permanente.* ~The REGULAR staff. *El personal permanente.* || **4.** ~Frequent. *Frecuente.* The IRA carried out REGULAR bombings. *El IRA llevó a cabo frecuentes atentados con bombas.* ~Don't be surprised, that's a REGULAR occurence. *No te sorprendas, eso es muy frecuente.* || **5.** Steady. *Fijo.* ~John has been Mary's REGULAR escort. *Juan ha sido el acompañante fijo de María.* ~To be in REGULAR employment. *Tener empleo fijo.* ~A steady income. *Una renta fija.* || **6.** Real. *Cabal, verdadero, total.* A REGULAR feast. *Un verdadero banquete.* ~A REGULAR disaster. *Un verdadero desastre.* ~A REGULAR genius. *Una verdadera lumbrera.* || **7.**

[Soldier, officer]. *De carrera.* The REGULAR army. *El ejército profesional.* || **8.** Evenly or uniformly arranged, symmetrical. *Parejo.* ~REGULAR teeth. *Dientes parejos.* || **9.** Methodical, organized. *Metódico, ordenado.* ~To keep REGULAR hours. *Llevar una vida ordenada (metódica).* ~A man of REGULAR habit. *Un hombre ordenado en sus costumbres.* || **10.** PHRASES. || •To make a REGULAR thing of arriving late. *Tener la costumbre de llegar tarde.* || •In the REGULAR course of events. *En circunstancias normales.* || •To have a REGULAR time for doing something. *Tener hoja fija para hacer algo, hacer algo siempre a la misma hora.* || •To make REGULAR use of something. *Usar algo con regularidad.* || •A REGULAR guy. *Un tío simpático.* || •As REGULAR as clockwork. *Como un reloj.* ⇨ REGULAR

REGULATION. *n.* Rule. *Norma, regla, reglamento.* ~Traffic REGULATIONS. *Normas de circulación.* ~It's against the REGULATIONS. *Va en contra del reglamento.* ⇨REGULATION

RELATION. *n.* [Family]. *Pariente.* ⇨RELACIÓN

RELAX [RELAJAR]. *v.* To loosen up, rest. *Descansar, esparcirse, expansionarse.* ~Now there is time to RELAX a little. *Ahora hay tiempo para esparcirse un poco.* ~We RELAXED in the sun of Majorca. *Nos expansionamos bajo el sol de Mallorca.* || **2.** Loosen (grip, muscles). *Aflojar.* ~To RELAX one's muscles. *Aflojar los músculos.* || **3.** [Restrictions, severity], *Suavizar.* || **4.** [Efforts]. *Cejar.* ~We must not RELAX in our efforts. *Es preciso no cejar en nuestro empeño.* || **5.** [Pain]. *Mitigar.* || **6.** [Bowels]. *Soltar.* To RELAX the bowels. *Soltar el vientre.* || **7.** •To RELAX one's hold on something. *Soltar.* || **8.** •RELAX! *¡Cálmate¡, ¡No te apures!, ¡tranquilo!* ~RELAX, I'll take care of everything. *Quédate tranquillo que yo me encargo de todo.*

RELEVANT. *adj.* Fitting. *Adecuado, apropiado, oportuno.* ~Bring the RELEVANT papers. *Traiga los documentos perti-*nentes. ~We have all the RELEVANT data. *Tenemos todos los datos que hacen al caso.* || **2.** Related. *Pertinente, relacionado con, aplicable a.* ~It's not RELEVANT. *No viene al caso.* ~The RELEVANT details. *Los detalles pertinentes.* ~Details RELEVANT to this affair. *Detalles relacionados con este asunto.* ~That's hardly RELEVANT. *Eso apenas tiene que ver (con lo que estamos hablando).* || **3.** •The RELEVANT authorities. *Las autoridades competentes.* ⇨ RELEVANTE

REMIT. *v.* [Fine, debts]. *Perdonar.* || **2.** [Sentence]. *Perdonar.* ~The judge REMITTED six months of his sentence. *El juez le redujo la pena en seis meses.* || **3.** Forgive (sins). *Perdonar.* God GRANTED his apostles the power to remit sins. *Dios concedió a sus apósteles el derecho de perdonar los pecados.* || **4.** Relax (efforts). *Moderar.* || **5.** [Vigilance]. *Aflojar.* || **6.** To return to a lower court. *Devolver (referir) a un tribunal inferior.* || **7.** To postpone. *Aplazar.* ~REMIT consideration of the matter until the next session. *Aplazar el estudio del tema hasta la próxima reunión.* || **8.** [Pain]. *Aliviar.* ~A sweet peace that REMITTED pain. *Una dulce paz que aliviaba el dolor.* ⇨REMITIR

REMODEL [REMODELAR]. *v.* Renovar. Su compañía se se encargará de RENOVAR el edificio. *His company will be responsible for remodeling the building.*

REMOVE. *v.* Take off. *Sacar, quitar.* Please REMOVE (take off) your hat. *Sáquese el sombrero por favor.* ~Reference books many not be REMOVED from the library. *No se puede sacar libros de consulta de la librería.* || **2.** Dismiss. *Despedir.* He was REMOVED from his job for theft. *Fue despedido por haber robado.* || **3.** [Obstacle]. *Eliminar.* ~These reforms will not REMOVE poverty and injustice. *Estas reformas no eliminarán ni la pobreza ni la injusticia.* || **4.** [From a list]. *Tachar, borrar.* || **5.** [Problem]. *Solucionar.* || •Remove oneself (from a place). *Salir.* ~Please REMOVE yourself from this room. *Salga de aquí, por* *favor.* ⇨REMOVER

RENDITION. *n.* Interpretation (role, piece of music). *Interpretación, ejecución.* ~He gave us an excellent RENDITION of the piece. *Nos ofreció una excelente interpretación de la pieza.* ‖ **2.** Translation. *Traducción.* ~The first RENDITION of the work into English. *La primera traducción de la obra en inglés.* ⇨RENDICIÓN

RENEGE. *v.* Break (promise). *Faltar a.* ~He RENEGED on his promise. *Faltó a su promesa, no cumplió su promesa.* ‖ **2.** [Cards]. *Renunciar.* ‖ **3.** [Agreement]. *Dar marcha atrás, volverse atrás.* Both had RENEGED on paying off the loan. *Ambos se volvieron atrás y no quisieron pagar el préstamo.* ⇨RENEGAR

RENEW. *v.* Resume (friendship, negotiations). *Reanudar.* ~I hoped that we could RENEW our friendship. *Esperaba poder reanudar nuestra amistad.* ‖ **2.** New. *Nuevo.* ~With RENEWED vigor. *Con nuevas fuerzas.* ~RENEWED outbreak of rioting. *Nuevos brotes de disturbios.* ~There have been RENEWED calls for an inquiry. *Se ha vuelto a pedir que se lleve a cabo una investigación.* ‖ **3.** [Lease, loan]. *Extender, prorrogar.* ‖ **4.** [Promise]. *Reafirmar.* ‖ **5.** [Effort]. *Redoblar.* ~He RENEWED his efforts to escape. *Redobló sus efuerzos para escapar.* ‖ **6.** [Attack]. *Volver a.* ~To RENEW the attack on someone. *Volver a arremeter contra uno.* ~They RENEWED the attack on the town. *Volvieron a atacar la ciudad.* ‖ **7.** [One's strength]. *Restablecer, cobrar.* ~To RENEW one's strength. *Restablacer sus fuerzas, cobrar nuevo vigor.* ‖ **8.** To resume. *Seguir con.* ~He got up and RENEWED his speech. *Se levantó y siguió con su discurso.* ‖ **9.** Replace, change. *Cambiar.* ~To RENEW water in a tank. *Cambiar el agua de un depósito.* ⇨RENOVAR

RENOVATE. *v.* [Painting, furniture]. *Restaurar.* ⇨RENOVAR

RENT. *n.* Rental, lease. *Alquiler.* ~Flat for RENT. *Se alquila piso.* •For RENT. *Se alquila.* FIG ~It pays the RENT. *Me da de comer (vivir).* ‖ **2.** [Of land]. *Arriendo.* ⇨RENTA

REPLACE [REEMPLAZAR]. *v.* Substitute. *Substituir.* ~The Matisse was REPLACED for a Klee. *El Matisse fue sustituido por un Klee.* ~Nobody can ever REPLACE you, my darling. *Nadie podrá nunca ocupar tu lugar, cariño.* ‖ **2.** To provide a substitute or equivalent in the place of. *Reponer.* ~She had to REPLACE the cups she had broken. *Tuvo que reponer las tazas que había roto.* ‖ **3.** To dismiss. *Destituir.* ~He has to be REPLACED. *Tuvo que ser destituido.* ‖ **4.** Pay. *Pagar.* ~We will REPLACE the broken glasses. *Nosotros pagaremos los vasos rotos.* ‖ **5.** Change. *Cambiar.* ~The batteries need REPLACING every week. *Hay que cambiar las pilas cada semana.* ~The frames were REPLACED for plastic ones. *Cambiaron los marcos por unos de plástico.* ‖ **6.** Put back. *Colocar, volver a poner.* ~She REPLACED the book on the shelf. *Colocó (volvió a poner) el libro en el estante.* ~REPLACE the receiver and redial. *Cuelque el auricular y vuelva a marcar.* ‖ **7.** Return (money). *Devolver.* ~You need to REPLACE the money you borrowed. *Tiene que devolver el dinero que pediste prestado.*

REPORT[1] [REPORTE]. *noun.* [General]. *Informe.* When you get back write a REPORT on everything that was said and done at the conference. *Cuando vuelva redacte un informe sobre todo que se ha dicho y lo que se ha hecho en la conferencia.* ‖ **2.** Piece of news. *Noticia.* ~The REPORT of his death affected all of us. *La noticia de su muerte nos conmovió a todos.* ‖ **3.** Rumor. *Rumor.* ~There are REPORTS that ... *Corre el rumor de que ...* ‖ **4.** Account. *Relato, relación.* ‖ **5.** [Weather}. *Boletín del tiempo.* ‖ **6.** [School]. *Papeleta, nota, certificado escolar.* ~She got a good REPORT. *Tuvo buenas calificaciones (notas).* ‖ **7.** [Press, radio, TV]. *Reportaje, crónica, información.* ‖ **8.** [Medical]. *Parte.* ‖ **9.** [Of gun]. *Estampido, detonación, explosión.* ‖ **10.** [Written school assignment]. *Reseña.* ~A book REPORT. *Una reseña sobre un libro.*

REPORT[2]. *v.* Relate, announce, declare,

tell. *Anunciar, declarar, informar, comunicar.* ~Several people REPORTED seing the tiger. *Varias personas dijeron haber visto al tigre.* ~He is REPORTED to own several wells. *Se dice que es dueño de varios pozos de petróleo.* ~Many companies REPORTED increased profits. *Muchas empresas anunciaron un incremento en sus beneficios.* ~The news was widely REPORTED. *La noticia fue ampliamente divulgada.* What have you to REPORT? *¿Qué tiene que decirnos?* James Blorgs REPORTS from New York. *James Blogs informa desde Nueva York, James Blogs desde Nueva York.* ‖ **2.** To complain. *Denunciar, acusar, quejarse.* She REPORTED him to the teacher. *Se quejó de él a su profesor.* I shall have to REPORT this. *Tendré que denunciar eso.* ‖ **3.** Present oneself. *Presentarse.* To REPORT for work. *Presentarse al trabajo.* ~REPORT to me when when you are better. *Venga a verme cuando se haya repuesto.* ~He is to REPORT to the court tomorrow. *Tiene que personarse mañana ante el tribunal.* ~REPORT to the reception desk. *Preséntese en recepción.* ‖ **4.** Notify (police). *Dar parte, denunciar.* ~To REPORT a theft to the police. *Dar parte a la policía de un robo.* ‖ **5.** Investigate. *Investigar.* A committee was set up to REPORT on the pill. *Se creó una commision para investigar la píldora.* ‖ **6.** To write for a newspaper. *Ser corresponsal (de un periódico).* ~She REPORTS for the Post. *Es corresponsal del Post.* ‖ **7.** To be accountable to (business). *Estar bajo las órdenes de, ser responsable a.* He REPORTS to the marketing director. *Es responsable al director de mercadeo.* ‖ **8.** To interview. *Hacer una entrevista.* The newspaper sent one of their best writers to REPORT on the famous visitor. *~El periódico envió a uno de sus más hábiles redactores a entrevistar al ilustre visitante.* ‖ **9.** PHRASES. ‖ •To REPORT sick. *Darse de bajo por enfermo.* ‖ •He's REPORTED to have said. *Parece que dijo que, habría dicho que.* ‖ •She is REPORTED to be in Italy. *Se cree que está en Italia.* ‖ •Nothing to REPORT. *Sin novedad.* ~Nothing to REPORT

from the front. *Sin novedad en el frente.* ⇨REPORTAR

REPUDIATE [REPUDIAR]. *v.* To reject, deny (charge, accusation). *Rechazar, negar.* ‖ **2.** To refuse to acknowledge (liability, debts). *Negarse a reconocer.* ‖ **3.** [Possibility]. *Descartar.* ‖ **4.** [A contract]. *Negarse a cumplir.*

REQUIRE. *v.* Need. *Necesitar.* ~You can draw cash as NEEDED. *Puede retirar dinero cuando lo necesite.* ~How many copies to you REQUIRE? *¿Cuántos ejemplares necesita?* ‖ **2.** To be needed. *Hacer falta.* ~We have all we REQUIRED. *Tenemos todo lo que nos hace falta.* ~What is REQUIRED to make an omelette? *¿Qué hace falta para hacer una tortilla?* ‖ **3.** Compulsory. *Obligatorio.* ~Attendence is not REQUIRED. *La asistencia no es obligatoria.* ‖ **4.** •The law REQUIRES that all criminals be punished. *La ley dispone que todos los criminales sean castigados.* ‖ **5.** •The radiator REQUIRES constant filling. *Hay que rellenar el radiador constantemente.* ⇨REQUERIR

RESERVATION. *n.* Misgiving. *Reserva.* ~Without RESERVATIONS. *Con ciertas reservas.* ~To accept something withour RESERVATIONS. *Aceptar algo sin reserva.* ‖ **2.** Booking. *Reserva.* ~To make a RESERVATION. *Hacer la reserva.* ‖ **3.** [In contract]. *Salvedad.* ‖ **4.** [In argument]. *Distingo.* ‖ **5.** [Land]. *Reserva.* ⇨RESERVA

RESIGN [RESIGNAR]. *v.* To give up an office or position. *Dimitir, renunciar a.* ~He RESIGNED from the committee. *Dimitió de la comisión.* ‖ **2.** Forfeit. *Renunciar a.* ‖ **3.** To give or sign over, as to the control or care of another. *Ceder.* ~To RESIGN a task to another. *Ceder un cometido a otro.* ‖ **4.** [Chess]. *Abandonar.*

RESIGNATION [RESIGNACIÓN]. *n.* Act of resigning. *Dimisión, renuncia.* ~His RESIGNATION was not accepted. *Su dimisión no fue aceptada.* ~To hand in one's RESIGNATION. *Presentar la (su) dimisión.*

RESOLUTION. *n.* (of the New Year type). *Propósito, decisión.* ~She made the

RESOLUTION to give up smoking. *Tomó la determinación (hizo el propósito) de dejar de fumar.* •Good RESOLUTIONS. *Buenos propósitos.* || **2.** [Character]. *Determinación, firmeza.* ~He show a great deal of RESOLUTION. *Se mostró muy decidido.* ⇨ RESOLUCIÓN

RESOLVE. *v.* Decide. *Decidir.* ~I RESOLVED to stay. *Decidí quedarme.* ⇨RESOLVER

RESPONSABILITY [RESPONSABILIDAD]. *n.* Obligation, duty. *Obligación, deber.* Every citizen has the RESPONSABILITY to vote. *Es deber de todo ciudadano votar* ~That was our RESPONSABILITY as a great nation. *Era nuestro deber, como corresponde a una gran nación (Cit. Prats).* ~That's his RESPONSABILITY. *Eso le incumbe a él, eso le toca a él.* || **2.** Job, duties. *Tarea, labor, trabajo.* ~It's his RESPONSABILITY to order the stationary. *Él es el encargado de hacer los pedidos de papelería.* ~I'm not willing to take any more RESPONSABILITES. *No estoy dispuesto a asumir más tareas.* ~The head of a large company has many RESPONSABILITIES. *El encargado de un compañia tiene muchas tareas que cumplir.* || **3.** Reliability, dependability,. *Formalidad, seriedad.* ~Try to show some RESPONSABILITY. *Procure tener un poco de seriedad.* || **4.** Management, direction. *Dirección.* ~The work is presently under the RESPONSABILITY of an expert. *La obra está bajo la dirección de un especialista.* || **5.** Blame. *Culpa.* ~He denied all RESPONABILITY in the matter. *Declaró no saber nada del asunto.* ~The RESPONSABILITY was not mine. *No tuve la culpa.* ~The RESPONSABILITY was laid at his door. *Lo culparon a él.* || **6.** •To take RESPONSABILITY. *Encargarse de, hacerse cargo de.* ~My husband tood full RESPONSABILITY for organizing the trip. *Mi marido se encargó de todos los preparativos del viaje.*

RESPONSIBLE [RESPONSABLE]. *adj.* Sensible, trustworthy. *Serio, formal.* ~He's a fully RESPONSIBLE person. *Es una persona de toda formalidad.* ~To act in a RESPONSIBLE fashion. *Obrar con seriedad (forma-*

lidad). || **2.** Guilty, to blame, at fault. *Culpable.* ~The window is broken, who's RESPONSIBLE? *La ventana está rota, ¿Quién tiene la culpa?* •To hold somebody RESPONSIBLE for an accident. *Echar a uno la culpa de un accidente.* || **3.** In charge. *Encargado.* ~He will be RESPONSIBLE for maintenance. *Se hará cargo del mantenimiento.* ~Each nurse is RESPONSIBLE for five patients. *Cada enfermera tiene cinco pacientes a su cargo.* || **4.** Important (post). *De importancia.* He plays a RESPONSIBLE role in the running of the company. *Desempeña un papel importante en la administración de la compañia.* ~She has a RESPONSIBLE job. *Desempeña un cargo importante.* || **5.** Cause. *Causa.* A build-up of gas was RESPONSIBLE for the explosion. *Una acumulación de gas fue la causa de la explosión.* || **6.** •To be RESPONSIBLE to somebody. *Tener que dar cuentas a alguien, estar bajo las órdenes de alguien.*

RESUME. *v.* Continue, carry on, pick up (where one left off). *Empezar de nuevo, volver a, continuar.* ~We will RESUME at ten o'clock. *Seguiremos a las diez.* ~To RESUME one's seat. *Volver a sentarse.* || **2.** [Control, duties]. *Reasumir.* ~To RESUME command. *Reasumir el mando.* || **3.** [Journey, work, negotiations]. *Reanudar.* ~We stopped for lunch, and RESUMED an hour later. *Paramos para almorzar y reanudamos el trabajo al cabo de una hora.* ~To RESUME talks. *Reanudar las conversaciones.* || **4.** [Conversation]. *Seguir.* || **5.** •To RESUME possession of something. *Recobrar la posesión de algo.* ⇨ RESUMIR

RETAIN. *v.* To keep. *Conservar.* ~It RETAINS something of its past glories. ~*Conserva una parte de sus viejas glorias.* ~He RETAINED his British sense of humor to the end. *Conservó el sentido de humor británico hasta el final.* || **2.** Keep in one's possesion. *Guardar, quedarse con.* ~A copy of the invoice should be RETAINED by the customer. *Es aconsejable que el cliente se quede con una copia de la factura.* || **3.** Employ. *Contratar.* ~To RETAIN the services of a lawyer. *Contratar a un abogado.* || **4.** [Control]. *Mantener.* ~To RETAIN control of. *Mantener el control sobre algo.* ⇨RETENER

RETICENT. *adj.* Reserved, restrained. *Reservado, callado, discreto, poco comunicativo.* ~She is rather RETICENT about her emotional life. *Es un tanto reservada en cuanto a su vida afectiva.* ⇨RETICENTE

RETRIBUTION. *n.* Just punishment. *Justo castigo, merecido.* || **2.** Retaliation. *Desquite, represalia.* ~In RETRIBUTION, they executed all the prisoners. *Como represalia, ejecutaron a todos los prisoneros.* || **3.** The Day of RETRIBUTION. *El Día del Juicio Final.* ⇨RETRIBUCIÓN

REVERSE. *adj.* ~In REVERSE order. *En orden inverso.* || **2.** •The REVERSE side. *El revés.*

REVERSE [REVERSO]. *n.* Opposible. *Contrario.* ~(Quite) the REVERSE. *(Todo) lo contrario.* ~It was the REVERSE of what we expected. *Fue todo lo contrario de lo que habíamos esperado.* || **2.** Other side (of cloth). *Revés.* ~The REVERSE side of a fabric. *El revés de una tela.* || **3.** [Of coin]. *Cruz.* || **4.** [Of medal]. *Reverso.* ~That's the REVERSE of the medal. *Es el reverso de la medalla.* || **5.** [Of page, check]. *Dorso.* ~Endorse the check on the REVERSE. *Endose el cheque al dorso.* || **6.** [Auto]. *Marcha atrás.* || **7.** [Direction]. *Contrario, opuesto.* || **8.** Setback. *Revés, contratiempo.* ~They suffered many REVERSES. *Sufrieron muchos reveses.* || **9.** Defeat. *Derrota.*

REVERSIBLE [REVERSIBLE]. *adj.* [Decision, verdict]. *Revocable.*

REVISE. *v.* [Exams, lesson, subject, notes]. *Repasar.* ~I need to REVISE my lessons for tomorrow's exams. *Necesito repasar mis lecciones para los exámenes de mañana.* || **2.** To change, alter (policy, plan, figures, estimate, opinion). *Modificar, cambiar.* ~Many people will have to REVISE their opinion. *Mucha gente tendrá que modificar su punto de vista.* ~I had to REVISE my opinion of her. *Tuve que cambiar de opinión respecto a ella.* || **3.** [Proofs].

Corregir. ~Third edition, REVISED and expanded. *Tercera edición, corregida y aumentada.* || **4.** To make a new version. *Refundir.* To REVISE a dictionary. *Refundir un diccionario.* ⇨REVISAR

REVISION. *n.* [For exam]. *Repaso.* || **2.** [Of text]. *Corrección.* || **3.** [Of a lesson]. *Repaso.* || **4.** [Of a dictionary]. *Refundición.* || **5.** [Opinion]. *Modificación.* ⇨REVISIÓN

REVOLVE. *v.* Rotate. *Girar, hacer girar.* ~To REVOLVE around a planet. *Girar alrededor de un planeta.* || **2.** Center on, depend on. *Girar en torno a, depender de, centrarse en.* ~All the discussion REVOLVED round three topics. *El debate se centró en tres temas.* ~The world doesn't REVOLVE around you, you know. *No te creas que eres el centro del mundo.* ~All the conversation REVOLVED around politics. *Toda la conversación giró alrededor de la política.* ⇨REVOLVER

RICH. *adj.*
❶ FOOD, WINE. Sumptuous (banquet). *Suntuoso, opulento.* || **2.** [Con alto contenido de grasas, huevos, etc.]. *Pesado, fuerte, indigesto.* ~Avoid RICH foods. *Evite las comidas pesadas (indigestas).* || **3.** Overly sweet. *Muy dulce, empalagoso.* ~I found the dessert too RICH. *El postre me pareció empalagoso.* || **4.** [Wine]. *Generoso.*
❷ ABOUNDING IN, PLENTIFUL. *Abundante, numeroso.* ~A gallery RICH in Impressionists. *Un museo que posee gran caudal de impresionistas.* ~A style RICH in metaphors. *Un estilo en el que abundan las metáforas.* ~Her autobiography is RICH in anecdotes. *Su autobiografía abunda en anécdotas.* ~This cereal is RICH in vitamins. *Estos cereales contienen abundantes vitaminas.* || **2.** Abounding in natural resources. *Abundante.* ~The soild is RICH in nitrates. ~*El suelo tiene abundantes nitratos.*
❸ VARIOUS. Fertil (soil). *Fértil.* || **2.** [Harvest]. *Abundante.* || **3.** [Voice]. *Sonoro.* || **4.** [Color]. *vivo, brillante, cálido, intenso.* || **5.** [Perfume]. *Fuerte.* || **6.** [Style]. *Copioso.*

‖ **7.** [Furnishings]. *Suntuoso, lujoso.* ‖ **8.** [Reward]. *Generoso.* ‖ **9.** [Fuel mixture]. *De alto octanaje.* ‖ **10.** Spendid (gift). *Magnífico, espléndido.* ~He was showered with RICH gifts. *Le dieron numerosos regalos de gran valor.* ‖ **11.** [Tradition, history]. *Largo, importante.* A RICH literary tradition. *Una larga tradición literaria.* ⇨RICO

RICHNESS. *n.* Sumptuousness. *Suntuosidad.* ‖ **2.** [Of soil]. *Fertilidad.* ‖ **3.** Abundance. *Abundancia.* ‖ **4.** [Of voice]. *Sonoridad.* ‖ **5.** [Of color]. *Viveza, brillantez.* ‖ **6.** [Of food]. *Alto contenido de grasas, huevos, azúcar, etc.* ‖ **7.** [Of fuel octane]. *Alto octanaje.* ‖ **8.** [Beauty]. *Preciosidad.* ⇨RIQUEZA

ROMANCE [ROMANCE]. *n.* Love affair. *Idilio, asunto amorosa, amor, amores, amorío.* ~Even though the novel does not contain a single ROMANCE, it is still very interesting. *Aunque la novela no presenta un solo asunto amoroso, resulta muy interesante (Prats).* ~Their ROMANCE lasted exactly six months. *Sus amores duraron exactamente seis meses.* ~She was my first ROMANCE. *Fue mi primer amor.* ‖ **2.** Charm, glamour, magic. *Hechizo, embrujo, encanto, lo romántico, lo pintoresco.* ~The ROMANCE of Spain is on every plane. *El encanto de España le acompaña (Cit. Prats).* ~The ROMANCE of the sea. *El encanto del mar.* ~The ROMANCE of travel. *Lo romántico del viajar.* ~The ROMANCE of history. *Lo bello (poético) de la historia.* ‖ **3.** Tale. *Novela*

sentimental, cuento de amor.* ‖ **4.** [Tale of chivalry]. *Libro de caballerías, poema caballeresco, libro de aventuras.* ‖ **5.** [Music]. *Romanza.* ‖ **6.** •ROMANCE language. *Lengua románica.*

ROUTINE [RUTINA]. *n.* [Skater, comedian]. *Número.* ~Let's go through that ROUTINE again. *Volvamos a ensayar ese número.* ‖ **2.** [Formula, pattern]. ~Don't give me that old ROUTINE. *No me vengas con la misma cantinela.* ~Don't give me that oppressed female ROUTINE! *¡No me vengas con eso de las mujeres oprimidas!* ~The usual sale ROUTINE. *El típico discurso de vendedor.* ‖ **3.** Custom, practice. *Costumbre, procedimiento acostumbrado.* ~A a matter of ROUTINE, she never allows interviews. *Acostumbra no conceder entrevistas.*

RUDE. *adj.* Impolite. *Descortés, grosero, mal educado.* ~Don't be RUDE to your mother. *No le faltes respeto a tu madre.* ~They made very RUDE comments on my cooking. *Hicieron comentarios muy poco amables sobre mi manera de cocinar.* ~It's RUDE to speak with your mouth full. *Es mala educación hablar con la boca llena.* ‖ **2.** Harsh, sudden. *Brusco, inesperado, repentino.* ~It was a RUDE shock. *Fue un golpe inesperado.* ~A RUDE awakening. *Un despertar repentino, una sorpresa desagradable.* ‖ **3.** Obscene. *Obsceno, verde (joke).* ‖ **4.** Rudimentary (tools). *Rudimentario, tosco.* ~A RUDE plough. *Un arado tosco.* ⇨RUDO

S

SALARY [SALARIO]. *n.* Compensation for work. *Sueldo.*

SALUTE[1]. *v. fig.* To acknowledge, pay tribute (courage, achievement). *Aclamar, aplaudir, rendir homenaje.* I can only SALUTE your single-mindedness. *No puedo sino aplaudir su determinación.* ‖ **2.** •To SALUTE the flag. *Jurar bandera.* ⇨SALUDAR

SALUTE[2]. *v.* Tribute. *Homenaje, reconocimiento.* ‖ **2.** [Firing of guns]. *Salva.* ~A 21-gun SALUTE. *Una salva de 21 cañonazos.* ‖ **3.** •To take the SALUTE. *Presidir el desfile.* ⇨SALUDO

SANCTUARY [SANTUARIO]. *n.* Asylum. *Asilo, refugio.* Refugees fleeing from the advancing army found SANCTUARY in Geneva. *Los refugiados huyendo del ejército en marcha encontraron refugio en Ginebra.* ‖ **2.** [For birds, animals]. *Reserva.* ~This park is the most important vulture SANCTUARY in Spain. *Este parque es la reserva de buitres más importante de España.* ‖ **3.** •To take SANCTUARY. *Refugiarse.*

SANE. *adj.* [Person]. *Cuerdo.* ~In the doctor's opinion he was SANE at the time of the murder. *Según la opinión del médico estaba cuerdo cuando cometió el asesinato.* ‖ **2.** [Judgement]. *Sensato, discreto.* ~A sane solution to a delicate problem. *Una solución sensata para resolver un problema difícil.* ‖ **3.** [Policy]. *Prudent.* ~The campaign for a SANE nuclear policy. *Una campaña para un programa nuclear prudente.* ‖ **4.** •To be SANE. *Estar en su cabales, estar en su sano juicio.* ~I began to wonder whether he was entirely SANE. *Empecé a preguntarme si estaba en sus cabales, si estaba en su sano juicio.* ‖ **5.** •It's the only thing that keeps me

SANE. *Es lo que impide que me vuelva loco.* ⇨SANO

SANITY. *n.* Mental health, soundness of mind. *Cordura, juicio, razón.* ~To loose one's SANITY. *Perder la razón.* ‖ **2.** Good sense. *Sensatez.* ⇨SANIDAD

SATISFY [SATISFACER]. *v.* To meet, comply with (requirements). *Llenar, reunir, cumplir.* ~If you SATISFY the basic criteria. *Si reune los requisitos básicos.* ‖ **2.** To convince. *Convencer.* ~I'm not SATISFIED of her innocence. *No estoy convencido de su inocencia.* ~I had to SATISFY myself that he was right. *Tuve que asegurarme de que tenía razón.* ‖ **3.** To suffice. *Bastar, ser suficiente.* ~I offered him ten thousand dollars to keep him quiet, but that didn't SATISFY him. *Le ofrecí 10 mil dólares para que no dijera nada, pero no fue suficiente.* ‖ **4.** [Debt]. *Liquidar.* ‖ **5.** To quench (one's thirst). *Aplacar.* ‖ **6.** Appease, satiate (one's hunger). SACIAR. ~And SATISFY his omnivorous appetite for reading in the village library. *Y saciar su voraz apetito por la lectura en la biblioteca del pueblo.* ‖ **7.** [A creditor]. *Reembolsar.* ~He had to sell his land to SATISFY his creditors. *Tuvo que vender su tierra para reembolsar a los acreedores.* ‖ **8.** To compensate. *Indemnizar.* ~They concluded a treaty to SATISFY Indians deprived of their inherited land. *Pactaron un tratado para indemnizar a los indios privados de las tierras que habían heredado.* ‖ **9.** To counter (argument, objection). *Responder satisfactoriamente.* ~To SATISFY one's objections. *Responder satisfactoriamente a las objeciones de uno.* ‖ **10.** To be contented with. *Contentarse con.* ~I'm afraid you'll have to be SATISFIED with that. *Lo siento, pero usted tendrá que contentarse con eso.* ‖ **11.**

To please. *Complacer.* ~He felt that nothing he did would SATISFY his boss. *Pensó que por mucho que lo intentara no podría complacer a su jefe.* ~Any good painting should SATISFY the eye. *Cualquier buen cuadro debe resultar agradable a la vista.* || **12.** To pay for. Pagar. ~The property would be insufficient to SATISFY the mortgage. *La casa no valía lo suficiente para cubrir la hipoteca.* ~He felt helpless to defend himself because he has no money to SATISFY court fees. *Se veía totalmente imposibilitado de defenderse por no disponer de dinero para pagar los gastos del pleito.* ⇨SATISFACER

SATURATE [SATURAR]. *v.* Drench (clothes). *Empapar.* ~The tablecloth is SATURATED with wine. *El mantel está empapado de vino.* || **2.** •To SATURATE oneself with. *Empaparse de.* ~I attended the meeting to SATURATE myself with what was going on. *He asistido a la reunión para empaparme de lo que pasaba.*

SAVAGE. *adj.* Ferocious, fierce (attack). *Feroz, furioso, violento.* ~The victim of a SAVAGE attack that left him crippled. *Víctima de un ataque feroz que lo dejó lisiado.* || **2.** [Punishment]. *Cruel, severo.* ~The punishment seems too SAVAGE. *El castigo me parece demasiado cruel (severo).* || **3.** [Blow]. *Violento.* ~He died from a SAVAGE blow on the head. *Murió de un golpe violento en la cabeza.* || **4.** [Persecution, criticism]. *Feroz, despiadado, virulento.* ~A SAVAGE attack on the President. *Una crítica virulenta (despiadada) en contra del presidente.* || **5.** [Character]. *Violento.* ~To have a SAVAGE temperament. *Tener un carácter violento.* ⇨SALVAJE

SAVE. *v.* [Money, time]. *Ahorrar.* ~That way we'll SAVE ourselves an hour. *Así nos ahorramos una hora.* || **2.** [Food]. *Almacenar.* ~We are SAVING canned food in case of an emergency. *Estamos almacenando alimentos enlatados en caso de urgencia.* || **3.** [Stamps]. *Coleccionar.* ~I've been SAVING stamps for more than 25 years. *Hace más de 25 años que colecciono sellos.* || **4.** To keep, put aside. *Guardar, apartar.* ~SAVE a slice for me. *Guárdame un trozo.* ~SAVE my space.

Guárdame el sitio. ~Don't eat it now; SAVE it for later. *No te lo comas ahora; déjalo para más tarde.* || **5.** Spare, avoid (trouble, expense, embarrassment). *Ahorrar, evitar.* ~We shall SAVE a lot of trouble if we take the bus. *Evitaremos muchos problemas si tomamos el autobus.* || **6.** [Computer]. *Guardar, salvaguardar.* || **7.** Protect. *Proteger.* ~These COVERS will save the chairs. *Estas fundas protegerán los sillones.* ~God SAVE the queen! *¡Dios guarde a la reina!*|| **8.** [A goalkeeper]. *Parar.* || **9.** [One's eyes]. *Cuidarse la vista.* You should not read without your glasses if you wish to SAVE your eyes. *Si quieres cuidarte la vista no debes leer sin anteojos.* || **10.** Reserve, conserve. *Reservar.* ~He's SAVING his strength for tomorrow. *Se reserva para mañana.* || **11.** Prevent. *Impedir.* ~He SAVED me from falling. *Impidió que yo me cayera.* ~He SAVED me from making a fool of myself. *Gracias a él no pasé por un idiota, no hice el ridículo.* ⇨SALVAR

SCENARIO. *n.* [Theatre]. *Argumento.* || **2.** [Cin. TV). *Guión.* ~He submitted a SCENARIO which would have resulted in a film of seven hours. *Presentó un guión que habría dado lugar a una película de siete horas de duración (Cit. Prats).* || **3.** Forecast. *Pronóstico, marco hipotético, hipótesis, supuesto.* ~What is most depressing is that unless air fares rise to the point where demand for air travel decline (not a likely SCENARIO, given the airlines need to fill their big new jets) there's no apparent solution to the problem of congestion. *Lo que resulta más deprimente es que a menos que las tarifas aéreas aumenten hasta el punto de hacer bajar la demanda de transporte aéreo (hipótesis poca probable dada la necesidad de las líneas aéreas de llenar sus nuevos reactores de gran capacidad), no se ven soluciones para el problema de la congestión (Cit. Prats).* || **4.** [Of future]. *Panorama, perspectiva.* ~She outlined the worse-case SCENARIO. *Esbozó el peor de los panoramas.* ⇨ESCENARIO

SCENE [ESCENA]. *n.* Place. *Lugar, esce-*

nario, teatro. ~The SCENE of the crime. *El lugar del crimen.* ~The SCENES of one's early life. *Los lugares frecuentados por uno en su juventud.* ~Golden Square, the SCENE of violent demonstrations. *Golden Square, escenario de violentas manifestaciones.* ~The police were on the SCENE within minutes. *La policía llegó al lugar de los hechos en pocos minutos.* ~The SCENE of operations. *El teatro de operaciones.* || **2.** View. *Panorama, vista.* ~The SCENE from the top is marvelous. *Desde la cumbre se abarca un panorama maravilloso.* || **3.** Fuss. *Escándalo.* ~To make a SCENE. *Armar un escándalo.* || **4.** Quarrel. *Riña, pelea.* || **5.** Action. *Acción.* The SCENE takes place in a castle. *La acción se desarrolla en un castillo.* || **6.** Sight, vision. ~It's a lonely SCENE. *Es un paisaje solitario.* ~A change of SCENE would do you good. *Le vendría bien un cambio de aire.* || **7.** Environment, sphere. *Ambiente, movida, mundo.* ~The pop SCENE. *El mundo del pop.* ~To be part of the Madrid SCENE. *Estar en la movida madrileña.* ~To set the SCENE for a love affair. *Crear el ambiente para una aventura sentimental.* || **8.** Stage setting. *Decorado.* ~SCENE change. *Cambio de decorado.* || **9.** Landscape. *Paisaje.* ~A wooded SCENE. *Un paisaje arbolado.* || **10.** Situation. *Panorama.* ~The present political SCENE. *El panorama político actual.* || **11.** •The SCENE was set for a tragedy. *Todo estaba preparado para la tragedia.* || **12.** •To come on the SCENE. *Aparecer.* || **13.** •To disappear from the SCENE. *Desaparecer.*

SCHOLAR [ESCOLAR]. *n.* Learned person. *Erudito.* ~A very SCHOLARLY man. *Un hombre muy erudito.* || **2.** [Specialist]. *Especialista, experto.* ~SCHOLARS have been unable to agree on a date. *Los especialistas (estudiosos) no se han puesto de acuerdo en cuanto a la fecha.* || **3.** •Greek SCHOLAR. *Helenista.* || **4.** •Roman SCHOLAR. *Latinista.* || **5.** •I'm no SCHOLAR. *Yo no soy nada intelectual.*

SCIENTIST [CIENTÍFICO]. *n.* An expert in science. *Hombre de ciencia.*

SECRETARY [SECRETARIO]. *n.* [Government]. *Ministro.* ~SECRETARY of the Interior. *Ministro del Interior.* ~SECRETARY of the

Treasury. *Ministro de la Hacienda.*

SECTION [SECCIÓN]. *n.* [Document]. *Artículo.* ~SECTION two, subsection one. *Artículo dos, punto (inciso) primero.* || **2.** [Of a book]. *Capítulo, parte.* ~The first SECTION of the book. *La primera parte del libro.* || **3.** [Of road, track]. *Tramo.* || **4.** [Population, community]. *Sector.* || **5.** [Of a city]. *Barrio.* || **6.** [Of a country]. *Región.* || **7.** [Of opinion]. *Sector.* || **8.** [Of a drawer]. *Casilla.*

SECULAR. *adj.* [School, teaching]. *Laico.* ~Secular school. *Escuela laíca.* || **2.** [Music, art]. *Profano.* || **3.** [Clergy, priest]. *Seglar.* || **4.** [Life]. *Mundana.* ~A very SECULAR life. *Una vida muy mundana.* ⇨SECULAR

SECURE [ASEGURAR]. *v.* To fasten, fix. *Sujetar, fijar (rope, knot, hair); afianzar (object to floor); cerrar bien (window, door); atar bien (animal, prisoner).* ~She SECURED her hair with pins. *Se sujetó el pelo con horquillas.* || **2.** To obtain. *Conseguir, obtener.* ~To SECURE the services of someone. *Obtener los servicios de uno.* || **3.** To guarantee. *Garantizar, avalar.* ~SECURED by mortgage. *Garantizado por una hipoteca.* || **4.** [Boat]. *Amarrar.* ~The boat was SECURED with a thick rope. *El bote estaba amarrado con una soga.* || **5.** [Area, building]. *Proteger, fortificar (contra algo).* || **6.** To put in a safe place. *Pone a buen recaudo.*

SENSIBLE. *adj.* Of sound judgement. *Sensato.* || **2.** Reasonable. *Razonable, prudente, lógico.* ~He made a REASONABLE offer. *Hizo una propuesta razonable (acceptable).* ~It's the SENSIBLE thing to do. *Es lo más indicado.* ~That's very SENSIBLE of you. *Eso me parece muy lógico.* ~Be SENSIBLE, you can't do it all on your own. *Sé razonable, no lo puedes hacer tú solo.* || **3.** [Choice, reply, taste]. *Acertado.* || **4.** [Clothing]. *Práctico, cómodo.* || **5.** [Precios]. *Módicos.* ~Quality goods at SENSIBLE prices. *Artículos de calidad a precios módicos.* ⇨SENSIBLE

SENSITIVE [SENSITIVO]. *adj.* [Document, information]. *Confidencial.* || **2.** [Skin]. *Delicado, sensible.* || **3.** [Market]. *Volátil, inestable.* || **4.** Touchy, easily offended.

Susceptible. ~He's very SENSITIVE to criticism. *Es muy susceptible a la crítica.* || **5.** [Teeth]. *Sensible.* || **6.** [Instrument, film]. *Sensible.* || **7.** Requiring tact. (topic, situation, subject). *Delicado.* ~Sorry, I didn't realize it was such a SENSITIVE issue. *Disculpe, no sabía que era un punto tan delicado.* ~The SENSITIVE border region. *La conflictiva zona fronteriza.* || **8.** Able to react to very small changes in heat, light, etc. *Sensible.* ~SENSITIVE to light. *Sensible a la luz.* ~The scar is still SENSITIVE. *La cicatriz está todavía sensible.* ~SENSITIVE scale. *Balanza sensible.* || **9.** Responsive to, understanding of (someone's needs or problems). *Tener presente, ser conciente de.* ~We must be SENSITIVE to the community's needs. *Debemos tener presentes las necesidades de la comunidad.* || **10.** Involving work, duties, or information of a highly secret or delicate nature (especially in government). *De confianza.* ~He holds a SENSITIVE post in the Ministry. *Ocupa un puesto de absoluta confianza en el Ministerio.* || **11.** Preoccupied. *Preocupado.* ~He's very SENSITIVE about his spots. *Vive preocupado por los granitos.* || **12.** •To be SENSITIVE to cold. *Ser friolento.* || **13.** •To be SENSITIVE to music. *Tener sensibilidad por la música.*

SENTENCE. *n.*
❶ GRAMMAR. *Oración, frase.* ~He writes very long SENTENCES. *Escribe frases larguísimas.*
❷ LAW. •To pass SENTENCE on somebody. *Imponer una pena a alguien.* || **2.** •Death SENTENCE. *Pena de muerte.* || **3.** •Life SENTENCE. *Cadena perpétua.* || **4.** •To be under SENTENCE of death. *Estar condenado a muerte.* || **5.** •The judge gave him a 6-month SENTENCE. *El juez lo condenó a seis meses de cárcel.* || **6.** •To serve one's SENTENCE. *Cumplir su condena.* ⇨SENTENCIA

SENTIMENT [SENTIMIENTO]. *n.* View, opinion. *Opinión, parecer, sentir.* ~He echoed the SENTIMENTS of the majority. *Se hizo eco del sentir de la mayoría.* ~My SENTIMENT exactly. *Estoy totalmente de acuerdo.* || **2.** Sentimentality. *Sensiblería, sentimentalismo.* ~To wallow in SENTIMENT. *Nadar en el sentimentalismo.*

SEPARATE [SEPARADO]. *adj.* Different. *Distinto, diferente.* ~They sleep in SEPARATE rooms. *Duermen en habitaciones distintas.* ~Could we have SEPARATE bills? *Queremos cuentas individuales.* ~I wrote it on a different sheet. *Lo escribí en otra hoja* ~The word has three SEPARATE meanings. *La palabra tiene tres significados distintos.* || **2.** [Of organization]. *Independiente.* ~A SEPARATE entity. *Una organización independiente.* || **3.** Private (entrance, room, personal property). *Particular.* ~Each one has his SEPARATE cup. *Cada uno tiene su taza particular.* || **4.** [Interest]. *Propio.* ~We have our SEPARATE interests. *Tenemos nuestros propios intereses.* || **5.** Physically apart. *Aparte, otro.* The gym is in a SEPARATE building. *El gimnasio está en un edificio aparte.* ~Could I have the salad on a DIFFERENT plate? *¿Me podría servir la ensalada en un plato aparte.* ~Answer each question on a SEPARATE sheet of paper. *Conteste cada pregunta en una hoja aparte.* || **6.** PHRASES. || •To go out our/their SEPARATE ways. *Irse cada uno por su lado.* ~After the divorce, they went their SEPARATE ways. *Después del divorcio cada uno se fue por su lado.* || •Keep your passport SEPARATE from your wallet. *No guarde juntos el pasaporte y la billetera.* || •The subject deserves SEPARATE treatment. *El tema merece ser tratado por separado.* || •Send it under SEPARATE cover. *Mándelo por separado.*

SEQUENCE [SECUENCIA]. *n.* Succession. *Sucesión.* ~The SEQUENCE of events that led to his downfall. *La sucesión de acontecimientos que lo llevaron a la caída.* || **2.** Series. *Serie.* ~A SEQUENCE of sonnets. *Una serie de sonetos.* || **3.** [Historical]. *Orden.* ~In historical SEQUENCE. *En orden cronológico.* || **4.** Result. *Resultado, consecuencia.* || **5.** [Of cards]. *Escalera.* || **6.** [Of tenses]. *Concordancia.* || **7.** Order. *Orden.* ~It's better to look at the pictures in SEQUENCE. *Es mejor ver las fotos por orden.*

SERIOUS [SERIO]. *adj.* Grave, severe (illness, injury, accident, problem). *Grave.* ~A SERIOUS mistake. *Un grave error.* ~The water shortage is getting SERIOUS. *La escasez* *de agua se está convirtiendo en un problema grave.* ‖ **2.** Of importance, major. *Grande, importante.* ~It doesn't need SERIOUS alterations. *No necesita grandes arreglos.* ~I have SERIOUS doubts about him. *Tengo muchas dudas acerca de él.* ‖ **3.** Earnest. *Decidido.* ~He's SERIOUS about leaving the country. *Está decidido a dejar el país.* ‖ **4.** •She's SERIOUS about your brother. *Está enamorada de tu hermano.* ‖ **5.** •To make a SERIOUS attempt to. *Esforzarse realmente por.*

SERVE. *v.* Provide with. *Equipar.* ~The area is SERVED by both bus and subway. *En la zona hay autobús y metro.* ~In towns SERVED by this line. *En las ciudades donde pasa esta línea.* ~These villages used to be SERVED by buses. *Antes en estos pueblos había servicio de autobuses.* ‖ **2.** To complete, carry out. *Cumplir, hacer.* ~To SERVE a prison sentence. *Cumplir una condena.* ~To SERVE one's apprenticeship. *Hacer el aprendizaje.* ~He had SERVED only a month of his presidency. *Sólo había cumplido un mes de su mandato presidencial.* ‖ **3.** [Tennis]. *Sacar.* ~It's your turn to SERVE. *Te toca a ti sacar.* ‖ **4.** To sell (goods). *Vender, despachar.* ‖ **5.** [Summons, writ]. *Entregar.* To SERVE a summons on somebody. *Entregar una citación a alguien.* ‖ **6.** To treat. *Tratar.* ~He SERVED me very ill. *Me trató muy mal.* ~Fate SERVED him badly. *El destino lo trató muy mal.* ‖ **7.** To deserve. *Merecer.* ~It SERVES him right. *Se lo ha buscado, se lo tiene merecido.* ~It SERVES him right for being so greedy. *Se lo merece por ser tan glotón.* ‖ **8.** To help, be useful. *Ayudar, ser útil.* ~If my memory SERVES me right. *Si mal no recuerdo, si no me falla la memoria.* ‖ **9.** Supply (person, area). *Abastecer.* ~Our company SERVES the entire area. *Nuestra compañia abastece toda esta zona.* ‖ **10.** Spend time, do duty. *Actuar, desempeñar, ejercer.* ~To SERVE on a committee. *Ser miembro de una comisión.* ~To SERVE on the council/in parliament. *Ser consejal/diputado.* ~He SERVED 14 years as mayor of the city. *Fue alcalde de esta ciudad por 14 años.* ‖ **11.** To prove, turned out. *Resultar.* His car SERVED him very well. *El coche le resultó muy bueno.* ‖ **12.** To be sufficient. *Ser sufi-*

ciente, bastar. ~This amount SERVES him for two months. *Esta cantidad le basta para dos meses.* 'SERVES four' (on a recipe). *Para cuatro.* ‖ **13.** Present itself. *Presentarse.* ~When the occasion SERVES. *Cuando se presente la ocasión.* ‖ **14.** •To SERVE mass. *Ayudar en misa, hacer de monaguillo (en la misa).* ⇨SERVIR

SERVICE [SERVICIO]. *n.* Favor. *Favor.* ~She has done us all a SERVICE. *Nos ha hecho a todos un favor.* ‖ **2.** [Maintenance]. *Revisión, mantenimiento.* ‖ **3.** [Coche]. *Puesta a punto.* ~My car is in for a SERVICE. *Mi coche necesita una puesta a punto.* ‖ **4.** Mass. *Misa.* ~To say mass. *Celebrar misa.* ‖ **5.** [Wedding]. *Ceremonia.* ‖ **6.** •Funeral SERVICE. *Funeral.* ‖ **7.** •The SERVICE. (I) [Military]. *El ejército.* (II) [Airforce]. *Aviación.* (III) [Navy]. *La marina.*

SEVERE. *adj.* Grave, critical, serious. *Grave, serio, crítico.* ~A SEVERE illness/wound. *Una grave enfermedad/herida.* ~The scarceness of rain presents a SEVERE problem for this region. *La escasez de agua presenta un serio problema para la región.* ~We're in a SEVERE situation. *La nuestra es una situación crítica.* ‖ **2.** Large, sizable, considerable, massive. *Grande, considerable.* ~A SEVERE loss of blood. *Una gran pérdida de sangre.* ~There's a SEVERE food shortage. *Hay una gran escasez de alimentos.* ~Our company suffered SEVERE losses last year. *Nuestra compañía sufrió pérdidas elevadas el año pasado.* ‖ **3.** Demanding, exacting. *Minucioso.* ~My car will have to undergo a SEVERE test. *Habrá que someter mi coche a una revisión minuciosa.* ‖ **4.** Simple, plain, austere (style, color, clothing). *Austero, adusto.* ~The only decoration to an othewise SEVERE facade. *El único adorno que ostentaba la fachada, que por lo demás ofrecía un aspecto austero.* ~In his SEVERE black garb. *En su austero vestido negro.* ‖ **5.** Arduous, difficult. *Difícil, duro.* ~A SEVERE test of endurance. *Una dura prueba de resistencia.* ‖ **6.** Extreme, drastic, harsh, strict. *Riguroso.* ~The SEVERE discipline of military life. *La rigurosa disciplina de la vida militar.* ~To take SEVERE measures. *Tomar medidas rigurosas.* ~The penalties will become more SEVERE. *El castigo resultará más rigoroso.* || **7.** [Weather]. Extreme, harsh, intense. *Riguroso.* ~The snows of a SEVERE New England winter. *Las nieves de un riguroso invierno en Nueva Inglaterra.* || **8.** Painful. *Agudo, fuerte, intenso.* ~A SEVERE pain in the shoulder. *Un fuerte (agudo) dolor en la espalda.* ~A SEVERE headache. *Un dolor de cabeza intenso.* || **9.** Painful (fig.). *Duro, fuerte.* ~A SEVERE blow. *Un duro golpe.* || **10.** Violent. *Violento, intenso, fuerte.* ~A SEVERE storm is expected tomorrow. *Se anticipa una violenta tormenta para mañana.* || **11.** Vehement, energetic. *Aspero.* ~A SEVERE scolding. *Una reprimenda áspera.* || **12.** •To be SEVERE with someone. *Ser muy duro con alguien.* ⇨SEVERO

SHOCK. *n.* [Of earthquake, explosion]. *Sacudida.* ~Everyone was alarmed by the SHOCK of the earthquake. *Todo el mundo se alarmó a causa de la sacudida que produjo el terremoto.* || **2.** [Electric]. *Descarga.* || **3.** [Distress, surprise]. *Impresión.* ~I nearly died of SHOCK. *Por poco me muero de la impresión.* || **4.** Scare. *Susto.* ~What a SHOCK you gave me! *¡Qué susto me diste!* ⇨CHOQUE

SIGNIFY [SIGNIFICAR]. *v.* To make known, denote. *Indicar, señalar.* || **2.** [Opinion, approval, consent, pleasure]. *Comunicar, hacer saber, expresar, dar a conocer.* ~To SIGNIFY one's approval. *Indicar su aprobación.*

SILENT. *adj.* Not talkative, not speaking. *Callado.* ~She was SILENT for a moment. *Se quedó callada un momento.* || **2.** [Film, consonant]. *Mudo.* ~A SILENT movie. *Una película muda.* ~In Spanish the h is SILENT. *La letra h en español es muda.* || **3.** Secretive, uncommunicative, reserved. *Reservado.* ~She told me a great deal about her children but was SILENT on the subject of her own activities. *Me contó muchas cosas acerca de sus hijos pero estuvo reservada (poco comunicativa) en lo que respecta a sus propias actividades.* ~The law is SILENT on this matter. *La ley no se pronuncia en esta materia.* || **4.**

Unsaid, implicit, tacit (agreement, understanding). *Tácito.* ~There was a SILENT agreement among the islanders not to reveal their secret customs. *Había un acuerdo tácito entre los habitantes de la isla de no divulgar sus costumbres secretas.* || **5.** PHRASES. || •SILENT partner. *Socio comanditario.* || •A SILENT order. *Una orden religiosa que observa voto de silencio.* || •To be SILENT. *Callarse.* ~He asked us to be SILENT. *Nos pidió que nos calláramos,* || •You have the right to be SILENT. *No está obligado a contestar.* || To keep (remain) SILENT. *Guardar silencio.* ~We must be SILENT during the ceremony. *Debemos guardar silencio durante la ceremonia.* ⇨SILENCIOSO

SIMPLE. *adj.* Plain, unsophisticated (person, thing, style). *Sencillo .* ~A SIMPLE person. *Una persona sencilla.* ~A SIMPLE dress. *Un vestido sencillo.* ~The SIMPLE life. *La vida sencilla.* •To be a SIMPLE soul. *Ser un alma de Dios.* || **2.** Easy. *Fácil, sencillo.* ~Let me show you how to do it, it's very SIMPLE. *Déjame mostrarte como hacerlo, es muy fácil (sencillo).* ~The machine is very SIMPLE to use. *La máquina es fácil de manejar.* ~Keep it SIMPLE. *No lo compliques, no compliques la cosa.* || **3.** Naive. *Ingenuo, inocente.* ~I'm not so SIMPLE as to believe that ...* No soy lo bastante ingenuo como para creer que ...* ~The worldwide story of the conquest of SIMPLE peoples by a dominant race. *La historia universal de la conquista de pueblos indefensos por una raza dominadora.* •SIMPLE Simon. *Simón el Bobito.* || **4.** Dim. *Corto de alcances, de pocas luces.* || **5.** Pure, sheer. *Puro.* ~The SIMPLE truth. *La pura verdad.* || **6.** Complete. *Ni más ni menos.* ~It's SIMPLE madness. *Es una locura ni más ni menos.* || **7.** Only. *Sólo.* Completing the race is not a SIMPLE matter of physical fitness. *El terminar la carrera no sólo depende de la condición física de una persona.* ~We can't do it, for the SIMPLE reason that we don't have enough time. *El único motivo por él que no podemos hacerlo es que no disponemos de suficiente tiempo.* || **8.** Wanting in power or importance. *Pobre.* ~A SIMPLE woman, much to weak to oppose the cunning of men. *Una pobre mujer, demasiado débil para oponerse a la astucia de los hombres.* || **9.** •SIMPLE fraction. *Fracción ordinaria.* ⇨SIMPLE

SIMPLICITY. *n.* Lack of sophistication. *Sencillez, naturalidad.* I think of Jennie, her SIMPLICITY and careless grace. *Pienso en Jennie, su naturalidad y su despreocupada finura.* || **2.** Foolishness. *Simpleza.* ~Because of his political SIMPLICITY, he can still be the prey of extremists. *Por su simpleza política, todavía puede llegar a ser víctima de los extremistas.* || **3.** Naiveté. *Ingenuidad, credulidad.* In spite of numerous hardships, he retained a great SIMPLICITY and kindliness of character. *A pesar de numerosas dificultades, nunca perdió su carácter sumamente ingenuo y amable.* || **4.** Incomplexity. *Sencillez.* ~The advantage of the plan is its SIMPLICITY. *El atractivo del plan es su sencillez.* ~The examination was SIMPLICITY itself. *El examen fue de lo más sencillo.* || **5.** Innocence. INOCENCIA. ~The combination of great intellect with childlike SIMPLICITY. *La combinación de un gran intelecto con la inocencia de un niño.* ⇨SIMPLICIDAD

SOBER. *adj.* [Expression]. *Grave.* || **2.** Serious. *Serio, formal.* ~A SOBER and intelligent young man. *Un joven inteligente y serio.* ~He was in a very SOBER mood. *Estaba muy serio.* || **3.** Rational, moderate, sensible, realistic (attitude, view). *Sensato.* ~A SOBER assessment of the facts. *Una seria valoración de los hechos.* ~SOBER habits. *Costumbres moderadas.* || **4.** [Color]. *Discreto.* ~A SOBER grey suit. *Un traje gris discreto.* || **5.** •The SOBER facts. *Los hechos tan cual son.* || **6.** •The SOBER truth. *La pura verdad.* ⇨SOBRÍO

SOCIALIZE [SOCIALIZAR]. *v.* Spend time with other people in a friendly way. *Circular, alternar, mezclarse, conversar, charlar con la gente, llevar (hacer) una vida social.* ~He's good at SOCIALIZING. *Tiene mucho don de gente.* ~We don't SOCIALIZE much these days. *No salimos mucho estos días.* ~He doesn't SOCIALIZE with his employees. *No tiene trato social con sus empleados.*

SOLICIT. *v.* Annoy. *Importunar.* || **2.** [Beggars]. *Mendigar, pedir.* || **3.** Collect money (for charity). *Pedir dinero para obras de caridad.* || **4.** [Prostitute]. *Buscar clientes.* ~She was arrested for SOLICITING in the streets. *Fue detenida por buscar clientes en la calle.* || **5.** [Business]. *Buscar clientes, ofrecerse.* ~He sent out leaflets soliciting business. *Envió folletos ofreciendo sus servicios.* || **6.** •No SOLICITING. *No se admiten vendedores.* ⇨SOLICITAR

SOLID [SÓLIDO]. *adj.* Unbroken (line, row). *Continuo, interrumpido.* ~A SOLID line. *Una línea continua.* || **2.** Not hollow (rubber ball, tire). *Macizo.* || **3.** Pure (metal, wood, muscle). *Puro, macizo.* ~Touch this arm, SOLID muscle! *Toca este brazo ¡puro músculo!* ~A SOLID gold watch. *Un reloj de oro macizo.* || **4.** Dense (fog, jungle). *Denso, espeso.* || **5.** [Building, structure]. *Fuerte, resistente.* || **6.** Full (period of time, distance). *Entero, seguido, largo.* ~We waited for two SOLID hours. *Esperamos dos horas enteras, más de dos horas.* ~We walked 14 SOLID miles. *Caminamos 14 millas largas.* ~For four SOLID hours. *Durante cuatro horas seguidas.* ~A SOLID day's work. *Un día entero de trabajo.* ~It rained for three SOLID weeks. *Llovió sin parar durante tres semanas.* || **7.** Unanimous (vote, support). *Unánime.* ~You have our SOLID support. *Tiene nuestro apoyo unánime.* || **8.** Firm. *Firme.* ~We're SOLID in our resolve. *Nos mantenemos firmes en nuestra resolución.* ~As SOLID as a rock. *Tan firme como una roca.* || **9.** [Meal]. *Fuerte, consistente.* || **10.** [Supporter, friend]. *Incondicional.* || **11.** Full. *Lleno, repleto, atestado.* ~The streets were packed SOLID. *Las calles estaban abarrotadas (llenas, repletas) de gente.* ~The square was SOLID with cars. *La plaza estaba totalmente llena (atestada) de coches.* || **12.** [Arguments, reasons]. *Bien fundado, poderoso.* To have SOLID grounds for thinking that. *Tener buenos motivos para creer que.* ~SOLID reasons. *Razones poderosas.* || **13.** [Typography]. *Sin interlíneas.* || **14.** Compact. *Compacto.* A SOLID mass. *Una masa compacta.* || **15.** Reliable, responsible (worker, person). ~A good SOLID worker. *Un trabajador serio y responsable.* ‖ **16.** •A man of SOLID build. *Un hombre fornido, bien plantado, un hombre de complexión robusta.*

SOMBER [SOMBRÍO]. *adj.* Gloomy. *Umbrío, lúgubre.* ‖ **2.** Pessimistic. *Pesimista.* ~He was SOMBER about our chances. *Se mostró pesimista acerca de nuestras posibilidades.* ‖ **3.** Melancholic. *Melancólico.*

SOPHISTICATED [SOFISTICADO]. *adj.* Experienced. *Enterado.* ~Today's British voters are much more SOPHISTICATED then they were twenty years ago. *Los votantes ingleses de hoy están mucho más enterados que hace veinte años.* ‖ **2.** Highly complicated, complex. *Complicado, complejo.* ~A SOPHISTICATED mechanism. *Un mecanismo complejo.* ‖ **3.** Elegant, refined. *Elegante, refinado, mundano. Una mujer sofisticada. An elegant, refined woman.* ‖ **4.** [Person]. Wordly, knowing. *Muy culto, refinado, sútil, fino.* ‖ **5.** Advanced (machine, method, system). *Ultra moderno, muy perfeccionado.* ‖ **6.** Intelectually appealing. *Que tiene sustancia, de calidad.* ~A SOPHISTICATED novel. *Una novela de calidad, una novela no para todo el mundo.*

SPECIAL [ESPECIAL]. *adj.* [Edition]. *Extraordinario.* ‖ **2.** [Agent]. *Secreto.* ‖ **3.** [On menu]. *Del día.* ~Today's SPECIAL. *Plato del día.* ~The chef's SPECIAL. *La especialidad del día.* ‖ **4.** [Poderes]. *Extraordinario.*

SPECIFIC [ESPECÍFICO]. *adj.* Definite (plans, proposal, ideas, date). *Concreto, determinado, definido.* ~Give SPECIFIC examples. *Dé ejemplos concretos.* ~They seem to have no SPECIFIC plans to deal with the problem. *No parece que tuvieron planes concretos para solucionar este problema.* ~They have fixed no SPECIFIC date for the wedding. *No han fijado una fecha concreta para la boda.* ~To be SPECIFIC. *Concretar.* ‖ **2.** Precise, exact. *Preciso.* ~At two fifteen, to be more SPECIFIC. *A las dos y cuarto, para ser más preciso.* ‖ **3.** Clear in meaning. *Explícito, detallado.* The manual gives very SPECIFIC instructions. *El manual contiene instrucciones detalladas.* ‖ **4.** Special, parti-

cular. *Especial, particular.* Have you a SPECIFIC reason for asking? *¿Me preguntas por algún motivo en especial (en particular)?* Is this game meant for any SPECIFIC age-group? *¿Es este juego orientado a personas de cierta edad?* ~Are you doing something SPECIFIC this weekend? *¿Haces algo en particular este fin de semana?* ‖ **5.** Characteristic. *Característico, propio.* Each individual has SPECIFIC traits. *Cada individuo tiene rasgos propios (característicos).* ~He has a SPECIFIC way of doing things. *Tiene su manera propia de hacer las cosas.* ‖ **6.** •SPECIFICS. *Datos, detalles, aspectos (concretos).*

SPECIFICATION [ESPECIFICACIÓN]. *n.* Condition. *Condiciones.* ~The only SPECIFICATION was that the women should be unemployed. *La única condición que se estipulaba era que las mujeres debían estar desempleadas.* ‖ **2.** Requirement. *Requisito.* ~Any student can apply for a loan, the only SPECIFICATION being that you must be 21. *Cualquier estudiante puede solicitar un préstamo. El único requisito es que debe haber cumplido los 21 años de edad.* ‖ **3.** [Of a contract]. *Estipulación.* All the SPECIFICATIONS of the agreement have been agreed upon. *Todas las estipulaciones del convenio han sido aceptadas.* ‖ **4.** Plan. *Plan detallado.* ~A SPECIFICATION has been drawn up for a new military aircraft. *Se ha elaborado un plan detallado para un nuevo avión militar.* ‖ **5.** Proposal. *Propuesta detallada.* ‖ **6.** •SPECIFICATIONS. *Datos específicos.* ~If you give the store the exact SPECIFICATIONS, they'll make the curtains for you. *Si Ud. quiere cortinas, lo único que tiene que hacer es proporcionar a la tienda los datos específicos.*

SPIRIT [ESPÍRITU] *adj.*
❶ LIVELINESS, VITALITY, VIVACITY, ZEST, FIRE, GAITY, VIGOR. *Ánimo, alegría, animación, vivacidad, brío.* ~To sing with SPIRIT. *Cantar con brío.* ~To be full of SPIRIT. *Estar lleno de ánimo.* ~To be in high SPIRITS. *Estar animadísimo, estar muy alegre.* This horse has plenty of SPIRIT. *Este caballo tiene mucho brío.* ~He tried to put

more SPIRIT into the team. *Intentó infundirle más ánimo a los jugadores.* ~To be in low SPIRITS. *Estar abatido.*

❷ ATTITUDE, DISPOSITION. *Actitud, disposición.* ~To come in the SPIRIT of peace. *Venir en son de paz.* He took what I said in the wrong SPIRIT. *Se tomó a mal lo que dije.* ~In a friendly SPIRIT. *De una manera amistosa.* ~That's the SPIRIT! *¡Así me gusta!* ~It's very important to play the game in the right SPIRIT. *Es importante jugar con la debida disposición de ánimo.* ~We acted in a SPIRIT of cooperation. *Actuamos dispuestos a colaborar.*

❸ MOOD. *Humor, gana.* ~In good SPIRIT. *De buen humor.* ~I'll do it when the SPIRIT moves me. *Lo haré cuando me dé la gana.* ~I could see she was in a fighting SPIRIT. *Veía que estaba con ganas de pelear.* ~Everyone is in a party SPIRIT. *Todo el mundo quiere divertirse.*

❹ PERSON, SOUL, GHOST. [Soul]. *Alma, ánima.* ~An unquiet SPIRIT. *Un alma en pena.* ~The SPIRIT leaves the body at the moment of death. *El alma se separa del cuerpo en el momento de la muerte.* || **2.** [Person]. *Ser, persona, alma.* ~The leading SPIRIT in the party. *El alma del partido, la persona más destacada del partido.* ~She was one of the weakest SPIRITS among us. *Era una de las personas más débiles entre nosotros.* ~They realized they were kindred SPIRITS. *Se dieron cuenta de que eran almas gemelas.* || **3.** [Ghost]. *Fantasma, aparecido.*

❺ PERSONAL QUALITY. Strength, fortitude, mettle. *Temple, entereza, fuerza.* ~They showed their SPIRIT in the hour of defeat. *Mostraron su entereza (temple) a la hora de la derrota.* || **2.** Character. *Carácter.* ~He lacks SPIRIT. *No tiene carácter.* || **3.** Courage. *Valor.* || **4.** •Community or public SPIRIT. *Civismo.* || **5.** Will. *Voluntad.* ~To break someone's SPIRIT. *Quebrar la voluntad de uno.*

❻ OTHERS. Alcohol. *Alcohol.* ~SPIRIT lamp. *Lámpara de alcohol.* || **2.** Surrounding influence or condition; ambience, atmosphere, climate. *Ambiente.* ~They went to the tennis club a few times, but they never

entered (got into) the SPIRIT of it. *Fueron al club de ténis en algunas ocasiones, pero nunca entraron en ambiente, nunca se entusiasmaron.* || **3.** •The SPIRIT is willing but the flesh is weak. *A pesar de las buenas intenciones, la carne es débil.*

SPOUSE [ESPOSO/ESPOSA]. Person's husband or wife. *Cónyuge.*

STAMP. *n.* [Postage]. *Sello, estampilla (Latin America).* || **2.** [Rubber]. *Estampilla.* || **3.** [Fiscal, revenue]. *Timbre, poliza.* || **4.** [Trading]. *Cupón.* || **5.** [For free food]. *Vale, bono.* || **6.** [In dancing]. *Zapateo.* || **7.** [Die]. *Cuño.* || **8.** [Mark]. *Marca, huella, impresión.* ~A principal who left her STAMP on the institute. *Una directora que dejo su huella en el instituto.* || **9.** [Of foot]. *Paso.* ~We could hear the STAMP of marching feet. *Oimos pasos de marcha.* || **10.** [Figurative]. *Sello.* ~It bears the STAMP of genius. *Lleva el sello de la genialidad.* || **11.** •A man of his STAMP. *Un hombre de su temple, un hombre de su calaña (derogatory).* ⇨ESTAMPA

STATION [ESTACIÓN]. *n.*

❶ PLACE/POSITION. *Sitio, lugar, posición, puesto.* ~From my STATION near the window. *Desde el sitio donde estaba junto a la ventana.* || **2.** Habitat. *Sitio.* ~The only STATION for this rare plant. *El único sitio donde existe esta planta tan poco frecuente.*

❷ PLACE OF OPERATION. *Puesto.* ~The policeman took up his STATION near the door. *El policía ocupó su lugar junto a la puerta.* || **2.** [Bombero]. *Cuartel de bomberos.* || **3.** Gas (filling) STATION. *Gasolinera.* || **4.** [Coastguard]. *Puesto.* || **5.** [Military]. *Puesto.* ~Action STATIONS¡ *¡A sus puestos (de combate)!* || **6.** [Police]. *Comisaría.* || **7.** [Power]. *Central.* || **8.** [Radio]. *Emisora.* || **9.** [Service]. *Area de servicio.* || **10.** [Wagon]. *Camioneta.* || **11.** [First aid]. *Casa de socorro.* || **12.** •Research STATION. *Centro de investigación.* || **13.** •To take up one's STATION. *Colocarse (irse) a su puesto.*

❸ SOCIAL STANDING. *Condición, clase social, posición.* ~Her STATION in life forbids such action. *Una mujer de su condición no puede hacer tal cosa.* ~Of humble STATION.

De baja posición social. ~A man of exalted POSITION. *Un hombre de clase social elevada.* ~To marry below one's STATION. *Casarse con alguien de posición inferior (a la de uno).*

STORY. *n.*

❶ FOR ENTERTAINMENT. Tale, short story. *Cuento.* ~Tell me a STORY. *Cuéntame un cuento.* ~She chose her favorite book of bedtime STORIES. *Eligió su libro predilecto de cuentos para leer antes de dormir.* || **2.** Account. *Relato, relación.* ~The STORY of their travels. *La relación de sus viajes.* || **3.** Plot. *Argumento, trama.* || **4.** Joke. *Chiste.* || **5.** Anecdote. *Anécdota.*

❷ FALSE OR UNFOUNDED INFORMATION. Rumor. *Rumor.* ~I've heard a STORY that you may be retiring next year - Is it true? *Me han dicho que Ud. piensa jubilarse el año que viene - ¿Es cierto?* His 'uncle' was really his father, or so the STORY goes. *El 'tío' era en realidad su padre, o eso dicen.* || **2.** Lie. *Mentira, cuento.* ~He made up some STORY about having to go to his aunt's wedding. *Me hizo el cuento de que había tenido que asistir a la boda de su tía.* ~A likely STORY! *¡Puro cuento!.* || **3.** Gossip. *Chisme.* || **4.** Version, contention, assertion. *Versión, explicación.* According to his STORY. *Según él.*

❸ NEWS. Newsworthy event. ~A reporter with a nose for a good STORY. *Un periodista con buen olfato para lo que es noticia.* || **2.** (Press, TV). *Artículo, reportaje, noticia.* A STORY about China appears on page 3. *En la página 3 aparece un artículo sobre la China.*

❹ EXPRESSIONS. || •But that's another STORY. *Pero eso es otro cantar, pero eso es harina de otro costal.* || •That's not the end of the STORY. *Pero ahí no termina.* || •It's the STORY of my life. *Siempre me pasa lo mismo.* || •He gave me the STORY on the new models. *Me dió información sobre (me habló de) los nuevos modelos.* || •It's the same old STORY. *Es lo de siempre.* || •The marks tell their own STORY. *Las señales hablan por sí solas.* || •What a STORY this house could tell! *¡Cuántas cosas nos diría esta casa!* || •It's a long STORY. *Sería largo de contar.* || •To make a long STORY short. *En resumidas cuentas, en pocas*

palabras. || •If you're poor it's a different STORY. *Si eres pobre es muy distinto, es otro cantar.* ⇨HISTORIA

STRANGE [EXTRAÑO]. *adj.* Unknown. *Desconocido.* ~Don't speak to any STRANGE men. *No hables con ningún desconocido.* || **2.** Unfamiliar, unaccostumed. *Nuevo, no acostumbrado, ajeno.* She was STRANGE to city life. *No estaba acostumbrada a la vida de la ciudad.* ~I never sleep well in a STRANGE bed. *No duermo nunca bien en una cama que no sea la mía.* ~It tastes STRANGE. *Tiene un gusto raro.* || **3.** Out of place. *Molesto, incómodo.* She felt a bit STRANGE at first. *Al principio se sentía un poco desplazada.* ~I feel STRANGE wearing a suit. *Me siento molesto (incómodo) con traje.* || **4.** Exotic (land). *Exótico, peregrino.* || **5.** Unusual, curious, odd, queer. *Raro.* ~How STRANGE! *¡Qué raro!* ~It's STRANGE that he didn't say anything about it. *Es raro (me extraña) que no me haya dicho nada.* ~What a STRANGE thing to say! *¡Qué cosa más rara de decir.* ~STRANGEST of all. *Lo más raro del caso es que ...* || **6.** [Person]. *Raro.* He's a STRANGE person. *Es un tipo (medio) raro.* || **7.** Unexpected. *Inesperado.* ~These were STRANGE results. *Aquellos resultados fueron inesperados.* || **8.** •Truth is STRANGER than fiction. *La realidad supera a la ficción.* || **9.** •STRANGE to say ... *Aunque parezca mentira.* ~I know all of her friends but I've never met her, STRANGE to say. *Conozco a todos sus amigos pero a ella, aunque parezca mentira, no la conozco.*

STRANGER [EXTRAÑO]. *n.* Unknown person. *Desconocido, extraño.* ~Never speak to STRANGERS. *No hables nunca con desconocidos.* || **2.** Outsider. *Forastero.* ~I'm a STRANGER here. *No soy de aquí, soy nuevo aquí.* || **3.** Hi, STRANGER! *¡Cuánto tiempo sin vernos!* || **4.** •To be a STRANGER to. *Conocer bien.* ~He's no STRANGER to vices. *Conoce bien los vicios.* ~She's no STRANGER to New York. *Conoce bien a Nueva York.* ~She's a relative STRANGER to the publishing world. *Tiene poca experiencia en el mundo editorial.* ~He's no STRANGER to fear. *Sabe perfectamente lo que es el miedo.* ~I am a

STRANGER to the subject. *Soy profano en la materia, no conozco el tema.*

STRICT [ESTRICTO]. *adj.* Exact, precise (discipline, accuracy, order). *Riguroso.* ~We need STRICT accuracy here. *Aquí es necesario emplear la más rigurosa exactitud.* ~In STRICT order of arrival. *Por riguroso orden de llegada.* || **2.** Severe, stern (ban, order). *Terminante.* ~He gave me a STRICT order not to go to that place without his permission. *Me prohibió de forma terminante entrar en ese lugar sin su permiso.* || **3.** [Person]. *Severo, riguroso, escrupuloso.* ~They're terribly STRICT here. *Aquí son terriblemente rigurosos.* ~To be STRICT with someone. *Ser severo con uno, tratar a uno con severidad.* || **4.** Complete. *Absoluto.* ~In the STRICTEST confidence. *En el más absoluto secreto.* ~In STRICT seclusion. *En un aislamiento completo.*

STUDY [ESTUDIAR]. *adj.* [University subject]. *Cursar.* ~He STUDIED philosophy at the university. *Cursó estudios de filosofía en la universidad.* || **2.** [Facts, proposal]. *Examinar, investigar.* ~Let's first STUDY the facts. *Primero vamos a examinar los hechos.* ~I haven't had time to STUDY the proposals yet. *Todavía no he tenido tiempo de examinar las propuestas.* || **3.** [Behavior]. *Observar.* ~He STUDIED himself in the mirror. *Se observaba en el espejo.* || **4.** •To STUDY for an exam. *Prepararse para un examen.*

STUPENDOUS. *adj.* [Effort, strength]. *Tremendo.* ~He's a man of STUPENDOUS strength. *Este hombre tiene una fuerza tremenda.* || **2.** [Success]. *Formidable.* ~A STUPENDOUS achievement. *Un éxito formidable.* || **3.** [Failure, problem]. *Mayúsculo.* ~I really don't see any solution to this STUPENDOUS problem. *Es un problema MAYÚSCULO al que no veo solución.* || **4.** Unusual. *Extraordinario.* The main character is a young woman of STUPENDOUS beauty. *La protagonista es una muchacha de extraordinaria belleza.* ⇨ESTUPENDO

STYLE [ESTILO]. *adj.* ❶ CLOTHES, HAIR. [Of dress, suit]. *Modelo.* || **2.** [Hairstyle]. *Peinado.* || **3.** [Fashion]. *Moda.* ~Long skirts are back in

STYLE. *Las faldas largas vuelven a estar de moda.* ~To go out of STYLE. *Pasar de moda.* ❷ VARIOUS. Elegance. *Elegancia, clase.* ~She has a lot of STYLE. *Tiene clase.* || **2.** Kind. *Tipo.* ~An american-STYLE comedy. *Una comedia de tipo americano.* || **3.** Cut of clothes. *Hechura.* ❸ EXPRESSIONS. || •A general in the old STYLE. *Un general de la vieja escuela.* || •To cramp somebody's STYLE. *Cortar los vuelos a uno.* || •To live/travel in STYLE. *Vivir/viajar a lo grande.* ~They were married in STYLE. *Se casaron a lo grande.* || •To live in STYLE. *Vivir con todo el lujo.* || •Telling lies is not my STYLE. *Decir mentiras no va conmigo.*

SUBJECT [SUJETO]. *n.* ❶ MATTER TALKED ABOUT. *Tema, materia, asunto.* This is a delicate SUBJECT. *Es un asunto delicado.* ~While we're on the SUBJECT of holidays. *Ya que hablamos de vacaciones.* ~On the SUBJECT of work. *Hablando de trabajo.* ~Enough on that SUBJECT. *Dejemos de hablar de eso (de este tema).* || **2.** •On the SUBJECT of. *A propósito de.* || **3.** •SUBJECT matter. *Contenido.* || **4.** •SUBJECT index. *Índice de materias (in a book), catálogo de materias (in a library).* || **5.** •To drop the SUBJECT. *Dejar el tema.* || **6.** •To get on the SUBJECT of. *Abordar, empezar a hablar de un tema.* || **7.** •To keep off a SUBJECT. *No aludir a un tema, evitar un tema, no tocar un tema.* || **8.** •To raise the SUBJECT of. *Plantear.* ~I'd like to raise the SUBJECT of finance. *Quisiera plantear el problema de la financiación.* ~To raise the SUBJECT of the war. *Introducir el tema de la guerra, empezar a hablar de la guerra.* ~This raised the whole SUBJECT of money. *Esto plantea el problema general del dinero.* || **9.** •To change the SUBJECT. *Cambiar de tema.* || **10.** •To get back to the SUBJECT. *Volver al tema.* ❷ MOTIVE/CAUSE/GROUND. *Motivo, objeto.* ~A SUBJECT for complaint. *Un motivo de queja.* ~That crime is now the SUBJECT of a detailed investigation. *Ese crimen es ahora objeto de una minuciosa investigación.* ~To be the SUBJECT of criticism/controversy. *Ser objeto de crítica/polémica.* The number of planes flying over the town has been the

SUBJECT of concern since last summer. *El gran número de aviones sobrevolando la ciudad ha sido un motivo de gran preocupación desde el verano pasado.* ❸ OTHER MEANINGS. Citizen. *Súbdito.* A British SUBJECT. *Un súbdito británico.* || **2.** [School]. *Asignatura.* He studied four SUBJECTS in his first year at college. *Cursó cuatro asignaturas en el primer año de la universidad.* ~My favorite SUBJECT at school was English. *La asignatura que más me gustaba en la escuela era el inglés.* || **3.** Experiment. *Sujeto.* ~Rats are often the SUBJECTS of scientific experiments. *Con frecuencia se usan ratas como sujetos de experimentos científicos.* || **4.** [Medicine]. *Caso.* ~He's a nervous SUBJECT. *Es un caso nervioso.* || **5.** [Of a painting]. *Motivo.* ~Monet often used his gardens as SUBJECTS. *Frecuentes motivos de los cuadros de Monet eran sus jardines.*

SUBMISSION. *n.* [In wrestling]. *Rendición.* || **2.** [Plan, proposal]. *Propuesta.* ~To make a SUBMISSION to someone. *Presentarle una propuesta a alguien.* || **3.** Report. *Informe, ponencia.* || **4.** [Law]. *Alegato.* || **5.** Presentation (documents). *Presentación.* || **6.** Contention. *Opinión.* ~It is our SUBMISSION that. *Sostenemos que.* || **7.** [Of evidence]. *Entrega.* || **8.** Resignation. *Resignación, conformidad.* || **9.** [To an examination]. *Sometimiento.* || **10.** •To beat into SUBMISSION. *Someter a alguien a base de golpes.* || **11.** •To starve into SUBMISSION. *Reducir por hambre.* ⇨SUMISIÓN

SUBMIT. *v.* [Application, proposal, claim]. *Presentar, entregar.* ~All applications have to be SUBMITTED by Friday. *Todas las solicitudes deben entregarse para el viernes.* ~I have SUBMITTED my manuscript to the publisher. *He entregado mi manuscrito al director.* || **2.** [Law]. *Alegar.* || **3.** Surrender. *Rendirse, ceder.* ~He SUBMITTED to his son's wishes and bought him a car. *Cedió a las peticiones de su hijo y le compró un coche.* || **4.** Contend. *Sostener, afirmar.* ~I SUBMIT that it was the wrong decision. *Sostengo que adoptamos una decisión equivocada (Cit. Prats).* || **5.** [Theory]. *Exponer, proponer.* ||

6. To suggest. *Sugerir, proponer.* || **7.** To point out. *Señalar, indicar.* ~I SUBMIT that there's another point of view. *Señalo que existe otro punto de vista.* || **8.** To resign oneself. *Conformarse.* || **9.** [Resignation]. *Ofrecer.* ~He SUBMITTED his resignation. *Ofreció su renuncia.* || **10.** [Interview]. *Otorgar.* ~To SUBMIT to an interview. *Otorgar una entrevista.* || **11.** •To SUBMIT to an operation. *Dejarse operar.* ⇨SOMETER

SUBSCRIBE. *v.* Support, agree with (opinion, theory). *Estar de acuerdo con.* ~I SUBSCRIBE to the view that. || **2.** [Signature]. *Poner.* || **3.** [Document]. *Firmar, poner su firma en.* || **4.** To contribute. *Contribuir.* || 5. To pay. *Pagar.* ⇨SUSCRIBIR

SUBSEQUENT [SUBSIGUIENTE]. *adj.* [Events, developments]. *Posterior, siguiente, ulterior.* ~On a SUBSEQUENT visit. *En una visita posterior.* ~SUBSEQUENT to our discussions I contacted him again. *Tras nuestras conversaciones, me volví a ponerme en contacto con él.* ~Incidents SUBSEQUENT to her departure. *Incidentes posteriores a su partida.*

SUBSTANTIAL [SUSTANCIAL]. *adj.* Sturdy, solid (furniture, building). *Sólido, fuerte.* || **2.** Firm, stout, strong (body). *Robusto.* || **3.** [Sum, loss, income, damage]. *Importante, considerable.* ~A SUBSTANTIAL sum of money. *Una considerable cantidad de dinero.* ~The document requires SUBSTANTIAL changes. *El documento necesita cambios radicales.* ~Many factories suffered SUBSTANTIAL damages. *Muchas fábricas sufrieron considerables daños.* || **4.** [Difference, improvement, change]. *Notable.* ~The findings show a SUBSTANTIAL difference between the opinions of men and women. *Las encuestas demuestran una notable diferencia entre las opiniones de los hombres y de las mujeres.* ~We need SUBSTANTIAL improvements in public transport. *Necesitamos notables mejoras en los medios de transporte.* || **5.** [Meal]. *Abundante, copioso.* ~After such a SUBSTANTIAL lunch, he decided to have a rest. *Después de tan abundante comida resolvió tomar una siesta.* || **6.** Wealthy, well-to-do. *Acaudalado, acomodado, adinerado.* || **7.**

[Law]. •SUBSTANTIAL damages. *Daños y perjuicios generales.* ‖ **8.** •[Law]. SUBSTANTIAL evidence. *Pruebas de peso.* ‖ **9.** [Contribution]. *Importante.* ‖ **10.** Nourishing, filling. *Sustancioso.* Do you have anything more SUBSTANTIAL than salad? *¿Tiene algo mas sustencioso que una ensalada?* ‖ **11.** Real, true. *Real, verdadero.* ~The SUBSTANTIAL world. *El mundo real.* ‖ **12.** Sound (argument). *Razonable, lógico, bien fundado.* ‖ **13.** [Error]. *Grave.* ~A SUBSTANTIAL error. *Un grave error.* ‖ **14.** [Penalty]. *Severo.* ‖ **15.** •To be in SUBSTANTIAL agreement. *Estar de acuerdo en gran parte, en principio, fundamentalmente.* ~We have reached a SUBSTANTIAL agreement on the terms of the deal. *Hemos llegado a un acuerdo sobre los puntos esenciales (fundamentales) del trato.*

SUBTLE. adj. [Perfume, taste]. *Delicado, tenue.* ~It was painted the SUBTLEST of pinks. *Estaba pintado de una rosa muy tenue.* ~A subtle FLAVOR of oranges. *El delicado sabor de una naranja.* ‖ **2.** Ingenious (remark, analysis). *Ingenioso, agudo.* ‖ **3.** [Irony, joke]. *Fino.* ~There was SUBTLE irony in his voice. *Lo dijo con fina ironía.* ‖ **4.** [Charm]. *Misterioso.* ‖ **5.** Crafty, cunning. *Astuto.* ~A SUBTLE mind. *Una mente astuta.* ‖ **6.** [Smile]. *Leve, ligero.* ‖ **7.** Not obvious, not easily noticeable. *Imperceptible.* ~His whole attitude has undergone a SUBTLE change. *Su actitud ha sufrido un completo aunque imperceptible cambio.* ‖ **8.** Tactful. *Discreto.* ~You could have been more SUBTLE. *Podrías haber sido más discreto.* ~A more SUBTLE approach is necessary. *Tienes que abordar el tema de una forma más discreta.* ‖ **9.** Perceptive, discriminating, keen, clever (mind, intellect, remark). *Perspicaz, agudo.* ‖ **10.** Insidious. *Insidioso.* ~A SUBTLE poison. *Un veneno insidioso.* ‖ **11.** Slight. *Leve.* ~There's a SUBTLE distinction between these two words. *Hay una leve diferencia entre estas dos palabras.* ⇨SÚTIL

SUBURB [SUBURBIOS]. n. Outskirt(s). *Barrio residencial, afueras, cercanías, alrededores.* ~A London SUBURB. *Un distrito en las afueras de Londres.* ~He lives in the SUBURBS. *Vive en las afueras.*

SUFFER. v. [Hunger]. *Padecer, pasar.* ~During the war years he SUFFERED great hunger. *Durante la guerra padeció mucha hambre.* ‖ **2.** Endure, bear, tolerate. *Aguantar, tolerar.* ~He doesn't SUFFER fools gladly. *No aguanta a los imbéciles.* ~I had to SUFFER her insults. *Tuve que soportar sus insultos.* ‖ **3.** LIT Permit. *Permitir, dejar.* ~She would not SUFFER him to come near. *No dejaba que se le acercara.* ~SUFFER the little children to come unto me. *Dejad que los niños se acerquen a mí.* ‖ **4.** Be affected, deteriorate. (I) [Health, eyesight]. *Resentirse,* (II) [Business, performance, relationship]. *Verse afectado, resentirse.* ~Sales have SUFFERED badly. *Las ventas se han visto afectadas seriamente.* ‖ **5.** Be afflicted. *Padecer.* ~He SUFFERS from asthma. *Padece de asma.* ⇨SUFRIR

SUFFOCATE. v. To choke, breathe with difficulty. *Asfixiar, ahogar.* ~Can you open a window? I'm SUFFOCATING. *¿Puedes abrir la ventana? Me estoy asfixiando.* ⇨SOFOCAR

SUFFOCATION. n. Choking. *Asfixia, ahogo.* ⇨SOFOCACIÓN

SUGGEST [SUGERIR]. v.
❶ PROPOSE, OFFER, SET FORTH. *Proponer.* ~I SUGGEST we leave at once. *Propongo que nos vayamos en seguida.* ~He SUGGESTED dinner the next evening. *Propuso que cenaramos juntos al día siguiente.* ~I SUGGESTED three alternatives. *Propuse tres posibilidades.* ~They have SUGGESTED him as president. *Lo han propuesto para presidente.* ❷ INDICATE, POINT TO. *Indicar, dar a entender.* This SUGGESTS that he came alone. *Esto hace pensar que vino solo.* ~It doesn't exactly SUGGEST a careful man. *No parece indicar un hombre prudente.* ~His reaction SUGGESTED a guilty conscience. *Su reacción daba a entender que se sentía culpable.* ~All the evidence SUGGESTS that he was involved. *Todas las pruebas indican que estaba involucrado.* ‖ **2.** Imply, hint. *Insinuar, hacer pensar, dar a entender.* ~Are you trying to SUGGEST that my son is a thief? *Insinua Ud. que mi hijo es un ladrón?* ~I'm not SUGGESTING that everyone in Britain is rich. *No*

quiero dar a entender (no digo que) toda la gente en Inglaterra sea rica. ‖ **3.** Evoke. *Evocar, hacer pensar en.* ~What does this poem SUGGEST to you? ~*¿En qué te hace pensar este poema?*

❸ TO BELIEVE, THINK, CONSIDER, SAY. *Ocurrir, decir, pensar.* ~Can you SUGGEST a possible source for this rumor? *¿Se le ocurre quien puede haber empezado este rumor?* ~I SUGGEST that he's lying. *Yo diría que está mintiendo.* ~No one is SUGGESTING (that) you stole the money. ~*Nadie está diciendo que robaste el dinero.* ~I SUGGEST to you that you're not telling the whole truth. *Hasta diría que no está diciendo toda la verdad.* Can you SUGGEST where we might meet? *¿Se te occure algún lugar donde encontrarnos.* ‖ **2.** Theorize, suppose. *Suponer, imaginarse.* This, I SUGGEST, is what happened. *Supongo que lo que pasó es lo siguiente.* ‖ **3.** •I SUGGEST that ... (in law speeches). *¿No es cierto que ...?*

❹ ADVISE, RECCOMMEND. *Aconsejar.* ~He SUGGESTED we (should) look for alternative accomodations. *Nos aconsejó que buscáramos otro alojamiento.*

❺ INSPIRE, PROMPT. *Dar la idea.* It was a magazine article that SUGGESTED the idea to me. *Fue un artículo en una revista que me dio la idea.* ~He told me a story which SUGGESTED a plot for a novel. *Me contó una historia que me dio la idea del argumento para una novela.*

SUGGESTION. *n.* [Proposal]. *Sugerencia.* ~I'm open to SUGGESTIONS. *Accepto sugerencias.* ~Have you any SUGGESTIONS for speeding up the process. *¿Se le ocurre algo para acelerar el proceso.?* ~It was your SUGGESTION to have a picnic. *Fuiste tú quien propuso ir de picnic.* ~I bought it at my wife's SUGGESTION. *Lo compré a instancias de mi mujer.* •To make a SUGGESTION. *Hacer una sugerencia.* •If I may make a SUGGESTION. *Si me permite proponer algo.* •My suggestion is that. *Propongo que.* ‖ **2.** [Insinuation]. *Insinuación.* ‖ **3.** Hint, slight trace. *Sombra, traza, pizca.* ~A dish with just a SUGGESTION of garlic. *Un plato con un poquetín de ajo, un plato con un leve dejo (saborcillo) a ajo.*

~With a SUGGESTION of irony in his voice. *Con un punto de ironía en la voz.* ~There was a SUGGESTION of a smile on his face. *Apenas esbozó una sonrisa.* ‖ **4.** Indication, evidence. *Indicio.* ~There's no SUGGESTION of corruption. *Nada indica que haya corrupción.* ~There is no SUGGESTION of any change in policy. *No hay ningún indicio de un cambio de política.* ~There was no SUGGESTION of foul-play. *No había indicios de que se hubiera cometido un crimen.* ‖ **5.** Hypnotic. *Sugestión.* ‖ **6.** Explanation, theory. *Teoría.* His SUGGESTION is the most plausible. *Su teoría es la más probable.* ‖ **7.** •Following your SUGGESTION. *Siguiendo sus indicaciones.* ‖ **8.** •I'm writing at the SUGGESTION of a friend of mine. *Le escribo siguiendo las indicaciones de un amigo mío.* ‖ **9.** •SUGGESTION box. *Buzón de sugerencias.* ⇨SUGESTIÓN.

SUGGESTIVE. *adj.* Indecent, risqué, off-color, offensive (remark). *Indecente, subido de tono.* ~Some of his lyrics are somewhat SUGGESTIVE. *La letra de algunas de sus canciones es algo subida de tono.* ~A magazine of smutty jokes and SUGGESTIVE pictures. *Una revista con chistes de mal gusto y fotos indecentes.* ‖ **2.** [Gesture, look]. *Provocativo, provocador.* ~A sly, SUGGESTIVE wink. *Un guiño malicioso y provocador.* ‖ **3.** Which stimulates thought (theory, commentary). *Que llama a la reflexión.* A great variety of SUGGESTIVE ideas. *Una gran variedad de ideas estimulantes.* ‖ **4.** •To be SUGGESTIVE of something. (I) *Parecer indicar algo.* ~The figures are SUGGESTIVE of an upturn in the economy. *Las cifras parecen indicar un repunte en la economía.* (II) Reminiscent. ~The design is SUGGESTIVE of a Roman villa. *El diseño hacer pensar (evoca) una villa romana.* ⇨SUGESTIVO

SUMMARY. *n.* Resumé. *Resumen.* News SUMMARY. *Resumen de las noticias.* ⇨SUMARIO

SUPPORT. *v.*

❶ HOLD UP. [Roof, structure]. *Sostener, apoyarse en, descansar en.* The beams SUPPORT the roof. *Las vigas sostienen el tejado.* ‖ **2.** To sustain or withstand (weight, pressure, strain, etc.). *Resistir, aguantar.*

~The chair couldn't SUPPORT his weight. *La silla no pudo resistir, aguantar su peso.* ~The bridge is not strong enough to SUPPORT so much weight. *Este puente no es suficiente fuerte para aguantar tanto peso.* || **3.** [Physical]. *Sostener.* Her legs can't SUPPORT the weight. *No le sostienen las piernas.*

❷ UPHOLD, BACK, BE IN FAVOR OF. Endorse, vote for (motion}. *Aprobar, votar en favor de.* ~Delegates voted to SUPPORT the resolution. *Los delegados votaron a favor de la resolución.* || **2.** Shore up (economy, finance). *Mantener, sostener.* ~A move to SUPPORT the dollar. *Una medida para mantener la cotización del dólar, para proteger el dólar.* || **3.** To agree with. *Apoyar, estar de acuerdo con.* Mary doesn't agree with me, but John SUPPORTS me. *María no esta de acuerdo conmigo, pero Juan me apoya.*

❸ ENCOURAGE, STAND BY. *Apoyar, respaldar.* ~We SUPPORT him whole-heartedly. *Lo apoyamos sin reserva.* || **2.** To sustain (a person, the mind, spirits, courage, etc.) under trial or affliction, comfort, strengthen. *Reconfortar, dar ánimo.* ~My wife SUPPORTED me during the entire ordeal. *Mi esposa me dió ánimo durante todo este difícil trance.* || **3.** Encourage. *Animar, alentar, ayudar.* ~My parents SUPPORTED me all through my studies. ~*Mis padres me animaron durante todos mis estudios.*

❹ CONFIRM, SUBSTANTIATE, CORRO-BORATE. [Theory]. *Sustentar, respaldar.* ~This SUPPORTS your theory. *Esto respalda su teoría.* || **2.** Corroborate, substantiate. *Confirmar, corroborar.* ~His alibi that he had been home all afternoon was SUPPORTED by his neighbors. *Todos los vecinos suyos atestiguaron que había estado en casa toda aquella tarde.*

❺ PROVIDE FOR. *Mantener.* ~He makes just enough to SUPPORT his family. *Apenas gana lo necesario para mantener a su familia.* ~She had to go to work to SUPPORT her parents. *Tuvo que ir a trabajar para mantener a sus padres.* || **2.** •To SUPPORT oneself. *Ganarse la vida.*

❻ TO PAY THE COST OF. Maintain,

sustain (financially). *Financiar.* ~The hospital is SUPPORTED entirely by private donations. *El hospital está completamente financiado por donaciones de particulares.* ~His campaign was SUPPORTED by private funds. *Su campaña electoral fue financiada por particulares.*

❼ SPORT. To be a fan of, back, encourage. *Seguir, ser hincha de, apoyar, animar.* ~Which team do you SUPPORT? *¿De qué equipo eres (hincha)?* ~They went along to SUPPORT their team. *Fueron a animar a su equipo.*

❽ MUSIC, CINEMA, THEATER. *Secundar, respaldar.* ~He's SUPPORTED by a splendid cast. *Lo secunda (respalda) un magnífico elenco de actores.* || **2.** •SUPPORTING role. *Un papel secundario.*

❾ VARIOUS. Tolerate, permit. *Tolerar, permitir.* ~The teacher told the student that he would not SUPPORT that kind of behavior. *El maestro les dijo a los estudiantes que no toleraría esta clase de conducta.* || **2.** To lean. *Apoyarse.* ~She had to SUPPORT herself on a chair. *Tuvo que apoyarse en un silla.* || **3.** Endure, bear. *Aguantar, tolerar.* ~She could not SUPPORT the heat any longer. *No pudo aguantar más el calor.* || **4.** To accompany. *Acompañar.* ~The mayor will attend the ceremony, SUPPORTED by a host of dignitaries. *El alcalde asistirá a la ceremonia, acompañado por un gran número de altos funcionarios.* ~The orchestral sound was needed to SUPPORT the voices. *Era necesaria la música de una orquesta para acompañar a los cantores.* || **5.** •To SUPPORT oneself. *Apoyarse en algo.* She held on to the door to SUPPORT herself. *Se apoyó en la puerta para no caer.* ⇨SOPORTAR

SUPPOSE. *v.* Believe, think. *Creer.* ~What do you SUPPOSE he'll do? *¿Tú qué crees que hará?* ~When do you SUPPOSE we can go? *¿Cuándo crees que nos podemos ir?* || **2.** (When making a suggestion or proposal). *What about if ...?* ~SUPPOSE we change the subject? *¿Qué tal si cambiáramos de tema?* ~SUPPOSE we leave now? *¿Y si nos fuéramos ya?* || **3.** [Obligation]. *Deber.* ~He's the one who's SUPPOSED to do it. *Es él quien debe* *hacerlo.* ~You're SUPPOSED to be in bed. *Deberías estar en la cama.* ~You're not SUPPOSED to eat those. *No deberías comer aquellos.* || **4.** Imagine. *Imaginar.* ~As you can SUPPOSE. *Como te puedes imaginar.* || **5.** •To be SUPPOSED to. (I) *To be expected to, to be allowed to.* ~Aren't you SUPPOSED to be at home? *¿No tendrías que estar en casa?* ~You're not SUPPOSED to tell anyone. *No se lo tienes que decir a nadie.* ~It's SUPPOSED to be kept in a cool place. *Hay que guardarlo en un lugar fresco.* ~You're not SUPPOSED to smoke in here. *No está permitido fumar aquí,* (II) [Indicating intention]. ~What's that SUPPOSED to mean? *Y que quieres decir con eso (si se puede saber)?* Where are we SUPPOSED to meet? *¿Dónde tenemos que encontrarnos?,* (III) indicating general opinion). *Dicen que ..., se considera.* ~It's SUPPOSED to be a very interesting book. *Dicen que es un libro muy interesante.* ~It's SUPPOSED to be the best restaurant in town. *Dicen que es el mejor restaurante de la ciudad.* ~This tower is *supposed* to be the highest in the world. *Se considera que esta torre es la más alta del mundo.* ⇨SUPONER

SUPPRESS. *v.* [Yawn]. *Ahogar.* || **2.** [Emotion]. *Contener.* ~She could barely SUPPRESS her delight. *Apenas podía contener su gran alegría.* || **3.** [Scandal]. *Disimular.* || **4.** [Newspaper]. *Retirar de la circulación.* || **5.** [Secret, news, facts, evidente, truth]. *Callar, no revelar, ocultar.* ~Attempts by the army to SUPPRESS documents related to the trial. *El intento por parte del ejército de ocultar unos documentos relacionados con el juicio.* A famous penal institution the name of which I prefer to suppress. *Una conocida penitenciaría cuyo nombre prefiero no mencionar.* || **6.** [Publication]. *Prohibir.* ~The government tried to SUPPRESS the book. *El gobierno intentó prohibir el libro.* || **7.** [Blood]. *Contener.* || **8.** [Passion]. *Dominar.* ~She could hardly SUPPRESS her anger. *Apenas podía dominar su ira.* || **9.** [Revolt, rebellion]. *Reprimir, sofocar.* ~The Hungarian revolt was SUPPRESSED by the Russian army. *La rebelión húngara fue sofocada por el ejército ruso.* ⇨SUPRIMIR

SUPPRESSION. *n.* [Of feelings, revolt]. *Represión.* || **2.** [Of fact, truth, evidence]. *Ocultación.* || **3.** [Of book]. *Prohibición.* || **4.** [Of passion]. *Dominio.* ⇨SUPRESIÓN

SUSCEPTIBLE. *adj.* [To illness]. *Propenso.* ~To be SUSCEPTIBLE to disease. *Ser propenso a enfermedades.* || **2.** [To beauty, flattery]. *Sensible.* ~SENSIBLE to beauty. *Sensible a la belleza.* || **3.** Impressionable. ~SUSCEPTIBLE to suggestion. *Sugestionable.* || **4.** Easily moved. *Impresionable.* ~A SUSCEPTIBLE young boy. *Un muchacho impresionable.* || **5.** [To women]. *Enamoradizo.* || **6.** SUSCEPTIBLE of. *Dar lugar a, prestarse a, estar expuesto a.* ~The style is very SUSCEPTIBLE to parody. *El estilo se presta a la parodia.* || **7.** Vulnerable. *Vulnerable, expuesto.* ⇨SUSCEPTIBLE

SUSPEND. *v.* [Pupil, student]. *Expulsar.* ~He was SUSPENDED for cheating. *Lo expulsaron por hacer trampas en el examen.* || **2.** Defer, hold over (decision). *Posponer.* || **3.** [Judgement]. *Reservar.* ~I'm SUSPENDING judgement on the book. *Reservo mi opinión sobre el libro.* || **4.** To hang. *Colgar.* ~The lights were SUSPENDED from the ceiling. *Las luces colgaban del techo.* || **5.** •Two year SUSPENDED sentence. *Libertad condicional de dos años.* ⇨SUSPENDER

SUSPENSION [SUSPENSIÓN]. *Adj.* Deferment. *Aplazamiento, postergación.* || **2.** [Employee, student]. *Expulsión.* || **3.** [Player]. *Sanción.*

SUSPICION [SOSPECHA]. *n.* Mistrust. *Recelo, desconfianza.* ~She looked at them with SUSPICION. *Los miraba con desconfianza (recelo).* || **2.** Doubt. *Duda.* ~I have my SUSPICIONS about his loyalty. *Dudo de su lealtad.* || **3.** Trace, hint. *Pizca, poco, atisbo (of a smile).* ~A SUSPICION of garlic. *Una pizca de ajo.* ~A SUSPICION of a smile. *Un atisbo de sonrisa.* ~He hadn't a SUSPICION of the truth. *No tenía la más ligera idea de la verdad.* || **4.** Aftertaste. *Dejo.* ~There's a SUSPICION of corruption about it. *Eso tiene un dejo de corrupción, eso huele un poquito a corrupción.*

SUSPICIOUS [SOSPECHOSO]. *adj.* Mistrustful. *Suspicaz, desconfiado, receloso.* || **2.** •To be SUSPICIOUS of someone. *Desconfiar de uno.* ~She was always SUSPICIOUS of his intentions. *Siempre desconfió de sus intenciones.* ~I can't help feeling SUSPICIOUS about them. *No puedo menos que desconfiar de ellos.*

SUSTAIN [SOSTENER]. *v.* Nourish, maintain, support (body, life). *Sustentar, preservar.* || ~SUSTAINING himself with lemon juice and vegetables. *Sustentándose con jugo de limón y verduras.* **2.** Confirm, uphold. (objections). *Admitir.* ~Objection SUSTAINED. *Se admite la protesta.* || **3.** To suffer (damage, loss, defeat, injury). *Sufrir.* ~They SUSTAINED minor injuries. *Sufrieron heridas leves.* || **4.** [Wound]. *Recibir.* ~He SUSTAINED a serious wound in the battle. *Recibió una grave herida en la batalla.* || **5.** Keep up, prolong (pretense, conversation). *Mantener, continuar.* ~She found it impossible to SUSTAIN the role of a submissive housewife. *Le resultó imposible continuar en el papel de la esposa sumisa.* ~A work which SUSTAINS the reader's attention. *Una obra que mantiene el interés del lector.* || **6.** [Charge, theory, claim]. *Confirmar, corroborar,* respaldar, apoyar. ~There was no proof to SUSTAIN his view. *No había prueba para respaldar su punto de vista.* || **7.** [Hope]. *Mantener.* || **8.** To endure. *Soportar, aguantar.* ~I couldn't SUSTAIN such an act. *No podía aguantar tal cosa.* ~A man bravely SUSTAINING the burden of fear. *Un hombre soportando con valor el oneroso peso del miedo que pesaba sobre él.* ~He wondered if he could ever again SUSTAIN a year's teaching. *Se preguntó si alguna vez podría volver a aguantar enseñar todo el año.*

SYMPATHIZE. *v.* Show pity, compassion; feel sorry for. *Compadecerse.* ~I SYMPATHIZE with him but there's nothing I can do. *Lo compadezco pero no puedo hacer nada.* ~I SYMPATHIZE with the poor. *Compadezco a los pobres.* || **2.** Express condolences. *Dar el pésame.* || **3.** Understand. *Comprender, entender.* ~I SYMPATHIZE with your point of view. *Comprendo tu punto de vista.* || **4.** Support. *Apoyar, mostrarse favorable a.* Those who SYMPATHIZE with our demands.

Los que apoyan nuestras reclamaciones. ~I fully SYMPATHIZE, but this cannot go on. *Lo entiendo perfectamente pero esto no puede continuar.* ⇨SIMPATIZAR

SYMPATHY. *n.* Pity, compassion. *Compasión, lástima.* ~She has my deepest SYMPATHY. *La compadezco.* ~You won't get any SYMPATHY from him. *El no mostrará ninguna compasión por tí.* ~I have no SYMPATHY for drunks. *No tengo compasión por los borrachos.* || **2.** Condolences. *Condolencia, pésame.* ~Our deepest SYMPATHIES. *Nuestro más sentido pésame, nuestras más sinceras condolencias.* || **3.** Understanding. *Comprensión.* ~SYMPATHY for someone's problems. *Comprensión de los problemas de alguien.* ~SYMPATHY between two people. *Comprensión entre dos personas.* || **4.** *Acuerdo, apoyo.* Support, approval. ~I was out of SYMPATHY with the majority. *No estaba de acuerdo con la mayoría.* ~To strike in SYMPATHY. *Declararse en huelga por solidaridad.* ⇨SIMPATÍA

SYNDICATE. *n.* Group, cartel. *Agrupación.* ~A SYNDICATE of leading businessmen. *Una importante agrupación de hombres de negocio.* ~A crime SYNDICATE. *Una organización mafiosa.* || **2.** News agency. *Agencia de prensa.* || **3.** Chain of newspapers. *Cadena de periódicos.* ⇨SINDICATO

SYSTEM [SISTEMA]. *n.*

❶ BODY. *Cuerpo, organismo.* ~My SYSTEM can't cope with that much food. *Mi cuerpo (organismo) no puede con tanta comida.* || **2.** •To get something out of one's SYSTEM (physically). *Eliminar.* ~It will help get the toxins out of your SYSTEM. *Te va a ayudar a eliminar las toxinas.* || **3.** •To get something out of one's SYSTEM (figuratively). (I) *Desahogarse.* ~I had to say it; I had to get it out of my SYSTEM. *Se lo tuve que decir; tenía que desahogarme,* (II) *Olvidar.* ~It took years to get her out of my SYSTEM. *Me llevó años sacármela de la cabeza (olvidarla),* (III) *Cumplir un deseo.* ~I've always wanted to go Disneyland; now I finally got it out of my SYSTEM. *Siempre quise visitar Disneylandia; finalmente se ha hecho realidad.* || **4.** •Digestive SYSTEM. *El aparato digestivo.* || **5.** •It was a shock to her SYSTEM. *Fue un* *golpe muy duro para ella.*

❷ NETWORK. *Red, cadena.* ~The railway SYSTEM. *La red de ferrocarriles.* ~Parliament has voted the necessary funds for the development of the RAILWAY system. *El Parlamento ha aprobado los créditos necesarios para la ampliación de los ferrocarriles (Prats).* ~In this town the outline of the road SYSTEM is still visible. *En este pueblo todavía se puede advertir las huellas de la antigua red de carreteras.* ~There is a complex SYSTEM of canals connecting Texas ports. *Una compleja red de canales enlazan los puertos del estado de Tejas.*

❸ DEVICE. *Diapositivo, mecanismo.* || **2.** Motor. *Motor.* ~Jet engine SYSTEM. *Motor a reacción.* || **3.** [Audio]. *Equipo (de sonido).* ~They stole the stereo SYSTEM and the television set. *Robaron el equipo de estéreo y el televisor.* || **4.** [Electric, heating]. *Instalación.* ~The electric SYSTEM of a car. *La instalación eléctrica de un coche.*

❹ VARIOUS. Establishment, status quo, regime. *Régimen, orden (estructura, organización) social.* || **2.** Method. *Procedimiento, técnica.* This SYSTEM has proven successful for a number of years. *Por muchos anós este método ha dado buenos resultados.* || **3.** Order. *Organización.* ~There has to be some sort of SYSTEM around here so we can function. *Necesitamos alguna organización en este lugar, sino no podemos trabajar.* || **4.** Service. *Servicio.* ~In Greece the postal SYSTEM has been improved in recent years. *En Grecia, el servicio de correos ha mejorado en los últimos años.* || **5.** Company, enterprise, firm. *Empresa, sociedad, compañía.* ~Columbia Broadcasting SYSTEM. *Sociedad de Radiofusión «Columbia» (Prats).* || **6.** [In gambling]. *Fórmula.* || **7.** •Feudal SYSTEM. *Régimen feudal.*

T

TABLET. *n.* [Of stone]. *Lápida.* ‖ **2.** [Of soap]. *Pastilla.* ‖ **3.** [Of writing paper]. *Bloc.* ‖ **4.** Plaque. *Placa.* ⇨TABLETA

TANK [TANQUE]. *n.* [On trucks, rail wagons]. *Cisterna.* ‖ **2.** [Fermentation tanks]. *Cubas.* ‖ **3.** [Developing tank]. *Cubeta.* ‖ **4.** [Fish tank]. *Pecera.* ‖ **5.** [Fuel tank]. *Depósito.* ~To fill up the TANK. *Llenar el depósito.*

TARIFF. *n.* Tax. *Arancel.* ‖ **2.** Price list (in a hotel, bar). *Lista de precio.* ⇨TARIFA

TEMPORARY [TEMPORARIO]. *adj.* Short-term. *Provisional.* ~As a TEMPORARY measure. *Como medida provisional.* ~These arrangements are purely TEMPORARY. *Este arreglo es provisional, nada más.* ‖ **2.** [Setback, improvement]. *Momentáneo, pasajero.* ‖ **3.** [Teacher]. *Suplente.* ‖ **4.** [Job, work, worker]. *Eventual.* A TEMPORARY secretary. *Una secretaria eventual.*

TENTATIVE [TENTATIVO]. *adj.* Not definite (plan, arrangement). *De prueba, provisional, provisorio.* ~A TENTATIVE arrangement. *Un arreglo provisional.* ‖ **2.** Hesitant. *Indecisivo.* ‖ **3.** [Gesture]. *Vacilante, de indecisión.*

TERM . *n.*
❶ PERIOD OF TIME. *Período, duración.* A five-year TERM. *Un período de cinco años.* ~He was condemned to a long TERM in prison. *Le condenaron a muchos años de cárcel, le impusieron una pena muy larga.* ‖ **2.** [Politics]. *Mandato.* ~The President's first TERM in office. *El primer mandato del presidente.* ‖ **3.** [Education]. *Trimestre.* ~The academic year has three TERMS. *El año escolar tiene tres trimestres.* ‖ **4.** [Jury]. *Período de sesiones.* ‖ **5.** •In the long/short TERM. *A largo/corto plazo.* ‖ **6.**

•To come to its TERMS. *Terminar.* ‖ **7.** •TERM loan. *Préstamo a plazo fijo.*
❷ CONDITIONS. *Condiciones.* ~According to the TERMS of the contract. *Según las condiciones del contrato.* ~Not on any TERMS. *Bajo ningún concepto.* ~What are your TERMS. *¿Cuáles son sus condiciones?* ~You may name your own TERMS. *Puede estipular las condiciones que quiera.* ~We offer easy TERMS. *Ofrecemos facilidades de pago.* ‖ **2.** •TERMS of payment. *Condiciones de pago.* •To dictate TERMS. *Imponer condiciones.* ‖ **3.** •TERMS of sales. *Condiciones de venta.* ‖ **4.** •TERMS of surrender. *Capitulaciones, condiciones de la rendición.* ‖ **5.** •To accept somebody on his own TERMS. *Acceptar a uno como es.* ‖ **6.** •To come to TERMS with a situation. *Adaptarse a (conformarse con) una situación.*
❸ RELATIONSHIP. *Relaciones.* •To be on familiar TERMS with. *Tener confianza con uno.* ‖ **2.** •To be on good/bad TERMS. *Mantener buenas/malas relaciones, llevarse bien/mal con uno.* ‖ **3.** •We're on the best of TERMS. *Somos muy amigos.* ‖ **4.** We're not on speaking TERMS. *No nos hablamos.*
❹ WORD, EXPRESSION. Word. *Palabra.* To choose one's TERMS carefully. *Elegir sus palabras.* ~She speaks about him in glowing TERMS. *Habla de él con gran admiración.* ~I told him in no uncertain TERMS. *Se lo dije claramente (bien a las claras).* ~He described it in graphic TERMS. *Lo describió en forma muy gráfica.* ‖ **2.** •A TERM of abuse. *Un insulto.* ‖ **3.** •A TERM of endearment. *Un apelativo cariñoso.* ‖ **4.** •In simple TERMS. *En lenguaje sencillo.* ‖ **5.** •They protested in the strongest possible TERMS. *Protestaron en forma sumamente enérgica.*

❺ WAY OF LOOKING AT THINGS. *En cuanto a, desde el punto de vista de, a nivel de.* ~The enormous cost of war, in human TERMS. *El enorme costo de la guerra desde el punto de vista humano.* ‖ 2. •In TERMS of. (I) In regards to. *En cuanto a.* ~In TERMS of money we're doing well. *Por lo que se refiere a (en cuanto a) la producción vamos bien,* (II) with a view to. ~He was talking in TERMS of buying it. *Hablaba de la posibilidad de comprarlo.* (III) From the point of view of. He sees everything in TERMS of profit. *Lo enfoca todo en función del beneficio que pueda producir.* ~He sees novels in TERMS of sociology. *Considera la novela en su función sociológica.* ~In international TERMS. *A nivel internacional.*
❻ VARIOUS. Price. *Precio, tarifa.* ~Our TERMS for full board. *Nuestro precio (tarifa) para pensión completa.* ~We bought it on advantageous TERMS. *Lo compramos a buen precio.* ‖ 2. •To come to TERMS with (somebody). *Llegar a un acuerdo con alguien.* ‖ 3. •To come to TERMS with (something). *Aceptar algo.* ~It's difficult to come to TERMS with being unemployed. *No es fácil hacerse a la idea de que uno no tenga trabajo, no es fácil acostumbrarse a no tener trabajo.* ⇨TÉRMINO

TIME [TIEMPO]. *n.*
❶ TIME OF DAY, TIME TO DO SOMETHING. *Hora.* What TIME is it? *¿Qué hora es?* ~She usually calls about breakfast TIME. *Suele llamar a la hora del desayuno.* ~At dinner TIME. *A la hora de la cena.* ~It was TIME for tea. *Era la hora del té.* ~We have to arrange a TIME for next meeting. *Tenemos que fijar la hora y fecha para la próxima reunión.* ~It's TIME to get up! *¡Es hora de levantarse!* ~Call me any TIME between nine and eleven. *Llámame a cualquier hora entre las nueve y las once.* ‖ 2. ~Greenwhich Mean TIME. *La hora Greenwhich.* ‖ 3. •In good TIME. *Con anticipación, temprano, puntualmente.* ‖ 4. •It's TIME I left. *Es hora de que me vaya.* ‖ 5. •TIME's up. *Ya es la hora.* ‖ 6. ~A watch that keeps good TIME. *Un reloj exacto.* ‖ 7. •TIME bomb.

Bomba de relojería. ‖ 8. •TIME switch. *Interruptor electrónico automático.* ‖ 9. •TIME clock. *Reloj registrador.* ‖ 10. To keep good TIME. *Estar siempre en hora.* The watch keeps good TIME. *Este reloj siempre está en hora.* ‖ 11. •Departure TIME. *Hora de salida.* ‖ 12. Estimated TIME of arrival. *Hora aproximada de llegada.* ‖ 13. •Against TIME. ~*Carrera contra el reloj.* ~To work against TIME. *Trabajar contra reloj.* ‖ 14. Not give someone the TIME of day. *No darle a alguien ni la hora.* ‖ 15. To be behind. *Llevar atraso.* ~We are an hour behind TIME. *Llevamos una hora de retraso.*
❷ OCCASION, INSTANCE, OCCURRENCE (with *first, next, last, many, once, another, every, one more,* etc.). *Vez, ocasión, oportunidad.* ~That was the last TIME I saw him. *Esa fue la última vez que lo vi.* ~I've told him a thousand TIMES. *Se lo he dicho mil veces.* ~At TIMES I feel like leaving him. *Algunas veces me dan las ganas de dejarlo.* ~Next TIME you can do it. *La próxima vez, lo haces tú.* ~I've been there many TIMES. *He estado allí en varias ocasiones.* ‖ 2. •Once upon a TIME. *Érase una vez.* ‖ 3. •TIME and TIME again, time after time. *Una y otra vez.* ‖ 4. •From TIME to TIME. *De vez en cuando.* ‖ 5. •(At) any TIME (you like). *Cuando quieras.* ‖ 6. •If I said this once I said it a hundred TIMES. *Ya lo debo de haber dicho mil veces.* ‖ 7. •Nine TIMES out of ten. *En el noventa por ciento de los casos, la gran mayoría de las veces.* ‖ 8. Third TIME is a charm! *¡La tercera es la vencida!* ‖ 9. •Better luck next TIME. *A ver si la próxima vez tienes más suerte.* ‖ 10. •Four TIME running. *Cuatro veces seguidas (consecutivas).* ‖ 11. •Every TIME (whenever). *Cada vez.* ~Every TIME we have a picnic it rains. *Cada vez que organizamos un picnic, llueve.*
❸ MOMENT, POINT IN TIME. *Momento.* ~He may turn up at any TIME. *Puede llegar en cualquier momento.* ~I was away at that TIME. *Estaba ausente en aquel momento.* ~Now is the TIME to ... *Ahora es el momento de ...* ~Now is a good TIME to tell him. *Ahora es el momento oportuno para decírselo.*

~There comes a TIME when nothing else can be done. *Llega un momento que no se puede hacer nada.* ~Have I called at an awkward TIME? *¿Llamo en mal momento?* ‖ **2.** Season, period. *Temporada, estación.* ~It will soon be strawberry TIME. *Pronto será la temporada de las fresas.* ~Spring is the nicest TIME of the year. *La primavera es la estación más agradable del año.* ~At his TIME in life. *Con los años que tiene.* ‖ **3.** •At the TIME of. *Cuando.* ~At the TIME of his death. *Cuando murió.* ‖ **4.** •By the TIME. *Cuando.* ~By the TIME the waiter brought the coffee she had fallen asleep. *Cuando el mozo sirvió el café ella se había dormido.* ~It'll be dark by the TIME we get there. *Cuando lleguemos ya estará oscuro.* ~By that TIME we were really worried. *Para entonces ye estábamos preocupadísimos.* ~They should have been back by this TIME. *Ya deberían estar de vuelta.* ‖ **5.** •At one TIME. *En cierto momento, habia momentos en que ...* ‖ **6.** •At this TIME of. [Year] *En esta época del año,* [Night] *A estas horas de la noche,* [Month] *A esta altura del mes.* ~I never have much money lef at this TIME of the month. *A esa altura del mes no me suele quedar mucho dinero.* ‖ **7.** •At the present TIME. *Actualmente, en la actualidad, en este momento.* ‖ **8.** •At no TIME. *Nunca, en ningún momento.* ~At no TIME was that my intention. *En ningún momento (nunca) fue ésa mi intención.* ‖ **9.** •At all TIMES. *Siempre.* ~It should be kept closed at all TIMES. *Debe mantenerse siempre cerrado.* ~At all TIMES of the day and night. *Las veinticuatro horas del día.* ~At all TIMES of the year. *Todo el año.* ‖ **10.** •At the TIME. *En aquel entonces (momento).* ~Who was president at the TIME? *¿Quién era presidente en aquel entonces?* ~He said nothing about it at the TIME. *En aquel momento no dijo nada al respecto.* ‖ **11.** •This TIME (yesterday). *Ayer a estas horas,* [*Next year*] *El año que viene para estas fechas.* ‖ **12.** •From that TIME on. *A partir de entonces, desde entonces.* ‖ **13.** •To be a good/bad TIME. *Ser un buen/mal*

momento. ‖ **14.** To be about TIME (for someone to do something). *Ser hora.* ~It's about TIME you learn some manners. *Ya es hora que aprendas modales.* ~It's high TIME somebody did something. *Ya es hora de que alguien haga algo.* ‖ **15.** •The TIME has come. *Ha llegado el momento.* ~The TIME has come for us to make a decision. *Ha llegado el momento de que tengamos que tomar una decisión.* ‖ **16.** •It CAME time when ... *Llegó el momento en que ...* ‖ **17.** •There's a TIME and place for everything. *Hay un momento y un lugar para todo.* ‖ **18.** •To be the TIME to. *Ser el momento de.* ~This is not the TIME to complain. *Este no es el momento para quejarse.* ‖ **19.** •Until such TIME. *Hasta que.* ~No decision can be taken until such TIME as we've seen the report. *No se puede tomar una decisión hasta que (no) hayamos visto el informe.* ‖ **20.** •To be the TIME (to do something). *Ser el momento de hacer algo.* ~Now is the TIME to buy a house. *Este es el momento (indicado) para comprar una casa.* ‖ **21.** •To be the best TIME. *Ser el momento más indicado.* ~This is not the best TIME to approach him. *Éste no es el momento más indicado para hablarle.* ‖ **22.** •My TIME has come. *Ha llegado mi hora.* ‖ **23.** •To bid one's TIME. *Esperar el momento oportuno.* ‖ **24.** Wrong time. *Mal momento.* ~He came at the wrong TIME. *Llegó en un mal momento.*

❹ WITH NUMBERS (in multiplications and comparisons). [Multiplication]. *Por, multiplicado por.* ~Three TIMES four is twelve. *Tres (multiplicado) por cuatro es igual a doce.* ‖ **2.** [Comparison]. *Vez.* ~Their garden is three TIME bigger than ours. *Su jardín es tres veces más grande que el nuestro.* ~She earns five TIMES as much as I do. *Gana cinco veces más que yo.*

❺ EXPERIENCE. ~To have a good/bad TIME. *Pasarlo bien/mal.* ~We had a marvelous TIME. *Lo pasamos en grande.* ~We had a lovely time. *Lo pasamos la mar de bien (lo más bien) .* ~A good TIME was had by all. *Todo el mundo se divirtió de lo lindo.* ~She's out for a good TIME. *Se propone divertirse*.|| **2.** •Thank you for a lovely TIME (set phrase). *Gracias por todo, lo hemos pasado estupendamente.* || **3.** ~To give someone a good TIME. *Hacer que uno se divierta.* || **4.** •Bad TIMES. *Malos momentos (ratos).* ~It's best to forget the bad TIMES and remember the good ones. *Lo mejor es olvidarse de los malos momentos (ratos) y recordar los buenos.* || **5.** •To have a difficult TIME (with someone). *Tener problemas con.* ~He's having a difficult TIME with his son. *Tiene problemas con su hijo.* || **6.** •Don't give me a hard TIME. *No me mortifiques.* || **7.** •Looking for a good TIME? (said by a prostitute). *¿Quieres pasarlo bien?*

❻ PERIOD, AGE, ERA. *Época, tiempos.* ~In our TIME. *En los tiempos en que vivimos.* ~In TIMES to come. *En el futuro.* ~A tradition which goes back to Medieval TIMES. *Una tradición que se remonta a la época medieval.* ~These are hard TIMES. *Estos son tiempos difíciles.* ~Then they fell on hard TIMES. *Entonces les tocó la época de las vacas flacas.* || **2.** In former TIMES. *Antiguamente.* || **3.** •The life and TIMES of Jane Austen. *Vida y época de Jane Austen.* || **4.** •To be ahead of one's TIME. *Adelantarse a su época.* || **5.** •To be behind the TIMES. [Ideas]. *Ser anticuado, ser chapado a la antigua.* [Not well informed] *Estar atrasado de noticias.* || **6.** •To keep up with the TIMES. *Mantenerse al día.* || **7.** [In respect to a person's life] That was before my TIME. *Eso fue antes de que naciera (empezara a trabajar aquí, etc.).* It won't happen in our TIME. *No viviremos para verlo.* ~I've seen some funny things in my TIME but ... *He visto cosas raras en mi vida pero ...* ~She was a great athlete in her TIME. *Fue una gran atleta en su época.*

❼ WITH RESPECT TO WORK. *Hora, jornada, sueldo.* || **2.** •On company TIME. *En horas de trabajo.* ~You shouldn't be doing this on company TIME. *No deberías hacer eso en horas de trabajo.* || **3.** •In one's own TIME. *Fuera de horas de trabajo, en tu tiempo libre.* || **4.** •To be on short TIME. *Estar trabajando una jornada redu-*

cida. || **5.** •To take (have) TIME off. *Tomarse tiempo libre.* || **6.** •We get TIME and a half. *Nos pagan hora y media de sueldo por cada hora de trabajo.* || **7.** •To pay double TIME. *Pagar doble sueldo.* ~On Sundays they pay double TIME. *Los domingos pagan doble (sueldo).* || **8.** •In one's spare TIME. *En el tiempo libre.*

❽ MUSIC. [Music]. *Compás.* To clap in TIME to the music. *Batir palmas al compás con la música.* || **2.** •Out of TIME. *Fuera de compás, descompasado.* || **3.** •To beat/keep TIME. *Marcar/seguir el compás.* || **4.** •They marched past in slow/quick/double TIME. *Pasaron marchando a paso lento/rápido/redoblado.* || **5.** •In double-quick TIME. *En un periquete, en un santiamén.* || **6.** •To mark TIME. [March on the spot] *Marcar el paso.* [Make no progress] *Hacer tiempo.* || **7.** •TIME signature. *Llave de tiempo.*

❾ VARIOUS. [For race]. Marca. ~What is your fastest TIME over 400 mm? *¿Cuál es tu marca en los 400 metros?* || **2.** Limit. *Plazo.* ~He paid within the required TIME. *Pagó la cuenta dentro del plazo fijado.*

❿ PHRASES.

•A SHORT TIME AFTER. *Al rato.* ~He woke up a short TIME after going to sleep. *Se despertó al rato de haberse dormido.*

•AHEAD/BEHIND TIME. *Adelantado/atrasado.* ~We're behind TIME on our project. *Vamos atrasados con el proyecto.*

•ALL IN GOOD TIME. *Despacio, sin prisa, cuando está listo uno, cuando le parece a uno.* ~She will make up her mind all in good TIME. *Decidirá cuando esté lista, decidirá cuando le parezca.*

•ALL THE TIME [Constantly] *Constantemente,* [from the beginning] *desde el principio.* ~I knew it all the TIME. *Lo supe desde el principio (desde el primer momento).*

•ANY TIME. (I) [By far]. *Toda la vida.* ~I rather work for John any TIME. *Prefiero trabajar para Juan toda la vida,* (II) [Whenever you're ready]. *Cuando quieras,* (III) [Don't mention it]. Thank you for your help. –Any TIME~. *Gracias por su ayuda.*

–*¡A sus órdenes, encantado!*

•AT A GIVEN TIME. *En un momento dado (determinado).*

•AT A TIME. (I) *A la vez.* ~I can only concentrate on one thing at a TIME. *Solo me puedo concentrar en una cosa a la vez.* ~He works at six places at a TIME. *Trabaja en seis sitios a la vez.* (II) ~We'll interview them four at a TIME. *Los entrevistaremos de cuatro en cuatro.* (III) ~She disappears for months at a TIME. *Desaparece y no se la ve por meses enteros.* ~He'd sit and stare into space hours at a TIME. *Se quedaba horas enteras (horas y horas) mirando al vacío.*

•AT ONE TIME. *En otros tiempos.*

•AT SOME TIME or another. *En un momento u otro.*

•AT THE BEST OF TIMES. *En el mejor de los casos.*

•AT THE SAME TIME. *A la vez.* They were all talking at the same TIME. *Todos hablaban a la vez.*

•AT THE TIME (OF his death). *Cuando (murió).*

•BETWEEN TIMES. *Entre una cosa y otra.*

•BY THAT TIME. *Para entonces.* ~By that TIME he had already gone. *Para entonces ya se había ido.*

•BY THE TIME THAT. *Cuando.* By the TIME that I got there it was over. *Cuando llegué ya se había acabado.*

•EVERY TIME. (I) *Cada vez.* ~Every TIME he comes we fight. *Cada vez que viene nos peleamos.* (II) ~Give me whisky every TIME. *Para mí, wisky, toda la vida.*

•FOR ALL TIME. *Para siempre.*

•FOR SOME TIME. ~He won't be here for some TIME yet. *Va a tardar en llegar.*

•FOR THE TIME BEING. *Por el momento, de momento, por ahora.*

•IN NO TIME (at all). *En un abrir y cerrar de ojos.* ~They arrived in next to no TIME. *Llegaron prácticamente en seguida, llegaron en menos de lo que canta un gallo.*

•IN THE NICK OF TIME. *En el momento preciso (oportuno).*

•IN THREE WEEKS' TIME. *Dentro de tres semanas.*

•IN TIME(s) TO COME. *En el futuro.*

•IT's ABOUT TIME. *Ya es hora.* ~It's about TIME you wrote to your mother. *Ya es hora que le escribas a tu madre.*

•NEAR HER TIME (a pregnant woman). *A punto de dar a luz.*

•OF YOUR TIME. Could I have five minutes of your TIME? *¿Podría concederme cinco minutos.*

•ON TIME. ~The buses hardly ever run on TIME. *Los autobuses casi nunca pasan a su hora (puntualmente).* ~She's never on TIME. *Nunca llega a tiempo, siempre llega tarde.*

•ONE AT A TIME. *Uno por uno, de a uno.*

•ONE STEP AT A TIME. *Paso a paso.* ~Take it one step at a TIME. *Hazlo paso a paso.*

•SOME TIME LATER. *Al rato.* Some TIME later I saw them leave. *Al rato los vi salir.*

•TIME AFTER TIME. *Una y otra vez.*

•TO BE BEHIND THE TIMES. *Tener ideas anticuadas.*

•TO BUY/SELL TIME (Radio, TV, cine). *Comprar/vender espacio.*

•TO BUY ON TIME. *Comprar a plazos.*

•TO DIE BEFORE ONE'S TIME. *Morir prematuramente.*

•TO DO TIME. *Cumplir una condena.*

•TO HAVE NO TIME (for something). *No gustarle (interesarle) a uno algo.* I have no TIME for sports. *No me gustan (interesan) los deportes.* ~She's got no TIME for traditional medicine. *No le tiene fe a la medicina natural.*

•TO HAVE TIME/NO TIME (for someone). *Caerle bien a uno una persona/No aguantar a uno.* ~I have TIME for you, baby. *Me caes muy bien, muchacha.* ~I have no TIME for people like you. *No aguanto (soporto) a gente como tú.*

•TO LOOSE NO TIME IN. *No tardar en.* ~She lost no TIME in replying. *Su repuesta no se hizo esperar.*

•TO MAKE TIME. *Darse prisa, apresurarse.*

•TO PASS THE TIME OF DAY (with someone).

No saludarlo a alguien. ~Now she doesn't even pass the TIME of day with me. *Ahora ni siquiera me saluda.* ~We just pass the TIME of day when we meet. *Cuando nos vemos, nos saludamos ¿qué tal? y nada más.*

•To SERVE ONE'S TIME. *Servir de aprendiz.*

•To SERVE TIME. He served his TIME in the Navy. *Hizo el servicio en la Marina.*

•To TAKE ALL ONE'S TIME. *Costarle trabajo (hacer algo).* It will take all your TIME to ... *Te costará trabajo ...* ~It took me all my TIME to understand what he was saying. *Me costó mucho (trabajo) entender lo que decía.*

•To TAKE ONE'S TIME. *Hacer las cosas con calma, ir despacio, no darse prisa.* ~I like to take my TIME over breakfast. *Me gusta desayunar con calma.* ~He certainly took his TIME answering! *¡No se apresuró mucho en contestarte que digamos!* ~You took your TIME! I've been waiting for half an hour. *¡Cómo has tardado! Hace media hora que te estoy esperando.*

•To TAKE ONE'S TIME (over something). *Hacer algo con calma.*

•WHEN MY TIME COMES. *Cuando llegue mi hora.*

•To TAKE TIME IN. *Tardar en.* ~What's the cooking TIME for an egg? *¿Cuanto tarda un huevo en cocerse?*

TOPIC. *n.* Theme, subject, point. *Tema, asunto.* The environment is a popular TOPIC these days. *El ambiente es un tema muy común en la actualidad.* ⇨TÓPICO

TRAIN [ENTRENAR]. *v.* Teach. *Formar, capacitar, preparar.* || **2.** To housebreak. *Enseñar, educar.* ~You've TRAINED your dog very well. *Tiene el perro muy bien enseñado.* || **3.** To teach (an animal to do tricks). *Amaestrar, adiestrar.* These dogs are TRAINED to detect explosives. *Adiestran a estos perros en encontrar explosivos.* || **4.** [Voice]. *Educar.* || **5.** [Soldier]. *Adiestrar.* || **6.** [Child]. *Enseñar.* || **7.** Accustom. *Acostumbrar, habituar.* || **8.** [In new skills]. (employee, worker). *Capacitar.* ~They're being TRAINED to use the machine. *Los*

están capacitando en el uso de la máquina. || **9.** [Teacher]. *Formar.* || **10.** Study. *Estudiar.* ~He was TRAINED as a painter. *Estudió pintura.* ~She's TRAINING to be a nurse. *Estudia enfermería.* || **11.** To aim. *Enfocar (camera), apuntar (gun).* ~She had her sights TRAINED on stardom from the first. *Ha tenido las miras puestas en el estrellato desde el principio.* ~He kept the pistol TRAINED at me all the time. *Me estuvo apuntando con la pistola todo el tiempo.* ~Last week all eyes were TRAINED on Geneva. *La semana pasada todos los ojos estuvieron puestos en Ginebra.* || **12.** [Horse]. *Domar.* || **13.** [Military]. *Instruir.* || **14.** •To TRAIN oneself in. *Ejercitarse en.*

TRANCE. *n.* Hypnotic sleep. *Estado hipnótico.* || **2.** FIG Reverie, transport. *Arrobamiento, éxtasis, rapto.* ⇨TRANCE

TRANSFER [TRANFERIR]. *v.* Change. *Cambiar.* ~She TRANSFERRED schools when she was twelve. *Se cambió de colegio cuando tenía doce años.* || **2.** [Call]. *Pasar, comunicar.* ~Can you TRANSFER me to Sales. *¿Me puede comunicar con el departamento de ventas?* || **3.** [Design]. *Calcar.* || **4.** [Football]. *Traspasar.* || **5.** [Funds]. *Girar.* || **6.** [Object]. *Pasar.* ~TRANSFER the meat to a serving dish. *Pase la carne a una fuente.* || **7.** [Prisoner]. *Trasladar.* They TRANSFERRED the prisoner to another cell. *Trasladaron al preso a otra celda.* || **8.** [Property, rights]. *Traspasar.* ~He TRANSFERRED ownership of the firm to his daughter. *Traspasó la compañia a su hija.* || **9.** [Rail]. *Transbordar, trasbordar, hacer transbordo.* ~You have to TRANSFER at Chicago. *~Tiene que hacer transbordo en Chicago.* || **10.** [To new post, place]. *Trasladar.* ~The firm is TRANSFERRING to Quito. *La compañia se traslada a Quito.* || **11.** •A TRANSFERRED charge call. *Una conferencia a cobro revertido.*

TRANSPORTATION [TRANSPORTACIÓN]. *n.* Transit. *Transporte.* ~The TRANSPORTATION system. *El sistema de transportes.*

TREATMENT [TRATAMIENTO]. *n.* [Person]. *Trato.* ~Our TREATMENT of foreigners. *El*

trato que damos a los extranjeros. ~The TREATMENT they received at the hands of the guards. *El trato que recibieron por parte de los guardias.* ~What have I done to deserve such TREATMENT? *¿Qué he hecho yo para merecer ese trato.* ~His TREATMENT of his friend. *La forma de portarse con los amigos.* ~His TREATMENT of his parents. *Su conducta con sus padres.* || **2.** Interpretation. *Interpretación.* ~The orquestra's TREATMENT of Bach. *La interpretación de Bach por la orquesta.* || **3.** Adaptation. *Adaptación.* ~The director's TREATMENT of the script. *La adaptación del texto por el director.* || **4.** •Preferential TREATMENT. *Trato preferencial.* || **5.** •To get/give the full TREATMENT. ~I got the full TREATMENT from him. *Se desvió para atenderme.* ~I got the full TREATMENT from the boss for my mistake. *El jefe me dijo de todo por haberme equivocado.* ~We were given the full TREATMENT. *Nos trataron a cuerpo de rey.*

TREMENDOUS [TREMENDO]. *adj.* Huge. *Inmenso, enorme.* ~There was a TREMEN-DOUS crowd. *Había una inmensa multitud.* ~A TREMENDOUS difference. *Una enorme diferencia.* || **2.** [Success]. *Arrollador.* || **3.** Marvelous, very good, formidable. *Estupendo, fabuloso, formidable.* ~Her performance was TREMENDOUS. *Su actuación fue formidable (fantástica).* || **4.** Great. *Muchísimo.* ~She has TREMENDOUS charisma. *Tiene muchísimo carisma.* ~She was a TREMEN-DOUS help. *Nos ayudó muchísimo.*

TRIBUTE [TRIBUTO]. *n.* [In flowers]. *Ofrenda.* || **2.** Acknowledgement. ~The movie is a TRIBUTE to the courage of these men. *La película rinde homenaje a la valentía de esos hombres.* ~This is a TRIBUTE to his loyalty. *Eso acredita su lealtad, eso hace honor a su lealtad.* ~To pay TRIBUTE to. *Rendir homenaje a, elogiar, pronunciar elogios de.*

TUTOR [TUTOR]. *n.* Private teacher. *Preceptor, profesor particular.* || **2.** [Book]. *Método.* ~A guitar TUTOR. *Un método para la guitarra.*

U-Z

ULTIMATE. *adj.* Eventual, final (aim, goal, destination). *Final.* ~What is the ULTIMATE purpose of this project? *¿Cuál es el objetivo final de este proyecto?* ~What's your ultimate ambition in life? *¿Qué es lo que ambiciona en última instancia?* ~Who has ULTIMATE responsibility? *¿Quién es el responsable en última instancia?.* ‖ **2.** [Reason, purpose, truth]. *Fundamental, primordial.* ~The ULTIMATE truth. *La verdad fundamental.* ~The ULTIMATE cause of the problem. *La raíz del problema.* ‖ **3.** Furthest. *Más remoto, extremo.* ~The ULTIMATE frontiers of science. *Los confines de la ciencia.* ‖ **4.** [Decision]. *Definitivo.* ‖ **5.** Utmost, supreme. *Máximo.* ~He's the ULTIMATE authority on the subject. *Es la máxima autoridad en el tema.* ~This is the ULTIMATE irony. *Es el colmo de la ironía.* ~The ULTIMATE sound system. *Lo último en sistemas de sonido.* ~It's the ULTIMATE in hair-styling. *Es el último grito del peinado.* ⇨ÚLTIMO

UNION [UNIÓN]. *n.* [Marriage]. *Enlace.* ‖ **2.** Harmony. *Armonía.* ~To live in perfect UNION. *Vivir en perfecta armonía.* ‖ **3.** [Trade]. *Sindicato, gremio.* ~The student's UNION. *El sindicato estudiantil.* ‖ **4.** •The UNION. *Los Estados Unidos.*

UNUSUAL [-SUAL]. *adj.* Uncommon, rare. *Insólito, inusitado, raro, poco común.* ~It's UNUSUAL for her to be so late. *Es raro que llegue tan tarde.* ~That's UNUSUAL! *¡Qué raro!* ~He spoke with UNUSUAL frankness. *Habló con inusitada franqueza.* ‖ **2.** Original. *Original.* ‖ **3.** *Exceptional.* Excepcional. ~Of UNUSUAL interest. *De excepcional interés.* ▶Aunque empleado con frecuencia, no existe en castellano la palabra *unusual* o *inusual.*

URGE. *n.* To press, insist on. *Instar.* ~They URGED the government to take immediate action. *Instaron al gobierno a que tomara medidas inmediatas.* ‖ **2.** Plead. *Exhortar.* ~He URGED the soldiers to put down their arms. *Exhortó a los soldados a que dejaran las armas.* ‖ **3.** To URGE somebody on. (I) Incite. *Darle cuerda a uno,* (II) Encourage. *Animar a alguien.* ~Their fans URGED them on to victory. *Los hinchas le animaron (alentaron) a conseguir la victoria.* ‖ **4.** Entreat. *Pedir con insistencia, rogar encarecidamente.* ~I URGE you to reconsider. *Le pido encarecidamente que lo reconsidere.* ⇨URGIR

USE [USAR]. *v.*

❶ EMPLOY FOR, APPLY TO A GIVEN PURPOSE. *Utilizar, emplear. valerse de, usar.* ~He USED a pair of pliers to remove the nails. *Utilizó unas tenazas para sacar los clavos.* ~He USES his car to go to work. *Emplea el coche para ir al trabajo.* ~They learned how to USE a fork and a knife to eat. *Aprendieron a servirse del tenedor y del cuchillo para comer.* ~I don't USE glasses. *No llevo lentes.* He USED a stick to help him walk. *Se valía de un bastón para andar.* ~I don't USE a car. *No tengo coche.* ~USE your shoe to knock the nail in. *Clávalo con el zapato.* ~I USE the bones to make soup. *Con los huesos hago la sopa.* ‖ **2.** [Purpose, function]. *Servir.* ~I USE it as a hammer. *Me sirve de martillo.* ~What is it USED for? *¿Para qué sirve.* ‖ **3.** Handle. *Manejar.* Have you USED a gun before? *¿Has manejado una pistola alguna vez?* ~Can you USE this tool? *¿Sabes manejar esta herramienta?* ~This camera is easy to USE.

Esta cámara es de fácil manejo. ~To gain proficiency in the USE of the typewriter. *Aprender el manejo de la máquina de escribir.* ‖ **4**. Need. *Necesitar.* ~They have more staff than they can USE. *Han contratado a más gente de la que necesitan.* ‖ **5**. Avail oneself. *Hacer uso de.* ~Only members can USE these facilities. *Sólo los socios pueden hacer uso de las instalaciones.* ‖ **6**. Practice, exercise. ~USE your head! *¡Piensa un poco (utiliza tu cabeza)!* ~USE your eyes. *Abra los ojos.* ~To USE one's influence. *Ejercer su influencia.* ‖ **7**. Apply. *Emplear.* ~To USE every mean. *Emplear todos los medios.* ~To use force. *Hacer uso de la fuerza.* ‖ **8**. Give (name). *Dar.* ~You can USE my name as a reference. *Puedes dar mi nombre si te piden referencias.* ‖ **9**. [Library]. *Frecuentar.* ~I often USE the library. *Frecuento la biblioteca a menudo.* ‖ **10**. [Book]. *Consultar.* ~What book did you USE? *¿Qué libro consultaste?* ‖ **11**. To speak or write in (a language). *Hablar escribir.* ~He can USE the language fairly well. *Habla y escribe el idioma bastante bien.* ~Don't USE bad language. *No digas palabrotas.* ‖ **12**. •Word which is no longer USED. *Palabra que ha caído en desuso.* ‖ **13**. •May I USE your phone? *¿Puedo hacer una llamada?* ‖ **14**. •May I USE YOUR toilet? *¿Puedo pasar al baño?* ‖ **15**. •Be careful how you USE this razor! *¡Cuidado con la navaja esa!*

❷ CONSUME, TAKE. *Consumir, tomar.* ~To USE drugs. *Consumir (tomar) drogas.* ~The school does not give scholarships to those who USE tobacco. *La escuela no ofrece becas a las personas que fuman.* ~Do you USE sugar in your coffee. *~¿Toma Ud. el café con azucar?* ~'USE by february 3, 1996'. *'Consumir antes del 3 feb 96.'* ~We USED all the bread. *Nos comimos todo el pan.* ~An increase in the USE of intoxicating liquors. *Un aumento en el consumo de las bebidas alcohólicas.*

❸ USE UP, GO THROUGH, SPEND. *Consumir.* ~This heater USES a lot of electricity. *Este calentador consume mucha electricidad.* ~This fire USES one ton of charcoal a week. *Este fuego consume una tonelada de carbón por semana.* ‖ **2**. [Product]. *Comprar.* ~I always USE the same soap. *Siempre compro el mismo jabón.* ‖ **3**. Exhaust, run out of (energy, funds, patience, supplies). *Agotar, acabar.* ~I USED all my shampoo. *Se me acabo el champú.* ~They USED all topics of conversation. *Agotaron todos los temas de conversación.* ~I USED all my strength. *Se me agotaron las fuerzas.* ‖ **4**. Spend. *Gastar.* ~I USED all the money you gave me. *Gasté todo el dinero que me diste.*

❹ VARIOUS. Take advantage. *Aprovechar.* ~She could USE her free time to better purpose. *Podría aprovechar mejor su tiempo libre.* ~He USED his political influence to get the job. *Aprovechó su influencia en la política para conseguir el puesto.* ‖ **2**. Manipulate, exploit. *Aprovechar(se).* ~Can't you see that they're USING you? *¿No ves que se están aprovechando de tí?* ‖ **3**. Requires. *Basarse en, llevar, tener.* ~The system USES a standard battery set. *El dispositivo lleva (funciona con) un juego de pilas normales (Prats).* ‖ **4**. To be in need of, to benefit from. *Venirle bien (algo a alquien).* ~I could USE a drink. *No me vendría mal un trago.* ~This room could USE some paint. *No le vendría mal a este cuarto una mano de pintura.* ~I could USE some of that money right now. *Este dinero me vendría bien en este momento.* ‖ **5**. To call. *Llamar.* ~It tooks his friends a while to acquire the habit of USING 'doctor' after he received his Ph.D. *Sus amigos tardaron algún rato en acostumbrarse a llamarle 'doctor' después de que consiguiera su título de Doctor en Filosofía y Letras.* ‖ **6**. •USE more care. *Tenga más cuidado.* ‖ **7**. •We USE first names in the office. *En la oficina nos tuteamos.*

USUAL [USUAL]. Normal, expected, routine, typical. *Normal.* ~This is the USUAL weather for this time of the year. *Este es el tiempo normal en esta época del año.* ~It's not USUAL for people to leave so soon. *No es normal marcharse tan pronto.* ~It's the USUAL practice. *Es lo normal.* ~It is USUAL for candidates to apply in writing. *Lo normal es que los candidatos hagan sus solicitudes por escrito.* ‖ **2.** Customary, regular. *Habitual, acostumbrado, de siempre.* ~Let's meet at the USUAL restaurant. *Nos encontramos en el restaurante habitual.* ~My USUAL walk in the hills. *Mi paseo habitual por los cerros.* ~You'll find the cutlery at it's USUAL place. *Los cubiertos están en su lugar habitual.* ~He replied with his USUAL irony. *Respondió con su habitual ironía.* ~With her USUAL calmness. *Con su acostumbrada tranquilidad.* ~The train arrived with its USUAL delay. *El tren llegó con el retraso acostumbrado.* ~I'll meet you at the USUAL time. *Nos encontramos a la hora acostumbrada.* ~The USUAL problems. *Los problemas de siempre.* ‖ **3.** Everyday. *De todos los días.* ~My USUAL clothes. *Mi ropa de todos los días.* ‖ **4.** [In comparisons (followed by: *earlier than, more than, less than,* etc.)]. *Que de costumbre, de lo normal.* ~We had more snow than USUAL this winter. *Este invierno ha nevado más que de costumbre, más de lo normal.* ~Earlier than USUAL. *Más pronto que de costumbre.* ‖ **5.** Common, ordinary. ~It's not USUAL for her to be late. *No suele llegar tarde.* As is USUAL at these events. *Como suele ocurrir en estas ocasiones.* ~With all the facilities USUAL to a military base. *Con todas las instalaciones que suelen tener las bases militares.* ‖ **6.** Typical. *Característico.* As is USUAL with women. *Como todas las mujeres.* ‖ **7.** PHRASES. ‖ •As USUAL. *Como siempre, como de costumbre.* Everybody was grumbling about the weather, as USUAL. *Todo el mundo se quejaba del mal tiempo, como de costumbre.* ‖ •The USUAL (drink}. *Lo de siempre, la misma bebida de siempre.* ‖ •The USUAL thing. *Lo de siempre.* ~The USUAL thing is for everybody to participate. *Lo normal es que todos participen.* ‖ •She wasn't her USUAL self. *No era la de siempre.* ‖ •Business as USUAL. *Estamos abierto.*

VAGUE [VAGO]. Indistinct, shadowy, hazy. *Borroso, indistinto (outline), poco claro*

(sound). ~A VAGUE outline. *Una silueta borrosa.* ~The VAGUE outline of a ship. *El perfil indistinto de un buque.* ‖ **2.** Light, faint. *Ligero, leve.* ~There was a VAGUE note of suspicion in his voice. *Había una leve nota de sospecha en su voz.* ~There's a VAGUE likeness between them. *Existe un ligero parecido entre ellos.* ~I have a VAGUE idea of how it works. *Tengo una ligera idea de como funciona.* ~There was a VAGUE scent in the air. *Había un leve aroma en el aire.* ‖ **3.** Unclear. *Poco explícito, poco preciso.* ~She was very VAGUE about her involvement. *Fue poco explícita acerca de su participación.* ~The book is very VAGUE on some points. *El libro es muy poco preciso en algunos puntos.* ~Some dictionaries are very VAGUE in describing the word 'vague'. *Algunos diccionarios dan definiciones muy imprecisas sobre la palabra 'vague'.* ~She was VAGUE about it. *No dio detalles.* ~He was VAGUE about the date. *No quiso precisar la fecha.* ‖ **4.** Uncertain. *Indeciso, dudoso.* ~When he answered my question he was very VAGUE. *Fue muy indeciso en contestar a mi pregunta.* I'm a little VAGUE about what happened next. *No me acuerdo muy bien de lo que pasó después.* ~The outlook is somewhat VAGUE. *La perspectiva es algo incierta.* ‖ **5.** Ignorant. *Falto de conocimiento.* ~I'm a bit VAGUE about structuralism. *Sé muy poco de estructuralismo.* ~I am VAGUE on the subject of ants. *Sé muy poca cosa en concreto de las hormigas.* **6.** ‖ Absent-minded. *Distraído, despistado.* ~To look VAGUE. *Tener aire distraído.* ‖ **7.** Least. *Mínima.* I haven't the VAGUEST idea. *No tengo la menor (más mínima) idea.*

VARIOUS [VARIOS]. Different, diverse. *Diversos, distintas, diferentes.* ~Let us consider the VARIOUS alternatives. *Consideremos las diversas opciones.* ~For VARIOUS reasons. *Por diversas razones.* ~In VARIOUS ways. *De diversos modos.* ~The VARIOUS authorities on the subject. *Las distintas autoridades en el tema.* ‖ **2.** •At VARIOUS times in the past. *En determinados momentos del pasado.*

VARNISH. *n.* [Nails]. *Esmalte* (para las uñas). ⇨BARNIZ

VERSATILE [VERSÁTIL]. Having various skills. *Polifacético, con muchas facetas.* ~A VERSATIL artist. *Un artista con muchas facetas.* ~His works shows Marañón as a very VERSATILE man. *En sus obras Marañón se revela como hombre de conocimientos variados (Prats).* || **2.** [Mind]. *Ágil, flexible.* || **3.** Having many different uses. *Dúctil, de múltiples aplicaciones, muy útil.*

VICIOUS. Violent. *Virulento.* || **2.** Malicious, nasty, hateful. *Malicioso.* ~VICIOUS gossip. *Chismes maliciosos.* || **3.** Depraved. *Depravado, perverso.* || **4.** [Dog]. *Bravo, fiero, malo.* ~Keep away from that dog, he can be VICIOUS. *No te acerques a ese perro, a veces se pone bravo.* || **5.** [Horse]. *Resabiado, arisco.* || **6.** [Criminal]. *Despiadado, sanguinario.* || **7.** [Attack, blow]. *Feroz, salvaje.* || **8.** [Crimen]. *Atroz, horrible.* || **9.**

Unpleasantly strong. *Fuerte.* A VICIOUS headache. *Un fuerte dolor de cabeza.* ~He landed a VICIOUS right. *Le asestó un fuerte derechazo.* || **10.** Malicious. *Malicioso, despiadado.* ~A VICIOUS smear campaign. *Una despiadada campaña de difamación.* || **11.** *PHRASES.* •To have a VICIOUS temper. *Tener muy mal genio.* || •To have a VICIOUS tongue. *Tener una lengua viperina.* || •With VICIOUS intent. *Con malas intenciones, con intención criminal.* ⇨VICIOSO

VILLAIN. [Theater, Cinema]. *Malo.* ~He plays the VILLAIN. *Hace papel de malo.* || **2.** Criminal. *Maleante.* || **3.** Cause. *Causa.* ~The major VILLAIN in cancer is smoking. *La mayor causa del cáncer es el cigarrillo.* || **4.** Scoundrel. *Sin vergüenza.* ⇨VILLANO

VULGAR. In poor taste. *De mal gusto.* || **2.** Indecent. *Grosero, mal hablado, ordinario.* || **3.** [Joke, song]. *Verde.* ~A VULGAR joke. *Un chiste verde.* ⇨VULGAR

SPANISH-ENGLISH

A

ABANDONADO [ABANDONED]. *adj.* Descuidado. *Neglected.* ~El jardín está ABANDONADO. *The garden is neglected, has not been looked after.* ~Tiene a su familia muy ABANDONADA. *He neglects his family.* ‖ **2.** Desaseado, dejado, desaliñado. *Untidy, unkempt.* ~Es muy ABANDONADO en el vestir. *He dresses very sloppily.* ~Últimamente está muy ABANDONADA. *She really let herself go lately.* ‖ **3.** [Piso]. *Vacant.* ‖ **4.** Despreocupado, descuidado. *Negligent, slack, careless.* ¡Qué ABANDONADO es! Hace años que no va al dentista. *He doesn't look after himself, he hasn't been to the dentist in years.* ~Es tan ABANDONADO, lo deja todo para mañana. *He's so slack about everything, he's always putting things off.* ‖ **5.** •Nos tienes ABANDONADOS. *You never come and see us anymore.*

ABANDONAR[1] [ABANDON]. *v.* Dejar, marcharse de cierto sitio. *To leave.* ~El público ABANDONÓ el teatro. *The audience left the theater.* ~Las tropas han empezado a ABANDONAR la zona. *The troops have started to pull out of the area.* ~ABANDONÓ la reunión en señal de protesta. *He walked out of the meeting in protest.* ‖ **2.** Dejar cierta actividad. *Pull out, withdraw, give up.* ~ABANDONÓ la carrera. *He pulled out of (withdrew from) the race.* ‖ **3.** Soltar. *To let go of.* ~ABANDONÓ la cuerda y el globo se escapó. *He let go of the string and the balloon flew away.* ‖ **4.** Dejar de favorecer. *To desert, forsake, leave to one's fate.* ~La suerte lo ha ABANDONADO. *His luck has run out (deserted him).* ~Nunca lo ABANDONA el buen humor. *He's always good-humored (his good humor never deserts him).* ~Me tienes ABANDONADO. *You have forgotten about me (you have deserted me).* ‖ **5.** Darse por vencido (competición). *To resign, concede defeat, throw in the towel.* ‖ **6.** Dejar de utilizar cierta cosa. *To leave behind.* ~Allí ABANDONAMOS la carretera y seguimos por un camino. *There we left the highway and followed a road.* ‖ **7.** Renunciar (trabajo). *To resign.* ~Tuvo que ABANDONAR el cargo. *He had to give up (resign from) the post.*

ABANDONARSE[2] [ABANDON]. *vr.* Descuidarse. *To let oneself go, to get slovenly.* ~Desde que tuvo hijos se ha ABANDONADO. *Since she had her children she let herself go.* ~No te ABANDONES y ve al médico. *Don't neglect your health, go see the doctor.* ‖ **2.** Entregarse. *To give in to, give way to, yield to, slip in.* ~Se ABANDONÓ al sueño. *He gave in to sleep (he let sleep overcome him).* ~ABANDONARSE a la tentación. *To yield to temptation.* ‖ **3.** Desanimarse. *To loose heart, get discouraged.*

ABANDONO [ABANDONMENT]. *sm.* [Actividad, idea]. *Giving up.* ~El ABANDONO de su carrera. *The giving up of his studies.* ‖ **2.** [Descuido]. *Neglect, lack of care.* ~El edificio se halla en un lamentable estado de ABANDONO. *The building is in a sorry state of neglect.* ~Da lástima ver el ABANDONO en que se encuentran estos jardines. *It's terrible to see how these gardens have fallen into neglect.* ‖ **3.** [Dejadez]. *Apathy, carelessness, laziness.* ‖ **4.** [Deporte]. *Withdrawal.* ~Ganar por ABANDONO. *To win by default.* ‖ **5.** [Ajedrez]. *Resignation.* ~El ABANDONO del campeón se produjo en la jugada número 30. *The champion's resignation came on move 30.* ‖ **6.** •Darse al ABANDONO. *To go morally downhill, to indulge in one's vices.* ‖ **7.** •Viven en el mayor abandono. *They live in* *utter degradation.* || **8.** •ABANDONO del hogar. *Desertion.*

ABISMAL. *v.* FIG Enorme, profundo. *Huge, enormous, vast, unbridgeable.* ~Una differencia ABISMAL. *A huge difference, a world of difference.* ~Entre los dos partidos políticos hay diferencias ABISMALES. *There are unbridgeable differences between the two political parties.* ⇨ABYSMAL

ABNEGACIÓN. *sf.* Sacrificio que alguien hace de su voluntad, de sus afectos o de sus intereses de forma desinteresada. *Care, dedication, self-denial.* ~Un médico ABNEGADO. *A dedicated physician.* ⇨ABNEGATION

ABORTAR. *v.* [Involuntariamente]. *Miscarry, have a miscarriage.* || **2.** Fracasar. *To fail, miscarry.* ⇨ABORT

ABORTO. *nm.* [Espontáneo]. *Miscarriage.* || **2.** [Provocado]. *Abortion.* || **3.** Engendro. *Freak, ugly person.* ⇨ABORTION

ABRAZAR. *v.* Abarcar. *To include, comprise, take in.* || **2.** Oportunidad. *To seize.* || **3.** [Empresa]. *To take charge of.* ~ABRAZÓ entusiasmada el nuevo proyecto. *She fervently undertook the new project.* || **4.** [Doctrina]. *To espouse.* || **5.** [Profesión]. *To adopt, enter, take up.* || **6.** [Tronco, columna]. *To encircle.* ⇨EMBRACE

ABREVIAR [ABBREVIATE]. *vt.* Hacer breve, acortar, reducir a menos tiempo o espacio. *To cut short.* ~Tuvo que ABREVIAR su visita. *He had to cut short his visit.* || **2.** *vi.* Acelerar, apresurar. *To hasten, to be brief, make it short.* ~ABREVIA, que no tengo mucho tiempo. *Be brief, I haven't got much time.* || **3.** •ABREVIAR los trámites. *To speed up formalities.* || **4.** •Para ABREVIAR. *To make a long story short.*

ABRUPTO. *adj.* [Montaña, pendiente]. *Steep.* ~Un sendero muy ABRUPTO ascendía por la montaña. *There was a steep path going up the mountain.* || **2.** [Terreno]. *Rugged, rough.*

ABSORBENTE [ABSORBENT]. *adj.* [Exigente]. *Demanding.* ~Ella es muy ABSORBENTE. *She demands so much of his time and attention.* || **2.** Que tiene un carácter

dominante. *Domineering.* ~Su madre es demasiado ABSORBENTE. *His mother is overly domineering.* || **3.** Que ocupa del todo la mente y el tiempo de una persona (trabajo). *Engrossing, demanding.* ~Tiene un trabajo demasiado ABSORBENTE. *His work is extremely demanding.* || **4.** [Hobby, tarea]. *Time-consuming.* ~Es un trabajo ABSORBENTE. *It's a job which takes a lot of time and energy.*

ABSTINENCIA [ABSTINENCE]. *sf.* Conjunto de síntomas orgánicos y psíquicos producidos por la cesación brusca de un tóxico. *Withdrawal.* ~Síndrome de ABSTINENCIA. *Withdrawal symptoms.* || **2.** [Religion]. *Fast, fasting.* ~Los católicos practican la ABSTINENCIA durante la Cuaresma. *Catholics fast during Lent.*

ABSTRACCIÓN [ABSTRACTION]. *sf.* Concentración mental. *Concentration.* ~Tiene gran capacidad de ABSTRACCIÓN. *He has great powers of concentration.* || **2.** Despiste, distracción. *Absent-mindedness.* ~El timbre de la puerta lo sacó de su ABSTRACCIÓN. *The doorbell brought him back to reality.* || **3.** Ensueño. *Reverie.* || **4.** •ABSTRACCIÓN hecha de este libro. *Leaving that book aside, with the exception of that book.*

ABUSAR. *v.* Hacer uso excesivo de una cosa en perjuicio propio o ajeno. *Overindulge in, misuse.* ABUSAR del tabaco. *To overindulge in smoking.* || **2.** Usar mal, excesiva, injusta, impropia o indebidamente de algo o de alguien, aprovecharse. *To take unfair advantage of, exploit.* ~ABUSARSE de la generosidad, hospitalidad, buena voluntad de uno. *To impose on someone's generosity, hospitality, good-will.*~María Juana se sintió indignada de que ABUSARAN de él de aquel modo. *María Juana was furious that they should take advantage of him in such a way.* || **3.** •ABUSAR de la confianza de alguien. *To betray one's trust (confidence).* ~Gritaré y todo el mundo sabrá que eres un ladrón y has robado a tus amos ABUSANDO de su confianza. *I'll scream and then everyone will know that you are a thief and that you have betrayed your employers' trust by stealing from them.* || **4.** ABUSAR (de una mujer, de un niño). *To molest.* ‖ **5.** •¡Sin ABUSAR! *Don't push it too far!* ⇨ABUSE

ABUSIVO. *adj.* [Precio, interés]. *Outrageous, exorbitant, excessive.* No sé cómo pueden cobrar estos precios ABUSIVOS. *I don't know how they can charge such exorbitant prices.* ‖ **2.** Que se aprovecha de una situación en beneficio propio. *Unfair, unjust, going too far, improper.* ~El contrato incluye dos cláusulas francamente ABUSIVAS. *The contract has two clauses which are blatantly unfair.* ‖ **3.** •Tratos ABUSIVOS. *Ill-treatment.* ⇨ABUSIVE

ABUSO. *sm.* [De confianza]. *Betrayal (of trust), breach of faith.* ‖ **2.** Injusticia. *Injustice, outrage.* ~Es un ABUSO que nos traten así. *It's outrageous that we should be treated in this way.* Es un ABUSO cobrar tanto dinero. *It's disgraceful to charge so much money.* ‖ **3.** •ABUSO deshonesto. *Indecent assault.* ‖ **4.** •ABUSO del tabaco. *Excessive smoking, smoking too much.* ‖ **5.** •Se ha hecho uso y ABUSO de esta metáfora. *This metaphor has been used time and again.* ⇨ABUSE

ACARICIAR [CARESS]. *v.* [Perro, gato]. *To stroke.* ‖ **2.** [Esperanza, sueño]. *To cherish.* ~ACARICIAR grandes ambiciones. *To cherish great ambitions.* ‖ **3.** [Idea, project]. *To have in mind, toy with, nurture.* ‖ **4.** Rozar. *To brush, touch lightly.* ~La brisa le ACARICIABA el rostro. *The breeze touched his face lightly.*

ACCEDER. *v.* Consentir en lo que otro solicita o quiere. *To consent, agree.* ~ACCEDIÓ a mi demanda. *He agreed to my request.* ACCEDIÓ a contestar preguntas del público. *He agreed to answer questions from the audience.* ▸También se puede emplear el parónimo inglés *accede,* pero es de uso poco común. ‖ **2.** Tener acceso, paso o entrada a un lugar. *To gain access to.* Un jardín al cual se ACCEDE por dos entradas. *A garden which you can enter from two points.* ‖ **3.** Ingresar (universidad). *To gain admittance to, enter.* ⇨ACCEED

ACCESIBLE [ACCESSIBLE]. *adj.* [Person]. *Approachable.* ~Un jefe ACCESIBLE. *A very approachable boss.* ‖ **2.** [Precio]. *Affordable.* ~ACCESIBLE a todos los bolsillos. *Within everyone's price range.* ‖ **3.** [Explicación]. *Easily understandable.* ~Es un libro ACCESIBLE para los estudiantes. *It's an easy to understand text.*

ACCESO [ACCESS]. *sm.* [De un avión]. *Approach.* ‖ **2.** [De tos]. *Fit.* ‖ **3.** [De fiebre]. *Attack, bout.* ‖ **4.** [De generosidad]. *Surge, moment.* ‖ **5.** [Ira, celos]. *Fit, outburst.* ~En un ACCESO de ira. *In a fit of rage.* ‖ **6.** [A un curso]. *Entrance.* ~Prueba de ACCESO. *Entrance exam.* ‖ **7.** •Estos están al acceso de todos. *These are within reach of everyone.* ‖ **8.** •Prohibido el ACCESO. *No admittance.*

ACCIDENTE. *sm.* [De superficie]. *Irregularities, unevenness.* ‖ **2.** [De terreno]. *Roughness, ruggedness, hilliness.* ‖ **3.** [Geográfico]. *Feature.* ~ACCIDENTES geográficos. *Geographical features.* ‖ **4.** [De avión]. *Crash.* ‖ **5.** [Desmayo]. *Faint, swoon.* ‖ **6.** •Una vida sin ACCIDENTES. *An uneventful life.* ⇨ACCIDENT

ACCIÓN *nf.* Acto, hecho (calificable moralmente). *Act, deed.* ~Hacer una buena/mala ACCIÓN. *To do a good/evil deed.* ACCIONES dignas de elogio. *Praise-worthy acts (deeds).* ‖ **2.** Influencia, efecto. *Influence, effect.* ~Está bajo la ACCIÓN de un sedante. *She's under sedation.* ‖ **3.** Cada una de las partes en que se divide el capital de una sociedad anónima. *Share, stock.*~ Esta empresa cuenta con más de diez millones de ACCIONES. *This company has more that 10 million shares.* ‖ **4.** Gesto, movimiento (mano). *Gesture, movement.* ‖ **5.** LOCUCIONES. ‖ •Novela de ACCIÓN. *Adventure story.* ‖ •ACCIÓN de gracias. *Thanksgiving.* ‖ •ACCIÓN de guerra. *Act of war.* ‖ •Radio de ACCIÓN. *Operating range.* ⇨ACTION

ACENTUADO [ACCENTUATED]. *adj.* [Con acento tónico]. *Stressed.* ~Sílaba ACENTUADA. *Stressed syllable.* ‖ **2.** Marcado (diferencia, cambio). *Strong, marked.* ~Una tendencia social muy ACENTUADA. *A very marked social tendency.*

ACEPTACIÓN [ACCEPTATION/ACCEPTANCE]. *sf.* Éxito. *Success.* Tener poca ACEPTACIÓN. *Not to be popular, to have little success.*

~Este producto tendrá una ACEPTACIÓN enorme. *This product will be a great success, will be very popular.* || **2.** Aprobación. *Approval.*

ACLARAR[1.] *v.* [Color, pelo]. *To lighten, make lighter.* ~La ropa blanca se aclara si se lava con LEJÍA. *Bleach brightens clothes.* || **2.** [Líquido]. *To thin (down).* ~Si la salsa ha quedado muy espesa, ACLÁRALA con un poco de agua. *If the sauce is too thick, thin it down with a little water.* || **3.** Enjuagar. *To rinse.* ~Esta LAVADORA no aclara bien la ropa. *This washing machine doesn't rinse clothes well.* || **4.** Explicar. *To explain, clarify.* ~Quiero ACLARAR una cosa. *I'd like to clarify something.* || **5.** Despejar (duda). *To resolve, remove.* || **6.** Empezar (día). *To dawn, break.* ~Ya está ACLARANDO y pronto saldrá el sol. *Dawn is already breaking and soon the sun will come out.* || **7.** MET [Tiempo]. *To clear up.* En cuanto ACLARE el tiempo saldremos. *We'll leave as soon as the weather clears up.* || **8.** [Throat]. *Clear.* ~He comprado pastillas para ACLARARME la voz. *I bought some cough drops to clear my throat.* ⇨CLARIFY

ACLARARSE[2]. *vr.* Entender. *To understand.* ~Es que no me ACLARO. *I don't really know what's going on.* || **2.** Explain. *Explicarse.* ¡A ver si te ACLARÁS! *Explain yourself!* || **3.** Decidirse. *To make up one's mind.* ⇨CLARIFY

ACOMODACIÓN. *sf.* Colocación conveniente. *Arrangement.* ~La ACOMODACIÓN de los invitados al banquete. *The seating arrangement for the banquet.* || **2.** [Vivienda, piso]. *Preparation.* || **3.** Adaptación. *Adaptation.* ~La ACOMODACIÓN de los hechos a la realidad. *The adaptation of theory to practice.* ⇨ACCOMMODATION

ACOMODAR[1]. *vt.* FIG Amoldar, armonizar o ajustar a una norma, adaptar. *To adapt.* ~ACOMODAR la ley a las realidades sociales. *To adapt the law to social reality.* ~No puedes ACOMODAR las reglas a tu antojo. *You can't bend the rules just to suit you.* || **2.** Colocar o poner en un lugar conveniente o cómodo. *Arrange, organize.* ~ACOMODA tus

juguetes en el armario. *Put your toys away in the cupboard.* || **3.** Conseguir sitio para. *Fit in, find room for.* ~Conseguimos ACOMODAR la nevera en el rincón de la cocina. *We manage to find room for, fit the refrigerator in the corner of the kitchen.* || **4.** Proporcionar empleo. *To give a job to, take on, fix up (with a job).* ACOMODÉ a mi primo. *I fixed my cousin up with a job.* || **5.** [Persona]. Poner en un lugar apropiado o adecuado. *To settle, make comfortable.* ACOMODARON al niño en un sillón. *They settled the child (made the child comfortable) in an armchair.* ~Déjame ACOMODARTE la almohada. *Let me fix the pillow (so you can be comfortable).* || **6.** Colocar en el lugar que corresponda o que esté disponible (persona). *To show to one's seat, find place for.* La azafata nos ACOMODÓ en nuestros asientos. *The flight attendant showed us to our seats.* ~Nos ACOMODÓ en la segunda fila. *She found us a seat in the second row.* || **7.** Convenir. *To be suitable.* ~Te enviaré una señorita que te ACOMODE para secretaria. *I'll send you a girl that may be appropriate as a secretary.* || **8.** Venir bien. *To suit, be convenient.* ~Si te ACOMODA, puedes venir mañana. *If it's convenient, you can come tomorrow.* ⇨ACCOMODATE

ACOMODARSE[2]. *vr.* Ponerse en la postura conveniente. *To settle down, make oneself comfortable.* ~No te ACOMODES, que hay mucho trabajo que hacer. *Don't make yourself too comfortable, there's a lot of work to be done.* || **2.** Amoldarse, adaptarse. *To adjust, adapt.* Se tendrá que ACOMODAR a nuestra manera de hacer las cosas. *He will have to adjust to our way of doing things.* ⇨ACCOMODATE

ACOMPAÑAR [ACCOMPANY]. *v.* [En carta]. *To enclose, attach.* ~En el folleto que le ACOMPAÑAMOS. *In the enclosed brochure.* ~Nos es grato ACOMPAÑARLE la información por usted solicitada. *We are pleased to enclose the information you requested.* || **2.** [En el dolor, la desgracia]. *To join.* ~Todos ACOMPAÑAMOS a la familia en su dolor. *We all join with the family in their grief.* || **3.** [A una señorita]. *To escort.* ‖ **4.** [A un enfermo]. *To keep company.* ~ACOMPAÑAR a un enfermo. *To keep a sick person company.* ‖ **5.** [A casa, a la puerta). *To take, to see.* ~Le ACOMPAÑARÉ a su casa porque es tarde. *I'll take you home because it's late.* ~Le ACOMPAÑO hasta la puerta. *I'll see you to the door.* ‖ **6.** [A un entierro). *To follow.* ~ACOMPAÑAR a un entierro. *To follow a funeral.* ‖ **7.** Comer, beber con. *To eat, drink with.* ACOMPAÑARON la comida con un buen vino. *They served the meal with a good wine.* ‖ **8.** Participar. *To join.* ~Mañana organizamos un bridge en casa. ¿Quiere Ud. ACOMPAÑARNOS? *We're having a game of bridge at home. Would you like to join us?* ‖ **9.** Participar de. *To share, agree with.* ~Le ACOMPAÑO en sus idea. *I share your ideas.* ‖ **10.** *Estar dotado (de ciertas cualidades). To be endowed with (certain qualities, ability].* ~Siempre le ha ACOMPAÑADO un gran sentido de humor. *He has always possessed a great sense of humor.* ‖ **11.** *LOCUCIONES.* ‖ •No quiero que me ACOMPAÑE. *I'd rather go alone.* ‖ •Le ACOMPAÑO en el sentimiento. *Please accept my condolences, my deepest simpathy.* ‖ •ACOMPAÑÓ a la madre en su dolor. *He comforted his mother in her grief.* ‖ •Gracias por ACOMPAÑARNOS en este coloquio radiofónico. *Thank you for being with us on the show.* ‖ •Siempre lo ACOMPAÑÓ la buena suerte. *He has always been lucky.* ‖ •El tiempo no nos ACOMPAÑÓ. *We were not very lucky with the weather.*

ACONDICIONAR. v. Arreglar. *To prepare, arrange, make suitable, equip, fit out.* ~ACONDICIONARON la sala para congresos. *They fitted (equipped) the hall for conferences.* ~Un centro sanitario debidamente ACONDICIONADO. *A properly equipped health center.* ~ACONDICIONAR un sótano para tienda. *To fit out a basement as a shop.* ‖ **2.** [Sala]. *To air-condition.* ‖ **3.** Mejorar. *To improve.* ~ACONDICIONAR la red ferroviaria. *To improve the railway network.* ⇨CONDITION

ACRE [ACRID]. *adj.* [Sabor]. *Sour, bitter.* ~Este vino tiene un sabor ACRE. *This wine*

has a sour (bitter) taste. ‖ **2.** [Palabras]. *Bitter, harsh, rude.* Su lenguaje siempre is ACRE. *He always speaks rudely.* ‖ **3.** [Crítica]. *Biting.* ‖ **4.** [Temperamento]. *Sour.* ~Tiene un carácter ACRE. *He has a sour disposition.* ‖ **5.** [Humor, tono]. *Caustic.*

ACREDITAR[1] [CREDIT]. *v.* [Probar, avalar]. *To prove, support, give proof of.* ~Este documento lo ACREDITA como único heredero. *This document proves him to be the only heir.* ~Los documentos que le ACREDITAN como residente. *The papers which prove that you are a resident.* ‖ **2.** Abonar en cuenta. *To credit.* ‖ **3.** Avalar. *To vouch for, guarantee.* ~ACREDITAR una firma. *To vouch for a signature.* ‖ **4.** [Por seguridad]. *To clear, give security clearance to.* ‖ **5.** Sancionar (representante). *To sanction, authorize.* ~Este documento me ACREDITA para entrar. *This paper authorizes me to enter.* ‖ **6.** Establecer. *To establish, confirm, recognize.* ~Este libro le ACREDITA como un gran pensador. *This book confirms him as a great thinker.* ~Una empresa ACREDITADA como líder en su campo. *A firm recognized as the leader in its field.* ‖ **7.** Dar fama o reputación. *To add to the reputation of.* ~Un producto que ACREDITA al fabricante. *A product which adds to the manufacturer's reputation.* ‖ **8.** •ACREDITAR su personalidad. *To establish one's identity.*

ACREDITARSE[2] [CREDIT]. *vr. To make one's name, gain a reputation.* ~Antes de que este bar se ACREDITE habrá que esperar mucho tiempo. *We shall have to wait a long time before this bar gains a reputation (makes it's name).*

ACTIVAR. *v.* [Market, economy]. *Stimulate, revitalize.* ~Medidas que ACTIVARÁN la economía. *Measures to stimulate the economy.* ‖ **2.** [Trabajo]. *To expedite, speed up, hurry along.* ~El alcalde ACTIVÓ las negociaciones. *The mayor speeded up the negotiations.* ‖ **3.** [Informática]. *To unable.* ‖ **4.** Avivar. *To liven up, quicken.* ⇨ACTIVATE

ACTO. Hecho público o solemne. *Function, ceremony.* ‖ **2.** *LOCUCIONES.* ‖ •ACTO de presencia. *Formal attendance, appea-*

rance; token appearance. ~Ni siquiera, hizo ACTO de presencia. *He didn't even make a token appearance.* || •ACTO sexual. *Sexual intercourse.* || •ACTO fallido. *Freudian slip.* || •ACTO religioso. *Church service.* || •ACTO de clausura. *Closing ceremony.* ~Mañana se celebrará el ACTO de clausura. *The closing ceremony will take place (be held) tomorrow.*|| •ACTO inaugural. *Opening ceremony.* || •ACTO reflejo. *Reflex action.* || •ACTO judicial. *Writ.* || •ACTO social. *Social event.* || •ACTO jurídico. *Legal transaction.* || •ACTO publíco. *Public ceremony.* || •ACTOS de violencia. *Assault and battery.* || •Celebrar un ACTO. *To hold a function.* || •En el ACTO. *While you wait, on the spot.* Reparaciones en el ACTO. *Repairs while you wait.* ~Fotocopias en el ACTO. *Photocopies while you wait.* ⇨ ACT

ACTUAL. *adj.* Que existe, sucede o se usa en el tiempo presente o en el momento que se habla. *Today, present-day, current.* La tecnología ACTUAL. *Present-day technology.* ~La legislación ACTUAL. *The current legislation.* ~En las circunstancias ACTUALES. *Under the present circumstances.* || **2.** Que está de moda o que tiene actualidad. *Fashionable, modern, up-to-date, trendy.* ~Estos trajes tiene un diseño muy ACTUAL. *Those suits have a very modern design.* || **3.** •Su carta del 6 del ACTUAL. *Your letter of the 6th of this month.* ⇨ ACTUAL

ACTUALMENTE. *adv.* Ahora, en la actualidad. *Nowdays, at the present time, currently, at the moment, at present, presently.* ~Antes era un lujo pero ACTUALMENTE es una necesidad. *It used to be a luxury but nowadays it's a necessity.* ~Se encuentra ACTUALMENTE en Italia. *He's in Italy at the moment.* ~ACTUALMENTE la situación es mucho más grave. *The situation today is far more serious.* ~ACTUALMENTE está fuera. *He's away at the present.* ⇨ ACTUALLY

ACTUAR [ACT]. *v.* JUR Formar autos, proceder judicialmente. *To prosecute, bring an action against.* || **2.** Realizar un ejercicio en una oposición. *To take an examination.* || **3.** Desempeñar con arte y facilidad alguna

cosa, ejecutar, interpretar (obra artística). *To perform.* ~ACTUÓ mágnificamente. *He performed brilliantly.*

ACUMULAR [ACCUMULATE]. *v.* [Gente]. *To gather.* ~La gente se ACUMULÓ delante del escaparate. *The people gathered in front of the window.* || **2.** [Recuerdos]. *To store up, collect.* || **3.** [Preocupaciones, cargos]. *To pile.* ~Acumular PREOCUPACIONES sobre alguien. *To pile worries onto someone.* || **4.** [Experience]. *Gain.* || **5.** [Trabajo]. *To pile up, mount up.* ~El trabajo se iba ACUMULANDO. *The work was piling (mounting) up.*

ACUSACIÓN [ACCUSATION]. *sf.* JUR Charge, indictment. ~Negó la ACUSACIÓN. *He denied the charge, he pleaded not guilty.* ~Un crimen sobre el cual no existe ninguna ACUSACIÓN formal. *A crime for which no one has ever been charged.* || **2.** •Formular una ACUSACIÓN en contra de alguien. *To bring charges against someone.*

ACUSADO [ACCUSED]. *adj.* Fuerte, marcado (tendencia, cambio). *Marked, pronounced, noticeable.* ~Un ACUSADO descenso de la temperatura. *A marked drop in temperature.* || **2.** [Característica, rasgo]. *Strong, prominent.* ~Los rasgos más ACUSADOS de su personalidad son el tesón y la alegría. *The prominent features of his personality are his cheerfulness and his determination.* || **3.** [Contraste, semejanza]. *Striking, marked.* || **4.** [Color]. *Deep.* || **5.** •Un ACUSADO sentido competetivo. *A strong (keen) competitive spirit.*

ACUSAR [ACCUSE]. *v.* Comunicar, generalmente a una autoridad, la falta o delito de alguien. *Denounce, report.* Han ACUSADO al presunto ladrón. *They reported the alleged thief (to the police).* || **2.** Revelar, manifestar. *To show, denote, reveal, register, betray, indicate, reflect.* ~ACUSABAN el cansancio del viaje. *They were showing signs of fatigue after the journey.* || **3.** Mostrar, indicar. *Indicate, show, register.* El termómetro ACUSA un cambio de temperatura. *The thermometer shows a change of temperature.* || **4.** Acentuarse (tendencia, costumbre). *To get stronger, become clear, pronounced, marked.* ~Esta tendencia se ACUSA cada vez más. *This tendency gets stronger all the time.* || **5.** Exponer en juicios los cargos contra el acusado. *To charge, bring charges against.* || **6.** Delatar. *To point to.* Todo parece ACUSARLA. *All evidence seems to point to her.* || **7.** Notarse, advertirse. *To be evident.* ~Se ACUSA una falta de organización. *The lack of organization is evident.* || **8.** *LOCUCIONES.* || •ACUSAR alegría, cansancio. *To look happy, tired.* || •ACUSAR el golpe. *To feel the blow.* || •ACUSAR recibo. *To acknowledge receipt.* || •ACUSAR retraso. *To be late.* ~ACUSAMOS cierto retraso. *We're a bit late.*

ADECUADO. *adj.* Apropiado, que cumple las características oportunas para el fin al que se destina, conveniente. *Suitable, fitting, appropriate, satisfactory, right, proper.* Es el hombre ADECUADO para el cargo. *~He's the right man for the job.* Es el hombre ADECUADO para nuestra hija. *~He's the suitable man for our daugher.* ~No me parece ADECUADO que vayas sin corbata a la reunión. *I don't think it is proper for you to go to the meeting without a tie.* ~Éste no es el momento más ADECUADO. *This is not the right moment.* ~Los documentos ADECUADOS. *The appropriate, the relevant papers.* ⇨ADEQUATE

ADEPTO. *sm.* Partidario de alguna persona o idea. *Supporter, fan, follower.* ⇨ADEPT

ADHERENCIA. *sf.* Pegajosidad. *Adhesion, sticking.* || **2.** [De un coche]. *Grip, roadholding, road-holding qualities.* •Tener adherencias. *To have good roadholding, to hold the road well,* FIG *To have connections.* ⇨ADHERENCE

ADICTO. *sm.* Partidario o seguidor de algo. *Supporter, follower, member (of a political party), partisan, devotee.* ~El director y todos sus ADICTOS abandonaron la reunión en señal de protesta. *The director and all his supporters left the room in protest.* || **2.** *adj.* •Ser ADICTO a. (I) Apoyar. *To support.* Sólo hay una minoría ADICTA a las propuestas de reforma. *Only a minority supports the*

reform proposals, (II) Fond of, keen on. *Aficionado.* Es ADICTO a la caza. *He's very fond of (keen on) hunting.* ⇨ADDICT

ADJUDICACION. *n.f.* Ortorgamiento, entrega, concesión (premio). *Award.* ⇨ADJUDICATION

ADJUDICAR[1]. *v.* Conceder. *To award.* ~Le ADJUDICARON el primer premio. *They awarded him the first prize.* ~Después de un largo pleito le han ADJUDICADO a él la finca. *After a long trial, he was awarded the ranch.* ~ Le fue ADJUDICADO el contrato. *He was awarded the contract.* || **2.** Asignar. *To allot, allocate.* El número de minutos ADJUDICADO a cada candidato. *The number of minutes alloted to each candidate.* || **3.** Vender (subasta). *To sell (auction).* ~Le ADJUDICARON la alfombra al anticuario. *The carpet was sold (went) to the antique dealer.* ⇨ADJUDICATE

ADJUDICARSE[2]. *vr.* Ganar. *To win.* ~El equipo chileno se ADJUDICÓ la victoria. *The Chilean team won.* ~Se ADJUDICÓ el premio por tercera vez. *She won the prize for the third time.* || **2.** Hacerse dueño, apropiarse, apoderarse (de una cosa). *To appropriate, take over.* ~Se ADJUDICÓ todos los libros para su uso exclusivo. *He took all the books for his exclusive (own) use.* || **3.** •¡ADJUDICADO! *Sold!* (en una subasta). || **4.** •ADJUDICAR daños y perjuicios. *To award damages.* ⇨ADJUDICATE

ADMINISTRACIÓN [ADMINISTRATION]. *sf.* [De una empresa, organización]. *Running, management.* Es el contable encargado de la ADMINISTRACIÓN del restaurante. *He's the accountant in charge of (running, managing) the restaurant.* || **2.** Conjunto de personas. *Management.* ~Este edificio está ocupado por la ADMINISTRACIÓN. *The administrative office is in this building.* || **3.** Oficina. *Headquarters, central office.* ~Para conseguir este documento debe ir a la ADMINISTRACIÓN. *To obtain this document you need to go to the central (main) office.*

ADMINISTRAR[1]. *v.* Dirigir (organización, empresa, asuntos). *To run, manage.* ~Su hijo ADMINISTRA la empresa. *His son runs*

(manages) the company. ~Sabe ADMINISTRAR sus asuntos. *He knows how to manage his affairs.* || **2.** Dar. (I) [Inyección, medicamento]. *To give.* ~Le ADMINISTRÓ un antibiótico. *He gave him an antibiotic,* (II) [Paliza, golpes]. *Hand out, dish out.* ~ADMINISTRAR una paliza. *To hand out a beating.* || **3.** Suministrar. *To supply.* ~ADMINISTRAR los víveres disponibles a quienes los necesiten. *To supply food to those in need.* || **4.** [Alimento]. *To ration.* || **5.** [Fuerzas, energía]. *To reserve.* ~ADMINISTRA tus fuerzas para mañana; las vas a necesitar. *You'd better reserve your energy for tomorrow; you'll need it.* ⇨ADMINISTER

ADMINISTRARSE[2] *vr.* *To manage one's own money or affairs, organize one's life, to get one's priorities right.* ~Tengo que ADMINISTRARME mejor si quiero tener tiempo para todo. *~I must organize myself better if I wish to have time for everything.* ⇨ADMINISTER

ADMIRACIÓN [ADMIRATION]. *nf.* •Signo de ADMIRACIÓN. *Exclamation mark.*

ADMIRAR. *v.* Asombrar. *To surprise, amaze, astonish.* ~Me ADMIRO que todavía no le hayan metido en la cárcel. *I'm surprised (amazed) that they haven't jailed him yet.* ~Me ADMIRA la ignorancia de la gente. *I'm amazed how ignorant people are.* || **2.** •Quedarse ADMIRADO. *To be amazed at, to marvel at.* || **3.** •No es de ADMIRAR que... *It's not (really) surprising that...* ⇨ADMIRE

ADMISIÓN. *sf.* Aceptación, recibimiento, entrada. *Acceptance, entrance.* ~Edad de ADMISIÓN. *Entrance age.* ~Reservado el derecho de ADMISIÓN. *We reserve the right to refuse entrance to anyone.* || **2.** •Prueba (exámen) de ADMISIÓN. *Entrance examination (test).* ~El plazo de ADMISIÓN de solicitudes finaliza mañana. *The closing date for receipt of applications is tomorrow.* ⇨ADMISSION

ADMITIR. *v.* Tener capacidad. *To hold.* ~El auditorio ADMITE diez mil personas. *The auditorium holds (has seating capacity for) ten thousand people.* || **2.** Suponer. *To suppose.* ADMITAMOS que tenga razón. *Let's suppose he's right.* || **3.** Aceptar. *To accept.*

~No se ADMITEN propinas. *No tips allowed.* ~Se ADMITEN tarjetas de crédito. *We take (accept) credit cards.* 'ADMITE monedas de 100pts'. *This machine accepts 100 peseta coins.* ~En correos no ADMITEN paquetes voluminosos. *Bulky parcels are not accepted by the post office.* ~Esta palabra está ADMITIDA por la Academia. *This word is accepted by the Academy.* || **4.** Permitir, tolerar. *To allow, permit.* ~No pienso ADMITIR que llegues a estas horas. *I will not have you coming home at this hour.* ~No ADMITO este tipo de conversación. *I will not tolerate this kind of conversation.* || **5.** Dar cabida. *Allow, grant, permit, be susceptible of, lends itself to, to be open to.* Un discurso que ADMITE varias interpretaciones. *A speech which lends itself to various interpretations.* ~Lo que dijo no ADMITE discusión. *There can be no arguing with what she said.* ~El asunto no ADMITE demora. *The matter must be dealt with immediately.* ~Esta afirmación no ADMITE dudas. *This statement leaves no room for doubts.* ~No ADMITE otra explicación. *There's really no other explanation for this.* || **6.** •ADMITIR por. *Accept as.* Esta teoría no se puede ADMITIR por válida. *This theory cannot be accepted as valid.* ⇨ADMIT

ADOPTAR. *v.* [Medidas]. *To take.* ~Habrá que ADOPTAR medidas enérgicas. *Drastic measures will have to be taken.* ~ADOPTÓ la decisión de no volver a verla. *He resolved (took the decision) not to see her again.* ⇨ADOPT

ADQUISICIÓN [ACQUISITON]. *sf.* Compra. *Purchase.* ~La ADQUISICIÓN de la casa. *The purchase of the house.*

ADVERSO. *adj.* [Suerte]. *Bad.* ~La suerte le fue ADVERSA. *He had bad luck.* || **2.** Opuesto. *Opposite.* ~Ella vive en el lado ADVERSO de la calle. *She lived on the OPPOSITE side of the street.* || **3.** [Adversario]. *Opposing.* ~El equipo ADVERSO. *The opposing team.* ⇨ADVERSE

AFECCIÓN. *sf.* Enfermedad. *Disease, trouble, condition.* Una AFECCIÓN de garganta. *A throat complaint.* ~Una AFECCIÓN cardíaca. *Heart trouble, a heart condition.* ~AFECCIÓN lumbar. *Back trouble.* ‖ **2.** Afición, inclinación, apego, atracción (por algo o alguien). *Fondness, attraction, attachment.* ~La amistad entre mujeres jóvenes suele ser una AFECCIÓN efímera. *The friendship which is common among young women is normally short-lived.* ⇨AFFECTION

AFECTAR. *v.* Pretender. *To pretend, feign.* AFECTÓ indiferencia. *He pretended to be indifferent.* ‖ **2.** Asumir, adquirir (apariencia, forma). *To adopt, take on.* ~AFECTAR la forma de estrella. *To adopt the shape of a star.* ‖ **3.** Afligir. *To upset, sadden, trouble.* ~La enfermedad de su madre lo AFECTA mucho. *His mother's illness upsets him a lot.* ‖ **4.** Dañar. *To damage.* ~Le AFECTÓ a los ojos. *It damaged his eyes.* ‖ **5.** Sufrir. *To suffer from.* ~Está AFECTADO de una grave enfermedad pulmonar. *He's suffering from a serious lung disease.* ‖ **6.** [Bienes]. *To encumber.* ‖ **7.** Concernir. *To concern.* ~Por lo que AFECTA a esto. *With regard to this.* ‖ **8.** •Las lluvias AFECTAN al sur. *It's raining in the south.* ⇨AFFECT

AFIRMACIÓN [AFFIRMATION]. *sf.* Aseveración. *Statement, assertion.* ‖ **2.** Afianzamiento. *Strengthening, securing.*

AFIRMAR[1]. *v.* Aseverar, declarar. *To state, declare, assert.* ~Un portavoz del gobierno ha AFIRMADO que habrá elecciones. *A spokesman for the government has stated that there will be elections.* ~AFIRMÓ haberla visto allí. *He stated (said, declared, asserted) that he had seen her there.* ‖ **2.** Afianzar. *To reinforce. strengthen, secure.* ~Poner unos clavos para AFIRMAR un estante. *To put in a few nails to secure a shelf.* ‖ **3.** [Escalera]. *To steady.* ~Asegúrate de que está bien AFIRMADA. *Make sure that it's steady.* ‖ **4.** Asegurar. *To assure.* ~Le AFIRMO que es verdad. *I assure you that it is the truth.* ‖ **5.** [Lealtad]. *To declare.* ‖ **6.** *LOCUCIONES.* ‖ •AFIRMAR bajo juramento. *To swear under oath.* ‖ •Ni AFIRMÓ ni negó que fuera así. *She neither confirmed nor denied that this was the case.* ‖ •AFIRMÓ con la cabeza. *He*

nodded with his head.* ⇨AFFIRM

AFIRMARSE[2]. *vr.* Afirmarse (opinión). *To maintain.* ~Se AFIRMÓ en su negativa. *He insisted on refusing.* ~AFIRMARSE en lo dicho. *To maintain one's opinion.* ‖ **2.** Imponerse. *To assert oneself.* ~La necesidad de AFIRMARSE como persona. *The need to assert oneself.* ‖ **3.** Recobrar el equilibrio, apoyarse. *To steady oneself.* ~AFIRMARSE en los estribos. *To settle one's feet firmly in the stirrups.* ⇨AFFIRM

AFLUENCIA. *sf.* [De gente, público]. *Inflow, influx, flow.* La AFLUENCIA del público al estreno desbordó todas las previsiones. *The number of people the first night surpassed all expectations.* ~La AFLUENCIA de turistas. *The influx of tourists.* ~La AFLUENCIA de coches al estadio. *The flow of cars towards the stadium.* ~La AFLUENCIA de capital extranjero al país. *The influx of foreign capital into the country.* ‖ **2.** [En reuniones]. *Attendance.* ‖ **3.** [Agua, sangre]. *Flow.* ‖ **4.** Elocuencia. *Eloquence, fluency.* ‖ **5.** Tropel. *Rush.* ⇨AFFLUENCE

AFLUENTE. *adj.* Caudaloso. *Flowing, inflowing.* ‖ **2.** [Persona]. *Verbose, wordy.* ~Estuvimos más de una hora escuchando a este afluente ORADOR. *We had to listen for over an hour to this verbose speaker.* ‖ **3.** [Discurso]. *Fluent, eloquent.* ⇨AFFLUENT

AGENCIA. *sf.* Oficina. *Office.* ‖ **2.** Branch. Sucursal. ~Este banco tiene varias AGENCIAS repartidas en todo el país. *This bank has many branches all over the country.* ⇨AGENCY

AGENDA. *sm.* Libro o cuaderno en que se apuntan, para no olvidarlas, aquellas cosas que se han de hacer. *Diary, notebook, address-book (de direcciones).* ~Voy a mirar en la AGENDA la fecha de la próxima reunión. *I'm going to check my notebook to see when is the next meeting.* ‖ **2.** ACAD. Relación de los temas que han de tratarse en una junta. *Agenda.* ⇨AGENDA.

AGITADO. *adj.* Preocupado. *Worried, upset.* ‖ **2.** Excitado. *Excited.* Los niños están muy AGITADOS esperando el viaje. *The children are very excited about the*

coming trip. ‖ **3.** Ajetreado. *Hectic.* ~Una vida muy AGITADA. *A very hectic life.* ‖ **4.** [Mar]. *Rough, choppy.* ‖ **5.** [Vuelo]. *Bumpy.* ‖ **6.** [Aire]. *Turbulent.* ‖ **7.** •Una época AGITADA. *A period of unrest.* ⇨AGITATED

AGITAR[1]. *v.* Sacudir. *To shake.* 'AGÍTESE antes de usarlo'. *'Shake before use'.* ~Me AGITÓ para despertarme. *He shook me to wake me up.* El viento AGITABA las hojas. *The wind rustled (shook) the leaves.* ‖ **2.** [Brazo, handkerchief]. *To wave.* ~AGITABA los brazos. *He was waving his arms.* ~AGITABA un pañuelo. *She was waiving her handkerchief.* ‖ **3.** [Ala]. *To flap.* ~El pájaro AGITABA las alas. *The bird was flapping its wings.* ‖ **4.** [Arma]. *To brandish.* ‖ **5.** [Con cuchara]. *To stir.* ‖ **6.** Excitar. *To excite, rouse, stir up.* Los niños están muy AGITADOS esperando el viaje. *The children are very excited about the coming trip.* ‖ **7.** Inquietar. *To worry, upset, make anxious.* ~La noticia del accidente me AGITÓ mucho. *The news of the accident upset me a great deal.* ‖ **8.** [Sociedad, país]. *To cause unrest in.* ⇨AGITATE

AGITARSE[2]. *vr.* (I) [Barco]. *To toss.* (II) [Toldo]. *To flap.* (III) [Inquietarse]. *To get worked up.* ‖ **2.** •El niño se AGITABA en su silla. *The baby was fidgeting in its chair.* ‖ **3.** •Los árboles se AGITAN en el viento. *The trees sway in the wind.* ⇨AGITATE

AGLOMERARSE. [AGGLOMERATE]. *v.* Amontonarse. *To pile up.* ~Coches que se AGLOMERAN en la plaza. *Cars which are piling up in the square.* ‖ **2.** Agruparse. *To form a crowd, to crowd round.* ~Curiosos que se AGLOMERAN. *Inquisitive people who crowd round.* ‖ **3.** *To crowd.* La gente se AGLOMERA en las ciudades. *People are crowding the towns.*

AGONÍA. *sf.* [De un moribundo]. *Death throes, dying breath, last gasp.* ~En su AGONÍA. *On his deathbed.* ~Tener una larga AGONÍA. *To die after a long illness.* ‖ **2.** Sufrimiento. *Suffering.* ~Las AGONÍAS de las tropas. *The suffering of the troops.* ‖ **3.** [De las campanas por un moribundo. *Knell.* ‖ **4.** Deseo. *Yearning, desire.* ⇨AGONY

AGONIZAR. *v.* Estar muriéndose. *To be dying, to be in the throes of death.* ~Está AGONIZANDO. *He could die any moment now.* ‖ **2.** •En su AGONÍA. *On his death-bed.* ‖ **3.** Extinguirse (luz). *To fade.* ‖ **4.** Molestar a alguno con instancias y prisas. *To bother, pester.* ~Déjame estar, no me AGONICES. *Leave me alone, don't bother me.* ‖ **5.** Desear vivamente una cosa. *To be dying to.* AGONIZO por salir. *I'm dying to go out.* ⇨AGONIZE

AGRAVAR. *v.* Aumentar (pena, castigo, multa). *Augment, increase.* ‖ **2.** Oprimir con gravámenes o tributos. *Increase taxation.* ‖ **3.** Aumentar el peso de alguna cosa, hacer que sea más pesada. *To weigh down, make heavier.* ‖ **4.** AGRAVARSE. Hacerse mas grave, empeorar (enfermo, situación). *To get (become) worse, worsen.* ~El problema del paro se ha AGRAVADO en los últimos meses. *The unemployment problem has gotten worse in these last months.* Este clima puede AGRAVAR la enfermedad. *This kind of weather can worsen the illness.* ⇨AGGRAVATE

AGRESIVO. *adj.* Propenso a faltar al respeto o a provocar a los demás. *Quarrelsome, hostile, offensive.* ~El estaba siempre AGRESIVO, dispuesto a herir. *He was constantly hostile and ready to offend.* ⇨AGGRESSIVE

AJUSTAR. *v.*
❶ ESTAR EN CONSONANCIA, CONFORMARSE CON, ATENERSE A. *To correspond, be consistent with, to fit in, comply with, be in keeping with.* ~Lo que me dices se AJUSTA a la verdad. *What you say is consistent with the truth.* ~Esta decisión no se AJUSTA a su política de apertura. *This decision is not in keeping with their policy of openness.* ~Tenemos que AJUSTARNOS al horario. *We must keep (work) within the timetable.* ‖ **2.** [Condiciones, reglas]. *To comply with, abide by.* ~Deberá AJUSTARSE a las condiciones aquí descritas. *It will have to comply with the conditions laid down.* ~CONFORMARSE a las reglas. *To Abide by the rules.* ‖ **3.** •AJUSTARSE a razones. *To yield to reason.*

❷ ARREGLAR, RESOLVER. [General]. *To arrange, fix.* || **2.** [En costura]. *To take in.* || **3.** Determinar (precio, sueldo, alquiler). *To fix, decide on, establish.* ~AJUSTARON el precio en 20.000 pesetas. *They fixed the price at 20.000 pesetas.* ~Todavía falta AJUSTAR el alquiler. *We still have to agree on (fix, set) the rent.* || **4.** [Matrimonio]. *To arrange.* || **5.** [Acuerdo]. *To make.* || **6.** Concertar (cuentas) *To settle, fix.* •AJUSTAR las cuentas a alguien. *To settle a score with someone.* •AJUSTARLE las clavijas a uno. *To put the pressure on someone.* •AJUSTARSE en sus costumbres. *To settle down.* || **7.** [Abuso, error]. *To make right.* || **8.** [Diferencias]. *To settle, reconcile.* || **9.** [Trato]. *To strike.* || **10.** Acordar. *To come to an agreement.* || **11.** [Tratado]. *To draw up.*
❸ ADAPTAR, AMOLDAR, ACOPLAR. *To fit.* ~AJUSTAR bien. *To fit well.* || **2.** [Pieza]. *To make fit.* ~AJUSTAR dos piezas. *To make two pieces fit.* || **3.** Encajar. *To insert, fit into or together.* ~AJUSTARSE el cinturón. *To tighten one's belt.* || **4.** •AJUSTAR el paso al de alguien. *To keep pace with someone.*
❹ VARIOS. [Criado]. *To hire, engage, take on.* || **2.** [Golpe]. *To strike.* || **3.** Apretar (tornillo, freno). *To tighten (up).* || **4.** Saldar (cuenta). *To balance.* || **5.** Liquidar. *To settle.* ⇨ADJUST

AJUSTE. *sm.* [De precio]. *Fixing.* Sólo falta el AJUSTE del precio. *All that remains is to fix the price.* || **2.** Apretamiento. *Tightening.* || **3.** [De páginas]. *Makeup, composition.* || **4.** [De gastos, horarios]. *Readjustment.* ~AJUSTE de plantilla. *Redeployment of labor.* || **5.** [De costura]. *Fit, fitting.* || **6.** [De una cuenta]. *Settlement, payment.* || **7.** Reconciliación. *Reconciliation.* || **8.** Acuerdo. *Compromise.* ~Llegar a un AJUSTE. *To come to an agreement.* || **9.** Sobrepaga. *Bonus.* || **10.** TECN Asemblaje. *Assembly.* || **11.** [Cinema]. *Spicing.* || **12.** •AJUSTE de cuenta. Settling of scores. ⇨ADJUSTMENT

ALIVIAR[1] [ALLEVIATE]. *v.* Aligerar. *To lighten, make lighter.* ~Deberías ALIVIAR un poco la carga de esa estantería, si no quieres que se venga abajo. *You shouldn't have so many things on that shelf; it may*

collapse. FIG ~Han hecho lo posible por ALIVIARNOS del peso del trabajo. *They've done everything possible to lighten our workload.* || **2.** Calmar, suavizar, disminuir (enfermedad, padecimiento). *To sooth, calm, ease, relieve, make more bearable.* ~Intenta ALIVIAR sus penas con la bebida. *He's trying to relieve his sorrows by drinking.* || **3.** Consolar. *To comfort, console.* ~Me ALIVIA mucho saber que me comprendes. *It's comforting to know that you understand me.* || **4.** Darse prisa. *To hurry.* ~Como no ALIVIES, no llegarás a tiempo. *If you don't hurry you won't get there in time.* || **5.** Acelerar. *To speed up.* || **6.** [Paso]. *To quicken.* || **7.** Robar. *To steal.* ~Le ALIVIARON la cartera. *He had his wallet lifted, they relieved him of his wallet.* || **8.** Ayudar. *To help out.* ~ALIVIARLE a uno en el trabajo. *To help someone out with his work.*

ALIVIARSE[2] [ALLEVIATE]. *vr.* [Dolor]. *To diminish, get better, recover (paciente).* || **2.** [Figurado]. *To unburden oneself.*

ALTERACIÓN. *sf.* Sobresalto, inquietud, agitación. *Agitation, uneasiness, restlessness.* ~Me produjo gran ALTERACIÓN recibir carta tuya. *I was greatly disturbed by your letter.* || **2.** Putrefacción. *Spoiling.* ~La rápida ALTERACIÓN de algunos alimento en verano. *The quick spoiling of certain foods at summertime.* || **3.** Alboroto. *Row, quarrel.* ~ALTERACIÓN del orden público. *Breach (disturbance) of the peace, disorderly conduct.* || **4.** •Una ALTERACIÓN del pulso. *An irregularity of the pulse.* || **5.** •ALTERACIÓN digestiva. *Digestive upset.* || **6.** •ALTERACIÓN de la salud. *Deterioration of health, change for the worse.* ⇨ALTERATION

ALTERAR[1]. *v.* Perturbar, trastornar (orden, silencio, paz). *To disturb.* ~Fue acusado de ALTERAR el orden público. *He was charged with disturbing the peace.* || **2.** Permanecer impasible. *To remain unmoved.* ~Siguió sin ALTERAR. *He went on unabashed, unmoved.* || **3.** Pasmar, desconcertar. *To be shaken by (event, news).* La noticia del golpe ALTERÓ visiblemente al embajador. *The ambassador was visibly shaken by the news of the coup.*

4. Estropear, dañar, descomponer (alimento). *To turn bad, spoil (food), sour (milk).* ~El calor ALTERA los alimentos. *Heat makes food go bad.* ‖ **5.** Adulterar, por ejemplo, la leche, con alguna mezcla. *Adulterate.* **6.**Tergiversar, torcer, deformar (verdad, hechos). *To distort misinterpret.* ~Está alterando los hechos. *He's distorting the facts.* ⇨ALTER

ALTERARSE². *vr.* Perturbarse, trastornarse, inquietarse. *To become upset, to be disturbed.* ~Le ALTERA cualquier ruido. *The least little noise upsets him.* ~No se ALTERA por nada. *Nothing ever upsets him.* ‖ **2.** Enojarse, excitarse, agitarse. *To get upset, excited, to loose one's temper.* ~No te ALTERES. *Don't get excited.* ~No se ALTERA por nada. *He never looses his temper.* ‖ **3.** Asustar. *To frighten.* Le ALTERA cualquier ruido. *The least little noise scares her.* **4.** Desfallecer, empañarse (voz). *To falter.* Con la emoción se le ALTERÓ la voz. *Her voice shook (faltered) with emotion.* ‖ **5.** Cambiar. *Change, affect.* ~La exposición al sol puede ALTERAR el color. *Exposure to sunlight can affect the color.* ~Se ALTERA con la humedad (medicina, etc.). *Store in a dry place.* ‖ **6.** •Se le ALTERÓ el pulso. *Her pulse became irregular.* ⇨ALTER

ALTERNAR. *v.* Relacionarse, tratarse. *To mix with, be sociable, associate with, socialize with.* ~Suele ALTERNAR con personajes famosos. *She often mixes with famous people.* ~Tiene pocas ganas de ALTERNAR. *She doesn' feel like socializing.* ‖ **2.** Turnarse. *To take turns.* ~Se ALTERNAN para cuidarla. *They take turns to look after her.* ‖ **3.** •ALTERnar en sociedad. *To rub shoulders with.* ‖ **4.** •ALTERNAR de igual a igual. *To be on an equal footing.* ⇨ALTERNATE³

ALTERNATIVA. *sf.* Necesidad en que se encuentra alguien de elegir entre dos acciones incompatibles entre sí e igualmente malas o desagradables. *Alternative, choice.* ~A Heidi le quedaba la ALTERNATIVA de ceder su cuarto o aceptar a la pequeña en su compañía. *Heidi had the alternative (choice) of either relinquishing her room or accepting the*

company of the child. ‖ **2.** •Tomar una ALTERNATIVA. *To decide, choose.* ⇨ALTERNATIVE

ALUVIÓN [ALUVION]. *sm.* Gran cantidad. *Flood.* ~Le llovió un aluvión de cartas. *He was inundated with a flood of letters.* ‖ **2.** [De gente]. *Horde.* ‖ **3.** [Preguntas, insultos]. *Barrage, shower.* ~Después de la conferencia hubo un ALUVIÓN de preguntas. *After the lecture he was bombarded with (there was a barrage of) questions.* ~Un ALUVIÓN de improperios. *A shower of insults, a torrent of abuse.*

AMBICIOSO. *adj.* Egoísta, codicioso. *Self-seeking, overambitious.* ⇨AMBITIOUS

AMENIDAD. *sf.* Atractivo. *Pleasantness, agreeableness.* ~Sus clases carecen de AMENIDAD. *His classes lack sparkle, interest.* ⇨AMENITY

AMOROSO. *adj.* Cariñoso. *Loving, afectionate.* ~En tono AMOROSO. *In an affectionate tone.* ~Un padre AMOROSO. *A loving father.* ‖ **2.** [Tierra]. *Workable.* La finca estaba rodeada de terreno AMOROSO. *The farm was surrounded with workable land.* ‖ **3.** Templado, apacible (tiempo). *Mild.* ~El tiempo se va haciendo más AMOROSO. *The weather is getting milder.* ‖ **4.** Relacionado con el amor. *Love (used as adjective).* ~Cartas AMOROSAS. *Love letters.* ~Hizo un estudio sobre la poesía AMOROSA de Pedro Salinas. *He wrote an article on the love poems of Pedro Salinas.* ⇨AMOROUS

AMPLIO. *adj.* Espacioso, extenso (espacio físico, extensión, dimensión). *Spacious, roomy.* ~Una vivienda AMPLIA. *A spacious (roomy) home.* ~Una calle AMPLIA. *A wide street.* ‖ **2.** [Sentido no espacial]. Completo, vasto, extenso. *Broad, wide, extensive, considerable.* ~Una AMPLIA gama de colores. *A wide range of colors.* ~Por AMPLIA mayoría. *By a large majority.* ~Tener AMPLIOS poderes. *To have extensive powers.* ~Tener un AMPLIO conocimiento de la historia. *To have an extensive knowledge of history.* ~El AMPLIO desarrollo de la economía. *The considerable development of the economy.* ~Fue elegido por AMPLIA margen. *He won the election by a wide margin.* ~Un tema que tuvo una AMPLIA difusión. *An issue that received wide media coverage.* ~Un AMPLIO programa de reformas. *A wide-ranging (comprehensive) program of reforms.* ~Un AMPLIO cambio de impresiones. *A wide exchange of views.* || **3.** Holgado, no ceñido. *Loose-fitting, baggy.* Una falda AMPLIA. *A loose-fitting skirt.* || **4.** No restringido. *Full, unrestricted.* ~En el sentido AMPLIO de la palabra. *In the broad (fullest) sense of the word.* || **5.** Total, absoluto. *Full, fullest.* ~Les ofrecemos las más AMPLIAS garantías. *We offer the fullest possible guarantees.* ~Un criterio AMPLIO. *A broad criteria.* || **6.** •Una AMPLIA sonrisa. *A broad smile.* || **7.** •Tener AMPLIAS facultades. *To be fully competent.* ⇨ AMPLE

AMPUTACIÓN [AMPUTATION]. *sf.* Supresión (en un texto). *Cutting out, deletion.*

AMPUTAR [AMPUTATE]. *v.* Suprimir una parte (de un texto, una obra). *To cut out, delete.* || **2.** Créditos]. *To curtail.*

ANGINA. n.f. •ANGINA de pecho. *Angina,* MED *angina pectoris.* •ANGINAS. *Tonsillitis, throat inflammation, sore throat.* ~Estar con ANGINAS. *To have a sore throat.* ⇨ ANGINA

ÁNGULO. *sm.* Esquina, rincón. *Corner.* ~En un ÁNGULO del salón. *In a corner of the lounge.* || **2.** Curva. *Bend, turn.* || **3.** [De tiro]. *Elevation.* || **4.** •ÁNGULO del ojo. *Corner of one's eyes.* || **5.** •ÁNGULO muerto. *Blind spot.* ⇨ ANGLE

ANGUSTIA [ANGUISH]. *sf.* Desasosiego. *Anxiety.* ~Vive con la ANGUSTIA de que algún día la despidan. *She's constantly worried that one day she's going to loose her job.* || **2.** Malestar físico. *Sickness, nausea.*

ANGUSTIADO [ANGUISHED]. *adj.* Afligido, acongojado. *Distressed.* || **2.** Preocupado. *Worried.* ~Vive ANGUSTIADA. *She lived in a constant state of anxiety.*

ANIMOSIDAD. *sf.* Valor, ánimo, esfuerzo. *Courage, spirit.* || **2.** ACAD. Aversión, ojeriza, hostilidad. *Animosity.* ⇨ ANIMOSITY

ANSIOSO. *adj.* Avaricioso, codicioso. *Greedy.* || **2.** Ambicioso. *Overambitious.* ~Es muy ANSIOSO y lo quiere todo para él. *He's very greedy and wants everything for himself.* || **3.** Voraz. *Gluttonous.* ⇨ANXIOUS

ANTICIPACIÓN. *sf.* •Con ANTICIPACIÓN. *Early, in advance.* ~Llegar con 5 minutos de ANTICIPACIÓN. *To arrive 5 minutes early.* ~Tienes que reservarlo con mucha ANTICIPACIÓN. *You have to reserve it a long time in advance.* ~¿Con cuánta ANTICIPACIÓN hay que sacar las entradas? *How far in advance do you have to buy the tickets?* ~Debe pagar el billete con ANTICIPACIÓN. *To have to pay the ticket in advance.* || **2.** •Con suficiente ANTICIPACIÓN. *In good time, enough in advance.* ~Llegó con bastante ANTICIPACIÓN. *He arrived early.* ⇨ANTICIPATION

ANTICIPAR[1]. [ANTICIPATE]. *v.* Pagar por adelantado. *To pay in advance.* ~ANTICIPAR el alquiler. *To pay the rent in advance.* || **2.** Fijar tiempo anterior al regular o señalado para hacer alguna cosa. *To do something ahead of time, advance, hasten, move up (date, event).* ANTICIPARON la reunión. *The date of the meeting was moved up.* || **3.** Prestar, adelantar (dinero, préstamo). *To lend, loan, advance (money).* || **4.** Adelantar, poner al tanto, comunicar, participar. *To inform, tell, notify, disclose.* No quiso ANTICIPARME el tema del debate. *He refused to tell me what the discussion was about.* || **5.** Anunciar. *To be a sign of, mean.* Estas nubes ANUNCIAN lluvia. *These clouds are a sign of rain.* || **6.** •ANTICIPAR las gracias. *To thank in advance.* ⇨ANTICIPATE

ANTICIPARSE[2]. *vr.* Precipitarse. ~No te ANTICIPES, hay que ir poco a poco. *Don't get ahead of yourself, you need to do this slowly.* || **2.** Manifestarse algo antes de lo habitual. *To be or come early.* La primavera se ha ANTICIPADO este año. *Spring came early this year.* || **3.** To get there before, to beat (someone) to it. *Tomar la delantera.* Fui a coger un trabajo, pero se me ANTICIPARON. *I went for a job but someone beat me to it.* || **4.** •ANTICIPARSE a un rival. *To be one step* *ahead of a rival.* ‖ **5.** •ANTICIPARSE a su época. *To be ahead of one's time.* ‖ **6.** •No ANTICIPEMOS acontecimientos. *We'll cross that bridge when we get there.* ⇨ANTICIPATE

ANTIGÜEDAD [ANTIQUITY]. *sf.* [En un empleo, cargo]. *Seniority.* ~Por orden de ANTIGÜEDAD. *By order of seniority.* ‖ **2.** [Objeto]. *Antique.* ~Tienda de ANTIGÜEDADES. *Antique shop.* ‖ **3.** Edad. *Age.* ~La fábrica tiene una ANTIGÜEDAD de 200 años. *The factory is 200 years old.* ~Esas ruinas tienen varios siglos de ANTIGÜEDAD. *Those ruins are several centuries old.* ‖ **4.** •En la ANTIGÜEDAD. *In olden days, in former times.*

ANULAR. [ANNUL]. *v.* [Pedido]. *To cancel.* ‖ **2.** [Goal]. *To disallow.* ~El árbitro ANULÓ el tanto. *The referee disallowed the goal.* ‖ **3.** [Ley]. *To repeal, revoke.* ~Una nueva orden ANULÓ las disposiciones anteriores. *The previous regulations were repealed by a new law.* ‖ **4.** [Sentencia]. *To overturn, squash.* ‖ **5.** [Persona]. *To deprive of authority, remove from office.* ‖ **6.** [Informática]. *To delete.* ‖ **7.** [Decision]. *To overule, to override.* ‖ **8.** [Efecto]. *To nullify, cancel out.* ‖ **9.** [Contrato]. *To rescind.* ‖ **10.** Dar orden de no pagar (cheque). *To stop, put a stop-payment.* ~ANULÓ el cheque. *He had the check stopped.* ‖ **11.** [Viaje, compromiso]. *To cancel.* ~He ANULADO mi cita de esta tarde porque no me siento bien. *I cancelled my appointment for this evening because I don't feel well.* ‖ **12.** Hacer perder personalidad. ~Su carácter autoritario ANULABA la personalidad de su hijo. *His domineering character dwarfed his son's personality.* ‖ **13.** Incapacitar, desautorizar. *To overshadow, to dominate.* Es una persona tan dominante que ANULA a cuantos trabajan con ella. *She's such a domineering person that she overshadows whoever she works with.* ‖ **14.** •ANULARSE. Perder autoridad. *To be overshadowed, diminished, to feel intimidated.* ~No te ANULES ante ellos porque puedes hacerlo mejor que ellos. *Don't let them intimidate you; you can do it better than they can.*

ANUNCIAR. *v.* Dar publicidad a alguna cosa con fines de propaganda comercial. *To Advertise.* ~Es un producto que han ANUNCIADO mucho. *It's a product that's been advertised a lot.* ‖ **2.** Prometer ser. *To promise to be.* La temporada de ópera se ANUNCIA muy interesante. *The opera season promises to be very interesting.* ‖ **3.** Presentarse. *Report.* Sírvase PRESENTARSE en recepción. *Kindly report to the reception office.* ‖ **4.** Presagiar, pronosticar. *To augur, bode.* No nos ANUNCIA nada bueno. *It augurs (bode) ill for us.* ‖ **5.** Indicar, señalar. *To be a sign of.* ~Las golondrinas ANUNCIAN la primavera. *Swallows are a sign of spring.* ~El tiempo ANUNCIA lluvia. *It looks like rain.* ⇨ANNOUNCE

ANUNCIO. *sm.* Sign, omen. *Presagio.* ~Un ANUNCIO de muerte. *An augur of death.* ‖ **2.** Anuncio publicitario. *Advertisement (en un periódico), commercial (en la televisión).* ~Los ANUNCIOS de un diario. *The advertisement in a daily paper.* ~Insertar un ANUNCIO en el periódico *To place an ad (advertisement) in the newspaper.* ~ANUNCIO a página completa. *Full-page advertisement.* ~ANUNCIO de trabajo. *Job advertisement.* ~ANUNCIOS breves (económicos, por palabras). *Classified ads.* ‖ **3.** Cartel. *Poster, bill (theatre), notice, sign.* ‖ **4.** Cartelera, anuncio mural. *Billboard.* ‖ **5.** LOCUCIONES. ‖ •Prohibido fijar ANUNCIOS. *Post no bills.* ‖ •Tablón (tablilla) de ANUNCIOS. *Bulletin board.*‖ •Hombre ANUNCIO. *Sandwichman.* ⇨ANNOUNCEMENT

APARECER [APPEAR]. *v.* [Revista, producto]. *To come out.* ‖ **2.** [Objeto perdido]. *Come up, show up.* ~¿APARECIERON tus llaves? *Have your keys turned up, did you find your keys?* ‖ **3.** [Person]. *Show up.* Esperé unas dos horas pero no APARECIÓ. *I waited over two hours but he didn't show up.* ~No suele APARECER por la oficina. *He usually doesn't turn up at the office.* ‖ **4.** Parecer. *To seem.* Todo APARECÍA como un sueño borroso. *It all seemed like a hazy dream.* ~El río Amazonas APARECE como un mar inmenso. *The Amazon river looks like an immense sea.* ‖ **5.** •Hacer APARECER. *To* *produce.* ~Hizo APARECER un ramo de flores. *He produced a bouquet of flowers.*

APARENTE. *adj.* Que parece y no es, ilusorio, irreal, engañoso. *Seeming, unreal, deceptive.* || **2.** Vistoso, de buena aparencia. *Showy, colorful, eye-catching, nice, beautiful, flashy (derog.).* El vestido es muy barato pero muy APARENTE. *The dress is very cheap but it looks very good.* ~Tiene una casa muy APARENTE. *He has a very elegant home.* ~Un restaurante APARENTE. *A stylish (chic) restaurant.* || **3.** Conveniente, oportuno, adecuado. *Suitable, fitting, convenient, proper, apt.* ~Esto es APARENTE para el caso. *This is suitable for my particular purpose.* ~Siempre encuentras las palabras más APARENTES. *She always finds the right (proper, fitting) words.* ⇨APPARENT

APERITIVO. *sm.* Porción de comida que se sirve de forma gratuita y acompañando una bebida. *Appetizer.* ~En este bar cuando pedimos cañas (vasos de cerveza), siempre nos ponen APERITIVOS. *In this bar everytime we order beer they throw in appetizers.* || **2.** ACAD. Bebida que se toma antes de una comida principal. *Aperitif.* ⇨APERITIF

APLICADO [APPLIED]. *adj.* Diligente. *Studious, diligent, hard-working, industrious.*

APLICAR. *v.* Utilizar, destinar. *To devote, assign.*~ Los bomberos APLICARON todos sus efectivos en sofocar el incendio. *The firemen devoted (assigned) all their contingent to put out the fire.* || **2.** Asignar cierto nombre a algo o alguien. *To name, give the name of.* ~Se le APLICÓ el nombre de heliotropo por la cualidad que tiene de ... *It has been given the name of heliotrope because of its characteristic of...* || **3.** Adjudicar. ~APLICAR bienes o efectos. *To award.* | | **4.** [Impuesto]. *To impose, levy.* || **5.** [Inyección]. *To administer, give.* || **6.** [Descuento]. *To allow.* || **7.** [El oído]. *To listen attentively.* || **8.** Emplear. *To be used for.* ~El agua se APLICA al riego. *Water is used for irrigation.* ⇨APPLY

APRECIABLE. *adj.* Digno de estima. *Worthy, esteemed.* ~Una persona APRECIABLE. *A worthy, esteemed person.* || **2.** •APRECIABLE Señor (en cartas). *Dear Sir.* ⇨APPRECIABLE

APRECIACIÓN. *adj.* Enfoque, percepción. *Interpretation.* ~Es cuestión de APRECIACIÓN. *It's a matter of interpretation.* || **2.** Juicio. *Assessment, appraisal.* || **3.** JUR. •APRECIACIÓN de la prueba. *Weighing of the evidence.* || **4.** JUR. •APRECIACIÓN del trabajo. *Job evaluation, merit rating.* ⇨APPRECIATION

APRECIAR[1]. *adj.* Estimar. *To like, to be fond of.* Un amigo al que APRECIO mucho. *A very dear friend.* || **2.** Estimar, valorar. *To value.* ~No VALORA la vida. *He get's little pleasure out of life.* || **3.** Percibir, observar, distinguir. *To see, notice, observe, make out.* ~En la radiografía se APRECIAN unas manchas oscuras. *Some dark areas are visible (can be seen) on the X-ray.* ~Desde lejos no puedo APRECIAR los detalles. *From afar I can't make out the details.* || **4.** Notar, advertir, captar, percibir. *Detect, sense.* Le aprecio cierta ironía en el tono de su voz. *~I seem to detect certain irony in your voice.* || **5.** Calcular o determinar el valor de una manera aproximada. *To determine, assess.* Trataba de APRECIAR el tamaño del local. *He was trying to determine the size of the site.* ~Fue difícil APRECIAR la magnitud de los daños. *It was difficult to determine the extent of the damage.* || **6.** Marcar. *To register.* ~Este cronómetro APRECIA centésimas de segundos. *This cronometer registers hundredths of a second.* || **7.** Tasar, valorar, estimar. *To appraise, value.* ~APRECIAR una pintura. *To appraise, value a painting.* || **8.** Detectar. *To detect.* El tumor le fue APRECIADO hace unos meses. *The tumor was discovered (detected) a few months ago.* || **9.** •Apreciar la DIFERENCIA. *To tell the difference.* ⇨APPRECIATE

APRECIARSE[2]. *vr.* Ser notable. *To be noticeable.* ~Se APRECIA un cambio notable. *A remarkable change can be seen.* ⇨APPRECIATE

APREHENDER. *v.* [Mercancías, contrabando]. *To seize.* ~La policía ha APREHENDIDO un alijo de droga valorado en más de cien millones de pesetas. *The police has seized a consignment of drugs valued at more than a hundred million pesetas.* || **2.** [Idea, concepto]. *To grasp.* ~No consiguió APRE-HENDER las explicaciones del profesor. *He was unable to grasp the teacher's explanations.* || **3.** Concebir. *Conceive, think.* || **4.** Concretar. *To pin down.* ⇨APPREHEND

APROBAR. *adj.* Pass (exam, test). APROBÉ en francés. *I passed my French exam.* ⇨AP-PROVE

APROPIAR. *v.* To adapt, fit. APROPIAR las leyes a las costumbres. *To adapt laws to customs.* || **2.** FIG To borrow, use. *Pedir prestado, usar.* ~APROPIÁNDOSE de una frase del Presidente. *Using (borrowing) one of the President's phrases.* ⇨APPROPRIATE

APROXIMACIÓN. *sf.* Acercamiento, enfoque, tratamiento (a un problema, texto). *Approach.* || **2.** [Política]. *Rapprochement.* || **3.** [Lotería]. *Consolation prize, prize for runners-up.* || **4.** Proximidad. *Nearness, closeness.* ~No parece ni por PROXIMACIÓN que vaya a ceder. *He seems nowhere near giving up.* || **5.** [Barco, avión]. *Approach.* La nave comenzó las maniobras de APROXIMACIÓN. *The plane began its approach.* || **6.** •Un intento de APROXIMACIÓN. *An attempt to improve relations.* ⇨APPROXIMATION

APTO. *adj.* Adecuado, útil. *Suitable, fitting, appropriate.* Esta película es APTA para menores. ~*This film is suitable for minors.* ~APTO para todos los públicos. *Rated 'G'.* ~APTO para el servicio militar. *Fit for military service.* || **2.** Capacitado, capaz. *Skilfull, suitable, good at.* ~Es muy APTA para los negocios. *She very good at business.* ⇨APT

ARBITRAR [ARBITRATE]. *v.* Reunir (fondos). *To collect.* ~ARBITRAR fondos. *To raise funds.* || **2.** [En fútbol, boxeo]. *To referee.* || **3.** [En tenis, béisbol]. *To umpire.* || **4.** [Medios, recursos]. *To furnish, to provide, contrive.* ~ARBITRAR los medios para lograr algo. *To work out the ways to achieve something.* || **5.** [Medidas]. *To introduce.* || **6.** [Solución]. *To find.* ~El gobierno tuvo que ARBITRAR una solución para resolver el problema de los agricultores. *The government was forced to find a solution to solve the farmers' problems.*

ARCADA. *sf.* [De puente]. *Arch, span.*

~Puente de una sola ARCADA. *Single-span bridge.* || **2.** Náusea. *Nausea, sickness.* || **3.** •ARCADA dentaria. *Denture.* ⇨ARCADE

ARDOR. *sm.* Calor. *Warmth, heat.* ~En el ARDOR del sol. *In the heat of the sun.* || **2.** [De estómago]. *Heartburn.* || **3.** [Argumento, batalla]. *Heat.* ~En el ARDOR de la batalla. *In the heat of battle.* || **4.** Escozor. *Burning, burning sensation.* || **5.** Quemazón. *Burn.* ⇨ARDOR

ARGUMENTO. *adj.* Tema, trama. *Plot, story line.* El ARGUMENTO de la obra está basado en hechos reales. *The movie is based on actual facts.* ⇨ARGUMENT

ARMAR. *v.* [Mueble, estantería]. *To assemble, put together.* ~Están ARMANDO los módulos de la nueva estantería. *They're assembling the modules of the new bookcase.* || **2.** Disponer, preparar. *To arrange, prepare, organize.* ~ARMARON un baile para todos los antiguos alumnos. *They prepared (set up, organized) a dancing event for all the former students.* || **3.** [Lío]. *To cause, make, start, stir up.* ~Sigan jugando pero sin ARMAR alboroto. *Keep on playing but don't make a racket.* ~ARMARON un escándalo porque no quise devolverle el dinero. *They caused a commotion because I wouldn't give them their money back.* || **4.** [Tienda]. *To pitch, set up.* ~Tardaron sólo diez minutos en ARMAR la tienda de campaña. *They only took 10 minutes to set up the tent.* || **5.** [Náutica]. *To equip, fit out, put into comission.* ~ARMARON el velero y partieron rumbo al sur. *They equipped the ship and set out southward.* || **6.** Proporcionar. *To provide, equip.* ~Le ARMARON de buenos consejos para que se comportara debidamente. *They gave him (provided him with) good advice so he would behave.* Cargar (arma de fuego). *To load.* ~ARMÓ la pistola y puso el dedo en el gatillo. *He loaded the gun and put his finger on the trigger.* || **7.** [Bayoneta]. *To fix.* || **8.** [Arco]. *To brace.* || **9.** [Escándalo]. *To create.* || **10.** [Trampa]. *To set.* || **11.** [Hormigón]. *To reinforce.* || **12.** [Costura]. *To stiffen.* || **13.** [A un caballero]. *To knight.* || **14.** [Cama]. *To put up.* || **15.** [Trampa]. *To set.* ⇨ARM

ARMARSE. *vr.* Disponerse, prepararse. *To prepare.* ~ARMARSE una nación. *To prepare for war.* || **2.** Disponer el ánimo para lograr cierto fin. *To muster.* ~Se ARMÓ de valor y decidió pedir aumento de sueldo. *He plucked up his courage and decided to request a raise in salary.* ~ARMARSE de paciencia. *To muster one's patience.* || **3.** [Lío, discusión, riña]. *To break out.*

ARRESTAR. *adj.* Arrestar (en cuartel). *To confine to barracks.* ⇨ARREST

ARROGANTE [ARROGANT]. *adj.* Valiente y noble. *Brave, courageous, noble.* ~Un joven ARROGANTE se ofreció para defender a la dama. *A brave young man came to the defense of the woman.*

ARSENAL. *adj.* Astillero. *Shipyard.* ~En un ARSENAL construyen barcos. *In a shipyard they build boats.* || **2.** Conjunto. *Array.* Tiene un gran despacho con un ARSENAL de libros técnicos sobre la materia. *He has a large office with an array of technical books on the subject.* ⇨ARSENAL

ARTEFACTO [ARTEFACT]. *sm.* Dispositivo, aparato. *Appliance, device.* ~ARTEFACTO explosivo. *Explosive device, bomb.* ~ARTE-FACTOS de alumbrado. *Light fittings.* ~Un ARTEFACTO incendiario. *An incendiary device.* ~ARTEFACTOS de baño. *Bathroom fixtures.* ~ARTEFACTOS eléctricos. *Small electrical appliances.*

ARTÍFICE. *sm.* Autor, creador. *Author, maker, responsible,* FIG *Architect.* Fue el ARTÍFICE y ejecutor material del secuestro. *He planned and carried out the kidnapping.* ~El ARTÍFICE de la victoria. *The architect of victory.* ~Era el ARTÍFICE de su felicidad. *She was the person responsible for his happiness.* ~Dios es el ARTÍFICE de la Creación. *God is the author of Creation.* ~Ha sido el ARTÍFICE de su fortuna. *He's a self-made man.* || **2.** Artista, virtuoso, experto, maestro. *Artist, craftsman.* ~Es un verdadero ARTÍFICE en la restauración de muebles. *He a real expert in furniture refinishing.* ⇨ARTIFICE

ARTIFICIO. *sm.* [Arte, habilidad]. *Art, craft, skill, dexterity.* || **2.** [Hechura]. *Work-*manship, craftmanship.* || **3.** Aparato. *Contrivance, device, appliance.* || **4.** [Truco, artimaña]. *Trick, artful device.* ~Una belleza sin ARTIFICIOS. *Natural beauty.* ~Emplea muchos ARTIFICIOS para disimular su edad. *He uses lots of tricks to hide his age.* || **5.** •ARTIFICIO pirotécnico, fuego de ARTIFICIO. *Fireworks.* ⇨ARTIFICE

ARTISTA [ARTIST]. *s.m&f.* [Del cine]. *Actor, actress.* ~En esta película actúa su ARTISTA de cine predilecto. *Her favorite actor plays in this movie.*

ASALTO. *sm.* Robo. *Holdup, robbery.* ~El ASALTO del banco. *The bank robbery.* ~Un ASALTO a mano armada. *An armed robbery.* || **2.** [En boxeo]. *Round.* ~Lo puso fuera de combate en el segundo ASALTO. *He knocked him out in the second round.* || **3.** [En esgrima]. *Bout.* || **4.** Fiesta. *Party.* ⇨ASSAULT

ASCENDER. *v.* Promover. *To promote.* Lo han ASCENDIDO a capitán. *He's been promoted to captain.* || **2.** Cifrarse (gastos, pérdidas). *To amount, add up to, total, come to.* La cuenta ASCIENDE a diez mil pesetas. *The bill comes to (totals) ten thousand pesetas.* ~Sus deudas ASCIENDEN a un millón de dólares. *His debts amount to (runs to) a million dollars.* ~El número de detenidos ASCIENDE a 300. *There's been more than 300 arrests.* || **3.** Aumentar (temperature, precios). *To increase, rise.* ~La temperatura ha ASCENDIDO durante la tarde. *Temperature has risen in the afternoon.* || **4.** Ser ASCENDIDO (deporte). *To be promoted, go up to.* Málaga ASCIENDE a primera división. *Málaga goes up to the first division.* || **5.** Alcanzar. *To reach.* ~La producción de acero ASCIENDE a cinco mil toneladas. *Steel production reaches five thousand tons.* ~El número de muertos ASCIENDE ya a 48. *The number of deaths has now reached 48.* || **6.** Mejorar de situación social. *To rise socially.* ~Ha ASCENDIDO rápidamente en su carrera. *He has risen (advanced) rapidly in his career.* ⇨ASCEND

ASEQUIBLE. [ACCESSIBLE]. *adj.* [De comprar]. *Within (everybody's) reach, moderate, reasonable, affordable.* ~Libros ASEQUI-BLES a todos. *Books within everybody's*

reach. || **2.** [De entender]. *Easy to understand.* || **3.** [Finalidad, meta]. *Attainable, achievable.* || **4.** [Plan, proyecto]. *Feasible.* || **5.** [Servicios]. *Available.* ~Estos tratamientos no son ASEQUIBLES para nosotros. *These treatments are not available to us.* || **6.** [Persona]. *Approachable, easy to get along with.*

ASESINAR [ASSASSINATE]. *v.* Matar. *To kill, murder.* ~La víctima fue ASESINADA a sangre fría. *The victim was murdered in cold blood.* || **2.** Molestar. *To pester, plague to death.* ~Me estás ASESINANDO con tantos disgustos. *You'll be the death of me.* || **3.** Mutilar. *To butcher, mutilate.* ~La adaptación ASESINA la obra de Lorca. *The adaptation mutilates Lorca's play.*

ASESINO [ASSASSIN]. *sm.* Que asesina, homicida. *Murderer.* ~El ASESINO fue detenido por la policía. *The murderer was arrested by the police.* ▶La palabra *assassin* se aplica al asesino de personajes políticos.

ASIGNACIÓN. *sm.* [Paga]. *Allocation, allowance, pocket money.* ~ASIGNACIÓN semanal. *Weekly allowance.* ~La beca supone una ASIGNACIÓN mensual de ... *The grant provides a monthly allowance of ...* ~Cuenta con una ASIGNACIÓN mensual de sus padres para hacer frente a sus gastos. *He receives a monthtly allowance from his parents to meet his expenses.* || **2.** [Sueldo]. *Wage, salary.* ~Tiene una ASIGNACIÓN mensual bastante elevada. *His monthly salary is very high.* || **3.** [Porción]. *Share, portion.* || **4.** Cita. *Appointment, rendezvous.* || **5.** [De fondos]. *Allocation.* ~Le han conseguido una ASIGNACIÓN para trabajos de investigación. *He has received an allocation for conducting reasearch work.* ~Este departamento tiene una ASIGNACIÓN anual de dos millones. *This department has an annual allocation of two million a year.* || **6.** Pensión. *Pension.* ⇨ ASSIGNATION

ASIGNAR. *v.* Determinar lo que corresponde a alguien, conceder, destinar. *To grant, bestow, award.* ~Le han ASIGNADO un sueldo de cien mil pesetas. *They have granted him a salary of a hundred* *thousand pesetas.* ~Le ASIGNARON una beca. *He was awarded a grant.* || **2.** Dar, atribuir, conceder. *Attach, ascribe.* Dos hechos a las que se ASIGNA especial importancia. *Two facts to which special importance is attached (ascribed).* || **3.** •ASIGNAR fondos. *To make an appropriation.* ⇨ ASSIGN

ASIGNATURA. *sf.* EDUC Materia. *Course.* ~Le faltan tres ASIGNATURAS para licenciarse en informática. *He needs three more courses to obtain his master's degree in computer science.* || **2.** EDUC •ASIGNATURA pendiente. *Failed subject.* Todavía arrastra una ASIGNATURA pendiente del curso anterior. *He still must pass a course which he failed last year.* ⇨ ASSIGNMENT

ASILO. *sm.* [De viejos]. *Home, institution.* ~Asilo de ancianos. *Old people's home.* || **2.** •ASILO de huérfanos. *Orphanage.* || **3.** •ASILO de pobres. *Poorhouse.* || **4.** Refugio. *Shelter.* ~Dormía en un ASILO para vagabundos. *He was sleeping in a shelter.* ~Nos dieron ASILO por la noche. *They gave us shelter for the night.* || **5.** Remanso. *Haven.* ASILO de la paz. *Haven of peace.* ⇨ ASYLUM

ASISTENCIA. *sf.* Concurrencia. *Attendance.* ~La ASISTENCIA es obligatoria. *Attendance is compulsory.* || **2.** Público, auditorio. *Public, audience.* ~La reunión se celebró con mediana ASISTENCIA. *There was a moderate attendance at the meeting.* ~El día del estreno hubo poca ASISTENCIA en el teatro. *On opening-day the attendance was very poor, few people showed up at the theater on opening-day.* || **3.** Presence. *Presencia.* Contamos con su ASISTENCIA a la recepción. *We are counting on your presence at the reception.* ~Con la ASISTENCIA de. *With the presence of.* || **4.** Acción de pasar la pelota a otro jugador (baloncesto). *Pass.* ~Este jugador ha dado diez ASISTENCIAS a su compañero y éste ha metido 20 puntos. *This player has made 10 passes to his teammate who scored 20 points.* || **5.** Medios que se dan a alguien para que se mantenga. *Allowance, maintenance, alimony.* || **6.** Conjunto de los mozos de plaza. *Bullring* staff. || **7.** LOCUCIONES. || •Falta de ASISTENCIA al trabajo. *Absence from work.* ~No se permite la falta de ASISTENCIA al trabajo. *Absence from work will not be allowed.* || •ASISTENCIA intensiva. *Intensive care.* || •ASISTENCIA médica. *Medical care.* || •ASISTENCIA sanitaria. *Health care.* || •ASISTENCIA en carretera. *Road-side service.* || •ASISTENCIA técnica. *After-sales service.* || •ASISTENCIA pública. *Public Health System.* || •ASISTENCIA social. *Social Welfare.* ⇨ASSISTANCE

ASISTENTE. sm. MIL Soldado adscrito al servicio de un superior. *Batman, orderly.* || **2.** Criada. *Servant (masc.), maid (fem.).* || **3.** •ASISTENTE social. *Social worker.* ⇨ASSISTANT

ASISTIR. v. Acudir, hallarse presente en. *To be present at (meeting), attend.* ~Diversas celebridades ASISTIERON a la ceremonia. *Various celebrities attended the ceremony.* ~ASISTE a la clase de inglés. *He attends an English class.* ~ASISTIR a misa. *To attend mass.* || **2.** Presenciar. *Witness.* Hemos ASISTIDO a cambios profundos en este campo. *We have witnessed great changes in this field.* || **3.** Acompañar en un acto público. *To accompany (at a public event).* ASISTE a los reyes en la ceremonia. *He accompanies the king in the ceremony.* || **4.** Socorrer, auxiliar (como médico, enfermero, etc.). *Care for, treat, attend.* ~El médico que le ASISTE. *The doctor who attends him (in whose care he is).* ~Le ASISTE un buen médico. *He is being treated by a good doctor.* ~En el hospital ASISTIERON a los heridos. *The wounded were treated at the hospital.* || **5.** JUR Tener (derecho), estar de parte de alguien. *Have, possess.* ~Me ASISTE el derecho a ser escuchado en esta reunión. *I have a right to be heard at the meeting.* ~Le asiste el derecho de. *You have the right to.* || **6.** Prestar servicio en una casa como sirvienta accidental. *To work as a cleaning lady.* || **7.** Servir. *To serve, wait on.* ~Los criados ASISTIERON a los invitados durante la reception. *The servants waited on the guests during the reception.* || **8.** Asistir un parto. *To deliver a baby.* || **9.** JUR Representar. *To represent, appear for.* ~ASISTIDO por su abogado. *With*

his lawyer present. || **10.** Arrastrar (naipes). *To follow suit (cards).* || **11.** Attender, ocuparse de. *To take care of, attend, help (formally).* ~En el consulado lo ASISTARÁN debidamente. *You will receive the necessary assistance at the consulate.* ~Respira ASISTIDA por una máquina. *She is breathing with the help of a respirator.* || **12.** •Dios nos ASISTA. *May God help us.* ⇨ASSIST

ASOCIARSE. vr. [Empresas, comerciantes]. *To collaborate.* || **2.** [Con alguien]. *To team up, join forces with.* ~Los trabajadores se ASOCIARON para defender sus derechos. *The workers teamed up in order to fight for their rights.* || **3.** [Negocio]. *To go into partnership.* ~Se ASOCIÓ con su cuñado para montar el negocio. *He went into partnership with his brother-in-law to start the business.* || **4.** [Hechos, factores]. *To combine.* ~El granizo y las heladas se han ASOCIADO para destruir la cosecha. *Between them the hail and ice have combined to ruin the harvest.* || **5.** [A un grupo, club]. *To become a member of.* ~Se ASOCIÓ a un grupo ecologista. *He became a member of (joined) an ecologist group.* || **6.** Compartir. *To share.* ASOCIARSE a la alegría de uno. *To share someone's joy.* ~Nos ASOCIAMOS al duelo nacional. *We share in the nation's grief.* ⇨ASSOCIATE

ASPECTO [ASPECT]. sm. [De una persona, objeto, lugar]. *Appearance, look.* ~Un hombre de ASPECTO distinguido. *A man of distinguished appearance, a distinguished-looking man.* ~La barba le da ASPECTO de intelectual. *His beard gives him an intelectual look.* ~La casa tenía un ASPECTO austero. *The house had an austere appearance.* ~Por su ASPECTO exterior la casa parecía deshabitada. *The house looked unoccupied from the outside.* || **2.** [Problema, asunto]. *Way.* ~No me gusta el ASPECTO que van tomando las cosas. *I don't like the way things are going (looking).* || **3.** •Tiene buen ASPECTO, no parece enfermo. *He looks fine, he doesn't look sick at all.* || **4.** •Esta herida tiene muy mal ASPECTO. *That's a nasty-looking wound.*

ASPIRACIÓN. sf. Acción de respirar.

Breathing-in, inhalation. ~La ASPIRACIÓN del aire fresco del campo es muy sana. *Breathing the fresh air of open country is very healthy.* ⇨ASPIRATION

ASUMIR. *v.* Aceptar, tener conciencia, admitir, responsabilizarse. *Accept, be aware of, come to terms with, admit.* Tienes que ASUMIR tus propias limitaciones y actuar de acuerdo con ellas. *You must accept your own limitations and act accordingly.* ~Debe ASUMIR las consecuencias de sus errores. *He must accept the consequences of his mistakes.* ~Ya tengo totalmente ASUMIDO el problema. *I've learned to live with (I have come to terms with) the problem now.* ‖ **2.** [Riesgo]. *To take.* ~No estaban dispuestos a ASUMIR ese riesgo. *They were not prepared to take that risk.* ‖ **3.** [Compromiso]. *To undertake.* ~Han ASUMIDO el compromiso de reconstruir la ciudad. *They have undertaken to rebuild the city.* ‖ **4.** [Mando]. *To take over.* ‖ **5.** [Cargo]. *To take up.* ‖ [Actitud]. *Adopt.* ~Asumió un aire de indiferencia. *He adopted an air of indifference.* ‖ **6.** •ASUMIR la dirección. *To take control.* ‖ **7.** •El incendio ASUMIÓ grandes proporciones. *It turned into a major fire.* ‖ **8.** •Asumió la defensa del presunto asesino. *He took on the defense of the alleged murderer.* ⇨ASSUME

ATACAR. *v.* [Dificultad, problema]. *To grapple, tangle with.* ‖ **2.** Emprender. *To begin, start upon.* ~ATACAR la ascención del Aconcagua. *To begin the ascent of Aconcagua.* ‖ **3.** [Nota]. *To strike.* ~La cantante tomó aire ante de ATACAR la nota final. *The singer took a breath before striking the final note.* ‖ **4.** [Una prenda de vestir]. *To button, to fasten.* ~Empezó a hablar mientras ATACABA su chaqueta. *While he was buttonning his jacket he began to speak.* ~Se ATACÓ fuertemente el cinturón. *She fastened her belt tightly.* ‖ **5.** [Sueño, enfermedad]. *To overcome.* ~En invierno me ATACA la gripe. *In winter time I always catch the flu, the flu gets the best of me.* ‖ **6.** Pegar. *To attach, fasten.* ‖ **7.** [Bolsa]. *To stuff, pack, cram.* ‖ **8.** [Carga de arma de fuego]. *To ram, ram home.* ‖ **9.** [Pieza musical]. *To launch into.*

~La orquesta ATACÓ el movimiento final. *The orquestra launched into the final movement.* ‖ **10.** [Nervios]. *Irritar, alterar.* ~Este ruido me ATACA los nervios. *This noise gets on my nerves.* ⇨ATTACK

ATAQUE. *sm.* Acceso. *Fit.* Un ATAQUE de celos. *A fit of jealousy.* ~Le va a dar un ATAQUE cuando vea eso. *You're going to have a fit when you see this.* ~Si la ves te va a dar un ATAQUE de risa. *You'll die laughing if you see her.* ~Le dio un ATAQUE de llanto. *He burst into tears.* ~Me dio un ATAQUE de rabia al ver tanta injusticia. *I was enraged to see so much injustice.* ‖ **2.** •ATAQUE cerebral. *Brain hemorrhage.* ‖ **3.** •ATAQUE fulminante. *Seizure, stroke.* ⇨ATTACK

ATENCIÓN [ATTENTION]. *sf.* Amabilidad. *Kindness, civility.* ‖ **2.** Servicio. *Service.* ~No nos podemos quejar de la ATENCIÓN. *We can't complain about the service.* ~Departamento de ATENCIÓN al cliente. *Customer service department.* ‖ **3.** Cortesía. *Courtesy.* ~Nos colmaron de ATENCIONES durante nuestra visita. *They were extremely courteous to us during our visit.* ~Lo importante es tener una ATENCIÓN. *It's the thought that counts.* ~¡Cuántas ATENCIONES! Estoy abrumado. *How kind! I'm overwhelmed.* •En ATENCIÓN a. *As a sign of respect.* ‖ **4.** Detalle. *Nice thought.* ~Ha sido una ATENCIÓN por su parte. *It was very kind of him.* ‖ **5.** Respeto, consideración. *Respect, consideration.* ~Tener ATENCIONES con las personas de edad. *To show respect toward the elderly.* ~Me tratan con mucha ATENCIÓN. *They are very considerate towards me.* ‖ **6.** Ocupaciones. *Affairs, duties, responsabilities.* ~Tengo ahora otras ATENCIONES más urgentes. ~*At this moment I have more important matters to take care of.* ‖ **7.** Necesidades. *Necessities, needs.* ~¡Hay tantas ATENCIONES que cubrir? *There are so many needs to take care of!* ‖ **8.** •Horario de ATENCIÓN al público. *Hours of business.* ‖ **9.** •Llamar la ATENCIÓN. *To be striking.* ~Llama la ATENCIÓN por su original diseño. *The originality of the design is striking.* ~Es una chica que llama la ATENCIÓN. *She's a very striking girl.* ~Me llamó la ATENCIÓN un detalle. *I was struck by a detail,* (II)

Apetecer. *To be fond of.* ~Lo dulce no me llama la ATENCIÓN. *I'm not very fond of sweet things,* (III) Interesar. *To interest.* ~Nada le llama la ATENCIÓN. *Nothing seems to interest him,* (IV) Sorprender. *To surprise.* ~Me llamó la ATENCIÓN no verlo allí. *I was surprised not to see him there,* (V) Despertar la curiosidad. *Catch the eye, notice.* ~Al principio no me llamó la ATENCIÓN. *At first I didn't notice anything unsual.* || **10.** •¡ATENCIÓN! (para avisar de un peligro). *Look out, careful!.* ~¡ATENCIÓN a los pies! *Mind your feet!* ~¡ATENCIÓN! Frenos potentes. *Beware! Powerful brakes.* ~¡ATENCIÓN a la velocidad! *Watch you speed!* ~ATENCIÓN, carretera en obras. *Danger, roadwork ahead.* || **11.** •En ATENCIÓN a. *In view of, bearing in mind that.* ~En ATENCIÓN a sus circunstancias familiares. *In view of his family circumstances.*

ATENDER. *v.* Pay attention. *Prestar atención.* ~No atendía a la conferencia, sino a lo que decían los que estaban a su lado. *He was not paying attention to the lecture, but to what people next to him had to say.* ~Atiende, que eso es importante. *Pay attention, this is important.* Lo explicó pero nadie lo atendió. *He explained it, but nobody paid any attention.* ~Atiéndeme cuando te hablo. *Listen (pay attention) when I'm talking to you.* ~Atiende a tu trabajo. *Pay attention to your work.* || **2.** Hacer caso, tomar en cuenta, considerar (opinión, deseo, consejo). *Heed, listen to, pay attention to.* ~No atiende a razones. *He doesn't listen to reason.* ~Atender a la edad. *To take age into account* || **3.** •Atendiendo a. *Considering, taking into account, on the basis of, in view of, in the light of.* ~Atendiendo a su estado de salud, se le hizo pasar en seguida. *Given his state of health they let him in immediately.* ~Los premios fueron otorgados atendiendo únicamente a la calidad de las obras. *The prizes were awarded strictly on the basis of the quality of the works.* ~Atendiendo a sus instrucciones. *In accordance with your instructions.* ~Atendiendo a las circunstancias. *In view of the circums-*

tances. || **4.** Cumplir con. *To meet, fulfill, carry out.* ~No tiene tiempo de atender a todos sus compromisos. *He doesn't have time to fulfill all of his obligations (commitments).* ~No pudo atender a sus deberes. *He wasn't able to carry out his duties.* ~No disponemos de recursos para atender a estos gastos. *We do not have the resources to meet these costs.* ~El dinero alcanzará para atender sus necesidades más urgentes. *The money will be sufficient to meet their most pressing needs.* || **5.** Esperar. *To wait.* ~Atiende un momento. *Wait a moment.* || **6.** Prestar un servicio. *To render a service, minister to.* ~El doctor no atiende los martes. *The doctor does not see anyone on Tuesdays.* ~En esa tienda atienden muy mal. *The service is very bad at that store.* ~¿Quién atiende aquí.? *Who's helping here?* ~Bien atendido (servicio, negocio). *Well staffed, well organized, well-administered.* || **7.** Satisfacer, acoger favorablemente. *To meet, satisfy, accomodate a demand, a request, grant, agree to.* ~Atendieron a mi petición. *They granted my request.* || **8.** Ocuparse, despachar (cliente). *Wait on (a customer).* ¿Alguien le atiende? *Is someone waiting on you?* || **9.** Agasajar. *Entertain.* ~Se atendió mágnificamente a los invitados. *The guests were treated (entertained) like royalty.* || **10.** Recibir, acoger (persona). *To receive, see.* El señor Sánchez no lo puede atender en este momento. *Mr. Sánchez cannot see you at this moment.* || **11.** Cuidar, asistir (niño, inválido). *Take care of, look after.* || **12.** MECH Mantener, revisar, reparar. *To service, maintain.* || **13.** LOCUCIONES. || •Atender por. *To answer to the name of.* ~El perro perdido atiende por Canelo. *The lost dog answers to the name of Canelo.* || •Atender al teléfono. *To mind, answer the telephone.* || •Atender un pedido. *To fill an order.* || •Atender un giro. *To honor a draft.* || •Atienda a lo suyo. *Mind your own business.* ⇨ ATTEND

AUDIENCIA. *sf.* [Entrevista]. *Formal interview.* || **2.** [De periódico]. *Readership.* || **3.** [Tribunal]. *Court.* || **4.** Sesión. *Hearing.* ⇨ AUDIENCE

AUDITORIO [AUDITORIUM]. *s.* [Personas]. *Audience.* ~El AUDITORIO en pie aplaudió al cantante. *The audience gave the singer a standing ovation.*

AUTOR [AUTHOR]. *sm.* [De un delito]. *Perpetrator, person responsable for.* ~Los AUTORES del atraco. *The perpetrators of the robbery.* || **2.** [Teatro]. *Manager.* || **3.** [De una idea, proyecto]. *Originator, creator, inventor.* ~El AUTOR del proyecto. *The originator of the plan, the person who conceived the idea.* || **4.** [De una canción]. *Writer.* || **5.** [De un gol]. *Goalscorer.* || **6.** •Una obra de AUTOR anónimo. *An anonymous work.*

AUTORIZAR. *v.* Justificar. *Justify, warrant.* ~El futuro no AUTORIZA optimismo alguno. *The future doesn't justify (warrant) the slightest optimism.* || **2.** Permitir, dejar, consentir. *Permit, give permission.* ~El juez le AUTORIZÓ a asistir al funeral. *The judge granted him permission to attend the funeral.* ~Mi padre me AUTORIZÓ a emplear su coche. *My father let me (gave me permission to) use his car.* || **3.** Admitir, aprobar. *To accept.* ~Palabra AUTORIZADA por su constante uso. *Word accepted through its constant use.* || **4.** Facultar, acreditar, justificar. *To warrant, justify, give the right to (do something).* ~Eso no le AUTORIZA para hablarme de este modo. *That doesn't give you the right to talk to me that way.* ⇨AUTHORIZE

AVANZAR. *v.* MIL Ascender. *To promote.* || **2.** [Propuesta]. *Put forward.* || **3.** [Noche, invierno]. *Draw on.* ~Avanzaba el verano. *Summer was drawing on.* || **4.** [En los estudios, el trabajo]. *To make progress.* ~Desde que estuviste en Inglaterra AVANZASTE mucho en tu inglés. *Since you went to England your English has improved a great deal.* || **5.** [Negociaciones, proyecto]. *To progress.* || **6.** Mover. *To move forward.* ~Hay que AVANZAR su silla. *You must move your chair forward.* ~AVANZAR un pie. *To*

put one foot forward. ⇨ADVANCE

AVENTURA [ADVENTURE]. *sf.* Riesgo. *Risk, danger, hazard.* ~Una AVENTURA peligrosa. *A dangerous venture.* ~Invertir en un negocio es una aventura. *Starting a business can be risky.* || **2.** Relación amorosa. *(Love) affair, fling.* ~Fue sólo una AVENTURILLA de verano. *It was just a holiday romance.* || **3.** Azar, casualidad. *Chance, contingency.* || **4.** •AVENTURA sentimental. *Love affair, affair of the heart.* || **5.** Historia, anecdota. *Story.* ¿Te conté la AVENTURA que me sucedió con las maletas en París? *Did I tell you the story of what happened to me in Paris with my suitcases?* || **6.** •A la aventura. *At random.*

AVISAR. *v.* Advertir, llamar la atención, prevenir. *To warn.* ~Le avisaron que venía la policía. *They warned him that the police was coming.* ~No me habían AVISADO de que la carretera estaba en mal estado. *He did not warn (caution) me that the road was in bad condition.* || **2.** Informar, comunicar, anunciar. *Inform, notify, tell, let someone know.* ~¿Por qué no me AVISASTE que venía? *Why didn't you tell me he was coming?* ~AVÍSAME con una semana de anticipo. *Let me know a week in advance (give me a week's notice).* ~Hay que AVISAR con tiempo a los socios. *We need to notify the members well in time.* || **3.** •AVISAR a. *To send for, call.* ~AVISAR al médico. *To send for the doctor.* ~AVISAR un taxi. *To call a taxi.* ~AVISAR a la policía. *To call the police.* || **4.** •Llegó sin avisar. *He showed up without any prior warning (unexpectedly).* ⇨ADVISE

AVISO. Advertencia. *Warning.* ~El ataque del país es un AVISO. *The attack on the country is a warning.* || **2.** Anuncio. *Announcement.* ~Aviso al público. *An announcement to the public.* || **3.** Notificación. *Notice.* ~Con 15 días de AVISO. *With 15 days notice.* ~Hasta PREVIO aviso. *Until further notice.* ⇨ADVICE

B

BACHILLER. Persona que ha obtenido el grado de segunda enseñanza. *High School graduate.* ~Una vez que fue BACHILLER, decidió cursar estudios universitarios. *When he finished High School, he decided to go to college.* ⇨BACHELOR

BAGAJE. *sm.* Caudal, acervo, patrimonio. *Cultural knowledge, cultural heritage.* ~El BAGAJE cultural de un pueblo. *The cultural heritage of a nation.* || **2.** [De experiencia]. *Wealth.* ~Su BAGAJE de experiencia en este campo. *His wealth of experience in this field.* || **3.** [Intelectual]. *Background.* ~BAGAJE intelectual. *Intellectual background.* ⇨BAGGAGE

BALANCE. *s.* Vaivén. *To-and-fro, rocking.* ~El BALANCE es más fuerte cuando el barco navega de través a las olas. *The rocking of a ship is more pronounced when it is sailing against the flow of the waves.* ~El BALANCE del andamio le hizo perder el equilibrio. *The shaking of the scaffold made him loose his balance.* || **2.** Cálculo. *Estimate.* ~El BALANCE provisional de heridos. *The provisional estimate of casualties.* || **3.** Inventario. *Stocktaking.* || **4.** Vacilación, inseguridad. *Hesitation, vacilation.* ~Vive en perpétuo BALANCE, sin dedicirse por ninguna opción. *He never seems to make up his mind about anything.* || **5.** [Accounting]. *Balance-sheet.* ~A fin de mes siempre hacemos BALANCE para controlar las ganancias. *We always make a monthly balance-sheet to see how the business is doing.* || **6.** •Hacer BALANCE de una situación. *To take stock of a situation.* ~Hizo BALANCE de su vida y se sintió satisfecho. *He took stock of his life and felt pleased with himself.* ⇨BALANCE[1]

BALANCEAR. *v.* Mecer. *To rock.* ~Si no BALANCEAS la cuna, llora. *If you don't rock his cradle, he starts crying.* ⇨BALANCE[2]

BALANCEARSE. *vr.* [En una mecedora]. *To rock.* ¡Deja de BALANCEARTE en la silla! *Stop rocking your chair!* || **2.** [En un columpio, hamaca]. *To swing.* ~Se BALANCEABA en la hamaca. *She was swinging (herself) in the hammock.* || **3.** [Barco]. *To roll.* ~El barco se BALANCEABA entre las olas. *The ship was rolling in the waves.* || **4.** [Péndulo]. *To move to and fro, oscillate.* || **5.** Vacilar. *To hesitate, waver.* ~Lo decidió en seguida sin BALANCEAR. *He made up his mind right away without hesitating.* || **6.** [Arbol, ramas]. *To sway.* || **7.** •Caminaba BALANCEÁNDOSE de lo cansado que estaba. *He was so tired that he swayed from side to side as he walked.* ⇨BALANCE[1]

BALANZA. *sf.* [Para pesar]. *Scales.* ~BALANZA de baño. *Bathroom scale.* ~BALANZA de cocina. *Kitchen scale.* FIG ~Esto inclinaría la BALANZA a favor de los visitantes. *This would tip the scales in favor of the visitors.* || **2.** •Poner en la BALANZA. *To weigh, to compare.* ~Hay que poner los pros y los contras en la BALANZA. *You must weigh the pros and cons.* ⇨BALANCE[2]

BALÓN. *sm.* Pelota. *Ball, football.* || **2.** Recipiente. *Cylinder.* || **3.** [Gases]. *Bag.* ~Un BALÓN de oxígeno. *An oxygen bag.* || **4.** Copa. *Brandy glass.* || **5.** FAM Fuerza que reanima. *Shot in the arm, boost.* || **6.** Fardo. *Bale.* ⇨BALOON

BARNIZ. *sm.* [En cerámica]. *Glaze.* || **2.** [En metal]. *Polish, gloss.* || **3.** Makeup. *Afeite.* || **4.** FIG Cualidad superficial. *Smattering,* veneer, superficial knowledge. ~Tener un BARNIZ de cultura. To have a veneer of culture. ~Su amabilidad es puro BARNIZ. Her kindness is just a veneer. ⇨VARNISH

BARRA. sf. [De bicicleta]. Crossbar. || **2.** [De labios]. Lipstick. ~No me gusta el rojo de tu BARRA de labios. I don't like the color of your lipstick. || **3.** [De pan]. French loaf, baguette. ~He comprado dos BARRAS y una docena de huevos. I purchased a couple of baguettes (French loaves) and a dozen eggs. || **4.** [Del acusado]. Dock. || **5.** [De testigo]. Witness box. || **6.** Barandilla. Rail, railing. || **7.** Palanca de hierro. Rod, lever, crowbar. || **8.** [Para cortinas]. Rod, pole. ~Las cortinas cuelgan de una BARRA de metal. The curtains hang from a metal rod (pole). || **9.** [Larga y delgada: en un armario]. Rail. || **10.** [De turrón, helado]. Block. || **11.** [De desodorante]. Stick. || **12.** [Signo de puntuación]. Slash. ~En la fecha 3/7/90, la BARRA separa el día, el mes y el año. In the date 3/7/90, the slash separates the day, the month and the year. || **13.** [Joya]. Pin. || **14.** [De hielo]. Block. ~Trajo dos BARRAS de hierro para enfriar las bebidas. He brought two blocks of ice to keep the drinks cold. || **15.** [De barco grande]. Helm. || **16.** [De arena]. Sandbank. ~Esa BARRA puede ser peligrosa para la navegación. This sandbank can be very dangerous for the ships that pass by. ⇨BAR

BARRACA. sf. (En Valencia y Murcia). Thatched farmhouse (typical of Valencia and Murcia). || **2.** Puesto de feria. Stall, booth. ~En la feria había una BARRACA con tiro al blanco. There was a booth with a shooting gallery at the fair. || **3.** LAT. AM. Almacén. Warehouse. || **4.** Cabaña. Hut, cabin. ~Eran tan pobres que vivían en una BARRACA hecha por ellos mismos. They were so poor that they lived in a self-made hut. || **5.** [De obreros]. Workmen's hut. ~Mientras duren las excavaciones, utilicen la BARRACA. During the digging use the workmen's hut. ⇨BARRACK

BASE. s. Fundamento. Basis. ~Arroz es la BASE de su alimentación. Rice forms the basis of their diet, their diet is based on rice. ~La BASE de una buena salud es la alimentación. The basis of good health is a balanced diet. ~Sobre la BASE de estos datos podemos concluir que ... On the basis of this information we can conclude that ... || **2.** Fundamento. Foundation, grounds. ~Su argumento carece de BASE. His argument has no foundation. ~No tiene suficiente BASE para asegurar eso. You don't have sufficient grounds to claim that. || **3.** Principio, conocimientos básicos. Basis, grounding. ~Este libro nos dará una buena BASE en astronomía. This book will give us a good grounding in astronomy. ~Tiene una sólida BASE científica. He has a sound basic knowledge in science. ~Llegó sin ninguna BASE. He hadn't mastered the basics when he arrived. || **4.** Premisa. Premise. ~Si partimos de la BASE de que. If we start with the premise that. || **5.** [De maquillaje]. Foundation. ~BASE de maquillaje. Make-up foundation. || **6.** pl. [De concurso]. Conditions, rules. || **7.** Fondo. Background. ~Sobre una BASE de tonos claros. Against a background of light tones. || **8.** Origen. Source. ~La BASE de su fortuna fue. The source of his wealth was. || **9.** LOCUCIONES. •A BASE de. By, on the basis of, by means of. ~A BASE de hacer nada. By doing nothing, with the idea of not doing anything. ~A BASE de 50 toneladas al año. On the basis of 50 tons a year, at 50 tons a year. ~A BASE de descansar se fue recuperando. By resting he gradually recovered. ~Lo consiguió a BASE de muchos sacrificios. He had to make a lot of sacrifices to achieve it. ~Vive a BASE de pastilla. Pills are what keeps her going. ~Traducir a BASE de diccionarios. To translate with the help of dictionaries. ~A BASE de muchos esfuerzos. Thanks to all his efforts. || •Alimento BASE. Staple food or diet. || •BASE de operaciones. Field headquarters. || •BASE espacial. Space-station. || •Comida a BASE de verduras. Vegetarian meal. || •En BASE a. With regard to, with a view to. || •Militante de BASE. Rank and file member. || •Opinión de BASE. Grass-roots opinion, rank-and-

file opinion. ‖ •Partir de una BASE falsa. *To start from a false assumption.* ‖ •Sentar las BASES. *To do the groundwork, lay the foundations of.* ‖ •Sueldo BASE. *Minimum wage.* ‖ •Tomar algo como BASE. *To take something as a starting point.* ⇨BASE

BATERÍA. Conjunto de instrumentos de percusión en una banda u orquesta. *Drums, percussion.* ‖ **2.** Músico que toca la batería. *Drummer.* ~El BATERÍA del conjunto es holandés. *The group's drummer is Dutch.* ‖ **3.** Grupo, juego, serie. *Set, collection, row (filing cabinets), fleet (truck), bank (lockers).* ‖ **4.** Brecha. *Breach.* ‖ **5.** DEP Pareja de lanzador y recibidor. *The pitcher and catcher (in baseball).* ‖ **6.** Fila de luces del proscenio. *Footlights* (in a theater). ~Los actores estaban deslumbrados por la BATERÍA y no veían al público. *The actors were blinded by the footlights and could not see the audience.* ‖ **7.** LOCUCIONES. ‖ •BATERÍA de cocina. *Kitchen utensils, pots and pans.* ‖ •Aparcar en BATERÍA. *To park at an angle to the curb.* ‖ •Tocar la BATERÍA. *To play the drums.* ~Su gran ilusión era tocar la BATERÍA. *His greatest dream was to play the drums.* ‖ •Entrar en BATERÍA. *To prepare for action.* ⇨BATTERY

BATIR. *v.* [Metal]. *To hammer, pound on.* ~El herrero BATE el metal con el martillo. *The blacksmith hammers the metal with a hammer.* ‖ **2.** [Palmas]. *To clap.* ‖ **3.** [Alas]. *To flap.* ~El pájaro herido BATÍA las alas, pero no podía volar. *The wounded bird flapped its wings, but he was unable to fly.* ‖ **4.** CUL [Nata, claras, crema]. *To whip.* ~BATIÓ la leche hasta convertirla en nata. *He whipped the milk into cream.* ‖ **5.** [Marca, récord]. *To break.* ~BATIÓ el récord mundial de los 100 metros libres. *He broke the world's 100 meters freestyle record.* ‖ **6.** Derribar (casa, muro, fortaleza). *To break down, knock down.* ~BATIR una puerta. *To break down a door.* ~La artillería BATIÓ las murallas enemigas. *The artillery broke down the enemy walls.* ‖ **7.** Desmontar, desarmar (tienda, toldo). *To take down.* ~BATIÓ el toldo para que el viento no lo rompiera. *He took down the awning so*

that the wind would not rip it (tear it apart). ‖ **8.** MIL [Reconocer]. *Reconnoiter.* ~Los soldados BATIERON la zona en busca de una patrulla emboscada. *The soldiers reconnoitered the region to make sure that none of their patrols had been ambushed.* ‖ **9.** [Moneda]. *To mint, coin.* ‖ **10.** [Pelo]. *To come back.* ‖ **11.** [Privilegio]. *To do away with.* ‖ **12.** [Viento]. *To sweep.* ~El viento BATIÓ la región durante tres días. *The wind swept the region for three days.* ‖ **13.** [Lugar]. *To comb, search.* ~A pesar de que BATIERON la ciudad entera, no encontraron al ladrón. *Although they combed the city through and through, they were unable to find the thief.* ⇨BEAT

BAUTIZAR [BAPTIZE]. *v.* Poner nombre. *To name.* ~BAUTIZAR un barco/una calle. *To name a ship/street.* ‖ **2.** Poner mote. *To knickname.* ~Le BAUTIZARON con el mote de 'El Alto'. *He was knicknamed 'El Alto'.* ‖ **3.** Mezclar con agua (vino, leche). *To water down, dilute.* ~Si quieres darle vino al chico, primero BAUTÍZALO un poco. *Mix in the wine with a little water before giving it to the boy.* ‖ **4.** [Persona]. *To drench, soak.*

BENEFICIO. *s.m.* Función benéfica. *Charity performance.* ~Un concierto a BENEFICIO del asilo de ancianos. *A concert in aid of the old people's home.* ‖ **2.** COM Ganancia. *Profit.* ~Este negocio produce grandes BENEFICIOS. *This business yields large profits.* ~Una inversión que reportó importantes BENEFICIOS. *An investment that brought significant profits.* ~Margen de BENEFICIO(s). *Profit margin.* ‖ **3.** Advantage. *Ventaja.* ~Los BENEFICIOS del empleo. *The advantages of the job.* ‖ **4.** LAT.AM [Ganado]. *Slaughter.* ‖ **5.** LOCUCIONES. ‖ •En BENEFICIO de todos. *In everyone's interest.* ‖ •En BENEFICIO propio. *In one's interest.* ~Todo lo hace en BENEFICIO suyo. *Everything he does is for his own gain (advantage).* ‖ •En BENEFICIO tuyo/suyo. *For your/his own good.* ‖ •BENEFICIO social. *Fringe benefit.* •BENEFICIO bruto. *Gross profit.* ⇨BENEFIT

BESTIA. *adj.* Ignorante, estúpido. *Stupid.* ~Es tan BESTIA que no reconoce un Picasso de un Velázquez. *He's so ignorant he can't tell a Picasso from a Velazquez.* ~¡No seas BESTIA, que vas a chocar! *Don't be so stupid (reckless), you're going to crash!* || **2.** Grosero. *Rude.* Mira si es BESTIA, entra sin saludar a nadie. *He's so rude, he just comes in without saying hello to anyone.* || **3.** Violento, brusco. *Brute, animal.* ~¡Qué hombre más BESTIA!, ha vuelto a pegarle. *What a brute (animal), he's hit her again.* || **4.** Clumsy. *Torpe.* ¡Ay, perdón! ¡que BESTIA que soy! *Oh, sorry!, I'm so clumsy!* || **5.** [Expresando admiración, asombro]. FAM *Amazing.* ~¡Qué BESTIA! ¡Metió seis goles! *That's amazing, he scored six goals!* ~¡Qué BESTIA! Se ha comido dos platos enteros de lentejas. *This guy is incredible! He's just eaten two whole plates of lentils.* || **6.** •A lo BESTIA. ~Comen a lo BESTIA. *They eat an incredible amount.* ~El público se puso a gritar a lo BESTIA. *The crowd began to shout like crazy.* ~Todo lo hace a lo BESTIA. *He's so slap-dash in everything he does.* ~Conducen a lo BESTIA. *They drive like madmen.* || **7.** •Estar hecho un BESTIA. *To be as strong as a horse.* || **8.** •Ser una mala BESTIA. *To be a nasty piece of work.* ⇨BEAST

BONANZA. *s.* [Tiempo]. *Fair weather.* || **2.** [Marítimo]. *Calm at sea.* ~El barco de vela avanzaba con suavidad porque había BONANZA. *Since the sea was calm the boat sailed smoothly.* ⇨BONANZA

C

CABINA. *sf.* Locutorio telefónico. *Telephone booth.* ⇨CABIN

CALCULAR. *v.* Evaluar. *To make an estimate, figure out.* CALCULA lo que necesitas. *Figure out how much you need.* ~CALCULÉ mal la distancia. *I misjudged the distance.* ~CALCULANDO por lo bajo. *At the lowest estimate.* ~Se CALCULA que asistirán más de 50 personas a la reunión. *It is estimated that over 50 people will be present at the meeting.* ‖ **2.** Hacer conjeturas. *To think, suppose, figure, guess.* ~CALCULO que llegará tarde. *I don't expect him until late.* ‖ **3.** Imaginar. *Imagine.* CALCULA el disgusto que se habrá llevado. *Imagine (just think) how upset he must have been.* ‖ **4.** •CALCULAR que ... *To reckon, anticipate, expect that ...* ~CALCULO que estaremos de vuelta a eso de la diez. *I expect to be back at about ten o'clock.* ~Yo le CALCULO unos 60 años. *I reckon he's about sixty years old.* ⇨CALCULATE

CALIDAD. *sf.* Condición. *Status.* Los documentos que CERTIFIQUEN su calidad de estudiante. *The document that proves your student status.* ~En su CALIDAD de presidente electo. *In his capacity as president elect.* ‖ **2.** Clase, categoría. *Type, kind.* ~Las distintas CALIDADES de tomates. *The various types of tomatoes.* ~Naranjas de primera/segunda CALIDAD. *First-class/second-class oranges.* ‖ **3.** Cláusula (de contrato). *Stipulation, term, condition.* ~A CALIDAD de que. *Provided that.* ‖ **4.** Importancia. *Importance.* ~Un asunto de CALIDAD. *A matter of importance.* ‖ **5.** •En CALIDAD de. *As.* ~El dinero que recibió en CALIDAD de préstamo. *The money he received as a loan.* ⇨QUALITY

CALIFICACIÓN. *sf.* Nota (en la escuela). *Mark.* ~En junio saldrán las CALIFICACIONES finales. *The grades for the final exams will be announced in June.* ⇨QUALIFICATION

CALIFICAR. *v.* Considerar, tildar, llamar. *To describe, consider, call, rate.* ~CALIFICARON sus ideas de progresistas. *They labelled his ideas as progressive.* ~Lo CALIFICÓ de inmoral. *He called him immoral.* ~La CALIFICARON de pintora genial. *They rated her a brilliant painter.* ‖ **2.** [Examen, ejercicio]. *To grade.* ~CALIFICÓ mi examen con un notable. *He gave me an A on my exam.* ⇨QUALIFY

CAMARADA. *sm.* [De trabajo]. *Colleague, fellow worker.* ~Se fue de juerga con sus CAMARADAS de la oficina. *He went out partying with his fellow workers at the office.* ‖ **2.** [De colegio]. *Schoolmate, school friend, classmate.* ~Lo conozco muy bien. Fuimos CAMARADAS de colegio. *I know him very well. We were schoolmates.* ⇨COMRADE

CANAL [CANAL]. *sm.* [Natural]. *Channel.* ~CANAL de la Mancha. *English Channel.* ‖ **2.** CANALÓN (de tejado). *Gutter.* ~Tenemos goteras en la casa porque se ha roto el CANAL. *We have leaks in the house because the gutter is broken.* ‖ **3.** Vía, medio. *Channel.* ~Por otros CANALES. *Through other channels.* ~Si no lo consigo de esta manera, tendré que probar por otros CANALES. *If I don't obtain it this manner, I'll have to try some other ways.* ~CANALES de distribución. *Distribution channels.* ‖ **4.** [TV]. *Channel.* ~Con esta antena veo seis CANALES. *With this antenna I can watch six channels.* ~CANAL de pago. *Pay channel, subscription channel.* ‖ **5.** [De cinta]. *Track.* ‖ **6.** Tubo. *Pipe, conduit.* ~El agua pasa por CANALES de plomo. *Water flows through lead pipes.* || **7.** Ranura. *Groove.*

CANCELAR. *v.* Saldar, pagar del todo una deuda. *Pay off, settle.* || **2.** Pagar (una cuenta). *To pay.* ~Quiero CANCELAR esta factura. *I wish to pay this bill.* || **2.** En el banco, cerrar una cuenta corriente. *To close off (an account).* || **3.** [Préstamo]. *Pay off.* ~Si ahorro, el año que viene podré CANCELAR el préstamo. *If I save enough, next year I'll be able to pay off the loan.* || **4.** Borrar de la memoria. *To dispel, banish (from one's mind), to do away with.* ⇨ CANCEL

CÁNDIDO. *adj.* Ingenuo, sin malicia, fácil de engañar. *Simple, naive, ingenuous.* || **2.** Innocent. *Puro.* ~La mirada CÁNDIDA de un niño. *The innocent look of a child.* ⇨ CANDID

CANTIDAD [QUANTITY]. *sf.* [Suma de dinero]. *Sum, amount.* ~CANTIDAD a abonar. *Amount due.* || **2.** Gran número, volumen. *Large number, great amount, lot of.* ~Había una CANTIDAD de mosquitos impresionante. *There was an incredible number of mosquitoes.* ~No te puedes imaginar la CANTIDAD de gente que había. *You wouldn't believe how many people were there.* ~Mira la CANTIDAD de comida que hay. *Look how much food there is.*

CAPTURAR. *v.* Cazar, pescar. *To catch.* ~El cazador logró CAPTURAR un magnífico ejemplar de leopardo. *The hunter was able to catch a beautiful specimen of a leopard.* || **2.** [Drogas, contrabando]. *To seize, confiscate.* ⇨ CAPTURE

CARÁCTER. *sm.* Índole. *Nature, kind.* ~Por razones de CARÁCTER privado. *For private reasons.* Una visita de CARÁCTER oficial. *An official visit.* ~El CARÁCTER superficial del estudio. *The superficial nature of the survey.* ~Con carácter gratuito. *Free of charge.* ~Con CARÁCTER devolutivo. *Retroactively.* Heridas de CARÁCTER leve. *Minor wounds.* || **3.** BIOL Feature, characteristic. ~CARÁCTER adquirido. *Acquired characteristic.* ~CARÁCTER hereditario. *Inherited characteristic.* || **4.**

•CARÁCTER de imprenta. *Type, typeface.* || **5.** •Tener buen (mal) CARÁCTER. *To be good-natured (bad-tempered).* || **6.** •Con CARÁCTER de. As. ~Con CARÁCTER de invitado. *As a guest.* ⇨ CHARACTER

CARBÓN. *sm.* [De leña]. *Charcoal.* ~Los trenes antes funcionaban con CARBÓN. *Trains use to run on charcoal.* || **2.** [Mineral, de piedra]. *Coal.* || **3.** [Para dibujar]. *Charcoal.* ⇨ CARBON

CARGO. *sf.* Carga, peso. *Load, weight, burden.* || **2.** FIG *Burden.* ~CARGO de conciencia. *Burden on one's conscience, remorse, guilty feeling.* ~No tengo ningún CARGO de conciencia por no haber ido a visitarlo. *I don't feel at all guilty for not having been over to visit him.* || **3.** Puesto. *Post, position. office.* ~Desempeña un importante CARGO en la empresa. *He holds an important position in the company.* ~Hoy toma posesión de su CARGO. *He takes up his post (position, office) today.* || **4.** [Teatro]. *Role, part.* ~Vestir el CARGO, *To look the part, dress the part.* || **5.** [Persona]. *Office-holder, highly-placed official.* •Altos CARGOS. *People in authority, top people, senior officials.* •Altos CARGOS directivos. *Senior management, top management.* || **6.** Deber. *Duty, obligation, responsability.* ~Dejo a su CARGO la solución del problema. *It's up to you to solve the problem.* || **7.** LOCUCIONES. || •Correr a CARGO de. *To be paid by.* ~Los gastos corren a CARGO de la empresa. *The expenses will be paid by the company.* || •El papel principal corre a CARGO de Fernando Arias. *The main part (leading role) is played by Fernando Arias.* || •Jurar el CARGO. *To take the oath of office.* || •Me hago CARGO de la gravedad de la situación. *I'm aware of the gravity of the situation.* || •Mi abuela se hizo CARGO de mí. *My grandmother took care of me.* || •Tiene cuatro hijos a su CARGO. *He has four children to support.* || •Un concierto a CARGO de la Orquesta Nacional. *A concert performed by the National Orquestra.* ⇨ CHARGE

CARRO [CAR]. *sm.* Carruaje de dos ruedas, carreta. *Cart, wagon.* ~El labrador llevaba la paja en un CARRO tirado por una mula. *The farmer carried the hay in a cart pulled by a mule.* || **2.** [De una máquina de escribir]. *Carriage.* || **3.** Carga. *Cartload.* ~De este campo hemos sacado tres CARROS de patatas. *We gathered three cartloads of potatoes from this field.* || **4.** Armazón con ruedas que se emplea para transportar objetos. ~En el aeropuerto cogí un CARRO para llevar las maletas hasta el coche. *At the airport I used a cart to take my suitcases to the car.* ~CARRO de supermercado. *Shopping cart.* || **5.** *LOCUCIONES.* •CARRO de guerra. *Charriot.* || •CARRO alegórico. *Float.* || •CARRO de combate. *Tank.* ~Los primeros CARROS de combate se construyeron en Francia. *The first tanks were built in France.* || •CARRO correo. *Mail van.* || •CARRO fúnebre. *Hearse.* || •CARRO de golf. *Golf buggy.* || •CARRO de bombero. *Fire engine.*

CASO. *sm.*
❶ ASUNTO, CUESTIÓN. *Thing, point.* ~El CASO es que están todos bien. *The important (main) thing is that everybody is all right.* ~No viene al CASO. *That's not the point.* ~Lo que dijo no venía (hacía) al CASO. *What he said had nothing to do with it.* ~El CASO es que no sé si aceptar o no. *The thing is that I don't know whether to accept or not.*
❷ ATENCIÓN. *Notice, attention.* ~Hacer CASO a o de alguien. *To heed, notice, pay attention to somebody.* ~No me hacen CASO. *They don't pay any attention to me.* ~Maldito el CASO que me hace. *She doesn't take the slightest notice of what I say.* ~¡No haga usted CASO! *Take no notice!, don't worry!* ~Hacer CASO omiso de. *Disregard, brush aside, dispense with.* ~Hizo CASO omiso de mis consejos. *He took no notice of my advice.* ~Sin hacer CASO de eso. *Regardless of that.*
❸ *LOCUCIONES.* || •CASO de conciencia. *Question of conscience.* || •CASO de fuerza mayor. *Dire necessity.* || •CASO fortuito. *Unavoidable accident, act of God.* || •CASO ilustrativo. *Case in point.* || •Cuando llegue el CASO. *In due course.* || •Dado el CASO que,

darse el CASO de que. *Supposing that.* ~Si se diera el CASO de que tuvieras que quedarte en Londres. *If you should have to stay in London.* || •El CASO es que... *The fact (thing) is that...* || •El CASO Mattei. *The Mattei affair.* || •En CASO afirmativo. *If this should be the case, if so.* || •En CASO contrario. *Otherwise.* ~En CASO contrario nos veremos obligado a cerrar. *Otherwise (if not), we will have no option but to close down.* || •En CASO de necesidad. *(I) If need be, (II) When required.* || •En el mejor/peor de los CASOS. *At best/worse.* ~En el peor de los CASOS te pondrán una multa. *The worst they can do is fine you.* || •En último CASO. *As a last resort.* ~En último CASO puedes acudir a tu tío. *As a last resort you could always go to your uncle.* ~En último CASO nos vamos a pie. *If worse comes to worse, we'll just have to walk.* || •Llegado el CASO. *If it comes to it.* ~Llegado el CASO podemos tomar el tren. *If it comes to it (if we have to) we can always take the train.* || •Para el CASO es igual. *What difference does it make?* || •Pongamos por CASO. *Let's take an example.* || •Ponte en mi CASO. *Put yourself in my position.* || •Por si ACASO. *Just in case.* || •Se dio el CASO de que ... *It so happened that ...* || •Según el CASO. *As appropriate.* || •Servir para el CASO. *To serve one's purpose.* || •Verse en el CASO de. *To be compelled to.* || •Venir al CASO. *To be relevant.* ~Lo que dijo no venía (hacía) al CASO. *What he said had nothing to do with it.* || •Yo en su CASO aceptaría. *I'd accept if I were you.* ⇨CASE

CASTIGAR. *v.* [A un criminal]. *To punish.* ~Serán CASTIGADOS de acuerdo a la ley. *They will be punished according to the law.* || **2.** Dañar. *To harm, ruin, affect.* ~La zona más CASTIGADA por la sequía. *The area hardest hit by the drought.* ~CASTIGÓ duramente su ya débil organismo. *It severely affected his already weakened body.* ~Las inundaciones CASTIGARON mucho la región. *The floods caused a lot of damage to the area.* || **3.** Afligir (enfermedad). *To afflict.* || **4.** [A un jugador]. *To penalize.* || **5.** DEP Derrotar. *To beat.* ~El equipo visitante CASTIGÓ duramente al equipo local. *The visiting team beat the local team badly.* || **6.** FAM. Enamorar. *To seduce.* ~Le dirigía insistentes miradas, con el objeto de CASTIGARLA. *He directed long seducing glances at her.* || **7.** [Carne]. *To mortify.* || **8.** [Físicamente]. *To strain, used hard.* ~CASTIGAR mucho a un caballo. *To ride a horse hard.* ~CASTIGAR a un toro. *To inflict a great deal of punishment on a bull.* || **9.** Corregir. *To refine (estilo); correct, revise (text).* || **10.** [Gastos]. *To reduce, cut.* || **11.** Mortificar. *To mortify.* ⇨CASTIGATE

CASUAL. *adj.* Fortuito, ocasional. *Chance, fortuitous, accidental, unexpected.* ~Fue un encuentro CASUAL. *It was a chance encounter (an accidental meeting), we met by chance.* ⇨CASUAL

CASUALMENTE. *adv.* Por casualidad. *By chance, accidentally.* Me topé con ella CASUALMENTE. *I met her by accident.* ~CASUALMENTE, lo vi ayer. *I happened to see him yesterday.* ⇨CASUALLY

CATEGORÍA [CATEGORY]. *sf.* Clase. *Class.* ~Hotel de primera CATEGORÍA. *First-class hotel.* || **2.** Rango. *Rank.* ~Tiene la CATEGORÍA de profesor ayudante en la Universidad de Madrid. *He holds the rank of assistant professor at the University of Madrid.* || **3.** Status. *Rank, standing.* ~CATEGORÍA social. *Social class.* ~En la sociedad capitalista, la CATEGORÍA social de los banqueros es muy elevada. *In a capitalistic society, the social standing of bankers is very high.* || **4.** Calidad, nivel, importancia, prestigio. *Quality, importance, prestige.* ~Un actor de mucha CATEGORÍA. *A distinguished actor.* ~Una revista de poca CATEGORÍA. *A second-rate magazine.* ~El hotel de más CATEGORÍA de la ciudad. *The finest hotel in town.* || **5.** Clase, grupo. *Type, class.* ~De la misma CATEGORÍA. *Of the same type.* || **6.** •De CATEGORÍA. *First-rate.* ~Un espectáculo de CATEGORÍA. *A fine (excellent, first-rate) show.* ~Un producto de CATEGORÍA. *A quality product.* ~Un coche de CATEGORÍA. *A luxury car.*

CAUSA. *sf.* Pleito. *Lawsuit.* ~En la CAUSA los dos hermanos luchan por la herencia. *In the lawsuit the two brothers are fighting for the inheritance.* || **2.** Juicio. *Trial.* ⇨CAUSE

CAUSAR [CAUSE]. *v.* Hacer, dar. *To make, give.* ~Me CAUSA un gran placer. *It gives me great pleasure.* ~Me CAUSÓ muy buena impresión. *He made a good impression on me.* || **2.** [Ira]. *To provoke.* || **3.** CAUSAR risa. *To make someone laugh.*

CELEBRACIÓN. *sf.* Cumplimiento, realización. *Holding.* ~La CELEBRACIÓN del juicio tendrá lugar hoy. *The trial will be held today.* ~El mal tiempo impidió la CELEBRACIÓN del concurso. *Bad weather prevented the contest form being held.* || **2.** Elogio, alabanza, aplauso. *Praise, applause, welcome.* Los vencedores fueron recibidos con ruidosas CELEBRACIONES. *The winners were warmly acclaimed (applauded, welcomed).* || **3.** [De ventajas]. *Preaching.* || **4.** Misa. *Mass.* ~Toda la familia del sacerdote asistió a su primera CELEBRACIÓN. *The entire priest's family attended his first mass.* ⇨CELEBRATION

CELEBRAR. *v.* Aprobar, ver con buenos ojos. *To welcome, applaud.* ~CELEBRO esta noticia. *I welcome this news.* ~CELEBRO su conducta. *I applaud his conduct.* || **2.** Realizar, llevar a cabo. *To take place, be held (reunión, elecciones).* ~El partido se CELEBRARÁ en Cádiz. *The match will be held in Cádiz.* || **3.** Finalizar, concretar. *To enter into, sign (contract, transaction), reach (acuerdo).* || **4.** Alabar, elogiar. *To pay compliment, praise.* ~Todos CELEBRARON su elegancia. *They all praised his elegance.* || **5.** Ensalzar. *To praise, extol (virtudes, belleza), sing (hazañas).* ~CELEBRABA las ventajas de vivir en el campo. *He was singing the praises of country life.* || **6.** Estar contento, alegrarse. *To be happy, to be delighted.* ~CELEBRO que todo haya salido bien. *I'm delighted that everything went well.* || **7.** Caer en (cumpleaños). *To fall on.* Su cumpleaños se CELEBRA el 8 de abril. *His birthday falls* on the 8th of April. || **8.** Mantener (conversación, charla). *To have, hold.* || **9.** Mostrar que lo que alguien dice es gracioso. *To laught at, find amusing (chiste).* ~CELEBRAR las gracias del niño. *To laugh at the child's remarks.* || **10.** Oficiar (boda). *To perform.* ⇨CELEBRATE

CELESTIAL. *adj.* [Placer]. *Heavenly.* ~Lo que me dijo fue música CELESTIAL para mis oídos. *His words were sweet music to my ears.* ⇨CELESTIAL

CERTIFICADO. *adj.* [Paquete, carta]. *Registered.* ~Mandé la carta por correo CERTIFICADO. *I sent the letter by registered mail.* ⇨CERTIFIED

CERTIFICAR [CERTIFY]. *v.* Asegurar el envío de una carta mediante un resguardo. *To register.* ~He CERTIFICADO el paquete para asegurarme de que llegue a su destino. *I registered the package to make sure it arrives safely.*

CHOQUE. *sm.* [General]. *Impact.* || **2.** [Auto]. *Crash, collision.* ~El CHOQUE se produjo en el cruce. *The collision occurred at the crossroad.* •CHOQUE múltiple. *Pile-up.* •CHOQUE de frente. *Head-on collision.* || **3.** MIL Escaramuza. *Skirmish.* El CHOQUE entre los dos ejércitos produjo un gran número de bajas. *Many were wounded in the skirmish between the two armies.* || **4.** [De vehículo en movimiento]. *Jolt, jar.* || **5.** [De explosión]. *Blast, shock wave.* || **6.** Ruido. *Clash.* || **7.** [De platos]. *Clatter.* || **8.** [De vasos]. *Clinking, clink.* || **9.** [Conflicto]. *Clash.* ~Se produjeron algunos CHOQUES violentos. *There were some violent clashes.* FIG ~Se produjo un CHOQUE entre ellos sobre el tema de las subvenciones. *They clashed over the question of subsidies.* ~Estar en abierto CHOQUE con. *To conflict openly with.* || **10.** •La policía de CHOQUE. *Riot police.* ⇨SHOCK

CÍNICO. *adj.* Descarado. *Impudent, brazen.* ~¡Qué CINISMO! *What nerve!* ⇨CÍNICO

CIRCULACIÓN. *sf.* Tráfico. *Traffic.* ~A esta hora la CIRCULACIÓN es muy intensa.

At this time of day the traffic is very heavy. ⇨CIRCULATION

CIRCULAR [CIRCULATE]. *v.* [Líquido, electricidad]. *To flow.* ~La corriente CIRCULA por el circuito. *The current flows through the circuit.* ~El agua CIRCULA por la cañería. *Water flows through the pipes.* ~La sangre CIRCULA por las venas. *Blood flows through the veins.* || **2.** [Trenes, autobuses]. *To run, operate.* ~Hoy no CIRCULAN trenes. *There are no trains running today.* ~CIRCULAN muchos coches por esta calle. *There's a lot of traffic on this street.* || **3.** [Rumor, noticias]. *To spread.* ~El rumor CIRCULÓ rápidamente. *The rumor spread quickly.* || **4.** Conducir. *To drive.* ~CIRCULAR por la derecha. *To drive on the right.* || **5.** No quedarse parado (personas). *To move about, walk, walk around.* ~Apenas CIRCULABA gente por las calles. *There was hardly anybody walking in the streets.* ~¡CIRCULEN, por favor! *Move along, please!* || **6.** [Tráfico]. *Travel.* ~El tráfico CIRCULABA a 25 km/h. *The traffic was travelling at 25 kp/h.*

CLARIFICAR. *v.* Poner transparente un líquido. *To purify, refine.* ⇨CLARIFY

CLARO. *adj.* Bien iluminado (cuarto). *Bright, light, well-lit.* ~Una habitación CLARA. *A bright room.* || **2.** Luminoso. *Bright.* ~El día apareció CLARO. *The day dawned bright and clear.* || **3.** [Color]. *Light.* ~Una tela verde CLARO. *A light-green cloth.* ~A los niños les sientan muy bien los colores CLAROS. *Light-colored clothes are becoming to children.* || **4.** [Piel]. *Fair, white.* || **5.** [Líquido, salsa]. *Thin.* || **6.** [Café, té]. *Weak.* || **7.** [Cerveza]. *Light* || **8.** Poco abundante. *Thin, sparse.* ~Pelo CLARO. *Thin hair.* || **9.** Ilustre. *Famous, illustrious.* ~CLAROS varones de Castilla. *Ilustrious men of Castile.* || **10.** [Tela]. *Threadbare.* || **11.** Nítido (fotos). *Sharp.* ~¿Cómo consigues estas fotografías tan CLARAS? *How do you get such sharp pictures?* ⇨CLEAR

CLIENTE [CLIENTE]. *s.* [General]. *Customer.* ~Este fontanero tiene muchos CLIENTES. *This plumber has many customers.* || **2.**

[Medical]. *Patient.* || **3.** [De un hotel]. *Guest.* || **4.** [Restaurante]. *Customer, patron.* || **5.** [En un taxi]. *Fare, customer.*

COINCIDIR [COINCIDE]. *v.* [En gustos, opiniones]. *To agree, be in agreement, share someone's views.* ~COINCIDIMOS los dos en ir al cine. *We both agreed to go see a movie.* ~COINCIDEN en sus gustos. *They share the same tastes.* ~Todos COINCIDIERON en que. *Everyone agreed that.* || **2.** [Encontrarse]. *To meet.* ~A veces COINCIDIMOS en el supermercado. *We sometimes meet at the supermarket.* || **3.** Estar en un lugar al mismo tiempo. *To be at a place at the same time.* ~COINCIDÍ con él en París. *I was in Paris at the same time that he was.* || **4.** [Dibujos]. *To line up, match up.* Calca bien el dibujo para que, al superponerlo al original, todos los trazos COINCIDAN. *Trace the drawing so that when you superimpose it on the original it will line up.*

COLEGIO. *sm.* Establecimiento privado de primera o segunda enseñanza. *Private school.* Llegó a ser profesor del mismo COLEGIO en que, de pequeño, aprendí las primeras letras. *He became a teacher at the same school where I first learn to read when I was a child.* ⇨COLLEGE

COLLAR. *sm.* Adorno que se pone alrededor del cuello. *Necklace.* ~Lleva un COLLAR de perlas. *She's wearing a pearl necklace.* || **2.** •COLLAR de fuerza. *Stranglehold.* ⇨COLLAR

COLORADO [COLORED]. *adj.* Rojo (cara). *Red.* ~Es un niño tan tímido que en cuanto le preguntas algo se pone COLORADO. *He's such a timid child that when you ask him a question he turns red.* || **2.** Súbido de color (chiste, anécdota). *Risqué, off-color.*

COMBATIR [COMBAT]. *v.* [Soldado, ejército]. *To fight.* ~COMBATIÓ con los Nacionales. *He fought on the Nationalist side.* ~Tuvieron que COMBATIR contra un enemigo numéricamente superior. *They had to fight an enemy far superior in numbers.* || **2.** [Viento]. *To blow.* || **3.** [Proyecto, propuesta]. *To fight.* ~El diputado COMBATIÓ el proyecto de ley presentado por el gobierno. *The*

representative fought against the bill. || **4.** Atacar. ~El ejército COMBATIÓ la fortaleza al amanecer. *The army attacked the stronghold at dawn.*

COMEDIA [COMEDY]. *sf.* Obra de teatro. *Play.* ~Lope de Vega escribió más de 500 COMEDIAS. *Lope de Vega wrote over 500 plays.* || **2.** Farsa. *Farse, put on, make-believe, act.* ~Su enfermedad fue una COMEDIA. *His illness was an act.* || **3.** Teatro. *Theater.* ~La COMEDIA del Siglo de Oro. *Golden Age drama.*

COMEDIANTE. *sm.* Actor. *Actor.* ~Los COMEDIANTES iban de pueblo en pueblo con sus trajes y sus comedias. *The actors would go from town to town with their costumes and their plays.* || **2.** Persona que finge lo que no siente en realidad. *Fraud.* La COMEDIANTE ésta nos ha hecho creer que estaba enferma para no ir a la clase. *She's playacting. She made us believe she was sick so she would not have to attend class.* || **3.** Farsante. *Joker.* ~¡Qué COMEDIANTE! *What a joker!* || **4.** Hipócrita. *Hypocrite.* ⇨COMEDIAN

COMENTARIO [COMMENTARY]. *sm.* Observación. *Comment, remark.* ¿Quiere hacer algún COMENTARIO? *Do you have any comments?* ~Ese COMENTARIO fue de mal gusto. *That remark was in very bad taste.* || **2.** *pl.* Murmuración. *Gossip.* ~Dar lugar a COMENTARIOS. *To cause gossip.* ~No te fíes de él, siempre esta haciendo COMENTARIOS a tus espaldas. *Don't trust him, he's always talking against you behind your back.*

COMETER. *v.* [Error, falta]. *To make.* ~COMETÍ la estupidez de decírselo. *I made the stupid mistake of telling him.* ~COMETIÓ cinco faltas de ortografía. *He made five spelling mistakes.* || **2.** Encargar. *To entrust, charge.* ~COMETER a uno la ejecución de algo. *To entrust someone with the execution of something.* ⇨COMMIT

COMODIDAD. *sf.* Calidad de cómodo. *Comfort, convenience.* Compre desde la COMODIDAD de su casa. *Shop in the comfort of your own home.* ~Vivir con COMODIDAD. *To live in comfort.* || **2.** Bienestar. *Well-*

being, welfare. ~Sólo piensa en su propia COMODIDAD. *He only thinks of his own well-being.* || **3.** *pl.* Conjunto de cosas para vivir con gusto y con descanso. *Amenities, pleasant things, comforts.* ~COMODIDADES de la vida. *The good things in life.* || **4.** Aspectos ventajosos que algo posee. *Facilities.* Un piso con todas las COMODIDADES. *A well-appointed (well-equipped) apartment.* || **5.** •A su COMODIDAD. *At your convenience.* ~Venga a su COMODIDAD. *Come at your convenience.* || **6.** •Siéntate con COMODIDAD. *Make yourself comfortable (in the chair).* ⇨COMMODITY

COMPAÑERO. *sm.* [De equipo]. *Teammate.* ~Este jugador ha dado diez asistencias a su COMPAÑERO (de equipo) y éste ha metido 20 puntos. *This player has made 10 passes to his teammate who scored 20 points.*

COMPENSACIÓN. *sf.* Indemnity. *Indemnización, reparación.* || **2.** •En COMPENSACIÓN. (1) En pago. *In payment,* (2) En cambio. *In exchange, in return.* ~Tú me enseñas español y en COMPENSACIÓN yo le enseñaré inglés. *You teach me Spanish and in return I'll teach you English.* || **3.** •COMPENSACIÓN por despido. *Severance pay.* ⇨COMPENSATION

COMPENSAR [COMPENSATE]. *v.* Valer la pena. *To be worthwhile.* ~No me COMPENSA hacerlo por tan poco dinero. *It's not worth my while doing it for so little money.* ~RESULTADOS que compensan. *Worthwhile results.* || **2.** [Error]. *To make amends for, to redeem, to make up for.* || **3.** [Efecto]. *To offset.* || **4.** [Cheque]. *To clear.*

COMPETENCIA. Rivalidad (en el comercio). *Competition.* ~En ese campo la COMPETENCIA es atroz. *Competition is fierce in that field.* La COMPETENCIA frena la subida de los precios. *Competition checks rising prices.* || **2.** Incubencia, jurisdicción, autoridad. *Scope, field, province, jurisdiction..* ~Eso no es de mi COMPETENCIA. *This is beyond my scope.* || **3.** Responsabilidad. *Jurisdiction, area of responsibility, authority.* ~La limpieza de las calles

es COMPETENCIA del Ayuntamiento. *The City is responsible for street-cleaning.* || **4.** Autoridad. *Expert knowledge.* ~Esta mujer tiene COMPETENCIA en materia de derecho. *She's a legal expert.* || **5.** Conjunto de personas representando la competencia. *Competitors, opposition.* La COMPETENCIA se nos adelantó. *Our competitors got us first.* ~Se fue a trabajar para la competencia. *He went to work for the opposition.* || **6.** Responsabilidad. *Responsibility.* Es COMPETENCIA directa del consejo. *The council has direct responsibility for it.* || **7.** Autoridad, poder. *Authority, power.* Tienen COMPETENCIA plenas en materia educativa. *They have complete authority (absolute power) regarding educational issues.* || **8.** *LOCUCIONES.* || •En COMPETENCIA con. *In competition with.* || •COMPETENCIA desleal. *Unfair competition.* || •COMPETENCIA tecnológica. *Know-how.* || •Hacer la COMPETENCIA. *To compete with.* ~Has sacado muy malas notas, ¿Le estás haciendo COMPETENCIA a tu hermana? *You received very low grades, are you trying to compete with your sister?* ⇨COMPETENCE

COMPLACIENTE. *adj.* Amable. *Obliging, ready to please, pleasing, helpful, kind, accomodating.* ~Es una persona COMPLACIENTE y si no te ayuda es que no puede. *He's a very obliging person and if he doesn't help you it's because he's not able to.* || **2.** Indulgente. *Indulgent.* ~Tiene una actitud demasiado COMPLACIENTE con él. *She overindulges him.*|| **3.** •Ser COMPLACIENTE con. *To be helpful to, be well disposed towards.* ⇨COMPLACENT

COMPLETO. *adj.* Lleno. *Full.* ~El tren iba COMPLETO. *The train was full.* ~El hotel está COMPLETO. *The hotel is full (booked up).* || **2.** Acabado, perfecto. *Perfect.* ~La falsificación era tan COMPLETA que era difícil advertirla. *The forgery was so perfect that you could hardly notice it.* || **3.** [Busca]. *Thorough.* || **4.** [Pensión, precio]. *Inclusive.* ~Pensión COMPLETA. *Full board.* || **5.** [Comida]. *With all the trimmings.* || **6.** •'Completo'. *No vacancies (en un hostal); sold out (en una taquilla).* ⇨COMPLETE

COMPLEXIÓN. *sm*. Constitución (física), temperamento. *Constitution, make-up, temperament, build*. ~Es de COMPLEXIÓN débil/robusta. *He has a weak/robust constitution*. ~Es una chica de COMPLEXIÓN atlética y juega al baloncesto. *She has an athletic build and plays basketball*. ⇨ COMPLEXION

COMPONENTE [COMPONENT]. *sm*. [De bebida, comida]. *Ingredient*. ~El COMPONENTE esencial de la paella es el arroz. *The most important ingredient in the 'paella' is the rice*. ‖ **2.** [De un equipo, una comisión]. *Member*. ~Hoy llegan los COMPONENTES del equipo de fútbol. *The members of the soccer team will be arriving today*.

COMPOSICIÓN. *sf*. De riña. *Settlement*. ‖ **2.** [De persona]. *Reconciliation*. ‖ **3.** Arreglo. *Arrangement*. ‖ **4.** [Medicamento]. *Mixture*. ‖ **5.** Creación. *Creation*. ~El Quijote el la mayor COMPOSICIÓN de Cervantes. *El Quijote is Cervantes' greatest creation*. ~La COMPOSICIÓN de un buen libro lleva tiempo. *Writing a good book takes time*. ‖ **6.** •COMPOSICIÓN de lugar. *Stocktaking*. ‖ **7.** •Hacerse una COMPOSICIÓN de lugar. (I) Determinar lo que va a hacer uno. *To make a plan of action*, (II) Formarse una idea. *To get a picture of a situation*. ⇨ COMPOSITION

COMPRENSIVO. *adj*. [Persona, actitud). *Understanding, tolerant, kind*. ~Si no quieres alejarte de tus hijos debes tener una actitud mas COMPRENSIVA. *If you wish to be closer to your children you must try to be more understanding*. ⇨ COMPREHENSIVE

COMPROMETER[1]. *v*. Arriesgar. *To endanger, risk, jeopardize*. El acuerdo COMPROMETE la soberanía del país. *The agreement jeopardizes national sovereignty*. ‖ **2.** Empeñar. *To commit oneself*. ~Ya me he COMPROMETIDO para salir esta noche. *I've already arranged to go out tonight*. ~Se ha COMPROMETIDO para empezar en enero. *He has committed himself to starting in January*. ‖ **3.** Obligar. *Compel, oblige, force, commit*. ~No le

COMPROMETE a nada. *It doesn't commit you to anything*. ~Esto no te COMPROMETE a aceptarle. *This does not commit you to accept it*. ‖ **4.** Involucrar. *To involve*. ~No te COMPROMETAS. *Don't get involved*. ‖ **5.** Poner en un aprieto. *To embarrass*. ~Compórtate con más discreción, me estás COMPROMETIENDO. *Please try to behave, you're embarrassing me*. ‖ **6.** [Complice]. *To involve, implicate*. ~Esa carta COMPROMETE al alcade en el asunto. *The letter implicated the mayor in the case*. ~Esos documentos te pueden COMPROMETER; es mejor que los quemes. *These documents could implicate you; you had better burn them*. ‖ **7.** [Habitación, plaza]. *To reserve, book*. ‖ **8.** [Pulmón, hígado]. *To affect*. La puñalada le COMPREMETIÓ el pulmón. *The stab wound affected his lung*. ~El cáncer ya le ha COMPROMETIDO el riñón. *The cancer has already affected (spread to, reached) the kidney*.

COMPROMETERSE[2]. *vr*. Dar su palabra. *To promise*. ~Se COMPROMETIÓ a terminarlo para el sábado. *She promised to finish it by Saturday*. ~Me COMPROMETO a cuidarlo como si fuera mío. *I promise to look after it as if it were my own*. ‖ **2.** [Novios]. *To get engaged*. ~Se COMPROMETIÓ con Juan. *She got engaged to Juan*. ‖ **3.** •COMPROMETERSE a hacer algo. *To undertake (to do something)*. ⇨ COMPROMISE[2]

COMPROMISO. *sm*. Obligación contraída. *Obligation, commitment, engagement*. ~Ella siempre cumple sus COMPROMISOS. *She always meets her obligations*. ~Tener muchos COMPROMISOS. *To have many commitments*. ~Solicite, sin COMPROMISO alguno, nuestro folleto informativo. *Send for our brochure without obligation*. ‖ **2.** Cita. *Appointment, date*. ~No pudo ir porque tenía otro COMPROMISO. *He was unable to go because of a prior engagement*. ~Si no tiene ningún COMPROMISO para esta noche, podríamos cenar juntos. *If you're not doing anything tonight, we could go out for dinner*. ‖ **3.** Situación apurada, aprieto. *Predicament, awkward situation*. ~No me pongas en este

COMPROMISO. *Don't put me in that difficult (embarrassing) situation.* ~¡Vaya COMPROMISO!, lo invité a cenar en un restaurante y se me olvidó el dinero! *What a predicament! I invited him for dinner and I left my wallet at home.* || 4. Promesa. *Pledge, undertaking, promise.* Ha contraído el COMPROMISO de educarlos en la fe católica. *She has undertaken (pledged) to bring them up in the Catholic faith.* || 5. Acuerdo. *Agreement.* ~Un COMPROMISO verbal. *A verbal agreement, a gentleman's agreement.* ~Entre ambas firmas existe el COMPROMISO tácito de respetarse los clientes. *Both companies have tacitly agreed not to try to steal each other's customers.* || 6. LOCUCIONES. •COMPROMISO matrimonial. *Engagement (to marry), betrothal.* ~Han anunciado su COMPROMISO matrimonial. *They have announced their engagement.* || 7. •¡Qué COMPROMISO! *What a nuisance!* || •Hacer honor a sus COMPROMISOS. *To meet one's obligations.* || •Libre de COMPROMISOS. *Without obligation.* || •Por COMPROMISO. *Out of a sense of duty.* ~Los invitó por COMPROMISO. *She invited them out of a sense of duty.* || •Soltera y sin COMPROMISO. *Single and unattached.* || •Poner a alguien en el COMPROMISO de. *To put someone in the position of.* No le regales nada, lo pones en un COMPROMISO. *Don't buy him anything or you're making him feel that he has to buy you something in return.* || •Salir de un COMPROMISO. *To get out of a difficulty.* || •Contraer un COMPROMISO. *To assume an obligation.* ⇨COMPROMISE[1]

COMPULSIVO. *adj.* Obligatorio. *Compulsory.* || 2. [Necesidad, impulso]. *Pressing, urgent.* ⇨COMPULSIVE

COMÚN [COMMON]. *adj.* Compartido. *Shared, mutual, communal.* ~Amigos COMUNES. *Mutual friends.* ~Cuarto de baño COMÚN. *Communal bathroom.* ~Gastos COMUNES. *Shared expenses.* || 2. Conjunto. *Joint.* || 3. Público. *Public, belonging to all, held in common.* ~Estas son la tierras COMUNES del pueblo y aquellas las particulares. *These are the public lands of the town and those are the private ones.* ~Cada

uno tiene su casa, pero el patio es COMÚN. *Each one has his own house, but the patio belongs to everyone.* || 4. Mayoría. *Majority, most.* ~El COMÚN de la gente aspira a la felicidad. *The majority of people seek happiness.* || 5. LOCUCIONES. •Fuera de lo COMÚN. *Out of the ordinary.* || •Hacer algo en COMÚN. *To do something jointly.* || •Lugar COMÚN. *Cliché, commonplace.* || •Poco COMÚN. *Unusual.* || •Por lo COMÚN. *Generally.*

COMUNICAR. Hacer saber, informar. *To inform, convey, tell.* ~Siento mucho COMUNICARLE que ... *I regret to inform you that ...* ~Le COMUNICARON la noticia por teléfono. *They informed him of the news over the telephone.* || 2. Transmitir (calor). *To transmit, impart (heat).* ~Este material COMUNICA calor a todas las habitaciones. *This material transmits heat to all the rooms.* FIG Celia COMUNICA a todos su alegría. *Celia transmits her good disposition to all.* || 3. Tener paso una cosa a otra. *To connect, link, join.* Un pasillo COMUNICA su despacho con el mío. *A corridor connects his office with mine.* Los dos lagos se COMUNICAN. *The two lakes join.* || 4. Dirigirse. *To contact, get in touch with.* Estoy tratando de COMUNICARME con él. *I'm trying to get in touch with him.* ~Hace mucho que no me COMUNICO con mi familia. *I haven't been in touch with my family for some time.* || 5. Estar ocupado (teléfono). *To be busy.* ~Está COMUNICANDO. *The line is busy.* || 6. Informar. *To send a report.* ~COMUNICAN desde Lisboa que ... *It is reported from Lisbon that ...* || 7. Transmitir (sentimientos, costumbres, enfermedades). *To spread, infect.* || 8. Extenderse, propagarse. *To spread.* El incendio se COMUNICÓ a la casa de al lado. *~The fire spread to the house next door.* || 9. •Cuartos COMUNICADOS. *Connecting rooms.* || 10. •¿Me COMUNICA con el Sr. Gómez? *May I speak to Mr. Gómez?* ⇨COMMUNICATE

CONCEDER. *v.* Otorgar, dar. *To give, grant.* ~Concédeme cinco minutos. *Give me five minutes.* ~Le CONCEDEREMOS un plazo de diez días. *We'll give you ten days*

(to pay). ~Me CONCEDIERON permiso. *They gave me permission.* ~No quiso CONCEDERLE el divorcio. *She refused to grant him a divorce.* ~Les CONCEDIERON a los empleados un mes de vacaciones. *They granted their employees a month's vacation.* || **2.** [Premio, beca, victoria]. *To award.* ~Los jueces CONCEDIERON el triunfo al irlandés. *The judges awarded victory to the Irishman.* || **3.** [Honor]. *Confer, bestow.* ~El honor que me CONCEDIERON. *The honor they conferred (bestowed) on me.* || **45.** [Atención]. *To pay.* || **5.** [Descuento, préstamo]. *To allow, grant.* ~Le hemos CONCEDIDO el crédito. *Your credit has been granted.* || **6.** [Importancia, valor]. *To give.* ~No hay que CONCEDERLE tanta importancia. *It's really not that important.* ~No le CONCEDIÓ demasiada importancia. *She did not give it too much importance, she did not attach too much importance to it.* ⇨ CONCEDE

CONCENTRACIÓN [CONCENTRATION]. *sf.* Reunión, manifestación pública. *Rally, mass meeting.* ~Una CONCENTRACIÓN de jóvenes en la plaza cantaba por la paz. *A rally of young people sang for peace in the city square.*

CONCENTRAR [CONCENTRATE]. *v.* [Atención]. *To focus.* || **2.** Reunir. *To hold.* El presidente CONCENTRA todos los poderes. *The president holds absolute power.* ~El poder está CONCENTRADO en manos de tres personas. *All the power is held by three persons.* || **3.** Congregar. *To assemble (multitud, tropas).* || **4.** [Interés]. *Center, focus.*

CONCEPTO [CONCEPT]. Juicio, opinión. *View, opinion, judgement.* ~¿Qué CONCEPTO has formado de él? *What do you think of him?* ~Tengo un mal CONCEPTO de su trabajo. *I have a very low opinion of her work.* ~En mi CONCEPTO. *In my view.* ~Formarse un CONCEPTO de uno. *To form an opinion of someone.* ~Tener buen CONCEPTO de uno. *To think highly of someone.* ~Como empleado me merece el mejor de los CONCEPTOS. *I have a very high opinion of him as an employee.* ~Bajo todo

(los) CONCEPTOS. *~From every point of view.* || **2.** Idea. *Idea, notion.* Tiene un CONCEPTO equivocado de lo que es la caridad. *He has a mistaken idea (notion) of what charity is all about.* ~No tengo un CONCEPTO claro de lo que es esta doctrina. *I don't have a clear idea of what this doctrine is about.* || **3.** Agudeza, dicho ingenioso. *Pun, witticism.* ~Su estilo abusa de los CONCEPTOS *She uses too many puns in her style.* || **4.** (De narracción). *Heading, section.* || **5.** Partida. *Item.* En este presupuesto hay tres cantidades por distintos CONCEPTOS. *In this estimate there are three quantities for different items.* || **6.** LOCUCIONES. || • Bajo (por) ningún CONCEPTO. *Under no account, under no circumstance.* || •Por dicho CONCEPTO. *For this reason.* || •En (por) CONCEPTO de. *By way of.* Se le pagó está cantidad en (por) CONCEPTO de derechos. *He was paid that amount as royalties.* ~Deducciones por CONCEPTO de seguros. *Deductions for social security.* ~Un complemento salarial (por) en CONCEPTO de dedicación plena. *An incentive payment for full-time work.* || •En su (más) amplio CONCEPTO. *In its broadest sense.*

CONCESIÓN [CONCESSION]. *sf.* [De un premio]. *Awarding.* La CONCESIÓN del premio Cervantes ha recaído en Miguel Delibes. *The Cervantes prize was awarded to Miguel Delibes.* || **2.** [De un préstamo]. *Granting.*

CONCLUIR. *v.* Terminar, finalizar. *To finish, complete.* ~Es tiempo de CONCLUIR. *It's time to finish.* ~Otra firma se encargó de CONCLUIR el proyecto. *Another company undertook to finish (complete) the project.* || **2.** [Negocio, trato, plazo]. *To close.* ~El plazo de inscripción CONCLUYE el próximo lunes. *Registration closes next Monday.* || **3.** [Trámite]. *To complete.* || **4.** Solucionar. *To settle.* || **5.** Convencer. *To convince.* || **6.** [Obra de arte]. *Put the finishing touches to.* || **7.** CONCLUIR con (en). *To end.* ~Las conversaciones CONCLUYERON en un acuerdo. *The talks ended in an agreement.* ~CONCLUYÓ con una concentración delante del cuartel. *It ended with a rally in front of the barracks.* || **8.** •CONCLUIR por. *To end up doing something.* ~CONCLUYERON por pedir un armisticio. *They eventually requested an armistice.* ⇨CONCLUDE

CONCRETO [CONCRETE]. *adj.* Determinado, específico. *Actual, particular, specific, precise.* ~La cantidad CONCRETA no es alta. *The actual amount is not high.* ~Buscaba un tipo de vestido CONCRETO. *She was looking for a particular type of dress.* ~En este caso CONCRETO. *In this particular instance.* ~No me dijo ninguna hora CONCRETA. *He didn't tell me any definite (particular) time.* || **2.** •En CONCRETO. *In brief, in short.*

CONCURRIR. *v.*
❶ JUNTARSE, UNIRSE. Juntarse (gente). *To meet, gather, assemble.* ~Los fieles CONCURREN a la iglesia. *The faithfuls gather at church.* || **2.** [Líneas]. *To cross, intersect.* || **3.** [Avenidas, calles)]. *To meet, come together, converge.* Las tres carreteras CONCURREN en Madrid. *The three roads converge in Madrid.*
❷ COMPETIR. Competir (en un mercado). *To compete.* ~CONCURRIR a un mercado. *To compete in a market.* || **2.** Concursar, tomar parte. (I) [En un concurso]. *To compete.* ~Al premio CONCURRIERON cien trabajos. *A hundred works competed for the prize,* (II) [En elecciones, examen]. *To be a candidate.* || **3.** [Deporte]. *To compete, take part in.* || **4.** Tomar parte. *To take part.* ~Todos los partidos que CONCURREN a los comicios. *All the parties taking part in the election.*
❸ ACUDIR, ASISTIR. *To attend.* ~Todos CONCURRIERON a la boda. *Everybody attended the wedding.* ~Los que no CONCURRAN al acto. *Those who do not attend the ceremony.* || **2.** Ir por costumbre a un mismo sitio. *To belong, be part of, to assiduously go somewhere, go somewhere as a group.* ~CONCURREN a la misma tertulia. *They go to the same group.*
❹ CONFLUIR, DARSE (factores, circunstancias). *To combine, come together.* ~Varios factores CONCURREN para que

ocurra. *A number of factors combine for this to occur.* ~Si CONCURREN circunstancias agravantes. *In the event of aggravating circumstances.* ~Las circunstancias que CONCURREN en cada caso particular. *The combination of circumstances surrounding each individual case.*
❺ COINCIDIR. Estar de acuerdo. *To agree* (also *to concur*). Todos CONCURRIERON en la necesidad de mejores equipos. *They all agreed on the need for better equipment.* ~Concurro con el senador en dos puntos. *I agree with the senator on two points.* || **2.** Juntarse ciertas cualidades (en una persona). *To be found, to be present.* ~CONCURREN en ella muy buenas cualidades. *She has many good qualities.*
❻ CONTRIBUIR. *To contribute.* ~Varios factores CONCURRIERON a la pérdida de la cosecha. *Several factors contributed to the failure of the harvest.* ~CONCURRIR a la derrota. *To contribute to the defeat.* ~CONCURRIR al éxito de una empresa. *To contribute to the success of an enterprise.* ~Diversos factores han CONCURRIDO en el fracaso de las negociaciones. *Many factors contributed to the breaking off of the negotiations.* ⇨CONCUR

CONDENAR. *v.* Declarar culpable (de). *To convict, find guilty (of).* ~Le CONDENARON por ladrón. *He was found guilty of robbery.* || **2.** Sentenciar. *To sentence.* Fue CONDENADO a tres meses de cárcel. *He was sentenced to three months in jail.* || **3.** Fallar (plan). *To doom.* ~El proyecto estaba CONDENADO al fracaso desde el principio. *The project was doomed from the start.* || **4.** Inutilizar, inhabilitar. *To block, wall off (puerta, ventana], to board up (con tablas), close up (habitación, sala).* ~Hemos tenido que CONDENAR el ático porque tiene goteras. *Since there were many leaks we had to close up the attic.* || **5.** [Al infierno]. *To damn.* || **6.** Obligar. *To compel, force, oblige,* (also *condemn*). ~El desempleo los CONDENA a vivir en la mendicidad. *Unemployment forces them to live by begging.* || **7.** Fastidiar. *To vex, annoy.* ~Este niño es tan pesado que me

CONDENA cada vez que estoy con él. *This child is so annoying he gets me out of my wits everytime I'm with him.* ⇨CONDEMN

CONDESCENDER [CONDESCEND]. *v.* Ceder. *To comply (with), yield, agree, consent.* ~CONDESCENDER a los ruegos de uno. *To agree with someone's request.* ~CONDESCENDER a los deseos de uno. *To yield to someone's wishes.*

CONDESCENDIENTE [CONDESCENDING]. *adj.* Transigente. *Helpful, obliging, willing to help.* ‖ **2.** Comprensivo. *Understanding.* ~Eres muy poco CONDESCENDIENTE. *You're not very understanding.* ~El entrenador ha sido CONDESCENDIENTE con las sugerencias de los jugadores. *The trainer has listened willingly to the suggestions of his players.*

CONDICIÓN.
❶ APTITUD, TALENTO. *Ability, aptitude.* ~Tener CONDICIONES para la música. *To have an aptitude for music.* ~No tiene CONDICIONES para este trabajo. *He's not suited for this job.*
❷ CLASE, CATEGORÍA SOCIAL. *Rank, social position.* ~Persona de CONDICIÓN. Person of rank. ~Una boda de personas de distintas CONDICIONES. *A wedding between people of different social scales.*
❸ CHARÁCTER, GENIO. *Nature, temperament.* ~De CONDICIÓN rebelde. *Of a rebellious nature.* ~De buena condición. *Good-tempered.* ~De mala CONDICIÓN. *Ill-tempered.* ~Tener CONDICIÓN. *To have character.*
❹ CALIDAD, SITUACIÓN. *Capacity.* ~En su CONDICIÓN de sacerdote. *As a priest.* ~En su CONDICIÓN de jefe de la delegación. *In his capacity as head of the delegation.*
❺ LOCUCIONES. ‖ •En CONDICIONES. *In working order.* ‖ •Poner en CONDICIONES. *To mend, repair.* ‖ •Estar en CONDICIONES (físicas) de hacer algo. *To be fit (to do something).* ~Estará en CONDICIONES de jugar el lunes. *He will be fit to play on Monday.* ‖ •Estar en CONDICIONES (morales) de hacer algo. *To be in the position of (doing something).* ~No estás en CONDICIONES de venir con exigencias. *You're not*

in a position to make demands. ‖ •Estar en malas/buenas CONDICIONES. *To be in a bad/ good state.* ~El coche está en malas CONDICIONES. *The car is in bad shape.* ‖ •No estamos en CONDICIONES de resolverlo. *We are not able to resolve it.* ‖ •Ayuda sin CONDICIONES. *Help with no strings attached.* ‖ •Rendición sin CONDICIONES. *Unconditional surrender.* ~Se rindieron sin CONDICIONES. *They surrendered unconditionally.* ‖ •CONDICIONES de pago. *Terms of payment.* ‖ •No estamos en CONDICIONES de comprar casa en este momento. *We can't afford to buy a house at this time.* ‖ •CONDICIONES requeridas. *Prerequisites, requirements.* ⇨ CONDITION[1]

CONDICIONAR. Influir, determinar. *Determine, govern, dictate.* ~Su aceptación CONDICIONA la mía. *His acceptance determines mine.* ~La publicidad CONDICIONA lo que compra la gente. *Publicity determines what people buy.* ‖ **2.** Ajustar. *To suit, to adapt, to be or make dependent, to be contingent upon.* ~Ha CONDICIONADO su decisión a la opinión de los demás. *He suited his opinion to the opinion of the others.* ‖ **3.** Supeditar, subordinar. *To make something conditional on something.* ~Estará CONDICIONADO a una mayor productividad. *It will be conditional on increased production.* ⇨ CONDITION[2]

CONDUCIR. Manejar un vehículo. *Drive.* ~Aprender a CONDUCIR. *To learn to drive.* ‖ **2.** Gente, ejército. *To lead.* ~El capitán del equipo nos CONDUJO a la victoria. *The team's coach lead us to victory.* ‖ **3.** [Líquido]. *To convey, carry, take.* ~Una pequeña acequia CONDUCE el agua al molino. *A narrow irrigation ditch carries the water to the windmill.* ‖ **4.** Transportar. *To carry, transport.* ~Un autobús CONDUCE a los pasajeros hasta el avión. *A bus carries the passengers to the airplane.* ‖ **5.** •CONDUCIR a algo. *To lead (to something).* ~Este sendero CONDUCE a la playa. *This path leads to the beach.* ~Puede CONDUCIR a error. *It can lead to mistakes.* ~No CONDUCE a ninguna parte. *This is getting us nowhere.* ~Esto ha de CONDUCIR al* desastre. *This is bound to lead to disaster.* || **6.** •¿A qué CONDUCE? *What's the point?* ⇨CONDUCT

CONDUCTOR. Persona que conduce un vehículo. *Driver.* ~El CONDUCTOR del autobús es muy joven. *The bus driver is very young.* || **2.** [Orquesta]. *Director.* ~Es CONDUCTOR de la Orquesta Sinfónica de Madrid. *He directs the Madrid Symphony Orquestra.* || **3.** Caudillo. *Leader.* Un CONDUCTOR de masas. *A leader of the masses.* ⇨CONDUCTOR

CONECTAR. *v.* Enchufar (radio, secadora). *To plug in.* ~Ya hemos CONECTADO la lavadora nueva. *We've already plugged in the new washing machine.* || **2.** Poner, encender (la radio). *To switch on.* ~CONECTA la radio para oir las noticias. *Switch the radio on so we can hear the news.* || **3.** [Radio, TV]. *To tune into a station.* || **4.** Llevarse bien, entenderse. *To get along, relate well.* ~Un cantante que CONECTA bien con la juventud. *A singer who relates well with young people.* || **5.** Enterarse. *To understand, be tuned in.* || **6.** Relacionar. *To put in touch with.* ~Yo les puedo CONECTAR. *I can put you in touch.* ⇨CONNECT

CONFECCIÓN. *s.* Actividad de hacer prendas de vestir. *Tailoring (de trajes), dressmaking (de vestidos).* ~Voy a una academia de corte y CONFECCIÓN para aprender a hacer mi propria ropa. *I'm taking classes at a dressmaking school so that I can learn to make my own clothes.* || **2.** [De artefactos]. *Making.* || **3.** [De un folleto, periódico]. *Producción.* || **4.** [De una lista]. *Drawing up.* || **5.** [De una maqueta]. *Construcción.* || **6.** [De una medicina]. *Preparación, making up.* || **7.** [Presupuesto]. *Drawing up, preparation.* ~La CONFECCIÓN del presupuesto. *The drawing up of the budget.* || **8.** *LOCUCIONES.* || •Industría (ramo) de la CONFECCIÓN. *Clothing (garment) industry.* || •De CONFECCIÓN. *Ready-to-wear.* || •CONFECCIONES. *Fashions.* || •Corte y CONFECCIÓN. *Dressmaking.* || •Es una CONFECCIÓN Pérez. *It's a Pérez creation.* ⇨CONFECTION

CONFERENCIA. Disertación pública. *Lecture, address.* ~Dar una CONFERENCIA. *To give a lecture, talk.* || **2.** Comunicación telefónica interurbana. *Long-distance call.* ~Operadora, quisiera poner una CONFERENCIA con París. *Operator, I would like to make a long distance call to Paris.* || **3.** •CONFERENCIA cumbre. *Summit, summit meeting.* || **4.** •CONFERENCIA de desarme. *Arms talks.* ⇨CONFERENCE

CONFERIR. Atribuir o añadir una calidad. *To give, lend.* ~Las canas le CONFERÍAN un aire digno. *His gray air gave him an air of dignity.* ⇨CONFER

CONFIANZA. *sf.* Confiabilidad. *Trust, reliance, trustfulness.* ~Persona de toda CONFIANZA. *Reliable person, trustworthy person.* ~Puesto de CONFIANZA. *Responsible post.* ~Es de confianza. *He's all right, you can speak freely in front of him.* ~Poner su CONFIANZA en. *To put one's trust in.* || **2.** Intimidad, amistad. *Intimacy, familiarity.* Creía que teníamos bastante CONFIANZA para que te dijera la verdad. *I thought we were sufficiently good friends for me to tell you the truth.* ~Tratar a uno con CONFIANZA. *Not to stand on ceremony with someone.* ~Tenemos mucha CONFIANZA. *We're close friends.* || **3.** [Libertades]. *Liberties.* ~Tomar demasiadas CONFIANZAS. *To take liberties.* ~No les des tanta(s) CONFIANZA(s) a los alumnos. *Don't let your pupils be so familiar (take liberties) with you.* ⇨CONFIDENCE

CONFIAR [CONFIDE]. *v.* Encomendar. *Entrust.* ~Le CONFIARON una misión difícil. *They entrusted him with a difficult mission.* ~CONFIÓ la educación de sus hijos a una institutriz. *He entrusted the education of his chidren to a governess.* || **2.** Estar seguro de. *To be confident.* ~El equipo CONFÍA en la victoria. *The team is confident of a victory.* ~CONFIAMOS en poder llevarlo a cabo. *We are confident that we can do it.* || **3.** Tener fe. *To trust.* ~CONFÍO en ella. *I trust her.* ~Debemos CONFIAR en Dios. *We must trust in God.* ~No CONFÍO en sus palabras. *I don't trust what she says.* || **4.** Contar con. *To count on, rely on, depend* *on.* ~No CONFÍES en su ayuda. *Don't count on his help.* ~CONFIAMOS en su discreción. *We rely (depend) on you to be discreet.* || **5.** Esperar. *To hope.* ~CONFIEMOS que llegue a tiempo. *Let's hope she arrives on time.* || **6.** Hacerse ilusiones. *To be over-confident.* ~No te CONFIES demasiado. *Don't be over-confident.* || **7.** Desahogarse, abrirse. *To open one's heart to somebody.* || **8.** •CONFIAR algo al azar. *To leave something to chance.*

CONFIDENCIA. Secreto. *Secret, confidential remark.* ~Te voy a hacer una CONFIDENCIA. *I'm going to tell you a secret.* || **2.** [A la policía]. *Tip-off.* || **3.** •Hacer CONFIDENCIAS a uno. *To tell secrets to someone, to confide in someone.* ⇨CONFIDENCE

CONFLICTO. Apuro, aprieto. *Difficulty, fix, jam.* ~Cuando estoy en algún CONFLICTO, pido ayuda a mis amigos. *When I'm in a jam I turn to my friends for help.* || **2.** Lo más recio de un combate. *The height of battle.* || **3.** Combate y angustia del ánimo. *Anguish.* || **4.** •Un CONFLICTO laboral. *A labor (trade) dispute.* ⇨CONFLICT

CONFORMAR[1]. *v.* Formar. *To shape, fashion, form.* ~Necesitaban CONFORMAR un ejército moderno. *They needed to form (shape) a modern army.* ~La educacion CONFORMA el carácter. *Education shapes character.* || **2.** TECH. *To mold, shape, form.* || **3.** Ajustar. *To adjust to, adapt to, bring into line with.* ~CONFORMAR los gastos con los ingresos. *~To adjust spending to income.* || **4.** Constituir. *To constitute, make up.* ~Las capas que CONFORMAN la superficie de la Tierra. *The layers which make up (constitute) the Earth's surface.* ~Estos once jugadores CONFORMAN el equipo. *These eleven players make up the team.* || **5.** Concordar. *To agree with.* || **6.** Contentar. *To satisfy.* Nos los vas a CONFORMAR con tan poco. *You're not going to satisfy them (keep them happy) with so little.* || **7.** [Cheque]. *To authorize payment of.* || **8.** [Enemigos]. *To reconcile.* ⇨CONFORM

CONFORMARSE[2]. *vr.* [Regla, will]. *To comply with, abide by, observe.* ~CONFORMARSE con la voluntad de Dios. *To comply with God's will.* || **2.** Contentarse (situación difícil). *To resign oneself, to accept.* ~Se CONFORMA con cualquier cosa. *He agrees to anything, he puts up with anything.* ~Se CONFORMÓ con una recompensa insignificante. *He agreed to a small compensation.* ~No se CONFORMA con nada. *He's never satisfied.* || **3.** Resignarse. *To resign oneself.* ~El niño es anormal y ellos no logran CONFORMARSE. *The child is handicapped and they cannot accept this fact.* ~No tienes más remedio que CONFORMARTE. *You'll just have to accept it (resign yourself to it).* || **4.** Concordar. *To agree with.* ~Sus ideas se CONFORMAN a las mías. *His ideas agree with mine.* ⇨CONFORM

CONFRONTAR. *v.* Cotejar (textos). *To compare.* || **2.** Lindar. *To border.* || **3.** [Testigos]. *To bring face to face.* || **4.** [Dificultad, peligro]. *To face.* ~CONFRONTAR la realidad. *To face up to reality.* ~Este país CONFRONTA la situación más difícil de su historia. *This country is facing the most difficult situation in it's history.* ⇨CONFRONT

CONFUNDIR. *v.* Equivocar (cosa). *To confuse with, mistake for.* ~CONFUNDIMOS el camino. *We mistook our way, we took the wrong road.* ~Me CONFUNDÍ de puerta. *It was the wrong door.* || **2.** [Persona]. *To mislead, confuse, mix up.* Nos CONFUNDEN la voz por teléfono. *People get our voices mixed up on the phone.* ~La CONFUNDIÓ con su prima. *He mistook her for his cousin.* || **3.** Mezclar. *To mingle, mix.* ~Ha CONFUNDIDO todos los sellos. *He has mixed up (jumbled up) all the stamps.* ~Al encuadernar el libro se CONFUNDIERON las páginas. *When they bound the book they got all the pages mixed up.* || **4.** [Acusador]. *To put to shame.* || **5.** [Con atenciones]. *To overwhelm.* || **6.** Perder. *To loose.* ~Me has CONFUNDIDO este libro otra vez. *You've lost that book of mine again.* || **7.** Borrar. *To blur, confuse.* || **8.** [Algo con algo]. *To mistake (something for something else).* ~CONFUNDIÓ el pimentón dulce con el picante. *He mistook the sweet paprika for the hot one.* || **9.** [Alguien con alguien]. *To mistake (someone for someone else).* ~La gente siempre me CONFUNDE con mi hermano gemelo. *People always mistake me for my twin brother.* ~Creo que se CONFUNDE señor; a Ud. no lo conozco. *You must be mistaken; I've never seen you before.* || **10.** Desconcertar. *To confuse.* No CONFUNDAS al pobre chico con tantos detalles. *Don't confuse the poor boy with so many details.* ~Tantas cifras CONFUNDEN a cualquiera. *All these numbers are enough to confuse anyone.* || **11.** Humillar. *To humble, to humiliate.* || **12.** [Dejar sin argumentos]. *To floor, to crush.* ⇨ CONFOUND

CONFUSO [CONFUSED]. *adj.* [Formas, recuerdos, idea, opinión, explicación]. *Blurred, vague, hazy.* ~Tiene una opinión algo CONFUSA sobre el tema. *He has a somewhat hazy opinion on the subject.* || **2.** Mezclado. *Mixed up.* || **3.** [Ruido]. *Indistinct.* || **4.** [Discurso, estilo]. *Obscure.*

CONGREGACIÓN. Sociedad. *Brotherhood, guild.* ⇨ CONGREGATION

CONJUGAR [CONJUGATE]. *v.* Combinar, reunir, unir, relacionar, coordinar. *To combine, bring together.* Ha logrado CONJUGAR elegancia y sencillez. *She has managed to combine elegance with simplicity.* ~La obra CONJUGA cualidades y defectos. *The work has both qualities and defects.*

CONJURAR. *v.* [Peligro, crisis]. *To ward off, stave off, avert* ~El gobierno ha tomado medidas para CONJURAR la crisis. *The government has taken measures to avert the crisis.* || **2.** Rogar. *To beseech, entreat, beg.* ~Les CONJURO que venga. *I beg you to come.* || **3.** Conspirar. *To conspire, plot.* ~Sentíamos que hasta los elementos se habían CONJURADO en contra de nosotros. *We felt that even the elements had conspired against us.* ~CONJURAR contra la República. *To conspire against the Republic.* || **4.** [Pensamiento]. *To rid oneself of, to get rid of.* ~Su sonrisa tiene el poder de CONJURAR los pensamientos tristes. *His smile has the power to chase away bad thoughts.* ⇨ CONJURE

CONMOCIÓN. Terremoto. *Shock, tremor,*

earthquake. || **2.** Fuerte transformación o cambios sociales. *Upheaval, unrest.* ~Una CONMOCIÓN social. *A social upheaval.* || **3.** Trastorno, agitación. *Shock, upset.* ~El siniestro produjo una profunda CONMOCIÓN en el país. *The disaster left the country in a state of profound shock.* ~La separación de Marta produjo una CONMOCIÓN familiar. *Martha's separation caused a great upset in the family.* ~La noticia de su muerte me produjo una gran CONMOCIÓN. *The news of his death was a great shock to me.* || **4.** •CONMOCIÓN cerebral. *Concussion.* ⇨ COMMOTION

CONQUISTAR. *v.* [A un hombre, mujer]. *Win over, win the heart of.* ~Acabó CONQUISTÁNDOLA. *He won her heart in the end.* || **2.** [Puesto, título, victoria]. *To win.* ~Había CONQUISTADO el puesto de director a los 30 años. *He had achieved the position of director by the age of 30.* || **3.** [Éxito, fama]. *To achieve.* ~Con este libro CONQUISTÓ la fama. *With this book he achieved fame.* || **4.** [Sentimiento, respeto]. *To win.* ~Los payasos CONQUISTARON a los niños. *The children were captivated by the clowns.* ~El actor CONQUISTÓ el corazón del público. *The actor won the affection (captured the heart) of the audience.* ⇨ CONQUER

CONSAGRAR [CONSECRATE]. *v.* Confirmar, establecer, acreditar, dar fama (a una persona). *To confirm, establish, prove.* ~Este triunfo lo CONSAGRA como un cirujano excepcional. *This success confirms him as a really exceptional surgeon.* ~La película que la CONSAGRÓ como una gran actriz. *The movie that established her as a great actress.* || **2.** [Palabra, expresión, costumbre]. *To establish.* ~Una expresión CONSAGRADA por el uso. *An expression which has established itself through usage.* || **3.** [Esfuerzo, tiempo, vida]. *To dedicate, devote, put in.* ~CONSAGRÓ su vida a sus hijos. *She devoted (dedicated) her life to her children.* || **4.** [Monumento, edificio]. *To dedicate.* ~El Ayuntamiento ha CONSAGRADO un gran monumento al poeta. *The Municipal government has*

dedicated a great monument to the poet. ‖
5. [Programa, publicación]. To devote, dedicate. ‖ 6. [Nueva palabra]. To accept, recognize. ~CONSAGRAR una nueva palabra. To accept a new word.

CONSCIENTE. adj. Responsable. Reliable. ~Es un niño muy CONSCIENTE para su edad. This child is very grown up for his age. ‖ 2. Sensato. Sensible. ~Ha sido una repuesta CONSCIENTE. It was a sensible answer. ⇨CONSCIOUS

CONSENTIR [CONSENT]. v. Tolerar. To tolerate, allow, permit. ~No CONSIENTAS que haga eso. Don't allow him to do that. ‖ 2. Mimar. To spoil, pamper. ~Su madre lo CONSIENTE demasiado. His mother spoils him to much. ‖ 3. Aguantar, soportar (peso, esfuerzo). To bear, admit, stand. ~La plataforma no CONSIENTE más peso. The platform will not bear anymore weight. ‖ 4. Aguantar (persona). To bear, put up with. ‖ 5. Ceder (mueble, pieza). To weaken. ~Al sentarse CONSINTIERON las patas de las silla. When they sat down the legs of the chair became loose.

CONSERVACIÓN [CONSERVATION]. sf. [General]. Preservation. ~Instinto de CONSERVACIÓN. Self-preservation. ~El cuadro se halla en un lamentable estado de CONSERVACIÓN. The painting is in a terrible state of preservation. ‖ 2. Mantenimiento. Maintenance, upkeep. ~Gastos de conservación. Upkeep costs, maintenance expenses. ‖ 3. [De alimentos]. Preserving.

CONSERVAR[1]. Guardar, tener guardado. To keep. ~Conservo una carta autógrafa de él. I have in my possesion a letter autographed by him. ~Consérvese en lugar fresco. Keep (store) in a cool place. ‖ 2. Tener o hacer todavía. To have still, to continue (to do something). ~Conservar la calma/el buen humor. To keep calm, to keep one's spirits up. ~Conserva una cicatriz de la guerra. He still bears a scar from the war. ~Conservo buenos recuerdos de aquella época. I have good memories of that time. ~Aún conserva buenos amigos

de la infancia. He still has (has kept) good friends from his childhood. ~Un régimen para CONSERVAR la línea. A diet to keep you in shape. Conserva intactas sus facultades mentales. He is still in full possession of his mental faculties. ~Todavía CONSERVA vivos los ideales de su juventud. He has kept alive the ideals of his youth. ~Conserva la costumbre de bañarse temprano todo los días. He continues to take an early shower every day. ‖ 3. Retener. Keep, retain. La arcilla CONSERVA el calor. Clay retains heat. ‖ 4. Cuidar de. Maintain, sustain. ~Conservar la salud (haciendo ejercicio). To maintain one's health (through excercise). ‖ 5. Mantener, preservar. To preserve (alimentos), retain (sabor, calor), preserve (costumbre, tradiciones). ~El frío CONSERVA los alimentos. Cold preserves foods. ‖ 6. Proteger, cuidar. To protect, care for, keep up (propiedad). ~Un producto para CONSERVAR los muebles. A product to protect your furniture. ~No sabe CONSERVAR los libros. He doesn't take care of his books. ⇨CONSERVE

CONSERVARSE[2]. vr. [Costumbre, ruinas]. Perdurar. To survive, remain, still exist; be retained, be kept. Aún se CONSERVAN restos del palacio. Some remains of the palace still survive. ~Tradiciones que se CONSERVAN en el sur. Traditions which still endure (survive) in the south. ‖ 2. No estropearse (alimentos). To keep. ~Las manzanas todavía se CONSERVAN. The apples are still good (to eat). ‖ 3. [Persona]. To keep well, to take good care of one's self. ~Se CONSERVA ágil (joven). He keeps trim/young. ~¡CONSÉRVESE bien! Look after yourself, take care of yourself? ‖ 4. •CONSERVE su derecha. Keep to your right. ⇨CONSERVE

CONSERVATIVO [CONSERVATIVE]. Que sirve para conservar (alimento, etc.). Preservative. ⇨CONSERVATIVE

CONSIDERACIÓN. sf. ‖ 2. Respeto. Regard, respect, esteem. ~Tengo una gran CONSIDERACIÓN por él. I hold him in high esteem. ~Un hombre que merece nuestra mayor CONSIDERACIÓN. *A man worthy of our highest esteem.* || **3.** Importancia. *Importance.* ~Una casa de cierta CONSIDERACIÓN. *A sizeable house.* ~Una herida de CONSIDERACIÓN. *A serious wound.* ~De poca CONSIDERACIÓN. *Of little importance.* ~No es de CONSIDERACIÓN. *It's not important.* || **4.** •CONSIDERACIONES. *Kindness.* ~Tener CONSIDERACIONES con alguien. *To be kind to someone.* || **5.** •En CONSIDERACIÓN de sus méritos. *In recognition of his merits.* || 6. •Es una falta de CONSIDERACIÓN. *It's not very considerate.* ⇨ CONSIDERATION

CONSIDERAR. Tratar con educación y respeto. *To treat with consideration, respect.* || **2.** Tener aprecio o estima a una persona. *To regard highly.* ~Se le CONSIDERA mucho en los círculos literarios. *He's highly regarded in literary circles.* ⇨ CONSIDER

CONSIGNAR. *v.* Asignar (cantidad). *To assign, allocate.* El Ayuntamiento ha CONSIGNADO poco dinero para la conservación de los parques. *The city council has allocated very litttle money for the maintenance of parks.* || **2.** Hacer constar. *To record.* ~El hecho no quedó CONSIGNADO en ningún libro. *The fact was not recorded in any book.* ~CONSIGNE en su envío el código postal. *Use the zip code.* || **3.** Anotar. *To take down, jot down.* ~CONSIGNÓ en el acto todo lo acordado en la junta. *He jotted down in the minutes all the decisions of the board.* || **4.** Depositar (en una cuenta bancaria). *To deposit.* ~CONSIGNÉ la paga en mi cuenta. *I deposited my paycheck in my account.* || **5.** Poner en depósito (equipaje). *To check.* ~CONSIGNÓ las maletas en el aeropuerto. *He checked his suitcases at the airport.* || **6.** Escribir. *To write in.* ~Olvidé CONSIGNAR mi nombre. *I forgot to write down my name.* ⇨ CONSIGN

CONSISTENCIA. Firmness, strength. *Solidez, fuerza, firmeza.* ~Tela sin CONSISTENCIA. *Flimsy material.* ~Esta estructura no tiene CONSISTENCIA, se derrumbará. *This structure is not strong enough, it will crumble.* ~El acero tiene mucha CONSIS-TENCIA. *Steel is very strong.* || **2.** [Teoría]. *Soundness.* ~Un argumento sin CONSIS-TENCIA. *A flimsy argument.* ~No se hizo caso de sus propuestas porque carecían de CONSISTENCIA. *They didn't take his proposals into consideration because they did not appear very sound.* || **3.** •Tomar CONSIS-TENCIA. *To materialize, to take form (idea), to thicken (crema, mayonesa).* ⇨ CONSIS-TENCY

CONSISTENTE. *adj.* Firme. *Firm, solid, strong.* Un pegamento CONSISTENTE. *A strong glue.* ~La estantería no es muy consistente. *The bookcase is not very solid.* || **2.** [Argumento, razón]. *Sound.* ~El confereciante presentó un grupo de ideas CONSISTENTES. *The lecturer's ideas were very sound.* || **3.** [Salsa, crema, masa]. *Thick.* ~La masa todavía no es muy CONSISTENTE. *The dough is still not thick enough.* ⇨ CONSISTENT

CONSPICUO. *adj.* Notable, sobresaliente (persona). *Eminent, famous, prominent, outstanding, distinguished, ilustrious.* ~Fue operado por un cirujano CONSPICUO. *He was operated on by an eminent surgeon.* ⇨ CONSPICUOUS

CONSTANCIA. *sf.* Testimonio. *Proof, evidence.* ~No tengo CONSTANCIA de que haya venido a verme. *I have no proof that he came to see me.* || **2.** Seguridad. *Certainty.* Tengo CONSTANCIA de que es cierto lo que dice. *I know for certain that what he says is true.* || **3.** •Dejar constancia. (I) Registrar. *To put something on record.* ~Una carta en que dejaba CONSTANCIA de su agradecimiento. *A letter in which she expressed her gratitude.* ~Que quede CONSTANCIA de que me opuse. *I would like the record to show that I was opposed,* (II) Probar, atestiguar. *To prove, show evidence of something.* ~Para que quede CONSTANCIA de la fecha. *In order to give proof of the date.* ⇨ CONSTANCY

CONSTIPADO. Resfrío, catarro. *Cold, blocked nose.* ⇨ CONSTIPATION

CONSUMIR[1]. *v.* Destruir. *To destroy.* ~El fuego CONSUMIÓ el edificio. *The fire*

destroyed the building. || **2.** [En un restaurante]. *To take, have.* ~En mi casa CONSUMIMOS mucha leche. *At home we drink a lot of milk.* || **3.** [Material]. *To wear away.* || **4.** [Paciencia]. *To wear down.* ~La larga espera me CONSUMÍA. *The long wait was wearing me down.* || **5.** [Tiempo]. *To take up.* ~Esta tarea CONSUMÍA todo mi tiempo. *This task was taking up all my time.* || **6.** [Person]. *To wear away.* ~Las preocupaciones lo CONSUMÍAN. *Worry was wearing him away.* || **7.** Agotar. *To wear out.* ~Tanto viajar lo CONSUME. *All that travelling wears him out.* || **8.** Poner nervioso. *To get on one's nerves.* ~Me CONSUME que estés perdiendo tanto tiempo. *Your loosing so much time bothers me.* ⇨CONSUME

CONSUMIRSE². *vr.* Extinguirse. *To burn out.* || **2.** [Persona]. *To waste away.* ~Se CONSUMÍA poco a poco debido a una gran enfermedad. *A long illness was wasting him away.* || **3.** Secarse (líquido). *To dry up, evaporate.* || **4.** Apenarse. *To mope, pine away.* || **5.** Achicarse. *To shrink.* || **6.** LOCUCIONES. •CONSUMIRSE de envidia. *To be eaten up by jealousy.* || •CONSUMIRSE de rabia. *To fume with rage.* || •La ambición la CONSUME. *She's burning with ambition.* ⇨CONSUME

CONTEMPLAR. *v.* Tomar en cuenta. *To take account of, deal with, provide.* ~La ley CONTEMPLA los siguientes casos. *The law provides for the following cases.* || **2.** Tratar bien, complacer. *Show (extra) consideration for, to be considerate towards.* || **3.** Mimar, consentir *To spoil.* ~No CONTEMPLES tanto a tu hijo. *You're spoiling your child too much.* || **4.** REL Meditar. *To meditate.* || **5.** [Obra, artista]. *To examine, study.* ⇨CONTEMPLATE

CONTENCIÓN. *sf.* Moderación. *Moderation, control.* ~Su capacidad de CONTENCIÓN le impidió que hiciera una tontería. *His sense of moderation prevented him from doing a foolish thing.* || **2.** Juicio. *Lawsuit.* || **3.** Acción de contener. *Containment, restriction.* ~La CONTENCIÓN del desempleo es nuestro principal objetivo. *Our main aim is to contain unemployment.* ~Medidas de

CONTENCIÓN del gasto público. *Measures to restrict public spending.* •Sin CONTENCIÓN. *Without restraint, freely.* || **4.** [De pasiones]. *Continence.* || **5.** [Agua, tierra]. *Containment.* ~Este muro de cemento sirve para la DETENCIÓN del agua de la presa. *This cement wall is used to contain the waters of the dam.* || **6.** [Military]. *Containing, containment.* ~Operación de CONTENCIÓN. *Holding operation.* || **7.** •Muro de CONTENCIÓN. *Retaining wall.* ⇨CONTENTION

CONTENDER. *v.* Competir. *To compete, fight.* ~CONTENDER en unas elecciónes. *To fight an election.* ~CONTENDER en unas oposiciones. *To take part in a competitive examination.* || **2.** Disputar. *To quarrel, argue.* ~Todos CONTENDÍAN sobre el partido de fútbol. *They were all arguing about the soccer game.* ⇨CONTEND

CONTENER [CONTAIN]. *v.* Reprimir (risa, lágrimas). *To contain, hold back, supress.* No pudo CONTENER la risa. *He couldn't hold back his laughter.* || **2.** Parar, controlar (infección, epidemia). *To contain.* ~CONTENER la sangre de una herida. *To stop the flow of blood from a wound.* || **3.** [Respiración]. *To hold.* || **4.** [Inovación, revuelta]. *To contain, hold back. keep in check.* La policía intentaba CONTENER a la gente. *The Police tried to hold back (contain, restrain) the crowd.* || **5.** [Tendencia]. *To curb, check.* || **6.** CONTENERSE. Dominarse. *To control oneself.* ~No me pude CONTENER y me eché a llorar. *I couldn't contain myself and I burst into tears.* ~Tuve que CONTENERME para no insultarlo. *I had to control myself to keep from insulting him.*

CONTRATAR [CONTRACT]. *v.* [Servicio, mercancía]. *To sign a contract for.* ~Ha sido CONTRATADO por seis meses. *~He has been given a six month contract.* || **2.** [Empleado]. *To hire, engage.* ~CONTRATÓ a dos albañiles para terminar la obra. *He hired two bricklayers to complete the work.* || **3.** [Deportista, artista]. *To sign up.* || **4.** [Arriendo]. *To take on.*

CONTRATO [CONTRACT]. *sm.* [De alquiler]. *Lease, leasing agreement.*

CONTRIBUCIÓN. *nf.* Impuesto]. *Tax, rates.* ~Pagar las contribuciones. *To pay one's taxes.* || **2.** •Exento de CONTRIBUCIONES. *Tax free, tax-exempt.* ⇨CONTRIBUTION

CONTROLAR. *v.* [Tema]. *To know about.* ~Estos temas no los CONTROLO. *I don't know anything about these subjects.* || **2.** Comprobar. *To check.* ~Sería conveniente que se CONTROLARA el tiempo que se tarda en hacer este trabajo. *Perhaps we should check to see how long it takes to do this work.* || **3.** COM Intervenir, revisar. *To audit.* || **4.** Vigilar. *Supervise, keep an eye on.* ~Tiene que CONTROLAR su peso. *He needs to watch (monitor) his weight.* ~Deja de CONTROLAR todos mis gastos. *Stop checking up on how much I spend the whole time.* ~El portero CONTROLABA las entradas y salidas. *The doorman kept a check on everyone who came in and out.*

CONVENIENCIA. Utilidad. *Advisability.* ~No dudo de la CONVENIENCIA de hacer lo que tu me dices. *There's no doubt in my mind that it would be advisable to do what you say.* Dudo de la CONVENIENCIA de estas medidas. *I don't feel these measures are advisable.* || **2.** Convencionalismo. *Convention.* ~CONVENIENCIAS sociales. *Proprieties, decencies.* || **3.** Conformidad entre cosas. *Conformity (of tastes, opinions), compatibility.* || **4.** Aptitud. *Suitability, fitness.* || **5.** Provecho, interés. *Usefulness, expediency.* ~Sólo piensa en su CONVENIENCIA personal. *He only thinks of his own interests.* ~Te hizo el favor por CONVENIENCIA. *He only did you the favor because it was in his own interest.* || **6.** Acuerdo. *Agreement.* || **7.** Puesto. *Domestic post, job as a servant.* || **8.** *pl.* Propriedad. *Property.* || **9.** Renta. *Income.* || **10.** •Atender a la propia CONVENIENCIA. *To think of how something will affect one.* ⇨CONVENIENCE

CONVENIENTE. Aconsejable. *Advisable, fit, proper, suitable.* ~No juzgó CONVENIENTE acceptar. *She did not think it advisable to accept.* ~Sería CONVENIENTE que guardaras cama. *It would be advisable for you to stay in bed.* || **2.** Deseable.

Desirable, proper. ~Una conducta CONVENIENTE. *Proper behavior.* ~No es la respuesta CONVENIENTE. *That's not the proper answer.* ~Si me ofreces una cantidad CONVENIENTE te lo vendo. *If you give me the right price, I'll sell it to you.* || **3.** Ser apto. *To suit, be suitable.* Este trabajo me CONVIENE. *This jobs suits me.* || **4.** Provechoso, útil. *Advantageous, useful.* ~Es CONVENIENTE comer frutas. *Eating fruits is very good (for your health).* || **5.** Adecuado, apropriada. *Fitting, right, appropriate.* ~Un actor CONVENIENTE para la película. *An actor just right for the film.* || **6.** •En el momento CONVENIENTE. *At the right time.* ⇨CONVENIENT

CONVENTO [CONVENT]. *sm.* [De monjes]. *Monastery.*

CONVICCIÓN. Persuasión. *Persuasion.* ~Tiene un gran poder de CONVICCIÓN. *He has great powers of persuasion.* ⇨CONVICTION

CONVICTO. Reo a quien se le ha probado su delito. *Person that has been convicted, condemned, found guilty; prisoner.* ~Visitó al CONVICTO en la cárcel. *She visited the prisoner at the jail.* ⇨CONVICT

CONVOCATORIA. *sf.* Llamamiento. *Call, summons.* ~CONVOCATORIA de huelga. *Strike call.* ~Hubo una CONVOCATORIA para una asamblea. *A meeting was called.* || **2.** Período de exámenes. *Examination.* ~Aprobó cinco asignaturas en la CONVOCATORIA de junio. *She passed five subjects in the June exams.* || **3.** Anuncio (de exámenes, concursos). *Official announcement.* ~CONVOCATORIA de premio. *Announcement of a prize competition.* ⇨CONVOCATION

COPIA. *sf.* [Persona]. *Image.* ~Es una COPIA de su madre. *She's the image of her mother.* || **2.** [Cine]. *Print.* ~Hacer una COPIA de una fotografía. *To make a print of a photograph.* || **3.** Abundancia. *Abundance.* || **4.** Reproducción. *Reproduction, replica, duplicate (llave).* Después de firmar me dieron una COPIA del contrato. *After signing the contract they gave me a copy of it.*

~Necesito una COPIA de la llave de esta casa. *I need a duplicate of the key for this door.* || **5.** •Máquina para sacar COPIAS. *Printer, copying machine.* ⇨COPY

CORAJE. Cólera, rabia. *Anger, rage, irritation.* ~Me da CORAJE pensar cómo me engañaron. *It makes me mad to think how I was tricked.* || **2.** Desfachatez. *Audacity, nerve.* ¡Qué CORAJE! *What nerve!* || **3.** •Me da CORAJE. *It makes me angry.* ~Le dio CORAJE llegar tarde. *He was angry at himself for arriving late.* ⇨COURAGE

CORONACIÓN [CORONATION]. *sf.* Culminación. *Crowning, completion, culmination.* ~La CORONACIÓN de su carrera. *The crowning moment (culmination) of his career.* || **2.** [Ajedrez]. *Queening.*

CORPULENTO. *adj.* [Persona]. *Burly, heavy-built.* ~GUARDABA la puerta un muchacho corpulento. *A heavy-built young man was guarding the entrance.* || **2.** [Tree]. *Solid, massive, sturdy.* ~GRABARON sus iniciales en el árbol corpulento. *They carved their initials on the giant tree.* || **3.** [Animal]. *Hefty, bulky, big.* ~Se me acercó un perro CORPULENTO. *This hefty (big) dog came to me.* ⇨CORPULENT

CORRECCIÓN. *sf.* [De pruebas]. *Proof-reading.* ~Julio se encargará de la CORRECCIÓN de las pruebas de imprenta de la revista. *Julio will proofread the magazine.* || **2.** Cortesía. *Courtesy, correctness, politeness, good manners.* ~Tratar a la gente con CORRECCIÓN. *To be polite.* ~Es un hombre de una gran CORRECCIÓN. *He's very well mannered.* ~Nos trató con CORRECCIÓN, pero con frialdad. *He was courteous, but cold.* || **3.** Reprimenda. *Rebuke.* || **4.** Castigo. *Punishment.* || **5.** •Hablar con CORRECCIÓN. *To speak well, to speak fluently (idioma extranjero).* ~Habla los dos idiomas con CORRECCIÓN. *He speaks both languages fluently.* ~Se preocupa mucho por la CORRECCIÓN de su lenguaje. *He constantly tries to speak well.* ⇨CORRECTION

CORRECTO. *adj.* Cortés, educado. *Polite, courteous.* ~Estuvo muy CORRECTO conmigo. *He was very polite to me.* || **2.** [Conducta]. *Proper.* ~Tiene un comportamiento CORRECTO y atento. *He always conducts himself in a proper and courteous manner.* || **3.** [Ropa]. *Suitable.* || **4.** [Rasgos]. *Regular, well-formed.* ⇨CORRECT

CORRESPONDENCIA [CORRESPONDENCE]. Correo, cartas. *Mail.* ~¿Llegó la CORRESPONDENCIA? *Has the mail come in yet?* || **2.** Enlace. *Commuting, connection (trenes).* ~En esa estación hay CORREPONDENCIA con autobuses urbanos. *At that station you can make connection with city buses.* || **3.** Equivalent. *Equivalente.* ~Esta palabra no tiene CORRESPONDENCIA en español. *There is no translation (equivalent) for this word in Spanish.*

CORRESPONDER. Encajar. *To fit.* ~La llave CORRESPONDE a la cerradura. *The key fits the lock.* || **2.** Concernir. *To concern.* ~A quien CORRESPONDA. *To whom it may concern.* || **3.** Tocar. *To be one's turn.* ~Ahora te CORRESPONDE a tí saltar. *Now it's your turn to jump.* || **4.** Incumbir. *To be someone's responsability, to be incumbent upon.* ~Esta tarea te CORRESPONDE a tí. *It's your job to do this.* ~No me CORRESPONDE criticarle. *It's not for me (it's not my job) to criticize him.* ~CORRESPONDE al Estado velar por la salud pública. *It's the responsability of the State to look after public health.* || **5.** Tocar, pertenecer. *To belong, to be one's due.* A él le CORRESPONDE la mitad de la herencia. *Half of the inheritance goes to him.* ~Esta es la parte que te CORRESPONDE. *This is your share.* || **6.** Devolver. *To return, reciprocate, repay (a favor).* ~El le regaló un bolso y ella le CORRESPONDIÓ con una corbata. *He gave her a purse and she gave him a tie in return.* ~Amor no CORRESPONDIDO. *Unrequited love.* ~CORRESPONDER a la amabilidad de alguien. *To repay someone's kindness.* || **7.** To be in harmony. *Armonizar.* || **8.** [Cifras]. *To tally.* ~Esta cifra no CORRESPONDE con ésa. *This figure doesn't tally with that one.* || **9.** Ser propio a. *To become, to befit, be fitting.* Fue recibido con los honores que CORRESPONDEN a su rango. *He* *was received with the honors befitting his rank.* ~Esa conducta no CORRESPONDE a una persona bien educada. *That behavior does not become a well-mannered person.* || **10.** Proceder de una forma razonable, natural o conforme a lo establecido. *To be the right or proper thing to do.* ~Si no puedes ir, lo que CORRESPONDE es que le avises. *If you can't go, you should let him know.* ~Ahora vas y te disculpas, como CORRESPONDE. *Now go and apologize, as it is right and proper.* || **11.** Cuadrar, encajar, responder. *To match.* Su aspecto CORRESPONDE a la descripción que me han dado. *His appearance fits (matches) the description I have been given.* ~Su versión no CORRESPONDE con la de los demás testigos. *His version doesn't match that of the other witnesses.* || **12.** Pertenecer. *To belong.* ~Este mueble no CORRESPONDE a esta habitación. *This piece of furniture doesn't belong in this room.* ~Este tornillo CORRESPONDE a esta pieza. *This screw belongs to this part.* ~Esos sillones CORRESPONDEN a este despacho. *Those chairs belong in this office.* || **13.** [Color, mueble]. *To match.* Estos botones no CORRESPONDEN. *These buttons don't match.* ~Las cortinas no CORRESPONDEN con los muebles. *The curtains do not match the furniture.* || **14.** Estar a la altura. *To come up to, to meet.* ~El éxito no CORRESPONDIÓ a mis esperanzas. *The success did not come up to my expectations.* || **15.** Ser adecuado. *To be appropriate, suitable.* ~Le contesté como CORRESPONDÍA. *I gave him a suitable reply.* || **16.** Ser el tiempo oportuno para hacer una cosa. *To be opportune, timely, the right time.* Todavía no CORRESPONDE sembrar la violeta. *It's still to early to sow the violets.* || **17** -se. Tener aprecio por una persona. *To have mutual affection, have regard for one another.* ⇨ CORRESPOND

CORRESPONDIENTE [CORRESPONDING]. *adj.* Apropiado. *Appropriate, suitable.* ~Haga la solicitud rellenando el impreso CORRESPONDIENTE. *To apply, complete the relevant form.* || **2.** Oportuno. *Convenient.* || **3.** Respectivo. *Respective, own.* ~Cada

uno con su CORRESPONDIENTE etiqueta. *Each one with its own label.* || **4.** [Palabra]. *Equivalent.*

CORRIENTE[1]. *adj.* Ni bueno, ni malo; ni bonito, ni feo; nada especial. *Ordinary, average, run-of-the mill.* ~Un vestido CORRIENTE. *An ordinary dress.* ~Una tela muy CORRIENTE. ~El inglés CORRIENTE. *The average Englishman.* •CORRIENTE y moliente. *Ordinary.* ~Nos hizo una comida CORRIENTE y moliente. *The meal he cooked for us was run-of-the-mill (nothing out of the ordinary).* || **2.** [Agua]. *Running.* ~Agua CORRIENTE. *Running water.* || **3.** De curso legal (moneda). *Valid, accepted.* || **4.** Fluido (estilo). *Flowing, fluent, easy, smooth.* || **5.** En regla. *In order.* ~Tiene CORRIENTE la documentación. *His papers are in order.* ~Todo está CORRIENTE para la partida. *Everything is ready for your departure.* || **6.** Normal, no extraño, extendido, frecuente. *Common, normal, frequent.* ~Es un error muy CORRIENTE. *It's a very common mistake.* ~Este tipo de robo es muy CORRIENTE en esta zona. *Robberies like that are very common in this area.* ~Lo CORRIENTE es efectuar el pago por adelantado. *The normal procedure is to pay in advance.* ~Lo CORRIENTE es no pintarlo. *The usual thing is not to paint it.* || **7.** *LOCUCIONES.* || •Salirse de la CORRIENTE. *To be unusual.* || •El cable está con CORRIENTE. *The wire is live.* || •Al CORRIENTE. (I) *Up to date.* ~Estoy al CORRIENTE en el pago de los recibos. *I'm up to date with all the payments.* ~Empezó el curso con retraso pero se ha puesto al CORRIENTE. *She started the course late but she has caught up.* (II) *Enterado.* ~No estaba al CORRIENTE de lo que occurría *He did not know what was happening.* || •Tener (mantener) al corriente. *To keep informed.* ~Quiero que me tengan (mantengan) al CORRIENTE de todas las noticias que reciban. *I want to be kept informed about any news that comes in.* || •Poner (alguien) al CORRIENTE (de algo). *To fill (somebody) in (on something).* ⇨ CURRENT

CORRIENTE². n.
❶ DE AGUA. *Flow, stream.* ~Corriente del Golfo. *Gulf Stream.* ~Corriente de lava. *Stream of lava.* || **2.** •Corriente sanguínea. *Bloodstream.* || **3.** •Corriente abajo. *Downstream.* || **4.** Corriente arriba. *Upstream.* || **5.** En sentido figurado. || •Ir (nadar, navegar) contra la corriente. *To swim (fig. go) against the tide.* || •Seguir (dejarse llevar, arrastrar por) la corriente. *To follow the crowd, to go along with.* || •Ir en contra de la corriente. *To go against the grain.* || •Seguirle (llevarle) la corriente a alguien. *To humor someone, play along with somebody.* || •Corriente de la conciencia (del pensamiento). *Stream of consciousness.*
❷ DE AIRE. *Draft.* ~Cierra la ventana que hay mucha corriente. *Shut the window, there's a terrible draft.* ~Corriente de aire caliente. *Flow of warm air.*
❸TENDENCIA. *Trend, current.* ~La corriente pro unidad europea. *The trend towards European unity.* ~Las corrientes modernas del arte. *The modern trends in art.* ~Una fuerte corriente inovadora. *A strong innovating tendency.* ⇨current

CORROMPER¹ [CORRUPT]. Sobornar. *To bribe.* ~Corromper a un funcionario. *To bride an official.* || **2.** Estropear (lenguage, costumbre). *To spoil.* ~La falta de lectura corrompe el lenguaje. *Not reading enough can impoverish one's language.* || **3.** Arruinar, echar a perder. *To spoil, ruin, cause damage to.* ~El calor corrompe la fruta. *Fruits spoil in the heat.*

CORROMPERSE² [CORRUPT]. *vr.* Pudrir. (I) [Alimentos]. *To turn bad, spoil,* (II) [Madera]. *To rot.* ~El pescado se corrompe con facilidad. *Fish spoils easily.*

CORRUPCIÓN [CORRUPTION]. *sf.* Putrefacción. *Rot, decay.* || **2.** Soborno. *Bribe.* || **3.** Perversión. *Seduction.*

CRÉDITO. *sm.* Buena fama. *Reputation, standing.* ~Una persona de crédito. *A reliable person.* ~Un médico que goza de mucho crédito. *A doctor of good standing.* || **2.** Cuenta. *Account.* || **3.** Préstamo. *Loan.*

~Me concedieron un crédito. *They gave me a loan.* ~Crédito hipotecario. *Mortgage loan.* He solicitado un crédito en el banco para comprarme una vivienda. *I've applied at the bank for a home loan* || **4.** Credibilidad, fe. *Reliability.* ~Fuentes dignas de crédito. *Reliable sources.* ~No di crédito a sus palabras. *I didn't believe what he said.* || **5.** •No dar crédito a sus ojos/oídos. *Not to believe one's eyes/ears.* ~No daba crédito a lo que estaba viendo. *He couldn't believe his eyes.* ⇨CREDIT

CRIATURA. *sf.* Crío, niño pequeño. *Baby, child.* ~A sus veinte años todavía se comporta como una criatura. *Although he's twenty years old he still behaves like a child.* ~¿Casarse?, pero si es una criatura. *She's getting married? but she's hardly more than a child.* ~Pero criatura ¿cómo te has podido creer eso? *You silly thing, fancy falling for that!* || **2.** teol Creación. *Creation.* ~El hombre es una criatura de Dios. *God created man.* || **3.** •Llorar como una criatura. *To cry like a baby.* ⇨CREATURE

CRIMEN. Asesinato. *Murder.* || **2.** Homicidio. *Manslaughter.* ⇨CRIME

CRIMINAL. Asesino. *Murderer.* ⇨CRIMINAL

CRISIS [CRISIS]. *sf.* Ataque. *Attack, fit.* ~Crisis de asma. *Asthma attack.* ~Crisis de llanto. *Fit of tears.* ~Crisis nerviosa. *Nervous breakdown.* || **2.** Escasez. *Scarcity, shortage.* ~Crisis de la vivienda. *Housing shortage.* || **3.** •Crisis de gobierno. *Cabinet reshuffle.*

CRISTAL [CRYSTAL]. *sm.* [Vidrio]. *Glass.* ~Botella de cristal. *Glass bottle.* ~Copa de cristal. *Wine glass.* ~Vaso de cristal. *Drinking glass.* ~El cristal de un reloj. *The glass of a watch.* || **2.** Lente (de gafas). *Lens.* ~Cristal de contacto. *Contact lens.* || **3.** [De ventana]. *Window (pane).* ~Una gamuza para limpiar los cristales. *A chamois for cleaning the windows.* || **4.** -es. *Piece of glass.* ~Ella se cortó el pie con unos cristales. *She cut her foot on some broken glass.* ~Había cristales rotos por el suelo. *There were pieces of broken glass* *all over the floor.* || **5.** Vaso (latinoamérica). *Drinking glass.* || **6.** Espejo. *Mirror, looking-glass.* || **7.** [Figurado y poético]. *Water.* ~El CRISTAL de la fuente. *The water of the fountain.* || **8.** *LOCUCIONES.* •CRISTAL ahumado. *Smoked glass.* || •CRISTAL antibalas. *Bullet-proof glass.* || •CRISTAL cilindrado. *Plate glass.* || •CRISTAL de aumento. *Magnifying glass.* || •CRISTAL de Murano. *Venetian glass.* || •NAUT CRISTAL de patente *Bull's eye.* || •CRISTAL de seguridad. *Safety glass.* || •CRISTAL delantero. *Windshield.* || •CRISTAL esmerilado. *Ground glass.* || •CRISTAL hilado. *Fiberglass.* || •CRISTAL inastillable. *Splinter-proof glass.* || •CRISTAL soplado. *Blown glass.* || •CRISTAL tallado. *Cut glass.* || •CRISTAL trasero. *Rear windshield.*

CRITERIO [CRITERION]. *sm.* Juicio. *Discernment, discrimination, judgement.* ~Lo dejo a tu CRITERIO. *I leave it to your discretion.* ~Tener buen CRITERIO. *To have sound judgement.* ~Tiene buen CRITERIO. *He has good taste.* || **2.** Opinión. *Opinion.* ~Cambiar de CRITERIO. *To change one's mind.* ~No comparto este CRITERIO. *I do not share that view.* ~Formar un CRITERIO sobre. *To form an opinion of.* || **3.** Enfoque. *Viewpoint, attitude, approach.* ~Depende del CRITERIO de cada uno. *It depends on the individual's point of view.* ~Le hace falta tener un CRITERIO más maduro. *One needs a more mature approach.* •CRITERIO estrecho. *Narrow viewpoint.* •Persona de amplios CRITERIOS. *Broad-minded person.* •Por cualquier CRITERIO. *By any standard.*

CRUDO. *adj.* [Invierno, clima]. *Severe, harsh.* ~Este invierno ha sido muy CRUDO. *This has been a very harsh winter.* || **2.** [Lenguaje]. *Harsh, raw.* || **3.** [Imágenes]. *Harsh.* ~La película tiene unas escenas muy CRUDAS. *The film has some very harsh scenes in it.* ~Es la CRUDA realidad. *Its the harsh truth.* || **4.** [Carne]. *Raw.* ~La carne está todavía un poco CRUDA. *The meat is not quite done.* || **5.** [Pollo]. *Undercooked.* ~Este pollo está CRUDO. *This chicken is undercooked.* || **6.** [Legumbres]. *Raw, uncooked.* || **7.** [Fruta]. *Unripe.* || **8.** [Agua].

Hard. || **9.** •Seda CRUDA. *Raw silk.* || •De color CRUDO. *Natural, unbleached.* ⇨CRUDE

CRUEL [CRUEL]. *adj.* [Clima]. *Harsh, severe.* ~Un cruel invierno. *A severe winter.*

CRUZAR. *v.* [Línea, calle]. *To intersect.* ~Esta calle no CRUZA Serrano. *This street doesn't intersect Serrano.* || **2.** [Palabra, mirada]. *To exchange.* ~No CRUCÉ ni una palabra con él. *We didn't say a single word to each other, we didn't exchange a single word.* || **3.** [Bets]. *To make.* ~CRUZAR apuestas. *To make bets.* || **4.** [Brazos]. To fold. ~CRUZAR los brazos. *To fold one's arms.* || **5.** Poner atravesado. ~CRUZAR algo con una raya. *To draw a line across or through.* || **6.** [Naútica]. *To cruise.* || **7.** To lay or place across. ~CRUZAR el camino con un árbol. *To lay a tree across the road.* ~CRUZAR un palo sobre otro. *To place a stick across another.* || **8.** •CRUZAR a nado. *To swim across.* || **9.** •CRUZARLE la cara a alguien. *To slap somebody's face.* ⇨CROSS

CUESTIÓN. *sf.* Asunto. *Matter.* ~En la reunión se discutieron, entre otras CUESTIONES, ... *Discussed at the meeting, among others matters, ...* ~Otra CUESTIÓN sería que estuviera enfermo. *If he were ill, that would be another matter.* ~Una CUESTIÓN jurídica. *A legal matter.* ~CUESTIÓN de vida y muerte. *A matter of life and death.* ~En CUESTIÓN de unas horas. *In just a few hours.* ~No es CUESTIÓN de enfadarse. *It's nothing to get angry about.* || **2.** [Discusión]. *Disagreement.* || **3.** [Problema]. *Problem, trouble, complication.* ~La CUESTIÓN es que ... *The trouble is that ...* ~No quiero CUESTIONES con los empleados. *I don't want trouble with the staff.* || **4.** *LOCUCIONES.* || •Llegar al fondo de la CUESTIÓN. *To get to the heart of the matter, to get to the root of the problem.* || •En CUESTIÓN de. *In a matter of.* Aprendió inglés en CUESTIÓN de meses. *He learned English in a matter of months.* || •La CUESTIÓN es. *The thing is.* ~La CUESTIÓN es que no tengo tiempo. *The thing is that I don't have time.* ~La CUESTIÓN es divertirnos. *The main thing is to have a good time.*

CULMINACIÓN [CULMINATION]. *sf.* Clímax. *Crowning achievement.* ~La CULMINACIÓN de su obra. *The crowning achievement of his literary career.* ~La procesión fue la CULMINACION de los festejos. *The procession was the high point of the celebrations.* || **2.** Realización. *Fulfillment.* || **3.** [Astronomía]. *Zenith.*

CULMINAR [CULMINATE]. *v.* [Objetivo]. *To reach, attain.* || **2.** [Acuerdo]. *To conclude, put the finishing touches to.* || **3.** [Tarea, carrera, vida]. *To finish, end.* ~Con su muerte CULMINA una etapa trágica de nuestra historia. *His death marks the end of a tragic chapter in our history.* || **4.** [Astronomía]. *To reach the zenith.* || **5.** Llegar una cosa a su punto culminante o de perfección. *To reach a climax, to reach a peak or its highest point.* ~La novela CULMINA cuando. *The novel reaches its climax when.*

CULTIVAR [CULTIVATE]. *v.* [Memoria]. *Develop, improve.* ~CULTIVAR la memoria. *To improve (develop) one's memory.* || **2.** [Bacterias, perlas]. *To culture.* || **3.** [Cultivo]. *To grow.* ~Un huerto bien CULTIVADO. *A well-tended vegetable garden.* || **4.** [Talent]. *To develop.* || **5.** [Artes]. *To encourage, promote.* || **6.** [Interés]. *To encourage, foster.* ~Para CULTIVAR un espíritu de solidaridad. *To foster a spirit of solidarity.* || **7.** Practicar. *To practice.*

CUMPLIMENTAR. *v.* Felicitar. *To congratulate.* ~En el día de su cumpleaños, CUMPLIMENTÓ a su suegra. *He congratulated his mother-in-law on her birthday.* || **2.** [Orden]. *To fulfill, carry out.* ~CUMPLIMENTÓ la orden del juez de citar al testigo. *He carried out the judge's order to call the witness.* || **3.** [Visitar, ir a saludar]. *To pay one's respects to, pay a courtesy call on.* ~El alcalde CUMPLIMENTÓ al rey. *The mayor paid his respects to the king.* || **4.** [Deber, actividad]. *To perform, do.* ~Después de CUMPLIMENTAR los trámites en la aduana, recogimos nuestras maletas y salimos a buscar un taxi. *After going through customs, we picked up our bags and went outside to look for a taxi.* || **5.**

Rellenar (formulario). *To fill in, complete.* Los alumnos CUMPLIMENTARON los impresos de matrícula. *The students filled in the registration forms.* ⇨ COMPLIMENT²

CUMPLIMIENTO. Ejecución. *Execution, carrying out.* ~CUMPLIMIENTO de una orden. *Execution of an order.* || **2.** Aplicación. *Enforcement, application.* ~El CUMPLIMIENTO de un decreto. *The application of a decree.* || **3.** Acatamiento. *Observance.* ~CUMPLIMIENTOS de los requisitos legales. *Observance of statutory provisions.* || **4.** Realización. *Fulfillment, honoring, performance.* ~CUMPLIMIENTOS de los compromisos. *Fulfillment of one's commitments.* ~Falleció en el CUMPLIMIENTO del deber. *He died in the course of duty.* || **5.** *LOCUCIONES.* || •CUMPLIMIENTO de la ley. *Observance of the law.* || •Falta de CUMPLIMIENTO. *Non-fulfillment, non-compliance.* || •Dar CUMPLIMIENTO a. *To fulfill.* || •En CUMPLIMIENTO con. *In compliance with.* ~En CUMPLIMIENTO con lo dispuesto por la legislación vigente. *In compliance with current legislation.* || •Dar CUMPLIMIENTOS a los nuevos estatutos. *To put the new statutes into operation, to enforce the new statutes.* || •Por CUMPLIMIENTO. *Out of courtesy, politeness.* ⇨ COMPLIMENT

CUOTA [QUOTA]. *sf.* [De un club, una asociación]. *Membership fees.* ~Ha subido la CUOTA del club de golf. *The golf club membership fees have increased.* || **2.** [De un sindicato]. *Dues.* || **3.** [De un seguro]. *Premium.* || **4.** [Precio, cantidad]. *Amount.* ~Pagan una modesta CUOTA por alimentación y hospedaje. *They pay a modest amount for board and lodging.* || **5.** Costo, gastos. *Charge.* ~La CUOTA de instalación de teléfono. *The cost of installing a telephone.* || **6.** Proporción. *Share.* ~Ya pagó su CUOTA de mala suerte. *She's already had her share of bad luck.* ~La CUOTA que pertenece a cada socio son 400 pesetas. *Each member's share comes to 400 pesetas.* || **7.** LAT. AM. Plazo. *Payment, installment.* ~En cómodas CUOTAS mensuales. *In easy monthly installments.* || **8.** Contribución. *Contribution.*

CUPÓN [COUPON]. *sm.* [Comercio]. *Trading stamp.* || **2.** [De lotería]. *Ticket.* ~El CUPÓN de los ciegos. *The lottery ticket for the benefit of the blind.* || **3.** •CUPÓN obsequio. *Gift certificate.* || **5.** •CUPÓN federal. *Food stamp.*

CURAR. *v.* Tratar (herida). *To treat, dress.* ~No le habían CURADO la herida. *The wound had not been dressed.* || **2.** Tratar (enfermedad). *To treat.* ~CURAR con medicamentos. *To treat with medication.* ~CURAR a un enfermo con antibióticos. *To treat a patient with antibiotics.* || **3.** Curtir (piel, cuero). *To tan.* || **4.** [Madera]. *To season.* ~En el almacén se guardan las tablas para que se CUREN. *The boards are kept in storage until they season.* || **5.** Recuperarse. *To recover, get well.* ~Una vez CURADO de la enfermedad. *Once he had recovered from his illness.* || **6.** [Herida]. *To heal.* ~El tiempo lo CURA todo. *Time heals all wounds.* || **7.** [Mal]. *To remedy, put right.* || **8.** [Paño, hilos. lienzos]. *To bleach.* ~Trabaja en una fábrica donde CURAN y tiñen algodón. *He works in factory where they bleach and dye cotton.* ⇨CURE

CURIOSO. *adj.* Ordenado, aseado. *Clean, neat, tidy.* ~Tiene la habitación muy CURIOSA. *His room is very tidy.* || **2.** Extraño. *Strange.* ~Es curioso que a este niño no le guste el chocolate. *It a little strange that this child doesn't like chocolate.* Es CURIOSO lo poco que se conoce la gente a sí misma. *It's strange how little people know themselves.* || **3.** *n.* Fisgón. *Busybody, nosey person.* || **4.** •Abstenerse CURIOSOS. *No timewasters.* || **5.** •Los CURIOSOS de la literatura. *Those interested in literature.* ⇨CURIOUS

CURSO. Año académico. *Year.* Este CURSO empieza en septiembre y termina en junio. *The school year begins in September and ends in June.* ~Está en el tercer CURSO. *He's in the third year.* ~Los del segundo CURSO. *Those in the second year.* •CURSO escolar. *School year.* •CURSO lectivo. *Academic year.* || **2.** •Dar CURSO a su indignación. *To vent one's indignation.* || **3.** •Dar CURSO a su imaginación. *To give free reins to one's imagination, let one's imagination run wild.* || **4.** •Dar CURSO a sus llantos. *To let one's tears flow.* || **5.** •Dar CURSO a una carta. *To dispatch a letter.* || **6.** •Dar CURSO a una solicitud. *To handle, start processing an application.* || **7.** •Dar CURSO a un pedido. *To attend to an order.* || **8.** •Dar CURSO a una petición. *To grant a request.* || **9.** •Estar en CURSO. *To be under way.* || **10.** •Año/mes en CURSO. *Current year/month.* || **11.** •Moneda de CURSO legal. *Legal tender.* || **12.** •Exámenes de fin de CURSO. *Final exams, finals.* || **13.** •Compañeros de CURSO. *Classmates.* || **14.** •Trabajo en CURSO.*Work in progress.* ⇨COURSE

D

DAMA. *sf.* Señora. *Lady.* ~DAMAS y caballeros. *Ladies and gentlemen.* ~Es toda una DAMA. *She's a real lady.* ‖ **2.** Mujer. *Woman.* ~La DAMA de sus sueños. *The woman of his dreams.* ‖ **3.** [Naipes, ajedrez]. *Queen.* ‖ **4.** [En damas]. *King.* ‖ **5.** •DAMAS. *Checkers.* ⇨ DAME

DEBATIRSE. *vr.* Luchar. *To struggle.* ~Se DEBATE entre la vida y la muerte. *He's fighting for his life.* ~La región se DEBATE en una masa de problemas.*The region is struggling to overcome a whole series of problems.* ~Se DEBATÍA entre sus sentimientos personales y las presiones que recibía. *She was torn between her personal feelings and the pressures which were being put on her.* ⇨ DEBATE

DECENTE. *adj.* Honrado. *Honest, respectable.* ~Puedes confiar en Ricardo, es una persona muy DECENTE. *You can trust Richard, he's a very honest person.* ‖ **2.** Limpio, aseado. *Neat, tidy.* ⇨ DECENT

DECEPCIÓN. *sm.* Disappointment. *Desengaño, desilusión.* ~Me llevé una DECEPCIÓN con esta película. *I was terribly disappointed in the film.* ~¡Qué DECEPCIÓN! *What a disappointment!* ⇨ DECEPTION

DECEPCIONAR. Desengañar. *To disappoint.* Este libro me DECEPCIONÓ. *This book was very disappointing.* ⇨ DECEIVE

DECIDIDO [DECIDED]. *adj.* Resuelto, enérgico. *Determined, resolute.* ~Adversario DECIDIDO. *A determined opponent.* ~Está DECIDIDO a hacerlo. *He's determined to do it.*

DECLARACIÓN [DECLARATION]. *sf.* Afirmación. *Statement.* ~El gobierno no ha emitido ninguna DECLARACIÓN al respecto.

The government has issued no statement on the matter. ~Se negó a hacer DECLARACIONES a la prensa. *He refused to make a statement to the press.* ‖ **2.** [Law]. *Statement, evidence, deposition.* •Hacer (prestar) una DECLARACIÓN. *To make a statement, to give evidence.* •DECLARACIÓN jurada. *Sworn statement.* •Tomar la DECLARACIÓN a uno. *To take a statement from somebody.* ‖ **3.** Explicación. *Explanation.* ‖ **4.** [De amor]. *Proposal (of marriage).* ‖ **5.** [Naipes]. *Bid, call.* ‖ **6.** •DECLARACIÓN de culpabilidad. *Confession of guilt.* •DECLARACIÓN de derechos. *Bill of rights.* ‖ **7.** •DECLARACIÓN de renta (impuestos, ingresos). *Income-tax return.*

DECLINAR. v. Disminuir. *To diminish, lessen.* ‖ **2.** [Fiebre]. *To abate, diminish.* ‖ **3.** Terminar (el día, la tarde). *To draw to a close.* ~Al DECLINAR el día. *When the day draws to a close.* ‖ **4.** [Terreno]. *To slope downwards.* ‖ **5.** [Brújula). *To vary from the true meridian.* ‖ **6.** [Belleza]. *To fade, to be on the wane.* ‖ **7.** Debilitarse. *To get weaker.* Ha DECLINADO mucho desde la última vez que lo vi. *He has gotten weaker since I last saw him.* ‖ **8.** Apartarse. *To depart.* ~DECLINAR del camino derecho. *To depart from the straight and narrow.* ⇨ DECLINE

DEDICAR. [Tiempo]. *Devote, spend.* ~DEDICÓ la tarde a escuchar discos. *He spent the evening playing records.* ~Los fines de semana se DEDICA a la pesca. *On weekends she spends her time fishing.* DEDICO mucho tiempo a la lectura. *I devote a lot of time to reading.* ‖ **2.** Ponerse a, empezar a. *Pursue (an activity), get down to.* ~Apagó la radio y se DEDICÓ a hacer su tarea. *He switched off the radio and got down to doing his homework.* || **3.** Dirigir. *Address.* DEDICÓ al público unas palabras de agradecimiento. *He addressed a few words of thanks to the audience.* || **4.** [Libro]. *To autograph.* ~Me regaló un ejemplar DEDICADO. *He gave me a signed copy.* || **5.** Entregarse a. *Go in for, take up.* ~Se DEDICÓ a la cerámica. *She took up pottery.* || **6.** Destinar algo para un fin determinado. *Set aside, reserve, use as.* DEDICA el salón para biblioteca. *He uses the sitting-room as a library.* ~Vamos a DEDICAR este cuarto para los archivos. *We're going to set this room aside for the files.* || **7.** Tener, demostrar. *To have, show.* Le DEDICA mucha admiración. *He has great admiration for him.* || **8.** •Dedicado a. *Concerning.* Emisión DEDICADA a España. *Program about Spain.* || **9.** •DEDÍCATE a lo tuyo. *Mind your own business.* || **10.** •¿A qué se DEDICA Ud? *What do you do (for a living)? What's your line?, what business are you in?* || **11.** •Se DEDICA a hacerme la vida imposible. *He does his best to make my life impossible.* ⇨ DEDICATE

DEFICIENTE. adj. Defectuoso. *Faulty, poor.* ~El DEFICIENTE estado de las carreteras. *The poor (unsatisfactory) state of the roads.* Este mueble tiene un acabado DEFICIENTE. *This piece of furniture has a faulty finish.* || **2.** Insuficiente. *Lacking, insufficient, poor, inadequate.* ~Una alimentación DEFICIENTE en vitaminas. *A diet lacking in vitamins.* ~Su conocimiento de la materia es DEFICIENTE. *His knowledge of the subject is inadequate.* ~Una iluminación DEFICIENTE. *Poor lighting.* || **3.** [Mentalmente]. *Retarded, handicapped.* || **4.** Insatisfactorio (trabajo). *Poor, inadequate.* Su rendimiento en clase es muy DEFICIENTE. *His class performance is very poor.* || **5.** [Salud]. *Poor.* || **6.** [Inteligencia]. *Low.* ⇨ DEFICIENT

DEFORMAR. v. [Madera]. *To warp.* ~La puerta de madera se ha DEFORMADO por la humedad. *Humidity has warped the wooden door.* || **2.** [Cara]. *To disfigure.* || **3.** [Realidad, verdad, imagen, palabras,

hechos]. *To distort.* ~El abogado DEFORMÓ las palabras del acusado. *The lawyer distorted the defendant's words.* ~Este proyector DEFORMA las imágenes. *This projector distorts the pictures.* ~Información que DEFORMA la realidad. *Information which distorts reality.* || **4.** [Chapa, riel]. *To distort, twist out of shape.* ~La percha ha DEFORMADO la chaqueta. *The hanger has pulled the jacket out of shape.* ~La lluvia ha DEFORMADO el sombrero. *The rain has put the hat out of shape.* || **5.** [Conciencia]. *To twist, warp.* || **6.** [Física]. *To strain.* ⇨ DEFORM

DEFORME [DEFORMED]. adj. [Cara, imagen]. *Distorted.* ~El monstruo, con su cara DEFORME, espantaba a cuantos lo miraban. *The monster, with its hideous face, scared all those looking at him.* ~La propaganda dirigida a turistas puede dar una imagen DEFORME de España. *Travel promotion can present a distorted image of Spain.* || **2.** [Objetos]. *Misshappen, shapeless.*

DEFRAUDAR. Decepcionar. *To let down, disappoint, dash someone's hopes.* ~Me has DEFRAUDADO. *You've disappointed me.* || **2.** •DEFRAUDAR la confianza de uno. *To betray someone's confidence.* || **3.** DEFRAUDAR al fisco. *To evade taxes.* ⇨ DEFRAUD

DEGRADAR. v. [Militar]. *To demote.* ~DEGRADARON al capitán por su comportamiento cobarde. *The captain was demoted for his cowardly conduct.* || **2.** Empeorar (calidad, valor]. *To diminish, lessen.* ~El suelo está excesivamente DEGRADADO. *The soil is too impoverished.* ~El tráfico ha DEGRADADO el bosque de esta zona. *Traffic has greatly affected the trees in this region.* || **3.** [Artes]. *To degrade (el color).* ⇨ DEGRADE

DELEGACIÓN [DELEGATION]. Cargo. *Post.* ~Le ofrecieron la DELEGACIÓN en Burgos. *He was offered the post of director at the Burgos office.* || **2.** Office. Oficina. •DELEGACIÓN de Hacienda. *Local tax office.* || **3.** Sucursal. *Branch.* ~La compañía tiene una DELEGACIÓN en Madrid. *The company has a branch in Madrid.* || **4.** Conjunto de delegados. *Body of delegates.* ‖ **5.** •DELEGACIÓN comercial. *Trade mission.*

DELICADO. Exigente (comida, gustos). *Particular, fussy.* ~¡Qué DELICADA eres! ¿Qué más da si está un poco quemado? *You're so fussy! So it's a little burned!* •Hacerse el DELICADO. *To be overfussy.* ‖ **2.** Remilgado. *Squeamish.* ‖ **3.** [Lenguaje, modales, gustos]. *Refined.* ~Eduardo tiene gustos muy DELICADOS. *Edward has very refined tastes.* ‖ **4.** Atento. *Considerate, thoughtful.* ‖ **5.** Que requiere cuidados. *Fragile (cerámica, cristal).* ~Cuidado con el jarrón de porcelana, que es muy DELICADO. *Be careful with the porcelain vase, it very fragile.* ‖ **6.** [Piel]. *Sensitive.* Una crema para pieles DELICADAS. *A cream for sensitive skin.* ‖ **7.** Susceptible. *Touchy, sensitive.* ¡Qué DELICADO eres¡ No lo dije para ofenderte. *Don't be so touchy! I didn't say it to offend you.* ‖ **8.** Débil. *Weak.* ~Tiene el corazón DELICADO. *He has a weak heart.* ~Después de la operación quedó muy DELICADO. *He was very frail (weak) after the operation.* ⇨DELICATE

DELICIOSO. *adj.* [Perfume]. *Exquisite.* ‖ **2.** Encantador (chica, niño, sonrisa). *Charming, delightful.* ~Es una mujer DELICIOSA. *She's a charming woman.* ‖ **3.** Agradable (clima, día, lugar). *Lovely, beautiful, delightful.* Está haciendo un tiempo DELICIOSO. *It's really lovely weather we're having.* ~Aquel es un lugar DELICIOSO. *This is a lovely place.* ⇨DELICIOUS

DEMANDA. Pleito, litigio. *Lawsuit.* ‖ **2.** •Presentar una DEMANDA en contra de. *To bring an action against, to take legal proceedings against.* ‖ **3.** Petición. *Request.* ~Lo siento mucho, pero no puedo acceder a su DEMANDA. *I'm very sorry but I cannot agree with your request.* ~DEMANDA de extradición. *Request for extradition.* ‖ **4.** •En DEMANDA de. *Seeking, in search of.* ~Se volvió hacia ella en DEMANDA de ayuda. *He turned to her for help.* ‖ **5.** Intento, empeño. *Attempt, try.* ~Lo conseguiré o pereceré en la DEMANDA. *I'll obtain it or I'll die in the process.* ⇨DEMAND²

DEMANDAR. Reclamar por medio de la justicia. *To sue, file a lawsuit.* ‖ **2.** JUR •DEMANDAR a uno por daños y perjuicios. *To sue someone for damages.* ⇨DEMAND¹

DEMOSTRACIÓN. *sf.* [De un teorema]. *Proof.* ‖ **2.** [De fuerza, cariño]. *Show, display.* ~Lo recibieron con grandes DEMOSTRACIONES de cariño. *They welcomed him with a great show (display) of affection.* ~Una DEMOSTRACIÓN de fueza. *A show of strength.* ‖ **3.** Señal. *Sign.* ~Las lágrimas son una DEMOSTRACIÓN de dolor. *Tears are a sign of grief.* ⇨DEMONSTRATION

DEMOSTRAR. Comprobar, indicar. *To show, to prove.* ~Lo mal que vive DEMUESTRA que no tiene mucho dinero. *The poor way in which he lives shows he hasn't much money.* ~DEMOSTRAR su ignorancia. *To show one's ignorance.* ~DEMOSTRAR interés. *To show one's interest.* ‖ **2.** [Matemáticas]. *To prove.* ‖ **3.** Establecer, probar. *To prove.* ~Ud. no puede DEMOSTRARME nada. *You can't prove anything against me.* ~La expedición de Magallanes DEMOSTRÓ la redondez de la tierra. *The Magellan expedition proved that the earth was round.* ⇨DEMONSTRATE

DENOMINACIÓN. *sf.* [Acto]. *Naming.* ~Mañana procederemos a la DENOMINACIÓN de las nuevas calles. *Tomorrow we will begin to assign names to the new streets.* ‖ **2.** Nombre. *Name.* ~Con el nuevo régimen se cambió la DENOMINACIÓN de muchas calles. *With the change of government, many of the streets' names have been changed.* ~Denominación social. *Company name.* ⇨DENOMINATION

DENUNCIAR [DENOUNCE]. Indicar. *Denote, point to, reveal, indicate.* ~Su escritorio bien ordenado DENUNCIABA un hombre de hábito metódicos. *His tidy desk denoted a man of methodical habits.* ~El retraso DENUNCIA la falta de planificación. *The delay points to a lack of planning.* ‖ **2.** [Delito]. *Report.* ~DENUNCIARON los precios abusivos a las autoridades. *They reported the exorbitant prices to the authorities.*

DEPARTAMENTO. [Tren]. *Compartment.* || **2.** [Objeto]. *Compartment.* ~La caja de herramientas tiene un DEPARTAMENTO para los tornillos. *The tool box has a compartment for screws.* ⇨DEPARTMENT

DEPENDER. *v.* Estar subordinado a una autoridad. *To be, come under; to be answerable to, to report to.* ~DEPENDÍAN directamente del director financiero. *They reported directly to the finance director.* ~La comisión DEPENDERÁ del Senado. *The commission will report, will be accountable, will be answerable to the Senate.* ~El museo DEPENDE de otro ministerio. *The museum is run by another ministry.* ⇨ DEPEND

DEPONER [DEPOSE]. v. [Dejar]. *To abandon, set aside.* ~Al final DEPUSO su actitud hostil. *In the end he set aside his hostility.* || **2.** Destituir (gobierno, presidente). *To remove from office, overthrow, topple.* ~A raíz del escándalo fue DEPUESTO de su cargo. *As a result of the scandal he was removed from office.* || **3.** [Derecho]. *To testify, give evidence about, make a statement (deposition).* || **4.** [Las armas]. *To lay down.* Decidieron DEPONER las armas. *They decided to lay down their arms.* || **5.** [Temor]. *To banish.* DEPONER EL TEMOR. *To banish fear.*

DEPOSITAR. *v.* Colocar *To place, put.* ~DEPOSITÓ una corona en el monumento de los caídos. *He placed a wreath at the war memorial.* ~DEPOSITÓ los libros en el suelo. *He placed the books on the floor.* || **2.** Almacenar. *To store.* ~DEPOSITARON las mercancías en un almacén. *The goods were placed in storage.* || **3.** Dejar. *To leave.* ~Se ruega DEPOSITAR las bolsas en la entrada. *Please leave all bags at the door.* || **4.** FIG [Confianza, ilusiones, esperanzas]. *To put (place) one's trust in someone.* ~Han DEPOSITADO en mi toda su confianza. *They have placed all their trust in me.* || **5.** [Cariño]. *To bestow.* ~DEPOSITÓ en él todo su cariño. *She bestowed all her love on him.* || **6.** •DEPOSITAR algo en manos de alguien. *To entrust someone with something.* || **7.** •DEPOSITÓ una fianza en favor

del acusado. *She stood bail for the accused.* || **8.** •DEPOSITARSE (posos, polvo). *To settle.* ~Cuando los posos se DEPOSITARON, sirvió un poco de vino. *After the dregs had settled, he served a little wine.* ~La arena se DEPOSITABA en el fondo del estanque. *The sand settled at the bottom of the pond.* ⇨DEPOSIT²

DEPÓSITO. *sm.* [De basuras]. *Dump.* || **2.** [Almacén]. *Store, warehouse, depot.* ~Nuestra empresa tiene un DEPÓSITO de mercancías en esa ciudad. *Our company has a warehouse in that city.* || **3.** Contenedor. *Tank.* ~Tiene en el jardín un DEPÓSITO de agua. *He has a water tank in his garden.* || **4.** [De objetos perdidos]. *Lost-and-found department.* || **5.** [De municiones]. *Dump, depot.* || **6.** [De gasolina]. *Tank.* ~Llenó el DEPÓSITO de gasolina *en la estación de servicio.* *He fill his gas tank at the gas station.* || **7.** [De madera, carbón]. *Yard.* || **8.** [En una caldera, conducto]. *Scale.* || **9.** [De cadáveres]. *Morgue.* ⇨DEPOSIT¹

DEPURACIÓN [DEPURATION]. *sf.* [Del agua]. *Purification, treatment.* || **2.** [De aguas residuales]. *Treatment.* || **3.** [De la sangre]. *Cleansing.* || **4.** [Política]. *Purge, purging.* || **5.** [De lenguaje, estilo]. *Refinement.* || **6.** [Informática]. *Debugging.*

DERIVACIÓN. *sf.* [De una carretera, río, canal]. *Turn-off, diversion.* || **2.** [Origen]. *Origin, source.* || **3.** [Composición]. *Word formation, compounding.* || **4.** [De palabra]. *Derivative.* || **5.** [De un problema, enfermedad]. *Consequence.* ~El médico estudiará la enfermedad y todas sus DERIVACIONES. *The doctor will study the illness and all its implications.* || **6.** Cambio. *Change, deviation.* ⇨DERIVATION

DESARROLLAR. *v.* Exponer (teoría, idea). *To explain, expound.* || **2.** [Tema]. *To explain.* ~Tiene que DESARROLLAR más ampliamente los puntos de su lección. *He has to explain the points of his lesson more clearly.* || **3.** Llevar a cabo (actividad, labor). *To carry out.* ~DESARROLLAR actividades subversivas. *To carry out subversive acti-*

vities. || **4.** [Coche, motor]. *To reach.* ~DESARROLLA una velocidad de ... *It can reach a speed of ...* || **5.** Desplegar. *To unfold.* ~DESARROLLAR un mapa. *To unfold a map.* FIG ~DESARROLLAR una gran inteligencia. *To show (reveal) great intelligence.* || **6.** MAT [Ecuación]. *To expand.* || **7.** [Rollo]. *To unroll, unwind.* ~DESARROLLÓ la alfombra. *He unrolled the carpet.* ⇨DEVELOP

DESARROLLARSE. *vr.* [Entrevista, acontecimiento]. *To take place.* ~La acción se DESARROLLA en una aldea gallega. *The actions takes places in a Galician village.* ⇨DEVELOP

DESARROLLO. *sm.* Incremento. *Growth.* ~Índice de DESARROLLO. *Growth rate.* ~La industría está en pleno DESARROLLO. *The industry is making rapid growth.* || **2.** MAT Ecuación. *Expansion.* || **3.** [Problema]. *Working out.* || **4.** [De bicicleta]. *Gear.* || **5.** [Mapa]. *Unfolding.* DEVELOPMENT

DESCARTAR. *v.* Rechazar. *Reject, turn down.* No debemos DESCARTAR su ayuda, porque puede sernos necesaria en cualquier momento. *We should not turn down their offer for help, we may need it at any time.* || **2.** [Plan, posibilidad]. *To rule out, dismiss.* ~Lo de ir en tren ha quedado DESCARTADO. *We've ruled out the idea of going by train.* || **3.** [Candidato]. *Reject, rule out.* ⇨DISCARD

DESCENDER. *v.* Bajar, pasar de una lado a otro. *To go down.* ~Se ayudaba con el bastón para DESCENDER poco a poco las escaleras. *With the help of a cane he slowly went down the stairs.* || **2.** [De categoría]. *To be demoted.* ~Ha DESCENDIDO de categoría en la empresa. *The company demoted him.* || **3.** [Fiebre, nivel, temperatura]. *To drop, fall, go down.* ~Mañana DESCENDERÁN las temperaturas. *Tomorrow the temperature will drop.* || **4.** [Líquido]. *To run, flow.* ~Las lágrimas DESCENDÍAN por su rostro. *The tears were running down his cheeks.* || **5.** [Cortina]. *To hang.* || **6.** [Persona, fuerza]. *To fail, get weak.* || **7.** FIG *To stoop to, to lower oneself to.* || **8.**

Originar, provenir. *To originate, come from.* ~La tribu DESCIENDE de la región central. *The tribe originated in the central region.* || **9.** Derivar. *To derive.* ~De esa palabra DESCIENDEN muchas otras. *Many other words derive from that one.* || **10.** [Pasajeros]. *To disembark.* ⇨DESCEND

DESCIFRAR [DECIPHER]. [Misterio]. *To solve.* ~DESCIFRAR un enigma. *To solve a mistery.* || **2.** [Motivos, causas, problema]. *To figure out.* ~El profesor PLANTEÓ un difícil problema, que ninguno de los alumnos logró DESCIFRAR. *The teacher set forth a difficult problem which none of the students were able to figure out.* ⇨DESCIFRAR.

DESCONECTAR. *v.* [Radio, TV]. *Switch off, turn off.* ~DESCONECTARON la calefacción antes de irse. *They switched (turn) the heating off before leaving.* || **2.** Desenchufar. *To unplug.* ~DESCONECTÓ la televisión y la cambió del lugar. *He unplugged the television set and moved it to another place.* || **3.** [Enchufe]. *Pull out, take out.* || **4.** •DESCONECTARSE. FAM *To be cut off, lose touch with.* ~Me había DESCONECTADO de mis antiguas amistades. *I had lost touch with my old friends.* ⇨DISCONNECT

DESCONTAR. *v.* Restar. *To deduct.* ~Te DESCUENTAN el 20% de impuestos. *You get 20% deducted for taxes.* ~Tienes que DESCONTAR las dos horas de la comida. *You have to deduct two hours for lunch.* ~DESCONTARSE años. *To pretend to be younger than one is.* || **2.** Exceptuar. *To leave out, disregard.* ~DESCONTANDO los gastos. *Excluding the expenses.* ~Si DESCONTAMOS los sábados y domingos, faltan sólo 15 días. *If we don't count Saturdays and Sundays, there are only 15 days left.* || **3.** •Dar por DESCONTADO. *To take for granted.* ~Doy por DESCONTADO su éxito. *I am taking his success for granted.* ⇨DISCOUNT

DESCUBRIR. *v.* [Conspiración]. *Uncover.* || **2.** Delatar. *To give away, expose.* ~No me DESCUBRAS a la policía. *Don't tell the police about me.* Lo DESCUBRIÓ su escritura. *His*

writing gave him away (betrayed him). ||
3. Devisar. *To make out, see, glimpse.*
~Desde la cima de la montaña se DESCUBRÍA
todo el pueblo. *From the mountain top,
you could see the entire city.* || **4.** Destapar
(placa, estátua). *Uncover, unveil.* ~El rey
DESCUBRIÓ una placa conmemorativa. *The
king unveiled a commemorative plaque.* ||
5. [Criminal, fraud]. *To find, detect, spot.*
DESCUBRIERON el fraude cuando ya era
tarde. *The fraud was detected when it was
already too late.* || **6.** Revelar. *To show,
reveal, disclose, expose.* ~DESCUBRIR el
estómago. *To bare (uncover) one's
stomach.* Se levantó levemente la falda
DESCUBRIENDO la rodilla. *She lifted up her
skirt slightly exposing her knee.* ~DESCU-
BRIR sus intenciones. *To reveal one's
intentions.* || **7.** [Petróleo]. *To find, strike.* ||
8. [Naipes]. *To lay down.* || **9.** DESCUBRIRSE.
Quitarse el sombrero. (I) *To take off one's
hat,* (II) [Boxeo]. *To lower one's guard.* ~El
soldado se DESCUBRIÓ al entrar en el
despacho del coronel. *Upon entering the
colonel's quarter, the soldier took off his
cap.* || **9.** •DESCUBRIR su pecho a uno. *To
open one's heart to somebody.* ⇨DISCOVER

DESERTAR. *v.* [Hogar]. *Abandon, leave.*
~DESERTAR del hogar. *To abandon one's
home, leave home.* || **2.** [Deberes, obliga-
ciones]. *Neglect.* ~DESERTAR de sus
deberes. *To neglect one's duties.* || **3.**
[Fiesta]. *To leave, to stop going.* ~DESERTAR
de una tertulia. *To stop going to a
gathering.* || **4.** [De un partido]. *To defect.*
~Cuando el partido perdió las elecciones,
muchos de sus miembros DESERTARON.
*When the party lost the election many of
its members defected.* || **5.** •DESERTAR al
campo contrario. *To go over to the enemy.*
⇨DESERT

DESESPERADO. *adj.* [Caso, situación].
Hopeless. ~En situación DESEPERADA. *In a
hopeless situation.* || **2.** [Esfuerzo].
Furious, frenzied. || **3.** Exasperado.
Exasperated. ~Me tiene DESESPERADO. *He
exasperates me.* || **4.** •Está DESESPERADO por
verte. *He's dying to see you.* ⇨DESPERATE

DESFIGURAR. *v.* [Cuerpo]. *To deform.* || **2.**

[Cuadro, momumento]. *To deface.* || **3.**
Borrar, confundir (contorno, formas). *To
blur.* ~El cristal DESFIGURABA el paisaje. *The
glass blurred the scenery.* || **4.** [Voz]. *To
alter, disguise.* || **5.** [Sentido, verdad,
hechos]. *To distort, twist, misrepresent.* ~El
gobierno afirma que la prensa ha DESFI-
GURADO los hechos. *The government claims
that the press has distorted the facts.*
⇨DISFIGURE

DESGRACIA. *sf.* Adversidad, infortunio.
Misfortune. ~Sufrió muchas DESGRACIAS en
su juventud. *He suffered many misfortunes
in his youth.* || **2.** Percance. *Mishap,
accident.* || **3.** Mala suerte. *Piece of bad
luck, setback, blow.* ~El accidente ha sido
una DESGRACIA. *The accident was a
setback.* || **4.** •¡Qué DESGRACIA! *What a
shame!, what bad luck!* ~¡Qué DESGRACIA,
se me ha quemado la sopa! *What a shame
(what bad luck), I burned the soup!* || **5.**
•DESGRACIAS personales. *Casualty.* ~En el
accidente no hubo que lamentar DESGRACIAS
personales. *There were no casualties in
the accident.* ⇨DISGRACE

DESHONESTO. *adj.* Grosero, descortés,
indecoroso. *Rude, discourteous.* || **2.** Obs-
ceno. *Indecent, lewd, improper.* ~Una
mujer DESHONESTA. *A loose woman.* ~Una
vida DESHONESTA. *A promiscuous life.* || **3.**
Mal, no correcto. *Wrong, unethical.* ~Ocul-
tarle la verdad me parece una acción
DESHONESTA. *It seems to me that it would
be unethical (wrong) not to tell him the
truth.* || **4.** •Palabras DESHONESTAS. *Obscene
language.* ⇨DISHONEST

DESHONRAR. *v.* Ofender. *To insult.* || **2.**
Ultrajar. *To slander, defame.* || **3.** Despres-
tigiar. *To bring disgrace on.* ~Estas acusa-
ciones DESHONRAN a todo el cuerpo de
policía. *These accusations bring disgrace
to the entire police department.* ⇨DISHONOR

DESISTIR. *v.* Abandonar, renunciar. *Give
up, abandon.* ~No DESISTÍA en su empeño.
*He would not give up the pursuit of his
objective.* ~Nada me hará DESISTIR de este
propósito. *Nothing will make me abandon
this goal.* || **2.** [Derecho]. *To waive, relin-*

quish. ~Desistir de una demanda. *To relinquish a claim*. ‖ **3**. Dejar (de hacer algo). *To stop (from doing something)*. ~Desistió de ir a la escuela. *He stopped going to school.* ⇨ desist

DESMONTAR [dismount]. *v*. Desarmar (mueble, estante). *To take down, dismantle, strip down, take apart.* ~Antes de pintar la pared hay que desmontar la estantería. *Before we can paint the wall we'll have to disassemble the bookcase.* ‖ **2**. Derribar (edificio, casa). *To knock down, demolish.* ~Los niños habían construido un castillo de arena en la playa, pero una ráfaga de viento lo desmontó. *The children had built a sandcastle on the beach, but a gust of wind knocked it down.* ‖ **3**. [Zona, selva]. *To clear (of trees).* ~Hemos desmontado los árboles de la sierra. *We cleared the mountain range of trees.* ‖ **4**. Allanar (terreno). *To level.* ~Antes de plantar el parque hubo que desmontar el terreno. *Before the park could be planted with trees the ground had to be leveled.* ‖ **5**. [Escopeta]. *To uncock.* ~Es conveniente desmontar las armas cargadas para evitar que se disparen. *It's a good idea to uncock loaded firearms to prevent them from going off.* ‖ **6**. [Tienda, vela, andamio]. *To take down.* ~Desmontamos la tienda de campaña. *We took down the tent.* ‖ **7**. [Artillería enemiga]. *To silence, knock out.* ‖ **8**. [Basura]. *To take away.* ‖ **9**. [Jinete]. *To throw, unseat.* ‖ **10**. [Motor]. *To strip.* ~Desmontaron el motor para arreglarlo. *They stripped the motor so they could fix it.* ‖ **11**. Separar (forro, pieza). *To remove, detach.* ‖ **12**. Sacar, quitar, separar. *To remove, take off.* ~Desmontar una rueda. *To remove a wheel.* ‖ **13**. [Diamante, piedra]. *To unset, unmount.* ‖ **14**. [Puerta]. *To unhinge.* ‖ **15**. [Traje]. *To unstich.* ‖ **16**. [Timón]. *To unship.* ‖ **17**. Rebatir (un argumento, teoría). *To refute.* ~Desmontó la teoría de su rival. *He refuted the theory of his competitor.* ‖ **18**. Deshacer (un montón de tierra, broza). *To scatter (a pile of dirt or wood).*

DESORDEN. Falta de orden. *Untidiness, mess.* ~El cuarto estaba en desorden. *The room was in a mess.* ~¡Qué desorden! *What a mess!* ~Perdona el desorden. *Please excuse the mess.* ‖ **2**. Desarreglo. *Irregularity.* ~Evite el desorden en las comidas. *Take meals at regular times.* ‖ **3**. *pl*. Excesos. *Excesses.* ~Ahora paga los desórdenes de su vida. *Now she's paying for the excesses in her life.* ‖ **4**. •Con el pelo en desorden. *With untidy, ruffled hair.* ⇨ disorder

DESPACHAR. *v*. Terminar (tarea, asunto). *To finish, complete, take care of, get through, get out of the way.* ~El orador despachó su conferencia en menos de media hora. *The speaker got his lecture out of the way in less than half an hour.* ~Yo ya he despachado mi tarea. *I've completed my task.* ‖ **2**. Tratar (asunto, problema). *To deal with.* ~Debo despachar un asunto con el director. *I must settle a matter with the director.* ‖ **3**. [En tienda]. *To serve, attend to.* ~Todavía no me han despachado. *I haven't been served yet.* ~Me despachó el dependiente de siempre. *The usual clerk served me.* ‖ **4**. [Entradas, localidades]. *To issue, sell.* ~Despachar localidades. *To sell tickets.* ‖ **5**. Comer. *To polish off, get through.* ~Despachar un bocadillo, una botella de vino. *To polish off a sandwich, a bottle of wine.* ‖ **6**. Despedir, echar. *To fire, let go, sack, send packing.* ~Despachó a la criada. *He dismissed the maid.* ~Vino pidiendo limosna y lo despaché. *He came begging and I sent him packing.* ‖ **7**. fam Matar. *To kill.* ‖ **8**. [Correspondencia]. *To deal with, attend to.* ‖ **9**. Acelerar. *To expedite, hurry along.* ‖ **10**. [Comercio]. *To sell, deal in.* ‖ **11**. Enviar. (I) [Carta, paquete]. *To send,* (II) [Mercancias, pedido]. *To ship.* ~Enseguida le despacho el pedido. *Your order will be shipped immediately.* ‖ **12**. Conversar. *To meet, consult with, speak to.* ~Despacha los viernes con sus asesores. *He meets with his advisors on Fridays.* ~La secretaría está despachando con el jefe. *The secretary is talking to the boss.* ‖ **13**. Deliberar. *To discuss.* Despa-

CHARON sobre asuntos de gobierno. *They discussed government matters.* || **14.** [Una historia]. *To reel off.* || **15.** Parir una mujer. *To give birth.* ⇨DISPATCH

DESPLAZAR[1]. *v.* Mover, correr. *To move, to shift.* ~DESPLAZAR una mesa. *To move a table.* ~El aluvión DESPLAZÓ todo lo que encontró a su paso. *The flood washed away everything in its path.* ~Chocó contra el vehículo estacionado, DESPLAZÁNDOLO unos 20 metros. *It collided with the stationary vehicle, pushing it at a distance of some 20 meters.* || **2.** [Informática]. *To scroll.* || **3.** To remove. *Quitar.* || **4.** [Tropas]. *To transfer, to move.* ⇨DISPLACE

DESPLAZARSE[2]. *vr.* Viajar, recorrer. *To travel.* ~Tiene que DESPLAZARSE seis kilómetros cada día. *He has to travel six kilometers every day.* || **2.** [Votos, tendencias]. *To swing, shift.* ⇨DISPLACE

DESTILAR. *v.* [Sangre, pus]. *To exude, ooze, secrete.* ~La herida DESTILA sangre. *The wound secretes blood.* || **2.** Revelar, denotar. *To exude, reveal.* ~Sus ojos DESTILABAN odio. *The look in her eyes were full of hatred.* ~La carta DESTILABA odio. *The letter exuded hatred.* ~Sus palabras DESTILABAN veneno. *His words exuded venom.* ~Su poesía DESTILA tristeza. *His poetry reveals sadness.* || **3.** Gotear. *To drip, to trickle.* ~El panal DESTILABA miel. *Honey trickled from the honeycomb.* || **4.** Filtrarse. *To filter through.* || **5.** [Charcoal, wood]. *To char.* ⇨DISTILL

DESTINO [DESTINY]. Suerte. *Luck.* || **2.** Puesto. *Post, job, position, placement, assignment. (de un funcionario).* ~Ése fue su primer DESTINO como diplomático. *That was his first diplomatic assignment.* ~Buscaba un DESTINO de cartero. *He was looking for a job as a postman.* ~¿Qué DESTINO tienes? *Where have you been placed?* || **3.** Fatalidad, fortuna. *Destiny, fate.* ~Quién sabe lo que nos depara el DESTINO. *Who knows what fate has in store for us.* ~Su DESTINO era acabar en la cárcel. *He was destined to end up in prison.* || **4.** Uso, fin. *Use, utility.* ~No se sabe qué DESTINO se les va a dar a esos fondos. *It is not known what those funds will be allocated to.* ~Debería darle un mejor DESTINO a esto. *This should be put to better use.* || **5.** •Dar DESTINO a algo. *To put to good use.* || **6.** •A franquear en DESTINO. *Postage will be paid by the addressee.* || **7.** •Salir con DESTINO a. *To leave for.* ⇨DESTINATION

DETALLE. Rasgo de cortesía, delicadeza. *Nice thought (gesture), nicely, token of appreciation.* ~¡Qué DETALLE! *How nice, how sweet!* ~Tiene muchos DETALLES. *He's very considerate.* ~Eso fue un DETALLE de su parte. *That's was a nice thought on his part.* || **2.** Toque decorativo. *Touch, ornament.* || **3.** Pequeño regalo. *A little gift, a little something.* ~Siempre que viene trae algún DETALLE. *Whenever he comes he brings a small gift (a little something).* || **4.** Sin perder DETALLE. *Closely.* ~Me observaba sin perder DETALLE. *He was watching me very closely, he watched my every move.* || **5.** Estado de cuenta. *Statement.* || **6.** Factura. *Bill.* || **7.** LOCUCIONES. || •Ahí está el DETALLE. *That's the secret.* || •No perder DETALLE. *Not to miss a thing, to miss nothing.* ~No perdimos DETALLE de lo que pasó. *We didn't miss a thing.* || •Un mal DETALLE. *A rotten thing to do.* || •Para más DETALLES. *What's more.* Es muy simpática y para más DETALLES soltera. *She's very nice and, what's more, she's single.* || •En DETALLE. *Fully.* ⇨DETAIL

DETENCIÓN. *sf.* Parada. *Stopping, halting.* ~Provocó la DETENCIÓN del tren. *It brought the train to a halt.* ~La falta de fondos PROVOCÓ la detención del proyecto. *The project was halted because of a lack of funds.* || **2.** Alto, detenimiento. *Stop, halt.* Una DETENCIÓN en el crecimiento del niño puede deberse a carencias vitamínicas. *Lack of vitamins may stunt a child's growth.* || **3.** Retraso. *Holdup, delay.* ~Lo llamé y vino sin DETENCION. *I called him and he came right away (without delay).* || **4.** Cuidado, detenimiento. *Care, thoroughness.* ~Examinó al enfermo con DETENCIÓN. *He examined the patient carefully (thoroughly).* || **5.** [En el juego].

Stoppage (of play). ‖ **6.** Estancamiento. *Stoppage, standstill.* ⇨ DETENTION

DETENER[1]. *v.* Parar (persona, balón, epidemia, vehículo). *To stop, halt.* ~DETENER las negociaciones. *To hold up negotiations.* ~Se DETUVO y la miró. *He stopped and looked at her.* ~La policía DETUVO el coche. *The police stopped the car.* ‖ **2.** Entretener (a una persona). *To delay.* ~No quiero DETENERTE más. *I won't keep you any longer.* ‖ **3.** Retener. *To hold back, keep, hold (respiración).* ‖ **4.** •DETENER la mirada en. *To settle one's gaze upon.* ⇨ DETAIN

DETENERSE[2]. *vr.* Entretenerse. *To hang about, linger.* ~Ven directo a casa, sin DETENERTE en el camino. *Como straight home, without stopping off on the way.* ~Me DETUVE arreglando el escritorio y perdí el tren. *I hung around tidying my desk and I lost the train.* ‖ **2.** Dedicar tiempo a pensar en explicar un asunto. *To stop to* (+ INF). ¿Te has DETENIDO en pensar en las consecuencias? *Have you stop to consider the consequences?* ⇨ DETAIN

DETERIORAR. *v.* Empeorar (relaciones, salud, situación). *To worsen, damage.* ~Los conflictos laborales han DETERIORADO nuestras relaciones. *The labor disputes have damaged our relations.* ~La situación económica se ha visto DETERIORADA por estos conflictos. *The economic situation has been considerably worsened by these conflicts.* ‖ **2.** Gastar. *To wear out.* ‖ **3.** Estropearse. *To get damaged.* ~Las mercancías se habían DETERIORADO durante el viaje. *The goods had been damaged in transit.* ⇨ DETERIORATE

DETERMINADO. Osado, valeroso. *Daring, bold, audacious.* ‖ **2.** [Fecha, tiempo]. *Given, appointed.* ~Van a tomar café todos los días a DETERMINADO bar del barrio. *They have coffee everyday at the same neighborhood bar.* ~En el día DETERMINADO. *On the appointed day.* ‖ **3.** [Precio]. *Definitivo, específico.* ‖ **4.** *Specific. Particular.* ~En este DETERMINADO caso. *In this particular case.* ⇨ DETERMINED

DETERMINAR. Decidir. *Decide.* Han DETERMINADO salir el lunes. *They decided to leave on Monday.* ‖ **2.** Indicar. *Detect, grasp.* Podemos DETERMINAR las razones de su conducta. *We can see the reason for his behavior.* ‖ **3.** Disponer. *To stipulate.* ‖ **4.** Fijar. *To fix, set.* ~DETERMINARON la fecha de la boda. *They fixed the date of the wedding.* ‖ **5.** Motivar. *Cause, provoke, bring about.* La nieve DETERMINÓ el accidente. *The accident was caused by the snow.* ~Las grandes manifestaciones DETERMINARON un cambio en la legislación. *The massive demonstrations brought about a change in the law.* ~Las circunstancias que DETERMINARON la caída del imperio. *The circumstances which brought about the fall of the empire.* ~Ha DETERMINADO un desplazamiento hacia las afueras. *It has lead many people to move to the outskirts.* ‖ **6.** Establecer, precisar (contrato). *To state.* Aún no han DETERMINADO las pautas que se deben seguir. *The guidelines still haven't been established (stated).* ~La ley DETERMINA que ... *The law stipulates (states) that ...* ‖ **7.** •Determinarse. *To bring oneself to, to make up one's mind.* ~No se DETERMINABA a irse. *He couldn't make up his mind to leave.* ⇨ DETERMINE

DIARIO. Periódico que se publica todos los días. *(Daily) newspaper, paper.* ~Todos los DIARIOS de hoy recogen la noticia del acuerdo de paz. *Today all the newspapers are announcing the peace agreement.* ‖ **2.** Libro DIARIO. *Journal, daybook.* ‖ **3.** •DIARIO de la mañana/tarde. *Morning/evening newspaper.* ‖ **4.** DIARIO dominical. *Sunday paper.* ‖ **5.** DIARIO de a bordo (de navegación). *Logbook.* ‖ **6.** DIARIO hablado. *News program.* ‖ **7.** DIARIO de sesiones. *Record of parliamentary proceedings, parliamentary report.* ‖ **8.** Gastos cotidianos. *Day-to-day expenses.* ~Con ese sueldo apenas alcanza para el DIARIO. *On his salary he barely makes enough for his everyday expenses.* ⇨ DIARY

DICTAR. *v.* [Ley]. *To enact, decree.* El Ayuntamiento DICTÓ unas normas sobre la recogida de basuras. *The City has enacted*

certain regulations on trash collection. ||
2. Aconsejar, indicar (conciencia, sentido
común, prudencia). *To suggest, say, advise.*
~Haz lo que el sentido común te DICTE. *Do
what common sense tells you.* ~El sentido
común nos DICTA cautela. *Common sense
advises caution.* || **3.** [Conferencia, dis-
curso]. *To give, deliver.* || **4.** [Sentencia].
To pronounce, pass. ~El tribunal DICTARÁ
sentencia mañana. *The court will pass
sentence tomorrow.* || **5.** LAT. AM. [Clase].
To give. DICTA inglés en un instituto
privado. *She teaches English at a private
school.* || **6.** LAT. AM. [Conferencias]. *To
deliver.* ~DICTÓ conferencias en varias
universidades. *She delivered lectures at
various universities.* || **7.** Ordenes. *To give,
issue.* || **8.** [Decreto]. *To promulgate, issue,
proclaim.* || **9.** •DICTAR disposiciones. *To
take (adopt) measures.* || **10.** •DICTAR la ley.
To lay down the law. ⇨DICTATE

DIFERIR. Aplazar. *Postpone, put off.* ~Han
DIFERIDO la boda. *The wedding has been
posponed.* || **2.** JUR [Sentencia]. *To reserve.*
⇨DIFFER

DILATADO [DILATED]. *adj.* Vasto, extenso.
Vast, extensive. ~Un hombre de DILATADA
experiencia. *A man of vast experience.* || **2.**
Largo. *Long.* Un DILATADO período de
tiempo. *A long period of time.* ~Una DILA-
TADA proyectoria política. *A long political
career.* || **3.** FIG Sin límite. *Limitless, wide.*
Horizontes DILATADOS. *Unlimited pros-
pects, wide horizons.* || **4.** [Estómago].
Distended. || **5.** Numeroso. *Numerous.* || **6.**
[Discurso]. *Long-winded, discursive.*

DILATAR [DILATE]. *v.* [Metal, calor]. *To
expand.* ~El calor DILATA los cuerpos. *Heat
expands bodies, heat causes object to
expand.* || **2.** Prolongar (en tiempo). *To
prolong, protract, stretch out.* ~Las
preguntas DILATARON el debate. *The
questions prolonged the debate.* ~El
concierto se DILATÓ. *The concert took
longer than expected.* || **3.** Retrasar, diferir.
To delay, put off, postpone. ~No puedo
DILATAR más mi viaje. *I can't postpone my
trip any longer.* || **4.** Ampliar. *To enlarge,
widen.* ~DILATÓ sus dominios hasta llegar

al mar. *He widened his domains until it
reached the sea.* || **5.** Difundir (fama). *To
spread.* ~Durante estos años su fama se
ha DILATADO. *In the last few years his fame
has spread.*

DILIGENCIA [DILIGENCE]. *sf.* Gestión.
Measure, step, piece of business, errand.
Activas DILIGENCIAS del gobierno. *Active
steps by the government.* ~Voy al centro a
hacer algunas DILIGENCIAS. *I have a few
errands to do in town, I have some
business to attend to in town.* || **2.** [Dere-
cho]. *Procedures, formalities.* ~DILI-
GENCIAS judiciales. *Judicial procedures
(formalities).* ~Instruir DILIGENCIAS. *To
institute proceedings.* || **3.** [En un docu-
mento oficial]. *Acknowledgment, stamp.* ||
4. Rapidez, prontitud. *Speed, rapidity.*
~Gracias a su DILINGENCIA, el asunto ha
quedado resuelto antes de lo previsto. *Due
to his quick action, the matter was
resolved promptly.*

DILIGENTE. *adj.* Activo, rápido. *Quick,
speedy, prompt.* ~Es un joven muy
DILIGENTE y lo tendrá terminado en seguida.
*He's very quick and he'll have it ready in
no time.* ⇨DILIGENT

DIMENSIÓN [DIMENSION]. Area de una
superficie. *Measurements.* ~El decorador
tomó las DIMENSIONES de la sala. *The
interior decorator took the measurements
of the room.* || **2.** Tamaño. *Size.* ~De gran
DIMENSIÓN. *Very large.* ~Un gasómetro de
enormes DIMENSIONES. *A gasometer of
enormous size.* || **3.** Alcance, magnitud. (I)
[De un problema]. *Magnitude, scale,
importance,* (II) [De una tragedia]. *Scale,*
(III) [De un artista]. *Stature, standing.* ~Un
matemático de DIMENSIÓN universal. *A
mathematician of world stature.*

DIRECCIÓN. Señas, domicilio. *Address.*
~Escriba en este formulario su nombre,
DIRECCIÓN y su teléfono. *Write down your
name, address and telephone number on
this form.* || **2.** Conjunto de piezas que sirve
para dirigir un auto. *Steering (mechanism).*
•Alinear la DIRECCIÓN. *To align the wheels.*
|| **3.** Volante. *Steering wheel.* || **4.** Cuerpo

directivo de una empresa. *Management.* ~Esto ha sido ordenado por la DIRECCIÓN. *This was ordered by the management.* ~Le dieron la DIRECCIÓN del proyecto. *They put him in charge of the project.* •Llevar la DIRECCIÓN de algo. *To run.* •Por orden de la DIRECCION. *By order of the management.* || 5. Despacho u oficina del director. *Manager's office, head office.* ~Tengo que ir a la DIRECCIÓN a hablar con el jefe. *I need to go to the head office and speak to the manager.* || 6. Junta. *Board of directors.* || 7. Destino. *Destination.* ~Salieron ayer con DIRECCIÓN a Soria. *They left yesterday for Soria.* || 8. Rumbo, trayectoria. *Line.* ~No puedo seguir la DIRECCIÓN de su razonamiento. *I can't follow his line of reasoning.* || 9. [Cine, teatro]. *Production.* || 10. Cargo de director. *Directorship, post of manager.* ~La DIRECCIÓN está vacante porque el antiguo director ha dimitido. *The post of manager is vacant because the former manager resigned.* || 11. [De un partido]. *Leadership.* ~Habrá cambios en la DIRECCIÓN del partido. *There will be changes in the party leadership.* || 12. [De un colegio]. *Headship.* || 13. [De un periódico]. *Editorship, editorial board.* || 14. [Oficina en una escuela]. *Principal's office.* || 15. Sentido. *Way.* •Calle de DIRECCIÓN única. *One-way street.* || 16. *LOCUCIONES.* || •DIRECCIÓN de ideas. *Train of thought.* || •[Orquesta]. Bajo la DIRECCIÓN de Campomar. *Conducted by Campomar.* || •DIRECCIÓN asistida. *Power steering.* || •DIRECCIÓN prohibida. *«No entry», «Do not enter».* || •DIRECCIÓN del remitente. *Return address.* || •DIRECCIÓN general. *Head office, headquarters.* ⇨ DIRECTION

DIRECTORIO. Junta. *Board of directors.* || 2. [Gobierno]. *Governing body.* || 3. [Normas]. *Instructions, directive.* ~El nuevo gerente estableció el directorio por el que debía regirse la empresa. *The new manager set the rules which the company must follow.* ⇨ DIRECTORY

DIRIGIR. *v.*
❶ ESTAR AL FRENTE (de una empresa, colegio, partido, expedición, orquesta,

país). [General]. Intervenir, gobernar, presidir, encabezar, conducir, guiar, administrar, regir. || 2. [Empresa]. *To manage, run, operate.* || 3. [Colegio]. *To run.* || 4. [Orquesta]. *To conduct.* ~DIRIGE la orquesta muy bien. *He's a very good conductor.* || 5. [Partido]. *To lead.* || 6. [Expedición, revuelta]. *To head, lead.* ~Él DIRIGIO a los amotinados. *He lead the rioters.* || 7. Guiar, dar consejo. *To guide.* ~No permite que nadie le DIRIJA. *He doesn't want anyone to tell him what to do.* ~El padre DIRIGIÓ a su hijo en la elección de una carrera. *The boy's father guided him in choosing a profession.* || 8. [Juego]. *To control, referee.* || 9. [Periódico, revista]. *To edit.* || 10. [Investigación, tésis]. *To supervise.* || 11. [Debate]. *To lead, head.* || 12. [Tráfico]. *To control.* || 13. [Asuntos públicos]. *To administer.* || 14. [Un país]. *To govern.* ~DIRIGIR una nación. *To govern a country.*

❷ DAR DETERMINADO DESTINO A ALGO (obrar de forma que cierta actividad tenga determinada finalidad). DEDICAR, ENCAMINAR, ORIENTAR, DESTINAR. *To aim.* ~Consejos DIRIGIDOS a los jóvenes. *Advice aimed at young people.* ~Estas palabras no van DIRIGIDAS a mí. *These words are not intended (meant) for me.* ~El folleto va DIRIGIDO a padres y educadores. *The booklet is aimed at parents and teachers.* || 2. [Acusación]. *To level.* || 3. [Carta, protesta, pregunta, observación, palabras]. *To address.* ~Esta noche el presidente DIRIGIRÁ un mensaje a la nación. *The president will address the nation tonight.* ~La carta venía DIRIGIDA a mí. *The letter was addressed to me.* ~DIRIGIÓ unas palabras de bienvenida. *He addressed a few words of welcome.* || 4. Encaminar, dedicar (esfuerzos, acciones). *To aim.* ~Acciones DIRIGIDAS a aliviar el problema. *Measures aimed at alleviating the problem.* ~DIRIGIREMOS todos nuestros esfuerzos a lograr un acuerdo. *We shall channel all our efforts to reach an agreement.* ~DIRIGE todos sus esfuerzos para constituir una familia. *He's dedicating all his efforts to form a family.* [Libro]. *To*

dedicate. ~DIRIGIÓ su libro a las amas de casa. *He dedicated his book to all homemakers.*
❸ PONER UNA COSA EN CIERTA DIRECCIÓN. Apuntar (cañon, telescopio). *To aim, point at.* ~DIRIGIR un telescopio hacia la luna. *To aim, point a telescope at the moon.* ‖ **2.** [Arma]. *To level, point, aim.* ~DIRIGIÓ la pistola hacia el ladrón. *He pointed the pistol at the thief.* ‖ **3.** [La mirada]. *To look towards.* ~DIRIGIÓ la mirada hacia el horizonte. *She looked (turned his eyes) towards the horizon.* ~DIRIGIÓ la mirada al cielo. *He looked towards the sky.* ‖ **4.** Encaminar (los pasos). *To walk towards.* DIRIGIÓ sus pasos hacia la esquina. *He walked towards the corner.* ‖ **5.** [Los ojos]. *To look down.* ~DIRIGIÓ los ojos hacia el suelo. *He looked down at the ground.*
❹ VARIOS. [Coche]. *To drive.* ~DIRIGIÓ el coche hacia la izquierda. ‖ **2.** [Atención]. *Concentrate.* ‖ **3.** [Barco, avión]. *To steer, to pilot.* ‖ **4.** •Se DIRIGIÓ a los periodistas. He addressed the reporters. ⇨DIRECT

DISCERNIR. *v.* Distinguir. *Distinguish.* DISCERNIR el bien del mal. *To distinguish (tell) good from evil.* ‖ **2.** Conceder, otorgar (premio). *To award.* ~El jurado DISCERNIÓ el premio por unanimidad. *The awarding of the prize by the jury was unanimous.* ‖ **3.** JUR [Tutela]. *To award, appoint as guardian.* ⇨DISCERN

DISCÍPULO [DISCIPLE]. Alumno. *Student, pupil.* ~Un DISCÍPULO aplicado. *A studious pupil.* ‖ **2.** (Filosofía). *Follower.*

DISCO [DISK]. *sm.* [Música]. *Record.* ~Le regalé un DISCO de música clásica. *I gave him a record of classical music as a present.* ~Grabar un DISCO. *To make a record.* ‖ **2.** [Teléfono]. *Dial.* ‖ **3.** [Semáforo]. *Traffic-light.* ~DISCO rojo/verde. *Red/green light.* ‖ **4.** [Deporte]. *Discus.* ~Lanzamiento de DISCO. *Throwing the discus.* ‖ **5.** [Ferrocarril]. *Signal.* ‖ **6.** [Conversación repetida]. *Same old story.* ~Siempre estás con el mismo DISCO. *You're always telling the same old story.* ‖ **7.** Señal de tráfico. *Sign, road sign.* ‖ **8.** •Cambiar de DISCO. *To*

change the record. ‖ **9.** •DISCO volante. *Flying saucer.*

DISCRECIÓN. Ingenio. *Wit.* ‖ **2.** Secreto. *Secrecy.* ‖ **3.** •Rendirse (entregarse) a DISCRECIÓN. *To surrender unconditionally.* ‖ **4.** MIL •¡Fuego a DISCRECIÓN! *Fire at will!* ‖ **5.** MIL •¡Descanso a DISCRECIÓN! *Stand easy!* ‖ **6.** •Vino a DISCRECIÓN. *Unlimited wine, wine as much as you like.* ‖ **7.** •Añadir pimienta y sal a DISCRECIÓN. *Add pepper and salt to taste.* ⇨DISCRETION

DISCREPANCIA [DISCREPANCY]. *sf.* Desacuerdo. *Disagreement.* ~MANIFESTARON su DISCREPANCIA con la resolución. *They expressed their disagreement with the resolution.*

DISCRETO. *adj.* Que no es extraordinario (persona, cosa). *Average, undistinguished (persona).* ~Un alumno DISCRETO. *An average student.* ~Viven en un piso discreto, no lujoso pero cómodo. *They live in a modest apartment, not very luxurious but comfortable.* ‖ **2.** [Moderado]. *Average, reasonable.* ~De dimensiones DISCRETAS. *Rather small.* ~Un sueldo DISCRETO. *A moderate salary.* ‖ **3.** [Color]. *Sober.* ‖ **4.** [Prenda]. *Modest, sober.* ~Viste de forma DISCRETA. *He dresses soberly.* ‖ **5.** Discernidor. *Discriminating.* ‖ **6.** Sagaz. *Prudent, wise, shrewd.* ~Habló con palabras DISCRETAS. *He spoke wisely.* ‖ **7.** [Plazo]. *Reasonable.* ‖ **8.** Ingenioso. *Witty.* ⇨DISCREET

DISCUSIÓN. *sn.* Disputa. *Argument.* ~Fue una DISCUSIÓN estúpida. *It was a stupid argument.* ⇨DISCUSSION

DISCUTIR. *v.* Reñir. *Argue.* ~No quiero DISCUTIR sobre este asunto. *I don't wish to argue on this point.* ⇨DISCUSS

DISGUSTAR. *v.* Molestar. *To upset, displease.* ~Está DISGUSTADA con la actitud de su padre. *She's upset about her father's reaction.* ~Me DISGUSTA que hables así. *It upsets me to hear you talk like that.* ‖ **2.** Enemistarse. *To quarrel.* ~Se DISGUSTARON por un malentendido y ahora no se hablan. *They had a misunderstanding and now they don't talk to each other.* ⇨DISGUST²

DISGUSTO. Desagrado. *Displeasure, annoyance, anger.* ~No pudo ocultar su DISGUSTO. *He was unable to hide his displeasure.* || **2.** Shock, blow. *Golpe.* ~La muerte de su madre le causó un gran DISGUSTO. *The death of this mother was a great blow to him.* || **3.** Revés. *Trouble, sorrow, misfortunes.* ~Su vida ha sido una serie de DISGUSTOS. *His life has been a long string of misfortunes.* ~Ha tenido muchos DISGUSTOS. *He has suffered many misfortunes, ha has had a lot of bad luck.* || **4.** Desavenencia, discusión. *Argument, minor quarrel.* ~Ha tenido un DISGUSTO con su cuñada. *She had an argument with her sister-in-law.* || **5.** *LOCUCIONES.* || •Estar (sentirse) a DISGUSTO. *To be (feel) ill at ease.* || •Matar a DISGUSTOS a uno. *To make one's life miserable.* ~Esos hijos me van a matar a DISGUSTOS. *These children will be the death of me.* || •Para mi DISGUSTO. *Much to my displeasure.* || •Dar un DISGUSTO. *To upset.* || •Llevarse un DISGUSTO. *To be (get) upset.* ~No sabes el DISGUSTO que me llevé. *You can't imagine how upset I was.* || •No gano para DISGUSTOS. *It's one thing after another.* || •A DISGUSTO. *Unwillingly, reluctantly, against one's will.* ~Lo hizo a DISGUSTO. *He did it reluctantly.* ~Si te vas a quedar a DISGUSTO es mejor que te vayas. *If you're going to stay against your will, you might as well go.* ⇨DISGUST[1]

DISIMULAR [DISSIMULATE]. *v.* Ocultar. *To conceal, hide.* ~Con la pintura se DISIMULAN las manchas. *Stains don't show under the paint.* ~Ella DISIMULA su pena. *She hides her sorrow.* || **2.** [Emoción, intención]. *To conceal.* || **3.** Disculpar. *To excuse.* ~Le ruego DISIMULAR la indiscreción. *Please pardon the liberty.* ~DISIMULA mi atrevimiento. *Forgive me if I've been too bold.* || **4.** Pasar por alto. *To condone, overlook.* ~La madre DISIMULABA las travesuras del hijo para que el padre no le castigara. *The mother would overlook her son's pranks so that the father would not punish him.* || **5.** Tolerar. *To tolerate.* || **6.** [Persona]. *To be lenient to, behave tolerantly towards.* || **9.** •DISIMULA, que nos

están mirando. *Act normal, we're being watched.*

DISIPACIÓN. *sf.* [De temores, dudas, ilusiones, niebla]. *Dispelling.* ~Un sol radiante ha producido la DISIPACIÓN de la niebla. *A burning sun dispelled the fog.* ⇨DISSIPATION

DISIPAR[1]. *v.* [Humo, niebla]. *To clear away.* El sol DISIPA la niebla. *The sun clears away the fog.* || **2.** [Esperanza]. *To shatter (hopes).* || **3.** Derrochar (dinero, fortuna). *To squander.* DISIPARON toda su herencia. *They squandered all of their inheritance.* || **4.** [Energía, fuerzas]. *To use up, waste.* || **5.** [Malentendido]. *To clear up.* || **6.** [Sospechas]. *To allay.* ⇨DISSIPATE

DISIPARSE[2]. *vr.* [Alcohol]. *Evaporate.* ~Dejó el frasco abierto y se DISIPÓ el alcohol. *He left the jar open and all the alcohol evaporated.* || **2.** [Nubes, niebla]. *To clear.* || **3.** [Esperanzas, ilusiones]. *To vanish, disappear.* || **4.** [Energías]. *To fail, flag.* ⇨DISSIPATE

DISMINUIR [DIMINISH]. *v.* [Número, cantidad]. *Decrease, drop, fall.* ~El número de fumadores ha DISMINUIDO. *The number of smokers has dropped (fallen, decreased).* || **2.** [Desempleo, exportaciones, gastos]. *To decrease, drop, fall.* || **3.** Reducir (Gastos, costos). *To reduce, bring down.* || **4.** [Velocidad]. *To reduce.* ~DISMINUIMOS la velocidad. *We reduced speed.* || **5.** [Importancia]. *To play down.* ~Es un asunto muy grave y se intenta DISMINUIR su importancia. *It's a very serious matter, and its importance is being played down.* || **6.** [Reflejos]. *To slow down.* El alcohol DISMINUYE la rapidez de los reflejos. *Alcohol slows down your reactions.* || **7.** [Temperatura]. *Lower, cause to fall, drop.* || **8.** [Dolor]. *To relieve.* || **9.** [Pena]. *To lighten.*

DISPENSAR. *v.* [Honor]. *To give, grant, accord.* ~Le DISPENSARON el honor de inaugurar el museo. ~*He was given (accorded) the honor of inaugurating the museum* || **2.** [Atención]. *To pay.* || **3.** [Ayuda]. *To give.* || **4.** Eximir, librar de una obligación. *To excuse, exempt, pardon.* ~Me DISPENSARON

la multa. *They exempted me from the fine.*
~Fue DISPENSADO del servicio militar. *He was
exempted from military service.* || **5.** [Acogida]. *Give, extend.* ~Le DISPENSARON un
caluroso recibimiento. *He was given a
warm welcome.* || **6.** Perdonar, disculpar.
To forgive, excuse, pardon. ~DISPÉNSEME
por llegar tan tarde. *Forgive me for arriving
so late.* || **7.** [Honores]. *To bestow.* ⇨DISPENSE

DISPONER[1]. Tener. *To have available (at
one's disposal).* ~El sindicato DISPONE de
fondos considerables. *The trade union
has considerable funds at its disposal.*
~DISPONE de poco tiempo. *He has little
time (at his disposal).* || **2.** Utilizar. *To make
use of, avail oneself of.* ~Todavía no puede
DISPONER de sus bienes. *He cannot yet
have the use of his assets.* || **3.** Ordenar,
establecer. *Provide, arrange, stipulate,
decide.* ~En cumplimiento con lo DISPUESTO
en el artículo primero ... *In accordance with
the provisions of article one ...* ~La junta a
DISPUESTO aumentar la cuota de los socios.
*The committee has decided to increase
membership fees.* || **4.** Ordenar (tratamiento
médico). *Order.* El médico ha DISPUESTO
reposo absoluto. *The doctor ordered complete rest.* ⇨DISPOSE

DISPONERSE[2]. *vr.* Prepararse. *To prepare,
make ready to.* ~Mientras se DISPONÍAN a
tomar un tren. *While they were preparing
to catch a train.* ~La tropa se DISPUSO a
atacar. *The troops prepared to attack.* || **2.**
•DISPONGA de mí cuando guste. *I'm at your
complete disposal (whenever you need
me).* ⇨DISPOSE

DISPOSICIÓN. *v.* Norma. *Regulation.*
~Disposiciones administrativas. *Administrative regulations.* ~No cumplía con las
DISPOSICIONES legales. *It did not comply
with the regulations.* || **2.** Talento. Aptitud.
~No muestra DISPOSICIÓN para la música.
He has no aptitude for music. ~Tiene
DISPOSICIÓN para idiomas. *He has a gift for
languages.* || **3.** Inclinación, voluntad.
Willingness, readiness. ~Demostraron su
DISPOSICIÓN a mejorar las condiciones. *They

showed the willingness (readiness) to
improve conditions.* || **4.** [De un bien].
Disposal. ~Pondremos un despacho a su
DISPOSICIÓN. *We will place an office at your
disposal.* || **5.** Colocación, arreglo. *Arrangement, layout.* ~No me gusta la DISPOSICIÓN de los muebles. *I don't like the way
the furniture is arranged.* ~La DISPOSICIÓN
de los cuartos. *The layout of the rooms.* ||
6. Cláusula. *Provision.* || **7.** [De tropas].
Formation. || **8.** •DISPOSICIÓN de ánimo.
Attitude, frame of mind. || **9.** •Estar a
DISPOSICIÓN de alguien. *To be at someone's
disposal.* ~Quedo a su entera DISPOSICIÓN
para cualquier consulta. *I am at your
disposal for any questions you may have.*
⇨DISPOSITION

DISPUTA. *sf.* Discusión, pelea. *Quarrel,
argument.* ⇨DISPUTE

DISPUTAR. *v.* Discutir. *To argue.* || **2.**
Pretender (premio, posesión). *To contend
for, fight for.* ~DISPUTAR el primer puesto a
uno. *To contend with someone for first
place.* || **3.** [Partido]. *To play.* || **4.** [Combate].
To fight. ⇨DISPUTE[2]

DISTINTOS. *adj.* Varios. *Various, several.*
~Hay DISTINTAS maneras de matar pulgas.
There's more than one way to skin a cat.
~Comimos DISTINTOS platos de queso. *We
ate various kinds of cheese.* || **2.** Diferente.
Different. ~Son gemelos, pero son muy
DISTINTOS. *They're twins, but they are very
different.* ⇨DISTINCT

DISTRACCIÓN. Distraimiento. *Absentmindedness.* ⇨DISTRACTION

DISTRAER [DISTRACT]. *v.* Divertir. *To
entertain, amuse, relax.* ~La música me
DISTRAE. *Music relaxes me.* || **2.** Robar. *To
embezzle.* ~El cajero DISTRAJO varios miles
de pesetas del banco. *The bank clerk
embezzled thousands of dollars from the
bank.* || **3.** [De una pena, de un dolor]. *To
take someone's mind off.* ~DISTRAER a uno
de sus preocupaciones. *To take someone's
mind off his worries.*

DISTRIBUCIÓN [DISTRIBUTION]. *sf.* Entrega. *Delivery.* ~La DISTRIBUCIÓN del correo.

Mail delivery. ‖ **2.** [De una casa, jardín]. *Layout, arrangement.* ~La DISTRIBUCIÓN de este apartamento. *The layout of this apartment.*

DIVERSOS. Varios. *Various.* DIVERSAS personas han solicitado nuestros servicios. *Various people have requested our services.* ⇨ DIVERSE

DIVINO [DIVINE]. *adj.* Bonito, precioso. *Wonderful, fantastic, gorgeous.* ~Tiene una casa DIVINA. *They have a fantastic house.*

DIVISIÓN. *sf.* POL [De partido]. *Split.* ‖ **2.** [De país]. *Partición.* ‖ **3.** [En familia, entre amigos]. *Strife, discord, split.* ~Sembrar la DIVISIÓN en una familia. *To sow discord within a family.* ‖ **4.** [Del átomo]. *Splitting.* ‖ **5.** Diferencia. *Difference, divergence.* ~Hay DIVISIÓN de opiniones. *Opinions are divided.* ‖ **6.** GRAM Guión. *Dash, hyphen.* ⇨ DIVISION

DIVULGAR [DIVULGE]. *v.* Difundir. *To disclose, reveal.* ‖ **2.** [Radio]. *To broadcast.* Las emisoras de radio DIVULGARON la noticia. *The radio stations broadcast the news.* ‖ **3.** Propagar. *To popularize.* ‖ **4.** [Noticia, información]. *To spread, circulate.* ~DIVULGAR una noticia. *To spread a piece of news.* ‖ **5.** [Cultura, ideas]. *To spread, disseminate.* ~La radio ha DIVULGADO la música clásica. *Radio has popularized classical music.*

DOBLAR. *v.* Plegar (tela, papel, camisa, servilleta). *To fold, crease.* ~DOBLAR un papel en dos. *To fold a piece of paper in two.* ~Ayúdame a DOBLAR las sábanas. *Help me fold the sheets.* ~DOBLÓ la hoja y la metió en un sobre. *He folded the sheet and put it in an envelope.* ‖ **2.** Torcer. *To bend.* ~DOBLAR una vara de hierro. *To bend an iron bar.* ‖ **3.** [Película]. *To dub.* ~Una película DOBLADA al castellano. *A film dubbed into Spanish.* ‖ **4.** [Esquina]. *To go around.* ~DOBLAR una esquina. *To turn a corner.* ‖ **5.** Girar. *To turn.* DOBLA a la izquierda. *Turn left.* ‖ **6.** [Campanas]. *To toll.* ~¿Por quién DOBLAN las campanas? *For Whom the Bells Toll.* ‖ **7.** Someterse, ceder. *To yield, give in.* Tuvo que DOBLARSE ante

las circunstancias. *He had to give in due to the circumstances.* ‖ **8.** [Cabeza, rodilla]. *To bend.* ~DOBLAR la rodilla. *To bend one's knee.* ‖ **9.** [Náutica]. *To round.* ~DOBLAR un cabo. *To round a cape.* ‖ **10.** Alcanzar (un auto). *To overtake.* ‖ **11.** Vencer. *To beat (up).* ‖ **12.** Ablandar (con ruegos). *To win over.* ‖ **13.** [Camino]. *Bend, turn.* ~En este punto la carretera DOBLA hacia el río. *At that point the road turns towards the river.* ‖ **14.** [Toro]. *To collapse.* ‖ **15.** [Los bajos de un pantalón]. *To turn up.* ~DÓBLATE los puños hacia arriba. *Turn the cuffs up.* ‖ **16.** Dominar. *To subdue, reduce to submission.* ‖ **17.** Disuadir. *To make someone change his mind.* ‖ **18.** Cansar mucho. *To wear out.* ‖ **19.** [Persona]. *Stoop, bend down.* ‖ **20.** Inclinarse. *To give, buckle.* ~Las ramas se DOBLAN por el peso de la fruta. *The branches give under the weight of the fruits.* ‖ **21.** •DOBLARSE por la cintura. *To be in stitches (por la risa).* ⇨ DOUBLE

DOMINAR[1] [DOMINATE]. *v.* Contener, detener. *To control, contain.* ~DOMINAR el fuego. *To contain the fire.* ~No logró DOMINAR su ira. *She couldn't contain (control) her anger.* ‖ **2.** Conocer a fondo. *To master, have a good command of, to be fluent in (language).* ~DOMINAR el francés. *To have a good command of French.* ~DOMINAR la fotografía. *To be very good at photography.* ~Nunca voy a poder DOMINAR el inglés. *I'll never be able to master English.* ‖ **3.** Abarcar con la vista. *To see.* Desde el balcón se DOMINA la llanura. *From the balcony one can see the plain.* ‖ **4.** Apoderar. *To overpower, overcome.* ~Le DOMINÓ la rabia. *He was overcome by rage.* ‖ **5.** Resaltar. *To stand out, prevail, predominate.* ~El azul era el color que DOMINABA. *Blue was the predominant color.* ~En la tela DOMINABA el color verde. *The prevalent color of the fabric was green.* ‖ **6.** [Rebelión]. *To subdue, put down, supress.* ‖ **7.** [Pasión]. *Control, master.* ‖ **8.** [Dolor, pena]. *To get over.* ‖ **9.** [Envidia, ambición]. *To rule, consume.* ~Lo DOMINABA la envidia. *He was ruled by envy.* ~DOMINADO por los celos. *Consumed by jealousy.*

‖ **10.** [Coche, caballo]. *Bring under control.* No logró DOMINAR el vehículo. *He couldn't bring the car under control.* ‖ **11.** [Adversario]. *Overpower.* ‖ **12.** Prevalecer. *To prevail.* ~El es quien DOMINABA en su familia. *In his family he was the one to prevail.*

DOMINARSE[2] [DOMINATE]. *vr.* Contenerse. *To control oneself.* Tuve que DOMINARME para no contestarle mal. *I had to restrain myself from answering him angrily.*

DOMINIO [DOMINANCE/DOMINATION]. *sm.* Control. *Control.* ~Bajo el DOMINIO árabe. *Under Arab control (rule).* ~En pleno DOMINIO de sus facultades. *In full command of her faculties.* ‖ **2.** Conocimiento profundo de algo (idioma, tema). *Command.* ~Se requiere perfecto DOMINIO del inglés. *Perfect command of English required.* ~El escritor tiene un gran DOMINIO del lenguaje. *This writer has a good command of the language.* ‖ **3.** [Público]. *Knowledge.* ~Ser del DOMINIO público. *To be public knowledge.* ~Su boda es ya del DOMINIO público. *Their wedding is public knowledge.* ‖ **4.** Ambito, campo. *Scope, sphere, field.* ~El DOMINIO de la ciencia. *The field (sphere) of science.* ~Entra en el DOMINIO de la fantasía. *It moves into the realm of fantasy.* ~‖ **5.** Territorio. *Domain, possessions.* ~La pérdida de sus DOMINIOS americanos supuso el fin del Imperio español. *The loss of its American domains (possessions) was responsable for the downfall of the Spanish Empire.* ‖ **6.** [Del aire, de los mares]. *Supremacy, command.* ~El DOMINIO de su país sobre los mares. *Their country's naval supremacy.* ~Dominio del mar. *Command of the sea.* ‖ **7.** [De las pasiones]. *Control, restraint.* ~En ningún momento perdió el DOMINIO de si mismo. *At no time did he loose his self-control.* ‖ **8.** Derecho de propriedad. *Ownership.*

DORMITORIO [DORMITORY]. *sm.* [De una casa]. *Bedroom.* ~Una casa de tres DORMITORIOS. *A three-bedroom home.*

DROGA. *sf.* [Limpieza]. *Household product.* ⇨ DRUG

DUPLICAR. *v.* [Ventas, precio]. *To double.* Las pérdidas DUPLICAN las de 1995. *The losses are double what they were in 1995.* ~Casi me DUPLICA la edad. *He's nearly twice my age.* ⇨ DUPLICATE

E

EDICIÓN. *sf.* Publicación. *Publication.* ~EDICIONES Sánchez. *Sanchez Publications.* || **2.** [De sellos]. *Issue.* || **3.** [Industría]. *Publishing.* ~EDICIÓN de sobremesa. *Desktop publishing.* ~El mundo de la EDICIÓN. *The publishing world.* || **4.** [Informática]. *Editing.* ~EDICIÓN en pantalla. *On-line editing.* || **5.** Reimpresión. *Reprint.* || **6.** FIG *Event, occasion.* ~Es la tercera EDICIÓN de este festival. *This is the third occasion on which this festival has been held.* ⇨EDITION

EDIFICAR [EDIFY]. *v.* Construir. *To build.* ~En este terreno van a EDIFICAR un banco. *On this lot they're going to build a bank.*

EDITAR. *v.* Publicar. *To publish.* ~¿Quién editó este libro? *Who's the publisher of this book?* ⇨EDIT

EDITOR. *sm.* Persona o entidad que publica una obra. *Publisher.* ~¿Quién es el EDITOR de este libro? *Who is the publisher of this book?* ⇨EDITOR

EDITORIAL. *sf.* Casa editorial. *Publisher, publishing house.* ~Un grupo de EDITORIALES exhibirán sus libros. *A group of publishers will display their publications.* ⇨EDITORIAL

EDUCACIÓN. *sf.* Buenos modales, crianza. *Upbringing.* ~No tiene EDUCACIÓN. *He has no manners.* || **2.** •Falta de EDUCACIÓN. *Lack of breeding, rudeness, discourtesy, bad manners.* ~Nunca he visto tal falta de EDUCACIÓN en la mesa. *I have never seen such bad table manners.* ~Es una falta de EDUCACIÓN hablar con la boca llena. *It's bad manners to talk with your mouth full.* || **3.** •¡Qué falta de EDUCACIÓN! *How rude!* || **4.** •Gastos de EDUCACIÓN. *School or college fees.* || **5.** •EDUCACIÓN a distancia. *Correspondence course.* || **6.** •EDUCACIÓN cívica.

Citizenship training. || **7.** •EDUCACIÓN vial. *Driver education.* || **8.** •EDUCACIÓN de la voz. *Elocution lessons, voice training.* ⇨EDUCATION

EDUCADO. *adj.* De buenos modales. *Polite, well-mannered.* ~Un niño bien EDUCADO. *A well-behaved (well brought up) child.* || **2.** •Mal EDUCADO. *Ill-manered, rude.* ⇨EDUCATED

EDUCAR. *v.* Criar, enseñar buenos modales. *To bring up, raise.* || **2.** [Voz]. *To train.* ⇨EDUCATE

EFECTIVAMENTE. *adv.* Realmente. *Really, actually, in fact.* ~Si EFECTIVAMENTE es así, hay que hacer algo. *If that is really the case, something must be done.* ~Sí, EFECTIVAMENTE, así fue. *That's right, that's how it was.* ~Dijo que estaría a las siete y, EFECTIVAMENTE, allí estaba. *He said he'd be there at seven and, sure enough, there he was.* || **2.** En efecto. *Quite, yes indeed, exactly, precisely, sure enough, you were right.* EFECTIVAMENTE, estaba donde tu has dicho. *You were right, it was just where you said it would be.* ⇨EFFECTIVELY

EFECTIVO[1]. *adj.* Cierto, verdadero. *Real, true, actual.* || **2.** •Hacer efectivo. *To cash (check), collect (bills), recover (cost), enforce (penalty), carry out (plan, threat), take effect (resignation).* ~Hice EFECTIVO el cheque ayer. *I cashed the check yesterday.* ~El abono se hará EFECTIVO por mensualidades. *Payment will be made in monthly installments.* ~Su dimisión se hará EFECTIVA a partir del 15 de enero. *His resignation will become effective from January 15th.* ⇨EFFECTIVE

EFECTIVO[2]. *nm.* Plantilla. *Personnel.* || **2.**

mil. Tropas, fuerzas. *Forces.* Numerosos EFECTIVOS de la policía rodearon el colegio. *A large police contingent surrounded the school.* || **3.** [Empleo]. *Regular, permanent.* || **4.** *LOCUCIONES.* || •Dinero en EFECTIVO. *Cash.* || •Pagar en EFECTIVO. *To pay cash.* || •EFECTIVO en caja. *Cash in hand.* || •En EFECTIVO. *Cash.* ~Sorteamos miles de premios en EFECTIVO. *Thousands of cash prizes to be won.* ~Pagó la cuenta en EFECTIVO. *She paid the bill in cash.* ~Nunca lleva dinero en EFECTIVO. *He never carries cash.* ⇨EFFECTIVE

EFECTO. *sm.* Fin práctico, finalidad. *Aim, object, purpose.* ~A tal EFECTO. *To that end.* ~A efecto de. *With the object of.* ~A EFECTO de máxima seguridad. *For the purpose of ensuring the tightest security.* ~A EFECTOS fiscales. *For tax purposes.* || **2.** DEP Movimiento rotario. *Spin.* ~Le dio a la bola con EFECTO. *He put some spin on the ball.* || **3.** DEP Desvío. *Swerve.* ~Tiró la pelota con EFECTO. *He made the ball swerve.* || **4.** Impresión. *Impression.* Su conducta causó muy mal EFECTO. *His behavior gave a very bad impression.* ~Me hace el EFECTO de que ... *It gives me the impression that ...* || **5.** [De un comercio]. *Stock, merchandise, goods, articles.* || **6.** [Contabilidad]. *Assets.* || **7.** Valores. *Bill of exchange, draft.* ⇨EFFECT

EFERVESCENCIA [EFFERVESCENCE]. *sf.* [De bebida]. *Fizziness.* || **2.** Alegría, vivacidad, exitación. *High spirits.* ~La EFERVESCENCIA de los jóvenes. *Youthful high spirits.* || **3.** Alboroto. *Commotion, agitation.* ~La EFERVESCENCIA política de la región. *The political turmoil in the area.*

EFERVESCENTE [EFFERVESCENT]. *adj.* Gaseoso (bebida). *Carbonated, sparkling, fizzy.* || **2.** [Situation]. *Volatile.* || **3.** Vivaz. *Vivacious, bubbly.* || **4.** Excitado. *High-spirited.*

EJECUCIÓN. *sf.* [Orden]. *Carrying out.* ~Poner en EJECUCIÓN. *To carry out.* ~Un proyecto de difícil EJECUCIÓN. *A plan which will be difficult to carry out (implement).* || **2.** [Música]. *Performance.* || **3.** [Derecho]. *Seizure.* ⇨EXECUTION

EJECUTAR. *v.* [Orden]. *To carry out.* ~Su empresa EJECUTARÁ la renovación del edificio. *His company will carry out the remodeling of the buiding.* ~El robo se EJECUTÓ en menos de cinco minutos. *The robbery was carried out in less than five minutes.* || **2.** [Sinfonía, himno nacional]. *To perform, play.* ~La orquesta EJECUTÓ la sinfonía con perfección. *The orquestra performed the symphony magnificently.* || **3.** [Derecho]. *To seize.* || **4.** [Informática]. *To run.* || **5.** [Ejercicio, salto]. *To perform.* ~EJECUTÓ el ejercicio sin cometer ningún error. *He performed the excercise without making any mistakes.* ~EJECUTÓ limpiamente el triple salto mortal. *He performed the triple somersault cleanly.* ⇨EXECUTE

EJERCER [EXERCISE]. *v.* Practicar. *To practice.* ~No puede EJERCER la medicina en este país. *She cannot practice medicine in this country.* || **2.** [Influence]. *Exert, use, bring to bear.* ~La televisión EJERCE un poder enorme sobre la juventud. *Television exerts enormous influence on young people.* || **3.** [Función]. *To perform, carry out.* ~EJERCE su trabajo de enfermera con entrega. *She's a dedicated nurse (she performs her duties as a nurse with dedication).*

ELABORACIÓN [ELABORATION]. *sm.* [De un producto, vino]. *Manufacture, production, making.* ~Disponer de todos los ingredientes necesarios para la ELABORACIÓN de una buena paella. *To have all the necessary ingredients to make a good paella.* ~De ELABORACIÓN casera. *Homemade.* ~Elaboración propia. *Made (baked, etc.) on the premises.* || **2.** [Del pan]. *Baking, making.* ~Para la ELABORACIÓN del pan se necesita levadura. *Yeast is used in the baking (making) of bread.* || **3.** [Del metal, de la madera]. *Working.* || **4.** [De una idea, plan]. *Development, working out.* ~Los responsables de la ELABORACIÓN del plan. *Those responsible for drawing up (working out, devising) the plan.* || **5.** [De un informe, estudio]. *Preparation.* ~La ELABORACIÓN del informe le llevó varios meses. *Preparation of the report took him several months.* || **6.** [Biología]. *Production.* || **7.** [De la miel].

Production. ~La abejas utilizan el néctar de las flores para la ELABORACIÓN de la miel. *Bees use the nectar in flowers to produce honey.*

ELABORADO. *adj.* Preparado por medio de un trabajo adecuado. *Processed, manufactured, made, produced.* ~ELABORADO en España. *Made (manufactured) in Spain.* ~Una plato ELABORADO con los mejores ingredientes. *A dish prepared using the finest ingredients.* ⇨ELABORATED

ELABORAR. *v.* Preparar un producto por medio de un trabajo adecuado. *To process, produce, make.* Estas galletitas han sido ELABORADAS con ingredientes de primera calidad. *These cookies are made of the finest ingredients.* ~El pan se ELABORA con harina, agua y levadura. *Bread is made of flour, water and yeast.* || **2.** Idear (doctrina, plan, proyecto). *To devise, draw up, work out.* ~Los presos ELABORARON un plan para escapar de la cárcel. *The prisoners devised a plan to escape from prison.* || **3.** [Metal, madera]. *To work.* || **4.** [Hormona, savia]. *To produce.* ⇨ELABORATE

ELECCIÓN [ELECTION]. *sf.* Acción de escoger. *Choice.* ~Lo dejo a tu ELECCIÓN. *I leave that up to you.* ~Una ELECCIÓN acertada. *A sensible choice.* ~Su patria de ELECCIÓN. *His chosen country.* ~El formato es a ELECCIÓN del cliente. *The choice of format is left up to the client.*

ELEGIR. *v.* Escoger. *To choose.* ~ELEGí el más caro. *I chose the most expensive one.* ~Te toca a tí ELEGIR. *It's up to you to choose.* ⇨ELECT

ELEMENTAL [ELEMENTAL/ELEMENTARY]. *adj.* Básico (curso, nivel). *Elementary, basic.* ~Tiene nociones ELEMENTALES del inglés. *He has a basic knowledge of English.* ~Desconoce las más ELEMENTALES normas de urbanidad. *He doesn't know the most basic (elementary) norms of civilized behavior.* ~Una gramática ELEMENTAL. *A basic grammar.* || **2.** Muy fácil. *Elementary.* ~Todo lo que estás diciendo es ELEMENTAL. *Everything you are saying is common sense.* || **3.** Esencial. *Fundamental.* ~Un rasgo ELEMENTAL de su poesía. *An essential (fundamental) feature of his poetry.*

ELEMENTO [ELEMENT]. *sm.* Individuo. *Type, individual.* ~Es un buen ELEMENTO. *He's a good sort.* || **2.** Pieza, componente (de una máquina). *Part, component.* || **3.** Medios. *Means, resources.* ~No disponemos de los ELEMENTOS básicos para llevar a cabo la tarea. *We lack the basic resources to carry out the task.* ~Yo te proporcionaré los ELEMENTOS necesarios para este trabajo. *I'll provide you with the necessary tools for this job.* || **4.** [Muebles]. *Section, unit.* ~Una biblioteca de siete ELEMENTOS. *A seven-section bookcase.* || **5.** Miembro. *Member.* ~Los ELEMENTOS de una junta. *The members of a board.* ~Un buen ELEMENTO del equipo. *A good member of the team.* || **6.** Tipo (persona). *Type, character.* Juntarse con ELEMENTOS sospechosos. *To join up with suspicious characters.* || **7.** Factor. *Factor.* ~ELEMENTOS que contribuyen al desorden. *Factors which contribute to the confusion.* ~La lectura de los clásicos fue un ELEMENTO decisivo en su formación literaria. *His reading of the classics contributed much to his literary education.* || **8.** [De una batería]. *Cell.*

ELEVAR. *v.* Levantar (objeto). *To raise, lift.* ~La grúa ELEVÓ el cajón hasta la cubierta. *The crane raised (hoisted, lifted) the crate onto the deck.* ~Elevó los brazos al cielo. *He raised his arms to heaven.* || **2.** *To uplift.* ~Música que ELEVA el espíritu. *Spiritually uplifting music.* || **3.** [Muro, nivel]. *To raise, make higher.* || **4.** Aumentar (precios, impuestos). *To raise.* ~ELEVAR el nivel de vida. *To raise the standard of living.* || **5.** [Voz, tono, moral]. *To raise.* ~ELEVAR el moral de alguien. *To raise one's moral.* || **6.** Presentar, dirigir (protesta, queja, informe). *To present, submit.* ~ELEVARON una protesta a las autoridades. *They presented (submitted) a letter of protest to the authorities.* ~ELEVARON el recurso al Tribunal Supremo. *They presented (submitted) an appeal to the Supreme Court.* || **7.** [Producción]. *To step up.* || **8.** [Electricidad]. *To boost.* || **9.** [Persona]. *To promote.* ~ELEVAR a alguien a un alto cargo. *To promote someone to a high position.* || **10.** [Edificio, monumento]. *To* *erect, put up.* || **11.** •ELEVEMOS nuestros corazones al Señor. *Let us lift our hearts to the Lord.* ⇨ELEVATE

ELEVADO [ELEVATED]. *adj.* [Edificio]. *Tall.* || **2.** [Pensamiento]. *Lofty, noble.* || **3.** [Tono, voz]. *Angry.* || **4.** [Precio, impuestos]. *High.* ~A precios ELEVADÍSIMOS. *At terribly high prices.* || **5.** [Terreno, montaña]. *High.* || **6.** [Cantidad]. *Large.* ~Un número ELEVADO de casos. *A large number of cases.* || **7.** [Categoría, calidad]. *High, important.* Tiene un puesto muy ELEVADO. *He has a very important (high) position.* || **8.** Estilo. *Lofty.* || **9.** [Matemática]. *Raised.* ~Diez ELEVADO a tres es mil. *Ten (raised) to the power of three is a thousand.*

EMBARAZADA [EMBARRASSED]. *adj.* Encinta. *Pregnant, expecting.* ~Dejar EMBARAZADA a una. *To get a girl pregnant.* ~Estar EMBARAZADA de 4 meses. *To be 4 months pregnant.*

EMBARAZAR. *v.* Dejar pregnada. *To make pregnant.* || **2.** Dificultar, estorbar. *To hinder, hamper.* Su abrigo le EMBARAZABA. *His overcoat hampered him.* ~Esto EMBARAZABA sus movimientos. *This hampered his movements.* || **3.** [Paso]. *Block, obstruct.* ~EMBARAZAR el paso. *To block the way.* ⇨EMBARRASS

EMBARCAR. *v.* [Aviación]. *To board.* || **2.** [Mercancías, equipajes]. *To load.* ~EMBARCARON las maletas en el avión. *They loaded the suitcases on the plane.* || **3.** [En un asunto, negocio]. *To involve.* ~EMBARCAR a alguien en un asunto. *To involve someone in an affair.* ⇨EMBARK

EMBARGO [EMBARGO]. Retención de bienes por mandamiento de juez competente. *Seizure of property.* ~El juez ordenó el EMBARGO de sus bienes. *The judge ordered the seizure of his assets.*

EMISIÓN [EMISSION]. *sf.* [Finanzas, filatelia]. *Issue.* ~EMISIÓN de bonos. *Bond issue.* || **2.** [Radio, TV]. (I) Programa. *Broadcast,* (II) [Transmission]. *Broadcasting.* ~La EMISIÓN de la tarde. *The afternoon broadcast.* || **3.** [Informática]. *Output.* || **4.** •EMISIÓN en directo. *Live transmission.* || **5.** •Director de

EMISIÓN. *Producer (radio).*

EMITIR. *v.* [Luz, calor]. *To give off.* ~El sol EMITE rayos luminosos. *The sun gives off bright rays.* || **2.** Manifestar. *To express.* ~EMITIR un juicio. *To express an opinion.* ~El director no quiso EMITIR ninguna opinión. *The manager refused to express an opinion.* || **3.** JUR [Sentencia, fallo, veredicto]. *To pronounce, return, hand down.* ~EMITIR el fallo (sentencia). *To pronounce judgement, to pass sentence.* || **4.** [Radio, TV]. *To transmit, broadcast.* ~La entrevista se EMITIRÁ el lunes. *The interview will be broadcast on Monday.* ~EMITIR en onda corta. *To transmit on short wave.* || **5.** [Moneda, títulos, sellos, bonos). *To issue.* ~El Banco de España ha EMITIDO una nueva serie de billetes. *The Bank of Spain has issue a new series of banknotes.* || **6.** [Dinero falso]. *To put into circulation.* || **7.** [Señal]. *To send out.* || **8.** [Voto]. *To cast.* || **9.** [Olor]. *To give off.* ⇨EMIT

EMOCIÓN [EMOTION]. *sf.* Sentimiento. *Feeling.* ~Nos comunica una EMOCIÓN de nostalgia. *It gives us a nostalgic feeling.* || **2.** Excitación. *Excitement, thrill.* ~¡Qué EMOCIÓN! *How exciting!* ~Al abrirlo sentí una gran EMOCIÓN. *I felt very excited on opening it.* || **3.** Tensión. *Tension, suspense.* ~La EMOCIÓN de la película no disminuye. *The excitement of the film does not flag.*

EMPLEAR[1] [EMPLOY]. *v.* Gastar (dinero). *To spend, invest.* ~EMPLEAR su fortuna en fincas. *To invest one's fortune in real estate.* || **2.** [Tiempo]. *To invest, spend, occupy, take.* ~EMPLEARON tres años en la construcción del puente. *It took them three years to build the bridge.* || **3.** Colocar (hijo, sobrino). *To fix up with a job.* Su padre le EMPLEÓ en una tienda. *His father got him a job in a shop.* || || **4.** •EMPLEAR mal. *To misuse.* ~EMPLEAR mal el tiempo. *To waste time.*

EMPLEARSE[2] [EMPLOY]. *vr.* [Palabra]. *To be used.* ~Esta palabra ya no se EMPLEA. *This word is no longer used.*

EMPLEO [EMPLOYMENT]. *sm.* Puesto, oficio. *Job, work, occupation.* ~Tiene un buen EMPLEO. *He has a good job.* ~Está sin EMPLEO. *She's without work.* || **2.** [Del tiempo].

Spending. ‖ **3.** Uso. *Use.* ~El EMPLEO del ordenador nos facilita mucho el trabajo. *Using a computer makes work much easier.* ~Modo de EMPLEO. *Instructions for use.* ~El EMPLEO DE una palabra. *The use of a word.*

ENCONTRAR. *v.* Hallar. *To find.* ~No lo ENCUENTRO. *I can't find it.* ~Lo ENCONTRÓ bastante fácil. *He found it pretty easy.* ~Por fin ENCONTRÓ el vestido que quería. *She finally found the dress she wanted.* ‖ **2.** [Persona]. *To bump into, come across.* ~Me ENCONTRÉ con Pilar. *I bumped into Pilar.* ‖ **3.** [Dificultades]. *To run into, come up against.* ~Nos ENCONTRAMOS con muchos problemas. *We ran into a lot of trouble.* ‖ **4.** Pensar. *To find, think.* ~ENCUENTRO que no es justo. *I don't think it's fair.* ⇨ENCOUNTER[1]

ENCONTRARSE[1]. *vr.* [Cosas, personas]. *To meet.* ¿Dónde nos ENCONTRAMOS? *Where shall we meet?* ‖ **2.** Sentirse. *To feel, be.* ~Dijo que no se ENCONTRABA bien y se fue a acostar. *He said he did not feel well and went to bed.* ~ENCONTRARSE a gusto. *To feel, be comfortable.* ~Encontrarse con GANAS de. *To feel like doing something.* ‖ **3.** Estar. *To be, find oneself.* ~Me ENCONTRABA en París. *I was in Paris.* ~Me ENCUENTRO en apuros. *I am in a bit of trouble.* ‖ **4.** [Vehículos]. *To crash, collide.* ‖ **5.** [Opiniones]. *To clash, conflict.* ~Las dos alas del partido acabaron ENCONTRÁNDOSE a la hora de elegir un nuevo presidente. *When the time came to elect a new president, the two wings of the parties clashed.* ‖ **6.** ⇨ENCOUNTER[1]

ENCUENTRO. *sm.* Choque. *Collision.* ‖ **2.** Competición deportiva. *Meeting, match, clash.* ~El ENCUENTRO de baloncesto tendrá lugar el martes próximo. *The basketball game will take place next Tuesday.* ~ENCUENTRO amistoso. *Friendly match.* ‖ **3.** Escaramuza. *Skirmish.* ‖ **4.** Oposición, contradicción (de opiniones, intereses, ideas). *Clash.* ~ENCUENTRO de opiniones. *Clash of opinion.* ‖ **5.** Reunión. *Meeting.* ~Se celebrará un encuentro sobre creación de empleo. *There will be a meeting dealing with employment oportunities.* ‖ **6.** Congreso, simposio. *Conference.* ‖ **7.** Cita. *Rendezvous.* ~El

ENCUENTRO de los astronautas en el espacio. *The astronauts' rendezvous in space.* ‖ **8.** Descubrimiento. *Discovery.* ‖ **9.** Hallazgo. *Find.* ‖ **10.** Discusión. *Fight, argument.* ⇨ENCOUNTER[2]

ENÉRGICO [ENERGETIC]. *adj.* Firm, forceful, bold (carácter, medida). *Firme, resuelto.* ~Tienes que ponerte ENÉRGICO. *You have to be firm.* ~El gobierno tomará medidas ENÉRGICAS para evitar la huelga. *The government will take firm measures to prevent a strike.* ‖ **2.** [Ademán, habla, tono]. *Emphatic.* ~Me dijo de forma ENÉRGICA que no pensaba abandonar el proyecto. *He declared emphatically that he did not intend to withdraw from the project.* ~En tono ENÉRGICO. *Emphatically.* ‖ **3.** [Esfuerzo]. *Determined, vigorous.* ‖ **4.** [Ejercicio]. *Strenuous.* ‖ **5.** [Campaña]. *Vigorous.* ‖ **6.** [Ataque]. *Vigorous, strong.* ~Lanzó un ENÉRGICO ataque contra ellos. *She launched a vigorous (fierce, strong) attack on them.* ‖ **7.** [Golpe]. *Heavy.* Le atestó un ENÉRGICO golpe en la cabeza. *He dealt him a heavy blow to the head.* **8.** [Protesta]. *Vigorous.* ~Un ENÉRGICO desmentido. *A vigorous denial.* ‖ **9.** Que produce mucho efecto (medicina, detergent). *Powerful.* ~Este detergente es muy ENÉRGICO contra las manchas. *This detergent is very powerful in getting rid of stains.*

ENFOCAR. *v.* Iluminar. *To shine a light on.* ~Le ENFOCÓ con una linterna. *He shone his flashlight on him.* ‖ **2.** Considerar. *To approach, look at, consider.* ~ENFOCAR un tema desde otro punto de vista. *To look at a subject from another angle.* ~Podemos ENFOCAR este problema de tres maneras. *We can approach this problem in three ways.* ⇨FOCUS

ENSAYO. *sm.* Prueba, experimento. *Test, trial, experiment.* ~Ensayo NUCLEAR. *Nuclear test.* ~Se pondrá en ENSAYO. *It will be tried out (tested).* ~Aprendizaje por ENSAYO y error. *Learning by trial and error.* ~A modo de ENSAYO. *As an experiment.* •Pedido de ENSAYO. *Trial order.* •Vuelo de ENSAYO. *Test flight.* •De ENSAYO. *Tentative.* •Tubo de

ENSAYO. *Test tube.* ‖ **2.** Intento. *Attempt.* ‖ **3.** Ejercicio. *Practice, exercise.* ‖ **4.** [Teatro]. *Rehearsal.* ~Ensayo general. *Dress rehearsal (de una obra teatral), final rehearsal (de un concierto).* ‖ **5.** [Rugby]. *Try.* ⇨ESSAY

ENTIDAD [ENTITY]. *nf.* [Comercial]. Firma, empresa, compañía. *Concern, company.* •ENTIDAD privada. *Private concern.* •ENTIDAD de seguros. *Insurance company.* •ENTIDAD bancaria. *Bank.* •ENTIDAD crediticia. *Credit company.* •ENTIDAD financiera. *Financial institution.* ‖ **2.** Importancia. *Significance.* •De ENTIDAD. *Important, of importance.* ~Un asunto de poca ENTIDAD. *A matter of little significance.* •De menor ENTIDAD. *Less important, not so large.* ‖ **3.** Reputación. *Reputation.* ~El equipo tiene mucha ENTIDAD. *The team has a very solid reputation.* ‖ **4.** Organización. *Organization, body.* ~La Real Academia es una ENTIDAD cultural. *The (Spanish) Royal Academy is a cultural organization.*

ENTRADA. Billete (espectáculo). *Admission, ticket.* ~Ya he sacado las ENTRADAS. *I've already bought the tickets.* •La ENTRADA es gratuita. *Admission is free.* •ENTRADA libre. *Free admission.* ‖ **2.** Plato ligero que se sirve antes de los principales. *Starter.* ‖ **3.** Inicio. *Beginning, onset.* ~La ENTRADA de la primavera. *The beginning of Spring.* ‖ **4.** Entrega, pago inicial. *Down payment.* ~Pagas $50.00 de ENTRADA y el resto en 48 mensualidades. *You pay a $50.00 down payment and the rest in 48 monthly installments.* ‖ **5.** Vestíbulo. *Hall.* ~Compró un espejo para la entrada. *He purchased a mirror for the hallway.* ‖ **6.** [Béisbol]. *Inning.* ‖ **7.** Ingreso. *Earnings.* Ésa es su única ENTRADA. *This is his only income.* ~Entre unas cosas y otras, él tiene unas buenas ENTRADAS. *All in all he makes good money (has a good income)* ‖ **8.** Público, concurrencia. *Audience.* ~Un espectáculo de poca/mucha ENTRADA. *A performance (show) with a small/large audience.* •ENTRADA floja. *Thin audience.* •Gran ENTRADA, ENTRADA llena. *Full house.* ‖ **9.** Recaudación. *Takings, receipts.* ‖ **10.** [Libro, discurso]. *Opening.* ~La novela tiene varias citas como ENTRADA. *The novel opens with various quotations.* ‖ **11.** Pórtico. *Porch, doorway.* ~El paragüero está en la ENTRADA. *The umbrella stand is in the doorway.* ‖ **11.** [Guerra]. *Invasion.* ‖ **12.** [De pelo]. *Where the hair is thinning.* ~Tiene ENTRADAS. *He's got a receding hairline.* ‖ **13.** Oportunidad. *Opportunity, chance.* ~Te lo explico si me das ENTRADA. *I'll explain it to you if you give me a chance.* ‖ **14.** [Mecánica]. *Inlet, intake.* ~ENTRADA de aire. *Air intake.* ‖ **15.** Admisión. *Admission.* ~Su ENTRADA en la Academia. *His admission to the Academy.* ‖ **16.** Ingreso. *Inflow.* La ENTRADA masiva de divisas. *The huge inflow of foreign currency.* ‖ **17.** Afluencia (turistas). *Influx.* ‖ **18.** LOCUCIONES. ‖ •Derechos de ENTRADA. *Import duty.* ‖ •De ENTRADA. *From the start (outset), right away, as a start, for a start, to begin with.* ~Nos dijo que no de ENTRADA. *She said no from the outset.* ~Lo calé de ENTRADA. *I sized him up from the beginning.* ‖ •Dar ENTRADA. *To let or allow in.* ‖ •Tener ENTRADAS (en la frente). *To have a receding hairline.* ‖ •ENTRADA de capital. *Capital inflow.* ‖ •ENTRADA en vigor. *Coming into effect.* ~Después de la ENTRADA en vigor del nuevo impuesto. *After the new tax comes into effect.* ‖ •ENTRADA a viva fuerza. *Forced entry.* ‖ •Prohibida la ENTRADA. *No admission, keep out.* ‖ •De primera ENTRADA. *At first sight.* ‖ •Entrada en materia. *Introduction.* ‖ •Vigilaba sus ENTRADAS y salidas. *She watched his comings and goings.* ‖ •ENTRADA de artistas. *Stage door.* ‖ •ENTRADAS y salidas. *Income and expenditures.* ‖ •De primera ENTRADA. *At first sight.* ‖ •ENTRADA general. *Standing room.* ‖ •Tener ENTRADA en una casa. *To be always welcome in a house.* ⇨ENTRY

ENTRETENER[1]. *v.* Retrasar, dar largas. *To delay, put off, hold up.* ~Están ENTRETENIENDO la resolución de la cuestión. *They're putting off the resolution of the matter.* ‖ **2.** Detener. *To hold up, detain, keep waiting.* ~No te ENTRETENGO más. *I won't keep you any longer.* ‖ **3.** Engañar (hambre). *To kill, stave* *off, ward off.* ‖ **4.** Hacer más soportable el tiempo de una cosa (espera, soledad). *To while away.* ~Encima de la mesa había revistas para ENTRETENER la espera. *There were some magazines on the table to while away the time, to make the waiting more bearable.* ‖ **5.** Tener suspenso. *To keep in suspense.* ‖ **6.** [Dolor]. *To allay.* ‖ **7.** Dedicarse sin seriedad a cierta ocupación. *To enjoy doing something.* ~Me ENTRETENGO tocando el piano. *I enjoy playing the piano.* ~Pintar me ENTRETIENE. *I enjoy painting.* ~La película ENTRETUVO a chicos y grandes. *The movie was enjoyed by both young and old.* ~Me ENTRETIENE mirar los escaparates. *I enjoy window-shopping.* ‖ **7.** Distraer. *Distract, keep occupied.* ~Mientras uno lo ENTRETENÍA, el otro le robó la cartera. *While one kept him occupied, the other stole his wallet.* ‖ **8.** Mantener atareado. *To keep busy, occupied.* Estas gestiones me han ENTRETENIDO toda la mañana. *These transactions have kept me busy all morning.* ‖ **9.** [Acreedores, muerte]. *To keep at bay.* ~ENTRETENER a los acreedores. *To keep one's creditors at bay.* ~ENTRETENER la muerte. *To keep death at bay.* ‖ **10.** [Enemigo]. *To ward off, divert (the enemy).* ‖ **11.** [Fuego]. *To keep alive, to keep going.* ~He puesto un tronco para ENTRETENER el fuego. *I've added a log to the fire to keep it burning (going).* ⇨ENTERTAIN

ENTRETENERSE[2]. *vr.* Distraerse. *To amuse oneself, while away the time.* ~Sólo para ENTRETENERME. *Just for fun.* ‖ **2.** Retrasarse. *To be delayed, held up.* ‖ **3.** Tardar. *To delay, loiter (on the way).* ~¡No te ENTRETENGAS! *Don't loiter on the way!* ‖ **4.** •Nos ENTRETUVO en conversación. *He engaged us in conversation.* ⇨ENTERTAIN

EPOCA [EPOCH]. *sf.*
❶ PERÍODO. *Time, age, period, era.* ~Una ÉPOCA de grandes cambios sociales. *A period (time, age) of great social changes.* ~Durante la ÉPOCA victoriana. *In Victorian times, in the Victorian age (era).* ~En aquella ÉPOCA había dos pretendientes. *During that period there were two pretenders to the throne.* En la ÉPOCA de Franco. *In Franco's times, under Franco.* ~Un Picasso de primera ÉPOCA. *An early (period) Picasso.* ~La ÉPOCA azul del pintor. *The painter's blue period.* En aquella ÉPOCA trabajaba en la fábrica. *In those days I was working at the factory.* ~En ÉPOCAS de crisis. *In times of crisis.* ~En la ÉPOCA del cine mudo. *In the era of silent films.*
❷ TEMPORADA, PARTE DEL AÑO. *Season, time.* ~La ÉPOCA de las fresas. *The strawberry season.* ~Durante la EPOCA de lluvias/sequía. *During the rainy/dry season.* ~No es ÉPOCA de naranjas. *Oranges are not in season.* ‖ **2.** •ÉPOCA del año. *Season, time of the year.*
❸ LOCUCIONES. •Muebles de ÉPOCA. *Period furniture.* ‖ **2.** •Coche de ÉPOCA. *Vintage car.* ‖ **3.** •Hacer ÉPOCA. *To be a landmark, to make history.* ~Eso hizo ÉPOCA en nuestra historia. *That was a landmark in our history.* ~Un grupo musical que hizo ÉPOCA. *A group which marked a new era in musical history.* ‖ **4.** •De los que hacen ÉPOCA. *To beat all.* Un gol de los que hacen ÉPOCA. *A goal to beat all goals.* ‖ **5.** Todos tenemos ÉPOCAS así. *We all have spells like that.* ‖ **6.** •Adelantarse a su ÉPOCA. *To be ahead of one's time.* ‖ **7.** •ÉPOCA glacial. *Ice-age.*

EQUIPAR. *v.* [Casa]. *To furnish.* ~Una casa muy bien EQUIPADA. *A well-furnished house.* ‖ **2.** [Local]. *To fit out.* ‖ **3.** [Barco]. *To fit out.* ~EQUIPARON la embarcación antes de zarpar. *Before sailing, they fitted out the ship.* ‖ **4.** [De víveres]. To provision. ‖ **5.** [Ropa]. *To fit out.* ⇨EQUIP

EQUIPO. Conjunto de personas que realizan una tarea determinada. *Team.* ‖ **2.** Grupo completo de jugadores. *Team.* ~Un EQUIPO de baloncesto. *A basketball team.* ~El EQUIPO local ganó el partido. *The local team won the game.* ‖ **3.** Ajuar. *Trousseau.* ⇨EQUIPMENT

ERRAR [ERR]. *v.* Equivocarse. *To be mistaken, to be wrong.* ~ERRÓ en su decisión. *He was mistaken in his decision, he made the wrong decision.* ~ERRAR el camino. *To take the wrong road, to loose one's way.* ~ERRAR la respuesta. *To give the wrong answer.* ‖ **2.** LIT Vagar. *To wander, rove, roam.* ‖ **3.** [Tiro]. *To miss, aim badly.* ~ERRÓ el tiro y la flecha salió fuera del campo. *He aimed badly and the arrow went out of the field.* || **4.** [Blanco]. *To miss.* || **5.** [Vocación]. *To miss, mistake.* ~ERRÓ su vocación. *She chose the wrong career.* || **6.** LIT [Mirada]. *To wander.* Su imaginación ERRABA por lugares lejanos. *His thoughts wandered (drifted. strayed) to far-off places.* || **7.** •ERRAR y porfiar. *To persist in error.*

ESCÁNDALO [SCANDAL]. *sm.* Alboroto. *Fuss, racket, din, uproar.* ~ARMAR un escándalo. *To kick up a fuss.* ~Cuando le presentaron la cuenta ARMÓ un escándalo. *When they gave him the bill he kicked up a fuss.* ~No hagan tanto ESCÁNDALO. *Don't make such a racket.* ~Nada de escándalos DENTRO del local. *We don't want any trouble in this store.* || **2.** Asombro. *Shock, astonishment.* ~Fue un ESCÁNDALO que se casara con alguien que le doblaba la edad. *Everyone was shocked to learn that he had married someone twice his age.*

ESCAPAR[1]. *v.* [Un ciclista]. *To break away.* || **2.** •Dejar ESCAPAR. (I) [Carcajada, suspiro]. *To let out, give.* ~Dejó ESCAPAR un grito de sorpresa. *He let out a cry of surprise,* (II) [Oportunidad]. *To pass up,* (III) [Persona, animal]. *To let get away.* ⇨ ESCAPE

ESCAPARSE[2]. *vr.* [Animal, niño]. *To run away.* ~Siempre te ESCAPAS cuando hay que arrimar el hombro. *You always disappear when there's some work to be done.* ~Se ha ESCAPADO de casa. *She's run away from home.* ~El canario se ha ESCAPADO de la jaula. *The canary got out of his cage.* ~Ven aquí, no te me ESCAPES. *Come here, don't run away (from me).* || **2.** [De una situación]. *To get out of.* ~De ésta si que no te ESCAPAS. *You're not getting out of this one.* || **3.** [Suspiro, grito, carcajada]. *To let out.* ~Se le ESCAPÓ un grito. *He let out a cry.* || **4.** [Gas, aire, agua]. *To leak.* El depósito tiene una grieta por donde se ESCAPA el agua. *The water tank has a crack and is leaking.* || **5.** Irse discretamente. *To slip away.* || **6.** [En deportes]. *To break away.* || **7.** Olvidarse. *To slip one's mind.* ~Se me ESCAPÓ su cumpleaños. *His birthday slipped my mind.* || **8.** [Palabra].

Slip out. ~Se me ESCAPÓ la palabra. *The word slipped out.* || **9.** •ESCAPÁRSELO algo a alguien. *To get away (something from someone).* ~Se me ESCAPÓ la cometa y el viento se la llevó. *The kite got away from me and the wind blew it away.* ⇨ ESCAPE

ESCENARIO. *sm.* [Teatro]. *Stage.* ~Había varios niños en el ESCENARIO. *There were several children on the stage.* || **2.** [De un suceso]. *Scene.* ~Los bomberos llegaron al ESCENARIO de los hechos. *The firefighters arrived on the scene.* ~La ceremonia tuvo por ESCENARIO la catedral. *The ceremony was held in the cathedral.* ⇨ SCENE/SCENARIO

ESPECTADOR [SPECTATOR]. *sm.* [De un accidente, espectáculo imprevisto]. *Onlooker.* || **2.** [Teatro, cine]. *Member of the audience.* ~LOS ESPECTADORES. *The audience, TV viewers.* || **3.** Testigo. *Observer.* Fui como simple ESPECTADOR. *I just went as an observer.* || **4.** •Una sala que tiene cabida para dos mil ESPECTADORES. *A theater that seats two thousand.*

ESPONTÁNEO [SPONTANEOUS]. *adj.* [Persona]. *Natural, unaffected.* || **2.** [Discurso, actuación]. *Impromptu, unprepared.*

ESTABLECER. *v.* Fundar (monarquía, orden). *To set up, found.* || **2.** [Gente]. *To settle.* ~Se ESTABLECIÓ en un pequeño pueblo cerca de Madrid. *He settled in a small town near Madrid.* || **3.** [Record, moda]. *To set.* || **4.** [Alegato]. *To justify, substantiate.* || **5.** Decretar, disponer (ley, reglamento). *To state, provide.* ~La ley ESTABLECE que. *The law provides (states) that.* ~Tres veces el precio ESTABLECIDO por la ley. *Three times the legal price.* || **6.** •Copérnico ESTABLECIÓ que la Tierra era redonda. *Copernicus proved that the Earth was round.* ⇨ ESTABLISH

ESTADO [STATE]. *sm.* [De enfermedad]. *Condition.* ~Su ESTADO es grave. *His condition is serious.* || **2.** [Relación]. *Summary.* || **3.** [De cuentas]. *Statement.* || **4.** Orden social. *Status, rank.* ~ESTADO civil. *Marital status.* || **5.** [Clase]. *Class.* ~En la sociedad medieval la nobleza constituía uno de los ESTADOS privilegiados. *In medieval society the nobility belonged to a* *priviledged class.*

ESTAMPA. *sf.* [En un libro]. *Picture, illustration.* ~A los niños les gustan los libros con ESTAMPAS. *Children like books with pictures.* || **2.** Aspecto, porte, presencia, aire (de una persona). *Aspect, look, appearance.* ~Ser la viva ESTAMPA de. *To be the spitting image of.* ~Un caballero de fina ESTAMPA. *A fine-looking gentleman.* || **3.** Marca. *Hallmark.* ~La ESTAMPA del genio. *The hallmark of genius.* || **4.** Imagen. *Print.* || **5.** Huella. *Imprint, footprint, track.* ~Dejó sus ESTAMPAS en la tierra mojada. *He left his footprints on the damp ground.* || **6.** Tarjeta religiosa. *Card bearing a religious picture.* || **7.** LIT Escena. *Scene.* ~El autor pintó muchas ESTAMPAS madrileñas. *The artist painted many scenes of Madrid.* || **8.** Litografía. *Litograph.* || **9.** Impresión. *Printing.* ~Dar una obra a la ESTAMPA. *To publish a book.* ⇨STAMP

ESTAMPAR [STAMP]. *v.* Imprimir (tela, diseño). *To print.* ~Una tela ESTAMPADA a mano. *A hand-printed fabric.* || **2.** Escribir. *To write.* ~ESTAMPÓ su firma al pie del documento. *He appended his signature to the document.* || **3.** Dejar impreso. *To engrave, imprint.* || **4.** Arrojar. *To hurl.* ~Estampó el libro contra la pared. *He hurled the book at the wall.* || **5.** Dar. *To plant, place.* ~Le ESTAMPÓ un beso en la frente. *She planted a kiss on his forehead.* || **6.** FIG •Aquellas escenas quedaron ESTAMPADAS en su memoria. *Those scenes remained engraved in his memory.*

ESTIMAR. Apreciar. *To esteem (hold in high esteem), respect, admire.* ~Era ESTIMADO por todo el mundo que lo conocía. *He was held in very high esteem by those who knew him.* || **2.** Tener sobre una cosa cierta opinión, considerar. *Consider, find that, deem.* ~No ESTIMO necesario que vayas tú. *I don't consider it necessary for you to go.* ~ESTIMÉ conveniente que otra persona lo sustituyera. *I considered advisable for someone else to replace him.* || **3.** Valorar (algo). *To be fond of, like, value.* ~ESTIMO mucho este reloj porque era de mi madre. *I value this clock*

very much because it belonged to my mother. ~ESTIMO su amistad. *I value your friendship.* | **4.** Sentir afecto por alguien. *To like, be fond of someone.* ~ESTIMO mucho a ese muchacho. *I'm very fond of this boy.* || **5.** Tener en gran estima. *To be highly prized.* ~Su piel es muy ESTIMADA. *It's skin is highly prized.* || **6.** Valorar, tasar. *To appraise, value.* ~Los peritos han ESTIMADO este cuadro en medio millón de pesetas. *Experts have appraised this painting at half a million pesetas.* ⇨ESTIMATE

ESTUPENDO [STUPENDOUS]. *adj.* Fantástico, maravilloso. *Super, marvelous, great, wonderful, terrific.* ~Tiene un coche ESTUPENDO. *He's got a marvelous car.* ~Hay chicas ESTUPENDAS. *There are some smashing girls.* ~Es ESTUPENDO para tocar la trompeta. *He's great on the trumpet.* ¡Estupendo! *Great!*

EVADIR. *v.* Eludir (respuesta, pregunta). *To avoid, sidestep.* || **2.** Responsibility. *To shirk, avoid.* || **3.** Evitar [daño, peligro]. *To avoid.* ⇨EVADE

EVALUAR. *v.* [Daños, pérdidas, situación]. *To assess.* ~Fue difícil EVALUAR la magnitud del suceso. *It was difficult to assess the importance of the event.* || **2.** [Alumno]. *To assess.* ~El profesor EVALÚA a sus alumnos cada tres meses. *The teacher assesses the work of his students every three months.* ⇨EVALUATE

EVENTO. Contingencia, eventualidad, Caso. *Occurrence, case.* ⇨EVENT

EVENTUAL [EVENTUAL]. *adj.* Casual. *Chance, unforeseen.* Circunstancias EVENTUALES modificaron el curso previsto de los acontecimientos. *Unforeseen circumstances altered the expected course of events.* ~Circunstancias EVENTUALES. *Chance circumstances.* || **2.** [Trabajo, obrero]. *Casual, temporary, provisional.* ~En esa empresa, los trabajadores EVENTUALES cobran por hora. *In that company, part-time workers are paid by the hour.* || **3.** [Oficial]. *Acting.* || **4.** [Solución]. *Stopgap.* || **5.** [Gastos, ingresos]. *Incidental, extra.* ~No declaró al fisco los* ingresos EVENTUALES que percibía en un segundo trabajo. *He did not declare on his income tax return the extra income derived from a second job.* || **6.** [Riesgos, pasivos]. *Contingent.* || **7.** Posible. *Possible.* ~Ante una EVENTUAL perdida. *Faced with a possible loss of.*

EVENTUALMENTE. *adj.* Casual o inciertamente. *Possibly, sometimes, on occasions, should the case arise, if and when, from time to time.* ~Las dificultades que EVENTUALMENTE podrían surgir. *The difficulties which might (possibly) arise.* ⇨EVENTUALLY

EVIDENCIA. *nf.* A la vista. *Obviousness.* ~Su carta estaba bien en EVIDENCIA sobre la mesa. *Her letter was lying on the table for everybody to see.* || **2.** •Poner alguien en EVIDENCIA. *To make a fool of somebody, to show somebody up.* ⇨EVIDENCE

EVOLUCIÓN [EVOLUTION]. *sf.* Desarrollo. *Development.* ~La EVOLUCIÓN científica ha permitido llegar a la luna. *Scientific development has made possible to go to the moon.* || **2.** Conjunto de movimientos (de un baile, etc.), giros, vueltas. *Movements, turns.* ~Las EVOLUCIONES de la bailarina. *The movements of the dancer.* || **3.** MIL Movimiento. *Maneuvers.* || **4.** Mejora, estado (de un enfermo). *Progress, condition.* || **5.** [De un avión, pájaro]. *Circle.* ~Viejos y niños contemplaban la EVOLUCIÓN de las palomas en torno a la plaza. *Young and old were contemplating the circling of doves around the square.* || **6.** Cambio. *Change.* La EVOLUCIÓN de la moda. *The change in fashion.*

EXAGERADO [EXAGGERATED]. *adj.* [Historia]. *Far-fetched.* || **2.** [Castigo]. *Excessive.* || **3.** [Precios]. *Exorbitant, steep, outrageous.* || **4.** [Gesto]. *Flamboyant.* || **5.** [Moda]. *Extravagant.* || **6.** •Ser EXAGERADO. *To overdo, go too far.* Es muy EXAGERADA con la comida. *She always makes far too much food.*

EXAGERAR [EXAGGERATE]. *v.* Pasarse de la raya. *To go too far.* Creo que eso sería EXAGERAR. *I think that would be going a bit too far.* || **2.** Abusar. *To overdo.* ~EXAGERAR

con los baños de sol. *To overdo one's sunbathing.* ~Tampoco hay que EXAGERAR, no tienes que acabarlo todo hoy. *There's no need to overdo it, you don't have to finish it all today.*

EXALTADO [EXALTED]. *adj.* [Discusión, discurso]. *Impassioned, heated.* || **2.** [Person]. *Excitable, hot-headed.* ~Un chico muy EXALTADO. *A very excitable boy.* || **3.** [Politics]. *Lunatic, hothead, extremist.* || **4.** [Estado, humor]. *Over-excited, worked up.* ~Los ánimos estaban EXALTADOS. *Feelings were running high.* ~Los EXALTADOS manifestantes profirieron insultos contra la policía. *The angry demonstrators hurled insults at the police.* ~Estaba muy EXALTADO y no sabía lo que decía. *He was really worked up and he didn't know what he was saying.*

EXALTAR[1] [EXALT]. *v.* Elevar. *To promote, raise.* ~EXALTAR al grado de general. *To promote to the rank of general.* || **2.** Ensalzar, elogiar, alabar. *Praise, extol.* EXALTÓ sus hazañas. *He extolled their feats.* || **3.** [Imaginación]. *To fire.* || **4.** Excitar (persona). *To excite.* || **5.** [Pasión, ira]. *To arouse.* ~Sus palabras *exaltaban* la ira de los asistentes. *His words aroused the anger of those present.*

EXALTARSE[2] [EXALT]. *vr.* Enardecerse. *To get overexcited, get carried away, get worked up.* ~Se EXALTA cuando habla de política. *He gets overexcited when he talks about politics.* || **2.** [En discusión]. *To get heated.* || **3.** [Emoción]. *To run high, become very intense.* ~¡No te EXALTES! *Don't get so worked-up!*

EXAMEN. *sm.* Análisis, reconocimiento. *Search, study.* ~Efectuaron un detallado EXAMEN de la zona. *They carried out a detailed search of the area.* ~Realizaron un minucioso EXAMEN de la situación. *They carried out an in-depth study of the situation.* || **2.** [De problema]. *Consideración.* || **3.** [De conducir]. *Test.* || **4.** [Médico]. *Checkup.* || **5.** Inspección. *Inspection.* || **6.** Indagación. *Survey, inquiry, investigation.* || **7.** [De testigos]. *Interrogatorio.* || **8.** [Cus-

toms]. *Registro.* || **9.** [Accounts]. *Revisión.*
⇨EXAMINATION

EXAMINAR. *v.* [Poner a prueba]. *To test.* ||
2. Inspeccionar. *To inspect, look through,
go over.* || **3.** Indagar. *To inquire into,
investigate, look into.* || **4.** Mirar deteni-
damente. *Estudiar.* || **5.** [Situación, caso].
To study, consider. ⇨EXAMINE

EXCITAR. *v.* [Emociones]. *To arouse, stir
up.* ~El discurso EXCITÓ la ira de los
asistentes. *His speech aroused the anger
of the audience.* || **2.** [Duda, esperanza]. *To
raise.* || **3.** Incitar. *Incite, urge on.* ~EXCITAR
el pueblo a la rebelión. *To incite the populace
to rebellion.* || **4.** [Deseo, apetito, curiosity].
To arouse. ~El ejercicio físico EXCITÓ nuestras
ganas de comer. *The physical exercise aroused our appetite.* ~Estas palabras misteriosas
EXCITARON todavía más su curiosidad. *Those
mysterious words aroused his curiosity even
more.* ⇨EXCITE

EXCUSAS. *nf* Disculpas. *Apologies.*
~Presentó sus EXCUSAS. *He apologized.*
⇨EXCUSE²

EXCUSAR. *v.* Evitar. *Avoid, prevent.* ~Así
EXCUSAMOS problemas. *This way we avoid
problems.* ~Se lo contó EXCUSANDO los
detalles más desagradables. *He told them but
spared them the most unpleasant details.*||
2. Olvidar, no tomar en cuenta. *Forget, pass
over.* ~Podemos EXCUSAR lo otro. *We can
forget about the rest.* || **3.** Ahorrar (sacrificio,
esfuerzo). *Not to have to, to save the
trouble of.* EXCUSAMOS decirle que. *We don't
have to tell you that.* ~Por esto EXCUSO
escribirte más largo. *So I can save myself
the trouble of writing at greater length.* ||
4. •EXCUSO decirle que. *Needless to say
that.* || **5.** •El que se EXCUSA se acusa. *To
excuse oneself is to accuse onself.* ⇨EXCUSE¹

EXHIBICIÓN. *sf.* [Cine]. *Showing, screen-
ing.* || **2.** Demostración. *Display.* ~Haciendo
EXHIBICIÓN de su fuerza. *Displaying (showing
off) his strength.* ~No le gusta hacer
EXHIBICIÓN de sus sentimientos. *He doesn't
like to reveal his feelings.* ⇨EXHIBITION

EXHIBIR. *v.* [Película]. *To show, screen.*

~Una película que EXHIBIERON en Madrid
hace un par de años. *A movie which was
shown in Madrid a couple of years ago.* ||
2. Mostrar con orgullo (regalo, trofeo). *To
show, show off.* || **3.** [Modelos, colección].
To show, display. ~Los modelos que EXHI-
BIERON en el desfile. *The designs on display
at the show.* ⇨EXHIBIT

EXPANDIR. *v.* [Ropa]. *To spread out.* || **2.**
Propagar, difundir (noticia). *To spread.* ~La
noticia se EXPANDIÓ rápidamente. *The news
spread rapidly.* || **3.** Divulgar. *To spread.*
~EXPANDIR la afición a la lectura. *To spread
the love of reading.* ⇨EXPAND

EXPANSIÓN [EXPANSION]. *sf.* Crecimiento.
Growth. ~La EXPANSIÓN económica. *Econo-
mic growth.* || **2.** Difusión (de una noticia,
doctrina). *Spreading.* || **3.** Diversión. *Relaxa-
tion, recreation.* || **4.** Efusión. *Expansiveness.*
~Su EXPANSIÓN de alegría contagió a toda la
familia. *His outburst of joy spread to the
entire family.* || **5.** Franquesa. *Frankness,
openness.* || **6.** Propagación. *Spreading.*
~La EXPANSIÓN de la epidemia produjo
numerosas muertes. *The spreading of the
epidemic caused many deaths.*

EXPECTACIÓN. Emoción, gran curiosidad
o interés. *Excitement, suspense,
anticipation.* ~La EXPECTACIÓN crece de un
momento a otro. *The excitement is growing
every moment.* ~Su visita produjo una gran
EXPECTACIÓN. *The prospect of her visit
created a great deal of excitement.* ⇨EXPEC-
TATION

EXPEDICIÓN [EXPEDITION]. *sf.* Envío.
Dispatch, shipping. ~Empaquetaban las
mercancías para su EXPEDICIÓN. *They
packaged the merchandise to be shipped.*
~Gastos de EXPEDICIÓN. *Shipping charges.* ||
2. Conjunto de mercancía. *Shipment.*
~Mandó la EXPEDICIÓN por vía aérea. *He sent
the shipment by air mail.* || **3.** Prontitud.
Speed. || **4.** [De documentos, billetes,
pasaporte]. *Issuing, issue.* ~Lugar y fecha de
EXPEDICIÓN. *Place and date of issue.* ~Venta
de billetes, EXPEDICIÓN inmediata. *Tickets sold
and issued on the spot.* || **5.** [De un telegrama,
carta]. *Sending.* ~¿Cuál es la fecha de

EXPEDICIÓN?. *On what date was the letter sent?* || **6.** [De un asunto]. *Dispatch.* •EXPEDICIÓN de salvamento. *Rescue mission, rescue party, search party.*

EXPEDIENTE [EXPEDIENT]. Legajo. *File, dossier.* ~Ponga este documento en el EXPEDIENTE del Sr. Gómez. *Put this document in Mr. Gómez's file.* || **2.** Investigación. *Investigation, inquiry.* ~Se abrirá un EXPEDIENTE informativo. *An inquiry will be held.* || **3.** Medidas disciplinarias. *Disciplinary action (proceedings).* || **4.** LOCUCIONES. || •Abrir un EXPEDIENTE. *To take disciplinary action.* || •El EXPEDIENTE del paciente. *The patient's (medical) record.* || •EXPEDIENTE académico. *Student record.* || •Un arquitecto con un brillante EXPEDIENTE profesional. *An arquitect with a brilliant track record.* || •Cubrir el EXPEDIENTE. *To do enough to get by.*

EXPEDIR. *v.* [Pasaporte, título]. *To issue.* ~Pasaporte EXPEDIDO en París. *Passport issued in Paris.* || **2.** [Contrato, documento]. *To draw up.* || **3.** Despachar (carta). *To send, dispatch.* || **4.** [Mercancías]. *To send, dispatch, ship, forward.* ~Para EXPEDIR paquetes certificados, hay que rellenar un impreso. *To ship registered packages, you must fill out a form.* || **5.** [Asunto]. *To deal with, dispatch, dispose of.* ⇨EXPEDITE

EXPERIMENTAR [EXPERIMENT]. *v.* Sentir. *Feel.* ~EXPERIMENTÉ un gran pesar cuando supe que te marchabas. *I was very sad when I heard that you were leaving.* || **2.** [Pérdida]. *Suffer.* ~La Bolsa ha EXPERIMENTADO fuertes pérdidas. *The stock market has suffered great losses.* || **3.** [Aumento]. *To show.* ~Las cifras han EXPERIMENTADO un aumento de un 5 por 100%. *The figures show an increase of 5%.* || **4.** [Cambio]. *To undergo.* || **5.** •EXPERIMENTAR una mejoría. *To improve, make progress.* || **6.** Probar. *To try out.* ~EXPERIMENTÓ la nueva batidora y se dio cuenta que no funcionaba. *He tried out the new mixer (blender) and realized it wasn't working.* || **7.** [Precios]. *To increase, go up.* ~El precio de la gasolina ha EXPERIMENTADO una subida. *The price of gasoline has increased.*

EXPLORAR. *v.* [Herida]. *To probe, examine.* ~El médico EXPLORÓ el pecho del paciente. *The doctor examined the patient's chest.* || **2.** [Radar]. *To scan.* || **3.** [Mina, yacimiento]. *To prospect, drill.* || **4.** MIL Reconocer. *Reconnoiter, scout.* || **5.** [Situación]. *To examine, investigate.* || **6.** [Con la vista]. *To scan.* || **7.** •EXPLORAR el terreno. *To see how the land lies.* ⇨EXPLORE

EXPLOTAR [EXPLOIT]. *v.* [Mina, veta]. *To work.* ~Van a volver a EXPLOTAR esta antigua mina de carbón. *They're going to work this old coal mine again.* || **2.** [Recursos]. *To tap.* || **3.** [Fábrica, negocio]. *To operate, run.* || **4.** [Tierra]. *To cultivate, to farm.* || **5.** [Bomba]. *To explode, go off.* ~La bomba EXPLOTÓ en una calle céntrica de Barcelona. *The bomb exploded in one of the main streets of Barcelona.*

EXPONER. Poner a la vista. *Display.* ~EXPUSIERON los trofeos en la vitrina. *They displayed the trophies in the showcase.* || **2.** To explain. *Dar a conocer (ideas, parecer).* Nos EXPUSO las razones de su dimisión. *He explained the reasons for his resigning.* || **3.** Presentar (una obra). *Exhibit.* ~El pintor EXPONDRÁ sus últimas creaciones en una galería de arte. *The painter will exhibit his latest paintings in an art gallery.* || **4.** Arriesgar, comprometer. *To risk, endanger, jeopardize.* ~En este asunto EXPONES tu reputación. *In this affair you are risking your reputation.* ~EXPONER la vida. *To risk one's life.* ⇨EXPOSE

EXPOSICIÓN [EXPOSITION]. *sf.* [Muestra de cuadros, esculturas]. *Exhibition, show, display, showing.* ~Hemos ido a ver una EXPOSICIÓN de pintura. *We went to see a painting exhibition.* || **2.** [De productos, maquinaria]. *Show.* ~Una EXPOSICIÓN de flores. *A flower show.* ~EXPOSICIÓN del automóvil. *Motor show.* ~EXPOSICIÓN canina. *Dog show.* EXPOSICIÓN de modas. *Fashion show.* || **3.** Explicación. *Account, claim, explanation.* ~Hizo una EXPOSICIÓN detallada de lo ocurrido. *She gave a detailed account of what had happened.* ~El periódico hace una EXPOSICIÓN clara de los hechos. *The paper gives a clear explanation of the facts.* || **4.** [De hechos, ideas]. *Exposé.* || **5.** [Fotografía]. *Exposure.* || **6.** [Al aire, sol]. *Exposure.* La prolongada EXPOSICIÓN de la piel al sol puede provocar graves quemaduras. *Prolonged exposure of the skin to the sun can cause serious burns.* || **7.** Riesgo. *Risk, danger.* ~Quiere ganar dinero sin EXPOSICIÓN. *He wants to make money without getting caught.* || **8.** •EXPOSICIÓN universal. *World fair.* || **9.** •EXPOSICIÓN comercial (industrial). *Trade fair.* || **10.** •Sala de EXPOSICIONES. *Gallery.*

EXTENDER[1]. *v.* [En general]. *To spread.* || **2.** Abrir, desdoblar. *Spread (out).* ~EXTENDIO un pañuelo sobre el pasto para sentarse. *He spread out a handkerchief on the grass so he could sit down.* ~EXTENDIÓ el mapa. *He spread out the map.* ~El ave EXTENDIÓ las alas. *The bird spread its wings.* || **2.** Dar (la mano). *To hold out, stretch out.* ~EXTENDIÓ la mano. *He held out his hand.* || **3.** [Pasaporte, certificado]. *To issue, grant (certificate of merit).*~Le EXTENDIERON un certificado. *They issued (granted) him a certificate.* || **4.** Escribir (cheque). *Write out.* ~¿A nombre de quién EXTIENDO el cheque? *To whom do I make the check payable?* || **5.** [Documento]. *Draw up.* || **6.** [Recibo]. *To make out.* || **7.** Tender (ropa). *Hang out.* || **8.** Poner una capa de barniz. *To apply a coat (of varnish, paint).* || **9.** Esparcir, repartir en más espacio. *To spread.* ~EXTENDÍA mantequilla sobre el pan. *He was spreading butter on his bread.* ~EXTENDER bien la crema por todo el rostro. *Spread the cream over the entire face.* || **10.** Derramar. *To scatter.* ~El viento EXTENDIÓ las hojas por todo el jardín. *The wind scattered the leaves all over the garden.* ~EXTENDIÓ los papeles por toda la mesa. *He scattered the papers all over the table.* || **11.** [Conocimientos]. *To expand.* ~Al estudiar los estudiantes EXTIENDEN cada vez más sus conocimientos. *By studying students increasingly expand their knowledge.* ⇨ EXTEND

EXTENDERSE[2]. *vr.* || Propagarse, difundirse (noticia). *Spread.* ~El rumor se EXTEN-

DIÓ rápidamente. *The rumor spread quickly.* ~La humedad se ha EXTENDIDO a la habitación de al lado. *The dampness has spread to the next room.* ~El incendio se EXTENDIÓ al tejado. *The fire spread to (reached) the roof.* ~Han EXTENDIDO la fe cristiana por todo el mundo. *They have spread the Christian faith throughout the world.* || **2.** Abarcar, ocupar (terreno). *Spread out, stretch (also extend).* Sus propiedades se EXTIENDEN hasta el río. *His property stretches down to the river.* || **3.** Dilatarse, explayarse, aparecer a la vista (una gran extensión). *Open up, widen, stretch out.* ~Delante de nosotros se EXTENDÍA el mar. *The sea lay spread out before us.* ~El campo se EXTENDÍA hasta el horizonte. *The countryside stretched to the horizon.* || **4.** Hablar detenidamente (sobre un tema). *To enlarge upon, go on about, expand on.* ~Siempre se EXTIENDE demasiado en sus clases. *He always goes on too long in his classes.* Ya nos hemos EXTENDIDO bastante sobre este tema. *We've already spent enough time on this subject.* ~¿Quisiera EXTENDERSE sobre ese punto? *Would you like to expand (enlarge) on that point?* ~Se EXTENDIÓ en la descripción de su viaje. *He expanded on the description of his trip.* || **5.** [Cartas]. *Lay down.* || **15.** [Guerra]. *Widen, escalate.* || **6.** Durar (tiempo). *To last.* ~El periodo que se EXTIENDE hasta la Revolución Francesa. *The period ending with the French Revolution.* ~El invierno se ha EXTENDIDO mucho. *This winter has lasted a long time.* || **7.** Echarse, tenderse, tumbarse. *To stretch out.* ~Se EXTENDIÓ en el suelo. *He stretched out on the ground.* || **8.** Derramarse, dispersarse. *To scatter.* Todos los papeles se han EXTENDIDO por el suelo. *All the papers were scattered on the floor.* || **9.** •EXTENDERSE a (cantidad). *Amount, reach, go as high as.* ~El libro se EXTIENDE a 400 páginas. *The book runs to 400 pages.* ~La deuda se EXTIENDE a dos mil millones de pesetas. *The debt amounts to two thousand millon pesetas.* || **10.** •EXTENDERSE en consideraciones sobre algo. *To expound something at length.* ⇨EXTEND

EXTENSIÓN. *sf.* [Tierra, mar]. *Stretch,*

expanse, surface area. ~Una EXTENSIÓN de tierra. *A stretch of land.* || **2.** [Discurso, obra, programa]. *Duration, length.* ~Debido a la EXTENSIÓN de la obra, no habrá intermedio. *Due to the duration of the performance, there will be no intermission.* ~Escribir un ensayo cuya EXTENSIÓN no supere las 200 palabras. *To write an essay of no more than 200 words.* || **3.** Dimensión, tamaño. *Extent, size.* ¿Qué EXTENSIÓN tiene la finca? *How large (what is the size) of the farm?* || **4.** [Music]. *Range.* || **5.** [Conocimiento]. *Extent, range.* ~La EXTENSIÓN de mis conocimientos. *The extent of my knowledge.* || **6.** Alcance, importancia (plan, programa, poder). *Scope.* ~La EXTENSIÓN de su poder es inimaginable. *The scope of his power is unimaginable.* || **7.** •En toda la EXTENSIÓN de la palabra. *In every sense of the word.* ⇨ EXTENSION

EXTENUARSE. *vr.* Agotarse, debilitarse, cansarse. *To waste away, get exhausted.* ~Le han EXTENUADO la caminata y el calor. *He's worn out with the heat and the long walk.* ⇨ EXTENUATE

EXTERIOR² [EXTERIOR]. *adj.* Fuera. *Outside.* ~Salgamos al EXTERIOR para tomar un poco de aire. *Let's go outside for a little air.* || **2.** [Pared]. *Outer.* ~La pared EXTERIOR de la iglesia es de granito. *The outer wall of the church is made of granite.* || **3.** [Cuarto]. *Outward.* ~Quisiera alquilar una habitación EXTERIOR que tenga mucha luz. *I would like*

to rent an outside-facing room which is well-lighted. || **4.** [Política, deuda, relaciones]. *Foreign.* ~El tratado estrechó las relaciones EXTERIORES entre los países europeos. *The treaty improved foreign relations between the European countries.* ~Asuntos EXTERIORES. *Foreign affairs.* ~Comercio EXTERIOR. *Foreign trade.*

EXTERIOR²· *sm.* [Aspecto]. *Outside.* ~Me gusta más el EXTERIOR del palacio que el interior. *I prefer the outside of the palace to the inside.* || **2.** [De una persona]. *Outward appearance.* Aunque su EXTERIOR resulta agradable, realmente es antipático. *Although he's outwardly friendly, he's really an unpleasant person.*

EXTINGUIR¹. *v.* [Deuda, raza]. *Wipe out, exterminate.* || **2.** [Sublevación]. *To put down (a rebellion).* || **3.** [Sentencia]. *To serve.* || **4.** [Violencia, injusticia]. *To put an end to.* ⇨ EXTINGUISH

EXTINGUIRSE². *vr.* [Sonido]. *To die away.* || **2.** Morir. *To die.* ~Su amor se EXTINGUIÓ. *His love died away.* || **3.** Apagarse. *To go out (fuego).* || **4.** [Especie]. *To become extinct, die out.* || **5.** Vencer. *To expire.* ~El contrato se ha EXTINGUIDO. *The contract has expired.* ⇨ EXTINGUISH

EXTRAVAGANTE. *adj.* Estrafalario, excéntrico. *Excentric.* || **2.** Raro. *Odd, strange, weird.* ⇨ EXTRAVAGANT

F

FABRICACIÓN. *sf.* Producción. *Manufacture, production, making.* ~De FABRICACIÓN propia. *Our own make, made on the premises.* ~FABRICACIÓN de tejas. *Tile making.* ~Televisores de FABRICACIÓN japonesa. *Japanese-made televisions.* ~De FABRICACIÓN casera. Home-made. ⇨FABRICATION

FABRICAR. *v.* Producir, manufacturar. *To manufacture, make.* ~FABRICAR automóviles. *To manufacture cars.* ~FABRICADO en España. *Made in Spain.* ~FABRICAR en serie. *To mass-produce.* FABRICAR cerveza. *To brew beer.* || **2.** Elaborar. *To produce.* ~La seda es FABRICADA por un gusano. *Silk is produced by a worm.* ~La abeja FABRICA la miel. *Bees produce honey.* || **3.** Conseguir, lograr. *To make.* ~En pocos años FABRICÓ una fortuna. *In the span of a few years he managed to make a fortune.* || **4.** Edificar. *To build, construct.* ⇨FABRICATE

FÁBULA [FABLE]. *sf.* Mito. *Myth, legend.* ~Existen muchas FÁBULAS sobre los dioses griegos. *There are numerous myths about Greek gods.* || **2.** Mentira. *Invention, fabrication.* ~Esta historia es una FÁBULA. *The story is an invention.* ~Déjate de FÁBULAS y dinos la verdad. *Stop inventing things and tell us the truth.* || **3.** Argumento. *Plot, story, action.* || **4.** Rumor. *Rumor.* Suena por la oficina una FÁBULA sobre varios despidos. *There are rumors going around the office that there's going to be some layoffs.* || **5.** Chisme. *Piece of gossip.* || **6.** Hazmerreír (persona). *Talk of the town, laughing-stock.* ~Fulano es la FÁBULA de Madrid. *So-and-so is the laughing-stock of Madrid.* || **7.** •De FÁBULA. *Fabulous.* ~Vamos a bañarnos, que el agua hoy es de

FÁBULA. *Let's go for a swim, the water today is fabulous.*

FACCIÓN. *sf.* Grupo de insurrectos. *Breakaway group, hostile group, troublemaker.* || **2.** Rasgos (de la cara). *Features.* ~Hermosas FACCIONES. *Beautiful features.* ⇨FACTION

FACILIDAD. *sf.* Cualidad de fácil. *Ease.* ~Se rompe con FACILIDAD. *It breaks easily.* ~Ahora tiene mayor FACILIDAD para viajar. *Now it's easier for him to travel.* ~Con gran FACILIDAD. *Easily.* ~Dar FACILIDADES. *To make things easy.* ~FACILIDADES de pago. *Easy terms.* || **2.** Talent. *Abilidad, aptitud.* ~Tiene FACILIDAD para los idiomas. *He has a gift for languages.* ~Tiene FACILIDAD para los números. *She's very good with numbers.* ~Tiene FACILIDAD de palabra. *He has a way with words.* || **3.** Posibilidades, oportunidades. *Chance, opportunities.* ~Se le dieron todas las FACILIDADES del mundo. *They gave him every chance.* || **4.** •¿Dan FACILIDADES? *Do you give credit?* ⇨FACILITY

FACILITAR [FACILITATE]. *v.* Simplificar. *To make easy, easier, simplify.* ~Tu actitud no FACILITA las cosas. *Your attitude doesn't make things any easier.* ~El satélite FACILITARÁ las comunicaciones. *The satellite will make communications easier.* || **2.** Proporcionar, suministrar. *To provide, supply, furnish.* ~Nos FACILITARÁN todo el equipo. *They'll provide us with all the equipment.* ~¿Quién FACILITÓ el dinero? *Who provided the money?* ~Me FACILITÓ un coche. *He provided me with a car.* || **3.** [Entrevista]. *To arrange (an interview).* || **4.** Agilizar. *To expedite.* || **5.** [Documento]. *To issue.* || **7.** •Se le FACILITA física. *He's good at physics.*

FACULTAD. *sf.* Universidad. *University.* ~Fue compañero mío en la FACULTAD. *He was at the University with me.* ~Quedarse a comer en la FACULTAD. *To have lunch at the University.* || **2.** Autoridad. *Power, authority.* ~Eso no está dentro de sus FACULTADES. *That is beyond the scope of your powers.* || **3.** MED Fuerza, resistencia. *Strength, resistance.* ~El estómago no tiene FACULTAD para digerir el alimento. *The stomach does not have the strength to digest food.* || **4.** •Tener FACULTAD para hacer algo. *To be authorized to do something.* || **5.** [Universidad]. *Department.* ~Es catedrático en la FACULTAD de Filología Románica. *He's a professor in the Romance Philology department.* || **6.** •FACULTADES mentales. *Mental power.* ~Cuando escribió su testamento estaba en plenas FACULTADES mentales. *When he wrote his will he was mentally competent.* ⇨FACULTY

FALACIA. *sf.* Falsedad, mentira. *False-hood.* ~¿Cómo has podido creer tal FALACIA? *How could you believe such a falsehood?* || **2.** Engaño, fraude. *Deceit, fraud, trick.* || **3.** Hábito de engañar. *Deceitfulness.* ⇨FALLACY

FALLAR. *v.* To miss. *Errar.* ~FALLAR el blanco. *To miss the target.* || **2.** [Derecho]. *To pronounce sentence on, pass judgement.* ~FALLAR en favor/contra de alguien. *To rule in favor/against somebody.* || **3.** [Premio, concurso]. *Award, decide on.* ~FALLAR un premio literario. *To award a literary award.* || **4.** Ceder (apoyo, cuerda). *To break, snap, give way, collapse.* ~FALLÓ la rama en que se sostenía y cayó a tierra. *The branch he was leaning on gave way and he fell down.* || **5.** [Piernas]. *To give way.* || **6.** [Fusil]. *To misfire, fail to go off.* || **7.** [Motor]. *To miss.* || **8.** Decepcionar. *To let down.* ~Prometió ayudarnos pero nos FALLÓ. *He promised he would help us but he let us down.* || **9.** No funcionar, andar mal. *Not to work properly, go wrong.* ~Algo FALLÓ y se estrellaron. *Something went wrong and they crashed.* || **10.** No acertar. *To prove wrong.* ~Sus pronósticos FALLARON. *His forecasts proved wrong.* ⇨FAIL

FALSIFICACION [FALSIFICATION]. *sf.* [De cuadros, firma]. *Forging, forgery.* ~Se le acusa de haber cometido FALSIFICACIÓN de documentos. *He's accused of forging documents.* || **2.** [De moneda]. *Counterfeiting.* ~Han desarticulado una banda que se dedicaba a la FALSIFICACIÓN de billetes. *They've broken up a counterfeiting ring.* || **3.** [Objeto]. *Forgery.*

FALSIFICAR. *v.* [Cuadro, firma]. *To forge.* ~FALSIFICÓ la firma de su padre en el cheque. *He forged his father's name on the check.* || **2.** [Dinero]. *To counterfeit, forge.* ⇨FALSIFY

FALSO. *adj.* [Persona]. *Insincere, hollow, dishonest.* ~María es muy FALSA; promete cosas que no tiene intención de cumplir. *Mary is very insincere; she makes promises she doesn't intend to keep.* || **2.** [Cuadro, sello]. *Forged, fake, bogus.* || **3.** [Joya]. *Imitation, fake.* ~Todas las joyas que lleva son FALSAS. *All the pieces of jewelry she's wearing are fake.* || **4.** [Caballo, mula]. *Vicious.* || **5.** [Opinión, teoría]. *Unsound.* || **6.** [Medida]. *Incorrect, wrong, inexact.* Una medida FALSA. *An incorrect measurement.* || **7.** LOCUCIONES. || •Puerta FALSA. *Concealed door.* || •Jurar en FALSO. *To commit perjury.* || •Dar un paso en FALSO. (I) [Tropezar]. *To trip, stumble,* (II) [Cometer un error]. *To make a blunder (wrong move).*|| •Golpear en FALSO. *To miss the mark.* || •Esta tabla está en FALSO. *This board isn't properly supported.* || •La maleta cerró en FALSO. *The suitcase didn't shut properly.* || •El tornillo giraba en FALSO. *The screw wouldn't grip.* ⇨FALSE

FALTA. *sf.* Carencia. *Lack.* ~Por FALTA de fondos. *Owing to a lack of funds.* ~No pudo terminar for FALTA de tiempo. *We couldn't finish it because we ran out of time.* || **2.** Escasez. *Shortage.* ~FALTA de agua. *Water shortage.* || **3.** Ausencia. *Absence.* ~He notado tu FALTA en la fiesta. *I noted you were absent at the party.* ~Tiene más de 30 FALTAS. *She has been* absent over 30 times. ‖ **4.** Error. *Mistake.* ~Tu redacción está llena de FALTAS. *Your composition is full of mistakes.* ~FALTA de ortografía. *Spelling mistake.* ‖ **5.** Mala acción, fechoría. *Misdeed.* ~Confesó sus FALTAS al sacerdote. *He confessed his sins to the priest.* ‖ **6.** [Infracción]. *Misdemeanor.* ~Incurrir en una FALTA grave. *To commit a serious misdemeanor.* ‖ **7.** DEP Infracción. *Foul.* ~El jugador cometió una FALTA y el árbitro lo expulsó del campo. *He committed a foul and the referee ejected him.* ‖ **8.** Fallo. *Failure, shortcoming.* ‖ **9.** [De fabricación]. *Flaw, defect.* ~Esta tela es más barata porque tiene una FALTA en la manga. *This fabric is cheaper because there's a flaw on the sleeve.* ‖ **10.** Tiro libre. *Free kick (en fútbol), free throw (en balónmano).* ‖ **11.** LOCUCIONES. ‖ •Hacer FALTA. *To be necessary.* ~Ahora sólo hace FALTA que llueve. *All we need now is for it to rain.* ~FALTA una escalera. *We need a ladder.* ‖ •Echar en FALTA. *To miss.* ‖ •Sin FALTA. *Without fail.* ‖ •FALTA de educación. *Bad manners.* ~Es FALTA de educación poner los codos en la mesa. *It's bad manners to put your elbows on the table.* ⇨FAULT

FAMA [FAME]. *sf.* Reputación. *Reputation.* ~Tiene FAMA de mentiroso. *He has a reputation of being a liar.* ~Tener FAMA de buen cazador. *To be known as a great hunter.* ~Tiene buena/mala FAMA. *He has a good/bad reputation.* ~Es un barrio de MALA fama. *It's a disreputable area.* ‖ **2.** Rumor. *Rumor, report.* ~Corre la FAMA de que ... *It is rumored that ...*

FAMILIAR. *adj.* De la familia. *Family, of the familiy.* ~Fiesta FAMILIAR. *Family reunion (get-together).* ~Los lazos FAMILIARES. *The family bonds, the ties of blood.* ~Subsidio FAMILIAR. *Family allowance.* ~Un restaurante de ambiente FAMILIAR. *A family restaurant.* Retrato FAMILIAR. ~*Family portrait.* ~Coche FAMILIAR. *Family car.* ‖ **2.** Informal (lenguaje). *Colloquial.* ~Expresión FAMILIAR. *Colloquial expression.* ‖ **3.** Casero. *Homely, domestic.* ‖ **4.** Sin ceremonia. *Informal, friendly.* ~Nos

dieron un trato FAMILIAR y estuvimos muy a gusto en su casa. *They treated us in a very friendly way and we enjoyed our stay at their home.* ‖ **5.** [Producto]. *Family-size.* ~Compra el gel FAMILIAR, que nos durará más de lo normal. *Buy the family-size gel, which will last us longer.* ⇨FAMILIAR

FANTASÍA [FANTASY]. *sf.* Imaginación. *Imagination.* ~Era sólo un producto de su FANTASÍA. *It was just a product (figment) of his imagination.* ~Los niños tiene una enorme FANTASÍA. *Children have a great deal of imagination.* ‖ **2.** Bisutería. *Item of custom jewelry.* ‖ **3.** Capricho. *Whim, fancy.* ‖ **4.** Afectación, presunción. *Conceit, vanity, airs.* ‖ **5.** •De FANTASÍA. (I) [Joya]. *Imitation* (used as adjective). ~Una joya de FANTASÍA. *A piece of imitation jewelry,* (II) [Artículos]. *Fancy.* Artículos, chaleco de FANTASÍA. *Fancy goods, waistcoat.*

FASTIDIOSO. *adj.* Molesto. *Annoying, vexing, bothersome, irksome, irritating, getting on somebody's nerves.* ¡Qué ruido más FASTIDIOSO! *What an irritating noise.* ~Este niño está muy FASTIDIOSO. *This child is getting on my nerves.* ~Es un tipo FASTIDIOSO. *He's an irritating sort of person.* ‖ **2.** Dañado. *Damaged, in bad condition.* ~Tiene el estómago FASTIDIADO. *He's got a bad stomach.* ~Su padre está FASTIDIADO. *Her father is in a bad way.* ‖ **3.** Aburrido (trabajo). *Tedious, tiresome, boring.* ~Es FASTIDIOSO tener que trabajar hasta tan tarde. *It's tiresome (tedious, boring) to have to work that late.* ‖ **4.** Asqueroso. *Sickening, disgusting.* ⇨FASTIDIOUS

FATAL. *adj.* Inevitable, ineludible. *Unavoidable, fated.* ~El paso por su casa para ir a la mía es FATAL. *Passing her house to go to mine is inevitable.* El destino FATAL así lo había escrito. *It was destined to happen.* ‖ **2.** Pésimo, muy malo. *Awful, terrible.* ~Tiene un inglés FATAL. *He speaks terrible English.* ~Lo pasaron FATAL. *They had a terrible time.* ~La obra estuvo FATAL. *The play was really bad.* ~Los niños están FATALES hoy. *The children are behaving terribly today.* ~Tener una suerte FATAL. *To have terrible luck.* ‖ **3.** Muy desacertado.

Wrong, mistaken. Ha estado FATAL en su intervención. *His involvement was misguided.* ⇨FATAL

FATALIDAD. *sf.* Destino. *Fate.* ~La FATALIDAD desempeñó un importante papel en la antigua religión griega. *Fate played an important role in ancient Greek religion.* || **2.** Desgracia, desdicha. *Misfortune, ill-luck.* ~Fue una FATALIDAD que no pudieras venir. *It was unfortunate that you could not come.* ~Tuvo la FATALIDAD de caerse por las escaleras. *He had the misfortune of falling down the stairs.* ⇨FATALITY

FATUO. *adj.* Engreído, vanidoso. *Conceited, vain.* ⇨FATUOUS

FELONÍA. *sf.* Deslealtad. *Disloyalty.* || **2.** Betrayal, treachery. *Traición.* ⇨FELONY

FENOMENAL [PHENOMENAL]. *adj.* Fantástico, estupendo. *Great, terrific.* ~Es un tipo FENOMENAL. *He's a fantastic guy.* || **2.** Enorme. *Collosal, huge.* ~Mi diste un susto FENOMENAL. *You scared me to death.* || **3.** Extraordinario. *Extraordinary.* ~Un talento FENOMENAL. *An extraordinary talent.* || **4.** *adv.* Estupendamente. *Wonderfully, marvelously.* ~Lo pasamos FENOMENAL. *We had a wonderful time.*

FIGURAR[1]. *v.* Representar. *To represent.* ~¿Qué FIGURAN estas rayas rojas? *What do these red lines represent?* || **2.** Simular. *To simulate, feign, pretend.* ~FIGURÓ estar muerto. *He pretended to be dead.* || **3.** Destacar. *To stand out, be important.* ~Es la persona que más FIGURA en la alta sociedad. *He's the most important person in high society.* || **4.** Aparentar. *To show off.* ~Todo se debe al afán de FIGURAR. *It's the urge to be somebody that causes it all.* || **5.** [En una lista, documento]. *To appear.* ~Su nombre no FIGURA en la lista. *His name doesn't appear on the list.* ⇨FIGURE

FIGURARSE[2]. *vr.* Imaginarse. *Imagine, suppose, suspect.* ~Nunca me lo hubiera FIGURADO. *I would have never suspected it.* ~Ya me lo FIGURABA. *I thought as much.* ⇨FIGURE

FILA [FILE]. *sm.* [De cine, teatro]. *Row.* ~En la primera FILA. *In the front row.* || **2.** Hilera. *Line.* ~Una FILA de coches. *A line of cars.* ~Formen FILA aquí para comprar las entradas. *Form a line here to buy your tickets.* || **3.** [Política]. *Ranks.* Milita en las FILAS socialistas. *He's active in (the ranks of) the socialist party.* || **4.** [De gente esperando]. *Line.* ~¡Póngase en FILA! *Line up!* || **5.** *LOCUCIONES.* || •Alistarse en FILAS. *To sign up.* || •Aparcar en doble FILA. *To double-park.* || •Apretar las FILAS, cerrar filas. *To close ranks.* ~Cerraron FILAS en torno a su líder. *They closed ranks around their leader.* || •Estar en FILAS. *To be in active service, to be in the army.* || •¡En FILA! *Fall in!* || •FILAS. *Ranks.* •Formar FILAS. *To fall in.* || •Incorporarse a las FILAS. *To join up.* || •Llamar a uno a FILAS. *To call somebody up, to be drafted.* ~Lo llamaron a FILAS. *He was drafted.* || •Romper FILAS. *To fall out, dismiss, break ranks.* ~¡Rompan FILAS! *Dismiss!* || •Tenerle FILA a uno (familiar). *To have something against someone.*

FINAL. *sm.* Fin. *End.* ~Me quedé hasta el FINAL. *I stayed until the end.* ~Al FINAL de la película ella se muere. *She dies at the end of the movie.* ~Al FINAL del día. *At the end of the day.* ~Al FINAL de la calle. *At the end of the street.* || **2.** [Musica]. *Finale.* || **3.** Desenlace (de una película, historia). *Ending.* ~No me gustó nada el FINAL. *I didn't like the ending at all.* ~Tiene un FINAL feliz. *It has a happy ending.* || **4.** [List]. *Bottom.* ~Están al FINAL de la lista. *They're at the bottom of the list.* || **5.** *LOCUCIONES.* || •Al FINAL. *In the end.* ~Siempre protestando pero al FINAL nunca hace nada. *He spends his whole time complaining but he never actually does anything.* || •El Juicio FINAL. *The Last Judgement.* || •FINAL de línea. *Terminal.* || •A FINALES de junio. *At the end of June.* ⇨FINAL

FINALES. *sm.* [En béisbol, fútbol americano]. *Playoffs.* ⇨FINALS

FINALIDAD. *sf.* Propósito, utilidad. *Purpose, aim, object, reason, intention.* ~La FINALIDAD de este libro. *The aim of this*

book. ~¿Qué FINALIDAD tendrá todo eso? *What can be the purpose of all this?* ~¿Con qué FINALIDAD se convocó la reunión? *What was the purpose of calling the meeting?* || **2.** Meta. *Goal, objective.* ~Perseguir algo como FINALIDAD. *To set something as one's goal.* ⇨FINALITY

FINALIZAR. *v.* Terminar. *To end, finish, complete.* ~Debemos FINALIZAR este trabajo hoy. *We must finish (complete) this work today.* ⇨FINALIZE

FINO. *adj.* [Oro]. Pure. ~Oro FINO. *Pure gold.* || **2.** [Alimentos, bebidas]. *Choice, select, quality.* || **3.** [Sentido]. *Sharp, acute.* ~Olfato FINO. *Keen sense of smell.* || **4.** De poco grosor o espesor, delgado. *Thin.* ~Un papel FINO. *A thin piece of paper.* || **5.** Educado, distinguido. *Refined, polite, well-bred, refined.* || **6.** [Humor, ironía]. *Subtle.* ~Una FINA ironía. *A subtle irony.* ~Un FINO sentido de humor. *A subtle sense of humor.* || **7.** [Tabaco]. *Select.* || **8.** Slender, slight (person). *Delgado.* || **9.** [Tela, lencería]. *Thin, delicate, sheer.* || **10.** [Intelligence]. *Shrewd, acute, penetrating.* || **11.** [Loncha]. *Thin.* ~Una lonja FINA. *A thin slice.* || **12.** [Labios]. *Thin.* || **13.** [Cintura, talle]. *Slender.* ~Talle FINO. *Slender waist.* || **14.** Liso, suave, terso; sin asperezas. *Smooth, soft.* ~Los bebés tienen la piel muy FINA. *Babies have very soft (smooth) skin.* || **15.** •Jerez FINO. *Dry sherry.* || **16.** •Piedra FINA. *Semi-precious stone.* ⇨FINE

FIRME [FIRM]. *adj.* Estable (escalera, mesa, silla]. *Steady, secure, stable.* ~Una viga muy FIRME. ~*A secure beam.* || **2.** Duro. *Hard.* || **3.** Sólido. *Solid, compact.* || **4.** [Color]. *Fast.* || **5.** [Mercado]. *Steady, strong.* || **6.** [Persona]. *Steadfast, resolute, staunch.* || **7.** Rígido. *Rigid.* || **8.** Erguido. *Straight, erect.* || **9.** *LOCUCIONES.* || •Mantenerse FIRME. *To hold one's ground.* || •Sentencia FIRME. *Final judgement.* || •Trabajar de FIRME. *To work hard.* || •Andar con paso FIRME. *To walk with a determined step.*

FÍSICO. *sm.* [Científico]. *Physicist.*

⇨PHYSICIAN.

FLUJO [FLUX]. *sm.* [Circulación, corriente]. *Flow.* ~Flujo sanguíneo. *Blood flow, flow of blood, loss of blood.* || **2.** [Física]. *Flux.* FLUJO magnético. *Magnetic flux.* || **3.** MED Secreción. *Discharge.* || **4.** [Informática]. *Stream.* || **5.** [De votantes]. *Swing.* || **6.** [De conciencia]. *Stream.* ~FLUJO de conciencia. *Stream of consciousness.* || **7.** [De vientre]. *Diarrhea.* || **8.** MAR *Rising tide, incoming tide.* ~FLUJO y reflujo. *Ebb and flow.* || **9.** Exceso (en la cantidad o intensidad de una cosa). *Torrent, wave.* ~Su FLUJO de palabras me marea. *His torrent of words makes me dizzy.* ~Un FLUJO emigratorio. *A wave of immigrants.* || **10.** •FLUJO de fondos. *Cash flow.*

FORMA. *sf.* Modo, manera. *Way, means, method.* ~No hubo FORMA de convencerle. *There was no way we could convince him.* ~Es su FORMA de ser. *It's just the way he is.* ~No me gusta nada su FORMA de organizar las cosas. *I don't like his way of organizing things.* || **2.** [De pago]. *Method.* || **3.** [De sombrero]. *Hatter's block.* || **4.** [De zapatero]. *Last.* || **5.** Fórmula. *Formula.* ~Es pura FORMA. *It's a mere formality.* || **6.** Contorno, apariencia. *Shape.* Tiene FORMA circular. *It's circular (in shape).* ~Tiene la FORMA de un platillo. *It's the shape of a saucer.* ~Las tenemos de todas FORMAS y tamaños. *We have them in all shapes and sizes.* ~Logró dar FORMA a sus proyectos. *He finally managed to give some shape to his plans.* || **7.** Modales. *Manners, social conventions, appearances.* ~En público siempre guardan FORMAS. *They always keep up appearances.* || **8.** [De mujer]. *Curves.* ⇨FORM

FORMACIÓN [FORMATION]. *sf.* Educación. *Upbringing.* || **2.** Adiestramiento. *Training.* ~Sin la debida FORMACIÓN en la investigación. *Without the proper research training.* ~FORMACIÓN musical. *Musical training.* ~FORMACIÓN profesional. *Technical (vocational) training.* ~Centro de FORMACIÓN obrera. *Worker's training center.* || **3.** [Enseñanza]. *Education.* ~Se recibe una buena FORMACIÓN en ese colegio. *They give you a good education at that school.* ~Tiene una buena FORMACIÓN literaria. *She has a very good literary education.* ~FORMACIÓN universitaria. *University (college) education.* ~FORMACIÓN sexual. *Sex education.*

FORMAL. *adj.* Serio, cumplidor, responsable. *Reliable, dependable, trustworthy, serious-minded, correct.* ~Sólo tiene 21 años pero es un muchacho muy FORMAL. *He's only 21 but he is very serious-minded (responsible).* ~A ver si eres un poco más FORMAL la próxima vez. *Try to be more responsable next time.* || **2.** Cortés. *Polite.* Sed FORMALES. *Behave yourselves.* ⇨FORMAL

FORMATO [FORMAT]. *sm.* Tamaño. *Size.* ~¿De qué FORMATO lo quiere? *What size do you want?*

FORMIDABLE. *adj.* Maravilloso, terrific, estupendo (persona, película, idea). *Terrific, marvelous, great.* ~Tu padre es un tipo FORMIDABLE. *Your father is a terrific fellow (guy).* ~¡Formidable! *Great!* || **2.** Enorme. *Huge.* ~En esta playa se levantan olas FORMIDABLES. *Huge waves dash to the shore.* ⇨FORMIDABLE

FORMULA. *sf.* Manera, sistema. *Way.* Una nueva FÓRMULA para conciliar las diferencias. *A new way of settling differences.* || **2.** Frase, expresión. ~FÓRMULA de cortesía. *Polite expression.* ~Las FÓRMULAS que se emplean en la redacción de cartas comerciales. *The standard expressions (set phrases) used in writing business letters,.* || **3.** [De un alimento]. *Recipe.* ~Elaborado según nuestra FÓRMULA exclusiva. *Made with our own exclusive recipe.* || **4.** Receta médica. *Prescription.* || **5.** •Por FÓRMULA. *As a matter of form, for form's sake.* ⇨FORMULA

FORMULAR [FORMULATE]. *v.* [Petición]. *To make.* || **2.** [Deseo]. *To express.* ~Los condenados a muerte tienen el derecho de FORMULAR un último deseo. *Prisoners on death row have a right to express their last wish.* || **3.** [Pregunta]. *To ask.* || **4.**

[Protesta, queja]. *To lodge.* || **5.** [Receta]. To write. ~FORMULAR una prescripción médica. *To write a prescription.* || **6.** •FORMULAR una reclamación. *To make (put in) a claim.*

FORTUNA. *sf.* Suerte. *Luck.* ~Buena FORTUNA. *Good luck.* ~Mala FORTUNA. *Misfortune.* ~Golpe de FORTUNA. *Stroke of luck.* ~Probar fortuna. *To try one's luck.* || **2.** Destino. *Fate.* ~Quiso la FORTUNA que se salvara la vida. *As fate would have it she was saved.* || **3.** Borrasca. *Storm.* ~Correr FORTUNA. *To weather a storm.* ⇨FORTUNE

FORZAR. *v.* Violar. *To rape.* || **2.** [Casa]. *To break into, enter by force, force one's way into.* || **3.** [Bloqueo]. *To run.* || **4.** MIL *To storm, take (by force).* ~Forzaron la ciudadela y se llevaron a todos prisioneros. *~They stormed the fort and took everyone prisoner.* || **5.** [Ojos]. *To strain.* ~Estaba FORZANDO la vista. *I was straining my eyes.* || **6.** || [Puerta, cerradura]. *To break open.* ~Perdió la llave y tuvo que FORZAR la cerradura para entrar. *He lost the key and had to break the lock open to go in.* ~Me han FORZADO la puerta del coche para robarme la radio. *They broke open the door and stole my radio.* ⇨FORCE

FRANCO [FRANK]. *adj.* [De una cosa]. *Clear, obvious.* || **2.** [Comercio]. *Free, exempt.* ~FRANCO a bordo. *Free on board.* ~FRANCO de aduana. *Custom-free.* ~FRANCO de porte y embalaje. *~Post and packaging free.* || **3.** Familiar. *Familiar, intimate.* || **4.** Pleno, patente. *Full, marked.* ~Estar en FRANCA rebeldía. *To be in open rebellion.* ~Estar en FRANCA decadencia. *To be in full decline.* ~El paciente ha mostrado una FRANCA mejoría. *The patient has shown marked signs of improvement.* ~Un clima de FRANCA cordialidad. *An atmosphere of genuine warmth.* || **5.** Libre de obstáculos. *Clear.* ~Podemos salir por esta puerta, la salida está FRANCA. *We can go out through this door, the exit is clear.* || **6.** Que tiene relación con Francia. *French.* ~FRANCO-canadiense. *French-Canadian.* || **7.** •Mantener mesa FRANCA. *To keep open* house.

FRESCO. *adj.* [Agua, viento, agua, weather]. *Cool, cold.* ~El tiempo está más bien FRESCO. *The weather is a bit chilly (on the cool side).* ~Agua/bebida FRESCA. *Cold water/drink.* ~Viento FRESCO. *Cool wind.* || **2.** [Tela, ropa]. *Light, thin, cool.* ~Esta blusa es muy FRESCA. *This blouse is nice and cool.* || **3.** [Aspecto]. *Healthy.* || **4.** Impasible, sereno. *Cool, calm, unruffled, cool as a cucumber.* ~Yo estaba muerto de miedo pero él estaba tan FRESCO. *I was scared to death but he was totally unperturbed.* ~Se quedó tan FRESCO. *He didn't bat an eyelid.* || **5.** Desvergonzado, descarado. *Shameless.* ~La muy FRESCA se fue sin pagar. *She had the nerve to leave without paying.* ~¡Qué FRESCO! *What nerve!* || **6.** *LOCUCIONES.* || •Estar más FRESCO que una lechuga. *To be cool as a cucumber.* || •Ponerse FRESCO. *To put on light clothes.* || •Pintura FRESCA. *Wet paint.* || •Hacer FRESCO. *To be chilly.* || •¡Ahora sí que estamos FRESCOS! *Now we're in a fine mess!* ⇨FRESH

FRICCIÓN. *sf.* Friega, masaje. *Rub, rubbing, massage.* ~Date una FRICCIÓN (unas fricciones) con la loción. *Rub the lotion into your skin.* ⇨FRICTION

FRONTERA [FRONTIER]. *sf.* Límite. *Limit, bounds.* ~Su ambición no conoce FRONTERAS. *Her ambition knows no bounds.* || **2.** Área sin límites precisos. *Borderland.* || **3.** •Sus ademanes están en la FRONTERA de lo ridículo. *His gestures border on the ridiculous.*

FRUSTAR [FRUSTRATE]. *v.* [Planes]. *To thwart.* ~La lluvia FRUSTRÓ nuestros planes de ir al cine. *The rain thwarted our plans to go to the movies.* || **2.** Defraudar (a una persona). *To disappoint.* || **3.** [Esperanzas]. *To dash.* Con su conducta FRUSTRABA las esperanzas que sus padres habían depositado en él. *By his conduct he was dashing all the hopes that his parents had placed in him.* || **4.** [Atentado]. *To foil.* ~El atraco al banco se FRUSTRÓ por la llegada de la policía. *The arrival of the police scared the bank robbers away.*

FRUSTRADO [FRUSTRATED]. *adj.* [Atentado, intento]. *Failed, unsuccessful.* ~Un golpe de estado FRUSTRADO. *An unsuccessful takeover.* || **2.** Defraudado. *Disappointed.*

FUENTE. *sf.* Manantial. *Spring.* || **2.** Recipiente. *Dish, serving dish, platter.* ~Puso la carne en una FUENTE ovalada. *He put the meat on an oval platter.* ~Una FUENTE de porcelana. *A china dish.* || **3.** [Origen]. *Source.* ~De FUENTES bien informadas. *From reliable sources.* || **4.** [Información]. *Source.* ~Esta enciclopedia es una buena FUENTE de datos. *This encyclopedia is a good source of information.* || **5.** [Imprenta]. *Font.* || **6.** •FUENTE de los deseos. *Wishing well.* ⇨FOUNTAIN

FUERZA [FORCE]. *sf.* Energía, vigor. *Strength, energy.* ~Tiene mucha FUERZA en los brazos. *She has very strong arms.* ¡Qué FUERZA tiene! *You're really strong!* ~No tengo FUERZAS para andar más. *I haven't got the energy to walk any further.* || **2.** Autoridades. *Authorities.* ~Las FUERZAS vivas de la localidad. *The local authorities.* || **3.** [Electricidad]. *Power, current, energy.* Han cortado la FUERZA. *They've cut off the power.* || **4.** Presión. *Pressure.* || **5.** [De una máquina]. *Power.* || **6.** Resistencia. *Resistance.*

FULMINAR [FULMINATE]. *v.* Matar (por el rayo). *To strike by lightning.* ~Morir FULMINADO. *To be struck by lightning.* || **2.** [Bomba]. *To hurl.* || **3.** [Por la enfermedad]. *To strike down.* ~FULMINADO por la enfermedad. *Struck down by illness.*

FUNCIÓN. *sf.* Cargo. *Duties.* ~En el ejercicio de sus FUNCIONES. *In the performance of his duties.* ~Fue suspendido de sus FUNCIONES. *He was suspended from duty.* || **2.** [Teatro]. *Performance.* ~FUNCIÓN de noche. *Late performance.* ~FUNCIÓN de tarde. *Matinée.* || **3.** [De circo]. *Performance, show.* || **4.** [De cine]. *Showing, performance.* || **5.** [De máquina]. *Operation, functioning.* || **6.** [Fiesta]. *Party.* ⇨FUNCTION[2]

FUNCIONAR. *v.* [General]. *To work.* ~El reloj FUNCIONA a la perfección. *The clock*

works perfectly. ~No FUNCIONA el ascensor. *The elevator is out of order.* ~Su corazón FUNCIONA con normalidad. *His heart is beating normally, has a normal beat.* ~FUNCIONA con pilas. *It runs on batteries.* || **2.** [Coche]. *To perform.* || **3.** [Idea, película]. *To work, be a success.* || **4.** [Relación, amistad, matrimonio]. *To work out.* ~Su matrimonio FUNCIONA perfectamente. *Their marriage is working out perfectly.* ~La relación no FUNCIONABA. *Their relationship was not working out.* || **5.** •Así no podemos FUNCIONAR. *We can't go on like this.* •Hacer FUNCIONAR una máquina. *To operate a machine.* ⇨ FUNCTION[1]

FUNERAL. *sm.* En el aniversario. *Memorial service.*|| **2.** [Misa], *Requiem.* ⇨ FUNERAL

FURIOSO. *adj.* Intenso. *Violent, intense.* ~Se desató una FURIOSA tempestad. *A violent storm broke.* ~Sintió unos celos FURIOSOS. *He felt madly jealous.* ⇨ FURIOUS

FUSIÓN [FUSION]. *sf.* [De empresas]. *Merger.* ~Se ha producido la FUSIÓN de varios bancos. *Several banks have merged.* || **2.** [De partido, organizaciones]. *Merger, amalgamation.* || **3.** [De ideas, intereses]. *Combination, amalgamation.* || **4.** Fundición (de los metales). *Melting.* || **5.** [De la nieve]. *Melting, thawing.* || **6.** [Unión]. *Joining, uniting.* || **7.** [Informática]. *Merge.*

FÚTBOL [FOOTBALL]. *sm.* [Que se juega fuera de los Estados Unidos]. *Sóccer.*

G

GABINETE. *sm.* Sala de consulta (de médico). *Doctor's office.* ‖ **2.** Sala de investigación. *Lab (chemistry, physics).* ‖ **3.** *Section, room of a museum.* ~El GABINETE de monedas. *The coin section.* ~El GABINETE de Historia Natural. *The Natural History room.* ‖ **4.** Estudio, despacho (dentro de casa). *Study, library.* ‖ **5.** Muebles. *Suite of office furniture.* ‖ **5.** Conjunto de profesionales. *Department.* ‖ **6.** Boudoir. *Tocador.* ‖ **7.** Cuarto de estar. *Private sitting room.* ‖ **8.** *LOCUCIONES.* ‖ •GABINETE de estudios. *Engineering firm.* ‖ •Trabajo de GABINETE. *Desk work (as opposed to field work).* ‖ •GABINETE de lectura. *Reading-room.* ‖ •De GABINETE. *Theoretical.* ‖ •GABINETE de consulta. *Consulting-room.* ‖ •GABINETE de estrategia. *Think-tank.* ‖ •GABINETE fiscal. *Tax advisory office.* ‖ •GABINETE de imagen. *Public Relations Office.* ‖ •GABINETE de prensa. *Press office.* ‖ •Estratega de GABINETE. *Armchair strategist.* ⇨CABINET

GALA [GALA]. *sf.* [Traje de etiqueta]. *Full dress, best clothes.* ~Se puso sus mejores GALAS el día de la entrega del premio. *He put on his best clothes on award day.* ~De GALA. *Dressed up,* MIL *in full uniform.* ‖ **2.** [Ciudad]. *Decked out.* ‖ **3.** [Lo más selecto]. *Cream, pride, flower, jewel.* ~La GALA de la sociedad. *The cream of society.* ~La GALA del pueblo. *The pride of the village.* ‖ **4.** Elegancia, garbo. *Elegance, gracefulness.* ‖ **5.** Pompa. *Pomp, display.*

GALERÍA. *sf.* ARQ. *Covered balcony, veranda.* ‖ **2.** Paso subterráneo. *Underground passage.* ~GALERÍA secreta. *Secret passage.* ‖ **3.** [Para cortinas]. *Curtain rail, valance.* ‖ **4.** Pasillo. *Passage, corridor.* ‖ **5.** •GALERÍA comercial. *Shopping center, galle-*ria. ‖ **6.** •GALERÍA de la muerte. *Death row.* ⇨GALLERY

GANAR. *v.*
❶ MERECER. *To deserve, earn.* ~Te has GANADO unas buenas vacaciones. *You've earned yourself a good vacation.* ‖ **2.** •GANARSE algo a pulso. *To work hard for something, to earn.* El ascenso se lo ha GANADO a pulso. *He really worked hard for, he really earned his promotion.* ‖ **3.** [Con ironía]. *To bring upon oneself, to incur.* Te estás GANANDO una buena paliza. *You're going to get (you're asking for) a good thrashing.*
❷ PERCIBIR UN INGRESO. [Sueldo, interés, dinero]. *To earn, draw.* ~GANA mil pesetas la hora. *He earns one thousand pesetas an hour.* ~GANA un buen sueldo. *He earns (draws) a good salary.* ~GANÓ mucho dinero con su última novela. *He made a great deal of money with his last novel.* ‖ **2.** [Dinero]. *To earn, make.* ~Lo único que quiere es GANAR dinero. *All he's interested in is making money.* ¿Cuánto GANAS al mes? *How much do you earn (make) a month?* ~GANA algún dinero haciendo traducciones. *He ekes out a living doing translations.* ‖ **3.** •GANARSE el pan y los garbanzos. *To earn one's daily bread.*
❸ VENCER, CONQUISTAR, SUPERAR (victoria, premio, carrera, partido, elecciones, batalla, apuesta). [Deporte, juego, competición]. *To win, beat.* ~GANAMOS el partido. *We won the game.* ~Le GANÉ al ajedrez. *I beat him at chess.* ~No hay quien lo GANE. *Nobody can beat him.* ‖ **2.** Conquistar. *To capture, take.* ~Después de una dura lucha GANARON la ciudad. *After a hard battle they captured the town.* ~GANÓ a los moros la ciudad de

Valencia. *He captured Valencia from the Moors.* || **3.** FIG Conquistar (apoyo, partidarios). *To win over.* ~No se deja GANAR en ningún momento por la desesperación. *He never gives way to despair.* ~Le GANÓ para su causa. *She won him over to her cause.* || **4.** Aventajar, superar. *To beat, surpass.* ~Le GANA en inteligencia. *She is much brighter than he is.* ~Me GANA en estatura, pero no en fuerza. *He is taller than I am but I'm stronger, he beats me insofar as height is concerned, but I'm stronger than he is.* || **5.** [Premio, dinero] (En un juego o concurso). *To win.* ~¿Cuánto GANASTE en las carreras de caballos? *How much did you win at the race track?* ~Ha GANADO mucho dinero al póquer. *She's won a lot of money playing poker.* || **6.** •Ir GANANDO. *To lead, be winning.* ~Van GANANDO por tres a uno. *They're leading three-one.*

❹ VARIOS. Alcanzar. *To reach.* ~GANARON la cumbre del Everest. *They reached the summit of Mount Everest.* || **2.** Mejorar. *To improve.* ~GANA en destreza cada día. *He gets more skillful every day.* ~Has GANADO mucho con este corte de pelo. *You look much better with this new hairstyle.* || **3.** Reclamar. *To reclaim.* ~Tierras GANADAS al mar. *Land reclaimed from the sea.* || **4.** Prosperar. *To thrive, do well.*

❺ LOCUCIONES. || •Sabe GANARSE los amigos. *He knows how to make friends.* || •GANARSE la confianza de uno. *To win somebody's trust.* || •GANARSE la antipatía de uno. *To atract somebody's dislike.* || •Salir GANANDO en algo. *To come out on top.* || •Llevar las de GANAR. *To hold the winning cards.* || •No GANAR para disgustos. *To have fate against one, to have nothing but trouble.* ⇨ GAIN

GENERO [GENDER]. *sm.* Clase. *Kind, sort.* ~Este GÉNERO de vida no es para mí. *This sort of life is not for me.* ~Te deseo todo GÉNERO de felicidades. *I wish you all the happiness in the world.* || **2.** [Arte, literatura]. *Genre.* ~El GÉNERO novelesco. *The novel.* ~Género dramático. *Drama.* •GÉNERO chico. *Light opera.* || **3.** Mercancía. *Article, piece of merchandise.* ~GÉNEROS de punto. *Knit-*

wear. ~GÉNEROS de primera calidad. *Quality goods.* || **4.** Tela. *Cloth, material, fabric.* ~¿De qué GÉNERO está hecho este vestido? *Of what fabric is this dress made of?* || **5.** Raza. *Race.* •El GÉNERO humano. *Mankind, the human race.* || **6.** Manera. *Style, matter, way.*

GENIAL. *adj.* Dotado de genio creador. *Talented, brilliant.* ~Su última sinfonía es una obra GENIAL. *His latest simphony is a work of genius.* ~Un hombre GENIAL. *A man of genius.* || **2.** Ocurrente, gracioso, divertido. *Funny, witty.* ~Tiene unas salidas GENIALES. *She makes some very witty remarks.* || **3.** Estupendo. *Great, fantastic.* || **4.** •Una idea GENIAL. *A brilliant idea.* ⇨ GENIAL

GENIO. *sm.* Carácter. *Disposition, nature, temperament.* ~Genio alegre. *Cheerful nature.* ~Buen GENIO. *Good nature.* ~De GENIO franco. *Of an open nature.* ~Corto de GENIO. *Spiritless, timid.* ~Tener buen GENIO. *To be good-natured.* || **2.** Mal carácter. *Temper.* ~¡Qué GENIO tiene este niño! *This child has such a temper!* ~Es una persona de mucho GENIO. *He has a quick temper.* •Tener mal GENIO. *To be bad-tempered.* •Estar de mal GENIO. *To be in a bad mood.* || **3.** Espíritu (de un país, de una época). *Spirit.* ~El GENIO español. *The Spanish spirit.* ~El GENIO del Renacimiento. *The spirit of the Renaissance.* || **4.** Ser fantástico. *Genie.* || **5.** Ánimo para emprender cosas. *Initiative, drive.* Este niño tiene GENIO. *This child has initiative.* || **6.** Particularidades, características (lengua). *Peculiarities, characteristics.* || **7.** •GENIO y figura hasta la sepultura. *The leopard cannot change its spots.* || **8.** •Llevar el GENIO a uno. *To humor somebody, not to dare to contradict someone.* ⇨ GENIUS

GENTIL. *adj.* Encantador, agradable. *Charming, pleasant.* ~Esta GENTIL doncella. *This charming young girl.* || **2.** Amable, fino. *Obliging, kind, courteous.* ~Gracias, es usted muy GENTIL. *Thank you, you're very kind.* || **3.** Que no es judío. *Gentile.* || **4.** Elegante. *Graceful, elegant.* ~De GENTIL porte. *Of graceful deportment.* || **5.** Pagano.

Heathen, pagan. ⇨GENTLE

GLOBAL. *adj.* [Infome]. *Full, comprehensive.* ~Un estudio GLOBAL. *A comprehensive study.* ‖ **2.** [Resultado]. *Overall.* ‖ **3.** [Precio, cantidad, suma]. *Total.* ~Cantidad GLOBAL a abonar. *Total amount due.* ⇨GLOBAL

GLOBO [GLOBE]. *sm.* Bolsa de goma flexible llena de aire o gas. *Balloon.* ~Decoraron la habitación de GLOBOS de varios colores. *They adorned the room with balloons of all colors.* ‖ **2.** [Lámpara, pantalla]. *Glass lampshade.* ~La lámpara tiene un GLOBO tallado. *The lampshade is made of cut-glass.* ‖ **3.** [De chicle]. *Bubble gum.* ‖ **4.** [In comics]. *Speech balloon (bubble).* ~Cuando ese personaje del comic se enfada, en su GLOBO aparecen serpientes, hachas y fuego. *When this comic book character gets mad, the speech bubble is full of snakes, axes and fire.* ‖ **5.** [En beísbol]. *Fly.* ‖ **6.** [En tenis]. *Lob.* ~Dar un GLOBO. *To lob the ball.* ‖ **7.** Preservativo. *Condom, rubber.* ‖ **8.** Enfado. *Anger, annoyance.* ~Se agarró un GLOBO de mucho cuidado. *He had a fit, he hit the roof.* ~Anda con un GLOBO tremendo. *She's really in a bad mood.* ‖ **9.** Borrachera. *Drunkenness.* ~Anoche ibas con un GLOBO impresionante. *You were high as a kite last night.* ‖ **10.** LAT. AM Mentira, embuste. *Lie, tall story.* ‖ **11.** Esfera. *Sphere.* La luna tiene forma de GLOBO. *The moon has the shape of a sphere.* ‖ **12.** *LOCUCIONES.* ‖ •Echar GLOBOS. *To daydream.* ‖ •GLOBO aerostático. *Balloon.* ‖ •GLOBO dirigible. *Airship, dirigible.* ~Los personajes de Julio Verne viajaban en GLOBO dirigible. *The characters in Jules Verne's novels travelled on dirigibles.* ‖ •GLOBO ocular. *Eyeball.* ‖ •GLOBO de aire caliente. *Hot-air balloon.* ‖ •GLOBO terráqueo. *The earth.* ‖ •GLOBO de luz. *Espherical lamp.* ‖ •Montar en GLOBO. *To go in a balloon.*

GLORIA. *sf.* Fama. *Honor.* ‖ **2.** Personalidad. *Heroe, figure.* ~Es una de las GLORIAS del deporte nacional. *He's one of the country's great sport figures (heroes).* ~Las viejas GLORIAS de Hollywood. *The grand old names of Hollywood.* ‖ **3.** Cielo. *Heaven.* ~Ganarse la GLORIA. *To go to heaven.* ‖ **4.** Delicia. *Delight.* ~El día es pura GLORIA. *It's a delightful day.* ~Es una GLORIA oirla cantar. *It's a delight to hear her sing.* ‖ **5.** Éxtasis. *Bliss.* Aquí dentro se está en la GLORIA. *It's blissful (heavenly, wonderful) in here.* ~Aquí se está que es una GLORIA. *It's heavenly here.* ‖ **6.** TEAT Salida a escena (para saludar al público). *Curtain call.* ‖ **7.** *LOCUCIONES.* ‖ •Cubrise de GLORIA (irónico). *To make a fool of oneself.* ‖ •Dios lo tenga en su santa GLORIA. *God rest his soul.* ‖ •Estar en su GLORIA. *To be in one's element.* ~Él, rodeado así de niños, está en la gloria. *He's in his element when he's surrounded by children like that.* ‖ •Estar en la GLORIA. *To be in seventh heaven.* ‖ •Hacer GLORIA de algo. *To boast about something.* ‖ •Oler a GLORIA. *To smell divine.* ‖ •Por la GLORIA de mi madre. *By all that is holy.* ‖ •Saber a GLORIA. *To taste heavenly, delicious.* ‖ •Una vieja GLORIA. *A has-been, a great figure from the past.* ⇨GLORY

GRACIA. *sf.* Favor. *Favor.* ~Disfrutaba de la GRACIA del rey. *He enjoyed the king's favor.* ‖ **2.** Indulto. *Pardon.* ~Petición de GRACIA. *Petition of pardon.* ‖ **3.** Buen trato. *Graciousness.* ~Caer en GRACIA a alguien. *To make a good impression on someone.* ‖ **4.** Nombre. *Name.* ~Dígame usted su GRACIA. *Could you give me your name, please.* ‖ **5.** Chiste. *Joke, trick, prank.* A mí no me hace ninguna GRACIA. *I don't find it funny at all.* ~Me hizo una GRACIA que a mí me ha costado cien mil pesetas. *He played a dirty trick on me that cost me a hundred thousand pesetas.* ‖ **6.** Encanto, donaire. *Gracefulness.* ~Baila con mucha GRACIA. *She's a very graceful dancer.* ~Un vestido muy sin GRACIA. *A very plain dress.* ‖ **7.** Habilidad especial. *Special gift.* ~Tiene mucha GRACIA para arreglar flores. *She has a real gift for flower arranging.* ‖ **8.** Clemencia. *Clemency.* ‖ **9.** *pl.* Agradecimiento. *Thanks.* ~Muchas GRACIAS. *Thank you very much.* ⇨GRACE

GRACIOSO[1]. *adj.* Chistoso, divertido. *Funny, amusing.* ~Es el chiste más GRACIOSO que he oído. *This is the funniest joke I've ever heard.* ~Un chico muy GRACIOSO. *A very funny boy.* || **2.** Ingenioso. *Witty.* || **3.** Atractivo, encantador. *Graceful, attractive, pleasing, charming.* ~Mercedes tiene una sonrisa GRACIOSA. *Mercedes has a charming smile.* ~Sus GRACIOSOS ojos. *Her charming eyes.* ~Las pecas le dan un aspecto muy GRACIOSO. *Those freckles make her look very cute.* ~Tiene una manera muy GRACIOSA de reírse. *She's got a really cute laugh.* || **4.** •Lo GRACIOSO del caso es que ... *The funny thing about it is that ...* ⇨GRACIOUS

GRACIOSO[2]. *sm.* Persona que molesta y no tiene gracia, persona latosa, pesada. *Clown, smart aleck, pain in the neck, pest.* ~Algún GRACIOSO ha cerrado la puerta con llave y se ha marchado. *Some clown locked the door and left.* ~¡No te hagas el GRACIOSO! *I suppose you think you're very funny, don't try to be funny!* ~Hacerse el GRACIOSO. *To clown around.* ~Siempre se hace el GRACIOSO. *He's always clowning around.* || **2.** [Teatro]. *Comic character.* ⇨GRACIOUS

GRADO. *sm.* Fase, etapa. *Stage.* ~El GRADO que ahora hemos alcanzado. *The stage we have now reached.* ~Está en el segundo GRADO de elaboración. *It is now in the second stage of production.* ~El juicio se encuentra en GRADO de apelación. *The trial is at the appeal stage.* || **2.** Nivel. *Level, amount, degree.* ~No sé que GRADO de amistad hay entre esos dos. *I don't know what degree of friendship exists between these two.* ~Otro ejemplo del GRADO de confusión reinante. *Another example of the degree of confusion that prevails.* ~Depende del GRADO de libertad que tengan. *It depends on the degree of freedom they enjoy.* **3.** Diploma, título. *Degree.* ~Tiene el GRADO de doctor. *He has a Doctor's degree.* || **4.** Rango. *Rank.* Tiene el GRADO de capitán. *He holds the rank of captain.* || **5.** Peldaño. *Step.* || **6.** Medida. *Measure.* || **7.** Nivel. *Rate.* ~GRADO de velocidad. *Rate of speed.* || **8.** Ganas. *Willingness.* ~De buen GRADO. *Willingly.* ~De mal GRADO, mal de mi GRADO. *Unwillingly, against my will.* ~De GRADO o por fuerza. *Willy-nilly.* || **9.** [Física,

meteorología]. *Degree.* ~Estamos a tres GRADOS bajo cero. *It's three degrees below zero.* || **10.** [Matemática]. *Degree.* ~A un ángulo de 60 GRADOS. *At a 60 degree angle.* || **11.** [Vino]. *Degree.* ~Un vino de 12 GRADOS. *A 12% proof wine.* || **12.** *LOCUCIONES.* || •GRADO Farenheit. *Degree Farenheit.* || •De GRADO en grado, por grados. *Gradually, step by step, by degrees.* || •En sumo GRADO. *In the highest degree.* || • Primo en tercer GRADO. *Third cousin.* || •En tal GRADO que. *In such a degree that, so much so that.* || •Doce GRADOS de alcohol. *Alcohol content of twelve percent.* || •Quemaduras de tercer GRADO. *Third-degree burns.* ⇨GRADE

GRADUAR. *v.* Medir (alcohol, vino). *To measure.* || **2.** Clasificar. *To grade, classify.* || **3.** Evaluar. *To appraise.* || **4.** Marcar (instrumento, termómetro). *Calibrar.* || **5.** Regular. *To adjust, regulate.* GRADÚA la temperatura del radiador para que haga menos calor. *Regulate the temperature of the water heater so that it's not as hot.* ~GRADUAR la salida del agua por el grifo. *To regulate the flow of water from a faucet.* || **6.** •GRADUAR la vista. *To test somebody's eyes.* || **7.** •GRADUARSE la vista. *To have one's eyes tested.* ⇨GRADUATE

GRANO. *sm.* [De café]. *Bean.* || **2.** Tumorcillo en la cara. *Spot, pimple.* ~Te ha salido un GRANO en la nariz. *You've got a pimple on your nose.* || **3.** Semilla. *Seed.* ~GRANO de sésamo. *Sesame seed.* ~GRANO de mostaza. *Mustard seed.* || **4.** [De sal]. *Pinch.* || **5.** Punto. *Speck.* || **6.** [De uva]. *Grape.* ~Un rácimo de GRANOS. *A bunch (cluster) of grapes.* || **7.** [De pimiento]. *Peppercorn.* || **8.** GRANOS. *Cereales.* || **9.** •Poner su GRANO de arena. *To make one's contribution.* || **10.** •Ir al GRANO. *To get to the point.* ⇨GRAIN

GRATIFICACIÓN. *sf.* Bonificación, sobresueldo. *Bonus.* ~Por quedarme a trabajar dos tardes, me han dado una GRATIFICACIÓN económica. *Because I worked overtime a couple of nights, they gave me a bonus.* || **2.** Recompensa. *Reward.* ~El proprietario del perro perdido le dio una GRATIFICACIÓN a la persona que lo encontró.

The owner of the lost dog gave a reward to the person who had found it. ‖ **3.** Propina. *Tip, gratuity.* ‖ **4.** Subvencion. *Bounty.* ⇨GRATIFICATION

GRATIFICAR. *v.* Recompensar. *To reward.* ~El gerente nos GRATIFICÓ con medio millón de pesetas. *The manager rewarded us with half a million pesetas.* ⇨GRATIFY

GRAVE [GRAVE]. *adj.* Pesado. *Heavy.* ‖ **2.** [Enfermedad]. *Serious.* ~Su enfermedad no es GRAVE y saldrá pronto del hospital. *His illness is not serious and he should be out of the hospital shortly.* ~Está GRAVE. *He's seriously ill.* ‖ **3.** [De estilo]. *Solemn.* ‖ **4.** [Nota, tono]. *Low, deep.* ‖ **5.** [Voz]. *Deep.* ~Los hombres tienen la voz más GRAVE que las mujeres. *Men have a deeper voice than women.* ‖ **6.** Espinoso (situación). *Critical, serious.* ~Es una situación GRAVE y debemos darle un solución rápida. *It's a serious situation and we need to find a quick solution.* ‖ **7.** Importante. *Important, momentous.* ‖ **8.** [De carácter]. *Serious, sedate, dignified.* ~Y otros GRAVES hombres. *And other worthy men.* ‖ **9.** [Herida]. *Severe.*

GRAVITATE [GRAVITATE]. *v.* Apoyarse en, recaer en. *To rest on.* ~Sobre él GRAVITA el peso de las decisiones. *The onus of the decision rests on him.* ‖ **2.** Amenazar. *To loom, hang over.* El peligro GRAVITABA sobre nuestras cabezas. *Danger loomed over our heads.* ‖ **3.** Centrarse. *To be centered around.* ~El conflicto GRAVITABA en torno a la Capital. *The danger was centered around the capital.* ‖ **4.** [Factores]. *To influence.* ~Los factores que GRAVITAN sobre está disminución. *The factors affecting (influencing) this reduction.*

GUARDA [GUIDE]. *sm.* [En un jardín zoológico, parque, museo]. *Keeper.* ‖ **2.** [En un edificio público, monumento histórico). *Custodian.* ‖ **3.** Cobrador. *Tram conductor.* ‖ **4.** [Imprenta]. *End paper, flyleaf.* ‖ **5.** [Caza]. *Gamekeeper, game warden.* ‖ **6.** [De la ley]. *Observance.* **7.** Tutela. *Custody (of a child).* ~La madre es la encargada de la GUARDA de sus hijos. *The mother has the custody of her children.* ‖ **8.** Protección. *Safekeeping, protection.* La GUARDA de sus

derechos. *The protection of his rights.* ~Un notario es el encargado de la GUARDA de estos documentos. *A notary is in charge of the safekeeping of these documents.* ‖ **9.** Varillas (de un abanico). *Outer ribs.* ‖ **10.** •GUARDA forestal. *Forester, forest ranger, game warden.* ~Los GUARDAS forestales evitan muchos incendios en los bosques. *Forest rangers prevent many forest fires.* ‖ **11.** •GUARDA jurado. *Security guard.* ⇨ GUARD[2]

GUARDAR. *v.* Conservar. *To hold, keep.* ~GUARDAR un buen recuerdo de. *To have a pleasant memory of.* ‖ **2.** Observar (la ley). *To observe, abide by.* ‖ **3.** [La derecha, la izquierda, las distancias, secreto]. *To keep.* ~GUARDAR la derecha. *To keep to the right.* ~GUARDAR las distancias. *To keep one's distance.* GUARDAR silencio. *To remain silent.* ‖ **4.** Poner en un sitio. *To put away.* ~GUÁRDALO en el cajón. *Put it in the drawer.* ~Se lo GUARDÓ en el bolsillo. *He put it away in his pocket.* ~GUARDA los juguetes. *Put your toys away.* ‖ **5.** Reservar. *To save.* ~GUÁRDAME un sitio. *Keep a seat for me.* ~GUÁRDALE un pedazo de pastel. *Save him a piece of cake.* ~GUARDA esta botella para Nochebuena. *Keep this bottle for Christmas Eve.* ‖ **6.** Proteger. *To protect.* ~¡Dios GUARDE a la reina! *God save the queen!* ‖ **7.** [Rencor]. *To harbor.* ‖ **8.** [Informática]. *To save.* ‖ **9.** Ahorrar. *To save.* ‖ **10.** Mantener en un lugar, conservar. *To keep.* ~GUARDO los huevos en la nevera. *I keep the eggs in the refrigerator.* ~Los tengo GUARDADOS en el desván. *I got them stored away in the attic.* ~Siempre GUARDA las medicinas bajo llave. *She always keeps the medicine locked away.* ‖ **11.** Mostrar, manifestar. *To show.* ~Le GUARDARON el debido respeto. *He was treated with due respect.* ~Hay que GUARDAR la debida compostura en la iglesia. *You must show proper respect when in church.* ~GUARDAR las apariencias. *To keep up appearances.* ‖ **12.** [Fiesta]. *To observe.* ⇨GUARD[1]

GUARDIA. *sm.* Defensa. *Defense, protection.* ‖ **2.** •Estar de GUARDIA. *To be on guard duty (soldado), to be on duty or call (médico), to be on duty (empleado), to be on watch* *(marino).* ‖ **3.** Turno (de servicio). *Shift of duty.* ‖ **4.** Policía. *Police officer, policeman.* ‖ **5.** [Náutica]. *Watch.* ‖ **6.** Turno de vigilancia (de un médico). *Shift.* ‖ **7.** *LOCUCIONES.* ‖ •Angel de la GUARDIA. *Guardian Angel.* ‖ •Estar de GUARDIA. *To be on duty.* ~Tiene GUARDIA de noche. *She's on night duty.* ‖ •Farmacia de GUARDIA. *All-night drugstore.* ‖ •GUARDIA de tráfico. *Traffic policeman.* ‖ •GUARDIA de asalto. *Riot police.* ‖ •GUARDIA municipal. *Urban, traffic police.* ‖ •GUARDIA nocturno. *Night watchman.* ‖ •Médico de GUARDIA. *Doctor on call.* ‖ •Poner GUARDIA. *To warn.* ~Me puso en GUARDIA contra los peligros. *She warned me of the dangers.* ⇨GUARD²

GUÍA [GUIDE]. *sm.*
❶ LIBRO, FOLLETO (de informacíon). *Manual, handbook.* ~Se compró un GUÍA de jardinería. *He bought a handbook on gardening.* ‖ **2.** [De teléfono]. *Directory.* ~Encontré tu número en la GUÍA telefónica (de teléfonos). *I found your number in the telephone directory (telephone book).* ‖ **3.** •GUÍA turística. *Tourist guidebook.* ‖ **4.** •GUÍA de calles, guía urbana. *Street map.* ‖ **5.** Itinerario (de trenes, autobuses). *Timetable.*
❷ ASESORAMIENTO. [Norma]. *Guidance, guideline.* ~Para que te sirva de GUÍA. *For your guidance.* ‖ **2.** •GUÍA vocacional. *Vocational guidance.*
❸ VARIOS. *sm.* [De bicicleta]. *Handbar.* ~Sujeta el GUÍA con las dos manos. *Hold the handbar with both hands.* ‖ **2.** [De bigote]. *End, tip.* ‖ **3.** Documento. *Permit.* Le pidieron al camionero que le mostrara la GUÍA. *They asked the truck driver for his permit.* ~La GUÍA de una pistola. *A gun permit.* ‖ **4.** [Informática]. *Prompt.* ‖ **5.** [Caballo]. *Leader, front horse.* ~GUIAS. *Reins.* ‖ **6.** [De cortina]. *Curtain rail.* ‖ **7.** •GUÍA sonora. *Soundtrack.* ⇨GUIDE

GUIAR. *v.*
❶ CONDUCIR, LLEVAR, MANEJAR (coche, caballo, barco, avión). ‖ **1.** [Auto]. *To drive.* ‖ **2.** [Barco]. *To steer.* ~Nunca he intentado GUIAR una barca. *I never attempted to steer a boat.* ‖ **3.** [Avión]. *To pilot.* ‖ **4.**

[Caballo] *To ride.* ‖ **5.** Encauzar (agua). *To direct.* Un canal GUÍA el agua a la turbina. *A canal directs the water to the turbine.*
❷ VARIOS. Dirigir. *To lead, direct.* ~Las huellas les GUIARON hasta la cueva. *The tracks lead to the cave.* ‖ **2.** Controlar. *To manage.* ‖ **3.** Orientar. *To advise.* ~GUIAR a uno en sus estudios. *To direct someone in his studies.* ‖ **4.** Motivar. *To motivate, move, drive.* Le GUÍA sólo el interés. *He's driven only by personal interest.*

GUSTO. *sm.* [Sentido]. *Taste.* ~Este guiso tiene poco GUSTO. *This stew is tasteless.* ~Tiene un GUSTO amargo. *It has a bitter taste.* ~Resulta amargo al GUSTO. *It has a bitter taste.* ~Esta bebida tiene un extraño GUSTO. *This drink has a strange taste.* ~Tiene GUSTO a fresa. *It tastes of strawberry.* ~Tiene GUSTO a quemado. *It has a burned taste.* ~Esto no tiene GUSTO a nada. *This doesn't taste of anything.* ‖ **2.** [Figuratively]. *Taste.* ~Sus palabras me dejaron un GUSTO amargo. *Her words left me with a nasty taste in my mouth.* ‖ **3.** Sabor. *Flavor.* ~¿De qué GUSTO quieres el helado? *What flavor ice cream do you want?* ‖ **4.** Sentido estético. *Taste.* ~Tiene un GUSTO horrible. *She has awful taste.* ~Tiene mucho GUSTO para arreglar las flores. *She does very tasteful flower arrangements.* •Ser de buen o mal GUSTO. *To be in good/bad taste.* ~No me parece de buen GUSTO lo que dijiste. *I don't think that what you said was in very good taste.* ~Una broma de mal GUSTO. *A joke that was in very bad taste.* •Tener buen/mal GUSTO. *To have good/bad taste.* ~Tiene muy buen GUSTO para vestirse. *She has very good taste in clothes.* •Ser persona de GUSTO. *To be a person of taste.* •¡Qué GUSTO! *How lovely! (what taste!).* ‖ **5.** Afición, inclinación. *Inclination, liking, taste.* Nuestros GUSTOS son muy dispares. *We have very different tastes.* ~Tiene GUSTOS caros. *She has expensive tastes.* ~Ha heredado de su padre el GUSTO por la música. *He has inherited a liking (love) of music from his father.* ~Es difícil elegir un libro si no conocemos sus GUSTOS. *Its difficult to choose a book for him* *without knowing what he likes.* ~Un verde demasiado vivo para mi GUSTO. *Too bright a green for my taste (liking).* •Eso va a GUSTOS. *It's a matter of taste.* •Hay para todos los GUSTOS. *There's something to suit every taste.* •Sobre GUSTOS no hay nada escrito. *There is no accounting for taste, to each his own.* •Hay GUSTOS que merecen palos. *Some people have no taste.* •Nunca llueve a GUSTOS de todos. *One man's meat is another man's poison, you can't please everyone.* •En la variedad está el GUSTO. *Variety is the spice of life.* ‖ **6.** [Con fórmulas de cortesía]. *Pleasure.* Mucho GUSTO, tanto GUSTO. *How do you do?, glad to meet you.* Con mucho GUSTO. *With pleasure.* ~El GUSTO es mío. *The pleasure is mine.* ~Tendré mucho GUSTO en acompañarle al aeropuerto. *I'd be delighted to take you to the airport.* ~Tengo el GUSTO de comunicarle que. *It gives me great pleasure to inform you that.* ~Tener GUSTO en. *To be glad to.* ‖ **7.** Agrado. *Liking.* ~¿Está a su GUSTO el peinado? *Is the style to your liking?* ~Agregue azúcar a gusto. *Add sugar to taste.* ~Al GUSTO del consumidor. *However you like it.* •Al GUSTO de. *To the liking of.* •SER del GUSTO de uno. *To be to somebody's liking.* •Tomar el GUSTO a. *To take a liking to.* •Tener gusto por. *To have a liking for, have an eye for.* •Hay para todos los gustos. *There is something for everyone.* •Nunca llueve a GUSTO de todos. *You can't make everyone happy.* •Sobre GUSTOS no hay nada escrito. *There is no accounting for taste.* ‖ **8.** Antojo, deseo, capricho, *Whim, fancy.* Satisface todos los GUSTOS de sus hijos. *He indulges all his childrens whims.* ~No puedo permitirme esos GUSTOS tan caros. *I can't afford such luxuries.* ~Maneja al marido a su GUSTO. *She has her husband twisted around her little finger.* •A gusto. *At will, according*

to one's fancy. ~Maneja las cifras a su GUSTO. *He manages figures according to his fancy.* ‖ **9.** Voluntad. *Will.* ~Lo hizo por su GUSTO, sin que nadie le obligara. *He did it of his own free will.* ~El siempre hace su GUSTO. *He always does what he wants to.* •Quien por su GUSTO padece, vaya al infierno a quejarse. *One must face the consequences of his own actions.* ‖ **10.** Placer, agrado, *Pleasure. satisfaction.* ~Da GUSTO ver a tanta gente joven. *It's a pleasure to see so many young people.* •Dar GUSTO a alguien (complacer a alguien). *To please somebody.* •Darse el GUSTO. *To treat oneself.* ~Hoy sí voy a darme el GUSTO. *I'm really going to treat myself today.* ~Darse los GUSTOS en la vida. *To enjoy life.* •Hacer algo a GUSTO. *To enjoy doing something.* •Por GUSTO. *For fun, for pleasure.* ~Escribe por gusto, no por dinero. *He writes for pleasure, not for the money.* •Dar GUSTO. *To please.* ~Dáme gusto y estudia. *Do me a favor and study.* •No hay GUSTO sin disgusto. *There is no rose without a thorn.* ‖ **11** Satisfacción. *Satisfaction.* ~Me di el GUSTO de decírselo a la cara. *I took satisfaction in telling it to his face.* ~El asunto se resolvió por fin a GUSTO de todos. *To the satisfaction of everyone, the matter was finally resolved.* ‖ **12.** LOCUCIONES. •Que da GUSTO. *Wonderfully, beautifully.* Baila que da GUSTO. *She dances beautifully.* ‖ •A gusto en. *Confortable, at ease, happy.* ¿Estás a GUSTO en tu nuevo trabajo? *Are you happy at your new job?* ~No se siente a GUSTO entre gente tan distinguida. *He feels ill at ease among such distinguishd people.* ‖ •Acomodarse a su GUSTO. *To make someone feel at home.* ‖ •Estar a GUSTO. *To feel at ease, be comfortable, to feel at home.* ~Aquí me encuentro a GUSTO. *Here I feel at home.* ⇨GUSTO

H

HABILIDAD. *sf.* Destreza. *Skill.* Con gran habilidad. *With great skill.* ~Siempre ha tenido gran HABILIDAD para la carpintería. *He's always been very good (adept) at carpentry.* ~Los futbolistas tienen HABILIDAD en el manejo del balón. *Basketball players are very skillful at handling the ball.* ‖ **2.** Astucia. *Cleverness, smartness.* ~Tiene gran HABILIDAD para convencer a sus oponentes. *He's very clever at convincing his opponents.* ~La película está realizada con gran HABILIDAD. *It's a very cleverly made movie.* ‖ **3.** DER [De un testigo]. *Competence.* ‖ **4.** Talento. *Talent.* ~La niña tuvo que lucir todas sus HABILIDADES delante de la familia. *The girl had to display all her talents before the family.* ‖ **5.** Lo que alguien realiza con facilidad, gracia y destreza. *Trick, feat, sleight of hand (mago).* ~Hace muchas habilidades en el trampolín. *He does a lot of feats on the trampoline.* ~Los niños disfrutaron con las HABILIDADES del mago. *The children had a great time watching the magician's tricks.* ‖ **6.** LOCUCIONES. •Tener HABILIDAD manual. *To be good with one's hands.* ‖ •Tener HABILIDAD para. *To be good at.* ‖ •Habilidades. *Skills.* ⇨ABILITY

HISTORIA. *sf.* Cuento, narración. *Story, tale.* ~El libro cuenta la HISTORIA de su vida. *The book tells the story of his life.* ~Es una HISTORIA larga de contar. *It's a long story.* ‖ **2.** Lío amoroso. *Scene.* ~Tuvo una HISTORIA con una inglesa. *He had a scene with an English girl.* ‖ **3.** Cuento, excusa, cosa inventada. *Excuse, tale.* ~Ahora me viene con la HISTORIA de que le robaron la cartera. *Now he's come up with this tale about his wallet being stolen.* ~No me vengas con HISTORIAS. *Don't come to me with your tales, don't give me that, don't give me any of your stories.* ~Déjate de HISTORIAS y dime por qué no viniste ayer. *Stop making excuses and tell me why you didn't come yesterday.* ~Estoy harto de escuchar siempre la misma HISTORIA. *I'm fed up with hearing the same old excuse.* ‖ **4.** Asunto. *Matter.* ~Alquien se quejó de no sé qué HISTORIA. *Somebody complained about something or another.* ~Estuvo metido en una HISTORIA de drogas. *He was mixed up with something to do with drugs.* ‖ **5.** Lío, problema. *Fuss, problem, trouble.* ~Ya tuvimos una HISTORIA con ellos hace dos meses. *We've already had a problem with them a couple of months ago.* ~Armar HISTORIAS. *To make trouble.* ‖ **6.** Chisme, enredo. *Gossip.* ‖ **7.** LOCUCIONES. •Es una mujer con HISTORIA. *She's a woman with a past.* ‖ •La HISTORIA de siempre. *The same old story, the same old song.* ‖ •La HISTORIA es larga de contar. *It's a long story.* ‖ •Ser de HISTORIA. *To be famous, to be notorious (peyorativo).* ‖ •¡Déjate de HISTORIAS¡ *Get to the point!* ‖ •Ser HISTORIA. *To be a thing of the past, to become unimportant.* ~Los malos ratos que pasamos ya son HISTORIA. *The bad times we had are over.* ⇨HISTORY

HONESTIDAD. *sf.* Pudor, decencia, decoro, recato. *Modesty, decency, propriety, decorum.* ‖ **2.** Castidad. *Purity, chastity.* ‖ **3.** Fairness. *Justicia.* ⇨HONESTY

HONESTO. *ms.* Decente o decoroso. *Decent, decorous, proper.* ‖ **2.** Recatado, pudoroso. *Modest.* ‖ **3.** Casto. *Pure, chaste.* ‖ **4.** LOCUCIONES. •Estado HONESTO. *Celibacy (mujer).* •Poco HONESTO. *Indecent, immoral.* ►"Honesto se asocia primordialmente

con la idea de castidad, en tanto que *honra-do* denota probidad y rectitud." (Alfaro).
⇨ HONEST

HORA. *sf.*

❶ GENERAL. [Del reloj]. *Time (of day).* ~¿Qué HORA es? *What time is it?* || **2.** Momento. *Moment, time.* ~A la HORA de su muerte. *At the moment (time) of his death.* ~Ya es HORA de irse a la cama. *It's time for bed.* || **3.** Experience. *Experiencia.* || **4.** Antigüedad. *Seniority.*

❷ LOCUCIONES.

• A BUENA(S) HORA(S). (I) *In good time.* ~Has venido a buena HORA. *You've come at a good time.* (II) ~¿Llamó ayer y me lo dices ahora? *¡A buenas horas?* *He called yesterday? Now you tell me! (it's a bit late isn't it?)* ~A buenas HORAS llegas. *This is a fine time to arrive!*

• A ESTAS HORAS. (I) *At this moment, by this time, about now.* ~A estas HORAS debe de estar llegando a Nueva York. *About now he must be arriving in New York.* ~Normalmente a estas HORAS ya hemos cenado. *We're usually finished with dinner by this time.* (II) En este momento. *Right now.* ~A estas HORAS, todavía no sé si me voy o me quedo. *I haven't made up my mind if I should go or not.*

• A LA HORA. *On the dot, punctually, on time.* ~Las clases siempre empiezan a la HORA. *Classes always begin on time.* ~Los trenes nunca llegan a la HORA. *Trains never arrive on time.*

• A LA HORA DE. *When it comes to.* ~Seguro que van a tener problemas a la HORA de traducir eso. *You can be sure they'll have problems when it comes to translating this.*

• A LA HORA DE AHORA. *At this time of the day.*

• A LA HORA DE LA VERDAD. *When it comes down to it.* ~A la HORA de la verdad nunca hacen nada. *When it comes down to it they never do anything.*

• A LA HORA EN PUNTO. *Right on time.*

• A LA HORA JUSTA. *On the stroke of time.*

• A LAS HORAS (DE UNO). *At regular times.* ~El niño tiene que comer a sus HORAS. *The*

child has to have its meals at regular time.

• A ESTAS HORAS. *At this time.* ~No puedo tomar café a estas HORAS porque me desvelo. *I can't drink coffee so late in the day because it keeps me awake.*

• A PRIMERA HORA. *First thing in the morning, early.* ~The llamaré a primera HORA de la mañana. *I'll call you first thing (early) in the morning.*

• A SU HORA. *At the proper time.*

• A TODAS HORAS. *All the time.* ~Está a todas HORAS diciéndome que tiene mucho dinero. *He keeps telling me (repeating) how much money he has.*

• A ÚLTIMA HORA. *At the last moment; in the nick of time; at the eleventh hour; last thing at night.* ~A última HORA decidimos no ir. *At the last moment we decided not to go.*

• A ALTAS HORAS DE. ~A altas HORAS de la madrugada. *In the early hours of the morning.*

• ANTES DE HORA. *Too early.*

• ANTES DE SU HORA. *Earlier, ahead of schedule.* ~El avión llegó antes de su HORA. *The plane arrived ahead of schedule.*

• CERO HORAS. *Midnight.* ~Se ha convocado una huelga desde la cero HORAS. *A strike has been called starting at midnight.*

• DAR HORA. *To give an appointment.* ~El médico me ha dado HORA para mañana. *The doctor has given me an appointment for tomorrow, I've got an appointment with the doctor tomorrow.*

• DAR LA HORA. *To strike.*

• DE HORA EN HORA. *Gradually.* ~Se le ve mejorar de HORA en HORA. *He's gradually getting better.*

• DEJAR LAS COSAS HASTA LA ÚLTIMA HORA. *To leave things until the last moment.*

• EN BUENA HORA. ~En buena HORA se me ocurrió venir a este país. *What a mistake it was for me to come to this country,* (II) Ojalá sea así. En buena HORA lo digas. *Let's hope this is the case,* (III) *At the right time, luckily.* ~En buena HORA decidimos comprar esta casa. *We decided to buy this house at the right time, luckily we decided to buy the house.*

•EN MALA HORA. *At a bad time, at the wrong time.* ~En mala HORA se nos ocurrió meternos en este lío. *It was really a bad move getting ourselves involved in this mess.* ~En mala HORA se le ocurrió irse a bañar en el río. *It was unfortunate that he had to take a bath (go for a swim) in the river.*

•EN QUÉ HORA. *Why in heaven* ¿En qué HORA se me ocurrió dedicarme a eso? *Why in heaven did I decide to spend my time doing that?*

•EN SU HORA. *At the proper time.*

•ENTRE HORAS. ~Comer entre HORAS. *To eat between meals.* ~Se pasa el día picando entre HORAS. *She nibbles all day.*

•ES HORA. *It's high time.* ~Es HORA en que vayas pensando en el futuro. *It's high time you started thinking of your future.*

•GANAR HORAS. *To save time.*

•HACER HORAS. *To work overtime.* ~Esta semana hice HORAS porque tenía trabajo atrasado. *I worked overtime this week because I was behind in my work.*

•HORA DE RECREO. *Playtime.*

•HORA DEL CIERRE. *Closing time (de un negocio), news deadline (de un periódico), closedown (de una emisión).*

•HORA FATAL. *Fateful hour.*

•¡HORA INGLESA! *On the dot.*

•HORA LEGAL U OFICIAL. *Standard time.*

•HORA LIBRE. *Free period.*

•HORA PENINSULAR. *Time in mainland Spain.*

•HORA SUPREMA. *Supreme moment.* ~Lucharé contra ellos hasta la HORA suprema. *I'll fight them to the supreme moment.*

•HORAS DE ATENCIÓN AL PÚBLICO de ocho a una. *Open to the public from eight to one.*

•HORAS DE VUELO. *Flying time.*

•HORAS EXTRAS (extraordinarias, suplementarias). *Overtime.*

•HORAS LIBRES. *Free, spare time.*

•HORAS MUERTAS. *Most of the time.* ~Se pasa las HORAS muertas jugando al billar. *He whiles away his time playing pool, he spends most of this time playing pool.*

•HORAS VALLE. *Off-peak times.*

•LA HORA DE LA VERDAD. *The moment of truth.*

•LLEGARLE LA HORA A UNO. ~Sabía que le había llegado su (última) HORA. *He knew his time had come.*

•LLEVAR HORA. *To have one's watch.* ~No sé cuánto tiempo estoy esperando porque no llevo HORA. *I don't know how long I have been waiting because I don't have my watch with me.*

•MALDITA SEA LA HORA QUE ... *Curse the day that ...* ~Maldita sea la HORA en que decidió volver. *Curse the day he decided to come back.*

•NO DAR NI LA HORA. *Not to give the time of day.* ~Desde que la nombraron jefa, no nos da ni la HORA del día. *Now that she's been made boss, she doesn't even give us the time of day.*

•NO SER HORAS DE. *To be no time to.* Éstas no son HORAS de llamar. *This is no time to call people up.*

•NO VER LA HORA (de algo). *To look forward impatiently (for something).* ~No veo la HORA de que se vaya. *I can't wait for him to leave.* ~No veo la HORA en que lleguen las vacaciones. *I'm really looking forward to my vacation.*

•NOTICIAS DE ÚLTIMA HORA. *Last-minute news.*

•PASAR LAS HORAS EN BLANCO. *To have a sleepless night.*

•PASARSE LAS HORAS MUERTAS. *To while away one's time.*

•PEDIR HORA. *To make an appointment.* ~¿Hay que pedir HORA para ver al especialista? *Do I need to make an appointment to see the specialist?*

•PONER EN HORA (reloj). *To set one's watch.* ~Puso en HORA su reloj para no llegar tarde a la cita. *He set his watch so he would not be late for his appointment.*

•SER LA HORA DE. *To be the time to.* Es la HORA de volver. *It's time to come back.* ~La HORA de acostarse. *Bedtime.* ~La HORA de comer. *Lunchtime.* ~La HORA de cenar. *Dinnertime.*

•SONAR LA HORA (de hacer aglo). *To be time (to do something).*

•TENER HORA. *To have an appointment.* ~Tengo HORA con el dentista a las cuatro. *I*

have a dental appointment at four.
•TENER HORAS DE VUELO. *To be an old hand, to be all there.*
•TENER LAS HORAS CONTADAS. *To have one's days numbered.* ~Tiene las HORAS contadas en la oficina. *His days at the office are numbered.*
•ÚLTIMA HORA. *Stop the presses.* ~Última HORA: terremoto en Santiago. *Stop the presses: earthquake in Santiago.*
•¡VAYA UNAS HORAS PARA SALIR! *What a fine time to go out!*
•YA ERA HORA. ~¡Ya era HORA de que llamaras! *It's about time you called!*

HÚMEDO [HUMID]. *adj.* [Casa, ropa, suelo, pared]. *Damp.* ~Esta toalla está HÚMEDA, coge otra seca. *This towel is damp, get a dry one.* || **2.** Empapado. *Wet.* || **3.** [Labios]. *Moist.* || **4.** [Ojos]. *Wet.* ~Tenía los ojos HÚMEDOS. *His eyes were full of tears.* || **5.** [País, lugar]. *Rainy.* ~Galicia es una región HÚMEDA. *Galicia is a rainy country.*

HUMOR [HUMOR]. *sm.* Genio. *Temper.* ~Tiene HUMOR de perro. *He has a very nasty temper.* || **2.** Estado de ánimo. *Mood.* ~Siempre está de mal HUMOR. *He's always in a bad mood.* ~Espera que esté de buen HUMOR para decírselo. *Wait until he's in a good mood before you tell him.* ~No tengo HUMOR para ir al teatro. *I'm not in the mood to go to the theater.*

I

IDEA [IDEA]. *sf.* Opinión. *Opinion.* ~Cambiar de IDEA. *To change one's mind.* ~Es de ideas bastante conservadoras. *He's quite conservative in his outlook.* ¿Qué IDEA tienes de él? *What do you think of him?* || **2.** Intención. *Intention.* ~No era mi idea ofenderte. *I didn't mean to offend you.* ~Mi IDEA era terminarlo hoy. *My intention was to finish it today.*

IDIOMA. *ms.* Lenguaje. *Language, tongue.* Habla cuatro IDIOMAS a la perfección. *He speak four languages fluently.* ⇨IDIOM

IGNORAR. *v.* Desconocer, no saber cierta cosa. *Not to know, be unaware of, be ignorant of.* ~IGNORO sus señas. *I don't know his address.* ~IGNORABA que ella le quería. *He didn't realize (was not aware) that she was fond of him.* ~IGNORABA que ... *I had no idea that ...* ~IGNORAMOS su paradero. *We don't know his whereabouts.* ⇨IGNORE

IGUAL. *adj.* Idéntico. *Identical.* ~Son IGUALES en todo. *They're identical in every way.* ~Por tí no pasan los años, estás IGUALITO. *Time hasn't changed you a bit, you're just the same.* || **2.** Semejante. *Anything like it, such a thing.* ~Jamás había oído estupidez IGUAL. *I had never heard anything so stupid.* ~No había visto nada IGUAL en mi vida. *I'd never seen anything like it in my life.* || **3.** Lo mismo. *The same.* Nuestros pareceres son prácticamente IGUALES. *Our opinions are practically the same.* ~Cómo está el enfermo? -IGUAL. *How is the patient? -About the same.* || **4.** Constante. *Uniform, constant, unvarying, unchanging.* ~Lleva un ritmo de vida muy IGUAL. *He works at an even (steady) pace.* ~La fuerza aplicada debe ser siempre IGUAL. *The amount of force applied must remain constant (uniform).* ~La marcha IGUAL del tren. *The steady motion of the train.* || **5.** Semejante, parecido. *Similar.* ~Este discurso es IGUAL que el que pronunció el año pasado. *This speech is similar to, pretty much the same as, the one he delivered last year.* || **6.** DEP Empatados. *Even, tied.* ~Ir iguales. *To be even.* || **7.** [Llano, mesa]. *Even, level.* ~Necesitamos una tabla que tenga la superficie muy IGUAL, para usarla como mesa. *We need an even (level) board that we can use as a table.* || **8.** Liso. *Smooth.* || **9.** [Temperatura]. *Even.* ⇨EQUAL

IGUALAR [EQUAL]. *v.* Nivelar (superficie, terreno, camino). *To level.* ~IGUALARON la superficie de la carretera antes de asfaltarla. *They leveled the surface of the road before asphalting it.* || **2.** Pulir, alisar. *To smooth.* || **3.** MAT *To equate.* || **4.** Llegar a un acuerdo. *To agree upon, conclude.* ~IGUALAR una venta. *To conclude a sale.* || **5.** [Flequillo, dobladillo]. *To even up, make straight.* ¿Puedes IGUALARME las puntas? *Could you even up (trim) the ends for me?* || **6.** [Precios]. *To match.* ~Nadie puede IGUALAR nuestros precios. *Nobody can match our prices.* || **7.** Empatar. *To tie.* ~Roca IGUALÓ a los tres minutos. *Roca tied the score three minutes later.* || **8.** [Césped]. *To trim.* || **9.** [Pintura, color, beauty]. *To match.* ~El color del pantalón IGUALA con él de la chaqueta. *The color of the pants matches that of his jacket.* ~Ninguna mujer IGUALA su belleza. *No woman matches her beauty.*

ILUMINAR. Alumbrar. *To light.* ~Una tenue luz ILUMINABA la habitación. *A pale light lit the room* || **2.** [Rostro, ojos]. *To light up.* ~Una sonriso ILUMINÓ su rostro. *A smile lit*

up her face. ~La alegría ILUMINÓ su cara. *His face lit up with joy.* || **3.** Aclarar alguna materia. *To enlighten.* || **4.** [Tema]. *To throw light upon.* || **5.** [Un estadio]. *To floodlight.* || **6.** [Con fondo de color]. *To provide (prints, engravings, etc.) with colored background.* ⇨ILLUMINATE

ILUSIÓN. *sf.* Esperanza, sueño. *Hope, dream, wish.* ~Su mayor ILUSIÓN es de ver a su hija casada. *Her fondest wish is to see her daughter married.* ~Sus ILUSIONES se realizaron. *His hopes were fulfilled, his dream came true.* ~Tiene la ILUSIÓN de que. *He cherishes the hope that.* ~El hombre de sus ILUSIONES. *The man of her dreams.* No me hago muchas ILUSIONES de que me lo van a conceder. *I'm not very hopeful that they'll give it to me.* || **2.** Alegría, satisfacción. *Excitement, thrill.* •Hacerse ILUSIÓN. *To be thrilled about.* El viaje nos hace mucha ILUSIÓN. *We're getting very excited about the trip, we're looking forward to the trip.* ~Tu carta me hizo mucha ILUSIÓN. *I was thrilled to receive your letter.* || **3.** Entusiasmo. *Eagerness.* ~Todos empezamos con mucha ILUSIÓN. *We all started with great enthusiasm.* || **4.** *LOCUCIONES.* || •Forjarse, hacerse ILUSIONES. *To build one's hopes.* || •¡Qué ILUSIÓN! *How exciting!* ~¡Qué ILUSIÓN! ¡un mes de vacaciones. *How exciting! a month's vacation!* || •No te hagas ILUSIONES. *Don't bank on it, don't kid yourself, don't raise your hopes, don't get false ideas, don't build your hopes up.* || •Con ILUSIÓN. *Hopefully.* || •Vive de ILUSIONES. *He lives in a dream world.* ⇨ ILLUSION

ILUSTRACIÓN. *sf.* Erudición. *Learning, erudition, enlightenment.* ~Una persona de vasta ILUSTRACIÓN. *An extremely erudite (learned) person.* || **2.** Publicación. *Illustrated magazine.* || **3.** La Ilustración. *The Enlightenment.* ~La ILUSTRACIÓN culminó con la Revolución Francesa. *The Age of Enlightenment reached its peak with the coming of the French Revolution.* ⇨ILLUSTRATION

ILUSTRADO [ILLUSTRATED]. *adj.* Culto, docto, instruido. *Learned, erudite, enlightened.* ~Habla bien, denotando que es una persona ILUSTRADA. *He speaks well, which*

shows that he's an educated person.

ILUSTRAR[1] [ILLUSTRATE]. *v.* To enlighten. *Instruir.* ~¿Que no lo sabes? Pues te voy a ILUSTRAR. *Don't you know? Well, let me enlighten you.* || **2.** Hacer famoso. *To make famous, to make illustrious.*

ILLUSTRARSE[2] [ILLUSTRATE]. *vr.* Educarse. *To acquire knowledge, learn.*

IMAGEN. *sf.* [En la mente]. *Picture.* ~Sólo conservo una IMAGEN borrosa de él. *I only have a very vague picture of him.* ~Hizo una IMAGEN de cómo sería el cuarto después de decorarlo. *He tried to picture how the room would look after he redecorated it.* || **2.** Semejanza. *Likeness.* || **3.** [Foto, TV]. *Picture.* || **4.** [En un espejo]. *Reflection.* ~Contemplaba su IMAGEN en el agua. *He was contemplating his reflection in the water.* ~Miró su IMAGEN en el espejo y le pareció que había envejecido. *He looked at his reflection in the mirror and had the impression that he had gotten older.* || **5.** [Estampa]. *Picture.* ⇨IMAGE

IMPARTIR. *v.* [En general]. *To give.* IMPARTIR asistencia médica. *To give medical assistance.* || **2.** Enseñar, dar (clases). *To give (classes).* ~IMPARTIR clases de informática. *To give computer classes.* ~Durante la Edad Media las clases se IMPARTÍAN en latín. *In the Middle Ages classes were given in Latin.* || **3.** [Órdenes]. *To give, issue.* ~Las órdenes se IMPARTEN únicamente desde la comandancia. *Orders are issued solely from command headquarters.* || **4.** •IMPARTIR su bendición. *To give one's blessing to.* ⇨IMPART

IMPEDIR. *v.* Imposibilitar, prohibir. *To prevent. stop.* ~Una importante reunión me IMPEDIRÁ ir al bautizo. *An important meeting will prevent me from going to the christening.* ~El dolor le IMPEDÍA caminar. *The pain prevented him from walking.* ~No logró IMPEDIR el accidente. *She was unable to prevent the accident.* || **2.** Disuadir. *To deter.* || **3.** Obstruir. *To block.* ~IMPEDIR el tráfico. *The obstruct the traffic.* ~Nos IMPEDIÓ el paso. *He blocked our way.* ~Esta válvula IMPIDE el paso del gas. *This valve blocks the flow of gas.* || **4.** Frustrar. *To thwart.* || **5.** •Eso no IMPIDE que. *This does not alter the* *fact that.* || **6.** •¡Nadie te lo IMPIDE! *Nobody's stopping you!* ⇨IMPEDE

IMPENETRABLE [IMPENETRABLE]. *adj.* [Secreto, acción]. *Obscure.* || **2.** [Persona]. *Inscrutable.* || **3.** [Fortaleza], *Impregnable.* || **4.** [Ojos, expresión, mirada]. *Unscrutable.* Su mirada IMPENETRABLE no dejaba ver lo que en realidad pensaba. *His unscrutable look did not reveal what he was really thinking.* || **5.** [Misterio, secreto, engima]. *Unfathomable.*

IMPLICACIÓN. *sf.* Contradicción, oposición. *Contradiction (in terms).* || **2.** Consecuencia. *Consequence.* ~Esta decisión política tendrá sin duda IMPLICACIONES negativas. *~This political move will undoubtedly have negative consequences.* || **3.** Participación. *Involvement.* ~Su posible IMPLICACIÓN en el escándalo. *His possible involvement in the scandal.* ⇨IMPLICATION

IMPLICAR. *v.* Conllevar, significar, entrañar. *To imply, entail, mean.* ~Eso no IMPLICA que no seamos amigos. *That doesn't mean that we are not friends.* ⇨IMPLICATE

IMPONER[1]. *v.* Exigir. *To demand, exact.* || **2.** [Silencio, obedencia]. *To command, demand.* || **3.** [Nombre]. *To give.* ~Se le IMPUSO el nombre de 'Calle de los Mártires'. *It was given the name of 'Street of the Martyrs'.* || **4.** Instruir. *To instruct.* ~IMPONER a uno en contabilidad. *To instruct someone in bookkeeping.* || **5.** Informar. *To inform, acquaint.* IMPONER a alguien de los hechos. *To acquaint someone with the facts, to inform someone of the facts.* || **6.** [Dinero, fondos]. *To deposit.* ~IMPONER dinero en el banco. *To deposit money in the bank.* || **7.** [Edificio]. *To be impressive.* || **8.** [Respeto, admiración, miedo]. *To inspire.* || **9.** [Carga]. *To lay, thrust upon.* || **10.** [Moda]. *To set.* || **11.** [Impuesto]. *To put, levy.* || **12.** Achacar. *To impute falsely.* || **13.** [Condecoración, medalla]. *To confer, award.* ~Le IMPUSO la máxima condecoración. *He conferred the highest civilian award upon him.* || **14.** Requerir (tarea). *To exact, demand.* || **15.** Asumir. *To assume, take on.* ~IMPONER un

deber. *To take on, assume a duty.* ⇨IMPOSE

IMPONERSE[2]. *vr.* Prevalecer. *To prevail.* ~Se IMPUSO el sentido común. *Common sense prevailed.* || **2.** Ponerse de moda. *To be fashionable.* ~Se ha vuelto a IMPONER la falda corta. *Short skirts have become fashionable again.* || **3.** Hacerse obedecer. *To assert oneself, get one's way, exact obedience from* || **4.** [Horario]. *To set oneself.* || **5.** [Idea]. *To become established.* || **6.** [Cambio, decisión]. *To be imperative, necessary.* Se IMPONE tomar una decision hoy mismo. *It's imperative that a decision be made today.* || **7.** Vencer. *To win.* ~Se IMPUSO por puntos. *He won on points.* ⇨IMPOSE

IMPOSICIÓN. *sf.* [Dinero]. *Deposit.* ~Hacer una IMPOSICIÓN. *To deposit money.* || **2.** Impuesto. *Tax.* ~IMPOSICIÓN directa. *Direct taxation.* || **3.** [De un impuesto]. *Introduction.* || **4.** Exigencia, obligación. *Demand.* ~A mí no me vengas con IMPOSICIONES. *Don't you start telling me what to do.* ⇨IMPOSITION

IMPRESIONAR. *v.* Conmover. *To move, touch, affect (with emotion, feeling).* ~Sus cariñosas palabras me IMPRESIONARON. *His affectionate words touched me.* || **2.** [Foto]. *To expose.* || **3.** Grabar (discos). *To cut, press* || **4.** *To shock, stun.* ~Me IMPRESIONÓ mucho verla tan delgada. *It really shocked me to see her so thin.* ~Lo que más me IMPRESIONÓ fue el estado lamentable del edificio. *What struck me the most was the terrible state the building was in.* ⇨IMPRESS

IMPROPRIO. *adj.* [Comportamiento, actitud, respuesta]. *Inappropriate, unsuitable.* ~Un comportamiento IMPROPRIO de una persona educada. *Inappropriate behavior for (unbecoming to) an educated person.* ~Un libro IMPROPRIO para su edad. *An unsuitable book for his age.* || **2.** Incorrecto. *Incorrect.* ~Es un uso IMPROPRIO de la palabra. *It is an incorrect usage of the word.* ⇨IMPROPER

INADECUADO. *adj.* Inapropiado. *Inappropriate, unsuitable.* ~Este libro es INADECUADO para niños de esa edad. *This book is unsuitable for children of his age.* ⇨INADEQUATE

INALTERABLE [UNALTERABLE]. *adj.* [Color]. *Fast, permamemt.* ‖ **2.** Impasible. *Impassive, imperturbable.* ‖ **3.** [Valores]. *Immutable.* ~Una mujer de una serenidad INALTERABLE. *A woman of immutable serenity.* ‖ **4.** [Amistad]. *Undying.* ‖ **5.** [Alimentos]. *Imperishable.*

INAPELABLE [UNAPPEALABLE]. *adj.* Inevitable. *Inevitable, unavoidable, irremediable.* ~Si seguimos jugando así, nuestra victoria is INAPELABLE. *If we keep playing this way, we will inevitably win.* ‖ **2.** [Triunfo, victoria]. *Indisputable.* ‖ **3.** Irrevocable. *Final.* ~Las decisiones de los jueces serán INAPELABLES. *The judges' decisions will be final.* ~La decisión de mi padre fue INAPELABLE. *My father's decision was final.*

INAUGURAR. *v.* [Canal, puente, exposición]. *To open (formally).* ‖ **2.** [Estátua, placa]. *To unveil.* ‖ **3.** [Una casa]. *To have a house-warming party.* ‖ **4.** [Curso]. *Start.* Hoy se INAUGURÓ el curso universitario. *Classes at the university started today.* ‖ **5.** Marcar primero (en un partido). *To open.* Brasil INAUGURÓ el marcador a los tres minutos. *Brazil opened the scoring after three minutes.* ⇨INAUGURATE

INCIDENCIA. *sf.* Influencia, efecto. *Impact, repercussion, consequence, effect.* ~Su discurso tuvo una gran INCIDENCIA. *His speech made a great impact.* ‖ **2.** Suceso, episodio. *Incident, events.* ~Un resumen de las INCIDENCIAS del viaje real. *Highlights of the royal tour.* ⇨INCIDENCE

INCITAR [INCITE]. v. Alentar, entusiasmar, animar. *To encourage.* ~Películas que INCITAN a la violencia. *Movies which encourage violence.* ~México trata de INCITAR a los norteamericanos a visitar el país. *Mexico tries to encourage Americans to visit their country.*

INCLINACIÓN. *sf.* Pendiente. *Slope, incline, slant.* ~La INCLINACIÓN del terreno. *The slope of the land.* ‖ **2.** [Del cuerpo]. *Stoop.* ‖ **3.** Reverencia. *Bow.* ~Me saludó con una leve INCLINACIÓN. *He acknowledged me with a slight bow.* ‖ **4.** Señal de asentimiento. *Nod.* ~Asintió con una INCLINACIÓN de la cabeza. *He nodded (his head) in agreement.* ‖ **5.** [Náutica]. *Tilt, pitch, list.* ‖ **6.** Predilección. *Fondness.* ~Tiene una INCLINACIÓN especial por la chiquita. *He's especially fond of the youngest one.* ⇨INCLINATION

INCONDICIONAL [UNCONDITIONAL]. *adj.* [Obediencia]. *Unquestioning, absolute.* ~Necesito de todos ustedes su INCONDICIONAL obediencia. *I require absolute obedience from all of you.* ‖ **2.** [Apoyo]. *Wholehearted.* ~Ud. tiene mi apoyo INCONDICIONAL. *You have my wholehearted support.* ‖ **3.** [Amigo]. *Faithful.* ~Toda la vida ha sido para mí un amigo INCONDICIONAL. *As long as I have known him he has been a most faithful friend.* ‖ **4.** [Partidario]. *Staunch.* Un partidario INCONDICIONAL de los derechos de la mujer. *~A staunch supporter of women's rights.* ‖ **5.** [Fe]. *Implicit, complete.* ~Tengo una fe INCONDICIONAL en sus méritos. *I'm totally convinced of his worth.* ‖ **6.** [Afirmación]. *Unqualified.*

INCONSCIENCIA [UNCONSCIOUSNESS]. *sf.* Desconocimiento, ignorancia. *Unawareness.* ~INCONSCIENCIA del riesgo. *Unawareness of the risk.* ‖ **2.** Irreflexión, insensatez. *Toughtlessness, irresponsability, recklessness.* ~Actúa con una INCONSCIENCIA propia de los 15 años. *He's as irresponsible as a 15-year old.*

INCONSISTENCIA. *sf.* Falta de consistencia (duración, estabilidad, solidez). *Frailty, instability, flimsiness.* ~La inconsistencia del material hizo que se rompiera el juguete. *The material was so flimsy that the toy broke.* ‖ **2.** [De líquido]. *Runniness, watery.* ‖ **3.** [De tela]. *Flimsiness.* ‖ **4.** [De argumento]. *Weakness, flimsiness.* ~Si analizas detenidamente los hechos, comprobarás la INCONSISTENCIA de tu teoría. *If you look at the facts closely you will realize the weakness of your theory.* ⇨INCONSISTENCY

INCONSISTENTE. *adj.* Falto de consistencia, endeble, frágil. *Weak, fragile.* ~Esta jarra es INCONSISTENTE. *This vase is fragile.* ‖ **2.** [De líquido]. *Runny, watery.* ‖ **3.** [De tela]. *Flimsy.* ‖ **4.** [De argumento]. *Weak, unsub-*

stantial. ⇨ INCONSISTENT

INCONVENIENCIA. *sf.* Impropriedad. *Unsuitability.* ‖ **2.** [No aconsejable]. *Inadvisability, inappropriateness.* ~Hemos discutido sobre la conveniencia o INCONVENIENCIA de marcharnos ahora. *We have been debating the advisability or indavisability of leaving at this moment.* ‖ **3.** Incorrección, descortesía. *Impoliteness.* ‖ **4.** Dicho grosero, disparate, indiscreción. *Rude remark.* ~Cometer una INCONVENIENCIA. *To be tactless.* ⇨INCONVENIENCE

INCONVENIENTE[1]. *adj.* Inapropiado, de mal gusto (lecturas, chistes). *Unsuitable, in bad taste.* ~Contó una anécdota INCONVENIENTE. *He told an off-color story.* ‖ **2.** No aconsejable. *Inadvisable.* ~Estas palabras tuyas son totalmente INCONVENIENTES en este momento. *Your comments are totally out of place at this time.* ‖ **3.** Incorrecto. *Impolite.* ‖ **4.** Grosero. *Rude, coarse.* ⇨INCONVENIENT

INCONVENIENTE[2] [INCONVENIENCE]. *sm.* Objection. *Objeción.* ¿Tiene algún INCONVENIENTE para que me case con su hija? *Do you have any objections against my marrying your daughter?* ‖ **2.** Desventaja. *Drawback, disadvantage.* ~Todo tiene sus ventajas y sus INCONVENIENTES. *Everything has it advantages and disadvantages.* ~Los INCONVENIENTES de viajar. *The drawbacks when you travel.* ‖ **3.** Problema, dificultad, obstáculo. *Difficulty, problem, obstacle.* ~Si no surge ningún INCONVENIENTE llegaré mañana. *If there are no problems I'll be there tomorrow.* ~Tiene el INCONVENIENTE de que está muy lejos. *The problem (trouble) is that its rather far away.* ‖ **4.** •Tener INCONVENIENTE. *To mind, to be all right.* ~Si usted no tiene INCONVENIENTE preferería que lo pagara ahora. *I'd rather you'd pay now if you don't mind.* ~No tengo INCONVENIENTE en decírselo. *I don't mind telling him.* ~¿Tienes INCONVENIENTE en acompañarme? *Do you mind coming with me?* ‖ **5.** •El INCONVENIENTE es que (está en). *The trouble (problem) is that.* ‖ **6.** •Poner INCONVENIENTE.

To give a problem. Si te ponen algún INCONVENIENTE para pagarte, dímelo. *If you have a problem getting paid, let me know.*

INCORPORAR[1]. *v.* [Ingredientes]. *To mix, blend.* ~INCORPORAR las claras batidas a la mezcla. *Blend the egg whites into the mixture.* ‖ **2.** Levantar. *To help to sit up.* ~La enfermera INCORPORÓ al anciano para darle la medicina. *The nurse help the elderly man to sit up so that she could give him his medicine.* ‖ **3.** Incluir, agregar. *To include, add.* ~INCORPORÓ estos detalles a su informe. *He included these details in his report.* ~INCORPORÓ otro capítulo al libro. *He added another chapter to his book.* ‖ **4.** Involucrar. *To involve.* ‖ **5.** [Teatro]. *To play the part of.* ‖ **6.** [Empleado]. *To assign.* ‖ **7.** [Recluta]. *To draft, call up, induct.* ‖ **8.** [Cabeza]. *To lift.* ~El perro INCORPORÓ la cabeza cuando oyó a su amo. *When the dog heard his master coming he lifted his head.* ⇨INCORPORATE

INCORPORARSE[2]. [Sociedad, regimiento]. *To join.* ‖ **2.** [Trabajo]. (I) [Por primera vez]. *To start.* ~INCORPORARSE al trabajo. *To go to (report for) work.* ~El capitán se INCORPORÓ al regimiento al que había sido destinado. *The captain reported to the regiment to which he had been assigned,* (II) [Volver]. *To go back to one's job.* ‖ **3.** [En la cama]. *To sit up, raise oneself.* ~Se INCORPORÓ en la cama. *He sat up in his bed.* ‖ **4.** Unirse. *To join.* Muchos se INCORPORARON a la protesta de los trabajadores. *Many joined the workers in their protest.* ⇨INCORPORATE

INCORRECCIÓN [INCORRECTNESS]. *sf.* Error. *Mistake, error.* ~El artículo está lleno de INCORRECCIONES. *The article if full of errors (inaccuracies).* ‖ **2.** Descortesía. *Discourtesy.* ~Me parece una INCORRECCIÓN no invitarlo. *It seems impolite (bad manners) not to invite him.*

INCREMENTO[INCREMENT]. *sm.* Crecimiento. *Growth.* ~El INCREMENTO de un negocio. *The growth of a business.* ‖ **2.** Aumento. *Increase, rise.* ~INCREMENTO salarial. *Pay increase.* ~El precio del kilo de carne ha sufrido un INCREMENTO de cien pesetas. *The price for a kilo of meat has increased by a* *hundred pesetas.* ‖ **3.** [Temperatura]. *Rise.*

INCURRIR. *v.* Cometer. *To commit.* ~INCUR-RIR en delito. *To commit a crime.* ~INCURRIÓ en un delito de fraude. *He committed fraud.* ‖ **2.** [En un error]. *To make, fall into.* ~INCURRIERON en el mismo error. *They made the same mistake.* ‖ **3.** [Desastre]. *To bring on oneself, become a victim of.* ⇨INCUR

INDICACIÓN. *sf.* Sugerencia. *Hint, suggestion.* ~Fui a este dentista por INDICACIÓN de tu padre. *I went to that dentist at your father's suggestion.* ~Aprovechó la INDICA-CIÓN. *He took the hint.* ~Seguiré sus INDI-CACIONES. *I'll follow your advice (suggestion).* ~No dio ninguna INDICACIÓN de sus intenciones. *She gave no hint of her intentions.* ‖ **2.** Instrucción. *Instruction, direction.* ~INDICACIONES para el uso. *Instructions for use.* ~Le dio INDICACIONES de cómo llegar. *He gave her directions as how to get there.* ~Siguió las INDICACIONES del prospecto. *She followed the instructions on the leaflet.* ‖ **3.** [Informe]. *Data, figures.* ‖ **4.** [Medicina]. *Symptoms, signs.* ‖ **5.** [Termómetro, instrumento]. *Reading.* ‖ **6.** Nota. *Note.* ~Una INDICACIÓN al margen. *A note in the margin.* ‖ **5.** Observación. *Remark, observation.* ⇨INDICATION

INDICAR [INDICATE]. *v.* Señalar. *To show, point out.* ~Un muchacho me INDICÓ dónde estaba la parada del autobús. *A young boy showed me where the bus stop was.* ~Me INDICÓ el lugar en el mapa. *He showed me (pointed out) the place on the map.* ~¿Me podría INDICAR el camino? *Could you show me the way?* ‖ **2.** Marcar (termómetro). *To read.* ~¿Qué INDICA el termómetro? *What does the thermometer read?* ‖ **3.** Aconsejar. *To show, advise, recommend.* INDÍQUEME lo que tengo que hacer. *Tell (show) me what I should do.* ~El abogado INDICÓ el procedimiento que había que seguir. *The lawyer advised us of the procedures we had to follow.* ~Siga las instrucciones que se INDICAN al dorso. *Follow the instructions given on the back.* ~Le INDIQUE que llevara un buen abrigo. *I recommended that he wear a heavy overcoat.* ‖ **4.** Esbozar. *To outline.* ‖

5. Sugerir. *To suggest, hint, reveal.* ~Es, como su propio nombre INDICA, una flor azul. *It is, as its name suggests, a blue flower.* Su traje INDICA gran pobreza. *His suit suggests extreme poverty.* ~La presencia de un ave les INDICÓ la proximidad de la costa. *The presence of a bird revealed that the coast was near.* ‖ **6.** Mostrar, denotar. *To show, give, reveal.* ~El precio no está INDICADO en el catálogo. *The price is not shown (given) in the catalogue.* ~Su mirada INDICABA cansancio. *His face revealed tiredness.* ‖ **7.** Decir. *To tell. request, ask.* ~Le INDIQUE que viniera más puntualmente. *I told him to try to be more punctual.* ~Le INDICARON que su presencia no era grata. *They told him that he was not welcome here.* ~Le INDICARON que permaneciera en silencio. *They told him to be quiet.* ‖ **8.** •Todo parece INDICAR que. *All the indications are that, there's every indication that.* ‖ **9.** •A la hora INDICADA. *At the scheduled time, at the specified time.*

INDIVIDUAL. *adj.* [Caso]. *Isolated.* ‖ **2.** [Cama, habitación]. *Single.* ~Hemos reservado en el hotel una habitación doble y otra INDIVIDUAL. *We've reserved a double room at the hotel and also a single one.* ‖ **3.** DEP [Prueba, final]. *Singles.* ~Individual femenino. *Women's singles.* ‖ **4.** Particular. *Peculiar, special.* ~El optimismo es el rasgo INDIVIDUAL más destacado de su carácter. *Optimism if one of his most prominent characteristics.* ‖ **5.** *sm.* Mantel. *Place mat.* ⇨INDIVIDUAL

INEXCUSABLE [INEXCUSABLE]. *adj.* Inevitable, ineludible. *Necessary, unavoidable, inevitable, inescapable.* ~Una visita INEXCU-SABLE. *A trip which must not be missed, an absolutely essential visit.* ~Tengo que marcharme porque tengo una cita INEXCU-SABLE. *I have to leave because I have an appointment that I absolutely can't miss (an extremely important appointment).*

INFERIOR [INFERIOR]. *adj.* Más bajo. *Lower.* ~Labio INFERIOR. *Lower lip.* ~El Egipto INFERIOR. *Lower Egypt.* ~En los pisos INFERIORES.*On the lower floors.* ~Las capas INFERIORES de la atmósfera. *The lower layers of the atmosphere.* || **2.** [En cantidad]. *Lower, less, under, below.* ~Cualquier número INFERIOR a diez. *Any number lower than (under, below) ten.* ~Pero el número puede haber sido muy INFERIOR. *But the number may have been much lower.* ~El bebé nació con un peso INFERIOR al normal. *The baby was below average weight when it was born.* ~Este juguete no es recomendable para niños de edad INFERIOR a los ocho años. *This toy is not recommended for children under eight.* || **3.** •La parte INFERIOR. *The lower part.* ~En la parte INFERIOR de la montaña la vegetación es más abundante. *There's much more vegetation in the lower part of the mountain.* || **4.** •Una cantidad INFERIOR a. *A lesser, smaller quantity than.*

INFERIR. *v.* [Herida, puñalada, golpe]. *Inflict.* ~El asaltante le INFIRIÓ una puñalada. *The attacker stabbed him (inflicted a stab wound on him).* ~Puede INFERIR un daño irreparable a nuestra juventud. *It could cause irreparable harm to our young people.* || **2.** [Daños]. *To cause.* ~Sacó una navaja y INFERIÓ una grave herida al dueño de la tienda. *He took out a knife and seriously wounded the owner of the shop.* || **3.** [Insulto]. *To insult.* Está enfadada con él porque en la discusión le INFERIÓ algunos insultos. *She's angry at him because in the discussion she insulted him.* || **4.** [Castigo]. *Impose.* ⇨INFER

INFERNAL [INFERNAL]. *adj.* [Calor]. *Unbearably hot.* ~Hacía un calor INFERNAL. *It was unbearingly hot.* || **2.** Terrible. *Terrible, unbearable.* ~Tengo un dolor de muelas INFERNAL. *I have a terrible, unbearable toothache.*

INFLAMAR[1]. *v.* Encender. *To set on fire, ignite.* ~Una chispa eléctrica INFLAMA la gasolina en el motor. *En electrical spark ignites the gasoline in the motor.* || **2.** Exaltar. *To excite, arouse, stir up.* ~INCITAR las pasiones. *To arouse passions.* ~La arenga INFLAMÓ los corazones de los soldados. *The speech stirred the hearts of the soldiers.* ⇨INFLAME

INFLAMARSE[2]. *vr.* Incendiarse. *To catch fire.* ~La pólvora se INFLAMÓ y explotaron varios cohetes. *The powder caught fire and many rockets exploded.* ⇨IMFLAME

INFORMAL. *adj.* [Person]. *Unreliable, untrustworthy.* ~Es muy INFORMAL, nunca llega a la hora que debe llegar. *He's very unreliable; he never arrives on time.* || **2.** [Comportamiento]. *Bad, unmannerly, incorrect.* || **3.** Poco usual. *Unconventional.* || **4.** Incapaz. *Unbusinesslike, disorganized.* || **5.** Maleducado. *Bad-mannered.* || **6.** Frívolo. *Frivolous.* ⇨INFORMAL

INGENIOSO. *adj.* Con chispa, agudeza. *Witty, clever.* || **2.** •Dárselas de INGENIOSO. *To try to be witty.* ⇨INGENIOUS

INGENUIDAD. *sf.* Candor. *Naiveté.* ⇨INGENUITY

INGENUO. *adj.* Crédulo. *Naive.* ⇨INGENUOUS

INGRATO [INGRATE]. *adj.* [Epoca, noticia]. *Unpleasant.* ~La estancia en ese hotel fue muy INGRATA porque tuvimos problemas con la dirección. *We had a very unpleasant stay at that hotel since we had problems with the management.* || **2.** [Trabajo]. *Thankless, unrewarding.* ~Es un trabajo INGRATO porque le dedico muchas horas y está muy mal pagado. *It's a thankless job since I spend much time at it and it pays little.* ~Las labores domésticas siempre son INGRATAS. *Housework is unrewarding work.* || **3.** [Tierra]. *Unproductive.* || **4.** [Sabor]. *Unpleasant, disagreeable.* || **5.** Desagradable, difícil. *Hard, difficult.* ~La vida es muy INGRATA. *Life is very hard.*

INICIAR[1]. *v.* Empezar (curso, viaje). *To begin, start.* ~El invitado INICIÓ el debate. *The invited guest started the discussion.* || **2.** [Una cosa nueva]. *To pioneer.* || **3.** Originar. *To originate.* || **4.** [En un arte]. *To introduce.* ~Su madre le INICIÓ en la lectura cuando era muy pequeño. *His mother introduced him to reading when he was very young.* ⇨INITIATE

INICIARSE[2]. *vr.* Aprender. *To learn.* INICIARSE en algo. *To learn something.*

~INICIARSE en el arte de tocar la guitarra. *To learn to play the guitar by oneself.* || **2.** Empezar (ceremonias, negociaciones). *To begin, start.* ~Se INICIÓ el debate el lunes. *The debate began on Monday.* || **3.** [En un arte]. *To take one's first steps in.* ~Se INICIABA en el arte de la oratoria. *They were taking their first steps in the art of public speaking.* ⇨INITIATE

INMACULADO. *adj.* Superficie. *Spotless.* ~La blancura INMACULADA de la nieve. *The pure (LIT pristine) whiteness of the snow.* || **2.** [Fama]. *Impeccable.* || **3.** [Mujer]. *Chaste.* ⇨IMMACULATE

INMERSIÓN. *sf.* [Submarino]. *Dive.* ~Desde el barco observamos la INMERSIÓN de un submarino. *From the boat we could see the submarine dive into the water.* || **2.** [De un hombre-rana]. *Dive, plunge.* || **3.** •Muerte por INMERSIÓN. *Drowning, death by drowning.* ⇨IMMERSION

INSEGURO [INSECURE]. *adj.* Dubitativo. *Uncertain, doubtful.* ~No te hagas ilusiones; la noticia es todavía INSEGURA. *Don't build your hopes up; the news is not yet official.* || **2.** Peligroso. *Unsafe.* ~Vamonos de este barrio; me parece muy INSEGURO. *Let's get away from this neighborhood; it doesn't look very safe.* ~TERRENO inseguro. *Dangerous ground.* || **3.** Falto de firmeza, estabilidad. (I) [Cosa]. *Unsteady, unstable.* ~No te acerques a la barandilla de la escalera porque es muy INSEGURA y te puedes caer. *Don't go near the handrail; it's unstable and you could fall.* (II) [Persona]. *Unsteady.*

INSENSIBLE. *adj.* Indiferente. *Insensitive. callous, unfeeling.* ~Es INSENSIBLE a todo sentimiento humano. *He's cold to any human feeling.* || **2.** Inperceptible. *Imperceptible, unnoticeable.* ~Ha subido tan poco la temperatura que el cambio es INSENSIBLE. *The temperature has risen so little that you can't notice the change.* || **3.** [Miembro, nervio]. *Numb, insensitive.* ~INSENSIBLE al frío. *Insensitive to the cold, not feeling the cold.* ~Desde el accidente tenía los dedos INSEN-SIBLES. *Since the accident his fingers were*

numb. ⇨INSENSIBLE

INSIGNIA [INSIGNIA]. *sf.* Bandera. *Flag.* || **2.** Estandarte. *Banner, standard.* ~El teniente llevaba la INSIGNIA del regimiento. *The lieutenant carried the banner of the regiment.* || **3.** [Barco]. *Pennant.* || **4.** Prendedor. *Badge, button.* || **5.** [Policia]. *Badge.* ~El policía lleva una INSIGNIA blanca. *The policeman wears a white badge.* || **6.** FIG Emblema. *Badge.* ~La roja INSIGNIA del valor. *The Red Badge of Courage.* || **7.** •Buque INSIGNIA. *Flagship.*

INSTANCIA. *sf.* Petición. *Request.* Fui al parque zoológico a INSTANCIA(S) de mi profesor. *I went to the zoo at the request of my teacher.* •Presentar una INSTANCIA. *To present a request.* •A INSTANCIAS de. *At the request of.* ~A INSTANCIAS del fiscal se realizó una investigación. *At the request of the district attorney an investigation was launched.* || **2.** Solicitud (escrita), formulario. *Application form.* ~Ud. tiene que rellenar esta INSTANCIA para reclamar el dinero. *You need to fill this form in order to claim the money.* || **3.** Súplica. *Plea, petition.* •Pedir algo con INSTANCIA. *To request something urgently.* || **4.** Momento. *Moments.* Las INSTANCIAS decisivas de nuestra historia. *The decisive moments in our history.* || **5.** Autoridad. *Authority.* ~Las más altas INSTAN-CIAS de la nación. *The highest authorities in the land.* || **6.** LOCUCIONES. || •Tribunal de primera INSTANCIA. *Small claims court.* || •En última INSTANCIA. (I) [Como último recurso]. *As a last resort.* ~En última INSTANCIA podríamos vender el coche. *As a last resort we could sell the car,* (II) [En definitiva]. *In the final (last) analysis.* ~La responsabilidad es, en última INSTANCIA, mía. *I'm ultimately responsible.* || •INSTANCIAS del poder. *Corridors of power.* || •En (de) primera INSTANCIA. *First of all.* ⇨INSTANCE

INSTITUCIÓN. *sf.* Creación, constitución. *Establishment.* ~La INSTITUCIÓN de un fondo de pensiones. *The establishment (setting up) of a pension fund.* ~A esta editorial se le debe la INSTITUCIÓN de un importante premio novelístico. *This publishing house is*

responsible for the establishment of an important prize for the best novel. || **2.** Bases. *Principles.* || **3.** •INSTITUCIÓN benéfica. *Charitable foundation (organization).* ⇨ INSTITUTION

INSTRUCCIÓN. *sf.* Enseñanza. *Education.* ~Se ha hecho cargo de la INSTRUCCIÓN de los niños. *She has taken responsability for the children's education.* •Tener poca INSTRUCCION en. *To have little knowledge, know very little about.* ~Una mujer sin INSTRUCCIÓN. *An uneducated woman.* ~Han recibido INSTRUCCIÓN sobre estos métodos. *They have been trained in these methods.* •INSTRUCCIÓN primaria. *Primary education.* •INSTRUCCION pública. *State, public education.* || **2.** [Deporte]. *Coaching, training.* || **3.** [De una causa]. *Trying, hearing.* •La INSTRUCCIÓN de un sumario. *Preliminary investigation.* || **4.** [Militar]. *Drill, training.* •INSTRUCCIÓN militar. *Military training.* || **5.** Reglas, normas. *Directions.* •INSTRUCCIONES pare el uso. *Directions for use.* || **6.** •Juez de INSTRUCCIÓN. *Examining magistrate.* ⇨ INSTRUCTION

INTERIOR [INTERIOR]. *adj.* [General]. *Inside.* ~El patio INTERIOR. *The inside patio.* || **2.** [Más cerca del centro]. *Inner.* ~La parte INTERIOR de una rueda. *The inner part of a wheel.* || **3.** [Pensamiento, voz]. *Inner.* ~Oyó una voz INTERIOR que le recriminaba. *She heard an inner voice reproaching her.* || **4.** [Comercio, política]. *Domestic, internal.* ~Política INTERIOR. *Domestic policy.* || **5.** [Geografía]. *Inland, inner.* || **6.** Espiritual. *Spiritual.* ~Un bienestar INTERIOR. *A spiritual well-being.* || **7.** *LOCUCIONES.* || •Habitación INTERIOR. *Room without a view, inner room.* ~Tengo en el hotel una habitación INTERIOR. *In the hotel I have an inner room.* || •La parte INTERIOR. *The inside.* ~La parte INTERIOR del colchón. *The inside of the mattress.* || •Pista INTERIOR. *Inside track.* || •Ropa INTERIOR. *Underwear.*

INTERIOR [INTERIOR]. *sm.* [En la parte de adentro]. *Inside.* Pasemos al INTERIOR. *Let's go inside.* ~Veía lo que ocurría en el INTERIOR de la habitación. *She could see what was*

happening in the inside of the room. || **2.** [Figurativo]. *Mind, soul.* En su INTERIOR. *Deep down.* ~En su INTERIOR no estaba de acuerdo. *Deep down he disagreed.* ~Dije para mí. *I said to myself.* ~En el INTERIOR de su alma la amaba. *Deep down he loved her.* || **3.** [De un país]. *Inland.* ~El INTERIOR es muy montañoso. *Inland it is very mountainous.*

INTERPRETAR [INTERPRET]. *v.* [Un papel]. *To play.* || **2.** [Obra]. *To perform.* || **3.** [Concierto]. *To play, perform.* ~La orquesta INTERPRETÓ las obras de Falla. *The orquesta played to works of Falla.* || **4.** [Canción]. *To sing.* ~INTERPRETA la canciones de Frank Sinatra. *He sings Frank Sinatra's songs.* || **5.** •Interpretar mal. *To misunderstand, misconstrue.* ~No quiero que INTERPRETES mal mi actitud. *I don't want you to misconstrue my position.* ~Me INTERPRETÓ mal. *He misunderstood me.* ~Me INTERPRETÉ mal. *I didn't make myself clear.*

INTERVENCIÓN [INTERVENTION]. *sf.* [Del teléfono]. *Tapping.* || **2.** [De cuentas]. *Audit, auditing.* || **3.** [En una conversación]. *Participation.* || **4.** [De los precios]. *Control, supervision.* || **5.** [Medicina]. *Operation.* ~Realizar una INTERVENCIÓN quirúrgica. *To perform surgery.* || **6.** Contribución. *Contribution.* ~Su INTERVENCIÓN en la discusión. *His contribution to the discussion.* || **7.** Participación. *Participation, involvement.* ~Se ha probado su INTERVENCIÓN en el atraco. *His involvement in the robbery has been proved.* || **8.** [De droga, armas]. *Seizure, confiscation.* || **9.** •Su última INTERVENCIÓN en una película española. *Her last appearance in a Spanish movie.* || **10.** •Hacer una INTERVENCIÓN. *To take the floor.*

INTERVENIR. *v.* Participar, tomar parte. *Participate, have a hand in, to take part in, contribute.* En esta película INTERVIENEN 30 actores. *There are thirty actors in this film.* No INTERVINO en la discusión. *She did not take part in the debate.* Él no INTERVINO en la decisión. *He did not have a hand in the decision.* ~Una reyerta en que INTERVINO un marinero. *A brawl in which a sailor was involved.* Clark Gable INTERVINO en la película Lo que el viento se llevó. *Clark Gable appeared in the film Gone With the Wind.* ~Las naciones que INTERVINIERON en la guerra. *The countries that took part in the war.* ~INTERVENIR en una conversación. *To join in a conversation.* || **2.** [Teléfono]. Interceptar, escuchar. *To tap.* || **3.** Inspeccionar cuentas. *Audit.* || **4.** Intermediar. *Mediate.* || **5.** Confiscar, embargar. *Confiscate, seize.* ~El juez le ha INTERVENIDO su cuenta corriente. || **6.** Entrometerse. *Interfere.* INTERVENIR un país en la política interior de otro. *To interfere with a country's internal affairs.* || **7.** Operar. *Operate on (perform surgery).* ~Fue INTERVENIDO en una clínica privada. *He underwent surgery in a private clinic.* ⇨ INTERVENE

INTOXICADO. *sm.* Envenenado. *Poisoned.* ⇨ INTOXICATED

INTOXICAR [INTOXICATE]. *v.* Envenenar. *To poison.*

INTRODUCIR. *v.* Poner, colocar, meter. *To place, put in, insert.* INTRODUJO la papeleta en la urna. *He put (placed) his ballot paper in the ballot box.* ~INTRODUZCA la moneda en la ranura. *Insert the coin in the slot.* ~INTRODUJO la llave en la cerradura. *He put (inserted) the key into the lock.* ~INTRODUJO la moneda en el teléfono y marcó el número. *He inserted a coin into the telephone and dialed the number.* || **2.** [Contrabando, drogas]. *To bring in, smuggle.* || **3.** [En un ambiente]. *Transport, take back.* ~Su música nos INTRODUCE en un mundo mágico. *His music transports us to a magical world.* ~El escritor nos INTRODUCE en la Francia del siglo pasado. *The writer takes us back to the France of the last century.* || **4.** Provocar

(problema, discordia]. *To cause, create, bring about.* ~INTRODUCIR el desorden, la discordia. *To bring on disorder, discord.* || **5.** [Informática]. *To enter, input.* || **6.** Entrometerse. *To meddle, interfere.* || **7.** Acompañar (a una persona al interior de un lugar). *To show into, bring in, show in.* ~La criada nos INTRODUJO en el salón. *The maid showed us into the living room.* ⇨ INTRODUCE

INTRODUCIRSE. *vr.* Meterse. *To get into, enter.* ~El agua se INTRODUCÍA por las ranuras. *The water was coming in (seeping through) the cracks.* ~La moneda rodó hasta INTRODUCIRSE por una grieta. *The coin rolled along and dropped down a crack.* ~Se INTRODUJERON en la selva. *They wento into the jungle.* ~INTRODUCIRSE en la alta sociedad. *To work one's way into high society.* || **2.** [Persona]. *To gain access.* ~~Se INTRODUJERON en el banco por un túnel. *They gained access to the bank through a tunnel.* Me INTRODUJE en su casa cuando no había nadie. *I slipped into the house when there was no one in.* || **3.** [Ideas, costumbres, moda]. *To find its way, become known.* ~Ideas foráneas que se INTRODUJERON poco a poco en nuestra sociedad. *Foreign ideas which gradually found their way into our society.* ~Su obra se INTRODUJO en México a través de las traducciones de Sanz. *His works became known in Mexico through Sanz's translations.* ⇨ INTRODUCE

INVESTIGACIÓN. *sf.* [Científica]. *Research.* ~Su última publicación es producto de años de INVESTIGACIÓN. *His latest book is the result of years of research.* ⇨ INVESTIGATION

J

JORNADA. *sf.* Día de trabajo. *Working day.* ~Una JORNADA de siete horas. *A 7 hour (working) day.* || **2.** Camino recorrido en un día. *Day's journey.* ~De Bilbao a Sevilla hay dos JORNADAS de camino. *It's a two-day journey from Bilbao to Seville.* || **3.** [Military]. *Expedición.* ~La JORNADA de Orán. *The expedition against Oran.* || **4.** *pl. Conference, congress.* ~Las II JORNADAS de Moda Española. *The 2nd Conference of Spanish Fashion.* || **5.** Día (deporte). *Day.* ~Los resultados de la JORNADA del Sábado. *Saturday's results.* || **6.** Etapa. *Stage of a journey.* ~Hice el viaje en tres JORNADAS. *I did the journey in three stages.* || **7.** Turno. *Shift.* || **8.** FIG Vida. *Lifetime, span of life.* ~Está llegando al final de su JORNADA. *He's reached his final journey.* || **9.** [Universidad]. *Congress, conference.* ~JORNADAS Cervantinas. *Conference on Cervantes.* || **10.** [Teatro, arte]. *Workshop, course.* || **11.** [Militar]. *Battle, memorable event.* ~La JORNADA de Waterloo. *The Battle of Waterloo.* || **12.** [Cinema]. *Part, episode.* ~Películas en tres JORNADAS. *Film in three parts.* || **13.** Acto (teatro clásico). *Act.* ~Una comedia en tres JORNADAS. *A play in three acts.* || **14.** *LOCUCIONES.* Capítulo (libro). *Chapter.* || •Al fin de la JORNADA. *At the end.* || •JORNADA anual. *Working days in the year.* || •JORNADA completa. *Full-time work.* || •JORNADA de puertas abiertas. *Open day.* || •JORNADA inglesa. *Five-day week.* || •JORNADA intensiva. *(Working day with a short break or no break for lunch so as to finish earlier).* || •JORNADA laboral. *Working week (semana), working year (anual).* ~Mi JORNADA laboral es de 8 horas diarias. *I work an 8 hour day.* || •JORNADA media. *Part-time work.* || •JORNADA partida. *Working day with a lunch break, split shift.* || •JORNADA semanal. *Working week.* || •Trabajar en JORNADAS reducidas. *To work spare-time.* ⇨JOURNEY

JORNAL. *sm.* Sueldo. *Day's wages, day's pay.* ~Trabajar a JORNAL. *To be paid by the day.* || **2.** Trabajo. *Day's work.* ⇨JOURNAL

JUBILACIÓN. *sf.* [Acción]. *Retirement.* ~Le quedan cinco años para llegar a la JUBILACIÓN. *He has five years to go before retiring.* || **2.** [Dinero, pensión]. *Retirement pension.* Con la JUBILACIÓN que le queda no tiene lo suficiente para vivir. *With the pension money that he receives, he doesn't have enough left to live on.* || **3.** •JUBILACIÓN anticipada. *Early retirement.* || **4.** •JUBILA-CIÓN forzosa. *Compulsory retirement.* || **5.** •JUBILACIÓN voluntaria. *Voluntary retirement.* ⇨JUBILATION

JUSTO. *adj.* Apretado, ajustado (ropa). *Tight.* ~El traje me viene muy JUSTO. *The suit is rather tight on me.* ~Estos zapatos me quedan demasiado JUSTOS. *These shoes are too tight (for me).* || **2.** Exacto. *Right, exact.* Cuatro kilos JUSTOS. *Four kilos exactly.* ~Buscaba la palabra JUSTA. *He was looking for just the right word.* ~Un cálculo JUSTO. *A precise calculation.* ~El peso JUSTO. *The correct weight.* || **3.** Preciso. *Precise.* ~Llegamos en el momento JUSTO en que salían. *We arrived just as they where leaving.* || **4.** Suficiente, apenas. *Enough.* ~Tenemos el tiempo JUSTO. *We have just enough time.* ~Tenemos lo JUSTO para vivir. *We have just enough to live on.* ~La comida estuvo un poco JUSTA. *There was just enough food.* || **5.** Razonamiento. *Sound.* ||

6. *LOCUCIONES.* || •Estamos JUSTOS de tiempo. *We're pressed for time.* || •JUSTO! *That's it!, correct!, right!* || •Lo JUSTO. Just enough (right). || •Más de lo JUSTO. *More than enough, more than is proper, more than usual.* || •Muy JUSTO. *Not enough, insufficient.* La comida ha sido muy justa. *There was scarcely enought food.* || •Viven muy JUSTOS con su sueldo. *They just manage to make ends meet with her salary.* ⇨JUST

JUVENIL. *adj*. [Aspecto]. *Youthful, young.* ~Un traje JUVENIL. *A youthful suit.* ~Susana lleva hoy un peinado muy JUVENIL. *Susan is sporting a very youthful hairdo today.* ~De aspecto JUVENIL. *Young-looking.* || **2.** [Categoría, competición]. *Junior.* ~El equipo JUVENIL. *The junior team.* || **3.** •Obra JUVENIL. *Early work.* || **4.** •En los años JUVENILES. *In one's early years, in one's youth.* ⇨JUVENILE

L

LABOR. *sf.* Trabajo. *Work.* ~Después de su enfermedad volvió a sus LABORES periodísticas. *After his illness he went back to his work as a journalist.* || **2.** Contribución. *Contribution, achievement, work.* Su importante LABOR en el campo de la física. *His important work in (contribution to) the field of physics.* ~Por fin valoraron su LABOR. *They finally appreciated his work.* || **3.** Trabajo que se hace con hilo, a mano o con máquina de coser. [De costura]. *Needlework, sewing.* [De punto]. *Knitting.* [De bordado]. *Embroidery.* [De ganchillo]. *Crochet, crocheting.* || **4.** Labranza, cultivo. *Tillage (de la tierra).* ~El agricultor pasó el año entero dedicado a las LABORES del campo. *The farmer spent the entire year tilling the land.* || **5.** *LOCUCIONES.* || •Una LABOR de equipo. *Teamwork.* || •Profesión: sus LABORES. *Occupation: housewife.* || •LABORES de chino. *Tedious work.* || •LABORES domésticas (del hogar). *Housework.* || •Estar por la LABOR de. *To be in favor of.* ~Están por la LABOR de poner en marcha esas medidas. *They're in favor of putting these measure into action.* || •Caballo de LABOR. *Workhorse.* || •Cesta de LABORES. *Sowing basket (de costura), knitting bag (de punto).* || •Dar dos LABORES a un campo. *To plough a field twice.* ⇨LABOR

LABORIOSO. *adj.* [Persona]. *Diligent, industrious, hard-working.* ~Las abejas son insectos muy LABORIOSOS. *Bees are hard-working insects.* ⇨LABORIOUS

LAMENTAR. *v.* Sentir. *To regret, be sorry about.* ~LAMENTO molestarle. *I'm sorry to disturb you.* ~LAMENTO mucho que tengas que irte. *I'm very sorry you have to go.*

~LAMENTAMOS informarle (comunicarle) que. *We regret to inform you that.* || **2.** Quejarse. *To complain, grumble, moan.* ~¿De qué te LAMENTAS? *What are you complaining about?* ~De nada sirve LAMENTARSE. *There's no use grumbling (moaning) about it.* || **3.** Deplorar. *To deplore.* ~Se LAMENTA de la incomprehensión de la gente. *He deplores people's lack of understanding.* || **4.** •No hay que LAMENTAR víctimas. *Fortunately there were no casualties.* ⇨LAMENT

LARGO. *adj.*

❶ DURACIÓN, PROLONGACIÓN (espera, viaje, visita, conferencia). *Long, lengthty, prolonged.* ~La semana se me ha hecho muy LARGA. *It's been a long week.* ~Un juicio que se está haciendo muy LARGO. *A trial which is going on for a long time.* ~Les unía una LARGA amistad. *They had been friends for a long time.* ~Un retraso LARGO. *A lenghty delay.* ~Una visita LARGA. *A prolonged visit.* || **2.** Excesivo, más de la cuenta (con 'resultar', 'ser', 'hacerse'). *Too long.* ~Se hizo LARGO el día. *The day dragged on.* ~Resultó LARGA la conferencia. *The lecture was too long.* ~Se nos hizo LARGA la espera. *We had to wait a long time.* || **3.** Mucho (con sustantivos como 'tiempo', 'meses', 'horas', 'años'), *Long.* ~Hacía LARGO tiempo que no le veía. *I hadn't seen him for a long time.* ~Viví LARGOS años en el extranjero. *I lived many years abroad.* || **4.** •Ir para LARGO. *To drag on.* ~Parece que va para LARGO. *It's looks like it's going to go on for a long time.* ~No te impacientes, porque eso va para LARGO. *Don't get impatient because this is going to take a long time.* || **5.** •LARGO y tendido. *At great length.* ~Hablaron LARGO y tendido sobre el tema. *They discussed the topic at great length.* || **6.** •Ser LARGO de contar. *To be a long story.* ~Es muy LARGO de contar. *It's a long story.* || **7.** •Ser más LARGO que un día sin pan. *To take forever.* || **8.** •A LARGO plazo. *Long-term.* ~Previsiones a LARGO plazo. *Long-term forecasts.* || **9.** •Hacerse LARGO. *To drag.*

❷ LONGITUD, EXTENSIÓN (camino, pasillo; pelo, uñas, piernas; falda, pantalones). *Long.* ~Una camisa de mangas LARGAS. *A long-sleeved shirt.* ~De pelo LARGO. *Long-Haired.* ~Un camino LARGO. *A long road.* ~Un tren de LARGO recorrido. *A long-distance train.* || **2.** •LARGO para. *Too long (for).* ~Esta tabla es LARGA para este armario. *This shelf is too long for this cabinet.* ~Esta falda te está LARGA. *This skirt is too long for you.* || **3.** •LARGO de uñas. *Light-fingered.*

❸ ENTERO (tiempo, cantidad). *Good, full.* ~Pasamos un mes LARGO allí. *We spent a good month there.* ~Tardó media hora LARGA. *He took a good (full) half-hour.* ~Recorrimos dos millas LARGAS. *We traveled a full two miles.* Los aventajó en un minuto LARGO. *He beat them by a full minute.* ~Le costó 50 dólares LARGOS. *It cost him a good 50 dollars.* ~Una dama sesentañera LARGA. *A lady well in her sixties.*

❹ PERSONA. Alto y delgado (persona). *Tall, lanky.* ~Un tío muy LARGO. *A very tall (lanky) guy.* Cayó cuan LARGO era. *He fell full length.* || **2.** Astuto, perspicaz, listo. *Sharp, shrewd.* ~Es muy LARGO y lo resuelve todo rápidamente. *He's very clever and finds an easy solution to everything.* || **3.** Generoso, dadivoso, liberal. *Generous, free-spending, lavish.* ~Es una persona LARGA y cortés. *He's a very generous and polite person.*

❺ 'A LO LARGO DE'. •A lo LARGO. (1) [Cortar, partir]. *Lengthwise.* ~Partir un tablón a lo LARGO. *To split a plank lengthwise,* (II) [De un camino, río]. ~Anduvimos a lo LARGO del andén. *We walked along (alongside) the platform,* (III) [De una jornada, novela]. *Throughout, in the course of.* ~Los libros que publicó a lo LARGO de su vida. *The books he published during (in the course of) his lifetime.* ~Tras los incidentes que se han producido a lo LARGO de la semana. *Following the incidents which have taken place in the course of the week.* || **2.** •A lo LARGO y a lo ancho de. *All over, throughout the length and breath of.* ~Hay ríos trucheros a lo LARGO y ancho de toda la región. *There are trout rivers all over the area.* ~A lo LARGO y ancho del continente americano. *Throughout the length and breath of the American Continent.*

❻ CON 'LARGA'. •A la LARGA. *In the long run, eventually.* || **2.** •A la LARGA o a la corta. *Sooner or later.* || **3.** •Dar LARGAS a un asunto. *To delay a matter, put off making a decision about a matter.* ~El Ayuntamiento da LARGAS a su proyecto urbanístico cada vez que lo presenta. *The city council delays its urban project everytime it brings it up.* || **4.** •Saberla LARGA. *To be shrewd, to know one's way about.*

❼ VARIOS. Arriado, suelto [marina]. *Loose, slack.* ~Este cabo está LARGO. *This rope (cable) is slack (loose).* || **2.** [Vocal, sílaba]. *Long.* || **3.** Lento (música). *Slow.* || **4.** FIG Dilatado, extenso (libro, obra, relato, película). *Long.* ~Una obra LARGA. *A long book.* ~Ser LARGO de contar. *To be a long story.*

❽ LOCUCIONES. || •Pasar (seguir) de LARGO. *To pass by, go by (sin parar), go straight past, to pass over (un detalle).* || •Ponerse (vestirse) de LARGO. *To wear a long skirt or dress (para salir de noche), to come out (como debutante), to make one's debut in society.* ~Poner o vestir de LARGO a su hija. ~*To launch one's daughter into society, to give one's daughter her debut.* || •Puesta de LARGO. *Coming out, debut (de una chica en la sociedad).* || •Venir de LARGO. *To go back a long way.* ~Esa disputa ya viene de LARGO. *That dispute goes back a long way, has been going on for a long time.* || •Poner (tener una) cara LARGA. *To pull (have) a long face.* || •Tirar de LARGO. (I) [Dinero]. *To spend lavishly*, (II) [Pintura]. *Use freely.* ~Si usas de LARGO la pintura. *If you put on the paint freely*, (III) [Calcular]. *To estimate high.* ⇨ LARGE

LATITUDES. *sf.* Zona, lugar. *Parts, region, area.* ~La flora de otras LATITUDES. *The flora of other parts of the world.* ~En estas LATITUDES. *In this area, in these parts.* ⇨ LATITUDE

LAVATORIO. *sm.* [Medicina]. *Lotion.* ~El boticario preparó un LAVATORIO y limpió las llagas del herido. *The pharmacist prepared a lotion and cleaned the wounds of the injured man.* ‖ **2.** Palangana, lavamanos. *Washbasin.* ~El LAVATORIO estaba lleno de agua. *The washbasin was full of water.* ‖ **3.** [Misa]. *Lavabo.* ‖ **4.** [Limpieza con agua u otro líquido]. *Act of washing.* ~Todas las mañanas había un tiempo dedicado al LAVATORIO. *Every morning they took time to wash themselves.* ⇨ LAVATORY

LAZO [LASSO]. *sm.* Adorno. *Bow.* ~Se puso un LAZO en la cabeza. *She put a bow in her hair.* ‖ **2.** [De zapato]. *Shoelace.* ~Le hizo el LAZO del zapato. *He tied her shoelace.* ‖ **3.** Nudo. *Knot.* ~Ató el paquete, haciendo un LAZO con la cuerda. *He tied the package and made a knot with the string.* ‖ **4.** Trampa. *Snare, trap.* ~Caer en el LAZO. *To fall into a trap.* ‖ **5.** Vínculo. *Tie, bond.* ~LAZOS de amistad. *Bonds of friendship.* ~LAZOS familiares. *Family ties.* ‖ **6.** Cinta. *Ribbon.* ~Se compró un LAZO de raso. *She bought a satin ribbon.* ‖ **7.** [De un camino]. *Loop, bend.* ‖ **8.** Enlace. *Link.* España sirve de LAZO entre Europa y América del Sur. *Spain serves as a link between Europe and South America.*

LECTURA. *sf.* Acción de leer. *Reading.* ~Los niños disfrutan con la LECTURA de historias de aventura. *Children enjoy reading adventure stories.* ‖ **2.** Interpretación. *Interpretation.* ~Hizo una LECTURA marxista de la obra. *He gave the work a Marxist interpretation.* •Sala de LECTURA. *Reading-room.* ⇨ LECTURE

LETRA [LETTER]. *sf.*
❶ TIPOGRAFÍA. *Type.* •LETRA cursiva.

Italics, italic type, script. ‖ **2.** LETRA de imprenta (molde). *Print.* ~Escriba el nombre completo en LETRA de molde. *Please print your full name.* ~Le halaga ver su nombre en LETRAS de molde. *He feels flattered when he sees his name in big print.* ‖ **3.** •LETRA negrilla, negrita. *Bold type, boldface.* ~Las locuciones de este diccionario están escritas en LETRA negrilla. *The expressions in this dictionary are in bold type.* ‖ **4.** •LETRA pequeña. *Small print.* ‖ **5.** •LETRA versalita. *Small capital (cap).* ‖ **6.** •LETRA redonda. *Roman type.* ‖ **7.** •LETRA florida. *Ornamental capital, head letter.* ‖ **8.** •LETRA titular. *Type used in headings.*
❷ FINANZAS. *Bill, draft.* •LETRA bancaria, letra de cambio. *Bank draft, banker's draft.* ‖ **2.** •LETRA del Tesoro. *Treasury bill.* ‖ **3.** •LETRA a la vista. *Sight draft.* ‖ **4.** •Pagar a LETRA vista. *To pay on sight.* ‖ **5.** •Aceptar/girar una LETRA. *To accept/present a draft.* ‖ **6.** •Devolver/protestar una LETRA. *To dishonor/protest a draft.* ‖ **7.** •Me quedan tres LETRAS por pagar. *I still have three installments to pay (make).* ‖ **8.** •LETRA abierta. *Letter of credit (for an unlimited amount).*
❸ LETRAS. [Universidad]. *Arts.* •Facultad de LETRAS. *Faculty of Arts.* ‖ **2.** •Licenciado en Filosofía y LETRAS. *Arts graduate.* ‖ **3.** •Primeras LETRAS. *Elementary education, three R's.* ~Aprender, saber las primeras LETRAS. *To learn, know how to read and write.* ‖ **4.** [Carta breve]. *Lines.* ~Sólo cuatro (unas) LETRAS para decirte que te quiero. *Just a few lines to say that I love you.* ‖ **5.** •Bellas LETRAS. *Literature, belles lettres.* ‖ **6.** •Ciencia y LETRAS. *Arts and Sciences.* ‖ **7.** •Con todas sus LETRAS. *Written out in full.* ‖ **8.** •Escribir en LETRAS de molde. *To print.* ‖ **9.** •LETRAS divinas (sagradas). *The Bible, the Scriptures.*
❹ CALIGRAFÍA. *Handwriting, writing.* ~Tener buena/mala LETRA. *To have good/bad handwriting.* ~Escríbelo con buena LETRA. *Write neatly.* ~Tiene una LETRA muy clara. *She has a very clear handwriting.* ~No entiendo tu LETRA. *I can't understand your writing (handwriting).* ~Despacito

y buena LETRA. *Slowly and carefully.* ~Esta es la LETRA de tu hermano. *This is your brother's handwriting.* || **2.** •De su puño y LETRA. *In his own hand.*
❺ 'AL PIE DE LA LETRA'. Textualmente, literalmente. *Literally.* ~Ateniéndonos a la LETRA del texto, dice que ... *If we read absolutely literally, the text appears to say* ... || **2.** Según el sentido literal de las palabras (con verbos como 'interpretar', 'tomar') ~Tomó al pie de la LETRA lo que dije y se enfadó. *He took what I said literally and got angry.* || **3.** [Sin variación o restricción. *Word for word.* ~Copió el artículo al pie de la LETRA. *He copied the article word for word.* ~Cumplió mis instrucciones al pie de la LETRA. *He carried out my instructions to the letter (literally).*
❻ VARIOS. Texto (música). *Lyrics, words.* ~Me gusta mucho la LETRA de esta canción. *I like this song's lyrics.* || **2.** Lema. *Motto.* || **3.** [Poesía]. *Rondeau.* || **4.** Astucia. *Astuteness, cunning, Artfulness.* || **5.** [Máquina de escribir]. *Character.* ~Tengo que limpiar las LETRAS de mi máquina de escribir. *I need to clean the characters on my typewriter.*
❼ LOCUCIONES. || •Tener LETRA menuda. *To be artful or cunning.* || •Mándale cuatro LETRAS. *Drop her a line.* || •La LETRA con sangre entra. *Spare the rod and spoil the child.*

LEVE [light]. *adj.* Delicado, tenue (perfume, gasa). *Delicate.* || **2.** Ligero (sospecha, duda, parecido, sonrisa). *Slight, faint.* ~Tenía una LEVE sospecha. *She had a faint (slight) doubt, suspicion.* ~Hay un LEVE parecido entre ellos. *There's a faint (slight) resemblance between them.* || **3.** [Brisa, knock]. *Faint, gentle, light.* ~Soplaba una LEVE brisa. *There was a gentle (slight) wind blowing.* ~Sintió unos LEVES golpes en la puerta. *He heard a gentle knocking at the door.* || **4.** [Infracción, herida]. *Minor.* ~Cometió una infracción LEVE. *He committed a minor offense.* ~Sus heridas son de carácter LEVE. *He has only minor injuries.* || **5.** De poca importancia (equivocación, error). *Slight, unimportant, trivial, small.* ~Aprobé porque sólo cometí un

LEVE error. *I passed the exam since I only made a slight error.* ⇨LIGHT

LIBRERÍA. *sf.* Establecimiento donde se venden libros. *Bookstore, book shop.* "LIBRERÍA Buenos Aires". *"Buenos Aires Bookstore".* ⇨LIBRARY

LIBRERO. *sm.* Persona que se dedica a la venta de libros. *Book dealer.* ~Ha llamado el LIBRERO para decirnos que ya están en la tienda nuestros encargos. *The book dealer called and said our order had come in.* ⇨LIBRARIAN

LICENCIA. *sf.* [Militar]. *Leave (of absence).* ~Viene a casa con LICENCIA. *He's coming home on leave.* || **2.** [Universidad]. *Degree.* ~LICENCIA en Derecho. *Law degree.* || **3.** Permiso, autorización. *Permission.* ~Pidió LICENCIA para verlo. *She asked permission to see it.* ~Con LICENCIA de sus jefes. *With his bosses' permission.* || **4.** Permiso legal. *Permit.* ~LICENCIA fiscal. *Business permit.* ~LICENCIA de obras. *Building permit.* ~LICENCIA de caza. *Hunting permit.* || **5.** [Comercio]. *Leave.* ~LICENCIA por enfermedad. *Sick leave.* ~LICENCIA de maternidad. *Maternity leave.* ~Estar de LICENCIA. *To be on leave.* ~Ir de LICENCIA. *To go on leave.* || **6.** •LICENCIA absoluta. *Discharge.* || **7.** •LICENCIA honrosa. *Honorable discharge.* ⇨LICENSE

LICOR. *sm.* Bebida alcohólica dulce y aromática. *Liqueur.* ⇨LIQUOR

LIGERO. *adj.* Leve. (I) [Dolor, sabor]. *Slight, faint,* (II) [Inconveniente]. *Slight, minor,* (III) [Golpe, brisa]. *Gentle.* ~Le dio un golpe LIGERO en la mano. *She gave him a gentle smack on the hand.* ~Soplaba una brisa LIGERA. *There's was a gentle breeze blowing.* || **2.** De poca importancia. *Slight.* ~Cualquier ruido, por LIGERO que sea, lo despierta. *She wakes up at the slightest noise.* ~Tiene unos conocimientos muy LIGEROS del chino. *He has a very slight knowledge of Chinese.* || **3.** No serio (conversación). *Lighthearted.* ~Lo dijo en tono LIGERO. *He said it in a lighthearted tone.* || **4.** Poco serio (persona). *Frivolous.* ~Todo se lo toma a la LIGERA. *He doesn't* *take anything seriously.* || **5.** Ágil (salto, movimiento). *Agile, nimble.* De un salto LIGERO, cruzó el riachuelo. *She leaped nimbly across the stream.* || **6.** Rápido, veloz (persona, animal, vehículo). *Fast, swift, quick.* ~Un caballo LIGERO como el viento. *A horse that runs like the wind.* ~Así andamos más LIGERO. *We go quicker this way.* || **7.** [Bebida]. *Weak.* || **8.** Inconstante. *Inconstant, fickle.* ⇨ LIGHT

LIQUIDACIÓN [LIQUIDATION]. *sf.* [En una tienda]. *Clearance sale.* ~LIQUIDACIÓN de fin de temporada. *End of season sale.* || **2.** [De una cuenta]. *Settlement, final payment.* ~No puedo hacer la LIQUIDACIÓN hasta el mes próximo. *I can't settle this account until next month.* || **3.** Cálculo. *Calculation.* ~Se hizo la LIQUIDACIÓN de lo que correspondía a cada uno. *They calculated how much was due to each person.*

LIQUIDAR [LIQUIDATE]. *v.* Licuar. *To liquify.* || **2.** [Mercancías]. *To sell off.* ~En verano las tiendas LIQUIDAN las existencias que han sobrado. *During the summer the stores sell off their overstock.* || **3.** [Deuda]. To pay off (also: *liquidate*). ~Quiero LIQUIDAR todas las deudas antes de irme de vacaciones. *I want to pay off all my debts before going on vacation.* || **4.** [Cuenta]. *To settle.* Ya he LIQUIDADO lo que le debía al sastre.

I've already paid the tailor what I owe him. || **5.** [Problema]. *Resolve.* ~Hay que LIQUIDAR este problema antes de mañana. *We have to solve this problem by tomorrow.* || **6.** Eliminar. *To kill, bump off.* || **7.** [Sueldo, pago]. *To pay.* ~Mañana voy a LIQUIDAR al fontanero. *Tomorrow I'm going to pay the plumber.* ~Me LIQUIDARON lo que me debían. *They paid me what they owed me.* || **8.** [Comida]. *To polish off.* ~Los chicos se LIQUIDARON todas las galletas. *The kids polished off all the cookies.* || **9.** [Dinero, herencia]. *To blow.* ~Se LIQUIDA el sueldo de un mes en 15 días. *She blows a month's salary in two weeks.*

LÓGICO [LOGICAL]. *adj.* Natural. *Natural.* ~Era LÓGICO que ella se enfadara. *It was natural that she should get angry.* Es LÓGICO que quiera más libertad. *It's only natural that he should want more freedom.* ~Es LÓGICO que se haya ofendido. *It's understandable (not surprising) that he should be offended.* || **2.** LOCUCIONES. || •Lo más LÓGICO. *The most sensible thing.* || •Es LÓGICO. *It's only natural.* || •Como es LÓGICO. *As might be expected.* •Como es LÓGICO, vendrá con ellos. *Naturally, obviously he will come with them.* || •¡LÓGICO¡ *Obviously, naturally.*

MADURO. *sf.* [Fruta]. *Ripe.* ~Estas naranjas no están MADURAS. *The oranges are not ripe.* || **2.** •MADURO para algo. *Ripe for something.* ~La situación no estaba MADURA para la revolución. *The situation was not yet ripe for a revolution.* ⇨MATURE

MAESTRO [MAESTRO]. *sm.* Profesor. *Teacher.* ~La MAESTRA del pueblo. *The village schoolteacher.* ~La vida es la mejor MAESTRA. *Life is the best teacher.* || **2.** Autoridad. *Authority.* ~El profesor Moreno, MAESTRO de las letras españolas. *Professor Moreno, a leading authority (an expert) on Spanish literature.* || **3.** TAUR *Matador, bullfighter.*

MALICIA. *sf.* Astucia, sutileza. *Cunning, craftiness, slyness.* ~Sin una poca de MALICIA, le será difícil desenvolverse en el mundo empresorial. *Without a little cunning it's going to be difficult for him to get ahead in the business world.* || **2.** Sospecha, recelo. *Suspición.* ~Tengo mis MALICIAS. *I have my suspicions.* ~Tengo la MALICIA de que no ocurrió así. *I suspect (have the suspicion) that it didn't happen that way.* || **3.** [De mirada, chiste, dicho]. *Naughtiness, provocative nature.* ~Contó un chiste con mucha MALICIA. *He told a very naughty story.* || **4.** Picardía. *Mischief.* ~Es un chico sin ningua MALICIA. *He's completely without guile.* ~Me guiño con MALICIA. *He winked at me mischievously.* ~Tiene tan poca MALICIA que no se da cuenta de estas cosas. *He's so naive that he doesn't see these things.* || **5.** [De un animal]. *Viciousness.* ⇨MALICE

MALICIOSO. *adj.* Taimado. *Sly, crafty, cunning.* || **2.** Vicioso. *Vicious.* || **3.** Travieso. *Mischievous.* || **4.** Pícaro (comentario, mirada, sonrisa, chiste). *Roguish, naughty, provocative.* ~Una mirada MALICIOSA. *A provocative glance.* ⇨MALICIOUS

MANDATO [MANDATE]. *sm.* Orden. *Order, command.* ~El soldado cumplió fielmente el MANDATO de su sargento. *The soldier carried the sargent's order dilligently.* || **2.** [Derecho]. *Writ, warrant.* ~Mandato JUDICIAL. *Search warrant.* ~MANDATO de prisión. *Arrest warrant.* || **3.** [Informática]. *Command.* || **4.** Poder. *Power of attorney.* || **5.** Periodo (gobierno). *Term (of office).* ~Durante su MANDATO. *During his term of office.* || **6.** [De comisión]. *Brief, terms of reference.* ~Pero eso no forma parte de mi MANDATO. *But that is not in my brief.* || **7.** •Ejercerá este poder por MANDATO constitucional. *He will exercise this power in accordance with the constitution.* || **8.** •MANDATO internacional. *International money order.*

MANEJAR. *v.* Usar. *Use.* ~MANEJAN conceptos que me resultan incomprensibles. *They use concepts that I find incomprehensible.* ~¿Sabes MANEJAR este programa de ordenador? *Do you know how to use this computer program?* || **2.** Manipular (herramienta, arma). *Handle, use.* ¡Qué bien MANEJAS la aguja y el hilo¡ *You really handle the needle and thread beautifully!* ~El sastre MANEJA muy bien las tijeras. *The tailor is very good at handling scissors.* || **3.** [Idioma, situación, cifras, caballo]. *Handle.* ~MANEJAR bien el idioma. *To speak a language well.* ~No sabe MANEJAR el dinero. *He doesn't know how to handle money.* ~MANEJAR cifras. *To deal with numbers.* || **4.** LAT. AM. [Car]. *To drive.* || **5.** [Máquina]. *Operate, run work, use.* || **6.**

[Diccionario]. *To use.* ‖ **7.** [Explosivos]. *Handle.* ‖ **8.** Dominar. *To domineer, push around, boss about.* ~Ella DOMINA a su marido. *She bosses her husband around.* ~MANEJAR a uno a su antojo. *To lead someone by the nose.* ‖ **9.** [Sword]. *Handle, wield.* ‖ **10.** Manipular (una persona). *Manipulate.* Estos periódicos MANEJAN la información a su antojo. *These newspapers manipulate information just as they please.* ‖ **11.** Atacar, resolver (problema, situación). *To tackle, handle, deal with.* MANEJÓ la situación muy bien. *He handled (dealt with) the situation very well.* ‖ **12.** •MANEJAR con cuidado. *Handle with care.* ‖ **12.** •MANEJAR el tinglado. *To pull the strings.* ‖ **13.** •MANEJAR los cuartos. *To hold the purse strings.* ⇨MANAGE

MANERA. *sf.* Modo, forma. *Way.* ~Yo lo hago a mi MANERA. *I do it my way, I have my own way of doing it.* ~¿Qué MANERA de comer es ésa? *That's no way to eat your food.* ~¡Comimos de una MANERA! *You should have seen the amount (way) we ate!* ~¡Qué MANERA de malgastar el dinero!. *What a waste of money!* ~De esta MANERA iremos más cómodo. *We'll be more comfortable this way.* ~No me gusta su MANERA de hablar. *I don't like the way she speaks.* •A MANERA DE. *By way of.* ~A MANERA de ejemplo. *By way of example.* ~Se levantó el sombrero a MANERA de saludo. *He lifted his hat in greeting.* ~A MANERA de prólogo. *By way of a prologue.* •A MI (TU, ETC.) MANERA DE VER. *In my view, as I see it.* •CADA CUAL A SU MANERA. *To each his own.* •CON BUENAS MANERAS. *Politely.* •DE ALGUNA MANERA. (I) Sea como sea. *One way or another, somehow.* ~De alguna MANERA tendré que conseguir el dinero. *I'll have to get the money one way or another,* (II) Hasta cierto punto. *To a certain extent, in some ways.* ~Sus novelas son, de alguna MANERA, el reflejo de su propia juventud. *His novels are, to a certain extent, a reflection of his own youth.* •DE CUALQUIER MANERA. (I) Mal. *Carelessly.* ~No lo pongas así, de cualquier MANERA,

dóblalo. *Don't just put it any which way, fold it up,* (II) Con facilidad. *Easily,* (III) En cualquier caso. *In any case.* ~De cualquier MANERA ya tenía que lavarlo. *I had to wash it any way, in any case.* ~De cualquier MANERA prefiero que me llames por teléfono. *I'd rather you call me first anyway.* •DE ESTA/ESA MANERA. *This/that way.* •DE LA MANERA QUE SEA. (I) Pase lo que pase. *Whatever happens.* (II) No importa como. *Any way you like.* •DE MALA MANERA. (I) Mal. *Badly.* ~Lo trataba de mala MANERA. *He used to treat her badly,* (II) Groseramente. *Rudely.* ~Me contestó de muy mala MANERA. *He answered me very rudely.* •DE MANERA QUE. Para que. *So that.* ~Te lo advertí de MANERA que no te quejes. *I warned you so you won't complain.* ~¿De MANERA que te casas en julio? *So you're getting married in July?* Dilo en voz alta de MANERA que todos te oigan. *Say it out loud so that everyone can hear you.* •DE NINGUNA MANERA. *In no way, certainly not.* ~De ninguna MANERA te lo voy a permitir. *There's no way I'm going to allow it.* ~No son de ninguna MANERA inferiores. *They are in no way inferior.* •DE OTRA MANERA. (I) Si no es así. *Otherwise,* (II) De distinto modo. *In a different way.* •DE TAL MANERA QUE. *In such a way that.* •DE TODAS MANERAS. *Anyway, at any rate, in any case.* •DE UNA MANERA O DE OTRA. *One way or another.* ~De una MANERA o de otra habrá que terminarlo. *It will have to be finished one way or the other.* •EN CIERTA MANERA. En cierto modo. *In a way, to a certain extent, up to a point.* ~En cierta MANERA, me alegró de lo ocurrido. *To a certain extent I'm glad it happened.* •EN GRAN MANERA. *Extremely, a great deal, very much.* ~Contribuyó en gran MANERA al desarrollo del proyecto. *He contributed a great deal to the development of the project.* •ES MI MANERA DE SER. *That's the way I am.* •LA MANERA COMO. *The way, how.* ~No entiendo la MANERA como sucedió. *I don't*

understand how it happened.
•MANERA de obrar. *Way of doing things, line of conduct.*
•MANERA DE SER. *The way one is.* ~Es su MANERA de ser. *That's the way he is.*
•MANERA DE VER. *Outlook, point of view.*
•NO HAY MANERA. *It's impossible, There's nothing one can do.*
•¡QUÉ MANERA DE ... *What a way to ...*
•SOBRE MANERA. *Very much.*
•¡Y DE QUÉ MANERA! *And how!* ⇨MANNER

MANÍA. *sf.* Costumbre. *Habit.* ~Tiene la MANÍA de dejar el coche siempre abierto. *He's got the bad habit of leaving the car unlocked.* ~Ha dado en la MANÍA de salir sin abrigo. *He's taken to going out without a coat.* || **2.** Afición exagerada, moda. *Craze, rage, obsession.* La MANÍA de las motos. *The motorbike craze.* ~La MANÍA de la minifalda. *The craze for miniskirts.* ~Tiene la MANÍA de la limpieza. *She has an obsession about cleaning.* || **3.** Ojeriza, antipatía. *Dislike, ill will.* ~Cogerle (tomarle) MANÍA a alguien. *To take a dislike to somebody.* ~Me tiene MANÍA. *He can't stand me.* || **4.** Capricho. *Whim, fad.* || **5.** Peculiaridad, rareza, aprensión injustificada. *Peculiarity, oddity, idiosyncracies.* ~Tiene la MANÍA de mirar debajo de la cama antes de acostarse. *She has this peculiar habit of looking under the bed before going to sleep.* ⇨MANIA

MANIFESTACIÓN. *sf.* Expresión. *Expression, show, demonstration, sign.* ~Como MANIFESTACIÓN de su amistad. *As a sign of his friendship.* ~Una gran MANIFESTACIÓN de entusiasmo. *A great show of enthusiasm.* ~Las MANIFESTACIONES artísticas de la época. *The artistic expression of the era.* || **2.** Demostración colectiva. *Demonstration, mass meeting, rally.* ~La policía dispersó la MANIFESTACIÓN. *The police broke up the demonstration.* || **3.** *pl.* Declaración. *Declaration, comment.* ~Las MANIFESTACIONES que hizo a la prensa. *The statements he made to the press.* La MANIFESTACIÓN de la artista sobre su vida personal escandalizaron a la opinión pública. *The declaration of the actress regarding her*

private life shocked public opinion. ⇨MANIFESTATION

MANIFESTAR [MANIFEST]. *v.* Declarar. *To declare, state, express.* ~MANIFESTÓ públicamente su adhesión a la campaña. *He publicly declared his support for the campaign.* || **2.** Demostrar (emoción, actitudes). *To show, display.* ~MANIFESTÓ gran entusiasmo por el proyecto. *He showed (demonstrated) a great deal of enthusiasm for the project.*

MANTEL. *sm.* Lienzo que se pone en la mesa para comer. *Tablecloth.* || **2.** •MANTEL individual. *Place-mat.* || **3.** •Levantar los MANTELES. *To clear the table.* || **4.** •Poner los MANTELES. *To lay the table.* ⇨MANTLE

MANTENER. *v.*
❶ CONSERVAR, PRESERVAR. *Keep.* MANTENGA el fuego encendido. *Keep the fire burning.* ~Póngalo en la heladera para que se MANTENGA frío. *Put it in the refrigerator so that it keeps cold.* ~MANTENER la comida caliente. *To keep the food hot.* ~ 'MANTENGA limpia España'. *'Keep Spain clean'.* ~ 'MANTENGA su derecha'. *'Keep to your right'.* ~Sigue MANTENIENDO vivos sus ideales. *He still keeps his ideals alive.*
❷ SUSTENTAR ECONOMICAMENTE. *To support, feed.* ~Ella sola MANTIENE a su familia. *She supports the whole family on her own.* ~Cuesta un dineral MANTENER a este perro. *It cost a fortune to feed this dog.*
❸ MANTENERSE. [En cierto estado, en cierta situación]. *To keep.* ~Se MANTUVIERON en primera división. *They kept their place in the first division.* ~Se MANTIENE en forma haciendo bicicleta. *She keeps fit by using her bicycle.* Siempre se MANTUVO a distancia. *He always kept his distance.* || **2.** Sostenerse. *To stand.* ~Este edificio se MANTIENE en pie de milagro. *It's a miracle this building is still standing.* || **3.** Sustentarse. *To support oneself.* || **4.** [Fuego]. *Keep going.* || **5.** Alimentarse. *To sustain oneself.* ~Se MANTIENE con leche. *She keeps on going with milk.* ~Se MANTIENE a base de vitaminas. *He lives on vitamin pills.*

❹ REALIZAR CON CIERTA CONTINUI-DAD. Celebrar, sostener (entrevista, reunión, conversación). *To have.* ~MANTEN-DRÁN una reunión esta tarde. *They will have a meeting this afternoon.* || **2.** [Corres-pondencia]. *Keep up.* ~MANTUVIERON correspondencia durante muchos años. *They corresponded for many years.* || **3.** [Negotiations]. *To hold.* ~Durante las negociaciones MANTENIDAS en Ginebra. *During the negotiations held in Geneva.* || **4.** [Conversation]. *Hold.* ~Es incapaz de MANTENER una conversación. *Is unable to hold a conversation.* ~MANTUVO una conversación muy interesante con la escritora. *He had a very interesting conver-sation with the author.* || **5.** •MANTENER relación con. (I) [Amorosas]. *To be going out with,* (II) [Amistosas]. *To be on friendly terms with.*

❺ VARIOS. Sostener, sujetar (una cosa para que no se caiga). *To support, hold up.* Esta columna MANTIENE la pared. *This column holds the wall up.* MANTIENE el clavo con una mano mientras le da golpes con la otra. *He's holding the nail in one hand while he drives it with the other.* || **2.** [Promesa, palabra]. *Cumplir.* ~Debes aprender a MANTENER tus promesas. *You must learn to keep your promises.* || **3.** [Mujer]. *To keep.* || **4.** Defender (contra). *Defend (against).* ~MANTENER una plaza contra el ataque del enemigo. *To defend a position against an enemy attack.*

❻ LOCUCIONES. || •MANTENERSE firme. *To hold one's ground.* || •MANTENERSE tran-quilo. *To keep calm.* || •MANTENERSE en vigor. *To stand, remain in force.* || •MANTE-NERSE en contacto con. *To keep in touch with.* || •MANTENER el equilibrio. *To keep one's balance.* || •Mantener la línea. *To keep trim.* || •MANTENERSE en sus treces. *To stick to one's guns.* ⇨MAINTAIN

MARCA. *sf.*
❶ MARCA DE UN PRODUCTO. [Produc-tos del hogar y comestibles]. *Brand.* ~¿Qué MARCA de café/jabón/dentrífico compras? *What brand of coffee/soap/toothpaste do you buy?* ~Prefiero comprar artículos de MARCA. *I prefer to buy brand names.* || **2.** [Otros productos]. *Make* ~Hay muchas MARCAS de coches/neveras/ordenadores en el mercado. *There are many makes of cars/refrigerators/computers on the mar-ket.* || **3.** •Pantalones/zapatos/ropa de MARCA. *Designer trousers/shoes/clothes.* || **4.** •MARCA de fábrica. *Trademark.* || **5.** •MARCA registrada. *Registered trademark.* || **6.** •De MARCA. *Excellent, outstanding.* || **7.** •Una MARCA de prestigio. *A well-known brand.*
❷ DEPORTE. [Récord]. *Record.* || **2.** •Batir (mejorar, superar) una MARCA. *To break the record.* || **3.** •Establecer una MARCA. *To set a record.*
❸ VARIOS. [En el ganado]. *Branding.* || **2.** Huella (del pie). *Footprint, footmark.* ~Es fácil seguir las MARCAS del fugitivo en el suelo arenoso. *It's easy to follow the fugitive's footprins in the sandy ground.* || **3.** [En papel]. *Watermark.* || **4.** [Náutica]. *Buoy, landmark, marker.* || **5.** [Naipe]. *Bid.* || **6.** Herramienta. *Stamp.* || **7.** Cicatriz. *Scar.* ~La herida le dejó una MARCA en el brazo derecho. *The injury left a scar on his right arm.* || **8.** •MARCA de ley. *Hallmark.* || **9.** •De MARCA mayor. *Outstanding, enormous, terrible.* ~Me llevé un susto de MARCA mayor. *I got a terrible fright.* ⇨MARK[1]

MARCAR. *v.* [Ganado]. *To brand.* ~Este ganadero MARCÓ sus reses con un hierro en forma de trébol. *This rancher branded his cattle with a clover-shaped iron.* || **2.** [Cabello]. *To set, style.* ~En esta peluquería, por lavar, cortar y MARCAR te cobran poco. *This beauty salon charges very little to wash, cut and style your hair.* || **3.** [Apa-rato]. *To indicate, show, register, read.* ~El contador MARCA 1.327. *The meter reads 1,327.* ~Mi reloj MARCA la hora exacta. *My watch is showing the exact time.* || **4.** DEP [Gol, puntos]. *To score.* ~El delantero centro MARCÓ casí al final del partido. *The center forward scored just as the game was ending.* || **5.** [Telefóno]. *To dial.* ~Marca el 003 si necesitas información. *Dial 003 for information.* || **6.** [Ropa]. *To put one's name on, embroider a name on.* || **7.** [Tierra]. *To mark off (out).* || **8.**

[Números]. *To keep a tally (score)*. || **9.** MUS [Compás, ritmo]. *To keep the beat.* || **10.** [Naipes]. *To bid.* || **11.** [Tarea]. *To assign, set.* ~El maestro MARCÓ la lección para el día siguiente. *The teacher assigned the lesson for the following day.* || **12.** COM [Artículo]. *To put a price on.* ~Tienes que MARCAR los libros que llegaron hoy. *You have to price the books that came in today.* || **13.** [Ley]. *Specify.* ~Dentro del plazo que MARCA la ley. *Within the period specified by the law.* || **14.** Representar, señalar (comienzo, cambio, final, muerte). *To represent, signal.* ~Su muerte MARCA el final de una era. *His death signals the end of an era.* || **15.** Alcanzar. *To reach.* ~Hoy ha MARCADO un nuevo mínimo. *Today it has reached a new low.* || **16.** Establecer. *To establish, set.* ~Seguimos la pauta MARCADA por nuestro fundador. *We follow the guidelines established (set) by our founder.* || **17.** Hacer resaltar. *To accentuate, to cause to bulge.* ~El vestido le MARCA mucho el estómago. *The dress makes her stomach stick out, accentuates her stomach.* || **18.** DEP [Tiempo]. *To clock.* ~Marcó un tiempo de 2.08. *She clocked a time of 2.08.* || **19.** Subrayar (palabras en un texto). *To outline.* || **20.** [Golpe, caída]. *To bruise.* ~La caída le MARCÓ la cara. *The fall bruised his face.* || **21.** •MARCARSE un farol. *To boast, show off.* || **22.** •MARCARSE un tanto. *To score a triumph.* ⇨MARK²

MARCHA [MARCH]. *sf.*

❶ VELOCIDAD. *Speed.* ~Moderar la MARCHA de un coche. *To reduce the speed of a car.* ~Hay que accelerar la MARCHA, que vamos retrasados. *We have to speed up, we're getting behind.* || **2.** •A toda MARCHA. *At full speed, at full blast (fig.).* || **3.** •Disminuir la MARCHA. *To slow down.* || **4.** •'MARCHA moderada'. *'Drive slowly'.* || **5.** •A MARCHAS forzadas. *Rapidly.* ~Caminaron a MARCHAS forzadas. *They walked at a rapid pace.*

❷ AUTO, MECÁNICA. *Gear, speed.* ~El coche tiene 5 MARCHAS. *The car has 5 gears.* || **2.** •MARCHA adelante. *Forward gear.* || **3.** •MARCHA atrás. *Reverse gear.* || **4.**

•MARCHA corta. *Low gear.* || **5.** •MARCHA directa. *Top gear.* || **6.** •MARCHA larga. *High gear.* || **7.** •PRIMERA marcha. *First gear.* || **8.** •Dar MARCHA atrás, poner en marcha atrás, invertir la marcha. *To reverse, put into reverse.* || **9.** FIG •Dar MARCHA atrás. *To pull out, back out, withdraw.* ~Han dado MARCHA atrás al proyecto. *They have abandoned the project.* ~Esto supondría dar MARCHA atrás en la negociaciones de paz. *This would mean withdrawing from the peace negotiations.*

❸ CURSO, DESARROLLO. *Development, course, progress.* ~La MARCHA de los acontecimientos. *The course of events.* ~La MARCHA de las negociaciones. *The progress of the negotiations.* || **2.** Rumbo, tendencia. *Trend, course.* ~La enfermedad sigue su MARCHA. *The illness is following its course.* || **3.** [De un huracán]. *Path, track.* || **4.** •Sobre la MARCHA. *As one goes along.* ~Resolveremos este problema sobre la MARCHA. *We'll solve that problem as we go along (when we get to it).*

❹ PARTIDA. *Departure.* ~Hay que prepararlo todo para la MARCHA. *We have to have everything ready for the departure.* ~El día de su MARCHA. *The day he went away.* ~Una MARCHA precipitada. *A sudden departure.* || **2.** •Ponerse en MARCHA. *To set off.* || **3.** •¡En MARCHA! *Let's go!*

❺ FUNCIONAMIENTO. *Operation, running.* ~La buena MARCHA del vehículo. *The efficient running of your vehicle.* || **2.** •Estar en MARCHA. (I) [Motor]. *To be running,* (II) [Proyecto, gestiones]. *To be under way,* (III) [Maquinaria]. *To be in operation, to be working.* || **3.** •Poner en MARCHA. (I) [Coche, motor], *To start.* (II) [Negocio]. *To start up,* (III) [Plan, proyecto, sistema]. *To set in motion.* ~Las negociaciones se han puesto en MARCHA. *The negotiations have been set in motion.* || **4.** •Coger la MARCHA. *To get use to, get into the rhythm, get into the swing of things, to get the hang of it.* ~En cuanto cojas la MARCHA, te será más fácil. *Once you get into the rhythm of it, you'll find it easier.*

❻ ANIMACIÓN, AMBIENTE, ALEGRÍA.

Humor, good vibrations. ~En esta ciudad hay mucha MARCHA. *This city is very lively, has a lot of night life.* || **2.** Fiesta. *Party.* ~La MARCHA empezó después de la medianoche. *The party began after midnight.* || **3.** •Tener MARCHA. *To have a lot of energy, to be fun-loving.* •¡Qué MARCHA tiene! *He's so full of energy!* ~Los chicos jóvenes tienen mucha MARCHA. *Young people have a lot of energy.* || **4.** •Irle a alguien la MARCHA. *To be having a good time.* ~No la invites porque no le va la MARCHA. *Don't invite her because she's not into parties.*

MARCHAR[1]. *v.* Funcionar. *To work.* ~La radio no MARCHA. *The radio isn't working.* || **2.** Andar. *To go, proceed.* ~El negocio MARCHA muy bien. *The business is doing very well.* Su MATRIMONIO no marcha muy bien. *Her marriage is not going too well.* || **3.** [En un bar, restaurante]. •¡MARCHANDO! *Coming up!*|| **4.** •MARCHAR sobre ruedas. *To run like clockwork.* ⇨MARCH

MARCHARSE[2]. *v.* Irse. *To leave, depart.* ~Se MARCHÓ de casa a los 18. *She left home when she was 18.* ⇨MARCH

MARGEN[1] [MARGIN]. *sm.*
❶ GENERAL. Borde. *Border, edge, fringe.* ~Viven al MARGEN de la sociedad. *They live on the fringes of society, apart from society.* || **2.** [Literatura]. *Marginal note.* ~Ver notas al MARGEN. *See margin (marginal) notes.* || **3.** Intervalo. *Gap, space.* || **4.** Libertad de acción. *Leeway.* ~Me han dejado un MARGEN de acción muy reducido. *They have left me very little leeway.* || **5.** •MARGEN comercial. *Markup.* || **6.** Franja de terreno. *Strip of land.* || **7.** Período (de tiempo). *Amount of time.* ~Dame un MARGEN razonable de tiempo. *Give me a reasonable amount of time.* || **8.** Grado. *Degree.* ~Un MARGEN de autonomía más amplio. *A greater degree of autonomy.* || **9.** Límites. *Range.* ~Dentro de los MÁRGENES normales. *Within the normal range (limits).* || **10.** Medida. *Extent.* ~Los MÁRGENES de credibilidad de estos sondeos. *The extent in which these polls can be believed.* || **11.** •Mantener al MARGEN. *To keep out, stand*

aside, remain on the sidelines. || **12.** •Dar MARGEN para. *To give an opportunity for, give scope for.* ~Dale MARGEN para que te demuestre lo que es capaz de hacer. *Give him an opportunity to show you what he can do.*
❷ AL MARGEN DE. Apartado. *Away from.* ~Prefiero mantenerme al MARGEN de este enredo. *I prefer to keep out of that business.* || **2.** Excluir. *To exclude, leave out.* ~Lo dejan al MARGEN de todas las decisiones importantes. *They leave him out of all the important decisions.* || **3.** A parte de, a pesar de. *Outside, apart from, despite.* ~Al MARGEN de lo que digas. *Despite what you may say.* ~Al MARGEN de algunos cambios menores. *Apart from a few minor changes.*

MARGEN[2] [MARGIN]. *sf.* [De un río]. *Bank.* ~Fundada a las MÁRGENES del río Mapocho. *Founded on the banks of the Mapocho River.* ~En la MARGEN derecha del río. *On the right bank of the river.* || **2.** [De una carretera]. *Side.*

MARINA. *sf.* [Organización]. *Navy.* ~La MARINA española está de luto por la pérdida de su insigne almirante. *The Spanish navy is mourning the loss of its famous admiral.* ~Servir en la MARINA. *To serve in the navy.* || **2.** Barcos. *Fleet.* ~El acuerdo afecta a toda la MARINA española. *The agreement affects the entire Spanish fleet.* || **3.** ARTE Cuadro. *Seascape.* Sorolla atrapa en sus MARINAS el reflejo del sol en el agua. *In his seascapes Sorolla captures the reflexion of the sun in the water.* || **4.** Zona costera. *Seacoast.* ~Vive en una pequeña casita de la MARINA. *He lives in a small house by the sea.* || **5.** Arte de navegar. *Seamanship.* || **6.** •De NÁUTICA. *Nautical.* ~Un término de NÁUTICA. *A nautical term.* ⇨MARINA

MASA [MASS]. *sf.* [Para pan, pasta]. *Dough.* ~El pan se hace con MASA de harina, levadura y agua. *Bread is made from a mixture of flour, yeast and water.* || **2.** [Para empanadas, tartas]. *Pastry.* ~MASA de hojaldre. *Puff pastry.* || **3.** [Para bizcocho]. *Mixture.* || **4.** [Para crepes]. *Batter.* || **5.**

Argamasa. *Mortar, plaster.* || **6.** Total. *Total.* ~La MASA de bienes. *The total fortune.* || **7.** •Comunicación de MASAS. *Mass media.* || **8.** •Con las manos en la MASA. *Red-handed.* || **9.** •Llevar en la MASA de la sangre. *To have in one's blood.*

MATERNIDAD [MATERNITY]. *sf.* Estado o cualidad de madre. *Motherhood.* ~La MATERNIDAD es una experiencia maravillosa. *Motherhood is a wonderful experience.*

MATRIMONIO. *sm.* Pareja casada. *Married couple.* ~Un joven MATRIMONIO. *A young couple.* ~El MATRIMONIO y los hijos. *The couple and their children.* ~El MATRIMONIO Romero. *Mr. and Mrs. Romero, the Romero's.* || **2.** *LOCUCIONES.* || •Contraer MATRIMONIO. *To marry, to get married.* || •Cama de matrimonio. *Double bed.* || •MATRIMONIO religioso. *Church wedding.* || •Nacer fuera del MATRIMONIO. *To be born out of wedlock.* || •MATRIMONIO por poder. *Marriage by proxy.* || •Partida de MATRIMONIO. *Wedding certificate.* ⇨MATRIMONY

MERMELADA. *sf.* Dulce. *Jam, preserves.* ~MERMELADA de fresa. *Strawberry jam.* ⇨ MARMALADE

MISERABLE. *adj.* Sordid. Una choza miserable. *A sordid shack.* ~Vivieron una vida MISERABLE. *They lived a sordid life.* || **2.** Extremely poor. *Muy pobre.* ~Una familia MISERABLE. *A very poor family.* ~Los MISERABLES. Poor (indigent) people. || **3.** Stingy, miserly. *Tacaño.* ~Es tan MISERABLE que, si cobraran por respirar, se ahogaría. *He's so stingy that, if you had to pay to breathe, he would choke.* || **4.** Despicable. *Despreciable, infame.* El que te atracó era un MISERABLE sin escrúpulos. *The person that attacked you was a despicable, unscrupulous human being.* ⇨MISERABLE

MISERIA. *sf.* Estrechez, pobreza extremada. *Extreme poverty.* ~Viven en la MISERIA. *They live in extreme poverty.* ~En esta casa no hay más que MISERIA. *This family is exremely poor.* •Caer en la MISERIA. *To fall into abject poverty.* || **2.** Stinginess, miserliness. *Avaricia, mezquindad.* || **3.** Pittance, small quantity. *Cantidad pequeña.*

~Me paga una MISERIA. *He pays me a pittance.* ~Gana una MISERIA. *To earn next to nothing.* ⇨MISERY

MISIÓN. *sf.* Puesto. *Job.* ~Regular el tránsito es MISIÓN de la policía. *Traffic control is the job of the police.* || **2.** Deber. *Duty.* Sólo cumplía mi MISIÓN. *I was just doing my job.* ⇨MISSION

MISTIFICAR. *v.* Engañar. *To trick, cheat.* || **2.** Embromar. *To hoax, play a practical joke on.* || **3.** Falsificar. *To falsify.* ~En su novela el autor MISTIFICA la realidad. *In his novel the author falsifies reality.* || **4.** Confundir. *To mix up, make a mess of.* ⇨MYSTIFY

MOLESTAR. *v.* Importunar. *Trouble, bother, pester, disturb. inconvenience.* Todos los días me llama para MOLESTARME con sus problemas. *Everyday he calls me and pesters me with his problems.* || **2.** Doler, herir. *To hurt, bother.* ~La luz era tan fuerte que le MOLESTABA la vista. *The light was so bright that it bothered (hurt) his eyes.* ~Todavía le MOLESTA la herida en el brazo izquierdo. *The bruise on his left arm still hurts him.* || **3.** Ofender. *To offend.* ~Perdóname si the han MOLESTADO mis palabras. *Excuse me if I said something that offended you.* ~Le MOLESTA que le digan que se está haciendo viejo. *He gets offended when you tell him that he's getting old.* ⇨MOLEST

MONUMENTO [MONUMENT]. *sm.* Hermosura, mujer atractiva. *Good-looking person.* ~Su novia es un MONUMENTO. *His girlfriend is a beauty.* || **2.** Documentos. *Documents, source material.* ~En la excavación se descubrieron varios MONUMENTOS que aclaran el origen de este pueblo. *In the excavation many documents were found which shed light on the origins of this town.* || **3.** [Religión]. Altar (decorated for Holy Week). || **4.** Obra excepcional. *Masterpiece, classic.* Esta obra es un MONUMENTO de la épica española. *This work is a classic example of the Spanish epic.* ~El Quijote es un MONUMENTO de la literatura universal. *El Quijote is a classic* *of world literature.* || **5.** LOCUCIONES. || •A esa mujer le levanto un MONUMENTO. *That woman deserves a medal.* || •MONUMENTO funerario. *Commemorative stone.* || •Visitar los MONUMENTOS de una ciudad. *To see the sights of a town, to visit the places of interest in a city.* || •MONUMENTO a los caídos. *War memorial.* || •MONUMENTO histórico-artístico. *Conservation area, listed building.* || •MONUMENTO al soldado desconocido. *Tomb of the unknown soldier.*

MORAL. *sf.* Doctrina. *Doctrine.* ~La MORAL cristiana. *The Christian doctrine.* || **2.** Moralidad, ética. *Morality.* ~Un lugar de dudosa MORAL. *A place of dubious morality.* || **3.** Estado de ánimo. *Morale.* ~Han quedado con la MORAL por los suelos. *The morale has sunk to an all-time low.* || **4.** Arrojo, determinación. *Will.* Con una MORAL de acero. *With iron-willed determination.* || **5.** [Como estudio]. *Ethics.* ⇨MORAL

MÓRBIDO. *adj.* [Escena, historia]. *Gruesome.* || **2.** LIT Delicado, suave. *Soft, delicate, tender.* ⇨MORBID

MOTIVAR. *v.* Causar. *To cause, give rise to, bring about.* ~Este fue el principal factor que MOTIVÓ su derrota. *This was the main cause of his defeat.* ~Esto ha MOTIVADO la subida de los precios. *This has brought about (given rise to) the price increase.* ~La mala visibilidad MOTIVÓ el accidente aéreo. *Poor visibility caused the plane crash.* || **2.** Razonar, explicar. *To explain, justify.* ~Este fue el principal factor que MOTIVÓ su derrota. *This was the main cause of his defeat.* ⇨MOTIVATE

MOTIVO. *sm.* Razón. *Purpose, reason.* ~El MOTIVO de no escribirte. *The reason I didn't write to you.* ~Por MOTIVOS de salud. *For reasons of health.* || **2.** Propósito. *Purpose.* ~'MOTIVO del viaje' (en un formulario). *Purpose of visit.* || **3.** Causa. *Cause, grounds.* ~No le des MOTIVO para que se queje de ti. *Don't give him cause to complain about you.* ~Este hecho no debe ser MOTIVO de preocupación. *The fact that this has happened should not be cause for worry.* ~Hay suficientes MOTIVOS de divorcio. *There are sufficient grounds for divorce.* || **4.** [Arte]. *Motif.* ~El paisaje es un MOTIVO recurrente en los impresionistas. *Landscapes are a recurring motif in the works of the Impressionists.* || **5.** LOCUCIONES. || •Bajo ningún MOTIVO. *Under no circumstance, on no account.* || •Con MOTIVO de. *On the occasion of.* Fue allí con MOTIVO de la boda de su hija. *He went there for (on the occasion of) his daugher's wedding.* || •Con tal (este) MOTIVO. *For this reason.* || •Con mayor MOTIVO. *Even more so.* || •Dar a alguien MOTIVOS para hacer algo. *To give someone reason to do something.* || •Juan Segarra ha sido MOTIVO de homenaje. *A tribute was paid to Juan Segarra.* || •No ser MOTIVO para. *To be no reason to (for).* || •Se ha enojado con MOTIVO. *He has every reason to be angry.* || •Sin MOTIVO. *For no reason at all.* ⇨MOTIVE

MOTOR [MOTOR]. *sm.* [De un coche]. *Engine.* ~Calienta el MOTOR antes de arrancar el auto. *Warm up the engine before starting the car.*

MOTORISTA. *sm.* Persona que conduce una motocicleta. *Motorcyclist.* ⇨MOTORIST

MOVER[1]. *v.* Hacer funcionar. *To drive, work.* ~La máquina MUEVE el tren. *The engines pulls the train.* ~El agua MUEVE la rueda. *The water turns (drives) the wheel.* || **2.** Incitar, provocar. *To drive, incite, induce, stir up.* ~MOVIDO por la compasión. *Swayed by compassion.* ~Sólo le MUEVE su interés por el dinero. *It's only money that impels him to do anything.* || **3.** [La cabeza]. (I) [Negando]. *To shake,* (II) [Asintiendo]. *To nod.* || **4.** [Cola]. *To wag.* || **5.** Manejar (dinero). *To handle.* ~MUEVE enormes cantidades de dinero. *He handles huge amounts of money.* || **6.** [Las manos]. *To wave.* ~MOVÍA las manos para decir adios. *He was waving good bye.* || **7.** Remover (café, té). *To stir.* ~MOVÍA el café con la cuchara. *He stirred the coffee with his spoon.* ⇨MOVE

MOVERSE[2]. *vr.* Gestionar. *To take every step, make all possible efforts.* ~Si quieres conseguir el trabajo vas a tener que

MOVERTE. *If you want to get the job, you'll have to get going.* || **2.** Darse prisa. *To hurry up.* ~MUÉVETE, o no acabarás nunca. *Get a move on or you'll never finish.* || **3.** [Mar]. *To get rough.* || **4.** [Viento]. *To rise.* || **5.** Evolucionar. *To be on the move.* || **6.** No poder estarse quieto. *To wriggle, fidget.* ~Este niño no deja de MOVERSE. *This child never stops wriggling.*|| **7.** Desplazarse, caminar, andar, conducir. *To travel, go, drive, walk.* No me gusta MOVERME por el centro de la ciudad con el coche. *I don't like to drive downtown.*|| **8.** Frecuentar, desenvolverse (en determinado ambiente). *To frequent, hang out at.* Se MUEVE en círculos intelectuales. *She frequents intelectual circles.* ⇨MOVE

MUNDANO. *adj.* Del mundo (problemas, placeres). *Worldly, of the world.* ~Rechazó los placeres MUNDANOS para retirarse a un monasterio. *He rejected worldly pleasures to withdraw to a monastery.* || **2.** De alta sociedad (fiesta, people). *Society (as an adjective), fashionable, social, social-minded.* ~Son gente muy MUNDANA. *They're great society people.* ~Una reunión MUNDANA. *A fashionable gathering, a gathering of society people.* ~Su gusto por la vida MUNDANA. *His taste for high society (social life).* ~Llevar una vida muy MUNDANA. *To lead a very active social life.* ⇨MUNDANE

MURMURAR. *v.* Susurrar. *To whisper.* ~Le MURMURÓ algo al oído. *~He whispered something in her ear.* || **2.** Refunfuñar, hablar entre dientes. *To mutter, grumble.* || **3.** Criticar. *To criticize.* || **4.** [Abejas, multitud]. *To hum.* || **5.** [En son de crítica]. *To mutter.* ~Andan MURMURANDO que el hijo no es suyo. *There are rumors (mutterings) that the child is not his.* ~Son cosas que se MURMURAN en la oficina. *They are just rumors that go around the office.* || **6.** Cotillear. *To gossip.* ⇨MURMUR

N

NACIONAL. *adj*. [Flight, market, product]. *Domestic*. En el aeropuerto hay un terminal para los vuelos NACIONALES y otro para los internacionales. *At the airport there is a terminal for domestic flights and another for international travel.* ‖ **2.** De la nación, del país. *Of the country.* ~En todo el territorio NACIONAL. *Throughout the country.* ~Los niños aprendieron los nombres de los ríos NACIONALES. *The children learned the names of the country's rivers.* ‖ **3.** • A nivel NACIONAL. *Nationwide.* ~Una campaña a nivel NACIONAL. *A nationwide campaign.* ‖ **4.** •Carretera NACIONAL. *Interstate highway.* ⇨NATIONAL

NACIONALIZAR [NATIONALIZE]. *v*. [Persona]. *Naturalize.* ‖ **2.** •Naturalizarse. *To become naturalized.* ~NACIONALIZARSE español. *To take up Spanish citizenship, to become a naturalized Spaniard.*

NATURAL. *adj*. [Child]. *Illegitimate.* ‖ **2.** Sin elaboración. *Plain.* ‖ **3.** [Fruta]. *Fresh.* ~¿Piña NATURAL o de lata? *Fresh or canned pineapple?* ‖ **4.** [Agua]. *Plain.* ‖ **5.** [Flor]. *Real.* ‖ **6.** [Wiskey]. *Straight.* ‖ **7.** *LOCUCIONES.* •Agua NATURAL. *Tapwater.* ‖ •Al NATURAL. (I) [En la realidad]. *In real life.* ~Es mucho más bonita al NATURAL. *She's much prettier without makeup,* (II) [Culinario]. *In its own juice.* ~Una lata de tomate al NATURAL. *A can of tomatoes in its own juice,* (III) [Mejillones]. *In brine,* (IV) [Cerveza, gaseosa]. *Unchilled.* ~Se sirve al NATURAL. *Served at room temperature.* ‖ •Ser NATURAL de. *To come from, be a native of.* ~Juan Prieto, de 33 años, NATURAL de Alicante. *Juan Prieto, 33 years old, from Alicante.* ‖ •Luz NATURAL. *Daylight, sunlight.* ‖ •De tamaño NATURAL. *Life-sized, life-size.* ~Retrato de tamaño NATURAL. *Life-sized portrait.* ‖ •Fuerzas NATURALES. *Forces of nature.* ⇨NATURAL

NAVEGAR. *v*. [Barco]. *To sail.* ~Había NAVEGADO todos los mares del mundo. *He had sailed the seven seas.* ~NAVEGAN a 15 nudos. *They're sailing at 15 knots.* ‖ **2.** [Avión]. *To fly.* ‖ **3.** •NAVEGAR a la deriva. *To drift.* ~El buque NAVEGABA a la deriva. *The vessel was drifting.* ‖ **4.** •Saber NAVEGAR. *To know what one is doing.* ⇨NAVIGATE

NEBULOSO. *adj*. [Cielo]. *Cloudy.* ~El cielo está NEBULOSO y anuncia lluvia. *The sky is cloudy and it may rain.* ‖ **2.** [Aire]. *Misty, foggy.* ~Hoy el día está muy húmedo y NEBULOSO. *Today it's very humid and foggy.* ‖ **3.** Tétrico. *Dark, gloomy.* ‖ **4.** [Ideas]. *Hazy, vague, obscure.* ~Sólo recuerdo imágenes NEBULOSAS del accidente. *I only have vague recollections of the accident.* ⇨NEBULOUS

NECESIDAD [NECESSITY]. *sf*. Urgencia, falta. *Need.* ~Una imperiosa NECESIDAD. *An urgent need.* ‖ **2.** Pobreza. *Poverty, need.* ~Viven en la NECESIDAD. *They live in poverty.* ~Su muerte lo dejó en la más extrema NECESIDAD. *His death left him in extreme poverty.* ‖ **3.** Inevitabilidad. *Inevitability.* ~Tienen que hacer trasbordo en Irún por NECESIDAD. *They have no alternative but to change trains at Irún.* ‖ **4.** *pl*. Requerimientos. *Needs, requirements.* ~No podremos satisfacer sus NECESIDADES. *We will be unable to meet your needs (requirements).* ‖ **5.** Privaciones. *Hardship.* ~Sufrieron muchas NECESIDADES. *They suffered a great deal of hardship.*

NEGOCIAR. *v*. Comerciar. *To do business, deal.* ~NEGOCIA en (con) ganado. *He deals (trades) in cattle, he's in the cattle business.*

~NEGOCIABA con su cuerpo. *She used to sell her body.* ⇨NEGOTIATE

NERVIO. *sm.* Resistencia. *Stamina, toughness.* || **2.** Fondo. *Crux, core.* || **3.** Impulso, vitalidad, brío. *Spirit.* ~El caballo es un animal con mucho NERVIO. *The horse is a spirited animal.* || **4.** [De una hoja]. *Rib, vein.* || **5.** [De una bóveda]. *Rib.* || **6.** [De un libro]. *Rib.* || **7.** [Del ala de un insecto]. *Vein, rib.* || **8.** [En la carne]. *Sinew.* ~Esta carne está llena de NERVIOS. *This piece of meat is full of sinews.* || **9.** [Music]. *String.* || **10.** [Persona]. *Soul, leading light, guiding spirit.* ~Es el NERVIO de la sociedad. *He's the guiding spirit of the club.* || **11.** •Tener NERVIO. *To have character.* ~Un hombre sin NERVIO. A spineless man. ⇨NERVE

NERVIOSO. *adj.* Excitable. *High-strung, excitable.* || **2.** Impaciente. *Impatient, restless.* || **3.** Inquieto. *Upset, agitated.* ~Estás muy NERVIOSA hoy. ¿Qué te ha pasado? *You seem very agitated (jumpy, on edge) today. What's up?* || **4.** [Anatomía]. *Wiry, sinewy.* || **5.** [Estilo]. *Vigorous, forceful.* || **6.** •PONERSE nervioso. *To get excited.* || **7.** •¡Qué niño tan NERVIOSO! *What a fidgety child!* || **8.** •¡No te pongas NERVIOSO! *Take it easy, calm down!* ⇨NERVOUS

NOTA. *sf.*
❶ NOTICIA BREVE. •NOTAS sociales. *Society column.* || **2.** •Y ahora con la NOTA deportiva. *And now with the sports round-up.* || **3.** •Según una NOTA que acaba de llegar a nuestra redacción. *According to a report just in.*
❷ RASGO, CARACTERÍSTICA, DETALLE. •La NOTA dominante. *The dominant feature.* ~La NOTA dominante de su estilo. *The dominant feature of his style.* ~La humedad constituye la NOTA característica. *High humidity is the most characteristic feature.* || **2.** Detalle. *Touch.* ~Para agregar una NOTA de humor. *To add a touch of humor.* ~Fue una NOTA muy simpática. *It was a very nice touch (gesture).*
❸ MÚSICA (Sentido figurativo). •Dar la NOTA. *To stand out, make oneself noticed.* || **2.** •Dar la NOTA discordante. *To be difficult*

or different. || **3.** •Ser la NOTA discordante. *To strike a sour note.* || **4.** •Forzar la NOTA. *To go too far.* || **5.** •Entonar la NOTA. *To pitch a note, give a note (for singers to start).*
❹ COMERCIO. [En una tienda]. *Receipt.* || **2.** •En un restaurante. *Bill, check.* ~El camarero trajo la NOTA. *The waiter brought the check.* || **3.** •NOTA de gastos. *Expense account.*
❺ EDUCACIÓN. [Calificación]. *Mark, grade.* ~Me puso una NOTA muy baja. *She gave me a very low grade.* ~Mañana nos darán las NOTAS. *Tomorrow the grades will be in.* || **2.** •NOTA escolar. *Terminal report.* || **3.** •Obtener buenas NOTAS. *To get good grades.*
❻ REPUTACIÓN. *Reputation.* ~Tiene NOTA de tacaño. *He has a reputation for being cheap.* || **2.** •De NOTA. *Famous.* || **3.** •De mala NOTA. *Of ill repute.*
❼ LOCUCIONES. || •NOTA informativa. || **2.** *Press release.* || **3.** •NOTA de prensa. *Press release.* || **4.** •Tomar NOTA. *To take down.* ~Tomé nota del pedido. *I took (down) the order.* ⇨NOTE

NOTAR[1]. *v.* Sentir. *To feel.* ~NOTABA el frío por todo el cuerpo. *She felt cold all over.* ~Notó que alguien le TOCABA el brazo. *She felt somebody touching her arm.* || **2.** Apuntar. *To write down.* || **3.** Señalar. *To indicate, point out.* ~Hizo NOTAR esta falta de interés. *He pointed out this lack of interest.* || **4.** Parecer. *To seem, look.* Se le NOTABA muy preocupado. *He seemed very worried.* || **5.** •Hacerse NOTAR. *To be felt.* ~Los efectos de la sequía ya se hacen NOTAR. *The effects of the drought are already being felt.* ⇨NOTE

NOTARSE[2]. *vr.* Percibirse. *To be noticeable, to be evident, to show.* ¿Se NOTA que son de distinto color? *Can you tell (does it show) that they're different colors?* ~Se NOTA que es novato. *You can tell he's a beginner.* ~Se le NOTA el acento. *His accent is very noticeable.* || **3.** Sentirse. *To feel.* ~Se NOTÓ cansado. *He felt tired.* ~Me NOTO muy raro con este vestido. *I feel funny in this dress.* ⇨NOTE

NOTICIA[1]. *sf.* Comunicación de cierto

suceso. *A piece of news.* ¡Qué NOTICIA tan deprimente! *What a depressing piece of news!* [En periódico, TV]. *News item.* ~Circula la NOTICIA de que. *It is rumored that.* •Una buena NOTICIA. *Good news.* •Hacer noticia. *To make news, hit the headlines.* •NOTICIA bomba. *Bombshell.* ~Lo de su divorcio fue una NOTICIA bomba. *The news of their divorce was a real bombshell.* •Es la primera NOTICIA que tengo. *It's the first I've heard of it.* •Dar la NOTICIA. *To break the news.* ¿Quién le va a dar la mala NOTICIA? *Who's going to break the bad news to him?* •NOTICIA necrológica. *Obituary.* •NOTICIA remota. *Vague memory.* ‖ **2.** Conocimiento. *Knowledge, notion.* ~No tenía NOTICIA de que hubiera problemas. *I had no idea that there were problems.* •No tener la menor NOTICIA de algo. *To know nothing at all about a matter, be completely ignorant of something.* ⇨NOTICE

NOTICIAS². *sf.* Contenido de la comunicación de cierto suceso. *News.* ~Las NOTICIAS son alarmantes. *The news is alarming.* ~Traigo buenas/malas NOTICIAS. *I have some good/bad news.* ~Tengo que darte una mala NOTICIA. *I have bad news for you.* •Ultimas NOTICIAS. *Latest news.* •Según nuestras NOTICIAS. *According to our information.* ‖ **2.** *LOCUCIONES.* ‖ •Estar atrasado de NOTICIAS. *To be behind the times, lack up-to-date information, be out of touch.* ‖ •Tener NOTICIAS de uno. *To hear from someone.* ~Hace tiempo que no tenemos NOTICIAS suyas. *We haven't heard from you for a long time.* ‖ •Las malas noticias llegan primero. *No news is good news.* ‖ •NOTICIA falsa. *False alarm.* ⇨NOTICE

NOTORIO. *adj.* Famoso. *Famous, well-known, renown.* ~Dos de las figuras más notorias de la oposición. *Two of the best-known opposition figures.* ~Un hecho notorio. *A well-known fact.* ~Es notorio que. *It's well known that, it's common knowledge that.* ‖ **2.** Manifiesto, notable, pronunciado. *Manifest, downright.* ~Se ha registrado un notorio descenso de la natalidad. *There's been a marked drop in the birthrate.* ~Pone un interés notorio en lo que hace. *He shows*

a downright interest in what he does. ‖ **3.** Evidente. *Obvious.* ~Nunca fue procesado, aunque eran NOTORIOS sus fraudes. *He was never brought to trial, althought it was obvious he was a swindler.* ‖ **4.** [Error]. *Glaring, flagrant, blatant.* ⇨NOTORIOUS

NOVEDAD [NOVELTY]. *sf.* Innovation. *New feature, new development.* ~La última NOVEDAD en el campo de la informática. *The latest innovation in the field of computing.* ~En este modelo se han introducido algunas NOVEDADES. *Some new features have been introduced on this model.* ~La gran NOVEDAD para esta temporada. *The latest idea (fashion, etc.) for this season.* ‖ **2.** Cambio. *Change.* ~Sin NOVEDAD en el frente. *All quiet on the Western front.* ~No hay NOVEDADES. *There's nothing to report.* ~El enfermo sigue sin NOVEDAD. *The patient's condition is unchanged.* ‖ **3.** [Libros, discos]. *New (latest) books, records.* ‖ **4.** Noticias. *News.* ~No es ninguna NOVEDAD que viven juntos. *Everybody knows they're living together.* ¡Vaya NOVEDAD! *That's hardly news!* ~Tengo NOVEDAD. *I have some news.* ‖ **5.** Percance, contratiempo. *Mishap, setback, incident.* ~Llegamos sin NOVEDAD. *We arrived safely (without mishap).* ~Aterrizó sin NOVEDAD. *He landed without incident.* ‖ **6.** Últimos modelos. *Latest fashions.* ~Sólo vendemos NOVEDADES. *We sell only the latest fashions.* ‖ **7.** Extrañeza. *Strangeness.*

NÚCLEO [NUCLEUS]. *sm.* Grupo de gente. *Circle, group.* ~Pequeños NÚCLEOS de disidentes. *Small groups of dissidents.* ‖ **2.** [Botánica]. *Stone, kernel, pit.* ‖ **3.** [De un asunto]. *Core, essence, heart, most important part.* ~El NÚCLEO del curso serán las clases prácticas. *The course will focus on practical lessons.* ‖ **4.** [De una bobina]. *Core.* ‖ **5.** [De un reactor]. *Core.* ‖ **6.** Centro. *Center, area.* ~Núcleo urbano. *City center.* ~NÚCLEO de población. *Center of population.* ~NÚCLEO residencial. *Residential area.* ~NÚCLEO de cultura. *Cultural center.*

NULO [NULL]. *adj.* Inepto. *Useless, completely incapable.* ~Es NULO para idiomas. *He's useless (hopeless) at languages.* ‖ **2.** [Partido]. *Drawn, tied.* ‖ **3.** Inexistente. *Non-existent*. ~Mis conocimientos del tema son NULOS. *My knowledge about the subject is nil, I know absolutely nothing about the subject.* ~Su valor nutritivo es NULO. *It has no nutritional value whatsoever.*

NUMERACIÓN [NUMERATION]. *sf.* [Acción]. *Numbering.* ~La NUMERACIÓN de las páginas se hace automáticamente por ordenador. *The computer automatically numbers the pages.* || **2.** Números. *Numbers.* ~Han cambiado la NUMERACIÓN de la calle. *The numbers of the street addresses have been changed.* || **3.** [Sistema]. *Numerals.* ~NUMERACIÓN arábica/romana. *Arabic/Roman numerals.* || **4.** [Imprenta]. *Pagination.*

NUPCIAL [NUPTIAL]. *adj.* ~Que tiene relación con la boda. *Wedding, marriage.* ~Marcha NUPCIAL. *Wedding march.* ~El lecho NUPCIAL. *The marriage bed.* ~La ceremonia NUPCIAL. *The wedding ceremony.*

OBEDECER. *v.* Responder. *To respond to.* ~El volante no le OBEDECIÓ. *The steering wheel wouldn't turn.* ~La enfermedad OBEDECIÓ a los medicamentos. *The illness responded to the medicine.* ‖ **2.** Provenir. *To be due to.* ¿A qué OBEDECE esa actitud? *What's the reason for this attitude?* ~Su retraso OBEDECE a problemas auditivos. *Her backwardness is due to hearing problems.* ⇨ OBEY

OBLIGAR. *v.* Forzar. *To compel, force.* ~El deber me OBLIGA a actuar. *Duty forces me to act.* ‖ **2.** Forzar. *To force (cerradura), to force, stretch (zapatos).* ‖ **3.** Empujar. *To push.* ~El libro sólo entra allí OBLIGÁNDOLO. *The books goes in there but you have to force it in.* ‖ **4.** [Ley, disposición]. *To bind, apply.* ~Esta ley sólo OBLIGA a los mayores de edad. *This law only applies to adults, only adults are legally bound by this law.* ⇨ OBLIGE

OBSEQUIOSO. *adj.* Que se esfuerza en agradar. *Attentive, obliging, helpful.* ~OBSEQUIOSO con las damas. *Obliging with the ladies.* ⇨ OBSEQUIOUS

OBSTRUIR. *v.* [Progreso]. *To impede.* ‖ **2.** [Reforma]. *To stand in the way.* ‖ **3.** Dificultar. *To interfere with.* ~La nueva ley ha OBSTRUIDO nuestros planes. *The new law has interfered with our plans.* ⇨ OBSTRUCT

OCASIÓN. *sf.* Oportunidad. *Oportunity, chance.* •La OCASIÓN hace al ladrón. *Opportunity makes the thief.* •Escapársele la OCASIÓN. *To miss the chance.* ~Se me ha escapado la OCASIÓN de conocerle. *I have missed the chance of meeting* you. •A la OCASIÓN la pintan calva. *It's an offer you*

can't refuse, you have to strike while the iron is hot, make hay while the sun shines. ‖ **2.** Ganga. *Bargain.* ~Es una verdadera OCASIÓN. *It's a real bargain.* •Precios de OCASIÓN. *Bargain prices.* •Muebles de OCASIÓN. *Second-hand furniture, cut-price furniture.* •OCASIONES. *Bargain, special offer.* •De OCASIÓN. *Second-hand, used, old.* ⇨ OCCASION

OCASIONAL. *adj.* Fortuito (encuentro). *Chance, accidental.* Un encuentro OCASIONAL fue el principio de nuestra relación. *A chance meeting was the beginning of our relationship.* ‖ **2.** [Persona, trabajo]. *Part-time.* Sólo consigo trabajos OCASIONALES. *I can only find part-time work.* ⇨ OCCASIONAL

OCASIONALMENTE. *adv.* Accidentalmente, por casualidad. *By chance, accidentally.* ~Solemos encontrarnos OCASIONALMENTE un par de veces por año. *We run into each other a couple of times a year.* ~Si OCASIONALMENTE se encuentran, dígaselo. *If you happen to meet him, tell him.* ⇨ OCCASIONALLY

OCUPADO [OCCUPIED]. *adj.* Atareado. *Busy.* ~Es un hombre muy OCUPADO. *He's a very busy man.* ‖ **2.** [Asiento]. *Taken.* ~¿Este asiento está OCUPADO? *Is this seat taken?* ‖ **3.** [Aseos. teléfonos]. *Engaged.* ~La línea está OCUPADA. *The line is engaged (busy).* ‖ **4.** [Puesto de trabajo]. *Filled.*

OCUPAR[1]. *v.*
❶ TIEMPO, ESPACIO, POSICIÓN. [Space]. Llenar. *To take up.* ~La cama OCUPA toda la habitación. *The bed takes up the whole room.* ‖ **2.** [Tiempo]. *To spend, take up.* ¿En

qué OCUPAS tus ratos libres? *How do you spend your spare time?* ~Me OCUPA demasiado tiempo. *It takes up too much of my time.* ~Esto me OCUPA totalmente. *This takes up all my time.* ~La redacción de la carta me OCUPÓ toda la mañana. *It took me all morning to write the letter.* || **3.** Estar en. *To be.* ~María OCUPABA el asiento trasero. *María was sitting in the back seat.* ~¿Qué lugar OCUPAN en la liga? *What position are they in the division?* ~OCUPAN el primer puesto. *They're in first place.* || **4.** •Ya han OCUPADO la casa. *They've already moved into the house.* || **5.** •Los niños OCUPABAN la habitación del fondo. *The children slept in the back.*
❷ VARIOS. Desempeñar. *To hold, fill.* Luis OCUPARÁ la presidencia. *Luis will be president.* ~OCUPAR un cargo. *To hold a post.* || **2.** Emplear. *To hire, employ.* ~Esta empresa OCUPA un centenar de obreros. *The firm employs a hundred workers.* || **3.** [Atmósfera]. *To fill, pervade.* || **4.** Confiscar. *To seize, confiscate.* ~Les OCUPARON todo el contrabando. *They seized all the contraband from them.* ⇨OCCUPY

OCUPARSE[2]. *vr.* Atender. *To look after, to take care of.* ~Ella se OCUPA de la parte técnica. *She takes care of the technical side.* ~¿Quién se OCUPA de los niños? *Who takes care of the children?* ~Este departamento se OCUPA de la administración. *This department is in charge of administration.* ~En seguida me OCUPO de Ud. *I'll be right with you, I'll attend to you in a moment.* ~Nadie se ha OCUPADO de arreglarlo. *Noboby has bothered to fix it.* ~Ya me OCUPARÉ yo de eso. *I'll see to that in due course.* || **2.** Tratar. *To concern oneself, pay attention to.* Los críticos no se OCUPARON del libro. *The critics paid no attention to the book.* ~Tú, OCÚPATE de lo tuyo. *You mind your own business.* || **3.** [De un asunto]. *To deal with.* Me OCUPARÉ de ello mañana. *I'll take care of it tomorrow.* ~En esta sección el autor se OCUPA de los peces. *In this section the author deals with fish.* ~El caso que nos OCUPA. *The matter we're dealing with.* || **4.** Hacer. *To do.* ¿En qué se

OCUPA este señor? *What does this man do?* ⇨OCCUPY

OCURRENCIA. *sf.* Idea. *Idea, bright idea.* Me dio la OCURRENCIA de mirar en el cajón. *It crossed my mind to look in the drawer.* ~Has tenido una feliz OCURRENCIA. *That's was an excellent idea (that you had).* || **2.** Comentario gracioso, agudeza. *Witty remark.* ~Todos celebraban sus OCURRENCIAS. *They were all laughing at her witty remarks.* || **3.** Idea disparatada. *Crazy idea.* ~Qué OCURRENCIA! *What an absurd idea!* ⇨OCCURRENCE

OFENSA. *sf.* Injuria, agravio. *Insult, abuse.* ~Lo ha tomado como una OFENSA personal. *She has taken it as a personal insult (slight).* ~No le hagas la OFENSA de darle una propina. *Don't insult him by giving him a tip.* ⇨OFFENSE

OFICIAL. *adj.* [Ejército]. *Officer.* •Primer OFICIAL (náutica). *First officer, first mate.* •OFICIAL del día. *Orderly officer.* •OFICIAL de enlace. *Liason officer.* || **2.** Artesano. *Craftman.* || **3.** Obrero. *Worker, skilled worker (workman).* ~Se necesita OFICIAL tornero. *Experienced machinist needed.* || **4.** Empleado. *Clerk.* Trabaja de OFICIAL en el juzgado. *He works as a court clerk.* || **5.** Auxiliar. *Assistant.* ~OFICIAL de costura. *Dressmaking assistant.* ~OFICIAL de peluquería. *Barber's assistant.* || **6.** Empleada. *Female office worker.* ⇨OFFICIAL

OFRECER[1]. *v.* [Banquete, fiesta}. *To hold, give.* ~OFRECIERON una comida en su honor. *They gave a dinner in her honor.* ~OFRECIERON una recepción en el Hotel Suecia. *They held a reception at the Suecia Hotel.* || **2.** [Regalo]. *To give.* ~Nos OFRECIÓ un café y galletas. *He gaves us some coffee and cookies.* || **3.** Presentar. *To present, display, reveal.* ~La ciudad OFRECÍA un aspecto festivo. *The town looked in a holiday mood.* ~La cara de la muchacha OFRECÍA una hermosa sonrisa. *The girl's face revealed a beautiful smile.* || **4.** [Gracias]. *To give.* || **5.** [Respetos]. *To pay.* || **6.** [Bienvenida]. *To extend.* || **7.** Prometer. *To promise.* ~Me ha OFRECIDO no fumar más.

He promised me he won't smoke anymore.
‖ **8.** [Difficulty, problems, risks]. *Present, involve, have.* ~El plan OFRECE varias dificultades. *The plan presents a number of problems.* ~La situación OFRECE pocas posibilidades de éxito. *The situation has very little chance of success.* ~La operación ofrecía algunos riesgos. *The operation involved certain risks.* ‖ **9.** [Opportunity]. *To give, provide, afford.* ~Le OFRECE la oportunidad de entablar nuevas amistades. *It affords her the chance to make new friends.* ‖ **10.** [Aspecto, vista]. ~Su habitación OFRECÍA un aspecto lúgubre. *Her room was gloomy.* ~El balcón OFRECÍA una vista maravillosa. *There was a marvelous view from the balcony.* ~El año OFRECE buenas perspectivas. *Things look good for the coming year.* ~OFRECÍAN un espectáculo desgarrador. *They were a heart-rending sight.* ‖ **11.** • 'OFRECEN trabajo'. *'Help needed'.* ‖ **12.** Invitar (a la casa de uno). *To invite (to one's home).* ~Cuando supo que venía, me OFRECIÓ su casa. *When he found out I was coming he invited me to his house.* ~Todavía no nos ha OFRECIDO su casa. *He still hasn't invited us to see his new house.* ⇨OFFER

OCUPARSE². *vr.* Prestarse. *To volunteer.* ~Me OFRECÍ. *I volunteered.* ~Me OFREZCO para lo que sea. *If there's anything I can do.* ‖ **2.** Presentarse (espectáculo, panorama). *To present itself.* ~El valle entero se OFRECÍA ante nuestra vista. *The whole valley lay before us.* ~Las cumbres nevadas se nos OFRECÍAN en todo su esplendor. *The snowy peaks appeared (stood) before us in all their splendor.* ‖ **3.** Ocurrírselo a uno. *To want.* ~Aquí estoy para lo que le OFREZCA. *If there is ever anything you want, please let me know.* ~¿Qué se le OFRECE? *What can I do for you?* ~¿Se le OFRECE algo más? *Anything else?, will that be all?* ‖ **4.** Suceder, ocurrir. *To occur.* Se me OFRECE una duda. *A doubt occurs to me.* ‖ **5.** •Se OFRECE niñera con experiencia. *Experienced nanny seeks employment.* ⇨ OFFER

OMINOSO. *adj.* Despreciable. *Abonima-*

ble, dreadful. ~Nunca podré perdonar aquella OMINOSA afrenta. *I can never forgive this abonimable insult.* ⇨ OMINOUS

OPCIÓN [OPTION]. *sf.* Alternativa. *Alternative.* ‖ **2.** Derecho. *Right.* ‖ **3.** Posibilidad. *Opportunity, chance.* ~No tiene OPCIÓN real al triunfo. *She has no real chance of winning.*

OPORTUNIDAD [OPPORTUNITY]. *sf.* Vez, ocasión. *Time, occasion.* ~En dos OPORTUNIDADES. *On two occasions.* ‖ **2.** Momento oportuno. *Chance.* ~En cuando surja la OPORTUNIDAD, se lo diré. *I'll tell her as soon as I have the chance.* ~Aún no había tenido la OPORTUNIDAD de saludarlo. *I still hadn't had the chance to say hello to him.* •En la primera OPORTUNIDAD. *The first chance I get.* ‖ **3.** Posibilidad. *Chance.* Dame una nueva OPORTUNIDAD. *Give me another chance.* ‖ **4.** Lo oportuno. *Timeliness.* ~La OPORTUNIDAD de su llegada. *The timeliness of his arrival.* ~Tiene el don de la OPORTUNIDAD (dicho con ironía). *He has a knack of showing up at just the wrong time.* ‖ **5.** *pl.* Ganga. *Bargain.* ~Me salió muy barato porque lo compré en OPORTUNIDADES. *It was cheap because I bought it at bargain prices.*

ORDEN. *sm.* Campo, ámbito. *Sphere, field, front.* ~En el ORDEN económico. *In the economic sphere.* ~En otro ORDEN de cosas (en discurso). *Passing now to other matters.* ~Hemos hecho progresos en todos los ÓRDENES. *We're making progress on all fronts.* ~En el ORDEN económico se plantean ciertos problemas. *Certain problems arise in the economic field.* ‖ **2.** Carácter. *Character, nature.* Problemas de ORDEN económico. *Problems of an economic nature.* ‖ **3.** Clase, tipo, indole. *Type, kind.* ~En este ORDEN de cosas. *In this respect.* ~En otro ORDEN de cosas. *Meanwhile.* ~Todas sus ideas son del mismo ORDEN. *His ideas are all the same (of the same type).* ‖ **4.** [Público]. *Peace.* ~Alterar el ORDEN público. *To disturb the peace.* ~Las fuerzas del ORDEN. *The forces of law and order.* ‖ **5.** Organización. *Organization.* ~En esta casa no hay ORDEN; cada uno come cuando le parece. *Everything is very disorganized in this house; everyone eats when they feel like it.* || **6.** || *LOCUCIONES.* || •ORDEN de comparecencia. *Summons.* || •ORDEN de detención/de registro/de embargo. *A warrant for arrest, for attachment, search warrant.* || •Con ORDEN. *In an orderly manner.* ~La salida de los espectadores se realizó con ORDEN. *All the spectators exited the theater in an orderly manner.* || •Pon un poco de ORDEN en tu habitación. *Tidy (straighten) up your room a little.* || •Poner en ORDEN. *To sort.* ~Puso EN ORDEN las cuentas. *She sorted the accounts out.* ~Puso las páginas en ORDEN. *She sorted out the pages.* ~Tengo que PONER mis ideas en orden. *I have to sort out my ideas.* || •Por ORDEN de edad/estatura. *By age/height.* || •Por ORDEN de. *According.* ~Pónganse por ORDEN de estatura. *Line up according to height.* || •Sin ORDEN ni concierto. *Without rhyme or reason.* || •Vayamos por ORDEN. *Let's begin at the beginning.* || •ORDEN de antigüedad. *Seniority, length of service.* || • ¡A las ÓRDENES! *Yes sir?* || •A la ORDEN de. *To the order of.* ~Cheques a la ORDEN de Suárez. *Checks to be made out to Suárez.* || •A sus ÓRDENES. *At your service.* || •¡ORDEN y compostura! *Behave yourself!* || •Hasta nueva ORDEN. *Until further notice.* || •ORDEN del día. *Agenda.* ~El primer tema del ORDEN del día. *The first item on the agenda.* ⇨ ORDER²

ORDENAR. *v.* Arreglar (habitación, cajón, armario). *To tidy up, straigthen, put in order.* ~Pasó toda la mañana ORDENANDO su habitación. *He spend the entire morning tidying up his room.* || **3.** To direct. *Encaminar.* ~ORDENAR los esfuerzos a. *To direct one's efforts toward.* || **4.** [Religion]. *To ordain.* || **5.** Autorizar (un pago). *Authorize.* ORDENAR un pago. *To authorize a payment.* || **6.** Organizar. *To organize, arrange.* ~ORDENAR las ideas. *To collect one's thoughts.* ~ORDENAR su vida. *To put one's life in order.* ~Hay que ORDENAR los libros por materias. *The books have to be arranged according to subject.* ⇨ ORDER¹

ORDINARIO. *adj.* Grosero. *Rude, bad-mannered, uncouth.* ~Es un muchacho muy ORDINARIO. *He's a very rude boy.* || **2.** Bajo, vulgar, basto. *Common, unrefined.* ~Son gente muy ORDINARIA. *They're very common people.* || **3.** [No especial o excepcional]. *Normal, corriente, regular.* ~Correo ORDINARIO. *Regular mail.* ~Serán sometido a juicio ORDINARIO. *They will be tried in civil court.* ~Se puede ir con traje ORDINARIO. *You can wear your everyday suit.* || **4.** [En la manera de hablar]. *Vulgar.* || **5.** De mala calidad, basto. *Of poor (bad) quality.* ~Una tela ORDINARIA. *A poor-quality fabric.* ~Un vino ORDINARIO. *A very average wine.* || **6.** •De ORDINARIO. *Usually, ordinarily.* ⇨ ORDINARY

ORGANISMO [ORGANISM]. *sm.* Entidad pública. *Organization, body, institution.* ~Los ORGANISMOS internacionales. *International organizations.*

ÓRGANO [ORGAN]. *sm.* Conjunto de personas. *Body, organization.* ~ÓRGANO legislativo. *Legislative body.* || **2.** Medio, agente. *Agent, mean.* || **3.** [Técnología]. *Part, member.* ~ÓRGANO de transmisión. *Driving part.* ~ÓRGANO motor. *Driving member.*

ORIENTACIÓN [ORIENTATION]. *sf.* [De un edificio]. *Aspect, exposure.* ~Cuál es la ORIENTACIÓN de la casa? *Which way does the house face?* ~Una casa con ORIENTACIÓN sur. *A house facing south.* || **2.** [Enfoque]. *Approach.* ~Hay que darle una nueva ORIENTACIÓN al problema. *We have to look at the problem in a different way.* || **3.** Guía, información, instrucción. *Guidance, information.* ~Cursillo de ORIENTACIÓN. *Induction course.* ~Estos datos te servirán de ORIENTACIÓN. *This information will give you an idea.* ~ORIENTACIÓN profesional. *Career (vocational) guidance.* ~Me ayudó en la ORIENTACIÓN bibliográfica. *He helped me with bibliographic information.* || **4.** Dirección. *Direction, course.* ~La ORIENTACIÓN actual del partido. *The party's present course (direction).* ~Ha dado una ORIENTACIÓN correcta a sus estudios. *He has given his studies the right direction.* || **5.** Formación.

Training. ~Ayuda mucho en la ORIENTACIÓN de los maestros. *It is very important in the training of teachers.* ‖ **6.** Inclinación, tendencia. *Leaning.* ~Este partido es de ORIENTACIÓN conservadora. *This party has conservative leanings (tends to be conservative).* ‖ **7.** [En un lugar]. *Bearings.* ~Perdí la ORIENTACIÓN. *I lost my bearings.* ‖ **8.** [De una antena, aguja magnética, veleta]. *Pointing.* ~La ORIENTACIÓN de la antena. *The way the antenna is pointing.* ‖ **9.** Tendencia. *Tendency.* ~No me gusta la ORIENTACIÓN que están tomando las cosas. *I don't like the way things are going.*

ORIENTAR[1] [ORIENT]. *v.* Dirigir, encaminar. *To direct, aim, design.* ~Charla ORIENTADA a los padres. *Talk aimed at parents.* ~Hay que ORIENTAR las investigaciones en otro sentido. *You will have to change the direction of your inquiries.* Una política ORIENTADA a combatir la inflación. *A policy designed to fight inflation.* ~Educación ORIENTADA al logro académico. *Education geared to academic success.* ‖ **2.** [Edificios]. *To place, position.* ~Una casa ORIENTADA hacia el sur. *A house facing south.* ~ORIENTE la antena al (hacia el) este. *Position the antenna to face east.* ~Decidieron orientarlo hacia el sur. *They decided to build it facing south.* ‖ **3.** Guiar. *To guide.* ~La policía les ORIENTÓ. *The policeman gave them directions.* ‖ **4.** Aconsejar. *To advise.* ORIENTAR a los jóvenes en la elección de una carrera. *To give young people guidance on their choice of a career.*

ORIENTARSE[2] [ORIENT]. *vr.* Encontrar el camino. *To get one's bearings, find one's way about; to get into the swing of things (fig).* ~Es difícil ORIENTARSE en este terreno. *It's hard to get one's bearings in this country.* ~Los antiguos navegantes se ORIENTABAN por las estrellas. *In ancient times sailors steered by the stars.* ‖ **2.** Girar. *Turn towards.* Plantas que se ORIENTAN hacia el sol. *Plants that turn towards the sun.* ‖ **3.** Inclinarse. *To lean towards, opt for.* ~Las tres hermanas se ORIENTARON hacia las ciencias. *The three sisters opted for*

science. ~Se ORIENTA hacia la contabilidad. *He is going in for accounting.* ‖ **4.** Informarse. *To get information.*

ORIENTE [ORIENT]. *sm.* [Puntos cardinales]. *East.* ~Todas las ventanas de la casa miran hacia el ORIENTE. *All the windows in the house face east.* ‖ **2.** Origen. *Origin.* ‖ **3.** [Viento]. *East wind.* ‖ **4.** *LOCUCIONES.* ‖ •ORIENTE Medio. *Middle East.* ‖ •Cercano ORIENTE. *Near East.* ‖ •Extremo (lejano) ORIENTE. *Far East.* ‖ •Gran ORIENTE. *Gran Lodge (de la masonería).*

ORQUESTA [ORCHESTRA]. [De baile, jazz]. *Band.*

OSCURECER[1]. *v.* [Impersonal]. *To get dark.* ~Empezó a OSCURECER. *It began to get dark.* ‖ **2.** [Arte]. *To shade.* ‖ **3.** Ofuscar. *To cloud.* ~El odio le OSCURECÍA la razón. *Hate clouded his thinking.* ‖ **4.** Superar, deslucir. *To overshadow.* ~El mal tiempo OSCURECIÓ la ceremonia. *The bad weather put a cloud over the ceremony.* Su triunfo fue OSCURECIDO por la ausencia de buenos competidores. *His victory was overshadowed by the lack of competition.* ⇨OBSCURE[2]

OSCURECERSE[2]. *vr.* Nublarse. *To become cloudy.* ~El cielo se OSCURECIÓ de repente. *All of a sudden the sky became cloudy.* ‖ **2.** [Vista]. *To grow dim.* ‖ **3.** [Gloria]. *To wane.* ⇨OBSCURE[2]

OSCURO. *adj.* [Calle, habitación]. *Dark, gloomy.* ~Son la cuatro de la tarde y ya es OSCURO. *It's only four o'clock and it's already dark.* ~La OSCURA y triste celda. *The gloomy cell.* ‖ **2.** [Future]. *Uncertain, gloomy.* ‖ **3.** [Asunto, pasado]. *Shady, murky, dubious.* ~Aún quedan puntos OSCUROS sobre su desaparición. *There are still some unanswered questions regarding his disappearance.* ‖ **4.** [Nublado]. *Overcast, cloudy.* ~Hoy está el cielo muy OSCURO y quizás llueva. *The sky is overcast and it may rain.* ‖ **5.** [Color]. *Dark, deep.* ~Un hermoso azul OSCURO. *A beautiful dark blue.* ~Vestía de OSCURO. *She was wearing dark clothes.* ‖ **6.** •A OSCURAS. *In the dark.* ~Quedarse a OSCURAS. *To be left* *in the darkness.* || **7.** •OSCURO como boca de lobo. *Pitch-dark.* ⇨OBSCURE[1]

OXIDARSE [OXIDIZE]. *v.* Enmohecer. *To rust, get rusty.* ~El cerrojo se ha OXIDADO. *The bolt has rusted.*

P

PACIFICAR [PACIFY]. *v.* Apaciguar. *To appease, calm down.* Las Naciones Unidas intentan PACIFICAR el país. *The United Nations is trying to appease the country.* ‖ **2.** [Mediante la fuerza]. *To restore peace.* ~Enviaron tropas para PACIFICAR la region. *They sent troops to restore peace in the country.*

PÁGINA [PAGE]. *sf.* [Sentido figurado]. *Chapter.* ~Aquellos hombres escribieron una PÁGINA importante de la historia. *Those men wrote an important chapter in history.*

PALIDECER [PALE]. *v.* [Persona]. *To turn pale.* ~PALIDECIÓ al oír la mala noticias. *He turned pale upon hearing the bad news.* ‖ **2.** Color. *To fade.* ~Hasta los colores más vivos PALIDECEN bajo los fuertes rayos del sol. *The brightest colors fade when exposed to the bright rays of the sun.* ‖ **3.** [Luz]. *To grow dim.* ‖ **4.** [Día]. *To wane.* ‖ **5.** FIG Disminuir (fama, renombre). *To diminish, be on the wane.* La fama de este artista esta PALIDECIENDO. *This artist's fame is on the wane.*

PANFLETO. *sm.* Libelo, escrito difamatorio. ~En su registro la policía encontró varios PANFLETOS en contra del gobierno. *In their search the police found numerous pamphlets of defamatory nature against the government.* ‖ **2.** [En revista, periódico]. *Satire, lampoon, scandal sheet.* ⇨ PAMPHLET

PAPEL. *sm.* Representación. *Role, part.* ~Esta actriz interpretó (hizo) el PAPEL de Julieta. *This actress played the part of Juliet.* •Desempeñar un PAPEL. *To play a part.* ‖ **2.** Actuación. *Performance.* ~Hizo un PAPEL lamentable en el congreso. *His performance at the conference was abysmal.* ~Si no le regalas nada vas a hacer muy mal PAPEL. *You're going to look very bad if you don't give her anything.* ~¡Hizo un PAPEL tan ridículo! *He made such a fool of himself!* ~El PAPEL de la oposición en la política actual. *The role of the opposition in today's politics.* •Hacer buen/mal PAPEL. *To do well/badly (at something).* ~María hizo un buen PAPEL en el examen oral. *María did well in the written exam.* ‖ **3.** Deber, obligación. *Duty, obligation.* ~Tu PAPEL es obedecer. *Your role is to obey.* ‖ **4.** Función, quehacer. *Function.* •Hacer el PAPEL de. *To act as, serve as, undertake the job of.* ~Ese cartón hace el PAPEL de pantalla. *This cardboard serves as a screen.* Ella ha hecho con estos niños PAPEL de madre. *She has been a mother to these children.* ‖ **5.** •Blanco como el PAPEL. *As white as a sheet.* ‖ **6.** •Perder los PAPELES. *To loose one's touch.* ~El equipo visitante perdió los PAPELES en la segunda parte. *The visiting team lost their touch in the second half.* ‖ **7.** •PAPEL de diario. *Newsprint.* ~Envuélvelo en PAPEL de diario. *Wrap it in newspaper.* ⇨ PAPER

PAR. *sm.* [Dos unidades]. *Couple.* ~Un PAR de terrones. *A couple of lumps.* ~¡Puedo hacerte un PAR de preguntas? *Can I ask you a couple of questions?* ‖ **2.** [Número]. *Even.* ~El 44 es un numero PAR. *44 is an even number.* ‖ **3.** Igual, muy parecido. *Similar or identical, alike.* Estos dos chicos son PARES en todo. *These two boys are alike in every way.* ‖ **4.** Noble. *Peer.* ~Los doce PARES. *The twelve peers.* ‖ **5.** LOCUCIONES. ‖ •A la PAR. (I) Al mismo tiempo. *At the same time, together.* ~Casó a las dos hijas a la PAR. *He married his two daughters on the same day.* ~Hizo el servicio militar a la PAR que yo. *We did military service together,* (II) Juntamente, además. *As well as.* ~Baila a la PAR que toca la armónica. *He dances and plays the harmonica at the same time.* ~Una cocina imaginativa a la PAR que sana. *Cooking that is both imaginative and healthy.* || •A tres PARES. *Lengthy. Un discurso a tres pares. A lengthy speech.* || •A pares. *In pairs, in twos, two at a time, two by two.* ~Se comía los caramelos a pares. *He would eat candies two at a time.* || •Con el corazón abierto de PAR en PAR. *With open arms.* || •De PAR en PAR. *Wide open.* ¿Quién dejó la puerta abierta de PAR en PAR? *Who left the door wide open?* ~Abrió la boca de PAR en PAR. *She opened her mouth wide.* || •No tener PAR. *To have no parallel, be unique.* ~Como mecánico no tiene PAR. *He's an outstanding mechanic.* || •PARES y nones. *Odds and evens.* || •Sin PAR. *Matchless, unparalleled, without equal, unrivaled.* ~Una atleta sin PAR. *An athlete without equal.* ~Como ceramista no tiene PAR. *As a ceramist he is unrivaled.* ~Una mujer de una belleza sin PAR. *A woman of matchless beauty.* ~La sin PAR Dulcinea. *The one and only Dulcinea.* ⇨PAIR

PARIENTE. *sm.* Persona que pertenece a la misma familia. *Relative, relation.* ~Hizo un largo viaje para visitar a sus PARIENTES. *He traveled a long way so he could see his relatives.* || **2.** •PARIENTES políticos. *In-laws.* || **3.** •Medio PARIENTE. *Distant relative.* ⇨PARENT

PARSIMONIOSO. *adj.* Tranquilo. *Unhurried, calm, slow, deliberate.* ~Cualquier cosa que haga le lleva mucho tiempo, porque es tan PARSIMONIOSO. *He's so slow (COLL laid back), he takes forever in doing anything.* || **2.** Moderado (con el dinero). *Sparing, economical, careful.* ⇨PARSIMONIOUS

PARTE. *sf.*
❶ EN NEGOCIACIONES, CONTRATO. *Party.* ~Las PARTES contratantes. *The*

parties to the contract. ~Las PARTES firmantes. *The signatories.* ~Ambas PARTES están dispuestas a negociar. *Both parties (sides) are willing to negotiate.* ~Soy PARTE interesada. *I'm an interested party.* ~Ambas PARTES están de acuerdo. *Both parties agree.* •PARTE contraria. *Opposing parties.*
❷ INFORME. *Report.* •PARTE médico. *Medical bulletin (report).* •PARTE metereológico. *Weather forecast (report).* •PARTE de baja. *Sick note.* •PARTE de clase. *Class report.* •PARTE de defunción. *Death certificate.* •PARTE de guerra. *Military communiqué, war report.* •PARTE matrimonial/de nacimiento. *Wedding/birth announcement.* •Dar PARTE. *To report, inform.*
❸ VARIOS. Bando. *Side.* ~¿De qué PARTES estás? *Which side are you on?* •Ponerse PARTE de. *To side with.* || **2.** Parentesco. *Side.* Por PARTE de mi madre. *On my mother's side.* || **3.** [En una repartición]. *Share.* ~Quiero mi PARTE. *I want my share.* •La PARTE del león. *The lion's share.* ~A PARTES iguales. *In equal shares.* || **4.** [Deporte]. *Half.* ~Primera PARTE. *First half.* || **5.** Rincón. *Corner.* ~En las cinco PARTES del mundo. *In the four corners of the earth.* || **6.** Lado. *Side.* Por cualquier PARTE que lo mires. *From whichever side you look at it.*
❹ LOCUCIONES.
•A TODAS PARTES. *Everywhere.* ~Va a pie a todas PARTES. *She goes everywhere on foot.*
•A UNA Y OTRA PARTE. *On both sides.*
•DE ALGÚN TIEMPO A ESTA PARTE. *For some time past.*
•DE MI PARTE. *As far as I'm concerned.*
•DE NINGUNA PARTE. *From any quarter.* ~No esperes ayuda de ninguna PARTE. *Don't expect help from any quarter.*
•DE PARTE A PARTE. *From one side to the other, through and through.* ~Atravesamos la ciudad de PARTE a PARTE. *We crossed one side of the city to the other.*
•DE PARTE DE. *On behalf of, from.* Llamo de PARTE de tu tío. *I'm calling on your uncle's behalf.* ~Salúdale de mi PARTE. *Give him my regards.* ~Dale saludos de PARTE de todos nosotros. *Give him our best wishes from*

all of us. ~Muy amable de su PARTE. *That is (was) very kind of you.* ~De PARTE del director que subas a verlo. *The director wants you to go up and see him.* ~Vengo de PARTE del Sr. Díaz. *Mr. Díaz sent me.* ~¿De PARTE de quién? *Your name, please?*, [Telephone]. *Who's calling?*
• ¿EN QUÉ PARTE? *Where.* ~¿En qué PARTE lo dejaste. *Where did you leave it?*
• DE UN TIEMPO A ESTA PARTE. *For some time now.* ~De cinco meses a esta PARTE la situación se ha ido empeorando. *The situation has been deteriorating over the past five months.*
• DE UNA PARTE A OTRA. *Back and forth, to and fro.*
• EL QUE CORTE Y REPARTE LLEVA LA MEJOR PARTE. *He who cuts the cake takes the biggest slice.*
• EN ALGUNA PARTE. *Somewhere.* ~En alguna PARTE de Europa. *Somewhere in Europe.*
• EN CUALQUIER PARTE. *Anywhere.* ~Se consigue en cualquier PARTE. *You can get it anywhere.*
• EN GRAN (BUENA) PARTE. *To a great extent.* ~Eso se debe, en gran PARTE, al aumento de la demanda. *This is largely due to the increase in demand.*
• EN LA PARTE DE ARRIBA DE LA ESTANTERÍA. *On the top shelf.*
• EN LA PARTE DE ATRAS DE LA CASA. *At the back of the house.*
• EN OTRA PARTE. *Somewhere else.* ~Debe de estar en otra PARTE. *It must be somewhere else.*
• EN PARTE. *Partly.* ~En PARTE es culpa mía. *It's partly my fault.*
• En todas PARTES. *Everywhere.* ~En todas PARTES de España. *All over Spain.* || •En todas PARTES se cuecen habas. *It's the same the world over.*
• EN UNA U OTRA PARTE. *Somewhere or other.*
• FORMAR PARTE DE. *To belong to, to be a member of.* ~Forma PARTE de la delegación china. *She's a member of the Chinese delegation.* ~Forma PARTE del equipo nacional. *He's on the national team.* ~Entró a formar PARTE de la plantilla. *He joined the staff.*
• IR A OTRA PARTE. *To go somewhere else.*
• LA MAYOR PARTE. *Most of, the (great)*

majority of. ~Destruyó la mayor PARTE de la cosecha. *It destroyed most of the harvest.* ~La mayor PARTE de los participantes. *The majority of the participants.*
• LLEVAR(SE) LA MEJOR PARTE. *To have the advantage, to come off best.*
• LLEVAR LA PEOR PARTE. *To be at a disadvantage.*
• MIRAR A OTRA PARTE. *To look the other way, to look in another direction.*
• NO LLEVAR A NINGÚNA PARTE. *Not to lead anywhere, to get (someone) nowhere.* ~Este camino no lleva a ningúna PARTE. *This road leads nowhere.* ~Esta discusión no nos va a llevar a ninguna PARTE. *This discussion isn't going to lead us anywhere.*
• PONER DE SU PARTE. *To do one's best, do one's share.* ~Yo te ayudaré, pero tú también tienes que poner de tu PARTE. *I'll help you but you have to cooperate.*
• PONERSE DE PARTE DE. *To side with.* ~Se puso de su PARTE. *He sided with her.*
• POR AMBAS PARTES. *On both sides.* ~Con concesiones por ambas PARTES. *With concessions from both sides.*
• POR MI PARTE. *As far as I'm concerned.* ~Yo, por mi PARTE, no tengo inconveniente. *As far as I'm concerned, there's no problem.*
• POR NINGUNA PARTE. *Nowhere, anywhere.* ~No aparece por ninguna PARTE. *I can't find it anywhere, it's nowhere to be found.*
• POR OTRA PARTE. *On the other hand.*
• POR PARTE DE. *By.* ~Su interrogatorio por PARTE del fiscal. *His questioning by the prosecutor.*
• POR PARTES. *Step by step, systematically.* ~Revisémoslo por PARTES. *Let's go over it section by section.* ~Vayamos por PARTES ¿Cómo empezó la discusión? *Let's take it step by step, how did the argument start?*
• POR TODAS PARTES SE VA A ROMA. *All roads lead to Rome.*
• POR UNA PARTE ...por otra. *On the one hand ... on the other.*
• SE FUE POR OTRA PARTE. *He went another way.*
• SER JUEZ Y PARTE. *To be one's judge and jury.*
• TENER PARTE EN. *To share in.* ⇨PARTE

PARTICIPACIÓN [PARTICIPATION]. *sf.* Pago. *Contribution.* || **2.** Intereses. *Interest, investment.* ~Como tiene PARTICIPACIÓN en la empresa, puede intervenir en su gestion. *Since he has an interest in the company, he can have a voice in running it.* || **3.** FIN Acción. *Share, stock.* || **4.** [En lotería]. *Part of a lottery ticket.* ~Regaló a todos sus empleados PARTICIPACIONES para el sorteo de Navidad. *He gave his employees a lottery ticket for the Christmas draw.* || **5.** Notificación. *Notice, notification, announcement.* ~PARTICIPACIÓN de boda. *Wedding invitation (announcement).* || **6.** [En ganancias]. *Share.* ~Exigen PARTICIPACIÓN en los beneficios. *They are demanding a share in the profits.* ~Aumentaron su PARTICIPACIÓN en el mercado. *They increased their market share.* || **7.** [En un torneo]. *Entry.* || **8.** [En una elección]. *Turnout.* ~El índice de PARTICIPACIÓN en las elecciones. *The turnout for the elections.* || **9.** •PARTICIPACIÓN en los beneficios. *Profit-sharing.*

PARTICIPAR [PARTICIPATE]. *v.* [En ganancias]. *To have a share (interest).* || **2.** Compartir. *To share.* ~No PARTICIPA de nuestro entusiasmo. *He does not share our enthusiasm.* ~PARTICIPAR en (de) una herencia. *To share in an estate.* || **3.** Notificar. *To notify, inform.* ~Nos PARTICIPÓ las buenas noticias. *He notified us of the good news.* ~Nos PARTICIPÓ los sucesos de aquel día. *He informed us of the events of that day.* || **4.** [En una empresa]. *To invest.* || **5.** [En una lotería]. *To hold.* PARTICIPA con la cantidad de 500 pesetas en el número 43456. *He holds a 500 peseta share in ticket number 43456.* || **6.** Advertir (en primera persona). *To warn.* ~Te PARTICIPO que si viene él, no vengo yo. *I must tell you that if he comes, then I'm not coming.*

PARTICULAR[1]. *adj.* No público. *Private, personal.* ~No venga a mi despacho sino a mi casa PARTICULAR. *Don't go to my office but to my home.* ~Clases particulares. PRIVATE classes. ~He has a PRIVATE teacher. *Tiene un profesor particular.* || **2.** Personal, individual. *Personal, individual.* ~Cada

cual tiene su opinión PARTICULAR. *Everyone has his own personal point of view.* || **3.** Notable. *Remarkable.* ~Lo que tiene de PARTICULAR es que ... *What's remarkable about it is that ...* || **4.** Especial, extraordinario. *Special.* •Nada de PARTICULAR. *Nothing special.* ~La casa no tiene nada de PARTICULAR. *There's nothing special about the house.* || **5.** No oficial. *Unofficial.* ~El presidente va a París en viaje PARTICULAR. *The president is going on an unofficial visit to Paris.* || **6.** Raro. *Peculiar.* Esa persona tiene un acento muy PARTICULAR. *This person has a very peculiar accent.* Tiene un sabor PARTICULAR. *It has a peculiar flavor, it has a flavor of its own.* || **7.** Extraño, insólito. *Strange, unusual.* •Nada de PARTICULAR. *Nothing unusual.* No tiene nada de PARTICULAR que quiera ir. *There's nothing strange (unusual) in her wanting to go.* ⇨ PARTICULAR[1]

PARTICULAR[2]. *n.* Asunto. *Matter.* ~No dijo mucho sobre el PARTICULAR. *He didn't say much about the matter.* || **2.** Persona. *Individual, private individual.* ~No comerciamos con PARTICULARES. *We don't do business with individuals.* || **3.** •Iba vestido de PARTICULAR. *He was in civilian clothes.* ⇨ PARTICULAR[2]

PARTIR[1]. *v.*

❶ DIVIDIR, CORTAR. Dividir. *To split, divide.* ~PÁRTELO en dos. *Split it in two.* ~El rayo PARTIÓ el árbol por la mitad. *The lightning split the tree in two.* ~PARTIR una manzana por la mitad. *To cut an apple in half.* || **2.** [Cards]. *To cut.* || **3.** Cortar con cuchillo (tarta, melón). *To cut.* ~PARTIÓ la pera en dos (por la mitad). *He cut the pear in two (in half).* ~PARTE la empanada en cinco partes. *Cut the meat pie into five equal pieces.* || **4.** [Madera]. *To cut.* ~PARTIR leña. *To cut wood.* || **5.** •PARTIR la diferencia. *To split the difference.*

❷ ROMPER. Romper. *To break, snap.* ~PARTIÓ la vara en dos. *He broke (snapped) the stick in two.* || **2.** [Con un golpe]. (I) [Labio]. *Split, split open,* (II) [Cabeza]. *To split open,* (III) [Cara]. *To smash.* ~PARTIRLE la cara a alguien. *To smash somebody's* *face.* || **3.** [Nuez]. *To crack.* ~PARTIR nueces. *To crack nuts.* || **4.** [Pan]. *To break.* ~¿Me PARTES un pedazo de pan? *Can you break me off a piece of bread?* || **5.** [En sentido figurado]. •Me PARTE el corazón. *It breaks my heart.*

❸ VARIOS. Distribuir, repartir. *To distribute, divide.* ~PARTIR la finca. *To divide the estate.* || **2.** FAM Desbaratar, desconcertar. *To ruin, spoil.* ~PARTIR a alguien por la mitad (por el eje). *To mess things up for somebody.* || **3.** Marcharse. *To leave* ~PARTIÓ ayer con destinación a Londres. *He left for London yesterday.* ~PARTIREMOS a las ocho. *We will leave at eight.* || **4.** Arrancar (marcha, narración]. *Set out (off), depart.* ~PARTIERON del puerto de Cádiz. *They set off from the port of Cádiz.* || **5.** [Operación matemática]. *Divide.* || **6.** Dar por establecido (premisa, un supuesto}. *To start, assume.* ~PARTIENDO de esta hipótesis. *If we take this hipothesis as a starting point.* ~Debemos PARTIR de la base de que lograremos los fondos. *We should start from the assumption that we will obtain the funds.* ~PARTIMOS del supuesto de que todos tienen gusto en venir. *We assume that you are all happy to come.* || **7.** Clasificar. *To classify.* || **8.** Compartir. *To share.* ~PARTIR entre cuatro. *To share between four.* ~PARTIR como hermanos. *To share like brothers.* || **9.** •A PARTIR de. *Starting from.* ~A PARTIR de ahora. *From now on.* ~A PARTIR de hoy. *As of today.* ⇨PART²

PARTIRSE². *vr.* Romperse, quebrarse. *To crack, split, break in two.* || **2.** •PARTIRSE de risa. *To split one's sides laughing.* ⇨PART²

PASADO [PAST]. *adj.* Último. *Last.* ~El año/lunes PASADO. *Last year/Monday.* || **2.** Anticuado. *Dated, old-fashioned.* ~PASADO de moda. *Out of date.* ~Todo lo que lleva es de lo más PASADO. *All her clothes are old-fashioned.* || **3.** [Flor]. *Faded, whithered.* || **4.** Alimento. *Bad.* ~La carne está PASADA. *The meat is bad.* || **5.** [Noticia]. *Stale, old hat.* || **6.** Muy cocido (arroz, pasta). *Overcooked, well done (carne).* ~El filete muy PASADO, por favor. *I'd like my steak well*

done please. || **7.** [Fruta]. *Overripe.* || **8.** [Idea]. *Antiquated, out of date.* || **9.** [Ropa]. *Old, worn, threadbare.* ~Los codos de la chaqueta están PASADOS. *The jacket has worn through the elbows.* || **10.** [Pan]. *Stale.* || **11.** [Zapatos]. *Gastado, raído.* || **12.** [Leche]. *Sour.*

PASAJE. *sm.* LAT. AM. Billete (de un viaje). *Ticket.* ~Sacar un PASAJE de ida y vuelta. *To buy a round-trip ticket.* ~El PASAJE en avión sale más caro. *The airline ticket is more expensive.* || **2.** Tarifa. *Fare.* ~Mi madre me regaló el PASAJE. *My mother paid my fare.* •Cobrar el PASAJE. *To collect fares.* || **3.** Viajeros. *Passengers (collectively).* ~El PASAJE. *The passengers.* || **4.** Callejón. *Passageway, alleyway, alley, narrow street.* || **5.** Viaje. *Crossing, voyage.* || **6.** Estrecho. *Channel, strait, pass.* ⇨PASSAGE

PASAR. *v.*

❶ MOVIMIENTO. [Por un lugar]. *Go by, come by, go past.* ~¿Ha PASADO el autobús? *Has the bus gone by?* ~No ha PASADO ni un taxi. *~Not a single taxi has gone by.* ~¿A qué HORA pasa el lechero? *At what time does the milkman come?* •PASAR de largo. *To go by (without stopping).* ~El autobús venía completo y PASÓ de largo. *The bus was full and went right by.* || **2.** Pasar por. *To go through.* ~Al PASAR por la aduana. *When you go through customs.* ~Prefiero no PASAR por el centro. *I'd rather not go through downtown.* ~El Tajo PASA por Aranjuez. *The Tagus flows through Aranjuez.* ~No dejan PASAR a nadie. *They're not letting anyone through.* ~El país está PASANDO por unos momentos muy difíciles. *This country is going through some difficult times.* ||| **3.** Entrar (persona). *To come in.* ~PASA, no te quedes en la puerta. *Come in, don't stand there in the doorway.* ~Hazle PASAR. *Ask him to come in.* ~PASE por favor. *Please come in.* ~No se puede PASAR. *You can't go in.* ~Nos hicieron PASAR. *They showed us in.* || **4.** Caber, entrar (cosa). *To fit.* ~No PASARÁ por la puerta. *It won't go through the door.* ~Esta camiseta no me PASA por la cabeza. *I can't get this T-shirt over my head.* || **5.** Continuar. *Go on* *to, proceed to.* ~PASARON a discutir el siguiente punto. *They proceeded (went on) to the next issue.* ~Y luego PASARON a otra cosa. *And then they went on to something else.* ~PASE adelante. *Go on, proceed, continue.* ~PASANDO a otra cosa ... *To change the subject..* ~PASE a la página 98. *Continued on page 98. ...* ‖ **6.** Ir. *To go.* ~El hilo PASA por el agujero. *The thread goes through the hole.* ~El río PASA por la ciudad. *The river flows (goes, runs) through the city.* ~PASÓ de teniente a general. *He was promoted from lieutenant to general.* ~PASARÉ por tu casa. *I'll call on you, I'll drop in.* ‖ **7.** Trasladar. *Move.* ~Hemos PASADO el televisor al comedor. *We have moved the TV to the dining room.* ‖ **8.** Cruzar. *To cross.* ~Es imposible PASAR la frontera sin pasaporte. *One cannot cross the border without a passport.* ‖ **9.** Detenerse (en un lugar). *Stop by, drop in.* Podríamos PASAR por el mercado. *We could stop off at the supermarket.* ~De camino tengo que PASAR por la oficina. *I have to drop in (stop by) the office on the way.* ~PASE Ud. por la caja. *Please go over to the cashier.* ❷ SUCEDER, ACONTECER. *To happen.* ~¿Qué le ha PASADO? *What happened to her?* ~¿Qué PASA aquí? *What's going on here?* ‖ **2.** •Lo que PASA es ... *The thing is that ...* ‖ **3.** •PASE lo que PASE. *Whatever happens, come what may.* ‖ **4.** •¿Qué te PASA? *What's the matter?* ‖ **5.** •¿PASA algo? *Is anything wrong?* ‖ **6.** •¿Qué PASA que no entra? *Why on earth doesn't she come in?* ‖ **7.** •Algo le PASA al motor. *Something is wrong with the engine.* ‖ **8.** •Siempre PASA igual. *It's always the same.* ‖ **9.** •Siempre me PASA lo mismo. *I'm always having the same trouble.* ‖ **10.** •Eso le PASA a cualquiera. *That can happen to anybody.* ❸ TIEMPO. *Spend.* ~PASAMOS una semana solos. *We spent a week on our own.* ~Se PASÓ la tarde durmiendo. *He spent the entire afternoon sleeping.* ‖ **2.** •PASAR el rato. *To kill time.* ‖ **3.** •Pasarlo bien/mal. *To have a good/bad time.* ~¡Qué lo PASES bien! *Have a good time!, enjoy yourself!* ‖ **4.** Acabarse. *To be over.* ~Se te ha PASADO la hora. *Your*

time is up (over). ‖ **5.** Terminar. *To end, be over.* ~Ha PASADO la crisis.*The crisis is over.* ~Ya PASÓ aquello. *This is all over and done with.* ‖ **6.** Estar. ~Se PASA meses sin ver a su mujer. *He goes months without seeing his wife.* ~Es capaz de PASARSE el día sin probar bocado. *He can easily go the whole day without having a thing to eat.* ❹ EXCEDER, SOBREPASAR. *To exceed, go beyond, be over.* PASA de los cincuenta. *He's over fifty.* ~PASAN de cien. *There are more than a hundred.* ~Eso PASA los límites de lo razonable. *That goes beyond anything that is reasonable.* ~Ella ha PASADO los treinta. *She's over thirty.* ~Eso PASA de ser una broma. *This goes beyond a joke.* ‖ **2.** Excederse. *To go too far.* ~No te PASES *Don't overdo it.* ~No te PASES con la sal. *Don't add too much salt.* ‖ **3.** •PASAR(se) de la raya. *To go too far.* ‖ **4.** •PASAR de castaño oscuro. *To be too much.* ‖ **5.** •Se PASA de generoso. *He's too generous.* ‖ **6.** •PASAR de listo. *To be too clever by half.* ❺ CAMBIO. PASAR de algo a algo. *To go from one thing to another.* ~En poco tiempo ha PASADO del anonimato a la fama. *In a very short span of time he went from obscurity to fame.* ~PASÓ del quinto al séptimo lugar. *She dropped (went) from fifth to seventh place.* ‖ **2.** PASAR a. *Continue.* ~Ahora puedes PASAR a tercera (auto). *Now you can change into third gear.* ❻ VARIOS. Padecer, sufrir. *Suffer, endure.* PASARON muchos apuros. *They suffered great hardship.* •PASAR frío. *To be cold.* •PASAR hambre. *To go hungry.* ‖ **2.** Tolerar. *Stand, tolerate.* ~No la PASO a esta mujer. *I can't stand that woman.* ~El profesor no the deja PASAR ni una. *The teacher does not let you get away with anything.* Yo el Roquefort no lo PASO. *I can't stand (hate) Roquefort.* ‖ **3.** Terminar. *To come to an end.* Ya PASÓ lo peor. *The worst is over.* ~Ya se te PASARÁ. *You'll get over it.* •PASAR de moda. *To go out of fashion.* ‖ **4.** Escapar, dejar escapar, perder. *Escape, miss.* No se le PASA nada. *Nothing escapes him.* No dejes PASAR esta oportunidad. *Don't miss this chance.* ‖ **5.** Considerarse. *Be consi-*

dered. ~Pasa por sabio. *He is considered a wise man.* || **6.** [Visita]. *To make, carry out.* ~El médico pasará visita. *The doctor will call.* || **7.** [Película]. *Run, show, screen.* || **8.** Olvidar. *To forget.* ~Se me pasó llamarle. *I forgot to call him up.* || **9.** [Enfermedad]. *To give, infect with.* ~Me has pasado tu tos. *You have given me your cold.* || **10.** Arreglárselas. *To manage.* ~Sin electricidad podemos pasar, pero sin agua no. *We can manage (do) without electricity, but not without water.* || **11.** Transcribir. *Copy, write again.* ~Tendré que pasar la carta. *I'll have to write (copy) the letter out again.* ~¿Me pasas esto a máquina? *Could you type this for me?* || **12.** Entregar, hacer llegar. *Give, send.* ¿Ha pasado ya la factura? *Have they sent the bill yet?* ~El padre le pasa una mensualidad. *Her father gives her a monthly allowance.*
❼ LOCUCIONES. || •Pasar el cepillo por el pelo. *To run a brush through one's hair.* || •I pass. *Count me out.* •Pásale un trapo. *Wipe it with a cloth.* || •Pasar a mejor vida. *To pass away.* || •Pasar el hilo por el ojo de una aguja. *To thread a needle.* || •Pasar en limpio. *To make a clean copy of.* || •Pasar la sopa por un colador. *To strain the soup.* || •Pasar por encima de alguien. *To walk all over somebody.* || •Pasar por la cabeza (imaginación). *To cross one's mind.* ~Ni me pasó por la imaginación que iba a hacer eso. *It didn't even cross my mind that she would do that.* || •Pasar sin. *To do without.* || •Pasarlas canutas (moradas). *To go through hell, have a rough time.* ⇨PASS

PASTA [PASTE]. *sf.* [De madera, papel]. *Pulp.* || **2.** [Para pan, pasteles]. *Dough.* || **3.** [Pastelito]. *Pastry.* || **4.** FAM Dinero. *Dough, bread.* ~Soltar la pasta. *To cough up the money.* || **5.** [De muelas]. *Filling.* || **6.** [De lapicero]. *Lead.* || **7.** [Cartón]. *Cardboard.* || **8.** [Fideos]. *Noodles, spaghetti.* || **9.** [De un libro]. *Full binding.* || **10.** [Of a book]. *Cover.* •Libro en pasta. *Bound book.* •Media pasta. *Halfbinding.* || **11.** LOCUCIONES. || •Pasta de hojaldre. *Puff pastry.* || •Pasta española. *Marbled leather binding.* || •Ser de buena pasta. *To be good-natured.*

|| •Tener pasta de. *To have the makings of, to be cut out for.* ~No tengo pasta para negocios. *I'm not cut out for business.* ~Tiene pasta de actriz. *She has the makings of an actress.*

PATÉTICO. *adj.* Digno de lástima, conmovedor. *Moving, touching, poignant.* ~Fue un discurso de despedida patético. *It was a moving farewell speech.* ⇨PATHETIC

PATIO [PATIO]. *n.* Espacio de un edificio al descubierto. *Court, courtyard, yard.* ~Elena está tendiendo la ropa en el patio. *Helene is hanging out clothes in the yard.* || **2.** [De una escuela]. *Playground, schoolyard.* ~Los niños salieron al patio del colegio para jugar. *The children went out to play in the schoolyard (playground).* || **3.** [Theater]. *Pit.* •Patio andaluz. *Interior courtyard (typical of Andalusian houses).* || **4.** LOCUCIONES. || •Patio de butacas. *Orchestra.* || •Patio de luces. *Well (of a building).* || •Patio de Monipodio. *Den of thieves.* || •Patio de operaciones. *Floor (of the stock exchange).* || •Patio de armas. *Parade ground.*

PATRIMONIO [PATRIMONY]. Bienes. *Wealth.* ~Su patrimonio es uno de los más grandes del mundo. *He's one of the wealthiest man on earth.* ~Patrimonio nacional. *National wealth.* || **2.** [Cultural]. *Heritage.* ~Estas ruinas romanas son lo más destacado del patrimonio artístico de la región. *These Roman ruins are one of the greatest specimens of the cultural heritage of that region.* || **3.** [Comercio]. *Capital resources, net worth.* ~Las últimas deudas contraídas por la empresa hicieron disminuir notablemente su patrimonio. *The last debts which the company incurred reduced its net worth considerably.*

PATRÓN. *sm.* Jefe. *Boss.* ~Toda su vida trabajó en la misma fábrica y para el mismo patrón. *He worked all his life in the same factory and for the same boss.* || **2.** Dueño, proprietario. *Owner.* ~Es el patrón de una gran empresa. *He's the owner of a large company.* || **3.** [De un barco]. *Captain, skipper.* ~El patrón no quiso abandonar el barco. *The captain refused to abandon ship.* || **4.** [En costura]. *Pattern.* ~La modista primero hace el PATRÓN y luego corta la tela. *The dressmaker first makes the pattern and then cuts the fabric.* || **5.** Medida. *Standard.* ~El oro suele ser el PATRÓN internacional para las distintas monedas del mundo. *Gold is the common standard of currencies around the world.* || **6.** [De pensión]. *Landlord, landlady.* || **7.** [De esclavo]. *Master.* || **8.** •Cortado por el mismo PATRÓN. *Cast in the same mold.* ⇨PATRON

PAVIMENTO. *sm.* [De asfalto]. *Road surface.* || **2.** [De habitación]. *Flooring.* La habitación tenía un PAVIMENTO de mármol. *The room had a marble floor.* ⇨PAVEMENT

PECULIAR. *adj.* Característico. *Particular, individual, characteristic.* ~Es un rasgo PECULIAR de su personalidad. *It's a particular trait of his.* ~Su modo PECULIAR de escribir. *Her own particular (individual) way of writing.* ~Reaccionó con su PECULIAR buen humor. *He reacted with his characteristic (usual) good humor.* ⇨PECULIAR

PELAR. *v.* Cortar el pelo. *To cut the hair off, shear (animal).* ~Veo que te has PELADO. *I see that you had a haircut.* || **2.** [Animal muerto]. *To flay, skin.* ~He llevado a PELAR el jabalí que cacé a la carnicería. *I took the wild boar that I shot to the butcher to have it skinned.* || **3.** [Mariscos, guisantes]. *To shell.* || **4.** Desplumar (pollo, ave). *To pluck.* ~La vieja estaba PELANDO un pollo. *The old woman was plucking a chicken.* || **5.** [Caramelo]. *To unwrap.* || **6.** [En el juego]. *To clean out, fleece.* ~Me PELARON. *The cleaned me out.* || **7.** [Árbol, hueso]. *To strip.* || **8.** Despojar. *To strip, despoil.* || **9.** Criticar. *To tear to pieces, criticize.* ~Las dos vecinas estuvieron toda la tarde PELANDO al vecindero entero. *The two neighbors tore the entire neighborhood to pieces all evening long.* ⇨PEEL

PENALIDAD. *sm.* Trabajos, miseria. *Hardship, troubles, suffering.* ~Pasaron muchas PENALIDADES. *They experienced great hardship.* ⇨PENALTY

PENETRACIÓN [PENETRATION]. *sf.* Sagacidad. *Insight, perception.* ~Un investigador debe tener una gran capacidad de PENETRACIÓN. *Researchers must have great insight.*

PENETRANTE. *adj.* [Frío, viento]. *Bitter, biting.* ~Se abrigó para combatir el PENETRANTE frío que hacía. *He wrapped himself up in order to protect himself against the bitter cold.* || **2.** [Herida]. *Deep.* ~El torero recibió una herida muy PENETRANTE. *The bullfighter received a very deep gash.* || **3.** [Inteligencia]. *Sharp, acute.* ~Nada podía escapar a la mente PENETRANTE de aquel genio. *Nothing escaped the sharp mind of that genius.* || **4.** [Arma]. *Sharp.* Un cuchillo PENETRANTE. *A sharp knife.* || **5.** [Vista]. *Acute.* ~Tener una vista PENETRANTE. *To have good vision.* || **6.** [Aroma]. *Strong.* ~Este perfume tiene un olor muy PENETRANTE. *This perfume has a very strong scent.* || **7.** [Ironía]. *Biting, sharp, cutting.* || **8.** [Voz, grito, música, sonido]. *Piercing, shrill.* ~Los ritmos de la música actual son muy PENETRANTES. *Present-day music beats have shrill sounds.* ⇨PENETRATING

PENETRAR. *v.* [En un lugar]. *To go in.* La puerta por donde PENETRÓ el ladrón. *The door through which the thief entered.* ~El agua PENETRABA por entre las tejas. *Water was coming in between the tiles.* ~PENETRAMOS poco en el mar. *We did not go far out to sea.* ~El frío que PENETRA en los huesos. *Cold that gets into one's bones.* || **2.** Descubrir, descifrar (misterio, secreto, mente). *To grasp, understand, fathom, delve into, decipher.* ~No logró PENETRAR el sentido de este enigma. *He was unable to fathom this mistery.* || **3.** [Sonido]. *To pierce.* ~Un grito PENETRÓ la noche. *A scream pierced the night.* || **4.** [Intención]. *To see through.* || **5.** Sustancia. *To permeate.* ⇨PENETRATE

PENSIÓN [PENSION]. *sf.* Casa de huéspedes. *Boardinghouse.* || **2.** Alojamiento (en una casa de huéspedes). *Board and*

lodging, room and board. ‖ **3.** Hotel. *Guesthouse.* ‖ **4.** [Universidad]. *Scholarship, fellowship, travel grant.* ‖ **5.** •PENSIÓN alimenticia. *Alimony.* ‖ **6.** •PENSIÓN vitalicia. *Annuity.*

PERCEPCIÓN. *sf.* Cobro. *Receipt, collection.* ~Estoy arreglando los papeles para la RECEPCIÓN del subsidio de desempleo. *I'm processing the needed papers to receive unemployment benefits.* ‖ **2.** Cantidad cobrada. *Payment.* ~Los empleados se quejaban del atraso en la RECEPCIÓN de los sueldos. *The employees complained about the lateness in the payment of salaries.* ‖ **3.** Idea. *Notion, idea.* ⇨PERCEPTION

PERCIBIR. *v.* Cobrar. *To collect, earn, receive, get.* ~Los empleados PERCIBEN su salario mensual. *The workers receive their monthly salaries.* ⇨PERCEIVE

PERDONAR. *v.* Disculpar. *To forgive.* ~Te PERDONO, pero que no se vuelva a repetir. *I forgive you, but don't let it happen again.* ~PERDÓNANOS nuestras deudas. *Forgive us our trespasses.* ~No le PERDONA una. *She doesn't let him get away with anything.* ‖ **2.** [De obligación]. *To exempt, excuse.* ~Les he PERDONADO las clases. *I have excused them from classes.* ~Hoy the PERDONO el dictado. *I'll let you off dictation today.* ‖ **3.** [Deuda]. *To write off.* ~Me PERDONÓ la deuda. *He wrote off my debt.* ‖ **4.** Perder, dejar. *To miss.* ~No PERDONAR un baile, una ocasión. *Not to miss a dance, a chance.* ‖ **5.** Omitir. *Overlook.* ~Sin PERDONAR detalle. *Without omitting a single detail.* ‖ **6.** No aprovechar. *To shirk from, let go by.* ~No PERDONAR medio para. *To use all possible means to.* ‖ **7.** [Esfuerzo]. *To spare.* ~No PERDONAR esfuerzos. *To spare no efforts.* ‖ **8.** *LOCUCIONES.* ‖ •PERDONA las molestias que puedan causar las obras. *We apologize for any incovenience the work may cause you.* ‖ •PERDONAR la vida a alguien. *To spare somebody's life.* ‖ •PERDONE, pero me parece que. *Excuse me, but I think.* ‖ •Dios lo haya PERDONADO. *God have mercy on him.* ⇨PARDON

PERFECCIONAR [PERFECT]. *v.* Mejorar. *To improve.* Ha ido a Inglaterra para PERFECCIONAR su inglés. *He went to England to improve his English.* ‖ **2.** Terminar. *To complete, finish, give the finishing touch.* ~PERFECCIONÓ su obra dándole una capa de barniz. *He gave his work the finishing touch by adding a coat of varnish.*

PERFORACIÓN [PERFORATION]. *sf.* [Mina]. *Boring, drilling.* ~Fue preciso una PERFORACIÓN de veinte metros para obtener agua. *They had to drill some twenty meters to get water.* ‖ **2.** [De tarjetas]. *Punching.* Estaba encargado de la PERFORACIÓN de las tarjetas. *His job consisted of punching (holes in) the cards.* ‖ **3.** [Madera]. *Drilling, boring.* ~Con este taladro no tardarás nada en la PERFORACIÓN de la pared. *With this power drill you'll drill a hole in the wall in no time.*

PERFORAR [PERFORATE]. *v.* [Llanta]. *To puncture.* ‖ **2.** [Agujero]. *To drill, make, bore.* ~PERFORAR un agujero en la pared, un túnel en el monte. *To bore a hole in the wall, a tunnel through the mountain.* ‖ **3.** [Pozo]. *To sink.* ‖ **4.** [Tarjeta]. *To punch, punch a hole in.* ‖ **5.** [Ficha]. *To punch.* ‖ **6.** [Costilla]. *To pierce, puncture.*

PERIÓDICO [PERIODICAL]. *sm.* Diario. *Newspaper.* ~El ABC es un PERIÓDICO de Madrid. *The ABC is a newspaper from Madrid.*

PERMANENCIA [PERMANENCE]. *sf.* Estancia. *Stay.* Durante mi PERMANENCIA en el extranjero. *During my stay abroad.* ~Los cosmonautas han batido el record de PERMANENCIA en el espacio. *The cosmonauts have broken the record for the longest stay in space.* ‖ **2.** [En una organización]. *Continuance.* ~La PERMANENCIA de nuestro país en la asociación. *Our country's continuance in (continued membership of) the association.* ~Su PERMANENCIA en el cargo está en duda. *His continuance in the post is in doubt.* ‖ **2.** Perseverancia. *Perseverance, constancy.* ‖ **3.** Duración. *Duration.* ~Durante la PERMANENCIA de las hostilidades. *During* *the duration of the hostilities.*

PERMISO [PERMIT]. *sm.* Licencia, documento. *License, permit.* ~PERMISO de conducir. *Driver's license.* ~PERMISO de residencia. *Residence permit.* ‖ **3.** Días libres. *Leave.* ~Obtuvo PERMISO de tres días. *He got three days' leave.* ‖ **4.** [Del soldado]. *Leave, furlough.* ~Estar de PERMISO. *To be on leave.*

PERSEGUIR. *v.* Reprimir. *To persecute.* ~Diocleciano PERSEGUIÓ a los cristianos. *Diocletian persecuted the Christians.* ‖ **2.** Acosar. *To pester, annoy, harass.* ~Me PERSIGUE la mala suerte. *I'm dogged by bad luck.* ~Parece que te PERSIGUEN las enfermedades. *You seem to be plagued by illness.* ⇨PURSUE

PERVERSO. *adj.* Malvado. *Evil, wicked.* ~Una mente PERVERSA. *An evil mind.* ~La madrastra PERVERSA. *The wicked stepmother.* ‖ **2.** Depravado. *Depraved.* ~Es un hombre PERVERSO. *He's a depraved man.* ⇨PERVERSE

PESTE[1]. *sf.* [Medical]. *Plague, epidemic.* ~La PESTE Negra. *The Black Plague.* ~PESTE bubónica. *Bubonic plague.* ‖ **2.** ~Una peste de mosquitos. *A plague of mosquitoes.* ‖ **3.** Hedor, mal olor. *Stench, stink, foul smell.* ¡Qué PESTE hay aquí, abran las ventanas! *What a stink there is in here, open the windows!* ‖ **4.** •PESTE porcina. *Swine fever.* ⇨PEST

PESTES[2]. *sf.* Palabras de enojo. *Swearing, obscenities.* ~Decir (echar) PESTES. *To curse.* ~Se marchó echando PESTES y dando un portazo. *He slammed the door and left cursing.* ‖ **2.** •Hablar PESTES de una persona. *To speak ill of a person.* ~Dijo PESTES del profesor. *He severely criticized the teacher.* ⇨PEST

PETULANTE. *adj.* Presumido. *Arrogant, vain, smug.* ~Su papel es el de un jovencito PETULANTE. *His role is that of an arrogant young man.* ⇨PETULANT

PIEZA. *sf.* Habitación. *Room.* ~PIEZA amueblada. *Furnished room.* ~PIEZA de recibo. *Reception room.* ‖ **2.** Trozo, remiendo (de tela). *Patch.* ~Le puso una PIEZA a los pantalones. *He put a patch on the trousers.* ‖ **3.** [Técnica]. *Part.* ~Las PIEZAS de un reloj/motor/televisor. *The parts (components) of a watch/engine/television.* ‖ **4.** [De tela]. *Roll.* ~Era el final de la PIEZA. *It was a remnant of the roll.* ‖ **5.** [Caza]. *Specimen.* ~Ha cazado una buena PIEZA. *He has bagged a fine specimen.* ‖ **6.** [Obra de teatro corta]. *Play, sketch.* ~La PIEZA que acabamos de ver me ha parecido bastante aburrida. *The play we just saw was quite boring.* ‖ **7.** [Moneda]. *Change.* ~Me dio el cambio en PIEZAS sueltas. *He gave me the change in small change.* •¡Buena PIEZA estás tú hecho! *A fine one you are!* ‖ **8.** *LOCUCIONES.* ‖ •Buena PIEZA. *Rogue, villain.* ‖ •De una PIEZA (con *quedar* o *dejar*). *To leave speechless, dumbfounded, flabbergasted.* ~Esta noticia me dejo de una PIEZA. *This news left me speechless.* ‖ •¿Me permite esta PIEZA? *May I have the pleasure of this dance?* ‖ •PIEZA arqueológica. *Find, object.* ‖ •PIEZA de recambio. *Spare part.* ‖ •Por PIEZAS. *Individually.* ~Venden las manzanas por PIEZAS. *You can buy apples individually.* ‖ •Precio por PIEZA. *Price per item.* ‖ •Taladro y destornillador en una sola PIEZA. *Combined drill and screwdriver.* ‖ •Traje de dos PIEZAS, un dos PIEZAS. *Swimming suit (for women).* ⇨PIECE

PILA. *sf.* [Electrica]. *Battery.* ~Esta radio funciona con PILAS. *This radio works with batteries.* ~Cargar la PILA. *To recharge one's battery.* ‖ **2.** [Construcción]. *Pier.* ‖ **3.** [De la cocina]. *Sink.* ~Pon los platos en la PILA para fregarlos. *Clean the dishes in the sink.* ‖ **4.** [De baño, lavadero]. *Basin.* ‖ **5.** [De agua]. *Small fountain.* ~En el centro del patio habia una pequeña PILA, de la que manaba agua fresca. *There was a small fountain in the middle of the patio from which refreshing water flowed.* ‖ **6.** Abrevadero. *Drinking trough.* ‖ **7.** •Nombre de PILA. *Christian name.* ‖ **8.** •Una PILA de años. *A lot of years.* ⇨PILE

PINCHAR. *v.* Punzar. *To prick, prickle.* ~Las espinas PINCHAN. *Thorns prick.*

~Acabo de PINCHARME el dedo con la aguja. *I just pricked my finger with the needle.* || **2.** [Globo, balón]. *To burst.* ~PINCHAR un balón. *To pinch a ball.* || **3.** Incitar, estimular. *To prod.* ~Le PINCHAN para que se case. *They keep prodding him to get married.* ~Hay que PINCHARLA. *She needs prodding.* || **4.** Molestar. *To needle, rile.* ~Deja ya de PINCHARLE. *Stop needling him.* || **5.** [Medicina]. *To inject, give an injection.* ~El niño está llorando porque no quiere que la enfermera lo PINCHE. *The boy is crying because he doesn't want the nurse to give him an injection.* || **6.** [Neumático]. *To puncture.* ~PINCHARON las cuatro ruedas. *They punctured (slashed) the four tires.* || **7.** Fracasar. *To fail.* ~He vuelto a PINCHAR en los exámenes de este semestre. *I failed (flunked) again on this semester's exams.* || **8.** [Con navaja). *To stab, knife.* || **9.** Herir. *To wound.* Cuidado con esta planta, que PINCHA. *Be careful with that plant, it's prickly.* || **10.** Provocar. *To provoke, stir up.* ~Le gusta PINCHAR a su hermana diciéndole que está gorda. *He likes to provoke his sister by telling her she's fat.* || **11.** [Disco]. *To play, put on.* ~Jaime PINCHA discos en una discoteca los fines de semana. *On weekends, Jaime works as a disk jockey.* || **12.** Perder. *To fail, suffer a defeat, get beaten.* || **13.** [Carne]. *To prick.* ~PINCHAR la carne con el tenedor. *To prick the meat with a fork.* || **14.** [Para recoger]. *To spear.* ~PINCHÓ una aceituna con el palillo. *She speared an olive with the toothpick.* || **15.** [Teléfono]. *To tap, bug.* ~Han PINCHADO el teléfono del presidente. *They tapped the president's telephone.* || **16.** •No PINCHAR ni cortar. *To cut no ice.* ~Él en la oficina no PINCHA ni corta. *He doesn't have any clout in the office.* ~Yo aquí ni PINCHO ni corto. *I don't have any say in what goes on here.* ⇨PINCH

PINTAR [PAINT]. *v.* Dibujar. *To draw, sketch.* ~Píntame un perro. *Draw me a dog.* || **2.** [Con pistola]. *To spray.* || **3.** Importar. *To count.* (I) [Estar de más]. ~Yo aquí no pinto nada. *I'm out of place here.* (II) [No tener que ver]. *I have nothing to do with*

this.

PIPA. *sf.* [Of wine]. *Cask, barrel.* ~Añejado en PIPAS de roble. *Aged in oak casks (barrels).* || **2.** Semilla, pepita (de sandía, mandarina). *Seed.* ~Se atragantó con una PIPA de sandía. *He choked on a watermelon seed.* || **3.** [Música]. *Reed.* || **4.** [Del girasol]. *Sunflower seed.* ~Cuando sale de paseo se compra una bolsa de PIPAS. *When he goes out for a stroll he always buys a bag of sunflower seeds.* || **5.** Pistola. *Pistol, gun.* ~Uno de los atracadores apuntó al cajero con una PIPA. *One of the bandits pointed his gun at the teller.* || **6.** •El cuento de la buena PIPA. *It goes on and on.* || **7.** •No tener ni para PIPAS. *To be flat broke.* || **8.** •Pasarlo PIPA. *To have a great time.* ⇨PIPE

PLAN. *sm.* [Cita, compromiso]. *Date.* Si no tienes PLAN para esta noche, podemos salir a cenar. *If you're not doing anything tonight, we could go out for dinner.* || **2.** Actitud. *Attitude.* ~Hoy está en PLAN vago. *He's in a lazy mood today.* ~Lo dijo en PLAN de broma. *He meant it as a joke, he was just kidding.* ~Como siga en este PLAN, acabará mal. *If he carries on like this, he'll come to no good.* || **3.** Aventura. *Affair.* ~Tiene un PLAN con la mujer del alcalde. *He's having an affair with the mayor's wife.* || **4.** Ligue. *Pickup.* Salió en busca de PLAN para la noche. *He went out looking for a pickup for the night.* || **5.** Boyfriend/girlfriend. *Novio/novia.* Creo que está buscando un PLAN para el verano. *I think he's looking for a girlfriend for the summer.* || **6.** •A todo PLAN. *On a grand scale.* || **7.** •En PLAN de. *As.* ~En PLAN de vencedor. *As winners.* ~En PLAN de broma. ~*As a joke.* ~Vamos en PLAN de turismo. *We're going as tourists.* || **8.** •PLAN de estudio. *Course of study, curriculum.* ⇨ PLAN

PLANTA. *sf.* [Del pie]. *Sole.* ~Asentar sus PLANTAS en un lugar. *To make oneself at home.* || **2.** Piso. *Floor, story.* ~PLANTA baja. *Ground floor.* ~Una ventana de la PLANTA baja. *A downstairs window, a ground floor window.* || **3.** Plano horizontal de un edificio. *Ground plan.* ~La PLANTA y el alzado de un edificio. *The ground plan and elevation of a building.* || **4.** Proyecto. *Plan.* || **5.** [Baile, esgrima]. *Stance, position (of the feet).* || **6.** [En un almacén]. *Department.* ~Grandes ofertas en la PLANTA de señoras. *Big savings in the ladies' fashion department.* || **7.** [De empleados]. *Staff.* ~La PLANTA de obreros de la empresa. *The company's work force.* ~Nuestra PLANTA de profesores. *Our teaching staff.* || **8.** Plantío. *Field.* || **9.** •De buena planta. *Good-looking or well-built (man), attractive or shapely (woman), magnificent (animal).* Un animal de magnífica PLANTA. *A magnificent beast.* || **10.** •De nueva PLANTA. *New.* ~Han construído la iglesia de nueva PLANTA. *They have built a new church, they have completely rebuilt the church.* ⇨ PLANT

PLATAFORMA. *sf.* [Trenes]. *Turntable.* || **2.** FIG Punto de partida. *Springboard, stepping stone.* ~Le va a servir de PLATAFORMA para la fama. *It's going to serve him as a stepping-stone to fame.* ~Esta fiesta fue la PLATAFORMA para conseguir amistades influyentes. *This party served as a springboard to make influential friends.* || **3.** [De negociación]. *Package, offer, set of proposals.* || **4.** LOCUCIONES. || •PLATAFORMA continental. *Continental shelf.* ||•PLATAFORMA espacial. *Space-station.* || •PLATAFORMA petrolífera. *Drilling rig, oil-rig.* || •PLATAFORMA de lanzamiento. *Launching pad.* || •PLATAFORMA de salida (natación). *Starting block.* || •PLATAFORMA móvil. *Moving sidewalk.* || •PLATAFORMA rodante (cine). *Dolly.* ⇨ PLATFORM

PLATO. *sm.* Parte de una comida. *Course.* ~PLATO fuerte (principal). *Main course.* ~Una comida de tres PLATOS. *A three-course meal.* ~PLATO combinado. *One-course meal.* || **2.** Guiso. *Dish.* ~Hoy voy a preparar un PLATO de arroz. *Today I'm going to make a rice dish.* || **3.** Receta. *Dish.* ~Un PLATO español. *A Spanish dish.* ~Es mi PLATO favorito. *It's my favorite dish.* || **4.** [De balanza]. *Tray, pan, scale.* || **5.** [De tocadiscos]. *Turntable.* || **6.** Platito [para una taza]. *Saucer.* || **7.** Objeto de críticas. *Butt.* || **8.** Temas de hablillas. *Subject of gossip.* ||

9. [Tiro]. *Clay pigeon.* || **10.** LOCUCIONES. || •Comen del mismo PLATO. *They're great friends.* || •Lavar los PLATOS. *To wash the dishes.* || •No es PLATO de mi gusto. *It's not my cup of tea.* || •Pagar los PLATOS rotos. *To pay the consequences.* || •Ser PLATO de segunda mesa. *To be second-best, to feel neglected, to play second fiddle.* ⇨PLATE

PLAUSIBLE. *adj.* Digno de alabanza. *Commendable, praiseworthy.* ~Las investigaciones produjeron unos resultados PLAUSIBLES. *The research produced praiseworthy result.* || **2.** Admisible, justificado (motivo, razón). *Acceptable, valid.* ~Hubo motivos PLAUSIBLES para esta decisión. *There were justifiable reasons for this decision.* ⇨ PLAUSIBLE

PODER. *sm.* Fuerza, vigor, eficacia. *Strength, effectiveness.* ~El PODER de este detergente contras las manchas ha sido probado. *The effectiveness of this detergent is well established.* || **2.** Posesión. *Possesion.* ~La carta está en PODER de las autoridades. *The letter is in the hand of the authorities.* ~Hay que evitar que llegue a su PODER. *We have to stop it from falling into his hands.* || **3.** [Documento]. *Letter of authorization; power of attorney (hecho ante un notario).* ~Dar a uno PODER para. *To authorize, to allow someone to.* || **4.** Capacidad. *Capacity.* ~Tiene un gran PODER de trabajo. *He has a great capacity for work.* || **5.** Ability. *Facultad.* Esta sustancia tiene el PODER de disolver las grasas. *This substance has the ability to dissolve grease.* ⇨POWER

POLÍTICA [POLITICS]. *sf.* Estrategia, programa, postura, manera de obrar. *Policy.* ~La POLÍTICA de esta empresa. *The policy of this firm.* ~Una POLÍTICA de no agresión. *A non-aggression policy.* || **2.** Tacto. *Tact, skill.* ~Si llevas el asunto con POLÍTICA, conseguirás lo que te has propuesto. *If you handle this matter skillfully, you'll achieve your goals.* || **3.** Cortesía. *Politeness.* || **4.** [Educación]. *Good manners.* ~Tiene mucha POLÍTICA y sabe como comportarse con sus invitados. ~*He has very good manners and knows how to* *treat his guests.* ‖ **5.** *LOCUCIONES.* ‖ •Padre/hermano/hijo POLÍTICO. *Suegro, cuñado, yerno.* ‖ •POLÍTICA de buena vecindad. *Good neighbor policy.* ‖ •POLÍTICA de pasillo(s). *Lobbying.* ‖ •POLÍTICA de cañonera. *Gunboat diplomacy.* ‖ •POLÍTICA de mano dura. *Strong-arm policy.*

POLUCIÓN. *sf.* Derrame de semen. •Polución nocturna. *Nocturnal emission, wet dream.* ‖ **2.** ACAD Contaminación. *Pollution.* ⇨ POLLUTION

POMPA [POMP]. *sf.* Burbuja (de jabón). *Bubble.* ‖ **2.** [En la ropa]. *Billow.* ‖ **3.** Ostentación. *Show, display.* ~Hacer POMPA. *To make a show of.* ~En esta casa todo es POMPA. *In this house it's all show.* ‖ **4.** Boato. *Pageant, pageantry.* ‖ **5.** [Del pavo real]. *Spread (of a peacock's tail).* ‖ **6.** Bomba. *Pump.* ‖ **7.** •POMPAS fúnebres. (I) *Funeral, funeral ceremony, funeral procession.* (II) 'POMPAS fúnebres'. *'Funeral Parlor'.*

PONDERAR. *v.* Alabar. *To praise.* ~Le PONDERAN de inteligente. *They speak highly of his intelligence, he is deemed (considered) to be intelligent.* ‖ **2.** [Cálculo, índice]. *To weigh, adjust.* ~Antes de tomar una decisión, el banco deberá PONDERAR todos los aspectos financieros. *Before making a decision, the bank will need to weigh all financial aspects.* ⇨ PONDER

POPULAR. *adj.* Folklórico (canción, baile). *Folk, traditional.* ~Arte/música POPULAR. *Folk art/music.* ~El folclore POPULAR español es muy rico y variado. *Traditional Spanish folklore is very rich and varied.* ~El VILLANCICO es una canción popular de Navidad. *The 'villancico' is a traditional Christmas song.* ‖ **2.** [Costumbres]. *Traditional.* ‖ **3.** [Lenguaje]. *Colloquial.* ‖ **4.** [Precios]. *Economical, reasonable.* ~La función de la tarde tendrá precios POPULARES. *The evening show will be shown at economical prices.* ⇨ POPULAR

PORTENTO. *sm.* [Cosa]. *Marvel, wonder.* ~Canta que es un PORTENTO. *She has a wonderful (marvelous) voice.* ~Hace verda-

deros PORTENTOS con materiales realmente pobres. *She works wonders using the poorest materials.* ‖ **2.** [Persona]. *Genius.* ~Esta niña es un PORTENTO. *This girl is a prodigy.* ~Es un PORTENTO para la química. *He's a genius at chemistry.* ⇨ PORTENT

PORTENTOSO. *adj.* Que causa admiración o pasmo (fuerza, erfuerzo). *Extraordinary, prodigious.* ~Con un PORTENTOSO salto logró batir el record. *With a prodigious jump he succeeded in beating the existing record.* ~Hércules hizo gala de una PORTENTOSA fuerza. *Hercules displayed prodigious strength.* ‖ **2.** [Representación, voz]. *Magnificent, wonderful, marvelous.* ⇨ PORTENTOUS

PORTERO. *sm.* [De edificio público, hotel]. *Doorman.* ‖ **2.** [Soccer]. *Goalkeeper.* ‖ **3.** Guardián (de una vivienda). *Caretaker, concierge.* ~He dado un paquete al PORTERO para tí. *I gave the concierge a package for you.* ‖ **4.** [Que limpia la casa]. *Janitor.* ‖ **5.** •PORTERO automático. *Entryphone, answering device, interphone, intercom.* ⇨ PORTER

POSTULAR. *v.* [Dinero]. *To collect (for charity).* ~POSTULAR para la Cruz Roja. *To make a collection for the Red Cross.* ‖ **2.** Proponer (medidas, soluciones). *To propose.* POSTULABA un cambio en la directiva. *He proposed a change of management.* ⇨ POSTULATE.

POSTURA [POSTURE]. *sf.* [Del cuerpo]. *Position.* ~Tengo que haber dormido en una mala POSTURA. *I must have slept in an awkward position.* ~Llevo tantas horas sentado en esta silla, que no sé en que POSTURA ponerme. *I've been sitting in this chair for so long that I don't know what position to take.* ‖ **2.** Actitud. *Attitude, stand, position.* ~La POSTURA del gobierno en este asunto. *The government's position in this matter.* Adoptar una POSTURA. *To take (adopt) an attitude.* ~Adoptó una POSTURA crítica frente a esta propuesta. *She adopted a critical attitude towards this proposal.* ~Eso de no comprometerse es una POSTURA muy cómoda. *Not committing yourself like that is an easy way out.* ‖ **3.**

[En subasta]. *Bid.* ~Anularon la subasta porque no había POSTURAS. *They suspended the auction because there were no bids.* || **4.** [En el juego]. *Bet, stake.* ~Hacer una POSTURA. *To lay a bet.* || **5.** Opinion. *Opinion.* ~Hay POSTURAS enfrentadas en la organización. *There are opposing views within the organization.* || **6.** [De los huevos]. *Laying.* || **7.** Arbolillo. *Sapling.* || **8.** [De mercancías]. *Price fixed by the authorities.* || **10.** Convenio. *Pact, agreement.* || **11.** •Tomar POSTURA. *To take a stand.*

PRACTICAR. *v.* [Agujero]. *To make, cut, drill.* ~PRACTICAR un agujero. *To make (drill) a hole.* || **2.** [Deporte]. *To go in for, play.* ~No PRACTICA ningún deporte. *He doesn't play any sport.* ~PRACTICAR el fútbol. *To play football.* || **3.** Realizar. *To perform, carry ou, make (corte, incisión); to perform, do (autopsia, operación); To carry out (redada, actividad); to make (detenciones).* ~PRACTICARON unas obras de renovación. *They carried out some renovation work.* ~Hubo que PRACTICARLE una cesárea. *They had to perform a Cesarean section (on her).* ⇨ PRACTICE[2]

PRECINTO. *sm.* Señal sellada. *Seal.* ~El envase lleva PRECINTO para que el comprador sepa que no ha sido abierto. *This jar has a seal to indicate that it hasn't been opened.* ⇨ PRECINCT

PRECIOSO. *adj.* Hermoso. *Lovely, beautiful.* ~Tienen un niño PRECIOSO. *They have a lovely child.* ~Una edición PRECIOSA. *A beautiful edition.* ⇨ PRECIOUS

PREDICAMENTO. *sm.* Prestigio, fama. *Fame, prestige, standing.* ~La figura de mayor PREDICAMENTO. *The most prestigious figure.* ~Un pianista de enviable PREDICAMENTO. *A pianist of enviable prestige (standing).* || **2.** Influencia. *Influence, weight.* ~Este político tiene gran PREDICAMENTO entre los miembros de su partido. *This politician has a great deal of influence on the members of his party.* ⇨ PREDICAMENT

PREOCUPARSE [PREOCCUPY]. *vr.* Ocuparse. *To ensure, make sure that, to see to it that.* ~Me PREOCUPÉ de que no faltara nada. *I made sure that we had everything.* || **2.** Interesarse. *To take interest in.* ~No se PREOCUPÓ más del asunto. *He gave no further thought (he took no further interest in) the matter.*

PREPARADO. *adj.* Instruido, culto. *Educated.* ~Es una persona muy PREPARADA. *She's very well educated.* || **2.** Capacitado. *Trained, qualified.* ~Un profesional muy bien PREPARADO. *A highly-trained professional.* ⇨ PREPARED

PREPARACIÓN. *sf.* Formación. *Training.* ~PREPARACIÓN musical. *Musical training.* ~Le falta PREPARACIÓN matemática. *He lacks training in mathematics.* || **2.** Aptitud, competencia. *Capacity, competence.* || **3.** [Estado]. *Preparedness, readiness.* ~PREPARACIÓN militar. *Military preparedness.* || **4.** [De un deportista]. *Training.* ~Su PREPARACIÓN física es muy buena. *He's in peak condition (form).* ⇨ PREPARATION

PRESENTACIÓN. *sf.* Aspecto, apariencia. *Appearance.* Su PRESENTACIÓN es siempre impecable. *His appearance is always impeccable.* Este plato tiene una PRESENTACIÓN inmejorable; veremos qué tal sabe. *This dish looks terrific; now let's see how it tastes.* || **2.** Exposición (de una mercancía). *Display.* ~Hacer una PRESENTACIÓN de productos. *To display one's products.* || **3.** [De moda]. *Parade, show.* ~PRESENTACIÓN de modelos. *Fashion parade, fashion show.* || **4.** [De dos personas por una tercera]. *Introduction.* ~Todavía no has hecho las PRESENTACIONES. *You still have not introduced us.* ~Hizo las PRESENTACIONES. *He introduced everyone, he made the introductions.* •Carta de PRESENTACIÓN. *Letter of introduction.* || **5.** [En sociedad]. *Coming out, debut.* || **6.** Entrega. *Handing, submission.* ~El plazo de PRESENTACIÓN de solicitudes termina mañana. *Tomorrow is the last day for submitting applications.* ~El límite de tiempo para la presentación del trabajo. *The deadline for handing in the work.* || **7.** Nombramiento. *Nomination.* Su PRESENTACIÓN como candidato ha sido aprobada por la comisión. *His nomination* as a candidate has been approved by the committee. || **8.** •PRESENTACIÓN en directo, en vivo. *Personal appearance.* || **9.** •PRESENTACIÓN en pantalla. *(On-screen) display.* ⇨ PRESENTATION

PRESENTAR[1]. v. Mostrar. *To show, display.* ~PRESENTA señales de deterioro. *It shows signs of wear.* ~El paciente no PRESENTABA ningún síntoma de intoxicación. *The patient showed no signs of food poisoning.* || **2.** Ofrecer (ventajas, cualidades, novedades). *To offer.* ~El nuevo modelo PRESENTA algunas novedades. *The latest model offers some new features.* ~PRESENTA muchas ventajas para el consumidor. *It offers the consumer many advantages.* || **3.** Enseñar. *To show.* ~Hay que PRESENTAR el carné para entrar. *You have to show your membership card to get in.* || **4.** Exponer por primera vez (libro, disco, canción). *To launch.* ~El escritor ha PRESENTADO un nuevo libro de poemas. *The writer has launched a new book of poems.* || **5.** [Una persona a otra]. *To introduce.* ~Le PRESENTO al Dr. Ruiz. *May I introduce you to Dr. Ruiz.* || **6.** [Pruebas, tesis]. *To submit.* ~Para obtener el título de doctor hay que PRESENTAR una tesis. *In order to receive a doctor's degree you need to submit a thesis.* || **7.** [Queja]. *To lodge, file, make.* || **8.** [Dimisión]. *To tender.* || **9.** [Propuesta]. *To propose, put forward.* || **10.** [Obra de teatro]. *To perform.* || **11.** [Película]. *To show.* || **12.** [Testigo]. *To produce.* ⇨ PRESENT

PRESENTARSE[2]. [En un lugar de manera inesperada]. *To appear, turn up, show up.* ~El estudiante se PRESENTÓ cuando estaba por acabar la clase. *The student showed up when the class was almost over.* ~Se PRESENTÓ a mi casa a la tres de la madrugada. *He showed up at my house at three o'clock in the morning.* || **2.** Ofrecerse. *To volunteer.* ~Se PRESENTÓ en el hospital cuando se enteró de que se necesitaban donantes de sangre. *He volunteered at the hospital when he found out that they were looking for blood donors.* || **3.** [A un examen]. *To take.* ~Se PRESENTÓ al examen. *She took the exam.* || **4.** [A un concurso].

To enter. ~Me PRESENTÉ al concurso. *I entered the contest.* || **5.** [Para un cargo]. *To apply.* ~Se PRESENTÓ para el cargo de director. *He applied for the post of director.* || **6.** [Problema, opportunidad]. *To arise, come up.* ~Si se me PRESENTA la ocasión, pienso ir de vacaciones. *I plan to go on vacation should the occasion arise.* || **7.** Parecer. *To look.* ~El futuro se PRESENTA prometedor. *The future looks promising.* ~El asunto se PRESENTA muy mal. *Things are not looking well at all.* || **8.** [Criminal]. *To turn oneself in.* ~Se PRESENTÓ a la policía. *He turned himself in to the police.* || **9.** [Como candidato]. *To run, stand.* ~Se PRESENTA como candidato independiente. *He's running as an independent candidate.* || **10.** Ocurrir, darse (caso). *To come up.* ~Se PRESENTÓ un caso singular. *A strange case came up.* || **11.** [Ante una autoridad]. *To report.* Los que están en libertad provisional deben PRESENTARSE a la policía cada cierto tiempo. *Those on parole must report to the police periodically.* ~El soldado recibió la orden de PRESENTARSE al capitán de su regimiento. *He was ordered to report to the captain of his regiment.* ⇨ PRESENT

PRESIDENTE. *sm.* [Del gobierno]. *Premier, prime minister.* ~El PRESIDENTE del gobierno viajó a París. *The prime minister went to Paris.* || **2.** [De las Cortes]. *Speaker (of the Spanish Parliament).* || **3.** [De una reunión, comité, acto]. *Chair, chairperson.* ~Este año soy la PRESIDENTA de la comunidad de padres. *This year I'm the chairperson of the Parents' Association.* || **4.** [De un tribunal]. *Presiding judge, magistrate.* || **5.** [De un jurado]. *Chairman.* ⇨ PRESIDENT

PRESERVAR. *v.* Proteger. *To protect.* ~Intentaba PRESERVARLA de todo mal. *He tried to protect (keep) her from harm.* ~Los invernaderos sirven para PRESERVAR las plantas del frío. *Greenhouses are used to protect plants from the cold.* ⇨ PRESERVE

PRESUMIR. *v.* Vanagloriarse. *To show off, boast.* ~PRESUME de tener muy buena memoria. *He boasts of having a good very*

memory. ~P<small>RESUME</small> de guapo. *He thinks he's good-looking.* ~P<small>RESUME</small> de intelectual. *He fancies himself as an intelectual.* ~Se compra mucha ropa porque le gusta P<small>RESUMIR</small>. *He buys a lot of clothes because he likes to show off.* ~P<small>RESUME</small> de artista. *She likes to think she's an artist.* ~*Presume* de experto. *He prides himself on being an expert.* ‖ **2.** Ser vanidoso. *To be conceited, to be vain.* ⇨P<small>RESUME</small>

PRETENDER. *v.* Querer, desear. *To want, wish.* ~El P<small>RETENDE</small> que yo le escriba. *He wants me to write to him.* ~Sólo P<small>RETENDO</small> que sea feliz. *I just want her to be happy.* ‖ **2.** Intentar. *To try.* P<small>RETENDE</small> ayudarnos. *He's trying to help us.* ~¿Qué P<small>RETENDES</small> insinuar? *What are you getting at?* ~P<small>RETENDIÓ</small> convencerme. *He sought to convince me.* ~Han P<small>RETENDIDO</small> robarme. *They attempted to rob me.* ~P<small>RETENDÍA</small> hacerme cambiar de opinión. *He was trying to make me change my mind.* ‖ **3.** Afirmar. *To claim.* P<small>RETENDE</small> ser el más rico. *He claims to be the richest person around.* ~P<small>RETENDEN</small> haber visto un platillo volador. *They claim to have seen a flying saucer.* ‖ **4.** Esperar. *To expect.* ~Cómo P<small>RETENDE</small> Ud. que lo compre yo? *How do you expect me to buy it?* ~¿Cómo P<small>RETENDE</small> Ud. que haga yo todo el trabajo solo. ~*How do you expect me to do all that work by myself.?* ~¿Qué P<small>RETENDES</small> de mí? *What do you expect of me?, what do you expect me to do?* ~¿P<small>RETENDES</small> que crea esta mentira? *Do you expect me to believe this lie?* ‖ **5.** Tratar de conseguir. *To be after, try to achieve.* ~¿Qué P<small>RETENDES</small> con esa actitud? *What do you hope to gain with this attitude?* ‖ **6.** Aspirar a, proponerse. *To seek, to try for, aspire.* ~P<small>RETENDE</small> llegar a ser médico. *He hopes to become a doctor.* ~P<small>RETENDE</small> llegar a la cima. *He aspires to reach the top.* ‖ **7.** Tener la intención. *To intend.* ~No P<small>RETENDO</small> decir lo que tiene que hacer. *It's not my intention to tell you what to do.* ‖ **8.** [Cargo]. *To apply for.* ~Hay una plaza y la P<small>RETENDEN</small> diez personas. *There's one position open and ten people are applying for it.* ‖ **9.** [Objetivo]. *To aim at, try to achieve.* ‖ **10.**

[Honor]. *To aspire to.* ‖ **11.** Cortejar. *To court, woo.* El jefe P<small>RETENDE</small> a la secretaria. *The boss is courting the secretary.* ⇨ P<small>RETEND</small>

PRETENSIÓN. *sf.* Aspiración. *Aim, aspiration.* Mi única P<small>RETENSIÓN</small>. *The only thing I want.* ‖ **2.** Soberbia. *Pretentiousness.* ~Tiene la P<small>RETENSIÓN</small> de casarse conmigo. *He expects (thinks) he's going to marry me.* ~Con demasiadas P<small>RETEN-SIONES</small>. *Too pretentiously.* ~Tener muchas P<small>RETENSIONES</small>. *To be pretentious.* ‖ **3.** Convicción. *Conviction.* Tenía la P<small>RETEN-SIÓN</small> de que ganaría. *He was convinced he was going to win.* ‖ **4.** Deseo. *Hope, wish, desire.* ~Expresó su P<small>RETENSIÓN</small> de que ... *She expressed her hope that ...* ~Enviar curriculum indicando P<small>RETENSIONES</small> salariales. *Send resumé indicating desired salary.* ‖ **5.** Reclamación (derecho. herencia). *Claim.* ‖ **6.** Afirmación. *Claim.* ~Tiene P<small>RETENSIONES</small> sobre la finca porque dijo que hace siglos perteneció a su familia. *He claims that he has the right to the farm since centuries ago it used to belong to his family.* ‖ **7.** •Tener pocas P<small>RETENCIONES</small>. *To be undemanding.* ~Una película sin demasiadas P<small>RETENSIONES</small>. *An unpretentious film, a so-so film.* ⇨P<small>RETENSE</small>

PREVENCION [PREVENTION]. *sf.* Preparativo. *Preparation.* ~Las P<small>REVENCIONES</small> para la ceremonia. *The preparations for the ceremony.* ‖ **2.** [Estado]. *Readiness, preparedness.* ‖ **3.** Cualidad. *Foresight, forethought.* ~Obrar con P<small>REVENCIÓN</small>. *To act with foresight.* ‖ **4.** Medida. *Precaution, precautionary measures, safety measures.* ~Hemos tomado ciertas P<small>REVENCIONES</small>. *We have taken certain precautions.* ~Medidas de P<small>REVENCIÓN</small>. *Emergency measures, contingency plans.* ‖ **5.** Prejuicio. *Prejudice.* ~Tener P<small>REVENCIÓN</small> contra uno. *To be prejudiced against somebody.* ~Tiene P<small>REVENCIÓN</small> contra las mujeres independientes. *He has something (he's prejudiced) against independent women.* ‖ **6.** Comisaría. *Police station.* ~Llevar a alguien a la P<small>REVENCIÓN</small>. *To take someone to the police station.* ‖ **7.** [Military]. *Guardhouse.*

|| **8.** Aviso. *Warning.*

PREVENIR[1]. *v.* Advertir. *To guard, warn.* ~Pudieron PREVENIRLE a tiempo. *They were able to warn him in time.* ~PREVENIERON a los conductores del mal estado de la carretera. *Drivers were warned of the bad state of the roads.* ~Te PREVENGO que es un mentiroso. *I'm warning you that he's a liar.* || **2.** Disponer. *To prepare, get ready, make ready for.* PREVINO todo lo necesario para el viaje. *He got everything ready for the trip.* || **3.** Prever. *To foresee, anticipate.* ~Más vale PREVENIR que curar. *Prevention is better than cure.* ~Más vale PREVENIR que lamentar. *Better safe than sorry.* || **4.** Proveer. *To provide.* || **5.** Predisponer. *To prejudice.* ⇨PREVENT

PREVENIRSE[2]. *vr.* Disponerse. *To get ready, prepare for.* ~PREVENIRSE para un viaje. *To get ready for a trip.* || **2.** Proveerse. *Provide oneself with.* ~PREVENIRSE de ropa adecuada. *To provide oneself with suitable clothing.* || **3.** •PREVENIRSE contra. *To take precautions against, prepare for.* || **4.** •PREVENIRSE en contra de uno. *To adopt a hostile attitude towards someone.* ⇨PREVENT

PREVIO. *adj.* Tras. *After, following, subject to.* PREVIA consulta a los interesados. *The interested parties having been consulted, after the interested parties had been consulted.* ~PREVIO acuerdo de los demás. *Subject to the agreement of the others.* ~PREVIO pago. *After payment.* ~PREVIO pago de los derechos. *Upon payment of the fees.* || **2.** [Idea]. *Preconceived, traditional.* || **3.** [Cine]. *Playback.* || **4.** •PREVIO aviso. *Prior notice.* || **5.** •Autorización PREVIA. *Prior authorization (permission).* || **6.** •PREVIA cita. *By appointment only, appointment required.* || **7.** •PREVIO a. *Prior to, before.* ⇨PREVIOUS

PRIMITIVO. *adj.* [Temprano]. *Early.* || **2.** Original. *Original, first.* ~El texto PRIMITIVO. *The original text.* ~Es una obra PRIMITIVA. *It's an early work.* ~Devolver algo a su estado PRIMITIVO. *To restore something to its original state.* || **3.** [Color]. *Primary.*

⇨PRIMITIVE

PRINCIPAL [PRINCIPAL]. *adj.* De mayor importancia. *Main.* ~Interpretó el papel PRINCIPAL. *He played the main part.* ~El personaje PRINCIPAL de la obra. *The main character in the book.* ~Lo PRINCIPAL es que no se hizo daño. *The main thing is that he didn't get hurt.*

PROBAR. *v.* Comprobar. *To test, check, try.* PRUEBA la puerta a ver si está cerrada. *Check to see if the door is locked.* || **2.** Sentar. *To suit, agree with.* ~La humedad le PRUEBA mal. *Dampness is bad for him.* || **3.** Intentar. *To attempt, try to.* ~Por PROBAR no se pierde nada. *There's no harm in trying.* ~PRUEBA a levantarlo. *Try to lift it.* ~PRUEBA a meterlo de lado. *See if it fits sideways.* || **4.** [Arma, aparato]. *To test, try (out).* ~PRUEBA la aspiradora antes de comprarla. *Try the vacuum cleaner before buying it.* || **5.** [Comida]. *To try, taste, sample.* ~PRUEBA un poco de esto. *Try a bit of this.* ~No han PROBADO nunca un buen jerez. *They have never tasted a good sherry.* || **6.** [Ropa]. *Try on.* ~No le puedo comprar zapatos sin PROBÁRSELOS. *I can't buy shoes for him without trying them on him.* ~La modista sólo me PROBÓ el vestido una vez. *The dressmaker only gave me one fitting for the dress.* || **7.** Poner a prueba (empleado, honradez). *To test.* ~Dejaron el dinero allí para PROBARLO. *They left the money there to test him.* ⇨PROVE

PROCEDER. *v.* Provenir. *To come from.* PROCEDE del norte. *He's from the North.* ~Estas patatas PROCEDEN de Israel. *The potatoes come from Israel.* ~Esta palabra PROCEDE del árable. *This word comes from Arabic.* || **2.** Actuar. *To act, behave.* ~Siempre PROCEDE con cautela. *He's always cautious.* Ha PROCEDIDO precipitadamente. *He has acted hastily.* || **3.** Ser oportuno. *To be advisable or appropriate.* ~En estas situaciones PROCEDE tomar medidas enérgicas. *Under these circumstances, it is advisable to take drastic measures.* ~Táchese lo que no PROCEDA. *Cross out what does not apply.* ⇨PROCEDE

PROCESAR. *v.* JUR Juzgar. *To try, put on trial, prosecute.* ~PROCESARON al presunto asesino. *They prosecuted the alleged killer.* ‖ **2.** Demandar. *To sue, bring an action against.* ⇨ PROCESS

PROCURAR. *v.* Intentar. *To try, attempt.* ~Hay que PROCURAR no molestar a nadie. *We have to try not to bother anybody.* ~PROCURA no hacer ruido. *Try not to make too much noise.* ‖ **2.** Conseguir. *To obtain, get, secure.* ~Esto nos PROCURARÁ grandes beneficios. *This will bring us great benefits.* ‖ **3.** Lograr + inf. *To manage to + inf.* ~Por fin PROCURÓ dominarse. *He finally managed to control himself.* ⇨ PROCURE

PRODUCCIÓN. *sf.* Conjunto de obras. *Output.* ~Su PRODUCCIÓN dramática es escasa. *His dramatic output is small.* ~La PRODUCCIÓN pictórica de Picasso. *The works of Picasso, Picasso's paintings.* ⇨ PRODUCTION

PRODUCIR[1]. *v.* Causar, originar. *To cause.* ~Estas declaraciones PRODUJERON una gran conmoción. *These statements caused a great stir.* ~Le PRODUJO una gran alegría. *It made her very happy.* ~Los cambios bruscos de tiempo PRODUCEN enfermedades. *Sudden changes in the weather cause illnesses.* ‖ **2.** [Árboles, terreno]. *To yield, bear.* ‖ **3.** Rendir. *To be profitable.* ~El negocio no PRODUCE lo que esperábamos. *This business is not as profitable as we expected.* ‖ **4.** FIN [Interés]. *To bear.*

PRODUCIRSE. *vr.* Ocurrir. *To take place, happen.* ~En este momento se PRODUJO una explosión. *At that moment there was an explosion.* ~Se PRODUJERON varios incidentes. *Several incidents occurred.* ‖ **2.** [Heridas]. *To inflict on oneself.* Se PRODUJO heridas con un cuchillo. *She inflicted wounds on herself with a knife.* ⇨ PRODUCE

PROFESAR. *v.* [Admiración, amor]. *To have.* ~PROFESAR una gran admiración por alguien. *To have a great admiration for someone.* ~PROFESAR un amor profundo. *To have a deep love for.* ‖ **2.** Ejercer. *To practice.* PROFESA la medicina desde hace veinte años. *He's been practicing medicine for twenty years.* ‖ **3.** Enseñar. *To teach.* PROFESAR la medicina. *To teach medicine.* ⇨ PROFESS

PROFESOR. *sm.* Maestro. *Teacher.* ⇨ PROFESSOR

PROMOCIÓN. *sf.* EDUC Conjunto de personas que obtienen al mismo tiempo un título de estudio o empleo. *Class, year or group that graduates at the same time.* ~La PROMOCIÓN de 1995. *The 1995 class.* ~Somos de la misma PROMOCIÓN. *We graduated together, at the same time.* ‖ **2.** COM [Oferta, ganga]. *Special offer.* ~Voy a probar este maquillaje que está en PROMOCIÓN. *I'll try this makeup which is on sale.* ‖ **3.** [En fútbol]. *Play-off.* ⇨ PROMOTION

PROPAGANDA. *sf.* Publicity, advertising. *Publicidad.* ~La revista no trae más que PROPAGANDA. *The magazine has nothing but advertisements in it.* ~Repartía PROPAGANDA de la agencia de viaje. *He was handing out advertising leaflets for the travel agency.* •Hacer PROPAGANDA (de un producto). *To advertise (a product).* ‖ **2.** FIG Compliment. *Elogio.* A ver cuando lo conocemos, le has hecho tanta PROPAGANDA. *When are we going to meet him? You talked so much about him.* ⇨ PROPAGANDA

PROSPECTO. *sm.* [De un fármaco]. *Directions for use.* ~Antes de tomar estas pastillas lee bien el PROSPECTO. *Before taking these pills be sure to read the instructions.* ‖ **2.** [De propaganda]. *Pamphlet, leaflet, prospectus (finanzas).* ‖ **3.** Publicidad. *Publicity, advertising.* ~Estos libros se venden bien gracias a la PROPAGANDA. *These books are selling well because they have been well advertised.*

PROYECCIÓN. *sf.* [Cine]. *Showing.* ~La PROYECCIÓN de la película fue interrumpida. *The showing of the film was interrupted.* ~El tiempo de PROYECCIÓN es de 95 minutos. *The running time is 95 minutes.* ~Una PROYECCIÓN de diapositivas. *A slide show.* ‖ **2.** [De una sombra]. *Casting.* ~Aunque se escondió, la PROYECCIÓN de su sombra en el suelo hizo que lo descubrieran. *Although he tried to hide, the casting of his shadow on the floor gave him away.* || **3.** [De luz]. *Throwing.* || **4.** Difusión, alcance. *Coverage, scope.* La nueva ley tendrá una PROYECCIÓN mucho más amplia. *The new law will a have much wider scope.* ~Su figura ha adquirido una PROYECCIÓN internacional. *He has become a figure of international renown.* ~Las declaraciones han tenido una gran PROYECCIÓN en la prensa. *His declarations had wide press coverage.* || **5.** [De rocas, lava]. *Discharge, throwing out.* || **6.** Porvenir. *Future.* ~Este joven jugador tiene una gran PROYECCIÓN. *This young player has a great future.* || **7.** Influencia. *Influence, hold, sway.* ~LA PROYECCIÓN de los periódicos sobre la sociedad. *The hold of newspapers over society.* ⇨PROYECCIÓN

PROYECTAR. *v.* Planear. *To plan.* ~Están PROYECTANDO un viaje a París. *They're planning a trip to Paris.* ~PROYECTAN mudarse pronto. *They are thinking of moving out shortly.* || **2.** [Película]. *To show, screen.* ~Mañana PROYECTARÁN una película de Bertolucci. *Tomorrow they will screen a movie by Bertolucci.* || **3.** [Sombra]. *To cast.* Los árboles PROYECTABAN su larga sombra en el camino. *The trees cast their tall shadows on the road.* || **4.** [Luz]. *To throw.* ~Varios focos PROYECTABAN luz sobre el escenario. *Numerous floodlights illuminated (threw light on) the stage.* || **5.** Lanzar. *To throw, hurl.* ~El impacto del golpe lo PROYECTÓ hacia adelante. *The force of the collision threw him forward.* ~El volcán PROYECTABA las rocas a gran distancia. *The volcano hurled the rocks enormous distances.* ⇨PROJECT

PULIR[1]. *v.* [Madera]. *To sand.* ~Esta máquina PULE los suelos de madera. *This machine is used to sand wood floors.* || **2.** Refinar (estilo, trabajo). *To polish up, put the final touch to.* ~Fue a Inglaterra a PULIR su inglés. *She went to England to brush up her English.* ~Ha escrito un artículo, pero aún falta PULIRLO. *He's written an*

article, *but he still needs to polish it up (give the final touch to it).* || **3.** [Persona]. *To make more refined.* ~Ella no ha conseguido PULIRLE los modales. *She hasn't managed to improve (refine) his manners.* || **4.** Alisar. *To smooth.* ~Antes de barnizar el parqué hay que PULIRLO. *Before applying varnish, you need to smooth the parquet flooring.* || **5.** FAM Robar. *To steal.* ~Me han PULIDO la cartera en el metro. *They stole my wallet in the subway.* || **6.** Adornar. *To adorn, embellish.* ⇨POLISH

PULIRSE. *vr.* Refinarse. *To improve oneself, become more refined.* || **2.** [Comida]. *To polish off, finish off.* ~Nos hemos PULIDO un litro de coñac. *We polished off a liter of brandy.* || **3.** [Dinero]. *To spend, squander.* ~He PULIDO en un día mi sueldo semanal. *I've spent an entire week's pay in a day.* || **4.** Acicalarse. *To spruce oneself up.* ⇨POLISH

PUNTO. *sm.*
❶ COSTURA. *Stitch.* ~¿Cuántos PUNTOS pongo? *How many stitches do I cast on?* || **2.** [De tela]. *Mesh.* || **3.** •De punto. *Knitted.* ~Una chaqueta de PUNTO. *A knitted jacket,* ~Vestido de PUNTO. *Knitted dress.* || **4.** •Hacer PUNTO. *To knit.* || **5.** •Diseño a PUNTOS. *Design of dots, pattern of dots.* || **6.** •Artículo de PUNTO. *Knitwear.* || **7.** •PUNTO de cruz. *Crossed-stitch.* || **8.** •PUNTO del derecho/revés. *Plain/purl stitch.* || **9.** •PUNTO atrás. *Backstitch.* || **10.** •PUNTO cadena. *Chain stitch.* || **11.** •PUNTO cruzado. *Herringbone stitch.* || **12.** •PUNTO de media. *Stocking stitch.* || **13.** •PUNTO elástico. *Rib, ribbing.* || **14.** •PUNTO jersey. *Stocking stitch.* || **15.** •PUNTO Santa Clara. *Garter stitch.* || **16.** •PUNTO sombra. *Shadow stitch.* || **17.** •PUNTO por encima. *Overcast stitch.* || **18.** PUNTO de dobladillo. *Hem stitch.*
❷ PUNTUACION. [Sobre la 'i' y la 'j']. *Dot.* || **2.** [Signo de puntuación]. *Period.* || **3.** •Dos PUNTOS. *Colon.* || **4.** •PUNTO y aparte. *Full stop, new paragraph.* || **5.** •PUNTO y coma. *Semicolon.* || **6.** •PUNTO y seguido. *Full stop.* || **7.** [Fig.]. •Con PUNTOS y comas. *In full detail.* ~Hacer algo con PUNTOS y comas. *To get something right down to the last detail.* || **8.** [Fig.]. •Poner los PUNTOS sobre

las íes. *To make something crystal clear.* ||
9. [Fig.]. •Poner PUNTO final a algo. *To end.*
~Decidió poner PUNTO final a sus relaciones. *He decided to end their relation-
ship.* || **10.** [Fig.]. •... y PUNTO. *That's all
there is to it, period.* Si te parece mal se lo
dices y PUNTO. *If you don't like it, you just
tell him, that's all there is to it.* ~Lo harás
como yo te digo y PUNTO. *You'll do it the
way I tell you, period.* || **11.** [Fig.]. PUNTO y
aparte. *Another story.* ~Eso ya es PUNTO y
aparte. *That's another story.* || **12.** [Fig.].
•Sin faltar PUNTO ni coma. *Accurately,
faithfully, minutely, down to the last detail.*
❸ VARIOS. [Marca, señal, trazo]. *Dot.*
~Desde el avión la ciudad se veía como un
conjunto de PUNTOS luminosos. *From the
plane the city looked like a cluster of
bright dots.* ~El barco no era más que un
PUNTO en el horizonte. *The boat was no
more than a dot (speck) on the horizon.*
•Lineas de PUNTOS. *Dotted line.* || **2.** Grado.
Extent. ~Hasta cierto PUNTO tiene razón.
To a certain extent she's right. ~Hasta
cierto PUNTO me alegro de que se vaya. *In
a way I'm glad he's leaving.* ~Claro que
fue atento y amable, hasta tal PUNTO que
llegó a resultarnos pesado. *Of course he
was attentive and kind, so much so that it
got too much for us.* |||| **3.** [Plumaje]. *Spot,
speckle.* || **4.** [Carta, dominó]. *Spot.* || **5.** •[De
sutura]. *Stitch.* ~Una herida que necesitó
10 PUNTOS. *A wound which needed 10
stitches.* || **6.** [Examen]. *Mark.* || **7.** [Taxi].
Taxi stand. || **8.** [Música]. *Pitch.* || **9.**
[Asunto, aspecto]. Los PUNTOS por tratar
en la reunión de hoy. *The matters (items)
on the agenda for today's meeting.*
❹ LOCUCIONES.
•A PUNTO. *Ready.* ~Con su máquina a PUNTO
para disparar. *With their cameras ready to
shoot.*
•A PUNTO DE. *About to.* ~Estábamos a
PUNTO de cenar cuando llamaste. *We were
about to have dinner when you called.*
~Estuvo a PUNTO de matarse en el accidente. *He was nearly killed in the accident.* ~Se notaba que estaba a PUNTO de
llorar. *You could see she was on the verge
of tears.*

•A PUNTO FIJO. *Exactly, for certain.* ~No
sabría decírselo a PUNTO fijo. *I couldn't tell
you for certain.*
•AL PUNTO. *At once, instantly.*
•BAJAR DE PUNTO. *To decline, fall off, fall
away.*
•CALZAR MUCHOS PUNTOS. *To know a lot.*
•CALZAR POCOS PUNTOS. *To know very little,
be pretty dim.*
•CONOCER LOS PUNTOS QUE CALZA UNO. *To
know what somebody is capable of, to
know where one stands with someone.*
•DAR EN EL PUNTO. *To hit the nail on the
head.*
•DARSE DOS PUNTOS EN EL CINTURÓN. *To
overheat* (fig.).
•DE TODO PUNTO. *Completely, absolutely.*
~Eso es de todo PUNTO inaceptable. *This is
totally unacceptable.* ~Se negaba de todo
PUNTO a hacerlo. *She flatly refused to do it.*
•EN PUNTO (tiempo). *Sharp, on the dot.*
~Las seis en PUNTO. *6 o'clock sharp.*
~Llegaron a las tres en PUNTO. *They arrived
at exactly three o'clock.* ~Ella llegó en
PUNTO. *She arrived punctually.*
•EN PUNTO a. *With regard to.*
•EN SU PUNTO (culinary). *Just right.* ~El arroz
está en su PUNTO. *The rice is just right.*
•ESTAR A PUNTO (de hacer algo). *To almost
(do something).* ~Estuve a PUNTO de
caerme. *I almost fell.*
•ESTAR EN EL PUNTO DE MIRA DE UNO. *To be
in somebody's sights.*
•GANAR/PERDER (MUCHOS) PUNTOS (para
alguien). *To go up/down in somebody's
estimation.*
•LLEGAR A PUNTO. *To come just at the right
moment.*
•LLEGAR A SU PUNTO CUMBRE. *To reach its
peak.*
•NO PERDER PUNTO. *Not to miss anything.*
•PARA DEJAR LAS COSAS EN SU PUNTO. *To be
absolutely precise.*
•PONER A PUNTO. *To fine-tune.* [Motor].
Tune. ~Poner un motor a PUNTO. *To tune
an engine.*
•PONER EN SU PUNTO. *To bring something
to its perfection.*
•PUNTO ciego. *Blind spot.*
•PUNTO CULMINANTE. *Climax, culminating*

moment.

•PUNTO DE APOYO. (I) *Backup.* ~No hay ningún PUNTO de apoyo para la escalera. *There's nowhere to lean the ladder,* (II) *Cornerstone.* ~Constituía el PUNTO de apoyo de su defensa. *It formed the cornerstone of his defense.*

•PUNTO DE ATRAQUE. *Berth, mooring.*

•PUNTO DE COSTADO (med.). *Pain in the side.*

•PUNTO DE MIRA. (I) [De un rifle]. *Front sight,* (II) [Objetivo]. *Aim, objective.* (III) [Blanco]. *Target.*

•PUNTO DE OBSERVACIÓN. *Lookout.*

•PUNTO DE REFERENCIA. *Benchmark.*

•PUNTO DE REUNIÓN. *Meeting place.*

•PUNTO DE VERANEO. *Summer, holiday resort.*

•PUNTO DÉBIL (flaco). *Weak spot.*

•¡PUNTO EN BOCA! *Mum's the word!, keep it under your hat.*

•PUNTO FIJO. [Vigilante]. *Guard.* ~Está en PUNTO fijo toda la noche. *He's on guard duty all night.*

•PUNTO MEDIO. [Equilibrio]. *Balance.* ~Hay que buscar el PUNTO medio entre las dos cosas. *You have to srike a balance between the two things.*

•PUNTO MENOS QUE. *A shade less than, not quite.*

•PUNTO MUERTO [Coche]. *Neutral.* [Fig.]. *Deadlock, stalemate.* ~Las negociaciones están en un PUNTO muerto. *The negotiations are deadlocked, there's a stalemate in the talks.*

•PUNTO NEGRO. [En la carretera]. *Blackspot.* [En la piel]. *Blackhead.* [Fig.]. *Blemish, defect.*

•PUNTO NEURÁLGICO. [Anatomía]. *Nerve center.* [Organización]. *Nerve center.* ~Un accidente en uno de los PUNTOS neurálgicos de la ciudad. *An accident at one of the busiest spots in the city.* ~Uno de los PUNTOS neurálgicos de la economía. *One of the key elements of the economy.*

•SABER ALGO A PUNTO FIJO. *To know something for sure.*

•SUBIR DE punto. *To grow, increase; to get worse.*

•PONGAMOS LAS COSAS EN SU PUNTO. *Let's be absolutely clear about this.* ⇨ POINT

R

RACIÓN [RATION]. *sf.* [De comida]. *Helping, portion.* ~Las RACIONES son muy abundantes. *The helpings are very generous.* ~ 'Tres RACIONES'. *'Serves three'.* || **2.** Parte. *Share.* Ya ha tenido su RACIÓN de disgustos. *He's already had his share of misfortune.* || **3.** [En un bar]. *Order.* ~Una RACIÓN de patatas fritas. *An order of French fries.*

RAQUETA [RACKET]. *sf.* [De ping-pong]. *Paddle.* || **2.** [De nieve]. *Snowshoe.* || **3.** [De crupier]. *Rake.* || **4.** [Del limpiaparabrisas]. *Blade, squeegee.*

RARO. *adj.* Extraño. *Odd, weird, strange.* Es un tío RARO. *He's a strange fellow.* ~Es RARO que aún no haya venido. *It's strange that he has not arrived yet.* || **2.** •RARA vez. *Seldom, rarely.* || **3.** •¡Qué RARO! *How odd!* ⇨RARE

RAZA [RACE]. *sf.* [De animal]. *Breed, strain.* || **2.** Estirpe. *Stock.* || **3.** •De raza. *Pedigree (perro), thoroughbred (caballo).*

RAZÓN [REASON]. *sf.* Recado. *Message.* ~Llevar una RAZÓN. *To take a message.* || **2.** Justicia. *Justice.* Con RAZÓN o sin ella, el caso es que se enfadó. *The fact is that, rightly or wrongly, she lost her temper.* || **3.** Lo correcto, verdad, acierto. *Right, rightness.* ~Le asiste la RAZÓN. *He has right on his side.* ~Dar la RAZÓN a uno. *To agree that someone is right, to prove right, to side with someone.* ~La RAZÓN está de su parte. *He is right.* ~Esta vez tú tienes la RAZÓN. *This time you're right.* ~Tienes toda la RAZÓN del mundo. *You're absolutely right.* || **4.** Información. *Information.* ~No supieron darnos RAZÓN de su paradero. *They were unable to give us any information as to his whereabouts.* ~Se alquila. RAZÓN: portería. *For rent: inquiries to the caretaker.* ~Se vende bicicleta. RAZON: este establecimiento. *Bicycle for sale, inquire within.* || **5.** •RAZÓN social. *Trade name.*

REACTOR [REACTOR]. *sm.* [Avión]. *Jet (plane).*

REALIZAR. *v.* [Plan]. *Execute, carry out.* ~Las últimas encuestas REALIZADAS. *The latest survey carried out.* ~Ha REALIZADO una magnífica labor. *He has done a magnificent job.* || **2.** [Viaje, visit]. *Make.* ~REALIZAR un viaje. *To take a trip, make a journey.* || **3.** [Cine, TV]. *Produce.* ~La persona que ha REALIZADO esta película es un director desconocido. *The director of this film is an unknown.* || **4.** [Prueba, entrevista]. *Conduct.* || **5.** [Operation]. *Perform.* ~Los médicos que REALIZARON la operación. *The doctors who performed the operation.* || **6.** [Sueños, ambiciones, ilusiones]. *Fulfill, realize, achieve.* Afortunadamente todas mis esperanzas se han REALIZADO. *Fortunately all my hopes have been fulfilled.* || **7.** [Compra, venta, inversión]. *Make.* ~La empresa REALIZÓ ventas por valor de ... *The firm had sales in the amount of ...* || **8.** [Meta]. *Accomplish, achieve, attain.* || **9.** [Bienes]. *Sell, dispose of.* || **10.** •REALIZAR gestiones. *To negotiate, take the necessary steps, make (the necessary) arrangements.* Está REALIZANDO gestiones para conseguirlo. *They are taking the necessary steps to attain it.* ~Están REALIZANDO gestiones para comprar la casa. *They are making arrangements.* ⇨REALIZE

RECEPCIÓN. *sf.* [De carta, mercancía]. *Receipt.* La RECEPCIÓN de solicitudes será de nueve a cinco. *Applications will be accepted from nine to five.* || **2.** [En academia]. *Admission.* ‖ **3.** [Cuarto]. *Drawing-room.* ‖ **4.** JUR *Examination (of witnesses).* ⇨RECEPTION

RECIPIENTE. *sm.* Receptáculo, envase. *Vessel, container.* ⇨RECIPIENT.

RECOLECCIÓN. *sf.* Recogida. *Gathering, collection.* ~Se dedica a la RECOLECCIÓN de chatarra. *He collects scrap metal.* ‖ **2.** Cosecha. *Harvest, harvesting.* ~La RECOLECCIÓN del arroz se hace mecánicamente. *The harvesting of rice is done mechanically.* ‖ **3.** [Temporada]. *Harvest time.* ‖ **4.** [Literatura]. *Compilation, summary.* ‖ **5.** Recogida de dinero. *Collection.* El parroco hizo una RECOLECCIÓN para comprar juguetes a los niños pobres. *The parish made a collection to buy toys for indigent children.* ⇨RECOLLECTION

RECONOCER [RECOGNIZE]. *v.* Admitir. *To admit, acknowledge.* ~RECONOZCO que me he equivocado. *I admit I was wrong.* ~Hay que RECONOCERLO. *You have to admit it.* ‖ **2.** [Paciente]. *To examine.* ~El médico está RECONOCIENDO al paciente. *The doctor is examining the patient.* ‖ **3.** MIL *To reconnoiter.* ~Enviaron una avanzadilla para RECONOCER la zona. *They sent a scouting party to reconnoiter the area.* ‖ **4.** Agradecer (regalo, servicio). *To be grateful for.* ~Le estoy muy AGRADECIDO por su ayuda. *I'm very grateful for your help.* ‖ **5.** Registrar (persona, equipaje). *To search, inspect, examine.* ~En la aduana RECONOCIERON todo nuestro equipaje. *All our baggage had to go through customs.* ‖ **6.** [Terreno]. *To survey.* ~El capitán mandó RECONOCER el terreno para ver si había algún peligro. *The captain ordered the terrain surveyed for possible dangers.*

RECURSO [RECOURSE]. *sm.* Medio. *Resort.* ~Como último RECURSO. *As a last resort.* ~He agotado todos los RECURSOS. *I've tried everything I can.* ‖ **2.** [Derecho]. *Appeal.* ~Interponer RECURSO contra. *To lodge an appeal against.* ‖ **3.** *pl.* Medios. *Resources (de un país), means (de una familia).* ~Los RECURSOS naturales de un país. *The natural resources of a country.* ~Una familia sin RECURSOS. *A family with no means of support.*

REDUCCIÓN. *sf.* [De una ciudad]. *Conquest.* ~La REDUCCIÓN de la ciudad a manos de los insurgentes. *The conquest of the city by the rebels.* ‖ **2.** [De los rebeldes, enemigos). *Defeat.* ~El ejército consiguió la REDUCCIÓN de los sublevados. *The army defeated the rebels.* ‖ **3.** Descuento, rebaja. *Cut.* ‖ **4.** Simplificación. *Simplification.* ‖ **5.** MED [De un hueso]. *Setting.* ‖ **6.** [En un vehículo]. *Shift.* ~Hacer la REDUCCION de tercera a segunda. *To shift from third to second.* ⇨REDUCTION

REDUCIR[1]. *v.* Vencer, dominar, someter. *To subdue (un enemigo), overpower (una persona peligrosa), to overcome (rebeldes).* La policía REDUJO al grupo de alborotadores. *The police subdued the group of troublemakers.* ‖ **2.** [Discurso]. *To abridge, cut down.* ~Tengo que REDUCIR el discurso porque sólo tengo quince minutos para hablar. *I have to abridge my speech since I only have fifteen minutes to talk.* ‖ **3.** To convert. *Convertir.* ~REDUCIR las millas a kilómetros. *To convert miles into kilometers.* ‖ **4.** [Auto]. *To shift into a lower gear.* ~REDUCE a segunda; este camino está en muy mal estado. *Shift to second (gear); this road is in very bad condition.* ‖ **5.** [Texto]. *To abridge.* ‖ **6.** [Hueso]. To set. ⇨REDUCE

REDUCIRSE[2]. *vr.* Ahorrar. *To economize.* ~Tuvimos que REDUCIRNOS. We had to cut down on expenses. ‖ **2.** •REDUCIRSE a. *To come down to, to amount to no more than.* ~El escándalo se REDUJO a un simple chisme. *The scandal amounted to nothing more than a piece of gossip.* ‖ **3.** [Actividad, intervención]. *To limit oneself.* ~Tú te REDUCES a cumplir tu obligación. *Just limit yourself to carrying out your duty.* ⇨REDUCE

REFERIR. *v.* Contar. *To tell, relate, recount.* ~Nos REFIRIÓ sus experiencias en África. *He related his African experiences to us.* ~Me visitaba casi a diario para REFERIRME sus angustias. *He came to see me almost every day to tell me his tales of woe.* ⇨REFER

REFLEJO [REFLEX]. *sm.* Imagen. REFLECTION. ~Mirar su REFLEJO en el agua. *To look at one's reflection in the water.* || **2.** Destello. *Gleam, glint.* || **3.** Consecuencia, resultado, testimonio. *Reflexion.* ~Sus palabras son REFLEJO de su pensamiento. *His words reflect his thoughts.*

REFORMA [REFORM]. *sf.* [Construcción]. *Alterations, repairs, improvements.* ~Cerrado por REFORMAS. *Closed for alterations.* || **2.** [Costura]. *Alteration.* ~A este vestido hay que hacerle algunas REFORMAS. *This dress needs some alterations.*

REGISTRAR[1]. *v.* [Equipaje, persona, lugar]. *To search.* ~REGISTRARON sus maletas. *Their suitcases were searched.* ~Durante su ausencia la policía REGISTRÓ su apartamento. *During his absence the police searched his apartment.* || **2.** [Archivo, documento]. *Survey, inspect.* || **3.** [Cajón]. *To look through.* ~¿Quién ha estado REGISTRANDO mis cajones. *Who has been looking through my drawers?* || **4.** Grabar. *Record.* REGISTRAR la voz en una cinta. *To record one's voice on tape.* || **5.** Detectarse. *To be recorded or reported.* Se ha REGISTRADO un ligero temblor. *A sligh tremor has been recorded.* ~Se han REGISTRADO varios casos de tifus. *A few cases of typhus have been reported.* || **6.** Observar. *Note, notice.* ~Hemos REGISTRADO un aumento de la criminalidad. *We have noted a rise in the crime rate.* ⇨REGISTER

REGISTRARSE[2]. *vr.* Ocurrir. *To happen.* ~El cambio que se ha REGISTRADO en su actitud. *The change which has ocurred in his attitude.* ⇨REGISTER

REGULACIÓN. *sf.* Control. *Control.* ~REGULACIÓN de la natalidad. *Birth-control.* ~REGULACIÓN del tráfico. *Traffic control.* || **2.** Reducción. *Reduction.* ~REGULACIÓN de empleo. *Reduction of the workforce.* ~REGULACIÓN de plantilla. *Staff cut.* || **3.** [De una máquina, pieza]. *Adjustment.* ~El botón izquierdo sirve para la REGULACIÓN de la temperatura. *The left button is used to adjust the temperature.* ⇨REGULATION

REGULAR. *adj.* No muy bien, no tan malo.

All right (I guess), not bad, so-so, reasonable, average, run-of-the-mill, nothing to write home about. ~¿Qué tal van los estudios? –REGULAR. *How's school going? –So-so.* ~¿Qué tal la película? –REGULAR. *How was the movie? –Nothing special, nothing to write home about.* ~Su trabajo es bastante REGULARCITO. *His work is pretty run-of-the-mill.* || **2.** Entre los dos. *In between.* ~¿Te gusta el chocolate espeso o líquido? –REGULAR. *Do you like your chocolate thick or runny? –In between.* ⇨REGULAR

RELACION. *sf.* Lista. *List.* ~Leyó la RELACIÓN de los asistentes al congreso. *He read the names of those present at the conference.* || **2.** Relato. *Account, telling.* ~Hizo una larga RELACIÓN de su viaje. *He gave a lengthy account of his trip.* || **3.** Influencias. *Influential friends, contacts, connections.* ~Tener (buenas) RELACIONES. *To be well connected, have friends in the right places.* || **4.** Conexión. *Connection, link.* ~Una RELACIÓN causa-efecto. *A cause and effect relationship.* || **5.** Trato. *Relationship.* ~Las RELACIONES entre padres e hijos. *The relationship between parents and their children.* || **6.** •Mantener RELACIONES con. *To keep in touch with.* || **7.** •Estar en buenas RELACIONES con. *To be on good terms with.* ⇨RELATION

RELEVANTE. *adj.* Sobresaliente, excelente, importante. *Outstanding, remarkable, important.* ~En este hotel se hospedan personas RELEVANTES. *Many famous people live in this hotel.* ⇨RELEVANT

REMITIR. *v.* Referir (al lector, usuario). *To refer.* ~La nota nos REMITE a la página 3. *The note refers us to page 3.* ~La autora REMITE constantemente a su anterior obra. *The author keeps referring the reader to her previous work.* || **3.** Perdonar los pecados. *To forgive.* || **4.** Aplazar. *To postpone.* ~Tuvimos que REMITIR la reunión hasta el lunes. *We had to postpone the meeting until Monday.* || **5.** [Fiebre, temporal, violencia]. *To subside, abate.* ~La ola de violencia esta REMITIENDO. *The wave of violence is subsiding.* ~Dentro de unos días REMITIRÁ el calor. *The heat will abate within a few days.* || **6.** Enviar (por correo). *To send.* ⇨REMIT

REMOVER. *v.* [Objetos]. *To change over, shift about.* ~Arriba no paran de REMOVER los muebles. *Upstairs they keep moving the furniture.* || **2.** Agitar (un líquido). *To shake up.* || **3.** [Salsa, café]. *Stir.* ~REMUEVA bien el café para que se disuelva el azúcar. *Stir your coffee well so that the sugar dissolves.* || **4.** [Salad]. *Toss.* || **5.** Reavivar. *To revive.* ~REMOVER los recuerdos. *To bring back memories.* ~Lo mejor es no REMOVER este tema. *It will be best not to bring this matter up again.* || **6.** Alterar. *To change.* ~Este nuevo problema lo ha REMOVIDO todo. *This new problem has turned everything upside down.* || **7.** Tierra. *To turn over, dig up.* ~REMOVIERON los escombros en busca de víctimas. *They dug about in the rubble in search of victims.* || **8.** •REMOVER un asunto. *To turn a matter over.* || **9.** •REMOVER el pasado. *To stir up the past.* || **10.** •REMOVER cielo y tierra. *To move heaven and earth.* ⇨REMOVE

RENDICIÓN. *sf.* Acción de rendirse. *Surrender.* La RENDICIÓN se produjo después de esta batalla. *The surrender took place following this defeat.* ⇨RENDITION

RENEGAR. *v.* Renunciar. *To renounce, disown.* ~Ha RENEGADO de su familia. *He disowned his family.* ~Nunca RENEGARÉ de mis principios. *I'll never renounce my principles.* ~RENUNCIÓ de su fe cristiana. *He renounced the Christian faith.* || **2.** Negar. *To deny vigorously.* ~Negó y RENEGÓ su participación en el asunto. *He vigorously denied his involvement in the affair.* || **3.** Blasfemar, maldecir. *To swear, curse.* ~RENEGABA de todos aquellos amigos que le había dado la espalda. *He cursed all those friends who had turned their backs on him.* || **4.** Quejarse. *To grumble, complain, protest.* ~RENEGABA del tiempo. *He was complaining about the weather.* ~Se pasó el día RENEGANDO porque se le había estropeado el coche. *He spent the entire day grumbling because his car had*

broken down. || **5.** Odiar. *To abhor, detest.* ~RENEGÓ de su hija porque se había hecho monja. *He detested his daughter because she had become a nun.* ⇨RENEGE

RENOVAR. *v.* Modernizar [cuarto]. *Redecorate.* ~Quisiéramos RENOVAR el cuarto de estar. *We're thinking of redecorating the living-room.* || **2.** [Política]. *To reorganize, transform, remodel.* || **3.** [Pasaporte, contrato]. *To renew.* ~El partido tiene posibilidades de RENOVAR su mandato. *The party has a chance of renewing its mandate.* || **4.** Cambiar (mobiliario). *To change, replace.* ~Necesitamos RENOVAR la vajilla; esta es muy vieja y desportillada. *We need to replace the dishes; these are very old and chipped.* || **5.** Reformar, poner al día. *To reform, update.* ~RENOVARON el código de la circulación. *They updated the highway code.* || **6.** Reavivar, reanudar. *To renew.* ~Ha RENOVADO su ataque contra la oposición. *He renewed his attack on the opposition.* ~Volvió al trabajo con RENOVADAS fuerzas. *He returned to work with renewed energy.* || **7.** •RENOVAR la herida. *To open up an old wound.* ⇨RENOVATE

RENTA. *sf.* Ingresos. *Income.* •Vivir de sus RENTAS. *To live on one's income.* ~¿Has presentado la RENTA este año? *Have you filed your income tax this year?* || **2.** •Impuesto sobre la RENTA. *Income tax.* || **3.** Interés. *Interest, return, yield.* || **4.** •RENTA fiscal. *Taxable income.* ⇨RENT

RENUNCIAR [RENOUNCE]. *v.* [Corona, trono]. *To relinquish.* ~RENUNCIÓ a la corona para casarse con una plebeya. *He relinquished the throne in order to marry a commoner.* || **2.** Dimitir. *To resign.* ~RENUNCIÓ a su puesto en la dirección. *He resigned his position from the board.* || **3.** Abstenerse de algo. *To give up.* ~Debes RENUNCIAR al azúcar. *You'll have to give up sugar.* ~Su médico le aconsejó que RENUNCIARA al alcohol. *His doctor advised him to give up alcohol.* || **4.** [Demanda]. *To drop, waive.* ~RENUNCIÓ a su herencia en favor de sus sobrinos. *He waived his inheritance in favor of his nephews.* || **5.** [En una competición]. *To withdraw.* ~Cuando le tocaba jugar, RENUNCIÓ. *When it was his turn to play, he withdrew.*

REPARAR [REPAIR]. *v.* [Ofensa, injuria, agravio]. *To make amends for, make up for.* REPARÓ su ofensa pidiéndome perdón. *He asked for my forgiveness for having offended him.* || **2.** [Daño, perjuicio]. *To make good, compensate.* ~Debes REPARAR el daño que le causaste. *You must make up for the harm that you caused him.* || **3.** Reponer (fuerzas, energías). *To restore, renew.* ~Tus palabras REPARARON mi ánimo. *Your words boosted my spirits.* ~Necesito un descanso que me permita REPARAR fuerzas. *I need a rest to renew my strength.* || **4.** Considerar. *To take into account.* ~Hay que REPARAR en los pros y los contras. *You have to take into account the pros and cons.* || **5.** Darse cuenta. *To notice, realize.* ~Reparé en que no llevaba la cartera. *I realized I didn't have my wallet on me.* || **6.** Hacer caso. *To pay attention to.* ~No REPARAR en gastos. *To spare no expense.* ~Repara en lo que vas a hacer. *Reflect on what you're going to do.* || **7.** [Fortunas]. *To retrieve.* || **8.** [Consecuencia]. *To undo.* || **9.** [Golpe]. *To parry.* || **10.** Observar, notar. *To observe, notice.* ~No REPARÉ en su peinado. *I didn't notice her hairdo.* ~¿Has REPARADO que aquí no hay sillas? *Did you notice there are no chairs here?* || **11.** Corregir (error). *To correct, put right.* ~Hemos tratado de REPARAR los errores del libro. *We tried to correct the errors in the book.*

REPORTAR. *v.* [Beneficios, pérdidas]. *To produce, yield, bring.* ~El negocio le REPORTÓ grandes ganancias. *The business brought him large profits.* || **2.** [Fama, prestigio]. *To bring.* ~El cine le ha REPORTADO mucha fama. *Acting has brought him great fame.* || **3.** [En litografía]. *To transfer.* || **4.** Refrenar, moderar. *To restrain, check.* ~Repórtate y sé más amable. *Restrain yourself and try to be nicer.* Por favor, REPÓRTATE y no llames la atención. *Please get a hold of yourself and don't make a scene.* || **5.** [Problemas, preocupaciones]. *To cause, bring.* ~Este asunto sólo

te REPORTARÁ problemas. *This affair will only cause you problems.* ⇨REPORT

REPRESENTAR [REPRESENT]. *v.* [Obra]. *To perform, put on.* ~La compañía REPRESENTARÁ La Casa de Bernarda Alba. *The actor's group will perform (put on) The House of Bernarda Alba.* || **2.** [Paper]. *To play.* ~Representó el papel de Cleopatra. *She played the part of Cleopatra.* || **3.** Aparentar. *To look.* ~No REPRESENTA la edad que tiene. *He doesn't look his age.* || **4.** Simbolizar. *To symbolize.* ~La paloma REPRESENTA la paz. *The dove is a symbol of peace.* || **5.** Reproducir (dibujo, fotografía). *To show, depict, portray.* ~La medalla REPRESENTA a la Virgen. *The medallion depicts the Virgin Mary.* ~La escena REPRESENTA una calle de los arrabales. *The scene depicts a street in the poor quarters.* || **6.** Hacerse presente en la imaginación. *To picture (mentally), imagine.* No consigo REPRESENTARME esta casa donde pasé mi infancia. *I can't quite picture the house where I once lived as a boy.* ¿Te lo puedes REPRESENTAR sin barba? *Can you picture him without a beard?*

REQUERIR. *v.* [Mandar traer]. *To demand, call for.* ~El ministro REQUIRIÓ su presencia. *The minister summoned him.* || **2.** Solicitar. *To request.* ~Requirió nuestra ayuda y se la prestamos. *He requested our help and we gave it to him.* || **3.** JUR Avisar. *To summon.* ~El juez ha REQUERIDO a los revoltosos que se presenten. *The judge summoned the rebels to appear in court.* || **4.** Persuadir. *To persuade, convince.* ~Con su elocuencia REQUIRIÓ a todos. *With his eloquence he convinced everyone.* || **5.** Exigir. *To call for, demand.* ~Esta conducta REQUIERE castigo. *This behavior calls for punishment.* ⇨REQUIRE

RESERVA [RESERVE]. *sf.* [De una habitación, mesa, pasaje, billete). *Reservation.* ~La RESERVA de asientos no se paga. *There is no charge for seat reservations.* ~He hecho una RESERVA para el vuelo de las nueve. *I've made a reservation for the nine o'clock flight.* || **2.** Cautela. *Reservation.* ~Acepté su propuesta con RESERVA. *I accepted his proposition with reservation.* || **3.** [Vino].

Vintage. ~Un vino de RESERVA. *A vintage wine.* ‖ **4.** Terreno. *Reservation.* ~RESERVA de indios. *Indian reserve.* ‖ **5.** [Secreto, discreción]. *Privacy, confidence.* ~Escribir con la mayor RESERVA. *To write in the strictest confidence.* ~Se garantiza la más absoluta RESERVA. *All applications treated in the strictest confidence.* ~Pidió RESERVA de su nombre. *He asked that his name be kept secret.* ‖ **6.** *pl.* Dudas. *Reservation.* ~Lo aceptó, pero no sin RESERVAS. *He agreed, but not without reservations.* ‖ **7.** Provisiones. *Supplies.* ~En la alacena hay una RESERVA de legumbres y alimentos en conserva. *In the cupboard there are ample supplies of vegetables and canned foods.*

RESERVAR [RESERVE]. *v.* Guardar. *To keep, save.* ~Nos tenía RESERVADA una sorpresa. *He had a surprise in store for us.* ~RESERVÓ lo mejor para el final. *She kept the best till last.* ‖ **2.** Ocultar. *To withold, keep to oneself.* ~RESERVÓ la noticia para sí. *He kept the news to himself.* ~Se RESERVÓ su opinion. *He withheld his opinion.*

RESISTIR[1] [RESIST]. *v.* Soportar (peso, cuerda). *To hold (out).* ¿RESISTIRÁ este nudo? *Will this knot hold?* ~No RESISTIÓ el peso adicional. *It couldn't take the extra weight.* ‖ **2.** Aguantar, soportar, tolerar (agotamiento, decepción). *To tolerate, stand, put up with, endure.* ~No puedo RESISTIR este frío. *I can't stand this cold.* ~No lo RESISTO un momento más. *I'm not putting up with this a moment longer.* ‖ **3.** Sostener (peso). *To bear, withstand.* ~La tabla no podía RESISTIR tanto peso y se partió. *The board couldn't withstand such weight and it cracked.* ‖ **4.** Durar. *To last.* ~Este edificio RESISTE. *This building has stood the test of time.* ~El equipo no puede RESISTIR mucho más. *The team can't hold out much longer.* ~El secador RESISTE todavía. *The hairdryer is still working.* ‖ **5.** •RESISTIR la mirada de uno. *To stare back at somebody.*

RESISTIRSE[2] [RESIST]. *vr.* Costar esfuerzo. *To struggle.* ~Se le RESISTEN las matemáticas. *She's having a hard time with math, math isn't her strongest subject.* ‖ **2.** Negarse.

To refuse. ~Me RESISTO a creerlo. *I find it hard to believe.* ‖ **3.** Combatir. *To put up a fight, fight back.* ‖ **4.** Seguir resistiendo. *To hold out.*

RESOLUCIÓN. *sf.* Solución. *Solution.* ~La RESOLUCIÓN de un problema. *The solution to a problem.* ~Un problema de RESOLUCIÓN nada fácil. *A problem which is not easy to solve.* ‖ **2.** Finalización, terminación. *Finishing off, completion.* ~A la RESOLUCIÓN de sus actividades. *Upon completion of his activities.* ‖ **3.** Decisión. *Decision.* ~Tomaron la RESOLUCIÓN de cerrar el hospital. *They decided to close the hospital.* ‖ **4.** Determinación. *Determination, resolve.* ~Creo que le falta la RESOLUCIÓN necesaria para afrentar ese problema. *I think he lacks the sufficient determination to face up to that problem.* ‖ **5.** Cualidad de decisivo. *Decisiveness.* ~Debes hablar con RESOLUCIÓN si quieres convencer. *You must speak decisively if you wish to be convincing.* ⇨ RESOLUTION

RESOLVER. *v.* Solucionar. *Solve.* ~Unas dificultades que estoy tratando de RESOLVER. *Some difficulties which I am trying to solve.* ‖ **2.** Gestionar, tramitar. *To settle.* ~Tengo que RESOLVER lo del pasaporte. *I have to settle the question of my passport.* ‖ **3.** [Química]. *To dissolve.* ‖ **4.** [Duda]. *Clear up.* ~A ver si me resuelves una duda. *I wonder if you could clear up one point for me.* ‖ **5.** Decidir. *To decide.* ~RESOLVÍ quedarme. *I decided to stay.* ~He RESUELTO comprar un coche nuevo. *I decided to buy a new car.* ⇨ RESOLVE

RESONANCIA [RESONANCE]. *sf.* Eco. *Echo.* ‖ **2.** Notoriedad. *Importance, widespread effect.* ~Ha tenido gran RESONANCIA. *It had a huge impact.* ‖ **3.** Consecuencias. *Repercussion.* ‖ **4.** Fama, popularidad. *Renown.* ~El asunto ha alcanzado una RESONANCIA enorme. *The affair has attained great popularity.*

RESPONDER [RESPOND]. *v.* Contestar. *To answer.* ~RESPONDER a una carta. *To reply to a letter.* RESPONDER al teléfono. *To answer the phone.* ~Pero él me RESPONDE con injurias. *But he answers me with insults.*

~RESPONDER a una pregunta. *To answer a question.* || **3.** Corresponder. *To go by, answer.* ~RESPONDE al nombre de Ramón. *He goes by the name of Ramón.* ~RESPONDER a una descripción. *To fit a description.* ~RESPONDER a una necesidad. *To answer (meet) a need.* || **4.** Rendir. *To produce.* ~Cuando llueve este campo RESPONDE. *When it rains this field is productive.* || **5.** Avalar. *To guarantee.* ~RESPONDER de alguien. *To be responsible for someone.* ~RESPONDER por alguien. *To vouch for someone.* ~No RESPONDO de lo que hagan mis colegas. *I'm not responsible for what my colleagues may do.* || **6.** Replicar. *To answer back.* ~Es un maleducado; siempre tiene que RESPONDER. *He has no manners; he always answers back.*

RESULTAR [RESULT]. *v.* Ocurrir. *To turn out.* ~Ahora RESULTA que no puede venir. *Now it seems she can't come.* ~RESULTA que no tenemos dinero. *It so happens that we don't have any money.* || **2.** Llegar a ser. *To prove to be, turn out to be.* ~A pesar de todo, RESULTÓ muy simpático. *In spite of everything, he turned out to be very nice.* || **3.** Dar resultado, ser conveniente. *To work out, to be best to, be a good idea, to be worth.* ~No RESULTA comprar barato. *It doesn't pay to buy cheap.* ~Su idea no RESULTÓ. *His idea didn't work (out).* ~No RESULTA dejar el coche fuera. *It's best not (it's not a good idea) to leave the car outside.* ~No RESULTA comer a la carta. *It doesn't pay to eat a la carte.* || **4.** Venir a costar. *To cost, come to.* ~El coche me RESULTÓ por medio millón de pesetas. *The car cost me half a million pesetas.* || **5.** Parecer bien. *To look well, to have a pleasing effect.* ~Esa corbata no RESULTA con este traje. *That tie doesn't go with this suit.* || **6.** Ser. *To be.* ~Aquí la vida RESULTA muy barata. *The cost of living here is very low.* ~RESULTÓ herido en el accidente. *He was injured in the accident.* ~RESULTA difícil comprenderlo. *It's difficult to understand.*

RESUMIR. *v.* Recapitular. *Sum up.* || **2.** Condensar. *Summarize.* ~La situación puede RESUMIRSE en pocas palabras. *The situation can be summed up in a few words.* || **3.** Reducir. *To abridge, shorten.* ~Este párrafo se puede RESUMIR en cuatro líneas. *This paragraph can be shortened to four lines.* || **4.** Venir a ser. *To be reduced to, boil down to.* ~El examen se RESUME en cuatro preguntas tontas. *The test boils down to a few silly questions.* ~Toda la obra se RESUME en la eterna lucha entre el bien y el mal. *The entire works boils down to the never-ending struggle between good and evil.* ~Todo se RESUMIÓ en unos porrazos. *The affair amounted to no more than a few punches.* ⇨RESUME

RETENER. *v.* [Cosa prestada]. *To keep back, hold back.* ~Siempre RETIENE los libros prestados más de lo debido. *He always keeps books that he has borrowed more than he should.* || **2.** Descontar. *To deduct, withold.* ~RETIENEN veinte dólares semanales de mi sueldo. *They deduct (withold) twenty dollars a week from my salary.* || **3.** Detener. *To detain, arrest.* ~La policía RETUVO a los testigos para interrogarlos. *The police detained the witnesses for questioning.* || **4.** [Tesoros, víveres]. *To hoard.* || **5.** [Datos, información]. *To withhold, keep back.* || **6.** Hacer permanecer, impedir que se vaya. *To keep, keep back, hold.* No te RETENDRÉ mucho tiempo. *I won't keep you long.* ~El maestro nos RETUVO. *The teacher kept us after class.* ~Ya nada me RETIENE aquí. *There's nothing to keep me here now.* ~No sabe como RETENER a su marido. *She doesn't know what to do to hold on to (to keep) her husband.* ~RETÉN este caballo para que no se escape. *Hold this horse so he doesn't escape.* || **7.** *To hold hostage.* ~Tres reclusos RETUVIERON a un funcionario. *Three prisoners held a guard hostage.* || **8.** [Agua]. *To hold.* La esponja RETIENE el agua. *Sponge holds water.* || **9.** [Aliento, atención, lengua]. *To hold.* ~RETENER el aliento. *To hold one's breath.* RETENER la atención de alguien. *To hold someone's attention.* RETENER la lengua. *To hold one's tongue.* || **10.** Recordar, aprender de memoria. *To remember, memorize.* Tiene facilidad para RETENER fechas. *He's very good at remembering dates.* ⇨RETAIN

RETICENTE. *adj.* [Discurso]. *Full of hints (insinuations).* || **2.** Reservado. *Misleading, deceptive.* || **3.** Irónico. *Ironic, sarcastic.* ⇨RETICENT

RETIRADO [RETIRED]. *adj.* Alejado. *Remote.* ~Vive en las afueras, en una calle muy RETIRADA. *He lives in the suburbs, in an out of the way street.* || **2.** [Vida]. *Quiet.* || **3.** [Lugar]. *Remote, secluded, quiet, out-of-the-way.* ~En un barrio RETIRADO del centro. *In an outlying district, in an area some distance from downtown.* ~Una casa RETIRADA de la carretera. *A house set back from the road.*

RETRIBUCIÓN. *sf.* Recompensa. *Reward, compensation.* || **2.** Pago, sueldo. *Pay, payment, salary.* ~RETRIBUCIÓN a convenir. *Negotiable salary, salary to be agreed.* ⇨RETRIBUTION

REUNIÓN [REUNION]. *sf.* [Para discutir algo]. *Meeting.* ~El director tuvo una REUNIÓN con sus empleados. *The director had a meeting with his employees.* ~Celebrar una REUNIÓN. *To hold a meeting.* ~Punto de REUNIÓN. *Meeting place.* || **2.** [De carácter social]. *Gathering.* ~No hicieron una gran fiesta sino una pequeña REUNIÓN. *They didn't have a big party, just a small gathering (get-together).* || **3.** [De datos, información]. *Collecting, gathering.* ~La primera fase de mi investigación será la REUNIÓN de datos. *The first step in my investigation will consist of gathering information.* || **4.** •REUNIÓN ilícita. *Unlawful assembly.* || **5.** •REUNIÓN informativa. *Press conference.* || **6.** •REUNIÓN plenaria. *Plenary session.*

REVISAR. *v. fin* Cuentas. *To check, audit.* || **2.** Billetes. *To inspect.* || **3.** Examinar. *To check.* ~REVISA el coche antes del viaje. *Check the car before going on your trip.* ~REVISÓ el paquete a ver si estaba todo el pedido. *He checked the package to see that his order was complete.* || **4.** Hacer una revisión periódica (coche). *To service, overhaul.* || **5.** [Derecho]. *To review.* ~Pidieron al juez que REVISARA la sentencia. *They asked the judge to review the sentence.* || **6.** [Teoría]. *To re-examine, review.* || **7.** Leer (documento). *To go through, look through.*

|| **8.** Comprobar (traducción, cuenta). *To check, go through.* || **9.** [Frenos]. *To check.* ~REVISAR los frenos. *To check the brakes.* || **10.** LAT. AM. [Equipaje, bolsillos]. *To search, go through.* ~Alguien me estuvo REVISANDO los cajones. *Someone's been going through my drawers.* || **11.** LAT. AM. [Paciente]. *To examine.* || **12.** Examinar (dentadura, vista). *To check.* Cada seis meses se hace REVISAR la dentadura. *He has his teeth checked every six months.* ~Tengo que ir al oculista a REVISARME la vista. *I need to go to the oculist to check my eyes.* || **13.** Corregir (pruebas). *To correct.* || **14.** [Lección]. *To review.* ~REVISA bien la lección antes del examen. *Review your lesson well before the test.* ⇨REVISE

REVISIÓN [REVISION]. *sf.* [De cuentas]. *Audit, auditing.* || **2.** [Médica]. *Checkup.* ~Para que te den el carné de conducir, tienes que someterte a una REVISIÓN médica. *In order to get your driving license you must first undergo a medical exam.* || **3.** [De billetes]. *Inspection.* || **4.** [De coche]. *Service, overhaul.* ~Tengo que hacerle una REVISIÓN al coche. *I need to have my car serviced.* || **5.** [De sueldos]. *Review.* || **6.** [De un trabajo, documento]. *Check, checking.* ~Efectuaron una REVISIÓN minuciosa de los gastos. *They made a detailed check of the expenses.* || **7.** [De una instalación]. *Inspection.* ~La REVISIÓN del generador reveló varios problemas. *Inspection of the generator revealed several problems.* || **8.** [De frenos]. *Check.* || **9.** [Derecho]. *Review.*

REVOCAR[1] [REVOKE]. *v.* [Órden, ley]. *To cancel, rescind.* || **2.** [Construcción]. *To plaster, stucco.* || **3.** Encalar. *To whitewash.* || **4.** [Persona]. *To remove from his post.* || **5.** [Humo]. *To send in a different direction, to blow back, blow the wrong way.* ~El viento REVOCA el humo. *The wind blows the smoke back.* || **6.** Disuadir. *To disuade.* || **7.** Poner una nueva fachada. *To resurface.* ~Levantaron un andamio para REVOCAR la fachada del edificio. *They built a scaffold in order to resurface the front part of the building.*

REVOLVER[1]. *v.* [Salsa, guiso, líquido]. *To*

stir. ~REVUELVE bien el café, que tienes el azúcar en el fondo. *Stir your coffee well, the sugar is at the bottom (of the cup).* ‖ **2.** [Ingredients]. *Mezclar.* ~Se REVUELVE la harina con el azúcar. *Mix the flour and sugar.* ‖ **3.** [Ensalada]. *To toss (the salad).* ~REVUELVE bien la ensalada para que se mezcle el aliño. *Toss the salad well with the dressing.* ‖ **4.** Producir náusea. *Upset.* ~Eso me REVUELVE el estómago. *That's upsets (turns) my stomach, that makes me sick to my stomach (figuratively).* ‖ **5.** [Cajón]. *Rummage through (a drawer).* ~He REVUELTO todos los cajones para encontrarlo pero no está. *I rummaged through all the drawers to find it, but it's not there.* FIG Los periodistas han empezado a REVOLVER en el pasado de ese político. *The reporters have started to rummage through that politician's past.* ‖ **6.** [Bolsillo]. *Fumble (in one's pockets).* ‖ **7.** Desordenar. *Mess up, disturb, disarrange, mix up, mess up.* ~Además de robarme me REVOLVIERON toda la casa. *They just didn't steal things, they turned the whole house upside down.* ‖ **8.** Confundir, mezclar. *To entangle, confuse.* ‖ **9.** Volver a pensar, tratar, indagar. *To bring back.* ~Hay asuntos que no conviene REVOLVER. *There are things that are better left alone.* ‖ **10.** [Tierra]. *To turn over.* ‖ **11.** [Papeles]. *To look through.* ‖ **12.** [Recipiente]. *To shake.*

REVOLVERSE[2]. *vr.* Volverse en contra de alguien. *To turn against someone.* ~Se VOLVIERON en contra de su familia. *They turned against their own family.* ~El perro se REVOLVIÓ en contra de su dueño. *The dog turned againts his master.* ‖ **2.** Moverse de un lugar a otro. ¿Por qué te REVUELVES inquieto en la silla? *Why are you shifting around so nervously in your chair?* Se REVOLVÍA en la silla. *He was fidgeting about in his chair, he was squirming uncomfortably in his chair.* ‖ **3.** Ponerse tempestuoso el tiempo. *Turn stormy (the weather).* ~El tiempo se ha REVUELTO y no podremos salir de excursión. *It looks as though there's going to be a storm and we won't be able to go on a trip.* ‖ **4.** Dar la vuelta.

Turn around. ~Se REVOLVIÓ para que no le vieran las lágrimas. *He turned around so that they would see the tears in his eyes.* ~Hay tanta gente que no puede uno ni REVOLVERSE. *It's so crowded that you can't even turn around.* ‖ **5.** [Seas]. *Get rough.* ~A río REVUELTO, ganancia de pescadores. *It's an ill wind that blows nobody any good.* ‖ **6** [Sedimento]. *To be stirred up, be disturbed.* ‖ **7.** Enturbiarse (un líquido). *To become cloudy.* ‖ **8.** [Con dolor]. *To writhe, squirm (with pain).* ‖ **9.** Agitarse (en la cama). *To toss and turn.* ~Se REVOLVÍA inquieto sin poder dormir. *He tossed and turned, unable to sleep.* ⇨REVOLVER

RICO. *adj.* Sabroso. *Delicious, tasty.* ~Esta sopa es muy RICA. *This soup is delicious.* Estos pasteles son RIQUÍSIMOS. *These pastries are exceptionally tasty.* ‖ **2.** Bonito, mono (niño). *Lovely, adorable, cute.* ¡Qué niño más RICO! *What a lovely child!* ‖ **3.** [Mujer]. *Beautiful, georgeous.* ~¡Qué RICA es tu vecina! *Your neighbor is georgeous.* ‖ **4.** [Vegetación]. *Lush.* ‖ **5.** Lleno. *Full.* Un viaje RICO en aventuras. *A trip full of adventures.* ⇨ RICH

RICTUS [RICTUS]. *sm.* [De desprecio]. *Sneer.* ‖ **2.** [De burla]. *Grin.* ‖ **3.** •Rictus de dolor. *Wince of pain.* ~Con un RICTUS de dolor en el rostro. *Wincing (grimacing) with pain.* ‖ **4.** •RICTUS de amargura. *Bitter smile.*

RIGIDEZ [RIGIDITY]. *sf.* Severidad (de una ley, doctrina). *Strictness, inflexibility, firmness.* ~La RIGIDEZ de las normas. *The inflexibility of the rules.* ~La RIGIDEZ de su educación. *The strictness of her upbringing.* ‖ **2.** [De un miembro]. *Stiffness.* ~La RIGIDEZ de su brazo le impedía escribir. *The stiffness in his arm prevented him from writing.*

RÍGIDO [RIGID]. *adj.* Severo. *Strict, inflexible, firm.* ~Disciplina RÍGIDA. *Strict discipline.* ~Mi padre es muy RÍGIDO y no me perdona nada. *My father is very strict and he doesn't let me get away with anything.* ‖ **2.** [Mirada, cara]. *Wooden, expressionless.* ~Ni ante la más grave noticia se inmutaba; su rostro siempre permanecía RÍGIDO. *Even the worst news seems not to perturb him:*

his face would remain expressionless. ‖ **3.** [Educación, dieta]. *Srict.* ‖ **4.** [Regla]. *Inflexible.* ~Unas normas muy RÍGIDAS. *Very inflexible rules.* ‖ **5.** [Carácter]. *Inflexible, unbending.* ~Es muy RÍGIDO y no cambiará de opinión. *He's an inflexible fellow and he won't change his mind.* ‖ **6.** [Moral, principios]. *Strict.* ‖ **7.** [Horario]. *Inflexible.* ~Tiene un horario muy RÍGIDO. *Her timetable is very inflexible.* ‖ **8.** [Pierna, brazo]. *Stiff.*

RIGUROSO [RIGOROUS]. *adj.* [Dieta]. *Strict.* ‖ **2.** [Juez]. *Harsh.* ‖ **3.** [Maestro]. *Strict.* ~El profesor es muy RIGUROSO cuando califica los exámenes. *The teacher is very strict when it's time to grade the tests.* ‖ **4.** [Castigo]. *Severe, harsh.* ‖ **5.** [Clima, invierno]. *Harsh, severe, extreme, hard.* ~Recuerdo que aquel año el invierno fue muy RIGUROSO. *I recalled that it was a harsh winter.* ‖ **6.** [Medida]. *Severe, tough, stringent.* ‖ **7.** [Actitud, disciplina]. *Harsh, severe.* ~Su tratamiento riguroso de los empleados. *His harsh treatment of the employees.* ‖ **8.** Minucioso. *Meticulous.*

RIQUEZA. *sf.* [De bienes]. *Wealth, riches, fortune.* ~Repartió su RIQUEZA entre los pobres. *He distributed his wealth amongst the poor.* ~Tiene una enorme RIQUEZA en joyas. *She has a vast fortune in jewels.* ~La mala distribución de la RIQUEZA. *The uneven distribution of wealth.* Ni toda la RIQUEZA del mundo podría comprarlo. *All the riches in the world could not buy it.* ‖ **2.** [En obras de arte]. *Treasures.* ~Las RIQUEZAS del museo arqueológico. *The treasures of the archaeological museum.* ‖ **3.** [Recursos]. *Riches, resources.* ~La explotación de las RIQUEZAS del suelo. *The exploitation of the earth's riches.* ~Las RIQUEZAS naturales de un país. *A country's natural resources.* ‖ **4.** [De detalles). *Wealth.* ~Describió el acontecimiento con una RIQUEZA de detalles. *He*

described the event with a wealth of details. ⇨RICHNESS

RODEO [RODEO]. *sm.* Desvío. *Detour.* ~Tuve que dar un gran RODEO. *I had to make a long detour.* ‖ **2.** [Evasiva]. *Evasiveness.* No andes con TANTOS rodeos. *Stop beating about the bush.* ~No andar con RODEOS. *To get straight to the point.* ‖ **3.** Encierro de ganado. *Roundup.*

RUDO. *adj.* Tosco. *Coarse, uncouth, rough.* ~Su RUDO temperamento le impide tener muchos amigos. *His rough manners prevents him from having many friends.* ‖ **2.** [Madera]. *Unpolished (wood).* ~Un pavimento RUDO. *An unpolished floor.* ‖ **3.** Sencillo. *Simple, uneducated.* ~Es un RUDO campesino. *He's a simple country person.* ‖ **4.** [Golpe]. *Duro.* ~Fue un duro GOLPE para ella. *It was a cruel blow for her.* ‖ **5.** Áspero al tacto. *Rough, harsh.* ⇨RUDE

RUMOR [RUMOR]. *sm.* Murmullo (de agua, viento). *Murmur.* ~El RUMOR del agua. *The murmur of water.* ‖ **2.** [De los árboles]. *Rustle, whisper.* ‖ **3.** [De voces]. *Hum, buzz, murmur.* ~A lo lejos se oía el RUMOR de voces. *The murmur of conversation could be heard in the distance.*

RUPTURA [RUPTURE]. *sf.* Rotura. *Breaking, breakage.* ‖ **2.** [De contrato]. *Breaking, breach.* ~La RUPTURA del contrato traería consecuencias muy graves. *Breaking the contract would have very serious consequences.* ‖ **3.** [De relaciones, negociaciones]. *Breaking-off.* ~Esa fue la causa de la RUPTURA de las negociaciones. *That was what caused the negotiations to be broken off.* ‖ **4.** [De una amistad, matrimonio). *Breakup.* ~Su RUPTURA con Ernesto. *Her breakup with Ernesto.* ~Tras la RUPTURA de su matrimonio. *After the breakup of his marriage.* ‖ **5.** [Con el pasado]. *Break.* ~Esta RUPTURA con el pasado. *This break with the past.*

S

SABOREAR [SAVOR]. *v.* Probar. *To taste.*
~Tomó un sorbo de vino, lo SABOREÓ y manifestó su satisfacción. *He took a sip of wine, tasted it and expressed his satisfaction.* || **2.** Disfrutar. *To Enjoy.* ~Para SABOREAR la comida hay que comer despacio. *To enjoy your meal you have to eat slowly.* FIG ~El cantante está SABOREANDO los mejores momentos de su carrera. *The singer is enjoying the best moments of his career.*

SACIAR [SATIATE]. *v.* [Sed]. *To quench.* Bebió hasta SACIAR la sed que tenía. *He drank until he quenched his thirst.* || **2.** [Curiosidad, anhelo]. *To satisfy.* || **3.** [Ambiciones]. *To fulfill.* || **4.** [Deseos]. *To satisfy, appease.* ~No parará hasta SACIAR sus deseos de venganza. *He will not stop until his desire for revenge is satisfied.*

SACRIFICAR [SACRIFICE]. *v.* Matar reses. *To slaughter.* || **2.** [Perro, gato]. *To put to sleep.*

SAL [SALT]. *sm.* Gracia. *Wit, wittiness.* ~Tiene mucha SAL. *He has a great wit, he's very amusing, he's good company.* || **2.** Encanto. *Charm.* ~Ella tiene mucha SAL. *She's delightful, she's absolutely charming.* || **3.** •Esto es la SAL de la vida. *This is the spice of life.*

SALUDAR. *v.* [De palabra]. *To greet, say hello.* ~Se acercó a SALUDARLO. *She went up to greet him.* ~Nunca SALUDA a nadie cuando llega a la oficina. *He never says hello to anyone when he comes into the office.* || **2.** [Con un gesto]. ~Los SALUDÓ con la mano. *He waved to them.* ~Los artistas salieron a SALUDAR al público. *The performers came out to take a bow.* || **3.** Aplaudir (inovación, medida). *To welcome, applaud.* SALUDO esta

decisión del comité. *I welcome (applaud) this decision by the committee.* || **4.** LOCUCIONES. || •No SALUDAR a uno. *To refuse to acknowledge somebody.* || •Le SALUDA atentamente (en carta). *Sincerely (yours).* || •SALUDA de mi parte a. *Give my regards to.* || •No nos SALUDAMOS. *We're not on speaking terms.* ⇨SALUTE[1]

SALUDO. *sm.* Salutación. *Greeting.* Le dio un beso a modo de SALUDO. *He greeted her with a kiss.* || **2.** [En carta]. *Best wishes, regards, greetings.* ~Les envíamos muchos SALUDOS. *We are sending our warmest regards (best wishes).* || **3.** Inclinacion. *Bow.* ⇨SALUTE[2]

SALVACIÓN [SALVATION]. *sf.* Rescate. *Rescue.* ~La ayuda del helicóptero hizo posible la SALVACIÓN de los náufragos. *With the help of a helicopter they were able to rescue the shipwrecked people.* || **2.** •No tiene SALVACIÓN. *There's no hope for him.*

SALVAJE. *adj.* Silvestre (vegetación, terreno). *Wild, uncultivated.* ~Este campo está lleno de hierbas y arbustos SALVAJES. *This field is full of weeds and wild bushes.* || **2.** [Animal]. *Wild.* ~Las panteras son animales SALVAJES. *Panthers are wild animals.* || **3.** Incontrolado. *Wild.* ~Sintió una pasión SALVAJE por esta muchacha. *He felt an uncontrollable passion for this girl.* || **4.** [Construcción]. *Unauthorized, illegal.* || **5.** [Camping, construcción, carteles]. *Unauthorized, illegal.* ~Para controlar la colocación SALVAJE de carteles. *To control illegal bill posting.* ⇨SAVAGE

SALVAR[1]. *v.* Compensar. *To compensate.* ~Su simpatía lo SALVA todo. *Her kindness makes up for everything.* || **2.** Superar (un obstáculo). *To clear.* ~El caballo SALVÓ el obstáculo saltando por encima. *The horse cleared the hurdle.* || **3.** [Dificultad]. *To get round, overcome.* || **4.** Recorrer (distancia). *To cover.* ~SALVAMOS la distancia en menos de dos días. *We covered the distance in less than two days.* || **5.** Atravesar (barrera, línea, montañas, ríos). *To cross.* || **6.** Exceptuar. *To exclude, except.* ~SALVANDO algunos errores. *Except a few mistakes.* || **7.** [Arroyo]. *To jump over, clear, jump across.* ~SALVAR un arroyo. *To jump over a stream.* || **8.** [Árbol, edificio). *To rise above.* || **9.** [Nivel del agua]. *To reach, rise as high as.* ~El agua SALVABA el peldaño más alto. *The water came up to the topmost step.* || **10.** [Puente]. *To cross, span.* ~El puente SALVA el río. *The bridge spans the river.* || **11.** [Barco]. *To salvage.* ⇨SAVE

SALVARSE[2]. *vr.* Sobrevivir. *To survive, come out alive, escape.* ~Sólo se SALVARON tres personas. *Only three people got out (escaped) alive, only three people survived.* || **2.** Evitar. *To get out (of something), to avoid (doing something).* ~Se SALVÓ de hacer el servicio militar. *He got out of doing military service.* ⇨SAVE

SANIDAD. *sf.* Calidad de sano. *Health, healthiness.* ~Ministerio de SANIDAD. *Ministry of Health.* ~Medidas de sanidad. Health measures. || **2.** [Aguas residuales]. *Sanitation.* ⇨SANITY

SANO. *adj.* Bien de salud. *Healthy.* ~El niño creció SANO y fuerte. *The child grew up healthy and strong.* ~Tiene dientes SANOS, porque se los cuida. *He has healthy teeth because he takes good care of them.* || **2.** Saludable. *Healthful.* ~Comida SANA. *Wholesome food.* ~Hacer deportes es muy SANO. *Playing sports is very good for your health.* || **3.** [En sentido moral: ambiente, vida, humor, lecturas] *Wholesome.* ~Se divierten de una manera muy SANA. *They just have good clean fun.* ~Es una filosofía SANA. *It's a sound (sensible) philosophy.* ~Se alojó en casa de una familia de SANAS costumbres. *He stayed at the house of a family with a wholesome way of life.* || **4.** [Objeto]. *Intact, unbroken.* ~No ha quedado plato SANO en toda la casa. *There wasn't a plate left unbroken in the house.* ~Esa silla no es muy SANA. *That chair is not in too good a condition.* ~Guardó el plátano SANO y tiro los otros. *He kept the good banana and threw away the others.* || **5.** [Doctrina, enseñanza]. *Sound.* || **6.** [Deseo]. *Earnest, sincere.* || **7.** [Objetivo]. *Worthy.* || **8.** •SANO y salvo. *Safe and sound.* || **9.** •Cortar por lo SANO. *To take drastic action.* ⇨SANE

SAQUEAR [SACK]. *v.* [Casas, tiendas]. *To loot.* ~Los soldados SAQUEARON la casa del alcalde. *The soldiers looted the mayor's home.*

SATISFACER. *v.* [Cantidad, cuota]. *To pay.* || **2.** [Deuda]. *To settle, pay off.* ~Ha SATISFECHO su deuda y ya no nos debe nada. *He has settled his debt and no longer owes us anything.* || **3.** [Letra de cambio]. *To honor.* || **4.** [Gastos, requisitos, exigencia]. *To meet.* ~El candidato SATISFACE todos los requisitos. *The candidate meets all the requirements.* || **5.** [Pérdida, daño, ofensa, agravio]. *To make good.* ~¿Ahora quién va a SATISFACERME de todo este destrozo. *Let me ask you, who is going to make good all this damage?* || **6.** [Demanda]. *To accede to.* || **7.** Convencer. *To convince.* ~No me SATISFACE la excusa que has dado para no ayudarme. *Your excuse for not helping me doesn't convince me at all.* || **8.** Premiar (por una acción). *To reward.* ~Le ayudé en su trabajo y quiso SATISFACERME. *He wanted to reward me for helping him to do his work.* || **9.** Aclarar (pregunta, duda, explicación). *To clear up, clarify.* ~Dime que parte de la explicación no ha quedado clara y SATISFACERÉ tu pregunta. *Let me know what part of my explanation you didn't understand and I'll clear it up for you.* || **10.** Complacer. *To please, gratify.* ~Me SATISFACE ver que han hecho las paces. *I'm pleased (gratified) to see that you have made up.* || **11.** [Deseo, aspiración]. *To fulfill.* ~Ha SATISFECHO el sueño de su vida. *He fulfilled his life's dream.* || **12.** [Hambre]. *To appease.* ~Con toda esta comida he SATISFECHO mi hambre. *With all this food I've appeased my hunger.* ⇨SATISFY

SECUESTRAR [SEQUESTER]. *v.* [Personas]. *To kidnap, abduct.* ~SECUESTRARON a su hija y le pidieron dinero para su rescate. *They kidnapped his daughter and demanded money as a condition for her release.* ‖ **2.** [Aviones]. *To hijack.* ~Los terroristas SECUESTRARON el avión y exigieron la dimisión del presidente. *The terrorists hijacked the plane and demanded that the primer minister resign.* ‖ **3.** JUR [Artículos, bienes]. *To confiscate, seize.* ~Les fueron SECUESTRADAS todas sus posesiones por orden del juez. *The judge ordered all their assets confiscated.* ‖ **4.** [Periódico, revista]. *To seize.* ~Los alumnos protestaron porque el rector de la universidad SECUESTRÓ la revista que ellos editaban. *There's was a student protest against the university president for seizing the school magazine.*

SECUESTRO [Act of SEQUESTERING]. *sm.* [De personas]. *Kidnapping, abduction.* ‖ **2.** [De un avión]. *Hijacking.* ~El avión venía de Madrid, pero sufrió un SECUESTRO aéreo. *The plane originated in Madrid but was hijacked on the way.* ‖ **3.** [De artículos, bienes). *Seizure, confiscation.* ‖ **4.** [De una revista, periódico]. *Seizure.*

SECULAR. *adj.* Antiquísimo. *Ancient, age-old, centuries-old.* ~Un prejuicio SECULAR. *An age-old prejudice.* ‖ **2.** Que dura cien años. *Century-old.* ~Árbol SECULAR. *Century-old tree.* ⇨SECULAR

SEGURIDAD [SECURITY]. *sf.* [Física]. *Safety.* ~La SEGURIDAD en la carretera depende del estado de la calzada. *Road safety depends upon the state of the road surface.* ~Como medida de SEGURIDAD, mantengan los cinturones abrochados. *As a safety precaution please keep your seatbelts fastened.* ~Por razones de SEGURIDAD, no se permite fumar. *For safety reasons, smoking is not permitted.* ‖ **2.** Confianza. *Confidence.* ~Hablar con SEGURIDAD. *To speak with confidence.* ~Seguridad en si mismo. *Self-confidence.* ‖ **3.** Certeza, certidumbre. *Sureness, certainty.* ~En la SEGURIDAD de su victoria. *In the certainty of winning, being sure of winning.* ~No lo sabemos con SEGURIDAD. *We don't know for sure.* ~No te lo puedo decir con

SEGURIDAD. *I can't tell you with any degree of certainty.* ‖ **4.** Fiabilidad. *Reliability, trustworthiness.* ~La SEGURIDAD del frenado. *The reliability of the brakes.* ‖ **5.** Garantía. *Assurance, guarantee.* ~No me dio ninguna SEGURIDAD de tenerlo para mañana. *He didn't give me any assurance that it would be ready for tomorrow.* ~Me ha dado SEGURIDADES de que cumplirá lo que pone en el contrato. *He assured me that he would meet the conditions of the contract.*

SENTIMIENTO. *sm.* Emoción. *Feelings.* ~Los SENTIMIENTOS de culpa. *Feelings of guilt.* ~Es una persona de muy buenos SENTIMIENTOS. *She's a very feeling (caring) person.* ~Canta con mucho SENTIMIENTO. *He sings with a lot of feeling.* ‖ **2.** Pesar. *Sorrow, grief.* ~Le acompaño en el SENTIMIENTO. *My deepest sympathy.* ~Con mi mayor SENTIMIENTO. *With my deepest regret.* ‖ **3.** Sentido. *Sense.* ~Sentimiento del deber. *Sense of duty.* ⇨SENTIMENT

SEÑAL [SIGNAL, SIGN]. *sm.* Marca, seña. *Mark.* ~Pon una SEÑAL en la página para saber por dónde vas. *Mark the page so you know where you're at.* ‖ **2.** Vestigio. *Trace.* ~Lo hicieron sin dejar SEÑAL. *They did it without leaving a trace.* ‖ **3.** [Cicatriz]. *Scar, mark.* ~El cuerpo no presentaba SEÑALES de violencia. *There were no marks on the body which might point to the use of violence.* ‖ **4.** [Teléfono]. *Tone.* ~Descuelgue y espere la SEÑAL para marcar. *Lift the receiver and wait for the tone.* ~Señal de comunicar. *Busy signal.* ~Señal de llamada. *Dial tone.* ‖ **5.** Síntoma. *Symptom.* ‖ **6.** Indicio. *Token, indication.* ~Dar una SEÑAL de su talento. *To give an indication of one's talent.* ~En SEÑAL de. *As a token of (como muestra de), as proof of (como prueba de).* ‖ **7.** [Depósito]. *Deposit, token payment, pledge.* ~Dejar una SEÑAL. *To leave a deposit.* ‖ **8.** [En animal]. *Mark, marking, brand.* ‖ **9.** [Geografía]. *Landmark.* ‖ **10.** [En un libro]. *Bookmark.* ‖ **11.** Rastro, huella. *Trace, track.* ‖ **12.** Recordatorio. *Reminder.* ‖ **13.** [De distinción]. *Mark.*

SENSIBLE. *adj.* [Temperamento]. *Sensitive.* ~Es tan SENSIBLE que no se le puede decir nada sin que se ofenda. *He's so sensitive that he gets offended at anything you say.* ‖ **2.** [Aparato]. *Sensitive.* Es muy SENSIBLE a los cambios de temperatura. *It's very sensitive to changes in temperature.* ‖ **3.** Delicado (piel). *Sensitive.* Piel SENSIBLE. *Sensitive skin.* ‖ **4.** Perceptible. *Perceptible.* ‖ **5.** Lamentable. *Regrettable.* ~Lamentamos tan SENSIBLE pérdida. *We regret such a sad loss.* ‖ **6.** [Que duele todavía]. *Tender, sensitive, sore.* ‖ **7.** Considerable. *Considerable, sizable.* ~Una SENSIBLE mejoría. *A marked improvement.* ~Un SENSIBLE aumento en el precio del petróleo. *A considerable increase in the price of oil.* ~La sequía ha ocasionado SENSIBLES pérdidas. *The drought has caused significant losses.* ⇨SENSIBLE

SENTENCIA. *sf.* Aforismo. *Maxim, saying.* ⇨SENTENCE

SEPARACIÓN [SEPARATION]. *sf.* División. *Division.* ~El río sirve de SEPARACIÓN entre las dos fincas. *The river marks the division between the two estates.* ~La SEPARACIÓN de palabras por sílabas. *The division of words into syllables.* ‖ **2.** Distancia, espacio. *Gap, distance, space.* ~Deja una SEPARACIÓN conveniente entre las sillas y la pared. *Leave an appropriate space between the chairs and the wall.* ‖ **3.** [De un cargo]. *Dismissal, removal.* ~La junta directiva decidió su SEPARACIÓN del cargo. *The board of directors decided to dismiss him from the post.* ‖ **4.** [De una pieza]. *Removal.*

SEPARAR. *v.* Despegar. *To detach, remove, take off.* ~No SEPARE la etiqueta antes de rellenarla. *Do not remove (detach) the label before filling it in.* ‖ **2.** Guardar, reservar. *To set aside.* ~He SEPARADO un poco de comida para tí. *I've put aside some food for you.* ~SEPARA una tajada de sandía para mí. *Put a slice of watermelon aside for me.* ~He pedido al panadero que me SEPARE dos barras de pan. *I've asked the baker to set aside two loaves of bread for me.* ‖ **3.** Apartar (una cosa de otra). *To move away.* ~SEPARA la silla de la pared. *Move the chair away from the wall.* ‖ **4.** Destituir (de un puesto). *To remove, dismiss.* ~El secretario fue SEPARADO de su

puesto. *The secretary was removed from his post.* ‖ **5.** [Palabras, sílabas]. *To divide, break up, split.* ~Las consonantes dobles no se SEPARAN en español. *In Spanish, double consonants should not be split up (divided).* ‖ **6.** [Conexión]. *To sever, cut.* ‖ **7.** [Cartas, fichas] *To sort (out).* ~SEPARA las fichas por colores. *Sort out the chips by color.* ‖ **8.** [Pieza]. *To remove, detach.* ‖ **9.** [Del servicio militar]. *To discharge.* ‖ **10.** Tener apartado o alejado. *To keep away.* ~Su trabajo lo SEPARA de su familia. *His work keeps him away from his family.* ~No se le puede SEPARAR de sus libros. *You can't keep him away from his books.* ‖ **11.** •Bajo las piernas SEPARADAS de Gulliver pasó todo el pueblo. *The whole town passed between Gulliver's open legs.* ⇨SEPARATE

SERENO [SERENE]. *adj.* [Persona].*Calm.* ~Se mantuvo SERENO a pesar de todos los problemas. *He kept calm in spite of all the problems.* ‖ **2.** [Ambiente]. *Peaceful.* ~El ambiente en la oficina está muy SERENO ahora. *The atmosphere in the office is very peaceful now.* ‖ **3.** [Cielo]. *Clear.* ~Hace una mañana SERENA, perfecta para pasear. *It's a clear morning, perfect to take a stroll.* ‖ **4.** [Tiempo]. *Fine, good, beautiful.* ~Era un día SERENO y el sol brillaba en lo alto del cielo. *It was a beautiful day and high in the sky the sun was shining.* ‖ **5.** [Tarde]. *Still.* ‖ **6.** [Mar]. *Calm, tranquil.* ~El lago estaba SERENO. *The waters of the lake were still (placid).* ‖ **7.** Que no está borracho. *Sober.* ~Si no estás SERENO, no conduzcas. *Don't drive if you're not sober.*

SERIO. *adj.* Formal. *Reliable, dependable, responsible.* ~Es una casa SERIA. *It's a dependable firm.* ~Un empleado SERIO y trabajador. *A reliable, hard-working employee.* ‖ **2.** [Color]. *Sober.* ‖ **3.** [Traje]. *Formal.* ‖ **4.** Honrado. *Honest, upright.* ‖ **5.** Decente. *Proper.* ‖ **6.** •Como no obedezcas voy a tener que ponerme SERIO contigo. *If you don't do as I say, I'm going to get annoyed with you.* ⇨SERIOUS

SERVICIO. *sm.* Empleados domésticos. *Servants, domestic help (empleo no fijo).*

~Sólo hablan de los problemas del SERVICIO. *All they talk about is the problem of having servants.* ~Se quedaron sin SERVICIO. *They were left without any domestic help.* ~Un piso de cuatro habitaciones y SERVICIO. *A four-room apartment with servant's quarters.* || **2.** Juego, conjunto. *Set.* ~SERVICIO de té. *Tea set.* ~Este juego no tiene SERVICIO de pescado. *There are no fish knives in this set.* || **3.** Baño. *Restroom.* ¿Los SERVICIOS, por favor? *Can you tell me where the restroom is?* ~El camarero me dijo que el SERVICIO de señoras estaba al fondo del pasillo. *The waiter told me that the ladies' room was at the end of the hall.* || **4.** [De policia]. *Job, case, inquiry.* || **5.** [De una deuda]. *Servicing.* || **6.** [En un hospital, empresa]. *Department.* ~SERVICIO de urgencias. *Emergency department.* ~Es jefe del SERVICIO de cirugía. *He's the chief surgeon.* ~El SERVICIO de limpieza en el supermercado es muy eficaz. *The supermarket cleaning department is very efficient.* || **7.** [En ténis]. *Serve.* ~Tiene que mejorar su SERVICIO. *She needs to improve her serve.* ⇨SERVICE

SERVIR[1]. *v.* Prestar ayuda. *To help.* ~¿En qué le puedo SERVIR? *What can I do for you, how may I help you?* ~Para SERVIRLE. *At your service.* || **2.** Suministrar. *To supply with.* ~Le SERVIREMOS la mercancía lo antes posible. *We shall deliver your merchandise as soon as possible.* || **3.** Trabajar de criado. *To be a servant.* ~Trata mal a los que le SIRVEN. *He treats his servants very badly.* || **4.** Valer. *To be useful, suitable.* ~Tu consejo me SIRVIÓ de mucho. *Your advice was very useful to me.* ~De nada SIRVE hablar. *Talking is useless.* Mi paraguas no SIRVE. *My umbrella is no good.* ~Para lo que me va a SERVIR. *For all the good it will do me.* ~No creo que SIRVA para este trabajo. *I don't think he's suitable for this job.* || **5.** [Pedido]. *To attend to, fill, process.* ~SERVIREMOS el pedido a la mayor brevedad. *We'll process your order as soon as possible.* || **6.** [Libro en biblioteca]. *Issue.* ~El libro está SERVIDO. *The book is out, the book is in use.* || **7.** [Programa de TV]. *To show, put on, present.* || **8.** [Cargo]. *To hold, fill.* || **9.** [Responsabilidad]. *To carry out.* ||

10. [Cañón]. *To man.* || **11.** [Máquina]. *To tend, mind, man.* || **12.** [Cartas]. *To follow suit.* || **13.** Actuar de. *To act as (interpreter, go-between).* || **14.** Estar empleada una persona. *To be employed.* ~SIRVE en la embajada española en París. *She works at the Spanish embassy in Paris.* || **15.** Usar. *To use.* ~Este papel me SIRVE de pantalla. *I use this paper as a screen.* ~Las espinas SIRVEN de alfileres. *Thorns can be used as needles.* || **16.** •SERVIR de estorbo. *To get in the way.* Este piano sólo SIRVE de estorbo. *This piano only gets in the way.* || **17.** •No SERVIR (persona). *To be useless.* ~Yo no SIRVO para eso. *I'm useless at that.* ⇨SERVE

SERVIRSE[2]. *vr.* [Comida]. *To help oneself.* ~SÍRVETE tú mismo. *Help yourself.* ~Se SIRVIÓ patatas. *He helped himself to potatoes.* || **2.** [Mandato atenuado]. *To be kind enough to.* ~SÍRVASE comunicarnos su decisión. *Please inform us of your decision.* ~SÍRVASE sentarse. *Please take a seat.* ~Si la señora se SIRVE pasar por aquí. *If madam would care to come this way.* ~SÍRVASE darme su dirección. *Could you give me your address, please?* || **3.** Emplear. *To use.* ~Aprendieron a SERVIRSE del tenedor y el cuchillo. *They learned to use a fork and a knife.* || **5.** Abusar. *To use, make use of.* Se han SERVIDO de tí. *You have been taken advantage of.* ⇨SERVE

SESIÓN [SESSION]. *sf.* Reunión (Consejo, asamblea, corporación). *Meeting.* ~A esta SESIÓN del Congreso han asistido casí todos los diputados. *Most representatives attended this meeting of the Congress.* || **2.** [De fotografía, pintura]. *Sitting.* || **3.** [De poesía]. *Reading.* || **4.** [De espiritismo]. *Séance.* || **5.** [De cine, performance]. *Show, performance.* ~Los actores de teatro dicen que es cansador representar dos SESIONES diarias. *The players complain that performing twice a day is tiring.* ~SESIÓN continua. *Continuous performance.* ~SESIÓN de noche. *Late show.* ~SESIÓN de tarde. *Matinée.*

SEVERO. *adj.* Riguroso (padre, profesor). *Strict.* ~Es un maestro SEVERO con los alumnos. He's very strict with his students. || **2.** [Régimen]. *Strict.* ~Sigue un régimen muy

SEVERO. *He's on a very strict diet.* ‖ **3.** [Castigo]. *Harsh, severe.* ~Su padre le impuso un SEVERO castigo por haberle mentido. *His father punished him harshly for having lied to him.* ‖ **4.** [Estilo]. *Stark, severe.* ‖ **5.** [Condiciones]. *Stringent, harsh.* ‖ **6.** [Frío]. *Bitter.* ‖ **7.** [Cara, expresión, apariencia]. *Stern, grim.* La SEVERA fachada del monasterio. *The stern facade of the monastery.* ‖ **8.** •Ser SEVERO con alguien. *To be hard on somebody, to treat somebody harshly.* ⇨SEVERE

SIGNIFICAR. *v.* Querer decir (palabra, símbolo). *To mean.* ~Busca en el diccionario lo que SIGNIFICA esta palabra. *Look this word up in the dictionary (to see what it means).* ~La luz roja SIGNIFICA peligro. *The red light means danger.* ~Cuando se enciende esta luz, SIGNIFICA que hay que apagar el aparato. *When this light goes on it means you have to shut off the machine.* ‖ **2.** Suponer, representar. *To mean, represent, involve.* ~SIGNIFICA una mejoría del servicio. *It means (represents) an improvement in the service.* ~La tarea más simple SIGNIFICA un gran esfuerzo. *The simplest of tasks involve a great deal of effort.* ~Para mí no comer carne no SIGNIFICA ningún sacrificio. *I don't consider it a sacrifice not to eat meat.* ‖ **3.** Valer, importar. *To mean.* ¿Es que yo no SIGNIFICO nada para tí? *Don't I mean anything to you?* ~Tu opinión SIGNIFICA mucho para mí. *Your opinion means a lot to me.* ‖ **4.** [Condolencias]. *To express.* ‖ **5.** Importancia. *To stress.* ‖ **6.** [Opinion]. *To state, make clear.* ‖ **7.** Hacer presente. *To express, make known.* SIGNIFICAR a uno sus intenciones. *To make one's intentions known to someone.* ~En varias ocasiones ya SIGNIFIQUÉ mi oposición a esta norma. *I've already expressed on various occasions my opposition to this regulation.* ⇨SIGNIFY

SILENCIOSO. *adj.* [Persona]. *Quiet.* ~Es un chico muy SILENCIOSO, no habla mucho. *He's a quiet child, he seldoms speaks.* ‖ **2.** [Calle, barrio, casa]. *Quiet.* ~Una casa SILENCIOSA. *A quiet house.* ⇨SILENT

SIMPATÍA. *sf.* Agrado, cariño. *Liking, affection, fondness.* ~Ganarse la SIMPATÍA de

todos. *To win everyone's affection.* ~Le tengo mucha SIMPATÍA. *I'm very fond of him.* ~No le tengo mucha SIMPATÍA a José. *I don't really like José.* ‖ **2.** [De ambiente]. *Friendliness, warmth, congeniality.* ‖ **3.** Encanto (persona, lugar). *Charm, attractiveness, likeableness.* ~Pronto los conquistó a todos con su SIMPATÍA. *She soon won them all over with her warm and friendly personality.* ~La famosa SIMPATÍA andaluza. *The well-known Andalusian charm.* ‖ **4.** •SIMPATÍAS y antipatías. *Likes and dislikes.* ⇨SYMPATHY

SIMPATIZAR. *v.* Congeniar. *To get on (well together).* ~SIMPATIZARON al instante. *They hit it off right from the start.* ⇨SYMPATHIZE

SIMPLE. *adj.* Que no es inteligente. *Simple-minded.* ~Es tan SIMPLE que todos lo engañan. *He's so simple-minded that he gets taken in easily.* ‖ **2.** No importante. *Mere, ordinary, just.* ~Un SIMPLE soldado. *An ordinary soldier.* ~Somos SIMPLES aficionados. *We're just amateurs.* ‖ **3.** Mero. *Just, mere, sheer.* ~Es una SIMPLE formula. *It's a mere formality.* ~Por SIMPLE descuido. *Through sheer carelessness.* ~Con una SIMPLE palabra. *With just one word.* ‖ **4.** Solo. *Single.* Una SIMPLE capa de pintura. *A single coat of paint.* ⇨SIMPLE

SIMPLICIDAD. *sf.* Sinceridad. *Candor, frankness.* ~Habló con toda SIMPLICIDAD. *He spoke with complete candor, he spoke frankly.* ⇨SIMPLICITY

SIMULAR [SIMULATE]. *v.* [Sentimiento]. *To feign.* ~SIMULÓ tristeza. *She feigned sadness, she pretended to be sad.* ‖ **2.** [Accidente]. *To fake, rig.*

SINDICATO. *sm.* Agrupación de trabajadores. *Union, trade union.* ~Los SINDICATOS de obreros surgen en el siglo diecinueve a partir de la revolución industrial. *Trade unions began in the nineteenth century with the industrial revolution.* ⇨SYNDICATE

SINGULAR [SINGULAR]. *adj.* Excepcional. *Exceptional, unique, outstanding.* ~La admiro porque es una mujer SINGULAR, inteligente y culta. *I admire her because she's a remarkable, intelligent and very educated person.* ‖ **2.** Raro. *Peculiar, odd.*

~Lo dijo en un tonillo muy SINGULAR. *He said it in a very peculiar (odd, funny) way.* Sherlock Holmes era un detective SINGULAR. *Sherlock Holmes was an odd sort of detective.*

SOBRÍO. *adj.* [Persona]. *Moderate, restrained.* ~Es una persona SOBRÍA en el comer y en el beber. *He eats and drinks moderately.* || **2.** [Estilo]. *Concise.* || **3.** [Color]. *Quiet.* || **4.** [Moda, aspecto]. *Plain, sober.* ~Viste de forma SOBRÍA y elegante. *He dresses plainly but elegantly.* || **5.** [Comida]. *Frugal.* ~Una cena SOBRÍA asegura una buena digestión y un sueño tranquillo. *A frugal dinner guarantees good digestion and sound sleep.* || **6.** [Comida]. *Light.* || **7.** •SOBRÍO en la bebida. *Temperate in one's drinking habits.* ⇨SOBER

SOFOCACIÓN. *sf.* [Rubor]. *Blushing.* || **2.** [De un incendio]. *Extinction.* Las tareas de SOFOCACIÓN del incendio duraron toda la noche. *The task of extinguishing the fire took all night.* || **3.** [De una rebelión]. *Suppression.* ⇨SUFFOCATION

SOFOCAR. *v.* [Incendio]. *Extinguish, put out.* ~Los bomberos SOFOCARON rápidamente el incendio. *The firemen rapidly put out the fire.* || **2.** [Rebelión, motín, revolución]. *To put down, suppress, crush, stiffle.* ~El gobierno mandó tropas para SOFOCAR la rebelión. *Government troops were sent to suppress the uprising.* || **3.** Avergonzar. *To make blush.* || **4.** [Epidemia]. *To stop.* || **5.** Azorar. *To embarrass someone.* ⇨SUFFOCATE

SOFOCARSE. *vr.* Ruborizarse. *To blush.* ~Se SOFOCÓ cuando le insultaron de este modo en público. *When they insulted him in front of everyone, he blushed.* || **2.** Enfadarse. *To get angry or upset.* ~No vale la pena de que te SOFOQUES. *It's not worth upsetting yourself about it.* || **3.** Jadear. *To get out of breath (al hacer un esfuerzo).* || **4.** Atragantarse. *To choke.* ⇨SUFFOCATE

SOLICITAR. *v.* Pedir. *Request.* ~SOLICITAR una entrevista. *To request an interview.* ~A los interesados SOLICITAMOS el envío de historial personal. *Applicants are requested to send a full resumé.* ~Pueden SOLICITAR catálogos por teléfono. *You can request catalogues by telephone.* || **2.** [Persona]. *To chase after, be in demand.* ~Es una persona muy SOLICITADA. *He's much in demand.* || **3.** [Mujer]. *To woo, court.* ~A esa chica la SOLICITAN todos sus compañeros de curso. *Everyone in class is after her.* || **4.** [Aprobación]. *To seek.* || **5.** [Puesto, trabajo]. *To apply for.* ~Con tu preparación, si SOLICITAS el trabajo, lo consigues. *With you training (experience), if you apply for the job, you'll get it.* || **6.** [Votos]. *To canvass.* ⇨SOLICIT

SOLIDEZ [SOLIDITY]. *sf.* Firmeza. *Firmness.* ~El terremoto no deribó la casa gracias a la SOLIDEZ de los cimientos. *The earthquake did not knock down the building because of the firmness of its foundation.* || **2.** [De principios, argumentos]. *Soundness.* ~Estoy seguro de las SOLIDEZ de sus creencias. *I'm convinced of the soundness of his beliefs.* || **3.** [De color]. *Fastness.* || **4.** [De una empresa]. *Soundness.* || **5.** [De una relación, institución]. *Strength.* ~El fracaso del golpe de estado demostró la SOLIDEZ de las instituciones democráticas. *The failed attempt to overthrow the government attests to the strength of the democratic system.*

SOMBRÍO. *adj.* [Lugar]. *Dark.* ~El cuarto es pequeño, frío y SOMBRÍO. *The apartment is small, cold and dark.* || **2.** [Persona]. *Gloomy, sullen.* ~Tiene un carácter SOBRÍO. *He's a sullen person.* ~Su rostro tenía un aspecto SOMBRÍO. *There was a sullen look in his face.* || **3.** [Porvenir, perspectiva]. *Dismal.* ~Después de la bancarrota, pensó que le esperaba un SOMBRÍO porvenir. *When he went bankrupt, he couldn't help thinking that the future looked very dismal.* || **4.** Sombreado. *Shaded.* ~Siempre buscaba un lugar SOMBRÍO donde leer. *He always look for a place to read in the shade.* ⇨SOMBER

SOMETER. *v.* Dominar. *Subjugate, conquer.* ~Un puñado de hombres logró SOMETER a todo el país. *A handful of men managed to conquer the whole country.* ~Fue necesario usar la fuerza para SOMETERLOS. *They had to use force to subdue them.* || **2.** Subordinar. *Subordinate.* ~Quieren SOMETER nuestros intereses a los de una multinacional. *They are trying to subordinate our interests to those of a multinational.* || **3.** [A torturas, presiones]. *To subject.* Le SOMETIERON a un exhaustivo interrogatorio. *They subjected him to a thourough interrogation.* || **4.** [A un tratamiento, operación]. *To undergo.* ~Fue SOMETIDO a una intervención quirúrgica. *He underwent an operation.* ⇨SUBMIT

SOPORTAR. *v.* Aguantar, tolerar. *To put up with, stand, bear, endure.* ~No SOPORTO la lluvia. *I can't stand the rain.* ~No lo SOPORTÓ. *I can't stand him.* || **2.** [Presión]. *Withstand, resist.* || **3.** [Tormenta, huracán]. *To weather.* || **4.** [Dolor, enfermedad]. *To endure.* ~SOPORTA el dolor con resignación. *She endures the pain patiently.* ⇨SUPPORT

SORPRENDER [SURPRISE]. *v.* Coger desprevenido. *To catch in the act, catch unaware, to take by surprise.* SORPRENDIERON al ladrón. *They caught the burglar in the act.* Nos SORPRENDIÓ la lluvia. *We got caught in the rain.* || **2.** Descubrir. *To discover, find out.* ~SORPRENDIERON nuestro secreto. *They discovered our secret.* ~La policía SORPRENDIÓ la guarida de los ladrones. *The police discovered the thieve's hideout.* || **3.** Asombrar. *To amaze.* ~Me SORPRENDE su inteligencia. *Her intelligence amazes me.* || **4.** [Conversación]. *To overhear.* || **5.** [Escondrijo]. *To come across.* || **6.** [Mensaje]. *To intercept.* || **7.** Engañar. *To deceive, abuse.* ~SORPRENDER su buena fe. *To abuse one's good faith.*

SOSTENER. *v.* Mantener firme (una estructura). *To hold up, support.* SOSTENER con una viga. *To support (hold up) with a beam.* ~Columnas que SOSTIENEN la bóveda. *Columns that support a vault.* || **2.** [Carga, peso]. *To bear.* ~SOSTENÍA todo el peso del hombre en los hombros. *He bore the whole weight of the man on his shoulders.* || **3.** [Conversación, discusión, polémica, relación, reunión]. *To hold, carry on, have, be engaged in.* ~SOSTUVIERON una acalorada discusión. *They had a heated discussion.* ~No he SOSTENIDO nunca una relación duradera. *I've never had a lasting relationship.* ~La polémica que SOSTIENE con

Godoy. *The dispute that he and Godoy are engaged in.* || **4.** Mantener (en un estado). *To maintain, keep.* Su partido lo SOSTIENE en el poder. *His party keeps him in power.* ~Lo único que la SOSTIENE es la fuerza de voluntad. *What keeps her going is her sheer willpower.* || **5.** Aguantar (dificultades). *To endure, bear, put up with, stand.* ~SOSTENER una situación muy desagradable. *To tolerate a very disagreeable situation.* || **6.** [Afirmación, argumento]. *To support, back up.* ~No tienes pruebas para SOSTENER esa afirmación. *You don't have any proof to back up (support) that statement.* || **7.** Sustentar (una familia, los hijos). *To support, maintain, provide for.* ~SOSTIENE una familia numerosa y tiene que trabajar mucho. *He has a large family to support, so he has to work hard.* || **8.** Defender (teoría, punto de vista). *To uphold, defend, stand by, stick to.* || **9.** [Nota musical]. *To hold.* || **10.** [Acusación]. *To maintain.* || **11.** [Presión]. *To keep up.* || **12.** [Resistencia]. *To strengthen, boost, bolster up.* || **13.** [Gastos]. *To meet, defray.* || **14.** Opinar. *To hold.* ~Según sus investigaciones, SOSTIENE que hay vida en otros planetas. *Based on his research, he maintain that there's life on other planets.* ~Yo siempre he SOSTENIDO que ... *I have always maintained that ...* || **15.** Sujetar. *To hold.* ~No tengas miedo, yo te SOSTENGO. *Don't be afraid, I'm holding you.* || **16.** [Velocidad, precios, categoría]. *To maintain, keep up.* ⇨SUSTAIN

SUBSIDIO [SUBSIDY]. *sm.* [De enfermedad]. *Benefit.* || **2.** [De vejez). *Pension.* ~Todos los trabajadores esperaban un SUBSIDIO al jubilarse. *All the workers expected to receive a pension when they retired.* || **3.** [De desempleo]. *Compensation.* ~Está cobrando el SUBSIDIO de desempleo. *He getting unemployment compensation.* || **4.** [Familiar]. *Allowance.*

SUBURBIO. *sm.* Barrio pobre (on the outskirts of town). *Slums, slum quarters.* ~Al ganarse mejor la vida pudo cambiar de piso y abandonar el SUBURBIO donde vivía. *When he started to earn a better salary he moved away from the poor neighborhood where he lived.* ⇨SUBURB

SUBYUGAR [SUBJUGATE]. *v.* [Enemigo]. *To overpower.* || **2.** [Voluntad]. *To dominate, gain control over.* || **3.** Cautivar, fascinar. *To captivate, charm, enthrall.* || **4.** [Pasiones]. *To subdue, master.*

SUFICIENCIA [SUFFICIENCY]. *sf.* Aptitud. *Aptitude.* ~Prueba de SUFICIENCIA. *Aptitude test.* ~Demostrar su SUFICIENCIA. *To prove one's competence, show one's capabilities.* ~Ha demostrado su SUFICIENCIA para este trabajo. *He has shown his competence for this kind of work.* || **2.** Presunción, engreímiento, pedantería. *Smugness, complacency, self-importance, air of superiority.* ~Sonrió con SUFICIENCIA. *She smiled smugly (complacently).* ~Tener aire de SUFICIENCIA. *To look smug, to look cocksure.* ~Su aire de SUFICIENCIA le ha creado muchas enemistades. *Her cocksure attitude has won her many enemies.*

SUFRIR. *v.* Tener. *To have (an accident, heart attack), undergo (an operation), experience (problems, changes), sustain (a loss).* ~Parece que este plástico ha SUFRIDO cambios muy bruscos de temperatura. *It seems that this plastic has undergone abrupt changes of temperature.* || **2.** Aguantar, soportar. *To bear, put up with.* ~No puedo SUFRIR a Juan. *I can't stand John.* || **3.** Consentir. *To tolerate.* ~No SUFRIRÉ tus insultos. *I won't tolerate your insults.* || **4.** [Examen, prueba]. *To take, undergo.* || **5.** Sostener (peso, carga). *To hold up, support.* ~Los cimientos SUFREN el peso del edificio. *The foundation supports the building.* ⇨SUFFER

SUGESTIÓN. *sf.* Insinuación. *Hint.* || **2.** Estímulo. *Prompting, stimulus.* ~Las SUGESTIONES del corazón. *The promptings of the heart.* ~Un sitio de muchas SUGESTIONES. *A place rich in associations.* || **3.** Poder, influencia. *Hypnotic power, power to influence others.* ~Emanaba de él una fuerte SUGESTIÓN. *A strong hypnotic power flowed from him.* ~Tiene gran poder de SUGESTIÓN. *He's very persuasive.* || **4.** Imaginario. *Imaginary.* ~No estás enferma, es pura SUGESTIÓN. *You're not ill, it's all in your mind.* ⇨SUGGESTION

SUGESTIVO. *adj.* Fascinante. *Alluring, fascinating.* ~El tema de esta película es muy SUGESTIVO. *The theme of this movie is fascinating.* || **2.** Atractivo. *Attractive.* ~Tienen un plan muy SUGESTIVO para este fin de semana. *They have interesting (attractive) plans for this weekend.* || **3.** [Escote]. *Revealing.* || **4.** [Libro, idea]. *Stimulating.* ⇨SUGGESTIVE

SUMARIO. *sm.* [En lo penal]. *Indictment.* ~Abrir (instruir) un sumario. *To issue (present) an indictment, to institute legal proceedings.* || **2.** Juicio administrativo. *Disciplinary action.* || **3.** Indice. *Content, table of contents.* ~Busca en el SUMARIO si está aquí la aventura de los molinos. *Check the index to see if the adventure of the windmills is here.* ⇨SUMMARY

SUMERGIR[1] [SUBMERGE]. *v.* Hundir. *To sink, plunge.* ~Han SUMERGIDO el país en la miseria. *They have plunged the country into poverty.* || **2.** Hundir, meter de lleno, interesar hondamente. *To immerse.* ~El autor SUMERGE al lector en la vida rural. *The author immerses the reader in rural life.* || **3.** Agobiar. *To overwhelm.*

SUMERGIRSE[2] [SUBMERGE]. *vr.* [Submarino]. *To dive.* || **2.** Concentrarse, sumirse. *To immerse oneself.* ~Se SUMERGIÓ en un profundo sueño. *He sank into a deep sleep.* ~La novela nos SUMERGE en la vida de la sociedad medieval. *The novel immerses us into the life of medieval society.*

SUMISIÓN. *sf.* [Actitud]. *Submissiveness, docility.* ⇨SUBMISSION

SUPONER. *v.* Significar. *To mean.* El premio SUPONE mucho para mi. *The prize means a lot to me.* || **2.** Implicar, acarrear. *To entail, mean, require.* ~Eso va a SUPONER mucho trabajo para mi madre. *That will mean a lot of work for my mother.* ~El traslado le SUPONE muchos gastos. *The move involves a lot of expenses for him.* || **3.** Adivinar, imaginar. *To guess, imagine.* ~Me lo SUPONÍA. *I guessed that much.* ~¿Quién lo iba a SUPONER? *Who would have imagined it?* ~Le SUPONÍA más viejo. *I thought he was older.* || **4.** Atribuir. *To be credited with.* ~Se le SUPONE una gran antigüedad. *It is credited with great* *antiquity.* ~Se ve que el equipo no tenía tanta 'fuerza' como se le SUPONÍA. *It is clear that the team did not have the 'pull' it was credited with.* ⇨SUPPOSE

SUPRESIÓN. *sf.* [De dificultades]. *Elimination, removal.* || **2.** [De una ley, impuesto]. *Abolition.* ~Los ciudadanos pedían la SUPRESIÓN de ese impuesto. *The citizens asked that that tax be abolished.* || **3.** [De restricciones]. *Lifting.* || **4.** [De una palabra]. *Deletion.* ~Las SUPRESIONES que han efectuado en el texto lo han dejado ininteligible. *The deletetions made to the text left it unintelligible.* || **5.** [Voluntaria]. *Omission.* || **6.** [De un servicio]. *Withdrawal.* ⇨SUPPRESSION

SUPRIMIR. *v.* [Dificultades]. *To eliminate, remove.* || **2.** [Una ley, un impuesto]. *To abolish.* || **3.** [Restricciones]. *To lift.* || **4.** [Palabra, párrafo, capítulo]. *To delete, take or leave out.* ~SUPRIMIÓ un párrafo entero. *She cut out, deleted a whole paragraph.* || **5.** [Libro]. *To ban.* || **6.** [Servicio]. *To withdraw.* ~Se SUPRIMIÓ la salida de las 9h. *The 9 o'clock service was withdrawn.* || **7.** Eliminar (gastos, puestos). *To eliminate, cut out.* ~Debemos SUPRIMIR estos gastos supérfluos. *We must eliminate (cut out) these unnecessary expenses.* ~Los problemas económicos le obligaron a SUPRIMIR ciertos lujos. *The economic situation forced her to forego certain luxuries.* ~La empresa sigue SUPRIMIENDO puestos de trabajo. *The company continues to eliminate jobs.* || **8.** Parar, suspender. *To stop, suspend.* Le SUPRIMIERON la medicación. *They stopped his medication.* ~Queda SUPRIMIDA la parada en El Colorado. *The train no longer stops at El Colorado.* || **9.** Excluir. *To leave out, skip.* ~¿Por qué no le SUPRIMES el ajo? *Why don't you leave out the garlic?* || **10.** Omitir. *Omit, skip.* Suprima los detalles. *Skip the details.* || **11.** [Informática]. *To delete.* ⇨SUPPRESS

SUPUESTO [SUPPOSED]. *adj.* Pseudo. *So-called, self-styled, would-be.* ~El SUPUESTO presidente. *The self-styled president.* ~El SUPUESTO electricista resultó ser un ladrón. *The so-called electrician proved to be a thief.* || **2.** Falso. *Assumed, false.* ~Nombre SUPUESTO. *Assumed name.* || **3.** Creencia.

Supposition, assumption. || **4.** Hipótesis. *Hypothesis.* || **5.** Según se afirma. *Alleged.* || **6.** Imaginario. *Imaginary.* ~Su SUPUESTA enfermedad. *His imaginary illness.* || **7.** *sm.* Datos, información. *Data, information.* ~Carecemos de los SUPUESTOS más elementales. *We are lacking the most elementary data.*

SUSCEPTIBLE. *adj.* Sensible. *Oversensitive, touchy.* ~Es muy SUSCEPTIBLE a las críticas. *He's very sensitive to criticism.* || **2.** Susceptible de. (I) Capaz. *Capable of.* ~Es SUSCEPTIBLE a la mejora. *It can be improved, there's room for improvement.* ~Órganos SUSCEPTIBLES de ser transplantados. *Organs which can be transplanted,* (II). Tendente. *Liable to.* ~Grupos SUSCEPTIBLES de cometer actos de terrorismo. *Groups liable of committing terrorist acts.* ⇨SUSCEPTIBLE

SUSCRIBIR. *v.* [Contrato, petición, tratado, convenio]. *To sign.* ~El escrito fue SUSCRITO por los que participaron en el acuerdo. *The document was signed by those who took part in the agreement.* || **2.** [Promesa]. *To make, agree to, ratify.* || **3.** [Seguro]. *To underwrite.* || **4.** [Acciones]. *To take out an option on.* || **5.** Estar de acuerdo. *To agree with.* ~Tiene un punto de vista muy sensato y SUSCRIBO sus opiniones. *He has a very sensible point of view and I agree with his views.* || **6.** •El que SUSCRIBE. *The undersigned.* ⇨SUBSCRIBE

SUSPENDER. *v.* Colgar. *To hang, hang up.* ~Quedó SUSPENDIDO de una rama. *He was left hanging from a branch.* || **2.** Aplazar (Trabajo, acontecimiento, viaje). *To delay, postpone, put off.* ~Han SUSPENDIDO el trabajo hasta nueva orden. *They have delayed work until new orders.* ~SUSPENDER hasta más tarde. *To put off till later.* || **3.** [Reunión, sesión]. *To adjourn.* || **4.** [Servicios]. *To discontinue.* ~Queda SUSPENDIDO el servicio de autobuses hasta nuevo aviso. *Bus service has been discontinued until further notice.* || **5.** [Exam]. *To fail.* ~Me han SUSPENDIDO. *I've failed (the exam).* || **6.** [Proceso]. *To interrupt.* || **7.** Pasmar. *To astound, astonish.* ⇨SUSPEND

SUTIL. *adj.* Delgado (hilo, hebra). *Thin,*

fine. || **2.** [Aroma]. *Delicate.* || **3.** [Color]. *Soft.* || **4.** [Brisa]. *Gentle.* || **5.** [Tela]. *Light, thin.* ~Una SUTIL gasa. *A thin gauze.* || **6.** Ingenioso. *Keen, sharp.* ~Es muy SUTIL, no hace falta que se lo expliques dos veces. *He's very sharp, you really don't need to explain it to him twice.* ⇨SUBTLE

T-Z

TABLETA. *sf.* Tabla pequeña. *Small board.* || **2.** [De chocolate]. *Bar.* ⇨TABLET

TARIFA. *sf.* Precio. *Price, rate.* ~TARIFA reducida. *Reduced rate, special deal.* ~TARIFA turística. *Tourist class rate.* ~TARIFA de agua. *Water charges.* ~TARIFA de anuncios. *Advertisement rate.* ~TARIFA de subscripción. *Subsription rate.* || **2.** [En transportes]. *Fare.* ~Los niños pagan una TARIFA reducida. *Children pay a lower fare.* || **3.** Cobro. *Charge, rate.* ¿Cuál es su TARIFA? *How much do your charge, what are your rates?* ~Cobra una TARIFA fija. *He charges a fixed rate.* ⇨TARIFF

TEMA [THEME]. *sm.* [Asunto, materia]. *Subject, topic.* ~¿No tienes otro tema de conversación? *Don't you ever talk about anything else?* ~Nos estamos alejando del tema. *We're getting off the subject.*

TEMBLAR, [TREMBLE]. *v.* [De frío]. *To shiver.* ~No podía dejar de TEMBLAR de frío. *He couldn't stop shivering from the cold.* || **2.** [Voz]. *To quiver.* ~Le TEMBLABA la voz. *His voice was quivering.* || **3.** [Con sacudidas]. *To shake.* ~Le TIEMBLAN las manos. *His hands are shaking.* || **4.** Estar asustado. *To shake with fear.* ~TIEMBLO ante el futuro. *I shudder when I think of the future.* ~El soldado TEMBLABA por su vida. *The soldier shook with fear.* || **5.** [Edificio, tierra]. *To shake.* ~Sus gritos hicieron TEMBLAR las paredes. *His screams made the walls shake.* ~Durante el terremoto todas las casas TEMBLABAN. *During the earthquake all the houses were shaking.*

TENSIÓN [TENSION]. *sf.* [De materiales]. *Stress.* || **2.** [De gases]. *Pressure.* || **3.** [De una persona]. *Stress, strain.* ~Está sometido a una gran TENSIÓN en el trabajo. *He's under* a lot of stress (strain) at work.

TÉRMINO. *sm.* Final. *End, conclusion.* ~Al TÉRMINO de la reunión. *At the end (conclusion) of the meeting.* ~Llevar a buen TÉRMINO las negociaciones. *To bring the negotiations to a successful conclusion.* ~Dio TÉRMINO a sus vacaciones. *He ended his vacations.* ⇨TERM

TIEMPO. *sm.* Clima. *Weather.* ~Lindo TIEMPO. *Fine weather.* || **2.** DEP [En un partido]. *Half.* ~Primer/segundo TIEMPO. *First/second half.* ⇨TIME

TIPO [TYPE]. *sm.* [Banco]. *Rate.* ~TIPO bancario. *Bank rate.* || **2.** [Persona]. *Fellow, guy, character.* ~TIPO raro. *Weirdo.* || **3.** [De hombre]. *Build, physique.* ~Tiene buen TIPO. *He's well built.* || **4.** [De mujer]. *Figure.* ~Tiene buen TIPO. *She has a nice figure.*

TÓPICO. *sm.* Lugar común. *Commonplace, cliché.* El TÓPICO de la chica guapa y tonta ya está pasado de modo. *The cliché about the dumb blond is no longer true.* ⇨TOPIC

TRANCE. *sm.* Ocasión crítica o difícil. *Ackward, situation, difficult moment, critical juncture.* ~Están pasando por un TRANCE difícil. *They're going through a bad time.* ~En un TRANCE de tan singular gravedad. *At such a critical juncture.* ~En tal TRANCE sólo se me ocurrió subirme a un árbol. *At that moment of peril my only thought was to climb a tree.* || **2.** [Ultimo, postrer, mortal, de muerte]. *Dying moments.* || **3.** •A todo TRANCE. *At all costs.* || **4.** •Estar en TRANCE de muerte. *To be on the point of death.* || **5.** •Estar en TRANCE de. *To be on the point of, to be in process of.* Estos lugares está en TRANCE de desaparecer. *These places are in the process of disappearing.* || **6.** •Puesto en tal

TRANCE. *Placed in such a situation.* ⇨TRANCE

TRATAR[1] [TREAT]. *v.* [Asunto, tema]. *To discuss.* ~Eso no se puede TRATAR delante de los niños. *We can't discuss this in front of the children.* ~Vamos a TRATAR primero los puntos de mayor urgencia. *Lets first deal with (discuss) the more pressing issues.* || **2.** Gestionar. *To handle, run.* || **3.** [Informática]. *To process.* || **4.** Calificar de una forma despectiva. Me TRATÓ de vago y irresponsable. *He called me lazy and irresponsible.* || **5.** Cuidar. *To take care of.* ~Te dejo las llaves del coche, pero TRÁTALO con cuidado. *I'm leaving you the keys to the car, but take good care of it.* || **6.** [Tener contacto, relaciones]. *To deal with.* ~Prefiero TRATAR directamente con el fabricante. *I Prefer to deal directly with the manufacturer.* || **7.** [Libro, película]. *To deal with, be about.* ~La conferencia TRATARÁ de medicina alternativa. *The lecture will deal with (be on the subject of) altenative medicine.* || **8.** •Tratar de (a una persona). *To address as.* ~Le TRATAN de 'su excelencia'. *They address him as 'his excellency'.* ~TRATAR a uno de tú. *To address someone as 'tú'.* || **9.** COM •TRATAR en. *To deal in.* || **10.** •TRATAR con. *To handle.* El ingeniero TRATA con máquinas. *Engineers handle machinery.*

TRATARSE[2]. *vr.* Relacionarse, tener contacto. *To mix, socialize, to be friendly with, associate with.* ~No me gusta la gente con la que se TRATA. *I don't like the people he associates with.* ~¿Tu te TRATAS con los López? *Are you friends of the López's.* || **2.** Ser acerca de. *To be about.* ~¿De qué se TRATA? *What is it all about?* || **3.** Ser cuestión de. *To be a question (matter) of.* ~Si se TRATA de dinero, te lo presto. *If it's only a matter of money, I'll lend it to you.* || **4.** Ser. *To be.* ~Se TRATA de la estrella del equipo. *We're talking about the star of the team.* ~TRATÁNDOSE de usted, no creo que haya problemas. *Since it's you (in your case) I don't think there will be any problems.*

TUTOR. *sm.* [law]. *Guardian.* ~Cuando murieron sus padres, su tío se convirtió en su TUTOR. *When his parents died, his uncle*

became his guardian. ~Consentimiento del padre o TUTOR. *Consent of parent or guardian.* || **2.** Protector. *Protector, guide.* La Virgen es nuestro TUTORA espiritual. *Virgen Mary is our spiritual guide.* || **3.** [De una planta]. *Stake, prop.* ⇨TUTOR

ÚLTIMO. *adj.* [En orden, tiempo]. *Last.* ~La ÚLTIMA casa a mano derecha. *The last house on the right.* ~El ÚLTIMO día del mes. *The last day of the month.* ~Los ÚLTIMOS años de su vida. *The last years of his life.* || **2.** [Más reciente]. *Latest, most recent.* ~¿Cuándo fue la ÚLTIMA vez que lo usaste? *When did you last use it?* ~Su ÚLTIMO libro es muy bueno. *His latest book is very good.* || **3.** [De dos]. *Latter.* ~Éste ÚLTIMO/éstos ULTIMOS. *The latter.* || **4.** [En el espacio]. *Furthest, most remote.* ~En el ÚLTIMO rincón del país. *In the furthest corner of the country.* || **5.** Más abajo. *Bottom, lowest.* || **6.** Más arriba. *Top, last.* ~Vive en el ÚLTIMO piso. *He live on the top floor.* || **7.** [Más atrás]. *Back, last.* ~Siempre se sienta en la ÚLTIMA fila. *He always sits in the back row.* || **8.** Definitivo. *Final.* ~Es mi ÚLTIMA propuesta. *That's my final offer.* || **9.** [Precio]. *Lowest, bottom.* ~Dígame lo ÚLTIMO, dígame el ÚLTIMO precio. *Tell me the lowest price.* || **10.** [Calidad]. *Finest, best, superior.* ⇨ULTIMATE

UNIR [UNITE]. *v.* Juntar (dos cosas). *To join.* ~UNIÓ los cables con cinta aislante. *He joined the wires with insulating tape.* || **2.** Combinar. *To combine.* ~Ha UNIDO dos estilos muy diferentes. *He has combined two very different styles.* || **3.** [Dos personas]. *Attach.* ~Están muy UNIDOS. *They're very attached to one another.* || **4.** Comunicar. *To link.* La nueva carretera UNE los dos pueblos. *The new roads link the two towns.* || **5.** [Compañías]. *To merge.* || **6.** [Recursos]. *To pool.*

URGIR. *v.* Ser urgente. *To be urgent, be pressing.* ~Me URGE tenerlo. *I need it urgently.* ~URGE encontrar una solución. *An urgent solution is required.* ⇨URGE

VACILAR [VACILATE]. *v.* [Al andar]. *To sway, stagger, wobble.* ~VACILÓ pero enseguida recuperó el equilibrio. *She staggered but she regained her balance*

immediately. ~VACILABA al andar, como si estuviese borracho. *He swayed from side to side as he walked, as if he were drunk.* || **2.** [Voz]. *To falter.* || **3.** [Luz]. *To flicker.* || **4.** FAM Bromear, tomar el pelo. *To tease, joke, kid, fool around.* || **5.** [Mueble]. *To wobble, be unsteady, rock, move, shake.* || **6.** [Memoria]. *To fail.* || **7.** [Fe, determinación]. *To waver.*

VARIAR [VARY]. *v.* Cambiar. *To change.* ~El pronóstico no ha VARIADO. *The forecast hasn't changed.* ~El viento ha VARIADO de dirección. *The wind has changed direction.* || **2.** Hacer distinto de como era antes. *To do differently.* ~No hacer más que VARIAR de opinión. *She's always changing her mind.* ~Ha decidido VARIAR su forma de vestir. *She's decided to dress differently.* || **3.** [Rumbo]. *To alter.* En medio camino VARÍAMOS de curso. *Half-way there we altered our course.* || **4.** [De posición]. *To change Around, switch about.* ~Si VARIAMOS la colocación de los muebles, el salón parecerá más grande. *If we change the furniture around, the living-room will seem larger.* || **5.** [Versión]. *To differ.* ~Su versión VARÍA del de su vecino. *His version differs from that of his neighbor's.*

VENTILAR [VENTILATE]. *v.* [Ropa, colchón]. *To air.* || **2.** [Opinión]. *To air.* || **3.** [Cuestión]. *To discuss, clear up, talk over, talk about.* ~Todos tienen oportunidades de VENTILAR sus frustraciones. *Everybody has a chance to talk about their frustrations.* || **4.** [Asunto privado]. *To make public, reveal.* ~No quiero VENTILAR mi vida privada delante de todo el mundo. *I don't want to discuss my private life in front of everybody.* ~Si yo te confío un secreto no es para que lo vayas VENTILANDO por ahí. *If I tell you a secret I don't want you to go spreading it around.*

VICIO. *sm.* Afición o gusto excesivo por algo. *Bad habit.* ~El único VICIO que tiene es el cigarrillo. *The only bad habit he has is smoking.* ~Tiene el VICIO de comerse las uñas. *He has the bad habit of biting his nails.* || **2.** Lo que aficiona o gusta de una forma excesiva. *Downfall, weak point.* ~Los bombones son mi VICIO. *Candies are my weak point.* ||

3. [De dicción]. *Problem.* ~Tiene VICIOS de dicción. *He has problems with his diction.* || **4.** Defecto, error. *Flaw, defect.* ~El contrato no es válido porque tiene VICIOS de forma. *The contract is not valid since it wasn't properly drawn.* ~La puerta ha cogido VICIO y ahora no encaja. *The door is warped and it won't close.*

VICIOSO. *adj.* [Persona]. *Depraved, perverted.* ~La gente VICIOSA que frecuenta esos antros. *The dissolute people who frequent those dives.* || **2.** [Cosa]. *Faulty, defective.* || **3.** BOT Frondoso. *Luxuriant, lush, thick.* || **4.** [Niño]. *Spoiled.* || **5.** Que tiene vicios. *Having bad habits.* ⇨VICIOUS

VILLANO. *sm.* Persona rústica. *Peasant.* ~El joven conde se distraía persiguiendo a las VILLANAS. *The young count would spend his time going after peasant girls.* ⇨VILLAIN.

VIOLENTO [VIOLENT]. *adj.* Embarazoso, incómodo. *Awkward, embarrassing.* ~Fue un momento un poco VIOLENTO. *It was an awkward moment.* ~Se sentía VIOLENTO en esa casa. *He felt ill at ease in that house.* ~Le resulta VIOLENTO hablar del tema. *She finds it embarrassing to talk about it.* ~¡Qué situación más VIOLENTA! *How embarrassing!* || **2.** [Postura]. *Unnatural, forced, crampted.* ~Su cuerpo estaba en una postura demasiado VIOLENTA para permanecer mucho tiempo quieta. *She too crampted in that position to be able to stay still much longer.* || **3.** [Acto]. *Forced, unnatural.* ~Me es muy VIOLENTO consentir en ello. *It goes against the grain with me to agree with it.* || **4.** [Sentido de un texto]. *Twisted, distorted.* ~Es una conclusión VIOLENTA que saca de su obra. *His interpretation of the work distorted.* || **5.** [Ejercicios]. *Heavy.* ~Evita hacer ejercicios VIOLENTOS hasta que estés completamente recuperado. *Avoid heavy exercises until you're completly recovered.*

VOTO [VOTE]. *sm.* [De castidad, pobreza]. *Vow.* ~Las monjas de este convento han hecho VOTO de pobreza. *The nuns in this convent are under a vow of poverty.* || **2.** [Deseo]. *Wish.* ~Hago VOTOS por su éxito. *I sincerely want him to succeed.* || **3.** Blasfemia. *Curse, oath.* || **4.** Palabrota. *Swearword.*

VULGAR. *adj.* Corriente, común. *Common.* ~ No es más que un VULGAR resfrío. *It's just a common cold.* ~Se las da de ejecutivo pero tiene un empleito VULGAR y corriente. *He makes out that he's some sort of executive but in fact he just has a run-of-the-mill (ordinary) job.* ~Opinión VULGAR. *General (common) opinion.* `|| **2.** Popular. *Popular.* Canciones vulgares. *Popular songs.* || **3.** [No técnico]. *Lay, common, popular.* ~El término VULGAR. *The lay term.* ~¿Cuál es el nombre VULGAR de esta planta? *What's the common (popular) name of that plant?* || **4.** [Persona]. *Ordinario, common.* ~El hombre VULGAR. *The common man.* || **5.** [Succeso, vida]. *Ordinary, everyday.* || **6.** Rutinario. *Humdrum.* || **7.** [Observación]. Trivial, commonplace. ⇨VULGAR

Basic Bibliography

Agencia EFE. *Manual del español urgente*. Cátedra, Madrid, 1989.

Cambridge International Dictionary of English. Cambridge University Press, England, 1995.

Clave. Diccionario del uso del español actual. SM, Barcelona, Madrid, 1996.

Collins Cobuild English Language Dictionary. HarperCollins, Glasglow, 1987.

Cuenca, Miguel. *Diccionario de términos equívocos («Falsos Amigos»)*. Alhambra, Madrid, 1987.

Fitzgibbon. J.P. *Escollos del inglés*. E.P.E.S.A. Madrid, 1955.

García Pelayo y Gross, Ramón. *Gran Diccionario Inglés-español*. Larousse, Paris, 1993.

Harrap's Concise Spanish and English Dictionary. Harrap Book Ltd. England, 1991.

Longman Dictionary of Contemporary English. Longman Group Ltd., England, 1995.

Martínez de Sousa, José. *Diccionario de lexicografía práctica*. Biblograf, Barcelona, 1995.

Martínez de Sousa, José. *Usos y dudas del español actual*. Biblograf, Barcelona, 1996.

Merino, José. *Palabras inglesas engañosas*. C.E.E.I., Madrid, 1985.

Merino, José. *Diccionario de dudas inglés-español*. Paraninfo, Madrid, 1971.

Moliner, María de. *Diccionario del uso del español*. Gredos, Madrid, 1992.

Prado, Marcial. *Dictionary of Spanish False Cognates*. National Textbook Company, Chicago, 1993.

Real Academia Española. *Diccionario de la lengua española*. Espasa Calpe, Madrid, 1992.

Seco, Manuel. *Diccionario de dudas y dificultades de la lengua española*. Espasa Calpe, Madrid, 1993.

Smith, Colin. *Collins Spanish-English, English-Spanish Dictionary*. HarperCollins, Glasglow, 1993.

The Oxford Spanish Dictionary. Oxford University Press, New York, 1994.

Torrents dels Prats, Alfonso. *Diccionario de dificultades del inglés*. Juventud, Barcelona, 1989.

Vox. *Diccionario general ilustrado de la lengua española*. Biblograf, Barcelona, 1989.

Vox. *Diccionario ideológico de la lengua española*. Biblograf, Barcelona, 1995.

OTHER PUBLICATIONS BY BILINGUAL BOOK PRESS

Bilingual Dictionary of Mexican Spanish. Bernard H. Hamel, Ph.D. *Bilingual Book Press*. 2nd ed., 1995. Revised and augmented. ISBN 1-886835-01-2. 196 pgs. Trade paperback. $17.95.

Includes nearly 6000 entries and over 7000 definitions, with many examples to illustrate their use, and there is a Spanish and English translation for all Mexican words and expressions. Includes all entries listed in the Spanish Royal Academy Dictionary pertaining to Mexico and over 300 actual examples from the works of renown Mexican authors such as Carlos Fuentes, Elena Poniatowska, Juan Rulfo and many others. For this book the author has drawn from his experience in Mexico (he holds a Bachelor's degree from the Universidad de las Americas in Mexico City) and his three years residence in Madrid (from where he received his Ph.D. in Romance Philology) to differentiate between standard Spanish and the Spanish spoken in Mexico.

The Best of Latin American Short Stories (Bilingual). Selection and translation by Anthony Ramírez. *Bilingual Book Press.* 2nd ed., 1995. ISBN 1-886835-02-0. 116 pgs. 51/2 x 8. Paper. $10.95.

Extreme care was taken both in the selection of the stories (which represent a diverse cross-section of Latin American authors) and the quality of the translation. Mr. Anthony Ramirez, a librarian at the Oxnard Public Library System, who selected and translated the stories, was chosen for this project by virtue of his proficiency in both languages, his dedication to Hispanic culture and his skill in short-story telling.

Bilingual Dictionary of Latin American Spanish. Bernard H. Hamel, Ph.D. *Bilingual Book Press*, 1995.
ISBN 1-886835-03-9. 160 pags. 8.5 x 11. Trade paperback. $15.95.

Includes over 5000 entries and 6000 definitions of the most commonly-used Latin American words and expressions, with many examples to illustrate their use, and there is a Spanish and English translation for every entry. Includes all entries listed in the Spanish Royal Academy Dictionary pertaining to all, most or much of Latin America.

Comprehensive Bilingual Dictionary of Spanish False Cognates. Bernard H. Hamel, Ph.D. *Bilingual Book Press*,
1995. ISBN 1-886835-06-3. 416 pags. 8.5 x 11. Trade paperback. $29.95. (January, 1998)

False cognates are words which are similar in both languages but have different meanings. *Rent* (alquiler)/*Renta* (income). Those seemingly friendly words offer an easy but deceiving translation, and present the most frequent pitfalls to the bilingual-speaking person. An indispensable tool for translators, interpreters and serious students of Spanish. Includes close to 2,000 English and Spanish False Cognates. The most comprehensive work of this type to date. The dictionary is completely bilingual and has separate English and Spanish Sections.

Two Holiday Folktales from Mexico (Bilingual Edition). Anthony Ramírez. *Bilingual Book Press,* 1995.
ISBN 1-886835-04-7. 96 pgs. 81/2 x 11. Paper. $8.95.

Yerba Buena (The Mint Bush. A Memorable Christmas Tale). Ask anyone in Mexico, "What's good for a stomach ache?" Most likely the answer will be, "Yerbabuena, of course!" Indeed, next to the cactus plant, there's nothing else quite as familiar in Mexico. Mint is used to season food and it is the ingredient that gives gum and candy a truly distinctive taste, but why is this wonderful and fragrant plant called a "good" herb? Most people will reply, "It makes you feel better." The real answer, however, is most unexpected. You will greatly enjoy this unusual Christmas tale!

Las Desventuras del Diablo (The Devil's Halloween Misadventures). All sorts of mishaps occur when the Devil boasts one day that he can get children into all types of mischief. Obviously he never heard this wonderful Spanish saying: "*Bien dicen que a veces los niños son más diablo que el diablo*". Proverbs and sayings, as we know, share truths and impart bits of wisdom. Thus, can children be at times more devilish than the Devil himself ? Chachalaca, the witch in this story, seems to think so, and tells her friend, as much. This wonderful tale (which is not at all scary) evokes pleasant memories of special childhood Halloween celebrations. This tale shows the creative genius that all children have for mischief making!

BILINGUAL BOOK PRESS

Quality Bilingual Publications

10977 Santa Monica Blvd.

Los Angeles, CA 90025

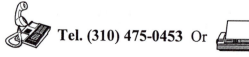 **Tel. (310) 475-0453** Or **Fax (310) 473-6132**